T0394616

FLAVIUS JOSEPHUS

VOLUME 8

JUDEAN ANTIQUITIES, BOOKS 18–20

FLAVIUS JOSEPHUS

TRANSLATION AND COMMENTARY

EDITED BY

STEVE MASON

VOLUME 8

JUDEAN ANTIQUITIES, BOOKS 18–20

TRANSLATION AND COMMENTARY

BY

DANIEL R. SCHWARTZ

BRILL

LEIDEN | BOSTON

The Library of Congress Cataloging-in-Publication Data is available online at https://catalog.loc.gov
LC record available at https://lccn.loc.gov/00022103

Typeface for the Latin, Greek, and Cyrillic scripts: "Brill". See and download: brill.com/brill-typeface.

ISBN 978-90-04-70368-1 (hardback)

This book is printed on acid-free paper and produced in a sustainable manner.

MIX
Paper | Supporting
responsible forestry
FSC
www.fsc.org   FSC® C004472

PRINTED BY DRUKKERIJ WILCO B.V. - AMERSFOORT, THE NETHERLANDS

In memory of Louis H. Feldman (1926–2017)—
a scholar, a gentleman, a mentor, and a friend

∵

CONTENTS

Series Preface: The Brill Josephus Project IX
Foreword XVI
Abbreviations XVIII
An Analytical Table of *Antiquities* 18–20 XXI

Introduction 1
   I   Expectations 1
   II   Disappointment 3
   III Nevertheless 12
   IV Intended Readership 16
   V   Josephus and His Sources 18
   VI Text 20
   VII Translation 27
   VIII Annotations 34

MAPS
Map of Roman Judea 38
Map of the Arsacid Kingdom in the First Two Centuries CE 39

TRANSLATION AND COMMENTARY
Book 18 43
Book 19 153
    Introduction to Book 19 155
Book 20 261

APPENDICES
   1   Chronological Survey of the Roman Governors of Judea, 6–66 CE 329
   2   On Possibilities, Probabilities, and Simon Cantheras's Pedigree (*Ant.* 19.297) 333
   3   An Ancient Table of Contents 340

Bibliography 344
Opening Note about the Indexes 377
Index of Subjects 378
Index of Ancient Persons and Places 379
Index of Modern Authors 382

Flavius Josephus (37–ca. 100 CE) was born Joseph son of Mattityahu, a priestly aristocrat in Jerusalem. For reasons explored in parts of this commentary, lethal conflict arose between Jerusalem and Roman authorities in 66 CE. When legions advanced into Galilee in the spring of 67, Josephus left a secure location in lakeside Tiberias to assist the imperiled town of Iotapata (Yodfat). Within a few weeks that town was overrun, and he surrendered under circumstances that have dogged his reputation ever since. After travelling to Rome with Titus, following Jerusalem's destruction (70 CE), he spent the balance of his life in the imperial capital writing about the war, Judean history and culture, and his own career. Four Greek works in thirty volumes have reached us.

Josephus boasts about the unique importance of his accounts, in a way typical of ancient historians (*War* 1.1–8; *Ant.* 1.1–4), but he could not have known how right that assessment would turn out to be. His corpus quickly became the indispensable source on Judea from 200 BCE to 75 CE, for Roman and later Christian and Jewish writers. For scholars today, analysis of other texts and physical remains occurs mainly in dialogue (if also disagreement) with Josephus, who provides the narrative spine. The importance of his work does not, of course, make it reliable. But anyone who wishes to use it must first try to understand it. That is the reason for this commentary series.

Josephus' works have been extensively cited and reworked ever since he wrote them. But his readers have usually had interests other than interpreting them as compositions. They have tended to look through them to underlying events, or to his sources. The most common questions asked even today are: "Is Josephus accurate, or reliable?" and "Where did he get his information?" The study of his works as efforts to communicate with ancient audiences—by examining their historiography, structures, plots, themes, diction, characterizations, and rhetoric, all in the context of audience expectations in Flavian Rome—was still lacking when a small group of Josephus experts from around the globe met in San

Miniato, Italy, in November 1992. Studies of Roman Judea and the New Testament's environment, which all depended on Josephus, were well known. But journal articles, monographs, essay collections, conferences, graduate seminars, or dissertations on Josephus' works were rare. That was the first such conference (of many), and the idea of an in-depth commentary to this author took shape in its wake. By 1996/1997, a team was in place. We were delighted that Brill, which had recently published major reference works on Josephus (below), agreed to produce the commentary.

Recent decades have witnessed the explosion of "Josephus studies," in this vein of interpreting his works in their ancient contexts. Everything that was missing a quarter-century ago is now routine: the conferences and dissertations resulting in numerous monographs, articles, and collected-essay volumes. Resources that inspired us in the 1990s included Heinz Schreckenberg's bibliographical, text-critical, and reception-historical studies (1970s), K. H. Rengstorf's *Complete Concordance to Flavius Josephus* (completed in 1983), and Louis H. Feldman's annotated bibliographies from the 1980s. These remain immensely valuable, and a growing array of complementary digital tools is opening new possibilities for intensive, methodical research on Josephus.

The time was and is right, therefore, for a full commentary. Already in antiquity, commentators on Homer or Aristotle differed in their aims and methods. Philo's goals were not those of the Qumran *Commentary on Nahum*, rabbinic *midrashim*, or Hippolytus and Origen. Our readers will have a better idea of what to expect if we explain the principles agreed upon by the original commentary team. They still guide our basic approach, though we have made adjustments in the intervening years.

The single most important thing to say is that we do not imagine that we are giving the last word on Josephus. Our aim is comprehensiveness only in the sense of covering the whole corpus. We hope that this resource will become a *catalyst* and reference point for further explorations of questions we may not have imagined. As the burgeoning research shows, no one could write an exhaustive commentary on this rich body of texts. We envisage our contribution as a pier from which to depart on countless journeys of exploration.

On the model of some classical counterparts, we had initially pondered writing a commentary alone, with a Greek phrase introducing each note. But we soon decided that an accompanying translation would help most readers and be more efficient for authors. Keeping a Greek text and/or a translation open alongside a volume of commentary alone would have been cumbersome, even for readers working at desks. And since the commentary would be on the Greek text, readers using an existing translation would have struggled to link our notes to it. Since we were making working translations for our private use anyway, it seemed sensible to include them. We could then attach comments as footnotes to a translation designed for the purpose, rather than printing Greek phrases that the reader would have to locate in another text.

Readers may wonder why we did not include a Greek text, then, with notes directly attached. We considered that too. A new critical text of Josephus remains a desideratum, however. That will require a new collation of available manuscripts and editorial decisions about what to print, a mammoth task quite apart from commentary, which was our concern. When we began, other projects were producing revised Greek texts, but only for sections of Josephus' work and with few manuscript variants indicated. We chose to base our translation on the standard Greek text for the whole corpus, which also provides the fullest critical apparatus: Benedikt Niese's *editio maior* (1885–1895). We also thought about printing Niese's text without apparatus, to anchor the commentary. But omitting an English translation would have severely limited our readership, whereas including both a Greek text and a translation would have unduly complicated the layout. And Brill confirmed that a Greek text would have made the volumes absurdly expensive. In any case, the Niese apparatus is at least as valuable as the text, which is famously problematic. The best solution seemed to be a commentary on the Greek text with a deliberately literal translation for reference, reflecting the Greek as far as possible.

Our translations sometimes adopt a more plausible reading than the one Niese printed: from among Niese's variants, the Loeb edition's revised Greek text, or one of those recent partial projects—the Michel-Bauernfeind edition of *Der jüdische Krieg*, the Münster editions of *Life* and *Against Apion* produced by Folker Siegert's team, or Étienne Nodet's French project (in Jerusalem) on *Antiquities'* biblical paraphrase. We have felt no iron loyalty to Niese's printed text, in other words, although it and its unmatched apparatus have been our starting point.

What does "literal" mean in this context? Granted that every translation is an interpretation, one can still imagine a spectrum between fidelity to the Greek source and a preference for idiomatic English. The former would produce a stilted translation, with multi-clausal sentences and exotic terminology; the other would be breezier, with punchy short sentences, perhaps using resonant words of our time (e.g., "terrorists") to match his "bandits" or "insurgents," even converting his *stadia* to miles or kilometers. In the abstract, one could make a good case for either pole, or for any stop between them, depending on one's aims and audience. "Accuracy" is a category best reserved for things that can be measured, not a useful criterion for literary composition. A translation may be *in*accurate, if faulty. But every translator faces countless choices about words, phrases, sentence structures, and tone or emphasis, none of which is simply accurate. Compare the dozens of translations of Homer's epics, which differ even in being verse or prose. Prose translations do not need to worry about meter, but the same problems face any effort to "carry over" into modern English a text composed in linguistic and social codes very different from ours.

Our choices were guided not by abstract considerations of how best to translate, but by the needs of the commentary. Translations meant to be read by themselves must include a great deal of implicit commentary. They make sense of ambiguous or cryptic terms, add clarifying phrases to complete thoughts, and replace pronouns with names. To keep a text lively for sustained reading, they usually vary the translation of oft-repeated terms, convert indirect to direct speech, give modern equivalents for ancient measures, and gloss over technical nomenclature. Since our translation is not intended to be read by itself, but to support the commentary, we had no reason to prioritize English readability. We could leave unclear terms as they were, while directing readers to the attached notes for elucidation.

Of the standalone translations,[1] we confess our admiration for the Loeb edition, the standard English-Greek text of Josephus for generations. Begun by Henry St. John Thackeray in the 1920s, it was completed in 1965 by the late Louis H. Feldman, who also prepared the splendid first volume of this Brill series (vol. 3: *Antiquities* 1–4, 2000). Both scholars were giants in the study of Josephus before that was a recognized subdiscipline. Our translation implies no criticism of the Loeb. Even if we could have negotiated copyright clearance to borrow it, however, most Loeb volumes would not have served our needs. Their charming variety of expression and often elegant renderings of Josephus' phrases make them superb for volume reading. Our commentary's interest in exploring his thematic lexicon, parallels in other ancient texts, and changing stylistic registers required a different approach.

Even a determined effort at literalness must, of course, yield to the demands of English readability. Robotically using the same English word because Josephus uses one Greek word, but in different senses, would have been counterproductive. If we can find a translation that works for most cases —as with "ancestry" for the six occurrences of γένος in *Life* 1–6 (Loeb uses five different words)—we use that to highlight Josephus' repetitive vocabulary. Where, however, Josephus exploits different senses of a word by reusing it in a short space—as with his only two occurrences of δημοσιόω, in *Life* 363, 370—the commentary discusses the wordplay but we translate differently as the context requires.

We also relinquish any effort to mirror Josephus' long sentences made of aorist-participle clauses. Whatever virtue there may be in rendering the 256 words of *War* 1.1–6 as a single English sentence is trumped by compassion for our readers. We can try to give a flavor of that highbrow opening without a confounding literalism. Readers with a background in Greek will see what lies behind the English: "After X had done Y," and "When [or Once] X had occurred," without our having to choose one phrase for consistency. Repeatedly saying "Having done

X, ..." would also have been falsely repetitive, since the Greek is not. Each participle sounded different, and Josephus apparently prided himself on his creativity. These constructions become a problem only in translation. Likewise, although his regular use of the present tense has a parallel in colloquial English ("A man walks into a bar and says ..."), he was not trying to be colloquial. We therefore usually render his narrative present as a past tense. Some volumes include an asterisk (*) to mark these cases. In short, because it serves a commentary on the Greek text, our translation must sit near the literal end of the spectrum, but not at any cost.

As for Josephus' versions of names, he wrote expecting his audiences to make do with what he gave them in Greek. They lacked knowledge of either Judean geography or Hebrew-Aramaic naming conventions. Interpreting Josephus means, in part, trying to recapture the situation of his ancient audiences. We avoid the temptation to use modern names in the translation; the commentary explains these. It is customary (though this practice is gradually changing) to Latinize Greek names in transliteration. Beyond that, our commentary uses American rather than British spelling conventions. Latinization renders Greek κ as *c*, αι and οι as *ae* and *oe*, and -ος as -*us*, while Americanization usually turns *ae* and *oe* into simple *e*. The -*os* / -*us* ending of male names in Greek and Latin is merely a formal feature of gendered declensions, and so can be dropped in principle. The result of all this is that in transliterating Josephus' names, to capture something of what his first audiences read or heard, we use a familiar English equivalent if that is what remains after the adjustments. For example, Ἄδαμος, Ἄβελος, Ἐλεάζαρος, Ἄβραμος, Λῶτος, Ἰάκωβος, and Δανίηλος yield Adam, Abel, Eleazar, Abram, Lot, Jacob, and Daniel. Where the adjustments leave an unusual form, however—Ῥουβῆλος for Reuben, Κάϊς for Cain, Κορῆς for Korah, Μωϋσῆς for Moses, Συμεών (as distinct from the more frequent Σίμων for Simon), or Ἱεροσόλυμα (rather than the Septuagint's Ἱερουσαλημ) for Jerusalem—or where Josephus gives various forms (Βαιθωροῦν, Βαιθωρώ, Βαιθώρων; Γουρίων, Γωρίων), we give his forms: Roubel, Kais, Kores, Moyses, Symeon, Hierosolyma. Again, the commentary discusses each case: how it might have resonated with ancient audiences, whether it agrees with the Septuagint or other Greek texts, his varying ways of representing Semitic words, or the meaning

---

1 The Loeb Josephus volumes include a light commentary, which expands considerably towards the end of *Antiquities*, but this mainly assists a reader curious about names or important manuscript differences. The translation is designed to be read on its own with a facing Greek text for comparison.

he assigns to a name (e.g., Ἱεροσόλυμα at *War* 6.438; *Ant.* 7.67). Where we transliterate his unfamiliar form, we also give the standard version in the commentary, sometimes also in square brackets at the first occurrence in the translation.

Here again, rigid adherence to abstract principle would serve no purpose. The guidelines above would yield Cores rather than Kores for Κορῆς, for example, but initial K looked better to the translator. The guidelines produce Judea and Idumea, but Achea and Galilea look needlessly odd to most contributors. If we transliterate as Kores, Achaea, or Galilee, Josephus' form remains clear enough. Likewise, although dropping -*os* (-*us* by Latinization) from biblical names is easy (above), it is not obviously desirable for all cases (Δαρεῖος, Κῦρος, Μονόβαζος, Ἄνανος, Στέφανος), or for Josephus' names ending in Greek -*as* (Ματταθίας, Ἀνανίας, Ἰούδας), even where the root is Semitic. Darius, Ananus, Ananias, and Judas are also familiar to readers and correspond to Josephus' versions, so there is no reason not to use them. A mechanical stripping of -*os* endings would affect also Latin names in Greek (Οὔαρος, Κέστιος, Γέσσιος Φλῶρος, Τίτος), which of course we leave as Varus, Cestius, Gessius Florus, and Titus—though Οὐεσπασιανός and Δομετιανός become Vespasian and Domitian, as if to drive home the limits of consistency.

Our concern to help readers understand Josephus' works in their ancient context leads us likewise to retain his units of measurement (*stadia, drachmas,* talents), place names, and titles (cohort, prefect, tribune, Caesar), rather than attempting modern equivalents, which the commentary can discuss.

In sum, we do not imagine that our effort at relative literalness is more *accurate* than other approaches. Translation is a complex phenomenon, arguably impossible in a strict sense. Different projects require different criteria. Because our translation serves the commentary, we have followed the principles above. The reader who cares mainly about the Greek text will want to have it open alongside. And although members of the team agree on the general principles of translation and transliteration, implementation rests with the judgment of the expert dealing with each volume.

Turning now to the commentary: it aims to include literary-interpretative and historical concerns, as they are relevant to the material being studied. The distinction requires explanation. If we understand history as the investigation of human

actions—events, institutions, or conditions of life—in the past, then the investigation of a historical problem will resemble the work of detectives. That is, we first gather and try to *understand* (or interpret) available evidence, before proceeding to test hypotheses that will explain it. In the study of the ancient past, historians quickly saw the value of what they called auxiliary sciences (*Hilfswissenschaften*), to support particular investigations into "what really happened." The idea of auxiliary research was to create an ever-expanding suite of resources that would make historical inquiries more efficient. Survivals relevant to Roman Judea, Syria, and Egypt include the remains of buildings, housewares and implements, coins, inscriptions, papyri, and full literary texts such as Josephus' works. Some of these remains have been handed down over generations; others have been discovered by diligent effort. Either way, auxiliary historical research involves the identification, collection, and interpretation of all such known survivals, in a preliminary way, and publishing the results in reference works. For the historian who then decides to open an inquiry into the causes of the Judean-Roman War, the nature of Jerusalem's governance in the 50s CE, or Pontius Pilate's governorship, these reference works are of inestimable value. They save us having to see each site or coin in person or interpret everything from scratch. Even if we end up proposing a new interpretation, they give us a solid place to begin.

A commentary to Josephus is an auxiliary reference work of the same kind, created to facilitate historical investigation. By sorting out manuscript variants, clarifying sources, weighing possible interpretations and offering preferred translations, noting conflicts within the corpus, and comparing Josephus' account with other surviving texts and archaeological finds, it aims to make historical inquiries into the realities behind the text more efficient. Contributors to the commentary also conduct such historical investigations into aspects of life in Roman Judea. So we have an interest in making the commentary useful for this work.

This preparatory function distinguishes the Josephus commentary from a reference work such as Emil Schürer's magisterial *History of the Jewish People in the Age of Jesus Christ* and other manuals on life in Roman Judea or New Testament backgrounds (*Umwelt*). Schürer has proven so valuable that, since its first appearance (1874 in German), it has gone through a century of updates. Its depth of scholarship and judiciousness in weighing evidence make it a valuable resource even today. It uses Josephus' compositions as a principal source, however, with little concern for interpreting them. It includes no discussion of the structures, themes, or characterizations in his writings, his situation as a writer in Rome, systematic comparison of his divergent accounts of the same events, or the possible reasons and implications. The Brill commentary complements Schürer and other manuals by working from the other direction. Instead of moving directly to constructing a reliable narrative of Hasmonean, Herodian, and Roman times or describing the main institutions and groups of the time, its primary task is to understand *Josephus' portraits*. Rediscovering the most famous Jewish author in this way is already a worthy exercise. In exposing the nature of Josephus' works and the freedom that he enjoyed in retelling stories, the project should help us to use Josephus more adeptly in historical investigations.

What we mean, then, by including both literary and historical issues is along these lines. Literary and philological questions in the strict sense have to do with uncovering the structures and plots of Josephus' narrative, thematically charged language, speeches and other digressions, the literary pitch or register of a work or section, allusions to literature then famous, rhetorical devices and approach to writing history, sources or inspirations, and Josephus' manuscript tradition. But we shall not get far in understanding any ancient text by studying it in isolation, no matter how sophisticated our methods may be. To put ourselves in the picture of Josephus' audiences, we need to consider what can be known of his environment in Flavian Rome, a body of knowledge that continues to grow through the study of texts and material remains. To have an idea of what he might have had in mind from his experience in Judea and environs, whether he conveyed this to his audiences or not, we also need to explore the events, places, institutions, and people he refers to there. Such historical content—when he mentions the gates or colonnades of Herod's temple, the later auxiliary garrison there, or the military standards that Pilate introduced—serves both to help us understand Josephus and to make his work useful for further inquiry. It is not the task of a commentary to conduct new investigations into the lost past, which require their own articles and monographs. But even as it tries to facilitate understanding of Josephus, it

must fuse historical with literary considerations. We are dealing with works written in ancient Greek, after all, in a time and social environment remote from ours. As a famous saying has it, "The past is a foreign country; they do things differently there."

All that said, Josephus' work is so diverse that readers should not expect the same proportion of literary and historical discussion throughout. Well over half of the corpus (*War* 1.31–2.180; *Antiquities* 1–18) deals with events before Josephus' lifetime. For those narratives, and often for later times, Josephus reworked source material. When commenting on his paraphrase of the Bible, the Letter of Aristeas, or 1 Maccabees, commentators focus mainly on literary-philological issues relating to both the source material, which we can often read for comparison (if not quite in the form he knew), and his techniques of adaptation. There would be little point in exploring what *really* happened with Adam and Eve, the Patriarchs, or the Exodus when analyzing Josephus' biblical paraphrase. The main concern there is to understand how he is adapting the source to his purposes, a task aided by comparison with how other contemporaries reworked the Bible. With much of *War*, the end of *Antiquities*, and *Life*, by contrast, the subject matter is the social-political landscape of Josephus' homeland and events that occurred while he was nearby. Since he was a knowledgeable eyewitness for these periods, or at least an informed judge of others' accounts, the commentary here includes much more historical and archaeological content, to facilitate the use of his narratives in reconstructing such events. The lively two-volume essay known as *Against Apion* is something else again. There, the commentary must take up issues ranging from the criticism of fragments by Alexandrian authors to philosophy in Josephus' time.

Although the literary-historical mix changes in accord with the subject matter, we aim at a roughly consistent proportion of commentary to primary text. When other translations of Josephus include light commentary, it tends to be disproportionate because famous passages, such as Josephus' account of the Essenes (*War* 2.119–61) or his references to Jesus or James (*Ant.* 18.63–64; 20.197–203), attract fuller comment. Commentary in the Loeb edition expands towards the end of *Antiquities*, partly because of the numerous textual difficulties. Our working assumption is that every part of the corpus, which Josephus wrote for expectant audiences and perhaps for performance or recitation (*War* 1.22), has roughly equal value for understanding the whole. Exceptions are programmatic passages such as the proems and conclusions, which ancient audiences knew to be pregnant by design. Their thematic density, especially in the case of *War*, calls for disproportionate space in the commentary. Where a passage has generated intensive modern study and debate, and so discussion would have created a lack of proportion (cf. *Ant.* 1.7), a commentator may devote an excursus to it.

Having outlined the reasons for the project and its basic principles, I close by observing that readers will nevertheless discover considerable variety in both the Josephan content of these volumes and the interests, language, and focus of our expert commentators. The original team worked out the principles in a year of discussions, but agreement about these did not then, and does not now, imply a *uniformity* of outlook. As humanists, we cherish individual insight, prize diversity, and enjoy lively discussions. As new colleagues have joined the project since the 1990s, the scope for discussion and debate has only widened to our collective benefit. The Josephus Seminar in the Annual Meeting of the Society of Biblical Literature provides one regular venue for our exchanges.

The Greek word *Ioudaios*, which Josephus uses about 1200 times, provides an example of our different inclinations. We all seek to understand the ancient environment of Josephus' works, but historians differ as to whether English "Judean" or "Jew" comes closest to what an ancient Greek or Roman (or *Ioudaios*) heard in this word-group. The original team agreed to use *Judean* for the volume titles of *War* and *Antiquities* but left the translation in each volume up to its author(s). Some have preferred to use *Judean* throughout. Others have favored *Jew / Jewish* as default. Others have opted to use either *Jew / Jewish* or *Judean*, depending on context. Each expert alone decides how to weigh relevant considerations: the particular content in question (from biblical paraphrase to philosophical debate), ancient parallels, audience assumptions ancient and modern, the nature of translation, and the role of transliteration. We hope that readers will appreciate all such individual differences, even as we seek to realize the goals and principles described above.

It remains to acknowledge and thank the many professionals outside the commentary team who have played important roles in the creation and continuation of this work: *amici* whose names may not otherwise appear. First, many specialists in Josephus and related fields offered welcome encouragement in early days. Though we cannot name them all, they include David Goldenberg, Erich Gruen, Gohei Hata, Tessa Rajak, Donna Runnalls, Pieter van der Horst, Tommaso Leoni, William den Hollander, Michael Helfield, and Reuben Lee. Some read work in progress, offering critique and suggestions. We thank them all, while absolving them of any responsibility for what went to press.

Second, we are immensely grateful to the staff at Brill for initiating this project and staying with it until now, with such élan, despite delays far beyond the originally planned completion date (2006). Elisabeth Erdman, Elisabeth Venekamp, Job Lisman, Sam Bruinsma, Jan-Peter Wissink, Anita Roodnat, and Ivo Romein provided crucial encouragement in early days. Loes Schouten, Mattie Kuiper, Tessa Schild, Marjolein van Zuylen, Peter Buschman, Gera van Bedaf, Tessel Jonquière, Laura Morris, and Nitzan Shalev have continued to absorb unavoidable delays with grace, while doing everything possible to keep the project alive. Their technical skill has turned our work into the durable and handsome volumes for which Brill is renowned, and now created an online version of the project: https://brill.com/view/db/fjo.

Finally, I record with gratitude the agencies and institutions that have made possible my work as both academic editor and contributor. These include York University, my long-time academic home and nurturing ground in Toronto, where the project took shape; the Social Sciences and Humanities Research Council of Canada (SSHRC), for funding in the early years; the Killam Foundation of Canada for a two-year leave fellowship; All Souls College and Wolfson College in the University of Oxford, for visiting fellowships; the Alexander von Humboldt-Stiftung, for a research year at the Humboldt University in Berlin; the University of Aberdeen (2011–2014); and the University of Groningen (2015–2020).

Steve Mason, *University of Groningen* (*Emeritus*)
General Editor, Brill Josephus Project

A Note on Volume Numbers (2024)

The project's volume numbers—some simple, others subdivided with letters—require an explanation. When the project began, we planned to follow the division in the Loeb edition of Josephus. With several times the amount of space available in Brill's large format, and without a Greek text on facing pages, we calculated that our translation and commentary (in smaller print and two columns below) should fit in the same number of volumes, which had been apportioned according to the amount of Greek text in each. The Loeb has in the meantime changed its divisions, but we planned to mirror its nine-volume structure at the time: 1 (*War* 1–3), 2 (*War* 4–7), 3 (*Antiquities* 1–4), 4 (*Antiquities* 5–7), 5 (*Antiquities* 8–10), 6 (*Antiquities* 11–13), 7 (*Antiquities* 14–17), 8 (*Antiquities* 18–20), and 9 (*Life, Against Apion*).

This plan worked as long as original members of the team were able to complete their work. *Antiquities* 1 through 10 (Brill volumes 3 to 5) reflect it. But life's twists and turns soon interfered. Some members had to leave the project and their large assignments were taken over by two or more colleagues, unavoidably working at different speeds in various environments. If one contributor was able to finish well ahead of the others, delaying publication only to keep to the numbering scheme would have made no sense. The first change came with *Life* (2001) and *Against Apion* (2006), though that was easily accommodated by designating *Against Apion* as volume 10. As other breaks occurred, the existence of volumes 9 and 10 required us to subdivide. Thus, *War* 2 appeared as 1b, *War* 4 as 2a, *Antiquities* 11 as 6a, and *Antiquities* 15 as 7b. For the interpretation of Josephus, these subdivisions hardly mattered. Any grouping outside the biblical paraphrase, including the old Loeb scheme, was mostly arbitrary. The *Life* and *Apion* are, for example, very different works. Nevertheless, Daniel Schwartz's willingness to prepare *Antiquities* 18–20 as a single Brill number (8) will be welcomed because these volumes, which describe events from 6 to 66 CE (cf. *War* 2) in Judea, Rome, and the Parthian empire, are of extraordinary interest to scholars from several disciplines.

FOREWORD

Some sixteen years have passed since I accepted Steve Mason's gracious invitation to prepare this volume, and close to a decade since I started giving overly optimistic estimates about finishing it "next year." In large measure, the delay requires no more explanation than the usual "life happened" and reference to numerous academic obligations, especially the administrative tasks entrusted to me by the heads of my academic home, the Hebrew University of Jerusalem, together with its most generous partner and funder, the Jack, Joseph and Morton Mandel Foundation.

But the delay also derived from the fact that during the same fifteen years I was working on my commentary on 1 Maccabees (which eventually appeared in 2022, ahead of the present volume). It was my assumption that working in tandem on the two main works of Jewish historiography in the Greco-Roman world, works written by authors from opposite poles of Jewish national experience (a court historian of a sovereign Jewish dynasty, writing in Hebrew, and a historian writing in Greek in the Diaspora in the wake of the destruction of the Temple, Jerusalem, and the last vestiges of Judean statehood), would engender perspectives that would fructify my work on both of them. Indeed, by 2014 my thoughts on the comparison had progressed to the point that I took some time off from both projects to write a small book, *Judeans and Jews*, that is devoted to the contrast exemplified by the two works. Readers may judge whether the delay was worth it.

Numerous people helped me along the way. First and foremost among them were three teachers. Menahem Stern (1925–1989) imparted a love for Josephus, for scholarly endeavor, and for the truth, that remains a living inspiration and challenge for my work. Louis H. Feldman (1926–2017), with whom I never studied, indefatigably lavished boundless generosity on a tyro who dared to bother him with questions about this or that detail; I have dedicated the present volume to his memory, in gratitude and specifically in recognition of my debt to his 1965 Loeb Classical Library edition of these same three books of *Antiquities*. In that connection I would underline that, given the very different format of the present series, in which (as Mason explains in his preface to the series) the translation is meant to be a platform for the commentary, my volume does not intend to supplant Feldman's; they serve different ends. When I just want to read Josephus in extenso, but with immediate access to the Greek, I will continue to prefer Feldman's volume. As for Lisa Ullmann (1922–2019), my stickling Greek teacher (and translator of Josephus's *War*) who demanded of herself as much as she demanded from me, if not more—I can only imagine how my work might have been improved had she lived to see my drafts. Of all three: תהא נשמתם צרורה בצרור החיים.

Among the many colleagues who helped me along the way, I will gratefully mention several patient and generous friends and colleagues here in Jerusalem who have gotten used, over the years, to being my consultants in their fields: Orit Peleg-Barkat and Zeev Weiss for archaeology; Deborah L. Gera for Greek; Ranon Katzoff for things Roman and Latin; Michael Shenkar for things Parthian; and Robert Brody, Yair Furstenberg, and Paul Mandel for rabbinic literature and law. Of friends abroad, I mention especially my fellow fans of Josephus, Jan Willem van Henten and Steve Mason. Over the years I have peppered them with questions large and small, and debated them with them, and their responses and advice have always been generous and instructive. Especially in the final stages of the project, in which Mason went over every jot and tittle of the first draft of this volume, he proved himself to be the most thorough editor one could imagine or hope for. Which is not to say that I always took his advice, or that of my other friends and consultants; responsibility for the volume is mine.

Sabbatical stays at the Netherlands Institute of Advanced Studies in 2008, and at the University of Toronto in 2010, were very instrumental in giving the project its initial impetus. Most of the work, however, was done at my desk at the Hebrew University's Mandel School for Advanced Studies in the Humanities, with all the wonderful support that afforded. I am also happy to thank Gila Emanuel and her staff at the Interlibrary Loan Department of the Hebrew University's Mt. Scopus library, whose friendly and efficient services I exploited incessantly over the past several years.

In moving toward the completion of the volume I was assisted by Anthony Ellis, who checked the translation of Book 18, and by Shlomo Brand, Sebastian Kenny, and Chananya Rothner, who helped with the proofreading. Their work was made possible by funding associated with the Herbst Family Chair in Judaic Studies, of which I was privileged to be the incumbent from 2014 until my retirement in 2022. I am also very grateful to Nadav Sharon, who worked extensively on the annotations to Book 19, and to Sarit Kattan Gribetz, who read drafts of the introduction and Book 20; both made numerous corrections and perspicacious suggestions. In the final stage of the project, generous and sharp-eyed Robert Brody read through the entire volume. Amicus fidelis protectio fortis.

The real beginning of this book came in a class in 1979 or 1980, when I wanted to teach something about *Ant.* 20.189 but mistakenly began reading to students from *Ant.* 20.179. That mistake directed my interest, and my students', to the fact that both passages (as also 20.211) begin virtually identically, κατὰ τοῦτον τὸν καίρον ὁ βασιλεὺς Ἀγρίππας ("At that time, King Agrippa …"), and led us to wonder what makes an author introduce stories in such a mechanical way. More than forty years later, it is appropriate to acknowledge that much of what I know, or think I know, about Josephus in particular or history in general, was generated or catalyzed in such interaction with students. I am very grateful to them; in the best tradition of research universities, they are very real partners in the genesis of this book. In giving the next generation of scholars a volume meant to help them in their own work on and with Josephus, I hope to give back some of what they have given me.

Finally, I join Steve Mason in thanking all the wonderful workers at Brill over the past many years. Their positiveness, professionalism, and patience are incomparable, and Gera van Bedaf, who is specifically in charge of the production of this volume, lives up admirably to the high standards set by her predecessors.

In conclusion, I will add a thought in light of the experience of one of my predecessors in Jerusalem: Abraham Schalit (1898–1979), a great scholar who devoted his life to the study of Josephus. He was a man of many projects, and a perfectionist, as is shown by the pearls that he managed to complete and publish, including his Hebrew translation of all of *Antiquities* and notes on its first decade, his *König Herodes*, and his *Namenwörterbuch zu Flavius Josephus*, works that I turn to frequently. However, Schalit's perfectionism came with a high price: given Psalm 90:10, much of what he worked on for decades, including the hundreds and hundreds of pages of his copious and erudite draft commentary on the second decade of *Antiquities*, which he expected to fill four volumes, was never completed and, tragically, ended up being discarded.

Perhaps such a fate was, and is, especially a hazard for a commentary, a work that has no agenda of its own apart from opening up an ancient book so as to facilitate its use by others—whose interests and needs could be endless, so every episode, every motif, and every word can occasion a dissertation. But as Steve Mason explains in his preface to the present series, its volumes too have that purpose: they aim to be "a pier from which to depart on countless journeys of exploration." In submitting the current volume to Steve and to Brill for publication, I am very cognizant that it is far from perfect, in many ways, but weigh that recognition against the lesson taught by Schalit's experience. I hope that, such as it is, others will find my work useful, and take things from here.

Daniel R. Schwartz
Jerusalem, March 2024

ABBREVIATIONS

1QS	Qumran *Community Rule*
AE	*L'année épigraphique*
AGAJU	Arbeiten zur Geschichte des antiken Judentums und des Urchristentums
AJEC	Ancient Judaism and Christianity
AJP	*American Journal of Philology*
ALGHJ	Arbeiten zur Literatur und Geschichte des hellenistischen Judentums
Ann.	Tacitus, *Annals*
Ant.	Josephus, *Antiquities*
ANRW	*Aufstieg und Niedergang der römischen Welt*
Apion	Josephus, *Against Apion*
ASOR	American Schools of Oriental Research
ASTI	*Annual of the Swedish Theological Institute*
b.	Babylonian Talmud, born, or *ben* (son of)
BMCR	*Bryn Mawr Classical Review*
BN	*Biblische Notizen*
CA	*Classical Antiquity*
CCFJ	K. H. Rengstorf 1973–1983[1]
CD	*Damascus Document*
CIIJ/P	*Corpus Inscriptionum Iudaea/Palaestinae*
CIL	*Corpus Inscriptionum Latinarum*
CJ	*Classical Journal*
Const.	Seneca, *De Constantia Sapientis*
CP	*Classical Philology*
CPJ	Tcherikover, Fuks, and Stern 1957–1964 and Hacham and Ilan 2020–.
CPR	*Corpus Papyrorum Raineri*
CQ	*Classical Quarterly*
CR	*Classical Review*
CRB	Cahiers de la Revue biblique
EI	*Eretz-Israel*
ÉtB	Études bibliques
FAT	Forschungen zum Alten Testament
FJTC	Flavius Josephus: Translation and Commentary
Flacc.	Philo, *In Flaccum*
GCS	Die griechischen christlichen Schriftsteller der ersten drei Jahrhunderte
GLAJJ	M. Stern 1974–1984
GR	*Greece and Rome*
GTRI	H. J. Mason 1974
HCS	Hellenistic Culture and Society
HDR	Harvard Dissertations in Religion
HJP	Schürer 1973–1987
HTR	*Harvard Theological Review*
HUCA	*Hebrew Union College Annual*
IAA	Israel Antiquities Authority

---

1 References in this format, in this list of abbreviations as elsewhere, refer to the bibliography at the end of the volume.

IEJ	*Israel Exploration Journal*
IGRR	*Inscriptiones graecae ad res romanas pertinentes*
ILS	Dessau 1892
INJ	*Israel Numismatic Journal*
JAOS	*Journal of the American Oriental Society*
JBL	*Journal of Biblical Literature*
JGRChJ	*Journal of Greco-Roman Christianity and Judaism*
JHS	*Journal of Hellenic Studies*
JJS	*Journal of Jewish Studies*
JLCL	LCL edition of Josephus
JQR	*Jewish Quarterly Review*
JRASS	Journal of Roman Archaeology Supplementary Series
JRS	*Journal of Roman Studies*
JSJ	*Journal for the Study of Judaism*
JSJSup	Supplements to JSJ
JSNTSup	Journal for the Study of the New Testament Supplement Series
JSP	Journal for the Study of the Pseudepigrapha
JSPSup	JSP Supplement Series
JSQ	*Jewish Studies Quarterly*
KP	*Kleine Pauly*
LCL	Loeb Classical Library
Leg.	Philo, *Embassy to Gaius/Legatio ad Gaium*
LSJ	Liddell-Scott-Jones 1992
LSTS	Library of Second Temple Studies
m.	Mishnah
MGWJ	*Monatsschrift für Geschichte und Wissenschaft des Judent(h)ums*
MJS	Münsteraner Judaistische Studien
MnemSup	Mnemosyne Supplementum
NEAEHL	E. Stern 1993–2008
NH	Pliny, *Naturalis Historia*
NovT	*Novum Testamentum*
NPNF	Nicene and Post-Nicene Fathers
NTOA	Novum Testamentum et Orbis Antiquus
NTS	*New Testament Studies*
OBOSA	Orbis Biblicus et Orientalis, Series Archaeologica
OCD	*Oxford Classical Dictionary* (3rd edition, 1996)
OGIS	Dittenberger 1903–1905
OLD	Glare 2000
PEQ	*Palestine Exploration Quarterly*
PIR¹	*Prosopographia Imperii Romani saec. I. II. III.* (3 vols; 1897–1898)
PWRE	*Paulys Real-Encyclopädie der classischen Altertumswissenschaft*
RAC	*Reallexikon für Antike und Christentum*
RB	*Revue biblique*
RGDA	*Res gestae divi Augusti*
RGRW	Religions in the Graeco-Roman World
RhM	*Rheinisches Museum für Philologie*
RPC	*Roman Provincial Coinage* (online)
RPCSup	*Roman Provincial Coinage Consolidated Supplement*, I–III, ed. P. P. Ripollès et al., 1992–2015 (online)
RQ	*Revue de Qumrân*
RSR	*Recherches de science religieuse*
RSV	Revised Standard Version of the Bible

SBB	Stuttgarter biblische Beiträge
SBLSCS	Society of Biblical Literature Septuagint and Cognate Studies
SBLSPS	Society of Biblical Literature Seminar Paper Series
SCI	*Scripta Classica Israelica*
SFSHJ	South Florida Studies in the History of Judaism
SIG	Dittenberger 1960
SJLA	Studies in Judaism in Late Antiquity
SNTSMS	Society for New Testament Studies Monograph Series
SP	Hunt and Edgar 1934
SPA	*Studia Philonica Annual*
SPB	Studia Post-Biblica
STDJ	Studies on the Texts of the Desert of Judah
Sup	Supplement(s)
TAPA	*Transactions and Proceedings of the American Philological Association*
ThLJ	Thackeray and Marcus 1930–1955
TLZ	*Theologische Literaturzeitung*
TSAJ	Texte und Studien zum antiken Judentum/Texts and Studies in Ancient Judaism
USQR	*Union Seminary Quarterly Review*
VT	*Vetus Testamentum*
VTSup	Supplements to Vetus Testamentum
WUNT	Wissenschaftliche Untersuchungen zum Neuen Testament
y.	Palestinian Talmud
ZDMG	*Zeitschrift der Deutschen Morgenländischen Gesellschaft*
ZDPV	*Zeitschrift des Deutschen Palästina-Vereins*
ZNW	*Zeitschrift für die neutestamentliche Wissenschaft*
ZPE	*Zeitschrift für Papyrologie und Epigraphik*
ZRGG	*Zeitschrift für Religions- und Geistesgeschichte*
ZWT	*Zeitschrift für wissenschaftliche Theologie*

References to biblical chapters and verses are according to the RSV. References to the Mishnah are according to the numbering in Danby 1933.

AN ANALYTICAL TABLE OF *ANTIQUITIES* 18–20

Note: for a more detailed table, with discussions of details, see Schwartz 1992: 188–193.

18.1   **The Beginning of Direct Roman Rule: Quirinius and Coponius**
      18.4   Judas the Galilean Incites Rebellion
      18.11   The Jewish Philosophies
      18.27   Herod's Heirs, apart from Archelaus
      18.29   An Incident in the Temple
18.31   **Early Roman Governors of Judea**
      18.36   The Foundation of Tiberias
      18.39   Parthian History, 3/2 BCE–17 CE
      18.53   Germanicus's Mission to the East and His Death
18.55   **Pontius Pilate's Tumultuous Governorship**
      18.63   Josephus on Jesus
      18.65   Two Roman Episodes
      18.85   End of Pilate's Governorship
18.90   Vitellius Visits Jerusalem, I
18.96   Rome, Parthia, and Herod Antipas, 35–37 CE
18.106   Death of Philip
18.109   Antipas and Aretas
      18.116   John the Baptist
      18.120   Vitellius Visits Jerusalem, II
18.126b   Agrippa I
      18.127   Herodian Genealogy
      18.143   Poor Agrippa in Judea
      18.161   Agrippa in Rome
           18.170   Tiberius's Style of Rule
           18.179   Agrippa's Imprisonment
               18.195   A German's Prophecy
      18.205   Tiberius's Arrangements for His Succession
      18.224   Death of Tiberius
      18.236   Gaius Succeeds to the Throne, Elevates Agrippa
18.238   Enter Woman, Enter Trouble, I: The Fall of Herod Antipas
18.256   Gaius's Attempt to Erect a Statue in the Temple of Jerusalem
      18.289   Agrippa's Intervention
      18.302   Renewed Crisis and Providential Denouement
18.310   The Jews of Mesopotamia: Two Episodes
      18.311   The Escapades of Asineus and Anileus
           18.340 Enter Woman, Enter Trouble, II: The Brothers' Fall
      18.371   The Jews' Troubles in Babylon and Seleucia
19.1   Gaius's Excesses
19.15   Josephus's Reason for Detailing the Assassination
19.17   The Conspirators
      19.32b   The Torture of Quintila
      19.37   Chaerea Enlists Fellow Conspirators

19.70   Delays
19.77   Chaerea's Speeches Impel to Action
19.84   The Assassination
         19.90   The Theater and Program
         19.96   Gaius Departs
         19.105   The Deed is Done
         19.111   Chaerea's Central Role
         19.114   The Assassins Make Their Getaway
19.119   The Germans' Rampage
19.127   Reactions in the Theater
19.138   The Germans at the Theater
19.153   Chaerea and Minucianus
19.158   The People and the Senate Deliberate
19.162   The Army Chooses Claudius
19.166   Sentius Saturninus's Speech in the Senate
19.190   Loose Ends: The Assassination of Gaius's Wife and Daughter
19.201   Gaius Caligula: Summing Up
19.212   Soldiers Kidnap Claudius to the Imperial Throne
19.229   Senators Talk, I
19.236   Agrippa Intervenes, I
19.248   Senators Talk, II
19.254   The Army Prevails
19.265   Agrippa Intervenes, II
19.268   Chaerea's Fate
19.272   The Aftermath
19.274   Claudius's Arrangements upon Succession to the Throne
19.278   Claudius and the Jews of the Empire
19.293   **Agrippa I, King of Judea**
         19.293b Agrippa's Opening Gestures and Arrangements
         19.300   The Dora Affair and Petronius's Intervention
         19.313   Agrippa and the High Priesthood
         19.317   Agrippa and Silas
         19.326   Agrippa vs. Marsus, I
         19.328   Agrippa the Benefactor
                  19.332   Gentle Agrippa
                  19.335   Agrippa's Projects in Berytus
         19.338   Agrippa vs. Marsus, II
         19.343   Agrippa's Death
         19.360   Claudius's Arrangements after Agrippa's Death
20.1   **Fadus's Governorship**
         20.9   Claudius, Agrippa II, and Herod of Chalcis
         20.17   The Conversion of the Royal House of Adiabene
                  20.49   Helena's Pilgrimage to Jerusalem
                  20.54   Izates Saves Artabanus
                  20.69   Izates vs. Vardanes
                  20.75   Izates vs. Grandees, Arabs, and Parthians
                  20.92   Deaths of Izates and Helena
         20.97   Theudas
20.100   **Tiberius Julius Alexander's Governorship**
         20.103   A Potpourri of Updates

20.105 **Cumanus's Stormy Governorship**
    20.125 Ummidius Quadratus Intervenes
    20.134 Claudius Adjudicates
20.138 Updates and Gossip about Herodians
20.148 Nero's Succession to the Empire
    20.154 Josephus's Reflections on His Own Mandate
20.158 More Updates about Herodians
20.160 **Felix's Governorship**
    20.173 The Caesarean Dispute, I
    20.179 Stasis in Jerusalem
    20.182 The Caesarean Dispute, II
20.185 **Festus's Governorship**
    20.197 The Death of Jacob ("James"), Jesus's Brother
20.204 **Albinus's Governorship**
    20.205 High Priests and Sicarii
    20.211 Agrippa II's Foreign Projects
    20.213 More High-Priestly and Herodian Violence
    20.215 Conclusion of Albinus's Governorship
    20.216 Agrippa II's Projects in the Temple and Jerusalem
20.224 Summary of the High Priesthood
20.252 **Florus's Governorship: The Conclusion of the Narrative**
20.259 Conclusion of *Antiquities*

INTRODUCTION

1. **Expectations.** Books 18–20 of Josephus's *Antiquities*, the last books of the work, are devoted to the years 6–66 CE. Whether one comes to them as literature or as history, they arouse high expectations. Readers may justifiably expect them to be the culmination and most important part of Josephus's magnum opus: they should be the high point of the work and are, moreover, devoted to a most important period.

As a work of literature, and especially as historiography, on the one hand, these three books bring the *Antiquities* to a close. We are, therefore, entitled to expect them to bring together, or to a conclusion, overarching themes and lines of thought developed earlier in the work in its first seventeen books. Indeed, we might expect Josephus to take the opportunity, offered by the conclusion of his work, to do his best as an author, so as to leave his readers with the very best impression of his talent as an author.

As history, on the other hand, expectations are raised by two outstanding advantages enjoyed by these three books in contrast to the first seventeen. First: they deal, for the most part, with a period for which Josephus himself was an eyewitness. Josephus was born in 37 CE, a point of the story reached already a quarter of the way into Book 18, with Tiberius's death and the end of Pontius Pilate's term of office as governor of Judea (18.89). Indeed, since Josephus's story is notably sparse from the end of Herod's reign (whereafter he could no longer depend on Nicolaus of Damascus) until the days of Agrippa I, but afterward becomes quite full, it is likely, as has often been noticed,[1] that the explanation is precisely the fact that, as a youth and young adult, he was able to depend on his own personal knowledge, as well as first-hand testimony of parents, friends, and other informants.

True, the testimony of witnesses who are near the events they describe is far from infallible. Even for events of their own day they may have no direct access, or access only to some part of the story or only to some particular perspective concerning it. Moreover, even when events are recorded by witnesses who had first-hand or otherwise good access to the events, the fact that they were so close and involved can lead them to tailor and skew accounts, consciously or unconsciously, in accordance with their tendencies. Such tendencies are likely to be more pronounced, and influential, than the ones at work when authors write about events that are more remote from themselves.

Nevertheless, ancient witnesses who were close to events are the modern historian's best guide to reconstructing and understanding them; often they offer the modern historian the only chance to do so. Historians, therefore, quite rightly prefer to depend on their testimony—applying to them all their experience, understanding, and skills, as well as the input of other relevant sources of all kinds, if available, in order to separate the wheat from the chaff and properly to understand and assess both.[2] *Antiquities* 18–20 may, therefore, be expected to be a valuable source for the history of the period.

---

1 See, for example, Bammel 1974a: 61 and *HJP* 1.51. Note that, with the exception of Pontius Pilate, Josephus has virtually nothing to report about the the Roman governors who ruled Judea prior to Agrippa. For Pilate, Josephus seems to have had special sources; see the annotations.

2 Note well: both the wheat and the chaff. Both that in our sources which points toward Ranke's "how things really were" and that which points away from it are grist for the historian's mill, for both, if properly recognized and analyzed, are evidence for what people in particular places and times did and thought, whether as actors,

The second advantage enjoyed by *Antiquities* 18–20, as a source of history, is its subject-matter. The preceding three books (15–17) were full of details, indeed frequently wallowing in gossip, about the reign of Herod—a king who, whatever his accomplishments, ended up being hated or despised by posterity, his kingdom dissected and thus set up for *divide et impera*. Yet earlier, Books 13–14 were devoted to the rise and fall of the Hasmonean state,[3] a kingdom that was finishing itself off in civil war even before Rome gave it the coup de grâce—a kingdom that Jews, until the modern period, were usually content to forget.[4] Our three books, in contrast, are devoted to events of world-historical importance, whose implications have shaped much of western history until today.

First of all, these three books are devoted to the history of Judea and the Jews in "the first century"—the chronological, geographical, and human context of the birth of Christianity. Although that particular story is told in detail in the Gospels and other books of the New Testament, and not by Josephus, our three books supply accounts of Herod Antipas and other Herodians, John the Baptist, Jesus, James, Pontius Pilate, and other figures important to the birth of Christianity, and also constitute, more generally, the main source of knowledge concerning the contexts of that story. So if, in general, it is the case that it was because of Christian interest that Josephus's works were preserved so exceptionally well in contrast to so much of ancient literature,[5] *Antiquities* 18–20 are, more than any other part of Josephus's oeuvre, at the heart of that explanation.

Moreover, the first century also saw the end of the last vestiges of Jewish statehood, of which the Temple of Jerusalem (destroyed in 70) was the linchpin,[6] and that story is told, in detail, by *Antiquities* 18–20. Just as clearly as Books 13–14 are devoted to the Hellenistic and Hasmonean period, and Books 15–17 are devoted to Herod's reign, Books 18–20 are devoted to Roman rule in Judea. From the institution of direct Roman rule at the outset of Book 18, to the end of the last Judean monarchy at the end of Book 19, and down to the allusion to the destruction of the Temple, which, as the "House of God," was the last vestige and symbol of the Jews' claim to have a place of their own in this world, at the end of Book 20 (§§257–258; cf. the opening brackets, as it were, at 18.8, 25), this is the process to which these three books are devoted. This process was just as seminal for the history of Jews and Judaism—which hardly remembered both the Hasmoneans and Herod—as the story of Jesus and the birth of Christianity was for that of the West in general. But for that story too, *Antiquities* 18–20 is our main source.

Finally, although the Principate was born already in the last third of the first century BCE, the six decades covered by *Antiquities* 18–20 are a major witness to the stabilization of the empire, from the death of the first Princeps early in Book 18 to that of Gaius Caligula, recounted at great length in Book 19, and down to the days of Nero, who ascends to the imperial throne in the middle of Book 20. It is to the twelfth year of Nero's reign that Josephus

---

authors, or copyists. They are both, therefore, topics for historical study. Indeed, usually one cannot study the one without studying the other as well, and much of an historian's task consists of determining which is which.

3 I take the basic structure of the second decade of *Antiquities* to be as follows: Books 11–12—introduction (note the correspondence of the introduction of "servitude" at 11.2 to its end at 12.434); Books 13–14—Hasmonean history; Books 15–17—Herodian history; Books 18–20—Roman rule. See D. R. Schwartz 2020a.

4 On ancient Jewish memory of the Hasmoneans, such as it was, see Alon 1977: 1–17; Noam 2018; and D. R. Schwartz 2022: 39. On the medieval period, see Flusser 2009. On the modern revival of interest, see Don-Yehiya 1992.

5 See Kletter 2016.

6 For the Temple as the linchpin of the Holy Land, comparable to a king's palace in his capital city from which sovereignty extends to the borders of his land, and thus as that which made war with Rome inevitable, see D. R. Schwartz 2009: 391–394.

twice dates the outbreak of the final catastrophe in the peroration of Book 20 (§§257, 259), just as prominently as at *War* 2.284.

Thus, students of Christianity, of Judaism, and of the Roman Empire may all rightly come to *Antiquities* 18–20 in the expectation that these books will enrich their knowledge about those topics, which are, for the West, among the most fundamental legacies of antiquity.

II. Disappointment. Anyone who comes to *Antiquities* 18–20 with such high expectations is quite likely to be disappointed. As literature, these books give the impression of being only half-baked. Sometimes the words that come to mind are merely "pedestrian" or "boring"; other times, too often, it is rather a matter of "unclear," "confusing," or "sloppy."[7] And that means that even when his work contains material that is very welcome to the historian, too frequently it comes in a way that makes it difficult to understand with any precision, and too frequently it positively misleads us.

Too often, first of all, it appears, even at the most basic level, that materials have merely been slapped down one after the other. Take, for example, the following two passages:

(a) At 19.342, after reporting some humiliating interference by Marsus, governor of Syria: "Agrippa took that with disgruntlement: toward Marsus, on the one hand, he was henceforth hostile, and, on the other hand, taking away the high priesthood from Matthias, he appointed Elioneus, the son of Cantheras, in his stead."

(b) At 20.139, after reporting that Claudius enlarged Agrippa II's kingdom: "Upon receiving this gift from Caesar, Agrippa married off his sister Drusilla to Azizus, King of Emesa, who was willing to be circumcised."

Both passages, using standard Greek formulations, clearly read as if the openings (down to "disgruntlement" and "from Caesar," respectively) are the conditions for the continuation; the first uses μέν and δέ to make both moves appear to be expressions of the same disgruntlement, and the second binds the two statements together by using a participle in the first statement, leaving a finite verb only in the second.[8] That is, readers are clearly guided to infer that Agrippa's disgruntlement about Marsus's intervention explains not only his hostility toward Marsus but also his decision to switch high priests, and that Agrippa's matchmaking resulted, somehow, from Claudius's gift of territories to him. But however natural those readings are, in fact there seem to be no such connections, and certainly Josephus points to none. Readers must choose between assuming Josephus knew of and meant to allude to such connections but failed to explain them to his readers, or that Josephus was merely listing unconnected items that were more or less contemporary but failed to indicate that to his readers.

Or, similarly, take 20.103–104:

> King Herod of Chalcis, having removed Joseph the son of Camei from the high priesthood, gave the succession to the office to Ananias the son of Nedebeus in his stead. Cumanus came as the successor of Tiberius Alexander. Herod, the brother of the elder king Agrippa, died in the eighth year of the reign of Claudius Caesar, leaving three sons: Aristobulus (who had been born to him by his first wife) and—of Berenice, his brother's daughter—Berenicianus and Hyrcanus. Claudius Caesar gave his reign to the younger Agrippa.

---

7 The latter adjective for Josephus's work was popularized by Cohen. See Cohen 1979: esp. 233 ("inveterate sloppiness … the narrative is frequently confused, obscure, and contradictory") and 276 (index, s.v. "Josephus: inconsistency and sloppiness").

8 As for 19.342: it has finite verbs in both statements, but my sense is nonetheless like that of Niese (1890a: 268), who separated the clauses only with a comma.

First, anyone who reads this will probably feel somewhat thrown around, as the three sentences, with no coordination or transitions from one to the next, choppily record changes of personnel in three different spheres (high priesthood, Judean governorship, Herodian family). Worse, however, is the fact that—as is shown by my experience with many readers, with whom I have tried it out over the years—most people who read these lines think, or suspect, that Josephus is carefully distinguishing between two Herods: "King Herod of Chalcis" and "Herod, the brother of the elder king Agrippa." That understanding derives from the use of differential identifiers and makes ready sense to readers, given their knowledge that in royal dynasties it is common for different people to bear the same name and therefore differentiation is needed.

In fact, however, the two Herods are one and the same. There is no doubt that King Herod of Chalcis was Agrippa I's brother (as is plainly stated, *inter alia*, at 19.277, 338). This passage, as we have it, seems therefore to be a mechanical juxtaposition of excerpts from at least two sources: one that chronicles the history of the high priesthood (and terms Herod "king"),[9] and another one that deals with Herodian family history (and identifies Herod by his relationship to Agrippa). Between the excerpts from those sources, Josephus informs us about a new Roman governor; perhaps that too came from some source, perhaps from Josephus's own inquiries or memory (he was around ten or eleven when Cumanus arrived). Be the latter as it may, the fact that Josephus could offer us two data about Herod of Chalcis without juxtaposing them or even coordinating their nomenclature is impressive support for the characterization of his work, in these books, as "hodgepodge"; any student who submitted such work would be sent home to rewrite, or to look for some profession that would not entail composition.

Again, sometimes plain sloppiness is evident. Does anyone believe that Josephus, had he proofread *Ant.* 18.160–161 even once, would have left the switch from "Dicearcheia" to "Puteoli" without explaining to readers (as *Life* 16 shows he thought requisite!) that they are names, in Greek and Latin respectively, for the same city? Is it not likelier that he was splicing together, here, excerpts from two sources, one that used the Greek name and one the Latin name, and failed to iron out even this minor difference between them (an hypothesis that other problems with the story support, as we shall see below)? Or can anyone really believe that Josephus, had he proofread the end of *Ant.* 20, would have left essentially the very same story at 20.181 and then again at 20.207, without even adding "again"? Is it not likelier that he had a story and, after inserting it in one context, decided it belonged in the other and inserted it there but forgot to delete it from the first? Anyone with experience in writing knows this happens all the time, but careful writers do enough proofreading to eliminate the problem.

Or note, for a more extended example, Tiberius's remarkable flitting between this world and the next, which fills a large part of Book 18. After his death is first reported at 18.89, he is alive and well for negotiations with the Parthians at 18.96–105, whereafter we hear first of Philip's death in Tiberius's twentieth year (i.e., three years before Tiberius's death), and then comes a long story about Herod Antipas that ends at §124 when news of Tiberius's death arrives in Jerusalem—just in time to be followed, at §§143–204, by a long story that moves back and forth between Agrippa's relations with Tiberius and an account of Tiberius's habits as emperor. That, in turn, is followed, beginning at §205, by another long story, this time about Tiberius's attempts to arrange the choice of his successor as emperor, and after that

9 Phrased like other such snippets in these books, "AA took the high priesthood from XX and gave it to YY" (such as 18.26, 34–35; 19.297; 20.179, 213), and probably all taken by Josephus from the same chronicle and placed at the points in his narrative where he thought they belonged. See the note on "Theophilus" at 18.123.

we again read of Tiberius's death, finalized this time by his funeral (§§224–236). These reports come from several different contexts, some of them probably supplied by different sources, and Josephus makes no attempt to coordinate among them or to indicate that they involve flashbacks or parallel events.[10]

The case of Gaius is similar, for his death too is reported three times: once in the context of Tiberius's death (18.223), once in the context of Judean events (18.305–307), and once in the course of an intensely detailed report of his assassination (19.1–211). I see no explanation other than negligence that can explain why, although Josephus quite properly informed readers of the second report, at §307, that he will report Gaius's death in detail later in his work, he did not so inform readers of the first report. Indeed, I believe that readers of 18.223, which reports "But Gaius too died not long thereafter, after a conspiracy was formed against him," may justifiably understand it as Josephus's way of taking final leave of that topic, which, after all, is not part of the mandate of the author of a book about Jewish history. Is the case of 18.223 not like that of 15.105, for example, where Josephus refers to a detail of Armenian-Roman history that "happened later" than his story, it is not reported elsewhere in *Antiquities*, and no one expects it to be reported? But readers who take 18.223 to be Josephus's taking leave of a subject—the conspiracy to assassinate Gaius—that is not his business, any more than Armenian-Roman history is, for his mandate is the history of the Jews, will be very surprised when they discover that the first more than two hundred paragraphs of Book 19 are devoted to that conspiracy and assassination. If such a text were submitted by a student, we would probably infer both that when writing 18.223 he did not yet plan to add 19.1–211, and that after doing the latter he never reread Book 18.[11]

Or what would we say of a student who did something like what Josephus did when introducing Petronius at 19.301: Josephus explains to his readers that Petronius was the Roman governor of Syria, failing to add even the slightest hint to the fact that Petronius had figured at length in that very capacity, and heroically, and with regard to a similar issue (pagan desecration of a Jewish holy site), in Book 18 (§§261–309)?

If, in those cases, Josephus's inattention to editing caused the same events or individuals to be mentioned time and again without any coordination, in other cases it made for his leaving us with loose ends. This happens even concerning events that, as opposed to Roman-Armenian history and the assassination of Gaius, are clearly within Josephus's mandate. Thus, for example, anyone who reads at 18.4–6 that Judas of Galilee stirred up a rebellion expects to hear about the Roman reaction and how the rebellion was put down, but nothing at all is said about it, apart from a peripheral cross-reference more than two books later, at 20.102, that adds no information. Readers of Gamaliel's statement in the

---

10 Compare, for example, Scherberich 2001: 148: after referring to the contradictions and repetitions in *Antiquities* 19 that Josephus engendered by juxtaposing excerpts from different sources, Scherberich concludes that Josephus's "qualities as an author appear, from this point of view, to be rather few."

11 Similarly, when at *Ant*. 20.54 Josephus begins a long story of Artabanus II's flight from hostile satraps to refuge with Izates in Adiabene, it is surprising that he makes no cross-reference back to the very similar story at 18.99–100. And if, as appears to be likely (see the note on "if he could" at 20.54), the two events are in fact the same, then the failure at 18.99–100 to include a promise to tell

the detailed story later suggests the same as the failure of 18.233 to allude to 19.1–211: that Josephus depended on different sources for these different parts of his work and when writing the earlier passages was not aware of the later ones or, in any case, not disposed to undertake even the modicum of work needed to coordinate them. For a somewhat similar case see *Ant*. 12.127, where Josephus refers to Nicolaus's *Universal History* rather than to his own report (based on Nicolaus) at 16.27–61, along with Czajkowski and Eckhardt 2021: 75, n. 6. However, that case is not as egregious, for at *Ant*. 12.127 Josephus, seeking to bolster his own credibility, needs to refer to other authors, not to himself.

Acts of the Apostles (5:37), that Judas perished and his followers were scattered, who turn to Josephus to fill out the story, will be completely disappointed. Similarly, anyone who reads at *Ant.* 18.105 that Vitellius postponed his revenge against Herod Antipas until Gaius ascended to the imperial throne may rightly expect to read what Vitellius did then, but in fact there is no follow-up.

If with regard to the deaths of Tiberius and Gaius we can at least be sure that the multiple reports all refer to the same event, in some cases Josephus left his text (probably: his extracts from sources or summaries of them) in such a state that we cannot really be sure whether his different reports refer to different events or, rather, to the same one from different points of view. Thus, for example (one cited above for another reason), when Alexander sends Agrippa to Dicearcheia and promises him money there (18.160), but Agrippa instead goes to Puteoli (§161) and eventually gets the money from Antonia Minor (§164), should we wonder why Agrippa did not follow up on the original promise? Or should we rather infer that what we have are simply two descriptions of the same loan, for Puteoli is the Latin name of Dicearcheia and Alexander was Antonia's agent (19.276) (see the note on "Puteoli" at 18.161)? When Vitellius visits Jerusalem twice (18.90–95, 122–125) and, given the details in Josephus's stories, historians find it impossible to assign dates to the two visits, should that be accepted simply as another detail about antiquity that we cannot know? Or is it rather reason to conclude the two visits were one and the same, described from two points of view (see the note on "Judea" at 18.90)? When the Senate sends Claudius messengers and after they present their case they get no response and their departure is not reported (19.234–235), while a few paragraphs later, in the course of a story in which Agrippa I stars, we read that the Senate sent delegates and they do get a response and do depart (§§244–247), should we wonder what happened to the first delegates, or, rather, infer that Josephus had two sources about the same set of delegates (see the note on "bestowed it" at 19.235)?

Similar to such questions about "doublets," numerous other issues have to do with the order of events. Three examples: it appears that Josephus created a continuous story at 18.109–125 although some fifteen years went by between §112 and §113 (see the note on "John" at 18.116);[12] that he reversed the order of the two stories about Parthian Jewry that conclude Book 18 (see the note on "this tragedy" at 18.310); and that the story Josephus begins at 19.292 about Agrippa's return to Jerusalem in 41 CE should actually have been told in the middle of Book 18, for it refers to his return in 38 CE (see the note on "better" at 19.294).

Moreover, although in general it is clear that Josephus arranged his narrative chronologically, with "chapters" devoted to the successive rulers of Judea (see the table that precedes this Introduction), two editorial procedures of his often confuse readers, and that means Josephus failed to make his procedure clear. The two practices are (a) reflection of the passage of time, when no ruler is present in Judea, by inserting secondary materials, and (b) collection of secondary materials at the ends of chapters.

Sometimes the first practice creates no confusion—either because the material that is inserted takes up no historical time, or because it clearly belongs, chronologically, where it is. Thus, on the one hand, while Quirinius is busy, as it were, with administering the census and registration of property announced at 18.1–3, Josephus amuses us by describing the Jewish sects (§§11–25); when he finishes that, he explicitly reverts to the Quirinius story and

---

12 The case is similar to that at *Ant.* 13.254. There, however, Josephus actually adds in "immediately" (εὐθύς) to link, chronologically and causally, the death of Antiochus Sidetes in 129/128 BCE to a campaign of conquests that, we now know from archaeological evidence unavailable to Josephus (Barag 1992/93), began more than a decade and a half later.

even gives a date (18.26), and so readers easily understand that, chronologically, Josephus is back where he was before the excursus about the sects, which filled no historical time.[13] Similarly, the summary of the high-priesthood (20.224–251), which fills up most of the space between the announcements of Florus's appointment (§215) and his arrival (§252), is obviously a topical excursus that takes up no historical time.

Again, when Josephus announces at 20.197a that Festus died in office and so Nero sent Albinus to govern Judea, and then fills up the time until Albinus arrived with the story of Ananus b. Ananus's execution of James, that story builds on the fact that Albinus was on his way but had not yet arrived. That is, no confusion is caused, because readers correctly understand that the story relates to the point in time in which it is located.

In other cases, however, readers may not realize that they are reading "fillers" meant to reflect the time needed for a new governor's arrival. Here are two examples: the appointments of Pontius Pilate (18.35) and Felix (20.138) precede, respectively by twenty and twenty-two paragraphs, the accounts of their Judean governorships (18.55; 20.160). Although it is obvious that Josephus did not mean to indicate that all the events reported in those intervals happened while the new governors were on their way, scholars have all too often assumed they happened after the new governor was appointed—and then condemned Josephus for carelessness when it became apparent that that was not the case. Thus, scholars who assume (following 18.35) that Pilate was appointed in 26 CE first inferred that Tiberias was founded (as reported at §§36–38) after that date and then, when numismatic evidence made it clear that the date was several years earlier, complained about Josephus's negligence, just as they inferred the same from the report of Germanicus's death at §§53–54, since they knew, from Tacitus and other Roman sources, that he died in 19 CE.

Similarly, scholars have assumed that the stories that follow the report of Felix's appointment, stories that refer to Claudius's two last years (53–54 CE) and even give details about Nero's accession to the throne in 54/55 (see 20.138, 148, 152–153), continue the story from Felix's appointment. That is a natural assumption, and is a major part of the argument for dating Felix's appointment to 52 CE. However, that dating runs into a number of problems, including the fact that, since Josephus reports Felix's appointment of Ishmael b. Phiabi to the high priesthood only at §179, it forces us to conclude (a) that Josephus erred when he reported, at *Ant.* 3.320, that there was a high priest named Ishmael in the days of Claudius, (b) that after the death of Herod of Chalcis in 48, Agrippa II waited more than five years before exercising his right to appoint high priests, and (c) that when the high priest Ananias was sent to Rome for judgment, no high priest was appointed to replace him.[14] It is much easier to avoid all of those problems and infer that the fact that Josephus reported the events of Felix's governorship after reporting the death of Claudius and accession of Nero means no more than that he used an update about Roman history to fill in readers about something of the background of his story and allow them to "feel" the time that passed while the new protagonist of his main story, the new Roman governor of Judea, made his way to his post.

The other editorial practice is not unrelated: even when there is no evident delay between the appointment of a new governor and his arrival, Josephus likes to bunch, at the end of the chapter on a governor, or just before the final event of a governor's term, "external"

---

13 This case is like one pointed out by Villalba 1986: 171–172: after Vespasian's men start building boats at *War* 3.505, Josephus entertains us with a fifteen-paragraph geographical excursus about the region, which allows us, as it were, to feel the passage of time needed for the construction of the boats. Thereafter we are, accordingly, ready for his announcement, at §522, that the boats were now ready and the story can move forward.

14 See the note on "retinue of" at 20.131.

events (events pertaining to Herodians, high-priests, Parthians...) that happened during his tenure. It is as if, in his mind, the main chapter was about the governor, but before closing the chapter and moving on to the next one, on the next governor, he needed to catch up by reporting other interesting events during the same period of time, often introduced as "at this time" or the like.[15] The result can be confusing, in at least two ways: (a) it leads unwary readers to infer that such external events happened only toward the end, or at the very end, of the governor's term of office, although in fact they may have happened at any earlier time during that period; (b) it leads unwary readers to infer that the external events that are bunched together happened at the same time, and that can lead to thoughts about the causal relationship between them, but in fact they may each have transpired at some different point in the governor's term.

Thus, for example, between Josephus's first three stories about Pontius Pilate's governorship of Judea (18.55–59, 60–62, 63–64) and the fourth and final one (18.85–89) he tells us about scandals at Rome "at that time" (§65, καὶ ὑπὸ τοὺς αὐτοὺς χρόνους). Similarly, just after the first two stories about Fadus's tenure as governor (20.1–5, 6–14), Josephus tells us about Herod of Chalcis's handling of the high priesthood "at that time" (κατὰ τὸν χρόνον ἐκεῖνον, §15) and then offers a long story (20.17–96) about the conversion to Judaism of the Adiabenian royal family, a story which, he assures us at its opening, happened "at that time" (κατὰ τοῦτον δὲ τὸν καιρόν, §17). Only after that story is completed does Josephus revert, at 20.97, to Fadus's governorship in Judea, reporting one more story about him before summarizing the chapter at §99: "These, then, were the events that happened to the Judeans while Cuspius Fadus was governor."

In neither of those cases, as others, should we assume that Josephus meant to date the external events specifically to the end of the governor's term of office in Judea. All too often, however, scholars do make such assumptions. Thus, for example, if above we saw that the location of *Ant.* 20.179 has led scholars to infer that Agrippa II appointed Ishmael b. Phiabi only after Claudius died and Nero succeeded him, now I will add that, since that appointment and its immediate aftermath is the last story in Josephus's chapter about Felix, it is common to conclude that Ishmael was appointed only in 59 CE, the last year of Felix's tenure as governor.[16] That conclusion exacerbates both problems mentioned above with regard to the 54 CE terminus post quem for Ishmael's appointment, but the problem evaporates if we realize that all Josephus meant by "at this time" (20.179) was "sometime during Felix's governorship."

In sum, while we can often determine the relative or absolute chronology of the events reported in these three books, and often we may even infer, or generously choose to assume, that Josephus was not confused about the chronology, his arrangement of the material is often confusing. If, for some prominent examples, Otto (1913: 186–187, cf. 180–181, n. *) opined that Josephus's use of "at this time" was often no more than a *Verlegenheitsphrase* (a phrase used by an author who was in the dark and could not be more specific), Hölscher (1916: 1983) concluded that the chronological order of the stories is "often very imperfect" (*vielfach sehr mangelhaft*) and Stern could roundly conclude that cases in *Antiquities* 18 in which early and late are reversed demonstrate "Josephus's failure to interweave his sources properly from a chronological point of view" (Stern 1991: 491–492), Josephus cannot be acquitted

---

15 Josephus's location of details about the Herodians at 20.139–147, between his reference to Claudius's twelfth year at §138 and his conclusion of Claudius's story beginning in §148, is a variation of this same practice.

16 So, for example, *HJP* 2.231 and VanderKam 2004: 463–475. For my response to the latter, see D. R. Schwartz 2024a.

of serious negligence. Whether that negligence was in the way he structured his narrative or "merely" in his failure to make his procedures clear to his readers, it is disappointing. As was observed, concerning both points of view we have taken, by a scholar whose study focused on the order of events in *Antiquities* 18, this product of Josephus's labor "ne permet de reconnaître ni un grand écrivain ni un historien capable de dominer parfaitement son sujet" (Giet 1956: 247).

That conclusion, which is interesting and inviting for "detective historians"[17] who seek to dissect Josephus's narratives and discover his original sources, and are thus happy to learn that he left them without too much retouching, has broader implications. A clear and prominent case in point is supplied by an aspect of the debate concerning the authenticity of the most famous passage in these books, namely the *Testimonium Flavianum* about Jesus at *Ant.* 18.63–64. As was argued by such great scholars as von Gutschmid, Niese, and Norden, the fact that the very next story opens at 18.65 with "Around those same times *another* terrible thing caused a tumult (ἕτερόν τι δεινὸν ἐθορύβει) for the Jews" indicates the current text of the *Testimonium* is not authentic, for—as opposed to the two stories that precede it and the three that follow it (§§55–59, 60–62, 65–80, 81–84, 85–89)—it includes no reference to anything "terrible" or any "tumult."[18] In response to that argument (as presented by Niese), however, one of the foremost modern scholars of ancient Christianity, Adolf von Harnack, was willing to defend the authenticity of the received text by declaring not only that the style of the Testimonium is "neutral" (i.e., does not point to Christian editing) but also that the editing of the last books of the *Antiquities* is so negligent and unsatisfying that we must ignore all arguments from style.[19]

Sometimes we can, it seems, be fairly confident in guessing the processes that led Josephus to leave us unsatisfactory prose. For a simple case, note the reference to "Tiberius Caesar" at 18.166, which readers who are not asleep should find jarring, for after the emperor's formal introduction to the story as "Tiberius Caesar" at §161 (after he had not been mentioned since §146) he was referred to either as plain "Tiberius" (§§162, 164, 165) or "Caesar" (§§163, 164), or simply assumed as the unnamed subject of a verb in the third person singular (§162). Why in the world should the end of §165, "his friendship with Tiberius was no longer inhibited," be followed by "Thereafter Tiberius Caesar (Τιβέριος ὁ Καῖσαρ) associated his grandson with Agrippa, urging him always to accompany him on his outings"?! The answer would seem to be that the present text was added secondarily: that at first it was not in Josephus's draft, but when he found later in his source, at §188, a reference to instructions that Tiberius had once given Agrippa, and realized that they had not been mentioned, he went back and inserted a reference to them at the appropriate place, §166. In doing so, however, Josephus failed, as so often happens, to formulate the new text in a way that sat comfortably in its surrounding context; frequently, as here, the roughness comes in the naming of individuals, for the original text used full names, short names, and pronouns naturally, but that was disturbed by the insertion. Who of us has never done such a thing, only to discover it upon proofreading, or to regret having missed it when seeing it in print?

Or, for a more complicated example, note the way Josephus concludes his account of Albinus at 20.215:

---

17 To borrow a phrase from Rajak 2002: xi, who attributed it to Mason.

18 See von Gutschmid 1893: 352–354; Niese 1894: iv–v; and Norden 1913a: 638–644.

19 "Der Stil [of 18.63–64] ist so 'neutral' und die Ausarbeitung der letzten Bücher der 'Altertümer' ist so flüchtig und unbefriedigend, daß man von stilistischen- und Kompositionsargumenten abzusehen gezwungen ist" (Harnack 1913: 1046). Concerning this generalization about the last books of *Antiquities*, even prior to Books 18–20, see below, at nn. 55–58.

When Albinus heard that Gessius Florus was arriving as his successor, he—desiring to be thought someone who had provided something [beneficial] for the Jerusalemites—brought out all the prisoners and ordered the execution of all of those who were clearly worthy of death, but freed, in return for money, those who had been imprisoned only on some minor and incidental charge. The result was that the prison was purged of prisoners, but the land was filled with brigands.

As Shaye Cohen noted, this passage is "peculiarly ambiguous or self-contradictory."[20] If Albinus freed only prisoners who had been imprisoned on some "minor and incidental charge," which means there was hardly reason to imprison them (cf. *Life* 13!), how could it happen that the land consequently became filled with brigands?![21] And if the first sentence praises Albinus for punishing those deserving of death but releasing those who were charged with only minor crimes, why sully his image both by saying he did it in order "to be thought" a positive ruler, which seems to imply that he in fact was not (an assessment that in fact is explicit at §§253–254), and by reporting, so it seems, that even the minor offenders were released only in return for bribes?[22]

Here too, as with the case of the "two" Herods, it appears that Josephus's text reflects failure to coordinate between input from two different sources. In that case, however, they merely used different nomenclature; in the present case they pulled in opposite directions. On the one hand, Josephus's account of Albinus, in *Antiquities*, focuses on Jewish villains (corrupt and self-seeking high priests; rebels), and for the most part, beginning with the very positive opening (§204), portrays the governor as dealing with them responsibly, as best he could, although he was overcome by the machinations of wicked Jews, be they high priests or Sicarii. In *War*, however, Josephus had portrayed Albinus terribly, and, quite artistically used that portrait of his tenure as part of the pronounced deterioration of Judean-Roman relations in the decade prior to the outbreak of the rebellion in 66 CE: the extended syncrisis at *War* 2.271–277 proclaims that Festus was just fine, Albinus was terrible but at least tried to keep his crimes secret, but Florus was terrible and actually paraded his crimes. All we need to suppose, in order to understand what happened at *Ant.* 20.215, is that Josephus, when composing this part of *Antiquities*, retained, in his memory, or perhaps even on his desk,[23] his earlier account of Albinus. If so, then by the time he got to the end of Albinus's term of office, at §215, he was on the verge of that extended syncrisis, which is a nice text, the type Josephus would want to reuse[24]—as we see he did, at *Ant.* 20.252–254, when he reverts to his narrative after digressing about the high priesthood. That syncrisis, however, requires readers to assume that Albinus was a villain. Accordingly, if Josephus's preceding narrative had portrayed Albinus as a good guy who did what he could in the face of Jewish villains, now Josephus had to do something, at least superficially, to make the transition to the opposite image. The blatant cacophony within §215 is, apparently, the result.

20 Cohen 1979: 62.

21 For the heinousness of brigands, in the Roman world and especially for Josephus in *Ant.* 20, see the note on "brigands" at 18.7.

22 Or if in fact Josephus means not bribes but, rather, the commutation of other penalties into fines, why did he not make that clear?

23 For a similar issue concerning *Ant.* 18.271//*War* 2.196 and *Ant.* 20.112/*War* 2.227, see Cohen 1979: 59–60.

24 For Josephus's use of this type of tripartite syncrisis, cf. *War* 7.262–270 and *Life* 32–41. As for reusing catchy formulations, cf. the note on "earlier said" at 20.110. In general, on Josephus's use of *War* as a guide when composing *Antiquities*, see Krieger 2002.

Finally, in this list of Josephus's failings as a composer when using his sources, note that *Antiquities* 18–20 have, among Josephus's books, more than their fair share of passages that exhibit the most "grotesque" example of Josephus's enslavement to his sources: promises to return to subjects to which, in fact he does not return and we can hardly imagine that he planned to return to them. Such promises are best understood as statements of the sources he was using.[25] True, it is *possible* that, when completing *Antiquities* 19, Josephus thought his account in *Antiquities* 20—which in fact goes no further than 66 CE—would include, as he promises at 19.366, a report of Vespasian's eventual disposition of the Palestinian auxiliary units after becoming emperor in 69 CE. But even that is not very likely; surely Josephus will have known by then, at the end of Book 19, that he was planning to close his narrative at the eve of the rebellion. Moreover, it appears to be downright impossible to imagine that, when composing the midst of *Antiquities* 20, he thought he would later relate, in *Antiquities*, events pertaining to the history of Herodians at least as late as the eruption of Vesuvius in 79 CE—as he promised he would in two back-to-back passages full of malicious gossip about Agrippa II and his sisters (20.144, 147).[26] The notion that he did intend to relate those events would require us to assume that, as late as the middle of *Ant.* 20, he did not plan to finish the work where he did, and where it made sense: at the outbreak of the rebellion of 66 CE, to which he had already devoted a detailed monograph. When the unlikelihood of that assumption is put together with the facts that those passages' vicious attitude vis-à-vis Agrippa II and his family is quite exceptional for Josephus, and that the story that ends at 20.144 is introduced at §141, into the midst of Josephus's main narrative, by two typical seaming devices,[27] it is difficult to avoid the conclusion that he took over the texts more or less wholesale, together with their attitudes and internal cross-references, from some other source, where they were at home.

One may wonder why Josephus left his work this way, with such manifold evidence of poor editing. Perhaps, as Thackeray thought, Josephus, who was born in 37 and nearing the age of sixty when he completed *Antiquities*, was simply tired.[28] Perhaps he viewed his text as something of a first draft, into which he roughly slapped his materials (what we used to

---

25 Drüner (1896: 92–94) lists eighteen passages in *Antiquities* that refer to non-existent future discussions, apart from those that refer to another composition that Josephus hoped to write (see the note on "laws" at 20.268). Of those eighteen, six are in Books 18–20 (19.366; 20.48, 53, 96, 144, 147). For an application of the theory that Josephus took over such internal cross-references from his sources, in which they were valid, see Büchler 1896/97 and Scott 1897. For the characterization of that theory as "grotesque," see Petersen 1958: 267. (It would be against the nature of a source-critic to suppress the hypothesis that Petersen took that adjective from a study on the same topic that he cites on the same page: Täubler's complaint [1916: 213] that Niese, in rejecting the hypothesis that Josephus's unverifiable references to what he wrote "elsewhere" in fact refers to a lost work of his, and positing in its stead that Josephus merely used such references as a convenient way to conclude discussions, avoided an improbable solution to the problem by suggesting, instead, one that is *grotesk*.)

26 Of course, it is is possible that Josephus thought he would write about those later events in another work.

But the references at 20.144, 147 read like internal cross-references (like our "see below"); when Josephus wants to express the hope to write a future composition, he does so explicitly (see the references in the note on "laws" at 20.268). Moreover, the list of planned works Josephus gives at 20.267–268 includes only two: one on details of Jewish practice and one that would "cursorily" update his *War* with "what has happened to us until the present day." Any discussion of the question, whether Josephus is dependent at §§144, 147 on some other source, must choose between assuming that he planned to detail in that cursory update the marriages of Agrippa I's daughters and their offspring, on the one hand, and building on the exceptionally hostile tone of these passages and their literary isolation, on the other.

27 Namely, "not long thereafter" and "under the following circumstances." Both are common in *Antiquities* 18 and 20. On them, see, for example, the first and last notes on 18.39; D. R. Schwartz 1981/82 and Williamson 1977.

28 Thackeray 1929: 106–107. Thackeray (1869–1930) was himself nearing sixty when he gave those lectures.

call "dumping index cards") in the hope of later returning to the materials, ironing them out and polishing them. It does not really matter. It is not our job to understand Josephus, nor is he waiting for us to give him grades for his work.[29] Rather, we have to know how to read his work and make the most, for our purposes, of what he left us.

III. Nevertheless. Despite all that has been said, things are not so bad; the cup that is half-empty is also half-full. From the point of view of history, Josephus's frequent failure to intervene in his sources can be a boon; and from the point of view of literature, he actually did more and better than one might think.

For those of us whose interests are mainly historical, namely, we wish to know what happened in the places and times described by Josephus and so we want to know how to derive reliable information from *Antiquities* 18–20, the fact that Josephus intervened so little into his sources is actually an advantage. For if, as it seems, Josephus used Roman material about the Jews of Rome, Roman material about Roman history and Parthian history, Jewish material from across the Euphrates about the Jews of Parthia and Adiabene, Herodian material about Herod Antipas, Agrippa, and their families, a Jewish source that was hostile to Agrippa II, reports by Roman governors, a high-priestly chronicle, and Roman material about the death of Gaius and the rise of Claudius to the imperial throne, then, to the extent he left them relatively undigested, his work is akin to an anthology of different testimonies and we thus have before us the reports of witnesses who were closer to the events they describe than Josephus was. To overstate the case in order to clarify it: if we can identify material Josephus took from his sources, we can hope to cover our desktops with the same materials and then to redo his work ourselves. In doing that, which obviously entails a measure of uncertainty, we can strive to evaluate the sources and put their testimonies together in the ways that seem to us, based on the information *we* have (which is often more, and better, than what Josephus had), to be closest to "how things really were."

Thus, for example, if today we know—from literary sources, inscriptions, coins, and excavations—more than Josephus did about the state of Parthia in the decades following 37 CE, we can depend on that knowledge, as scholars do, to reverse the order of the two stories that conclude *Antiquities* 18; see the note on "tragedy" at 18.310. Or, for another example, if we can read Tacitus, as Josephus could not, and so we know (as Josephus may not have known) that the Roman events reported in 18.65–84 occurred in 19 CE, we can use that, one way or another, in deciding what to do with Josephus's dating of Pontius Pilate's term of office; see the note on "same times" at 18.65.

The catch, or the challenge, of that type of work, is created by the condition stated above: "to the extent he left them relatively undigested." It is against the assumption, that that condition is fulfilled, that much of recent scholarship on Josephus has focused. Although above I gave several examples that support the notion that, indeed, Josephus did little with his sources apart from juxtaposing extracts from them, leaving him something of a compiler, and if in the last paragraph I pointed out how advantageous that is for historians of the period, much of modern scholarship has been devoted to rehabilitating Josephus as an author. And to the extent he was, then much of our confidence in our ability to get behind his work to his sources, and then use them independently, will be undermined. It is with serious consideration of this tension, between Josephus as a compiler and Josephus as an

---

29 For discussion of an egregious case in *Ant.* 14 (§§74–78) and the possible explanations, see D. R. Schwartz 2013: 13, 18–22.

author, that all work on these books, and on the history they report, must proceed. In Part V of this Introduction we will revert to Josephus's use of his sources in more detail.

Indeed, there is much in *Antiquities* 18–20 that, contrary to the examples assembled above, shows Josephus as an author. This applies to all levels of the book. First, at the most local level, within units, Josephus often strove to create flow and unity in his narrative. Note, for some examples:

a.   The repetition of virtually the same terms at 18.2 (ἀποτιμησόμενος ... ἀποδωσόμενος) and 18.26 (ἀποδόμενος ... ἀποτιμήσεων), where the latter, as a *Wiederaufnahme*, signals to readers that the story is reverting to its main line.

b.   In the account of the three Jewish sects, the fact that Josephus introduces each with a statement about its λόγος (18.12, 16, 18) lends the discussion a unified character, while the fact that the Fourth Philosophy (§§23–25) is not said to have had one functions as part of Josephus's case that it is not legitimate.

c.   Similarly, at 18.171 and 18.175 Josephus uses ὄχλος in order to bind up the case at hand with the parable illustrating it.

d.   The exchange at 18.264–265 between Petronius, the Roman governor of Syria charged with erecting a statue of Gaius in the Temple of Jerusalem, on the one hand, and Judean protesters, on the other, uses similar expressions to paint polarity. Namely, when the Jews assert that they cannot violate the laws for which their ancestors had voted ("raised their hands," χειροτονέω), Petronius responds that he cannot violate that upon which the emperor has "voted" (προαναψηφίζω), thus making the confrontation between the two sides totally diametric.

e.   Similarly, a little later Josephus uses the same verb to clarify that Petronius finally realized that his own need to "take care of" (διακονέω) the emperor's order (§§262, 265, 269, 277 [bis]) was met head-on by the Judeans' insistence upon "taking care" (διακονουμένον) of virtue (§280). Accordingly, and in deference to the Jews' sincerity, Petronius undertook not only to evade his orders but also, in the very last word of the episode, to "take care" (διακονεῖν) of everything for the Judeans (§283).

f.   At 19.79–80, Chaerea's move from "do we not see" (οὐχ ὁρῶμεν) in his first speech to "do you not see" in the second (οὐχ ὁρῶμεν ... οὐχ ὁρᾶτε) hints heavily, by dissociating himself from his audience, at his willingness to act alone, if needed. This hint then becomes explicit at the end of the second speech (§83), where he clearly distinguishes himself from his audience (ἐγω ... ὑμῶν).

g.   Note the humor at 18.89: Pilate "hurried" (ἠπείγετο) to Rome, but Tiberius "beat him" (φθάνει) to the finish line by dying.

h.   The ironic use of ἠνείχετο at 19.13 answers that of ἠνείχοντο at the opening of the preceding paragraph (§12), thus rubbing in the contrast between what the people "was compelled" to endure and the travesties of justice that Gaius, as it were, "was compelled" to commit. Similarly, at §§25–26, Josephus uses the same verb to contrast Gaius, who refused "to heed" the people, to the latter, who had "to heed" him.

i.   Josephus opens both 19.31 and 19.32 with the same verb, παρίστατο, prefacing it at §32 with καί ("also"), to make it clear that one impetus (Gaius's demeaning behavior) engendered two results: not only rage but also courage "came over" Chaerea.

j.   Frequently Josephus uses the same (or basically the same) term at the introduction of a story and at its end in order to indicate that what came in between was the details. See, for example, 19.66, 69 (προκαταθέμενος χάριν ... χάριτος κατάθεσιν), 19.162, 165 (ἁρπά-ζεται ...ἥρπαστο), 19.148, 151 (διασαφοῦντες ... σαφοῦς).

k.   At 19.230 the Senate instructs its messengers to call upon Claudius not to act "drunkenly," just as at 19.232 it asks them to relate to the possibility that Claudius will not be "sobered" by Gaius's death. The Senate's repeated employment of the same image lends unity to its appeal to Claudius.

Next, units of text are often coordinated in ways that give them meaning in their larger contexts. Sometimes this is only a matter of a word here or there at the opening of a paragraph. So, for example, when 18.39 opens a story about the death of a Parthian king (τελευτᾷ δὲ καὶ Φραάτης ὁ Παρθυαίων βασιλεὺς κατὰ τοῦτον τὸν χρόνον), the καί ("there *also* died") serves, apparently, to coordinate his death with that of Augustus, mentioned a few lines earlier (§32).[30] Similarly, the very next story, after the Parthian one ends at 18.52, opens at §53 with "There *also* died Antiochus, the king of Commagene" (ἐτελεύτησεν δὲ καὶ ὁ τῆς Κομμαγηνῆς βασιλεὺς Ἀντίοχος). This all gives readers a sense of continuity. Similarly, after 19.279–291 present two edicts by Claudius, Josephus tells three stories about Agrippa, and each of them begins by summarizing the preceding story: just as §292 summarizes the edicts before telling the first story in §§292–296, §297 summarizes that first story before telling the second in §§297–298, and §299 summarizes that second story before offering the third in §§299–311. These transitions create the impression, at least, that there is some meaningful relationship between the events; we are not just reading a concatenation of snippets.

Other times, Josephus uses a striking term to draw texts together. Thus, for example, anyone who wonders why Josephus, who wanted to state at 18.18 that the Essenes *consider* souls to be immortal, literally wrote, instead, that they "*make* souls immortal" (ἀθανατίζουσιν δὲ τὰς ψυχὰς) should realize that he does it in order to mirror his preceding statement about the Sadducees' doctrine (§16), which "makes souls disappear together with bodies" (τὰς ψυχὰς ὁ λόγος συναφανίζει τοῖς σώμασι).[31] The fact that both verbs colorfully refer, literally, to doing, rather than to believing, draws the two passages together—just as, in the same context, Josephus's use of another rare word, περιμάχητον, at both 18.12 and 18.18, compares what the Pharisees and the Essenes, respectively, thought it to be "worth struggling for."

Sometimes Josephus is even more heavy-handed. For example, when 20.105–112, 113–117, and 118–124 present, back to back, three violent episodes in the days of Cumanus, the second is introduced by "Their first mourning had not even ended when another descended upon them" and the third by "There was *also* [an outbreak of] hostility (γίνεται δὲ καὶ ... ἔχθρα) between the Samaritans and the Jews ... "—and readers are thus made to realize quite clearly (as noted by Norden 1913a: 642), that they are reading an integrated text with a theme that the times are very troubled, not just an assemblage of diverse reports. Other times, Josephus uses a leitmotif, which is not limited to the transitional lines, to impart unity to a sequence of paragraphs. The most famous example, alluded to above (at n. 18) in connection with the *Testimonium Flavianum*, comes in his account of Pilate, which consists of a series of episodes all characterized, whether by verb (θορυβέω) or noun (θόρυβος), as "tumults" (18.58, 62, 65, 85, 88). Josephus's concern to impart unity to this chapter is evident in the fact that the use of such terminology for two of the events, those in Rome (at §§65 [ἐθορύβει], 85 [θορύβου]), seems to be quite artificial.

But not only adjacent stories can be linked together this way. Josephus also uses, at times, common motifs that link together episodes that are far from one another, and they too give readers the satisfactory impression that they are reading a composition and not just an anthology. So, for example, readers of *Antiquities* 18 are offered, at wide intervals (§§42, 241–246, 360–362), three cases of the same stock figure: a nagging wife who moves the plot forward by pushing her husband further than he wants to go. Similarly, allusions to the biblical story of Joseph are applied to Agrippa in the middle of Book 18 (§§195–201, 237) and then

---

30 This would be all the more natural if the intervening section, §§36–38, on Tiberias, was added later. See the notes on "rabble" at 18.37 and on "also" at 18.39.

31 My thanks to Yair Furstenberg, who pointed out this example.

again at the end of *Ant.* 19 (§§319–322), and readers who recognize and appreciate them are thereby reassured that they are reading a single work, no matter how much it wanders and how disparate its themes and sources. And although, as noted above, Josephus seems to have reversed the historical order of his two Parthian stories that conclude Book 18, at least he was careful enough to both open the first and close the second with references to Nehardea and Nisibis (§§311–312//379), thus giving at least the impression of a complete unit.

Finally, at the macro-level, note that by opening Book 18 with a rebellion that allows Josephus to dilate on the evils of rebellion and point toward the one that, sixty years later, would bring about the destruction of the Temple (§§7–9), and by ending the book's prologue by dating that final rebellion specifically to the days of Florus (18.25), with whose advent the story of Book 20 ends (20.252–258), Josephus creates a pair of brackets that frame Books 18–20: at the outset they give readers a notion of where this final section of the *Antiquities* is to go, and at the end they indicate to readers that they have arrived, "a sense of an ending."[32] And Josephus does that thematically as well: if in the opening paragraphs of Book 18 he points especially to innovation concerning Jewish traditions (τῶν πατρίων καίνισις) as that which brings about culpability and destruction (§9), he reverts to the same claim at the very end of the narrative in *Antiquites* 20 (§216), where Agrippa II was convinced that innovation (καινοποιεῖν) in the Temple cult was a good thing but in fact all that he did was contrary to the ancestral laws (πάντα δ' ἦν ἐναντία ταῦτα τοῖς πατρίοις νόμοις) and therefore "it was impossible that judgment not be imposed" (20.216–218). Josephus's reversion to his opening theme announces to readers, in so many words, that the work's sorry tale has come to its conclusion.

Indeed, the three books seem to be organized in a way that is meant to give meaning to the sequence: if Book 18 depicts the inception of Roman rule in Judea, bringing it down to 41; and Book 20 depicts the continuation of Roman rule from 44 and brings it down to the onset of the catastrophe in 66; Book 19, which interrupts the story, creates some tension by pointing to ways not taken. Namely, if Books 18 and 20 tell the story of the troubles of the Roman province of Judea under the Roman Empire, Book 19 raises the possibilities that Rome might revert from empire to republic and that Judea might revert from province to autonomous kingdom. In the end, however, neither of those happened: whatever the assassins of Gaius wanted, the army saw to the preservation of the empire; and Agrippa I's kingdom did not last more than a few years. Thus, Books 18–20 tell a story from beginning to end, but the end is separated from the beginning by a diversion, Book 19, that creates some tension by suggesting that things could have been otherwise but explains, in the end, why they were not. That is a clear structure, one that readers can well understand, and one which continues to interest readers today—who continue to wonder and to debate whether the story of *Antiquities* 18–20, that is, the story of Roman direct rule of Judea, which began in 6 CE and engendered the catastrophe of 70 CE, could have ended otherwise.[33] With all the work's shortcomings, recognition for this basic achievement should not be denied Josephus.

---

32 He also reminds readers of the same trajectory by prominently referring to Florus again at the very end of Book 19. For other ways in which Josephus adumbrates the end, see the note on "the" at 20.184. More generally on Josephus's somewhat teleological presentation of events, in *War* as well, which fosters the tendency to think the catastrophe was inevitable, see Bilde 1979 and esp. Mclaren 1998.

33 See, for example, Goodman 2007a; S. Schwartz 2009/10 and idem 2014: 76–81; Mason 2016c: 199–280; Grabbe 2021: 384–386.

IV. **Intended Readership.** More than any other books of *Antiquities*, Books 18–20 raise the question of Josephus's intended readership. According to common wisdom, *Antiquities* was meant for non-Jewish readers, and, in general, that is surely correct.[34] It conforms to statements made by Josephus in the prologue to the work (see esp. 1.5, 9, and 10–17, where he compares his project to that of the Jews who translated the Torah for Ptolemy Philadelphus), and at 16.174 and in the work's conclusion (20.262), where he explicitly states his work is addressed to the Greeks, and anyway it is clear that a work of which the first half is a Greek paraphrase of the Jews' sacred scripture was not meant for Jews. Indeed, just as various other parts and aspects of *Antiquities* point to non-Jewish readers,[35] so too there is much in our three books that does that, and points, in fact, specifically to Roman readers. Thus, for example, when at 18.53–54 Josephus gives a brief account of Germanicus's mission to the East and his assassination there by Piso (§§53–54), he apparently saw no need to identify Germanicus or Piso. It is obvious that his purpose was simply to make Roman readers, who were familiar with that story, feel at home and to supply them with a point of reference that would allow them to realize when, in their own history, there transpired the events of Judean history that Josephus is about to recount. So too, when Josephus reports that an owl appeared over Agrippa I's head and takes the trouble of pointing out its Latin name was "bubo" (*Ant.* 18.195), it is clear that he is thinking of Roman readers. It is Roman readers who will know that the appearance of a bubo was, for such great men as Crassus, Julius Caesar, and Augustus, a portent of coming catastrophe,[36] and so its appearance over Agrippa's head—which his German fellow prisoner explained (18.197–201) to be a good sign the first time but a portent of Agrippa's death the next time (as it was at 19.346)—will suggest to them such associations with regard to the Judean king.

Indeed, more generally, there are passages in which it appears clear that the point of view is plainly Roman. Note, for example, that when Josephus refers at 18.51 and 18.53 to Parthian delegations that were "sent up" or "sent" he does not bother, in either case, to add "to Rome"; nor does he do so in the reference at 18.171 to embassies that might "come up." Where else would anyone want to send a delegation?! And who but Romans would be interested in the detailed account of Tiberius's attempted machinations and Gaius's succession to the imperial throne in Book 18 and, all the more so, in the lengthy accounts of the conspiracy to kill Gaius, and of Claudius's rise to the throne, that take up so much of Book 19?

Nevertheless, these three books do supply plenty of reason to think that Josephus, whether as an author or anthologizer, was also thinking of Jewish readers (or, less charitably, that he sometimes forgot that he meant to be thinking of non-Jewish readers). This is, perhaps, clearest in his allusions to biblical stories: the abovementioned use of the Joseph story with regard to Agrippa I at 18.195–201, 237 and 19.319–322, his playing with the Esther story at 18.289–301, and various biblical allusions in the Mesopotamian story that begins at 18.310. Given the clear fact that "the translation of the Holy Scriptures into Greek made

34 See esp. Mason 1998b; Feldman 2000: 397–398, n. 576; Höffken 2007; Pummer 2009: 62–64. True, some of them leave open some possibility that Josephus secondarily imagined Jewish readers too (and Feldman's note is on *Ant.* 4.197, where Josephus apparently says that), and Troiani 1986, S. Schwartz (1990: 177, 198), Sterling 1992: 298–308, and Huitink and van Henten 2009 urge much more openness concerning this issue. Nevertheless, with regard to the *Antiquities*, van Henten (2018: 127) correctly

observes that "The ongoing debate about this tends to lead to a consensus that this audience consisted primarily of the contemporary cultural elite in Rome" (van Henten 2018: 127). See also Mason 2005b, which argues the same for Josephus's *War*.

35 For a survey of these data, see Höffken 2007: 334–335.

36 See the note on "bubo" at 18.195.

no impression whatever in the Greek world, since in the whole of Greek literature there is no indication that the Greeks read the Bible before the Christian period,"[37] these all point to the expectation of Jewish readers, who would appreciate the allusions. So do various formulations that take for granted knowledge of details of Jewish law, such as 18.93, which, in the context of referring to the purity of the high priest's vestments, mentions that the storage room was built of stone, a detail that would mean nothing to non-Jewish readers; 18.136, where Josephus complains that Herodias married her first husband's brother *while the former was still alive*—a point that is otiose for readers who do not realize that Josephus is alluding to the biblical rules that forbid a woman from entering into such a relationship unless she is the childless *widow* of the first husband, in which case she is *required* to marry her late husband's brother (Deut 25:5–10; *Ant.* 4.254–256); and 19.294, where Josephus reports that that Agrippa "shaved" numerous Nazirites, without explaining what "Nazirites" are or that they are forbidden to cut their hair,[38] and without explaining that the verb, a literal translation of a Hebrew idiom, actually means that he financed their sacrifices so they could be allowed, finally, to be released from their vows and, therefore, to shave.[39]

But Josephus's orientation toward Jewish readers is also clear in the way that, when moving toward the end of his work and describing events of his own day as an adult in Jerusalem, he rewrites his narratives in *War*, about Felix and Albinus, in a way that moves the focus away from blaming Rome for sending corrupt governors who provoked the rebellion. Rather, Josephus blames the Jews for having brought on the catastrophe themselves, by their sinfulness. In doing so, Josephus, although writing as best he could as Flavius Josephus of Rome, clearly takes his place as part of the Judaic and indeed biblical historiographical tradition, comparable to other Jews of his day, and later, who contemplated the catastrophe and blamed it on Jewish sinfulness.[40] True, such preaching could have a welcome implication for a Roman audience, insofar as a Jewish proclamation that the Romans had done the Jewish God's work apparently entails the conclusion that Jews (should) accept Roman rule. However, it also undercut the Roman victory by implying that without the Jewish deity's support, the Romans could not and would not have been victorious.[41] Hence, the primary audience for such reflections on the reasons for the catastrophe will have been a Jewish one. Thus, although Josephus addressed his *Antiquities* mainly to non-Jews and specifically to Romans, by far not everything need be pushed into that mold—and whether we think that means that Josephus was not up to writing a book with a consistent orientation, or rather thought, like Emerson, that he need not be bound by the small-minded hobgoblin of consistency, the result, for those who want to know how to read the book, is the same.

---

37 So Tcherikover 1957: 177. So too, especially with regard to Romans, Radin 1917/18. For some details, see Stern, *GLAJJ* 1.361–362 and D. R. Schwartz 2008: 85, n. 194.

38 For both points, contrast *Ant.* 4.72: "all those—who are called 'Nazirites'—who have consecrated themselves by vowing to abstain from cutting their hair and from wine …" It is difficult to imagine that, when writing 19.294 without any such explanations, Josephus thought he could depend on readers to remember that reference to "Nazirites" (the only other time the term appears in his corpus) fifteen books earlier.

39 On these three examples, see the notes ad locc.

40 For a survey of such responses in apocalyptic and pseudepigraphic literature, see K. R. Jones 2011. On rabbinic literature, see Klawans 2010b.

41 This is also the case for the basic story in *War*, in which the Roman victories in the north (Gamala), the center (Jerusalem), and the south (Masada) were all by virtue of divine intervention (*War* 4.76; 6.252; 7.318); in the first and third cases the intervention was demonstratively of the very same type (a sudden, and catastrophic, change of the wind's direction). This fits in quite well with traditional Jewish theodicy but competes with, and thus qualifies, another basic theme of *War*, one that credits the Roman victory to the heroic Flavians. See D. R. Schwartz 2015b.

v. Josephus and His Sources. As is already suggested by their hodgepodge nature, mentioned above, the last three books of *Antiquities* are a happy hunting ground for source-critics. Despite the fact that many of the events that Josephus reports belonged to his own lifetime, he could not have witnessed most of them. He was, therefore, necessarily dependent on others; the obvious seams and jumps from topic to topic, which reflect the difficulty of fashioning a narrative out of disparate materials, merely confirm what anyway we should expect in the nature of things. As noted above, it seems, in fact, that Josephus used Roman material about the Jews of Rome; Roman material about Roman history and Parthian history; Jewish material from across the Euphrates about the Jews of Parthia and Adiabene; Herodian material about Herod Antipas, Agrippa, and their families; a Jewish source that was hostile to Agrippa II; reports of Roman governors; a high-priestly chronicle; and detailed Roman material about the death of Gaius and the rise of Claudius to the imperial throne. In the annotations to the respective sections of these three books I have pointed to the main indications for such sources and to relevant bibliography. Here I would add only two general observations.

The first is that it is, it seems, impossible to find direct external evidence for any of the sources used by Josephus in these three books, just as it is impossible to know the names of their authors. Even in the case of the one major putative exception, namely, Josephus's long story about the assassination of Gaius Caligula in Book 19, which (since Mommsen 1870) is often supposed to derive, at least in large measure, from an otherwise lost account by Cluvius Rufus, the ascription is quite hypothetical. It derives only from the apparent reference to Cluvius (or a member of his family) at 19.91–92; from our knowledge that Cluvius wrote a lost history; and from our reasonable conviction that Josephus must have had a detailed source for his story. That is all something, but not conclusive—and it leaves scholars ample room both for doubts about the identification of Cluvius as a source and doubts about his (or anyone else's) identification as Josephus's *sole* source for this long story. Fortunately, however, giving the author of the source a name would not matter much, for, as Timpe (1960: 474–475, n. 4) noted, all of Cluvius's works are lost,[42] so even if we were sure this narrative owed much to him, it would not point us to much in the way of other extant evidence for Cluvius's interests, biases, and the like.[43]

Rather, in that case, as in others, we are left—and this is my second general observation—with the Josephan text itself, as also, at times, others' parallel stories that show ways Josephus did not take in editing his sources. As I have attempted to indicate in annotations on relevant passages, this can yield meaningful results, which enrich our understanding both of what the sources said and of what Josephus wanted to do with them.

Take, for a simple example, Josephus's back-to-back stories at *Ant.* 18.65–80 and 18.81–84 about foreigners in Rome who took advantage of respectable Roman matrons. These juicy stories seem to derive from the first-century Roman equivalent of tabloid journalism,[44] and may share a source with Tacitus's stories at *Annales* 2.85. But be that as it may, it is obvious

---

42 For the fragments and testimonia, see Levick 2013: 2.1036–1041.

43 I qualify "much in the way of" in deference to theories about what Tacitus, Suetonius, or others may have derived from Cluvius. See, for example, Townend 1960 and 1964, along with my discussion of Mommsen 1870 in the introduction to Book 19. Such theories may well be true, but given the intervention of those other authors,

confidence about the ability to point to pristine Cluvian material, and then to use it together with such material distilled from Josephus, will hardly be high enough to justify such attempts.

44 Schemann 1887: 27–28 ("ein Stück aus der Skandalchronik des damaligen Rom"); Norden 1913a: 641, n. 2 ("chronique scandaleuse").

that the opening and end of the first story (§§65, 79) and the end of the second (§84), are Josephus's own contribution, meant to lead readers to conclude that the Egyptians were much worse than the Jews.

Josephus's accounts of the governorships of Pilate (18.55–89) and Cumanus (20.105–136) are more complex examples. They are longer than his accounts of all other governors, and given the fact that these are also the only two governors, of those described by Josephus, who were sent to Rome to defend themselves (*Ant.* 18.89; 20.132–136), it does not require much imagination to hypothesize, at least, that Josephus's accounts of them were so long because he had access to materials prepared in connection with their hearings.

That is, to begin with, just a hypothesis. But if readers of these accounts encounter tensions, namely statements or nuances that pull in different directions, then the hypothesis becomes useful, and that itself recommends it. Thus, for example, if *War* 2.176 reports that Pilate foresaw "tumult" and therefore armed his soldiers already prior to the Jews' protest, while the close parallel at *Ant.* 18.61 has him arming them only in response to abusive Jewish behavior, we might shrug the difference off as inconsequential. But suppose we note two more details in which *War*'s version of this story differs from the very parallel one in *Antiquities*: *War* (ibid.) portrays Pilate's fore-arming of the soldiers not as looking for trouble but, rather, as "foresight" (προήδει), and *War* emphasizes that Pilate ordered his soldiers not to use swords but only wooden clubs; while *Antiquities* too mentions the clubs (18.61), it notes neither that they were merely wooden (so less lethal than iron) nor that they were specifically told not to use swords. These two details in *War* point to an attempt to portray Pilate as a responsible governor who was both proactive and moderate.

Such a portrayal, however, constitutes a frontal contradiction of the way Josephus frames his account of Pilate in *War*: he opens the Pilate stories at §169 with Pilate bringing his troops to Jerusalem with no reason stated and introducing the offensive standards into the city "at night and under cover" (νύκτωρ καὶ κεκαλυμμένας), so as to create a fait accompli.[45] That seems to put readers on notice that Pilate was a villain, and therefore leaves us wondering why the body of his account would include details that tend, even more than their parallels in *Antiquities*, to exculpate Pilate.

Given the normal assumption that editors who are using extant materials are most active at the seams, the hypothesis suggests itself that, in preparing his account of Pilate in *War*, Josephus used a source that portrayed him more positively than Josephus wanted to, so he blackened Pilate in the introduction but let details congenial to Pilate remain in the body of the story. But that implies, in turn, that the less congenial details in Josephus's later version, *Antiquities*, reflect his effort to bring the body of the story into line with his own attitude. That would seem to me to be a reasonable hypothesis even if we could not point to any other reason to suspect the existence of a source favorable to Pilate; all the more so if, as suggested above with regard to Pilate's need to defend himself in Rome, we do have such reason.

In other words, a source-critical analysis of Josephus's parallel account in *War* has, unsurprisingly, its implication for our understanding of Josephus's work in *Antiquities*. Some of this is indicated in the notes to *Ant.* 18.55–62, some I have offered in more detail elsewhere (D. R. Schwartz 2007b: 132–143).

---

45 That they were brought into the city at night is also stated in *Ant.* 18.56, but not at the beginning of the story (§55). That, along with the absence of "under cover," allow readers of the story in *Antiquities* to think that Pilate was not devious but simply did not know that the introduction of the standards, which happened to have been after nightfall, would offend the Jews. Another possibility, even more favorable to Pilate, was suggested by Eck; see the note on "night" at 18.56.

The governorships of Felix and Albinus are characterized by other tensions, and they too are fruitful insofar as they point up a Josephan bias that is otherwise too easily missed. Take, for example, Josephus's sweeping reference at 20.182 to Felix's misdeeds (ἀδικήματα, "acts of injustice"), which sounds as if readers know they were numerous and heinous and characterized his rule. Feldman, in his note ad loc. (1965: 487, n. f), refers us to Tacitus in order to illustrate that characterization. That is legitimate, but it might also make us notice that apart from the murder reported in 20.163–164, it is, in fact, quite difficult to illustrate the characterization of Felix in 20.182 on the basis of Josephus's own account in *Antiquities*.[46] If we were to begin with that, 20.182 would in fact function as a pointer that directs our attention to the fact that Josephus's account of Felix's days focuses much more on Jewish villains and hardly portrays the governor as one. And the same goes for Albinus's days as well: although 20.253–254, almost forty paragraphs after the end of Josephus's account of Albinus, echoes a passage in *War* (2.277) that portrays Albinus as a terrible villain, that hardly corresponds to the picture painted by Josephus's narrative about that governor's term of office in *Ant.* 20.197–215. Rather, as with his narrative about Felix, it is Jewish villains who are the focus of Josephus's opprobrium and Albinus is portrayed as having done his best to deal with an impossible situation. Were it not for Tacitus on Felix, and for the remnants of *War* at 20.253–254 about Albinus, we might well not notice what in fact interests Josephus more in *Antiquities*—and thus we might miss the chance to consider what, for Josephus, changed between *War* and *Antiquities*, and why it changed.[47]

Finally, under this rubric of "sources," we should recall, more generally, that since *Antiquities* 18–20 cover the same period of time (6–66 CE) as *War* 2.117–279, it is natural that, as especially Krieger (2002) has shown via a detailed synopsis, Josephus related to his account in *War* as something of a skeleton outline while composing the much longer account in *Antiquities*. While there are manifold differences between the accounts, as well as numerous additions, it seems—as the abovementioned cases of 20.215, 253–254 illustrate—that Josephus would keep track of where he was in his narrative by referring to *War* as an outline. This is also suggested by the fact that although there is much in *Ant.* 18–20 that is without parallel in *War* 2.117–279, there is next to nothing in the latter that is without parallel in the former. In the annotations I discuss some of the differences and their possible explanations, just as Mason does in his annotations to *War* 2 in his 2008 FJTC volume on it. The present volume includes, therefore, scores of references to "Mason 2008," but readers should realize that that is just a drop in the potential bucket, for Mason's 150 pages on *War* 2.117–279 are all, in a very real way, part and parcel of any commentary on *Antiquities* 18–20.

VI. **Text.** It seems that three phenomena, one at each major stage of the book's history, conspired, as it were, to create significant difficulties for the text of *Antiquities* 18–20. Of them, one pertains to the creation of these books, one to their transmission, and one to scholarly reception of Niese's edition.

After H. St. John Thackeray noted in 1926, in the introduction to his Loeb edition of Josephus's *Life*, that there are numerous commonalities between the Greek of that little work and that of *Antiquities* 20,[48] in 1929 he proposed a theory to explain that phenomenon.

---

46 As is noted by Brunt 1961: 214, n. 77

47 For some thoughts in that direction, about Josephus's reorientation in *Antiquities* to a religious approach appropriate to the Diaspora, hence to a focus on Jewish sins rather than on the nature of Roman rule

in Judea, see Tuval 2013: 246–256 and D. R. Schwartz 2014: 48–61.

48 JLCL 1.xv–xvi. For a similar list, see *ThLJ* ix. For an illustration that is not among those listed by Thackeray, see Schalit 1968: 60, s.v. Ἱεροσολυμίτης: after appearing

Namely, he argued that an editor, who had a predilection for Thuycididean formulations but little talent, had revised Books 17–19, and that that accounts for the significant differences between the Greek of those three books, on the one hand, and Book 20 and the *Life*, on the other. According to Thackeray, the Greek of the latter two books is Josephus's own unretouched work, whereas that of Books 17–19 is the revision created by the "Thucydidean hack" (Thackeray 1929: 109–114). A year later, the year of Thackeray's death, this theory was reiterated and bolstered in the first fascicle of Thackeray's *Lexicon to Josephus*, in which he marked the words and formulations, in Books 17–19, that were especially attributed to that putative *Verschlimmbesserer*. In Book 20 and the *Life*, in contrast, "we probably come nearer than anywhere else to the *ipsissima verba* of the author" (*ThLJ* ix).

That theory, although it received some initial support, has not fared well in subsequent scholarship, for two complementary reasons. On the one hand, the past many decades have seen a decline in the respectability of source criticism, which is an attempt to get behind the present text of Josephus to more primitive stages of his text, and the theory of literary "assistants" is another type of such theory. Although not without protests, scholars have largely given up on that type of work, branding it with a German name in order to help delegitimize it;[49] in general, they assume that, at best, it can produce hypotheses that are too speculative to be worth their time. On the other hand, Josephus's stock as an author has risen in recent decades,[50] so scholarly willingness to ascribe him responsibility for his own work, and, accordingly, the wide reading in Greek literature (including Thucydides) that would allow him to produce it,[51] has grown. These two complementary trends underlie the main attacks on Thackeray's theory. Today, most scholars tend to ignore it or dismiss it.[52]

Nevertheless, the fact remains that the main datum on which Thackeray based his theory, one that is especially important to us here, has hardly been challenged. Too often, scholarly discussion has focused only on Thackeray's theory of a "Thucydidean hack": Thackeray had pointed to the frequency of Thucydidean formulations in Books 17–19, and that observation elicited the criticism of scholars who noted that such formulations can be found elsewhere as well in his corpus.[53] Even that response, however, is not very satisfying, for the preponderance of evidence still regards Books 17–19.[54] More important for our present discussion, however, is the fact that only meager attention has been given to the other pillar of Thackeray's case, which has remained in place: his observation that the Greek of Book 20 is very similar to that of *Life*. That observation, together with the differences between Josephus's language in those books and in Books 17–19, is what brought him to posit that the former show us Josephus's own style.

---

only once each in Books 16–19, it appears seventeen times in Book 20 and twenty-two times in *Life*.

49 See such protests as Syme 1984: 1393 ("'Quellenforschung,' to some a name of dread, is in this context not to be evaded without vexation or calamity") and Potter 1999: 90 ("*Quellenforschung* should not be a dirty word").

50 See S. Mason's editor's preface to this series.

51 See, for example, Price 2011.

52 Note, for example, Rajak 2002: 233–236.

53 See esp. E. Stein 1937: 2–3, 12–14, 66; Petersen 1958: 260–261, n. 5; Rajak 2002: 233–236; Bilde 1988: 132–134; Feldman 1998a: 178, n. 23. For other doubts about the theory, see Shutt 1961: 59–78.

54 As is emphasized by Smallwood 1963. Here I would emphasize that E. Stein (1937: 66) recognized that Thucydides's influence is significantly greater ("aanzienlijk grooter") in Books 17–19 than it is in the other books of *Antiquities*. He suggests explaining that on the basis of the assumption that in writing these books Josephus used his parallel account in *War*, which has many reminiscences of Thucydides. However, that cannot explain why *Antiquities* 20, which too parallels *War*, is so different. Here too, I would note that, *pace* Bilde (1988: 132), who writes, in rejecting Thackeray's theory, that "Stein showed that all of the books in Josephus's works are very uniform linguistically and stylistically," in fact Stein's dissertation

The fact that Thackeray characterized the Greek of Books 17–19 by reference to a Thucydidean hack is merely secondary. What is important for us, in the present context, is the way Thackeray characterizes the difference he observed: "a student who happened to make his first acquaintance with Josephus in this portion [Books 17–19] would pronounce him a difficult writer and perhaps be deterred by the involved and turgid language, whereas he would find the *Life* absurdly easy and crude."[55] That assessment, already expressed quite colorfully by von Destinon in 1904,[56] is one that cannot be so easily criticized by mere checking of where which words appear. It has not been attacked, and it was fully confirmed a decade after Thackeray wrote, by another British classicist who was very familiar with Josephus's writings. Namely, in his 1939 "The Composition of Josephus' *Antiquities*," G. C. Richards, although presenting a revision of Thackeray's theory (namely, he posited that the work of the assistants came in the course of the preparation of a second edition of *Antiquities*[57]), retained Thackeray's assessment of the current state of Books 17–19: in the course of the putative revision, he declared, "XVII–XIX were utterly ruined. XX was left alone."[58] Such an assessment of the difference between the Greek of Books 17–19, on the one hand, and that of Book 20 (and the *Life*), on the other hand, retains its validity whatever one thinks of the explanation.

Indeed, as one who has translated *Antiquities* 18–20 for the present project, and the *Life* for another one, I too can confirm, for what it might be worth, that while reading *Antiquities* 20 and *Life* is usually a very simple matter, as devoid of difficulty as it is of charm,[59] Books 18–19 can be quite a challenge. As the distinguished editor of the present series once e-mailed back, when I asked him what he thought about the translation of a certain passage in Book 18: "Ant. 18, huh? Well, it's a bit of torture, as you well know."[60] Yes, I do. That is the first issue: whatever explains it—and more than one explanation is possible[61]—the Greek of Books 18–19 is often quite difficult, and, as such, has invited copyists to do their best to improve it. Since it is so different from the Greek of Book 20 and the *Life*, and since the *Life* is by its nature such a personal book, it is difficult to avoid concluding that the latter is what Josephus himself could produce, while others—whether as assistants at the time of writing, or revisers at some later point—attempted to improve the Greek of Books 17–19 but actually ended up degrading it.[62]

---

does not at all address *Antiquities* in this connection, apart from the passage mentioned at the beginning of this note.

55 Thackeray 1929: 109–110.

56 As Destinon (1904: 18) put it, someone who has read the first fifteen books of *Antiquities* and then continues into Books 16–19 is comparable to someone who has been riding comfortably in a light carriage on a well-paved highway and suddenly finds himself continuing in a clumsy wagon on a bumpy rural road. For a yet earlier version of that impression, see Ritschl 1873: 599: "allem Anschein nach, um nicht zu sagen ganz augenscheinlich, der ganze spätere Theil des Iosephischen Archäologie nicht zu einer abschliessenden Redaction gelangt ist, sondern grossentheils nur eine unverarbeitete oder nicht genug verarbeitete Zusammenstellung angesammelter Materialien darbietet, vielleicht nur von der Hand eines Amanuensis."

57 Such theories were very popular at the time. See, in general, Emonds 1941; on Josephus, see esp. Laqueur

1920; Attridge 1976: 52, n. 2; and the note on "end my *Antiquities*" at 20.259.

58 Richards 1939: 40. Note also Feldman's assessment (1984b: 766) that in "the second half of the 'Antiquities' certain books, notably Book 18, are in much worse shape than others, while other books, notably Book 20, are in much better condition."

59 Recall Thackeray's characterization of the Greek of the *Life* as "absurdly easy and crude" (above, at n. 55), along with his observation at *ThLJ* ix, that it is quite similar to that of *Antiquities* 20.

60 For his phrasing of the same in a somewhat higher register, see his reference (Mason 2008: 91) to "the obfuscatory style of *Ant.* 17–19 in general."

61 Especially one might think here of the possibility that sections of Books 18–19, including the long account of the conspiracy to assassinate Gaius in Book 19, are based on sources in Latin.

62 Readers who write in languages that they learned only secondarily may well be familiar, as the present

The second problem, which concerns the work's transmission, has to do with the fact that although Josephus's *Antiquities* might be said to suffer, in general, from being preserved in too many manuscripts,[63] its last three books survive in too few. Manuscript P (a Palatine manuscript in the Vatican Library), of the ninth or tenth century, which Niese characterized as the oldest and best of all the witnesses,[64] does not include Books 18–20. Neither do the three next-best witnesses (FVL—Florence, Vatican, Leiden). That left Niese with only three manuscripts (AMW—Ambrosianus [Milan], Laurentianus [Florence], Vaticanus), ones that had been assessed as less trustworthy in the books for which other witnesses survived. Although he tended to prefer A, of the eleventh century,[65] nevertheless, too often this means that scholars have to choose between or among readings of which none is ideal or has a strong presumption of authenticity.

The third and final point, which concerns the reception of Niese's edition, is related to the second: since Niese took such a strong stand about the primacy of P, reviewers and subsequent scholars naturally tended to focus on that point. Moreover, that tendency was reinforced by the fact that Samuel Naber, in his own Teubner editions of *Antiquities* 11–20 (which appeared in 1892–1893, shortly after Niese's), pointed to his own more skeptical stance toward P as the main issue—virtually the only issue discussed in his preface—that distinguished between the two editions.[66] The natural result was that the appearance of the two editions was greeted by reviews that focused on this point: so Wendland (1892) and Frick (1893a) in their very detailed reviews of the third and fourth volumes of Niese's editio maior, which include *Ant.* 11–15 and 16–20 (with *Life*); so too Frick (1893b), Jacoby (1893), and Rühl (1893) in their reviews of Naber; so too Reinach (1893), in his review of Niese's third and fourth volumes—and so too, much more recently, Schreckenberg (1972: 39; 1977:

---

author is, with the need to choose between publishing in one's own style, which cannot compete with the best that practiced natives can produce, and entrusting one's work to well-meaning style editors, many of them "wannabe" authors who did not make the cut. Evidently, Josephus's assistants "for the Greek language" (*Apion* 1.50) in preparing *War* did a much better job than whoever undertook, prior to or following the completion of *Antiquities*, to work on Books 17–19.

63 As was observed by Schalit 1963: vii-viii: "Readers should know that, from one point of view, Josephus's good fortune was deleterious. As opposed to his rival, Justus of Tiberius, the writings of the Jerusalem priest survived until today. This was caused by the great affection for his writings evinced by the Christian Church, which viewed him, *inter alia*, as a witness to Jesus ... But this affection had its downside: the more copyists copied his writings, the more corruptions came to afflict their text. And not only that, but later copyists, who noticed corruptions introduced by earlier ones, attempted to correct the corruptions, and thereby corrupted the text all the more. The result is that there is no other ancient Greek text that has been corrupted and spoiled as much as Josephus's writings ..." (my translation). If this is true for Josephus

in general, it is true all the more for the books on the period that most interested Christian readers and copyists. Cf. Mommsen's comment, in an 1874 letter in support of Niese's application for governmental funding for the preparation of his critical edition of Josephus, that "giebt es in der klassisch-historischen Literatur keine schlimmere philologische Lücke als der kritisch noch bodenlose Josephus ist" (Bichler 2018: 83; "philologische" is the reading of the original letter, in Niese's file in the Geheimes Staatsarchiv Preußischer Kulturbesitz, Berlin-Dahlem). My thanks to Reinhold Bichler for his help with this note.

64 Niese 1890a: iii.

65 Niese 1892: xxxiii (apart from the Palatinus, "longe optimum esse apparet Ambrosianum eumque in libris XVIII, XIX, XX, qui non extant in Palatino, fundamentum recensionis esse"); so too Feldman 1965: 438, n. a: "the Ambrosian is definitely our best MS. for Books XVIII–XX, and one should be slow to depart from it." Feldman tended to follow that assessment more than Niese; see the note on "brought to him" at 20.5.

66 See Naber 1892: iv–v. There is no preface to Naber 1893, which includes *Ant.* 16–20 and the *Life*—perhaps because, in the absence of P, there was not much to argue about.

117–124[67]) and Leoni (2009: 165; 169, n. 94). Even Schürer, despite the very positive nature of his reviews of Niese's third and fourth volumes, felt the need to complain that Niese "over-estimated" the value of P.[68]

Such a focus of the discussion of Niese's and Naber's editions, on the merits of P, was quite natural. However, since P does not exist for Books 18–20, the result was that, even beyond the fact that, in general, "so far little attention has been paid to the second half of *Judean Antiquities* from a philological viewpoint" (Leoni 2016: 314), such discussion as there has been, of the textual tradition of the last decade of *Antiquities*, has marginalized our three books. Wendland (1892), for example, in his review of Niese's editio maior of Books 11–20, refers to more than fifty passages but of them only two are in *Antiquities* 18–20, and Frick (1893a), in his review of the same volumes, refers to ten specific passages, none of them in our three books.

Of course, scholars—not bound to allegiance to any particular manuscript for these books—have been all the more active in proposing emendations. Already Niese offered many, and if in his editio maior (1890a) he often restrained himself and confined them to his critical apparatus, in his editio minor (1890b), which allowed him only a very minimal apparatus, he often went the whole way and corrected the text accordingly.[69] Richards and Shutt (1937, 1939), quoted above, offered close to fifty emendations of Books 18–20 (more than twice as many as for Books 1–3); Feldman too offered numerous emendations, in his 1965 Loeb edition of these three books, some of them his own, some suggested by Levi Arnold Post, who was then among the editors of the LCL;[70] and in 2012, in support of his call for a new edition of *Antiquities*, Schreckenberg offered nearly seventy more in these three books.[71] Usually these emendations make the text smoother and easier to understand than the received text. Just as usually, however, they raise—as the skeptical Feldman repeatedly noted in response to Naber and Schreckenberg, whose Greek, he argued, was better than Josephus's—the question whether Josephus's original text was in fact smoother and easier than the received text.[72]

In choosing among extant readings, the usual rules of thumb, including preferences for the more difficult reading (*lectio difficilior*[73]) and shorter reading (*lectio brevior*[74]), apply. So does the general presumption that Niese knew the text and language of Josephus inside out, so as a rule we should adhere to his editio maior.[75] As for emendations, although here too each case must be discussed on its own merits, I will posit three more or less intuitive and banal rules of thumb that guided me in this volume. In the absence of direct manuscript

67 This long discussion is devoted to the evaluation of numerous passages in *Ant.* 12–17 in which P disagrees with other witnesses and Niese adopted its reading.

68 See Schürer 1890, 1892. The complaint that Niese is too dependent on P appears at 1892: 516.

69 So, for some examples, at 18.12, 19, 31, 66, 78, 173, 194, 219, 253, 330, 354, 368 and 19.12, 157, 302, 332. Cf. below, n. 75.

70 See, for example, Feldman 1965: 202–203, n. b and his textual apparatus to 18.18, 346.

71 Schreckenberg 2012: 53–55.

72 Feldman 1984a: 20, 26–27; 1984b: 765–767. See, for example, the note on "purchase" at 18.90.

73 See, for example, the note on "combination" at 18.13.

74 See, for example, the discussion below, after n. 78, of Feldman on 20.260–266.

75 As was noted above (at n. 69), Niese himself often departed from the editio maior in his editio minor, which appeared the same year. As he explained (Niese 1888: iii), having given the text according to the best manuscripts in his editio maior, in his editio minor he adopted readings of other manuscripts, or emendations of his own or of others, which appear to be quite certain ("satis certae uiderentur"). Indeed, in many of the cases in which Niese suggested such conjectures, it is difficult or impossible to understand the text of his editio maior. Nevertheless, it is unfortunate that the format of neither edition allowed him to explain the emendations. Many of Niese's, as those of others, are discussed in my annotations.

evidence, or even when it exists but is not unanimous and one may suspect a copyist emended his text, an emendation is all the more warranted: (a) the more difficult the unemended text is; (b) the less support Josephus's own writings offer for the unemended text, and the more they offer, especially in nearby context, for the proposed emendation; and (c) the more minimal the proposed emendation is; this includes, but is not limited to, the ease with which the extant text can be understood as a transcriptional error.

To illustrate these considerations, let us look at several suggested emendations in Books 18–19, moving from the most to the least warranted. At 18.170, first of all, Josephus reports, according to all the witnesses, that since Tiberius was typically a procrastinator, he was never in a hurry to receive embassies, and that, for the same reason (ὅθεν), he was περίοπτος about examining prisoners. That makes no sense, for περίοπτος means "highly visible, striking, remarkable" (CCFJ 3.396, s.v.). Accordingly, already Ernesti (1795: 162) suggested that we read ἀπερίοπτος—the same word but with a privative prefix; he pointed to Thucydides 1.41 for this adjective in the sense of "negligent." This is a very convincing emendation and has been universally accepted, because, following the three criteria listed above: (a) the text as is is apparently impossible, beyond what would be preferred as a *lectio difficilior*; (b) there is other Josephan evidence for the correction, both (i) in general, for there is abundant other evidence for Thucydidean formulations in this part of *Antiquities*[76] and, more importantly, (ii) in particular, for Josephus uses ἀπερίοπτος elsewhere in this sense (18.272; 19.72); and (c) the correction is minimal—just one letter. Thus, although it would be nice to have some manuscript that reads ἀπερίοπτος or some elegant explanation of how the mistake crept into the text (why or how the opening alpha disappeared), rather than merely to chalk it up to negligence, we may be fairly confident about this correction.

Perhaps slightly less cogent because it involves a few more letters, but nevertheless quite convincing, especially in light of support from nearby context, is von Gutschmid's suggestion of ὑβρίσματος instead of ὁρίσματος at 18.357. On the one hand, the latter is given by all of the witnesses, and although this is its only appearance in Josephus's oeuvre, the former appears (apart from this suggested emendation) nowhere in that corpus. But, on the other hand, μετὰ ... ὁρίσματος ("with border/limit") is quite difficult to fit into the context here; μετὰ ...ὑβρίσματος ("with outrage") fits it quite naturally; and, very importantly, the emendation is also supported by the use of the cognate verb, τοὺς ὑβρίσαντας, in allusions to this story, using the same root (περιύβρισται, ὑβρίσαντας), in the nearby context (§§358, 360). For a similar case, see the note on "bordering" at 18.293.

Turning to less convincing suggestions, contrast, for example, the case of 19.21, where the codices read οὐ πάντ' ἐλεύθερον and Hudson (Hudson and Havercamp 1726: 1.917, n. p), followed by others, suggests emending that into οὐκ ἀνελεύθερον. While it is definitely easier to construe the text as emended, (a) it is not impossible to construe the received text (see the note on "not inappropriate" at 19.21), (b) Josephus nowhere uses ἀνελεύθερον and neither does Thucydides, and (c) the correction entails omitting four letters and adding three. Thus, in all three respects the case is less convincing than that concerning 18.170, and one can well understand Niese's reluctance, in both of his editions, to depart from the unanimous testimony of the manuscripts. Nevertheless, most of his successors followed Hudson: Mathieu and Hermann (1929: 200), Feldman (1965: 224), Wiseman (2013a: 41), and apparently Schalit (1963: 320).

---

76 As Ernesti 1795 frequently noted. This was, of course, the starting point for Thackeray's theory about Josephus's "Thucydidean hack," who assisted him in Books 17–19; see *ThLJ* viii. The fact that ἀπερίοπτος appears in Josephus only in Books 18–19 was part of Thackeray's argument.

Or consider the case at 18.359, where Anileus expresses the fear that a certain course of action would lead to a massacre of the Jews in Babylon and there would be no ἀναστροφή if that happened. Ernesti (1795: 169–170), following a yet earlier editor, suggested that, despite the unanimity of the witnesses, we instead read ἀποστροφή. True, ἀποστροφή would be easier, for while ἀναστροφή usually means "conduct" or "comportment" (Danker 1982: 358–359; Spicq 1994: 1.111–114), as at 19.28 and Galatians 1:13, which does not fit the context here, ἀποστροφή would naturally mean "refuge," as it does at 19.131, and that would fit the context. However, if in the case of 18.170 περίοπτος was simply impossible, here the situation is different: ἀναστροφή literally means "a turn back/up" and so can mean "recovery" and fit 18.359; that sense is also in evidence at 18.173 and 19.90 ("respite"); and the emendation would require the change of two letters, not only one.

Similarly, at the end of 18.5 all the witnesses read φόνου: the rebels urged the masses not to shrink from the murder their struggle would require. Already Hudson (Hudson and Havercamp 1726: 1.870), however, emended that into πόνου ("hardship"), and that was followed by Niese (1890a: 141) and others. The motivation for this correction was probably the notion that those who encouraged rebellion would not use such a harsh word as "murder" to describe what their followers would have to do. Feldman, however, retained φόνου, and that appears preferable, although not precisely for the reason Feldman offers (1965: 7, n. b): "since, as can be seen from §8, the Fourth Philosophy did not shrink from murder to attain its aims." That argument, about what the rebels did, is not very relevant; what is relevant is that Josephus condemned what they did as murder. That makes it likely that here, at the end of §5, Josephus is ironically characterizing the rebel leaders as calling upon their followers to steel themselves to do even the crimes they will have to commit—crimes which Josephus himself, as author, then goes on to detail at §§6–8. True, had the witnesses read πόνου no one would have thought of substituting φόνου. Since, however, the witnesses read φόνου and it is possible to understand the statement as Josephan irony, it seems best to leave the text alone.

Finally, in this group, note that also the very next paragraph, 18.6, illustrates what is often the case: that considerations are not unambiguous, and so scholars do not always agree in their assessments of the degree to which the received text is impossible and how that stacks up against the "price" of emending it. Namely, while most witnesses read ἐπιβουλή ("plot, conspiracy"), there is also some evidence for ἐπιβολή ("attack, undertaking, project, plan, intention"), and that fits the context somewhat better. But ἐπιβουλή is not impossible and ἐπιβολή is not a perfect fit—and it is not surprising that scholars differ. See the note on "plot" at 18.6.

To illustrate the least convincing emendations, let us consider the case of 18.274, where the Jews ask Petronius "to write Gaius how relentlessly deadset they were against accepting the statue" (γράφειν πρὸς Γάιον τὸ ἀνήκεστον αὐτῶν πρὸς τὴν ἀποδοχὴν τοῦ ἀνδριάντος) and Richards and Shutt (1937: 176) suggest that a participle (corresponding to "telling him" after "Gaius") has fallen out of the text. For that suggestion they offer two arguments: the text without a participle is unusual ("γράφειν c. acc. is unusual in J[osephus]") and the Latin translation of Josephus[77] "shows a participle was once read." On the basis of those two arguments, they ask what that lost participle might have been, and answer their question on the basis of §281, where Petronius agrees to write Gaius "explaining" (διασαφῶν) the Jews' disposition. That easily led Richards and Shutt to posit that the original text of §274 read γράφειν πρὸς Γάιον τὸ ἀνήκεστον αὐτῶν διασαφοῦντα.

---

77 Which they do not quote. In ed. Frobenius (1524: 537) it reads: "quin potius scribendum Caio decerneret, *significans* immobilem animum iudaeorum."

That is quite an admirable argument: the Greek seems to be missing something here, the Latin seems to indicate there once was something, and there is, within Josephus, indeed very nearby within Josephus, suggestive evidence for what that something was. However, the text as is is not impossible; we do not know who, where, or when "once read" a participle here and the fact that the Latin translation has one need not mean it was there in the Greek; and for the loss of a word like διασαφοῦντα we should probably insist on more of an explanation than for the loss of a letter or two as in the first two cases discussed above. From all points of view, that is, this suggestion is much less cogent than either of them. Fortunately, for historians and most readers, however, if not for students of Josephus's Greek, the question whether "and tell him" was in the original text or only assumed by it does not seem to matter much.

Finally, in this connection, note simply that (a) these three rules apply not only to choices between sticking with the received text and emending it, but also to choices between or among proposed emendations even when all agree that the received text cannot be accepted, and (b) there can be conflicts between rules. A glance at 19.218 will illustrate both points. First of all, while many modern scholars (and, apparently, medieval copyists) agree that κατὰ φωνήν at 19.218 is impossible, Niese retains it. Moreover, among the many who reject it, we find that Naber considered solving the problem by changing two letters to create a fairly mundane text, but was unhappy with it and proposed something more radical; Feldman would solve the problem by changing only one letter and so creating a text that uses a rare word; and Schreckenberg makes a radical emendation based on a notion of what Josephus must have wanted to say, a notion that derives from other passages, elsewhere in Josephus's oeuvre, in which he says such things. See the note on "Gaius" at 19.218.

That is: when an unacceptable text can be made passable by a minimal emendation but completely satisfying by a more radical one, honest and experienced scholars, even those very familiar with Josephus's style, may differ, and we have to live with such uncertainties. As Reinach put it, in his review of Niese, they are often matters of taste and judgment.[78] Note, for example, that while Niese (1892: xxxiii) rejected, as parade examples of "pluses" in A(mbrosianus) that are "inepta aut inutilia," its additions at 20.94 and 20.113–114,[79] and Mathieu and Herrmann (1929) and Schalit (1963) followed Niese's lead in rejecting A's readings in both cases, Feldman (1965) adopts both of them—just as the notation "A: om. MWE" appears five times in Feldman's notes justifying his readings of *Ant.* 20.260–266 in which, contrary to the *lectio brevior potior* rule followed there by Niese, Feldman adopted "pluses" found only in A. As a rule, I stuck to Niese's editio maior, now and then relating, in the annotations, to emendations and the difficulties that elicited them.

VII. **Translation.** In his review of the first volume of the LCL *Josephus*, Max Radin observed that although, in comparison with William Whiston's classic translation (1737),[80] Thackeray's is "superior," "based on the far more accurate historical knowledge which the newer translator possesses," nevertheless "something has been lost in savor." Thackeray's translation, Radin observed, "sounds a little flat," and so "I am afraid that the new translation will never be issued in folio, bound in brass clasps, and read by sea-captains to their crews, as Kipling

---

78 Reinach 1893: 123: choosing among contradictory readings is an "affaire de goût et de bon sens."

79 For other cases, see the note on "brought to him" at 20.5.

80 The original edition is exceedingly rare, and subsequent editions were often revised. In the present volume I have used the 1878 edition listed in the bibliography, which is widely accessible, including online via Internet Archive.

tells us was done with Whiston's *Josephus*."[81] Here Radin expressed two assumptions, of which one is more obvious than the other.

The obvious one is that the more accurate the translation, that is, the more the translator strives to have his version conform precisely to the original, the less natural it will be in the target language. The more the translation conforms to the idiom of the target language, the more "savor" it will have—but that savor will be of the modern, target language, not of the ancient source. So to the extent Thackeray undertook to be more accurate than Whiston, he necessarily undertook to give up something of his fine English style.[82]

But everything is relative. Although Radin would not agree with the editor of the present series that the Loeb translation "makes idiomatic English the highest virtue,"[83] or with Feldman, who had, in preparing *Ant*. 18–20, access to a rough draft of Thackeray's translation and commented that "it often is hard to improve upon for sheer verve of style" (Feldman 1965: ix), it is obvious that, as Mason goes on to detail, the Loeb translations do make all sorts of concessions to English readability. This new Brill series leans in the other direction. That is in line with its goal to provide a translation that is a point of departure for the commentary.[84] Indeed, the new translations in this series are frequently quite close to the original.

On the one hand, that is useful, insofar as it directs readers of the text to the commentary for assistance in understanding the text, and also allows readers of the commentary to see, in the text, the issues that the commentary is addressing. Thus, for example, some translators render *Ant*. 18.18 loosely and quite roundly, using mundane verbs that gives readers no pause: "The doctrine of the Essenes *is* that all things are left in the hand of God"; "Les Esséniens *ont pour croyance* de laisser tout entre les mains de Dieu."[85] However, Josephus actually writes that the Essenes' doctrine φιλεῖ ("tends to," "is wont to," "likes") to leave all to God. While the abovementioned translators apparently thought that is simply a flourish and means no more than "their doctrine is," it can be interesting and possibly fruitful to consider the possibility that Josephus is hedging[86] and the reason he might be doing so (see the note on "tends to" at 18.18). The place for such discussion is the commentary. If, however, the loose translation were given, readers would have no reason to consult the commentary, and, if they nevertheless did that, they would not see, in the translation that was supplied to them, the issue that is being debated.

On the other hand, of course, a translation that hews closely to the original also has its price in terms of "flatness" and loss of "savor," or even—of downright intelligibility. Indeed, that potential price was recognized in advance: "Needless to say, even a determined literalness must yield to the ultimate commandment of basic readability in English."[87] As Barlclay put it in his introduction to his FJTC volume on *Against Apion*, he "attempted to keep the translation as close to the Greek (or Latin) as possible, *without unduly straining the English*"[88] (my italics, DRS). Given that different translators' and readers' may locate the bar for "*basic* readability" at different heights, and hold differing notions as to what is "as close *as possible*"

---

81 Radin 1927/28: 234. The reference is to the first chapter of Kipling's *Captains Courageous*.

82 Thackeray's "literary taste and sense of style" are emphasized by Burkitt 1931: 227, and may be appreciated in his independent writings, such as Thackeray 1929.

83 S. Mason in Feldman 2000: x.

84 As Mason explains, ibid. ix–x.

85 I added the italics into Whiston 1889: 267 and Mathieu and Herrmann 1929: 35–36.

86 Something like that is suggested by the formulation at Whiston 1878: 471: "The doctrine of the Essens (sic) is this: That all things are *best* ascribed to God" (my italics, DRS). Shilleto's revision of Whiston's translation, cited in the preceding note, which omitted "best," eliminated the suggestion.

87 Mason in Feldman 2000: x.

88 Barclay 2007: lxiv.

to the original Greek without "*unduly* straining the English," we find ourselves in the position of stating a basic tendency without the expectation that all would agree in every case. That seems to be the nature of the things. As the ancient rabbis noted, "he who translates a verse literally is a liar, while he who adds to the verse is a blasphemer" (*t. Megillah* 3:41, ed. Lieberman, 364). In preparing the present translation of *Ant.* 18–20, accordingly, I have always been aware of the basic desideratum of reflecting the Greek, but have not hesitated to move toward more idiomatic English (or what was such when I learned to write English some sixty years ago) when failure to do so seemed to be "unduly strained." Readers who want a more readable translation are urged to read Feldman's, and if they want a more elegant one—Whiston's; readers who prefer an English version even closer to the Greek might try it themselves, or use Google Translate.[89]

Radin's other assumption, which is less self-understood, is that a translation is more accurate if the translator possesses more accurate historical knowledge. If that refers to a translator's more accurate knowledge of the history of the original language, it is probably a truism but not very relevant, for one may doubt that much concerning the knowledge of ancient Greek, that is relevant to translation, progressed between Whiston and Thackeray. Rather, I assume that Radin means that Thackeray had, in the twentieth century, more accurate knowledge of the ancient world, in which and of which Josephus wrote, than Whiston did in the eighteenth. That is certainly the case, but its relevance to the quality of Thackeray's *translation* is not readily apparent. When a well-informed historian translates an ancient work, how should his or her historical knowledge impact upon the translation?

Here my basic position is that translators should stick to being translators, especially in a format such as FJTC that allows them another venue—the annotations—in which to be historians. That is, they should avoid allowing their historical knowledge to impact "unduly" upon their translations. This is for two reasons. On the one hand, sometimes the modern historian's notions will be wrong, or in dispute, and why should he or she, when translating, force them on the ancient source? At 19.332, for example, Feldman (1965: 370–371, nn.332 b–c) allowed his belief that, historically, it could not be that a Jew who was "very exacting about the [Judaic] regulations" would discriminate between converts to Judaism and Jews by birth, to dictate both an emendation of one word in the Greek text and recourse to an egregiously unusual translation of another. In doing so, Feldman depended on rabbinic literature, as his footnotes show, to guide him, and so to allow him to guide readers of his translation, about ancient Judaism. While Feldman was at work, however, and in the decades that followed that, it became apparent, from Dead Sea Scrolls, that there were indeed ancient Jews who, precisely because they were very exacting about the Judaic regulations, as they understood them, discriminated between converts and Jews by birth, both in general and in the specific context to which Josephus alludes (entry into the Temple).

---

89 The dilemma could be exemplified by any number of passages. Here are two, both from near the end of *Ant.* 20. On the one hand, at §256 Josephus refers to "devastations," in the plural (πορθήσεις), wrought by brigands. Feldman (1965: 523) uses the singular, in accordance with English style. Like Whiston (1878: 533), I left the plural, as that, although somewhat jarring, does not create any difficulty in understanding the sentence. At §264, in contrast, where Josephus opens with "among us [Jews]," next refers to others in the third-person plural (ἐκείνους ... ἐκμαθόντας), and then goes on to refer to "they," readers who correctly expect the latter to refer to the Jews will be confused because it is not in the first-person plural and, therefore, seems to refer to the others, who were referred to in the third-person plural. I think leaving that confusion is going too far, and therefore (like Schalit 1963: 373) I changed "they" to "we," within brackets. Feldman (1965: 523–525) agreed that the translation simply must deviate here, but handled it more radically by making several changes: he turned "among us" into "our people" and made it the subject of verbs that he changed, correspondingly, into the active voice.

It is unfortunate that the world's standard edition of *Antiquities* 18, for the past sixty years, has imposed another view on Josephus.[90]

Or, for another example, somewhat more complex, note Feldman's (1965: 460–463) handling of 20.137–138: Πέμπει δὲ καὶ Κλαύδιος[91] Φήλικα Πάλλαντος ἀδελφὸν τῶν κατὰ τὴν Ἰουδαίων προστησόμενον πραγμάτων. (138) τῆς δ' ἀρχῆς δωδέκατον ἔτος ἤδη πεπληρωκὼς δωρεῖται τὸν Ἀγρίππαν τῇ Φιλίππου τετραρχίᾳ καὶ Βαταναίᾳ προσθεὶς αὐτῷ τὴν Τραχωνῖτιν σὺν Ἀβέλλᾳ· Λυσανία δ' αὕτη γεγόνει τετραρχία· τὴν Χαλκίδα δ' αὐτὸν ἀφαιρεῖται δυναστεύσαντα ταύτης ἔτη τέσσαρα. Feldman, who as his predecessors at least as far back as Froben in 1524 (including Niese 1890a: 299) opens a new chapter at §137, translated as follows:

> Claudius now sent Felix, the brother of Pallas, to take charge of matters in Judea. When he had completed the twelfth year of his reign, he granted to Agrippa the tetrarchy of Philip together with Batanea, adding thereto Trachonitis and Lysanias' former tetrarchy of Abila; but he deprived him of Chalcis, after he had ruled it for four years.

Note three points about Feldman's translation: the first two pertain to the way it is dependent on Tacitus, while the third points to the way that dependence forced him to adopt a less than natural translation of a simple Greek conjunction and also contradicts an otherwise attractive historical hypothesis.

a.   Feldman reads Κλαύδιος in the nominative, as the name of the emperor, following the Epitome (Niese 1887–1896: 358), instead of the accusative (Κλαύδιον) offered by the manuscripts and followed by Niese (1890a: 299; 1890b: 252), according to which "Claudius" was Felix's gentilicium. Feldman's move derives (as he notes at [461, n. e]) from a consensus among historians, deriving from other evidence (beginning with Tacitus, *Hist.* 5.9.3), that Felix's gentilicium was in fact Antonius, not Claudius.[92] That does not prove, however, that Josephus did not think it was Claudius.

b.   By indenting at §137 in order to indicate a new paragraph (Book 20, Ch. 7), Feldman's translation separates §137 from §136 but links it closely to §138, which reports what Claudius did "when he completed his twelfth year", i.e., 51/52. That indenting, which associates Felix's appointment with that year, is in line with a widespread consensus among scholars (e.g., Feldman, loc. cit; *HJP* 1.458–460), that Felix was appointed in 52 CE. That consensus derives from the fact that Tacitus, in a story he tells about Cumanus and Felix (*Ann.* 12.54), seems to point to that year as the outset of Felix's governorship.

c.   Both editorial decisions about §137 deriving from Tacitus (reading "Claudius" in the nominative and indenting at §137) make it the beginning of a new story, one that is apparently unconnected to what precedes it. That, however, is problematic in two ways:

   i.   It requires translators to create continuity artificially, either with regard to the contents by inserting "as well" ("And Claudius sent Claudius Felix *as well*" [Schalit 1963: 363]) as if we had just heard that Claudius sent someone else (we did not) or temporally, by translating Josephus's nondescript conjunction καί ("and") as "now" (Feldman, loc. cit.), "ensuite" (Mathieu and Herrmann 1929: 274), or "allora" (Moraldi 1998: 2.1237). Contrast the very similar passage at 18.237, where after Josephus reports various arrangements by Gaius he adds ἱππάρχην δὲ

---

90 On this case, see the note on "by birth" at 19.332.
91 Here I am adopting Feldman's reading, following the Epitome (Niese 1887–1896: 358); see Feldman 1965: 461–462, n. e. and the next note.

92 See Stern, *GLAJJ* 2.52 and S. Schwartz 1984: 240; Kokkinos 1990; Brenk and De Rossi 2001: 410–411.

ἐπὶ τῆς Ἰουδαίας ἐκπέμπει Μάρυλλον and none of the four translations just mentioned with regard to 20.137 adds anything to Josephus's brief report,[93] precisely because its context is clear from the preceding lines, which it continues.

ii. It leaves those readers and historians who were under the impression that Cumanus, who was appointed around 48 CE (20.103–104), served no more than a year (see Appendix 1, §8), forced to choose between rejecting that impression, on the one hand, and concluding that Claudius let three years go by before appointing Cumanus's successor, on the other. Neither option is impossible, but neither is attractive.

In sum, were it not for Tacitus's input about Felix's gentilicium and the date of his appointment, Feldman, as Niese, probably would have left "Claudius" in the accusative and then chosen between one of two ways to deal with the fact that πέμπει, which traditionally opens a new paragraph here, was left with no subject, neither proper name nor pronoun: either, as Schalit (1963: 363, cited above), he would have inserted "Claudius" or "the emperor" as the subject of the verb or—as I have chosen, as already Buchon 1836: 532—he would have ignored the traditional paragraphing and attached §137 to the end of §136, so as to avoid, as at 18.237, the need to refer anew to Claudius as the subject of πέμπει. But connecting §137 to §136 would leave §138, with its reference to Claudius's twelfth year, to open a new story, just as, for example, a new story opens at 19.343 with "When he had completed (πεπλή-ρωτο) his third year as king of all of Judea" and another at 20.92 with "Not long after, having completed (πληρώσας) fifty-five years since his birth and twenty-four years of reign, he died …" In cases such as these, the use of a new date indicates a new start,[94] while the use of πληρόω (as πεπληρωκώς at §138) suggests to readers that some time has passed since the last-mentioned events.

Both points suggest that more weight be given to the alternative historical thesis, according to which Felix replaced Cumanus well before the end of Claudius's twelfth year.[95] According to that alternative reading, which seems to be natural, §§136–137 complete the preceding story, which is about the way Claudius handled Judea and ends by reporting whom Claudius appointed instead of Cumanus, and then §138, after the reflection of the passage of some time, opens up a discussion of a secondary topic: the Herodian family, its territories, and especially its family affairs, and that discussion continues until §147. The case is very similar to that at 18.237–238: at §237 Gaius finishes up his handling of Judean business, including the dispatch of a new administrator, and then at §238 Josephus gives a new dating ("In the second year of the reign of Gaius Caesar") and turns to extra-Judean Herodian affairs.

This is not the place to discuss the historical questions of how long Cumanus served as governor, when Felix replaced him, and what Felix's gentilicium really was. What is relevant here is merely to illustrate that historians' consensuses (which in this case derive from Tacitus) concerning such questions can affect the editing, translation, and even the paragraphing of the relevant text, and to recommend that such external influence be kept at a minimum, insofar as translation is concerned.

So much for illustrating the argument that a translator should, on the one hand, hew closely to the original even at the expense of letting it contradict our historical notions, for even if our notions are correct, the ancient author might not have shared them. Moreover,

---

93 Schalit 1963: 303; Feldman 1965: 143; Mathieu and Herrmann 1929: 173; Miraldi 1998: 2.1144.

94 As, for example, at *War* 2.284; Genesis 41:2; Luke 3:1–2; 1 Macc 1:10; Thucydides 2.2.

95 For that thesis, see Appendix 1, §8.

our notions might turn out, eventually, to be less than well-founded. But it is also the case, on the other hand, that even when the translator's historical knowledge *is* well-founded, it is usually better to supply a literal translation and then, as an historian, to use the annotations for other—even conflicting or ambiguous—information. That will occasion discussion of the issues (or references to such discussions), and that will, hopefully, add to the reader's knowledge about the ancient author—which is among the prime purposes of volumes such as this one.

Thus, for a fairly simple example, note that at 18.148, and again at 18.240, where Josephus refers to Herodias as συνοικοῦσα(ν) Ἡρώδη (lit. "cohabiting with Herod"), Mathieu and Herrmann, Feldman, and Schalit, in their translations, simply identify her as Herod's "wife," turning the Greek participle into an English noun. That certainly conforms to the real situation; Herodias was Herod's wife. Nevertheless, Josephus contented himself with a verb that states the facts of the matter, thus stopping short of stating Herodias's status; in this case, Whiston (1878: 480, 486) came closer, offering "who was now the wife" at 18.148 and going so far as "who now lived as wife" at 18.240. In fact, however, one can go further, for Josephus does not use the word "wife" of Herodias at all, although it would have been simple to do so; note especially, in contrast, that at 18.110 he refers to Herodias as having been the "wife" (γυνή) of her first husband (whom she left for Herod), just as at 18.148 he refers to Cypros as Agrippa's wife (γυνή) just a line or two before referring to Herodias as "cohabiting" with Herod.

True, Josephus is totally capable of using the same participial formulation of other women without, apparently, implying any reservation concerning the validity of their marriages,[96] just as married people, today, may note they have "lived together" for a number of years without implying they are not married. Nevertheless, neither in English nor in Greek does that show that the verb *means* marriage. Josephus's consistency in this case, in his use of this verb rather than "wife" for Herodias, thus seems to suggest, even apart from a general tendency to literal translation, that translators should think twice before doing what Josephus did not do.

Indeed, that would be the case even if translators had no idea as to why Josephus might be reluctant to call Herodias Herod's "wife"; all the more so since Josephus condemned their relationship both from the outset (18.109–110) and again at 18.136.[97] Translating "wife" denies readers the opportunity to see there is a question here, while a literal rendering of Josephus's formulation invites the reader, and therefore the annotator, to raise the question of Josephus's attitude concerning relationships like this. That is a topic of potential relevance both to Gospel evidence on the same subject (see the note on "his words" at 18.118) and, more generally, to Josephus's notions of legal status and the potential discrepancy between it and real status.

It is to another issue of the last-mentioned type that I will turn for one final example: when Josephus referred to gentiles who adopted Jewish practices, Feldman tended to refer to them as "converts" to "Judaism" or to the Jewish "religion." We, however, think of "religion" as something that includes more than practice, and of "conversion" as a formal process, supervised and controlled by others. Namely, just as, in the former example, the difference

---

96   Note, for example, 19.297; 20.147, 153.

97   After reporting at 18.109–110 that Herod "inso-lently" urged Herodias to leave her first husband and marry him, and she indeed promised to make the move, at 18.136 Josephus explicitly condemns their relationship as a violation of the ancestral laws concerning incest.

between "cohabiting" and "marriage" is the difference between what two people are doing and its definition by the law, so too we think of "converts" as people who have so been recognized by a formal process, not only as people who are doing what Jews do.

Thus, for example, at 20.17 we read that Helena and Izates εἰς τὰ Ἰουδαίων ἔθη τὸν βίον μετέβαλον but Feldman rendered "became converts to Judaism"; correspondingly, when Josephus reports, twenty paragraphs later (§38), that Izates learned that his mother πάνυ τοῖς Ἰουδαίων ἔθεσιν χαίρειν, Feldman reports that she "was very much pleased with the Jewish religion." That formulation indicates Feldman's assessment, as an historian, expressed elsewhere as well, that the adoption of Jewish practices amounted to what we would call conversion, namely the change of what we would call one's "religion." And it probably also went together with his recognition that, in the pre-rabbinic period, there was no formal process, so one could accomplish that change all by oneself.[98]

As an historian, I would say that both of those views are reasonable. And I am also willing to accept Feldman's use of "Jew" rather than "Judean" as a usual translation for Ἰουδαῖος, especially in connection with religion and with the Diaspora.[99] Feldman's translations of these passages, however, hide from readers the basic point here, namely, that Josephus's view of religion focused on practice, a point that can be of great interest in a number of contexts, just as they also obscure the fact that the "conversions" involved were effected by individuals without outside involvement or approval. Accordingly, in my translations of such passages I have adhered to Josephus's vocabulary, which refers to practice, and kept my discussion of "religion" and "conversion" to the annotations. Those point up, *inter alia*, such issues as whether or not ancient Jews were aware of the abstract entity we term "religion" or specifically, in this case, "Judaism"; whether they thought it was only a matter of practice or, rather, of belief as well; and whether conversion was a do-it-yourself process or, rather, one that was supervised by community authorities.

To round off this discussion of the relation of our historical notions to translation, I will note that it happens, albeit rarely, that the received text is so difficult that help must be sought wherever it may be found. Thus, for example, when the manuscript tradition of a proper name points to no one who is otherwise known, but a very appropriate candidate with a slightly different name is known from elsewhere, it often seems, despite the risk of circular argument, to be warranted to emend the text accordingly. A good and very certain example of this comes at 19.185, where all the manuscripts mention a senator named Στρεβέλλιος Μάξιμος but the Latin offers, instead, Trebellius. Since Strebellius is not otherwise known as a name, but Trebellius is fairly common, and since, specifically, there is evidence for an M. Trebellius Maximus who was active in public life a few years later (see the note on "Maximus" at 19.185), it seems to be warranted, or even trivial, to emend the name to Τρεβέλλιος (and, perhaps, to conjecture that the opening sigma resulted from someone reading the preceding word as τι rather than τις).

Note, however, that even that case would have been more difficult had Josephus repeated the name Στρεβέλλιος more than once, or had there been no other evidence for a likely candidate named Trebellius, or had the evidence concening the other candidate pointed, one way or another, away from the individual mentioned at 19.185—and that many or most of the suggested emendations, in Books 18–20, suffer from one or the other of those difficulties. In such cases, it usually seems best to refrain from emendation—especially in a format

---

98 On the development of the conversion procedure in the rabbinic period, see Cohen 1999: 198–238 and Lavee 2018.

99 See D. R. Schwartz 2014.

such as the present one, in which the annotations allow for discussion of the issues. See, for example, the notes on "cavalry commander" at 18.237 and 19.299, on "Regulus" at 19.1, on "Minucianus" at 19.18, on "[to the spectacles]" at 19.77, and on "Norbanus" at 19.123.

Note, finally, that, in the translation, words within parentheses (such as "reserved for the final shamelessness" at 18.8) are explicit in Josephus's Greek, while words within square brackets are my own addition—usually to fill out a thought or clarify or replace a pronoun without burdening readers with yet another footnote. In order to avoid the introduction of very numerous bracketed supplements, I tended to a somewhat liberal assessment of what is explicit in the text, but there are translators who would be even more liberal. Thus, for example, although usually I added in pronouns without brackets when the meaning is clear, even when they are not explicit in the Greek, I usually did use brackets when I added in even a little more, such as "he said" to clarify that something is part of an actor's statement, not a Josephan comment (e.g. 18.172, 279), or when I filled out the logic of a statement (e.g., "nonetheless" and "moreover" in 18.5), although perhaps many readers would have understood the same even had I not added it.

VIII. Annotations. If annotations are meant to aid readers to understand a book and to help them (as Steve Mason puts it in the series' preface) as a pier from which to push off toward whatever countless purposes and interests they may have, it seems that annotations on *Ant.* 18–20, that is, on three books that (a) are in ancient Greek, (b) frequently mention or take for granted names, institutions, notions and the like with which many modern readers will not be familiar, (c) are based on sources that have not survived, (d) were put together by an author who turned them, in large measure, into a work of his own in accordance with his own values and goals, and (e) recount events that are also reported or illuminated by other sources, should have, accordingly, five purposes.

First, as a philologist, I have attempted to justify my readings and translations when that seemed necessary—when Josephus's usage, and/or my take on it, are not as readers might expect. Most often, that entails comparison with Josephus's own usage, whether in order to explain that he is using a word surprisingly because he wanted to create some internal allusion or to show that he uses the same term or formulation the same way elsewhere. Very often the work has already been done by others; my debts to my predecessors and colleagues is much greater than is indicated by the numerous references to Thackeray's *ThLJ*, to Feldman's LCL edition of *Ant.* 18–20, to Rengstorf's *CCFJ*, and to the work of other commentators on Josephus, especially those in the present series. In this context, I will note that often, when I noticed, I noted the fact that a word is rare or appears nowhere else in Josephus; what, if anything, to make of that, I usually leave to others.

Next, as an antiquarian, I have striven to explain, to twenty-first century readers, the references to ancient *realia*: institutions, customs, individuals, toponyms, buildings, events, etc. Usually these explanations are brief, but include references to relevant bibliography.

Third, as a source-critic, I point out evidence for Josephus's use of sources and its implications. There are many types of such evidence, some more probative than others, including outright contradictions within Josephus's narrative that seem, to me, to be too difficult to imagine coming from the same mind and hand, differing points of view, confusing or misleading formulations, and differential vocabulary. Cf. Mason 2003a and Schwartz 2013: 94–109. In most cases, the annotations strive to give readers enough information to understand the problems and the way a source-critical hypothesis could explain how or why they came to be, along with references to studies that discuss the respective issues more thoroughly—whether or not they agree with my own proposal.

Fourth, however, as a composition critic, I attempt (in line with a major thrust of the present series) to point to Josephus's own hand—and so: intentions—as an author, even in cases in which he is using sources. Indeed, it is especially in cases in which he is following a source, so it would have been easy for him to stick to its formulations, that his deviations indicate what was important for him. Obviously, that is often speculative, for we do not have access to the original sources; would that we had, for *Ant.* 18–20, something even slightly comparable to the Hebrew Bible, which (whether in the original or in the Greek translation) underlies just about all of *Ant.*1–11; the *Letter of Aristeas*, which underlies a hundred paragraphs of *Ant.* 12; and 1 Maccabees, which underlies much of *Ant.* 12–13, to such an extent that one can print them in parallel columns and clearly see where and how Josephus went off on his own.[100] However, at times we can, it seems, be confident that we are reading Josephus's own formulations and thoughts. This is particularly the case in books like these, which relate to his own time, so he might be expected both to be less dependent on sources and to have more of his own thoughts and assessments. Moreover, comparisons with the parallel narratives in *War* 2 occasion much thought as to what changed, or how Josephus changed, between the two books.

Evidence of Josephus's own point of view is especially to be identified in parts of these books in which an author's hand is naturally to be expected—in first-person statements (such as 19.15–16 and 20.155–157, 166) and at the "seams" between passages devoted to different topics and, perhaps, built upon different sources—which means, in practice, at the beginnings and ends of large units. Thus, for a central example noted above, if at the opening of Book 18 Josephus chooses to characterize (and condemn) anti-Roman rebels as having introduced religious innovation and revolution (§9, καίνισις καὶ μεταβολή), just as he closes his account of the last governor whose term he recounts, Albinus, with an account of Agrippa II's villainous "innovation" (καινοποιεῖν) with regard to a detail of the Temple cult (§§216–218), readers may be sure that, however forced the former and however trivial the latter, they serve to make Books 18–20 into a unified composition. There is no reason not to credit that achievement to Josephus himself. And that, of course, points us to a theme that must have been very important for Josephus, and bolsters us in our expectation that other passages too, that underline the importance of observing Jewish law as received from the ancestors, are also to be understood as his own emphases. If, as is at times the case (see, for example, the notes on "make images" at 18.55 and on "forbidden to us" at 18.264), that expectation leads us to read carefully to see if there is any roughness or inconcinnity that indicates that Josephus has given special attention to formulating his account, all the better.

Fifth, and finally, as an historian, I attempt, in the notes, to deal with "what really happened." This requires—as the first three jobs do not, but the fourth often does (as shall be explained)—attention to other ancient evidence apart from Josephus's, be it literary (as it most often is), epigraphic, numismatic, or archaeological. Following the historian's usual rules, methods, and models of human behavior, it appears that examination of Josephus's testimony in light of the other evidence, which might corroborate it, expand upon it, nuance it, or contradict it, can lead us to judgments about what, probably, really happened. Here too, much has been done by others; the history of the Roman world in general, and of the Jews and Judea in particular, in the first-century (a.k.a. *neutestamentliche Zeitgeschichte*), are very well-plowed fields, and frequently my notes simply point readers to an established view or ongoing debate, underlining any special relevance of Josephus's evidence when I am aware of it.

---

100 On *Aristeas* and 1 Maccabees see, respectively, Pelletier 1962 and Sievers 2001. For the comparison of *Antiquities* to the Hebrew Bible, see the notes in the relevant volumes of JLCL, FJTC, and Schalit 1944, along with Feldman 1998a–b and Nodet 2018.

As stated at the opening of the preceding paragraph, the juxtaposition and comparison of Josephus's evidence to that of others (including his own evidence in *War*) is also of relevance to composition criticism. That is because often it is only the comparison of Josephus's evidence to that of other ancient sources that leads us to notice what is special about Josephus's. It shows "the ways not taken" that were possible, and, just by doing so, urges us to wonder why Josephus did something else. Who, for example, would notice that, after violating the sanctity of Jerusalem, Josephus's Pilate decided to back down out of respect for the Judeans' noble loyalty to their religion, were it not for the fact that Philo's very similar story (*Leg.* 299–305) portrays Pilate as cruel and corrupt and has him backing down only when compelled by Tiberius? Who would notice that Josephus's accounts of Felix and Albinus in *Ant.* 20 are basically positive, leaving sinful Jews the villains of their stories, were it not for the parallel accounts in *War* 2, which cast the governors as the main villains? Or who (to revert to an example brought two paragraphs ago) would notice that 18.55 and 18.264 do not quite make sense (for they have Jews protesting that Romans are doing things that Jews are forbidden to do) if there were no parallel accounts, that do make sense (for they have Jews protesting about Romans doing things that are forbidden to be done [i.e., *by anyone*] in the Holy Land or Holy City), at *War* 2.170, 195? But readers who do notice those ways not taken will, willy nilly, ask not only what really happened but also why Josephus's statements about that changed.

These, then, are the five goals the annotations attempt to serve, in the hope that they will help the next generation of readers of Josephus along in their pursuit of the topics that interest them.

MAPS

0   50 km

N

Tyre

Paneas (Casearea Philippi)

GALILEE

Gamala

Ptolemais

Tarichea

Hippos

Tiberias

Sepphoris

Abila/Raphana

Dora

Gadara

DECAPOLIS

Scythopolis

Caesarea

Ginae

Pella

Sebaste

Gerasa

Mt. Garizim

Jordan River

Apollonia

SAMARIA

Joppa

Philadelphia

Jamnia

Lydda

PEREA

Jericho

Azotus

Jerusalem

Qumran

JUDEA

Ascalon

Anthedon

Machaerus

Gaza

IDUMEA

Masada

NABATEA

Raphia

Malatha

Map of Roman Judea. Wikimedia Commons, Erik Gaba, licence CC BY-SA 3.0 / template mapping: from Aryeh Kasher, *Jews and Hellenistic Cities in Eretz-Israel* (T.übingen 1990) p. 47, with additions by Steve Mason and Chaim Schwartz/ mapping: Suzana Matešić, DLK / graphic: Nina Hardwig, HUND B

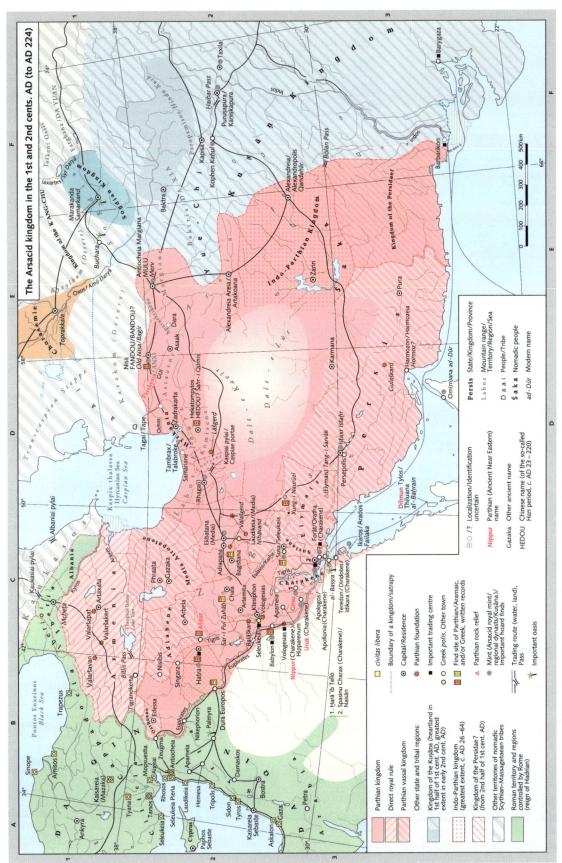

Map of the Arsacid Kingdom in the First Two Centuries CE. From: *Brill's Historical Atlas of the Ancient World* (ed. A-M. Wittke, E. Olshausen and R. Szydlak; English ed. by C. F. Salazar et al.; New Pauly Supplements; Leiden: Brill, 2010), p. 215

TRANSLATION AND COMMENTARY

BOOK 18

(1.1)[1] 1 Turning now[2] to Quirinius, who was one of those who had been admitted to the Senate,[3] after completing service in the other positions[4] and after going through them[5] all had become a consul,[6] and who in other ways too was respected more highly than all but a few:[7] when he came to Syria, having been sent by Caesar to be the administrator of justice[8]

The Beginning of Direct Roman Rule: Quirinius and Coponius

---

1 Quirinius's census has been studied intensively, especially because it is mentioned at Luke 2:2, among the circumstances of the birth of Jesus: Luke states the census happened to be carried out just as Mary was about to give birth, and that is what occasioned Joseph and Mary's visit to Bethlehem then, since the census required each person to be in his ancestral residence, and the family of Joseph, Mary's husband, was thought to be Davidic, hence from Bethlehem (see Matthew 2:5–6, quoting Micah 5:2). Two data supplied by Luke, when compared with Josephus's data, create the so-called "Quirinius Problem": since at Luke 1:5 Luke dates his story to "the days of Herod" and Mary becomes pregnant in ch. 1 but gives birth in ch. 2, at the time of the census, it follows that Luke dates Quirinius's census, and the birth of Jesus, to the days of Herod (or very shortly after his death), just as Matthew 2 (which does not mention the census) clearly dates Jesus's birth to the days of Herod. But Josephus just as clearly puts Quirinius's census after the end of Archelaus's decade-long rule of Judea after Herod's death; see esp. §26 and, for Archelaus's decade-long tenure, *War* 2.111–113, *Ant.* 17.342, 345–347, and *Life* 5. For some of the huge bibliography on this contradiction concerning the date of the census, and discussions of the question that conclude that the dating of the census in Herod's reign is impossible, if only because a Roman governor would not have conducted a census in the kingdom of an autonomous vassal king, see Schürer's classic demonstration that Herod died in 4 BCE and discussion of Quirinius's census (*HJP* 1.326–328, n. 165, and 399–427), also Ogg 1967/68; Boffo 1994: 182–203; Sherwin-White 1963: 162–171; Stern 1974a: 372–374; Schreckenberg 1980: 186; Fitzmyer 1981: 400–405; Syme 1984: 881–883; Brown 1993: 547–556; Dąbrowa 2011; Rhoads 2011; Gertoux 2015; and Mahieu 2012: 447–463, together with Sievers 2014. It might be that the simplest explanation of the genesis of the problem is the hypothesis that the section on Mary in Luke 1 is secondary, introduced in order to clarify (as Matt 3:13–17 and John 1:1–34 do in other ways), in accordance with Christian needs, that, from the earliest possible point in the story, John recognized Jesus's superiority; see D. R. Schwartz 2013: 110–115.

2 Opening a book of *Antiquities* with δέ is usual for Josephus, whether it answers a μέν at the end of the preceding book (as at *Ant.* 19.1) or, as here (as also at 20.1), does not. So too, for example, the opening of Xenophon's *Hellenica* and of the sixth and seventh books of Dionysius of Halicarnassus (cited by Schalit 1979:1–2).

For discussion of the precise sense (continuative? adversative? emphatic?), see Verdenius 1974 and van der Horst 1979. Here it seems simply to be a way of underlining the name of the character on whom the story will now focus; compare the note on "to Agrippa" at §195.

3 I.e., a senator; for the longwinded way of formulating that, cf. on "administrator of justice" later in this paragraph. For the use of βουλή for the Roman Senate, see *GTRI* 121 and, for Josephus, *ThLJ* 108.

4 For Quirinius's career, including his consulship in 12 BCE and his governorship of Galatia-Pamphylia ca. 5–3 BCE, see Tacitus's summary in *Ann.* 3.48.1–2, also *HJP* 1.258–259, and Dąbrowa 1998: 27–30. Dąbrowa 1998 gives many examples of the careers of the governors of Syria in the first two centuries; on their high status, reflected by the stationing of three or four legions in the province (see the note on "Roman" at §262), see Rey-Coquais 1978: 62 and Nitschke 2006: 93–95. As Nitschke emphasizes, virtually all were former consuls and in most cases the Syrian appointment was the peak of their careers. That itself constitutes an argument in the long debate (inspired by a desire to justify Luke 2:2) as to whether *ILS* 918 makes it likely that the governorship mentioned here was Quirinius's second in Syria; for that debate, see also *HJP* 1.425–426.

5 For the same expression with a different verb, see *Ant.* 19.32.

6 In 12 BCE. For the use of ὕπατος of a Roman consul, see *GTRI* 165–171.

7 For this sense of σὺν ὀλίγοις, see also 19.20, 125 and LSJ 1215, s.v. ὀλίγος, §3b. It is nevertheless possible that Josephus meant, as Whiston (1878: 470) thought, that Quirinius came to Syria "with a few" in his entourage; cf. the fuller, and unambiguous, formulation at §49: σὺν ὀλίγοις τοῖς περὶ αὐτόν, also §107. But in the present case it is difficult to see what the point of that observation would be.

8 As with "who had been admitted to the Senate" instead of "a senator," above, so too δικαιοδότης (which appears only here in Josephus) seems to be no more than a fancy formulation for "governor"; see Stern 1974a: 373. Here Stern responds to the suggestion that Josephus does not mean that Quirinius was governor of Syria at the time of this census, a notion that could open up the possibility that the time when Quirinius conducted a census as governor of Syria (as indicated more explicitly at Luke 2:2) was earlier, in the days of Herod, as Luke suggests, with Quirinius then having only some special assignment;

for the nation and to assess their possessions, 2 Coponius, of the equestrian order,[9] was sent along with him to be the governor of the Judeans with full authority.[10] Quirinius too came to Judea, which had become an appendix to Syria,[11] in order to evaluate the Judeans'[12] possessions and to dispose of Archelaus's property.[13] 3 Although at first they took the news of the registrations badly,[14] they settled down[15] after the high priest Joazar,[16] who was the son

---

Stern writes that that "seems far-fetched." For epigraphic evidence for the use of the term of provincial governors, see *GTRI* 37, s.v. δικαιοδότης, §4.

9 τάγματος τῶν ἱππέων; for this formulation, see *GTRI* 57, s.v. ἱππεύς. By introducing Coponius (who, apart from the brief parallel at *War* 2.107, is otherwise unknown) as an equite, paralleling his introduction of Quirinius as a senator, Josephus clarifies to his readers that the secondary status of Judea, in contrast to Syria, was paralleled by the difference in ranks of those sent to administer them. For the contrast between senators and equites, see the note on "was chosen" at 19.3.

10 Despite the preceding context, which sounds as if Quirinius were just administering the initial evaluation but Coponius was given full authority in Judea, the next sentence shows this is not what Josephus meant. Rather, the parallel narrative at *War* 2.117 explains what "full" means: the authority even to put subjects to death. See *HJP* 1.367–372 and 2.219–223; Bammel 1974b; Lémonon 2007: 70–86; Martin 2006: 175; and Mason 2008: 80–81, n. 722, also the note on "approval" at 20.202. For ἐξουσία as *legal* authority, *ius*, see *GTRI* 44.

11 This formulation, which echoes that of 17.355, seems to be contradicted by that in *War* 2.117, according to which Judea became a province. But that account also makes no reference to the fact that the Roman census of Judea in 6 CE was administered by the Roman governor of Syria—a point that supports the present formulation. Hence, it seems that the formulation in *War* should be viewed as a general statement, whereas here we learn that, although Judea had a separate administrator, who usually functioned as a governor, Judea was under the general supervision of the Roman governor of Syria. In any case, it is clear, from *War* as well (e.g., 2.185, 239–244, paralleled below at §261 and 20.125–133), that the governors of Syria exercised such a role when needed, as is only to be expected, given their higher rank and prestige and the legions at their disposal; this point leaves the question, whether Judea was part of Syria, largely formal. In general, see Ghiretti 1985; Cotton 1999: 76–81, who argues that Judea did not become "an independent province" until after the death of Agrippa I; and Eck 2007: 1–51, who puts that off until the revolt of 66, when (in 67) Vespasian, an ex-consul, was sent directly to Judea by the emperor, not by the Roman governor

of Syria. See also Mason 2008: 78–79, n. 718, and idem 2016c: 239–245.

12 Lit. "their." The use of "their" with reference to "Judea," as also "they" at the beginning of §3, indicates the assumption that *Ioudaioi* are to be understood, here, as "Judeans." For a similar passage, see §196.

13 The same two goals of Quirinius's mission are mentioned at §26, as already at 17.355. On property owned by Herod and inherited by Archelaus (termed "Archelaus's house/estate" in the same context at 17.355), see *War* 2.96–97//*Ant.* 17.319–320, also Wilker 2007: 76–78. On the sense of χρήματα, cf. the note on "labor" at §319. As for Luke's reference to what Quirinius did as an imperial census (ἀπογραφή) of "the entire inhabited world" (Luke 2:1), rather than as a measure related to Rome's particular needs in Judea after Archelaus's exile, note a Roman officer's report, preserved in an inscription (originally from Beirut?) found in Venice (Boffo 1994, no. 23 = *ILS* 2683), that he conducted a census ("censum egi") in Apamea on Quirinius's orders. This suggests that Quirinius, upon his arrival in Syria (to which Judea was now attached), conducted a census throughout all of its borders, and that could account for Luke's impression that it was universal.

14 For ἐν δεινῷ φέροντες see also, for example §§261, 354.

15 This verb, ὑποκαταβαίνω, appears elsewhere in Josephus only once, in a literal sense of "coming down" from the mountains to the coast (*Apion* 1.180).

16 This reference to Joazar as high priest is problematic, because according to *Ant.* 17.339 he was deposed about a decade earlier. This problem cannot be avoided by reference to the fact that Josephus and the New Testament often identify someone as "high priest" in the sense of belonging to that class, especially (but not only) if the individual was once *the* high priest, as is the case in such passages as 20.180–181, 207 and Acts 4:6 (on that general usage see Stern 1976: 600–603), for §26 reports that, in the wake of the present episode, Joazar was removed from office and replaced by another. That is, here Josephus means he was the incumbent. Perhaps he was reinstated sometime after the abovementioned deposition and Josephus failed to report that; this might be a case in which Josephus's move from Nicolaus (followed down to the end of *Ant.* 17) to other sources entailed some roughness. See VanderKam 2004: 417–419.

of Boethus,[17] convinced them not to oppose it any longer. So they, for their part, overcome by Joazar's words, evaluated their possessions without any equivocation.[18]

4 But Judas the Golanite,[19] a man from a city named[20] Gamala[21] who had associated with himself Sadok, a Pharisee,[22] pressed for rebellion, saying that the evaluation was nothing other than the imposition of outright[23] enslavement[24] and calling upon the nation to lay claim[25] to its liberty:[26] **5** if they were to attain it, they would achieve happiness, having established its foundation, while if they were to fail to bring about such success they would [nonetheless] garner for themselves the honor and good repute [that accrues to those who]

Judas of Galilee Incites Rebellion

---

17 "Son of Boethus" probably means "of the clan of Boethus"—a well-known family of Alexandrian origin that rose to prominence in Herod's days (*Ant.* 15.320–322); see esp. 19.297, also Smallwood 1962: 15 and 32–34; Stern 1976: 604–606; and Hachlili 1983/84: 202–203. Joazar's precise identity depends on the interpretation of *Ant.* 17.164. See VanderKam 2004: 413–414 and below, Appendix 2.

18 Josephus uses ἐνδοιάζω frequently in these books, usually, as here, with a negation (§§97, 132, 231, 329; 19.108, 242).

19 Better known as "Judas the Galilean"; that is how the leader of this rebellion, explicitly linked to the time of Quirinius's census, is named at 18.23; 20.102; *War* 2.433; and Acts 5:37. The fact that Josephus identifies him here as a Golanite, despite that usual practice and despite the fact that usually Josephus is content to refer generally to Gamala as if it were part of the nearby Galilee (see the note on "Gamala" later in this paragraph), seems to indicate a need specific to the present context: the desire to indicate to readers that this rebellious Judas is not to be identified with the Galilean rebel of about a decade earlier, Judas the son of Ezekias, to whom Josephus devoted several lines not too far back (*Ant.* 17.271–272). Josephus's efforts have not, of course, stopped historians from wondering whether the two were not in fact one; see Mason 2016c: 246, n. 171.

20 By adding "a city named" Josephus recognizes that his readers might not have heard of the city. Indeed, Josephus might not have remembered ever mentioning the city in *Antiquities*; the last (and only) times it is mentioned in the work are at 13.394, 396. Cf. the notes on "are called" at §11 and on "Nazirites" at 19.294.

21 Which was indeed in the Golan, as Josephus also states at *War* 4.2. Elsewhere, however, Josephus more generally includes Gamala in the Galilee: he includes Vespasian's conquest of Gamala (*War* 4.1–83) within his account of the fighting in the Galilee (see esp. ibid. 84 and 120), just as his survey of Gamala's affairs in *Life* 46–61 comes within his account of the cities of the Galilee (see *Life* 30, 61). Indeed, at *War* 2.568 Josephus roundly defines

Gamala as the largest city of the Galilee. On Gamala and Josephus's accounts of it, see Aviam 2007.

22 This conforms to Josephus's statement at §23 that the fourth philosophy, founded by Judas, agreed with the Pharisees about most things.

23 For ἄντικρυς in such a metaphorical sense ("downright, outright"), see also §302 and *Ant.* 4.150; *ThLJ* 53. For its basic locative sense ("opposite"), see 20.169 and *Life* 248. For echoes of Thucydides in the present phrase and the next paragraphs (§§5–8), see Feldman 1965: 6–7, n. a. Cf. the note on "slavery" at §47.

24 The basic notion seems to be that the assessment would allow for Roman taxation and that would be the embodiment of enslavement. But it should be noted that the very notion of the census itself, which patently reduces people to the status of objects, could easily be associated with enslavement, as in 3 Macc 2:28 ("reduced to *laographia* and servile status"; cf. Kasher 1985: 226–228). For Judas's fight being a refusal to accept "slavery," see the opening of his grandson's (?) speech at Masada, *War* 7.323, also, more generally, the first main section of Agrippa II's great anti-rebellion speech at *War* 2.348–357.

25 For similar usage of ἀντίληψις, see §215, also the use of the verb, ἀντιλαμβάνω, in the same sense, at 19.238.

26 "Liberty" is, of course, the standard opposite of "slavery"; see, for example, 12.434/13.1; 13.213; 19.42; 20.121; and *War* 7.255. Although sometimes, such as *Ant.* 12.281, 302–303 and 13.198 (in his paraphrase of 1 Maccabees), Josephus presents the freedom to live according to Jewish law as all the "liberty" the Jews want, here, as elsewhere, Josephus freely admits that, insofar as government is concerned, Roman rule means the end of the Jews' freedom. Affirmation of this conclusion, but with the call upon Jews to accept it and stop dreaming of "liberty," is a prime theme of Agrippa II's speech in *War* 2.345–401, just as both of Eleazar ben Yair's speeches at Masada argue repeatedly that those who want to remain free by evading Roman rule can do so only via suicide (7.326, 334, 344, 386). On Josephus on "liberty" see Gafni 2019: 21–22 and D. R. Schwartz 2002; on "Israel's freedom" more generally, see Hengel 1989: 110–122.

think great thoughts;[27] and [moreover] the deity[28] cannot do other than cooperate with that which they resolve,[29] and will indeed foster its success no less enthusiastically [than them] if with eagerness in their minds for great things they stand firm and do not back away from the murder[30] that will be incumbent upon them.

6 Since it was with pleasure that people received the news of their words,[31] the audacious[32] plot[33] made great progress[34]— and there is no evil that did not sprout forth from these men, and the nation was infected[35] [by them] beyond what words [can describe]: 7 with the instigation of wars of incomparable and unstoppable intensity; with the doing away of friends who could have alleviated[36] the suffering;[37] with assaults by large bands of brigands[38] and the annihilation of people of the first rank—all this with the claim to be establishing the common

---

27 Such positive usage of μεγαλόφρονος, of those who undertake rebellion, followed up by μεγάλων ("great things") later in this paragraph, is probably to be understood ironically, in light of the condemnation that begins more explicitly with the reference to "murder" at the end of the paragraph. Cf. 20.176 and *Life* 17, 43, where Josephus condemns rebels as μέγα φρονοῦντες, people who are "thinking (too) big," i.e., out of line, with arrogance or hubris, like Herodias at §255.

28 By using τὸ θεῖον rather than ὁ θεός, Josephus chooses a more universal-sounding nomenclature, as is appropriate for the presentation of Judaism as a "philosophy" (§§9, 11, 25) See also the notes on "deity" at §288 and 20.41. As Shutt (1980: 173–179) concludes his discussion, "The above investigation supports the conclusion that usually *to theion* is used by Josephus to mean 'the deity,' without necessarily any reference to the God of Israel." Correspondingly, note Haaland 1999: 46, n. 53: τὸ θεῖον is "underrepresented" in *Against Apion*, where Josephus avoids presenting Judaism as a philosophy (see the note on "philosophy" at §9).

29 On such "synergetism," rather than waiting for God to act himself, see Byron 2003: 84. The idea that God helps them who help themselves is akin to that ascribed to Chaerea at 19.56, 233; note also 18.363.

30 Reading φόνου, with the witnesses. Hudson, followed by Niese and Schalit, emended this into πόνου (suffering, burden), probably on the assumption that Josephus would not ascribe to Judas and Sadok such a pejorative designation of what their men would need to do. However, Josephus's point seems to be bitterly ironic, namely, that these wicked demagogues could convince their gullible followers that even murder is necessary; so too at §23. In §7, in contrast, it is the innocent who endure πόνος.

31 Here Josephus moves from his ironic presentation of the elevated formulations of the rebel leaders to their tragic consequences. On "receiving with pleasure," see the note on "pleasure" at §63.

32 For audacity (τόλμα/τόλμημα, θράσος) and the related verbs and adjectives as characteristic of rebels,

see, for example, *War* 2.238, 267, 303, 409, 412, as below, in what Mason (2008: 219, n. 1693) terms "the build-up to war" in *Ant.* 20 (§§108, 114, 165, 180–181, 199, 206, 213). Josephus considers it to be especially characteristic of youths; see 19.45 and the note on "youths" at §10.

33 Here I translate ἐπιβουλή, as in the main witnesses, and as in the same phrase at §181. Niese, here as in his conjecture at 16.332 (Niese 1890a: 55) and (in his editio minor) at *War* 4.154 (Niese 1895: 276), prefers ἐπιβολή, which, in the sense of "attack, undertaking, project, plan, intention" (the relevant definitions of ἐπιβολή in *CCFJ* 2.151), comes close to what we would expect. However, it only comes close; we would expect something like "movement." Given the near-unanimity of the witnesses, we should perhaps prefer to understand that Josephus is chacterizing the rebels as conspiring against both Rome and the Judean commonweal.

34 Josephus likes this collocation; see for example §§142, 181, 340.

35 For ἀναπίμπλημι (lit. "fill up") in the sense of "infect," "defile," see *ThLJ* 41 (s.v. ἀναπιμπλάναι, §3) and, for example, Feldman's translations of 19.172 and 20.160 (Feldman 1965: 295, 477). For similar usage with ἀναπίμπλημι see 20.160; with plain πίμπλημι, see also 20.124, 215. For the comparison of a state's deterioration to its suffering from a disease, cf. §25 and 20.214.

36 Josephus uses this verb, ἐπελαφρύνω, only one other time—*Life* 284.

37 Here Josephus may well have been thinking of Ananus, son of Ananus; see his eulogy of him in *War* 4.321, where Josephus emphasizes that had he not been murdered he would either have brought the war to an end or else postponed the Roman victory. For his murder as the main turning-point of the war, according to Josephus, and therefore of Josephus's *War*, see esp. Mason 2016b: 22–23.

38 For λῃσταί and bands of them (λῃστήρια) as heinous criminals (the Romans' "latrones") very familiar to Josephus's readers, see Grünewald 2004 (esp. 91–109 on Judea), also Brighton 2009: 60–62; Sharon 2017: 361–377; and Grabbe 2021: 138–145. Whatever the truth about them was (nationalist rebels? self-seeking criminals?,

welfare, but in reality in the hope of private gain.[39] 8 Out of these there sprouted [outbreaks of] civil strife[40] and political murder: while one man was slaughtered by members of his own community, in the madness of these people against one another and against themselves, so enthusiastic were they not to be inferior to those who opposed them, another man was slaughtered by their enemies, famine (reserved for the final shamelessness),[41] and the conquest and destruction of cities, until the civil strife consigned even the Temple of God[42] to the flames of the enemy. 9 So it is that innovation[43] and revolution concerning the ancestral usages[44]

––––––––––––––

"social bandits"?), it is clear that Josephus's terminology is quite pejorative. Note, however, that this is the only time Josephus refers to λῃσταί or λῃστήρια in Book 18 or 19, whereas in Book 20 they appear quite often and, indeed, references to their becoming more and more widespread are something of a refrain that marks steps along the way to the final catastrophe. Note esp. 20.124, 160, 172, 210, 215, 255–256. Thus this passage contributes significantly to the function of this introduction as an opening bracket meant to portray the start of direct Roman rule as the beginning of the end.

39 Like many authors, Josephus frequently contrasts the way things seem to the way they really are. Compare, for example, §260; 17.163, 241; and 19.101, 130, 156–157, 246; *Apion* 2.281. This is especially useful when, as here, it points up the falsity of villains' claimed justifications for their self-serving actions; so, for example, at 19.40–41, 130. The theme is prominent in the *Life*, which is full of double games, and in the long account of Gaius's assassination in Book 19, where the very nature of tyranny imposes on ruler (as here) and ruled the need for dissimulation; see the note on "ostensibly" at 19.157. For more on the Greco-Roman distinction between word and deed, see Danker 1982: 339–343.

40 True, στάσις "can best be defined as internal war between local groups of citizens" (Berger 1992: 10), and often Josephus indeed uses it that way, for factional violence within cities; see, for example, 18.374; 19.278; and 20.173 (on Seleucia, Alexandria, and Caesarea). In other cases, however, such as §63 and 20.227, and perhaps here as well, Josephus uses the term more broadly, of "rebellion"—the result being the portrayal of Jewish rebellion against Rome as the work of only a faction among the Jews, one that, as he insists in the present passage as elsewhere, in no way represents the Jews as a whole. On Josephus on "stasis," although especially in *War*, see Mason 2008: 319–320, n. 2627; Price 2011; and Chapman 2019. For Josephus's frequent interpretation of events in *Antiquities* in terms of "stasis" (e.g. 1.117, 4.140, 225; 13.291, 299), along with the argument that he did so in order to appeal to the interests of non-Jews and Jews who were familiar with the topos (e.g. from Thucydides's famous account of Corcyra [3.82–84]), see Feldman 1998a: 140–143.

41 This is the only occurrence of ἀναισχυντία in Josephus. For the hunger and shamelessness that characterized the depths of suffering during the Roman siege, see *War* 6.199 (ἀναίδεια) and the terrible story introduced there (§§201–213); on it, see D. R. Schwartz 2013: 87–89.

42 This move to very Jewish terminology, referring to "God" rather than "the deity" (see the note on "deity" at §5) and to the "Temple of God" rather than "the Temple of the Jews" (so Gaius at §297) or as "the Temple" simpliciter, as usual, is, just as the lesson stated in the next line, a clear self-positioning of Josephus as a Jewish author bespeaking the Jewish religion; so too 20.49, where he reflects the attitude of a Jewish pilgrim.

43 The same principle, that innovation with regard to ancestral practice is heinous and brings on catastrophe, reappears at 20.218, at the very eve of the end of the story. Together with the present passage, it thus frames the whole period of direct Roman rule. Cf. the Introduction, at n. 32. Other statements of this principle include 5.306; 15.267, 281. For the general ancient assumption that old things were legitimate and the concomitant condemnation of innovation, see Pilhofer 1990. Note also *Apion* 2.182–183 and 2.222, where Josephus condemns those who depend on "saying new things" (καινολογεῖν) to mislead fools, just as Acts 17:21 similarly pokes fun at Athenians who have nothing to do but talk all day about whatever happens to be new (there the condemnation of innovation comes along with scorn for Greek wordiness; cf. the note on "desire it" at 20.204). For the way Josephus's condemnation of innovation and proclaimed devotion (in the immediate continuation) to the ancestral laws resonated with Roman ideals, see esp. Goodman 1994: 334–335. On the equation of "new" gods with "strange, foreign" gods, especially in the imperial period, cf. Norden (1913b): 53, n. 3.

44 For Josephus's use of τὰ πάτρια, see esp. Schröder 1996. Usually it refers to the ancestral *laws*. Here, Josephus's polemic against the rebels is premised upon his account of them as a philosophy, one that claimed to be a variety of the Jewish religion, which allows him to denounce it as as such and to set it as a bracket parallel to the one supplied by another violation of the Jewish religion at 20.216–218. It could well be that the Sicarii would have been puzzled or amused by Josephus's presentation of them as a group of the same genus as the

can bring the scales[45] down to the destruction of those who gather together [to pursue them].[46]

Indeed, Judas and Sadok stirred up a fourth and invasive[47] philosophy[48] among us, and, once they were supplied with numerous devotees of it, they both filled up the state at that time[49] with tumults[50] and also laid the roots of the troubles that later overtook us—all of that because [their philosophy] was not previously accustomed to be among the [Jews'] philosophies.[51] 10 I would like to go on a little about it,[52] if only because the destruction of our state came about because of the enthusiasm of our youths[53] for them.[54]

---

schools of Jewish religious philosophy, but for Josephus, who by *Antiquities* was tending to view "being Jewish" as a matter of religion, which has various philosophies, that was the only point of view from which he could posit or condemn varieties of Jews.

45 For this image, see also §349 and 19.144.

46 I have translated τοῖς συνελθοῦσιν in accordance with the use of the verb at §20. Note that Josephus states only that punishment falls upon the perpetrators. In fact, however, his story frequently reports, both in *War* (e.g., 2.455) and the present volume (e.g., §§62, 84), that rebels' clashes with the government bring down suffering on innocent bystandbyers as well, if only because they failed to intervene; see the notes on "did not" at §62 and on "with them" at 20.180. Here in contrast, in this programmatic introduction, Josephus prefers to sign onto a simpler religious statement.

47 For a thorough demonstration that ἐπείσακτος, for Josephus and others, means "brought in from elsewhere" (compare, for example, the similar use of ἐπεισάγω for the introduction of foreign practices at 15.281), which in matters of religion, and customary practice in general, of course constitutes a condemnation, as is stated here, see van der Horst 2012.

48 For Josephus's use of φιλοσοφία and the verb φιλοσοφέω and φιλόσοφος, see Haaland 1999: 289–290. As he summarizes, "we see that in *Bellum* and *Antiquitates* the 'philosophy words' are almost exclusively employed in descriptions of Jews and Judaism." For *Antiquities*, see, apart from here, 13.289 (on the Pharisees) and 1.25; 8.44; 12.37, 99 (where the Jews engage in "philosophizing" with the king); 16.398. In *Against Apion*, in contrast, such words are used almost only of others: Greeks, Egyptians, and Chaldaeans. This is part of a general anti-Greek orientation of Josephus in *Against Apion*; note that some witnesses give the work's title as *Against the Greeks*. In other words, in the *Antiquities* Josephus enjoys portraying the Jews as having philosophies, for it makes them as respectable as the Greeks, while in *Against Apion*, in which he generally takes an anti-Greek stance (except for when it's convenient to cite Greeks who approve of the Jews), he portrays "philosophy" superciliously, as the type of prattle that would appeal only to Greeks, who excel in such nonsense but have little regard for truth, while the

Jews, like Romans, are serious and honest people. See esp. *Apion* 2.225, also *Life* 40, Acts 17:18–21 and Plutarch, *Life of Cato the Elder*, chs. 22–23. For thoughts as to what might have engendered such a move within what must have been no more than a couple of years (Domitian's persecution of philosophers?; Greek criticism of Josephus's *Antiquities*?), see Haaland 2005.

49 Josephus's use of τὸ παρόν ("the present") of 6 CE here means *their* present (cf. the fuller phrasing in 20.61), in contrast to the later period to which he next alludes.

50 In *Ant*. 17–20 Josephus often uses θόρυβος and θορυβέω to describe Jewish violence that he condemns; see the note on "tumult for the Jews" at §65.

51 This statement is seconded at the opening of §11, which grounds the other, legitimate, philosophies in "the earliest times." Josephus achieves the same deligitimizing end in *War* 2.118 by asserting that Judas's teachings had nothing to do with those of other Jewish schools (οὐδὲν τοῖς ἄλλοις προσεοικώς)—of which, he emphasizes at the opening of the excursus that follows that paragraph, as here at §11, there were three.

52 Namely, about the fourth philosophy.

53 Josephus frequently asserts that it was the intemperate nature of youths that brought about rebellion and, in its wake, suffering and destruction; see esp. *War* 2. 225, 284, 290, and 4.128, as well as Levine 1974: 394–395, n. 94; Eckstein 1990: 192–193 (esp. on the theme's Polybian background); and Mason 2008: 313, n. 2567. Both of the latter cite comparable material from elsewhere. Note that this is not a problem of Jewish youth alone; see *Ant*. 19.300. This is a useful apologetic claim, for it means that the older Jews, who were also wiser (on the need of youths to get idealism and extremism out of their system, see esp. Josephus, *Life* 12, also ibid. §80) and more representative of Judaism, tried to prevent rebelliousness. See, for example, *War* 2.290, 410–411; *Ant*. 20.123. Cf. *Ant*. 4.152 (on Phinehas): if a youth was hotheaded and violent for a good cause, he was exceptional.

54 I.e., for Judas and Sadok. Holwerda (1853: 113) suggested emending αὐτῶν into αὐτήν, which would have the advantage of describing the rebels of the 66–70 as devotees of the fourth philosophy, not of its founders, and would also allow us to avoid the problem that κατά

(1.2)[55] **11** The Jews have had, since the earliest times,[56] three[57] philosophies[58] concern- ing their ancestral usages: they are, as they are called,[59] that of the Essenes,[60] that of the Sadducees, and, a third, philosophized by the Pharisees. True, there is what I wrote about them in the second book of my *Judean War*,[61] but nevertheless I will make brief mention of them now as well.[62]

The Jewish Philosophies

---

with the genitive usually means "against." As so often, one wonders whether there is enough justification for the assumption that Josephus wrote a text better than the one that has come down to us—in this case, without vari- ants (Niese 1890a: 141).

55 As is the case with the long excursus on the Jewish sects (as they are conventionally termed) at *War* 2.119–166, which is introduced at the same place in the narrative, after mentioning Judas's rebellion against Rome in 6 CE, the basic point of the present excursus is to emphasize that Judas's approach was an illegitmate innovation, a departure from what was accepted, and therefore legiti- mate, among the Jews. But if that excursus began with a long account of the Essenes, who are presented, implic- itly, as respectable Jewish versions of Spartans/Romans (see Mason 2007a), the current one opens with the Pharisees and then follows it with an account of the Sadducees, who—as is especially shown by Main 1990— serve as foils for them. This highlighting of the Pharisees, whose devotion to the traditions and laws is emphasized, corresponds both to the local context (as opposed to the rebels' penchant for innovation, emphasized at §9) and, more generally, to a basic theme of *Antiquities*—the emphasis on Jewish law.

The massive corpus of scholarly literature on ancient Jewish "sects" (as they are conventionally termed) is closely linked to literature on Josephus's accounts of them—their sources, their functions, and their worth as evidence. On the function of Josephus's excurses on the sects, see Haaland 2007. In general, on Josephus and the sects, see Feldman's bibliographical survey (Feldman and Hata 1989: 420–429), McLaren 2000, Goodman 2007b: 33–46, and A. I. Baumgarten 2016. For Josephus on specific sects see, on the Pharisees, Mason 1991 and 2021 and Baumbach 1997; on the Sadducees, Main 1990, Poehlmann 1992, and virtually all studies of the Pharisees; on the Essenes, Beall 1988, Bergmeier 1993, Mason 2007a, Mason 2008: 84–95, Collins 2009, Krause 2017: 207–220. On the similarity of Josephus's account of the Essenes to those of Philo (*Hypothetica* 11.1–8; *Quod omnis probus liber sit* 75–91), which leads to hypotheses that Josephus followed Philo or they both followed a common source, see Collins 2009: 52–54, 58–60.

56 I.e., legitimately; see the note on "innovation" at §9.

57 For Josephus's penchant for presenting topics dia- lectically under three headings, of which frequently one is in the middle and one on either side, see, for example, *Ant.* 13.171–173 (on these three sects, of which, as here,

the Sadducees ascribe all to free will, the Essenes ascribe nothing to it, and the Pharisees take a middle position); there were three conspiracies against Gaius (19.17) and three murdered by the avenging Germans (19.123–126); *War* 5.539 (of the Romans some disdained the appeals of Jews who offered to surrender, some disbelieved them, but the majority simply ignored them); 6.237–241 (some wanted to destroy the Temple, some to preserve it, and some had a middle view); and *Life* 32, 124 (some favored war, some favored peace, some dissimulated). Cf. the note on "largest part" at §145.

58 See the note on "philosophy" at §9.

59 In the Greek, "as they are called" (λεγόμενοι) comes at the end of the sentence, but probably should be taken to relate to the names of all three sects. By using words like λεγόμενοι, Josephus reassures his readers, as it were, that indeed the word is strange and they are "allowed" not to know it. For similar usage, see e.g., §§4, 22, 90–91, 159.

60 As Mason notes (2008: 89), when writing of Essenes in the plural Josephus always uses Ἐσσηνοί, as here and at §18, while when referring to them in the sin- gular he prefers Ἐσσαῖος. While Bergmeier (1993) made this part of a source-critical analysis, probably we need see here only a matter of euphony, as is suggested by Mason. For further discussion of Bergmeier's analysis, see Frey 2022: esp. 335–346. As for what the name might mean: Josephus gives the topic no attention, and it still seems to be anyone's guess; see Kampen 1986 and Frey 2022: 349–351.

61 *War* 2.119–166. Although much of the narrative of *War* 1–2 is paralleled in *Ant.* 12–20, there are, alongside 13.72 and a possible hint at 18.129, only three passages in *Ant.* 12–20 in which Josephus refers explicitly to *War*. One comes at the end of *Antiquities* (20.257–258), where Josephus concludes his narrative in 66 CE and refers his readers to *War,* as a whole, for the continuation of the story, but the other two (13.171–173; 13.298) are, as the present one, cross-references to his detailed account of the sects in *War* 2 that are added to brief passages about them. It seems that this topic was especially salient in Josephus's mind as one on which he had written some- thing of a monograph in *War* 2. In one of his usual exas- perating inconsistencies, however, at *Ant.* 15.371 he refers to the Essenes, promises to write about them sometime in the future, but fails to refer to his account in *War* 2.

62 After promising at §10 to say more about the fourth philosophy, it is surprising that Josephus first announces and offers an account of the other three. Apparently, his

(1.3) 12 So, to begin: the Pharisees[63] conduct their lives very plainly, not giving themselves up to anything more luxurious, following the guidance of those things that their doctrine[64] has deemed good and passed on[65] to them and considering, as that for which they must primarily strive,[66] the observance of the things it[67] has preferred to prescribe. They step aside out of respect for those who are advanced in years,[68] exalting themselves neither to contradict the things[69] they introduced nor[70] in insolence.[71] **13** Although they posit that everything happens according to fate,[72] they do not deny human will[73] its influence upon them, from [influencing] that which it sets in motion,[74] for it seemed right to God that

---

tactic is similar to the one announced explicitly at §65, namely, that readers will understand the promised account the way he wants them to if he first presents something else, in light of which the promised account should be read.

63 On the meaning of "Pharisee," see A. I. Baumgarten 1982 and Morrison 2021.

64 Josephus opens his account of each of the three sects he presents as ancient and legitimate by referring to its λόγος (§§12, 16, 18). His failure to do so concerning the so-called "fourth philosophy" (§§23–25) is part of his case for its illegitimacy.

65 The verb here, παραδίδωμι, points to the Pharisaic adherence to their "tradition," *paradosis*; see the note on "indeed" at §16.

66 Josephus's emphasis on the Pharisees' adherence to tradition and abhorrence of deviation from it (those who do so are arrogant, "exalting themselves") makes them the precise opposite of the rebels he has been describing and condemning until now; see esp. §9. His use of the rare περιμάχητον binds this account, of the Pharisees, to that of the Essenes (§18).

67 Their doctrine.

68 Which should make them very respectable in Roman eyes and, by implication, set up the Sadducees, who like to contradict their teachers (§16), for the opposite evaluation. Compare, for example, Ovid's account at *Fasti* 5.57–78 of the way the elderly were respected in the good old days (cited by Parkin 2003: 100–107, along with a number of texts that express the widespread image of the Senate as an instiution in which old men ["senes"], who are wise and experienced, rule Rome. Parkin's doubts about the degree to which practice differed from the ideal do not matter here.)

69 Apparently: the teachings mentioned earlier in this difficult passage.

70 Reading according to Niese's conjecture (1890a: 142; 1890b: 123), ἤ, instead of the manuscripts' οἱ. Others (including Feldman 1965: 10, followed by Mason 1991: 288) simply omit these letters (as does the Epitome [Niese 1887–1896: 300]), rendering a simpler text: "nor are they inclined boldly to contradict the things that were

introduced [scil. by them]." But if that were the original text, it would be difficult to explain what generated the received text; it is easier to imagine the omission of this small word, especially if a copyist did not understand what two options Josephus was delineating. It seems, however, that Josephus means to distinguish between the Pharisees' failure both to reject things (probably he means laws) introduced by their elders and to argue with their elders out of insolence—and thereby sets them up as a match for the Sadducees, who, according to §16, do both: not only do they oppose laws introduced by their teachers (because they only accept laws, i.e. biblical laws [cf. the note on "laws" at §16]); they also consider it laudable to argue with their teachers.

71 Here, within the context of this excursus on sects, Josephus is preparing a contrast with the Sadducees; see §16. But readers of this book may also recall Josephus's emphasis on the youth of the rebels he condemned at §10; cf. esp. *War* 2.417, where the young rebels arrogantly reject the advice of their elders.

72 On εἱμαρμένη, and the fundamental correspondence of Josephus's report about the Pharisees and rabbinic notions, see Moore 1929; Shutt 1980: 183–186; Maier 1981; and Klawans 2012: 44–91. For a survey and critique of "scholarly interpretations of Josephus on fate and free will," see Mason 1991: 384–398.

73 On the construction here (τοῦ ἀνθρωπείου τὸ βουλόμενον), note Richards's complaint (1939: 37): "The neuter article with adj[ective] or participle is an overdone idiom in xvii–xix. Its use is pushed so far as to make the phrase *govern a genitive* [as here, DRS]. This is a solecism not to be attributed to a Greek assistant … Here J[osephus] seems to go astray in his desperate effort to improve his style" (original emphases).

74 Here I translate the text of the codices, ἀπ' αὐτῆς, on the assumption Josephus means that although, indeed, fate does set things into motion, the Pharisees do not deny all room for human will, a claim that he will explain in the remainder of the sentence. Niese (1890a: 142), followed by Thackeray (1932) and Feldman (1965: 13), reads ἐπ' αὐτοῖς with the Epitome (Niese 1887–1896: 2).

there be a combination[75] of both its[76] council[77] and of him among men who desires to proceed with virtue or vice. **14** It is also[78] their belief that souls have an undying power, and that under the earth there are rewards and punishments for those whose striving in life[79] was [respectively] for virtue or vice: eternal imprisonment is imposed upon the latter, while the former are given an easy return to life.[80] **15** Because of these [teachings] they are[81] extremely persuasive with the citizens,[82] and so it is the case that all divine things that happen—prayers and the performance of sacred rites—are done according to their teaching.[83] Such is the great extent to which the cities[84] bear witness to their striving

---

75 Reading χρᾶσιν, with three manuscripts and Feldman; cf. *War* 5.212 and 7.298. On the reading and translation here, see Mason 1991: 295 and Klawans 2012: 254–255, n. 94. Ambrosianus, followed here by Niese (1890a: 142), reads χρίσιν (judgment, decision), but, as Thackeray (who translates "a coalition") observed (1932: 93, n. 1), applying the *lectio difficilior* rule, "'transcriptional probability' (Hort's phrase) confirms this reading: χρίσιν would not have been altered to χρᾶσιν."

76 I.e., fate's.

77 That is, Josephus portrays the relationship between human will and fate as something of a debate in a council-chamber. For literal usage of βουλευτήριον, see for example 17.280 and 19.60.

78 This sounds as if Josephus is now turning to another doctrine of the Pharisees, having completed his discussion of free will vs. fate. But since the only importance of immortality, in his discussion here (as more explicitly in *War* 2.156–157), is the fact that it inspires concern for rewards and punishment for virtue and vice, his use, later in this paragraph, of the same two terms that concluded §13 (ἀρετῆς ἢ κακίας) links the two together.

79 For ἐπιτήδευσις as "striving after" virtue (ἀρετή), see also §§15, 66 and 19.49, also the note on "strove" at 19.32.

80 For Josephus on the sects' views of the afterlife, see Klawans 2012: 92–136.

81 For Mason's argument, based partly on comparison with other passages (such as 13.288; 17.41) where Josephus is critical of the Pharisees, that τυγχάνουσιν here means "happen to be," which he takes to mean "as merely a matter of chance," see Mason 1991: 301, 304. As he emphasizes, however, even if translated that way there is here no explicit criticism of the Pharisees, such as that found elsewhere, for Josephus's intention, here, is to present the Pharisees, as the Sadducees and Essenes, as respectable representatives of legitimate Judaism, as opposed to Judas's fourth philosophy. Moreover, τυγχάνω frequently

means (as Mason recognizes) nothing more than "is" (see, for example, §§11, 27), and even if one insists on "happen to be," that can be insistent, as in Feldman's translation: "they are, as a matter of fact" (Feldman 1965: 13). It seems that the fact that Josephus points, here, to their *teachings* as the reason for the Pharisees' popularity argues against a reading that has the latter coming about "as merely a matter of chance." Cf. below, the note on "better" later in this paragraph.

82 For this respectable translation of δῆμοι, in line with the reference to "cities" later in this paragraph, see *GTRI* 35, also *ThLJ* 134–135 and Mason 2008: 213, n. 1651. Contrast below, at §17, where, in the context of his account of the Sadducees, who are said to be "first in rank," the Pharisees' followers are instead characterized as being supported by the "masses," as aristocrats prefer (see the note on "multitude" at §26). Josephus, that is, is concerned to make each of the three sects appear respectable, so as to leave the "Fourth Philosophy" a total outsider. For the insistence that a reference to "citizens" (even in something as formal as 20.11, alongside ἄρχουσι βουλῇ) need not entail the notion that Jerusalem was a *polis*, according to Greek standards, see Tcherikover 1964: 66. But Josephus and others regularly refer to Jerusalem as a city (*polis*, urbs), whatever the institutional details.

83 For ἐξήγησις meaning not "exegesis" (of a text or tradition) but, rather, declaration (of law), see Mandel 2017: 145–168.

84 Of the use of the plural, when it is difficult to imagine Josephus was thinking of any city apart from Jerusalem, Horsley (2022: 83–84) comments that Josephus could mean towns and villages as well and observes that this formulation "is … just one more example of how Josephus is couching his account in terms typical of Hellenistic urban life in which various philosophies had influence across many cities."

after virtue,[85] which is better[86] than all others with regard both to conduct of life and to doctrines.[87]

(1.4) 16 The doctrine of the Sadducees,[88] in contrast,[89] has the souls disappear[90] along with the bodies,[91] and, with regard to observance, nothing at all obliges them apart from the laws;[92] indeed,[93] they account[94] it a virtue to contradict[95] the teachers of the wisdom[96] [of the school] to which they belong.[97] **17** This doctrine has come only to a few, and although they are first in rank,[98] nothing, so to speak, is done their way; for whenever they attain some

---

85 Cf. *Life* 12, where Josephus reports that after trying out different sects he eventually returned to the city (Jerusalem) and began to live like a Pharisee.

86 Cf. Mason 1991: 304–305, who deliberates whether κρείσσονος here means "better" or, rather, "more influential, predominant," a sense that is indeed easily documented; see, *inter alia*, 19.97, 112, 146, 173, 207 and 20.89. If, as Mason prefers, that translation is adopted, Josephus would not be recommending the Pharisees here, but only recognizing their influence, just as elsewhere in his work there are passages in which he recognizes their influence and complains about it; see esp. 13.288, 401–402, and 17.41. However, this passage does not complain about it, and in light of the explanation that their status derives from recognition of their virtue, the picture it gives is basically positive.

87 Here Josephus assumes that Judaism, like other philosophies, has two main elements: practices and doctrines. So too, for example, at *Apion* 2.179, 181. In the present context, which refers to Pharisaism as one of the Jews' "philosophies," readers should understand this as reflecting the standard distinction between theoretical and practical philosophy; see, for a prominent precedent, Aristotle, *Nicomachean Ethics* 2.2. (1103b). By evaluating the Pharisaic way as better than all others, Josephus sets us up for the coming account of the Sadducees, which is built to contrast them with the Pharisees.

88 Although there have been some other suggestions (see *HJP* 2.405–407), it is usually assumed that the name derives from Ṣadoq, the name of the high priest in the days of David and Solomon, whose progeny supplied high priests for centuries (see 1 Chronicles 6:8–15// *Ant.* 10.151–153). This hypothesis is based especially on the evidence for a close relationship between Sadducees and high priests; see the note on "rank" at §17.

89 I have used this heavy translation of δέ because the coming account is evidently built specifically to parallel that of the Pharisees. True, Josephus sometimes treats all three sects together; so in his three main accounts of them (here; *War* 2.119–166, and *Ant.* 13.171–173) and in *Life* 10. Nevertheless, just as a few passages in the New Testament (which never mentions Essenes) portray the Pharisees and Sadducees in parallel and in conflict with each other (Matthew 22; Acts 5:17//33 and 23:6–9), so too Josephus

takes them as a pair; so explicitly at *Ant.* 13.288–298 and implicitly at 20.199 (see the note there on "reported"). The same also emerges from *War* 2, where his long account of the Essenes (§§119–161) is followed by a very short one (§§162–166) that discusses the Pharisees and Sadducees, weaving them together as a pair of opposites.

90 Lit. "*makes* the souls disappear," a forceful formulation that sets readers up for the just as striking, but contrary, formulation about the Essenes at §18: they "make the souls immortal."

91 On the Sadducean denial of life after death, see Klawans 2012: 101–106. It is mentioned frequently in New Testament references to their hostility to the early Christians, whose belief focused on the resurrection of Jesus; see the note on "high priests of God" at 20.198. Cf. the note on "along with itself" at 19.325.

92 I.e., the written laws of the Torah, as opposed to traditions; see esp. *Ant.* 12.297. For a rabbinic claim, nonetheless, that the Sadducees also had other written laws (as opposed to the Pharisees, who kept their extra-biblical laws oral), see the scholion to *Megillat Ta'anit* to 4 Tammuz (Noam 2003: 77–79, with discussion at 206–216), along with Le Moyne 1972: 219–223.

93 By this use of γάρ to link the Sadducees' refusal to observe anything not ordained by "the laws" to their approbation of contradicting their teachers, Josephus makes it clear that his account of the Pharisees, at §12, which posits "tradition" as a source of legal authority apart from "the laws," refers to traditions beyond the written laws of Moses. So too *Ant.* 13.297. Cf. A. I. Baumgarten 1987.

94 For such non-numerical use of ἀριθμέω, see also §210 and 19.62

95 According to Thackeray (*ThLJ* 30), ἀμφιλογεῖν is not found elsewhere in Greek literature. But similar forms are found; see LSJ 92.

96 For Josephus's propensity to assert that Jewish laws embody wisdom, see also below, §§59, 81; cf. 19.172, on Roman laws.

97 I have supplemented and translated in line with Josephus's usage at 20.199. For another nuance of μέτειμι, see 19.253.

98 Here Josephus seems to be alluding to the high-priestly class; cf. the opening of his *Life* and, on the class

office[99] they yield—albeit unwillingly and under duress—to that[100] which the Pharisee[101] says, for otherwise they would not be tolerated by the masses.[102]

---

in general, Stern 1976. The assumption that the Sadducees are indeed, in general, to be associated with the rich high-priestly aristocracy, depends: on the derivation of "Sadducee" from Ṣadoq ("Zadok"), the name of the high priest in the days of David and Solomon and head of the high-priestly dynasty that lasted until the Hasmoneans (see *inter alia* Ben Sira 51 [MS B: "praise Him who chose the House of Zadok to serve as priests," parallel to the choice of David to be king]), and which is frequently associated with priests (e.g., Ezek 44:15; *1QS* 5:2, 9); on such texts as Acts 4:1 and 5:17, *Ant.* 20.199–200 (high priests and Sadducees), *Assumption of Moses* 7 and *Avot de Rabbi Natan* A5 (ed. Schechter, 26) (rich Sadducees), *Ant.* 20.206–207 and *b. Pesaḥim* 57a//*t. Menaḥot* 13:18–21 (ed. Zuckermandel, 533) (rich and powerful high priests); and on Sadducean legal positions that appear to be congenial to interests of the rich and high-priestly; see, for example, Finkelstein 1962: 1.138–141, 283–284 on Sadducean willingness to divide large estates and to view slaves as similar to animals, and ibid. 2.637–753 on their pro-priestly views. It is usually assumed, for example by Magness (2002: 93–94), that the rich who inhabited many of the opulent residences in the Herodian Quarter of Jerusalem's Old City were Sadducees. For a maximalist case about the relationship between Sadducees and the high priesthood, see Kokkinos 1998: 383–384.

99 Presumably Josephus is referring to the high priesthood; see the preceding note. For use of τιμή of a respected office, see, for example, §326; Josephus uses it frequently of the high priesthood (e.g. §§26, 35; 19.297; 20.16, 103, 225). As the present passage, so too *b. Yoma* 19b, as some others in rabbinic literature, claims that the Pharisees indeed enforced their will upon Sadducean high priests. But the historicity of these texts is not beyond doubt; many religious establishments like to claim that their authority was accepted by all in the good old days. True, at *War* 2.411 Josephus includes "the notables among the Pharisees," alongside the "powerful men" and the chief priests, among those who tried to dissuade the rebels from introducing a fateful change in the Temple praxis. Nevertheless, while in the rabbinic version of that story (*b. Giṭṭin* 56a) a rabbi is said to have been in charge and no priests are mentioned, Josephus's report (*War* 2.409), more plausibly, says that it was the high priest's son, who was serving as "captain of the Temple," who convinced those ministering in the Temple (§409) to take the decision, despite the opinions of the "chief priests and notables" (§410) and the priestly experts (§417); it is clear that they are in charge, and if the Pharisees really participated alongside of

them, it was only in a secondary role, "part of the élite's effort to reach and calm the masses by every available means" (Mason 2008: 315, n. 2583). The same is indicated by the equation of priests and decision-makers at §§29–30 and by Vitellius's decision, when relinquishing Roman authority over the high priests, to transfer the sacred vestments to the custody of the priests (§§90–95). Interesting vignettes illustrating continued priestly authority despite competition are supplied by *m. Rosh HaShana* 1:7 (courts of priests and of sages operating in Jerusalem at the same time, each following its own rules but making determinations about the same calendrical issue) and *m. Ketubbot* 1:5 (a "court of priests" making decisions, about marriage arrangments, which were not approved of by "the sages." For other sources on such a court, see D. Tropper 1972/73; he concludes that "the priests themselves directed the ritual ceremonials in the Second Temple at Jerusalem" [220]). In general, for the notion that the priests retained much of their religious authority until the Temple was destroyed, see Mason 1988. That goes hand in hand with a broad movement in modern scholarship that limits the influence of the Pharisees. See, for example, Goodblatt 1989.

100 Given the way Josephus makes his account of the Sadducees contrast with that of the Pharisees, we should probably infer that the vague references at §17 should be interpreted by §15: Josephus is referring to the conduct of divine rites.

101 This singular form is strange, and sounds resentful and menacing: "the best people" have views but "the Pharisee" stands in the way of implementing them, due to his popularity among those who, in the next line, are termed "the masses." That is not at all as respectful as the formulation at §15, where it is the "the citizens" and "the cities" that are loyal to the Pharisees. For such mass support of the Pharisees (παρὰ τῷ πλήθει) being taken as threatening, see also *Ant.* 13.288, 401–402 (along with the nasty passage at 17.41–45, where the Pharisees, who are hostile to Herod, are said to be very influential with another type of people unworthy of respect: women [see the note at §255 on "womanly words"]). Those passages seem to derive from Nicolaus of Damascus (D. R. Schwartz 1983b), and denounce the Pharisees, in harsh terms, as using their influence in opposition to properly established government. In the present case, in contrast, the Pharisees' influence (which, as Mason notes [1991: 304], is reported "in a resigned way"), is illustrated only with regard to religion, not state.

102 For the aristocratic disdain evinced by πλῆθος here, see the note on "multitude" at §26.

(1.5) **18** The doctrine of the Essenes tends to[103] leave everything to God,[104] but[105] they hold that souls are immortal[106]—believing, as they do,[107] that coming near to[108] righteousness[109] is something for which a man should strive.[110] **19** Although they send votive offerings[111] to the Temple they execute[112] sacrifices according to different rites of

---

103 For Josephus's use of φιλέω, which Feldman renders here as "is wont to," see *CCFJ* 4.299–300. The use of such a qualified verb, as opposed to the expected round statement as to what they believe (which some translators supply here), such as those given above for the Pharisees and Sadducees, is surprising. Note, for example, Josephus's use of φιλέω in his observation about what is usual in romance (15.84) and his snobbish references to the way crowds tend to behave (see the note on "mob" at 19.130); no one would suggest that those are rules as firm as philosophical doctrines are expected to be. One may suspect that Josephus is hedging in order to mitigate the contradiction between the present statement, about leaving everything to God, and the continuation of the sentence; see the note on "believing, as they do."

104 For this belief in Qumran see, for example, "For a man's way is [not] his own, and a man cannot direct his own steps, for judgment is God's and perfection of way is from his hand" (*Manual of Discipline* 11:9–11, echoing Jeremiah 10:23; see D. R. Schwartz 2013: 43–46). In general, see Sanders 1992: 373–376 and Klawans 2010a.

105 I render this δέ heavily in order to make clear (as, apparently, with Josephus's use of φιλέω just above) that there is some tension between attributing everything to God, on the one hand, and demanding that people strive for something, on the other. On that tension, or contradiction, and the ancient Jewish debates about "compatibilism" (the belief that the two can be reconciled, one way or another), see Wächter 1969, Klawans 2009, and a somewhat revised version of the latter: Klawans 2012: 44–91. Here Josephus posits that the Essenes' belief in immortality is meant to motivate people to strive for it, by doing what the righteous do. The same point about the moral implication of the belief (of Essenes as also Greeks) in immortality is made at greater length at *War* 2.154–157.

106 Lit. "they make the souls immortal"; see the note on "disappear" at §16. On Essene beliefs concerning the afterlife, see esp. Puech 1993.

107 Here I take the circumstantial participle ἡγούμενοι to be explaining the reason for their belief in immortality; compare, for example, 19.100. As Wächter (1969: 109) notes, attributing all to God could imply that the Essenes divested themselves of responsibility for their own actions, thus laying them open to a charge of "Libertinismus"; Josephus, who portrays the Essenes so positively, is carefully avoiding that by stating what it is for which they must strive, even at the cost of somewhat contradicting his opening statement.

108 Translators differ as to whether τὴν πρόσοδον here means "approach" or "reward." But "reward" is a stretch; the closest we come to that meaning is "profit" or "income" (as, for example, at §§22, 287, 293; 20.23). For "approach" see 17.292; 19.198. So too J. Strugnell (1958: 109) and Feldman (1965: 15–16).

109 For a long compilation of Josephus's use of τὸ δίκαιον for righteousness or justice, as for example at 19.273 and 20.181, see *ThLJ* 177–178, s.v. δίκαιος, §3. . Note that H. Lewy (1920–1945: 124) added after τὴν πρόσοδον, in a penciled interlineal note in his edition of Niese's editio minor, the gloss "sc[ilicet] τῆς ἀθανασίας." That apparently means that he derived τοῦ δικαίου from ὁ δίκαιος (which too is frequent; see *ThLJ* loc. cit.) and took Josephus to mean that the Essenes thought a righteous man should strive to approach immortality, i.e., to be worthy of attaining immortality. However, there is little reason to think Josephus would think that the Essenes prescribed only what the righteous should do, and at *War* 2.154–155 he states they believed that the souls of *all* people are immortal, the difference being between the comfort of the virtuous ones and the suffering of the wicked ones. Another option was taken by J. M. Baumgarten (2022: 166): he suggested that τοῦ δικαίου τὴν πρόσοδον means "approach of [= by] Righteousness," pointing to the personification of Ṣedeq (righteousness) in some Qumran texts. However, especially given the absence of capitalization, but even without it, it appears that Josephus could hardly expect his readers to understand that. For more on this difficult passage, see D. R. Schwartz 2024c.

110 Here, by using περιμάχητον, Josephus reminds readers to contrast the Essenes with the Pharisees (§12).

111 On ἀναθήματα see A. I. Baumgarten 1994: 174–175, also the note on "installation of the statue" at §272.

112 Reading θυσίας ἐπιτελοῦσιν in accordance with most witnesses (for the standard collocation see, for example, 10.43; 12.253; 18.234; 19.71), without the negation supplied by the Epitome (Niese 1887–1896: 300: οὐκ ἐπιτελοῦσι) and the Latin ("non celebrant"). For a defense of the omission of the negation, see esp. Hölscher 1916: 1991–1992, n. **. As J. Strugnell has shown (1958: 113–5), however, even if we add in the negation, the meaning hardly changes: since the end of the sentence clearly states the Essenes offered sacrifices, even if we read the negative here, the text could mean only that the Essenes do not execute sacrifices *there*, in the Temple, but rather—as the sentence goes on to explain—elsewhere, "by themselves." See D. R. Schwartz 2013: 58–60.

purity,[113] which they practice,[114] and for this reason they are excluded[115] from the common enclosure and execute sacrifices[116] by themselves.[117] Otherwise[118] they are people of the most excellent nature, and apply themselves with all their efforts to farming.[119] 20 And it is

---

113 By noting that the Essenes send votive offerings to the Temple, by stating that their refusal to sacrifice in it derives merely from different details concerning purity, and by claiming that the Essenes nevertheless sacrifice just as other Jews do, although by themselves, Josephus minimizes the extent to which they differ from other Jews concerning this central institution of Judaism. This reflects Josephus's general tendency to portray unity among the Jews, a tendency that passages like this pit against his desire to show that we too have our schools of philosophy. See M. Goodman 2007b: 33–46.

114 For this sense of νομίζομαι see, for example, §30.

115 For the argument that εἰργόμενοι here must be translated as reflexive ("sich absondernd"), for it is unlikely that the Temple police would have excluded (i.e., that Josephus would imply that they would exclude) pious people only because they did lustrations differently from others, see Hölscher 1916: 1991–1992, n. **. Others, however, assert that the middle of this verb is always passive, not reflexive, in Josephus; so Marcus 1954: 158, probably based on the data assembled at *ThLJ* 220, s.v. εἴργειν; see also the data assembled, in support of the same conclusion, by A. I. Baumgarten 1994: 171, including 19.267. That leads them to infer that "Essene exclusion from the Temple was a *punishment* imposed on them by those in charge" (A. I. Baumgarten, ibid.; original emphasis). That conclusion, however, creates a conundrum, "a paradoxical situation" as Baumgarten puts it: can we really imagine that the Essenes would go on sending votive offerings to the Temple, which amounts to recognizing its legitimacy, if the authorities of the Temple refused to allow the Essenes to perform their cult there and so they maintained a complete sacrificial cult elsewhere, as is indicated by ἐφ' αὐτῶν τὰς θυσίας ἐπιτελοῦσιν at the end of the present text? Baumgarten goes on to mitigate the problem by suggesting that the Essenes did not maintain a complete sacrificial cult elsewhere, but only sacrificed Red Heifers (Numbers 19), in order to take care of their purification needs. However, there is no apparent justification to so limit θυσίας, and anyway "understanding Josephus in this manner does not eliminate the paradox" (A. I. Baumgarten 1994: 180). Accordingly, it seems better to go another route: to recognize that often it is difficult to distinguish between reflexive and passive senses of the Greek middle, and—despite Baumgarten's doubts in his n. 8—one cannot really exclude the notion that Josephus means that the Essenes excluded themselves because they understood that the law—including their own law—prevents them from sacrificing along with everyone else. For the law as an external authority voluntarily taken upon themselves by Jews, see *Ant.* 17.151. Note also Josephus's formulations elsewhere, about what "the Law allows us" to do, e.g., §§55, 264.

116 In light of the generally spiritual nature of the Essenes it has been suggested that Josephus is referring, here, to some sort of metaphorical sacrifices for "worship" in general. However, the fact that the very same words appear in the first part of the sentence, with reference to real sacrifices, seems to exclude that possibility. For their usual usage with regard to real sacrifices, see also such passages as 10.43 and 19.71. See, in general, J. M. Baumgarten 1977: 52–54 (originally published in 1953) and 57–74, and A. I. Baumgarten 1994.

117 The contrast between "common" and "by themselves" clearly means that the Essenes did not sacrifice in the common court of the Temple but did do so by themselves, in a separate part of the Temple. So, for example, J. M. Baumgarten 1977: 62–63, 66. But since it is impossible to imagine a separate altar for their use within the Temple, and since anyway those who sacrificed at the Temple did not do so themselves but only passed on their sacrifices to the officiating priests, all Josephus need mean is that a separate section of the courtyard was set aside for the Essenes, so that, when they came to bring sacrifices, and when they ate those parts of them consumed by the offerers, they could avoid contact with other Jews, whom they considered to be impure (and who may have considered the Essenes impure). Whether this is indeed true, historically, is another question, but it is not difficult to imagine even temporary arrangements for such a separation, on occasion. So too Taylor 2012: 97–99. As she notes, perhaps the mysterious "Essenes' Gate," mentioned at *War* 5.145, had something to do with such special arrangements.

118 As A. I. Baumgarten (1994: 170–171) notes, this ἄλλως implies that the previous statement, about the Essenes' sacrifices, amounted to criticism—a point that he takes to contribute to his interpretation of that statement. For Josephus's use of ἄλλως to indicate a contrast, compare, for example, 17.273, 278; see also Baumgarten, loc. cit, n. 5, and *ThLJ* 25 s.v. ἄλλως. However, given the continuation here, this criticism is very mild, as is noted by Hölscher (1916: 1992, n. **, cited by Baumgarten) and by Taylor 2012: 99. Moreover, criticism of the Essenes for observing different rules of purity does not entail any conclusion about where they sacrificed "by themselves."

119 For this *topos* of the industrious and irenic life of agriculture, cf. also §283 and *Apion* 2.294; on its resonance in Rome, see Barclay 2007: 367.

appropriate to wonder at them, among all who strive after virtue,[120] for never has there been found the likes of them among the Greeks or the barbarians,[121] not even for a short time, while they have maintained their way of life since antiquity[122] without hindrance. Property is held in common among them, the rich man enjoying his own property no more than does he who owns nothing[123]—and that is done by men who number more than four thousand![124] **21** They neither admit[125] wives nor seek to own slaves, for they think the one engenders injustice while the other introduces the makings of internal strife.[126] Rather, they live self-reliantly and, for their additional needs,[127] they serve one another.[128] **22** They elect[129]

---

120 Same phrase: §278. Cf. the similar phrasing at §14.

121 A favorite Josephan way of referring to all of humanity. See, for example, *Ant.* 1.107; 4.12; 8.284; 15.136; 16.176. Cf. Galatians 3:28.

122 The Essenes' antiquity, which endows them with legitimacy (see the note on "innovation" at §9), was emphasized by Pliny as well (*NH* 5.73 [*GLAJJ*, no. 204]): "per saeculorum milia—incredibile dictum—gens aeterna est."

123 On the sharing of property among the Essenes, see also *War* 2.122, 127 and Philo, *Hypothetica* 11.4–5. At Qumran the central text is *Manual of Discipline* 6:18–23. In general, see Mealand 1975; Taylor 2001; and Mason 2008: 101, n. 762.

124 That is, Josephus emphasizes the Essenes' ability to adhere to common ownership of property although there are so many of them. The same number appears in Philo's account of the Essenes: *Quod Omnis Probus Liber Sit* 75. For the possibility of a common source (or of Josephus using Philo), see *HJP* 2.562, n. 1; Smith 1958: 279; Taylor 2012: 96. Some common points and vocabulary will be noted in the comimg notes. Given the size of the settlement and its water supply, it is normally assumed that no more than two hundred resided in Qumran itself at any given time, perhaps even fewer (see Meyers 2010: 32). Those who assume the Qumran=Essene equation suggest that the number here includes the numbers of Essenes in other "encampments" (as they are called in CD 7:6) as well; indeed, both Josephus (*War* 2.124) and Philo (*Hypothetica* 11.1) state that the Essenes live in many different cities and villages. But one may doubt that either of them had access to any hard data.

125 This is usually translated as if it refers to Essene abstinence from marriage; see the next note. However, the phrasing here, οὔτε γαμετὰς εἰσάγονται, which (as noted in *ThLJ* 222, s.v. εἰσάγειν) refers to "bringing in" (admitting) *wives* (not women), apparently includes the broader notion, that although married people might enter the sect, they could not bring their wives with them into the community. Cf. *War* 2.151 (on elderly Essenes) and 2.160–161 (even marrying Essenes separate from their wife when they are pregnant, which suggests they would do the same when they can no longer become pregnant),

along with *Damascus Document* 6:11–7:6 as explained by J. M. Baumgarten 2022: 115–118. In the wake of Guillaumont 1971, Baumgarten also compares the traditions (that build on Exod 18:2) concerning Moses, who was at first married but renounced conjugal relations when he became a prophet.

126 The structure is apparently chiastic (as above, §14): slavery engenders injustice and marriage engenders internal strife. For Philo's fuller expression of the latter point (marriage creates family units that disrupt the unity of the commune), see *Hypothetica* 11.14–17. For Josephus on slavery as unjust, see Gibbs and Feldman 1985/86; for it being the opposite of "liberty," see the notes on "enslavement" and "liberty" at 18.4. On women as troublemakers, see the note on "demands" at §42. Essene celibacy (although qualified at *War* 2.160–161), posited also by Philo (loc. cit.) and by Pliny (*NH* 5.73 [*GLAJJ*, no. 204]), is usually taken to be one of the main arguments for identifying the Qumran sect as Essene. However, debate continues about whether the Qumran sect was celibate. See, for example, J. M. Baumgarten 2022: 109–119; Regev 2008; and Cohen-Matlofsky 2020. Note also Moehring 1961.

127 This is the only occurrence of ἐπιχράομαι in Josephus. Niese suggested emending it into the more common ἀποχράομαι.

128 The obvious implication is that wives and slaves are meant to serve their masters. As we see, Josephus considers that to be unjust in the case of slaves; apparently he realizes that a free man today might be a slave tomorrow. As for women, however, Josephus apparently saw no such problem, for they are baser than men; see *Apion* 2.201, along with Barclay 2007: 284, nn. 805–806. The only problem, as Josephus saw it, was that all too often they fail to know their place, and, as a result, create strife and other calamities; see, for example, §§41, 255, 360–362, also *Ant.* 13.431.

129 As Josephus, Philo too (*Hypothetica* 11.10) uses χειροτονέω (lit. "stretching the hand," as in pointing or voting) of the choosing of the Essenes' treasurers. The verb could refer to appointment or election; I have preferred the latter both because no officials who might "appoint" have been mentioned, and because of the wordplay

good men to be receivers[130] of their income and of whatever the ground produces, and priests for the preparation of bread and [other] foods.[131] They live in a way[132] that is not at all bizarre;[133] rather, it is very similar[134] to that of those called the "Ktistae" among the Dacians.[135]

(1.6) 23 As for the fourth of the philosophies:[136] Judas the Galilean[137] became its leader.[138] They agree with the Pharisees' opinions about everything else,[139] but have a virtually

---

at §§264–265. At *War* 2.123 as well, in this same context, χειροτονητός spparently refers to election; see Mason 2008: 102–103, n. 779.

130 This is the only case of ἀποδέκτης in Josephus. For the Essenes' eschewal of money among themselves but willingness to take it from others, see J. M. Baumgarten 2022: 175–179.

131 Josephus distinguishes between the administration of property and the preparation of food; the entrustment of the latter to priests apparently reflects considerations of ritual purity, such as those implied at §19. This is, along with *War* 2.131, which also comes in the context of the Essene's food, the only place in which Josephus's narratives on the Essenes refer especially to priests, although they figure so prominently in the writings of the Qumran sect, including with regard to governance and property: "only the sons of Aaron shall rule with regard to law and property" (*Community Rule* 9:7).

132 Which is exotic, so Josephus feels the need to defend them by showing that it is not without parallel in the Greco-Roman world.

133 Apart from 11.217, such usage of παραλλάσσω reappears in the second half of *Antiquities* only in the next paragraph. For writers who "get stuck" on a word for a while, cf. Mason 2001: lii.

134 This is the only occurrence of ἐμφέρω in Josephus.

135 The manuscripts, followed by Niese (1890a: 144), read "the majority (πλείστοις) of the Dacians," and that, in light of Qumran usage of *harabbim* ("the many") of the members of the community, has led some to think that Josephus is comparing the Essenes to the Qumran sect. But that does not account for the reference to the Dacians (a Thracian people mentioned in *War* 2.369), nor have Josephus's readers heard of the Qumran "many." Accordingly, it seems preferable to adopt one of the emendations—of "Ktistae" or "Dacians" or both—that have been proposed; see Kruse 1959; Schalit 1968: 104, s.v. Σάκαι; and Mason 2011b: 239–240. As Feldman (1965: 20–21), here I have followed Ortelius's suggestion to leave "Dacians" in place but replace πλείστοις with Κτίσταις, based upon Strabo's reference (*Geog.* 7.3.3, citing Posidonius) to some exotic Thracians called "Ktistae," who live without wives; for this suggestion, see Beall 1988: 122 and Feldman 1984a: 616–617. True, our knowledge concerning Josephus's familiarity with Strabo's

writings applies only to his *Historica Hypomnemata* (see Albert 1902 and Stern, *GLAJJ* 1.261–262), but it may be either that Josephus was nevertheless familiar with the *Geographica* or that he heard about the "Ktistae" some other way. Another possibility, Mason's emendation of ΔΑΚΩΝ into ΛΑΚΩΝΩΝ, according to which Josephus compared the Essenes to "what are said to be the majority of the Spartans," has the advantage of linking this passage up with Josephus's apparent tendency to compare the Essenes to the Spartans (see Mason 2007a). However, it departs from Josephus's usual use of λεγόμενοι as "so-called" modifying an unfamiliar proper noun; see the note on "called" at §11. Moreover, although Λάκων does appear twice (*War* 1.513; 2.381), in the large majority of his references to Spartans Josephus calls them Λακεδαιμόνοι. Finally, however much Josephus compares the Essenes to Spartans with regard to their discipline and toughness, readers would be hard put to accept the statement that the Essenes' way of life, including their celibacy, was quite similar to that of the Spartans.

136 This fourth philosophy seems to be the movement that Josephus later condemns as the Sicarii; see the coming note on "manners" and the note on "Sicarii" at 20.186.

137 Judas is the only sectarian leader mentioned by name in this excursus on sects; by giving the name, Josephus reminds his readers of the historical context that occasioned the excursus. It is, however, surprising that he terms him "Judas the Galilean," for at §4 he introduced him as a Golanite. But elsewhere too he is termed a Galilean; see the note on "the Golanite" at §4. Probably Josephus was careful to be precise in his first reference to Judas, but later used his more usual sobriquet—which might reflect where he grew up, or was active, or perhaps some general notion that equated "Galilean" with "rebel"; for such a notion, see Loftus 1977/78, Hengel 1989: 56–59, and, more recently, Thiel 2020.

138 That is, he not only began a rebellion in 6 CE, as was reported in §§4–8, and founded a corresponding philosophy (§9); he also stood at its head.

139 This statement agrees with Josephus's reports that Judas's partner was a Pharisee (§4) and that in general the Pharisees' views were most popular (§§15, 17). But it contradicts the claim of *War* 2.118 that Judas of Galilee's new school had nothing in common with the others. Cf. Mason 2008: 83, n. 731.

immovable[140] passion for liberty, since they take upon themselves God alone as their leader and ruler.[141] They consider the suffering of death, even in bizarre manners,[142] to be a baga-telle, as also the bringing of retribution upon kinsmen and friends in order to avoid calling any man "ruler."[143] 24 I have omitted going on any further about the immovability of their steadfastness[144] in such matters since it has been observed by so many people, and so I have no fear that anything said about them will be received with disbelief. On the contrary, to talk about it might minimize the scorn with which they accept the suffering of pain.[145] 25 The nation began to suffer[146] from the mania that grew out of them when Gessius Florus, who was governor, provoked them in his madness, by his outrageous abuse of authority, into rebelling against Rome.[147]

So much, then, concerning the ways philosophy is done among the Jews.

(2.1) 26 Quirinius—having disposed of Archelaus's property, and the assessments being already completed,[148] which occurred in the thirty-seventh year after Antonius was defeated

---

140 The manuscripts read δυσκίνητος, but Niese (1890a: 144) adopted Bekker's (1856: 128) emendation: δυσνίκητος. As Anthony Ellis points out, however, the former fits the present context well, and the fact that it seems to be very rare (see LSJ 457–458, s.v.) suggests that it is the *lectio dif-ficilior.* The same notion, that they cannot be moved, is expressed in another way in §24.

141 For the argument that Josephus, here and else-where, has fashioned Judas as a straw man who held this view and is therefore to be condemned, a tactic Josephus employed in order to deflect criticism from himself and his fellow priests and others who in fact (as argued esp. by Goodblatt 1996) adhered to the same tenet at the begin-ning of the rebellion, see McLaren 2004. For a response, see Rappaport 2011: 332; while Rappaport may have gone too far in asserting that "James McLaren fiercely denies the historicity of Judas ... pure invention," McLaren comes very close to that insofar as he asserts that Josephus made up, for his own reasons, just about everything he reports about Judas.

142 The present passage (§§23–24), with its reference to all sorts of tortures, to the rebels' refusal to acknowl-edge any man as "ruler" (δεσπότης [see the next note]), and to the reaction of spectators, sounds as if Josephus is specifically thinking of *War* 7.417–418, where the refer-ence is explicitly to Sicarii. The same theme, namely, that even when they are rebellious and thus in the wrong, nevertheless Jewish rebels show no cowardice, reappears at §62. On bizarre Roman modes of torture and execu-tion, see the note on "the entire city" at 20.136.

143 On Josephus's use of δεσπότης, often with refer-ence to God, see *ThLJ* 130, s.v., also Fischer 1958/59; cf. the note on "despot's orders" at 19.68. There is something ironic and bitter about the passage, in this short sen-tence, from evident praise of them for their courageous willingness to die hard deaths to their willingness to let

others pay the price of their own constancy. Cf. the note on "murder" at §5, on their willingness to justify murder.

144 I have translated ὑπόστασις, according to LSJ 1895, s.v., §II.B.4. Elsewhere it appears in Josephus only in the opening paragraph of *Apion.* While Barclay (2007: 4, n. 9) renders it as a philosophical term, "essence," Siegert et al. (2008: 1.99) offer *Eigenständigkeit* ("independence"), which is close to "steadfastness." For that sense of ὑπόστα-σις see also Polybius 4.50.10 (on the resolute resistance of the population of Byzantium to the Rhodians) and 6.55.2 (of Horatius at the bridge).

145 A point especially underlined at *War* 7.417–419.

146 See the note on "infected" at §6. Here Josephus apparently means that the problem that was born already in 6 CE grew to catastrophic proportions sixty years later.

147 Here Josephus apportions responsibility for the rebellion. In his view, here, the Fourth Philosophy's innovative (and therefore: reprehensible; see the note on "innovation" at §9) teaching, about accepting no man as a ruler, was a mania, but what allowed its teaching to engender a rebellion was the abusive behavior of a Roman governor; see also the note on "four men" at §84. By inserting this reference at the end of this excursus, which basically ends the prologue of this book, Josephus adumbrates the end of his story, where Florus is intro-duced in the narrative's final chapter (20.252–258), thus suggesting—as does the reminder at the very end of Book 19 (§366)—that readers should view *Ant.* 18–20, namely his account of direct Roman rule in Judea, as a single unit. See the Introduction, at n. 32.

148 Here, by using ἀποδόμενος ... ἀποτιμήσεων, Josephus reminds readers of the two assignments mentioned at §2, in a *Wiederaufnahme* that indicates to readers that he is reverting to that story after an interval during which they were completed. By inserting the long excursus about sects Josephus allowed his readers to feel, as it were,

by Caesar at Actium[149]—removed Joazar the high priest from his high position, since he had been overcome by the multitude[150] in popular strife,[151] and appointed Ananus the son of Seth high priest.[152]

27 Herod and Philip[153] were appointed to their respective tetrarchies and took them over.[154] Herod, after building up the walls of Sepphoris, the pearl[155] of the entire Galilee,[156] named it Autocratoris.[157] As for Betharamaphta, which too is a city, he surrounded it with a wall and named it Julias, after the emperor's[158] wife.[159] 28 Philip, for his part,

Herod's Heirs, apart from Archelaus

---

the passage of time needed for Quirinius to accomplish his assignments. For similar cases, see the Introduction, at n. 13.

149 On 2 September 31 BCE. For dating according to the Actian era see also *War* 1.398 (and for memorialization of Actium in Judea, see on 19.343). For use of the Actian era on coins, with regard to Roman governors of Syria, see *HJP* 1.257, 259–260. In context, especially after the reference to Actium reminds readers of the Roman conquest of Egypt, readers might understand Josephus to be reminding them that Rome instituted direct rule in Judea only long after it did so in Judea's two massive neighbors: Syria (represented here by Quirinius) and Egypt.

150 Although sometimes neutral, as for example at §123, πλῆθος often conveys contempt, à la "mob," *hoi polloi*. Note, for example the contrast at §17 between the high-class few and the πλῆθος, also 19.202 and the pathetically gullible "urban multitude" at 20.169; cf. the note on "multitude" at 19.138.

151 That is, although Josephus had reported at §3 that the Jews, in general, accepted Joazar's call and abstained from opposing the assessment of their possessions, enough opposed him to produce the rebellion led by Judas— reason enough for Quirinius to have him replaced. See Bammel 1974a.

152 The witnesses split here between Σεθί and Σεέ. Stern (1976: 606) suggests that Ananus was the brother of Joshua the son of Σεέ, who was high priest prior to Joazar (*Ant.* 17.341). At 20.198 Josephus remarks on this Ananus's five sons who were to be high priests. On this family of high priests (known as "The House of Anan" in the list of high-priestly houses preserved in *b. Pesaḥim* 57a), see Stern 1976: 606–607 and VanderKam 2004: 422–424.

153 Herod's sons. It is usually assumed that their mothers were, respectively, Malthace and Cleopatra, although there is some room for doubt about the former; see the note on "the high priest" at §109. On them, see esp. *HJP* 1.336–353; Hoehner 1972; and Wilker 2007. Much of what is reported about them, in the next two paragraphs as also at §§36–38, has to do with their building of cities, as their father before them; what else was allowed to a client ruler? For a general survey of that long-term project and their role in it, cf. A. H. M. Jones 1931. Josephus's shift of focus from the high priesthood to the affairs of

the Herodians is jarring (note that Feldman 1965: 23 adds "meanwhile."). It seems to indicate that, from Josephus's point of view, he is merely bringing us up to date concerning topics ancillary to his main narrative, with no expectation of a continuous narrative; see our next note. For a similarly jarring passage, see 20.103–104.

154 They began their service in 4/3 BCE, after Augustus arranged the affairs of Herod's kingdom; see §106, where 33/34 CE is termed Philip's 37th year, just as his latest coin is dated to his 37th year; see Meshorer 2001: 85–90 and Strickert 1995. Similarly, Herod Antipas's dated coins go down to his 43rd year, and §§255–256 show, correspondingly, that his rule came to an end in 39 or 40; see Kogon and Fontanille 2018: 16–20. That is, having completed his story of Judea down to 6 CE, Josephus is now catching up on events—even as early as 2 BCE (see the opening note at 18.2.4 [§39])—that he considered peripheral to his main story but nevertheless important for it; see the table in D. R. Schwartz 1992: 189.

155 This seems to be the sense of πρόσχημα (usually: "ornament"/"outward appearance," as at 14.302, or "pretence/pretext," as at 4.146). See Kokkinos 2008: 241 "the pretence of every Galilean (i.e. in claiming primacy over othe cities)." On the competition between Sepphoris and Tiberias, which latter Josephus was happy to denigrate at §§36–38, see *Life* 37–38 and Miller 1987.

156 Cf. *War* 2.511: Sepphoris was "the strongest city in Galilee," and *War* 3.34: "the largest of the cities of Galilee, fortified in the strongest possible position." For Sepphoris in the first century, see Nagy 1996, Meyers 1998, Chancey 2001, and Weiss 2007: 392–407.

157 There seems to be no other evidence for this name. As Sepphoris's coins show, by the sixties it renamed itself Neronias and Eirenopolis ("city of peace"), but by the mid-second century both would be replaced by "Diocaesarea." See Meshorer 1985: 36–37, 113, and Chancey 2005: 102.

158 Augustus. In this translation I have, as a rule, used "emperor" for αὐτοκράτωρ, as is conventional. Cf. the note on "ancestors" at 19.23.

159 I.e., Livia, called "Julia" after she was adopted into the Julian gens in 14 CE. It appears that this city was originally called Livias (so Pliny, *NH* 13.44), and its name changed with hers; see *HJP* 2.176–178 and Stern, *GLAJJ* 1.494. Note that in the parallel to this passage at *War* 2.168,

renovated[160] Paneas, which is by the sources of the Jordan,[161] and called it Caesarea;[162] and to the village of Bethsaida,[163] near Lake Gennesaritis, he granted the status of *polis*[164] in recognition of the great number of its residents and its other might,[165] naming it by the same name as Julia, Caesar's daughter.[166]

An Incident in the Temple

(2.2) 29 While Judea was being administered[167] by Coponius (who, as I said,[168] had been sent out together with Quirinius), the following occurred:[169] While the festival of unleavened bread—which we call *Pascha*[170] —was being celebrated, it was the custom of the priests to open the gates of the Temple[171] in the middle of the night.[172] 30 This time, upon the first

---

this Julias is specifically said to have been in the Perea; that differentiates it from the Julias mentioned in the next paragraph, but identifies it with the Perean Julias mentioned at 20.159. Cf. M. D. Smith 1999.

160 Although κατασκευάζω can refer to the construction of buildings, as for example at §§91, 338 (where there is a clear contrast between forts that were newly built and those that already existed and were only fortified), 15.234 and 20.211 (theaters), and cultic buildings (20.228, 237), with regard to cities it seems to refer to something more secondary than the foundation and construction of a new city. Indeed, at 20.211 Josephus uses it of Agrippa II's work in the same city discussed here, and also qualifies it as μείζονα ... κατασκευάσας ("greatly built up"? "enlarged"?). Perhaps the reference is to the type of improvements Herod Antipas introduced in the cities mentioned in §27. For Herod's work in Paneas prior to Philip, see *Ant.* 15.363–364//*War* 1.404–406. For the archaeological evidence, which basically begins with Herod, see V. Tzaferis in *NEAEHL* 5.1687–1592.

161 On this claim, which Josephus repeats at *War* 1.404 and 2.168 but apparently doubts at *War* 1.406 and explicitly contradicts at *War* 3.509–515, see D. R. Schwartz 2020b.

162 On Caesarea Philippi, as it was called to distinguish it from other Caesareas, see *HJP* 2.169–171. For its foundation in 3/2 BCE, see Kokkinos 2008: 241. On its coins, of which one terms Philip as "founder" (κτίστης) and its era is clearly 3 BCE, see Meshorer 1984/85: esp. 38–40.

163 On this *polis* (which is how it is defined at 20.159 as well), where Philip would eventually die (§108), see Arav and Freund 1995–2009; Strickert 2010 and 2011; Ellens 2014; and Kuhn 2015.

164 As Kokkinos (2008: 243) paraphrased: "Philip provided (παρασχών) Bethsaida, previously a mere village (κώμην), with some status (ἀξίωμα), evidently city status, by adding multiple settlers (πλήθει οἰκητόρων) and some other strength (καὶ τῇ ἄλλῃ δυνάμει), either constitutional or of resources. A village-to-city upgrade would be the appropriate interpretation, with the important renaming after the Emperor's daughter." The city is not known to have minted coins.

165 For the argument that δύναμις here refers to a military garrison, see M. D. Smith 1999: 338–339.

166 Augustus's daughter was disgraced and exiled in 2 BCE, so that would be a terminus ad quem for this foundation. As has been noted by Kokkinos (2008: 245–246), who defends that date, Julia's fall must have taken Philip by surprise. The lack of evidence for the name in the coming decades may indicate that he found it wise to avoid it as long as Augustus and Tiberius were alive; the Gospels, referring to the 30s, call the city Bethsaida. For another possibility, namely, that Josephus meant to say the city was named after Augustus's wife, Livia Julia, see M. D. Smith 1999 and Strickert 2002 and 2010. That would go together well with the recognition that in fact Augustus's daughter was in disgrace well before her exile, at least since Tiberius divorced her in 6 BCE, so it is unlikely that anyone would have founded a city in honor of her after that. See Mason 2008: 137–138, n. 1046.

167 For διέπω of ruling a province, as also at §150 and 19.316, see esp. *GTRI* 131–132. In general, on Josephus's use of numerous terms and verbs to denote provincial governors, see Eck 2008, also Eck 2007: 27–31 (assemblage of data) and 39–45 (complaints about Josephus's ignorance, sloppiness, and "völlig chaotische Verwendung von Begriffe").

168 At §2.

169 On this incident, see Pummer 2009: 222–230 and—on a rabbinic memory (*m. ʿEduyyot* 8:5) of bones once having been found in the Temple, which may or may not have to do with this incident—Y. Fisch in Ilan and Noam 2017: 1.485–492.

170 Josephus pedantically makes this equation numerous times, including 14.21; 17.213; 20.106. For Josephus on Passover, see esp. Colautti 2002.

171 For τὸ ἱερόν in the general sense of "the Temple," not the inner courts, see, for example, §§8, 19, 60, 82; Joüon 1935. In this case it is clear, from the continuation, that the gates in question allowed entry to the porticos, not the inner sanctuary. Cf. the notes on "God" at §261 and on "sanctuary" at 20.233.

172 Apparently this reflects the large numbers of pilgrims expected; see the note on "twenty thousand" at 20.112. Presumably, however, whatever the logistical

opening of the doors, some Samaritan men[173] who had secretly[174] come to Jerusalem[175] began to scatter[176] human bones[177] in the porticoes[178] and throughout the Temple.[179] Although they[180] had never previously considered such things, they now began to manage the Temple with greater security in other ways as well.

———

reason, pilgrims would have understood such a midnight procedure in light of Exodus 12:29—which would heighten the intensity of the moment and, therefore, exacerbate the outrage concerning the offense reported here.

173 For Josephus's general hostility toward the Samaritans, see *Ant.* 9.288–291; 11.323, 340–347; 12.257–264; 13.74–79; 20.118–136; Pummer 2009. Pummer (2009: 226–227), however, doubts that Josephus means the perpetrators were Samaritans, for they too, as observers of biblical law, should have been concerned to keep away from human bones; this consideration leads him to discuss the possibility that Josephus's ἄνδρες Σαμαρεῖται means something else. However, one need not touch bones to be able to scatter them, and if they were bothered by the consideration, the Samaritans could have recruited perpetrators who were already impure. In any case, if readers do not take the reference to be to Samaritans, of whose hostility to Judeans and competition with the Temple in Jerusalem they have often read (see esp. 9.291; 11.114, 323, 340–346; 12.10, 257–264; 13.74–79), they will be at a loss to understand what motivated the perpetrators. In general, note that although modern scholars at times tend to distinguish between "Samarians" (who reside in Samaria) and "Samaritans" by religion, Josephus's nomenclature makes no such distinction; see, for example, *Ant.* 9.290 and 11.97 with 11.114–119.

174 "Secretly" presumably means they had hidden their identity as Samaritans. Accordingly, it appears to be unjustified to depend upon the present story as evidence for the latter half of the following statement: "Jerusalem hated Shechem, but since a Samaritan was a follower of the Torah he was admitted into the temple of Herod" (Bickerman 2007: 1.488). Rather, it seems that this story indicates that Samaritans were excluded from the Temple—which would correspond, in a general way, with the story at *Ant.* 11.306–310, that presumes that even a full-fledged Jewish priest, who married a Samaritan woman, would be excluded from ministering in the Temple. More specifically, moreover, we know that inscriptions forbade the entry of a "foreigner" (ἀλλογενής; *OGIS* 598 = Boffo 1994, no. 32; cf. *HJP* 2.285, n. 57) into the central court of the Temple. For Jewish use of ἀλλογενής of a Samaritan, see Luke 17:18; cf. the note on "by birth" at 19.332. In general, on the Samaritans' status in the eyes of Jews in antiquity, see Schiffman 1984/85.

175 Although Clearchus of Soli is said to have quoted Aristotle as commenting that the Greek name of Jerusalem (which he gives in transliteration, Ἰερουσαλήμη) is very odd (*Apion* 1.179), I have rendered the usual Hellenized form employed by Josephus, Ἰεροσόλυμα, by "Jerusalem" rather than a transliteration, on the assumption that by the late first century, after the Judean war and the ensuing Flavian triumph and propaganda, it (as its Latin equivalent, Hierosolyma) was as familiar to Josephus's readers as "Jerusalem" is to modern readers. See, for example, the references to Pliny and Tacitus in the note on "humanity" at 20.49. On the forms of the toponym, which have aroused interest especially in New Testament scholarship, see the data and bibliography assembled by Danker 2000: 470–471.

176 This is the only occurrence of διάρριψις in Josephus.

177 Which engender the most severe type of impurity according to biblical law; see Num 19, esp. v. 16; below, §38; and the commentaries to Luke 10:30. For the severity of this defilement of the Temple in Josephus's eyes, cf. the note on "impiety" at 20.165.

178 The Temple was surrounded by porticoes, στοαί, which, as is said at 20.192, 221, were in the outer part of the complex (the ἔξωθεν ἱερόν). Of them, "the Royal Stoa," on the south, was particularly impressive, and it was next to the main gates in the southern wall of the Temple enclosure. See *War* 5.190–192; *Ant.* 15.412–416; Schalit 2001: 380–382; van Henten 2014: 313–316; and Peleg-Barkat 2017.

179 Something about the discovery of the bones and reaction to it seems to be missing at this point; Niese (1890b: 126) suspects a lacuna. Perhaps there was reference both to greater care concerning Samaritans as well as more generally intensified supervision. For Temple police, see the next note. Mathieu and Herrmann (1929: 139) fill in the text here so as to have it refer here to an unprecedented prohibition of entry by Samaritans. However, Josephus's statement that in this case they entered Jerusalem "secretly" suggests that even earlier, before things were tightened up, they would have been excluded had their identity been known; see just above, the note on "to Jerusalem." Cf. Appendix 3, n. 3.

180 Apparently: the priests, mentioned at §29. On the Temple police, whose primary responsibility was to keep out people who are not allowed to enter, see esp. Philo, *Spec. leg.* 1.156 (Levites on guard duty at entrances and patrolling day and night); *m. Middot* 1:2; Acts 5:24, 26;

Early Roman
Governors of
Judea

31[181] Coponius returned to Rome not long thereafter,[182] and as his successor as ruler there came Marcus Ambivulus,[183] during whose tenure also[184] Salome, King Herod's sister, died,[185] leaving Jamneia[186] and its entire toparchy to Julia,[187] along with Phasaelis, which lies in the plain,[188] and Archeläis,[189] in which[190] numerous palms are planted[191] and their fruit is excellent. **32** He was succeeded by Annius Rufus, in whose days Caesar died—who had been the second[192] Roman emperor, for fifty-seven years, six months and two days of rule;[193] of that period of time, Antonius had ruled together with him for fourteen years.[194] He lived seventy-seven years.[195] **33** Caesar was succeeded in rule by Tiberius Nero, who was the son of his wife Julia and was the third emperor; Valerius Gratus, sent by him as prefect[196]

Fragment Oxyrhynchus 840 (Bovon 2000); and Safrai 1976: 872–873.

181 On the early years of Roman provincial rule, see *HJP* 1.357–398 and Lémonon 2007. The term "governor" is conventional, corresponding to Josephus's general ἡγεμών (e.g. §§25, 55–56); for their precise status, as "prefects" subordinate to the governor of Syria, see especially Eck 2007: 1–51. I use "prefect" for ἔπαρχος, "procurator" for ἐπίτροπος, and "governor" for ἡγεμών; cf. the note on "prefect" at §33. Of the terms of office of the first governors, prior to Pontius Pilate, very little is known (*HJP* 1.382–383; Smallwood 1981: 156–160; and Krieger 1993a), and Josephus skips them in his parallel narrative in *War* 2, where he goes straight from his account of the sects (§§119–166) to that about Herod's heirs (§§167–168) and then to Pilate (§169–177). It has frequently been pointed out that Josephus's narrative of the period from the death of Herod to the reign of Agrippa I is quite meager; see, for example, Täubler 1904: 5–6; *HJP* 1.51. This probably has to do with the end of Nicolaus's narrative in the wake of Herod's death. Although Josephus need not use everything his sources offered, he could not use what they did not offer, and—as Bammel (1974a: 61) points out—Josephus, born in 37 (*Ant.* 20.267), could not yet depend on his memory, nor hardly on that of his father (b. 5/6 CE [*Life* 5]), for those early decades of the first century.

182 We have no data concerning the length of the tenure of the first three Roman governors, mentioned here and in the next paragraph, who served between 6 and the death of Augustus (§32). The conventional allocation of three years to each (6–9; 9–12; 12–15; *HJP* 1.382) is only a guess. Cf. the note on "Tiberius Alexander" at 20.103.

183 This is Niese's conjecture, adopted in his editio minor (1890b: 126) and followed by others, including Feldman (1965: 26). The manuscripts read Ambibouchos.

184 This καί apparently means "in addition to his being governor." Cf. the notes on "also" at §39 and 20.223.

185 On Salome, see Kokkinos 1998: 177–192 and D. W. Roller 2018: 59–78. She was born in the 50s BCE and, according to the present passage, died ca. 10 CE.

186 On Jamneia (Jabneh) see *HJP* 2.109–110. For its status, deriving from its special history described here, as

an imperial enclave with its own procurator, see the note on "Jamneia" at §158.

187 Augustus's wife Livia, as is noted at §33. If, as is often assumed, Marcus Ambivulus served only until 12 CE, Josephus's nomenclature is somewhat anachronistic here, for Livia's name changed to Julia only in 14 CE, according to the terms of Augustus's will which had her adopted into the Julian *gens*; see the note on "wife" at §27.

188 I.e., the Jordan valley. For the location of Phasaelis, north of Jericho, see *HJP* 2.168–169.

189 On Archelais, which too was north of Jericho (but south of Phasaelis), see *HJP* 1.355, n. 12, and H. Hizmi in *NEAEHL* 1.181–182 and 5.1600–1602.

190 This probably includes Phasaelis too, as is made clearer by the parallel at *War* 2.167 (which ignores Archelais and mentions only Phasaelis and its palmgroves) and Pliny, *NH* 13.44 (*GLAJJ*, no. 214), where the palms of both sites are mentioned.

191 This is the only occurrence of φύτευσις ("planting") in Josephus.

192 Including Julius Caesar, as does, for example, Suetonius in his *Twelve Caesars*. So too below, §224.

193 Augustus died on 19 August 14. Josephus apparently counts, fairly accurately, from the death of Julius Caesar on 15 March 44 BCE, which was actually closer to 57 years and five months before Augustus's death. Below, Josephus will continue to keep track of such detailed data: see §224 (Tiberius), 19.201 (Gaius), 20.148 (Claudius), also *War* 4.491 (Nero).

194 Apparently Josephus again begins his reckoning from Caesar's death (15 March 44), and takes it down to Antonius's suicide on 1 August 30.

195 Actually, he died shortly before his seventy-sixth birthday, as is noted by Suetonius (*Aug.* 100), who earlier (ibid. 5) reported that he was born on 23 September 63 BCE.

196 This is the usual translation of ἔπαρχος; see *GTRI* 45, 138–140. Indeed, that the title of Gratus's successor, Pontius Pilate, was *praefectus Iudaeae* is shown by the Caesarean inscription that mentions him; see the opening note at §55. Presumably the same was the case for other governors of Judea whom Josephus termed ἔπαρχος

as Annius Rufus's successor, came to Judea. **34** He terminated the [high-]priestly[197] service of Ananus[198] and proclaimed Ishmael the son of Phabes high priest.[199] But then he removed him from office, not long after, and appointed Eleazar, the son of Ananus the high priest, to the high priesthood.[200] After the latter had lasted a year[201] he removed him too from office and transferred the high priesthood to Simon, the son of Camith.[202] **35** But after for him

---

(19.363; 20.193, 197). Elsewhere, however, in *Antiquities* with regard to governors in the days of Claudius (20.2, 132, 162, along with the verb at 20.97, 147), and more generally in *War* (2.117, 169, 220, 247, 252; 6.238; 7.216), Josephus often uses ἐπίτροπος ("procurator" [*GTRI* 49]) for Roman governors of Judea. One can debate whether this indicates a change in titulature (from one that sounds military to one that is more administrative) beginning with Claudius (for which perhaps other evidence can be adduced; see Jones 1968: 115–125; *HJP* 1.358–360) or only Josephan carelessness about titles (see *GTRI* 142–143; Eck 2008; Mason 2008: 79–80, n. 720). Perhaps, indeed, we should conclude that, in Josephus's world, which lacked capital letters and italics, his predilection for varying his vocabulary applied even to such terms. The latter is suggested both by his use of several other terms for governors (such as ἡγεμών [§55]) and by his use of different terms even for the same individual, even within the same book; see 19.363/20.2.

197 Apart from this passage, which uses ἱερᾶσθαι (as Niese notes, Eusebius, in quoting our passage at *Demonstration of the Gospel* 8.2 [399a, ed. Heikel, 386], reads instead a more exact verb: ἀρχιερᾶσθαι, which Josephus uses at 17.207), Josephus uses no such verb in Book 18: although the book reports the appointment and removal from office of numerous high priests, it does not interest Josephus to characterize them as having *served* as high priests. Rather, this book is organized according to the terms of Roman governors, and one of the things they did was appoint high priests. Contrast the high-priestly chronicle preserved at the end of Book 20, where ἀρχιερατεύω appears regularly (§§225, 228, 242, 243, 250) and the high priests are said to have "ruled" (see the note on "ruled" at 20.238). That illustrates that text's inner-Jewish orientation.

198 Ananus's appointment was recorded at §26.

199 This Ishmael b. Phabes is not to be confused with a later high priest of the same name; see the note on "Phabes" at 20.179. It seems that the Phiabi family (as it is called in Hebrew sources), like at least one other family of high priests that appeared under Herod (see the note on "Boethus" at §3), was of Egyptian origin. That reflected Herod's need, as a non-Aaronite who ousted the Hasmoneans, to foster a new high-priestly class without ties to the Hasmoneans—a class whose members, as Jews of the Diaspora, would have no deep ties in Judea

and were used to keeping their religion apart from the affairs of the state. See Stern 1974c: 274 and VanderKam 2004: 406.

200 That is, after a short interruption, Ananus's son was appointed to succeed him—the first of five of his sons to be appointed to the post, as is noted at 20.198. For the other four, see the note there, on "high priests of God." The fact that Josephus makes no comment on this here, and that he refers to Ananus as "Ananus the high priest" rather than as plain "Ananus" or "the aforementioned Ananus," as we would expect in a freely-composed narrative, suggests that Josephus is dependent here on a high-priestly chronicle with successive formal entries about high priests but no narrative. On such entries, see the note on "Theophilus" at §123.

201 Switching high priests after a year was contrary not only to the ancient practice, which lasted until the Hasmonean period, according to which high priests served until death (Numbers 35:25; Josephus, *Ant.* 15.41), but even to Herod's practice of appointing and removing high priests at will; some of them lasted for several years. But, as the present passage, various sources of the Roman period reflect the notion that high priests were appointed for one year; so John 11:49, 51; 18:3 ("the high priest of that year") and *b. Yoma* 8b ("for they would give money for the [high] priesthood and switch them every twelve months"). This may have not been a rule, but it was common enough to affect the image of the high priesthood, tarnishing its prestige (cf. 2 Macc 11:2–3!); see *b. Yoma* 9a, where it is claimed that there were so many high priests in the Second Temple period that, with a few exceptions, none lasted even a year, thus illustrating the biblical promise that "the years of the wicked will be short" (Proverbs 10:27). In general, see Holzmeister 1920 and Alon 1977: 61–65, 86. The result was the development of the notion, in this period, of a class of "high priests" rather than a single one for each generation; see the the note on "Joazar" at 18.3. It may be that such frequent switching of high priests was among the complaints of Judeans that had to be handled by Germanicus in 19 CE (see Tacitus, *Ann.* 2.42.5 [*GLAJJ*, no. 283]). That could explain the remarkable fact that, in contrast to Gratus, Pontius Pilate made no appointments at all to the high priesthood, Caiaphas lasting throughout his entire governorship.

202 On Simon b. Camith, see VanderKam 2004: 425–426. Like others, VanderKam supposes that this Simon is

too no more than a year passed in which he held the post, Joseph, known as Caiaphas,[203] succeeded him. And Gratus, having done these things, returned to Rome after having stayed eleven[204] years in Judea. Pontius Pilate came as his successor.

The Foundation of Tiberias

(2.3) 36 Herod the tetrarch,[205] his friendship with Tiberius having advanced considerably,[206] built a city named Tiberias after him, founding it in one of the best parts of the Galilee,[207] alongside Lake Gennesaritis.[208] There is a hot spring not far from it in a village called Ammathus.[209] 37 A hodgepodge rabble[210] settled [in it], not a few of them Galileans, and those who came from the territory subject to him who were coerced[211] and forcibly brought to the settlement; some of them were also of the highest rank.[212] He even accepted, as fellow

---

identical with the "Simon b. Qimḥit" mentioned in rabbinic sources, such as *t. Yoma* 3:20 (ed. Lieberman, 248), where Qimḥit, a woman's name, is apparently the name of the high priest's *mother*. See Ilan 1992. It may well be that Simon was of the same clan as Joseph b. Camei, whose appointment to the high priesthood is mentioned at 20.16, as well as Joseph b. Simon (*Ant.* 20.196), thus pointing to another family of the high-priestly oligarchy, Qimḥit, alongsde the better-known families of Boethus, Ananus, and Phiabi; see Schalit 1968: 70; Stern 1976: 608–609; Ilan 2002: 425–426.

203 "Caiaphas" is, apparently, an Aramaic version of the surname Cantheras ("porter," "carrier of burdens"), which is known both from Josephus and from an epigraphic find (see Greenhut 1992); see the note on "Ananus" at 19.297. On Caiaphas, who stayed in office for some eighteen years (see §95), see Bond 2004; VanderKam 2004: 426–436; and Metzner 2010. On the dating of his tenure, see the next note. On his family, see Appendix 2.

204 Although Niese (1890a: 146) noted no variants, the number "eleven" is quite surprising, for the account of Gratus's governorship, which consists of the successive appointments of four high priests—one upon his own arrival in Judea, one "not long after" and two more after a year each—instead leads readers to expect perhaps "three" or "four." This point is part of the dossier that leads to the suggestion that Gratus was in fact replaced in 18 or 19 CE, not 26; see the opening note at 18.3.1 (§55).

205 Herod Antipas; on him, see esp. Hoehner 1972; Jensen 2007 and 2010; Wilker 2007; and Kogon and Fontanille 2018. Josephus already gave a report of some of Antipas's building projects at §§27–28. The fact that Josephus broke up his narrative of this tetrarch's foundations and placed this item here suggests that he wanted to date it specifically to this part of his story; for a similar procedure, cf. *Ant.* 12.237, 387–388, and 13.62.

206 For such phrases, compare §§168 and 289, also 20.205. The theme of "cultivating" friends in high places is one that interests Josephus; see also §§161, 165–167, 19.66, 211; 20.205. In fact, however, we seem to have no evidence for any close relationship between Antipas and Tiberius,

and the story at §245 suggests he was content to keep his distance.

207 For Josephus's description of the Galilee, see *War* 3.35–48 and Weiss 2007.

208 On Tiberias in the first century, see Weiss 2007: 387–392. For the foundation of the city between 19 and 21 CE, established by numismatic evidence, see Avi-Yonah 1950/51; Jensen 2010: 136; Mahieu 2012: 410–413 (she defines the possible range as 16–22 CE); and Kogon and Fontanille 2018: 21–22. The fact that Josephus places the story here is part of the argument for the chronological suggestion made in the opening note at 18.3.1 (§55).

209 On the Ḥammat springs, just south of Tiberias, of which Josephus had bad memories from his days in the Galilee (see *War* 2.614//*Life* 85), see HJP 2.178–179, n. 512. On pre-Niese readings of the text here, which gave rise to hypotheses about another location, "in Tiberias" rather than near it (as here), see Schürer 1890: 645.

210 Greek σύγκλυδες; cf. 19.243. For the interpretation of Josephus's hostile account of the population of Tiberias on the background of his own problems with the city in 66/67 CE, recorded in great detail in his *Life*, beginning with the hostile presentation of the city at §§32–42, and colored by his personal competition with Justus of Tiberias, see Cohen 1979: 140 and Miller 2001. See also the note on "also" at §39.

211 This is the only occurrence of ἀναγκαστός in Josephus.

212 It is not clear whether Josephus means that even among the higher echelons of the newly founded Tiberias (the οἱ ἐν τέλει—often used of rulers, e.g., §284; 20.121; *Life* 79) there could be found riffraff and people forced to live there, or, rather, that he is admitting that among those forced to move to Tiberias there were some more aristocratic types. In the latter case, this would be a qualification of his general condemnation of the population of Tiberias, perhaps added so as to allow himself the option of denying that his statement was meant to be totally inclusive. For Josephus's recognition that the population of Tiberias was not homogenous, see *Life* 32–36.

settlers, indigent people[213] who gathered together from anywhere at all, including some who were not even clearly free.[214] **38** In many cases he liberated many of them and—while imposing upon them the requirement that they not leave the city—he gave them benefits, preparing residences for them at his own expense and adding in gifts of land. [He did this] for he knew that the settlement was against the law and departs from what is allowed by the Jews' ancestral usage, because Tiberias had been founded upon destroyed[215] graves, of which there were many there, and our regulation[216] declares that residents [of such a place] are impure for seven days.[217]

(2.4)[218] **39** Around this time[219] also[220] Phraates king of the Parthians died,[221] after his son Phraataces[222] fostered a plot against him under the following circumstances.[223] **40** Phraates,   *Parthian History, 3/2 BCE–17 CE*

---

213 Which made them despicable by definition, in Josephus's aristocratic eyes; cf. §315.

214 I.e., including fugitive slaves.

215 True, it is possible to imagine taking ἀναιρέω to mean that, before building the city, they "carried off" the bones and relocated them elsewhere. However, were that the case, readers would assume the problem had been solved. Since it is evident that Josephus had no desire to imply the problem had been solved respectably, we should probably conclude, instead, that he means that graves were simply destroyed, but left in place, during the building of Tiberias. On the senses of ἀναιρέω, see *ThJL* 36, s.v. (where our passage is aptly brought alongside 15.391, where Thackeray suggests "demolish" for Josephus's report that Herod ἀνελῶν ancient foundations on the Temple Mount and then built in their stead).

216 On the sense of τὸ νόμιμον, see the note on "regulations" at §274.

217 See Numbers 19:11, 16, and above, §30. Josephus assumes here that readers know that the Torah requires those who come in contact with human bones to be impure for seven days and then to undergo a purification ceremony—which means that continual contact with such bones is totally unacceptable. Compare the rabbinic story of the purification of Tiberias, in *Genesis Rabbah* 79 (ed. Theodor-Albeck, 941–945) and parallels, on which see esp. Levine 1978. For sensitivity to the possibility that there might be human remains in a building-site, see *m. Oholoth*, chs. 16–18. For Josephus on the impurity of those who come into contact with corpses, see *Ant.* 4.262 and *Apion* 2.203, 205.

218 For the following story, see von Gutschmid 1888: 116–119; Debevoise 1938: 143–153; and (on Thesmousa) Bigwood 2004; Gregoratti 2012: 184–187, and D. W. Roller 2018: 123–127. The story opens with the death of Phraates IV in 3/2 BCE, long before the foundation of Tiberias ca. 20 CE (see the note on "Lake Gennesaritis" at §36), not "around this time." Rather, Josephus is still filling in events peripheral to the period of Judean history that he has just narrated, down to the end of the governorship of Valerius Gratus (§35): after leaving the history of Judea there, he

then turned to Herod's other sons, bringing their story down to the foundation of Tiberias; now he is turning to other ancillary events of the same period, this time—in Parthia. For this usual system, also followed, for example, in the long story about Parthia at the end of this book (see the note on heading "this tragedy" at §310), see D. R. Schwartz 1992: 188–198.

219 For this convenient way ("das bekannte Verzahnungsstück" [Laqueur 1913: 199]) of stringing together narratives otherwise unconnected one to another, as for example already at Gen 38:1, and, for example, *Ant.* 20.179, 189, 211, see D. R. Schwartz 1981/82. The fact that the narratives are not otherwise connected often suggests—no more, but no less—that that they derive from different sources.

220 This καί seems to be meant to lend some continuity to the narrative by adding yet another death to those of Salome and Augustus (§§31–32). For such moves on Josephus's part, cf. §53 (the beginning of the very next story), §310, and, for example, 5.175 ("It happened that similar suffering also befell the tribe of Dan ...," just as it befell the tribe of Benjamin in the preceding story) and 11.302 ("he too had a brother," just as his predecessor). If so, however, that suggests that Josephus clumsily inserted the intervening stories, one on the basis of a high-priestly chronicle (§§33–35; cf. the note on "high priesthood" at §34) and one on the founding of Tiberias (§§36–38), into a text which went from §32 to §39. Composition critics who suspect the attack on Tiberias is part of Josephus's response to Justus, whose work appeared only twenty years after he wrote it (*Life* 360) and, therefore, probably after the composition of *Antiquities*, or at least of its first draft, may put this observation into the appropriate dossier. See the note on "rabble" at §37.

221 As the context will make clear, Josephus refers here to Phraates IV—who death came in 2 BCE. See Schippmann 2016.

222 According to Debevoise (1938: 143), this is a diminutive for Phraates.

223 For Josephus's use of this formula (with αἰτία for "circumstances" or "details") to introduce a new story

who already had legitimate[224] children, fell in love[225] with an Italian slavegirl named Thesmousa,[226] who had been sent to him by Julius[227] Caesar along with other gifts.[228] At first he used her as a concubine, smitten by her great physical beauty, but with the passage of time, and after she bore a son, Phraataces, he proclaimed the wench[229] his wife and treated her as of [that] status.[230] **41** Whatever she said persuaded the king, and she, eager to ensure that the son born to her should be ruler of the Parthians, saw that that would not happen unless she engineered[231] the elimination[232] of Phraates's legitimate children.[233] **42** Accordingly, she urged him to send his legitimate children off to Rome as hostages.[234] And so they were sent off to Rome,[235] as it was not easy for Phraates to resist Thesmousa's

---

concerning a topic unconnected with the preceding context, in which case he often, as here, prefaces the story with a brief summary of it, compare §§91, 152, 310; 20.17, 141. Frequently, and especially when as here it comes together with "around this time" (see the first note on this paragraph), this reflects the insertion of material based upon a discrete source, as if Josephus thought it useful to summarize the story, which he treated as a closed unit, before giving its details; see Williamson 1977: esp. 50–55 and D. R. Schwartz 1992: 271, n. 76. That is probably the case here as well. For the source's Roman nature, see the note on "by nature unstable" at §47.

224 That is, children by his wife. For such usage of γνήσιος, which, when used of offspring, clearly distinguishes such "legitimate" children from those born to servants or concubines, see, for example, *Ant.* 1.153, 344. Of siblings, it refers to those who share both parents, as at 19.204 and *Life* 8. On the adjective see, in general, Spicq 1994: 1.296–299.

225 Something is rough here, and Niese (1890a: 147) marks a lacuna. I have adopted Petersen's emendation recorded by Feldman (1965: 32, n. 4): ἦρα, for without such a new verb, the Greek (Φραάτης παίδων αὐτῷ γενομένων γνησίων Ἰταλικῆς παιδίσκης ὄνομα αὐτῇ Θεσμοῦσα) would mean that Phraates already had legitimate children by the Italian concubine. It is clear that Josephus means to contrast legitimate children to those borne by the concubine.

226 On the different forms of her name, here and at §42, see Bigwood 2004: 38. On coins she appears as Μοῦσα—a name that is common enough among slaves. Accordingly, Josephus's text, which offers θεσμοῦσα or θερμοῦσα, seems to reflect the use of the *title* θεά ("divine") which accompanies her name on coins.

227 Apparently a slip for Augustus; see the next note.

228 This came in the context of the Roman-Parthian arrangements of 20 BCE (see E. Strugnell 2008), or perhaps a few years earlier (Bigwood 2004: 39–40).

229 For such contemptuous use of ἄνθρωπος, see also §349, 351 and, apparently, *War* 1.578. Cf. the note on "poor woman" at §71.

230 Bigwood (2004: 40) notes that the fact that "Theamousa" figures as "queen" (βασίλισσα) on coins supports the claim that she was promoted to Phraates's "official wife."

231 Josephus likes to use μηχανή and μηχανάομαι not only of the plain way/mean/method of doing something (as, for example, at §§51, 125, 276), but, rather, specifically of the underhanded machinations of villains (e.g. 17.17; 20.153, 163, 239, 248).

232 Although usually ἀποσκευή refers to "baggage," as at §377, here Josephus uses it in a sense frequently indicated by the verb (ἀποσκευάζομαι): she meant to have the other sons killed (so ἀποσκευασάμενος at §306) or otherwise eliminated (cf. 19.274); cf. *ThLJ* 75 ("get rid of, make away of, kill"). That would be routine in royal families; see the note on "his death" at §187. But introducing the pushy and villainous mother makes this part of a special complex Josephus loves: Thesmousa is almost as wicked as Agrippina at 20.151, in contrast to the virtuous Helena at 20.29–30.

233 As Bigwood notes (2004, 41), it seems that Phraates was allowed to choose his successor. But we can understand that Thesmousa might fear that legitimate sons had better chances than hers.

234 This way of explaining the sending of royal hostages to Rome, as if it were part of a scheming woman's machinations, fits the nature of this story, just as it fits Josephus's stereotyping of women; see the note on "demands" later in this paragraph. But it does not make much sense, for sending sons to Rome does not eliminate them; rather, it could allow them to establish connections that would help pave their way to the throne or otherwise be useful (see esp. §52). In fact, the education of foreign princes in Rome—as for example, Agrippa I (§143) and perhaps Agrippa II (20.135)—was quite regular practice, with advantages for both sides. See Braund 1984: 9–21 ("The Making of the King: Education"), Allen 2006: 149–177, Wheeler 2007, and Nabel 2017.

235 For other sources on Phraates IV's children in Rome, beginning with *RGDA* 6.32, see Debevoise 1938: 144.

demands.[236] But Phraataces, who alone was being raised [to rule] the state, thought it terrible, as well as too time-consuming, to take over the rule [only] when his father gave it to him, so he conspired against his father with the cooperation of his mother,[237] with whom—so it was reported[238]—he also had sexual relations.[239] **43** However, he incurred hatred for both reasons, for his subjects viewed the abomination of having sexual relations with his mother as no less serious than patricide; compassed about by civil strife before he managed to prosper greatly, he fell from [rule] of the state[240] and so died.[241] **44** Since the most noble of the Parthians all agreed, on the one hand, that it would be impossible for the state to be maintained without a king, but also that, on the other hand, it was necessary[242] that the king be of the line of the Arsacids, for it was not legal for others to rule,[243] and they had had their fill by then of the frequently outrageous treatment of the kingdom as a result of the marriage with the Italian concubine and her offspring,[244] they sent a delegation to Orodes[245] and called upon him, for—although he was not so desired by the masses and was accused of[246] some excesses of cruelty, for he was very brutal[247] and also had a bad tendency to anger—he was a member of the [royal] family. **45** He was killed, however,[248] by

---

236 The husband who gives in to his pushy wife's nagging despite his own better judgment, and pays the price, is a favorite theme in this book; cf. §§241–246 (Herodias) and §§360–362 (Mithridates's wife), also §§343–352 on Anileus's wife. On nagging women, see also 15.239 (Mariamme brought on her own death by her "disproportionate freedom of speech") and Plato, *Laws* 5.731d; cf. 20.145, where Josephus condemns Berenice for manipulating Polemo to serve her own purposes. For Josephus on women, see also the note on "contemptible women" at 19.129. More generally, see Eder 2022.

237 As the continuation shows, we should understand that they not only "plotted against" Phraates but also killed him.

238 As "some say ... the more generally held account" at §45, this seems to indicate that Josephus heard the story from more than one source. As at 19.193 and 20.143, the present formulation also serves to allow Josephus to repeat a juicy and nasty story, such as he likes to tell about women, without taking responsibility for it.

239 This is something of the ultimate sin ("not found even among pagans," according to Paul in 1 Corinthians 5:1), one that, even concerning Nero and Agrippina, Cassius Dio (61.11) is prepared to report, but not to vouch for its veracity. One may, therefore, understand Bigwood's inclination (2004: 43–47), after reviewing the lack of other evidence for such a union and the propensity of authors to tell such stories in order to denigrate their enemies and amuse their readers, to view it as "a piece of slander concocted by Phraatakes's enemies. He certainly had plenty of those" (as Josephus goes on to report). Even the fact that she appears as "queen" in Phraataces's days need not imply they were married, for it could simply be a continuation of the title established in Phraates's days; see the note on "status" at §40.

240 For such use of ἐκπίπτω with πραγμάτων, see also 15.191 (and 15.189). For similar formulations with ἐκπίπτω and other nouns, see *inter alia* 10.216; 13,328; 20.66. τὰ πράγματα in the sense of "the state" is standard Hellenistic usage; see Bikerman 1938: 4.

241 In 4 CE, the year of his last coins, together with "Theamousa"; see Bigwood 2004: 36–37.

242 Reading, δέοι δὲ βασιλεύοντος—an emendation suggested by von Gutschmid, in his private copy of Josephus (see Niese 1892: lv; 1890a: 148) and adopted by Mathieu and Herrmann 1929: 141, Schalit 1963: 285, and Feldman 1965: 36. Niese retains the manuscripts' reading, οἱ δὲ τοῦ βασιλεύοντος, which is difficult to construe but, if anything, probably means the same.

243 This consideration might be merely novelistic. Note, however, that at *Ann.* 2.1, in telling the next stage of this story, namely Vonones's fall from favor, Tacitus summarized that, although he was of Parthian royal stock his Parthian subjects scorned him as if he were a foreigner ("quamvis gentis Arsacidarum, ut externum aspernabantur"). Cf. below, §47.

244 The plural here (τῶν γενέσεων) is surprising.

245 Orodes III. The details of his lineage are as unknown as the events of his short reign; see Olbrycht 2014: 92. After the reference to Orodes something is wrong with the text; Niese first (1890a: 148) offered the mysterious εἰς δάν and listed a number of readings and suggested emendations, then (1890b: 128) contented himself with an obelisk (indicating a lacuna) between the two words.

246 This is the only occurrence of ὑπαίτιος in Josephus.

247 For this same collocation of cruelty and brutality, see 9.232; 19.201, on Gaius Caligula, is similar. On Josephus's usage of σκαιός, see the note on "invidious" at 20.266.

248 In 6 CE, according to Debevoise 1938: 151.

some people acting together: some say this happened in the midst of drinking and eating, for it is customary for each person to carry a sword,[249] but according to the more generally held account [it happened when] they took him out to hunt.[250] **46** Then they sent envoys to Rome to ask for a king from among the hostages,[251] and Vonones was sent—picked out from among his brothers.[252]

It seemed that fortune had turned [his way], having been bestowed upon him by the two greatest powers under the sun—his own and a foreign one. **47** However, very quickly the barbarians[253] underwent a turnabout (just as [anyway] they are by nature unstable),[254] in light of this degradation (for they considered doing what a foreigner commanded to be enslaved to him) and [so] instead they called being a hostage "slavery,"[255] and [because of] the dishonor attached to that term; [they emphasized that] it was not by right of war that he had been given to the Parthians to rule as king, but, rather—and much worse!—as a peacetime insult.[256] **48** Therefore they immediately called upon Artabanus, king of the Medians, who was of the Arsacid line.[257] Artabanus was persuaded and advanced with an army. Vonones went out to meet him, and at first, with the masses of the Parthians supporting him,[258] he joined battle and was victorious; Artabanus fled to the borders of Media. **49** Not long thereafter, however, he gathered [his forces], attacked Vonones and was victorious; Vonones escaped on horseback, with [only] a few of his people, to Seleucia.[259] Artabanus, who wrought much slaughter during the rout in order to terrify the barbarians, returned with his multitude [of troops] to Ctesiphon.[260] **50** So now he ruled the Parthians, while Vonones managed to flee to Armenia; at first he aimed for [rule of] that country and sent delegates to Rome. **51** When Tiberius rejected his request,[261] because of a lack of manhood[262] and the threats of the Parthian king, for he too had sent up[263] a delegation, holding out the threat of war, Vonones—having no other practical means[264] to gain the kingdom,

---

249 Apparently this means that it was usual to carry swords even at dinner. For illustration from depictions of Parthian banquets, see Heyn 2008: 179 (to which I was kindly referred by Peter Zilberg).

250 Unfortunately, Josephus's account is (according to Lenschau 1939) the only surviving testimony concerning the death of Orodes.

251 That is, the legitimate sons of Phraates (above, §42).

252 Augustus took personal credit for this (*RGDA* 6.33: "A me ...").

253 See the note on "supporting him" at §48.

254 That is, barbarians in general are like the mob among cultured peoples. Instability as characteristic of the *hoi polloi* is a constant theme in *Life*; see §§40, 77, 103, 113, 149, etc., along with Mason 2001: 45, n. 242. This, together with the reference to the Parthians as "barbarians," sounds like a clear expression of Roman disdain; cf. the note on "sent up" at §51.

255 Destinon (1904: 31) proposes emending Niese's ἀντὶ δουλείας into ἄντικρυς δουλείαν, as above §4: the Parthians considered being a hostage tantamount to slavery.

256 Tacitus (*Ann.* 2.2) has the Parthians complaining that those who had defeated Crassus and driven Antonius away were now reduced to accepting the Roman emperor's lackey ("mancipium Caesaris").

257 Artabanus II, who reigned ca. 10/11–38 CE. In the past he was numbered Artabanus III. He will figure prominently below, §§96–103, 326–353, also at 20.37–69. On him, see Debevoise 1938: 152–166; Kahrstedt 1950; and Schippmann 2011.

258 This seems to indicate that the opposition to Vonones mentioned in §47 was mainly among the aristocrats. So too at §44, it is the aristocrats who insist on criteria for kings.

259 On Seleucia, see below, §372.

260 His usual winter quarters (§377), located on the Tigris south of modern Baghdad. On Josephus's use of ἀναχωρέω and ἀναχώρησις, see *ThLJ* 44–45.

261 Neither this nor the reason supplied by the next words is recorded anywhere else.

262 Apparently the lack of manhood was Vonones's, demonstrated by his defeat and flight. But it is possible that Josephus means that Tiberius was unmanly insofar as he feared Artabanus's threats, mentioned in the next line.

263 This is the only instance of ἀναπρεσβεύω in Josephus, and, like the references to "barbarians" (§§47, 49)—expresses a Roman point of view. Cf. ἀναπέμπω at 20.131 and the note on "up to Rome" at §246.

264 For such use of μηχανή ("means, tactic, device, contrivance"), compare §§276, 281; 20.153. Here I follow Feldman (1965: 40), who reads μηχανή ... ἑτέρα, following two manuscripts. Niese (1890a: 149), following other

for even the Armenian notables around the Niphates [mountains] had joined forces with Artabanus—52 gave himself up to Silanus, the governor of Syria.[265] He, in deference[266] to his having been brought up in Rome,[267] kept him under guard in Syria.[268] Artabanus gave Armenia to Orodes, one of his own children.[269]

(2.5) 53 There also died[270] Antiochus, the king of Commagene,[271] and the masses split with the nobles, each side sending a delegation:[272] the notables requested a reorganization of the structure of the state as a province,[273] the masses—that they be ruled by a king in accordance with ancestral practice.[274] 54 And the Senate voted to send Germanicus[275] to regulate affairs in the East, Fortune[276] making this the opportunity for his death. For when he was in the East and had regulated everything, he was killed by Piso,[277] by poison, as has been related elsewhere.[278]

Germanicus's Mission to the East and His Death

---

witnesses, read μηχανή … ἑτέρας βασιλειάς, as if Josephus were noting that Vonones could not find another kingdom to rule. That seems less likely.

265 On Q. Caecilius Metellus Creticus Silanus, consul in 7 CE and governor of Syria 11/12–17, see HJP 1.259–60 and Dąbrowa 1998: 30–32.

266 For this sense of κατὰ αἰδῶ, see Ant. 7.230 and 14.375.

267 See above, §42. For κομιδῇ here as "upbringing," see CCFJ 2.516, s.v.

268 According to Tacitus, Vonones was allowed to live in royal style, but within a few years was moved to Cilicia and then, in 19 CE, killed by his guards when trying to escape custody; see Ann. 2.4, 58, 68.

269 On this Orodes, hardly known from other sources, see Täubler 1904: 9–10. It seems that Orodes reigned until 18 CE, so this Parthian story has taken us to about the same time as the history of Judea (the appointment of Caiaphas in 18 or 19—§35) and of Herod Antipas (the foundation of Tiberias in 19—§§36–38). So does the very next story. See the opening note on 18.3.1 (§55).

270 This formulation affords the next narrative, which too is extraneous from the point of view of Jewish history, some semblance of continuity with the preceding story, since both deal with Roman relations with the East. Cf. the note on "also" at §39.

271 Antiochus III of Commagene, d. 17 CE. Tacitus too (Ann. 2.42–43) reports that his death was among the circumstances that occasioned Germanicus's mission to the East. See Sullivan 1977a: 783–785; Sartre 2005: 75.

272 To Rome; the fact that this need not be said reflects the same point of view as ἀναπρεσβεύω at §51. See also the next note.

273 I.e., similarly, a *Roman* province. For similar usage, note "legions" at War 1.157, which apparently reflects the Roman point of view of Josephus's editors for War (see Apion 1.50), as opposed to Nicolaus's Syrian point of view preserved at Ant. 14.79 ("Roman legions"), just as, a few lines earlier in both works, Ant. 14.76 has plain "province" for Syria while War 1.157 has "the Syrian province"; see D. R. Schwartz 2013: 18–22.

274 Sullivan (1977a: 784–785) thinks the local unrest reported by Tacitus (Ann. 2.42.5) probably reflects the same attitude. For a similar split between aristocrats and the population at large with regard to the annexation of Judea by Rome, compare 17.304–314 (and War 2.84–91), where we read, in the context of 4 BCE, of Jewish aristocrats who urged Augustus to establish provincial rule in Judea after Herod's death, to 17.271–285 and 18.1–9, where we read of contemporary rebels aspiring to kingship and of popular opposition to Roman rule when it was in fact established ten years later.

275 On Germanicus (son of Drusus the Elder, brother of Claudius, father of Gaius Caligula), his mission to the East, and his death in 19, see Koestermann 1958; Weingärtner 1969; Levick 1999: 154–156; Barrett 2019: 19–32; Lott 2012: 340–345; and Powell 2013.

276 Josephus frequently allows τύχη a role, for example at §§197, 239, 267. See esp. Lindner 1972: 89–94; Shutt 1980: 183–186; Villalba 1986: 51–58; and Klawans 2012: 85–86, 189–190.

277 On Piso, the Roman governor of Syria ca. 17–19, see HJP 1.260 and the Senatus Consultum de Cn. Pisone Patre published in 1996; for the latter, see Yakobson 1998; the studies in AJP 120/1 (Spring 1999); and Lott 2012: 125–157 (text and translation), 255–311 (commentary). For the rumor that Tiberius was behind the murder, see Tacitus, Ann. 2.43 and Suetonius, Tiberius 52 and Caligula 2. The way Josephus refers to Piso here, as if readers know who is meant, without explaining that he was the governor of Syria (nor even that he had replaced the last-named incumbent in that position, §52), indicates Josephus's dependence here on a Roman source—such as those to which he alludes at the end of this paragraph. Thus, Josephus's procedure here is very similar to that at Ant. 11.305; in that case too, as also at 20.154–157, Josephus refers to other authors in abstaining from going into any more detail about something that is extraneous to Jewish history.

278 Germanicus died on 10 October 19. His popularity (reflected at 18.206–210; 19.217, 223) engendered massive mourning upon his death; see Barrett 2019: 31 and esp.

Pontius Pilate's
Tumultuous
Governorship
(3.1)[279] 55 Pilate, the governor of Judea, when bringing his army from Caesarea[280] and transferring[281] it to winter quarters in Jerusalem, thought to abrogate[282] the Jews's regulations by bringing into the city busts of Caesar,[283] which were attached to the military

---

Fraschetti 1991. The main extant literary sources concerning his death (Suetonius, *Cal.* 3.2; Tacitus, *Ann.* 2.55–72; Cassius Dio 57.18) are later than Josephus, so his reference to "elsewhere" must be to their sources, which did not survive.

279 On Pilate, who is well known from the Gospels, and who is mentioned by Philo (*Leg.* 299–305; see the note on "Caesar" later in this paragraph), by Tacitus (*Ann.* 15.44), and by an inscription from Caesarea (Boffo 1994, no. 23 = *CII/P* II, no. 1277) that names him "praefectus Iudaeae," and for whose Judean governorship there is also numismatic evidence (Meshorer 2001: 170–173), see *HJP* 1.383–387, 438–440, Bond 1998, Boffo 1994: 217–233, and Lémonon 1992 and 2007. For relatively recent finds, see Szanton et al. 2019, concerning a monumental street in Jerusalem from Pilate's time and Amorai-Stark et al. 2018, concering a finger-ring thought to bear Pilate's name; for doubts about the latter, see Eck and Ecker 2023. Pilate's appointment, to replace Gratus, was mentioned at §35. The fact that Josephus postpones his narrative of Pilate's term of office until he finishes his account of events in 18–19 CE (down to the foundation of Tiberias and the deaths of Orodes of Armenia, Antiochus III of Commagene, and Germanicus) is, along with the fact that Roman events of §§65–84 are dated by Tacitus (*Ann.* 2.84) to 19 CE, part of the argument for dating Pilate's appointment to that time. For that argument, see Mason 2008: 139, n. 1054, and D. R. Schwartz 2013: 139–145. On the literary effect of the postponement, to reflect the time it took Pilate to make his way to Judea, see the note on "completed" at §26. On the "tumultuous" nature of Pilate's governorship, according to the present account, see the note on "tumult" at §58. On Josephus's account of Pilate in *War* 2, see Mason 2008: 138–150 and Stowasser 2008. For the suggestion that the account (§§55–62) is a Josephan revision of an originally pro-Pilate report, perhaps prepared in connection with some hearing in Rome (see §89), which aimed to portray the Judeans as tumultuous so as to justify Pilate's measures to maintain order, and which survived better in *War* 2.169–177, see several of the annotations on these stories and D. R. Schwartz 2007b: 132–143.

280 I.e., Caesarea Maritima, the Roman capital of Judea. Since the days of Herod's massive work there it was one of Palestine's two antipodes, over against Jerusalem, the Jewish capital; cf. Lémonon 2007: 113–114 ("Une province à deux centres") and Eck 2007:14–18; Beebe 1983:

206–207. Hence Pilate's move to Jerusalem of what was fine in Caesarea had, whether or not intended, special significance, as is indicated by the end of the story at §59. For the same contrast of the two centers in other contexts, cf. Acts 23–25 (Jewish Jerusalem, which is hostile to Paul, is repeatedly contrasted with Roman Caesarea, which protects him) and *b. Megillah* 6a ("Caesarea and Jerusalem—if someone tells you they are both desolate or both inhabited, do not believe him; [but if it is said that] Caesarea is desolate but Jerusalem inhabited, or Jerusalem desolate but Caesarea inhabited, believe him"). For Josephus's account of Caesarea's construction, which (like the city's name) makes its Roman orientation clear, see *Ant.* 15.331–341. On the history of Caesarea, see *HJP* 2.116–118; Levine 1975; Ringel 1975; Lifshitz 1977; Patrich 2011, also below, 20.173–178.

281 With the exception of a suggested emendation at 3.289, this is the only occurrence of μεθιδρύω in Josephus. But ἱδρύω is common enough, including in the next paragraph.

282 Josephus does not say why Pilate would undertake such a goal. Nor, indeed, does Josephus state that Pilate realized that bringing the busts into Jerusalem would be construed as abrogating Jewish regulations. Perhaps he did not know that; perhaps he thought it would not ruffle Jewish sensitives if the busts were confined to the army's quarters; perhaps he thought the Jews did not care if non-Jews made images (see the note on "images"); perhaps he thought the Jews would not even know about the busts in the army's quarters (see the note on "night" at §56). Thus, translations of ἐφρόνησε such as "took a bold step in subversion" (Feldman 1965: 43) or "conspired to violate" (Schalit 1963: 286) go too far. What is important for Josephus here is only that, once Pilate brought the busts in, for whatever reason, it was difficult to back down in the face of protest, but that he nevertheless did so, in the end, in recognition of the Jews' sincerity.

283 For Roman military standards and such busts, see esp. Domaszewski 1885. At *Leg.* 299–305, Philo has Agrippa I tell a similar story, but Agrippa emphatically denies the iconic nature of what Pilate brought into the city and, further differing from Josephus's story, has the emperor, Tiberius, personally involved in the story. For a comparison of Philo's and Josephus's accounts, see Smallwood 1987: 126–127; she concludes that "The differences between these two stories are so obvious that they cannot be treated as variants of a single story." That

standards, although the law forbids us to make images.[284] **56** And it was for this reason that the preceding governors had made their entry into the city with standards without such ornaments.[285] Pilate was the first who, without the people knowing it, for his entry was at night,[286] brought the images into Jerusalem and set them up. **57** When they knew of it, they went en masse to Caesarea and pleaded, for many days, for the removal of the images. When he did not agree, for that would amount to an offense vis-à-vis Caesar, but they did not give up[287] entreating him, on the sixth day he stationed his armed troop unseen and himself got up on his tribune.[288] This had been set up in the stadium,[289] where the ambushing force hid. **58** When the Jews besought him again, at a given signal he surrounded them with the soldiers and threatened to pronounce a death sentence[290] immediately,[291] if they did not cease their tumult[292] and depart to their homes. **59** But they threw themselves prostrate

---

is true, but one may nonetheless ask whether these different *stories* relate to two different *events* or, rather, to the same event. Usually the former option is adopted; so, for example, Smallwood, ibid., also Smallwood 1981: 161–167; *HJP* 1.384–386; Stern 1974a: 351–352; Lémonon 2007: 127–148, 188–213; and Mason 2008: 140, n. 1057. However, it appears likelier that Philo's story relates to the same event, but has been skewed to allow it to be rhetorically useful for Agrippa in the role he played in the story as told by Philo: Agrippa was referring to the episode in the context of his attempt to convince Gaius to back down from erecting a statue of himself in the Temple of Jerusalem (see below, §§261–309). Philo's way of doing that was by portraying Pilate's action as less heinous than it really was, and then by involving Tiberius and attributing to him a response that was very harsh, thus indicating to Gaius, in an *argumentum e minore ad maius* Philo makes explicit at §306, that the introduction of something iconic is all the more reprehensible. Such an argument would have lacked all force if the concession had been made, as Josephus reports, by a governor, not an emperor. See D. R. Schwartz 1983a and 2013: 115–121, including discussion of other cases, at *Leg.* 261 and *Flacc.* 26ff., in which Philo plays fast and loose with the facts in order to serve some greater purpose. For a similar case, see also the note on "be used" at §95. For some further discussion, which, however, seems not to take Philo's rhetorical needs, and willingness to serve them, sufficiently into account, see Lémonon 1992: 759–760, 765–768.

284 Note that Josephus's formulation here does not fit the case, for the fact that Jewish law (the Second Commandment [Exod 20:4–5//Deut 5:8–9]) forbids Jews not only to worship images but even to make them (a prohibition observed very widely during the late Second Temple period [Levine 2005b; Levine 2012: 37–61]) does not explain why or how Jews would claim that Roman soldiers could not carry images into Jerusalem. What is needed is something like what Josephus wrote in the parallel account in *War* 2.170, where it is said that such images were not allowed in the city. For another case of

the same contrast between *War* and *Antiquities*, see the note on "to us" at §264. The fact that Josephus's formulations link the prohibition to the Jews rather than (as in *War*) to a place, Judea, reflects his becoming a Jew of the Diaspora between his two works. On that theme, see Tuval 2013 and D. R. Schwartz 2014: 49–61.

285 For a similar claim, about all Judea and not only Jerusalem, see §121.

286 Josephus likes to report that sneaky moves were made under the cover of darkness; so, for example, at §§159, 355, 370; 20.208. See Drüner 1896: 45–46, on such Josephan embellishments of his versions of stories in the Pentateuch and 1 Maccabees. Note, however, that while Josephus apparently means us to understand that Pilate was deliberately provocative and exploited the darkness in order to create a fait accompli, it might be that, as Eck suggests (2007: 57–59), Pilate brought the images into the city at night so as to avoid Jewish knowledge of them; after all, the images were to be set up in the soldiers' quarters and perhaps he could hope that the Jews would not become aware of them—thus allowing him both to do his duty to the emperor and to avoid riling his subjects.

287 This verb, ἐξαναχωρέω, appears elsewhere in Josephus only at §245.

288 As Quadratus at 20.130; cf. Philip's "throne" (§107).

289 On the hippodrome/"stadium" in Caesarea, see Patrich 2001 and Weiss 2014: 24–28. For other evidence for use of stadiums for public meetings, such as *War* 2.618, see ibid. 202–203.

290 θάνατον ἐπιθήσειν ζημίαν; the formulation is virtually the same as at §226.

291 ἐκ τοῦ ὀξέος is quite common in Books 17–19, whether by itself, as here and at §§170–171, 173, 236, 277, 294, 299 (also 17.23, 256, 344; 18.170, 173, 236, 277; 19.47) or in combination with μηδὲν εἰς ἀναβολάς (as at 17.187, 312; 18.309; 19.197; see the note on "immediately" at 19.197).

292 This is the first appearance of θορυβ- in Josephus's account of Pilate; it recurs at §§62, 65, 85, 88 and, as §65 suggests, probably figured in the original version of §§63–64 as well. It well reflects the Roman point of view that

and, baring their throats,[293] said they would gladly accept death[294] rather than dare transgress the wisdom[295] of the laws. And Pilate, astounded by their fortitude in the observance of the laws,[296] immediately removed the images from Jerusalem and brought them back to Caesarea.

(3.2) 60 He also made an aqueduct to bring water from Jerusalem, at the expense of the sacred moneys,[297] the watercourse beginning around two hundred furlongs away.[298] But they did not like the works surrounding[299] the water,[300] and many

---

focuses not on the issue that gave rise to the protest but, rather, on disorder, delegitimizing the protestors as if they were merely a mob. Especially Norden (1913a: 638–645) underlined this leitmotif, "tumult(ous)," of Josephus's narrative on Pilate. For its function, in leading readers to think of "turbulent times" and thus prepare them for the final catastrophe, see especially McLaren 1998. Note that it is not found in the parallel narrative of Pilate's days in *War* 2.169–177; there, instead, the leitmotif is ταραχή (§§170, 175, 176).

293 It is not clear how prostrate people can bare their throats. Perhaps we should understand the two as sequential, or perhaps we should take σφαγή more generally as "neck," as is suggested at *CCFJ* 4.138, s.v. ("the spot where the sword strikes the neck, the throat"). In any case, here as at §271 the scene sounds very impressive, and that is the point.

294 For willingness to die rather than violate the laws, a diasporic motif that is very prominent in *Antiquities*, see also §§264–266, also, for example, 12.304; 14.66–68; 17.152; 20.116; *Apion* 2.271–272. Cf. the note on "people" at §278.

295 On the wisdom of the laws, see the note on "wisdom" at §16.

296 This point, so important for Josephus in *Antiquities* (see the preceding note and the note on "law" at §222), makes the juxtaposition of this story to the next one into a diptych: Jews who remain firm in their devotion to their own values, even up to willingness to die for them, win Roman respect, while Jews who misbehave and evince scorn for Rome and its representatives, as in the next story (§60), get what they deserve. For a similar point, see the note on "provoking them" at 20.175. The contrast between the two stories is made even more stark by the fact that while it is clear why the Jews opposed the introduction of busts of the emperor into the city, it is not at all clear why they opposed the use of sacred funds for the aqueduct (see the note below, on "water.")

297 That is, money that had been donated to the Temple, whether as special gifts or as part of the regular Temple-tax. Cf. *Ant.* 14.72, 105–113, also below, §§82, 312 and 20.220–222; Stern, *GLAJJ* 1.274; Mason 2008: 34, n. 304; and the note on "to God" at §312.

298 At *War* 2.75 the length is said to have been four hundred furlongs. For Josephus's furlong ("stade") being

around 200 meters, and attempts to identify the remnants of this aqueduct, see Mason 2008: 147–148, n. 1103; for the latter, see also Yechezkel et al. 2021. Note both that, as Mason observes, the length of an aqueduct can be, due to terrain, much longer than the distance as the crow flies, and that Josephus does not say that Pilate built along the entire distance; it may be that he only built an aqueduct along one section of the route. The aqueduct studied by Yechezkel et al. brought water from the Biar Spring (some fifteen km. southwest of Jerusalem) to "Solomon's Pools" south of Bethlehem (for a map of aqueducts around Jerusalem, see ibid. 2).

299 ἀμφί is one of the words that appear in *Antiquities* only in Books 17–19, often for those "around" someone (18.165, 248, 276; 19.70) but also a few times, as here, apparently, for "concerning" (17.172, 325, 354; 18.196). It may be that this vague term, rather than "they did not like the project," implies that their objection regarded something peripheral to the project itself; see the next note.

300 Josephus does not explain why the Jews opposed Pilate's project, which apparently served the public interest; if Agrippa II could be applauded for using sacred funds in order to pave Jerusalem's streets and thereby support indigent workers (20.219–222), why should Jews oppose Pilate's use of sacred funds to build an aqueduct that brings water to Jerusalem? To say that was because Pilate was using the money "for his own secular purposes" (Feldman 1965: 46–47, n. b) is hardly fair. For the use of temple funds for public works, 20.220–222 and *m. Sheqalim* 4:2 (which even specifically mentions "water-channel" [aqueduct?]). Perhaps the issue vis-à-vis Pilate had more to do with the question of principle and procedure, namely, who was entitled to decide how to use the funds; so Lémonon 2007: 154–155. Or perhaps there was some particular problem involved; for the possibility that the aqueduct went through a graveyard and that some Jews thought that desecrated the graves and/or impugned the water's purity (which would especially be a problem insofar as the water was used in the Temple cult), see the discussion in Patrich 1982. In any case, the very lack of reason for the Jews' opposition is among the reasons to think that the story, as we have it, goes back to a brief meant to defend Pilate; see the opening note at 18.3.1 (§55). In Josephus's narrative, however, it contributes to

myriads[301] of people assembled and cried out to him to stop that which he planned; some of them also employed insults and abused the man,[302] as a mob[303] often does.[304] **61** He, for his part, had a large multitude of soldiers wearing their [style of] clothing,[305] carrying clubs[306] under their garments, and sent them off to surround the Jews, while he himself ordered [the latter] to withdraw. When they, however, intensified their vilifications, he released[307] to the soldiers the prearranged sign. **62** They beat [the Jews] even more than Pilate had ordered them to, punishing both those who rioted and those who did not.[308] But they displayed no cowardice,[309] and—taken as they were, unarmed, by men who were attacking them well-prepared—many of them were even killed there, while the others, wounded, withdrew. Thus ended [this outbreak of] civil strife.

(3.3)[310] **63** Around this time there lived Jesus—a wise man, if indeed he should be called a man. For he was the performer of amazing deeds, [and] a teacher of such men who receive

Josephus on Jesus

---

building the diptych: if in the first story, the Jews protested on account of a plain violation of their law, in the present story they are not said to have any good reason.

301 Josephus likes this hyperbole; cf. §§270, 277, 279, 287, 313, 366 and 20.211.

302 Another major contrast with the first story, where the Jews' protest focuses on their own principles, not on denigrating Pilate.

303 For this pejorative connotation of ὅμιλος, cf. 4.37 and 19.222.

304 Josephus, an aristocrat, expresses similar scorn for "mobs" elsewhere as well; see the note on "the mob" at 19.130.

305 Apparently: the Jews' style of clothing. In the parallel at *War* 2.176, they are described as being ἐσθῆσιν ἰδιωτικαῖς—clothing which, whether Jewish or Roman, did not identify them as soldiers, a measure that was probably meant to avoid instilling panic in the crowd, such as that which ensued in a similar scene at 20.110–111. This, as the next item, that they carried only clubs (a point esp. underlined in the parallel in *War*; see the next note), contributes to the picture of Pilate as moderate but responsible, attempting to avoid provocation but nevertheless being prepared to use force if required. Together with the fact that the text condemns the Jews as having behaved like a mob and persisted in vilifying the Romans, on the one hand, and, on the other hand, claims that when the Roman soldiers turned to violence they went beyond their orders, the whole narrative sounds like it is based on an account composed in order to defend Pilate by blaming both the Jews and, for the abuses, insubordinate soldiers. See also the next annotation. For the proposal that such an account derives, ultimately, from materials prepared by or for Pilate in the context of the hearing for which he was sent to Rome (§89), see D. R. Schwartz 2007b: 132–143 (where the same suggestion is also made concerning Josephus's narrative on Cumanus in Book 20; see the note on "festival" at 20.109).

306 This is the only occurrence of σκυτύλη in Josephus. Note that in the parallel passage, at *War* 2.176, Josephus has specifically *wooden* clubs and emphasizes that Pilate ordered the soldiers not to use their swords. In both cases, that appears to reflect a defense of Pilate as having been restrained, which has been toned down here; see the preceding note.

307 The use of ἀποδίδωμι suggests that Pilate, despite the provocation, held the fatal order back as long as he could. See the preceding notation.

308 In his reports about clashes with the Roman forces, and warnings against them, Josephus frequently emphasizes that, once they begin, the victims are not limited to the villains who brought them on. See, for some examples, 20.123; *War* 2.305–307, 399, also below, the end of §84.

309 See the note on "bizarre manners" at §23.

310 The next two paragraphs, §§63–64, constitute the so-called *Testimonium Flavianum*, the most famous passage in Josephus. Although quoted as early as the fourth century, by Eusebius (*Church History* 1.11.7–8; *Demonstration of the Gospel* 3.5, 124), its authenticity has been the subject of debate for centuries; see Bardet 2002, Whealey 2003 and, for briefer surveys, Winter 1973, van Voorst 2000: 81–104, Mason 2003b: 225–236, and van Henten 2020, also above, Introduction, at nn. 18–19. For detailed comparison of its vocabulary and style to Josephus's, see esp. van Liempt 1927 and Gramaglia 1998. Basically, there are three options: it is authentic (so, for example, Harnack 1913 and Victor 2010); it is wholly inauthentic (so, for example, Olson 1999 and 2013, who ascribes it to Eusebius); or it is what is left after an originally authentic text underwent revision by Christian editors and/or copyists. Total authenticity seems to be ruled out not only by the general consideration, that the plain expression of Christian belief about Jesus, if authentic, would mean that Josephus had become a Christian; the suggestion that that is the case, although argued by

truth with pleasure,[311] and he drew after him[312] many Jews and many Greeks as well.[313] He was the Christ.[314] **64** After Pilate sentenced him to crucifixion[315] upon his denunciation[316]

Whiston (see Feingold 2015: 26–28), garnered virtually no support, for it has, apparently, no other support in his oeuvre. Total authenticity is also ruled out by a specific literary consideration, noted especially by Norden (1913a): the opening of §65 indicates that it follows a story that (as those that precede the *Testimonium*; see the note on "tumult" at §58), culminated in a "tumult." That is not the case for the *Testimonium* as we have it, but could well be imagined, given such texts as Luke 13:1, 23:2, and 24:21// Acts 1:6–8, and the very fact that Pilate had Jesus killed; probably he had good Roman reason to do that. However, it is likely that Josephus did write something about Jesus, for his readers would know Christianity came from Judea and expect him to say something about it, and that likelihood is supported not only by the reference to Jesus as 20.200, which is usually taken to be authentic (see the note there on "Christ"), but also by the appearance of various Josephan phrases in the *Testimonium*; see van Liempt 1927 and, for a list of fifteen words or phrases in the *Testimonium* that are common in *Ant.* 17–19 and not typical of Eusebius, Mason 2022a: 169. In general, moreover, we should prefer a more conservative conjecture, if possible. That is, the third option seems to be the likeliest, namely, that Josephus wrote something about Jesus, which probably included something about tumults associated with him (cf. Luke 13:1) but did not make affirmative statements about Jesus's messiahship and resurrection but rather reflected them as what Christians believed— and Christian copyists refashioned the text to their liking. Indeed, "the majority view still is that Josephus did write a passage about Jesus, which was later adapted by a Christian scribe or editor" (van Henten 2020: 365).

311 "Receive with pleasure" (δέχομαι ἡδονῇ) is, as Mason notes, a collocation that is distinctively characteristic of Books 17–19 (17.329; 18. 6, 59, 63, 70, 236; 19.127, 185; cf. the note on "endure" at 19.28), and so has often been seen as an indication that the *Testimonium* began as a Josephan composition. And even if "ἡδονή normally denotes sensual pleasure" (Winter 1973: 436), the abovementioned passages show that that is often not the case, and so there is little reason to see here any hint of criticism.

312 Van Liempt (1927: 111–112) lists forty occurrences of ἐπάγεσθαι in Josephus's writings and adds that it is not found in ancient Christian literature. That corresponds to von Gutschmid's (1893: 352–353) remark that the phrase πολλοὺς δὲ καὶ τοῦ Ἑλληνικοῦ ἐπηγάγετο has "ganz Josephische Färbung ... [and is] ganz Josephisch," just as Thackeray (1929: 146) would later comment that "the repetition of 'many,' the neuter τὸ Ἑλληνικόν, and the use of ἐπάγεσθαι for 'win converts' are all thoroughly Josephan." There seems, however, to be no good reason to follow Th.

Reinach (1897: 7) and Eisler (1929/30: 1.39) in reinforcing Josephan authorship here by ascribing a hostile sense ("mislead," "seduce") to ἐπάγεσθαι here; for details, and an explanation of how Reinach came to offer that interpretation, see D. R. Schwartz 2023. Rather, Josephus could well express pride in the popularity of this outgrowth of Judaism even if he did not subscribe to it, just as, at *Ant.* 20.197–203, he expresses outrage at Sadducean maltreatment of its devotees.

313 This statement, which cannot be justified on the basis of New Testament evidence concerning Jesus for, despite some ambiguities, his mission seems to have been confined to Jews (Matthew 10:6; 15:24; Acts 10; cf. Jeremias 1982 and Bird 2006), has been adduced as proof that it was composed by an outsider, such as Josephus. But it could just as well be an anachronistic statement by a Christian writer, who knew of and approved of the inclusion of gentiles and, aware or unaware of the anachronism, pointed to Jesus himself as its author. For discussion of this argument as part of the case for identifying Eusebius as the *Testimonium*'s author, see Olson 2013: 105–108 and Vitelli 2018: 12. Or perhaps it was inserted craftily by a Christian forger who wanted to make it look like a mistake that only an outsider, such as Josephus, could make. Arguments such as these can go on endlessly.

314 The plain unqualified nature of this declaration, in contrast to "Jesus called Christ" in the reference to him in connection with his brother James at 20.200, is among the reasons to assume the present text has undergone Christian editing.

315 Lit. "punished on a cross" (σταυρῷ ἐπιτετιμηκότος). Although this could refer to impalement or hanging on/ from a pale or wooden beam (see esp. J. M. Baumgarten 1982, and Hadas-Lebel 2002—both in connection with ἀνασταυρῶσαι in *Ant.* 13.380), in the Roman period it typically referred to crucifixion. See Danker 2000: 72, s.v. ἀνασταυρόω ("always simply *crucify*"), and 941, s.vv. σταυρός, σταυρόω. The Crucifixion is usually dated to 30 or 33 CE; see Brown 1994: 2.1373–1376 and Visi 2020: 16–19.

316 Often the use of ἔνδειξις and ἐνδείκνυμι implies the denunciation was malicious and/or unfounded; see, for example, 17.3l 19.33, 133. And this is especially the case if, as here, no reason has been supplied that might justify an indictment. This can function as an argument against the authenticity of the *Testimonium*, whether we assume that the original text supplied a good reason for the indictment (such as inciting insurrection; see the note on "the Jews" at §65) and a Christian scribe left that out, or because the original text did not blame the Jewish dignitaries but a Christian scribe did. Note (with Eisler 1929/30: 42, n. 2) that whoever produced the text of the *Testimonium* used

by some of the most important men among us,[317] those who had earlier come to love him did not give up, for he appeared to them, alive again, in the course of the third day [after his death],[318] the divine prophets having stated that[319] and myriads of other marvels about him. And until today the adherents of this religion,[320] called "Christians"[321] after him, have not died out.

(3.4) 65 Around those same times[322] another terrible thing caused a tumult for the Jews,[323] and that coincided with acts not at all devoid[324] of shame concerning the temple of

Two Roman Episodes

---

by Jerome (*De viris illustribus* 13 [on Josephus]), which says instead that Pilate executed Jesus on account of the envy (*invidia*) of the leading Jews, was, apparently, reacting to this problem.

317 Niese (1894: v) saw here (παρ᾽ ἡμῖν) evidence of non-authenticity, because, he observed, apart from introductory and closing passages (such as 1.4 and 20.259, 264) Josephus usually speaks of the Jews in the third-person plural. However, as van Liempt (1927: 112–113) and others responded, Josephus uses the first-person plural often enough to neutralize this argument. See, for example, §55, also 3.248; 14.77–78; 20.198; *Life* 10.

318 For belief in Jesus's resurrection on the third day after his crucifixion, see, for example, Luke 24:46, Acts 10:40, 1 Corinthians 15:4. For his appearance to his disciples on that same day, see Mark 16:9–14 (only in the longer ending of the gospel) and Luke 24.

319 For prophesy of resurrection on the third day, see Hosea 6:2 and 1 Corinthians 15:4, also Matthew 12:40, which alludes to Jonah 1:17; Cook 2019.

320 Josephus's use of φῦλον here has been the object of much attention, for it is usually translated "tribe" and taken to be derisive, and since that would not be expected from a Christian forger or reviser, it is usually taken to be an argument for the text's authenticity. See, for example, Harnack 1913: 1048–1049, 1057; Winter 1973: 434. I accept the argument that the term is not to be expected from a Christian, but, in leaving it Josephan, I do not see good reason to assume it is derisive. Rather, I would translate φῦλον here as "adherents of a religion," on the basis of such passages as *Ant.* 12.23, where Josephus has Aristeas emphasize that he is not a Jew by birth nor is he the Jews' ὁμόφυλος; that must mean he is a Jew neither by descent nor by religion. Similarly, at *Ant.* 14.115 Josephus quotes Strabo's complaint that the Jews' φῦλον has "taken over" all around the world; since Jews cannot impose their descent upon others, it must be their religion that is meant. So too *Ant.* 16.2, where Josephus refers to ἀλλόφυλοι as those who do things differently than Jews do and can require Jews enslaved to them to violate their own "religion," and 12.145//*War* 5.194, where, with regard to non-Jews excluded from the Temple, Josephus carefully replaces ἀλλογενής (the term used in the inscriptions in the Temple; see the note on "secretly" at §30) by ἀλλόφυλος, which avoids the

implication that proselytes (who are of foreign birth but share the Jews' religion) were excluded. See also the note on "own community" at 19.330. That is, Josephus is stating that Christianity is not a type of Judaism; it is another religion. For more on this, in the context of the *Testimonium*, see D. R. Schwartz 2002.

321 According to Acts 11:26, the name "Christians" appeared for the first time in Antioch, sometime in the fourth or fifth decade of the first century; cf. Bickerman 2007: 2.794–808. Among Roman sources, see esp. Tacitus, *Ann.* 15.44.2–3, along with Stern, GLAJJ 2.91–92.

322 As usual, these words serve to link together stories that are otherwise quite unconnected. Cf. above, §39. The Roman events reported in the next two stories (§§65–84) belong to 19 CE, as is clearly indicated by Tacitus, *Ann.* 2.85 (where, as here, promiscuity, Egyptians, and Jews are all juxtaposed) and is supported by the placement of the brief report in Cassius Dio 57.18.5a; see Stern, GLAJJ 2.70. True, it is often thought that the opening of the present story, and the placement of these stories, are incorrect, for Pilate's tenure is usually thought to have begun only in 26 CE, as emerges from the present text of 18.35. However, it seems more likely that Pilate began his governorship already in 19 CE, and that Josephus's placement of these Roman stories here actually supports that, alongside other considerations; see the opening note at 18.3.1 (§55).

323 This opening line implies that the preceding story was about some terrible thing that caused a tumult—which gives us an idea of what Josephus's original account of Jesus reported; see the introductory note on 3.3 (the Testimonium) at §63. It also emphasizes, for readers, that all of Josephus's narrative on Pilate is characterized by "tumult," whether as verb or as noun; see the note on "tumult" at §58. In this case, Josephus's move involves some craft, insofar as this opening reference to a "tumult" among the Ἰουδαῖοι allows readers to accept it without second thought as if they were about to read another item in the narrative about Pilate. It is only fifteen paragraphs later (§80) that they will be told that it actually pertains not to Judeans but, rather, to the Jews *of Rome* and so (although Josephus does not point this out) has nothing to do with Pilate. Cf. the note on "also" at §310.

324 The double negative ("litotes") intensifies: the acts were very shameful. Compare, for example, "not at

Isis[325] in Rome.[326] After first preserving the memory of the audacity of the adherents of
Isis, I will shift the narrative to what happened to the Jews.[327]

66 Paulina was quite highly respected, thanks both to the prestige of her ancestors among
the Romans and to[328] her own striving after virtue.[329] She also had power on account of
her wealth, and was pleasing to the eye, but although she was of the age in which women
tend to be proud,[330] the conduct of her life tended to self-restraint.[331] She was married to
Saturninus,[332] who was one of those who was totally on a par with her[333] in good reputation. **67** She was [however], passionately desired by Decius Mundus, one of the equites
who then enjoyed a high reputation. But she was above being conquered by him by gifts,
as was shown by the fact that even after very many of them had been sent [to her] she
ignored [him]. This inflamed him all the more, so that he even promised her 200,000 Attic
drachmas[334] for one opportunity in bed with her. **68** But when even that failed to bend her,
he—taking badly such lack of luck with his passion—thought it would be better to punish
himself with death by starvation and so put an end to the evil that had befallen him. Indeed,
he took the decision to die that way and was not at all averse to[335] fulfilling that decision.

69 But Mundus had from his father a freedwoman named Ida, who was skillful in all sorts
of evils, and she took badly the youth's decision to die—for that he was perishing was not
at all hard to see.[336] Going to him, she raised his spirits with her words, and was convincing in promises of certain hopes as to how intimate relations between him and Paulina

---

all unwilling" at §68, "not at all unfamiliar" at §259, "not
at all disobliging" at 19.24, and "not at all averse" at 19.58,
also the use of οὐκ ἄσημον at 16.243, 201; 20.247; and *Life* 1,
along with Paul's similar reference to Tarsus according to
Acts 21:39.

325 Four temples of Isis are known in first-century-
Rome. Apparently the reference here, as also at *War* 7.123,
is to the largest of them, namely, the one in the Campus
Martius, which was paired with a Serapeum; so Gasparini
2017: 387.

326 On Isis in Rome, see Takács 1995, with pp. 80–86
on the present story.

327 That is, Josephus will give the extraneous material first so as to allow his narrative to return, thereafter, to its main topic. For a similar case, cf. 5.341, where
Josephus, having reported a prophecy to Eli and Samuel
without earlier mention of Samuel, announces that
he will then digress in order to introduce the prophet
before continuing with the main story. In this case, the
arrangement has an apologetic point: by telling the Isis
story first, and at much greater length, Josephus allows
the Jews' misdeeds to pale in comparison. For a similar
move, see the note on "as well" at §11. Apart from setting
up readers for the following story, it has been suggested
that the present story is also meant to mock the preceding one, about Jesus, whether by mocking belief in the
virgin birth by referring to faked intercourse with a god
(Bell 1976/77) or by mocking those who believe in resurrection by referring to gullible dupes who will believe
anything (Gasparini 2017).

328 Reading τῷ τε with Hudson and Havercamp (1726:
1.877), followed by Feldman (1965: 52), rather than the
manuscripts' τῶν, which was retained by Niese (1890a:
152) but is difficult to construe. As so often, in his editio
minor (1890b: 131) Niese too adopted the emendation; see
the Introduction, at n. 69.

329 For this phrase, cf. §§14, 20, 278.

330 For Josephus's notion of the usual overweening
behavior of married women, cf. §§241–245 and 360–362.
For Josephus's assumption that there are ages at which
one tends to misbehave, cf. *Life* 80, also the note on
"youths" at §10.

331 For this virtue (σωφρονέω, σωφροσύνη as at §§73,
76), cf. 19.210 and, in general, North 1966 and Spicq
1994: 3.359–365 (esp. 363–365 esp. on women, as at §180
and at 6.296, concerning whom it corresponds to Latin
pudicitia—modesty, chastity, virtue). Cf. the note on
"chastity" at §180.

332 Paulina and Saturninus seem to be otherwise
unknown; see the note on "Saturninus" at §83.

333 This is the only occurrence of ἀντισόομαι in
Josephus.

334 It is usually assumed that 6000 drachmas = 1
talent = about 26 kilograms on the Attic standard, so
200,000 drachmas would be around 33 talents—a huge
sum; see Mason 2008: 34–35, n. 306.

335 On such usage of the verb, which amounts to
"quite prepared," see *ThLJ* 59, s.v. ἀπαλλάσσειν, §2.

336 Ida's role in this story is very similar to that played,
according to Plutarch, *Parallela minora* 22, by Myrrha's
nurse in the story to which Josephus refers at 19.94.

could be brought about. 70 After he received her appeal with pleasure,[337] she told him she would need only 50,000 [drachmas] for the conquest of the woman. Thus did she arouse the youth's spirits, and after receiving the money she had requested she did not follow the same paths as those who had attempted to arrange the matter before her, for she saw that the woman could not at all be conquered by money. Rather, knowing that she was very devoted to the cult of Isis, she concocted the following scheme.

71 Coming to some of the priests [of Isis] and, after giving them great assurances—and especially, that she would give them 25,000 up front and another payment of that size when the business was completed—she explained to them the youth's passion [for Paulina] and urged them to apply every effort to procure the poor woman.[338] 72 They, smitten and brought over by the money, promised [to do what was asked]. The oldest of them hurried to Paulina's house and, upon entering, asked to go speak with her privately. When this was granted, he said he had been sent by Anubis,[339] for the god had succumbed to passion for her and requested that she come to him. 73 This statement was quite welcome to her, and she both boasted to her women friends about this request by Anubis and also told her husband, that she had been summoned[340] to Anubis's dinner and bed. And he agreed, knowing very well his wife's self-restraint. 74 She went to the sacred enclosure, and after she ate there, when it was time to sleep, and the priest had shut the inner doors and taken away the lamps—Mundus was also there, having hidden there in advance. Nor did he fail to have intimate relations with her; she ministered to him the entire night, under the assumption that he was a god. 75 After he went off before the priests, who knew about the plot, had begun to stir, Paulina went early in the morning to her husband and reported to him in detail about the epiphany of Anubis; and she boasted[341] to her women friends by talking about him. 76 They, on the one hand, refused to believe [her report], considering[342] the nature of the business; but on the other hand they were cast into perplexity for, when they turned their gaze to her self-restraint and fine reputation, they could not adjudge the things unbelievable, as they should.

77 On the third day after the act, however, Mundus encountered her and said: "Paulina, I saved 200,000 drachmas that you could have added to your estate, although you performed, leaving nothing out, that which I had called upon you to do. True, you set out to insult Mundus, but I—concerning myself not with the names but only with the pleasure of the act—assigned him the name Anubis."[343] 78 Having said that he went off, but she, having for the first time come to understand the insolent act, tore her garment and, after explaining the magnitude of the whole plot to her husband,[344] she asked him not to forgo seeking aid—whereupon he reported[345] the matter to the emperor.

---

337 Cf. the note on "pleasure" at §63.

338 Here, as at §112 (as also at 15.231 and 19.34), the use of ἄνθρωπος of a woman seems to express sympathy rather than contempt. For the latter, see the note on "wench" at §40.

339 On Anubis in the Greco-Roman world, see Gasparro 2018 (on the present story: 541, n. 79).

340 This is the only occurrence of εἰσαγγέλλω in Josephus.

341 This is the only occurrence of ἐλλαμπρύνομαι in Josephus.

342 Lit. "looked at" (ὁρῶντες), answered "on the other hand" by ἀπίδοιεν ("turned their gaze") later in this sentence.

343 Here the witnesses differ. The translation follows Niese (1890a: 154; 1890b: 133), who adopted Ambrosianus's αὐτῷ ("for him"); this preserves the third person used earlier in the sentence ("to insult Mundus") and, despite the intervening use of first-person singular (μοι ... ἐθέμην), apparently winks at Mundus's joke of pretending he is not Mundus. Feldman (1965: 56–57) prefers the more pedestrian ἐμαυτῷ ("for me"), supplied by two other witnesses.

344 For the wife's exemption from punishment because she was deceived, see Digesta 48.5.11.12.

345 Niese (1890a: 154; 1890b: 133) suggests emending the manuscripts' ἐπεσήμηνε into ἀπεσήμηνε, whether simply because Josephus uses the latter much more

79 Tiberius, upon learning the details by interrogating the priests closely, crucified them as well as Ida,[346] for it was she who had caused the catastrophe and put together the whole scheme to outrage the woman; and he tore down the temple and ordered that the statue of Isis be thrown into the Tiber River. 80 But Mundus was punished [only] with exile, for Tiberius thought the fact that his crime had been done out of passion should preclude the imposition of a more severe penalty.[347]

So much for the outrageous things done by the priests of the temple of Isis. Now, as I announced earlier[348] in my account,[349] I will revert to the story of what happened at the same time to the Jews in Rome.[350]

(3.5) 81 There was a Judean man, who had fled his [country][351] after an accusation of transgressing certain laws and in fear of punishment on their account, and he was very wicked. Indeed,[352] at the time in question he was staying in Rome, giving himself out as an authority[353] in the wisdom[354] of the laws of Moses, 82 having associated with himself three men who were of just the same ilk. When Fulvia, one of the eminent women, who had associated herself with Jewish practices,[355] habitually met with them, they urged her to send via them purple[356] and gold for the Temple in Jerusalem,[357] which they then took and used up on their own personal expenses (which was their purpose in making the request in the first place.)[358] 83 When Tiberius was informed of the matter at his wife's behest by

---

frequently or also so as to make the phrasing here conform to that of the next story (§83), since Josephus treats the two stories—and perhaps received them—as a matched pair.

346 Under the terms of the *Lex Julia de Adulteriis* (*Digesta* 48.5.9–10); see Rogers 1932: 253–254.

347 As Lembi (2001: 55) notes, this novelistic motif, that being overcome by passion can excuse criminal behavior, reappears in the story of Asineus and Anileus (§350); it also recurs in that of Izates (20.22). (On the general theme of a man being enslaved by his passion for a woman, see the note on "passions for her" at 19.193.) As a matter of fact, Rogers (1932: 254) states that Mundus's exile was simply the regular punishment for adultery imposed by Augustus's *Lex Julia* (Paulus, *Sententiae* 2.26.14), which also mandates the confiscation of half the offender's property. See, in general, Corbett 1930: 139–143. However, the present case, in which the woman was misled, would seem to be more heinous than the usual adultery, and so might have been expected to entail a more severe punishment, especially if, as Josephus reports, those who merely facilitated the crime were executed.

348 At §65. This is the only occurrence of προαποση-μαίνω in Josephus. For formulation with the agent in the dative, cf. §§142, 202, 209, 222, 225, etc.

349 For such use of λόγος, see the note on "work" at §307.

350 On the Jews of ancient Rome see Leon 1995; Noy 1995; Barclay 1996; Rutgers 1998; and Rocca 2022.

351 For such use of τῆς αὐτοῦ cf. τῆς αὐτῶν at §97. As at §196, the country is defined by the man being called a Ἰουδαῖος, hence "Judean."

352 On καὶ δή as a way to introduce something that illustrates the preceding statement, see the note on "for example" at §257.

353 On Josephus's use of ἐξηγητής, for authoritative legal authorities rather than "exegetes" who interpret texts, see the note on "teaching" at §15.

354 For Josephus's emphasis on the wisdom of the laws, see the note on "wisdom" at §16.

355 On such "sympathizers" or "judaizers," who adopted Jewish practices, concerning which there is a huge literature, especially since the appearance of Reynolds and Tannenbaum 1987, see esp. Stern, GLAJJ 2.103–106 (a large collection of evidence apropos of Juvenal's complaint about such people at *Satires* 14.96–106) and Cohen 1999: 140–197. Cf. the notes on "revere" at 20.34 and on "god-fearing" at 20.195.

356 On the great value attached to purple dye and material in antiquity, see Reinhold 1970. For valuable purple tapestries among the Roman booty from the destruction of the Temple, see *War* 7.134, 162.

357 On such donations to the Temple, see for example *Ant.* 14.110. On donations specifically by gentiles, see HJP 2.312–313.

358 For Roman outrage at Jewish success in encouraging others to donate to the Temple in Jerusalem, which will have created fertile soil for suspicions that the money

Saturninus,[359] who was both his friend[360] and Fulvia's husband, he ordered the departure[361] of all of Roman Jewry.[362] **84** Of them, the consuls sent four thousand people into military service on the island of Sardinia;[363] and punished many who did not agree to serve in the army because of their observance of the ancestral laws.[364] And so they[365] were banished from the city on account of the wickedness of four men.[366]

---

would in fact be used to pad private pockets, cf. Tacitus, *Hist.* 5.5.1.

359 It is strange that Fulvia's husband has the same name as Paulina's (§66). For the somewhat speculative argument that the two women were one and the same, see Rogers 1932. Syme (1964: 165) prefers to content himself with "The problem of identities is puzzling." As Stern notes (1991: 511, n. 46), the text might simply be confused; one should not expect too much accuracy from a *Skandalchronik* (see the Introduction, n. 44).

360 Much has been written about Tiberius's "friends," especially occasioned by John 19:12; see Spicq 1994: 3.458–461. At times it seems to refer more to a semi-official position; see the note on "companions" at 19.268. In a gossipy text like this one, however, we probably should not assign the term any specific meaning.

361 Tiberius's expulsion of the Jews from Rome is mentioned by several ancient writers, especially Tacitus, *Ann.* 2.85 (who clearly dates the event to 19 CE) and Suetonius, *Tiberius* 36; both of them, like Josephus, juxtapose the punishment of the Jews to that of the Egyptians. According to Josephus, all the Jews were expelled, while some of them were also conscripted into army service or punished if they refused it. On this expulsion, see Stern, *GLAJJ* 2.68–73; Rutgers 1994; Gruen 2002: 29–36; and Lans 2015.

362 For τὸ Ἰουδαϊκὸν τῆς Ῥώμης compare Josephus's use of the same term for the Jewish population of a given city: for example, *War* 2.105 (Rome); 399; 478 (Syrian cities); 487, 492, 495 (Alexandria). On this usage, see D. R. Schwartz 2005: 76–77 and Mason 2008: 347, n. 2937. Cf. *CPJ* 1.5, n. 14, on a quarter called Συροπερσικόν in Memphis.

363 According to Tacitus (*Ann.* 2.85 [*GLAJJ*, no. 284]), they were sent to Sardinia to fight "bandits" there, on the assumption that if they failed and perished, little would be lost. On bandits in Sardinia, see Hengel 1989: 26. However, Woods (2008: 271–272) doubts that there was much of a problem there in 19 CE, and suggests, instead, that Tiberius's conscription of Jews into the army, however Josephus and Tacitus for their own reasons preferred to portray it, was actually part of a more general mobilization of forces to deal with a rebellion in Africa. Sardinia would then have been only a station along their way. On Jews in the Roman army, see Schoenfeld 2006; González Salinero 2022: 40–45.

364 It is not clear whether Josephus means that *of those who were sent to Sardinia* many were punished for this reason, or, rather, that apart from those who were sent there for army service there were many others who, for this reason, refused to go and were therefore punished. What was important for Josephus was to underscore the Jews' devotion to their laws even when that brings punishment upon them; cf. the note on "people" at §278.

365 Since this sentence concludes the entire story, it seems that "they" refers to "all of Roman Jewry" (§83), not only to those mentioned earlier in the present paragraph: Jews sent to Sardinia or those who refused service.

366 Here Josephus underlines just how unfair the collective punishment was: most Jews were guilty of no crime, and those few who were guilty were criminals from a Jewish point of view too (§81!), and, therefore, were not representative of the Jews of Rome at large. This is all in contrast to the story about the cult of Isis, where, as Josephus tells it, the criminals included the most representative figures of the cult: the priests themselves. For similar comments about the way disproportionate suffering can result from the misconduct of a single individual (in that case: a Roman), see 20.112 and *War* 2.399. This is all part of Josephus's general thesis, that the clashes—and eventual war—between Jews and Romans occurred because too much influence was achieved by a few Jewish troublemakers, who were not representative of the Jews, and by a few corrupt and cruel governors, who were not representative of the Romans. Compare §62's insistence that once a clash with the Romans begins there is no distinction between innocent and guilty, and esp. Agrippa II's speech at *War* 2.350–354: if only the responsible Jewish leaders (such as those of *War* 2.410–411 and of *Ant.* 18.121, 273; 20.123), and responsible Roman governors, such as Festus according to *War* 2.271 and Albinus according to *Ant.* 20.204, were allowed to control affairs, peace and stability would prevail. That is, there was nothing inherently wrong about Roman rule of Judea, as the rest of the world; things went wrong only due to glitches, when non-representative types, such as Jewish "bad apples," or corrupt secondary officials (but not the emperor), or people who, like Caligula, were simply insane, are, exceptionally, in control for some time. This thesis, shared by the author of 2 Maccabees with regard to Seleucid domination of Judea, is a prime element of diasporic historiography; see D. R. Schwartz 2008: 243–244.

End of Pilate's Governorship

(4.1) 85 Neither was the Samaritan[367] nation[368] free from tumult.[369] For a man who did not care much about lying, and who manipulated everything according to the pleasure of the mob, called them together and urged them to accompany him up Mt. Gerizim, which is considered by them to be the holiest of all mountains. He promised them that upon arriving there he would show them the sacred vessels that were buried there, Moses having deposited them there.[370] 86 Considering his statement plausible, they stationed themselves, armed, in a certain village, named Tirathana,[371] adding to their numbers those who joined them so that they could make the ascent to the mountaintop with a large multitude of people. 87 But Pilate forestalled their ascent, hindering it by dispatching cavalry and heavily armed infantry, who fell upon those who had gathered earlier in the village; a battle ensued, in which they killed some and forced others to flee.[372] Many were also taken prisoner, and of them Pilate killed those who were the most dominant and the most influential among the fugitives.

(4.2) 88 When this tumult had been put down, the council of the Samaritans went to Vitellius—a man of consular status[373] who was governing Syria[374]—and accused Pilate of the slaughter of those who had been killed. For, they said, it was not out of rebellion

---

367 On the present episode, see M. F. Collins 1972 and Pummer 2009: 230–243. It posed a problem for Josephus, for although he usually likes to condemn the Samaritans (see the note on "Samaritan men" at §30), here the needs of this "tumultuous" chapter require him to present them as Pilate's innocent victims.

368 This designation of the Samaritans as a separate ἔθνος is not to be taken for granted. Contrast 2 Macc 5:22–23 and 6:2, where the author considers them part of the same nation (γένος) as the Jews, although they worship at different temples; so too an inscription from Delos characterizes Samaritans as "Israelites who sacrifice at Mt. Gerizim" (Boffo 1994: 47–60). Probably the former should be understood as reflecting the diasporic author's lack of interest in the Temple of Jerusalem and therefore his lack of concern about its competition (see D. R. Schwartz 2008: 46–47), while the latter expresses the Samaritans's self-identification. Josephus, in contrast, formulates as we should expect from a priest of Jerusalem, just as elsewhere he mocks the Samaritans for claiming to be Jews only when that is convenient (9.290–291; 11.341; 12.257–264).

369 On this leitmotif of Josephus's account concerning Pilate, see the note on "tumult" at §58.

370 The notion that Moses buried vessels on Mt. Gerizim is strange for two reasons: according to the Bible he died in Transjordan (Deuteronomy 34) and so never was near Mt. Gerizim, and stories about hidden Temple vessels make sense only on the background of the destruction of a Temple. Note, however, that in one

of the earliest and most detailed versions of such stories, at 2 Macc 2:4–8, we read that, just prior to the destruction of the First Temple, Jeremiah brought the Ark of the Covenant and the altar of incense from Jerusalem *to the mountain from which Moses saw the land* before he died and hid them there, to await the day of God's mercy and restoration of the Temple. Although that mountain was in Transjordan, according to Deuteronomy 34, this juxtaposition of Moses-on-a-mountain and the hiding of Temple appurtenances, together with the competition between Gerizim and Jerusalem, might have been enough to generate the belief reflected by the present story—and, as elsewhere (e.g. 20.97–99, 167–172), the Roman government could well be worried about subjects who thought that the day of God's intervention was near. For a detailed study and a similar suggestion, see Collins 1972.

371 Other readings include "Tirathaba" or the like. "It is generally assumed that the place is to be identified with et-Tire, 6 km. south-west of Shechem" (Pummer 2009: 233, along with bibliography and discussion of possibly related later traditions).

372 This is a standard way to round out a battle report; compare, for example, §324; 8.294; 14.95; 20.79.

373 On the use of ὑπατικός for a *vir consularis*, in this case (as at §§104, 150) for a provincial governor of consular rank, see Mason, *GTRI* 169–171.

374 On L. Vitellius, consul in 34, proconsul of Syria between 35 and 39 CE, and father of one of the emperors in the *Vierkaiserjahr* (68/69 CE), see *HJP* 1.262–263 and Dąbrowa 1998: 38–41.

against Rome, but in order to escape Pilate's outrageous behavior, that they had come to Tirathana.[375] **89** Dispatching Marcellus, one of his friends,[376] to be the administrator[377] of the Judeans, Vitellius ordered Pilate to go to Rome to explain himself to the emperor in response to the Samaritans' accusations.[378] And so Pilate, having spent ten years in Judea,[379] hurried[380] off to Rome—obeying Vitellius's orders since it was impossible to oppose them. But before he made it[381] to Rome, Tiberius preempted him[382] by dying.[383]

---

375 There is a little cynicism here, because in fact, according to Josephus's story, the Samaritans had gone to Tirathana in the hopes of finding sacred vessels hidden by Moses. Compare 20.125–126; there too, the Samaritans are portrayed as telling the Romans what it was useful to say, not the truth.

376 On a Roman governor's friends (*amici*), as also at §§122, 269 and 20.117, see Walker 2000: 87.

377 Josephus's choice of ἐπιμελητής here, which otherwise he does not use of Roman governors of Judea, might well indicate that Marcellus, who is otherwise unknown, was considered a substitute pending Tiberius's decision concerning Pilate. In Roman contexts, the term usually refers to some type of "curator"; see *GTRI* 46–47, s.v.; for the usual Greek terms for Roman governors, see ibid. 142–143 and the note on "prefect" at §33. On Marcellus, including on the possibility that he is the same as Marullus (§237), see Appendix 1.

378 Presumably he would have had to defend himself against complaints from Jews as well; in a case like this, just as in those described at 17.342 and 20.132, every additional complaint would help, and the Samaritans will have been happy to join forces with them and throw the whole book at the governor. For the suggestion that Josephus's text reflects Pilate's efforts to defend himself against the Jews' accusations, see the note on "clothing" at §61.

379 Josephus's statement that Pilate served ten years, together with §35's statement that his predecessor served

eleven, corresponds well with his statement at §177 that together these two governors filled out Tiberius's entire tenure as emperor, which began after Augustus's death in August 14 and ended with Tiberius's in March 37. However, we have seen reasons to prefer the possibility that Pilate's term in fact began ca. 19 CE; see the opening note at 18.3.1 (§55).

380 Cassius Dio reports at 53.15.6 that governors were required to return to Rome within three months after the end of their tenures. Indeed, Smallwood notes (1954: 15) that Pilate will have wanted to hurry to Rome, so as to get there before his accusers.

381 Tiberius died on 16 March 37, and so we may infer that Vitelliuis sent Pilate not more than a few months earlier; had he been sent much earlier, he should have arrived at the capital prior to Tiberius's death. For discussion of the chronological issue, see the note on "Judea" at §90. Josephus does not mention Pilate any more, but subsequent legends more than made up for that. See Maier 1971 and Lémonon 2007: 231–254.

382 This reference to what Tiberius did, rather than to his death having intervened, sounds like a little joke: Pilate hurried but Tiberius finished the race sooner, by dying. For the competitive implication of φθάνω, see esp. *Life* 15 and Daube 1980: 18–20.

383 For similar cases, in which the emperor's death intervened just in the nick of time, cf. §§305–309 and 19.10, 107.

Vitellius Visits
Jerusalem, I

(4.3)[384] 90 Upon arrival in Judea,[385] Vitellius went up[386] to Jerusalem, for they were then celebrating an ancestral festival, named *Pascha*.[387] After being magnificently received,[388] Vitellius completely remitted,[389] for all those who resided there, the taxes on the purchase[390] of agricultural produce; and he agreed[391] that the priests should supervise the high priest's

---

384 A second report of a visit by Vitellius begins at §120. For the question, whether the two reports concen the same visit or two separate visits, see the next note.

385 This formulation is surprising, for nothing in the narrative has led us to expect Vitellius to visit Judea now. Such a visit is explained, however, by the narrative at §120ff.—which too culminates in a visit to Jerusalem during a Jewish festival, in the course of which news of Tiberius's death reached Vitellius (§124). It appears that what seem to be two visits are one and the same, Josephus supplying us with reports about it from two points of view: the first reflects the interests and notions of Jerusalemite priests and the second focuses upon Herod Antipas. This conclusion is invited by the chronological conundrum that confounds all efforts to allow for two such visits if we accept Josephus's statement here that the first of the two visits occurred on a Passover. In brief, that conundrum is as follows. If that Passover was that of 37 CE, which, we may assume, was ca. 20 April, then the second visit must have been on the next holiday, Pentecost (*Shavuot*). But that was fifty days later (Leviticus 23:15–16//*Ant.* 3.252), so in early June, and it is impossible to imagine that Rome's highest official in the East would not have heard, by then, of Tiberius's death in mid-March. Moreover, the report of the second visit apparently refers to the fourth day of the festival, and Pentecost was only one day long (Numbers 28:26; *Ant.* 13.251–252). But if, in order to allow the second visit to be on Passover 37, we suppose the first visit was on Passover 36, it would be impossible to accept Josephus's statement at §89 that Pilate, who set off to Rome before the visit, hurried to Rome but nevertheless failed to arrive prior to Tiberius's death in March 37; but it is indeed likely that he would want to hurry (see the note on "hurried" at §89). As *War* 2.203 shows, even three months would be long. So it is no easier to place the first visit on Passover 36 than on Passover 37. While various scholars suggest rejecting one or another of the data that construct this conundrum, as noted above it seems, as Otto (1913: 192–194, n. *) and Krieger 1992 recognized, simpler to think that there was only one visit, on Passover 37, of which Josephus offers two accounts. For objections, see the notes on "agreed" at §90 and on "Theophilus"at §123. On this problem see Holzmeister 1932; Smallwood 1954; Stern 1974b: 68–70; D. R. Schwartz 1992: 202–217; and idem 2013: 101–106.

386 As at §122 and 20.164–165, also e.g. 11.89, 93, 325; 16.169, 171; 18.313; *War* 2.16, 40, 244; etc., this is a standard phrase for travel to Jerusalem or the Temple, whether in general (e.g. *m. Taanit* 4:2) or specifically with regard to pilgrimage (e.g. Micah 4:2//Isaiah 2:3; Jeremiah 31:6; *m. Hallah* 4:11 and *m. Nedarim* 3:10). Cf. the note on "went down" at 20.50 and Mason 2008: 16, n. 109 (on *War* 2.16).

387 Passover; see the note on "*Pascha*" at §29. Compare a similar Passover visit by one of Vitellius's successors, after he in his turn put down violence between Judeans and Samaritans; *Ant.* 20.133 and *War* 2.244.

388 Just as at §123, where Vitellius's visit is reported along with its circumstances. On such receptions of visiting rulers, see the note there on "multitude."

389 For Josephus's use of ἀνιέναι for remitting taxes, see *ThLJ* 49, s.v., §3. Compare especially Archelaus's remission of taxes of various kinds, reported at *War* 2.4// *Ant.*17.204–205. It too came around the time of Passover (*War* 2.10//*Ant.* 17.213) and was not necessarily meant to extend beyond the holiday week. See also 12.142–144; 15.365; 16.64–65; 19.299; and Keddie 2019: 135–137.

390 Assuming that the tax was in fact paid by the seller, Naber (1893: xix) suggested emending Niese's ὠνουμένων, for which the apparatus shows no variants, into πωλουμένων. However, while it is true that it was easier for tax-collectors ("publicans") to collect from vendors, whose stores and stands were known and stationary, it does not seem difficult to understand the statement to mean that a tax on purchases was collected from vendors. Schalit, for example, translates (1963: 289) according to Naber but, when quoting the Greek text (2001: 287, n. 491), retains Niese's. For discussion of this tax and its precedents (including in the days of Archelaus [17.205]), see Schalit 2001: 286–288 and Udoh 2020: 175–177.

391 In a reference to this event at 15.405, in the course of a survey of the history of the custody of the vestments, Josephus states that Vitellius agreed only after first writing Tiberius about the issue and obtaining his approval. If so, Vitellius could not have agreed during the course of his visit, when the issue was first raised. If the datum is true, it could impact upon the chronological issue discussed in the note on "in Judea" at §90, allowing for the hypothesis that the visit reported at §§90–95 occurred well before Pilate was deposed from office, with Josephus telescoping events by reporting already there Vitellius's

vestment and all its ornaments,[392] which should be stored in the Temple, just as previously they had enjoyed this authority. **91** At this time, however, it had been on deposit in the Antonia (that being the name of a fortress) under the following circumstances. After one of the priests, named Hyrcanus (who was called "the first" because there were many who bore that name[393]) had built a large building[394] near the temple, most of his daily life was there and the vestment—of which he was the guardian because only he was allowed to wear it—was stored there, whenever he put on lay clothing in order to go down into the city. **92** His sons and grandsons adhered to the same practice. Herod, when he reigned as king,[395] built up this building—which was conveniently located—at great expense and named it Antonia after [Marcus] Antonius,[396] whose friend he was;[397] and he maintained the vestment there as he found it, trusting that for this reason the people would never revolt against him.[398] **93** As did Herod, so too did Archelaus his son, who was installed as king[399] after him. And when the Romans succeeded to rule after him, they took control of the vestment,

---

eventual approval of the gesture, which in fact occurred (with Tiberius's approval) only during his next visit, reported at §§123–124. However, on the one hand the report at 15.405 is riddled by mistakes (note its references to Vitellius instead of Longinus at §407 and to "one day" before each festival at §408 rather than seven; see the note on "holiday" at §94), and on the other hand the fact that 20.12 has Claudius rely on the precedent set by Vitellius, not by Tiberius, positively contradicts the report at 15.405. For the suggestion that the report at 15.505 reflects a lost account by Philo (the lost end of the *Legatio*?), who, in arguing with Gaius Caligula about his plan to defile the Temple, had every interest to credit earlier *emperors* (and not merely governors) with respect for the Temple, see D. R. Schwartz 1992: 214–217, also the note on "Caesar" at §55.

392 For the high priest's special vestments, termed "golden vestments" (e.g., *m. Yoma* 3:4 and 7:3), see Exod 28; *War* 5.230–237; and *Ant.* 3.159–178. Much symbolic significance was attached to them; cf. Wisdom of Solomon 18:24 and esp. Philo, *Life of Moses* 2.109–135 and *Special Laws* 1.84–97, also Schorch 2010: 191–194. For Josephus on the (high)-priestly vestments, see Grünbaum 1887: 37–55, Sanders 1992: 92–192, Castelli 2002: 263–272, and Gußmann 2008: 369–408. For some iconic representations of them, see Taylor 2016.

393 I.e., John Hyrcanus (son of Simon), a Hasmonean ruler and high priest ca. 135–104 BCE. But he did not have "many" successors of that name, but only one: his grandson, Hyrcanus II. See the note on "Hyrcanus" at 20.240.

394 On the meaning of *baris* (fortress? large house?), which is apparently here, as at *Ant.* 20.85, a common noun (but is a proper noun in *War* 1.75, 118, where it appears, as here, in the identification of the Antonia), see Welles 1934: 320–321 and Mandel 1992.

395 Although, as at §194, βασιλεύσας need not mean "[immediately] upon becoming king," nevertheless it is probable that Herod began working on it in the early years of his reign, while Antony was alive and perhaps even before he and Octavian became enemies. Schalit (2001: 366) places its construction in the mid-30s and van Henten (2014: 210, n. 1938) points to the Battle of Actium (31 BCE) as a definitive terminus ad quem.

396 On this fortress, which figures frequently in Josephus's writings, see Busink 1970–1980: 2.838–841 and Netzer 2018: 123–125.

397 The φιλία between Herod and Antonius is underlined at *Ant.* 15.162, 183, 189, where Josephus has Herod tell Augustus that he had had the greatest friendship (φιλίαν... μεγίστην) with Antonius, and also at 15.409, in the context of naming the fortress, as here. For the background, see *inter alia Ant.* 14.324–329, 381–387.

398 That is, Herod held the vestments hostage to the people's, and also the particular high priest's, good behavior.

399 Actually, Archelaus was not a "king," only an "ethnarch," and the difference was important (and is preserved, for example, at 20.251); Herod had recommended that Archelaus be enthroned as king after him but Augustus explicitly decided against that and appointed Archelaus ethnarch, although holding out hope that he might promote him to king at some later time (*Ant.* 17.317; *War* 2.93). Josephus's usage here is loose—just as Matthew 2:22 speaks of Archelaus as "reigning as a king" and Mark 6:14 speaks of Herod Antipas as "king." Use of the term here conforms well to the hypothesis that Josephus's source here was one with parochial Jewish interests, not so interested in the details of Roman rule and titles of Herodians. See D. R. Schwartz 1992: 207–209.

which was stored in a house built of stones[400] under the seal both of the priests and of the treasurers, the commander of the fortress lighting a lamp there every day.[401] **94** Seven days before each holiday[402] the commander of the fortress issued the vestment to them, and after it had been purified the high priest used it; one day after the festival[403] it was again deposited in the house where it had previously been stored. This was done on the three festivals of every year and on the Fast.[404] **95** But Vitellius dealt with the vestment according to our ancestral usage, directing the commander of the fortress not to concern himself with where the garment is stored or when it should be used. Having done those things for the benefit[405] of the nation, and having removed Joseph, known as Caiaphas, from the priesthood,[406] he appointed Jonathan, son of the high priest Ananus, to the high priesthood.[407] Then he set out on his way back to Antioch.

---

400 This phrasing is peculiar, both because Josephus does not tell us why this detail matters and because he has already told us that the garment was stored in the Antonia, which was a well-known fortress—so why refer to it this way here, and obliquely, as "the house, where it had previously been," in the next paragraph? It seems that Josephus's source here, which was very interested in priestly affairs but not in Roman and Herodian titulature and the like, assumes a readership familiar with some details of the Jewish cult, such as the rule that stone does not contract impurity (see Deines 1993; Magness 2011: 70–73; Miller 2015: 153–183) and the fact that one of the chambers of the Temple *was called* "house of stone" (*beit even*). Note especially *m. Parah* 3:1, which records that the high priest was sequestered there seven days prior to the preparation of the Red Heifer (on which see Numbers 19 and *Ant.* 4.79–81). It is likely that the high priest was also sequestered there in preparation for other appearances that required purity, such as the liturgy of the Day of Atonement. See D. R. Schwartz 2006.

401 The fact that no effort is made to explain this (which is evidently meant to be an expression of respect), is, as the above reference to "house built of stones," an aspect of the "insider" priestly nature of this account.

402 Cf. the preparations of the high priest "seven days before the Day of Atonement" (*m. Yoma* 1:1) and "seven days before the burning of the red heifer" (*m. Parah* 3:1). Cf. *Ant.* 15.408 and the note on "agreed" at §90.

403 Feldman (1965: 67) renders μετὰ μίαν τῆς ἑορτῆς ἡμέραν "after the first day of the festival" but given the facts that Josephus uses μίαν rather than πρώτην,

and that of the holidays two (Pentecost and the Day of Atonement) were only one day long so it would be strange to speak of their "first" days, it seems preferable to translate as above; so too Mathieu and Herrmann 1929: 150 and Schalit 1963: 290.

404 I.e., the Day of Atonement; for such usage of the definite article, see also *War* 5.236, Acts 27:9, and several other passages noted by Sharon 2014a: 198. Although the present passage suggests that the high priest usually officiated only on festivals, and *War* 5.230 agrees that the high priest did not officiate daily, the latter states he served not only on festivals but also on Sabbaths and new moons. Moreover, note that according to Lev 16:4 and *m. Yoma* 3:6–7 the high priest did not wear the "golden vestments" (but rather only linen ones) when entering the Holy of Holies on the Day of Atonement; on *War* 5.236, which seems to imply that he did, see D. R. Schwartz 2010. If, as the Mishnah reports, the linen garments he wore were indeed very expensive, it may be that they too were stored together with the "golden vestments."

405 On the "benefaction" (εὐεργεσία) expected from good rulers, as for example at §306 and 19.328, see Danker 1982; Spicq 1994: 1.107–113; Rajak 2001: 373–391; and Gardner 2007. On Josephus on euergetism, see S. Schwartz 2009.

406 On Caiaphas, see the note on "Caiaphas" at §35. It may be that his long tenure indicates that he got along especially well with Pilate, and so now fell along with him. See Metzner 2010: 74–88, 167–171.

407 I.e., a brother of Eleazar (§34); on the family, see the note on "high priesthood" at §34. Jonathan was not to last long; see §123 and the note on "once" at 19.314.

(4.4)[408] 96 Tiberius[409] also sent Vitellius a letter,[410] ordering him to establish friendly relations with Artabanus, the king of the Parthians,[411] for since Artabanus was hostile, and had taken over Armenia,[412] Tiberius feared him, lest he do any more harm. [And he wrote Vitellius that] he would trust an agreement of friendship only if [Artabanus] gave him hostages, especially—Artabanus's own son.[413] 97 Along with writing that to Vitellius,[414] Tiberius also attempted to convince, with large gifts of money,[415] the kings both of the Iberians and of the Albanians[416] to fight Artabanus without equivocation. They resisted [his appeal[417]],

---

408 On Rome's eastern front late in Tiberius's days, after King Artaxias III of Armenia died without an heir in 34/35 CE, inviting competing moves by Parthia and Rome, see Täubler 1904: 29–62; Debevoise 1938: 158–163; Garzetti 1956; Levick 1999: 145–147; Olbrycht 2012; and Schlude 2020: 92–115. Vitellius's meeting with Artabanus II, which is the main topic of the following section, is dated by Suetonius (*Gaius* 14.3) and Cassius Dio (59.27.3) to the reign of Gaius, and the same might be indicated by the fact that Tacitus does not mention the event, although his account of Tiberius's reign survives completely; that suggests that he too ascribed it to the days of Gaius, for which his account is lost. Josephus's dating of it to the days of Tiberius has, therefore, led to much scholarly debate, the three possibilities being ascription of the event to Tiberius's reign, to Gaius's, or to both, that is, given the fact that in any case Josephus's report comes near the end of Tiberius's reign (see §§89, 124), perhaps Vitellius began the negotiations under Tiberius but concluded them under Gaius. Some of those who ascribe the event to the days of Tiberius surmise that those who ascribed it to Gaius did so out of hostility to Tiberius, while those who prefer to date it to the days of Gaius point, *inter alia*, to Josephus's account of Antipas's and Vitellius's activities in Palestine as reason to think they could not have been at the Euphrates late in Tiberius's days. For a thorough review of the issues, see Garzetti 1956; he concludes by preferring the later date (as he puts it, at the end of his article, he prefers Tacitus's silence to Josephus's confusion). So do HJP 1.351 and Olbrycht 2012: 228–299. Täubler (1904: 39–62), followed by Stern (1974c: 285, n.2), upholds Josephus's dating, while Levick (1999: 147) took something of the middle position: "These negotiations came at the very end of Tiberius' principate, so near his death that they could be ascribed to the reign of Gaius [here she refers to Suetonius and Dio, as above. DRS]. But Tiberius deserves the credit."

409 True, Tiberius's death was reported, in the context of Judean history, at §89. Now Josephus is reverting to some external events of the preceding period. This is his usual procedure; see the notes on "Herod and Philip" at §27 and the opening note at 18.2.4 (§39).

410 For such use of γράμματα of a single letter, Danker (2000: 205, s.v. γράμμα, 2a) cites several passages, including Diodorus Siculus 13.93 and Acts 28:21, but neither of those is unambiguous. It is, however, frequent in Josephus, who at times (as Thackeray notes; see *ThLJ* 117, s.v. γράμμα, 2) uses it as the equivalent of singular ἐπιστολή; see, for example, *Ant.* 8.50–53, 9.99–100, 11.26–27. Cf. the note on "letter" at §105.

411 Artabanus II; see the note on "Arsacid line" at §48.

412 Although readers might think this picks up the story from §§50–52, which left Artabanus in control of Armenia in 18–19 CE, in fact that story had a continuation that is not offered by Josephus: one of the outcomes of Germanicus's tour of the East (to which Josephus refers only cursorily at §§53–54) was to oust Artabanus's son, Orodes, from Armenia. Instead of him, a Roman protégé, Artaxias III, was installed. The latter remained on the throne until his death in 35 CE, whereupon Artabanus made a new move, installing another son on the Armenian throne; see the note on "the king's son" at §98. It is that which elicited Tiberius's response described here. See Dąbrowa 2012: 174. The present story will fill in that background in the following paragraphs, culminating with Artabanus's reestablishment of his rule over Armenia (§100). See the note on "Artabanus" at §101.

413 Named Darius (§103).

414 It appears, however, that the events recounted from here until §100 occurred prior to, and explain, the peace initiative reported at §96 and detailed beginning at §101; see the note on "Artabanus" at §101.

415 For "convincing with money," see also §97 and 20.119, 164, 183.

416 States just east of the Black Sea, in modern Georgia.

417 This supplement seems to be required by the continuation. Täubler (1904: 32), whose understanding of the continuation differs, takes ἀντεῖχον to mean they fought. But the absence of an object, and the apparent contrast with the Alani (οἱ δέ ...Ἀλανοί δέ), who did something on behalf of the Romans (apparently), supports the interpretation that these two kings did nothing.

but the Alani[418] gave [the Romans] passage through their land and, opening before them the Caspian Gates,[419] allowed them to attack Artabanus. 98 So Armenia was retaken[420] and, since in these battles the land of the Parthians was filled with warfare, the most prominent men were killed; all of their land was devastated,[421] and the king's son[422] fell along with many myriads of soldiers. 99 As for his father, Artabanus: Vitellius, with the aid of a consignment of money to his relatives and friends, intended to kill him by the hand of those who accepted the gifts. Artabanus, however, having discovered the plot and that it was one from which he could not escape (for given the fact that it had been put together by so many men of the first rank it could not fail to achieve its end), 100 and now being convinced that whoever had sincerely stood beside him in the past was either corrupted and craftily only feigning goodwill toward him, or when an attempt upon his life was made would align himself with those who had rebelled, sought to save himself by [fleeing to] the upper satrapies.[423] Later, [however], after collecting a great army of Dahae and Scythians,[424] he made war on those who opposed him and [again] established his rule.[425]

(4.5) 101 When Tiberius heard this, he sought to establish friendship with Artabanus.[426] Since the latter willingly agreed, when invited to discuss these matters, Artabanus and Vitellius

---

418 On the Alani, see esp. *War* 7.244–251, where Josephus, with reference to the seventies of the first century, characterizes them as Scythians and locates them north of Parthia in the region of the Don River and the Sea of Azov. The text of this passage is somewhat doubtful. I have translated according to Niese (1890a: 158), who reads Ἀλανοί in accordance with the manuscripts (but in 1890b: 136 marks a lacuna after it). Cf. Täubler 1904: 31, n. 2 and Feldman 1965: 70–71, n. a, who argue for Ἀλανούς, that is, that the other kings let the Alani through the Caspian Gates. That fits the geography better, as Feldman notes, but collides not only with the manuscripts; it also makes "through their land" problematic, since "lands" or "realms" is expected for two kings. It is not at all clear that it is justified to give these considerations less weight than to an assumption of Josephus's accuracy concerning details of eastern geography and history and our desire to let his story be closer to Tacitus's (*Ann.* 6.33).

419 At the southeastern corner of the Caspian Sea. Josephus himself (*War* 7.245) seems to be the oldest source for the story that Alexander built iron gates to close off a pass there—a story that would have a long history because of the belief that identified the people of Gog and Magog as Scythians (*Ant.* 1.123) and explained that the gates were built to keep them out. See Feldman 2000: 43–44, n. 319, and Bietenholz 1994: 121–126.

420 This expresses a Roman point of view: the Roman protectorate was restored. See Dąbrowa 2012: 174.

421 Cf. the note on "devastation" at §275.

422 Named generically by the dynastic name, Arsaces, in the more detailed account in Tacitus, *Ann.* 6.31 (for such

generic usage, see, for example, Diodorus 34/35.18–19 and 1 Macc 14:2–3). His death is alluded to at 6.33.

423 "Upper" means inland, in the mountainous regions far from the sea; cf. the note on "went down" at 20.50. Usually αἱ ἄνω σατραπεῖαι is used without differentiation simply to mean "faroff hinterland" (12.147, 197; 13.185), and the addition of τι makes it all the more vague; why should Roman readers care where, precisely, in the remote Asian outback, Artabanus sought refuge? Details of this stage of the story, down to Artabanus's flight, are supplied by Tacitus, *Ann.* 6.36. What seems to be another version of Artabanus's flight appears in Book 20; see the note on "if he could" at 20.54.

424 For the juxtaposition of these peoples, at home east of the Caspian Sea, see also 20.91. According to Tacitus, *Ann.* 2.3.1, Artabanus had grown up among the Dahae, but at 6.41.2—among the Scythians, "which means the same in this context" (Olbrycht 2014: 95). Strabo, in fact, says most Scythians were called Dahae (*Geog.* 11.8.2). Probably many Romans saw no need to distinguish between all those Asians.

425 Over Armenia; this is the takeover alluded to at §96. See the next note.

426 As Lewy carefully noted in the margin of his copy (1920–1945: 136: "96=101; §96/101 Vorgeschichte"), this opening, which repeats the terms of §96, clarifies that the intervening story provides the background of the order announced at §96—and the story in between was a flashback to explain the circumstances. That is, §§97–100 are a flashback within a flashback (see the note on "Armenia" at §96).

both came to the Euphrates. 102 The river being bridged, they approached each other in the very middle of the bridge, each with his own guard surrounding him.[427] After words calling for an agreement were expressed,[428] Herod the tetrarch feasted them in the middle of the bridge, sheltering[429] the bridge with a very expensive tent.[430] 103 And Artabanus sent Tiberius his son Darius as a hostage,[431] along with numerous gifts, including a man seven cubits high[432]—a Judean by descent,[433] named Eleazar. Because of his height, he was called Gigas.[434] 104 Thereupon[435] Vitellius set out for Antioch; Artabanus—for Babylonia.[436] But Herod, who wanted to be the one who first gave Caesar the news about the taking[437] of the hostages, wrote up everything in full detail in a letter and sent it off with letter-bearers, leaving nothing for the consular [legate][438] to report. 105 After Vitellius's letter[439] too was sent and Caesar indicated to him that he already knew because Herod had already supplied him with the news, Vitellius was very upset and supposed that he had suffered more than was

---

427 Compare an eyewitness account of a meeting in the middle of the Euphrates, in 1 CE, between Gaius Caesar (Augustus's grandson) and King Phraataces of Parthia (on whom see above, §§39–43): Velleius Paterculus 2.101, quoted and commented upon by E. Strugnell 2008. (For such a solution to the diplomatic issue, compare the signing of the 1807 Treaty of Tilsit between Napoleon and Czar Alexander on a fancy raft in the middle of the Nemen River.) Suetonius (*Cal.* 14.3), however, specifically says that Artabanus crossed the Euphrates and adds that he paid homage to the Roman standards and busts of the Caesars.

428 This translation of καὶ λόγων αὐτοῖς συμβατικῶν γενομένων is based esp. on 14.60, where Pompey offered such terms to the defenders of Jerusalem. Cf. Thucydides 5.76.1 and 6.103.3. Josephus does not actually report that an agreement was reached, but the continuation clearly implies that, and Cassius Dio 59.27.3 explicitly refers to Vitellius having compelled Artabanus to make a treaty that was advantageous to the Romans (σπονδάς ... πρὸς τὸ τῶν Ῥωμαίων σύμφορον δούς).

429 Usually ἐπισκήπτω means "make to fall upon, direct against, charge" (*CCFJ* 2.174), for which reason Richards and Shutt (1939: 182) suggest emending ἐπισκη-ψάμενος here into ἐπισκεπασάμενος—"having covered over." Although that verb nowhere appears in Josephus, he does use σκέπη ("covering") some fifteen times; see, for example, its use of a shelter at *War* 3.169.

430 This is the only occurrence of σκηνίς in Josephus; usually he uses σκηνή.

431 On a young Parthian hostage of this name in Rome in the days of Gaius, see Suetonius, *Caligula* 19. In general, see the note on "hostages" at §42.

432 He might well be the Jewish giant seen by Columella, as he reports at *De re rustica* 3.8.2 (*GLAJJ* 1.426–428), which seems to have been completed in the seventh decade of the first century (Forster 1950: 123).

433 Josephus frequently identifies individuals as something "by descent," often so as to distinguish between their descent and their current status, between which there is some tension. See D. R. Schwartz 1981 and Cohen 1994. So, for example, at 10.22 Josephus refers to a servant of a Judean king who was, surprisingly enough, of Ethiopian descent. Since there is nothing surprising about a Parthian king owning a Jew, it may be that, in the present case, Josephus is, as at 10.22, alluding to the surprising gap between the slave's place of origin and his current location. Hence the translation of Ἰουδαῖος here as "Judean." For such usage, see the note on "descent" at §314.

434 That is, "Giant."

435 The use of ἐπὶ τούτοις points more to the reason than the timing; so too at 20.267. See LSJ 622a, §II; Haenchen 1971: 62–63, n. 6; and the note on "his" at 20.101.

436 Debevoise (1938: 163, n. 70) takes this to refer to the city of Babylon and thinks Seleucia must be intended; see ibid. 12, n. 51, where he states this error is frequent in later sources. But while Josephus often uses the short form, Βαβυλών, as the Hebrew *babel*, both for Babylonia (see Schalit 1968: 22) and for the city of Babylon (as at §§359, 373), it seems that when, as here (with Niese [1890a: 159] listing no variants), he uses the long form, Βαβυλωνία, he means Babylonia; cf. esp. §§313, 318, 337, along with the very fact that the story at §§310–379 uses Βαβυλωνία regularly but Βαβυλών only twice (§§359, 373), both of the latter regarding the city.

437 Josephus uses λῆψις only twice, both in *Ant.* 18 (here and §294).

438 See the note on "consular status" at §88.

439 Such use of ἐπιστολαί, in the plural, of only a single letter, is rare in this period; see Danker 2000: 381, s.v. ἐπιστολή. But it is not impossible. See, for example, 10.15–16 (where the biblical text, 2 Kings 19:9–13, has only one letter), 12.330–331 (where there is no reason to

really the case.[440] But he kept his wrath about it hidden until he got his revenge[441] when Gaius took over rule of the Romans.[442]

Death of Philip (4.6) 106 Then too Philip,[443] Herod's brother,[444] died in the twentieth[445] year of Tiberius's reign, having ruled the Trachonitis and Gaulanitis, as well as the nation of the Bataneans, for thirty-seven years.[446] During the years he ruled he had exhibited a moderate and inactive style.[447] 107 Indeed, he spent his whole life within the land subject to him, proceeding around it together with only a few chosen people, with the throne upon which he sat when he gave judgment following him along the way, so that whenever anyone who met

---

imagine more than one letter), and van Henten's (2014: 116, n. 1029) uncertainty concerning 15.175. Here, moreover, it corresponds to the plural γράμματα at §96; see the note on "letter" there.

440 That is, his resentment was greater than what was justified. This assessment betrays a point of view sympathetic to Antipas; for the use of a source here, cf. the note on "Romans" in the next sentence. For the same focus on Antipas, cf. the note on "Herod's brother" at §106.

441 For this sense of μετέρχομαι, see *CCFJ* 3.98, s.v.

442 Gaius took over the empire after Tiberius's death in March 37. Josephus never tells us about any such revenge by Vitellius. Perhaps we should assume that Vitellius, who as governor of Syria was responsible for Rome's Parthian front, seconded Agrippa's accusation against Antipas reported at §§250–251. For another guess, see *HJP* 1.351: Vitellius took his revenge by abrogating his campaign in support of Antipas at the earliest possible opportunity (§124). In any case, it is difficult to imagine that whoever was behind this line did not go on to report the sequel, although Josephus did not. Thus, this case is similar to cases in which Josephus explicitly promises sequels and fails to report them and the possibility arises that the reference has been taken over from the source he was using; see the Introduction, at nn. 25–27.

443 On Philip, see *HJP* 1.336–340 and Wilker 2007: 92–93. His coins: Strickert 1995; Meshorer 2001: 85–90.

444 This use of plain "Herod" for Herod Antipas reflects very clearly the fact that this whole chapter is devoted to the affairs of that tetrarch.

445 Equation of Philip's thirty-seventh year—which is also the date of his latest dated coin (see Strickert 1995)—with Tiberius's twentieth (33/34 CE) indicates a counting that began in 4/3 BCE, in the wake of Herod's death in 4 BCE. The use of that era is what we would normally expect, and the resultant early dating avoids the problem that would have arisen had Philip founded a city in honor of Augustus's daughter after her exile in 2 BCE; see the note on "daughter" at §28. That Philip's years were counted from Herod's death or shortly thereafter is also

supported, indirectly, by the fact that that is how Herod Antipas's years were counted, as is shown by his coins: his latest coins are dated to his forty-third year and we know he was dethroned in 39 CE. See the note on "took them over" at §27. True, the Latin version here (Niese 1890a: 160) reads *uicesimo secundo* ("twenty-second"), a reading that is found in many early printed versions; see Steinmann 2009: 23–25. Placing the event in Tiberius's twenty-second year is attractive, insofar as it would make the present passage fit better into its chronological context, since the events reported before it and after it happened around the death of Tiberius in 37 CE. However, there is no Greek support for this reading, and it may have originated in a scribe's desire to make the events fit into their context. For further discussion of this, and defense of the Greek reading, see Jachowski 2015.

446 Some Latin witnesses read 32 or 35; the latter fits the reading "twentieth year of Tiberius's reign" and the assumption (undercut by the preceding note), that Philip counted from 1 BCE, but the former does not seem to fit anything else. On Philip's territories, see the note on "Philip's tetrarchy" at 20.138.

447 Cf. the similar formulation at §256—but if Gaius was moderate and high-minded, Philip was moderate and ἀπράγμων ("inactive"), which more or less means that he was not cut out to be a ruler. Josephus uses this especially of Hyrcanus II (*Ant.* 13.408; 14.6, 13), and thus explains (presumably following Nicolaus of Damascus, who in turn was following a Thucydidean model [Marcus 1943: 432, n. a]) why it was justified and necessary that Antipater and his sons took over in his stead; see D. R. Schwartz 1994. Similarly, this criticism of Philip, along with the notice that he died childless, is part of *Antiquities'* account of how and why it happened that none of Herod's three heirs managed to maintain Herodian rule in Palestine and therefore it was a son of one of their deceased half-brothers, Agrippa I, who took over. As for the other two: even apart from the fact that Archelaus and Antipas were both guilty of incest (*Ant.* 17.341; 18.110), Archelaus proved to be a failure as a ruler (17.342) and Antipas was brought

him was in need of his assistance, immediately, without delay,[448] the throne was set up wherever it happened to be. Sitting upon it, he would hear what was said, fix punishments for those who were convicted, and release those who had been charged unjustly. 108 He died in Julias,[449] and there he was brought to rest in the tomb which he had himself built in advance, and there were costly funeral proceedings. As for the rule [of his tetrarchy]: since he left no children,[450] Tiberius took it over and attached it to the province of Syria.[451] But he ordained that the taxes collected in the tetrarchy that had been his should be kept on deposit.[452]

(5.1) 109 At this time, King Aretas of Petra[453] and Herod engaged in violent strife with one another, for the following reason.[454] Herod the tetrarch[455] had married Aretas's daughter[456] and been together with her for a considerable time. Once, going off to Rome,[457] he lodged with Herod—who was his brother, although of a different mother; for that Herod had been born to the daughter of Simon the high priest.[458] 110 Being seized by a passion for his wife, Herodias,[459] who was the daughter of Aristobulus[460] (who too was their brother[461])

Antipas and Aretas

---

down by his pushy wife (18.240–246, 255). Readers will note, and understand, that both were exiled to Gaul (17.344; 18.252). So it happened that Agrippa I came to be the only available Herodian heir, as Josephus will also flesh out from another point of view beginning at §126.

448 Josephus uses οὐδὲν εἰς ἀναβολάς in *Ant.* 17–19, but, apart from 7.224, nowhere else: see the note on "immediately" at §58.

449 Apparently his capital; see above, §28.

450 On his wife, Salome, see §137.

451 The same phrasing that Josephus used of Judea at §2.

452 That is, Tiberius did not finalize the status of Philip's territory, instead attaching it administratively to Syria but leaving the question of its future status undecided. Perhaps this indicates thoughts about restoring some measure of Herodian rule, as eventually happened; see §237. For the notion of a longterm Roman plan for Judea, worked out stage after stage by the three emperors who, one after another, gave Agrippa thirds of his grandfather's kingdom, see esp. Ciaceri 1916/17.

453 I.e., Aretas IV, king of the Nabateans, ca. 9 BCE–40 CE. On him, see *Ant.* 16.294–299, 337–355, also von Gutschmid 1885: 84–85, 87–89; HJP 1.581–583; and Barkay 2018.

454 On this combination of "at this time" and "for the following reason," see the first and last notes on §39.

455 This full identification, after he was just referred to as plain "Herod," seems to be meant to differentiate the tetrarch from his homonymous brother mentioned in the next sentence.

456 For an attempt to identify her on the basis of epigraphic and numismatic evidence, see Kokkinos 1998: 230–231.

457 Josephus gives no reason for his trip, which is of no import for his story. For some discussion of possibilities, see Saulnier 1984: 367–368. As Saulnier notes, the issue is potentially linked to the chronological one discussed in the note on "John" at §116.

458 That is, this Herod, who was visited by Antipas, had been born to Herod the Great and Mariamme II, the daughter of Simon ben Boethus (as is also reported at §136 and 17.19); Kokkinos (1998: 222–223) terms him "Herod III." Herod Antipas, correctly identified here as his half-brother, is usually assumed to have been the son of Herod the Great and his Samaritan wife, Malthace, hence Archelaus's full-blood brother, as is said explicitly in the genealogical list at *War* 1.562 and its parallel at *Ant.* 17.20. However, a few passages seem to assume that Antipas and Archelaus had different mothers: *Ant.* 17.188–9 (refers to Antipas, Archelaus, and Philip in that order and then notes that *Philip* was Archelaus's full brother), *War* 2.14, 21//*Ant.* 17.219, 225 (Archelaus and Antipas travel separately to Rome, each with his mother), *War* 2.39//*Ant.* 17.250 (in the context of the dispute between Archelaus and Antipas we read that "Archelaus's mother" died), and Nicolaus of Damascus's autobiography (Stern, GLAJJ 1.252, line 71) reports an appeal to Archelaus and Antipas to stop fighting in deference to their love for their common *father*. Whatever the truth, this difference may have source-critical implications; see D. R. Schwartz 2018.

459 On her, see esp. Gillman 2003 and Strickert 2014.

460 As is stated at §136 and *War* 1.552.

461 I.e., their half-brother, born to Herod the Great and the Hasmonean Mariamme I and executed in 7 BCE. That is, Herodias married first one uncle and then another. On marriages with nieces in Jewish antiquity, see the note on "brother Herod" at 19.277.

and sister of the elder Agrippa,[462] he dared to approach her with words about marriage. She accepted, and they made an agreement that she would move [from her husband] to him[463] upon his return from Rome. The terms of their covenant included that he would divorce Aretas's daughter. **111** He then went off to Rome, having entered into this agreement. When he returned, after taking care in Rome of the business for which he had set out,[464] his wife, who had learned of the covenant with Herodias, asked him—before he knew that she had learned the whole story, and without revealing her true intention—to send her to Machaerus,[465] which is on the border between Aretas's territory and Herod's.[466] **112** Herod sent her off, not at all anticipating that the poor woman[467] had any idea [of his plans]. She, however, had already, a considerable time earlier, sent ahead to Machaerus, and to one who was subject to her father,[468] so that all had been prepared for her trip, by that governor; once she arrived she pressed on to Arabia, being conveyed by the governors one after another,[469] so that she reached her father[470] as quickly as possible[471] and related what Herod had in mind. **113** Having made this the point of departure[472] for hostility concerning the border in the region of Gabalis,[473] both rulers assembled troops and entered into war, but sending

---

462 Given the desire to define Herodias's genealogy precisely here, this, and not "Agrippa the Great," seems to be the meaning of Ἀγρίππου … τοῦ μεγάλου here, as for example 20.104, where it serves to distinguish "the elder" from "the younger" Agrippa. Cf. the note on "the elder" at §142.

463 Josephus's formulation, μετοικίζασθαι, which stops short of defining her planned relationship with Herod Antipas as marriage, corresponds to other passages in which he denies the legitimacy of their marriage; see §§136, 148, and 240. For Josephus's concern with the distinction between legitimate marriage and lesser liaisons, see also §§40, 344.

464 Repeating the same verb as at §109.

465 On Machaerus, which was a fortress near the east coast of the Dead Sea, approximately at its middle, see Josephus's description in *War* 7.164–177; Netzer 2018: 75–76.

466 Similarly, *War* 7.172 states that Machaerus was in Herod's kingdom but adjacent to Arabia, and the same emerges from *War* 3.46–47. On the nuances of Josephus's use of "Arabia," at times as here of the kingdom in the south, and at time more broadly, up toward Damascus, see D. R. Schwartz 2024b.

467 Cf. the note on "poor woman" at §71.

468 I have translated according to Niese's text here, εἰς τὸν Μαχαιροῦντα τῷ τε πατρὶ αὐτῆς ὑποτελεῖ, which follows the manuscripts, as opposed to the text in the first (1544) edition (which still appeared in Dindorf 1865: 704): εἰς τὸν Μαχαιροῦντα τότε πατρὶ αὐτῆς ὑποτελῇ. Niese's text here was welcomed enthusiastically by Schürer (1890: 644–645), because by eliminating τότε and separating (via τε) Machaerus from the statement about being subject it eliminated the problematic statement of earlier editions, based on the first edition, that Machaerus was

then subject to Aretas. That statement, Schürer argued, made little sense here (would Antipas, without suspecting anything, have let his wife go to a fortress outside of his domain?!) and also conflicts with the evidence of §119, that Machaerus was subject to Antipas at the time. Moreover, it has been claimed that archaeological evidence too indicates that Machaerus, although on the frontier, was ruled by Antipas; see Hoehner 1972: 143–144 and *HJP* 1.344–345, n. 20 (both citing publications by Nelson Glueck). Following Niese's text, Josephus seems to mean that she wrote ahead not only to Machaerus, which was under her husband's control, but also to the first of the series of her father's governors who, according to the next lines, took care of her along her way to Petra. Nonetheless, Mathieu and Herrmann (1929: 154), Feldman (1965: 78–79), and Schalit (1963: 291) ignore Niese's resurrection of the manuscripts' reading. For discussion of the text and its implications, cf. Visi 2020: 8, n. 18.

469 On Aretas IV's governors (including the "ethnarch" mentioned in 2 Corinthians 11:32–33), and for first-century epigraphic evidence for Nabatean usage of the loanword 'STRG for governors, corresponding to Josephus's use of στρατηγοί here, see Taylor 1992: 722.

470 In Petra, some two hundred km. south of Machaerus.

471 For ᾗ τάχος cf. §§168, 321, also 17.261, 265; *Life* 65.

472 Note that Josephus does not say that Aretas immediately attacked, and the reference to a border dispute also raises the possibility that hostilities did not begin merely on account of, and immediately upon, his daughter's arrival—a possibility that may relate to the chronological issue discussed in the note on "John" at §116.

473 The text here is quite uncertain, the suggested readings reflecting attempts to identify the contested location; see Feldman 1965: 80–81, n. a, and the detailed

out generals instead of [leading the troops] themselves. **114** When it came to a battle all of Herod's army was destroyed, after an act of treachery by some fugitives who, although from Philip's tetrarchy,[474] had fought together with Herod. **115** Herod wrote this to Tiberius. He reacted with wrath at Aretas for having initiated [the hostilities] and wrote to Vitellius to make war and either bring Aretas up[475] in fetters [to Rome[476]], if captured, or send him his head, if he was killed. That, then, is what Tiberius instructed the governor of Syria to do.

(5.2)[477] **116** But to some of the Jews it seemed that Herod's army had been destroyed by God—and that quite justly, punishing him as requital for John,[478] who was nicknamed "the   *John the Baptist*

---

discussions in Schalit 1968: 32 (s.v. Γαμαλιτική) and Hoehner 1972: 254–255, n. 4. Feldman reads ἐν γῇ τῇ Γαβαλίτιδι, following a conjecture by Jones, and sees here a reference to Gabala. That reading is defended by Hoehner as well. However, *Ant.* 2.6 places Gabala in Idumea and Schalit doubts that Antipas could have claimed something so far to the south of the Perea (of which the southern boundary was at Machaerus; see *War* 3.46–47). Hence he prefers to stay closer to Niese's text (ἐν γῇ τῇ Γαμαλικῇ) and suggests identifying the area in dispute as that of Beth Gamul (Jeremiah 48:23), which Judeans might have claimed as having once been part of the territory of the Reubenites, before being conquered by Moab.

474 It is unclear whether this means "since they came from Philip's territory" or, rather, "although they came from Philip's tetrarchy." As at §105 (see the note there on "Romans"), the detail seems to imply knowledge (or perhaps: a prejudice) of which Josephus's readers are unaware, and thus points to a source that focuses on Antipas. For the suggestion that the men from Philip's territories, of which the population was mostly non-Jewish (*HJP* 1.448–338), tended to support their "Arab brethren," see Hoehner 1972: 255.

475 For Josephus's frequent use of ἀνάγω of being "brought up" to trial and punishment, as at 19.154 and 20.102, 168, 246, see *ThLJ* 32, s.v., §5. So too ἀναπέμπω; see *GTRI* 21 and D. R. Schwartz 2017: 379, n. 12. But see the next note.

476 Presumably the coming reference to the sending of Aretas's head to Rome indicates that here too that is what is meant; for similar practice, see 20.131, 161. For "going up" as a standard Roman formulation for travel to Rome, see the note on "sent up" at §51.

477 On this passage, which is usually assumed to be basically authentic, see Nodet 1985; Hartmann 2001: 254–355; Mason 2003b: 214–225; Tromp 2008, and D. R. Schwartz 2013: 106–109. For doubts, see Nir 2009. Note that the passage fails to suggest any connection between John and Jesus. Since, as especially Tromp argues, early Christians, who had to admit John's chronological

precedence, were concerned to overcome its apparent implication of superiority by arguing that John was in fact only paving the way for Jesus, à la Isa 40:3–5 (Mark 1:2–3; Luke 1:76 and 3:4–6; Matt 3:3; John 1; see esp. Tromp 2008 and D. R. Schwartz 2013: 66–70), the absence of such concerns here is one of the major reasons to assume the passage is basically authentic.

478 Some, for example Tromp 2008 and Visi 2020, would take the notional causal relationship between the death of John, on the one hand, and Antipas's defeat at the hands of Aretas ca. 36 CE, on the other, to indicate that the former came close to the latter, half a decade or more later than Tiberius's fifteenth year (28/29 CE), to which Luke dated John's appearance and imprisonment (Luke 3:1, 19–20), which presumably was soon followed by his death. Indeed, the dating of the defeat to the mid-30s is required by Vitellius's involvement (since his term as governor of Syria began only after his consulate in 34) and the reference to Tiberius's death in March 37 (§124). But it is very difficult to move John's death to the mid-30s for, as Visi admits (2020: 29), "Broadly speaking, the synoptic gospels are committed to the idea that John's mission and death preceded Jesus' mission and death," and that is very explicit at Mark 6:14–16, so moving John's death down to the mid-30s would entail making Jesus's career and death later than is usually assumed; for good reason, Jesus's death is usually placed in 30 or 33 (see the note on "crucifixion" at §64). Therefore it appears to be simpler to posit that even if John died in the late 20s, observers could view Antipas's defeat in 36 as divine punishment. God is allowed to be long-forbearing, so punishments can come long after crimes. Compare, for two examples, Genesis 42:21 (with ibid. 37:2 and 41:46) and the widespread Christian belief, beginning with Justin Martyr (Clements 2012), that the destruction of the Second Temple in 70 CE was divine punishment of the Jews for their role in the Crucifixion some four decades earlier. Note, however, that if John's criticism of Antipas focused on Antipas's illicit marriage, as the Gospels report (see the note on "words" at §118), it follows that, despite the

Baptist." 117 For Herod had killed him, [although he was] a good man and had instructed the Jews to value virtue highly[479] and—practicing justice toward one another and piety toward God—to join together in baptism. For it seemed to him that this is the way in which baptism is acceptable,[480] namely, they should not employ it to obtain forgiveness for sins of any kind, but, rather, for the purification of the body [alone], seeing that the soul had already been purified in justice. 118 When the others too flocked together, for they were greatly elated[481] when they heard his words,[482] Herod, afraid lest his considerable ability to sway people would give rise to rebellion (for it seemed that they would do everything he urged),[483] thought it much better to take the initiative and kill him before any revolt arose because of the man, than to wait for the rebellion to happen and then, falling into trouble, regret it.[484] 119 So on account of Herod's suspicions he was sent in fetters to Machaerus, the abovementioned fortress,[485] and killed there.[486] To the Jews it seemed that it was to avenge him that Herod's army was destroyed, God having desired to inflict a calamity upon Herod.

Vitellius Visits Jerusalem, II

(5.3) 120 Vitellius, having prepared himself for war against Aretas with two legions of infantry[487] and taking along, to fight alongside them, as much light-infantry and cavalry as he could get from kingdoms under Roman overlordship, set out quickly toward Petra

---

way the story flows here, a good number of years went by between Antipas's marriage to Herodias and the outbreak of his war with Aretas. The same also derives from the fact that Antipas and Herodias were already married when Agrippa returned from Rome to Judea after the death of Drusus the Younger in 23. See the notes on "departure" at §113 and on "together" at §148. For such telescoping, which can create temporal and causal connections between events that are separated by years, cf. the Introduction, at n. 12.

479 This is the only occurrence of ἐπασκέω in Josephus.

480 This is the only instance of ἀποδεκτός in Josephus.

481 Reading ἤρθησαν with the manuscripts (and Feldman 1965: 82), rather than Niese's (1890a: 162) ἤσθησαν ("delighted"). Niese thought that the latter was offered by Eusebius in his citation of this text at *Church History* 1.11.5. However, as Nodet (1985: 325–326) noted, the GCS edition of the latter (ed. Schwartz 1903: 78), which appeared around a decade after Niese's edition, shows that most witnesses, as those to Josephus here, read ἤρθησαν. Were Josephus thinking of delight or pleasure, we would have expected the collocation "receive with"; see the note on "pleasure" at §63. For the suggestion that there was, originally, no verb here, only the statement that many gathered together because of John's words, cf. Richards and Shutt 1937: 176.

482 Which, according to the Gospels (Matt 14:3–4// Mark 6:17–18//Luke 3:19–20), centered on condemnation

of Antipas for marrying his brother's wife. It is noteworthy that Josephus, who in the preceding paragraphs recounted that outright violation of propriety and law (Lev 18:16; 20:21), does not link it directly to John's teaching, thus leaving readers in the dark as to what, in John's innocuous message (§117), could have aroused Antipas's fear. This, however, corresponds to Josephus's usual diasporic approach in the *Antiquities*: Jewish religious leaders, especially those of whom he approves, are made to appear as unthreatening as possible to the state's authorities, even at the cost of leaving readers perplexed when the latter do, in fact, move against them. For other cases, see below, 20.97–99, 167–172. This point joins others (Thackeray 1929: 132; Mason 2003b: 214–215; D. R. Schwartz 2013: 107–108), that show that, whatever his source concerning John the Baptist (and one may well think of Baptists or Christians in Rome), Josephus was seriously involved in the formulation of this passage on John.

483 For the trope of rulers who are threatened by antagonistic religious leaders who are so influential with the masses, or with other dupes, that they enjoy support even if their charges are false, cf. 13.288 and 17.41.

484 For this type of consideration, cf. §318.

485 §111.

486 As is also reported at Matthew 14:3–1//Mark 6:17–30.

487 Of the three or four at his command; see the note on "two legions" at §262.

and arrived in[488] Ptolemais.[489] **121** After setting out to lead the army through the land of the Judeans, he was confronted by some of their people of the highest rank who besought him [not to take] the route through their land; for, [they said], it was not according to their ancestral usage to tolerate the introduction of images into it, and there were many [images] attached to the standards.[490] **122** Persuaded, he changed his original intention concerning these things and, having ordered the army to go [instead] via the Great Plain,[491] he himself, together with Herod the tetrarch and his friends, went up[492] to Jerusalem to sacrifice to God,[493] since an ancestral holiday of the Jews was then underway.[494] **123** After arriving there, and being received splendidly by the Jewish multitude,[495] he stayed there for three days, during which he took the [high] priesthood away from Jonathan and passed it on to his brother, Theophilus.[496] **124** When on the fourth day he received a letter reporting

---

488 A more usual translation of ἔσχε would be "occupied," and so it is translated by Feldman and others. However, there was no need for Ptolemais to be occupied; contrast §262, where Vitellius's successor, Petronius, simply "comes" (παρῆν) with his army to Ptolemais. Hence, I have translated here as at §89.

489 Acco (Acre). On it see, in general, *HJP* 2.121–125. For this port being the first stop of later Roman generals invading Palestine from Syria, see §262 and *War* 2.501; 3.29.

490 The issue is the same as at §55.

491 Probably the Esdraelon, as, for example, at 20.118. That is, Vitellius planned to have the army march south-eastward across Palestine, cross the Jordan around Scythopolis and Pella, and then continue southward. See Udoh 2002: 133–135. After quoting scholars (such as *HJP* 1.388, n. 247) who propose just that, in accordance with Josephus's usual usage of "great plain" (see esp. *Ant.* 8.36 and *War* 3.39), Udoh asserts that although that is "plausible," nevertheless, "Vitellius could also have continued to march his troops from Ptolemais down the coastal plain," of which the northern part is the Sharon, which would then be what is meant by "great plain" here. I do not see what justifies his move from that to his statement, a page later, that the latter is "likely." While it is true that Josephus also uses "great plain" for the Jordan Valley, that is not a possibility here, and Udoh's case for it ever being used of the Sharon is quite weak; see the chart on pp. 131–132 of his article, also Sharon 2017: 129–131

492 This is the standard formulation; see the note on "up" at §90.

493 Josephus likes to report such expressions of respect for the Jewish Temple and God on the part of gentile dignitaries. See *HJP* 2.309–313 and and Krauter 2007. Indeed, he likes it so much that he tends to hide its problematic nature from a monotheistic point of view; see D. R. Schwartz 1992: 102–116.

494 This is a strangely vague formulation. It might well reflect the fact that Josephus's source referred to Passover but he, on the false assumption that the present passage describes a visit later than the one mentioned at §§90–95, decided to leave the reference vague. See the note on "in Judea" at §90. For similar recourse to vagueness elsewhere, such as *Ant.* 11.22, 74, 326–339, and 14.285, see D. R. Schwartz 2013: 126.

495 Just as splendidly as Antiochus III (*Ant.* 12.138) and Antiochus IV (2 Macc 4:21–22) were welcomed to Jerusalem, and Jonathan to various cities including Ascalon (*Ant.* 13.148–149, elaborating on 1 Macc 11:60). On such "adventus" ceremonies, which demonstrate to rulers (and readers) the loyalty of Jewish subjects, see esp. Cohen 1982/83: 45–49, apropos of Alexander the Great's reception reported at *Ant.* 11.327–331.

496 No reason is stated for this move; for some guesses, see Smallwood 1981: 173. In any case, this item, if true, is the most concrete argument in favor of the thesis that Josephus's two accounts of Vitellius in Jerusalem indeed refer to two separate visits, for Jonathan was appointed during the first visit (§95). On this question, see the note on "Judea" at §90, where I explain my preference for the conclusion that there was only one visit. It seems that while Josephus was convinced that these were two visits, the two sources that he used did not include the details concerning the high-priestly appointments. Rather, as Krieger (1993a: 22–23) pointed out, Josephus seems to have had a list that recorded, in order, appointments and removals of high priests, giving the name of the relevant authority but no further narrative context; "associating these entries with other historical data was up to Josephus himself, and it is apparent that he was not always capable of doing so properly" (my translation). Note also the Introduction, at n. 9; the note on "high priesthood" at §34; and Krieger 2002: 91: "A synopsis can show us that the list of high priests, used by Josephus when he

Tiberius's death,[497] he administered to the multitude[498] an oath of loyalty to Gaius.[499] Then he recalled his army, each man to go to his own home for the winter, for he was no longer empowered, as he had been, to wage war[500] now that the state had passed into Gaius's hands.[501] **125** And it is said that Aretas, having consulted the flight of birds[502] when he heard of Vitellius's troops, said that it was impossible that the army should make its way to Petra, for one of the leaders would die—either the one who had ordered the expedition[503] or the

---

wrote *Antiquities* and unknown to him when writing *War*, had only an internal, not an absolute chronology." So if the list included successive items reporting Vitellius's two interventions and Josephus thought he knew of two separate visits to Jerusalem, it was only natural for him to place one item in his account of each visit. If, however, we tend to conclude there was only one such visit, we must assume that while one intervention probably took place during that visit, we do not know whether the other one too took place during that same visit, or during another (unrecorded) visit, or from afar.

497 On 16 March 37. This statement, that news of the emperor's death reached Vitellius only in the course of this visit, is one of the horns of the chronological dilemma discussed in the note on "in Judea" at §90, which leads to the conclusion that this visit is the same as the one described there, during Passover 37. That Vitellius received the news of Gaius's death during a visit to Jerusalem is corroborated by Philo (*Leg.* 231).

498 Although this somewhat vague term (πληθύς) often corresponds to Latin *plebs* (GTRI 76), and although Philo (*Leg.* 231), referring explicitly to Vitellius's presence in Jerusalem when news of Gaius's accession arrived, claims that the news was welcomed enthusiastically in Jerusalem, and although Josephus used πλῆθος of the Jewish "multitude" as recently as the preceding paragraph (§123), nevertheless it is perhaps simpler to assume that "the versatile word" (Mason 2008: 55, n. 494) refers, here as often elsewhere (e.g. §§48–49), to the army. On the one hand, we certainly would expect to hear that Vitellius administered the oath to his troops, and, on the other hand, had Josephus meant that all the Jerusalemites were asked to take the oath, we would expect—especially on the background of earlier reports of resistance to an oath of loyalty to Herod (15.368–371; 17.42) and to the introduction of symbols of the emperor in Jerusalem (§§55–59)—to hear how the Jews responded. Cf. §258, where Apion is said to have been able to point to general Jewish refusal to swear by the emperor. For the point that it was the soldiers' oaths that were especially important (as at 19.247 and *War* 4.617,

also Suetonius, *Claud.* 10.3–4), so if the present oath was demanded of the local population too it was probably in connection with the administration of the oath to the army, see Herrmann 1968: 106, 111.

499 For oaths of loyalty to emperors, which became routine beginning with Tiberius (as at Tacitus, *Ann.* 1.7), as at 19.247, 259, see Herrmann 1969, Briscoe 1971, and Wardle 1997. Literally εὔνοια is "goodwill," and so it can function with regard to free agents (so, for example, at §§206, 220; 20.20), but it is required of subjects (and wives—§254), hence "loyalty," as also at 19.151; see Spicq 1994: 2.123–128; Danker 1982: 327–328; and Herrmann 1968: 49, n. 99. Note, for example, the beginning and end of Nero's proclamation of freedom for the Greeks (67 CE [SIG 814]): in order to requite the Greeks for their εὔνοια to him, he acts out of εὔνοια toward them. Quite properly, Johnson, Coleman-Norton and Bourne (1961: 147) render the first "loyalty" and the second "goodwill." For English translations of two loyalty oaths at the opening of Gaius's reign, one from Portugal and one from the Troad (Smallwood 1967, nos. 32–33 = ILS 190 and SIG 797), see Johnson, Coleman-Norton and Bourne 1961: 136; for one to Augustus, in Paphlagonia in 3 BCE, see ibid. 127 (OGIS 532). The latter two, which are in Greek, use the verb εὐνοέω.

500 Because the verb opens with ἐκ, Feldman rendered πόλεμον ἐκφέρειν "to make war abroad," as if Vitellius's consideration applied specifically to the fact that he was acting outside of his own province, Syria. However, Josephus frequently uses the phrase in the simple sense of "wage war"; so, for example, at *Ant.* 5.186, 8.401, and 12.327.

501 Cf. *War* 4.498. For Schürer's conjecture about Vitellius, cf. the note on "the Romans" at §105.

502 This is the only occurrence of οἰωνοσκοπέω in Josephus. Frequently it is not clear whether this and related terms refer to augury in general, or rather, following the literal sense, to that based specifically upon observation of the flight of birds. On Greek and Roman ornithoscopy, see Bar-Kochva 1996: 57–69.

503 Tiberius.

one who set out[504] at the other's behest to carry out his decision, or the one against whom the army was prepared.[505] **126a** And so Vitellius returned to Antioch.

126b Agrippa, the son of Aristobulus, had gone up[506] to Rome a year before Tiberius died[507] in the hope of being able to do something for himself when near the emperor, should the opportunity present itself to him.[508]

Agrippa I

127 Now I would like to report at some length about what happened to Herod and his family,[509] both because their story is pertinent to this work of history, and because it constitutes testimony to the divine, namely, that neither being multitudinous nor any other prowess[510] achieved by men can bring benefit without piety toward the divine,[511] **128** [as must be the case], if it happened [as it did], that, although they had been numerous, all but a few of Herod's descendants perished in the course of a hundred years. Perhaps learning their unfortunate fate will contribute something to bringing humanity to being reasonable,[512] **129** just as it might be useful to recount the story of Agrippa, which is one that is in the highest degree worthy of amazement. For he rose from a totally undistinguished status, and contrary to the expectations of all who knew him, to quite a high power. Although I have previously said something about these things,[513] now they shall be reported in detail.[514]

Herodian Genealogy

504 Vitellius, using the same verb as at the opening of §121.

505 This translation follows Niese's text, which has the text refer to Tiberius, Vitellius, and Aretas himself, all three preceded by "or" (ἤ). Feldman (1965: 86–87, n. b) objects that that entails "the unlikely possibility of Aretas foretelling the possibility of his own death, an event which surely would not keep the Romans out of Petra," and therefore recommends an emendation suggested by H. Petersen. In fact, however, it seems that the war was essentially a private affair between Herod Antipas and Aretas, and might well have ended upon the latter's demise.

506 See the note on "sent up" at §51.

507 Tiberius died on 16 March 37. On the date of Agrippa's trip, see the note on "governing Syria" at §150.

508 I have translated as Mathieu and Herrmann (1929: 156) and Schalit (1963: 292), following the order of the clauses. Feldman (1965: 87), in contrast, took δύναμις to refer to "the means" that allowed Agrippa to make his trip to Rome.

509 On Herodian genealogy see esp. Kokkinos 1998. For detailed family trees, see *HJP* 1.614 and the foldout tables after p. 589 of JLCL 8 (1963) and in the back of Schalit 2001. The following summary of Herodian genealogy picks up precisely at the point the last major snippet ended—with the marriages of Mariamme I's two daughters (*Ant.* 17.22//*War* 1.566). Such an orientation of the summary is obviously built according to the interests of Agrippa's family, since Agrippa I's wife, Cypros, was the daughter of one of Mariamme's daughters, Salampsio, as is stated at §131, and Agrippa II was the product of that union. Thus, this list links Agrippa II to Mariamme,

and so to the Hasmoneans, via both his father (of whom Mariamme was paternal grandmother) and his mother (of whom Mariamme was maternal grandmother). See D. R. Schwartz 2018.

510 Compare esp. Samuel's speech at 6.21, where the prophet preaches (in line with Josephus's main thesis in *Antiquities*; see the next note) that righteousness and proper worship of God, not arms or physical prowess (σωμάτων ἀλκαῖς), will bring prosperity and other blessings. On ἀλκή, see also §323,

511 This is, Josephus stated at *Ant.* 1.14, the basic point of the entire work, one that is reiterated, although with reference to the ancestral tradition rather than "the divine," at the opening of this book too (§9), as at the beginning of the main story of the next one (19.16).

512 For Josephus's explicit hope to improve humanity by narrating object lessons related to God, cf. 1.14–15; 17.60; and 19.16, also the note on "suffering" at 20.166.

513 If this, as it seems, refers only to Josephus's account of Agrippa I in *War* 2 (beginning at §178), it is puzzling, for much of what is recorded in *Ant.* 18–20 has its parallels in *War* 2, but Josephus mentions this only here. Nevertheless, it does seem that the "compressed" account in *War* 2 (Mason 2008: 150, n. 1124) is based on the same sources Josephus used for this fuller account; see D. R. Schwartz 1990a: 1–38.

514 This usage of ἀκριβῶς, which does not mean that previously he was inaccurate but, rather, that previously he wrote more generally, is a good example of the sense "in detail." See A. I. Baumgarten 1982, Oakley 2019: 141–142 ("fullness and precision"), and esp. Fantasia 2004: 60–61, to which I was kindly referred by David Friedman.

(5.4) 130 Herod the Elder[515] had two daughters by Mariamme,[516] the daughter of Hyrcanus:[517] one was Salampsio, who was given by her father in marriage to Phasael, who was her cousin (the son of Phasael, who was Herod's brother), and the other was Cypros, whom too he married to a cousin—Antipater, the son of Herod's sister Salome.[518] 131 Phasael had five [children] by Salampsio: the sons[519] Antipater, Alexander, Herod, and daughters: Alexandra and Cypros. The latter was married by Agrippa, the son of Aristobulus,[520] while Alexandra was married by Timius, a prestigious Cypriot, with whom she also died, childless. 132 But Cypros had by Agrippa two male [children][521] and three daughters: Berenice, Mariamme, and Drusilla; the names of the boys were Agrippa and Drusus, of whom Drusus died before he grew up.[522]

---

515 I.e., "Herod the Great." See the note on "the Elder" at §142.

516 This opening of the list is clearly tailored to its point here—the genealogy of Agrippa, who, as Josephus will now explain, was born to the daughter of one of the two daughters mentioned here. This list is a direct continuation of the one presented in *Ant.* 17.19–22 (and its parallel at *War* 1.562–566), which begins as a table of Herod's nine wives and culminates with Mariamme I's two daughters. There, however, the list does not function well in its context, for it is presented as if it illustrates the fact that Herod had such a large family that he could easily find a new fiancée for Alexander's son, but in fact the list mentions no such woman and the question of that son's marriage arrangements simply disappears. Thus, we may conclude that Josephus had a summary of Agrippa's ancestry and he brought one segment of it, concerning Herod's wives and children, in *Ant.* 17 and the next segment here, when he turned to telling the story of Agrippa himself. Probably the same text supplied information used later as well, such as Josephus's notices at 19.277 and 20.104 about the subsequent history of Herod of Chalcis; note that those passages deal with him as Agrippa's brother, not as Aristobulus's son. In general, cf. D. R. Schwartz 2018.

517 Actually, she was the *granddaughter* of Hyrcanus II, born to his son Alexander. The same mistake appears elsewhere too (*War* 1.262). Probably it reflects

both the fact that Alexander died long before Hyrcanus, in 49 BCE (14.125), and the tendency of pro-Agrippan tradition to link Herod to the last Hasmonean ruler.

518 So too at 17.230 and *War* 1.566 he is identified merely as Salome's son. Schalit's (2001) detailed genealogical table lists him as the son of her first husband, Joseph, but Kokkinos (1998: 192) points instead to Salome's second husband, Costobar.

519 This specific meaning of παῖδες here seems implied by the contrast to "daughters" later in the sentence.

520 That is, Agrippa I married his cousin Cypros; she was the daughter of Salampsio, who was a full sister of Agrippa's father, Aristobulus.

521 As Thackeray notes (*ThLJ* 84–85, s.v. ἄρρην/ἄρσην), this adjective ("male") appears often in the sense of "son," especially when opposed, as here, to "daughter"— whether accompanied by a noun (such as παῖς at 20.92, also, for example 1.186 and 6.129; so too Revelation 12:5 and *m. Ketubbot* 4:10–11) or, as here, as a substantive, without any noun (7.190 and 14.300). Perhaps the formulation reflects the sense that υἱός might be used more generally and inclusively of members of a family; see the note on "Boethus" at §3.

522 Drusus was named in honor or in memory of Tiberius's son, with whom Agrippa was close; see §143. Probably πρὶν ἡβῆσαι means before reaching marriageable age, which is what would be of interest in a genealogical account such as this. So too ἡβήσαντες at §134.

133 Agrippa [I],[523] together with his brothers Herod and Aristobulus, was raised for his father[524] by Berenice. They were children of the son of Herod the Elder, while Berenice was the child of Costobar and Herod's sister, Salome. **134** Aristobulus had left them as infants when he died at his father's hands, together with his brother Alexander, as I reported earlier.[525] When they grew up, this Herod, Agrippa's brother,[526] married Mariamme, the daughter of Olympias (daughter of King Herod) and of Joseph (the son of King Herod's brother Joseph); by her he had a son, Aristobulus. **135** Aristobulus, the third brother of Agrippa,[527] married Iotape, who was the daughter of King Sampsigeramus of Emesa,[528] and they had from her a daughter who was deaf-mute;[529] her name too was Iotape. So much for the children of the males.[530] **136** Herodias, their sister, married Herod,[531] the son of Herod the Elder by Mariamme daughter of Simon the high priest, and Salome was born to them;[532] after her birth, Herodias—undertaking a gross violation of ancestral usage—decided to marry Herod,[533] thus leaving her husband, while still alive, for his brother of the same father.[534]

---

523 Having followed Cypros until now, and having introduced Agrippa as her spouse at §§131–132, Josephus now turns to him. This switch is somewhat confusing; Niese (1890b: 164) marked a lacuna here and Schalit (1963: 293) would fill it by inserting eight words; Feldman (1965: 90) has eight notes on the text, cataloguing manuscripts and emendations; and Kokkinos (1998: 188, n. 52) offers a radically revised text, beginning by turning the opening reference to Agrippa, which Niese has in the dative, τῷ δὲ πατρὶ τούτων Ἀγρίππας ἐτρέφετο ..., into the nominative: ὁ δὲ πατὴρ τούτων Ἀγρίππας. My translation, perforce a guess, retains Niese's opening text but assumes that the supplying of information about who "raised" Agrippa and his brothers reflects knowledge of their father's execution when they were young (as is recalled in the next paragraph), hence it cannot be that Josephus meant to say (as Feldman has it) that they were raised *by* their father. Rather, they were raised *for* their father, namely, by Berenice, their mother. I have begun a new paragraph here, since the next lines follow each of Agrippa I's siblings: Herod, Aristobulus, Herodias. Note, with Stern (*GLAJJ* 2.368 and 3.65), that we do not know which of them was the eldest.

524 Agrippa's father, Herod's son Aristobulus, was executed in 7 BCE, as Josephus reminds his readers in the next paragraph.

525 In the final chapter of *Ant.* 16.

526 Usually known as Herod of Chalcis (see 19.277). This identification, just as that at the opening of §135, shows again that this list is focused on Agrippa I; contrast, for example, the identification of Philip at §106, where the focus is on Antipas.

527 I.e., the third of the brothers, who was Agrippa's second brother. See §133a.

528 On this king of Emesa, see also *Ant.* 19.338; Sullivan 1977b: 212–214.

529 It is not clear whether κωφός means "mute" (as at *Apion* 2.173—its only other occurrence in Josephus) or deaf-mute; cf. LSJ 1019–1020 s.v. In rabbinic Hebrew too, a single word, ḥereš, can serve for both; note esp. *m. Terumot* 1:2.

530 Namely, the male children of Aristobulus and Berenice.

531 On this Herod, see the note on "high priest" at §109.

532 This Salome is usually thought to be the unnamed dancing daughter of Herodias mentioned in Mark 6:22, as emerges from her description there as Herodias's daughter, i.e., not the daughter of Herodias's current husband, Herod Antipas. See Hoehner 1972: 151–156, also Kokkinos 1998: 232–233.

533 Antipas. For Josephus's account of their scandalous marriage, see §§109–110.

534 Here Josephus apparently condemns Herodias for two sins. First, she left her husband, rather than being freed from him by divorce or death; as Josephus emphasizes at 4.253 and 15.259, Jewish law (Deuteronomy 24:1–3) requires that divorce be effected by the husband. This is a standard item in Josephus's condemnations of Herodian women; see the note on "ancestral rules" at 20.143. Second, Herodias married her husband's brother, although that is forbidden by Lev 18:16 and 20:21, also *Ant.* 17.341 (and see the note on "his words" at §118); the only exclusion from the latter prohibition recognized by Jewish law is that at Deut 25:5–10//*Ant.* 4.254–256 (cf. Mark 12:19), which allows, even requires, the "levirate" marriage of a childless *widow* to her late husband's brother. Perhaps Josephus had that in mind when emphasizing, here, that Herodias left her first husband while he was still alive, although one may doubt that many non-Jewish readers would realize that fine point. More generally, note that neither of the two sins delineated above was so heinous in Roman eyes.

He had the Galilean tetrarchy.[535] **137** Her daughter, Salome, married Philip, son of Herod [the Elder], the tetrarch of Trachonitis, and when he died childless[536] she was married by Aristobulus, son of Agrippa's brother Herod. They had three children: Herod, Agrippa and Aristobulus.[537]

138a That, then, was the line of Phasael and Salampsio.

138b As for Cypros,[538] she had a daughter by Antipater, named Cypros, and she was married by Alexas, who was also called Helcias, the son of Alexas[539] —and her daughter [too] was named Cypros.

Herod and Alexander, who were—as I said[540]—brothers of Antipater, died without children.[541] **139** Alexander, King Herod's son who was killed by his father, had sons—Alexander and Tigranes—by the daughter of King Archelaus of Cappadocia. Tigranes reigned as king of Armenia,[542] but when charges were brought against him in Rome he died childless.[543] **140** As for Alexander, he had a son named Tigranes (like his own brother), who was sent out by Nero as king of Armenia; he had a son named Alexander, who married Iotape, the daughter of King Antiochus of Commagene, and Vespasian installed him as king of Cietis[544] in

---

Divorce by the wife might have been acceptable to Roman readers (see Jackson 2005: 359) and marriage to one's former husband's brother was not forbidden by Roman law until the fourth century; see Codex Theodosianus 3.12.2 and Codex Justinianus 5.5.5. My thanks for those references to Ranon Katzoff, who also commented that this is "an example of the effect Jewish law had on Roman law via Christianity." That is, Josephus, who refers here to "a gross violation of ancestral usage," seems to be writing here more as a Jew and for Jews, or to have forgotten that he was writing for Romans. Cf. Introduction, at n. 34.

535 By noting that Herodias abandoned her first husband for one who had a tetrarchy, Josephus implies that that was the reason, thus condemning Herodias as a faithless gold-digger. Indeed, readers who realize that even a tetrarchy is only a second-rate realm might start to wonder where things might go from here. Such readers, if patient enough to wait for §240, will not be disappointed.

536 As we read at §108.

537 Thus the names of Herodias's three sons were the same as those of her three brothers.

538 Here Josephus reverts to the very opening of this family tree (§130) and begins to follow the second line mentioned there, which begins with the report that Herod's daughter Cypros married her first cousin, Salome's son Antipater. But as opposed to the first line, to which Josephus devoted seven-eight paragraphs, the second receives only four—two on childless death and two on apostasy. By ending the whole list this way, Josephus gives the impression of fulfilling his opening promise about showing how the line disappeared (§§127–129). In fact, however, his account of the first line ends (at §137) with Salome bearing three sons and no indication that they disappeared. Since that first line is Agrippa's, one

might imagine that Josephus received these details from that part of the family, which had little interest in documenting its distant cousins. Cf. *Life* 364–366.

539 This earlier Alexas was a "friend" of Herod (*War* 1.566) and executor of his will (*War* 1.660; *Ant.* 17.175), who eventually married Herod's sister Salome (17.10). In the present passage we read that one of his sons, evidently from an earlier marriage, here identified as "Alexas, who was also called Helcias," married Cypros, who was the granddaughter of both Herod and Salome. On the family, which would play an important role in the 30s (§273) and 40s (19.353), as also, apparently, the fifties and sixties (20.194) and even later (*Apion* 1.51), see Stern 1976: 612–613 and Kokkinos 1998: 185–186.

540 Josephus mentioned Herod and Alexander at §131.

541 From here until the end of this account, Josephus assembles evidence for his opening generalization (§127–129), that much of Herod's house disappeared within a century.

542 Actually, he was deposed by 12 CE, so Josephus formulated here "minus accurate" (*PIR*[1] 3.318); Tacitus, more accurately, refers to him, in the context of his downfall, as "Armenia quondam potitus." See the next note.

543 This sounds as if he was executed, and, indeed, Tacitus's report of his punishment (*Ann.* 6.40), although it refers only generally to punishment, comes in a list of deaths. See Kokkinos 1998: 262 and Stern, *GLAJJ* 2.73.

544 Here I follow Wilhelm 1894, as did Feldman (1965: 95, n. c); see also Kokkinos 1998: 253. Niese (1890a: 165) gives ἠσιοδός and lists a number of suggested emendations; at 1890b: 142, however, he adopts νήσιδος, the genitive of νησίς ("islet," as for example at Polybius 16.2.8), originally proposed by Ernesti 1795: 161. But an "islet" does

Cilicia. **141** The children of Alexander[545] abandoned the Jews' native cult immediately upon growing up[546] and went over to Greek ancestral practices.[547]

As for Herod's other daughters, it befell them to die without children.[548]

142 Of the descendants born to Herod, I have listed those surviving at the time that Agrippa the Elder[549] took over the kingdom. Having set out these particulars about the family in advance, it remains to me to go over the turns of fortune that accompanied Agrippa, and how he managed to steer through them and make his way forward to the highest prestige and power.

---

not sound like much of a kingdom, and, as Wilhelm (1894: 5–6) noted, anyway it seems more natural to expect a proper noun denoting the kingdom; he suggested that the reference is to the Cilician tribe/people ("natio") to which Tacitus refers as Cietae or Clitae at *Ann.* 6.41 and 12.55, which is also known from epigraphic and numismatic evidence. Wilhelm concludes that the relevant kingdom included most of western Cilicia.

545 Namely, those mentioned at §§139–140. For detailed accounts of them, see Stern 1991: 242–244 and Kokkinos 1998: 246–263. This is, therefore, a summary statement about this part of Herod's line. (As Kokkinos notes in his n. 37, it is just possible that Josephus is referring, here, to the children of the last-named Alexander, not to Herod the Great's son. But it seems to be superfluous to note that the children of a King of Cetis, who himself was married to a Commagenian princess and was the son of a king of Armenia, had no Jewish connections.)

546 Feldman renders εὐθὺς ἅμα τῷ φυῆναι "immediately from birth," so too Schalit (1963: 294), but Kokkinos (1998: 255, n. 37) suggests "as soon as they were physically developed" and *CCFJ* 4.340 offers "from earliest youth." Cf. ἔτι φυομένους κωλῦσαι ("nip in the bud") at §318.

547 Josephus's terminology concerning what we would call "conversion" and "apostasy" is usually quite tangible, focusing on practice. That is, rather than referring to a change of religion, he often focuses on practice, referring to "ancestral" practices (πάτρια), "customs" (ἔθη), quasi-legal practices (νόμιμα), or laws (νόμοι). Thus, here he refers to those who adopted Greek πάτρια, at 20.100 it is the Jews' "ancestral customs" (πατρίοις … ἔθεσιν) that Philo's nephew abandoned, at §82 it was Jewish νόμιμα to which Fulvia had "gone over" (προσεληλυῖαν!), at 20.34 we read of a Jew who taught the women of the court of Adiabene "to revere God as it was πάτριον for the Jews," and a little later (§38), looking back at that, we read that Izates learned that his mother was pleased with Jewish customs (ἔθη). Similarly, at *Ant.* 13.257–258 Josephus writes that the Samaritans adopted "circumcision and Jewish laws," which is then paraphrased as "circumcision and the rest of the Jewish way of life (δίαιταν)"; in contrast, Sylleus could not marry Herod's daughter because

he refused to "be enrolled in" Jewish ἔθη (16.225). So too, for example, Philo, *Life of Moses* 2.19–20: it is the Jews' νόμιμα that attract others. Although Josephus does seem to use the term θρησκεία to mean "religion" (see the note on "religion's" at §287), and can even refer to those who had "gone over" to it (*War* 2.560), such usage is rare; and although the abstract concept "Judaism" already existed by Josephus's day (2 Macc 2:21; 8:1; 14:38; Galatians 1:13–14), it was not yet very popular; neither Philo nor Josephus uses it. Indeed, it has been argued that even when it does appear, it refers not to "Judaism" but, rather, to "Judaizing" others; see Mason 2007b, along with the response in D. R. Schwartz 2014: 91–112. Be that as it may, it would take time before more inclusive and abstract concepts of conversion and apostasy would develop and become widespread. See esp. Cohen 1987 (on Josephus's usage) and, more generally, Cohen 1999 and Lavee 2018. Josephus's failure to conceptualize conversion as a change of an individual's identity should also be understood in light of his pride in his priestly descent (*Ant.* 16.187; *War* 1.3; 3.352; *Life* 1–6, 80; *Apion* 1.54; Tuval 2013: 260 ["Josephus' priestly status and origins seem to have constituted the most important ingredients of his self-identity …"]), for the more one ascribes significance to pedigree, the harder it is to admit a born gentile could become a Jew. Indeed, "neither the *De Bello Judaico* nor the *Antiquitates Judaicae* states that a 'convert' is equal to the native born or somehow joins the larger Jewish community" (Cohen 1987: 412). For the priests' difficulty with conversion, see also the note on "by birth" at 19.332.

548 Roxane and Salome II, daughters, respectively, of Herod's wives Phaedra and Elpis (Kokkinos 1998: 242). Both had been married to sons of Herod's brother, Pheroras (*Ant.* 17.322).

549 So, not "the Great"; the intention is to distinguish Agrippa I from Agrippa II; so too at §110; note also 20.9, 135, where Agrippa II is 'the younger Agrippa." Similarly, the use of μέγας of Herod seems to mean "Herod the Elder," as Otto noted (1913: 149–150), apparently to distinguish him from Antipas; the fact that the title appears only here (§§139, 133, 136), in this genealogical context, but nowhere else, argues against its meaning "the

*Poor Agrippa in
Judea*

(6.1) 143 A short time before the death of King Herod, Agrippa[550] had been staying in Rome, being brought up together with, and being very close to, Drusus, son of the emperor Tiberius.[551] He also became friendly with Antonia,[552] the wife of the elder Drusus, for Berenice, his mother, had been highly regarded by her and had asked her to help her son along.[553]

144 By his nature, Agrippa was magnanimous[554] and had a tendency to give expensive gifts. True, as long as his mother was alive he did not reveal his inner inclination,[555] considering it best to avoid the wrath she would have evinced about such things. **145** But when left to follow his own character after Berenice died, he squandered[556] his money: Some of it he spent for his own costly lifestyle, and some went for gifts without measure; but the largest part[557] he paid to Caesar's freedmen,[558] in the hope that they would act [to help him[559]], and within a short time he was beset by poverty. **146** That was a hindrance to going on living in Rome. Moreover, Tiberius forbade the friends of his deceased son[560] to appear before him, for the sight of them reminded him of his child and aroused his grief.[561]

Great" (although I have retained that conventional title for Herod in my own prose). See also the note on "the Elder" at §273. True, there is evidence for the use of βασιλεύς μέγας not only of Agrippa I (*Ant.* 20.104) but also of Agrippa II (*OGIS*, nos. 419–421; *Life* 33), who could not have been termed "the elder." See D. R. Schwartz 1990a: 136, also, more generally on the title, Wilhelm 1943: 160–162. But such usage, where μέγας modifies βασιλεύς rather than a proper name, is not what we have here, and even at 20.104, where we do have Agrippa I as βασιλεύς μέγας, the juxtaposition of father and son, of whom the latter is termed "the younger," makes it likelier that Josephus was distinguishing between them as elder and younger, rather than giving one an honorific title and denying it to the other. See D. R. Schwartz 1990a: 136 and Mason 2001: 40–41, n. 204 (on *Life* 33).

550 For bibliography, see the note on "He" at 19.293.

551 Drusus the Younger, son of Tiberius and Vipsania Agrippina. On him, see the note on "deceased son" at §146.

552 I.e., Antonia Minor—daughter of Marcus Antonius; wife of Tiberius's brother, Drusus the Elder; mother of Claudius and Germanicus, and grandmother of Gaius. See Kokkinos 1992. Born in 36 BCE, she was a grand old Roman matron by this time (§126); on her status, see §§180–182.

553 After Aristobulus was executed, in 7 BCE, Berenice took the children to Rome, and there they were raised in the highest circles. Indeed, according to §165, Agrippa was "raised together" with Claudius, the son of Antonia Minor; both were born ca. 10 BCE. Probably something similar could be said of Agrippa's brothers as well; see 20.13. For Berenice's closeness to Claudius's mother, Antonia Minor, see also §§156, 165, also the note on "friends" at 19.288. Antonia also took numerous other eastern princes under her wing; see Levick 1999: 268, n. 63 and Kokkinos 1992: 25. Cf. *CPJ* 156d, col. III, lines 11–12, where an Alexandrian

anti-Semite is said to have accused Claudius of being a "cast-off son of the Jewess Salome"—a slur that probably builds on common knowledge of his mother's closeness to the Herodian family.

554 According to Richards and Shutt 1939: 182, "μέγας cannot be right. μεγαλόφρων is probable." Although "cannot" might be overstated (and see μειζόνως, apparently in the same sense, at §194), it is the case that μεγαλόφρων, including in the sense of "generous," which fits the context here and in the next paragraph quite well, is common in Book 18 (§§5, 254, 255, 256).

555 For this translation of τὸ θέλον, here, see *CCFJ* 2.12, s.v. ἐθέλω.

556 For this pejorative sense of ἀναλίσκω, required by the context here, see the note on "squandering" at 20.211.

557 For such tripartite divisions (τά ... τά ... τά), in which Josephus points to two options (here: spending on himself and on gifts for others) and then focuses on a third (here: bribes to freedmen), cf. §§178, 239–240; 19.1–2, 19–21; *Apion* 1.3; *War* 5.539; and the extreme case that begins at *War* 2.119.

558 On Tiberius's freedmen, and their growing influence after the death of Drusus in 23 (mentioned in the next paragraph), see Levick 1999: 117.

559 Richards and Shutt (1939: 182) would eliminate the need for this parenthetical explanation by emending πράξεως into συμπραξεως.

560 Drusus Caesar ("Drusus the Younger") died in 23 CE. On him, and his death (which some included in the charges against Sejanus [see §181]), see Lott 2012: 345–347.

561 Although Suetonius (*Tib.* 52) prefers to claim that Tiberius was unaffected by Drusus's death—a standard slur, similar to those that Gaius showed no respect for Tiberius or Antonia upon their deaths; see Charlesworth 1933: 107–109. For Tiberius's oration at Drusus's funeral, see Tacitus, *Ann.* 4.12.

(6.2) **147** For these reasons he set sail for Judea, doing very poorly and being humiliated by the loss of all the money he had had and his lack of means to pay his debts to the money-lenders, who were numerous and who allowed him no way to avoid them.[562] Things went so far that, given his lack of practical options and in his shame about his circumstances, he retreated to a tower[563] in Malatha, in Idumea,[564] and there contemplated[565] committing suicide.[566] **148** However, his wife Cypros perceived his state of mind and applied herself in every way to keeping him away from such decisions.[567] She also sent a letter to his sister, Herodias, who was cohabiting with[568] Herod the tetrarch, and reported to her what Agrippa was contemplating and the duress that had brought him to such thoughts. **149** She urged her, being a family relation, to help him, seeing that she herself was doing her best to succor her husband, although on the basis of the same resources.[569] And so they sent for Agrippa and, arranging for him to reside in Tiberias, assigned him a defined sum for his livelihood and appointed him market-supervisor in Tiberias.[570]

150 Herod, however, did not long adhere to the terms that had been agreed upon, although even they were not sufficient.[571] For once when they were together in Tyre they came to insults, under the influence of wine, and Agrippa, considering Herod's abuse of him

---

562 ἀλεωρά (evasion, escape) appears in Josephus elsewhere only at *War* 3.163.

563 Apparently an abandoned fort that had once been part of Herod's defenses of the southern border of his kingdom. For the archaeological remains at Malatha (identified as Tell el-Milḥ), see Beit-Arieh 2008 and Beit-Arieh and Freud 2015; on the Roman period, see O. Tal, ibid. 18. For "towers" in this region see already 1 Macc 5:65 and Jubilees 36:20.

564 Malatha was about twenty-three km. east of Beersheva, thirty-six south of Hebron. It is noteworthy that a grandson of Herod, even one with quarter-Hasmonean lineage, sought refuge in Idumea; cf. Herod's flight to Idumea in 40 BCE (*Ant.* 14.353//*War* 1.263). For the conjecture that the fort remained from an estate that had belonged to Agrippa's Idumean ancestors, see Rappaport 2013: 366.

565 This is the only occurrence of περίνοια in Josephus.

566 Attentive readers might recall the similar story about Elijah at 8.348, where too Josephus mentions Idumea although his biblical source (1 Kings 19:3–4) does not.

567 Here we have the first piece of Josephus's contrast between Cypros and Herodias: the former urges her husband to avoid despair and death, while the latter will urge her husband to abandon tranquility and thereby drive him to his downfall (§§240–255). Note also §159.

568 Josephus is unwilling to call Herodias Herod Antipas's wife (γαμετή—cf. e.g., §§21, 40, 341, 344) because of the egregious illegality of their marriage, which he underlines at §136. See the note on "to him" at §110. The present notice, that Antipas was already married to Herodias shortly after Agrippa's return to Judea in the

wake of Drusus's death in 23 CE, is part of the argument offered in the note on "John" at §116, that their marriage came long before the war between Antipas and Aretas.

569 This translation follows Niese (1890a: 167), καὶ ταῦτα ἐξ ὁμοίων ἀφορμῶν. That is, Cypros emphasizes that she is doing her best to help her husband although her resources were the same as his, i.e. very meager. For this meaning of ἀφορμή see for example, *Ant.* 13.429; *ThLJ* 99, s.v. Her reference to her own lack of resources is meant, of course, to encourage Herodias (and Antipas), whose resources are greater, to step in and help. The text would be simpler if, with Mathieu and Herrmann (1929: 160), Schalit (1963: 294), and Feldman (1965: 98), we accept the negation (οὐκ) that appears in two witnesses after ταῦτα. That reading makes Cypros's point somewhat more explicit: in her appeal to Herodias she states that she is supporting her husband "although she does not have the same resources," inviting her to realize that it was only politeness that brought her not to complete the thought with "as you."

570 On the *agoranomos* (market supervisor) in Roman Palestine, see Sperber 1977 and Erdkamp 2005: 302–305. For lead weights of the *agoronomoi* of Tiberias, one perhaps of Agrippa I himself (and, if so, his full Roman name was Gaius Julius Agrippa), see Qedar 1986/87, Stein 1992, and Sigismund 2007: 332–334.

571 This is a remarkable case of parti pris that contributes to the characterization of Josephus's narrative (source?) as pro-Agrippan. For although the details of the story, in the next lines, amount to two men getting drunk and angry at each other and one stalking off, the present summary puts all of the blame on Antipas, who failed to adhere to his agreement with Agrippa, which anyway had

for his poverty and dependence upon a food-dole intolerable, betook himself to Flaccus, the consular [legate], who earlier, in Rome, had been a close friend of his; now he was governing Syria.[572]

(6.3) 151 Flaccus received him and he stayed with him, but he[573] had already been preoccupied[574] there by Aristobulus—who was Agrippa's brother and was hostile to him.[575] True, their mutual hostility did not damage them to the extent of depriving them of the honor due them as friends of the proconsul. **152** Nonetheless, Aristobulus did not desist from his ill-will toward Agrippa, until finally he was able to make Flaccus hostile to him,

---

been unfairly in his own favor, and was also arrogantly abusive. Cf. the notes on "stolen them" at §169 and "later" at §194.

572 On L. Pomponius Flaccus, governor of Syria since 32 CE, see Schürer, *HJP* 1.262, and Dąbrowa 1998: 37–38; specifically on the dating of his death, see also D. R. Schwartz 1990a: 183–184 and Stein 1992: 146–147. A consul ordinarius in 17 CE, he must have been more than a decade older than Agrippa, so one may wonder how close their friendship was. The reference to him here supplies a terminus ad quem for this story, for Tacitus reports, at *Ann.* 6.27, that Flaccus died in 33 CE. True, Schürer argued that, despite Tacitus's clear statement, Flaccus in fact served until 35. But, on the one hand, Tacitus's notice appears sandwiched between items explicitly said to have happened in that very year ("extremo anni … eodem anno"), so it seems that Tacitus was quite aware of chronology when he wrote it. On the other hand, Schürer's three arguments for 35 appear to be inconclusive. One argument is that since Vitellius was appointed only in 35 (Tacitus, *Ann.* 6.32), dating Flaccus's death to 33 would entail the governorship of Syria being vacant for a year. However, Tacitus in fact has Tiberius complaining, precisely in the context of Flaccus's death (*Ann.* 6.27), about the dearth of willing candidates for such positions, so Dąbrowa (1998: 38) lives easily with the hiatus in this case. Schürer's second argument is that if Agrippa arrived in Rome only in 36 (§126), after leaving Flaccus (see §§155–161), it is unlikely that he left no later than the end of 33. However, this point is, just as well or better, one of two arguments in support of the hypothesis that in fact Agrippa returned to Rome in 33/34, making a round trip prior to the one mentioned at §126 (the other argument being the time-consuming events that we would have to fit into half a year if Agrippa returned to Rome only a year before Tiberius's death and spent the last six months of Tiberius's reign in prison; see D. R. Schwartz 1990a: 51). Finally, Schürer argued that since Tacitus (*Ann.* 6.27), when reporting Flaccus's death, notes that at that time a decade ("decimum annum") had passed since the appointment of L. Arruntius as governor of Hispania Citerior, while we know from *Ann.* 4.45 that

L. Piso was governor there in 25, it follows that Arruntius was appointed later than that and so Flaccus died no earlier than 35. However, "decimum annum" might be a round datum, and anyway, as the new Schürer (loc. cit.) itself notes, Syme (1956: 20–21) has shown that Piso was not a governor but only a substitute, so it might be that Arruntius was appointed earlier.

573 Apparently: Flaccus (see the next note). This is also suggested by the repetition of Agrippa's name in the next line, as if otherwise "his brother" would refer to Flaccus's brother.

574 That is (it seems): Flaccus's attentions had already been given to Aristobulus. I have translated according to Niese's conjecture in his apparatus criticus (1890a: 167), προκατεσχηκότος; see LSJ 1485, s.v. κατέχω. The manuscripts (followed by Niese, loc. cit.) read παρακατεσχη-κότος, which is rendered "checked" by Feldman (1965: 100, n. a), in accordance with LSJ 1312, s.v. παρακατέχω: "keep back," "detain." The manuscripts' reading makes sense, insofar as the statement that Aristobulus "checked" Agrippa is immediately explained by the notice that Aristobulus was hostile to Agrippa. However, that reading is nonetheless jarring, for readers do not know that Aristobulus was already staying with Flaccus. To solve that problem, Feldman (1965: 100) adopted the Epitome's reading, προκατειληφότος (Niese 1887–1996: 311), which Feldman renders "had been anticipated by." That would make sense, but, as *CCFJ* 3.533 shows, it is quite difficult to justify that translation; after listing such meanings as "conquer (occupy) previously," "to seize first" for other appearances of προκαταλαμβάνω in Josephus, it offers only a question mark for the verb's meaning here. Hence it appears to be preferable to solve the same problem by adopting Niese's emendation, at least as the best of some bad options. Note, however, that, contrary to his frequent practice (see the Introduction, at n. 69), Niese did not adopt it in his editio minor (1890b: 144).

575 No reason is stated for the hostility. Given the fact that other elements in this story reflect the application to Agrippa of the biblical story of Joseph and his brothers (see the note on "in common" at §201), it may be that

exploiting the following circumstance to serve his ill-will: **153** When the Damascenes had a border dispute with the Sidonians, and Flaccus was about to hear their arguments, the Damascenes, learning that Agrippa could have great influence upon Flaccus, asked him to take their part and promised him a large sum of money. **154** And he indeed undertook eagerly to do whatever he could to help the Damascenes. But knowledge of the agreement concerning the money did not escape Aristobulus, and he accused him before Flaccus. When the matter was investigated and [the truth] was evident, he ejected Agrippa from his friendship with him. **155** Thus pushed around[576] [back] into extreme poverty, he came to Ptolemais,[577] and in light of the impossibility of living anywhere else he made up his mind to sail to Italy. But since that was prevented by his lack of funds, he asked Marsyas (a freedman of his) to procure for him the requisite means by borrowing them from someone. **156** Marsyas asked Protos—a freedman of Agrippa's mother Berenice, who in accordance with her[578] testament[579] had become subject to Antonia[580]—to supply him [the money] on the basis of a written commitment and promise from him. **157** But he, who accused Agrippa of having bilked him of some money, forced Marsyas to make up a promissory note for 20,000 Attic drachmas but receive 2,500 less.[581] Marsyas agreed because he had no other options. **158** Having received this money and come to Anthedon,[582] Agrippa took a ship and was about to set sail. However, Herennius Capito, the procurator of Jamneia,[583] upon learning [that Agrippa was there] sent soldiers to collect from him 300,000[584] pieces of silver that he owed Caesar's treasury in Rome; they forced him to stay put. **159** He pretended, then, to obey that which they ordered, but at nightfall he cut the mooring cables and set sail to

---

readers were expected to read this in light of Gen 37:2–4, or, more generally, in light of general expectations about jealousy among brothers, especially in royal families; cf. 18.41–42 and 20.29, 37.

576 περιωθέω appears in *Antiquities* only in Books 17–18, including below, at §§362, 375.

577 On this port city, see the note on "Ptolemais" at §120.

578 Reading τῆς ἐκείνης, Niese's conjecture; see Niese 1890b: 144, followed by Feldman 1965: 102. The manuscripts, followed by Niese 1890a:168, read ἐκείνου, but that masculine form is quite difficult to construe, if only because Marsyas and Protos are both still alive. Perhaps, as Deborah L. Gera suggested, if pressed we could take the masculine form to be a genitive of possession or contents ("by virtue of [the provision] of the testament that relates to him"), but that would require us not only to accept such an elliptic formulation but also to assume that Josephus did not tell us, explicitly, whose testament it was. Hence the emendation is very attractive. But see the next note.

579 On διαθήκη of a will (testament), which occurs very often in Josephus's accounts of Herod's in *War* 1 and *Ant.* 17, see Danker 2000: 228–229. As Danker indicates, whereas in the Hellenistic period the term meant exclusively "last will and testament," in the Roman period there is some evidence for "compact, contract." That could open up new possibilities about how Protos came to be

Antonia's. But that meaning seems not to be found in Josephus. See *ThLJ* 143–144.

580 On Antonia Minor, see the note on "Antonia" at §143.

581 That is, he lent the money at 14% interest, somewhat higher than the usual 12–12.5%. For manifold evidence for the latter, see *CPR* 7 (1979): 162–163.

582 A port near Gaza; see *HJP* 2.104.

583 As is reported at 17.189, 321 and 18.31, Jamneia (Jabneh), located near the coast between Tel-Aviv and Ashdod, had a history of its own; see *HJP* 2.109–110 and Kletter, Ziffer, and Zwickel 2011. Herod left it to Salome, she left it to Augustus's wife, Livia, and from the latter it eventually became a special domain of the imperial house, with its own procurator. On such procurators of imperial estates, see Jones 1968: 123–124. Here we see him functioning outside of his bailiwick, which gives some support to Philo's more general characterization of him as "collector of the imperial revenues in Judea" (*Leg.* 199). Capito, who is mentioned here and at §163, and is also known from an inscription (*AE* 1941: no. 105 = Smallwood 1967: no. 255) on a silver bust of Tiberius, which fills out his name as Gaius Herennius Capito, figures in a central role in Philo's *Legatio* (§§199–202), in his account of the antecedents of Gaius's attempt to Romanize the Temple of Jerusalem; cf. the note on "for example" at §257.

584 So too §163. But at §159 Agrippa asks for a loan of only 200,000.

Alexandria. There he besought Alexander the Alabarch[585] to give him a loan of 200,000.[586] He said he would not supply the money to *him*, but he did not refuse it to Cypros, so struck was he by her love for her husband and all her other virtue.[587] **160** She promised [to undertake responsibility for the loan], and Alexander gave them five talents[588] in Alexandria and promised to give them the rest when they arrived in Dicearcheia,[589] for he was wary of Agrippa's propensity for spending. And so Cypros, after sending off her husband on his sea voyage to Italy, returned with the children to Judea.

Agrippa in Rome **(6.4) 161** Upon coming to Puteoli,[590] Agrippa wrote a letter to Tiberius Caesar, who was staying in Capri; he explained to him that he had arrived in order to serve him and to see him and asked that permission be given him to come to Capri.[591] **162** Tiberius did not delay at all, in general writing him in friendly terms and especially indicating how grateful he was for his safe return to Capri. And when Agrippa arrived, Tiberius welcomed and hosted him in a manner that in no way fell short of his letter's enthusiasm. **163** The next day, however, after there reached Caesar a letter sent him by Herennius Capito, stating that Agrippa, after taking a loan totaling 300,000, had ignored the dates that had been agreed upon for payment, and then, when a demand [for repayment] was made he had absconded in flight[592] from the territory subject to him, leaving him powerless to use his authority to collect the money, **164** Caesar, upon reading the letter, was very indignant, and ordered that Agrippa's access to him be cut off until the debt was paid. But he, not at all cowed by Caesar's wrath, asked Antonia, the mother of Germanicus and of Claudius (who would later be the caesar[593]), to give him the 300,000 as a loan, so he would not lose Tiberius's friendship. **165** She gave him the money,[594] in memory of his mother, Berenice, for the two women had been very close

---

585 Philo's brother, according to §259. "Alabarch" (which also appears in *OGIS* 674) probably means "Arabarch," i.e., Alexander was responsible for the collection of customs on traffic with Arabia, which was very lucrative (see Tcherikover in *CPJ* 1.49, n. 4; Evans 1995: 590; and Schimanowski 2007: 123); and then there was also the family's import-export business, on which see A. Fuks in *CPJ* 2.197–200. For the resultant wealth, see also *Ant.* 20.100, *War* 5.205, and *CPJ* 420; for the family's links with Agrippa's, see 19.276–277, perhaps also 20.147. On Alexander, see esp. Evans 1995. On the family, see also Appelbaum 2018 and Sterling 2020; the latter doubts the identification of "alabarch" and "arabarch" but tends to agree he was some sort of customs official.

586 Presumably drachmas; see the note on "drachmas" at §67.

587 As above, §148.

588 That is, about 30,000 drachmas, leaving 170,000 to be turned over later.

589 Dicearcheia is the Greek name for Puteoli, as Josephus explains at *Life* 16. See the next note.

590 It is quite strange that Josephus uses this Latin name after using the Greek name in the preceding paragraph, without explaining to his readers that they denote the same city. Contrast *Life* 16, where Josephus uses both

names and explains that they refer to the same city. For the argument that the text here (just as the story of Agrippa's finances; see the note on "Tiberius's friendship" at §164) reflects the splicing of materials from two different sources, see D. R. Schwartz 2007b: 127–130.

591 Tiberius spent much of his last years in Capri; see Houston 1985.

592 Such an otiose but emphatic collocation (οἴχοιτο φυγάς), with an effect like "skedaddled," is common, beginning with Homer; see LSJ 1211, s.v. οἴχομαι, §I.

593 Here is a clear case of "Caesar" turning from a name into a title; so too below, at §194. As Mason (2008: 153, n. 1147 and 172, n. 1294) notes with regard to *War* 2.181, 206, this usage reflects Josephus's own times, in an age in which, since the days of Gaius, "Caesar" was no longer part of the emperor's name. The transformation is usually seen as complete by the "Four-Caesar-Year" (68/69).

594 The fact that Josephus makes no further reference to the 170,000 drachmas Agrippa was to collect in Dicearcheia, promised him by Alexander the Alabarch (§160), seems to point, as does the move from "Dicearcheia" to "Puteoli," to a shift of sources between §160 and §161. It is easy to understand the discrepancy about the loan, for 19.276 reports that Alexander the Alabarch was the guardian of Antonia's estate. That suggests that the

to one another,595 [and she was also close] to him, because he had been brought up with Claudius and his comrades; after using it to pay back the debt, his friendship with Tiberius was no longer inhibited.

166 Thereafter Tiberius Caesar596 associated his grandson597 with Agrippa, urging him always to accompany him on his outings. But598 Agrippa, having been received in friendship by Antonia, turned [instead] to cultivating his relationship with Gaius, who was her grandson, and who—thanks to the goodwill toward his father599—was one of the most respected people. **167** For there was another,600 a Samaritan by descent and a freedman of Caesar, from whom Agrippa found the way to borrow a million [drachmas]; Agrippa used [some of] it to pay Antonia the debt he owed her, and, by consuming601 the rest in cultivating his relationship602 with Gaius, he became quite highly regarded by him.

(6.5) 168 Once, during this period when Agrippa's friendship with Gaius was progressing greatly, it happened that while they were out riding they came to talk about Tiberius, and Agrippa, turning to prayer603—for the two of them were alone—[voiced the hope] that Tiberius would give up rule as soon as possible and turn it over to Gaius, who was in all ways more worthy of it. These words were heard by Eutychus, a freedman of Agrippa's, who was the carriage-driver. At first he kept quiet about it. **169** But when he was accused of stealing clothes from Agrippa (and indeed he had stolen them!604), and fled but was caught and brought before Piso, who was the guardian of the city,605 he said the reason that he had fled was to tell Caesar that he had some confidential words to say to him that bore upon his own safety. Putting him in chains, [Piso] sent him to Capri, but Tiberius, as was his wont, left him in chains. For he was more of a procrastinator than any other king or tyrant.606

---

money Alexander promised to lend Agrippa was actually Antonia's, which Alexander, knowing of Antonia's friendship for Berenice and Agrippa, or for some other reason, agreed to lend Agrippa. Some recalled that as Alexander's loan; others, as Antonia's.

595 On this friendship, see the note on "along" at §143.

596 The use of Τιβέριος ὁ Καῖσαρ is strange, coming as it does after several references to Tiberius simpliciter. It is likely that the present notice (§166a) was added by Josephus secondarily in order to adumbrate the report at §188.

597 Tiberius Gemellus, the son of Tiberius's late son, Drusus (on whom see §46).

598 I have used this strong translation of Ἀγρίππας δέ and added in "(instead)" because, as §188 clearly indicates, Agrippa's preference for Antonia's grandson was contrary to Tiberius's recommendation of his own grandson.

599 Josephus likes to recall Germanicus's popularity; cf. §206 and 19.217, 223.

600 Reading ἄλλος, with the manuscripts, followed by Niese (1890a: 170) and Feldman (1965: 107–108, n. f). On the assumption that this means "another Samaritan," this has been thought a problem, for no Samaritan was mentioned previously. That spurred scholars (such as Hudson and Havercamp 1726: 1.889) to emend the text into the proper name Θαλλός—the name of a first-century (?)

historian cited by Julius Africanus, Eusebius, and several other Christian writers; see Stern, GLAJJ 3.38–42; Holladay 1983:343–369; and van Voorst 2000: 20–22. However, on the one hand there is no apparent reason to think Thallos was a Samaritan or rich enough to make this loan, and on the other hand the text may be punctuated and translated as above, the reference being to "another" freedman, like Protos (§156), to whom Agrippa could turn for help.

601 As at §§144–145, 160; Josephus reminds us that this is what Agrippa did with money whenever he had it.

602 For such use of θεραπεύω of a calculated self-serving service of others, see also §§188, 294, 20.205, etc. On the phenomenon, see 6.341 and the note on "considerably" at §36.

603 For κατ᾽ εὐχὰς τραπομένου compare 3.25 and 6.22.

604 Confidence about this, and the desire to record it emphatically, may point to a source close to Agrippa. Cf. the note on "himself" at §150.

605 The praefectus urbi (GTRI 98, s.v. φύλαξ); so too below, §235. He was something like a manager of Rome and the surrounding territory, responsible for public order, water and grain supplies, and fire safety. On this Piso, who had been a consul in 27, see HJP 1.261.

606 This characterization of Tiberius is often adduced in connection with Tacitus's account, at Ann. 1.7 and 1.11–12, of his succession to the empire following Augustus's

Tiberius's Style of Rule

170 Thus [for example], he did not receive embassies immediately upon their arrival, nor did he send successors to governors and procurators that he appointed, unless they first died.[607] For the same reason he was neglectful[608] about interviewing prisoners. **171** When even his friends asked the reason he proceeded so lethargically, he said, concerning the embassies, that he kept them waiting because if they were handled and sent away immediately other embassies might be undertaken and come up[609] and then there would devolve upon him the burden[610] of receiving them and sending them again on their way. **172** As for the [appointments to] offices, [he said] that once he had appointed people to them he allowed them to maintain them,[611] out of foresightful regard for the subjects. For [he said], it is natural that governments of every type be characterized by greed, and when positions are not ancestral,[612] but might be taken away after a short period, and the length of the term is unknown [in advance], incumbents would feel even a greater urge to steal. **173** But if they remained in their positions for a longer time, they would have their fill of theft because of the magnitude of what they had already gained and would be rather sluggish[613] in such practice in the future. In contrast, if a position were to change hands without delay,[614] those exposed as the rulers' potential victims would never be able to recover,[615] for they would never be granted intervals of time in which those who had already taken what they wanted would be sated and [therefore] moderate[616] their enthusiasm to take more—because the moment of their departure would come before that could happen. **174** As proof[617] [for the

---

death, with scholarly discussion of it focusing on whether Tacitus's characterization of Tiberius's *cunctatio* (indecision) in that context was meant to be general or pertained only to that episode, and whether Tacitus was serious or, rather, ironic. See, for example, the discussion in Woodman 1998: 40–69.

607 Or even when they did; see §108. On this characterization of Tiberius's policy and practice concerning provincial governors, which was often explained as betraying a weakness of character, see esp. Tacitus, *Ann.* 1.80, also Gray 1972. Some, however, such as Levick 1999: 127–128, would interpret it more favorably—as Josephus has Tiberius himself suggest in the next lines.

608 The manuscripts read περίοπτος ("conspicuous" [as e.g. 13.211]) but that hardly fits the context, hence Ernesti's emendation, based upon Thucydides 1.41: ἀπερίοπτος ("unregarding, reckless" [LSJ 186, s.v.]). So too at §272 and 19.72. See the Introduction, at n. 76.

609 To Rome; on the Roman perspective revealed here, as at §§51, 53, see the Introduction, at n. 36.

610 Here ὄχλος—which is echoed in the parable at §175—might retain something of its usual nuance: "mass" (of bothersome embassies that would have to be handled).

611 For Tiberius's policy of allowing governors to remain long in office, and whether and to what degree it worked to the advantage of the provincial subjects, see Brunt 1961: 210–211, Orth 1970: 71–81, and Levick 1999: 125. Cf. Powell 1936: he would emend the present passage, reading ἀϊδίους ("everlasting," "eternal"), as at §§14, 252

and 19.16, instead of the manuscripts' αἰδοῦς ("regard") and taking the passage to refer to appointments "for life," as suggested by §170.

612 I.e., inherited and therefore held throughout one's lifetime. Compare 15.40–41 and 20.235. For doubts concerning the assumption that governors who lasted for long terms were less predatory, see Brunt 1961: 210–211. After reviewing the evidence, he concludes that "Long tenures may have satiated the avarice of the governors; they also postponed the day of reckoning. It is merely an *a priori* assumption that in themselves they testify to the worth of the men who enjoyed them." For similar debates today, as to whether shorter terms (for the officeholders are afraid of prosecution) or rather longer terms (as Tiberius would have it) better deter corruption, see Tsur 2021.

613 This adjective, ἀμβλύς, appears elsewhere in Josephus only at 19.206, there too in the comparative and applied to a sluggish ruler.

614 Lit. "immediately"; see the note on "immediately" at §58.

615 On the sense of ἀναστροφή, see the note on "recovery" at §359.

616 Reading ὑποδιδοῖέν, with Niese 1890a: 171. But as with the other appearance of this verb in *Ant.* (17.111), neither the text nor the sense is certain. See *CCFJ* 4.253, s.v. ὑποδίδωμι.

617 For Josephus's use of παράδειγμα not merely for "illustration" or "model" but in a stronger sense, as "proof on the basis of an example," see §§251, 304, 328.

validity of this policy] he told them the following story. Someone once lay wounded, with a multitude of flies swarming around his wounds. Someone who happened by, taking pity on the unfortunate man and assuming that it was on account of inability that he did not help [himself], was about to come up and shoo them away. 175 When [the wounded man] asked him to desist from doing that, he asked him, in response, the reason for his lack of interest in escaping the trouble that beset him.[618] He said: "You would be doing me even a greater injustice[619] if you drove them off. For these flies are already full of my blood and for them there is no longer such urgency to trouble[620] me. They are even somewhat ceasing. But if there were to come others with their hunger unassuaged, they would take over this already exhausted[621] body and consign it to its death." 176 For this reason, for him[622] too [so Tiberius said] it was considerate, for his subjects, who had been ruined by so many robbers, not to continually send out governors; for in the manner of flies they would attack them—for their natural tendency to profit-seeking would be reinforced by the prospect that that pleasure would soon be taken away from them. 177 Let Tiberius's actions themselves testify to the truth of what I have said about his nature in this regard:[623] for although he was emperor for twenty-two years he sent [only] two governors to Judea to administer the nation—Gratus and then Pilate, who succeeded him as the governor.[624] 178 Nor was he this way toward the Judeans alone, but different in his treatment of his other subjects.

But he also explained his delay in hearing prisoners:[625] being condemned to death would constitute relief from their current troubles, and it was not appropriate for them to enjoy such good fortune. For those who were being worn down by vexation about what hung over them, [the delay of trial] would weigh down their misfortune all the more.[626]

(6.6) 179 For this reason, Eutychus too did not obtain a hearing and was kept in chains. But after some time had gone by and Tiberius had come from Capri to Tusculum,[627] which is about a hundred furlongs from Rome,[628] Agrippa asked Antonia to bring it about that Eutychus have a hearing about those matters concerning which he had accused him. 180 Antonia was always held in high respect by Tiberius, both as was appropriate given their family relationship, for she had been the wife of his brother, Drusus, and thanks to

Agrippa's Imprisonment

---

618 This reference to his condition as κακοῦ τοῦ ἐφε-στηκότος recalls Tiberius's reference to governors who ἐφεστήκασιν εἰς πλέον (§173a).

619 By phrasing the problem this way (μειζόνως γὰρ ἂν ἀδικοῖς με), rather than more generally "you would put me in a worse position" (Feldman 1965: 113), Tiberius's parable reminds readers of the real issue the parable is meant to illustrate.

620 This ὄχλον echoes ὄχλος at §171, to link Tiberius's claim to that of the protagonist in the parable.

621 For governments that cruelly "exhaust" their subjects, cf. 19.246 (ὠμότητι τετρῦσθαι).

622 Reading according to Niese's conjecture, καὐτῷ (1890b: 148), rather than καὐτός (Niese 1890a: 172), which is retained by Feldman 1965: 112.

623 For this tendency of Tiberius, see the note on "maintain them" at §172.

624 This datum will have forced anyone who undertook to adjust the length of Gratus's and Pilate's terms of office to keep their sum constant; see the note on "eleven" at §35.

625 The third category of delay listed at §170, kept for the end because it is the most relevant in the present context. Cf. the note on "largest part" at §145.

626 The text of this paragraph is quite difficult, but the general sense is clear. It is closely paralleled by Philo's account, in *Flacc.* 128–129, of the deliberate delays of the trial of someone who had been accused of *maiestas* toward Tiberius.

627 On Tiberius's villa in Tusculum, southeast of Rome, where he stayed intermittently between 29 and 34, see McCracken 1940.

628 At about five furlongs per km. (see the note on "away" at §60), this comes to twenty km., which is quite accurate.

the virtue of her chastity[629]—for although she was widowed young[630] she remained [in that status], refusing to marry[631] another although Augustus[632] urged her to be married to someone; and she preserved her life free of all reproach. 181 Moreover, she had herself been a major benefactress[633] to Tiberius: when a great conspiracy had been put together against him by Sejanus,[634] who had been his friend and at that time held great power since he had been the commander of his troops, and most members of the Senate and many freedmen had joined [the conspiracy] and the army had been corrupted, the conspiracy made great progress and would have done the job for Sejanus had Antonia not exercised boldness that was cleverer than Sejanus's wickedness.[635] 182 For when she learned what had been organized against Tiberius, she wrote it all to him in detail and, giving the letter to Pallas, the most trusted[636] of her slaves,[637] sent him to Tiberius in Capri. He, upon learning [what was planned], executed Sejanus and his co-conspirators.[638] As for Antonia, although already he had respected her highly, now he honored her all the more and considered her reliable in all respects.

183 Now, however, when called upon by this Antonia to examine Eutychus, Tiberius said: "But [why should I do anything? For] if, on the one hand, Eutychus's report about what Agrippa said was a lie, then the punishment he has received from me is sufficient; but if upon interrogation[639] it becomes clear that what he said was true, let it not be that in his yearning to punish his freedman he summon justice down upon himself!" 184 When Antonia told him that, Agrippa began to demand with all the more pressure that the matter be examined, and so Antonia—for Agrippa did not let go and repeatedly made the request—found an opportunity, as follows.

629 On the translation of ἀρετῇ τοῦ σώφρονος see the note on "self-restraint" at §73. For the widespread notion that it was virtuous for a widow to remain unmarried, for a woman should ideally be *univira*, see *Ant.* 17.352, also, for example, Tacitus, *Germania* 19.2, Plutarch, *Tiberius Gracchus* 1.4, and much additional material assembled by Walcot 1991.

630 Drusus the Elder died in 9 BCE, when Antonia was twenty-seven.

631 For Josephus's approval of such loyalty to late husbands, cf. 17.352.

632 For Augustus's encouragement of widows to remarry, as part of his general policy concerning marriage, see also Suetonius, *Augustus* 34 and Kokkinos 1992: 15–16.

633 Cf. the note on "benefit" at §95.

634 On L. Aelius Sejanus, who was praetorian prefect under Tiberius and consul in 31 but executed for conspiracy that same year, see esp. Nicols 1975 and Hennig 1975. Nicols, who notes that according to Tacitus (*Ann.* 6.3) and Suetonius (*Tiberius* 61) it was against Germanicus's children, including Gaius Caligula, that Sejanus had been plotting, suggests that it was only post-Caligulan historiography, which did not want to arouse any sympathy for the tyrant, that preferred to recall Sejanus's conspiracy as one against Tiberius; perhaps, for example, it was only in that context that the murder of Drusus Caesar was added

to the charges against him (see Lott 2012: 347). But see the opening of Suetonius, *Tiberius* 65, also Philo, *Leg.* 160.

635 For doubts that Antonia had anything to do with Sejanus's downfall, mainly on the basis of the fact that the other sources make no mention of it, see Nicols 1975. Nicols suggests that the story derives, ultimately, from Agrippa's family tradition, which was interested in glorifying the memory of Antonia. For a similar attempt to profit from Sejanus's downfall, note Philo's claim (*Leg.* 159–160) that Sejanus conspired not only against Tiberius but also, and therefore, against the Jews of Rome, for he knew they were the emperor's most loyal supporters.

636 As also §325 and 20.163; cf. §205.

637 On the former, an influential Greek in Rome who in 31 was still a slave but was soon to be freed and to remain at the heights of court life in Rome until his death in 62, see Oost 1958 (p. 15 on the present episode, which indeed shows Antonia's great trust in him). Pallas will reappear at 20.137, 182.

638 This is the only occurrence of συνεπίβουλος in Josephus. For a single appearance of the verb, συνεπιβουλεύω, see 13.308.

639 Frequently βασανίζω involves torture (e.g., 19.34–35), but in this case we hear of none, just as at §154 it is used simply for the investigation of a matter. See *ThLJ* 102, s.v.

185 Once when Tiberius was being carried, reclining in a litter in front of which were walking her grandson Gaius and Agrippa, who had just had a meal, Antonia, who had been walking by the litter, called upon Tiberius to summon Eutychus and examine him. **186** To this he replied: "But let the gods know, Antonia, that it is not by my own will, but from the necessity of following your appeal, that I shall do what shall be done." Having said that, he ordered Macro,[640] who was Sejanus's successor, to bring Eutychus. He arrived without delay. Tiberius then asked him what he had to say against the man who had granted him his liberty.[641] **187** He said:

> O Lord, Gaius was riding in a carriage, he together with Agrippa, and I was sitting at the feet of the two of them,[642] and after many words had gone by between them, Agrippa said to Gaius: ""Would that the day soon come, when this old man steps aside[643] and appoints you to rule the world.[644] Surely his grandson Tiberius[645] would not at all stand in our way, for you would see to his death,[646] and thus the whole inhabited world would be happy and I myself more than anyone else!"

188 Tiberius, who thought the reported words credible, and also recalling his old grudge against Agrippa (for despite the fact that he had urged him to take care of Tiberius, who was his grandson and Drusus's son, he had acted disrespectfully by ignoring the orders and locating himself entirely at Gaius's side[647]), **189** said: "So, Macro—fetter him." Macro, however —both because he was not sure that he knew clearly concerning whom he had been ordered, and because he could not expect that Tiberius might ordain something like that concerning Agrippa—refrained, expecting [Tiberius] to clarify his words. **190** After Caesar had gone around the hippodrome and encountered Agrippa standing there, he said: "Look here,[648] Macro, I told you that that man should be chained!" When he asked, in response, which man [he meant], he said "Agrippa, of course." **191** Agrippa turned to

---

640 Q. Naevius Cordus Sutorius Macro, praetorian prefect after Sejanus. See van der Horst 2003a: 102–103. For a long account of his close relationship with Gaius, which led to his downfall and death by early in 38 (Smallwood 1970: 185–186; Bastianini 1975: 271), see Philo, *Leg.* 32–61.

641 As stated at §168, Eutychus was Agrippa's freedman.

642 This is apparently the sense of the dual here, τοῖν ποδοῖν; Eutychus's point, apparently, is to emphasize that he could hear both halves of the conversation.

643 This use of μεθίστημι is, it seems, meant to represent Eutychus as employing clever innuendo. For while at §168 Josephus had Agrippa referring to the possibility of Tiberius abdicating, here he has Eutychus using a verb that could imply that Agrippa was actually expressing the hope that Tiberius would soon die; see, for example, §§31, 89, 147, 352, and note that Mathieu and Herrmann (1929: 166) simply render "en quittant la vie." That, of course, makes the offense all the more heinous. Nevertheless, the verb is ambiguous, and that, together with the fact

that Eutychus has Agrippa go on to state the hope that Tiberius would appoint Gaius, would allow Eutychus deniability should anyone accuse him of explicitly and falsely ascribing to Agrippa the hope that Tiberius would soon die.

644 See the note on "earth and sea" at 19.1.

645 On Tiberius Gemellus, see the note on "grandson" at §166.

646 That this would be the natural corollary of Gaius's rise to the throne is apparently taken for granted; so too at §215. Compare §41, 5.234 (//Judges 9:5), 7.350 (//1 Kings 1:12, 21), and 20.29, along with Diodorus Siculus 17.5.4, Philo, *Leg.* 67–68 and Plutarch, *Life of Demetrius* 3.4: writing not long after Josephus, Plutarch declared that the rule, that rulers should kill off their brothers, is as hard and fast as the postulates assumed by geometricians. Cf. §215 and 20.29. In the Ottoman Empire such practice was even legalized (Ekinci 2018).

647 See §166.

648 On καὶ μὴν δέ, see Denniston 1954: 356–357.

beseeching [the emperor], reminding him of his son with whom he was raised[649] and the way he had brought up Tiberius,[650] but accomplished nothing, and was led off—chained in his purple robes.[651]

192 It was boiling hot, and since there had not been much wine at his meal he was also burning up with thirst, which made his anguish and humiliation grow all the more. Seeing one of Gaius's slaves by the name of Thaumastus bringing water in a jug, he asked him to let him drink. **193** After he held it out for him and Agrippa drank with gusto, he said: "O slave, if this service you rendered me turns out to be a good sign, when I am released from these bonds I will not delay to encourage Gaius to liberate you—you who, although I am in bonds, served me just as if I were still in my former status, omitting nothing of the dignity that was mine."[652] **194** And he did not lie;[653] for later, when reigning as king, upon receiving Thaumastus from Gaius after he became the caesar,[654] he magnanimously[655] set him free and appointed him curator of his property; and when he died he left him to his son Agrippa and daughter Berenice[656] to take care of the same stewardship. It was in that position that he died, in old age. But all that happened later.[657]

A German's Prophecy

(6.7) 195 To return to Agrippa:[658] he was then standing, in chains, in front of the palace, leaning dispiritedly against a certain tree along with many other prisoners. When a certain bird, which the Romans call "bubo,"[659] alighted upon the tree upon which Agrippa was leaning, one of the prisoners, a German, who had been watching, asked the soldier [who was guarding him] who it was who was wearing purple. **196** Learning that his name was Agrippa and that he was a Judean by birth and one of the most eminent people there,[660] he asked

---

649 Drusus, who was born ca. 13 BCE, was a little older than Agrippa (b. 10 BCE). For their close friendship, see §143.

650 That is, Agrippa argued that Tiberius was wrong to assume that he had ignored Tiberius Gemellus. But Josephus has already told us that he did (§166). Josephus has no problem about reporting Agrippa's willingness to lie, or otherwise to play around with words, when that was useful; it conforms to his more general portrayal of Agrippa as one who knows how to get along with important people. Cf. the note on "ours" at 19.243.

651 On purple as a sign of nobility, see the note on "purple" at §82.

652 This episode is quite similar to Josephus's account, at 20.54–68, of the relations between Izates and Artabanus.

653 At this point Ambrosianus and the Latin version supply an additional short sentence: "Rather, he did repay him." Niese first bracketed it (1890a: 175) and then omitted it (1890b: 150). Indeed, it adds nothing to the preceding sentence. Cf. the note on "brought to him" at 20.5.

654 Cf. above, note on "caesar" at §164.

655 On the sense of μειζόνως here, see the note on "magnanimous" at §144.

656 On such coupling of Agrippa II and Berenice, see the note on "her brother" at 20.145.

657 All this attention to Thaumastus and first-hand knowledge about his career have engendered the

hypothesis that he lies behind much of this material; see Schemann 1887: 4 and Feldman 1962: 333. In any case, it is the kind of story Josephus likes, about turns of fortune, just like Agrippa's own story.

658 Ἀγρίππας δέ. For such toggling between one protagonist and another, compare §§205, 289, also the notes on "turning now" at §1 and "with Petronius" at §288.

659 An owl, more specifically: eagle-owl. In antiquity it had a reputation for wisdom (and as such accompanied Athena). Of particular relevance here is its reputation as harbinger of death: appearance of owls presaged, it was said, *inter alia*, Crassus's debacle at Carrhae, the assassination of Julius Caesar, and the deaths of Claudius and Augustus, for, in general, "the *bubo* is a funereal bird, and is regarded as an extremely bad omen, especially at public auspices" (Pliny, *NH* 10.34, trans. H. Rackham [LCL]). This was especially the case insofar as it was a nocturnal bird, so daytime appearances were unsettling. For numerous sources on the Roman period, see Pease 1935: 375–377 and Swan 2004: 301. As Opelt (1966: 892–893) noted, in contrast, this motif is not at all common in Greek literature. Thus, with the help of a bird (cf. Gen 40:17–19!), Josephus has included a very Roman element in this story, one that meshes comfortably with the Jewish ones that are so prominent (see the note on "in common" at §201).

660 As with "they" after "Judea" at §§2–3, the use of "there" after *Ioudaios* here means it should be translated "Judean."

the soldier, to whom he was chained,[661] to move closer so they could converse. For, he said, he wanted to ask him something about his ancestral practices. **197** Upon his assent, when he stood near [Agrippa] he said, via an interpreter:

> O young man, you are depressed by the suddenness of your vicissitude, which was so great and at one fell swoop brought upon you by Fortune, and you will consider incredible words that interpret divine providence[662] as boding your release from the calamity that has come upon you.[663] **198** Nevertheless, know that I will—swearing by my ancestral gods and by those that are native here, who have ordained iron [chains] for us—tell you everything, not because saying it gives the pleasure of being garrulous, nor in the hope of cheering you up idly. **199** For predictions on such matters, when what really happens falls short of what was indicated, engender grief worse than what would have been felt if these things had never been heard to begin with.
>
> But even if I place myself in danger, I think it is proper to inform you of the gods' prediction: **200** It cannot fail to happen that you will immediately be released from these bonds and advance to the utmost dignity and power,[664] such that you will be envied by all who now observe your fortunes with pity, and your death will be a happy one, with children to whom you will leave your fortune. But remember, that whenever you again see that bird, your death will follow in five days. **201** That will happen as has been indicated by the god's dispatching of this bird. I thought it would be unjust to withhold from you the understanding that derives from foreknowledge of these things, for if you know the good things of which you are going to have the advantage you can belittle your present affliction. But when happiness comes to you, remember to see to our relief too from this misfortune, which we now have in common.[665]

---

661 Such chaining together is also mentioned by Seneca, *Epistle* 5.7 and Atheneus 5.213b; see Mommsen 1899: 300, n. 2. Cf. Acts 12:6.

662 For Josephus on divine providence, see the note on "of man" at 19.61.

663 The qualification of the calamity as τοῦ ἐφεσηκότος might be merely temporal, as it is rendered by Feldman (1965: 123 ["present']) and Schalit (1963: 299 ["of this hour"]). But literally, as C. Seeman kindly pointed out to me, it indicates that the calamity has "come upon" Agrippa, namely from somewhere/someone, and so in the present context, as elsewhere in Josephus where it is used of revelatory visions (such as *Ant.* 17.351 and *Life* 208), it may suggest divine involvement. See Spilsbury and Seeman 2017: 106, n. 999.

664 Reading ὄλβον, with most manuscripts. For this type of blessing, cf. 1.234. For a scene similar to this one, see 20.59.

665 It seems obvious that this scene and speech, including the reference to the bird above Agrippa's head and the request that Agrippa, upon release, attempt to help his fellow prisoners, is meant to recall the exchanges between Joseph and Pharaoh's officials in Genesis 40; note especially vv. 13–15, 17–19. The Joseph story is echoed elsewhere too in Josephus's account of Agrippa: §237a (cf. Gen 41:14), 237b (Gen 41:42), and 19.321 (cf. Gen 40:20); cf. the note on "hostile to him" at §151. On such typology in Josephus, including at 20.20–21, see Daube 1980. Apart from Josephus's love for the biblical Joseph story in general, perhaps on the background of the shared name or because he believed that he too was saved just as providentially as Joseph (Gen 45:5–8//*War* 3.351, 354, 404, cf. *Life* 204, 208–209; *Ant.* 11.237, and Daube 1976), here there is also a special point: Agrippa, just like Joseph, was a Judean *Wunderkind* who, after various troubles including imprisonment in the imperial capital, eventually, with the help of divine providence, received from the king an extremely high position. But we may doubt that Josephus's non-Jewish readers would recognize the allusions. See the Introduction, at n. 37. They might, however, remember Josephus's own prophecy to Vespasian (*War* 3.399–408, recalled in Suetonius, *Vespasian* 5.6 and Cassius Dio 66.1 [*GLAJJ*, nos. 313, 429]) and the fact that the Flavian emperors rewarded him graciously (*Life* 413–429).

202a The German who predicted these things was then consigned by Agrippa to laughter as much as later he appeared to be deserving of wonder.

202b Antonia was quite upset by Agrippa's misfortune. But seeing that discussing his case with Tiberius would be most difficult and anyway would come to naught, **203** she instead obtained for him Macro's agreement,[666] that the soldiers who guarded him, as also the centurion who would be in charge of them and would be chained together[667] with him, would be moderate people; that he would be allowed to bathe daily; that freedmen and friends would have easy access to him; and that [he would easily enjoy] whatever other bodily comforts might be relevant. **204** His friend Silas and his freedmen Marsyas and Stoecheus visited him, bringing the foods he liked and taking care of everything. They also brought him clothes, which they pretended to sell, and when night came they laid them out for him[668] with the cooperation of the soldiers, who had so been instructed in advance by Macro.[669] This went on for six months.[670] That, then, was Agrippa's situation.

Tiberius's Arrangements for His Succession

(6.8) 205 As for Tiberius:[671] upon returning to Capri he became ill. At first this was only moderately so, but as the illness got worse he had bad premonitions about himself and therefore ordered Euodus, who was the most valued[672] of his freedmen,[673] to bring the children to him, for he desired to converse with them before he died.[674] **206** He no longer had any sons of his own,[675] for Drusus, the only one he had had, was already dead. There survived the latter's son, Tiberius, nicknamed Gemellus,[676] and Gaius, who was the son of Germanicus (the

---

666 This translation is an attempt to follow Niese's suggestion (1890a: 177), approved by Destinon 1904: 28, that we read some noun, such as ἐκφρόντισιν, as the object of εὑρίσκετο ("found," "obtained"). The manuscripts read ἐν φρόντισιν, which is difficult to construe; cf. *CCFJ* 4.324, which offers two suggestions with question marks for this passage. But ἐκφρόντισιν too is not simple (which is probably why Niese hedges his conjecture with "vel sim." and does not adopt it in his editio minor), for although the verb ἐκφροντίζω appears at 18.290 and 19.171, there it means "think up," "devise," which hardly fit here, and the noun ἐκφρόντισις appears nowhere in Josephus and, indeed, there is no entry for it in LSJ.

667 Destinon (1904: 28–29), who assumed that the received text, συνδέτο ("chained together"), meant Agrippa was chained to a centurion who was a fellow prisoner, and considering that impossible, proposed to emend the text here into συνετοῦ ("intelligent," "clever"). That is, Antonia arranged for a supervisor who was smart enough to look the other way and allow Agrippa the special treatment reported in the next lines. It appears, however, that the other evidence for chaining a prisoner to a guard (see the note on "was chained" at §196) eliminates the difficulty.

668 I.e., as bedding. For the same procedure and phrasing, cf. 9.111//2 Kings 9:13.

669 As Mommsen (1899: 303, n. 6) documents, such private arrangements were not rare.

670 Apparently the last six months of Tiberius's life; he died on 16 March 37.

671 Τιβέριος δ'—cf. the note on "Agrippa" at §195. In this case, it is likely that the turn to another character reflects a shift of sources as well; see the notes on "Gemellus" at §206 and on "Euodos" at §211.

672 Cf. the note on "most trusted" at §182.

673 Perhaps to be identified with the freedman of the same name mentioned by Tacitus (*Ann.* 11.37) in the days of Claudius.

674 On Tiberius's attempt to arrange for his succession, see Barrett 2019: 51–53.

675 Here, as the continuation shows, the use of παῖδες γνήσιοι is meant to contrast the deceased Drusus (above, §146) with the two grandchildren—the former natural (unless one believed—as Suetonius [*Tiberius*, 62.3] states Tiberius did—rumors that he was the product of an adulterous affair of his mother, Livilla), the latter adopted. For other nuances of γνήσιος, see the note on "legitimate" at §40 and on "full sister" at 19.204. Already in 35, Tiberius had appointed them both as his heirs (Suetonius, *Tiberius* 76), thus postponing the decision that now had to be made.

676 The fact that he is fully identified here, although referred to a few times in the preceding narrative, which focused on Agrippa (see §§166, 187–188), suggests that the present detailed story about Tiberius's attempt to arrange for his own heir, which is quite detailed but makes no reference to Agrippa or Jews, is from a different source.

son of his brother),[677] who was already a young man;[678] he had gone through a demanding education, and enjoyed great goodwill of the populace thanks to the virtue of his father, Germanicus. 207 For he[679] had achieved great respect among the masses because, by virtue of the propriety of his bearing and the courtesy with which he dealt with people, he was never overbearing;[680] [rather], he acquired respect by wishing to be evenhanded to all. 208 For that reason not only the populace and the Senate thought very highly of him, but also every one of the subject nations—some of whom had met him and were taken by the charm of his social intercourse, while others drew their conclusions from the reports of those who had met him. 209 When he died,[681] the grief for him displayed by everyone was not feigned suffering that was really flattery of the government,[682] but, rather, the authentic grief of people who all considered that his death touched them—so unoverbearing[683] were his dealings with people. 210 As a result, he left to his son too a great advantage with all people; among others, especially the army was aroused on his behalf and reckoned it a virtue even to die, if need be, so as to make him the ruler.[684]

(6.9) 211 After Tiberius ordered Euodos[685] to bring him the children the next day around dawn, he prayed to the ancestral gods to give him some clear[686] sign as to who would inherit the empire. He had a strong tendency to leave it to his son's son,[687] but more than his own opinion and decision he trusted God[688] to make a revelation concerning them. 212 He

---

677 Germanicus was "the son of Tiberius's brother," Drusus the Elder. By taking the quoted words to be a parenthetical identification of Germanicus, rather than applying to Gaius, we may avoid the need, felt by Feldman (1965: 128, n. 1), to emend "son" (given by all the manuscripts) into "grandson."

678 Gaius, born in 12 CE, was around 25 when Tiberius died. For such usage of νεανίας, compare 20.144, where Josephus refers to Drusilla's son Agrippa as a νεανίας at the time of his death in 79 CE. Since Agrippa was the fruit of Drusilla's marriage to Felix (20.141), which came after her first marriage to Azizus no earlier than 53 CE (20.139), this Agrippa will have been in his mid-twenties in 79 CE. For νεανίας of men at the seventh of eight stages of life between infancy and being a "full adult" (τέλειος ἀνήρ), see Philo (Cherubim 114). Danker (2000: 667, s.v.), citing additional sources and discussions, assigns it generally to men between about 24 and 40.

679 Germanicus, as is made clear by the opening of §209.

680 "This is only the second attestation of the adjective ἀνεπαχθής, after Philo's lone example (Ebr. 215). Josephus will use the cognate adverb at 18.209, just below, and the adjective again at 19.218, of Claudius. It is part of the distinctive lexicon of this part of Antiquities. Since the adverb occurs once in Thucydides (2.37.3), and only there before Josephus except in ps-Dionysius (Ars rhet. 5.6), Thucydides is the likely inspiration" (Steve Mason).

681 In October of 19; see above, §§53–54.

682 On the expressions of grief over the death of Germanicus, see the note on "elsewhere" at §54.

683 As at §207. Cf. 19.218, about Germanicus's brother, Claudius.

684 On the young Gaius's popularity with the soldiers, see Suetonius, Cal. 9. Compare Ant. 19.217, where the soldiers termed Claudius "Germanicus" and thereby explained why he should rule.

685 Here, after the intervening explanatory digression, Josephus reverts to the story he began at §205.

686 This is the only occurrence of πρόφαντος in Josephus, but the same notion is picked up by ἀποφανού-μενον at the end of this paragraph.

687 I.e., to Gemellus. In fact, however, the sources are not at all unanimous as to which heir Tiberius preferred, and it may be that he had no clear preference. See the note on "before he died" at §205.

688 As at §212, I have translated Josephus's reference to ὁ θεός, especially in light of the power Josephus attributes to him, the way a Jew would refer to him. Josephus's easy passage here from "gods" (a few lines earlier) to "God" is noteworthy. True, polytheistic authors were entirely capable of referring to ὁ θεός in the singular, apparently in a collective sense; see Nilsson 1958 (a reference kindly supplied by Anthony Ellis). Similarly, there is nothing surprising about Josephus, although Jewish, referring to Tiberius's ancient gods, in the plural,

therefore arranged for an omen,[689] according to which the empire would go to the one who first came to him on the morrow. Having thus made up his mind, he sent to the tutor of his grandson and ordered him to bring the boy to him at the first hour, assuming that God would take no notice of this stratagem. But he [in fact] vetoed his decision. **213** Namely, when, with such things in mind, as soon as it was day he ordered Euodos to summon in the boy who came first, he went out and found Gaius in front of the bed-chamber. Since Tiberius was not there, for his breakfast was still unfinished, and Euodos did not at all know what his master wanted,[690] he said: "Your father[691] calls you," and showed him in. **214** When Tiberius saw Gaius, then for the first time he realized the power of the deity,[692] while as for his own hegemony—he saw himself entirely divested of the ability to see to what he had decided, for power from there[693] had not been given to him. He bewailed greatly his lot, that he had been deprived of the power to give effect to his own prior decision, **215** and that his grandson, Tiberius, would both fail to receive the rule of Rome and also be in need of salvation; for his salvation would depend upon others, stronger than him, and they would consider it[694] to be intolerable to associate with him, while his kinsmen would not be able to help him, on account of the fear and hatred towards him on the part of him who ruled them—whether because he was next in line for the throne or because he would never cease to counterplot [against Gaius],[695] both to save himself and to lay claim to the throne.[696]

---

as already at §186 and at §§219–221; for similar practice, cf. §§198–199 along with numerous cases in the Parthian history that concludes Book 18 (§§328, 334, 344, 348, 361) and the long Roman story in Book 19 (§§167, 169, 175, 182, 219, 233). But the passage from plural to singular here is jarring and, presumably reflects Josephus's monotheistic belief about the realities of divine power, as opposed to Tiberius's belief.

689 In accordance with his general tendency; see §§216–217. This is the only appearance of οἰώνισμα in Josephus, just as οἰώνισις at §218.

690 The implication is that, had he known, Euodos would have found a way to keep Gaius out.

691 Tiberius was, of course, not Gaius's father; he was the brother of Gaius's paternal grandfather, Drusus the Elder. But a few years after Drusus's death in 9 BCE Tiberius adopted Drusus's son, Germanicus, who was Gaius's father, and that could perhaps justify the use of "father" here; on such general usage, to express endearment and respect, see OLD 1308, s.v. pater, §5. Here, Euodos's use of "father," which (whether or not he is thought to have intended it) implies succession, functions as part of the narrative's basic claim, namely, that Tiberius's appointment of Gaius to succeed him was the product of forces beyond his control.

692 This scene is very reminiscent of Ant. 13.322–323, where John Hyrcanus attempts to prevent the fulfillment of God's will that his son Alexander Janneus would become king, but God had his way.

693 I.e, from on high, from the deity.

694 Reading Bekker's (1856: 161) emendation, εἰση-γησαμένων, with Niese 1890b: 154; Naber 1893: 195; and Feldman 1965: 132. Niese 1890a: 179 retains, as usual, the manuscripts' reading, εἰσηγησαμένω—a dual form (?) that appears to be impossible to construe here. It is, however, not clear how to translate εἰσηγησαμένων. Thackeray (ThLJ 223, s.v.εἰσηγεῖσθαι), who too follows Bekker here, and whom I have followed faute de mieux, suggests "consider" for the present passage, in line with the usual collocation of ἡγέομαι with ἀνεκτόν, as at §§150, 348; but he qualified his suggestion with a question mark in recognition of the fact that, as he shows, the usual meaning of the compound verb is rather "introduce," "propose" (so, for example, at §§12, 332). CCFJ 2.42 goes one further, offering only a question mark for our passage.

695 This compound verb, ἀντεπιβουλέω, appears elsewhere in Josephus only once (War 4.59), just as Josephus employs (creates?) many such compounds with ἀντε- and uses them once or twice each; CCFJ 1.138–139. This formulation assumes readers will think of Gaius as plotting against Tiberius.

696 That, already in 35, when he appointed them both heirs, Tiberius predicted that Gaius would kill Gemellus, is reported in a quotable anecdote preserved by both Tacitus (Ann. 6.46) and Cassius Dio 58.23; cf. the note on "his death" at §187. Indeed, the young Gemellus was murdered shortly into Gaius's reign; see §223. For "laying claim" (ἀντίληψις), see the note on "lay claim" at §4. Josephus's insight here, that it is likely that potential heirs will plot against a king (especially, but not only, if, as in

216 Tiberius indeed had a strong tendency to the interpretation of birthday-horoscopes,[697] and had derived from it information more correct than those who willingly devote their lives to it. Once [for example], when he saw Galba coming in towards him he told those who were his closest associates that the man who was coming would [someday] be the most honored in the Roman empire.[698] **217** Because [some] divinations came true, especially this man, of all rulers, believed that all were reliable, and he depended on them in running the state. **218** But now he was taking very badly the unfortunate way things had turned out, burdening himself as if his child's son's death had [already] occurred and reproaching himself[699] for having thought in advance to depend upon an omen. For although he could easily have died free from grief, in ignorance of that which would happen, now he must die while being worn away by the foreknowledge of the misfortune that would occur to those he most loved. **219** But although he was upset by the unexpected passage of the realm to those[700] whom he had not wanted, he did say to Gaius, however unwillingly and without desire:[701] "Child, although Tiberius is more closely related to me than you are,[702] it is by my own decision and with the gods' ratification of it that I convey the Roman empire to you and place it in your hands. **220** I request that, when you have become familiar with the empire, you forget neither my goodwill (for I appointed you to such a great dignity), **221** nor your family relationship with Tiberius.[703] Rather, in the knowledge that it was with the gods and in their wake that I provide you with such boons, requite my enthusiasm for them[704] and take care of Tiberius too, in view of the family relationship. Moreover, bear in mind that as long as Tiberius is alive he will be a bulwark protecting you[705]—both your rule and your safety—but if he dies it will be the prelude to misfortune.[706] **222** For those who are alone in such a peak status in a state are in a dangerous situation,[707] and things that are done contrary

---

this case, they could think their own claims to the throne more legitimate than that of the incumbent), and that it is therefore likely that they will be suspected of such plotting, so that, in consequence, even if they did not tend to plot it is likely that they would be forced to do so in order to protect themselves, is well illustrated by his account of Herod and his sons during the king's final decade.

697 On Tiberius's predilection for astrology, see Potter 1994: 158–160. "The noun γενεθλιαλογία occurs only here in Josephus and is found before him only in fragments of astrological writers. Rare cognates appear in Philo (2) and Strabo (1)" (Steve Mason).

698 Galba was indeed emperor for about seven months in 68/69 CE. This prediction is mentioned by other writers as well: Suetonius, *Galba* 4; Tacitus, *Ann.* 6.20.2; Cassius Dio 57.19.4.

699 Naber (1893: 176) and Feldman (1965: 134) read αὑτοῦ with rough breathing, which appears to be preferable.

700 The plural here is somewhat puzzling. Perhaps it reflects the assumption that whoever succeeds to the imperial throne will eventually be succeeded by his own son.

701 Same phrase: §362.

702 Niese's text (1890a: 189) has Tiberius telling Gaius that Tiberius Gemellus μοι συγγενεστέρου ἢ κατὰ σέ, but what is meant is not "although Tiberius (Gemellus) is more closely related to me than to you" but, rather, that "although Tiberius (Gemellus) is more closely related to me than you are." Hence Niese's conjectural reading of τοῦ instead of ἢ, adopted in his editio minor (1890b: 154). Tiberius Gemellus was Tiberius's grandson, the son of his son Drusus the Younger, while Gaius was Tiberius's grandnephew, the grandson of Tiberius's brother, Drusus the Elder.

703 I.e., with Tiberius Gemellus, Gaius's second cousin.

704 Apparently: the gods. Tiberius's point seems to be that since it was his own devotion to the gods that brought Gaius his good fortune, Gaius too should be devoted to the gods and behave properly, which includes abstaining from murdering his own cousin.

705 The same image reoccurs below, at §253.

706 Cf. *War* 2.454—προοίμιον ἁλώσεως. These are the only two occurrences of προοίμιον in Josephus (here spelled: φροίμιον).

707 Here Josephus has Tiberius warn Gaius not only about the wickedness of murder but also about the

to justice, and by doing away with the law[708] that enjoins us to behave otherwise, are not left unpunished by the gods." **223** That is what Tiberius said, but his words did not convince Gaius, although he promised [to obey them]. Rather, when he was appointed to office he put Tiberius [Gemellus] to death in accordance with his [great-uncle's] predictions.[709] But he too died not long thereafter, after a conspiracy was formed against him.[710]

Death of Tiberius

(6.10) 224 Tiberius,[711] having appointed Gaius heir to the empire, survived a few more days and died, having ruled for three days, five months, and twenty-two years.[712] Gaius was the fourth emperor.[713] **225** The Romans were happy at the good news when they heard of Tiberius's death, but they did not have the boldness to trust it[714]—not out of lack of desire, for they would have paid much money to assure the truth of the report, but rather out of fear that if the report were untrue and they had prematurely risen and displayed their joy it could ruin them if they were denounced. **226** For this one man had inflicted upon well-born Romans[715] more terrible things than any other, for he was always wrathful toward everyone and unstoppably cruel when he acted, even if there was no sense to his reason for turning to hate [somebody]; all those whom he judged he naturally dealt with savagely, imposing the death penalty even for the most trivial [offences].[716] **227** So it was that although the report they heard concerning him brought pleasure to their ears, they were inhibited from

---

moral perils faced by those who rule alone. This hints at Josephus's more general preference for aristocracy rather than monarchy, which tends to tyranny; see Mason 2012: 140–152.

708 Commenting on the use of the singular here (τοῦ νόμου), which he takes to be an obvious ("offenbar") allusion to the *Jewish* law, Free (2017: 600) sees here a statement by Josephus that even the Roman emperor must obey the law of the God of the Jews ("Mehr noch als auf die römische Rechtsordnung verweist Tiberius an dieser Stelle auf göttliches Recht im Sinne jüdischer Vorstellung. Auch ein römischer Herrscher hat sich somit dem einen wahren Gott unterzuordnen"). That seems to be overdone, and not only because of the reference to "gods" in the plural in this and the preceding paragraph; the use of "the law" is not absolute here, for the continuation indicates which specific law Tiberius means. But it does seem that, as Free argues, more generally in *Antiquities* 18–19 Josephus contrasts Tiberius, who recognizes that he is subject to the gods, to Gaius, who sets himself up as a god. The present passage, which more or less echoes Josephus's own statements about the Jews, their God and his laws (*Ant.* 1.14, 20, 23, 72; 6.307; 7.93; 17.60; 18.127; 19.16), is part of that.

709 Summarized at §215; cf. the note on "to his death" at §187. Tiberius Gemellus was killed late in 37; see *Philo, Leg.* 23–31; Dio 59.8.2; Suetonius, *Caligula* 23.3; Barrett 2019: 109–110.

710 It is quite remarkable that Josephus does not promise, here, to recount that story, which he does at such

length in *Ant.* 19; contrast §307 and see the Introduction, at n. 11.

711 The Latin translator felt a need to explain here, as Niese (1890a: 189) records, that the preceding lines had gotten ahead of the story ("sed haec postea, tunc autem"). In fact, in this case it does not seem to be difficult for readers to realize that. The notice illustrates, however, the ancient reader's assumption that the story is normally told in strict chronological order—an assumption that, in other cases, creates confusion that is much worse.

712 Tiberius died on 16 March 37, according to Suetonius, *Tiberius* 73 and Tacitus, *Ann.* 6.50. In *War* 2.180 Josephus gives the same figure as here, differing only about the months (here five, there six, as is also the reading [VI] of the Latin here, according to Niese [1890a: 180]). That difference could be an error, or perhaps reflects a lack of clarity about what date should be considered the beginning of Tiberius's rule, see Mason 2008: 153, n. 1145.

713 Josephus likes to keep track of such things. See §33 and 20.148.

714 For similar difficulties, see §§231–232 and, after the death of Gaius, 19.132–133.

715 On Josephus's aristocratic tendency to depict the persecution of the well-born (εὐπατρίδες) as a hallmark of tyranny, see the note on "good birth" at 19.2.

716 It seems, however, that the accusation that Tiberius was guilty of massive abuse of *maiestas* proceedings, depending on informants in order to run roughshod over his enemies, is in large measure a matter of hostile historiography, the type that may be seen so luridly in

enjoying it as much as they would have liked by their extreme fear[717] of the troubles that
were to be expected if it turned out their hope was false.

228 But Marsyas, Agrippa's freedman, learning of Tiberius's death, pushed his way and ran
to inform Agrippa. Catching him on his way out to the bathhouse, he motioned to him and
said to him, in the Hebrews' language, "the lion is dead."[718] **229** Understanding his meaning
and overcome with joy about it, he responded: "May a multitude of my thanks come upon
you for everything you have done for me, and for these good tidings—if [only] what has been
reported is true!" **230** Seeing the enthusiasm with which Marsyas had come and the joy that
his words had brought Agrippa, the centurion who was responsible for guarding Agrippa[719]
inferred from the words that something new had happened and asked them about the matter at hand. **231** For a while they stalled him, but when he pressed them Agrippa, who in the
meantime had become his friend, explained without delay.[720] He shared in the pleasure at
the news, for it redounded to Agrippa's benefit, and supplied him with dinner. While they
were feasting and their drinking was moving along, someone came and said that Tiberius
was alive and within a few days would return to the city. **232** The centurion was terribly
upset at the news, for death was the punishment for what he had done: he had joyfully eaten
together with a prisoner, and that—at the news of the death of the emperor! Knocking
Agrippa off the couch he said: "Do you imagine you will escape my notice after lying about
the emperor's death, and not make good for it[721] with your own head?!" **233** Having said
that, he ordered that Agrippa be bound (for previously he had freed him from the bonds)
and posted a stricter guard than before. Agrippa spent that night in such difficult circumstances. **234** But the next day word filled the city, confidently, that Tiberius had died, and
people took courage and already openly spread the report;[722] some even offered sacrifices;
and letters arrived from Gaius: one to the Senate, informing it of Tiberius's death and that
he himself had succeeded to the empire, **235** and the other to Piso, the guardian of the
city,[723] including that statement and also ordering to transfer Agrippa from the military
camp to the house in which he had stayed prior to his imprisonment. From then on Agrippa
could carry on his household activities[724] with confidence. True, there was a guard, but the
supervision of his daily activities was loosened up.

236 After Gaius came to Rome, bringing Tiberius's body, and held a sumptuous funeral
for him in accordance with the ancestral laws,[725] he was eager to release Agrippa on that

*Gaius Succeeds
to the Throne,
Elevates Agrippa*

Suetonius. For a more balanced picture, see Levick 1999:
182–200, Rutledge 2001: 89–103, and Yakobson 2003. For
Josephus's contrast between trivial offences and those
that deserve the death penalty, cf. 13.294 and 20.215.
Note, however, that at *Apion* 2.215 Josephus, in his effort
to make Jewish law appear to be very strict and uncom-
promising (i.e., so Roman, in contrast to wishy-washy
Greeks), insists that most violations of Jewish law entail
the death penalty.

717 For Josephus's use of δεῖμα (also in *Ant.* 19.49 and
20.78), see *ThLJ* 122, s.v.

718 How this was meant to refer to the emperor is
not clear. Lewy (1920–1945: 156) and Lembi (2001: 64)
suggested that the point is the similarity of the Hebrew
'aryeh to the latter half of "Tiberius." That is possible, but
it might suffice to note the natural comparison between
the lion, as "king of beasts," and the emperor—although

it is difficult to find evidence for that title prior to the
second century; see Aelian, *Nature of Animals* 5.39, the
opening line of the first chapter of the *Physiologus*, and
b. *Ḥagigah* 13b.

719 That is, he had overall responsibility; see §233 on
the guards he posted.

720 Same phrase as at §3.

721 For such usage of ἀναμάσσω (which reappears in
Josephus only at 16.26), *ThLJ* 39, s.v. refers to Homer, *Od.*
19.92: "that thy blood not be on thy head for this."

722 Interestingly, θροέω appears in Josephus only here
and at 19.137—where too the context is one of fearful
uncertainty as to whether the emperor was really dead.

723 See the note on "guardian of the city" at §169.

724 I take αὐτῆς to refer to his house.

725 On the funeral, see Levick 1999: 219–220. True,
as Charlesworth notes (1933: 107–108), Dio (59.3) makes

very same day. But Antonia held him back from that—not out of any antipathy toward the prisoner but, rather, out of consideration for Gaius's propriety, lest he engender, by immediately releasing a man who had been imprisoned by Tiberius, the impression that he received Tiberius's death with pleasure.[726] 237 But after not many days he sent for him to come to his house, had his hair cut and changed his clothes,[727] and then placed a crown upon his head and installed him as king of Philip's tetrarchy,[728] giving him also Lysanias's tetrarchy[729] as an additional gift. He also exchanged his iron chain for a gold one[730] of the same weight. As the cavalry commander[731] of Judea he sent out Marullus.[732]

Enter Woman, Enter Trouble, I: The Fall of Herod Antipas

(6.11)[733] 238 In the second year of the reign of Gaius Caesar,[734] Agrippa requested permission to set sail so as to organize his rule, then to return after arranging whatever had to be

---

it seem as if Gaius showed little respect for the dead Tiberius, bringing his body to Rome at night and laying it out at daybreak, but that is only part of his usual calumny of Gaius. In fact, epigraphic evidence shows that five days elapsed between the arrival of Tiberius's body on 29 March and his state funeral on 3 April; Suetonius (*Caligula* 15) says Gaius buried Tiberius in grand style and with much weeping; and there is epigraphic evidence that Gaius sacrificed in Tiberius's memory (Arval *Acta* for 25 May 38; ed. Henzen, xliv). Thus, whatever Gaius thought privately, in public he showed Tiberius due respect—as Josephus too indicates.

726 Both Dio (59.3) and Suetonius (*Caligula* 15.2; 23.2; 29.1) report that, after first honoring Antonia, Gaius then turned to humiliating her and drove her to suicide—which came already on 1 May 37, not much more than a month after Gaius rose to the throne. Thus, if indeed Gaius originally treated his grandmother with favor, that lasted, as Kokkinos (1992: 27–28) notes, only a few weeks.

727 Although such attention to hygiene and appearance was certainly in order when visiting the emperor, Josephus's need to report these details seems obviously meant to compare Agrippa to Joseph, upon his release from prison and first audience with Pharaoh; see Gen 41:14. As in other such cases, however, presumably non-Jewish readers would miss the point. See the note on "in common" at §201.

728 Which had been awaiting a permanent solution since 34 CE; see above, §108.

729 Abila, on which see *HJP* 1.567–569 and Boffo 1994: 172–174. Note also the more detailed wording at 19.275: "Lysanias's Abila." But it may well be that Josephus was wrong to include Abila here (just as indeed it is not mentioned in the parallel at *War* 2.181); see the note on "had given him" at 19.274.

730 This too is reminiscent of Joseph—Gen 41:42. So too Daniel (Dan 5:16//*Ant.* 10.240) and Mordechai (*Ant.*

11.254); this is part of the Jew-makes-good-in-a-foreign-court complex. See Meinhold 1976 and Wills 1990.

731 Some would emend ἱππάρχην, although supplied unanimously by the manuscripts and seconded by the Latin "magistrum equitum," into a term that more clearly denotes a governor (ἔπαρχον or ὕπαρχον, i.e. prefect or subordinate commander; see Niese 1890a: 183), on the assumptions that Gaius would not be involved in the appointment of a mere commander of cavalry and that Judea needed a governor. So too H. Mason (*GTRI* 56, s.v. ἱππάρχης) brands the reading here (as at 19.279, 299) a "falsa lectio." (Indeed, of the ten occurrences of ὕπαρχον listed in *CCFJ* 4.237, six are alternate readings for ἱππάρχης.) It seems, however, that after Pontius Pilate's stormy regime in Judea no new governor was appointed in his stead, and that the Roman governor of Syria administered affairs in Judea with the help of secondary officials—such as this commander of cavalry and the "tax-collector of Judea" mentioned by Philo at *Leg.* 199. See D. R. Schwartz 2013: 47–50. Given the absence of reference to commanders of infantry and other forces, however, it is likely that this "cavalry commander" enjoyed broader authority, just as, at 19.299, Silas is said, by most witnesses, to have been the ἱππάρχος of the entire army; see the note there, on "cavalry commander."

732 Marullus is never heard of again; cf. the note on "administrator" at §89.

733 For the heading, cf. §340. Traditionally the next two paragraphs (§§238–239) are the end of ch. 6 and a new chapter begins with §240. However, as Lewy (1920–1945: 157) noted, in fact we have here a triad of the type mentioned in the note on "the largest part" at §145: some reacted this way, some that way, but the reaction that interests us in particular is the third, Herodias's jealousy.

734 I.e., in the spring or summer of 38 CE. According to Philo's *Flacc.* 26, Agrippa sailed from Italy when the summer winds began.

done.[735] **239** When the emperor agreed, he went, and seeing him as a king surprised all men, proving to those who saw him—when they considered his earlier straits and his present happiness—the great power of Fortune over men. Some pronounced him blessed, for he had not failed to achieve his hopes, while others were in a state of disbelief about what had happened.

(7.1) 240 But[736] Agrippa's sister Herodias, who was cohabiting with[737] Herod, who was the tetrarch of Galilee and Perea,[738] was jealous[739] of her brother's authority, seeing that he had achieved a dignity much higher than that of her man, since although he had once left as a fugitive unable to settle his debts, now he had come back in high status and prosperity! **241** Aggrieved, and only with difficulty bearing such a turnabout of his lot, especially whenever she saw him going about before the masses in the customary honorific appurtenances of royalty, she was unable to restrain herself and hide her envy-driven distress; rather, she attempted to rouse her husband, demanding that he set sail for Rome and petition[740] for equal honors. **242** For [she said], life would not be tolerable if while Agrippa, who was the son of Aristobulus, who had been condemned to die by his father, and who had lived in such poverty and want that he had been totally dependent upon relief[741] for his daily necessities, and who had set sail in flight from his creditors, had returned as a king, he,[742] who was the son of a king, and who was summoned by the royal pedigree he shared to claim equal status, should settle for happily living out his life as a commoner.[743]

---

735 The specific references to the emperor's permission and to sailing by ship suggest that Josephus is aware of Philo's *In Flaccum*, which carefully tells the story of Agrippa's sea voyage to Judea in a way calculated to show that it was not Agrippa who was responsible for the violence that was occasioned by his visit to Alexandria. Philo emphasizes (§§25–28) that Agrippa went via Alexandria (once the favorable summer winds began) only because the emperor recommended that, and that Agrippa took care for his ship to remain out of the harbor until after nightfall, so as to ensure that the Alexandrians would not be aware of his visit—but Philo's story is patently unbelievable, if only because he is so emphatic about Agrippa's measures that he leaves us with no explanation of how his visit became known, much less how it elicited complaints and parodies concerning his flashy and pompous parading around the city (*Flacc.* 30, 39). See D. R. Schwartz 1989/90: 113–117. Josephus goes even further: he simply ignores Agrippa's role in the episode. On this issue, see esp. Sanders 2016.

736 This heavy translation of δέ seems to be warranted here, as it moves us from the two general outlying options (some unnamed people believed and were happy, some disbelieved) to the specific middle one upon which Josephus desires to focus: Herodias believed but was unhappy. Cf. the notes on "the largest part" at §145 and on "especially Rome" at 19.2.

737 Josephus's formulation, συνοικοῦσα, apparently expresses his denial of the legitimacy of their marriage; so too above, §§110 and 136.

738 Perea was the Jewish region of Transjordan, roughly between the Dead Sea and the Sea of Galilee, described at *War* 3.46–47 (between Machaerus and Pella, with Philadelphia's hinterland as its eastern border). On the extent of Antipas's territories, see Hoehner 1972: 43–51, 277–290.

739 For Josephus, jealousy of one's success, whether on the part of one's enemies or some general impersonal fate, is frequently that which moves things along; see e.g., *War* 1.208, *Life* 84–85, and *Ant.* 13.288, along with Shatzman 2002, who assembles more evidence for the motif in ancient literature. In the present instance, Josephus emphasizes it by mentioning it again at the conclusion of this episode (§255). Note also §340. Contrast the note on "envy" at 20.75.

740 Usually, μνηστεία and μνηστεύω are used of a man's "wooing" or betrothing a woman (e.g. 1.242, 245, 255; 4.246, 298; 17.15; *Apion* 2.200), so there is something abrasive, and therefore comical, about a woman urging her husband to do it vis-a-vis someone else. This contributes to Josephus's portrayal of her plan as misguided, even "frivolous" (§255).

741 Namely, upon them; see §§149–150. For ἐπικουρίζω in connection with tax relief, see 17.204 and 19.25.

742 I.e., Antipas.

743 At this point Josephus moves from indirect speech to the speech itself. This is not rare; at JLCL 3.32, n. 1, on *War* 4.102, Thackeray notes that "speeches tend to drift into *oratio recta* at the close." See, for example, §§263–264, §279, 294–295; 13.400–404; 19.40–41, 45.

243 For, Herod, even if previously you were not bothered by the fact that your status was lower than that of your father, who sired you, at least[744] now you should aspire to the dignity of your family. Do not tolerate being outdone and passed by the honor [given to] a man who once courted your money! Do not proclaim [by your inaction] that his poverty can demonstrate nobility better than our prosperity can![745] And never consider it non-disgraceful to take second seat to those who [only] yesterday, or the day before yesterday,[746] survived only thanks to your mercy! **244** No, let us go to Rome;[747] and let us spare no effort, nor expense of silver and gold. For it is not better to save them up for worthless things than to spend them in order to acquire a kingdom.

(7.2) 245 He resisted for a time; loving peace and quiet and leery of the Roman hustle-bustle, he tried to bring her about. But she—the more she saw him moving away [from her position], the more she exerted pressure, demanding that he not turn away from doing everything for a kingdom. **246** The end was that she did not give it up until she defeated him;[748] he shared her position, albeit unwillingly, since there was no other way to get away from her once she had made such decisions. Equipped as extravagantly as possible, sparing nothing, he went up to Rome,[749] taking Herodias with him.[750]

247 But Agrippa, learning of their intention and of their preparations, made preparations himself as well. After he heard that they had embarked,[751] he too sent someone to Rome—his freedman, Fortunatus, bringing gifts for the emperor and letters against Herod, things he himself would tell Gaius when the opportunity presented itself.[752] **248** He set out by ship after Herod's party and sailed very deftly, so close behind Herod that as the one was meeting Gaius, the other was landing and presenting his letters.[753] Both had sailed as far as Dicearcheia and found Gaius in Baiae. **249** This too is a small city[754] in Campania, located around five furlongs from Dicearcheia,[755] where there are extravagantly furnished royal residences, for each of the emperors, seeking fame, attempted to outdo his predecessors.[756] The area also has hot baths, springing[757] by their own power up from the ground; they are good for curing those who use them and in other ways as well are conducive to luxurious life.[758]

---

744 For such usage of γοῦν, as also at §349 and 19.169, see *ThLJ* 117, s.v.

745 Here is a good expression of the aristocratic assumption that wealthy people deserve their wealth since it points to their ἀρετή ("nobility" or "virtue"); cf. *Apion* 1.30. On Josephus's use of ἀρετή, see the note on "virtuous power" at §266.

746 For this collocation, (ἐ)χθὲς καὶ πρῴην, see also 2.348 and *Apion* 1.7; 2.14, 154.

747 This round phrasing says it all; to "go to Rome" is to try "to make it big." Cf. Acts 28:15.

748 Josephus is happy to make the nagging wife responsible for her husband's decision against his better judgment; cf. the note on "demands" at §42.

749 For this common phrasing, which betrays a Roman point of view, which may or may not have source-critical implications, compare 17.345; 18.51, 115, 126; 20.131, 134, 161, 182, also D. R. Schwartz 2017.

750 The last words sound ironic, as if now, having pushed him around until she got what she wanted, she played the role of the dutiful wife accompanying her husband.

751 So they would not hear of his own move.

752 For such usage of ἡ καιρός, see also §313, 17.51 and 19.99.

753 Although plain κατάγω is frequent in Josephus, this is the only occurrence of ἐπικατάγω. For the nuance, which emphasizes the competition between the two missions to the emperor, see Thucydides 3.49.4.

754 This is the only occurrence of πολύδριον in Josephus.

755 Josephus's furlong (stade) was roughly 200 meters; see the note on "away" at §60. The real distance by land is, in fact 5–6 km., so the present datum, approximately a kilometer, is "grossly underestimated" (Barrett 2019: 243). Since 18.179 and 19.6 show that Josephus was fairly familiar with distances in Italy, perhaps the text has been corrupted in transmission.

756 The remains of their efforts are now submerged under water; see Maione 2016.

757 Reading ἀνιόντα with MW and *ThLJ* 49, s.v. ἀνιέναι, rather than Niese's ἀνιέντα.

758 The town had the reputation of a center of vice and debauchery. See, for example, Sextus Propertius,

250 Gaius, at the time he was greeting Herod, who had gotten to him first, was going over Agrippa's letters, which were composed as an accusation of Herod, accusing him of complicity with Sejanus against Tiberius's rule[759] and now with Artabanus the Parthian against Gaius's rule.[760] 251 The proof[761] of this statement was the fact that Herod's armories contained equipment sufficient for 70,000 heavily-armed soldiers. Upset by what was reported, Gaius asked Herod if the statement about the arms was true. 252 When he said—for it was impossible to say otherwise, for that would contradict the truth[762]—that the weapons were indeed there, Gaius deemed the accusation of rebellion to be reliable. Taking the tetrarchy away from Herod, he added it to Agrippa's kingdom, giving also his property to Agrippa; as for [Herod] himself, Gaius punished him with exile in perpetuity, designating as his residence Lugdunum, a city in Gaul.[763] 253 Learning that Herodias was Agrippa's sister,[764] he said he would give her whatever of the property was her own and that she should consider[765] her brother the bulwark[766] who saved her from sharing her husband's suffering. 254 She, however, said: "Although you, O emperor, say these things magnanimously and in accordance with your dignity, I am prevented from enjoying your gracious gift by my loyalty[767] to my husband. Since I have shared happiness with him, it is not right that I should abandon him when he is down on his luck." 255 He, angered by her high spirit,[768] exiled her together with Herod and gave her possessions to Agrippa. This then, was the judgment with

---

Elegies 1.11 ("corruptas Baias") and esp. Seneca, *Moral Letters to Lucilius* 51 ("On Baiae and Morals").

759 See the note on "Sejanus" at §181.

760 For Gaius's generally good relations with Artabanus II, see Wilkinson 2005: 31–34. Hoehner (1972: 362–262) accepts the possibility that Antipas was in some alliance with Artabanus, but perhaps we should prefer to imagine that the accusation reflected no more than Agrippa's—or a vengeful Vitellius's (see §105)—extrapolation of a halfway credible accusation from Antipas's pushy intervention in Roman-Parthian relations a few years earlier (§§102–105).

761 See the note on "to prove" at §174.

762 Presumably Josephus means that while Antipas would have lied had it at all been possible, in this case the evidence was too clearcut.

763 But according to *War* 2.183 he was exiled to Spain. One can either compromise by concluding that he was exiled to Lugdunum Covenarum, which was in Gaul but on the Spanish border, and supposing that Josephus was either trying to reflect that or perhaps confused about the detail; or, given the fact that that Lugdunum was relatively obscure and plain "Lugdunum" normally referred to the much larger one, namely Lyon (capital of Gallia Lugdunensis), simply reject the datum in *War* and perhaps infer that Josephus is here correcting a mistake of which he became aware sometime after writing the latter.

For the second option see Braund 1983: 241–242, followed by Lembi 2001: 65. For a survey of the issue, see Mason 2008: 156, n. 1165.

764 Having grown up so closely with Agrippa, it is unlikely that he first learned this now. But it is possible that it was only now that he learned that she was Antipas's wife. In any case, the story is better this way.

765 Reading Niese's conjecture, νομίσαι (Niese 1890b: 160), adopted by Feldman (1965: 150) too. The manuscripts, and so Niese 1890a: 185, have νομίσας, which can hardly be construed.

766 Same image as §221.

767 On this sense of εὔνοια, cf. the note on "to Gaius" at §124.

768 This is quite striking: after Herodias opened her speech at §254 by praising the emperor for acting μεγαλοφρόνως, and at §256 Josephus himself will praise Gaius for acting that way, here Gaius condemns Herodias for doing the same. As at §362, the difference is, of course, that what is appropriate for a man, and especially for a ruler, is not appropriate for a woman—for whom "thinking big" can be rebellious, thinking *too* big; cf. the note on "emboldened" at 20.176. On magnanimity as an appropriate characteristic for rulers, see also the notes on "valor" at §326 and "wrath" at 19.334 and Arnhart 1983. On Josephus's usage see, in general, D. R. Schwartz 2025.

which God punished Herodias for her envy[769] of her brother, and Herod for having listened to frivolous[770] womanly words.[771]

256 As for Gaius:[772] he managed affairs in the first and second year very magnanimously[773] and, by practicing moderation,[774] he fostered the affection of the Romans themselves and of their subjects toward him. But as time went by, the magnitude of his rule led him to stop thinking of himself as a human being and, making a god of himself, he presumed to conduct all affairs of state without respect for the divine.[775]

(8.1) 257 Thus, for example,[776] when there was civil strife in Alexandria between Jews and Greeks residing there, three delegates chosen by each side in the strife came to Gaius. Among the Alexandrian delegates one was Apion,[777] who terribly badmouthed the Jews, among other things claiming that they ignore the honors due to Caesar. **258** Thus [he argued], of the subjects of Roman rule all had altars and temples for Gaius, receiving him in all ways as they receive the gods; only these people consider it unrespectable to honor him with statues and to take oaths by his name.[778] **259** After Apion spoke at length and harshly, hoping to arouse Gaius [against the Jews], as was indeed likely, Philo—the head of

---

769 Here Josephus rounds out this narrative by repeating the leitmotif used at its outset (§240). The theme is basically the same in the shorter parallel at *War* 2.181–183, but that makes no reference to God. This is typical of the contrast between *War* and *Antiquities*. See D. R. Schwartz 2014: 56–57.

770 This reference to women as characterized by κουφολογία (as already at 17.121), coming right after the condemnation of Herodias as having been too pushy, is reminiscent of 4.219, where Josephus points to the "frivolous" and overly "bold" (διὰ κουφότητα καὶ θράσος) nature of women as explaining why they are not allowed to give testimony in legal processes. Cf. 18.21 and the note on "contemptible women" at 19.129.

771 This formulation is similar to that at *Ant.* 1.49, where Josephus explains that God punished Adam for listening to Eve's γυναικείας συμβουλίας. At this point Antipas drops out of history, all the more so insofar as, it seems, he left no sons (Kokkinos 1998: 232).

772 On this episode, which opens here and ends at §309, see Bilde 1978; Smallwood 1987: 120–125; D. R. Schwartz 1990a: 77–89; Bernett 2007: 277–287; Gruen 2016; and—on a rabbinic echo of it (*Megillat Ta'anit* for 22 Shevat and its scholion [Noam 2003: 112–114])—V. Noam in Ilan and Noam 2017: 453–492.

773 See the note on "high spirit" at §255.

774 As did Philip (§106), but he was a do-nothing, not a "big thinker"; see the note there on "inactive style."

775 For the widespread notion that Gaius started off well but eventually, whether because of a disease or because power simply went to his head, took a severe turn for the worse, see also Philo, *Leg.* 8–14, 22, 67; Suetonius,

Cal. 22; Cassius Dio 59.8.1; Sidwell 2010; and Barrett 2019: 312–313. Contrast 19.201.

776 For καὶ δή introducing something that illustrates the preceding statement or what it implies, corresponding to "for example" or "indeed," see also 19.332 and 20.16, 81, 257; for the nuances in classical usage, cf. Denniston 1954: 248–253. These words, which make all of Gaius's actions derive from his self-deification, correspond to Josephus's omission of all reference both to Agrippa's visit to Alexandria, which (according to Philo, *Flacc.* 26ff.) touched off the violence reported by Josephus at §§257–260, and to the Jewish provocation in Jamneia, which (according to Philo, *Leg.* 199–203) touched off Gaius's attempt to erect his statue in the Temple, of which we shall read in detail. See D. R. Schwartz 2012a and Sanders 2016. On Gaius's self-deification, see the note on "mortal" at 19.4.

777 Josephus introduces Apion without τις ("a certain Apion") or the like, as if he assumes his readers know the name. On Apion, who was a prominent Alexandrian scholar, rhetor, and politician in the first half of the first century, one whose ability to make noise already brought Tiberius (according to Pliny, *NH*, preface §25) to call him *cymbalum mundi* and who achieved some notoriety teaching in Rome after this delegation, see Stern, *GLAJJ* 1.389–90 and Barclay 2007: 170–171, n. 7.

778 On the imperial cult in the eastern provinces in the days of Gaius, see Barrett 2019: 192–194; Gruen 2016: 404. Concerning the West, however, Fishwick (1978: 1215) roundly states that "no trace is discernible in the West of the absolutist tendencies of Gaius reported by the literary authorities," and, accordingly, his emperor-by-emperor

the Jewish delegation,[779] a man of high repute from every point of view who was the brother of Alexander the Alabarch[780] and not at all unfamiliar[781] with philosophy[782]—was about to[783] respond to the accusations. 260 But Gaius shut him out, demanding that he be gone; he was very angry,[784] and it was obvious that he was going to do something terrible to them. Philo left, having thus been treated outrageously, and told the Jews who were with him that they should bolster their spirits, for although nominally[785] Gaius was wrathful at them, in fact it was God that he was leading on against himself.[786]

(8.2) 261 Gaius, taking it very badly that the Jews alone so ignored him, sent out Petronius as the legate[787] of Syria to replace Vitellius as ruler [there],[788] ordering him to invade Judea with a large force;[789] if they accepted [Rome's demands] willingly, he should set up a statue

---

survey has no chapter on Gaius. There is, in any case, no need to suppose that Apion's generalization was based on research rather than antagonism. Nor, for that matter, is there much room for confidence that Josephus's report—perhaps ultimately from Philo?—accurately preserves Apion's argument.

779 For Philo's role as a Jewish community leader, see esp. Goodenough 1926 and Birnbaum 2004.

780 On Alexander, see the note on "Alabarch" at §159.

781 On such a double negative, see the note on "not at all devoid" at §65.

782 For "not unfamiliar (φιλοσοφίας ... οὐκ ἄπειρος) with philosophy," cf. Life 40, where Josephus writes that Justus was "not unfamiliar (οὐδ' ἄπειρος) with Greek culture," which is, in the context there that condemns Justus, an extremely backhanded compliment. However, Josephus's focus concerning Justus was on rhetorical virtuosity as opposed to truth; cf. the notes on "philosophy" at §9 and on "desire it" at 20.264. Concerning Philo, however, the present comment sounds wholly positive. On the question, whether Josephus was familiar with any of his writings, see esp. Barclay 2007: 353–361, along with the note on "four thousand" at 18.20.

783 This translation of οἷός τε ἦν fits the context. Feldman (1965: 154) translates similarly, "was prepared to," but, perhaps in deference to the distinction suggested by LSJ (1209, s.v. οἷος, §§III.1b vs. III.2) between οἷος ἦν ("intended ... was on the point of doing") and οἷός τε ἦν ("was fit or able to do"), omits τε; correspondingly, Mathieu and Herrmann (1929: 177) and Schalit (1963: 305) have Philo being "capable" of responding. However,

the opening of §260 assumes that Philo was not only capable of responding but also that he was about to do so, and Josephus's usage of οἷός τε ἦν at 14.105 and at Life 401 shows that such a distinction with regard to τε need not be assumed: in the former Crassus was about to strip all of the Temple's gold, were it not for the intervention of a Jewish priest, and in the latter Sulla was about to pursue Josephus's troops when Josephus sprang an ambush on him.

784 This is the only occurrence of περιοργής in Josephus. For Philo's account of his disastrous meeting with Gaius, see Leg. 349–367.

785 For this type of distinction, cf. the note on "private gain" at §7.

786 For a similar formulation, see 20.108.

787 For this usage of πρεσβευτής, see GTRI 153. On Publius Petronius, governor of Syria 39–42 CE, see HJP and Dąbrowa 1998: 42–43. Not much is known about him apart from his dealings with the Judeans, which are described at great length by Josephus (here, at 19.301–311 and War 2.184–203) and Philo, Leg. 207–260.

788 For a detailed account of Gaius's recall of Vitellius, see Cassius Dio 59.27.

789 For such usage of χείρ, see also 10.85 12.398; 17.156, 20.91. The fact that the coming story makes no mention of any Roman governor of Judea reinforces the conclusion that neither Marcellus (18.89) nor Marullus (18.237) served in that position. Rather, they were secondary Roman officials during the reign of Gaius, who preferred to allow the governor of Syria direct authority in Judea. See D. R. Schwartz 1990a: 62–66. Cf. the note on "Syria" at §2.

of him[790] in the sanctuary of God,[791] but if they acted out of folly,[792] he should do the same after overpowering them in war. **262** And so Petronius, upon taking over in Syria, hastened to fulfill Caesar's orders.[793] Having assembled as many auxiliary troops as he could, and taking two legions[794] of the Roman[795] army, he came to Ptolemais, planning to winter there so that, when spring came, he would not have far to go to make war.[796] He wrote to Gaius and told him what he planned to do, and the latter praised his energy and enjoined him not to hold back at all but, rather, to prosecute the war vigorously if they were not obedient.

263 But many myriads of Jews appeared before Petronius in Ptolemais, beseeching him not to force them into law-violation and transgression of their ancestral practice.[797] **264** "If," [they said], "you in any case are obligated to bring the statue and erect it, do what has been decided upon only after first doing away with us. For we cannot stand by and watch things [happen] that are forbidden to us[798] by the dignity of our lawgiver and our forefathers, who

---

790 Although *War* 2.185 refers, instead, to "statues," as does one version of the scholion to *Megillat Ta'anit* for 22 Shebat (Noam 2003: 283), Tacitus (*Hist.* 5.9.2) and Philo (*Leg.* 188) agree that one statue was planned, and so too the Mishnah (*Ta'anit* 4.6) refers to a single "image." According to Philo (*Leg.* 188, 346), it was to be named after Zeus: "Gaius, the New Zeus made manifest." On these varying formulations, see Stern, *GLAJJ* 2.51. For Gaius's self-equation with Zeus, see 19.4–5.

791 As here, so too the continuation of his story, at §§280 and 309, refers specifically to the ναός. For Josephus's use of this term for the *hekhal*, the inner sanctuary, as opposed to the Temple in general, see the note on "sanctuary" at 20.233. So too rabbinic versions of the present episode, beginning with *m. Ta'anit* 4:6, refer consistently to the *hekhal*; on those versions, see the note on "Gaius" at §256. Philo (*Leg.* 188, 306), ever the dramatist (D. R. Schwartz 1989/90), went one further, claiming that Gaius planned to have the statue erected in the innermost shrine, the "Holy of Holies."

792 On ἀγνωμοσύνη, see *ThLJ* 5, s.v. Here, as at 12.167 (where "arrogance" is suggested by Marcus at JLCL 7.83), the word expresses how the ruling power regards the obdurate refusal of subjects to accept its authority. So too, for example, 14.101.

793 Here and at §266 Niese has the text refer to ἐπι-στολαί, lit. "letters." Some would prefer ἐντολαί ("orders"; so the Epitome here [Niese 1887–1896: 320] and Naber at §266), but a letter from an emperor is obviously a command and such usage seems to be usual enough; see Schreckenberg 1977: 124. See, for example, 19.279, where Claudius "ordered" (ἐπιστέλλει) the prefect of Egypt to do something, and esp. 19.292 where he "ordered via writings" (διὰ γραμμάτων ἐπιστείλας); had ἐπιστέλλω meant "sent," "writings" would have been the object, not the means. Cf. the note on "orders" at §294.

794 Normally four were stationed in Syria in the first century; see Tacitus, *Ann.* 4.5; *HJP* 1.362, n. 42; Rey-Coquais 1978: 67. The statement here, that two legions were taken, conforms to Philo's statement (*Leg.* 207) that Petronius took "half the army of the Euphrates." *War* 2.186 states, instead, for whatever reason, that he took three legions; see Mason 2008: 158, n. 1185.

795 The need for the adjective here is to distinguish these legions from the auxiliary units. For a similar case, cf. 19.365. Otherwise (and even in some similar cases, such as 18.120), usually plain "legions" suffices for Josephus.

796 I.e., he would already be in Palestine, not have first to bring his troops down from Syria. Cf. §120 and *War* 2.499–500: Gallus's move of his troops, from Antioch to Ptolemais, at the outbreak of the rebellion of 66.

797 Although violation (παρανομία) of law and transgression (παράβασις) sound synonymous, it appears that Josephus distinguishes here between law and ancestral practice (esp. if we end the sentence with πατρίου, as in all manuscripts apart from Ambrosianus, which adds νόμου). This distinction reappears at §264b: Jewish law was given by the lawgiver but ratified by the ancestors. See the note there on "adopted." It is, however, possible that the reference to παρανομία might (also?) refer to Roman law, namely, that the Jewish spokesmen allude to the possibility of rebellion, similar to the warning about banditry at §274. For such ambiguity, which can be useful for subjects of an empire, cf. Acts 18:13–15.

798 This argument, about what is forbidden to Jews, is not really apposite here for the Jews were not being asked to do anything. Contrast the parallel at *War* 2.195, where Josephus has the Jewish protesters assert, relevantly, that the prohibition applied to the place, not to the perpetrators: it was not allowed for there to be such an image "not only in the Sanctuary but even in any non-sacred place within the country." The move in *Antiquities*, even

raised their hands and adopted[799] these [laws] as pertaining to virtue."[800] **265** Petronius became angry and said: "Were I the emperor and had taken it into my mind to do these things on the basis of my own considerations, it would have been justified for you to speak to me that way. Now, however, since I have been ordered by Caesar it is completely imperative to carry out his decrees,[801] for otherwise I would have to to suffer a more[802] irremediable punishment for disobeying them."[803] **266** But the Jews said:

> Just as you think, O Petronius, that it is impossible to disobey Gaius's orders, so too is it impossible for us to violate what the law proclaims. Trusting in the virtuous power[804] of God and in the labors of our ancestors, until now we have remained innocent of violation, and we would never dare to be so wicked as to violate, out of fear of death, prohibitions which he thought bring us measures of goodness.[805] **267** Rather, we shall endure and face our fortunes while preserving our ancestral practices, risking what is set out for us, undertaking the worst things for the glory of God, firm in the belief that whatever happens there is hope because God will stand by us; because [we know that] Fortune tends to both sides in public affairs; **268** and because if we were to obey you we would bring upon ourselves much censure as being unmanly (for that would be taken to explain our violation of the law) as well as great wrath of God, who even in your judgment must be considered greater than Gaius.

---

at the price of making the story less coherent, from what is forbidden in a particular place to what is forbidden to particular people, reflects Josephus's move, between *War* and *Antiquities*, from a Judean orientation to a Judaic, diasporic one—from a stance that endows one particular land with special religious significance to one that does not. For another instance of this, see the note on "make images" at §55.

799 Here, by using χειροτονέω (as, for example, at §22), Josephus implies that the laws oblige the Jews because they decided ("voted") to undertake them. So too at 17.151: the Law forbids *those who choose to live according to it* to erect images. See D. R. Schwartz 2014: 55–56. The present formulation is answered by Petronius's in the next paragraph.

800 For Jewish law's being meant to foster virtue (ἀρετή), see also, for example, *Apion* 2.226, 278, 286 and *Letter of Aristeas* 144, 150. On the same theme in Philo and its Platonic background, see Annas 2017. For the same concerning Roman law, see 19.57.

801 This is the only occurrence of προαναψηφίζω in Josephus. By having Petronius use, with reference to the emperor's order, language properly used of decrees (ψηφίζματα) "voted upon" by citizens or a representative body (in Roman context: of senatus consultum, decretum decurionum, or plebiscitum [*GTRI* 100]), Josephus artfully makes the legate respond directly to the Jews' claim at the end of §264.

802 This use of the comparative (ἀνηκεστοτέραν) seems to indicate that Petronius means the suffering that would be imposed upon him, if he disobeys, is worse than that which the Jews would suffer by witnessing the desecration of their temple.

803 This is the only occurrence of παρακρόασις in Josephus and the only evidence for this noun in LSJ 1314, s. v. The verb, παρακροάομαι, appears at §§188, 279, and that too is the only evidence for it cited in LSJ, ibid.

804 For Josephus's use of ἀρετή, see *ThLJ* 81–82 and *CCFJ* 1.223–226. Usually, of course, it means "goodness, excellence, virtue" or the like, and that is how it is usually translated here too. However, in context, here, it must entail the implication that God not only is virtuous but also has the power to protect those who remain loyal to him, and will do so. Note, in this connection, that Philo's *Embassy to Gaius*, dedicated to the present episode, was actually transmitted under the title Φίλωνος Ἀρετῶν πρῶτον ("Philo's First Work on 'Virtues'"), see already Eusebius, *Church History* 2.6.3; 2.18.8. On that meaning ("the specifically Jewish sense of ἀρετή = θεία δύναμις" [Smallwood 1970: 39–40]), see Danker 2000: 130 ("manifestation of divine power, *miracle*") and Reiter 1927; *inter alia*, Reiter points also to *Ant.* 17.130, where Josephus uses ἀρετή in parallel to ἰσχύς ("strength").

805 For the phrase ἀγαθοῦ ῥοπή, cf. §293—ῥωπή εὐδαίμονος, also Mason 2008: 37, n. 323 (on *War* 2.52).

(8.3) 269 Petronius, seeing from [their] words how difficult it would be overcome their will, and that it would not be within his power to carry out the dedication of the statue for Gaius without battle, and that there would be much bloodshed, assembled his friends and the entourage that accompanied him and hastened to Tiberias, eager to become cognizant of the disposition of the Jews as it was [there]. **270** Since [the] Jews, although they considered the danger of war against the Romans to be great, considered that of violating the law to be even greater, many myriads again came out to confront Petronius when he came to Tiberias. **271** When they supplicated him not at all to subject them to such duress nor to defile the city [of Jerusalem][806] by the dedication of the statue, Petronius said: "Would you, then, go to war against Caesar,[807] giving no thought to all he can bring to bear or to your own weakness?" They said: "In no way will we fight, but we will die before we violate the laws."[808] And lying upon their faces and proffering their throats[809] for slaughter they said they were ready to be killed. **272** And they went on that way for forty days, all the time ignoring their fields although it was the sowing season[810]—so great was their preference and firm resolve to die rather than look on at the installation of the statue.[811]

(8.4) 273 With matters in this state, Aristobulus (King Agrippa's brother) and Helcias the Elder[812] and others who were of the most powerful of that house,[813] along with the most prominent [Jews], came to see Petronius, appealing to him, **274** given the fact that he had

---

806 Such an easy move between the sanctity of the Temple and that of the city was natural, for the sanctity of "the holy city" (see the note on "holy city" at 20.118) derived from that of the Temple ("the house of God"). But phrasing of the threat as one to the *polis* would also resonate well among Josephus's Greek readers; cf. D. R. Schwartz 2008: 50–51 and Carlier 2008.

807 The same phrase appears verbatim at *War* 2.196 as well. While this suggests that Josephus was using *War* here, or a common source (Schemann 1887: 28–29), such verbal agreement is so rare, and this passage is so quotable, that, as Cohen (1979: 59–60) notes, it is possible that Josephus simply remembered the line. For similar cases, see the notes on "festivity" at 20.112, on "benefactor" at 20.253, and the Introduction, at nn. 23–24.

808 The use of "the laws" here, rather than "our laws," functions to explain both halves of their response. For an unsuccessful Jewish attempt to exploit the same ambiguity, cf. Acts 18:13–15.

809 See the note on "baring their throats" at §59.

810 That is, in the autumn (indeed, late enough in it that people could be worrying about a drought—§285); so too *War* 2.200. This contradicts Philo's report at *Leg.* 249, which places what seem to be the same negotiations at the time of the wheat-harvest, i.e. in the spring. The obvious solutions (one or the other is wrong, they refer to different events, they refer to a harvest in the fall or a sowing in the spring) have all been proposed; see Smallwood

1970: 281–283, D. R. Schwartz 1990a: 78–80, and Mason 2008: 166–167, n. 1258.

811 I have translated ἀνάθεσιν τοῦ ἀνδριάντος literally, with regard to physical introduction, for presumably the Jewish protesters, here as at 19.300, did not care whether the setting up of the statue was accompanied by a dedication of any sort. Nevertheless, this term was regularly used of "dedications"; see the note on "votive offerings" at §19, also *ThLJ* 35, s.vv. ἀνάθεσις, ἀνάθημα; 43, s.v. ἀνατιθέναι.

812 He was a member of the Herodian "house" (see immediately below) by marriage; see §138 and Stern 1976: 613. For his continued prominence in the days of Agrippa I, see 19.353. The use of "the Elder" here, which is evidently meant to distinguish this Helcias from a son of the same name (see the note on "the Elder" at §142), is the main reason to assume, as does Kokkinos (1998: 200), that the Helcias mentioned in 20.194, evidently an appointee of Agrippa II in his capacity of supervisor of the Temple (*Ant.* 20.16, 216–218) was his son. Another son of Helcias the Elder was Archelaus, mentioned at *Apion* 1.51 as prominent alongside Agrippa II; indeed, for a while the two were brothers-in-law (19.355; 20.140, 147).

813 As is indicated by §276, the "house" is Aristobulus's, or, more generally, the Herodian house. At *Leg.* 300, with regard to a similar but earlier episode, in the days of Pilate, Philo reports a similar appeal by "the king's [= Herod's] four sons." That report is, however, somewhat puzzling, for it is not easy to think who Philo was thinking of, apart

seen the multitude's zeal [for its cause], not to bring it to desperation. Rather, [they urged him] to write Gaius[814] how relentlessly[815] deadset the [protesters] were against accepting the statue, that they had upped[816] and left their farming so as to sit and protest, and that while they did not want to go to war about it since they could not,[817] they would gladly accept death rather than violate their regulations[818]—the result being that, with the land remaining unsown, brigandage would flourish because of [the inhabitants'] inability to make the tribute payments.[819] **275** Perhaps, [they urged], Gaius might be moved to pity and neither be cruel in attitude nor contemplate the devastation[820] of the nation. But if [Gaius] persevered in his earlier desire for war, let him undertake the project himself.[821] **276** That was what

---

from Antipas and Philip. For an attempt, see Smallwood 1970: 302–303.

814 As Richards and Shutt (1937: 176) note, γράφω + the accusative in the sense of "write about something' is rare. Therefore, in view of §281, and adducing the Latin translation, which indicates a participle, they suspect that διασαφοῦντα has fallen out. This suggestion is discussed in Part VI of the Introduction.

815 Probably the Jews' spokesmen would prefer "resolutely," but τὸ ἀνήκεστον, which is repeated at §278 in the description of Petronius's letter, has a more negative valence; Thackeray (*ThLJ* 47–48) offers "incurable, fatal, relentless."

816 Although frequently ἀφίστημι refers to rebellion, here the Jews' spokesmen would not present things that way, and the contrast with "sitting" in the continuation of the verse seems to indicate a contrast such as that denoted by "upped."

817 It is interesting that Josephus has Petronius proposing to explain the Jews' refusal to fight as deriving merely from inability, rather than from a willing acceptance of Roman rule. This is a theme that characterized Josephus himself in *War*. See esp. Stern 1987: 74–77; he emphasizes that Josephus avoids, in anti-war speeches in *War*, the claim—found elsewhere, e.g., in Aeliuis Aristides's "Roman Oration" and in Philo's *Leg.* 143–158— that Roman rule was beneficial for its subjects. Rather, he focuses on the unavoidability of Roman rule, hence on the folly of opposing it. That line apparently corresponded to what Romans wanted to hear from someone reflecting the thoughts of a people that had recently rebelled against them, and here Josephus has Petronius ascribe the Judeans the same position. In the *Antiquities*, in contrast, as Stern notes (1987: 77, pointing especially to the numerous documents in the *Antiquities* that testify to Roman protection of Jewish rights), Josephus himself tends more to the position that Roman rule was good for the Jews. Cf. the conclusion of Schalit's introduction to *Antiquities*: "*Antiquities* is the first composition after the destruction of the Second Temple that sees the future of

the Jewish people in the West as a positive political program" (Schalit 1944: lxxxi).

818 At times, especially when alongside νόμοι, νόμιμα can be used to denote norms of a lower and hence less-binding status; Philo (*Hypothetica* 7.6), for example, distinguishes among "unwritten practices, νόμιμα, and the νόμοι themselves." So too, at *Ant.* 13.297 Josephus explains that since the νόμιμα observed by the Pharisees are not written among the Mosaic νόμοι, but rest only on ancestral tradition, the Sadducees hold them not to be binding. But in the present passage there is, obviously, no reason to emphasize the second-rate status of νόμιμα. Rather, the case is like that at 14.65, 67, where νόμιμα are synonymous with νόμοι and Jews are ready to die rather than violate them. Similarly, the Jews' claim here is basically the same as at §59, but there νόμοι is used. Indeed, even at *Ant.* 13.297 Josephus says the Sadducean claim is that only written νόμιμα need be observed—a formulation that does not distinguish between them and νόμοι. For another case in which, for a different reason, no distinction is made, see the note on "customs" at 19.290.

819 Concerning this threat, cf. the note on "practice" at §263, also Tacitus's report (*Hist.* 5.9) that the Jews indeed took up arms against Gaius's project, until his death made that superfluous. For the normal assumption that people who could not pay taxes would flee and became bandits, or would at least be so defined by the ruling power, see Safrai 1963, McGing 1998: 172 ("the step from tax flight to banditry was a small one"), and Kloppenborg 2009: 471–479. On Roman taxes in Judea in this period, see Lémonon 2007: 91–94 and Udoh 2020.

820 For this sense of ἀνάστασις, see 16.278, also ἀνάστατος at §§98, 368; *ThLJ* 42. Note that §301 uses the same term to refer to the "installation" of the statue, thus making clear the starkly polar options in the present episode.

821 Although it is not clear whether this refers to Petronius or Gaius, the latter seems likelier, namely, that the Jews urged Petronius to refuse to carry out the orders and let Gaius fulfill them himself, if he wanted to persist. Cf. §278.

Aristobulus's people called upon Petronius to do. And Petronius, [a] because Aristobulus's people were exerting so much pressure because their appeal was for great things, and they were using every tactic in their supplications, and also [b] **277** beholding the Jews' resolve that was arrayed against him,[822] and [c] thinking it terrible to bring death upon so many myriads of people in executing Gaius's madness, holding them guilty for their reverence to God and then living the rest of his life in terrible expectation,[823] thought it much better to write Gaius [and report] their implacability and endure his wrath at his not having immediately fulfilled his orders.[824] **278** Perhaps, [he thought], he might even convince him; but if he remained in his original mania he[825] would undertake the war against them.[826] And if Gaius did turn some of his wrath against him it might be appropriate, for those who strive for virtue,[827] to die for such a multitude of people.[828] So he decided to deem his petitioners' request persuasive.

(8.5) 279 Summoning to Tiberias the Jews, of whom many myriads came, he stood up in front of them and declared to them that the present military expedition had not been his idea, the orders having come from the emperor, whose wrath would be endured not with delay, but rather immediately, by anyone who mustered the boldness to disobey the orders.[829] [He said:]

---

822 This is the only occurrence of ἀντιπαράταξις in Josephus. But the corresponding verb (ἀντιπαρατάσσω) appears often.

823 For Josephus's use of ἐλπίς, see *ThLJ* 249–250. Although usually it means "hope" (see esp. Spicq 1994: 1.480–492), often, as here, "expectation"—which can include the expectation of something unhoped for but nevertheless expected—is more appropriate. So, for example, *Ant.* 2.211 (destruction), 19.57 (suffering), 138 (destruction); see also 19.57, 138. For the fear of post-mortem suffering for crimes during one's lifetime, see also §287.

824 The text of this sentence is very uncertain; Niese (1890a: 190) indicates a lacuna after τὸ ἀνήκεστον αὐτῶν and others have emended. The main question is whether τὸ ἀνήκεστον (implacability) is the Jews' (as in two manuscripts, which read αὐτῶν, as already at §274), or rather Gaius's (emending to αὐτοῦ [so Feldman 1965: 162], as at §§265, 282, and 19.65). I have adopted the former option and, accordingly, added in "about." In any case, the diction points up how impossible Petronius's position was. Cf. the note on "taking care" at §280.

825 Apparently: Gaius. See the next note.

826 As the Jewish spokesmen suggested (§275), but if there it was possible to understand that they contemplate Petronius persisting against them, here, apparently, he associates himself with the Judeans, as the next words show.

827 Compare Philo's claim, at more or less the same juncture in the story (*Leg.* 245), that Petronius had

some interest in Jewish philosophy and piety. We know of no further data to support the claim, and in general it appears that Romans had next to no notion of Jewish literature (see the Introduction, at n. 37). Probably, therefore, Philo's statement about Petronius is simply the way a philosopher chooses to compliment a good man; so too, at *Leg.* 310 Philo has Agrippa underline Augustus's accomplishments as a philosopher.

828 Same phrase: §20. The willingness to die for one's values is a consistent theme in *Antiquities*, even as opposed to *War*; see esp. Gafni 2019: 22–24, who, referring to such passages as 12.267, 281–282, 304, 314–315 and 13.5–6, shows how, in his rewriting of 1 Maccabees, Josephus emphasizes the Hasmoneans' willingness to die as opposed their willingness to fight. See also, *inter alia*, *Ant.* 14.66–68; 18.59; and *Apion* 2.218–219. This emphasis on martyrdom, especially when the choice is violation of Jewish law, which *Antiquities* shares with 2 Maccabees as opposed to 1 Maccabees, is part of their diasporic orientation; see D. R. Schwartz 2014: 16–17 (on martyrdom in 1 and 2 Maccabees) and 59–60 (on *Ant.* 14.63–67), also Tuval 2013: 171, n. 177, on *Ant.* 6.149 (Josephus's addition to 1 Sam 15:17–23).

829 Reading προστάγμασι, as suggested by Thackeray (cited and followed by Feldman 1965: 164), rather than the manuscripts' πράγμασιν. In the parallel account in *War* 2, πρόσταγμα is Josephus's usual term for Gaius's order to erect the statue (§§186, 202, 203).

It is appropriate for someone who has attained so high an office by his approval not
to oppose his [will[830]] in any way. **280** But I do not consider it right not to give up
my safety and my honor in order that you not be destroyed—you who are so many,
[and] who are taking care[831] both of the virtue of your law, which, it being your ancestral law, you consider worth fighting for, and of God, who is above all authority and
power—whose sanctuary I would not be so bold as to ignore by allowing outrage[832] to
befall it at the behest of the ruling powers.

281 Rather, I am sending [a letter] to Gaius, explaining your positions, also defending, in a fashion, the good arguments you put forward by which I, against my [original]
opinion, was convinced.[833] And let God[834]—for his authority is greater than that of
any human contrivance[835] or power—give his support, ordaining[836] both for you the
preservation of the ancestral ways and, for himself, that he not fail, because of human
decisions but against the wishes [of the Jews[837]], to receive the usual honors [due
him]. **282** And if Gaius becomes embittered and turns his implacable wrath toward
me, I will endure[838] any danger and any misery that visits my body and my fortune
rather than look on as you, who are so many, are utterly destroyed for doing such good
things. **283** So go away now, each of you to his own affairs, and work the land.[839] And I
myself shall write to Rome, and neither I nor my friends will turn away from taking
care[840] of everything for you.

(8.6) 284 Having said that and dissolved the assembly of the Jews, he asked the leaders to
take care[841] of what was needed for agriculture and to win over the people by [spreading]
good expectations. Thus he, for his part, made an effort to raise the multitude's morale. And
God, for his part, demonstrated to Petronius his freedom of action[842] and that everything is

---

830 As Anthony Ellis notes, probably γνώμη is to
be understood after τῇ ἐκείνου; note the contrast with
Petronius's own γνώμη, which is mentioned explicitly
ealier in this paragraph.

831 Reading διακονουμένων (rather than διακνούμενον,
as the mss.), with Hudson and Cocceji, cited by Niese
(1890a: 190) and followed by Feldman 1965: 164. This use
of this verb is striking here, as it is the same used numerous times of the expectation that Petronius would "carry
out" Gaius's order (§§262, 265, 269, 277 [bis]). Same move:
§283. Cf. the note on "his orders" at §277.

832 Refusal to "ignore" (περιορά) ὕβρις is common,
e.g., at *War* 2.116 and *Ant.* 5.145; 7.120; and 18.360.

833 The last half of this sentence is somewhat
opaque, and has invited emendations; my translation is
no more than a guess. See Feldman's apparatus and notes
(1965: 164–165).

834 Here Josephus has Petronius speak reassuringly
to the Jews, using their nomenclature; cf. §288, where
Josephus has Petronius instead use "the deity" when writing to Gaius.

835 For such usage of μηχανή, cf. the note on "means"
at §51.

836 For such usage of πρυτανεύω, see also §198.

837 For παρὰ γνώμην as "against the wishes," see for
example 13.102; 14.245, 435; *Life* 67. Usually the person

whose wishes are flouted is named, hence my parenthetical expansion. Perhaps Petronius hints that he himself is
also among those who desire that God continue to receive
his customary honors.

838 This is the only occurrence of τλάω in Josephus.

839 For this being the way a ruler formulates his expectation that a restive or rebellious population give it up and
return to its routine way of life, compare, for some examples, 2 Macc 12:1 (with 11:23, 26, 29 on "tending to their own
affairs"), *War* 4.84; *Ant.* 16.271; 17.193; and the amnesty for
those who are "living quietly and attending to their own
farming" in a 154 CE edict of a Roman governor of Egypt:
Wilcken 1912: 33 (no. 19, col. 2, lines 13–15), in English in
Johnson, Coleman-Norton, and Bourne 1961: 214.

840 See the note on "taking care" at §280.

841 For such use of προμηθέομαι, cf. §§286, 360 and
19.153.

842 Reading παρρησίαν with the manuscripts and
Niese (1890a: 191). Thackeray 1919: 86, n. 2, who limits
παρρησία to "frankness," which does not fit here, prefers
instead to read παρουσίαν, "presence" with the Epitome
(Niese 1887–1896: 321) and the Latin ("praesentiam").
However, for a broader sense of παρρησία see 15.198 and
16.293, where, respectively, van Henten (2014: 132) and
Marcus and Wikgren (1963: 327) rendered "freedom
of action."

in his hands.[843] **285** For just as he finished his speech to the Jews, he let loose a heavy rain, which was against all human expectation, for that day had been clear since morning with nothing in the sky indicating rain.[844] Moreover, the entire year had been afflicted by such a severe drought that it made people despair of any water from above, even when they saw the sky was cloudy. **286** As a result, when there then came down so much rain, which was unusual and against all expectation, it gave the Jews hope that Petronius could not possibly fail in his petition on their behalf. Petronius himself, moreover, was totally stunned by seeing so palpably[845] that God was taking care of the Jews; he had indicated this with so great an apparition that not even those who in fact tended to hold the opposite position were left with any capacity to argue about it.[846] **287** When writing Gaius he wrote about this along with all the rest, bringing everything and appealing in every way not to drive so many myriads of people into desperation; and [he explained] that if he killed them (for it would not be without war that they would violate their religion's[847] regulation) he would both be denied the income normally received from them and be subjected to a curse[848] in the next era.[849] **288** Moreover, the deity[850] that stands at their head has shown that its power is unimpaired and has not left anything indicating any doubt about its power.

This, then, was how things stood with Petronius.[851]

Agrippa's Intervention

(8.7) 289 Turning now back to King Agrippa, who happened to be spending time in Rome: he had greatly advanced his friendship with Gaius.[852] Once he held a dinner for him,[853]

---

843 Feldman (1965: 167) renders καὶ τὴν ἐπὶ τοῖς ὅλοις σύλληψιν "and would lend His aid in all matters." However, although συλλαμβάνω (middle) can mean "to aid," in all other cases Josephus uses the noun σύλληψις for "capture," just as Philo regularly uses it for "arrest" (*Flacc.* 108, 116, 119, 145). Given that, and the fact that the immediate continuation, which justifies this statement (§285—γάρ), shows God's control of all, not his aid for Petronius, I have preferred to translate σύλληψις in a way close to Josephus's usual usage.

844 As in the case of the similar miracle reported at Herodotus 1.87.

845 See LSJ 556, s.v. ἐναργής: "esp. of the gods appearing in their own forms."

846 For God's control of rain and his use of it to communicate his pleasure or the opposite, as already in the Bible (Lev 26: 4, 19; Deut 11:14, 17; 1 Sam 12:17–18; 1 Kings 18), compare *Ant.* 14.22, 390–391, and 15.425; of the last three, the first and third have rabbinic parallels (*m. Ta'anit* 3:8 and *b. Ta'anit* 23a), discussed in Ilan and Noam 2017: 1.318–340, 411–416. The motif is not at all limited to Jews; see, for example, Herodotus 1.87, Diodorus Siculus 17.49.3–4, and Cassius Dio 72(71).8 (in the days of Croesus, Alexander the Great, and Marcus Aurelius, respectively). For a long list of Greek and Roman instances, see Kovács 2009: 145–147.

847 For the translation of θρησκεία (and so θρησκεύω) in this general sense (not just "cult"), see Spicq 1994: 2.200–204 and D. R. Schwartz 2014: 91–102. See also, however, the notes on "practices" at §141 and on "religions" at 19.270.

848 The text is evidently corrupt; see Feldman's (1965: 168) critical apparatus and Richards and Shutt 1939: 182.

849 For a similar notion of future retribution, see §277.

850 Note that above, at §§284–286, Josephus, in his own Jewish voice as narrator, states that it was God (ὁ θεός) who had demonstrated his providential care for the Jews. Now, in reporting a Roman governor's letter to the emperor, Josephus artfully has him use the less personal τὸ θεῖον. For Josephus's use of the latter, which as a reference to God is usually translated as "the deity" rather than "God," see the note on "deity" at §5.

851 Statements like this, which wrap up a stage of the story (καὶ NN ἐν τούτοις ἦν) and thus prepare us, often (as here) with the aid of μέν ... δέ, to a switch of view to another setting but with the implied promise to return to the first one, are quite common in Josephus. See, for example, 7.232; 8.354, 393; 13.267, 283;18.379/19.1; 19.263; 20.68, 99. Cf. the note on "To return to Agrippa" at §195.

852 Josephus frequently alludes to Agrippa's success in making friends in high places—§§145, 151, 167–168 (just as, in general, he likes the theme of "cultivating" such people; see the note on "considerably" at §36). His friendship with Gaius is also mentioned by Cassius Dio 59.24.1, who reports that the Romans viewed Agrippa, and Antiochus of Commagene as two "tyrant trainers."

853 The coming story of Agrippa's dinner for Gaius, the latter's offer of any gift Agrippa might choose to request, Agrippa's first refusal and finally his request that a decree against the Jews be abrogated, is meant to recall

and took care to outdo everyone both in his expenditure for the dinner and in supplying everything that is conducive to pleasure, **290** so that none of the others, not even Gaius himself, believed he could ever offer something equal to it, if he wanted to, not to mention outdoing it. So far did the man exceed everyone in preparing [the dinner] and in thinking out and supplying everything for Caesar.[854] **291** Gaius was struck by his intelligence and munificence, such that in order to satisfy him he had exerted himself to use an abundance of money even beyond his means,[855] and he wanted to imitate Agrippa's ambitious undertaking for his pleasure. Therefore, when feeling free under the influence of wine and transformed into an especially cheerful mood, he said at the symposium, when he had been called upon to drink:[856]

> **292** Agrippa, already in the past I have been conscious of the respect with which you relate to me and the great loyalty[857] you demonstrated, even when you were beset by dangers on its account in the days of Tiberius.[858] You never fail in any way to show goodness toward me, even beyond your means. Now, therefore, since it would be shameful for me to be behind you in enthusiasm, I would like now to make up for what I previously omitted; **293** for whatever gifts I have hitherto apportioned to you come to little. Anything that can add you a measure of happiness[859] shall be arranged for you through my enthusiasm and my strength.

Now, he said that supposing that [Agrippa] would ask for a large territory bordering[860] [his own] or the revenues of certain cities.[861] **294** He however, although he had prepared

---

chs. 5–7 of the biblical story of Esther. That story too, as that of Joseph (on which see the note on "have in common" at §201), was a paradigmatic example, for Jews (who read the Book of Esther every year, on Purim), of how Jews could succeed in the Diaspora. Cf. Meinhold 1976, Wills 1990, and Hacham 2007. One may wonder how many of Josephus's non-Jewish readers would notice the allusion, which would require them to recall it from Josephus's version of the story at 11.240–243, 260–268.

854 The text of this last clause is in doubt; Niese (1890b: 186) inserts an obelisk (indicating a "crux") before ἢ Καίσαρος ἐκφροντίσας and, as Niese (1890a: 193, first note) and Feldman (1965: 168, nn. 6–7) detail, witnesses differ concerning both ἐκφροντίσας and Καίσαρ. I have translated according to Hudson's emendation, Καίσαρι, which they cite. ἐκφροντίζω appears in Josephus only here and 19.171; cf. the note on "agreement" at §203.

855 The same point, that he used money ὑπὲρ δύναμιν, is repeated by Gaius at §292. It, and Agrippa's chronic impecuniousness, is a frequent theme in Josephus's account of Agrippa's early life; see §§144–147, 150, 154–160, 164–165.

856 I.e., to give a toast, as, for example, at *Flacc.* 113. On such ancient toasting, often with each participant of the symposium having a turn, see Cairns 2012: 264 (in connection with Horace, *Odes* 1.27); especially with regard to a guest's desire to praise a generous host, see Korzeniewski 1974. More generally, on drinking at Roman banquets (often alluded to as "comissatio"—reveling), see M. B. Roller 2017: 181–188.

857 On the translation of εὔνοια, see the note on "loyalty to Gaius" at §124.

858 The reference is to Agrippa's imprisonment after he was overheard expressing the hope that Tiberius soon die and be succeeded by Gaius; see above, §§186–189.

859 For ῥοπὴν ... τοῦ εὐδαίμονος, cf. the note on "measures of goodness" at §266.

860 That is, Josephus has Gaius assuming that Agrippa would want to enlarge his income from land, either by enlarging his own kingdom or by giving him the income from other cities. For the first option, as Feldman (1965: 170), I have adopted the Epitome's reading: τῆς προσόρου (Niese 1887–1896: 322). In his editio maior, Niese (1890a: 193) retains the manuscripts' τῆς προσόδου but comments that the Epitome's reading is possibly or probably correct ("fort. recte"), just as he inserts an obelisk here in his editio minor (1890b: 186). Schalit (1963: 308) retains Niese's text and renders "land of great income," but that is difficult, as is also the repetition of "income" later in the sentence: if both options mentioned "income," we would expect a formulation that includes the two options under that general heading. Cf. §300, where the two options mentioned here are formulated as the enlargement of his realm by enlarging either his monetary revenues or his other power; that bolsters the notion that only one of the two options was formulated as greater income, while the other was a gift in kind (such as the enlargement of his kingdom).

861 For the practice of bestowing the income of a city or a territory upon a recipient of royal favor, see,

everything concerning which he wanted to make his request, did not reveal his intention.[862] Rather, he immediately responded to Gaius that just as earlier it had not been in the anticipation of profit from him that he had served him against Tiberius's orders,[863] so too now nothing of what he did in order to grant him pleasure was in return[864] for any personal profits. **295** [He also said that] the gifts he had already received from Gaius were in fact great, beyond what he could hope for even when bold. "For even if they were less than what was in your power to give, they were greater than my expectations and than my status as recipient [deserves]." **296** Gaius, struck by his virtue, pressed him all the more to say what might make him happy if he granted it to him. He responded:

> Since, my lord, you have in your confidence [in me] proclaimed me worthy of receiving your gifts, I will not request anything that contributes to [my] prosperity, for I am very distinguished[865] by the things you have already granted me. **297** Rather, I will call upon you to [do something] that will bring you the reputation of piety and make the divine power your ally in all that you desire; and as for me, it will give me the good reputation among those who learn of it, that they know that I never failed to obtain your authority for anything I needed. Namely, I request that you no longer contemplate completing[866] the dedication of the statue that you ordered Petronius to make for the temple of the Jews.[867]

(8.8) 298 Although he was aware of the fact that it would be dangerous for him if Gaius decided not to accept the request, and it would do no other than get him killed, nevertheless, because he considered [the issue] to be of great significance, as it in fact was, he decided to cast the die[868] for them. **299** As for Gaius: being both [a] beholden to Agrippa for his service of him, along with the fact that it would have been inappropriate if, in the sight of so many witnesses,[869] he should immediately back down and break his promise about things that he himself had earnestly pushed[870] Agrippa into requesting, **300** and also [b] in awe of Agrippa's virtue, for he had given little thought[871] to enlarging his own realm through

---

for example, *Ant.* 12.154; 19.276; 20.138; 1 Macc 10:39, 89; 2 Macc 4:30; von Gutschmid 1885: 85.

862 For such building up of the tension, cf. 11.242–243//Esther 5:6–8.

863 Josephus refers here, literally, to Tiberius's letters (τὰς Τιβερίου ἐπιστολάς), but §§166 and 185, where the request is mentioned, make no reference to anything in writing. So we have to choose here among three possibilities: either we should infer that Tiberius wrote Agrippa; or we should read ἐντολάς, with several witnesses; or we should infer that Josephus used ἐπιστολαί for "orders" even if not written. Cf. the note on "orders" at §262.

864 Josephus uses λῆψις only here and at §194.

865 This is the only occurrence of ἐνδιαπρέπω in Josephus.

866 Lit. "doing." Cf. πράττειν διενοεῖτο at 17.4 and διανοοῖτο πράσσειν in *Life* 72.

867 If at §8 and at 20.49 Josephus, as a Jewish author and reflecting Helena's attitude as a Jewish pilgrim, refers

to the Temple as the "Temple of God," here he uses language that Gaius would have used.

868 For such use of κύβον ἀναρριπτεῖν, cf. Plutarch's *Life of Caesar* 32.6, whose Greek version of Caesar's famous "alea iacta est" at the crossing of the Rubicon was ἀνερρίφθω κύβος; as Plutarch comments, it was an image "with which men usually prelude their plunge into desperate and daring fortunes" (trans. Perrin, LCL). Presumably the only other appearance of ἀναρριπτέω in Josephus, at *War* 4.217, points to the same image. Dice games were very popular in Rome (and Claudius even wrote a treatise about them, according to Suetonius, *Claud.* 33); see Purcell 1995 and D. G. Schwartz 2006: 25–28.

869 Other participants in this dinner.

870 See the note on "insist" at 19.229.

871 In his editio maior, Niese (1890a: 194) read only ἐν ὀλίγῳ, but it appears that a verb, such as τίθημι (as at §23) or ποιέω (as at §367), is missing; accordingly, in his editio minor (1890b: 167) he noted a lacuna here. See the list of suggestions in Feldman 1965: 172–173, n. 6.

monetary revenues or other power;[872] rather, he had directed his attention to the general welfare, acting as if he were the ambassador of the laws and the divinity, he agreed, and wrote to Petronius, praising him for having assembled the army and for what he had written him about them,[873] [and then continuing];

> 301 Now, however, if you have already set up the statue, let it stand. If, however, you have not yet made the dedication, do not trouble yourself about it anymore. Rather, dismiss the army and, as for you, go back to the affairs I originally sent you to take care of. For I no longer require the installation of the statue; in this I am doing a favor for Agrippa, a man whom I honor so greatly that I cannot deny whatever he needs and requests.

302 Gaius wrote that to Petronius, however, before reading [Petronius's letter[874]], from which he wrongly inferred[875] that the Jews were hurrying into rebellion, as if their state of mind indicated nothing other than that they were threatening outright[876] war against Rome. 303 He was very troubled [by that], as if they had dared to put his rule to the test. He was a man who was in all circumstances[877] controlled by shame, one who overcame [any tendency to do] what was better; and once he had decided to direct his rage against someone he rushed [into it] more than all others[878] without imposing any control at all upon it. Rather, adjudging the pleasure he derived from his rage to be the criterion of happiness, he wrote to Petronius:

Renewed Crisis and Providential Denouement

> 304 Since you have considered whatever gifts the Jews have provided you to be weightier than carrying out my orders, and have in all ways presumed to give them pleasure in contravention of my orders, I order you to become your own judge[879] and consider what should be done to you, upon whom my wrath has descended. For you shall be made an example, for all [who live] today and those who are later to come, that the orders of a man who is emperor are never to be neglected.

(8.9) 305 That was the letter that he wrote to Petronius.[880] But Petronius did not receive it while Gaius was still alive, for the ship of those that brought it was so delayed that Petronius

---

872 On the first formulation of these options, see the note on "bordering" at §293.

873 Since §302 states that when Gaius wrote this letter he had not yet read Petronius's letter that implored him to back down (§§287–288), it must be that Gaius's praise mentioned here pertains to another, earlier, letter by Petronius—namely, the one mentioned at §262. Indeed, according to §262 that letter pertained to the army and its preparations, which fits the present reference. True, according to §262 Gaius answered that letter immediately. But that would not prevent the emperor from again referring to that letter when now writing Petronius to cancel his original order. For another reference to that letter, see Philo, *Leg.* 333. Philo, however, prefers to portray Gaius as being insincere, rather than to have him change his mind upon receipt of Petronius's next letter.

874 I.e., his new letter cited in §§287–288. Niese marks a lacuna after ἐντυχεῖν, here, one that should be filled by something like what the Epitome (Niese 1887–1896: 322) supplies: ταῖς αὐτοῦ ἐπιστολαῖς.

875 This verb, καταδοκέω (or, as Thackeray conjectures, καταδοξάζω), appears only here in Josephus. Both Whiston (1878: 490) and Schalit (1963: 309) take the text to mean that Petronius's letter informed Gaius that the Jews were hurrying into rebellion, but it seems that, in context, Josephus must mean that was a *false* inference, something like διαλαμβάνω in 2 Macc 5:11.

876 For this sense of ἄντικρυς, see the note on "outright" at §4.

877 For ἐπὶ πᾶσιν, cf. 17.147.

878 For παρ' ὁντινοῦν compare 19.65, 208.

879 For suicide so as to avoid judgment, see van Hooff 1990: esp. 111–114.

880 Philo does not report this second letter, but he too reports that Gaius changed his mind. According to Philo (*Leg.* 338), Gaius decided to have a new statue made and be brought secretly and suddenly to Jerusalem during a trip he was planning to make to the East; on the plan for such a trip, see the note on "Egypt" at 19.81. What both stories have in common, as Bilde (1978: 86–89) emphasizes, is

first received a[nother] letter, from which he learned of Gaius's death.[881] **306** For God was not about to forget the dangers that Petronius had undertaken in showing favor to the Jews and honor to him.[882] Rather, by eliminating Gaius, angry at what he had dared to do in order to have himself worshipped, God discharged his debt[883] [to Petronius. And] Rome and the entire realm too joined in considering Petronius a benefactor,[884] especially the most eminent members of the Senate, for Gaius had turned his unbridled wrath against them.[885]

307 So he, on the one hand, died not long after he wrote Petronius the letter imposing death upon him. Later in this work[886] I will recount the circumstances[887] in which he died, and the nature of the conspiracy against him. **308** As for Petronius, on the other hand: He first received the letter that informed him of Gaius's death, and not long after—the one commanding him to take his own life. He rejoiced at the good timing of the disaster that had overtaken Gaius **309** and marveled at God's providence,[888] which with no delay, but rather immediately,[889] remunerated him for having both proffered respect for the sanctuary[890] and aided in the salvation of the Jews. Thus it happened that, for Petronius, the danger of death was avoided in a way easier than possibly could have been imagined.[891]

---

the knowledge that Agrippa's intervention, one way or the other, brought Gaius to back down, along with the claim that he changed his mind again—so it was only the murder of Gaius that put an end to his project. As Bilde concludes, we may believe the part about Agrippa's success, but have doubts about Gaius again changing his mind. The latter may well be only the way tradition, although not forgetting what really happened (Agrippa's successful intervention), managed to maintain its schematic assessment of Gaius as having been so wicked that only the assassination could put an end to his plans. Moreover, for pious storytellers that put God back into the picture; the story would have been far less wondrous had Gaius himself backed down. Cf. *War* 4.75–76 and 7.317–319: at both Gamala and Masada the besieged Judeans were defeated not because of overwhelming Roman power, but rather because, at a critical point, a supernatural power changed the direction of the wind.

881 For other cases in which Gaius's death is said to have saved someone's life just in the nick of time, see 19.10 and Cassius Dio 59.29.4. Readers so inclined can read such cases in line with Josephus's explanation, which follows immediately.

882 For these two objects of Petronius's attention, see above §280. But note esp. that a few lines later, at §309, Josephus rephrases the two as *the Temple* and the Jews. For such a close identification of the Temple with God, see also 20.108, 166.

883 This verb, χρεολυτέω, appears in Josephus only here and at *Ant.* 7.387. Niese (1890a: 196) marks a lacuna

after this infinitive; my bracketed addition is an attempt to fill out the sense and flow.

884 Reading συνευεργετεῖται, as suggested by Niese ad loc. (1890b: 196). This is the only reference for συνευεργετέω cited in LSJ 1713, s.v., but nevertheless it approves it as probable. LSJ translates "join in doing good to." However, it seems likelier that the sense is "joined in proclaiming/considering him a benefactor" (εὐεργέτης); cf. the use of εὐργετέω of a person in the sense "proclaim as εὐεργέτης" in a first-century inscription from Patara (Hicks 1889: 76–77, cited in LSJ 712, s.v.). But there seems to be no literary or epigraphic evidence to bear out Josephus's statement here. In general, cf. the note on "benefit" at §95.

885 As Josephus will emphasize at 19.2; see the note there on "the Senate."

886 I.e, in Book 19. For such use of λόγος, cf. §80; 3.218; *Life* 40; Acts 1:1.

887 See the note on "circumstances" at §39.

888 As often, this closing reference to divine providence indicates the point of the story. Cf. the note on "of man" at 19.61.

889 For virtually the same phrase, οὐδὲν/μηδὲν εἰς ἀναβολὰς ἀλλ' ἐκ τοῦ ὀξέος, see the note on "without delay" at §107.

890 On ναός, see the note on "God" at §261.

891 This is the only occurrence of τοπάζω in Josephus. For similar comments, as here summarizing narratives, see 19.334 and *Life* 394.

(9.1) 310 The Jews of Mesopotamia too,[892] and especially those who reside in Babylonia,[893] were affected by terrible suffering, no less than any other, including murder of them in such great numbers as have never before been recorded.[894] I will recount everything about these events in detail, also setting out the circumstances[895] that caused them this tragedy.[896]

The Jews of Mesopotamia: Two Episodes

311 Nehardea is a Babylonian city that, in addition to being populous, also has a good and large territory,[897] which along with other advantages is also replete with inhabitants. Moreover, it is not at all easily reached by enemies, since it is completely enclosed by a turn of the Euphrates River and by walls constructed [around it]. **312** Nisibis[898] is another city at the same turn of the river —for which reason Jews, putting their trust in the nature of these places, used to deposit there[899] both the didrachmas,[900] which it is their ancestral practice for each to give to God,[901] as well as whatever other votive offerings there might be, using these cities as if they were a treasury. **313** From there the deposited offerings were sent up to

The Escapades of Asineus and Anileus

---

892 That is: just like the Jews of Judea. Josephus likes to coordinate chapters of his work with the help of such small words. Cf. the note on "also" at §39. Moreover, note that although these two Babylonian stories have nothing to do with Gaius, their very presence here, in the midst of Josephus's Gaius narrative, reinforces the impression that Gaius's days were terrible for the Jews; so too at 19.1. That was not an unwelcome outcome for Josephus. For a similar procedure concerning Pilate, cf. the note on "for the Jews" at §65. Cf. also the note on "others" at 19.193: when Josephus hates someone, insinuation, for which no responsibility need be taken, is an easy option.

893 On their history in this period, see Neusner 1984 and Herman 2012.

894 For such hyperbole, cf. the note on "recorded" at 19.1. Here it refers to the closing episode of the coming narrative—the massacre in Seleucia (§376).

895 See the note on "circumstances" at §39.

896 On the following two stories (§§310–370 on Asineus and Anileus; §§371–379 on the Jews of Seleucia), see Schalit 1965; N. G. Cohen 1975/76; Neusner 1984: 53–61; Goodblatt 1987a; Shaw 1993: 179–184; Lembi 2001; Rajak 2001: 280–286; Herman 2006. The second story, culminating in the massacre in Seleucia, is dated fairly firmly to ca. 41 (see the note on "no troubles there" at §373), which is why these stories appear here, following the death of Gaius in 41. For the same procedure regarding the preceding narrative on Parthian affairs, see the opening note at 18.2.4 (§39). However, note that although the story of Asineus and Anileus is placed here as if it preceded that of the massacre in Seleucia, the latter flowing from the former, Goodblatt (1987a: 616–622) argued that, in fact, their historical order is the opposite, for the anarchic conditions in Parthia, which the former reflects, more likely reflect the period after 41 than that before it. Goodblatt argues that the two stories are originally of different origins, and it was Josephus who juxtaposed them—a

presumption that can also build on some other differences between the two stories, especially two, noted by Goodblatt 1987a: 620–621 and Herman 2006: 267–268: (a) the story of Asineus and Anileus has novelistic features and also biblical allusions, while the one about Seleucia does not, and (b) the first story terms Parthian non-Jews "Parthians" (thirteen times between §313 and §362) or "Babylonians" (at §§318, 339, 368, 369, 370, 371 [bis], and the seam at §372), the second—"Syrians" (§§372, 374, 375, 378). Indeed, in the second story there is no reference to "Parthians" and only one (§378) to "Babylonians," while in the first story there is only one reference to a "Syrian," at §355—and note that he is, in fact, friendly to the Jews (giving them information to use against the Babylonians), as opposed to the "Syrians" of the second story. See also the note on "Babylonians" at §371, which is the clumsy beginning of the seam between the second stories.

897 Chora (χώρα)— the land surrounding a city and belonging to it. On Nehardea, on the east bank of the Euphrates some forty km. west of Baghdad, which was a major Jewish center until the mid-third century, see Oppenheimer 1983: 276–293.

898 Given the details here about its location, this Nisibis is to be distinguished from the famous city of the same name hundreds of miles to the north. According to Oppenheimer (1983: 333–334), "there are no other sources having clear reference to the Nisibis near Nehardǝ'a, though some of the talmudic ones could apply to that place." See also Oppenheimer 2005: 356–373.

899 Lit. "in it" (ταύτῃ), but the end of this sentence makes it clear that both cities were used.

900 I.e., two-drachma coin, the equivalent of a half a shekel (Exod 30:13) on the Tyrian standard (see *War* 2.592), which was the standard currency used in the Temple; see Mason 2008: 397, n. 3551; *HJP* 2.66–67, n. 210.

901 On this tax, see esp. Mandell 1984. For other evidence concerning Jews from Babylonia making the

Jerusalem whenever there was an opportunity[902] to do so, with many myriads[903] of people taking part in the conveyance of the moneys out of fear of the predations of the Parthians, to whom Babylonia was subject.[904]

314 Now Asineus and Anileus,[905] Nehardeans by descent,[906] were brothers.[907] After being orphaned by their father, their mother ordained that they learn how to work with looms,[908] for among the local inhabitants it is not considered inappropriate for men to spin wool.[909] [Once it happened, however,] that the man who supervised their labors upbraided and beat them on account of their late arrival [at work], although they had learned the craft from him.[910] **315** They, considering the punishment an outrage, dragged down as many weapons

---

pilgrimage to Jerusalem, see *Ant.* 17.26, Philo, *Leg.* 216, Acts 2:9, *m. Yoma* 6:4.

902 For this translation of καιρός see also §247 and 17.51; for similar usage, see §321.

903 "Many myriads" is a favorite phrase; cf. the note on "myriads" at §60. Nevertheless, see the note on "twenty thousand" at 20.112.

904 For the fear of brigands who might attack Babylonian Jewish pilgrims to Jerusalem, see esp. *Ant.* 17.23–28, where we read of Babylonian Jewish cavlarymen settled by Herod in the vicinity of Trachonitis in order to protect them. On brigands in that same general region, see also 16.271–281 and *OGIS* 424.

905 The latter name may well have been recognizable as a Jewish name; for the evidence, see Ilan 2002: 384.

906 Beginning at §319, however, it will become apparent that they are Jews. Here that is taken for granted, as is suggested by the focus on Jews beginning in §312, as well, perhaps, by the name of at least one of the two brothers (see the preceding note). For Josephus's use of τὸ γένος, when introducing a character, to indicate place of birth, see, for example, 13.131 and 20.142, 252, also Gruen 2020: 167–172. Elsewhere it refers, instead, to familial or ethnic descent; see the note on "by birth" at 19.332.

907 Josephus otiosely defines them as "brothers of each other," perhaps to create some balance alongside the preceding clause: καὶ ἦσαν γὰρ Ἀσιναῖος καὶ Ἀνιλαῖος— Νεερδᾶται μὲν τὸ γένος, ἀλλήλων δὲ ἀδελφοί.

908 Lit. "the manufacture of looms" (ἱστῶν), but the end of the sentence indicates that it is not such carpentry but, rather, *working with* looms, i.e. weaving, that is meant. Naber (1893: xxiv, 94) would solve the problem by reading ἱστίων ("of sails"), which is somewhat supported by the Latin: "ut nauium operarentur uelamina" (Niese 1890a: 197). But it is not likely that sails were made of wool or that readers would think they were. See Feldman 1965: 131–135, n. d.

909 This is the only occurrence of ταλασιουργέω in Josephus. Josephus's point here is somewhat ambiguous; on the one hand he explains how it could be that the boys' mother could apprentice them to a weaver, but on the other hand, §338 will show that is this is to be understood as a lowly beginning. Herman (2006: 251) shows that, indeed, weaving was considered very unmanly in Parthia—and therefore suspects that the statement here is a misunderstanding on the part of the tradent. Perhaps, however, it is sarcastic. In any case, the statement that in Parthia it is thought to be respectable for men to weave would be well-received by Roman readers who would be happy to learn how unmanly the Parthians were. For a very comparable passage, Mason points to Herodotus 2.35, where, with the same effect, a list of what are meant to be read as shocking role-reversals between Egyptian men and women includes men sitting at home and weaving; according to Lloyd (1976: 148), extant representations of weaving in Greece depict only women weavers. Probably we should assume that at *War* 7.438, where Josephus reports that a certain villain who informed against him was a weaver, that datum serves as part of Josephus's condemnation of the man. Cf. Vegetius 1.7 (Stelten 1990: 18–19: linen-weavers and all those who seem to have womanly professions [*linteontes omnesque, qui aliquid tractasse videbuntur ad gynaeces pertinens*] should not be inducted into military service) and John Chrysostomus's complaint (Homily 34 on 1 Corinthians, §7; Chrysostomus 1839: 480) about men who weave: "For it is God Himself who gave to woman-kind skill in woven work. Woe be it ... for men's general effeminacy hath gone so far as to introduce our men to the looms. ..."

910 The point of the last clause is not clear. Perhaps Josephus means that one could have expected the master-weaver would be nicer to them, given the length of their relationship, and that is why they took the punishment to be outrageous, as he reports in the next sentence.

as they could find stored above the house and went off to a place called "Splitting[911] of the Rivers," which by nature was capable of supplying good pastureland and enough green fodder[912] to put aside for the winter. The poorest of the youth[913] came to join them, and, arming them[914] with the weapons, they became their generals and leaders in doing wicked deeds without any hindrance. **316** Having progressed so far that they could not be opposed and had built themselves a citadel, they sent to those who used the pastures and demanded tribute from them from their livestock, enough to be sufficient sustenance [for them], promising to those who agreed both friendship and protection from enemies from wherever they might come, but, to those who refused, slaughter of their flocks. **317** The [victims of this extortion], who could do nothing else, agreed and sent as many sheep as were demanded. Thus it happened that their power increased all the more and they were fully capable of injuring whomever they wanted, assailing them[915] suddenly. All who came their way began to serve them, and they were fear-inspiring even for those who [only] thought of trying [their strength against them], so that word of them spread and made its way even to the king of the Parthians.

(9.2) 318 The satrap of Babylonia heard these things, and, having decided to nip them in the bud[916] before even worse calamities arose because of them, collected as large an army of both Parthians and Babylonians as he could and set out against them, hoping to attack them and wipe them out before it became known that he was preparing the army. **319** He stationed [his] men around the marsh[917] but kept quiet. On the morrow, however, which was the Sabbath—a day of rest for the Jews from every thing[918]—he advanced bit by

---

911 This is the only occurrence of διάρρηξις in Josephus.

912 This is the only occurrence of χιλός in Josephus.

913 As already at §37, being poor implies moral depravity. And being young made them all the worse; see the note on "our youths" at §10. Cf. the note on "inexperienced" at §367.

914 This is the only occurrence of φράγνυμι in Josephus.

915 Note that the same verb, ἐλαύνω, is used in the next paragraph of the satrap's forces, and in that case §320 makes it clear that they came on horseback.

916 This follows Niese's text (1890a: 198), which adopts von Gutschmid's conjecture, ἔτι φυομένους; for this metaphor, cf. *Life* 193, also below, §324, and the note on "growing up" at §141. For the same idea, cf. §118.

917 By ἕλος, Josephus is probably referring to what is known in Aramaic as *'agma'*; see Sokoloff 2002: 79, s.v.

918 I have translated παντὸς χρήματος literally; *CCFJ* 4.366 gives "matter, object, thing" as the main translation for χρῆμα in the singular, about the same as LSJ 2005, §II ("thing, matter, affair"). However, it may be that the Greek text reflects some misunderstanding, for Josephus and his readers know that Jews do not abstain from everything on the sabbath; it is, specifically, certain *actions*, defined as *labor*, from which they abstain. As H. Weiss (1998: 365) observed, "Josephus does not tire from reminding his readers that on the seventh day Jews 'abstain from labor' and 'rest from all work'"; nowhere is Josephus so vague as to refer to abstinence from "everything" or "all things" or the like. Moreover, "rest" (ἀργία) would not apply to abstaining from most "things." The closest Josephus comes to such vagueness comes, it appears, at *War* 2.396, and even there it is "actions" from which Jews are said to abstain. Usually, ἔργον ("work") is specified (1.35; 3.91, 281; 12.274), and elsewhere Josephus speaks either of the general requirement of "rest" (12.4; 18.354; *War* 2.456) or of specific prohibitions (engaging in warfare or marching—12.274–277; 13.252; 14.63, 226; *War* 2.392; appearance in court —16.163, 168). Moreover, many readers would presumably know the same from what they see of Jewish life, if not from literature; on the Jewish sabbath in Roman literature, see Michael 1924; Goldenberg 1979; and Stern, *GLAJJ* 2.102–103, 106–107. Accordingly, *CCFJ* (ibid.) suggests "undertaking" for this passage, as also for 19.67, 75. But that is quite a stretch from the usual meanings of the term, and it is possible to render with "matter" at 19.67, 75, as I shall. Elsewhere, Josephus uses χρῆμα in in the singular only a few times: five times where "thing" or the like is appropriate (11.56; 13.211; 15.336; 19.67, 75) and one or perhaps two that refer to money (18.158 and, perhaps, 4.285, given the latter's dependence on Exod 22:7, which opens with a reference to money). The latter meaning, which is also found at Acts 4:47, is related to the overwhelming usage of χρῆμα,

bit[919] [with his troops], in the hope of making a sudden attack, thinking that his enemies would not dare to oppose him and so he would be able to take them prisoner without a fight.[920] **320** Asineus, however, happened to be sitting together with his companions, with their arms lying next to them. "Men," he said, "There has come to my ears the neighing[921] of horses—not as if they are grazing, but as if they have men riding upon them, and I also notice some flapping[922] of bridles. I am afraid that our enemies have surreptitiously surrounded us. So—let someone go forward as an observer to bring us a clear picture of what is upon us. Would that the words I said prove false!"

321 After he said that, some men went off to scout out what was happening, and as soon as possible[923] they arrived [back] and said:

> You were not wrong. Rather, you were a true conjecturer[924] of what the enemy is doing—for they are not about to let us continue our outrages any longer. **322** We are caught in a trap, no different from grazing animals—for a large number of horsemen have ridden against us while we are at a loss to do anything due to the command of our ancestral laws that compels us into idleness.

323 But Asineus was not about to let the opinion of the scout decide what was to be done. Rather, he considered that instead of dying in inactivity, and thus making the enemies happy, it was more in conformance with the law to meet them [in battle] courageously[925] and make them pay the penalty for having coerced them to violate the law, dying [in the process] if need be. So he himself picked up his weapons and instilled among those who were with him the courage needed for the same kind of valor.[926] **324** Coming to close quarters

---

which is in the plural and relates to money; note that Danker (2000: 1089, s.v) offers only such meanings: "wealth in gener[al], *property, wealth, means*, any kind of currency, *money*." This is found hundreds of times in Joephus's oeuvre; see, for example, §§225, 252, 253, 291, 300. 313. But "money" does not fit the present text any better than "matter, object, thing."

Given the fact that the usual translations of χρῆμα ("thing," "money") do not work here, and given the possibility that the story derives from an eastern Jewish source, and especially given the juxtaposition here with "all" (ἀπὸ παντὸς χρήματος), one may wonder if the Greek text here is not a mistranslation of an original Hebrew text, which used the standard Hebrew collocation that denotes what is to be abstained from on the Sabbath: *kol melakhah* ("all labor," as in Exod 12:16; 20:1//Deut 5:14; Lev 23:30). Since *melakhah*, apart from "work," also has the sense of "property" (as in Exod 22:8, 11 [RSV: "goods," "property"]; 2 Chr 17:13 [RSV: "great stores"]), that could explain the mistranslation here. Even if the text was originally in Aramaic (see the note on "dead man" at §343), one might expect Jews to retain that Hebrew term. But if they used an Aramaic equivalent, the situation would be the same, for the likely term, *'avida*, has both senses. See Sokoloff 1992: 393 ("work, service, profession, trade, merchandise, needs [?]"). My thanks to Robert Brody for help with this note.

919 So ("little by little") LSJ 329, s.v. βραχύς, §2, citing the same phrase in Thucydides 1.64.

920 While it is perhaps remarkable that the satrap assumed that Jewish outlaws would be scrupulous about observing the Sabbath, it is not surprising that he thought scrupulous Jews would abstain even from defending themselves when attacked. For although the Hasmoneans had adopted a policy that allowed fighting in self-defense on the Sabbath (1 Macc 2:29–41//*Ant.* 12.275–277), gentiles might not have heard of that, and they may well have heard stories about Jews refusing to defend themselves on the Sabbath, whether totally (see *Ant.* 12.3–6 // *Apion* 1.209–211) or partially (*Ant.* 14.63). In general, see Goodman and Holladay 1986: 167–171.

921 This is the only occurrence of χρεμετισμός in Josephus.

922 This is the only occurrence of ἀνάκρουσις in Josephus.

923 Cf. the note on "opportunity" at §313.

924 This is the only occurrence of εἰκαστής in Josephus.

925 Reading ἀλκῇ with the Epitome (Niese 1887–1896: 323), followed by Niese 1890b: 171 and Feldman 1965: 186. The manuscripts, followed by Niese 1890a: 199, have ἀλκῆς, which is difficult to construe. On ἀλκή, see the note on "prowess" at §127.

926 I.e., for valor similar to his own.

with the enemy, they killed many of them, for they had come contemptuously, thinking that they would take them like ripe fruit,[927] and forced the others to flee.

(9.3) 325 The king of the Parthians, when he received a report of this battle, was struck by the brothers' audacity and desired that they come so he could see them and speak with them. He sent [to them] the most trusted of his bodyguards, saying:

326 King Artabanus,[928] although he has been treated unjustly by your attack upon his realm, has—having allowed his wrath to be overcome by your valor[929]—sent me to give you the right hand[930] and good faith, granting you immunity and inviolability on the roads in the desire that you come to him seeking friendship without guile and deceit; and he promises to give you gifts and honor,[931] from which you will henceforth benefit by his authority, along with that which is now yours by virtue of your own valor.

327 Asineus himself put off going there, but sent his brother Anileus with as many gifts as he could bring. He set off and was allowed in to the king. Artabanus, upon seeing that Anileus had come alone, asked the reason why Asineus had remained behind. 328 When he learned that he had remained in the marsh out of fear, he swore by his ancestral gods that he would do them no evil if they visited him in reliance upon him, and he gave his right hand,[932] which among all the barbarians there is the greatest proof of security for visitors.[933] 329 For no one would ever be false once he had given his hand, nor—once such a grant of security had been made—would anyone ever hesitate to trust [even] those whom he had suspected of desiring to do him wrong. So Artabanus, after doing that, dispatched Anileus to convince his brother to return [with him]. 330 The king[934] did this in the hope of curbing[935] the Jewish brothers' valor by turning it into friendship, for his satraps were rebellious or in a

---

927 As stated, using something of the same image, at §318.

928 Apparently the reference is to Artabanus II; see the note on "Arsacid line" at §48.

929 A ruler's ability and willingness to be large enough to ignore offense is, for Josephus, a standard example of "magnanimity" (μεγαλοφροσύνη); see 2.141; 12.122, 128. Cf. the note on "high spirit" at §255.

930 On this binding gesture, see the note on "for visitors" at §328. The present case is recalled at §334.

931 Perhaps τιμή means "an office," as often; see the note on "some office" at §17.

932 As he promised in his letter (§326).

933 For the evidence for this, see Herman 2006: 252. However, although the gesture is frequently mentioned in an eastern context (e.g. 8.387; 20.62; Tacitus, *Ann.* 11.9; Mason 2022b: 13–14, n. 16), Josephus takes it for granted in the Greco-Roman world as well; see, for example, *War* 2.451; 6.356, 378, 433; 7.102. It may be, therefore, that here he means that the gesture was respected *even* among the barbarians—a comment that betrays an outsider's point of view, be it Josephus's or that of his source. Cf. Shaw 1993: 192.

934 In the Greek there is, here, quite anomalously, no article; contrast, for example, at §§317, 325, 344, 377. But

so too at §359, and often enough elsewhere in Josephus (even where it could not be rendered by an indirect article, as at 6.67 and, perhaps, below at §360) to appear not to be mere scribal carelessness; so, for example, 2.101, 167; 10.6; 17.20, 36. Perhaps, as Anthony Ellis suggests, it is a remnant of classical usage esp. with regard to the kings of Persia; see LSJ 309, s.v., §III.1. Cooper (1998: 389–390, §50.2.18) offers much evidence for such Attic usage and explains that it amounts to treating βασιλεύς as a proper name. My thanks to Deborah L. Gera for her help with this note.

935 The image is one of putting a bit (ἐνστόμισμα) into the mouth of a horse in order to control it—another word from the equine world. For the familiarity with horses implied by the present story (§§15, 320, 322, 354), pointing to its Iranian background, see Herman 2006: 52. Although the manuscripts here read ἐνστομισμάτων, both the plural and the genitive are strange, and have occasioned emendations here, as has the appearance of the better-testified ἐπιστόμισμα, in the same sense, at §371 and 19.228. For such usage, from the literal "shut someone's mouth, muzzle, gag" (as in Titus 1:11) to "curb, restrain" (Philo, *Allegorical Interpretation* 3.155), as here, see Spicq 1994: 2.61–62.

rebellious mood and he was about to set out against them. **331** He was, therefore, afraid that, while the war was going on there,[936] in order to subdue the rebels, Asineus's men would grow greatly in strength and either make Babylonia subservient to them or, if they failed to achieve that, would not fail to work yet greater evils.

(9.4) 332 So he, with such thoughts in mind, dispatched Anileus, and he convinced his brother, adducing the king's enthusiasm and the oath that had been made, whereupon they set out quickly to Artabanus. **333** When they arrived he received them with pleasure,[937] and he marveled at Asineus's courage[938] in action, observing that he was altogether short in appearance and [therefore] gave those whom he met, at first sight, reason to scorn him and to think nothing of him. Indeed, he told his friends that Asineus's soul was, by comparison, greater than his body.

Once, while drinking, he pointed out Asineus to the chief of his army, Abdagases, telling him the man's name and of the valor he had displayed in war. **334** When Abdagases asked him for permission to kill him as repayment[939] for the way he had outraged the Parthian realm, the king said:

> But I cannot give you permission [to act] against a man who has depended upon my good faith, and whom, moreover, I convinced [to come] on my urging, by sending him my right hand[940] and making myself reliable by oaths to the gods. **335** But if you really are a good warrior, you can avenge the outrage of the kingdom of the Parthians without any breach of my oath: when he is about to return to his home, prove yourself superior to him with your own force and without my knowledge.

336 But at dawn,[941] he called for Asineus and said:

> Young man, it is time for you to return to your home, and no longer to stir up the wrath of even more of the generals here to kill you even without my consent. **337** I grant you as deposit the land of Babylonia, to be under your care so as to preserve it free from brigandage and from suffering other evils. And I am worthy of a good disposition on your part, having maintained blamelessly my own pledge [to you]—and that, not with regard to bagatelles, but, rather, with regard to [your very] survival.

338 With those words, and giving him gifts, he then[942] sent Asineus on his way. When he reached home he built forts and fortified those that had already [existed]. He had become great in a short period of time, and there was no one among his predecessors who from such a point of departure[943] had come, through boldness, to grasp control of affairs of

---

936 In the far-flung regions ruled by the rebellious satraps.

937 "Receive with pleasure" is a favorite collocation of Josephus; see the note on "pleasure" at §63.

938 For Josephus's admiration of soldiers for their courage, note especially 12.307, where he goes so far as to replace his source's (1 Macc 4:10) claim, that God will support Judas's forces because of his mercy and covenantal obligation, by his own claim that God will do so because he admires their εὐψυχία. Specifically for bravery in the face of death, see the note on "bravely" at 19.200.

In general, see Spicq 1994: 2.155–156 and Feldman 1998a: 308–309.

939 This is the only occurrence of ἄποινα in Josephus.

940 As is reported at §§325–326.

941 I.e., in secret. Josephus portrays Artabanus as quite wily: first he misleads Abdagases into thinking that he would be able to overcome Asineus, then he helps Asineus escape the danger.

942 This is the only occurrence of τηνίκα in Josephus.

943 See the note on "wool" at §314.

state.[944] **339** The Parthian generals who were sent down there paid him court, [to such an extent that] the honor he received from Babylonia seemed minor and less than his own valor itself.[945] He thus enjoyed dignity and power; all the affairs of Mesopotamia were up to him;[946] and their[947] good fortune went on growing for fifteen years.[948]

(9.5)[949] **340** But just when their good circumstances were coming to a peak the beginning of troubles took hold of them,[950] for the following reason: because the valor, by virtue of which they had risen to great power, they now redirected toward outrage, [namely], toward the violation of ancestral [laws], motivated by lusts and [the pursuit of] pleasure. Having met a certain Parthian, who had come to be the general of those regions, **341** and who was accompanied by his wife—who was praised beyond other women for other reasons too, but what gave her a special measure of influence upon him was her astounding beauty—**342** Asineus's brother[951] Anileus, learning of her beauty either by hearsay or by seeing her himself, became both her lover and her enemy: [her enemy] because he could not hope to be unified[952] with the woman unless he gained authority over her by possessing her, but also [her lover], because he considered his desire for her difficult to resist.[953] **343** Forthwith her husband was designated,[954] among them,[955] an enemy and a "dead man,"[956]

Enter Woman,
Enter Trouble,
II: The Brothers'
Fall

---

944 Contrast Josephus's comments about Agrippa, who too underwent a major jump in his status. But that was due to his good fortune (§197) or—as the biblical Joseph—divine providence (§§127–130; see the note on "in common" at §201), while for these Babylonian gangsters it was due only to their "boldness" or "strength" (§347). That explains their downfall, which begins in a few lines.

945 This seems to mean that the honors he received from Parthia, to which Babylonia was subject (§§313, 337), mimimized the relative significance of the honor he received from the latter.

946 Thackeray (*ThLJ* 13, s.v. αἴρειν) comments that the text here is doubtful; so is the sense.

947 This reading in the plural, αὐτῶν, supported by a few witnesses and followed by Niese 1890a: 202 and Feldman 1965: 192, fits the opening of the next paragraph and also §347. Other witnesses, followed by Schalit (1963: 313), maintain here the singular in use in the preceding lines.

948 As Goodblatt argues (1987: 616–622), followed by Herman (2006: 262–264), these were the years "from the disintegration of the rule of Artabanus in 36/7 till the consolidation of power by Vologases in 51/2."

949 For the heading, cf. §238.

950 This is a variety of a usual Josephan motif. See the note on "was jealous" at §240.

951 The need to identify him here reflects the fact that since §332, where Anileus was last mentioned, the story has concentrated on Asineus; cf. the note on "their" at §339.

952 For use of σύνοδος in a sexual context, see also 17.51—there together with συμπράσσω, just as here together with ἐκπράσσω.

953 This is the only occurrence of δυσαντίλεκτος in Josephus. For the idea that passion for a woman can be irresistible, cf. the note on "passion" at §350.

954 For Josephus's use of χειροτονέω (lit. "stretching out hands," i.e. voting), cf. the note on "elect" at §22.

955 Neither text nor meaning is secure here. Niese (1890a: 202), following Ambrosianus, read ἐπ᾽ αὐτῆς, perhaps meaning "on her account," but it is difficult to square that with the genitive, and Schalit's (1963: 313) translation of Niese's text, "together with her," suggests the gang wanted to kill the woman too, but it is plain that they did not. The above translation is, faute de mieux, a guess at the meaning of the reading according to three other witnesses: ἐπ᾽ αὐτοῖς.

956 Here Ambrosianus, followed by Niese (1890a: 202; 1890b: 174), reads κτείνων κιτιῶν, but other witnesses offer κτιλίων [or κτιλλίων] κιτίων or only some version of the second word, which remains obscure. This suggests that κτείνων, which clearly refers to killing, was born as a gloss for the obscure word that now follows it. Schalit (1965: 165–171; 1968: 75), followed by Feldman (1965: 533), suggests that κιτιῶν began as κτιλλίων or the like (found, as noted above, in two witnesses), which was a transliteration of the Aramaic *qᵉtila*. That is, Schalit argues, Josephus's source reflects the phrase (*gavra*) *qᵉtila* ("a killed [man]"), which is used in the Babylonian Talmud (including *Pesaḥ.* 110b and *Sanh.* 71b, 81a, 85a) to denote a person who, although alive, is considered dead, whether

and after he was drawn into battle and fell[957] and was killed, she was captured and married to her lover.[958]

But it was not without great misfortunes for Anileus, and for Asineus too, that she entered their house; rather, it was with a certain great tragedy, for the following reason.

344 After she was taken captive upon her husband's death she had concealed[959] the statuettes[960] of the gods, which were [worshipped] according to her husband's and her own ancestral custom, and thereby preserved their native custom (for it is the native custom of all people there to have objects of worship in their homes and to take them with them when traveling abroad).[961] At first she performed their cult secretly, but when she was designated wife[962] she began to worship them in her customary way, according to the same regulations that she had followed in the days of her first husband. **345** At first, the most respected companions among them [told Anileus[963]] that what he was doing was not at all in accordance with Hebraic practice or in conformance with their laws, for he had taken a gentile woman who deviated from the precise sacrifices and religious rites that were customary among them.[964] Let him take care [they said], lest too much indulgence of corporeal pleasure destroy the good regime and the authority that up until then had [under his leadership] flourished under the deity. **346** When that accomplished nothing,[965] and, on the contrary, [Anileus] even killed one of his most respected friends because he had spoken

---

because of a terminal medical condition or a death sentence. As such, he who kills such a person is not considered a murderer. That is, the brothers proclaimed the Parthian to be one who could be killed with impunity. For other putative evidence of an Aramaic source for the present story, see N. G. Cohen 1975/76. None of these suggestions is watertight (and see the reservations of Goodblatt 1987a: 619 and Lembi 2001: 67–68), but they are suggestive. For another such suggestion, cf. the note on "labor" at §319.

957 For such use of πίπτω of death in battle, see also §§98, 366–367; 20.176.

958 If, as has been suggested (Goodblatt 1987a: 620), this was thought to have been justified by the law of Deuteronomy 21:10–14//*Ant.* 4.257–259, the author sees no need to point that out; what is important is that conquest and unification come together, as stipulated in the preceding paragraph. This is an item in the case that this story began as a novella and the edifying comments at §§340 and 347 were added (by Josephus? or some predecessor?) only later.

959 This meaning of περιστέλλω, suggested for our passage by *CCFJ* 3.401, as also the bracketed reference to worship, seems to be warranted by the continuation of this paragraph. Usually the verb refers to wrapping something in order to protect or preserve it; cf. LSJ 1388, s.v., and, for example, 19.237.

960 This is the only occurrence of ἀφίδρυμα in Josephus.

961 Cohen (1999: 170, n. 93) commented that a wife's insistence on worshipping gods other than her husband's constitutes an "egregious exception" to the ancient norm formulated in Plutarch's *Advice to Bride and Groom* 19 (*Moralia* 140D), and also illustrates the assumption that if she did do so, it would be in secret: "It is becoming for a wife to worship and to know only the gods that her husband believes in, and to shut the front door tight upon all queer rituals and outlandish superstitions. For with no god do stealthy and secret rites performed by a woman find any favour" (trans. Babbitt, LCL). It is not clear, however, how widely that expectation was recognized and observed. In this case, moreover, since Anileus's wife had been taken captive, it was understandable that she might conclude that it need not bind her.

962 For Josephus's insistence on the significance of this change of status, cf. §40, also the note on "living together" at §148.

963 Niese (1890a: 208) marks a lacuna here, but it appears to be obvious that something like this is needed (and it is indeed supplied by the Epitome: ἔλεγον Ἀνιλαίῳ ὡς [Niese 1887–1896: 325]).

964 Note that Josephus has them phrase the problem not merely as one of intermarriage, but rather as a matter of the violations of the Jewish religion it would inevitably entail. So too in Josephus's main discussion of intermarriage: his version of Numbers 25 in *Ant.* 4; see esp. the Midianite women's speech at §§134–138 and its immediate results at §§139–140. On that episode, see van Unnik 1974.

965 Similar phrase: 17.252.

too openly,[966] and he, with his eyes on[967] loyalty to the laws and vengeance against him who killed him, called down a curse upon Anileus himself and also upon Asineus and all their companions, that they should suffer that the same end come upon them at the hands of their enemies: **347** [upon the brothers], as having been the authors of the wickedness, and upon the others, for they had not come to his assistance when he was undergoing such suffering because of his attempt to assert the laws. The others were upset about this, but restrained themselves, remembering that they had achieved their good fortune not by virtue of any cause other than [the brothers'] strength.

348 However, when they heard even of the worship of the gods that the Parthians revere, they considered that Anileus's offense against the laws was no longer tolerable, and so they went to Asineus and, by now in greater numbers, cried out against Anileus: **349** they said that although it was all right that previously he had not himself seen that which was expedient to do, at least[968] now he should turn things around before the sin tips the scales[969] and brings perdition upon him and every one else as well. As for [Anileus's] marriage with that wench,[970] they said it happened without their approval and was not in accordance with the laws they were accustomed to follow, and that the cult the woman practiced constituted a show of disrespect for the God of their religion.

350 [Asineus] himself knew that his brother's sin was, and would in the future be, the cause of great calamities, but he did not hold him back [from it] because he was won over by the goodwill deriving from family relationship; rather, he supplied him with the excuse of being overcome by the greater evil power of passion.[971] **351** But when great numbers continued to gather day after day and their complaining became more and more [intense], to such an extent that he spoke about them to Anileus, upbraiding him for those things that were already done and demanding that he stop them in the future by sending the wench back to her relatives, **352** he accomplished nothing through these words. But the woman, taking notice of the unrest[972] that gripped the people on her account and fearing lest Anileus be made to suffer because of his passion for her, put a drug into Asineus's food,[973] thus getting

---

966 A frequent motif: see 19.319–325 and 20.162. No one likes criticism.

967 Reading, with Niese, θεώμενος, which is normally plain "looking, watching." Perhaps for this reason, L. A. Post (cited by Feldman [1965: 196] in his apparatus ad loc.) suggested reading ἀποθεώμενος, which would yield something like "looking away (from his own fate) to ... ", similar to the description of another martyr at 2 Macc 7:11 (where ὑπεροράω is used in the same sense). However, the emendation does not seem to be warranted, for two reasons: (a) in the only other place in Josephus in which ἀποθεάομαι might appear, *War* 2.310, the sense must be just the opposite: "look attentively at" (so both *ThLJ* 68, s.v. ἀποθεᾶσθαι and LSJ 198, s.v. ἀποθεάομαι); and (b) there is no security that the verb indeed appears at *War* 2.310, where it is indeed offered by two manuscripts but rejected by Niese and even by Thackeray himself (JLCL 2.442), and LSJ 198 offers no evidence at all for the verb, apart from *War* 2.310.

968 On γοῦν, see the note on "at least" at §243.

969 For this image, apparently implied by the verb here (ἀνακειμένην), see also §9.

970 Cf. the note on "wench" at §40.

971 As Lembi (2001: 55) notes, this motif, that passion for a woman can excuse a man's crimes, already appeared at §80. This too suggests that, whatever the source, Josephus was at work as an editor. Cf. *War* 1.359 and *Ant.* 15.88, 93, on Antonius having been "enslaved" by his passion for Cleopatra (as men might be subjugated by a female slave [4.244] and Herod was by Mariamme [15.219]); as is noted by van Henten (2014: 60, n. 502), this view, which tends to excuse Antonius for his misdeeds, was "more or less the official one at Rome after Octavian's victory at Actium."

972 Lit. "murmuring," "grumbling." This is the only occurrence of θροῦς in Josephus.

973 Apparently she assumed that it was really competition between the brothers that lay behind the complaints; the readers know better.

rid of the man without fear of punishment, for [even if she were to be accused of the murder] it would be by her lover that she would be judged for what she had done.

(9.6) 353 Anileus, who now remained alone, took over the command and led his army out against the villages of Mithridates—one of the leading men of Parthia, who had married the daughter of King Artabanus. He looted them, taking much money and many captives,[974] as well as livestock and much else—whatever things contribute to the well-being of those who own them. 354 But when Mithridates, who happened to be there at the same time, heard of the capture of the villages, he took it quite badly that without any prior wrongdoing Anileus had begun to treat him unjustly, ignoring his dignity to his face. Collecting as much cavalry as he could and, [of the foot-soldiers[975]], those who were in their prime of life, he came to attack Anileus's men.[976] The latter was resting in one of his villages, so as to fight on the morrow; for that day was the sabbath, which the Jews pass in leisure.[977] 355 But when Anileus learned of this[978] from a Syrian man,[979] a gentile from another village who told him everything in detail, including the place where Mithridates was going to eat, he ate early[980] and marched out at night, hoping to fall upon the Parthians while they did not know what was happening. 356 Falling upon them around the fourth watch,[981] he killed some while they were still sleeping and drove the others into flight. Taking Mithridates alive, he led him to his [camp] seated naked on an ass, which is considered the greatest humiliation among the Parthians.[982] 357 After he had brought him down to the forest with such outrage[983] [to his dignity], his friends demanded that he kill Mithridates; but he heatedly argued with them, urging the opposite. For, [he said], it would not be appropriate[984] to kill a man of a first-ranked Parthian family, one who was even more eminent by virtue of his connection by marriage with the king. 358 What had so far been done was, [he claimed], still tolerable, for although Mithridates had been outraged, the preservation of his life would be remembered with gratitude to those responsible for it, by him who had been so benefited; 359 but if he were to suffer something irreversible, the king would not be content until he inflicted

---

974 For ἀνδράποδον referring specifically to prisoners of war, see Gibbs and Feldman 1985/86: 291–292.

975 Following Niese's (1890a: 205; 1890b: 176) emendation of ὁπλιτῶν instead of πλείστων, for the latter is difficult to construe and it is unlikely that we would be told of an attack by cavalry alone.

976 As often (see Danker 2000: 798, s.v., §h2δ), here too "οἱ περί NN" means "NN and his men," as we can see from the immediate continuation. Cf. the note on "retinue of" at 20.131.

977 As above, §319. Here, however, it is not said that the Jews would not dare to fight, only that they would be at leisure, which perhaps means only an expectation that their guard would be down.

978 Namely, of Mithridates's plan to attack them.

979 On this "Syrian," see the note on "this tragedy" §310.

980 As at 12.306, καθ' ὥραν apparently means "in a timely fashion," i.e., early.

981 Presumably Josephus is assuming the Roman system of dividing the night (roughly 6 p.m. to 6 a.m.) into four watches (Mark 6:48; Pliny, NH 10.46; Vegetius 3.8

[Stelten 1990: 154–155]). The fourth, before dawn (hence a.k.a. ἑωθινὴ φυλακή—War 3.251; 4.63), was a good time for surprise attacks; see War 3.319 (on the ἐσχατή φυλακή, when guards might be expected to be lax and slumbering) and 4.63–64, also, for example, Livy 4.9.13 and Caesar, Gallic War 1.21. For a rabbinic discussion of whether the night is divided into three watches (as is apparently assumed by "middle watch" at Judges 7:19) or four, see t. Berakhot 1:3 (ed. Zuckermandel, 1; 1:1 in ed. Lieberman, 1).

982 As Herman (2006: 257–260) documents, Persians considered even merely riding on an ass to be demeaning; to be forced into it, and while naked, made it all the worse.

983 Reading μετὰ ... ὑβρίσματος, von Gutschmid's emendation cited by Niese (1890a: 205) and adopted by Feldman (1965: 200); it is bolstered by περιύβρισται at §358 and τοὺς ὑβρίσαντας εἰς αὐτὸν at §360. The manuscripts here read μετὰ ... ὁρίσματος, but "border" seems impossible to construe here.

984 For this translation of μὴ καλῶς ἔχειν, which means more than the fear of the price to pay (§359), see, for example, 17.354 and 19.6–7.

a great massacre upon the Jews in Babylon.[985] It was right that they spare those [Jews] both on account of their common ancestry and because if they were to suffer a disaster there would be no recovery,[986] for they will have used up the multitude of those there who are in their prime.[987]

360 When he formed such considerations and set them forth in the discussion, he convinced them. So Mithridates was released. But when he came [home], his wife upbraided him, for, in ignoring [the need] to see to vengeance being taken upon those who had outraged him, *and being content with having been saved from captivity by Jewish people*,[988] he also failed to see to[989] vengeance for [the insult to] her too, he being the son-in-law of a[990] king.[991] **361**[992] "So now" [she said], "either you return to your manly valor, or else I swear by[993] the royal gods that I will dissolve my marital partnership with you."[994] **362** And he, who was unable to endure the daily renewed castigation by his wife[995] and fearful lest his wife's high spirit[996] might indeed lead her to dissolve her marriage with him, gathered up— however reluctant and unwilling[997] he was—an army as large as possible and set out. By now, he himself[998] was convinced[999] that survival was not to be endured if he, a Parthian, were to be pushed around[1000] by a Jew fighting against him.

---

985 Ἐν Βαβυλῶνι, that is, in the city of Babylon; cf. the note on "Babylonia" at §104. Assuming that, for which Niese (1890a: 205) reports no variants, is the correct reading, it is noteworthy that Josephus offers, here, no reason to expect the massacre in Babylon in particular, a city that has not been mentioned in this story. Apparently he, or already his source, has specified the city in light of what is reported later; see the note on "Babylon" at §373, where clearly the city is meant. For the Jews of the city of Babylon in the talmudic period, see Oppenheimer 1983: 44–62.

986 That is, there will be no recovery from a royal attack on the Jews of Babylon, which would "use up" their strongest men. On the text and translation, cf. Feldman 1965: 202–203, n. b. For this fairly literal sense of ἀνα- στροφή, see also §173. Usually, however, it means "conduct, comportment" (as at 19.28, Galatians 1:13 and Ephesians 4:22), and so it has been proposed to emend it into ἀπο- στροφή; see the discussion in Part v of the Introduction.

987 For this sense of ἀκμή, see *ThLJ* 18, s.v., citing, inter alia, *Ant* 3.8; 5.164; 7.78.

988 The italicized words render the opening of §361; I moved them to here so as to facilitate readability.

989 For such use of προμοθήομαι, cf. §§284, 286 and 19.153.

990 Cf. the note on "the king" at §330.

991 This convoluted sentence seems to mean that she complained that his willingness to abstain from avenging himself entailed ignoring his obligation to avenge the contempt shown to her as well (καὶ ταύτῃ τιμωρῶν), which was especially reprehensible since she was the king's daughter.

992 See the note on "people" at §360.

993 As above, §328.

994 A woman's threat to walk away from her marriage unilaterally is part of Josephus's standard hostile portrayal of a termagant. Cf. the note on "ancestral rules" at 20.143.

995 Cf. §245. As with Herodias (§§242–244), Josephus enjoys portraying a nagging wife who, taking an insult to her husband (that he is willing to accept) as an insult to her, rants and makes life impossible for him until he agrees to do something dangerous, against his better judgment. In the present case, however, her urging brings him to success, since his enemies are wicked; Herodias, in contrast, urged her husband to compete with Agrippa, who was Gaius's, and God's, fair-haired boy. The woman's pushy nature, in this case, is accentuated all the more by the explicit moderation not only of her husband, but also of Anileus (§§357–359), both of whom desired to avoid further conflict.

996 Again, as Herodias—§255. Cf. the note on "defeated him" at §246.

997 Same phrase: §219.

998 That is: not just his wife.

999 Here Josephus contradicts his comment a line earlier, where he emphasizes that Mithridates was reluctant and unwilling and gave in only due to his fear of his wife. For a similar situation, see the notes on "others" at 19.193 and on "drug" at 20.148. In those cases too, Josephus's antipathy to pushy women makes him loath to give up on blaming them, even when it creates tension within the story.

1000 Same verb below, at §375; cf. the note on "pushed around" at §155.

(9.7) **363** Anileus, when he learned that Mithridates was riding out against him with a large force, thought it would be dishonorable to remain in the marshes rather than seeking to preempt the enemy by going out to confront him. Hoping to do things similar to those he had successfully done in the past, and [hoping] that those who dare and practice being courageous would indeed be endowed with manly virtue,[1001] he led out his force. **364** Many came and joined his original army, looking forward to turning to pillaging the gentiles after terrifying the enemies altogether into flight[1002] by the [mere] sight of them.[1003] **365** When, however, they had advanced around ninety furlongs, and were—because of the dearth of water along the way and its being midday—beset by thirst, Mithridates appeared and attacked them, when they were in a miserable state for lack of drink, for which reason, as well as on account of the hour of the day, they were unable to carry their weapons. **366** A humiliating rout was thus imposed upon Anileus's men, for they were exhausted[1004] [troops] engaging fresh [troops]. There was much slaughter: many myriads of men fell. Anileus and those who remained with him retreated to the forest in flight, having afforded Mithridates great joy at his victory over them. **367** Anileus was joined by an inexperienced[1005] mob of wicked men who considered their survival cheap in exchange for fleeting ease, so that their influx was a compensation[1006] for the great number of those who had been killed. Because of their lack of training,[1007] however, they were not at all the equal of those who had fallen. **368** Nonetheless, using even them[1008] he was able to overrun the villages of the Babylonians, and they were all laid waste by Anileus's wantonness. **369** The Babylonians, and those who were involved in this war, sent to the Jews of Nehardea and demanded that they turn Anileus over, and when they refused this appeal—for even if they had wanted to turn him over they were not capable of doing so—[the Babylonians] called upon them to make peace. [The Jews of Nehardea] said that they too wanted negotiations to make peace,

---

1001 For similar thoughts, see the note on "resolve" at §5.

1002 This is the only occurrence of προεκπλήσσω in Josephus. He uses a number of προεκ- words only once each; see *CCFJ* 3.524.

1003 This portrayal of those who joined Anileus's army as being in it greedily for booty, and as arrogantly supposing that the mere sight of them would cause the enemy to flee, prepares readers quite pointedly for their coming debacle.

1004 Cf. 13.327: τῇ δυνάμει ἀπηγορευκότες ("exhausted in strength") and 19.192.

1005 Niese (1890a: 207) reads ἄπορον ("indigent"), with all the manuscripts. However, although scorn for the poor would fit the bias evinced at §315, it appears to be more natural to speak, when describing those who fill the ranks of an army, of an inexperienced mob than a "poor" mob, and that is what is also suggested by "lack of training" in the next sentence. Hence Hudson's suggestion (cited by Niese), ἄπειρον, "inexperienced" (as, for example, at 2.347; 5.118; *War* 1.650). Hudson's suggestion is bolstered, indirectly, by the Latin translation, *infinita multitudo hominum pessimorum* which gives no support for ἄπορον but can well be a mistranslation of ἄπειρον.

("Infinita" ["boundless"] apparently renders another sense of the Greek adjective, one that, although adopted by Schalit [1963: 315], does not fit the context). For the emphasis on training and experience as a necessary for military success, see the note on "training" later in the next sentence.

1006 This is the only occurrence of ἀντανίσωμα in Josephus.

1007 This is the only occurrence of ἀμελέτητος in Josephus. Josephus likes to underline the importance of military training. See, for example, 19.243; *War* 2.577–582; 3.72–75; and Eckstein 1990: 200. In this passage, as in the comment in §366 about exhausted troops fighting fresh troops, and in a similar passage at 19.243, Josephus takes the pose of the experienced general. For an imaginative recreation of Josephus's military career, see Hata 1994: 311–312, 318–319. On Roman military training, see esp. Vegetius 1.9–19 (Stelten 1990: 22–39) and Phang 2008: 37–53.

1008 Reading τούτοις with Lowthius, cited by Niese 1890a: 207 (where the manuscripts' ταύταις is retained) and later adopted by him (Niese 1890b: 178) and Feldman (1965: 204).

and sent men with the Babylonians to negotiate with Anileus.[1009] 370 But the Babylonians discovered, after making observations, the place where Anileus was encamped,[1010] and falling upon them surreptitiously at night, while they were drunk and overcome by sleep, they killed with impunity all whom they caught there, including Anileus himself.

(9.8) 371 The Babylonians, now freed of Anileus's heavy [hand]—for it had served to curb[1011] their hatred for the Jews (which existed because they were always greatly at odds on account of the contradictions between their laws,[1012] so that whichever happened first to be more confident would touch off mutual violence) so long as Anileus's men were not destroyed—the Babylonians[1013] now began to attack the Jews. 372 The latter were greatly outraged at the Babylonians' wantonness, but neither being able to respond in battle nor considering it tolerable to live together they departed[1014] for Seleucia, which was the most famous of cities there,[1015] founded by Seleucus Nicator.[1016] It was inhabited by numerous Macedonians[1017] and a majority of Greeks, but not a few Syrians too enjoyed civic status there. 373 It was there that the Jews fled, and for five years they suffered no troubles there.[1018]

The Jews' Troubles in Babylon and Seleucia

1009 The opposition between good and peace-seeking Jewish citizens, on the one hand, and Jewish brigands and rebels, on the other, against whom the former are powerless, is a standard Josephan theme. See, for example, 20.180 and the note there on "remonstrated with them."

1010 For ἰδρυμένος of a military force's encampment, see for example *Ant.* 14.467. Cf. μεθιδρύσας at 18.55.

1011 As above, §330.

1012 This interpretation of what makes for hatred of Jews is reminiscent of Esther 3:8//*Ant.* 11.212; perhaps Josephus had that in mind when writing here about this Babylonian episode. But it would resonate well in Rome as well; see Tacitus, *Hist.* 5.4.1 ("The Jews regard as profane all that we hold sacred; on the other hand, they permit all that we abhor ...").

1013 This clumsy first sentence of the new story, which adds so much information after the first mention of "the Babylonians" that it has to mention them again, reads like a seam, as if Josephus had a source that referred to Babylonians attacking Jews and he expanded its opening in order to create some continuity with the preceding story. This observation conforms to others, namely, that from this point on the narrative no longer reads like a novel and is also devoid of moralizing elements, and thus supports the conclusion that the two stories are of differing provenances. That conclusion, in turn, undermines, to some extent, the presumption that the order in which they appear in Josephus's work is their chronological order; see the note on "this tragedy" at §310.

1014 From the city of Babylon, as becomes clear, retrospectively, at §373. Josephus, perhaps already his source, apparently depends on readers to infer from "the Babylonians" that the attacks came in Babylon, as was already predicted at §359.

1015 On Seleucia on the Tigris, already mentioned at §49, see Held 2002: 221–236.

1016 The mss. read "Nicanor"; the same mistake occurs at 12.119 and 13.213. For the foundation of Seleucia by Seleucus Nicator, the first Seleucid king, see Pliny, NH 6.30, 122 and Appian, *Syrian Wars* 57. Strabo, *Geog.* 16.2.5 compares the city in size to such great metropolitan centers as Alexandria and Antioch.

1017 Indeed, its "Macedonian" character ("Macedonumque moris") was emphasized by Pliny, loc. cit. Josephus usually uses the term of the Seleucids, quite regularly in Book 13 (see 12.434 and 13.1, 3, 7, 29, 43, 62 etc.), but after that it hardly appears. Hence "Macedonians" is appropriate here, after the reference to the foundation of the city by the first Seleucid king; for the Seleucid kingdom as *Macedonicum Imperium*, see Bikerman 1938: 5. In contrast, Ἕλληνες is common throughout (including above, §§20, 141, 257). Although the coming reference to the latter might suggest a purist distinction between Macedonians and Greeks, it seems likelier that it means "other Greeks," since §374 ignores Macedonians and refers only to "Greeks" and Syrians.

1018 This datum is the foundation of all discussions of the story's chronology. Usually it is assumed that the civil strife (stasis) depicted in the coming paragraphs is the same as the conflict described by Tacitus at *Ann.* 6.42. Since Tacitus reports (ibid.), in the context of 36 CE, that Seleucia accepted Tiridates as its ruler, which amounted to a rebellion against Artabanus II, and at *Ann.* 11.9, in the context of 41, reports that the revolt of Seleucia lasted seven years, it follows that the stasis, and the revolt, began in 35 or 36 CE. For that reconstruction, see esp. Goodblatt 1987a: 605–616. Accordingly, if the Jews moved to Seleucia just before the stasis began, as the present passage suggests, it follows that the slaughter in their sixth year in

However, in the sixth year after they first suffered ruination in Babylon[1019] and established new settlements outside of that city, and therefore arrived in Seleucia, there befell them a greater calamity, for a reason that I shall [now] set forth.

(9.9) 374 The life of the Seleucians is to a large extent characterized by civil strife and discord between the Greeks and the Syrians, the Greeks [usually] prevailing. But now, when there was such strife at the time when the Jews were taking up residence together with them, the Syrians prevailed because of an agreement they made with the Jews—who were men unafraid of danger who enlisted enthusiastically to fight.[1020] 375 The Greeks, who were being pushed around[1021] in the civil strife, seeing that they had only one possible point of departure for restoring their prior status, namely, if they could put an end to the unanimity[1022] of the Jews and the Syrians, each spoke with those Syrians who had been their friends before what had happened, promising them peace and friendship. 376 They were happy to be convinced, so both sides put together statements and, after the leaders of each side brought about a reconciliation,[1023] the negotiations were quickly concluded. When they were all of one mind, they both thought fit to put forth, as great proof of their mutual goodwill, their hatred of the Jews:[1024] falling upon them suddenly they killed more than 50,000 men. All of them perished, apart from some who were allowed to escape by the mercy of friends or neighbors. 377 For those, escape was to Ctesiphon, a Greek city located not far from Seleucia,[1025] where the king winters every year[1026] and most of his baggage[1027] happens to be stored there. But it was not wise for them to settle there, for the people of Seleucia gave no consideration to the respect[1028] due the monarchy. 378 So the entire Jewish people there now was in fear of the Babylonians and the Seleucians, for even those Syrians

---

the city, with which the coming story ends, came in 40 or 41. That conclusion dovetails readily with the fact that Josephus places the story just after reporting the death of Gaius in 41. That is, just as elsewhere, Josephus tells some story that is peripheral to the history of Judea after concluding the history of Judea in that same period. See the note on "took them over" at §27.

1019 As at §359, ἐν Βαβυλῶνι refers to the city of Babylon itself; cf. the note on "departed" at §372.

1020 This fits Josephus's usual concern to portray the Jews as brave; see the note on "courage" at 18.333.

1021 Same verb as above, §362.

1022 The manuscripts read τὸν λέγοντα ("that which was said"), which makes little sense; Niese (1890a: 208) adopts the first edition's colorful reading, ταὐτὸν λέγοντας, which is supported by its (re)appearance at §378; so too at 10.107 and 17.35.

1023 This is the only occurrence of ἐπιδιαλλαγή in Josephus; the verb ἐπιδιαλλάττω also appears once (16.175).

1024 This sounds like bitter irony, reminiscent of 18.5.

1025 The two faced each other on opposite sides of the Tigris, so close that later they were considered one city.

1026 As is also noted by Strabo, Geog. 16.1.6. Cf. above, §49.

1027 On ἀποσκευή, which can include both property and dependent people, see Lee 1972. Cf. the note on "elimination" at §41.

1028 This renders the text as emended by Hudson (1726: 1.913), τιμῆς ...μὴ πεφροντικότων, followed by Feldman 1965: 210 and Schalit 1963: 316. Niese 1890a: 209 retains the manuscripts' τιμῇ ... πεφροντικότων in the dative and with no negation, which is difficult to construe. (The verb usually takes the genitive; see, for example §221 and numerous examples in CCFJ 4.323, s.v. φροντίζω.) What Josephus seems to mean is that while one might have thought that the royal presence in Ctesiphon would keep the local population, including that in nearby Seleucia, in line and therefore life would be safe for Jews who resided there, in fact that was not the case, for, when it came to the Jews, at least, the locals disregarded the king's expectations. This is a typical stance of diasporic history: the king is just fine, so when there are troubles it must be caused by those who flout the king and disregard his will. Cf. 20.135, 182; Esther 7; 2 Macc 4:3–31, 36–38; 3 Macc 6:20–28 (satire); Philo, Leg. 159–160; and Yerushalmi 1976: 2–3, 17–34 ("'And the king of Portugal was a gracious king,'" so if Jews were massacred he must have been out of town, like Antiochus at 2 Macc 4:30–36).

who were citizens of those places were unanimous[1029] with the Seleucians about making war against the Jews. **379** And so they gathered together in great numbers in Nehardea and Nisibis, attaining safety by virtue of the strength of these cities and also because they were inhabited by a large number of people[1030] who were all fighting men.[1031]

This, then, was the way things were for the Jews residing in Babylonia.[1032]

1029 Same phrase as above, §375.

1030 For the large Jewish communities of Nehardea in later generations, see Oppenheimer 1983: 276–293. As for Nisibis, see the note on "Nisibis" at §312.

1031 As was stated at §374. Thus, this long story ends neatly, as it began at §§311–312, with emphasis on the security provided the Jews by these two cities—which have now been contrasted with Seleucia. This is an impressive achievement by Josephus, esp. if we assume that the historical order of the stories is the reverse; see the note on "this tragedy" at §310.

1032 For such rounding out of stories, see the note on "with Petronius" at §288. For such a conclusion of an entire book, cf. Books 13 ("Such, then, was the death of Alexandra"), 14 ("This, then, was the end of what we received about the end of the Hasmonean family"), and 15 ("This, then, is, on the one hand, the tenor of what pertains to the construction of the sanctuary").

BOOK 19

INTRODUCTION TO BOOK 19

This is quite an exceptional book, insofar as three-quarters of it are devoted to Roman history: well more than the first half offers a long and detailed account of the assassination of Gaius (§§1–211), and then another sixty paragraphs tell the story of Claudius's ascent to the imperial throne (§§212–273). Only thereafter does the last quarter of the book (§§274–366), on the Judean monarchy of Agrippa I, pick up the story of Jewish history from the point it reached in Book 18 with the death of Gaius in 41 (18.305–309). The extensive and detailed attention devoted to the first two topics is obviously surprising in a book on the history of the Jews; contrast 20.156–157, where Josephus explains that he will not write much about Nero because his concern is with the history of the Jews.[1]

The length and detail of the Gaius and Claudius stories, along with the fact that they are by far the most detailed surviving accounts of these events, have spawned a great deal of scholarship. See esp. Schemann 1887: 31–56, Destinon 1904: 7–14, Henning 1922 (non vidi), Momigliano 1932, Charlesworth 1933, Timpe 1960, Feldman 1962, Ritter 1972, D. R. Schwartz 1990a: 23–30, Goud 1996, Wiseman 1992, Scherberich 2001, Free 2017, and Flatto 2020: 98–100. For a very useful annotated translation of 19.1–273, see Wiseman 2013a, along with Mason 2016a's critique from the point of view of Josephan scholarship. Much, perhaps too much, of the scholarship on Book 19 has been source-critical. In this introduction to the book I will seek something of a balance between that and a composition-critical approach.

The source-critical orientation of most scholarship on these narratives derives from the natural assumption of numerous scholars that Josephus must have used a Roman source or Roman sources for the story, if only because he could not have known of these events first-hand (he was a child in Jerusalem when they occurred). Moreover, it is usual to assume that Josephus, as historian of the Jews, had no real interest in the details of these stories. Accordingly, if such basically irrelevant narratives are nevertheless allowed so much space—regularly assessed as "disproportionate"[2]—in his work, Josephus must have found them ready to go. He inserted them, so it is often posited, merely as "padding" to fill out his work,[3] and may be presumed to have followed his Roman source or sources very closely, even slavishly.

These interlocked assumptions have led to sweeping assertions about Josephus's dependence on his Roman source(s) for these narratives, indeed to a willingness to relate to these narratives as if they reproduce the formulations and views of others, not of Josephus.[4] That,

---

1 So too *War* 4.492–496. Similarly, note 11.305 and 18.54, where Josephus gives bare summaries of events external to Jewish history and simply notes that others have written more extensively about them.

2 So, for example, Hölscher 1904: 66 ("unverhält-nismäßige Ausführlichkeit") and Syme 1958: 1.287 ("disproportionate amplitude").

3 "Füllstoff" (Destinon 1904: 4–5), "padding" (Charlesworth 1933: 114), "to eke out his scanty materials" (Thackeray 1929: 69). As for why Josephus wanted to fill out his materials—while Syme (1958: 1.287) notes merely that "his reasons are not clear," others offer motivations:

perhaps Josephus felt his coverage of the years prior to Agrippa I's reign was too thin (see the Introduction, at n. 1); perhaps Josephus wanted, specifically, to fill out twenty books, in imitation of Dionysius of Halicarnassus's *Roman Antiquities* (Thackeray 1929: 68–69; cf. Cowan 2018); or perhaps he thought his work would sell better in Rome if it included these stories (Destinon 1904: 6–7).

4 For prominent examples, see the passages from Syme and Wiseman cited below, before n. 11, about Josephus having "stuck pretty close to," or even "reproduced" and "with fidelity transcribed," his Latin source. So too Thackeray 1929: 69: "all this is obviously drawn

of course, dampened interest in asking about whether and how they function in Josephus's own work, a question that would, willy-nilly, encourage us to think more about Josephus's own involvement in composing the story. Such thinking would suggest that Josephus was, in these narratives, an active editor of his sources, perhaps even worthy of being called an "author."

Two circumstances reinforced earlier scholarship's tendency to avoid the latter. The first is the fact that, as mentioned above, Josephus's narratives about Gaius's death and Claudius's ascent to the throne are by far the most detailed surviving accounts of these events (alongside the much briefer ones found in Suetonius, *Cal.* 56–58 and *Claud.* 10; Cassius Dio 59.29–30 and 60.1; and Josephus's *War* 2.204–214). As such, they have attracted much scholarly interest among students of Roman history. But historians who deal with Roman emperors are not, by and large, at home in Josephus's writings and Josephan scholarship, and, as so often happens, scholars in one field often prefer to extract from another's sources the material they want and then insert it into the dossiers and contexts with which they are familiar, on the basis of considerations with which they are familiar. The result can be a scholarly tendency to build on something from *Ant.* 19 without consideration of what it meant for Josephus.[5]

The second circumstance is the fact that, for a long time, scholars thought that Josephus used only one source for these narratives, and that we can name its author. That made it all the easier to view these narratives as non-Josephan, and thus to justify a willingness to view them without reference to the rest of *Antiquities*, or the rest of Josephus's oeuvre. I refer to a theory that had quite a remarkable history—one that might be paradigmatic about one way scholarship sometimes works.

Namely, in 1870 Theodor Mommsen published an article on Tacitus and Cluvius Rufus. It began, in the best tradition of philological labor, with several pages of detailed and meticulous comparison of parallel passages in Tacitus's Latin to passages in Plutarch's Greek. Mommsen concluded that while neither was dependent on the other, the similarities are so great that both writers must have used a common source, which, he suggested, was the lost Latin history by Cluvius Rufus. Cluvius was active under Nero and somewhat later, and is known to have written a history of Rome; on him and his work (which Tacitus, *Hist.* 4.43.1 assumes to be well known), see esp. Levick 2013.

Mommsen's interest in Cluvius Rufus went a bit further. As far as we know from the few surviving testimonies and fragments (Levick 2013: 2.1036–1041), Cluvius wrote only about the days of Nero and, perhaps, the civil war preceding Vespasian's rise to the throne. Mommsen, nevertheless, nearing the end of his study, briefly raised the question whether we can point to other ancient writers who used Cluvius's work. That serves as the opening for his opinion, stated in a single sentence, that Josephus, "to the extent he followed Roman annals, probably followed Cluvius" (Mommsen 1870: 322).

Mommsen said no more about this. He did not even say anything about where (not to mention how, or to what extent) Josephus probably followed Cluvius. But the sole passage in *Antiquities* to which he referred (in the continuation of that sentence) in support of his suggestion is the reference to Cluvius at 19.91–92, in Josephus's account of the assassination of Gaius. That, of course, indicates Mommsen was thinking of that narrative.[6]

---

from a Latin source," which Josephus "has not hesitated to incorporate entire, not withstanding its irrelevancy to his proper subject."

5 Compare Sandmel's complaint (1962: 8–9) about scholars of rabbinic literature, and of the New Testament,

who behave as if they think that their expertise in one corpus allows them to extract and use tidbits from the other.

6 Mommsen's full text on the subject is as follows: "Dass Josephus für seine 93 n. Chr. abgeschlossene Archäologie und ebenso für den jüdischen Krieg,

Interesting, and, perhaps paradigmatic, are the differential fates of Mommsen's main thesis about Tacitus, Plutarch and Cluvius, on the one hand, and of his aside about Josephus and Cluvius, on the other. In support of the former, Mommsen supplied, as noted, a long and detailed argument. That gave scholars something to bite into, they did, and, as Syme noted about a century later, "not many concurred" (Syme 1958: 2.675). In contrast, concerning Josephus's use of Cluvius, Mommsen's suggestion rested, apart from Cluvius's appearance at 19.91–92, only on Mommsen's own authority. But that seems to have been enough: given Mommsen's stature, it is perhaps not surprising that his suggestion, although hardly more than a brief obiter dictum, was widely accepted, broadened, and turned into near certainty. While some writers were content to remain close to Mommsen's "probably," in general his thesis was taken to be both more certain and broader than it was when first offered. It was taken for granted by many, and by 1913, for example, a prominent German Latinist could write quite generally that "That Cluvius Rufus was Josephus's source for Roman affairs until the days of Nero is just about certain, for Mommsen, as is well known, demonstrated that with regard to [Josephus's] report of the assassination of Gaius and Claudius's rise to the throne."[7] For a compilation of similar citations, see Feldman 1962: 320–321.

Apart from Mommsen's authority, what made his suggestion attractive is not only the general point that we know Cluvius wrote a history. It is, rather, the reference to Cluvius at 19.91–92: a report of a very private conversation between one Bathybius (who is otherwise unknown) and Cluvius, who is defined as a ὑπατικός, that is, a *vir consularis*, one who had been a consul. The assumptions that such a private conversation would not have been known to others, nor (even if they did hear of it) would it interest them enough to record it, are the main pillars of the hypothesis that Cluvius is Josephus's source here.

Sic transit gloria mundi. It appears that a century after his Nobel Prize and his death, a Mommsenian obiter dictum carries less weight than it once did. Doubts have sprung up, and recent generations have seen scholars backing away from Cluvius; see esp. Timpe 1960: 500–501; Feldman 1962; Goud 1996; Levick 2013: 1.555; Barrett 2019: 263–264; Mason 2016a; and Free 2017. There are various reasons for this skepticism.

First, a fundamental textual issue. Mommsen, writing in 1870, took it for granted that Cluvius was mentioned at *Ant.* 19.91. Indeed, that was all he would find, with no notes pointing to any issue, whether he was using Bekker's Teubner edition of 1856, which offers Κλούδιος (i.e., Κλούουιος), or Dindorf's bilingual Didot edition of 1865, which offers Κλούβιος and "Cluvius."[8] However, that is an emendation, as would soon be noted by Niese (1890a: 226): he traced the emendation (with β) to Hudson[9] and indicated (as Hudson did) that,

---

insoweit er dabei römische Annalen gebrauchte, sich an Cluvius gehalten hat, ist wahrscheinlich schon wegen der Erwähnung desselben, die er, wie bemerkt, in die Erzählung von Caligulas Tode einlegt" (Mommsen 1870: 322). Mommsen's "wie gemerkt" refers to p. 318 of his study, where, in summarizing the known data about Cluvius, he points to *Ant.* 19.91 to document both that Cluvius was among the senators present when Gaius was killed and that he had earlier been a consul. Apart from those passages, Mommsen refers to Josephus in this study only in a note on p. 322, where, in support of his suggestion that Cassius Dio too followed Cluvius, he notes that a certain number of casualties appears both in Dio 65.19.3 and in Josephus's *War* 4.653, and infers that they both had

a common source. Referring as it does to the very late sixties, when we know Cluvius was active, that observation cannot bolster any conclusion about Josephus's use of Cluvius in *Ant.* 19, and Mommsen indeed abstained from using it as if it did.

7 Norden 1913a: 641, n. 2 ("Als Quelle des Josephus für seine Ῥωμαϊκά bis in die Zeit Neros ist Cluvius Rufus so gut wie sicher, da Mommsen das für den Bericht über die Ermordung des Gaius und die Erhebung des Claudius auf den Thron bekanntlich erwiesen hat.") Norden puts this to work with regard to the Roman stories at 18.65–84.

8 Bekker 1856: 204 (unchanged in Naber 1893: 222); Dindorf 1865: 740.

9 Hudson and Havercamp 1726: 1.924, n. k.

in fact, the manuscripts instead offer κλούιτον or κλαύιτον, and the Latin, cluitum. See esp.
Ritter 1972 and Wardle 1992b: 467. Although there seems to be no good candidate other
than Cluvius (for Goud's admittedly tentative and unprovable suggestion [1996: 481] that
the reference is in fact to Claudius would require not only another emendation but also
our willingness to imagine that Josephus would identify Claudius merely generically, as a
vir conularis), realization that "Cluvius" is an emendation necessarily creates some doubt.
That doubt is compounded, moreover, by Timpe's observation (1960: 500, pointing to *Ann.*
11.11 as the only time Tacitus mentions himself and then it is both without his name and in
a context in which he held an important office) that it is not at all to be taken for granted
(*selbstverständlich*) that a Roman historian would mention himself, and that by name, in
such a trivial context as that of §§91–92.

And then there is a chronological issue. As indicated above, we know that Cluvius Rufus
was alive and well and active in the late 60s, and all that is known of his writing pertains to
the days of Nero and later. The assumption that he wrote about events of 41 is no more than
that, and the assumption that he was a consul a quarter-century before his floruit is possible
but not what we would expect,[10] not to mention the lack of other evidence for it. True, Syme
(1958: 1.294) suggests that we resolve this problem by assuming that Josephus's reference
to him as a consular, in the context of 41, is anachronistic; so too Gallivan 1978: 423. That is
possible, but accepting that into the web of assumptions required to shore up the Cluvius
hypothesis weighs it down all the more. The same is true of Levick's suggestion (2013: 1.551,
555) that we solve this problem by assuming that the consular of 19.91 was Cluvius's father.
That would solve the chronological problem without denying the younger Cluvius access to
knowledge of the private exchange, of which his father could have told him. However, we
do not have other evidence for the elder Cluvius having been a consul, and if the reference
at §§91–92 is to him, the link between the story and the historian, which is the main prop of
the theory, would be at least attenuated.

A third doubt pertains to the thesis that most of *Antiquities* 19 is based on a Latin text. In
cases in which there is no explicit evidence for such proposals, we would expect the proof
to come from mistranslations, and from comparison of our Greek text to the surviving Latin
of the putative source. But of Cluvius's prose only a few inconsequential lines have survived (Levick 2013: 2.1038–1041), all second-hand, and in my reading of numerous studies
of Josephus's narratives here I have not noticed any suggestions of mistaken translations.
The closest one comes to that is, apparently, the pun on the name "Lupus" at 19.270, which
is based on knowledge that the common noun means "wolf" in Latin. However, despite
Levick's claim (2013: 1.555) that "the source is rightly concluded to be Latin because of the
pun on *lupus* (wolf)/Lupus (name) at 19.270–1," in fact it seems that anyone writing in Greek
in Rome might well take such knowledge of basic Latin for granted. Hölscher's more careful
conclusion (1904: 67), that the author understood Latin, is all that is required.

True, Syme declared that "Josephus reproduces a Latin original, the style of which shows
through" and refers to "the Roman historian whom that learned Jew (or his team of literary
collaborators) with such fidelity transcribed" (Syme 1958: 1.287), and Wiseman (2013a: xvi),

---

10 This consideration was pointed out by Groag
(*PWRE* IV/1 [1900]: 121) and by Wardle 1992b: 467, whose
doubts Levick (2013: 1.551) terms "cogent." Goud (1996:
481) adds yet another reason to doubt Cluvius was consul prior to 41: the fact that Tacitus (*Hist.* 2.37) refers to
Suetonius Paullinus, who was *legatus praetorius* in 42, as
the oldest (*vetustissimus*) of the consulars in 69 CE. Goud

considers this "decisive." However, the adjective might
mean only "oldest" rather than "most senior." Moreover,
the context seems to refer not to all surviving consulars
but only to those whom Otho might have considered taking as a general, and so, since Cluvius seems to have had
no military experience (Wiseman 2013a: 109), we probably should not ascribe much weight to this consideration.

who translated the text, said the same: "Fortunately for us, Josephus stuck pretty close to his Roman sources (even traces of their Latin may sometimes be detected in his Greek)." But although one should hesitate to doubt the impression of such great Latinists, it may be noted that Syme offered no examples, and of the three Wiseman cited in addition to "Lupus" none pertains to style; as "Lupus," all pertain to individual words and none, it appears, is any more probative.[11] When one adds, moreover, the fact that any Greek author describing Roman affairs on the basis of Latin sources might well endow his text, here and there, consciously or not, with Latin color, and retain Latin toponyms or terminology, and the fact that the Greek of any writer of Greek in Rome, such as Josephus, might easily become colored by Latin (see esp. Ward 2007), confidence that such impressions about style show that Josephus's narrative is a slavish translation of a written source can hardly be robust. To ice that cake, I will add that the only fairly suggestive cases I myself have noted, namely (a) the appearance of the anomalous συμπολίτης at 19.175 (see the note ad loc. on "fellow citizens"), and (b) περιπεσὼν τῷ ξίφει μέχρι δὴ καὶ τὴν κώπην τῷ τραύματι συνελθεῖν at 19.273, where the anomalous Greek (lack of τοῦ after μέχρι) and the ready availability of the Latin *capulo tenus* (*Aeneid* 2.553 and 10.535–536) make the translation hypothesis attractive, are at best only suggestive and, in any case, far from being enough to support a more general hypothesis. Anyone used to living in a society in which people use more more than one language encounters such phenomena daily.

Finally, although some scholars who have noted the frequent difficulty of the Greek in Book 19 have suspected it points to the book being a translation, the fact—too easily ignored by scholars who focus only on Book 19—that similar difficulties plague Books 17–18 as well, for whatever reason, as noted above (at nn. 55–58 to the Introduction) undermines the justification for positing such a special explanation for one of those books.

In sum, from a philological point of view, the hypothesis that most of Book 19 closely follows a Latin original is neither bolstered by the type of evidence we would normally expect nor a solution to a problem in need of one.

A fourth doubt pertains to the argument (e.g., Hölscher 1904: 67; Wiseman 2013a: 46, on §16), that the frequent references to "gods" in the Gaius story (§§167, 169, 175, 182, 219, 233) show that the author had a "Roman-pagan way of thought," as Hölscher put it, i.e., that Josephus was slavishly following a Roman source. In fact, however, of those six occurrences, the first four are in Sentius Saturninus's speech, §219 is in the direct speech of a Roman soldier, and §233 is part of the indirect speech of delegates of the Senate. Josephus need have no monotheistic qualms about reflecting the parlance of pagans, be they Romans, Germans, Alexandrians, or Parthians; compare, for example, 18.186, 198, 219, 258, 334. In fact, one might suspect that Josephus was happy to point out that respectable non-Jews took their religion seriously, just as respectable Jews.

The fifth doubt about the Cluvius theory is that although earlier scholars thought that the entire story, including the assassination of Gaius and Claudius's ascent to the throne, derived from a single Roman source, numerous scholars have posited Josephus's use of more

---

11 Namely, Wiseman refers to his notes on §§130, 202, 214, and 270 ("Lupus"). At §130 he asserts that Josephus's use of δόσις (in the plural) renders *munera* and, in his translation, offers "gladiatorial shows." However, the word seems common enough (*ThLJ* 188 marks it as characteristic of *Antiquities*), and the sense of donation, which is absent from Wiseman's translation, is required, for at §130 Josephus is referring to the way Gaius bought the support of women and children, parallel to the way he paid mercenaries according to §129. At §202 Wiseman renders θείου καὶ νομίμου "laws of gods and men" and comments that "J's phrase looks like a translation of *fas iusque* in his Latin source" (Wiseman 2013a: 30, 82); but if so, the passage testifies to the translation being rather free, which

than one source.[12] There are some doublets, and contradictions—be they details such as the way familiarity with the Palatine is taken for granted at §75 but the site is introduced and explained at §223, or the dating of the end of the Republic to the days of Pompey (§228) or, rather, to Julius Caesar (§§173, 187), along with such larger issues as the army's "kidnapping" of Claudius (which is debated and decided upon, and executed by soldiers, at §§162–165, but then again, mysteriously, happens by chance at §§212–220) and, more generally, the image of Claudius[13]—that suggest that different sources lie behind different parts of the long narrative. Note also that Josephus explicitly acknowledges, several times (§§60, 88, 95,106–107, 110, 196), his awareness of more than one opinion (although that need not imply his use of more than one source). Similarly, the Agrippan material at 19.236b–245 seems to be inserted into a context that does not need it and reads more smoothly without it: already by §236a Claudius was prepared to respond to the Senate's envoys to him, but first Josephus has a flashback introducing Agrippa I into the story and then briefly reporting his advice to Claudius about how to respond to the envoys (§§236b–245), and only thereafter does Claudius do so—continuing the way he could have directly after §236a.[14] Moreover, the very fact that Josephus says here nothing about what Agrippa was doing in Rome, although the last time he had been mentioned (18.301) was more than fifty Niese-pages earlier, reinforces the suspicion that the inserted passage is based on a source that dealt with Agrippa. But the more we abandon the notion that Josephus was dependent on a single source for the Gaius and Claudius stories, and rather envision him creating his own narrative on the basis of sources, the more we must posit that he was involved in the narrative as it now stands.

All in all, then, there is, today, as part of a general reaction to older doctrinaire versions of source-criticism, more willingness to entertain the notion that Josephus was active and auctorial in these narratives. And once that willingness is given a chance, its fruits are not at all negligible. So let us now turn away from the Cluvius-hypothesis to that opposite approach and see where, and how far, it can take us.

A brief summary of the stories will point up their main motif. The story of the assassination focuses on Gaius and those who conspired to assassinate him, while that of Claudius's ascent to the throne focuses on the contest between the Senate, which, as the assassins, dreamed and talked of restoring the Republic, and other more practical actors. The latter, namely the army and Agrippa I (who is portrayed as having successfully functioned as a duplicitous mediator), instead brought on, within a day of the assassination, a new emperor: Gaius's uncle (brother of his father, Germanicus), Claudius. The two stories are linked together by Cassius Chaerea, a tribune of the Praetorian Guard who was the main conspirator and assassin but whose execution, at the end of the story, exhibits the ultimate

---

undermines our ability to recognize any original Latin. As for §214, where Wiseman comments that Josephus's οἱ περὶ τὸ στρατηγικὸν καλόυμενον "no doubt translates *in praetorio* in his Latin source," it seems, instead, that the phrase shows only, as 18.195, 19.3–4, and 20.186, Josephus's awareness that he has non-Romans among his readers. Similarly, elsewhere he uses the same or similar formulations to indicate his awareness that other non-Greek names are not familiar to his readers (so, for example, 18.29, 90; 20.2, 80).

12 See esp. D. R. Schwartz 1990a: 23–30; Goud 1996; 477–478; and Wiseman 2013a: xiv–xvi.

13 On this, see esp. Goud 1996: 477–478, who emphasizes the tensions between the pathetic and laughable Claudius of the second kidnapping story, in which he is kidnapped by a soldier at the spur of a moment (§§216–220), on the one hand, and the respectable Claudius of §§162–165, whose kidnapping came after serious deliberation by an assembly of soldiers.

14 Cf. Timpe 1960: 502, who thinks the Agrippa passage ends not at §245, before Claudius's response to the envoys, but, instead, after it, with §246, so the "seam" (*Nahtstelle*) comes after Claudius's response, at §247. The detail matters little. Timpe's conclusion is as mine: "Man

futility of the hope to roll history back and reestablish the Republic. And so the relationship between the two parts of the story is clear: the noble story of the conspiracy and assassination, which ends with Gaius's death and the opening up of hope for a return to the Republic, is dashed by the practical story of Claudius's ascent to the throne, which shows those hopes collapsing against the realities of military power and the manipulations of a clever Jewish powerbroker. Readers are left with the memory of the gallant Chaerea, who was executed by the new emperor (§§268–272), and the contrasting image of senators, who are good at proclaiming high-sounding words and hopes about "liberty" (ἐλευθερία appears thirteen times down to 19.263, including four in Sentius Saturninus's speech at §§166–184, which is undermined immediately by a scene demonstrating his servility vis-à-vis Gaius [185]), but incapable of doing anything effective. First they exasperate Chaerea by hesitating and delaying (§§28, 47, 70, 74–80); then they can do no better than pretend to be upset at Gaius's death (§158) but nevertheless think, in their arrogance, that power had already come into their hands (§161); eventually, since the army (which had the real power) decided that it was impossible for the Senate to rule the empire effectively (§§162, 225), and that the senators were arrogant (§§161, 236) and greedy (§224), they are left to choose among sending Claudius empty threats (§§229–236), pathetically pinning their hopes on divine intervention in recognition of their virtue (see the note on "fortune" at §233), hiding and scattering (§248), being "stymied" (§255), and, in the end, abjectly accepting the new emperor (§266). The moral of the story, as Syme put it (1958: 1.287), is that "the lethargy of the aristocracy is blamed for the despotism of the Caesars, while soldiers and people accept the new dispensation because the Senate's rule had been unjust and oppressive." These are, as he notes, "opinions that emerge about state and society not inappropriate in one of the annalistic predecessors of Cornelius Tacitus."

However, the source-critical question is not whether these opinions are not inappropriate to someone else's work. Rather, it is whether they are appropriate to a Josephan work, where they are found. And the fact is that the story's lesson is quite reminiscent of the way Josephus, in his *War*, brackets the Judeans' rebellion against Rome: just before the rebellion, Agrippa II scornfully rejects the Jewish rebels' hope for "liberty" in the Roman world (*War* 2.348–357), and just after it Eleazar ben Yair realistically explains to his fellow holdouts at Masada that in this (Roman) world liberty can be attained only in death (*War* 7.323–336, 341–350). Agrippa II's scorn for rebels who talk big about "liberty" and Eleazar's recognition that it is not to be attained in this world, under the Roman emperors, are, essentially, the same as our story's scorn for the big talkers in the Senate who give high-sounding speeches while the army, Claudius, and his clever Jewish kingmaker makes real things happen on the ground.

Similarly, the story's focus on "liberty" is characteristic of *Antiquities* too; "one might almost say that liberty is the leitmotif of the history of the Jewish people as Josephus sees it" in *Antiquities* (Feldman 1998a: 148).[15] So the numerous occurrences of ἐλευθερία in the story of Gaius's murder should point those uncommitted to an extreme source-theory to Josephus himself, whatever his source(s) included. Correspondingly, the opposite of liberty is tyranny, and it too is written large in Book 19—but, as Mason emphasized, no larger than elsewhere in *Antiquities*, where it plays the same role; "the *AJ* thematises tyranny (fifty-two

---

erkennt hier, wie ungeschickt die Agrippageschichte in den alten römischen Zusammenhang eingefügt ist."

15 Feldman assembles examples from Josephus's paraphrase of the Bible, concluding his discussion by

noting that "Roman readers would recall that in the conspiracy to assassinate the mad Gaius Caligula, the password adopted by the conspirators was the same word, 'Liberty' (ἐλευθερία) (*Ant.* 19.54)."

occurrences of the word-group), as the greatest constitutional calamity, and uses Gaius as crowning example" (Mason 2016a: cliii–cliv; see also Flatto 2020: 98–100).

Moreover, it is not only the case that Josephus condemns them all generally as tyrants. As Mason emphasizes, Josephus also characterizes the tyranny of Herod and Tiberius the same specific way, the way that speaks most to an aristocrat like Josephus (not just like Cluvius!): tyrants persecute the well-born (εὐπατρίδες; *Ant.* 17.307; 18.226). That is, tyranny is especially opposed to "rule by the best people," i.e., aristocracy—which is the best type of rule, no less for Josephus (see *Ant.* 4.223; 6.36) than for supporters of rule by the Roman Senate.[16] Accordingly, when one gets to the same complaint about Gaius, at 19.2, "it feels like the same narrative" (Mason 2016a: cxlvi), and we should demand strong evidence before we assume that it is not the same narrator at work, whatever his sources. So much for the main motifs of the Gaius and Claudius stories.

Beyond that, note that Book 19's Roman stories are well at home in *Antiquities* in three ways. First, they fulfill the promise offered at 18.307. Second, the book has a clear structure that goes beyond the Roman materials. Third, the book, as a whole, plays a very clear role within the structure of *Antiquities* 18–20.

The first of those points is obvious, and the second is almost as self-evident: *Antiquities* 19 begins with the story of a Roman emperor who thought himself a god and died a miserable death, and ends with the story of a Jewish king who was thought to be a god (§345) and died a miserable death. Indeed, both of them die in the context of public events in memory of Augustus (§§75, 343)! It is difficult to imagine that, whatever his sources, Josephus, as an author, was not interested in making the point, in line with his general statements at §16 and §347, about man's need to remember that he is beneath God. And the fact that that is a thesis that Josephus underlines elsewhere as well,[17] in his oeuvre, bolsters that conclusion all the more.

As for the third point, Book 19's place in the structure of Books 18–20: to see it we should realize that after Book 18 showed just how difficult Roman rule was under Pilate and Gaius, but the Roman part of Book 18 ended with the death of Gaius (§§305–307), readers could hope for an improvement. And, indeed, Book 19 raises the possibility of an improvement, in two ways. First, by emphasizing Gaius's wickedness and demonstrating that noble Romans opposed him, the long opening of the book lets readers hope for the restoration of the Republic. Second, the shorter but nevertheless substantial story of Agrippa I, which ends Book 19, similarly holds out hope for an improvement: a return to autonomous Judean rule under a king who united, through his pedigree, both the proud Hasmonean line that embodied the memory of independence, and the realistic Herodian line that epitomized acceptance of Roman rule. However, in both theatres the stories end with dashed hopes: Gaius is replaced by another yet emperor, who proclaimed his allegiance to the imperial system by opening his rule with the execution of Gaius's noblest assassin, and Agrippa dies suddenly after only a brief reign, whereupon Claudius restored Roman provincial rule in Judea. Indeed, for those—first-century Judeans or modern readers of Josephus—who had pinned their hopes on Agrippa introducing a reversal of the course of history, back

---

16 My position is similar to Free's (2017: 605) with regard to Sentius Saturninus's speech (§§183–189): while it is, at least in its meaning (although perhaps not in its phrasing) a reproduction of the views of a certain group of senators, it nevertheless corresponds well to Josephus's own views; see Mason 2012: 147–152. For Josephus's understanding of "tyrants" as, especially, aristocrats who betray their peers in order to usurp authority for themselves, see esp. Ben-Yishai 2021.

17 See, for example, *Ant.* 9.196–201, 296, on kings of Judah whose disrespect for God brought on their downfall, as well as 18.127–128 on the Herodian line in general.

from Roman rule to Herodian autonomy or even (given his descent from Mariamme I) to Hasmonean independence, the irony was that the main legacy of Agrippa's reign was the fact that his reunification of all of Herod's kingdom under one ruler facilitated the subjugation of all of it to a Roman governor upon his demise. That leaves it to Book 20 to continue the story of Judea under direct Roman rule that had begun in Book 18. If already there that story was "turbulent" and "tumultuous," full of conflict, now, with nothing essential having changed in Book 19, certainly not for the better, the story reverts to its original downward course—all the more so, until it works its way down to the final catastrophe. That catastrophe, promised at the opening of Book 18, is ushered in at the end of Book 20, where the last paragraphs of the narrative (§§252–258) are devoted to excoriating the Roman governor under whom the rebellion broke out and to referring readers to the *War* for the dismal continuation of the story.

• • •

In drawing up a balance, I would observe that, on the one hand, it is obvious that Josephus used Roman sources for these Roman stories. How else could he have learned such details? Indeed, as noted in the Introduction (at n. 11) it even seems likely that, at one point (when composing 18.223), he did not intend to write up the story of Gaius's death; that suggests that, at that point, he did not yet have access to the relevant sources or, at least, did not yet plan to undertake the labor necessary to use them in his work. On the other hand, however, attempts to say anything specific about the identity of those sources, and the suggestion that Josephus's account be viewed as a slavish translation, founder on numerous difficulties, while the accounts' motifs are characteristically Josephan and the stories, as a whole, fit well into Book 19 and, more broadly, Books 18–20. That these Roman stories are longer and more detailed than we would expect, a fact that points to the extent of source-material available, does not change the basic fact that, in the end, although based as an historian's work must be on sources, Book 19 should be viewed as a Josephan composition.

(1.1) 1 As for Gaius,[1] he did not exhibit the insanity[2] of his hubris[3] only toward the Jews of Jerusalem and wherever else they might live.[4] Rather, he sent it out to be in the entire earth and sea,[5] wherever people were subject to Rome, filling it[6] with myriads of evils, the likes of which have never previously been recorded.[7] **2** But it was especially Rome[8] that knew the horror of the things he did, for he did not at all consider it with any more respect than the other cities, harrying and plundering[9] everyone in general but especially the Senate[10]

1 For Josephus's opening of a book with δέ, see the note on "turning now" at 18.1.

2 Josephus regularly employs the term "insanity" or "madness" (μανία) with reference to Gaius in this book (§§5, 11, 39, 50, 69, 130, 193, 196, 258; cf. §284), having employed it already with regard to his order to erect his statue in the Jerusalem temple (18.277–278). Gaius's "madness" is also reported by Seneca (*Const.* 18.1), Philo (*Leg.* 34), Tacitus (*Ann.* 13.3), and Cassius Dio (59.29.1); cf. Suetonius, *Cal.* 50.2–3. Below, at §193, Josephus mentions a tradition attributing Gaius's madness to a love-potion given to him by his wife Caesonia (so also Suetonius, *Cal.* 50.2). Although early modern research generally accepted this depiction of Gaius as a madman, later research has been more critical of it. For skeptical reviews of the ancient sources, and of scholarship bent on diagnosing a mental condition, see Schrömbges 1988 and Sidwell 2010. Such skepticism leaves it to us to choose between an evil Gaius and a much more positive assessment of him. Indeed, some scholars would go far in the latter direction, offering a more positive assessment of Gaius's personality and rejecting or belittling claims of wickedness as intentional calumny by hostile and later sources, influenced especially by senators; see Barrett 2019: 284–291 and Winterling 2011: 2–7, 187–194. For the argument, however, that such revisionism can swing the pendulum too far to the other side, and an analysis of some of its modern contexts, see Yavetz 1996. On imperial insanity in general, see Winterling 2018.

3 In *War* 2.184 Josephus, auctorially, speaks of Gaius's hubris (ἐξύβρισεν εἰς τὴν τύχην) in regard to his considering himself divine and his plan to erect a statue of himself in the Jerusalem temple, and above at 18.280 Josephus has Petronius do the same about that plan. Now, in Book 19, it is mentioned often (e.g., §§22, 42, 82, 129).

4 By this brief introduction Josephus builds a bridge from the preceding book to this one, and in doing so artfully creates the impression that even the suffering of the Jews of Babylonia, said at 18.310 to be the topic of the last long section, was Gaius's fault. On such insinuation, see the note on "also" at 18.310.

5 Despite the immediate continuation, which somewhat limits this phrase, it appears that Josephus is alluding to a common Roman perception of Rome's universal rule, *terra marique*. For that perception see also Josephus's prophecy to Vespasian at *War* 3.402 (ruler of "land and sea and all of the human race"), also, for example, Polybius 1.2; 1 Maccabees 8:32; Diodorus 40.4; Dionysius of Halicarnassus, *Ant. Rom.* 1.3.3–5; Philo, *Flacc.* 104 and *Leg.* 44, 141; and Cicero, *Pro. Man.* 56 ("[O]ne law, one man, and one year ... caused us again at length to appear really to be the masters of all nations and countries by land and sea"). For a passage like the present one, that condemns the Roman ruler (there: Pompey) in the same context, see the *Psalms of Solomon* 2:26, 29. See Nicolet 1991: 29–56, Shatzman 1999: esp. 54–58, 78–80, and Berthelot 2021: 127–132. In relation to Gaius, note also Philo's description of the extent of the sovereignty he inherited from Tiberius in *Leg.* 8: "... he succeeded to the sovereignty of the whole earth and sea" (τὴν ἡγεμονίαν πάσης γῆς καὶ θαλάσσης); cf. ibid. §§10, 309. For similar formulations, see 18.187 and below, §§14, 40, 193.

6 The Roman empire.

7 Similar hyperbole: *Ant.* 11.299; 15.396; 18.310; 19.204; *War* 6.199.

8 For such tripartite structures as this, in which Josephus turns to focus upon his central topic after first addressing two relevant but outlying possibilities (in this case: Jews on the one hand, and provincial subjects of Rome around the world, on the other), see the note on "largest part" at 18.145.

9 ἄγοντος καὶ φέροντος, as at 2.239, 16.277, 17.272, and *War* 7.91, also, for example, Xenophon, *Hellenica* 3.2.2 (φέρωσι καὶ ἄγωσι τὴν χώραν); "frequent in Herodotus and Attic prose" (LSJ 17, s.v. ἄγω, §I,3). The notion of attrition under Gaius's unrelenting tyranny recurs several times in this book (§§173, 192, 246).

10 A similar generalization about Gaius's relation to the senators is expressed above at 18.306. Cassius Dio (59.6) writes that at the beginning of his reign Gaius "showed great deference to the senators," and was generally rather fair and positive in relation to the Senate and prominent people (cf. Suetonius, *Cal.* 17). But his treatment of the senators soon turned demeaning and abusive. Suetonius (*Cal.* 26.2–3) reports that he had senators run for miles in their togas beside his chariot and serve

and those of its members who were of good birth[11] or honored because of the fame of their ancestors. 3 He invented myriads [of measures] against the equites too,[12] as they were called—people who in terms of prestige and financial power were considered, in the city, to be on the same level as the senators, since it was from them that the Senate was chosen.[13] Their lot was deprivation of office[14] and exile, or else they were killed and their property plundered—for even the killings occurred, in the main, so as to allow for the confiscation of their property.[15] 4 He also deified himself and demanded, from his subjects, honors that were no longer mortal.[16] On his frequent visits to the temple of Jupiter,[17] which they[18] call

---

as his waiters. See also ibid. 30.2, as well as Seneca, *De Ira* 3.18.3–19.2; *Ben.* 2.12. For Gaius's abuse of some of the most distinguished families, see also Suetonius, *Cal.* 35, and note Aurelius Victor, *De Caesaribus* 3 (Bird 1994: 3), who emphasizes the "widespread murders of senators and nobles." For the argument that, nevertheless, most senators had nothing to fear and that later sources exaggerated the hostility between Gaius and the Senate, see Barrett 2019: 307–312.

11 Εὐπατρίδης, as below, §§75, 132, 136. In a Roman context, the term is used of "patricians"; see *GTRI* 50. Josephus's description here, of Gaius's terrible treatment of them, recalls that of Tiberius (18.226) and of Herod, who too was "wont to kill members of the nobility (εὐπα-τρίδας) upon absurd pretexts and then take their property for himself" (17.307). That is, it is a standard element in the aristocratic Josephus's list of complaints about tyrants. See S. Mason 2003c: 583; idem 2016a: cxlv–cxlvi; and Ben-Yishai 2021.

12 Philo too reports Gaius's battle against the Senate and the equestrian order (Philo, *Leg.* 74–75).

13 The equites were distinct from and of a lower status than those of the senatorial class; see the note on "equestrian order" at 18.2. Nevertheless, "they intermingled socially with senators; they married into senatorial families; like senators they could be summoned to serve on the emperor's *consilium*. Sons of leading equestrian officials were the prime source of recruitment of new senatorial families" (F. G. B. Millar and G. P. Burton in *OCD* 552). In general see, on the equites' relations with emperors, Brunt 1983. On Gaius's attitude toward them, which seems to have been much more balanced than the present attack on him indicates, see Barrett 2019: 305–307. For the promotion of equites to the Senate, see Maecenas's speech in Dio 52.25.6–7, also Dio 53.15.2: "the emperor himself selects equites to be sent out as military tribunes, both those who are prospective senators and the others ..." Similarly, regarding Gaius, Dio reports that "some of them [scil., the equites] he even permitted to wear the senatorial dress before they had held any office through which we gain admission to the Senate, on the strength

of their prospects of becoming members later, whereas previously only those, it appears, who had been born into the senatorial order were allowed to do this" (59.9.5).

14 This term, ἀτίμωσις, appears in Josephus elsewhere only at 18.349, where, in reference to God, it can only mean degradation, lack of respect. So too, here Wiseman (2013a: 3, 44) offers "dishonour." Here, however, the context seems to indicate something more specific. On τιμή, see the note on "office" at 18.17.

15 The same notion, taken for granted at §65, is found in Dio 59.21.4, which, however, refers to provincials. Suetonius reports an episode in which Gaius arbitrarily had two rich equites, who happened to pass by, arrested and their property confiscated (*Cal.* 41.2). For his brutal treatment of the equites see also ibid, 26.4. Elsewhere Suetonius reports that Gaius criticized the equestrian order "as devotees of the stage and the arena" (ibid. 30.2). On Gaius's plundering and various methods of financial extractions see especially Suetonius, *Cal.* 38–42 and Dio 59.10.7; 59.14–15. Both Suetonius and Dio explain these extractions as due to his urgent need for funds because he had squandered vast sums to pay for his extravagant lifestyle (see esp. Suetonius, *Cal.* 37.1–38.1); Dio (59.21.1) asserts that Gaius's monetary extractions were so great that he eventually "spent practically all the money in Rome and the rest of Italy, gathered from every source from which he could in any way get it" and that given that "his expenses were pressing him hard, he set out for Gaul ... with the purpose of exploiting both Gaul with its abounding wealth and Spain too." See also Dio 59.21.1–6 and Barrett 2019: 297–302.

16 On his divine or semi-divine pretensions, see Philo, *Leg.* 75–80, 93–114; Suetonius, *Cal.* 22.2–4, 52; Dio 59.4.4 and 26.5–28.8; and, of course, his attempt to erect a statue of himself in the Temple of Jerusalem (18.256–309). See the discussions in Yavetz 1996: esp. 125–127 and Barrett 2019: 190–205.

17 As is conventional, here, as elsewhere in Roman contexts, I render Josephus's "Zeus" as "Jupiter."

18 This shows a foreigner's perspective, as do §§24, 214. So does the very fact that Josephus troubles, here,

the Capitolium[19] and is the most honored of temples among them, he was so audacious that he addressed Jupiter as "brother."[20] 5 And also the other things he did left nothing to miss in insanity. [Thus, for example], given the fact that he thought it too much to have to use a trireme to make the crossing from Dicearcheia[21] (a city located in Campania) to Misenum[22] (which is another city on the sea), 6 and since anyway, being ruler of the sea,[23] he thought it [appropriate] to demand from it the same as from the land: he connected promontory to promontory, which measured thirty furlongs of sea,[24] thus enclosing the entire gulf,[25] and rode his chariot over the bridge.[26] For, [he said], being a god it was appropriate[27] for him

to identify and describe this temple; elsewhere (see the next note) he mentions it without any such explanations, taking the readers' familiarity with it for granted.

19 As at §§11, 71, also, for example, 12.416; 14.36; 16.48; *War* 7.153. The Temple of Jupiter Optimus Maximus was, according to tradition, initially planned by Tarquinius Priscus during his war with the Sabines (Livy 1.55) and completed by Tarquinius Superbus, and dedicated in the first year of the Republic, but the temple of Gaius's time was the one rebuilt—following its destruction by fire in 83 BCE—by Q. Lutatius Catulus in 69 BCE (e.g., Pliny, *NH* 19.23; Suetonius, *Jul.* 15; Tacitus, *Hist.* 3.72) and repaired by Augustus (*RGDI* 20). For the hill and the temple see Richardson 1992: 68–70 and 221–224, respectively. For this temple being called simply "the Capitol" see Pliny, *NH* 33.19. The Temple served, *inter alia*, as the archives of Rome from its earliest days (Suetonius, *Vesp.* 8.5; Josephus, *Ant.* 14.186–188, 266, 16.48), and was the site of numerous public events.

20 Accordingly, Philo reports (*Leg.* 188, 346) that the statue of himself that Gaius wanted to erect in the Temple of Jerusalem was to be named "Gaius, the New Zeus made manifest." Indeed, Gaius is said to have called himself "Jupiter Latiaris" (Cassius Dio 59.28.5; similarly, Aurelius Victor, *De Caesaribus* 3 [Bird 1994: 3]; cf. Suetonius, *Cal.* 22.2). Suetonius also writes that Gaius would engage in conversations with Jupiter Capitolinus, and reports that—saying that Jupiter invited him to live with him—Gaius built a bridge to connect his palace to the Capitol, over the temple of Augustus. Then, however, feeling he was still too far from Jupiter, he began to build himself a house on the Capitol itself (*Cal.* 22.4; cf. Cassius Dio 59.28.2). See also the note on "of him" at 18.261. For a somewhat skeptical review of the evidence, including the hostile literary sources but dearth of epigraphic evidence concerning Gaius's self-deification, concluding that "Caligula had no desire for the world to identify him as

a god, even if, like most people, he enjoyed being treated like one," see Barrett 2019: 195–199.

21 I.e., Puteoli; see the note on "Puteoli" at 18.161.

22 Misenum (modern Miseno) is at the southern tip of the peninsula at the west of what is known today as the Gulf of Pozzuoli, a northern extension of the Gulf of Naples. Suetonius (*Cal.*19.1) and Dio (59.17.1) agree that the bridge began at Puteoli, but report a different location of its other end, closer to Puteoli. Suetonius points to Baiae, which is located between Puteoli and Misenum, and is where Gaius received the embassies of Herod and Agrippa (see above at 18.248–249, which includes a description of Baiae). Dio locates its end at Bauli, of which the location is uncertain; for details, see Barrett 2019: 242–243 and H. Lindsay 1993: 94.

23 For his supposed conquest of the ocean, see Suetonius, *Cal.* 46. Dio (59.26.6) reports his posing as Neptune (cf. ibid. 17.11), and, speaking of his dressing up in general and in the likeness of gods in particular, Suetonius (*Cal.* 52) mentions that he often held a trident—Neptune's symbol—when thus dressing up. On his dressing up as a god or goddess, see also below, §30, and the note on "earth and sea" at §1.

24 Ca. 6 km. Cassius Dio 59.17.1 gives the length of the bridge, between Puteoli and Bauli (not Misenum) as 26 furlongs, i.e., ca. 5 km, while Suetonius (Cal. 19.1) gives 3,600 paces, i.e., ca. 5.3 km. Cf. H. Lindsay 1993: 94–95.

25 Of Puzzuoli.

26 In further describing this bridge of boats, Dio 59.17.2–3 writes that it included resting places and rooms for lodging, and that they had running drinking water. The dimensions of the project are illustrated by Dio's report (ibid.) that the drafting of so many ships for the building of this bridge caused a famine; so too Aurelius Victor, *De Caesaribus* 4 (Bird 1994: 5).

27 On καλῶς ἔχειν, see the note on "be appropriate" at 18.357.

to make his trips that way.[28] 7 Of the Greek temples there was none that he left unlooted,[29] ordering that whatever paintings or sculptures[30] they had and all other statues and dedicatory offerings with which they were furnished be brought to him; for, [he said], it was not appropriate that beautiful things be located anywhere apart from the most beautiful place, which happened to be the city of the Romans. 8 With the things brought from there he ornamented the palace[31] and gardens as well as all his residences throughout the land of the Italians.[32] He even had the audacity to order the transfer to Rome of the Zeus honored by the Greeks at Olympus and therefore called "Olympian," which had been made by Pheidias the Athenian.[33] 9 That, however, he did not do, for the master builders told Memmius Regulus,[34] who had been assigned the task of moving the Zeus, that to move the work would ruin it. It is said that for this reason, and also because of major portents that occurred, such that no one could fail to believe them,[35] Memmius put off transporting [the statue]. 10 He wrote these things to Gaius, explaining his leaving of the order unfulfilled—and was saved from the ensuing danger of perishing [only] because it was preempted[36] by Gaius's death.[37]

---

28 This story alludes, of course, to Herodotus's story (7.22–24, 34–36) of Xerxes's attempt to bridge the Hellespont, a famous exemplum of arrogance; cf. *War* 2.358, also, *inter alia*, Isocrates, *Panegyricus* 89 and 2 Macc 5:21. Gaius himself is reported to have compared his project with those of Xerxes and Darius; see Dio 59.17.11 (cf. Suetonius, *Cal.* 19.3; Seneca, *De Brev. Vit.* 18.5)—a comparison that will have fit right into Greek and Roman notions of tyrannical oriental despots. On this project, for which various explanations have been suggested, including three suggested already by Suetonius, *Cal.* 19.3, see Barrett 2019: 240–242 and Malloch 2001; Malloch's own suggestion is that Gaius was asserting a similarity to Alexander the Great (cf. Dio 59.17.3). Dio reports this project in his narrative for 39 CE, and although some scholars have questioned that and proposed that it took place in 40, Dio's date has been upheld by Wardle 2007.

29 Robbing temples is one of the typical sacrilegious acts attributed to ancient tyrants; see Dunkle 1971: 15–16. When perpetrated against one's own temples, it is often thought to be among the most heinous of crimes, comparable to treason; see Xenophon, *Hellenica* 1.7.22 and *Apion* 2.263. Here, however, the reference is to a Roman emperor's robbery of Greek temples, a focus that will have especially interested Josephus's Greek readership.

30 Pliny (*NH* 35.17–18) mentions Gaius's failed attempt to remove portraits of Atalanta and Helen from a temple at Lanuvium. According to Pausanias 9.27.3–4, Gaius took a sculpture of Eros from Thespiae, which was later returned by Claudius, only to be taken again by Nero to Rome, where it was later destroyed by fire.

31 Lit. "the house," but the use of the definite article (τὴν τε οἰκίαν) and the coming contrast with the plural "residences" points to something special. So too below, §162.

32 On Gaius's pursuit of art, see Barrett 2019: 223–224. Barrett emphasizes that Gaius was not exceptional in this pursuit; for great Greek works of art adorning imperial palaces, see Millar 1977: 145–146.

33 Pheidias (or: Phidias) was a famous Athenian sculptor, who was active in the mid-fifth century BCE. His most famous works were this Zeus of Olympia and Athena Parthenos (Quintilian 12.10.9). The former was especially large; on it, see Strabo, *Geog.* 8.3.30; and esp. Pausanias 5.10.2, 5.11. On Phidias himself, see Plutarch, *Per.* 13.4, 9; 31.2–5; Stewart 1990: 1: 257–263; Spivey 2013: 176–193. According to Suetonius (*Cal.* 22.2) and Dio (59.28.3), Gaius wanted to bring this statue to Rome in order to remove its head and replace it with his own.

34 Publius Memmius Regulus was suffect consul in 31 CE (Tacitus, *Ann.* 5.11), and in 35–44 CE he was legate in Moesia, Achaia, and Macedonia. In 38 CE, Gaius recalled Memmius to Rome and forced him to give him his wife, Lollia Paulina, in marriage, only to divorce her soon thereafter (Suetonius, *Cal.* 25.2; Dio 59.12.1; Tacitus, *Ann.* 12.22). Memmius was later proconsul of Asia, probably in 48/49.

35 Dio (59.28.4) does not report the logistical problem, but reports such portents: the ship specially built to bring the statue was shattered by thunderbolts and loud laughter was heard anytime anyone approached the statue (cf. Suetonius, *Cal.* 57.1).

36 On such usage, cf. the note on "beat him" at 18.89.

37 On such fortuitous timing, just in the nick of time, see the note on "Gaius's death" at 18.305.

(1.2) 11 So far did Gaius's madness go, that when a daughter[38] was born to him he brought her up to the Capitolium[39] and deposited her on the knees of the image,[40] saying that the child was jointly his and Jupiter's and that he designated both as her fathers, and that he would leave open[41] the question as to which of the two was the greater[42]—**12** even with such things that he did did the people have to put up! He also permitted[43] servants to bring against their masters whatever charges they wanted;[44] and all accusations had severe consequences, because the things that were said were usually [said] in order to please him or at his direction. **13** So it happened that Polydeuces, who was Claudius's slave, dared to denounce Claudius,[45] and Gaius put up with[46] going to the hearing of his own uncle in a capital case in the hope of receiving the authority to execute him. But[47] it did not turn out for him that way.

14 And since he had filled the whole world,[48] which he ruled, with malicious accusations[49] and wicked deeds, and had greatly elevated the power of slaves[50] over their masters,

---

38 Julia Drusilla was born a month after Gaius's marriage to her mother Caesonia, probably in the summer of 39 (Barrett 2019: 133–134). She was named after Gaius's favorite sister Drusilla, who had died the preceding year; on her, see the note on "full sister" at §204.

39 I.e., the Temple of Jupiter on the Capitoline hill; see above, §4.

40 I.e., Jupiter's statue. Dio (59.28.7) too mentions Gaius's placing her on Jupiter's knees and adds that he appointed Minerva as her nurse. For the question of the Roman, or possibly Egyptian, background of this procedure, see Barrett 2019: 134–135. Suetonius (*Cal.* 25.4) does not mention Jupiter, but does agree that Gaius, who took her "to the temples of all the goddesses," eventually brought her to Minerva, whom he put in charge of her nurture and training.

41 For ἐν μέσῳ in the sense of "placing before the public," cf. the more usual εἰς μέσον—e.g. §§246, 261, also, for example, *Ant.* 4.29, *Apion* 2.197, and *Life* 334, 359.

42 Compare Josephus's closing comments on Gaius, where he is said to have been "anxious both to be and to seem greater than the deity" (§202). Suetonius reports that Gaius once sat beside the statue of Jupiter and "asked the tragic actor Apelles which of the two seemed to him the greater" (Suetonius, *Cal.* 33).

43 Reading ἐπεχώρησε, as is conjectured by Niese (1890a: 212 and 1890b: 183) and adopted by Feldman (1965: 220), rather than ἐπεχείρησε with the manuscripts, which are followed by Wiseman 2013a: 12. The latter—as also the Latin—would apparently imply that Gaius actually incited servants to bring charges. That would be a welcome sense, but the use of that verb for inciting others, rather than undertaking something oneself, is difficult to establish.

44 Accusations of slaves against their masters are also mentioned below at §131, and readers of Josephus will recall Agrippa's troubles with Eutychus (18.168–169, 185–187). Gaius's elevation of slaves over their masters is mentioned shortly below (§14) as a major motivation of conspiracies against him. As another first-century Jewish aristocrat would comment, "Nothing is harder for those who were once superiors than to be accused by their former inferiors or for those who were once rulers by their former subjects, which is just as if masters were to be accused by slaves born in their house or purchased with their money" (Philo, *Flacc.* 127, trans. van der Horst 2203a: 77).

45 Suetonius (*Claud.* 9.1) states that Claudius "was continually harassed by all kinds of accusations, brought against him by strangers or even by the members of his household" (trans. Rolfe, LCL), but does not implicate Gaius in those matters. However, Suetonius (ibid.) does report another episode in which Gaius raged at Claudius and almost had him killed. Cf. ibid. 38.3 and below, §§67, 221.

46 The same verb (ἀνέχω) is used at the outset of §12, but here it is ironic: they had to suffer Gaius's nonsense, and he "had to endure" committing travesties of justice. For such bitter irony, cf. the note on "murder" at 18.5.

47 As at the opening of §9.

48 See the note on "earth and sea" at §1.

49 This is the only occurrence of συκοφαντία in Josephus, but he uses related words often enough, e.g., συκοφόντημα at 16.349 and συκονφοντέω at 10.114, 16.170, and *Apion* 2.42. Usually the term implies that the accusations are made in the hope of profit, whether by extortion of the victim or in order to find favor with the victim's enemy. For the history and Athenian usage of the term, see Lofberg 1917: vii–xi.

50 Lit. "slaveocracy" (δουλοκρατία); in Josephus, this appears only here and below at §261, and no other ancient author uses it; perhaps it's Josephus's own coinage.

conspiracies frequently began to be formed[51]—some in anger, for the sake of vengeance for what they had suffered, while others set out to handle[52] the man before they fell [from grace] and suffered great troubles.[53]

Josephus's Reason for Detailing the Assassination

15 Therefore, since his death made a major contribution both to the laws[54] and the security of happiness of everyone, and also to those of our own nation, which was on the verge of being ruined and would have perished had not his death speedily intervened,[55] I wish to go through the entire account[56] of it in detail[57]—16 also[58] because it affords much reason to believe in the power of God,[59] consolation for those who are down in their fortunes, and sobriety for those who think that good fortune is eternal and will not take a turn for the worse[60] if it is without virtue.[61]

Josephus's complaint here, about slaves ruling or having more power than their masters, is similar to Cassius Dio's at 60.2.4, using the cognate verb, that Claudius "was slave-ruled and women-ruled (ἐδουλοκρατήθη καὶ ἐγυναικοκρατήθη)."

51 Here Josephus starts to get to the point. Suetonius (*Cal.* 56.1) speaks of "several" who thought of assassinating him, and says that, at the time that the successful plot that he will describe began to take shape, "one or two had been detected, and the rest were waiting for favourable opportunity." Suetonius also mentions "conspiracies," ibid. 24.3 and 26.3. Dio (59.25.5b, 6–7) mentions conspiracies that were discovered. For the various conspiracies, see further Barrett 2019: 247–253; he argues that, however disparate, the various conspiracies were parts of one single process.

52 Such euphemistic use of μεταχειρίζομαι (lit. "have in hand," "handle," as at 7.48 and 14.245) for killing is widespread; see 15.186, 17.79, 18.264, and below, §§68, 197, 270. This is part of a general tendency to avoid direct references to killing and death, especially when the perpetrators are casted positively. See, for example, Parker 2002 (a reference for which I am grateful to Jan Willem van Henten).

53 E.g., both Vinicinianus and Chaerea; see below, §§20 and 21, respectively. For the same distinction as here, between those who were already Gaius's victims and those who had to fear when their turn would come, see also §§42, 181.

54 For a tyrant, by definition, threatens or violates the laws. According to the Roman view, "Liberty is based on the laws," as Cicero writes (*Agrarian Law* 2.102; see also his *Pro Cluentio* 146 and Wirszubski 1950: 7–9, 83–87), and tyranny is the opposite of rule based on the laws; see Wiseman 1992. In the present book, Josephus takes up this view most prominently in the long speech of Sentius Saturninus, below at §§167–184; see also §§156 and 230–231. Elsewhere too Josephus contrasts life under a tyrant

to life according to the laws (e.g., *War* 5.429–441; 7.259–261; *Ant.* 5.234, 339; 15.321; 16.4; 17.304).

55 Here Josephus alludes to his long account of Gaius's order to erect his statue in the Jerusalem Temple (18.261–309).

56 For such use of λόγος, cf. the note on "account" at 19.66. This passage amounts to something of an apology for the great length of the coming account, given the fact that its details—apart from the bare fact of Gaius's death—have virtually no relevance to Jewish history as such. Contrast 20.154–157, where Josephus explains that, as an historian of the Jews, he has no need to expand upon the events of Nero's reign.

57 For this sense of ἀκρίβεια as the historian's standard, see the note on "in detail" at 18.129. For the present phrasing, cf. *Ant.* 1.214, also, for example, Thucydides 1.22.2 and 5.26.5 (cited by Wiseman 2013a: 46).

58 For Josephus's use of ἄλλως, see the note on "otherwise" at 18.19.

59 In the body of the story there is hardly a hint of God's involvement (note only §§61), but Josephus was explicit about it at 18.306–309 and here, in his introduction to the story, he similarly makes an effort to allow it to serve a—or rather: the—basic theme of his work; see the note on "virtue" at the end of this paragraph. Similarly, in the body of the story Josephus allows pagan speakers opposed to Gaius to involve "the gods" time and again (§72, 167, 182, 219, 233), and that too supports his theme; cf. the note on "law" at 18.222.

60 As Mason notes, the double compound ἐπιμεταφέρω occurs only here in Josephus (if here, for the manuscripts diverge), and this is, in fact, the only instance of it in all surviving Greek literature. There are a number of such cases in *War* 4; see, *inter alia*, Mason 2022b: nn. 106, 356, 329, 354, 393.

61 This is standard Josephan preaching in *Antiquities*, beginning with the prologue (1.14, 20). See esp. 17.149 and 18.127 (which too, as here [§15], opens with βούλομαι).

(1.3) 17 There were three paths being prepared for his death,[62] all of them directed by good men. Aemilius Regulus,[63] originally of Cordoba in Iberia, had gathered certain people together and was eagerly looking forward to doing away with Gaius, whether through them or by himself. **18** Another group was organizing to join them, of which the military tribune Chaerea Cassius[64] was the leader. And Annius Minucianus[65] was no small part of those organizing against the tyranny.[66] **19** The reasons that brought them together in their hatred of Gaius [were as follows].

Regulus, for his part, was affected by anger and hatred of all things that transpired unjustly.[67] And he had something of a passionate[68] and free mind, for which reason he did not even support concealing the plots; he certainly shared [information about them] with

The Conspirators

---

62 Triadic introductions like these are standard for Josephus; see the note on "three" at 18.11.

63 He is not mentioned again by Josephus, apart from §19, or in any other source. Willrich (1903: 456) suggested that his name be corrected to Aemilius Rectus, and that he is to be identified with the Rectus who was a friend of a well-known Stoic opponent of Gaius, Julius Canus; see Plutarch, *Moralia*, frag. 211. According to that account, Rectus was executed by Gaius three days after his philosopher friend. Thus, this suggestion fits well with the apparent "philosophical" opposition to Gaius of Josephus's Regulus (see §19), and explains his disappearance from Josephus's narrative. Willrich (ibid. 456–457) further conjectured that this Rectus was a relative of Seneca, who also came from Cordoba; for more on that, see Kavanagh 2001b.

64 Chaerea was a tribune of the Praetorian Guard. His central role in the assassination is recorded in all of the other sources: Dio 59.29.1–7, Suetonius, *Cal.* 56–58, Tacitus, *Ann.* 1.32, and Seneca, *Epistle* 4.7, *Const.* 18.3. Tacitus (*Ann.* 1.32) records his heroics during the riots that broke out in Germany in 14 CE, following the death of Augustus. Since Tacitus says he was "adulescens" then, he must have been past forty by the end of Gaiuis's reign; indeed, Suetonius (*Cal.* 56.2) characterizes him as already old (*senior*) by then.

65 The manuscripts consistently have Μινουκιανός both for this conspirator, who is mentioned several other times, and for Marcus Vinicius below at §102, so, as Wiseman notes (2013a: 47) that is presumably what Josephus wrote. However, the correct name is Vinicianus, as is shown by Cassius Dio's reference to him (60.15.1) in his account of the conspiracy, as also by epigraphic evidence (Smallwood 1967, nos. 4 and 10); the confusion of M and V would seem to imply a written source. I retain "Minucianus" in the translation but use either "Vinicianus" or, with scare quotes, "Minucianus" in the annotations. L. Annius Vinicianus was the son of Annius

Pollio, and together they were charged with treason by Tiberius in 32 CE (Tacitus, *Ann.* 6.9). In 42 he was involved in a plot against Claudius, and committed suicide after its failure (Dio 60.15); see Swan 1970. His son, Annius Vinicianus, Corbulo's son-in-law, would die after his failed conspiracy against Nero in 66.

66 This is the first explicit reference in Book 19 to Gaius's rule as tyrannical but, clearly, throughout this narrative, his being a tyrant is the underlying justification for the assassination. In Josephus as elsewhere, τύραννος need not have a pejorative connotation, and could simply refer to a minor ruler (as at *Ant.* 13.235; 14.40, 297), where the implied contrast with βασιλεύς relates to magnitude of the realm, not to its quality. When used, however, of someone who could be a βασιλεύς, the contrast is qualitative. Compare, for example, *Ant.* 14.157 (Hyrcanus could become ἀντὶ βασιλέως τύραννον) and Philo's discussion in *On Providence* 2.2, where God is said to be not a cruel and violent τύραννος but, rather, a benevolent βασιλεύς; later (2.24–32) the text enlarges on the evils of tyrants. For an assemblage of ancient evidence for the virtue of assassinating a tyrant, see Wiseman 1992: 5–8. On Josephus's views on tyrants, see van Henten 2011 and Ben-Yishai 2021. More generally, see Luraghi 2018.

67 It is perhaps surprising that here and above at §17 Josephus lists this Regulus-Rectus (see the note on "Regulus" at §17) first, despite the fact that he disappears from the narrative hereafter and that Chaerea was known as the main conspirator. Perhaps this fact has no significance, but perhaps Josephus (or his source) intentionally listed him first given that, of the three, he is the only one who had no personal motivations and rather acted out of pure ideological motives of hatred of the regime and love of liberty.

68 Θυμοειδής ("passionate, high-spirited, high-tempered" [LSJ 810, s.v.]). This is its only occurrence in Josephus.

many[69]—friends and others whom he considered men of action.[70] 20 Minucianus,[71] for his part, was out both to avenge Lepidus,[72] who had been his best friend and an exceptional[73] citizen, whom Gaius had killed, and also due to fear for his own life. For when Gaius gave free rein to his wrath's propensity for murder, he went about it treating all the same way.[74] 21 As for Chaerea, he was bearing the shame of the insults of unmanliness addressed to him by Gaius.[75] Moreover, apart from the fact that he was endangered by daily intimacy and service [of the emperor] he considered Gaius's death [to be a goal] not inappropriate[76] to a free man.

22 [They said] that the matter should be presented to the consideration of all who had witnessed Gaius's hubris and all who were desirous of escaping, by eliminating him, the pointed [sword] that was at the brink of[77] [attacking] others. Perhaps they would be successful,[78] and it would be noble to be successful in bringing such boons for the salvation of the city and the empire, undertaking the project[79] although it entailed suffering and even perdition. 23 Above all Chaerea was pushing forward, both because of a desire to improve his reputation and also because, on account of the fearlessness that was greater [than usual] thanks to his being a tribune, it would be easy for him to get close to Gaius and kill him.[80]

---

69 For the plot becoming known to people, see below §§62, 91–92, 132–133, 197.

70 Josephus's conviction that only the δραστήριος should be involved in public affairs is especially explicit in his contrast between the brothers Aristobulus II and Hyrcanus II; see 13.407 and 14.8, 13, 44; D. R. Schwartz 1994.

71 Above, "Minucianus" was the third conspirator mentioned, but now Josephus turns to him second, prior to Chaerea rather than after him. This allows Josephus to emphasize Chaerea by putting him last. On such triads, cf. the note on "Rome" at §2. Throughout this account, Josephus will emphasize Chaerea's centrality; see, *inter alia*, §§23, 111, 182–184, along with Destinon's suggestion cited in the note on "hands" at §113.

72 Marcus Aemilius Lepidus, son of M. Lepidus (consul in 6 CE), had been married to Gaius's favorite sister, Drusilla (Dio 59.11.1), and was—according to Dio—repeatedly declared by Gaius to be his chosen successor (59.22.6). Philo (*Flacc.* 151, 181) reports his successful support for Flaccus in 38/39. It is also reported that Lepidus had adulterous relations with Gaius's other sisters, Agrippina and Julia (Dio 59.22.6; Suetonius, *Cal.* 24.3; Tacitus, *Ann.* 14.2), and allegedly also with Gaius himself (Suetonius, *Cal.* 36.1; Dio 59.11.1). Gaius executed him in 39 on a charge of conspiracy against him (Suetonius, *Cal.* 24.3; *Claud.* 9.1; cf. Seneca, *Epist.* 4.7). For Lepidus's genealogy and relationship to Gaius and the imperial family see further, Barrett 2019: 115–116; for analysis of the allegation

of his involvement in conspiracy against Gaius, see ibid. 144–146 and H. Lindsay 1993: 110–111.

73 For such use of σὺν ὀλίγοις, see the note on "a few" at §18.1.

74 That is, apart from the widespread general fear mentioned at §14, Vinicianus's friendship with Lepidus gave him particular reason to be fearful—as will be reiterated at §49.

75 For Gaius's taunting of Chaerea for his supposed effeminacy see below, §29, as well as Suetonius, *Cal.* 56.2 and Cassius Dio 59.29.2.

76 That is, quite appropriate. The translation here follows Hudson's emendation, οὐκ ἀνελεύθερον; see the discussion in Part VI of the Introduction. For the intensifying function of the double negative ("litotes"), see the note on "not at all devoid" at 18.65. Niese, who retains the manuscripts' reading, οὐ πάντ᾽ ἐλεύθερον, would apparently translate "he considered Gaius's death something not at all appropriate for a free man [to desist from]," but that is quite a stretch.

77 This image (ἀκμὴν ἀκμάζουσαν), which characterizes the danger posed by Gaius as being both sharp and at its peak of readiness, adumbrates, as poetic justice, the swords that will eventually kill Gaius (§§105–110).

78 For similar reasoning, see 18.278.

79 As at §27.

80 It is not clear whether ὑπὸ τοῦ ἀδεέστερον means that Chaerea, since he was a tribune and therefore allowed

(1.4) 24 Meanwhile the hippodrome races came around.[81] The Romans[82] are very excited about this spectacle: they assemble enthusiastically in the hippodrome[83] and, having come together as a multitude, make their requests of the emperors concerning whatever they yearn for[84]—and those of the latter who decide that the requests are not to be rejected are not at all disobliging.[85] 25 So this time they asked Gaius, with fervor and supplication, to remit imposts and give some relief from the taxes imposed [upon them].[86] He, however, gave no heed,[87] and the more they shouted, the more he sent people out this way and that, ordering them to arrest those who were shouting and, bringing them forward,[88] to kill them without delay. 26 That is what he ordered, and that is what those ordered did, and numerous people died as a result. The populace, seeing what had happened, gave heed[89] and stopped shouting, for they saw with their own eyes that the request about money had quickly brought death upon them.[90]

27 This moved Chaerea even more to undertake the project, and to put an end to Gaius, who behaved so bestially toward people. Frequently at banquets he had been about to put his hands into action, but restrained himself on account of rational calculation; for although he no longer had any doubts about killing the man, he was looking for the right moment, so that he would use his hands not to no avail,[91] but, rather, to accomplish what he had decided upon.

---

to approach Gaius, would be less fearful than others, or rather that Gaius, for the same reason, would be less fearful (and therefore more easily overcome) when Chaerea approached him. The practical result is the same.

81 There were several games in Rome in which races took place. For a survey of Roman chariot racing, see Bell 2014. Wiseman suggests that the present reference is to the *ludi Romani*, held September 4–19.

82 This comment, like §§4 and 214, shows an awareness or anticipation of non-Roman Greek readers.

83 I.e., the Circus Maximus—the largest of all Roman circuses (hippodromes), between the Palatine and Aventine hills. On it, see Dodge 2014: 562–564, and the detailed account in Humphrey 1986: chapters 3–5.

84 For this translation of χρήζω, see also §47. For such petitions to emperors at venues of entertainment see Suetonius, *Aug.* 34.2, *Tib.* 47; Tacitus, *Ann.* 6.13. As Cicero put it, "the opinion and feeling of the Roman People in public affairs can be most clearly expressed on three occasions, at a meeting, at an Assembly, at a gathering for plays and gladiatorial shows" (Cicero, *Pro Sestio* 106, trans. Gardner, LCL; cf. ibid. 115). See further, Millar 1977: 368–375 and Cameron 1976: 157–192.

85 For this translation here, similar to Schalit's (1963: 321), see *ThLJ* 99, s.v. ἀχαριστεῖν and *CCFJ* 1.285, s.v. ἀχαριστέω. Feldman (1965: 227) and Wiseman (2013a: 6) take it to mean the populace is not ungrateful, but that requires switching the subject.

86 Such tax relief was a standard gesture; cf. 17.204–205, 18.90, and 19.299. The distinction between τέλος and φόρος, in a Roman context, is usually thought to be

between, respectively, indirect taxes and tribute. See Danker 2000: 999 and 1064, s.vv. Suetonius (*Cal.* 40–41) reports that Gaius had "levied new and unheard-of taxes," that he taxed all goods and services, and that these new tax regulations were originally not published, leading to many offenses due to ignorance. When the people urgently requested that he publish the regulations, he had them posted "in a very narrow place and in excessively small letters, to prevent the making of a copy." Cassius Dio (59.28.11) reports that he had the regulations inscribed in very small letters on a tablet which he had hung at a very high place, "so that it should be read by as few as possible and that many through ignorance ... should lay themselves liable to the penalties provided," and that the people then rushed to the hippodrome to complain. Cf. the note on "ground" at §291, about Claudius's proper practice in this regard, just as Dio (60.4.1) reports that Claudius abolished the taxes that were introduced by Gaius.

87 See the note on "gave heed" at §26.

88 I.e., to make a public spectacle of their deaths. Cf. the note on "entire city" at 20.136.

89 The same verb (ἀνέχω) as at §25, i.e., Gaius did not heed their demands, but forced them to heed his response. For a similar move with the same verb, cf. above, §§12–13.

90 Cf. Cassius Dio 59.28.11: "Once when the people had come together in the Circus and were objecting to his conduct, he had them slain by the soldiers; after this all kept quiet" (trans. Cary, LCL).

91 For εἰς κενόν, cf. §96 and *War* 1.275.

(1.5) 28 [Chaerea] had been a soldier[92] for a good bit of time already, and he did not endure[93] Gaius's conduct[94] with pleasure. When Gaius appointed him to see to the collection of taxes or whatever other sums were supposed to come into the imperial treasury and were in arrears because the rate had been doubled,[95] he took his time[96] in exacting them, following his own[97] nature rather than Gaius's order. **29** Because he behaved mercifully, viewing with pity the misfortune of those who were being forced to pay, he drove Gaius into rage; he called his laxity in collecting the moneys for him [evidence of] effeminacy.[98] Indeed, he also insulted him in other ways, and whenever he asked him for the password, when it was his day,[99] he would give him womanly words, **30** such as were totally shameful,[100] although he himself was not devoid [of effeminacy]: in certain mystery rites,[101] which he had created, he wore women's robes and contrived wigs of curls[102] or other ways to make himself

---

92 This translation follows the mss., which read ἐστρατεύετο; that is retained by Niese in both of his editions and followed by Mathieu and Herrmann (1929: 201), Schalit (1963: 321) and Wiseman (2013a: 6: "As a long-serving soldier, Chaerea did not enjoy ..."). Josephus's notion seems to be that career soldiers are men of action, so the need to bide his time was especially difficult for him—esp. given Gaius's behavior reported in the coming lines. Naber (1893: xxvi), however, followed by Feldman (1965: 228–229)—perhaps because στρατεύομαι usually refers to the movements of an army ("to take the field, undertake a campaign (military expedition], invade ..." [CCFJ 4.50]), not something done by an individual, and given the fact that the motif of delay is frequent in this story (§§47–48, 70, 74, 77, 78, 84, 89 ...)—adopted Holwerda's emendation: ἐστραγγεύετο; "things had been going slowly." That is quite a rare verb, so if Josephus used it here we might understand that copyists turned it into the more familiar ἐστρατεύετο (for the suspicion of the same confusion at 2 Macc 15:17, see D. R. Schwartz 2008: 503). However, στραγγεύομαι never appears in Josephus; the context seems to require something about Chaerea; and στρατεύομαι can refer to an individual's serving as a soldier; cf. 3.287; 7.320; 14.226; 18.84.

93 This phrase (ἡδονῇ φέρων) appears later in this story (§§83, 246), as also in Books 17–19 (17.148, 183, 211; 18.227, 289) and is, as Mason notes, characteristic of those three books, just as "receive with pleasure" (see the note at 18.63).

94 On ἀναστροφή, see Danker 1982: 358–359 and Spicq 1994: 1.111–114; cf. the note on "recovery" at 18.359. Two manuscripts have συναναστροφήν ("living with"), and accordingly Wiseman translates: "Chaerea did not enjoy his intimacy with Gaius."

95 Wiseman notes that neither the doubling of the rate nor Chaerea's role in collecting these payments is attested elsewhere.

96 As others, I have ignored the puzzling ἐκεῖ (usually: "there") here. ThLJ 231, s.v.: "'on that occasion' (?)."

97 Here Niese (1890a: 215) offers αὐτοῦ with smooth breathing, Naber (1893: 212) with rough. The latter ("his own") fits the context better. Niese seems often (although not always; cf. e.g. 17.58 and 18.169) to have preferred to reserve the rough breathing for cases with the fuller orthography, ἑαυτοῦ, as, for example, at 18.52 and 19.88.

98 For this nuance of μαλακία ("softness"), which is especially warranted by §21 and by the watchwords mentioned in the next sentence, see Danker 2000: 613, s.v. μαλακός, §2.

99 The watch of the Praetorian Guard appears to have changed in the eighth hour of the day (cf. Martial. Epigrams 10.48.1–3), and its commander would then be given the daily password by the emperor, an act perhaps symbolizing control of the empire; see Bingham 2013: 83–84 and Barrett 2019: 262. Other recorded instances of the giving of such passwords include Tacitus, Ann. 1.7 and Suetonius, Claud. 42, Nero 9.

100 The same is reported by Seneca, Const. 18.3 and Suetonius, Cal. 56.2, who say that Gaius gave passwords such as "Venus" and "Priapus," and Cassius Dio 59.29.2, who mentions "Love" and "Aphrodite" (Venus). Cf. Pausanias 9.27.4. Cf. Sossius's calling the last Hasmonean king, upon his surrender, "Antigone" instead of "Antigonus" (Ant. 14.481).

101 For Gaius's celebrating mysteries see also below, §§71, 104; cf. Barrett 2019: 292–293.

102 This is the only occurrence of πλοκαμίς in Josephus. "It is a poetic word, hardly found before Josephus's time in extant literature. Cf. Dionysius, Ant. rom. 7.9.4: Aristodemus, the tyrant of Cumae (6th cent. BCE), nicknamed Malakos, undertakes to feminize the boys in his territory, forcing them to wear women's clothes and hairstyles" (Steve Mason).

falsely appear feminine.[103] And yet he dared to address such shameful things to Chaerea![104]
31 Rage came over Chaerea whenever he received the password, and even more when he passed it on, for he was laughed at by those who received it, so that his fellow tribunes too jested about him: whenever he was about to get the password from Caesar, they would predict which [word] conducive to jesting [Gaius would give him]. **32a** For this reason there also[105] came upon him the courage to take some partners, for he was angry about matters that were truly not trivial.[106]

32b For there was Pompedius,[107] a senator, who had gone through almost all the official positions;[108] but otherwise he was an Epicurean,[109] and for that reason one who strove[110] [to lead] an inactive life.[111] **33** He was informed upon by Timidius,[112] who was his enemy,

The Torture of Quintilia

---

103 All of the sources mention Gaius's habit of dressing up in women's attire; see Seneca, *Const.* 18.3; Pliny, *NH* 37.17; Suetonius, *Cal.* 52; Cassius Dio 59.26.6–8, the latter saying that he did so in order to impersonate female divinities. Cf. Barrett 2019: 195–196. Josephus similarly accuses John of Gischala's followers of dressing up like women (*War* 4.561), and that seems to be part of his invective against them as "tyrants"; see von Ehrenkrook 2011.

104 The same contrast between Gaius's derision of Chaerea as feminine and the fact that he himself dressed femininely is made by Seneca, *Const.* 18.3.

105 This καί coordinates the use of παρίστατο here, of his courage, with the appearance of the same verb in the preceding paragraph, of his rage, underlining that the same impetus (Gaius's demeaning behavior) engendered both a negative result and a positive one.

106 That is (as the coming γάρ indicates), Chaerea's resentment concerning effeminate passwords (which, although bothersome, were not of essential importance) was not the only problem, as Josephus will now explain.

107 Cassius Dio tells a similar story at 59.26.4, but names the accused Pomponius, and Suetonius briefly mentions it without naming those involved (*Cal.* 16.4). Swan 1976 identifies him as P. Pomponius Secundus (*OCD* 1219), who survived prosecution under Tiberius in 31 (Tacitus, *Ann.* 5.8), was at some point governor of Crete and Cyrene, and was suffect consul in 44. That Pomponius is referred to by Pliny (who also wrote his biography, according to Pliny the Younger, *Ep.* 3.5), as a "consular poet" (*NH* 7.80). Pomponius also wrote pieces for the theater (Tacitus, *Ann.* 11.13), which would account for his acquaintance with the actress Quintilia. For the present episode see also Barrett 2019: 251. Pomponius's brother figures in §§263–264.

108 The formulation is similar to Josephus's introduction of Quirinius at 18.1.

109 Neither Suetonius nor Cassius Dio describes him as a senator, as one who held offices, or as an Epicurean.

110 This is the only occurrence of ἐπιτηδευτής in Josephus, and he is the earliest known user of this word. He also uses other forms of the word often, including 18.14, 15, 20, 21, 66, 92, 349; 19.49, 147; 20.264. For the notion, as here, that adherence to a particular school or sect leads people to "strive" (ἐπιτηδεύω) for some particular way of life, cf. 18.14–15, 20–21.

111 I.e., a life unconcerned with public affairs; cf. §§221, 231 and the note on "inactive style" at 18.106. For the Epicurean doctrine of non-involvement in political life, see Diogenes Laertius 10.119: "... nor will he [i.e., the wise man] take part in politics, as is stated in the first book *On Life* [by Epicurus]." For examples of the implementation of this ideal, see Plutarch, *Brutus* 12.3; Philo, *Spec. leg.* 3.1–2; Schofield 2000: 437–443; and Goodenough 1926. By portraying Pompedius as both a senator and active public figure and also as an Epicurean who led an inactive life, Josephus has it both ways: he condemns Gaius both for persecuting senators (as above, §2) and for persecuting innocent people.

112 The name Timidius is unparalleled (Wiseman 2013a: 51). Cassius Dio (59.26.4) does not name the accuser, and rather says that Pomponius "had been betrayed by a friend." Birley (2000: 620–622), pointing to manuscript evidence for "Tummidius," suggests that Ummidius Quadratus is meant. But Ummidius has not yet been mentioned by Josephus; he appears only in Book 20 (§§125–133), so it would be surprising, although not impossible, for Josephus to mention him without introduction here. Is it too wild to suggest that Josephus, or his source, has mistaken the Latin adjective "timidius," which denounced the informer as cowardly, for his proper name? Or that he or his source deliberately played that way with the informer's real name (perhaps "Timinius,"

as if he had used inappropriate invective against Gaius;[113] he brought, as witness to that, Quintilia[114]—a woman of the stage who, thanks to her conspicuous beauty, was adored by many, including Pompedius. **34** Since [the charge] was false, the poor woman[115] thought it would be terrible to give testimony that would lead to the death of her lover. Timidius expressed the desire that she be tortured, and Gaius, who was enraged, ordered Chaerea to torture Quintilia at once, without delay.[116] For he used Chaerea for murder cases[117] and whenever torture[118] was needed, on the notion that he would proceed all the more cruelly so as to evade the accusation of softness.[119]

35 When Quintilia was led in for torture, she stepped on the foot of one of the conspirators,[120] signaling to him to be brave and not to fear her torture, for she would endure it with manly virtue.[121] Chaerea, unwillingly but under compulsion from on high, tortured her cruelly, and after she did not at all give in he led her into the sight of Gaius, in a state that gave no pleasure[122] to those who saw her. **36** Even Gaius suffered at the sight of Quintilia, who was in a terrible state on account of her suffering; he acquitted both her and Pompedius of the charge, and also honored her with a gift of money[123] as the price of consoling her for the outrage that had been inflicted upon her beauty and for the unbearability of the pains.

Chaerea Enlists Fellow Consirators

(1.6) 37 These events distressed Chaerea greatly, for he had been—to the extent it was dependent upon him[124]—the agent of evil to people whom even Gaius [held to be] deserving of comfort.[125] So he said to Clemens[126] and Papinius[127] (Clemens was commander of the Praetorian Guards and Papinius too[128] was a military tribune):

---

as Wiseman suggests, or "Ummidius")? For the use of *Spitznamen* that play with names in order to condemn, such as "Antiochus Epimanes" ("crazy Antiochus") for Antiochus Epiphanes at Polybius 26.1a, Hierosyla ("temple-robbing") for Hierosolyma (Jerusalem) at *Apion* 1.311, and "Biberius Caldius Mero" ("drinker of hot wine") for Tiberius Claudius Nero at Suetonius, *Tiberius* 42.2, see Bruun 1999.

113 According to Cassius Dio (59.26.4), the accusation was of plotting against Gaius.

114 Quintilia is not named in the other sources. Dio (ibid.) says she was Pomponius's mistress, and Suetonius identifies her as a "freedwoman" (*Cal.* 16.4).

115 For this translation of ἡ ἄνθρωπος of a woman, cf. the note on "poor woman" at 18.71.

116 For μηδὲν εἰς ἀναβολάς, see the note on "without delay" at 18.107.

117 Φονικός. In *Antiquities*, the word appears only here and below at 19.201; in *War*, however, it appears half a dozen times.

118 Στρέβλωσις occurs only here in Josephus. The same root is used twice in the next paragraphs, στρεβλόω at §38 and στρέβλη at §41, and both are the only occurrences in *Antiquities*.

119 As above, §29.

120 Barrett (2019: 251) assumes this was Chaerea himself, but Josephus apparently distinguishes between the two.

121 For the topos of women who endure torture with manly virture, cf. 2 Macc 7:21; 4 Macc 15:30 and 16:14; and D. R. Schwartz 2008: 309.

122 That is, as the sight of a beautiful woman should; see §33.

123 800,000 sesterces, according to Suetonius, *Cal.* 16.4.

124 Reading, as Feldman (1965: 232–234) and Wiseman (2013a: 41), with Hudson and Havercamp (1726: 1.919): κακῶν ὅσον ἐπ' αὐτῷ γενόμενον.

125 On παρηγορία, see esp. *Ant.* 15.277–278. Here it apparently refers to the παραμυθία mentioned at §36.

126 M. Arrecinus Clemens. His daughter, Arrecina Tertulla, would later be Titus's first wife (Suetonius, *Titus* 4.2), and his son, Arrecinus Clemens, held the same position as his father under the Flavians and was suffect consul in 73 and again in 83 or 84. At first he was close to Domitian and favored by him, but eventually Domitian executed him (Tacitus. *Hist.* 4.68; Suetonius, *Dom.* 11.1).

127 He is unknown, but may have been related to Sextus Papinius, who had been executed by Gaius (Seneca, *De Ira* 3.18.3).

128 I.e., like Chaerea.

38 Look, Clemens,[129] we haven't omitted anything in guarding our emperor completely. For of those who conspired together against his rule[130] we have—applying foresight and effort—killed some of them, while others we have tortured so well, that even he was moved by pity.[131] With such great virtue do we do the army's business!

39 Clemens remained silent, and although the fact that he was shamed by the orders was apparent in the look and in the blush that came upon him,[132] out of a concern for [their] safety he did not think it justified for them to refer to the emperor's madness in words. **40** Chaerea, in contrast, already emboldened and turning to words,[133] heedless[134] of the dangers to him, went over with him, in detail, the terrible things that were overwhelming the city and the empire, saying that while nominally[135] it was Gaius who was responsible for such things, **41** for those who attempt to investigate the truth,

It is I, O Clemens, and this Papinius, and before both of us—you, who are imposing these tortures upon the Romans and all of humanity.[136] For we are not carrying out Gaius's orders but, rather, our own opinions, **42** if when it is possible to stop him from so outraging the citizens and subjects we go on administering [on his behalf], appointed as it were to be bodyguards and executioners instead of soldiers and bearing these arms not for liberty, nor for the Romans' rule, but rather to preserve him who enslaves their bodies and minds.[137] And we defile ourselves daily with the blood of massacring and torturing them, until such time as someone will do the same to us in fulfillment of Gaius's orders.[138] **43** For he will not rule vis-à-vis us with goodwill on account of these things [that we have done for him]; rather, out of suspicion, and certainly when the number of those killed has already grown.[139] For Gaius's acts of rage will never cease, for its goal is not justice but pleasure,[140] and so [eventually] we too shall be set up as targets. What is necessary is that we secure[141] for everyone immunity from conspiracy[142] as well as liberty, and for ourselves—escape from danger.

(1.7) 44 Although it was clear that Clemens approved of Chaerea's position, he urged him to keep silent, lest—if word circulated widely and things that should be hidden were spread about—before they were able to do anything the plot be discovered[143] and they

---

129 Although Chaerea is said to be speaking here with both Clemens and Papinius, his first speech is addressed to Clemens, who is of higher rank, as is made clear here and at §41.

130 For such conspiracies, see the note on "formed" at §14.

131 As is reported at §36.

132 Along with §§31 and 32, this is the third time that παρίστημι has been used in a few paragraphs.

133 See the note on "by Gaius" at §21.

134 This translation here is offered by *CCFJ* 1.133, s.v. ἀνίημι.

135 On such distinctions, which are very common in this book, see the note on "private gain" at 18.7.

136 For this Roman point of view, compare the note on "earth and sea" at §1.

137 That is, the complete opposite of "liberty," *libertas*. Cf. Wirszubski 1950: 1–3 and the note on "liberty" at 18.4.

138 For the expectation that this would come sooner or later, cf. §14.

139 Given the coming reference to pleasure, the point seems to be "l'appetito vien mangiando"—the assumption that, over time, a tyrant will want increasingly more victims in order to satiate his appetites. This assumption is the opposite of the one Tiberius expressed in his parable about flies at 18.172–176.

140 See the note on "pleasure" at §201.

141 For this sense of ψηφίζω, see also §193. Contrast the note on "decrees" at 18.265.

142 Ἀνεπιβούλευτος appears in Josephus only in *Ant.* 19 (here and §§150, 178), and only as a substantive with τό. Here it is very apt: Chaerea's point is that they need to conspire against Gaius in order to save the people from the emperor's conspiracy against it.

143 Similar wording at 17.193 and 18.111.

be punished.[144] Rather, he left everything to time and to the hope it afforded,[145] trusting that some fortunate accident[146] would come to their aid. **45** For [he said], he himself was excluded by his age[147] from such an audacious project,[148] "but although I could possibly propose something safer than what you, Chaerea, have put together and spoken about, how could anyone [propose] anything more splendid?!" **46** And so Clemens went home, distracted[149] by his thoughts about what he had heard and what he himself had said. Chaerea, for his part, was worried[150] and hurried off to Cornelius Sabinus,[151] who too was a military tribune—someone he well knew[152] to be both highly esteemed and a lover of liberty,[153] and therefore hostilely disposed toward the state of the government—**47** since he yearned to undertake immediately what he had decided upon. Although he thought it well to add others [to his team], he was afraid that through Clemens things would be bandied about, and anyway he assumed that postponements and delays would redound to the advantage of those who had the upper hand.

(1.8) 48 But since Sabinus was happy about the whole thing, for he was not at all lagging behind [Chaerea] but, rather, had come to the same opinion, and it was only for lack of someone with whom he could speak safely that he had kept silent with regard to these matters—now that he had at his disposal a man who would not only hide what he learned after he joined him but also made his own opinion clear, he was very optimistic and urged Chaerea not to delay. **49** They then turned to Minucianus, who was akin to them in his

---

144 Although, as we soon learn (§47), Chaerea did not fully trust Clemens himself to keep quiet.

145 For such a portrayal of time (here: χρόνος) as playing an active role in history, compare Nero's speech at the Isthmian Games in 67 (Oliver 1989: 573; no. 296, line 19), in which he complains about Time (ὁ αἰών) not having allowed him to live in a day in which he could have been even more generous than he was. See also §227 and *Apion* 2.279.

146 For τυχαῖος, compare τυχαίως at §125 and τυχούσης at 20.215.

147 If the identification with M. Arrecinus Clemens is correct (see the note on "Clemens" at §37), it seems rather unlikely that he was indeed too old at this time, for his children were active in the 70s (see the note on "Clemens" at §37). Moreover, Chaerea too was no youth; see the note on "Chaerea Cassius" at §18. So, it seems, Clemens is to be understood as begging off with a flimsy excuse. While cynical readers may take this to indicate that he was "shrewd enough to distance himself from the actual mechanics of the assassination and let his subordinates run the real risks" (Barrett 2019: 253), readers are probably meant to see Clemens as a fearful foil for Chaerea. For more of that, see §57.

148 On τόλμα, and its association with youth, see the note on "audacious" at 18.6.

149 For such metaphorical usage of περιφερόμενος ("bounced around") see also §§57, 109; while Clemens and Gaius could be distracted, the heroic Chaerea could not.

150 The next paragraph (§47) will explain why.

151 According to Suetonius (*Cal.* 56, 58) and Cassius Dio (59.29.1), Cornelius led the conspiracy together with Chaerea. He is, apparently, otherwise unknown.

152 This verb, ἐξεπίσταμαι, appears frequently in this narrative (§§46, 65, 133, 177). Here and at §65, it indicates that, alongside his other virtues, Josephus's Chaerea is also a good judge of character.

153 Τοῦ ἐλευθέρου ἐραστήν. Josephus uses similar language of the Israelites in Egypt: τῆς ἐλευθερίας ἐρῶντας (*Ant.* 2.281), but also in his description of the Fourth Philosophy, above, at 18.23: "[they] have a love for liberty that can hardly be overcome (δυσνίκητος δὲ τοῦ ἐλευθέρου ἔρως)." In his encomium of Ananus in the *Jewish War*, he writes "unique in his love of liberty and passion for democracy" (φιλελεύθερος τε ἐκτόπως καὶ δημοκρατίας ἐραστής; *War* 4.320), and φιλελεύθερος is used by Josephus several other times in *War*.

virtuous habits and equally devoted to high-thinking,[154] but suspected by Gaius on the background of the death of Lepidus.[155] For Minucianus and Lepidus had been great friends, and he was in great fear of dangers to himself.[156] 50 For Gaius was terrifying to all who were in high positions, as one who would not hold back from unleashing his madness against each one of them, whoever they might be. 51 Therefore, although their revulsion at the way things were happening was evident to all of them, they held back from directly expressing their opinion, and their hatred for Gaius, out of fear of dangers. One way or another, however, they ascertained their mutual hatred for Gaius and for that reason they did not cease to relate to one another with goodwill.

(1.9) 52 When they met together, there were norms of dignity to respect,[157] just as, earlier too, whenever they met, they were accustomed to show honor to Minucianus, both in light of his preeminent dignity (since he was the most noble of citizens) and because he was praised by all, 53 especially when he took up discussion of a matter.[158] He indeed opened [the discussion], asking Chaerea what password he had received that day; for the outrage done to Chaerea by the giving of passwords was the talk of the city.[159] 54 But the latter, totally ignoring the humor of his words,[160] requited[161] Minucianus for having enough trust to meet with him about such matters, and said:

> You give me the password "Liberty,"[162] and you are to be thanked for arousing me to more than my usual energy. 55 I do not need any more words to encourage me, if indeed you too are of the same opinion [as me]; for we shared the same view even before we met together. I am girded with one sword, and it will suffice for both of us.[163] 56 So come: let us take the work into hand! You be the leader: order me to go wherever you desire, and thither I shall take myself, relying[164] on the aid supplied by your making common cause [with me]. There is no lack of weapons[165] for men who have thrown their souls into the work;[166] indeed, usually it is actually by virtue of the latter that the weapon becomes active.[167] 57 I have jumped into this action without being distracted[168] by the prospect[169] of what I myself might suffer. For I do not have the time to consider the dangers to myself, since I am in grief[170] over the enslavement of my fatherland, which was the

---

154 On the nuances of τὸ μεγαλόφρων, see the note on "high spirit" at 18.255.

155 On Lepidus, see the note at §20.

156 For Vinicianus, his relationship with Lepidus, and his current dangerous position, see above §§18, 20.

157 As Thackeray notes (*ThLJ* 57, s.v. ἀξίωσις), "meaning doubtful."

158 For λόγου ἅπτεσθαι, see also 18.110.

159 See §§29–31. Josephus uses ἀοίδιμος elsewhere only at 6.165.

160 I.e., although it was at his own expense.

161 That is, he repaid his confidence by putting himself on the line. For such usage of ἀμείβω in the middle voice, compare §151 and 20.93.

162 As Wiseman notes, the same password was used by Brutus at Philippi, according to Cassius Dio 47.43.1. See also below, at §186.

163 See the end of the note on "with Gaius" at §270.

164 This is the only occurrence of πίσυνος in Josephus.

165 For σίδηρος (lit. "iron") as "weapon," see also §148 and 20.165, also 10.118; 11.283; 19.56; at *War* 2.619, Mason (2008: 408, n. 3688) notes that the choice of this term, rather than the more "prosaic" and usual ξίφος, "poeticizes the drama." So too here, the fancier word fits the hortatory context.

166 For similar thoughts, see §233 and 18.363.

167 Cf. the saying quoted by Seneca (*Epistle* 87): "a sword kills no one; rather, it is the slayer's weapon" (*gladius neminem occidit; occidentis telum est*).

168 See the note on "distracted" at §46.

169 For ἐλπίς referring not only to "hope" but also to an unwelcome prospect, cf. the note on "expectation" at 18.277.

170 ἐπαλγέω. "Only here in Josephus. Since he is only the third attested user of the verb, after Euripides (*Suppl.* 59) and Strabo (*Geog.* 11.3.2), this may be an allusion to the tragic situation of the former" (Steve Mason).

most free of all, the abolition of the laws[171] of virtue,[172] and the ruin of all of humanity undertaken by Gaius. **58** Let me be worthy, in your eyes as judge, to be entrusted with these things, given the fact that we think the same about these matters and you are not at all averse[173] to me.

(1.10) 59 Minucianus, observing the intense flow of his words, greeted him happily and encouraged his boldness. After he praised and embraced him, they took leave [of one another] with prayers and supplications.

60 And there are some who insist that what was said was well-founded,[174] namely, that when Chaerea came into the Senate building, someone's voice was heard out of the crowd, urging him to persevere to the end—thus encouraging him to proceed and do what had to be done, with the divine power being on his side. **61** [And they go on to report] that at first Chaerea suspected that he had been caught, one of the conspirators[175] having turned traitor;[176] but in the end he realized that it was in fact intended to encourage him from the outset, whether it was a warning from one of those in the know who was signaling him, or rather God, who oversees the affairs of man,[177] who was encouraging him.[178]

62 [Knowledge of] the plot had circulated among many people[179] and everyone present was armed—those who were senators and equites and whatever soldiers there were who knew about it—for there was not even one, who would not reckon[180] the elimination of Gaius as good fortune. **63** For this reason all were eager, each in whatever way he could, not to fall behind willingly in any way from the courage needed for these things; rather, they undertook the tyrannicide[181] with as much enthusiasm and power, in words and in actions, as they could.

---

171 See the note on "tyranny" at §177.

172 For law as meant to foster virtue, cf. the note on "virtue" at 18.264.

173 On such usage of ἀπαλλάσσω in the passive and negative, see *ThLJ* 59, s.v., §2.

174 Apparently βεβαίως here means that some who tell the following anecdote insist that it is authentic, i.e. true; see the note on "full-fledged" at 20.38. However, the text is not simple and has invited emendations (see Feldman 1965: 244, nn. 2–3); Niese (1890a: 221) suspects a lacuna.

175 Συνωμοτῶν. Lit. "those who took an oath together"—Josephus's usual term in this book for the conspirators (§§61, 73, 78, 101, etc.). Cf. συνόμνυμι at §38.

176 "Traitor" (προδότης) is quite a harsh term, to which Josephus must have been sensitive. See his pious denial at *War* 3.354 (cf. §§361, 381) and especially *Life* 416, where καὶ αὐτῶν means that both Jews and Romans accused Josephus of being one. Above, at §§45–47, Chaerea worried about Clemens possibly revealing a secret, if only by indiscretion; now, as the story nears its climax, things are becoming more polarized.

177 In *Antiquities* Josephus loves to underline divine providence. See esp. his explicit conclusions on the

subject at the end of Books *Ant.* 10, 15, and 17, as well as *War* 7 (§453), also above, §16, and such passages as 18.127–128, 199, and 20.18, 49, 91; Attridge 1976: esp. 71–107; and Klawans 2012: 81–90.

178 For heavenly voices in Josephus's writings see *Ant.* 13.282, and—preceding the destruction of the Temple—*War* 6.299 (paralleled in Tacitus, *Hist.* 5.13.1). In Roman sources see Cicero, *Div.* 1.99, 101. They are reminiscent of the rabbinic notion of the heavenly *bat kol* (lit. "daughter of the voice," i.e., echo); for one that is said to have presaged the death of Gaius, see *t. Soṭah* 13:6 (ed. Zuckermandel, 319; ed. Lieberman, 232) and parallels, along with Noam in Ilan and Noam 2017: 1.469–472.

179 Wiseman (2013a: 53) asserts that this stage of the narrative is equivalent to §22 above, therefore pointing to their origins in different sources. However, in context, the present passage assumes that some time has passed since the first expressions of discontent related in the earlier passage.

180 For such usage of ἀριθμέω, see also 18.16, 210.

181 Τυραννοκτονία ("killing of a tyrant, tyrannicide") appears in Josephus only in *Ant.* 19, here and below at §§92, 184, and 191. On Josephus on "tyrants," see the note on "tyranny" at §18.

64 And then there was Callistus.[182] He was a freedman of Gaius but this one man had come into the highest power;[183] his power was no less than that of the tyrant himself, being feared by all on account of the great wealth that was his.[184] **65** For he was very venal[185] and behaved more outrageously than anyone else,[186] exercising his authority improperly. Moreover, he knew Gaius's nature thoroughly: that it was impossible to mollify him; that when he had decided on something he would never allow any distractions;[187] and that he himself was, for many and sundry reasons (not least: the magnitutde of his wealth), in danger.[188] **66** Accordingly, he even paid court[189] to Claudius, secretly re-aligning himself with him[190] in the hope that when and if Gaius were out of the way and the empire would pass to [Claudius], he would have laid down the basis for the same honor and power by having made a down payment of favor and goodwill into his account.[191] **67** [In support of this claim I can adduce] at least[192] the fact that he was so audacious as to say that although he had been ordered to kill Claudius with a drug,[193] he continually found myriads of delays for the matter.[194] **68** It seems, however,[195] that Callistus made this story up in order to curry Claudius's favor.[196] For neither would Gaius, had he been set upon killing Claudius, have heeded[197] Callistus's excuses, nor would Callistus, had he ever been commanded to do it, have thought it desirable [to delay[198]]; nor was it possible that, had he violated the despot's orders,[199] he would not have immediately paid the price. **69** Rather, concerning Claudius it was thanks to some divine power that he was able to escape Gaius's madness, while as

---

182 Apparently C. Iulius Callistus, to whom the physician Scribonius Largus dedicated his *Compositiones*. Cf. Millar 1977: 75–76; Barrett 2019: 116–117. Tacitus (*Ann.* 11.29.1) and Cassius Dio (59.29.1) also mention him among the prime conspirators. Callistus's daughter, Nymphidia, was said to have had intimate relations with Gaius, and her son, Nymphidius—a claimant to the principate following Nero's death—even claimed to be Gaius's son (Tacitus, *Ann.* 15.72; Plutarch, *Galba* 9).

183 Suetonius (*Cal.* 56.1) writes that the plot enjoyed the connivance of Gaius's most influential freedmen, but does not name any of them. Pliny identifies Callistus as "the freedman of Claudius," and also emphasizes his wealth and influence (*NH* 36.60), and Cassius Dio 59.19.5–6 illustrates Callistus's influence over Gaius in the case of Domitius Afer.

184 On the growing influence of freedmen under Gaius, see Yavetz 1996: 105–106. For Callistus's rise to power, see also Seneca, *Epistle* 47. On Josephus's sharing in Roman aristocratic hatred of wealthy and influential freedmen (such as Pallas and Beryllus—*Ant.* 20.182–184, also, more generally, 20.135), see the note on "friends" at 20.135.

185 Δωροδόκος. This is the only occurrence of this word in Josephus.

186 For such usage of παρ᾽ ὁντινοῦν, see also §208.

187 Josephus uses ἀντίσπασμα elsewhere only at 17.36.

188 See the note on "property" at §3.

189 For such use of θεραπεύω of calculated self-serving cultivation of others, see the note on "relationship" at 18.167.

190 For doubts about this, see the note on "himself" at §69.

191 Using λόγος in the sense of a financial "account," as at 11.102 and 17.223; see also Bickerman 2007: 1.437–438.

192 Here γοῦν indicates that the following story (§§67–69) is meant to illustrate the statement that concludes §66, a point that is made clear by the repetition, at §69, of the banking image (προκαταθέμενος χάριν and then χάριτος κατάθεσιν). Cf. the note on "at least" at 18.243.

193 See the note on "denounce Claudius" at §13. For Gaius's collection of poisons, see Suetonius, *Cal.* 49.3.

194 On χρῆμα, here as at §75, see the note on "labor" at 18.319.

195 For a similar comment, cf. below, §107.

196 For similar criticism of Nicolaus, cf. 14.9 and 16.183–187.

197 So *CCFJ* 1.121 (s.vv. ἀνέχω, ἀνίσχω) of this passage; so too above, §§25–26. For the verb's range of meanings, including "to restrain oneself" at 18.241, 347, see also *ThLJ* 47.

198 This parenthetical addition seems to be the simplest way to make sense of this passage, which has perplexed editors and attracted emendations.

199 Here δεσπότης seems to have a negative connotation, as also at §179; 7.390; and 13.330. Usually, however, it

for Callistus: nothing was in fact done by him, and he fabricated [the story] to store up goodwill[200] for himself.[201]

Delays

(1.11) 70 Day after day there were many many delays for those around Chaerea,[202] for many were hesitant. For Chaerea [himself] would not willingly have delayed action; rather, he thought any time at all was appropriate for the act.[203] 71 Indeed, he often had an opportunity, when he went up to the Capitolium[204] when sacrifices were being offered by Gaius for his daughter.[205] For when Gaius stood up above the palace[206] and scattered gold and silver money upon the people,[207] he could have pushed him headlong[208]—and the roof is high above the Forum; or [he could have killed him] at the productions he instituted at the mysteries.[209] 72 For he gave no attention to anything [else], being taken up in planning how to do properly that which he had to do,[210] and in his despair of the belief that anyone [else]

---

simply means "ruler" or "master" (see, for example, 18.187, 213, 296; 19.6, 14, 131), just as Josephus can use it of God (on which see Fischer 1958/59). Cf. the long entry at *ThLJ* 130.

200 Josephus reverts here, with χάριτος κατάθεσιν, to the financial image he introduced at §66, thus indicating to readers that this story ends here.

201 Indeed, Callistus remained prominent under Claudius (see Pliny, *NH* 33.134, 36.60; Tacitus, *Ann.* 11.38, 12.1–2). This has been taken by some as one of the reasons to suggest that Claudius himself was involved in the plot, and that together with one group of conspirators their original plan was to replace Gaius with Claudius (see Levick 1990: 35–39). That suggestion is rejected by Wiseman 2013a: 53–54, because the evidence indicates that, prior to the assassination of Gaius, Claudius was not a likely candidate to succeed him to the Principate (see Suetonius, *Claud.* 2–10).

202 This phrasing (τοῖς ἀμφὶ τὸν Χαιρέαν) does not exclude Chaerea (see the note on "retinue of" at 20.131). But it does put the onus on the others, a point the text goes on to make explicit. For a similar move, see the note on "you" at §80.

203 This repeated emphasis on Chaerea's resolve to do the deed as quickly as possible (see also above, §§23, 28, 47), and the contrast with the other conspirators' hesitancy, clearly make Chaerea the main hero of this narrative. Note, however, that at §27 above, Chaerea himself is also said to have been hesitant to kill Gaius when he calculated his chances of success as not great.

204 See above, §§4, 11.

205 See above, §11. It is unclear what the occasions for these sacrifices were. They could not have been her birthday, given that the account speaks of it occurring "often."

206 Although various scholars have assumed a palace on the Palatine was meant, Wiseman (2013a: 55) notes that, in that case, we would expect βασίλειον, as

at §§75, 103, etc. Given the unanimity of the witnesses for βασιλική here, the reference is probably, instead, to the Basilica Julia, at the southwestern side of the Forum, which Suetonius (*Cal.* 37.1) also mentions as the building from the roof of which Gaius would scatter money to the people. On that basilica, see Richardson 1992: 52–53.

207 Gaius's scattering of money among the people from a basilica's rooftop is mentioned by Suetonius, *Cal.* 37.1, as well as Cassius Dio 59.25.5, who also reports that many people died in the scramble for the money, and that Gaius mixed small pieces of iron with the coins. For similar scattering by emperors, see below §93. also, *inter alia*, Suetonius, *Nero* 11.2; Cassius Dio 61.18.1–2 (Nero), 66.25.5 (Titus); Suetonius, *Dom.* 4.5; and Millar 1977: 137.

208 The collocation κατὰ κεφαλῆς has been the object of much discussion apropos of its occurrence, in another sense, in 1 Corinthians 11:4; see, *inter alia*, Massey 2007 and Brown 2013. As Brown notes (367, n. 4), there is some papyrological evidence for the collocation being used, specifically, of a blow to the head. Here, however, the reference to the height, from which Gaius would fall if pushed, seems to point to falling down head first, "headlong."

209 On these, see above, §30.

210 It seems that the subject of this sentence is Chaerea, and the point is that he knew he had these options because he was devoting all of his thought to the topic of how to kill Gaius. Others think that Josephus means that Gaius was so attentive to performing the cult properly that he would easily fall prey to an assassin; so, for example, Schalit 1963: 325, *CCFJ* 1.110 (on this passage), and, perhaps, Wiseman 2013a: 12. But that is both to ignore Gaius's bodyguards and also to agree that Josephus (or his source) would use such a nice adverb as εὐπρεπῶς for anything Gaius did.

would undertake anything.[211] But if no worthy power of the gods brought death to him,[212]
73 he himself[213] would have enough strength to do away with Gaius, even if he were not carrying a sword.[214] To such an extent was Chaerea angry at[215] his fellow conspirators, fearing
that the opportunities would slip away.

74 They, although seeing that the things he wanted were indeed requisite,[216] and that
what he was urging was for their own good, nonetheless asked him to delay things at least
for a little while, lest somehow, if some mishap occurred when they came together for
the undertaking, they would both create turmoil in the city with searches for those who
had been party to the deed and also make it impossible for those who would in the future
again[217] undertake such a daring deed, because Gaius would have secured himself better
against them. **75** [They said] it was best to handle the matter when spectacles were being
held on the Palatine.[218] Those are celebrated in honor of the first Caesar, who transferred
the government of the populace to himself.[219] Not far in front of the palace a tent[220] was

---

211 The construction of the last clause goes hand in
hand with the one that precedes it. Schalit (1963: 325) and
(apparently) Wiseman (2013a: 12) take it to mean that
Gaius "confidently refused to believe that anyone would
attack him," and that gave Chaerea confidence that he
could successfully assassinate Gaius. However, ἀπόγνω-
σις usually means "despair"; see, for example, 18.285 and
19.199, also *ThLJ* 66. Moreover, the notion that Chaerea
thought his attack on Gaius would be without risk would
undercut his heroism, while the notion that no one else
would do it fits the context here (§70).

212 I.e., to Gaius. That is, Chaerea is represented
as thinking that he will kill Gaius unless some superior
divine force steps in and does the job; see the next note.

213 This sentence is difficult and has attracted several
emendations; see *CCFJ* 4.110, s.v. τίμιος. Feldman (1965:
250) notes "The MSS. yield little sense," and Niese, who
followed the manuscripts in his editio maior (1890a: 223),
marked a lacuna in his editio minor (1890b: 192) just
before the text quoted immediately below. Here, faute de
mieux, I have attempted to render Niese's text: εἰ δὲ μηδὲν
τίμιον ὡς τῶν θεῶν αὐτῷ δύναμιν τοῦ θανάτου παρατυγχάνειν.
Feldman followed Petersen in reading τὸ κωλῦον instead
of τίμιον and Γαΐῳ instead of αὐτῷ, thus taking the sentence to mean that Chaerea would kill Gaius "if no divinity prevented Gaius from meeting his death," and Hudson,
followed by several including Mathieu and Herrmann
(1929: 207) and Wiseman (2013a: 41, 55), suggested σημεῖον
instead of τίμιον, the result being Chaerea's readiness to
kill Gaius even without any "sign" from the gods. Apart
from the radical nature of those emendations, however,
it also seems that Josephus's Chaerea should not be contemplating that eventuality; Chaerea is portrayed as being
so sure that Gaius should die that, for him, there was no
reason to imagine the gods would want to save him, nor
any need for any sign from them. The only question was
whether the gods would preempt him.

214 Lit: "an iron." See the note on "weapons" at §56.

215 Reading δι᾽ ὀργῆς εἶχε with two witnesses—a common formulation; see 3.12, 33; 5.155; 6.150; 7.147, 321. So
too Feldman 1965: 250 and Wiseman 2013a: 12, 55. Niese
(1890a: 223) adhered to the other witnesses, which offer
εὐχῆς εἴχη, omitting the preposition and offering another
noun. But how that can be rendered, without an inordi-
nate amount of parenthetical supplementation, is not
apparent.

216 Josephus uses νομίμων, "of that which law
requires," but it seems that a broader sense is needed here.

217 Reading αὖθις with Holwerda (cited by Naber
1893: xxvii), instead of the codices' αὐτοῖς.

218 Namely, during the *Ludi Palatini*, as stated by
Suetonius, *Cal.* 56.2 and Cassius Dio 59.29.4. These *ludi*
were established in memory of Augustus (as is said at §87)
by Livia, shortly after his death in 14 CE. They began on
Jan. 17, the anniversary of the wedding of Augustus and
Livia (see Degrassi 1963: 161, 400–401), and are said to
have lasted three days (Cassius Dio 56.46.5), but see the
note on "[to the spectacles]" at §77. As for the Palatine,
see the note on "to be settled" at §223.

219 I.e., Augustus, as is said explicitly at §87, and see
the previous note. As Wiseman (2013a: 55) notes, the
observation that Augustus was the first to transfer the
government of the people to himself contradicts the view
reflected at §§173 and 187, which point, instead, to Julius
Caesar. Indeed, it is obvious from 18.32–33 that Josephus
considered Augustus the second emperor. However,
while §§173 and 187 are complaints about Julius Caesar,
here there is no criticism of Augustus, so perhaps we
should understand that the former violated the extant
legal order (§173!) while the latter is, here, said to have
instituted the change of it.

220 This translation of καλύβη, here and at §90, its
only other occurrence in Josephus, is adopted from *CCFJ*
2.426. Feldman (1965: 251) states that "hut" is the literal

constructed,[221] and the Romans of best birth[222] watch the show together with their children and wives, and so does Caesar. **76** Then it would be easy for them, with so many myriads of people crowding themselves into a small place, to execute the attack upon him as he entered[223]—and the power of his shield-bearers,[224] even if some of them were eager [to try to save him], would not be available to aid him.

Chaerea's Speeches Impel to Action

(1.12) 77 Chaerea did hold off, but although it was decided to carry out the job on the first day of the spectacles, when they came, the delays[225] granted by fortune were stronger than what they had earlier decided upon, and although three days were added [to the spectacles],[226] they were just barely able to do the job on the final day.[227] **78** After calling together the conspirators, Chaerea said:

---

meaning (although he prefers "stage"), and Wiseman (2013a: 12, 56) indeed offers "wooden hut" and suggests, as Feldman, that it was part of the theater. However, it seems that the reference here is to where the audience was, not where the actors performed, and it also seems that (as Feldman apparently recognized) "hut" is too shabby a word to use of something erected for lavish imperial celebrations.

221 As with καλύβη, Josephus uses πηκτός only here and at §90.

222 I.e., patricians; see the note on "good birth" at §2.

223 In fact, however, the attack on Gaius came only after he left; see §101–105. The current statement about original plans contributes to the oft-repeated theme that the assassins' plans were often delayed; see the note on "delayed" at §28. That, of course, heightens the drama of the story.

224 On Gaius's German bodyguards, see the note on "bodyguards" at §119. True, given the use of ὑπασπιστής here (which Josephus uses elsewhere only once, at *Ant.* 5.252), rather than δορυφόροι as at §119 or the usual σωματοφύλαξ (as at 19.214, 221, 237, 247), Wiseman (2013a: 56), pointing to the use of ὑπασπιστής for elite forces of Alexander the Great's army, suggested that the reference is to the Praetorian Guard—Chaerea's and Clemens's (§37) comrades-in-arms. However, §§119–121 and §§149–150 make it clear that the bodyguards, from whom opposition might be expected, were the Germans, and the allusion to Alexander, if there is one, could be, as that at §95, only part of the story's critique of Gaius for elevating himself to the status of a Macedonian monarch.

225 Here fortune (τύχη) is compared to a judge who grants "stays of execution." On such delays, see the note on "entered" at §76. On Tyche in Josephus, see the note on "Fortune" at 18.54.

226 This translation follows the manuscripts, which read ὑπερβαλλομένου. Wiseman (2013a: 56) renders that as "exceeding the three by the scheduled days," observes that that is unintelligible, and assumes the reference is to Gaius's three-day extension of the games that year, reported by Cassius Dio (59.29.6). Accordingly, he takes the text to mean "Even though three days were added to the scheduled programme" (Wiseman 2013a: 13). Other scholars, however, finding it difficult to take the verb to mean "having been added," especially in the absence of reference to the subject, Gaius, emend to ὑπερβαλλομένοις and take the text to mean "having let pass the three days" (so Feldman 1965: 253, defended by Wardle 1991: 161). Given the unanimity of the manuscripts here on the one hand, and the frequency of difficulties with the Greek of *Ant.* 19 on the other, I tend to ascribe less weight to that argument than to the way the unemended text can be coordinated, as Wiseman noted, with Dio's evidence—a move that also allows both to agree with Suetonius (see the next note).

227 There is some debate about the date of the assassination. Suetonius (*Caligula* 58.1) clearly dates it to "VIIII Kal. Feb.," i.e., January 24, and although Cassius Dio does not supply a date, he does state (at 59.30.1) the length of Gaius's reign and his datum brings us to January 23–24 (Wardle 1991: 158–159). This poses a difficulty, because, as noted above (on "Palatine" at §75), the spectacles were originally held for only three days, beginning on January 17, so will have ended on January 19. The only way to reconcile the data, if not by positing that Suetonius's datum is erroneous, is to assume the spectacles were lengthened to eight days (January 17–24). Indeed, that seems to be stated by Cassius Dio 59.29.5–6, where we read that the conspirators planned to kill Gaius at the spectacles, waited five days, and then, when Gaius added three more

185

The long time that has gone by shames us for still delaying the execution of what was decided upon so courageously. And it is terrible [to imagine] that if we are informed[228] against the whole project will fall through and Gaius will act all the more outrageously. **79** Or do we not see that every day that we grant as an addition to Gaius's tyranny is subtracted from those of liberty? We must henceforth be fearless and, after supplying others with reason for happiness, establish ourselves, in turn, for ever and ever, in great admiration and honor.

80 When [he saw] that they could neither oppose what he had said as if it were not completely correct, nor directly take the business into hand, but rather remained silent, overwhelmed, he said:[229]

Why, my good men, do we hesitate? Or do you[230] not see that today is the last day of the spectacles[231] and Gaius is about to set sail?! **81** (For he had prepared to sail to Alexandria to inspect[232] Egypt.[233]) Is it proper that we let this blemish on the vaunted greatness[234] of the Romans slip out of our hands[235] and go parading across land and sea? **82** How could we not condemn ourselves, justly, out of shame at what happened,

---

days, they made their move. If we accept that statement about the length of the festival, and also Josephus's datum (here) that they did their deed on its last day, Suetonius's date is confirmed. True, that requires that we read Dio 59.29.5–6 to mean they acted at the conclusion of the additional three days, not when they were announced, and that is not necessarily the most natural meaning, and an additional problem would arise if we thought that Josephus, here, stated the conspirators waited only three days. But the reading of Dio is possible and, as explained in the preceding note, Josephus seems to mean something else, namely, that (as Dio reported) Gaius added three days. But even if we take Josephus to mean that the conspirators waited only three days, that would seem to be the weakest item in the dossier; perhaps it would reflect only the knowledge, of Josephus or of a copyist, that the festival usually lasted three days (Dio 56.46.5). For the entire debate see also Degrassi 1963: 400–401, who prefers to correct the text of Suetonius; Wardle 1991, who upholds January 24; and Barrett 2019: 261–262, who leaves the issue unresolved.

228 Μήνυμα. Josephus uses this term only here and at *War* 7.223.

229 For a very similar scene, in which one brave member of a deliberative body urges his fellows to overcome their fear of a tyrant and rise to the occasion, see *Ant.* 14.172–174 (which has a parallel at *b. Sanhedrin* 19a–b). As at *War* 7.323–336, 341–388, however, in the present case Josephus has the speaker give two speeches: after the first moves the crowd but insufficiently, the second carries the day.

230 Note that in his first speech, at §79, Chaerea, with οὐχ ὁρῶμεν, politely included himself with the others who might not see what should be seen. Now, in the more insistent second speech, with the move to the second-person

οὐχ ὁρᾶτε he creates—as explicit in §83—a gap between him and any who do not follow him.

231 See the note on "final day" at §77.

232 For this translation of θεωρία here, see *CCFJ* 2.344, s.v.

233 Philo too mentions a planned trip to Alexandria (*Leg.* 172–173, 250–253, 338). Those passages, however, seem to imply that the intended expedition was to take place significantly earlier than what Josephus says here, possibly in the late summer, which would also be more reasonable than a sea-expedition in January (cf. Barrett 2019: 267, n. 57). Suetonius (*Cal.* 49.2) writes that just prior to his death Gaius "had made up his mind to move to Antium [Gaius's birthplace (ibid. 8.2, 5)], and later to Alexandria." Yet, as scholars have noted, this should be taken with a grain of salt; such an accusation would have been "an easy way to discredit him" (Barrett 2019: 292; H. Lindsay 1993: 152).

234 It is difficult to render μεγαλαυχία here. On the one hand, Chaerea evidently means that as long as Gaius is alive he sullies the good name of Rome; perhaps, then, we should imagine him referring to Rome's *magnificentia* or the like. For μεγαλαυχία as *magnificentia*, see Goetz 1888: 365; on the *magnificentia* of Rome, see Dyson 2010: 206.. On the other hand, however, when Josephus uses μεγαλαυχία or its cognates elsewhere, it has a pejorative sense, "boasting" or "arrogance." See *War* 1.477, *Ant.* 4.62, and *Apion* 2.126 (also αὔχημα at §§174, 250). Perhaps, then, readers are to understand Chaerea to mean that as long as Gaius is alive, he shows that all the Romans' talk of their own greatness is no more than empty and unjustified boasting. I have tried to capture this ambiguity by adding "vaunted" to "greatness."

235 For προέσθαι τῶν χειρῶν, see also §236.

if some Egyptian[236] were to kill him, considering that his hubris was not to be tolerated by free men? **83** I, for my part, will no longer tolerate your excuses. Rather, I will face the dangers this very day,[237] immediately, enduring with pleasure[238] whatever shall ensue from them, and I would not postpone any more even if it were possible! For what could be more vexing[239] for a man of élan than for another to kill Gaius while I am still alive, thus depriving me of the virtue of the deed?!

The Assassination

(1.13) **84** Having said that, he himself stormed out to do the job, having emboldened all the others, so there was passion to put the project into motion without further delay.

85 At daybreak he made his way as customary to the Palatine, girded with an equite's sword. For it was the practice of the military tribunes to be girded with one when asking the emperor for the password, and it was his day to receive the password.[240] **86** A multitude was already gathering at the Palatine, in expectation of the spectacle, with much hustle and bustle, and Gaius was happy to see the mob so enthusiastic, and [that] for that reason[241] no separate section had been set aside for the Senate or for the equites,[242] so that all sat mixed together—both men together with women and slaves mixed in alongside the free.[243] **87** When way had been made for Gaius, he sacrificed to Augustus Caesar, in whose honor the spectacles were celebrated, and when one of the sacrificial victims fell it happened that the robe of Asprenas[244]—one of the senators—was drenched with blood.[245] That made Gaius laugh, but for Asprenas it was to be, indeed, a manifest ill omen; for he was cut down along with Gaius.[246] **88** And it is reported that Gaius was, contrary to his nature,

---

236 As Reinhold (1980: 103) put it, "for centuries" the Romans "treated the masses of Egyptians as the 'rubbish of society.'" See, for example, Juvenal, *Satire* 15; Tacitus, *Hist.* 1.11.1; Dio Chrysostom, *Orat.* 32 ("Ad Alexandrinos"). See also Berthelot 2000: 196–202.

237 This translation of ὁμοῦ σήμερον is suggested for this passage at *CCFJ* 3.209, s.v. ὁμοῦ.

238 On this phrase see the note on "endure" at §28.

239 Josephus uses σχέτλιος only here and at *Apion* 2.33.

240 For the tribune's receiving of the password, see the note on "his day" at §29. Chaerea carried out this task of asking for the password later that day, and it was immediately followed by the assassination (below, §105). The sword "appears to have identified him as the individual responsible for this duty on that particular day" (Eaton 2011: 54).

241 This is the only occurrence of παρό in Josephus apart from *War*.

242 Aristocratic outrage is palpable here; cf. §§2–3. Cf. Suetonius, *Cal.* 26.4: Gaius induced the general public to take the seats of the equites in the theater in order to produce discord between the two groups.

243 Separate seating at the games was decreed by the Senate under Augustus, according to Suetonius, *Aug.* 44. He wrote that Augustus "put a stop to the disorderly and indiscriminate fashion of viewing the games"; that is, the

exact opposite of Gaius's policy here. For details about the separate seating arrangements, see Rawson 1987: 89–110.

244 Probably P. Nonius Asprenas, who was consul in 38 (Frontinus, *Aq.* 13; Dio 59.9.1), although it is surprising that Josephus, in contrast to 19.91 (and 18.1), does not characterize him as having been a consul but only as "one of the senators." Assuming that the reading "Asprenas" at §98 is correct (see there), he was involved in the conspiracy.

245 According to Suetonius (*Cal.* 57.4), however, it was Gaius whose clothing was soiled by the blood. For the argument that the original tradition was deliberately ambiguous, as reports of such omens often were, and that this omen actually presaged the death of both and Gaius did not understand that, see Woods 2018. Ibid. 875 Woods assembles evidence that the splattering of blood on someone was often taken to be an omen of death. On ambiguous omens, and "the delight that ancient authors often took in describing the initial misinterpretation of an omen by the relevant figure before he eventually realises, all too late, that he has got it wrong," see ibid. 878. For a similar case, see the note on "Gaius" at §270.

246 This is the only occurrence of ἐπικατασφάζω in Josephus. Feldman (1965: 257) takes it locatively: "over Gaius' dead body," but that notion is not supported in the report of Asprenas's death, below at §123. Rather, ἐπί here probably is temporal ("to be slaughtered immediately

most conversational[247] that day, and that he amazed all those whom he encountered with the affability of his conversation with them. **89** After the sacrifice, turning to the spectacle he sat down. Around him were his most honored friends.

90 Now the theater, which was set up each year, had the following design:[248] it had two doors, of which one led outside, the other into a portico with entrances and exits, in order that those who were inside would not be bothered, and from the tent[249] itself another was closed off inside it, by partitions, in order to give the competitors, as well as whatever musicians[250] there were, a place of respite.[251] **91** When the crowd too sat down, Chaerea (together with the [other] military tribunes) was not far away from Gaius. Caesar had the right wing of the theater. Bathybius,[252] a man of senatorial rank who had been praetor, asked Cluvius,[253] who was seated beside him (he too a man of consular rank), whether information had reached him concerning anything new in public affairs; in saying this, he took care lest he be overheard. **92** When [Cluvius] said no sign of anything had come to his attention, Bathybius said: "Well, Cluvius, we have before us a tyrannicide show."[254] Cluvius responded: "'Quiet, my good man, lest some other Achaean hear the story.'"[255]

The Theater and Program

---

after, be killed at the same time" [*CCFJ* 2.161]), or perhaps even causative ("on Gaius's account").

247 This is the only occurrence of εὐπροσήγορος ("conversational"?) in Josephus. Cf. below on "familiarity" at §131.

248 "Josephus' description of the arrangements for the games is one of the most confused of his whole narrative and rendered even more incomprehensible by textual corruption. It has so far eluded coherent explanation" (Barrett 1989: 170). Moreover, the fact that the whole of the Palatine hill was burned in the great fire of 64 CE (Tacitus, *Ann.* 15.39.1; Cassius Dio 62.18.2) makes reconstruction even more difficult. For an attempt, see Wiseman 2013a: 103 (Figure 2b, where "Augustan forecourt?" marks the assumed site of the temporary theater); more generally, see idem 1987 and 2013b.

249 See the note on "tent" at §75.

250 This is the only occurrence of ἀκρόαμα in Josephus. LSJ 56, s.v. offers "lecturers," "singers," and "players" as, for example, at Polybius 4.20.10. As Walbank (1957–1979: 1.468) notes ad loc., this sense passed into Latin (*acroama*); he cites Cicero *Pro Sestio* 116 and *Pro Archia* 20.

251 On ἀναστροφή, see the note on "recovery" at 18.359.

252 For the suggestion that Bathybius, "whose identity is a complete mystery" (Kavanagh 2010: 1007), be identified with one Pacuvius mentioned by Seneca in *Epistle* 12.8, who seems to have been both an ex-praetor and a connoisseur of things Greek, see Birley 2000: 622–623.

253 This is the conventional reading, since Hudson and Havercamp (1726: 1.924, n. k), despite the variety of readings supplied by various witnesses; see Wardle 1992b: 467 and Free 2017: 589, n. 10. Beginning with Mommsen 1870, moreover, it has often been suggested that no one but this Cluvius would have known of this conversation or cared to report it, which led to the conclusion that Josephus's source was a known historian, Cluvius Rufus. However, there remain doubts about the name, and, even if it is Cluvius, it may be that the chronological context is too early, for Cluvius Rufus is known mostly from the 60s, so perhaps the individual mentioned here is his father, from whom the story could have made its way to any historian, not only to his own son. For more discussion of this source-critical issue, see the introduction to Book 19. Specifically on the date of Cluvius's consulship, apparently sometime under Nero, see Gallivan 1978: 423 (where, however, "too old" should apparently be "born too late").

254 Given the ease with which both kings and bandits could be viewed as "tyrants" (on bandits, see Ben-Yishai 2007), this is apparently to be understood as a clever comment which, if overheard by the wrong people, could be explained as referring to the forthcoming performances; see the notes on "ruler" and "Myrrha" in §94. Cluvius's response, however, shows that he understood it to be referring to the planned assassination of Gaius. So should readers, esp. since they have not yet learned what shows were on the program.

255 The quotation is from the *Iliad* 14.90–91, nearly identical with the received text.

93 When a great quantity of fruit was poured out among the spectators and also numerous birds of species that are valued, for their rarity, by those who manage to catch them, Gaius observed with enjoyment the fights over them and plundering [from one another] as the spectators snatched them.[256] **94** And then it happened that omens signifying two things occurred. For a mime was presented, in which a ruler[257] was caught and crucified,[258] and the dancing pantomimist[259] presented the tragedy *Cinyras*,[260] in which both [Cinyras] and his daughter Myrrha[261] are killed.[262] Thus much artificial blood was poured out—both around the crucified man and around Cinyras.[263] **95** It is also agreed that the day it happened was the same date[264] that Pausanias[265] (one of the "Companions"[266]) killed Philip the son of Amyntas, king of the Macedonians,[267] when he entered the theater.[268]

---

256 This is reminiscent of the practice described at §71 and by other writers; see the note on "upon the people" at §71.

257 The reference is, apparently, to a chief of bandits; see the next note. Josephus, however, uses the general term ἡγεμών in order to make the relevance of the omen clear.

258 Suetonius (*Cal.* 57.4) mentions this omen, as a performance of "a farce called *Laureolus*, in which the chief actor falls as he is making his escape and vomits blood." The present story is, according to Coleman (1990: 64), the earliest testimony to this popular Roman story about a bandit, Laureolus, who was caught and crucified; it is also mentioned by Martial (*Spectacles* 7) and Juvenal (8.187). The latter identifies its composer as a certain Catullus—whom Wiseman (1985: 192–198) proposed to identify as the well-known Roman poet of the first century BCE.

259 This is this only occurrence of ὀρχηστής in Josephus, although he used ὀρχηστρίς (female dancer) in the "Tobiad romance" (12.187, 188). LSJ translates: "dancer; later esp. pantomimic dancer." From Suetonius, *Cal.* 57.4, we know that it was a pantomime dance, and that the dancer's name was Mnester—one of Gaius's favorites, whom he would often kiss even in public (ibid. 55.1; cf. Dio 59.27.1), and who is elsewhere said to have been one of Gaius's male sexual partners (Suetonius, *Cal.* 36.1; Cassius Dio 60.22.3–4).

260 Suetonius, *Cal.* 57.4 does not name the tragedy. Cinyras was a legendary king of Cyprus, mentioned already in the *Iliad* (11.20–22). The mythical tragic story that was the subject of the pantomime is recounted in detail in Ovid, *Met.* 10.298–502, and more briefly in Plutarch, *Parallela minora* 22 and Hyginus, *Fabulae* 58. According to the legend, one of Cinyras's daughters, Myrrha, had an uncontrollable passion for her father—a story of unlawful lust, attempted suicide, and incest.

261 In Plutarch, *Parallela minora* 22 and Hyginus, *Fabulae* 58 and 242, she is named Smyrna.

262 In none of the various versions of the myth is Cinyras said to have been killed. Only Hyginus, *Fabulae*

242 says that he committed suicide because of the incest. As for his daughter, no version of the story has her being killed; rather, she is transformed into a tree. Wiseman (2013a: 60) suggests that Josephus misunderstood the omen: that its point was not the amount of blood spilled, but rather the play itself, since, as Suetonius reports (*Cal.* 57.4), the play presented (*Cinyras*) was also presented the day Philip was killed.

263 Suetonius (*Cal.* 57.4) too writes that "the stage swam in blood."

264 The belief that this type of coincidence is significant, suggesting some guiding hand that, for whatever reason, deliberately "roll good things to a good day and bad things to a bad day" (*b. Ta'anit* 29a), was widespread. Note, for example, the belief that Ventidius defeated the Parthians in 38 BCE on the same date that they defeated Crassus fifteen years earlier (Eutropius 7.5); that Herod conquered Jerusalem on the same date as Pompey, twenty-seven years earlier (*Ant.* 14.487); that Herod completed the renovation of the Temple on the same date as his ascent to the throne (*Ant.* 15.423); that massacres of Romans in Jerualem and of Jews in Caesarea, in 66 CE, happened "the same day and hour, as if due to supernatural providence" (*War* 2.457); that both the first and second temples of Jerusalem were destroyed on the same date (*m. Ta'anit* 4:6) but also that the messiah was born on that date (*y. Berakhot* 2:4); etc. For a variation on this theme, see the note on "precisely" at §187.

265 As is noted at 11.304, "as has been told elsewhere" (§305); for his name and the story, see Aristotle, *Politics* 5.1311b and Diodorus Siculus 16.93–94.

266 On ancient usage of *hetairoi* with regard to Philip II and Macedonia, both for courtiers and for heavy cavalry, see Rzepka 2012.

267 That is, Philip II, the father of Alexander the Great. Philip, whose father was Amyntas III, was killed in 336 BCE.

268 That murder is also reported at 11.304–305, where Josephus depends upon "as has been related elsewhere." The occasion was the celebration of Philip's daughter's marriage to Alexander of Epirus. However, while Philip

96 Gaius was of two minds as to whether he should remain until the end of the spectacle *Gaius Departs* because it was the final day, or, rather, bathe and eat and then return as he had done on the preceding days.[269] Minucianus, who was sitting above Gaius and was afraid that the opportunity might be piddled away to no avail, got up when he saw that Chaerea had already gone out and hurried to catch up with him and encourage him. **97** Gaius, however, taking hold of his robe in a seemingly friendly way, said: "Where to, my dear sir?"[270] And so he sat down [again], seemingly out of regard for Caesar. However, his fear[271] was stronger, and after a short time he again arose. **98** Gaius did not at all prevent him in his departure, thinking he was making his departure for some necessity. [Asprenas],[272] who was desirous of fulfilling what had been decided upon, himself urged Gaius to go out for bathing and a meal,[273] as had previously been his practice, and after that to come back.

(1.14) 99 Chaerea's men had stationed one another as the opportunity allowed,[274] and each was bound to stand where he had been stationed, making every effort not to leave. Now, however, they were upset with the delay and with the postponement of the matter at hand, for already it was around the ninth hour of the day.[275] **100** And since Gaius was still hesitating, Chaerea was eager to go back in and fall upon [Gaius] in his seat; but he foresaw that that would entail slaying along with him many of the senators and equites who were present. Although he was afraid of that, he was also eager [to go ahead with the assassination], believing that it was proper to consider those killed to be a small price to pay in purchasing safety and liberty for all. **101** In fact, they[276] had already turned to entering the theater when it became apparent[277] that Gaius had stood up. That stirred up a tumult, and the conspirators went back and also tried to push the crowd back,[278] saying that was so as [not to]

---

was murdered in the summer (Wiseman 2013a: 60), around July (Hammond and Griffith 1979: 726), Gaius was killed in January. Since Suetonius reports (*Cal.* 57.4) that the same play was performed at the games at which Philip was executed, but does not say it was the same date, we should conclude either that Josephus's formulation here is simply confused and that he (or his source) meant, as Suetonius, to refer to the play, not to the date, or else that folk memory, which tends to like such coincidences, has had its way. For the comparison of Gaius here to a Macedonian monarch, cf. the note on "shield-bearers" at §76.

269 Suetonius (*Cal.* 58.1) explains that Gaius hesitated whether or not to go for lunch because he had an upset stomach on account of excessive eating the previous day.

270 For "My dear Sir" (suggested for μακάριος here by *CCFJ* 3.50, s.v.), see Dickey 1996: 140.

271 Namely, Vinicianus's fear that the opportunity would be missed (§96).

272 The manuscripts give various versions of the name, but unless we are to assume that Josephus is emphatically referring (αὐτός, "himself") to someone unknown to his readers, which would be perplexing, it makes sense, as most scholars agree, to read Asprenas, as at §87. If he was close enough to Gaius to be splashed by the blood of his sacrifice, as is reported there, he could

indeed be close enough to talk with Gaius, as is reported here. Asprenas would soon be the first to be killed by Gaius's German bodyguards, after the assassination (below, §123).

273 Suetonius (*Cal.* 58.1) writes that he went "at the persuasion of his friends," without identifying them.

274 For ἡ καιρός, cf. 17.51 and 18.247, 313.

275 Since sunup (§85), i.e., mid-afternoon. According to Suetonius (*Cal.* 58.1), it was about the seventh hour when Gaius began debating whether to leave to eat; that is more in line with the assumption that the eighth hour was the time of the change of the watch of the Praetorian Guard (cf. Martial. *Epigrams* 10.48.1–3)—which is when its commander would get the watchword from the emperor, as Chaerea will soon do.

276 Chaerea and his men.

277 Perhaps the use of σημαίνω here points to trumpets, as for example at *War* 6.68 and *Ant.* 7.279, 12.307, 338, 410, 427—some sort of fanfare that accompanied the emperor's move to depart. Such an official departure would probably entail, however, more of an entourage than the continuation of the story assumes. More usually, the verb simply means "mean" or "indicate"—namely, in this case, via the "tumult."

278 In Suetonius's second version of the assassination (see the note on "severe blow" at §105) the crowd

offend Gaius, but in fact for their own safety: they wanted to carry out the murder after first rendering Gaius deprived of defenders. 102 His uncle Claudius,[279] and his sister's[280] husband, Marcus Minucianus,[281] as well as Valerius Asiaticus,[282] had already gone out—people whose departure no one could have prevented even if they wanted to do so, out of respect for their dignity—and then he came himself, along with Paullus Arruntius.[283]

103 But when he was within the palace,[284] he turned away from the direct paths, along which were stationed, at intervals, those of the slaves who served him, and down which Claudius's party had preceded him. 104 Instead, he turned down a narrow and deserted

---

is likewise said to have been pushed back by "centurions who were in on the plot" (Suetonius, *Cal.* 58.3; cf. Suetonius, *Claud.* 10.1). However, in Suetonius's version, that appears to take place later in the course of the assassination—after Gaius had left the theater and met the Asian boys' choir (on which see below, §104).

279 The next emperor; the younger of the two sons of Drusus, the older being Gaius's father, Germanicus. Cassius Dio 60.1.3, in contrast, just after his much less detailed account of the assassination, states that Claudius was with Gaius when he came out of the theater.

280 Julia Livilla (cf. §251). The youngest of Gaius's sisters (Suetonius. *Cal.* 7), she was born in 18 CE (Tacitus, *Ann.* 2.54.1). In 39 she was banished to the Pontic islands along with her sister Agrippina, on the charge of adulterous relations with Lepidus and involvement in his alleged conspiracy (Suetonius, *Cal.* 24.3; Dio 59. 22.6–9; see further the note on "Lepidus" at §20). The two were called back to Rome by Claudius (Dio 60.4.1). However, she was soon banished again (41 CE) after being accused by Messalina of having an adulterous relationship with Seneca the Younger, and was killed shortly thereafter (Dio 60.8.5; Suetonius, *Claud.* 29.1; Tacitus, *Ann.* 14.63).

281 As in the case of Annius Vinicianus (see the note on "Minucianus" at §18), so too here, as also at §251, the manuscripts consistently read "Minuc-" but the true reading should be "Vinic-"; Tacitus (*Ann.* 6.15) gives the name of Julia's husband as Marcus Vinicius. They were married in 33. Vinicius was consul in 30 CE, and the historian Velleius Paterculus dedicated his history to him as consul (e.g., 1.8.1, 12.6, 13.4; 2.7.5). In 36 he was appointed to the committee established to evaluate the damage caused by a serious fire in Rome (Tacitus, *Ann.* 6.45), in 41 he considered himself a candidate to replace Gaius (below, §251), and in 45 he was made consul for a second time (Dio 60.25.1). However, according to Dio (60.27.4), during the following year he was killed by Messalina, who had had Vinicius's wife, Julia, banished a few years earlier (see the previous note).

282 D. Valerius Asiaticus was a senator from Vienne in Gallia Lugdunensis. Although a provincial, he became

highly respected and influential in Rome, serving twice as consul (Dio 60.27.1): suffect consul in 35 and ordinarius in 46 (Dio 60.27.1). His prestige and influence were certainly due to his great wealth (Tacitus, *Ann.* 11.1; Dio 60.27.2–3), but also to his close relationship with Antonia (Tacitus, *Ann.* 11.3). Seneca mentions his close friendship with Gaius (*Const.* 18). According to Tacitus, *Ann.* 11.1, Asiaticus was later accused of being one of the leaders of the plot against Gaius. If he was involved, probably that was, as Seneca implies, because of Gaius's insults, including his criticism of the sexual performance of Asiaticus's wife, Lollia (Seneca, *Const.* 18; Barrett 2019: 254–255). Josephus does not mention him as partaking in the conspiracy, but does mention Asiaticus's retrospective approval of the assassination (below, §159; also Dio 59.30.1), thus implying that he had not been involved. For more on Asiaticus, his family background, and his descendants, see Kavanagh 2001a: 109–117; as Swan (1970: 156, n. 25), Kavanagh argues against the notion that Asiaticus was involved in the conspiracy.

283 On the illustrious Arruntius family, see Syme 1986: 260–269. However, a Paullus Arruntius is not otherwise known; see ibid. 262. Kavanagh (2010) argues that the name should be emended into Aquila Arruntius, thus identifying him with the otherwise unknown Aquila who is said below (§110) to have given the final blow to Gaius. The twin advantages of identifying our Arruntius as that Aquila are that thereby Josephus did not introduce Arruntius without any relevance (the fate of the other people mentioned here as being with Gaius, apart from Arruntius, is reported later), and that Aquila, mentioned below without any introduction, would indeed be known to readers. Noting, furthermore, that prior to his death Gaius was in the company of former consuls, Kavanagh suggests that this M. Arruntius Aquila, who would deliver the final blow, is to be identified with the consul of 38 by the name of M. Aquila Iulianus (*CIL* 6:811; Dio 59.9.1; Frontinus, *Aq.* 102).

284 For a suggested reconstruction of Gaius's path to his death, see Wiseman 2013a: 106.

passageway,[285] a shortcut, in order to go to the baths and also to observe the youths[286] who had come from Asia.[287] These had been dispatched from there for the hymns of the mysteries that he had held[288] and some of them were to take part in the Pyrrhic dances,[289] which were to be held in the theaters.[290]

105 Chaerea came up to him and asked for the password. When he said one of those meant to elicit mockery,[291] Chaerea did not hesitate at all; rather, pouring out abuse against Gaius, he drew his sword and dealt him a severe blow.[292] But it was not completely well-placed.[293]   *The Deed is Done*

106 True, there are some who say that Chaerea deliberately abstained from doing away[294] with Gaius with a single blow, so as to take all the more vengeance from him with a multitude of wounds.[295] **107** But this notion does not convince me,[296] for, in such affairs, fear does

---

285 This στενωπός, narrow passage, alley (see *Life* 304), is also mentioned at Dio 59.29.6. Suetonius's description (*Cal.* 58.1) is slightly different, speaking of "a *crypta* (a concealed, subterranean passage) through which he had to pass," and not mentioning the baths.

286 Suetonius (*Cal.* 58.1) writes that these youths were rehearsing their performance in the passageway.

287 According to Dio 59.29.6, however, the youths were highborn boys whom Gaius had collected in Greece and Ionia.

288 See the note on "mystery rites" at §30. Cassius Dio (59.29.6) writes that the boys were there to sing a hymn composed in Gaius's honor. However, at 60.7.2 he says they had been practicing the Pyrrhic dance (just as the same is reported at 60.23.5, in Claudius's days), which accords with their second role in Josephus's version here. For Suetonius's version, see the note on "theaters" at the end of this paragraph.

289 Suetonius reports its performance in Rome both well before Gaius and well after his day (*Jul.* 39.1; *Nero* 12.1–2). Although the dance, which is said to have originated in Crete (Pliny, *NH* 7.204), once had a warlike character (Plato, *Laws* 814e–815b), by the first century, in Rome, it was more of a dramatic ballet, representing mythological themes, often associated with Dionysus (Bacchus), and at times involving animals (e.g., Pliny, *NH* 8.5). The dance is described in Apuleius, *Met.* 10.29–34.

290 Suetonius (*Cal.* 58.1), ratcheting up the tension, adds that Gaius wanted to return to the theater and have the performance begin immediately, but that did not happen because the choir's leader complained that he had a chill. Dio 60.7.2 reports that later they indeed gave a performance of the Pyrrhic dance and were rewarded by Claudius with citizenship.

291 For this repeated type of insult toward Chaerea see above, §§29–31.

292 Suetonius (*Cal.* 58.2–3) provides two versions of the actual assassination. According to the first, as Gaius was talking to the boys, Chaerea came up behind him and shouted "hoc age!" ("do it") and cut Gaius deeply in the neck, whereupon Sabinus, who was in front of Gaius,

stabbed him in the chest. Although often it is thought that "hoc age!" was an allusion to a sacrificial rite, in which it was the priest's response to the sacrificer's question, "shall I do it?," Rolfe (1933) argued that there is insufficient evidence for such a rite, and prefers to render Cheraea's statement simply as the equivalent of "take that!" For the view that indeed the sacrificial allusion is intended, see Woods 2018: 878. Suetonius's second version is closer to that of Josephus, but nevertheless varies in some significant details. In this version, the centurions are said to have first gotten rid of the crowd (see the note on "back" at §101), and then Sabinus, not Chaerea, asked for the password. Gaius gave the password "*Iovem*" (Jupiter), and Chaerea replied "*Accipe Ratum!*"—"so be it," or "accept the fulfilment of your vow" (Barrett 2019: 259)—and, as Gaius looked around, "he split his jawbone with a blow of his sword." Seneca (*Const.* 18.3) reports that Chaerea cut Gaius down with the first blow, to his neck, but does not say if he did so from the front (as in Josephus) or from the back (as in Suetonius's first version).

293 I.e., not mortal. For such use of καίριος, cf. 8.415 and 9.105. All the sources agree that the initial blow was not fatal. Josephus now digresses from the report about the assassination, in order to discuss assertions that Chaerea deliberately did not kill Gaius with the first blow; the description of the course of the assassination will be resumed at §109.

294 Διεργάζομαι is used in *Antiquities* only here and at §350, pertaining to the death of Agrippa.

295 For these multiple wounds see below, §110. Charlesworth 1933: 112 suggests that this type of explanation arose out of a moralizing measure-for-measure tradition often employed for tyrants. For Suetonius (*Cal.* 30.1) reports that Gaius "seldom had anyone put to death except by numerous slight wounds, his constant order, which soon became well-known, being: 'Strike so that he may feel that he is dying.'" Thus, killing him by inflicting numerous wounds would be poetic justice. For a pronounced case of this, see the very end of Philo's *In Flaccum*.

296 For a similar type of Josephan evaluation of his sources see above, §§68–69.

not allow for the making of such calculations. Indeed, if Chaerea did have such a notion, I would hold that he stood out from all others in idiocy, preferring the enjoyment of his anger to favoring the immediate rescue of himself and his fellow conspirators from danger. For there were many ways in which Gaius could have been succored, had he not preempted[297] them by giving up the ghost,[298] and had that happened Chaerea would have had to deal not with the punishment of Gaius but, rather, with that of himself and his friends. 108 Indeed, even he who succeeded should have kept quiet about it so as to escape the wrath of those who would oppose them, so certainly when it was unclear if the act would succeed it would have been foolish for him to seek to destroy both himself and the opportunity. But let those who so desire view these things however they like.[299]

109 As for Gaius, who was dazed[300] by the pain of the blow (for the sword had carried into the area between[301] the shoulder and the neck, where the collarbone[302] kept it from going any further), he neither screamed out in alarm nor called out to any of his friends, whether out of disbelief or because he was anyway[303] unable to think straight.[304] Groaning on account of the extremity of the pain, he threw himself forward in flight[305]—110 only to be met by Cornelius Sabinus,[306] who had already worked out[307] his plan. He pushed him [down] upon his knee, and then, at a single command,[308] the many people standing around chopped at him with their swords, urging each other on; it was a regular contest for them

---

297 Josephus likes this ironic usage; cf. the note on "beat him" at 18.89.

298 For this phrase, τὴν ψυχὴν ἀφεῖναι, see also 8.325; cf. ἀποψύχω at §114.

299 For similar statements, see *War* 5.257, and several with regard to miracles and the like, including *Ant.* 2.348, 10.281, 17.354, along with Begg and Spilsbury 2005: 317, n. 1192 (on 10.281). Cf. the note on "I believe" at 20.166.

300 See the note on "distracted" at §46.

301 This is the only occurrence of μεσσηγύς in Josephus.

302 This is the only occurrence of κλείς in Josephus.

303 One may wonder whether this ἄλλως means only "anyway, because of the blow" or, rather, "anyway, even without any blow." Cf. the note on "otherwise" at 18.19.

304 The manuscripts read ἀφρονήσει—the only appearance of ἀφρονέω ("act senselessly") in Josephus. Niese and Naber both proposed emendations, although maintaining the same root; see *CCFJ* 1.284, s.v.

305 This is in contrast to Suetonius's account (*Cal.* 58.3). He writes that after the initial blows, Gaius was writhing on the ground and called out that he was still alive, and that his litter-bearers came to his aid with their poles.

306 On Cornelius, see above, §46, also the note on "Chaerea" at §111.

307 This is the only occurrence of προκατεργάζομαι in Josephus.

308 Scholars differ as to how to render ἀφ᾽ ἑνὸς ἐγκελεύσματος. Evidently it refers to something that was said, but the term ἐγκέλευσμα is very rare; see Mason 2008: 149, n. 1114 and 375, n. 3304. The latter comments on *War* 2.549, the term's only other appearance in Josephus; Mason renders "encouragement," a meaning that fits that passage and the only earlier evidence, where the verb (ἐγκελεύω) appears: Xenophon, *Cynegeticus* 6.25. So too LSJ 471. However, "at a single encouragement" is impossible, for the reference is obviously to something that was uttered; at *War* 2.549, for example, Mason (2008: 375) translates "what sang out in response from the Judean side was encouragement." Here, in contrast, there is no such accompanying reference to anything uttered, a fact pointed up by translators' need to add it: "sur un seul *cri* d'exhortation" (Mathieu and Herrmann 1929: 212), "at a single *word*" (Wiseman 2013a: 16 [he prefers to introduce "word" instead of "encouragement"]), "at a single *word* of encouragement" (Schalit 1963: 328 and Feldman 1965: 269; my emphases, DRS). Moreover, it is somewhat surprising to think that "encouragement" could be a single word, but an order is typically brief, and it is an order that is expected in the context of an armed attack by a number of men, of whom several, if not all, were soldiers. Accordingly, it appears preferable to translate "command, signal" (so *CCFJ* 2.7, s.v.), in line with the sense of the verb ἐγκελεύεσθαι, "to command" (*ThLJ* 211, s.v.); so, for example, at *War* 2.176 ("directed" [Mason 2008: 149];

[to see, who could hit him more].[309] Finally, as all agree, it was Aquila[310] who delivered the blow that actually[311] finished him off.

111 But one should attribute the act to Chaerea.[312] For even if the job was done together with many others alongside him, he was the first to ponder how to do it, preceding the others by far. **112** He was also the first to speak out boldly about it to others,[313] and once the scattered people had adopted the notion of the assassination, he gathered them together and organized everything intelligently. When the time came to express opinions he was far superior [to others], and, captivating [those to whom he spoke] with well-chosen words, he forced everyone [to act] even when they did not dare to do so. **113** Moreover, when the time came to take things into hand, then too he was clearly the first[314] who moved and took the assassination in hand courageously, thereby presenting Gaius to the others in a state in which he was easily overcome[315] and already on the verge of dying.[316] Therefore it is just that whatever the others did should be accounted to the credit of Chaerea's will, his virtue, and the work of his hands.[317]

Chaerea's Central Role

(1.15) 114 Gaius, on the one hand, having met his end that way, lay there lifeless, having expired[318] due to his many wounds.[319] **115** Chaerea's people, on the other hand, once they were finished with Gaius, saw that it would be impossible to save themselves by going

The Assassins Make Their Getaway

"with orders" [Thackeray JLCL 2.391]), a translation that does not require supplementation by "word[s] of." Cf. Suetonius (*Cal.* 58.3): everyone joined in stabbing Gaius, "for the signal (*signum*) to all was 'do it again.'" Here "signal" amounts to "order," just as, for example, Pilate's σημεῖον to his soldiers at *War* 2.172 amounts to an order.

309 Seneca (*Const.* 18.3) writes that, following Chaerea's initial blow, "from all sides blades showered upon him, avenging public and private wrongs," whereas Suetonius (*Cal.* 58.3) reports that "the others dispatched him with thirty wounds," adding that some aimed their swords at his genitals—which would again be poetic justice given Gaius's alleged immoral sexual behavior. Cassius Dio (59.29.7) has a more gruesome report, that these assailants kept "stabbing him savagely, even though he was dead," and even adding the sensational detail that "some even tasted of his flesh." For Dio's predilection for such lurid details, cf. Cassius Dio 62.7, 68.32.1, and [72].4.1 cited by Stern, GLAJJ 2.387.

310 Despite Josephus's assertion that all agree about this, Aquila is not even mentioned in the other surviving narratives of the assassination, and is not otherwise known. For more on him, see the note on "Arruntius" at §102.

311 "Actually" is Thackeray's suggestion for this occurrence of ἀκριβῶς (ThLJ 20). Cf. the note on "in detail" at 18.129.

312 Seneca (*Const.* 18.3) too found it important to emphasize that Chaerea was entitled to most of the credit, writing that "among the conspirators he was the first to lift his hand" and that he felled Gaius by a single blow, and emphasizing it again after describing the subsequent

blows landed on Gaius from other assailants: "but the first hero was Chaerea ..." Cassius Dio (60.29) and Suetonius (*Cal.* 56.2; 58.2) split the credit more evenly between Chaerea and Sabinus.

313 True, Seneca (*Const.* 18.3) writes that Chaerea "had a way of talking that ill-accorded with his prowess; his voice was feeble and, unless you knew his deeds, was apt to stir distrust" (trans. Basore, LCL). But that description of his skill as a speaker hardly fits Josephus's account of him in the next lines; see also his speeches at §§38–43, 54–58, 78–83.

314 Again, compare this to Seneca's emphasis on Chaerea's priority, quoted in the note on "Chaerea" at §111: "he was the first to lift his hand," "but the first hero was Chaerea."

315 In Josephus, εὐεπίβατος appears only here and in *War* 6.51.

316 Apart from *War* 1.79, this verb too, προθνῄσκω, appears in Josephus only here.

317 For the argument that especially §§111–113 indicate that Josephus's story is based on a Roman pamphlet (*Flugschrift*) dedicated to demonstrating Chaerea's primacy in the plot and the deed itself (especially in light of his less than impressive performance according to §105 and the excuses presented immediately thereafter), see Destinon 1904: 8–14.

318 This is the only occurrence of ἀποψύχω in Josephus, apart from one doubtful case (see the note on "very long" at 20.94). Cf. the note on "ghost" at §107.

319 For this kind of transitional phrase, which wraps up one scene before toggling to another, cf. §§263, 272b, 274, and 292a, also, for example, *Ant.* 8.393 and *War* 2.654;

through the same passages they had used in coming, and were in apprehension[320] on account of what had been done. For the danger to those who had killed the emperor was not at all small, since he was honored by the populace, in its inanity,[321] and was beloved,[322] and the soldiers who would look for him would not do so without bloodshed. **116** Moreover, since the passages in which they had done the deed anyway were narrow[323] and were blocked up by the large multitude of servants and those soldiers of the emperor's guard[324] who were in attendance that day, **117** it was via other routes that they arrived at the house of Germanicus, the father of the Gaius whom they had just now killed. This was adjacent to that,[325] for although the palace was one building it had been expanded bit by bit, with buildings for each of those people who had been in power;[326] these buildings were named for those who built them or even for those who only gave them their names after starting the construction one day or another.[327] **118** Having gotten out of the way of the mob's onslaught, for the moment they had no reason for fear, for the height of misfortune that had befallen the emperor was still unknown.

6.192. When the reference is to the death of an historical figure it can introduce, or even amount to, an obituary, as with Judas Maccabeus at 12.433–434 (see Wiseman 2013a: 64, citing Currie 1989), but that need not be the case. Josephus's "obituary" for Gaius will come at §§201–211.

320 For ὄκνος, which is somewhere between hesitation and fear, compare §70; 20.157; and *Life* 251.

321 For Josephus's contempt for the masses, see the note on "the mob" at §130.

322 For Gaius's popularity among the general populace see also below, §158. However, as Wiseman notes (2013a: 71), elsewhere Josephus, as also Dio 59.30.1a, speaks of popular support for the assassins (§§189, 191; cf. 272), which suggests the use of more than one source; see the note on "meantime" at §158.

323 For the narrow alley in which the assassination took place, see above §104.

324 These soldiers were members of the Praetorian Guard (either Chaerea's soldiers, or those of Sabinus, or both) who were not privy to the plot and should be distinguished from the German bodyguards who will soon seek the assassins (§§119–126); see Millar 1977: 62–63.

325 Namely, the imperial palace, where Gaius was killed (§103); it is mentioned in the immediate continuation.

326 As Richardson (1992: 281) observed: "By the last century of the republic [the Palatine] had become the most fashionable place in Rome to have a house," and houses there were tightly packed. See also Wiseman 1987: 168–169. Wiseman writes: "[B]efore Domitian's rationalization of the site, the 'palace' was not an organic whole but the combination of several originally independent neighbouring houses, acquired by Augustus and his successors in an increasingly extensive area of contiguous property" (ibid. 168). Cf. Barrett 2019: 234–238.

327 The last words are problematic. The translation here follows Niese who, following Ambrosianus, reads τι τῶν ἡμερῶν, although he marks a corruption here in his editio minor (1890b: 198); Feldman (1965: 270) instead reads τι τῶν μερῶν with the editio princeps and renders "started some part of the structure." One way or another, Josephus is referring to people whose contribution was only limited (in duration or extent) and nevertheless the whole building was named after them. Aside from the house of Germanicus mentioned here, some of these named houses on the Palatine are attested: the house of Hortensius, in which Augustus lived (Suetonius, *Aug.* 72.1); the house of Catulus, which already in Augustus's day constituted a part of the palace (Suetonius, *Gramm.* 17); the house of Gelos (Suetonius, *Cal.* 18.3); and the

119 The first people reached by the news of Gaius's death were the Germans. They[328] were bodyguards[329] who comprise the Celtic[330] cohort,[331] which was called by the name of the nation from which they were recruited.[332] **120** It was their ancestral [nature][333] to be governed by their tempers to an extent rare even among certain other barbarians, for they hardly take rational calculation into consideration. They are also very strong, bodily, and whenever they storm and engage their enemies—whomever they consider them to be—they are successful from the outset. **121** When they, then, learned that Gaius had been killed, full of indignation (for they did not judge things, as it is virtuous to do, with regard to all, but only with regard to their own interests, and Gaius had been greatly beloved by them because by giving them moneys he had purchased their loyalty)[334] **122** they drew their swords—led by Sabinus,[335] a military tribune who had gained virtue[336] in the eyes of this

The Germans' Rampage

---

house of Tiberius (Tacitus, *Hist.* 1.27; Suetonius, *Vit.* 15.3; Plutarch, *Galba* 24.7). See Wiseman 1987: 168.

328 As Mommsen (1910: 18, n. 1 [originally published in 1882]) notes, the text of the following sentence is in a ruinous state ("zerrüttet"); he reports his correspondence with Niese about it and Niese's suggestion about restoring its text. Niese's suggestion as reported by Mommsen, the reading in his ed. maior (1890a: 281), and the reading in his ed. minor (1890b: 198) all differ slightly from one another.

329 Note that here, as at §42, Josephus uses δορυφόροι, in contrast to §§214, 221, 237, 247, 267, where he uses σωμα-τοφύλακες—which at §214 he defines as the Praetorian Guards, as is usual in Roman Greek (*GTRI* 90, s.v.). German horsemen were already employed by Julius Caesar as his personal guard (Caesar, *B.G.* 7.13.1; Speidel 1994: 12–15). German bodyguards of the emperor were undoubtedly employed by Augustus as well (Suetonius, *Aug.* 49.1), and also later by Tiberius and Nero (Tacitus, *Ann.* 1.24, 13.18, 15.58), and Gaius himself is said to have gone to Germany in order to recruit more of them (Suetonius, *Cal.* 43). Even King Herod had a German-Gallic-Thracian bodyguard, thanks to his Roman friends (*War* 1.672). For a survey of the evidence, see Mommsen 1910: 17–19; ibid. 18, n. 1, he identifies the unit mentioned here as the "Batavian" one known from inscriptions, from Suetonius, *Cal.* 43, and from Cassius Dio 55.24.7. The unit—which was called *Germani corporis custodes* (e.g., Suetonius, *Cal.* 55.2, 58.3) and, informally "Batavian" (Dio 55.24.7)—was disbanded by Galba in 68/69 (Suetonius, *Galba* 12.2). At times, they took part in military campaigns even when the emperor stayed in Rome. See further, Millar 1977: 62–63 and especially Speidel 1994, 12–31 and Bellen 1981.

330 On ancient usage of "Celts," in general, see Cunliffe 2011; on loose Roman usage of "Celts," "Gauls," and "Germans," see Boatwright 2012: 34–35. For "Celts" of Gauls, see, for example the very first sentence of Caesar's *Gallic Wars*. True, Josephus himself (*War* 7.75–76) distinguished between Gauls and Germans, as did some

others, such as Caesar (e.g. the openings of *Gallic Wars* 6.21 and 6.24) and Strabo (*Geog.* 4.4.2). However, even the latter admits (ibid.) their similarity, and so it is not surprising that "the ancient writers in general regarded the Germans as Gauls (Celts)," as Oldfather (1939: 163, n. 1, on Diodorus 5.24.3) observes in explaining why Diodorus fails to mention Germans in his account of western Europe.

331 In support of this translation of τάγμα, here, Bellen (1981: 52, n. 130) cites Tacitus, *Hist.* 3.69.1 (*cohortes Germanicae*) and an inscription (*CIL* 14.2960: *cohors Germanorum*). Cf. the note on "units" at 20.122.

332 For καταλέγω of recruiting, cf. *War* 2.268, 576; *Ant.* 15.109.

333 Josephus gives no noun here. For his assumption, that each nation has its characteristic nature (ἦθος), see Mason 2007a: 223–225.

334 This is perhaps meant to contrast with Romans, who supposedly could not be bought by gifts and would rather oppose a tyrant. Compare Tacitus's characterization of the Parthian king Artabanus's foreign bodyguards as "members of a class neither comprehending good nor regarding evil but feed and fed as the agents of crime" (Tacitus, *Ann.* 6.36, trans. Jackson, LCL). See Speidel 1994: 28.

335 Not to be confused with Cornelius Sabinus, who was among the assassins (above §§46–48, 110). This Sabinus was apparently one of the Thracian gladiators that Gaius put at the head of his German bodyguard (Suetonius, *Cal.* 55.2)—an anomalous appointment (Weaver 1983: 439) that Suetonius views as an example of his madness. Cf. Cassius Dio 60.28.2: he too mentions this Sabinus's command of the gladiators under Gaius when he reports that, in 46, Claudius and many others wanted to see him killed in a gladiatorial match, but Messalina—whose lover he was—saved him.

336 Josephus's phrase here, κτησάμενος ... ἀρητήν ("having acquired virtue"), although supplied by all the

type of men not through the virtue and nobility of his ancestors,[337] for he had been a gladiator, but because of his bodily strength—and criss-crossed[338] the palace in search[339] of
Caesar's assassins.

123 They cut Asprenas[340] into pieces[341] because he was the first one they came
upon—it was he whose robe had been stained by the blood of the sacrificial animals, as
I said above[342]—an incident of which the occurrence did not indicate any good luck. The
next one to run into them was Norbanus,[343] who was one of the most noble citizens and
had had many generals among his ancestors.[344] **124** When they did not show any respect for
his dignity,[345] with his greater strength he grabbed away the sword of the first to come upon
him when they clashed, and it was obvious that he would not be killed passively—but when
he was surrounded by many assailants he fell under a multitude of wounds. **125** The third
was Anteius, one of the outstanding[346] members of the Senate.[347] Unlike his predecessors,
who fell to the Germans by chance, [he was caught] because of his love of a spectacle and

---

witnesses, is so strange that Feldman (1965: 272–273)
and Wiseman (2013a: 42) emend to κτησάμενος ... ἀρχήν
("achieved his command"). However, the text as it is reads
well (as apparently recognized by Schalit 1963: 328, from
whom I borrowed "this type of men") as a snide comment
by the aristocratic author who observes that, although
Sabinus was not of respectable stock, uncouth barbarians, such as the Germans (§120), considered him "virtuous" (manly) because he had been a gladiator.

337 In contrast, regular military tribunes were normally equites by birth; see Brunt 1983: 43, 47. For the virtues of one's ancestors as a respectable justification for
authority, see cf. §164.

338 For the nuances of διεξιέναι, here as at §§226 and
318, see *ThLJ* 173, s.v.

339 This is the only occurrence of ἀνερευνάω in
Antiquities.

340 See the note on "Asprenas" at §87. As mentioned there, if the reading "Asprenas" at §98 is correct
it implies that he was involved in the plot, and thus, in
his case, the Germans indeed found and punished one
of the assassins. But they had no way to know that, and
Josephus explains his death simply by the fact that he
was the first person they happened to encounter; the
two victims mentioned in the coming lines seem to have
been innocent. Similarly, Suetonius (*Cal.* 58.3) reports
that the Germans "slew several of his assassins, as well as
some inoffensive senators."

341 Apart from here, Josephus uses κρεουργέω only at
13.345, in an equally cruel scene.

342 §87.

343 Reading, with several manuscripts and Niese,
δεύτερος Νωρβανός. However, two manuscripts read βάρβαρος instead of δεύτερος, and the search to make sense

of that has led scholars, such as Wiseman 2013a: 66, to
posit that the reference is to L. Norbanus Balbus (consul
in 19) or his son of the same name. Ignoring βάρβαρος, one
might also think of C. Norbanus Flaccus, who was consul
in 15. See Barrett 2019: 267, n. 54. Whoever he was, there
is nothing in the present story that suggests that he was
among the conspirators. Rather, the Germans (who had
no way to know who was part of the conspiracy) are pic-
tured as running wild, killing whomever they met, as is
stated at §126.

344 A C. Norbanus was consul in 83 BCE; C. Norbanus
Flaccus was consul in 24 BCE (and is the proconsul of Asia
mentioned at *Ant.* 16.166, 171 and by Philo at *Leg.* 314–315);
and the latter's father, of the same name, was consul in 38
BCE after having fought alongside Anthony and Octavian
against the assassins of Julius Caesar (Appian, *B. Civ.*
4.87.1; 102–107; 130; Plutarch, *Brut.* 38.2; Dio 47.35–36)—
which could account for the present reference to "generals." See Smallwood 1970: 309–310 and Atkinson 1958:
319–323. For Josephus's usage of αὐτοκράτωρ (*imperator*),
when not of emperors (e.g. 18.27, 32–33, 79, 89), then of
Roman generals (as here and at 14.164, 225, 306), see *ThLJ*
94, s.v. and *GTRI* 118–120. Cf. the note on "commander"
at §256.

345 Readers might note that the Germans' total disregard for proper norms is underlined by the contrast
between this μηδὲ αἰδουμένων ... ἀξίωσιν and αἰδοῖ τῆς ἀξι-
ώσεως at §102.

346 On σὺν ὀλίγοις, see the note on "a few" at 18.1.

347 This Anteius is not otherwise known. Wiseman
(2013a: 66) suggests he was related to Publius Anteius,
who—at some later point—was supposed to become
the governor of Syria, but eventually remained in Rome
(Tacitus, *Ann.* 13.22; cf. ibid. 16.14).

the pleasure he took in seeing, with his own eyes, Gaius lying on the ground—thus satisfying his hatred of him. For he had driven Anteius's father[348] (who bore the same name) into exile and, not content with that, had sent out soldiers after him and killed him.[349] **126** So he had come and was for those reasons happy at the sight of the corpse. However, when the palace became filled with tumult, he escaped—although he resolved to hide himself—neither the thoroughness of the Germans' search nor their murder, wildly enraged as they were, of guilty and innocent alike.[350] So these men died there.[351]

(1.16) 127 As for the theater: when word of Gaius's death reached it there was shock and disbelief. For some, although receiving with great pleasure[352] [the report] of his death, for already long ago they had thought of its happening as a boon for themselves, were in disbelief on account of fear.[353] **128** And there were others for whom it was very much unhoped for; for they did not wish such a thing to happen to Gaius, nor did they accept [the report] as true, for [they thought] there was no person capable of acting with such bravery. **129** Those were the contemptible women[354] and children, whatever slaves there were, and some of the soldiers: the [soldiers] because they were serving as mercenaries[355] and no less because they shared in the tyranny:[356] by ministering to his hubris they were able to intimidate[357]

Reactions in the Theater

---

348 Perhaps, as Wiseman notes (2013a: 66), to be identified with an officer of that name who served under Germanicus in 16 CE (Tacitus, *Ann.* 2.6.1).

349 As Barrett (2019: 148) notes, his fate (exile followed by execution by soldiers sent after him) is the same as that of Flaccus, according to the end of Philo's *In Flaccum*. Indeed, ibid. 180–191 Philo reports that Gaius ordered the execution of many of his exiles (with Flaccus at the head of the list). For similar reports, see Suetonius, *Cal.* 28 and Cassius Dio 59.18.3.

350 As mentioned above, Suetonius (*Cal.* 58.3) too reports that the German bodyguards killed some of the assassins, along with some innocent senators. Cassius Dio (59.30.1b), reports not that they searched for the assassins, but rather that they fell "to rioting and quarreling, with the result that there was some bloodshed" (trans. Carey, LCL).

351 Feldman and Schalit translate "thus," as if Josephus is merely summarizing their death. But ταύτη may mean "there" (as, for example, at 18.62, 90–91, 123; 19.200) and that sense would prepare readers for the switch of scene at the opening of §127. Readers may note that, as usual, Josephus rounds out his story after giving three examples; cf. the note on "three" at 18.11.

352 A common Josephan phrase; see the note on "pleasure" at 18.63.

353 For a similar situation at the time of Tiberius's death, see 18.225. Suetonius (*Cal.* 60) likewise writes that at first people could not believe that Gaius was dead and suspected that the report was made up by the emperor himself in order to find out how people felt about him.

354 For Josephus's contemptuous use of γύναιον rather than γυνή, see *ThLJ* 119, s.v. For Josephus's scorn for women in general, see *Ant.* 4.219: "Let the testimony of women not be accepted because of the levity and boldness of their gender," and 3.5; 5.294—all non-biblical notions—as well as 1.49 (with Feldman 2000: 17–18, n. 101), *Apion* 2.201, and the notes on "demands" at 18.42 and on "frivolous" at 18.255; Feldman 1998a: 188–192; and Ilan 2016: esp. 218–219. Josephus himself was married once while still in Judea (if *War* 5.419 is not only tear-jerking rhetoric) and three times thereafter (*Life* 414–415, 426–427), and his experience was not the best: he reports that, of those three, the first left him and he divorced the second because he was not happy with her habits; the third's character was superior, he emphasizes, to that of many women.

355 That this simple fact is adduced as reason to expect loyalty from mercenaries reflects, apparently, the recognition that they are dependent upon the ruler who pays their wages and, since they are foreigners, have little reason to consider what might otherwise be best for the state. On mercenaries and tyranny see, in general, Kiernan 1957. Here, however, it is not clear whether Josephus is referring to foreign mercenaries or, rather, to soldiers in general as if they were no better than mercenaries, for they only cared about their wages.

356 This rare compound verb, συντυραννέω, which also appears at Strabo, *Geog.* 13.1.57, occurs nowhere else in Josephus.

357 Apart from here, Josephus uses ἐπανασείω only at §143.

the most powerful citizens, thus achieving honor and also profits; **130** while the women and the youth were, as is usual for the mob,[358] taken in[359] by the spectacles and the gladiatorial games[360] he presented, as well as by the pleasure of some meat-distributions[361] that he provided[362]—nominally for the benefit of the public, but really in order to satiate[363] Gaius's cruel madness;[364] and **131** the slaves, because they had achieved familiarity[365] and scorn for their masters, [Gaius's] support allowing them refuge from abuse. For it was easy for those who lied against their owners and informed about their property to gain credence,[366] and so both to become free and to gain wealth as wages for the accusations, for the prize to which they were entitled was an eighth of [the victim's] possessions.[367]

132 As for the well-born:[368] even if some of them thought the report was reliable, whether because they knew about the plot in advance or because they wanted to believe it, considering it desirable, they consigned to silence not only their joy about what had been reported, but even the appearance of having heard [the report]. **133** The latter were afraid lest their hope turn out to be false and they would be punished for having prematurely exhibited their opinion,[369] while the former, who knew with certainty of the plot because they had participated in it, hid from one another even more, both out of lack of knowledge and fearing that, if they spoke about it to someone for whom the tyranny, when in force, had been advantageous,[370] if Gaius were still alive they would be informed against and punished. **134** For there was another story that had made its way around:[371] while admitting that Gaius

---

358 Josephus, the aristocrat, takes it for granted that his readers share his scorn for the masses and how they tend to behave (ὅπερ ὄχλος φιλεῖ); see also 6.81; 7.287; 17.156, 204; 18.60; 19.115. On his disdain for the masses, see also Rajak 1998: 239–240 and Mason 2001: 38, n. 188.

359 Lit. "taken up"; for such use of ἀναλαμβάνω, cf. 18.299. Neither Suetonius nor Dio reports anything of this type. Dio (59.30.1a), in fact, writes that, following the assassination, the people actually dragged Gaius's statues and images from their pedestals, "for the people in particular remembered the distress they had endured." Yavetz explains Gaius's early popularity among the general populace as due to his antagonism toward, and humiliation of, the upper classes, but concludes that by 39 the people became "disillusioned with Caligula" because of his cruelty and "completely antagonistic towards him." See Yavetz 1969: 113–118, also Barrett 2019: 302–305.

360 See the note on "considerable number" at §253.

361 This is the only occurrence of κρεανομία in Josephus. For the manifold evidence for such *viscerationes*, as they were called, in ancient Rome, often in connection with public spectacles, see esp. Kajava 1998.

362 Wiseman notes the similarity of the motives of the lowest classes in 69, as reported by Tacitus (*Hist.* 1.4): "The lowest classes, addicted to the circus and theatre, and with them the basest slaves, as well as those men who had wasted their property and, to their shame, were wont to depend on Nero's bounty, were cast down and grasped at every rumour" (trans. Moore, LCL). Gaius is said to have given the people generous gifts, added a day to the Saturnalia, given several gladiatorial shows and races at

the circus, and exhibited numerous plays (Suetonius, *Cal.* 17.2–18.3; Dio 59.2.2, 6.4).

363 In Josephus, ἐκπίμπλημι, with the prefix that makes the verb emphatic, appears only here and, perhaps, in 12.187.

364 Dio (59.10.2) writes that Gaius had an "insatiable desire for the sight of blood." This is related to his general tyrannical *saevitia*, for which see Suetonius, *Cal.* 27–32; Dio 59.10. For that tyrannical trait in Roman historiography, see Dunkle 1971, esp. 14–15.

365 For this meaning of προσηγορία, see LSJ 1512, s.v. True, Josephus uses it only in the sense of "designation, name, title," which leads CCFJ 3.558–559 to mark the present instance as doubtful; it lists three emendations that have been offered. I have translated in light of εὐπροσήγορος ("conversational") at §88.

366 As above, §§12–14.

367 According to the Augustan law, it was a quarter (Tacitus, *Ann.* 4.20; cf. Suetonius, *Nero* 10.1). On informers (*delatores*) in the days of Gaius, see esp. Rutledge 2001: 103–105.

368 On εὐπατρίδης ("patrician"), see the note on "good birth" at §2.

369 See the note on "fear" above at §127.

370 Such as those listed in §§128–131. For a survey of Gaius's friends and associates, which identifies few Roman aristocrats who survived him although "there was no shortage of close acquaintances at the lower end of the social scale," including gladiators, actors, and, especially, imperial freemen, see Barrett 2019: 111–117.

371 ἐπιφοιτάω. Also below, at §197.

had been wounded, it denied that he had died, and claimed that he was alive and being treated by physicians.[372] **135** And so no one trusted anyone, to whom he might be bold enough to reveal his own opinion; for if the man was a friend [of Gaius] he was suspected of goodwill toward the tyranny, but if he related to Gaius with hatred he destroyed the credibility of the things he said because of his failure to receive with goodwill anything said by anyone else. **136** And it was reported by some (and they banished the optimistic hope especially of the well-born) that [Gaius], ignoring the dangers and totally[373] disregarding[374] his wounds, had, though bleeding severely, made his way to the Forum and was making a speech to the people [there].[375] **137** These, then, were the things imagined in the unthinking desire of those who undertook to bandy things about,[376] and they were taken one way or the other by those who heard them. But no one left his seat,[377] out of fear of the accusation that would be brought against[378] those who went out first. For judgment concerning them would be made not according to the intention which they would claim had been in their mind, but, rather, according to whatever those who would accuse them and judge them would choose to imagine.

(1.17) 138 When a multitude[379] of Germans[380] surrounded the theater, their swords drawn, all the spectators expected[381] to perish, and whenever anyone entered they were gripped by panic, as if then and there they were going to be totally chopped up.[382] They were totally helpless, for they neither dared to leave nor believed that remaining in the theater would keep them safe from danger. **139** When [the Germans] stormed into the theater, a clamor broke forth from the theater, everyone turning to beg the troops—claiming that they knew nothing about anything, neither of what had been contemplated by the rebels, if in fact there had been an uprising,[383] nor of what had actually happened. **140** And [they called upon the Germans] to spare them and not punish those who were not guilty for the audacity of others, and to let [them alone][384] in instituting the search for those who had done whatever it was that had been done. **141** And [they said] all those things and more, with

The Germans at the Theater

---

372 According to Josephus below, at §237, this type of story was circulated by Agrippa.

373 For this sense of κομιδῇ, as also at §362 (//*War* 1.203), see LSJ 975, s.v.

374 This is the only occurrence of ἄφροντις in Josephus.

375 This is the only occurrence of δημηγορία in Josephus. For the people gathering in the Forum after the assassination, in a zealous attempt to find Gaius's murderers, see below at §§158–159.

376 Josephus uses θροέω only one other time; see the note on "spread the report" in 18.234.

377 In the theater.

378 For ἐπιφέρω with αἰτία see also, for example, §193 and 11.117; LSJ 670, s.v., §13.

379 The use of πλῆθος tends more toward "gang" than "unit," thus intensifyng the fear; see the notes on "mob" at §130 and on "multitude" at 18.26.

380 The emperor's German bodyguards; see above, §§119–122.

381 On ἐλπίς, see the note on "expectation" at 18.277.

382 This verb, συγκόπτω, appears in Josephus only here and at 15.306, but is common elsewhere.

383 ἐπανάστασις. This term appears only here in *Antiquities*, but a few times in *War*.

384 This translation and bracketed supplement take παρέντας to be the crowd's appeal to the Germans to leave the innocent alone and confine themselves to instituting a search (ἐρεύνην ... καταστῆναι) for the guilty alone. So too Mathieu and Herrmann 1929: 216 and Wiseman 2013a: 21. This seems to be what the context requires. Feldman (1965: 281), in contrast, takes παρέντας, in and of itself more naturally, to mean they called on the Germans to abandon the idea of instituting a search. But nothing in the context suggests that could be a reasonable request under the circumstances.

tears and beating[385] of their faces,[386] praying[387] and wailing as the danger which was near taught them to do, each one of them speaking as one who is struggling for his own life.

142 Faced with that, the soldiers' wrath subsided,[388] and they contritely gave up their intention to attack the spectators, which would have been cruel and so it indeed appeared to them,[389] despite the fact that they were so wildly enraged[390] that they affixed[391] the heads of Asprenas and his men[392] upon the altar.[393] **143** At the sight of them, the spectators suffered all the more, thinking of the dignity of the men and pitying their suffering, so that they too were intimidated[394] almost to the same degree by the very close contact with danger, for it was unclear whether in the end they would be able to avoid suffering. **144** So it was that even those who hated Gaius passionately and justly were denied the opportunity[395] for mirth about him, for the question whether they too would perish was still in the balance;[396] even then it was still the case that no reliable guarantee of survival had materialized.[397]

(1.18) 145 Euarestus Arruntius[398] was one of those people who announce sales; accordingly, using his loud voice and accumulating as much money as the richest of the Romans, he possessed so much power that he could do whatever he wanted throughout the city, both then and later. **146** He posed as if he were in the deepest mourning; although he hated Gaius as much as anyone else did, the lesson taught by fear and the strategy required to secure safety took precedence over the pleasure of the moment.[399] **147** After taking care to adorn himself just as if preparing for [mourning] the most honored of all dead, he entered the theater and announced the death of Gaius, thus putting an end to the people's being tossed about[400] in their ignorance as to what had happened.

---

385 This is the only occurrence of τύψις in Josephus. Mason compares Nicander's use (coinage?) of it with regard to attacks by wild creatures (*Theriaca* 921, 933); on the term, see Overduin 2015: 522.

386 Apparently a gesture of self-affliction that expresses lamentation and probably expresses the hope to forestall worse at another's hands. See Sittl 1890: 20, n. 8 (referring *inter alia* to Juvenal, *Satires* 13.128, Curtius 7.2.5). My thanks to Yona Gonopolsky for his help with this note.

387 Josephus uses ἐπιθειάζω a few times: *War* 1.656; *Ant.* 2.338, 4.118, 8.109.

388 Cf. the note on "pity" at 20.255.

389 This moral calculation does not correspond to the characterization of these German bodyguards at §§120–122. Cf. the note on "back" at §149.

390 As at §126.

391 This is the only occurrence of ἀπερείδω in *Antiquities*.

392 As is usual, this formulation (οἱ περί NN) includes NN; see the note on "retinue of" at 20.131. And this is confirmed in the present case by §216. However, the initial story of this murder (§123) speaks of Asprenas being killed alone. This might have a source-critical implication; see the introduction to Book 19.

393 Apparently the same altar on which Gaius sacrificed before the day's spectacles, at the beginning of the assassination scene, where Asprenas was drenched with the sacrifice's blood (above, §87)—thus completing the fulfillment of the omen.

394 In Josephus, ἐπανασείω appears only here and at §129.

395 Reading τῆς χώρας with Niese (1890a: 235); 1890b: 201), in accordance with the manuscripts, and, faute de mieux, taking χώρα metaphorically: they were not in the position to experience mirth. Cf. LSJ 2015, s.v. χώρα, §I.4. For centuries editors have considered emending to some form of "joy" (χαρά). Among those who accept the latter, note esp. Wiseman 2013a: 42, 68: Niese's text cannot be salvaged because "deprived of the place of pleasures" is "meaningless."

396 For something being "in the balance," cf. 18.9, 349 and *War* 4.399 (ἐν πολέμου ῥοπαῖς).

397 For such use of συνελθεῖν for parts coming together into a whole, cf. §127.

398 This Arruntius is not otherwise known, but not to be confused with the Arruntius mentioned at §102. Wiseman (2013a: 68) suggests, on the basis of the Greek cognomen (which means "well-pleasing," "very suitable"), that he was a freedman.

399 That is, he had his priorities right; cf. §§107, 125.

400 *CCFJ* 4.95, s.v. συμπεριφέρω, suggests only "to be" for this passage, but it seems that a more literal translation fits the context better; Schalit (1963: 332) offers "hurled this way and that." For the way uncertainty about the emperor's death could toss people around, see also 18.231–234.

148 In the meantime, Arruntius Stella[401] came[402] and calmed things down, together with the military tribunes recalling the Germans, ordering them to put their weapons away, and making it thoroughly clear[403] [to them] that Gaius was dead. **149** That most certainly saved the people gathered in the theater and everyone who in any way at all met up with the Germans; for had [the Germans] had any hope that Gaius was still breathing, there is no evil deed from which they would have held themselves back.[404] **150** Their loyalty[405] to him was so boundless that they were willing to purchase his immunity from conspiracies[406] against him, and keep such misfortune from befalling him, even at the cost of losing their own lives. **151** But once they had received clear[407] notice of his death, their wrathful quest for vengeance ceased, for it was now pointless for them to display their enthusiastic loyalty, for he who would have rewarded them had perished.[408] They also feared that if they went any further in their outrageous behavior they might become the object of attention of the Senate, if power devolved upon it, or of whoever managed to come into power.[409] **152** So the Germans, if only just barely, desisted from the frenzy that had overtaken them upon the death of Gaius.

---

401 Niese (1890a: 235) read καὶ Στήλας Ἀρούντιος, i.e., (L.) Stella Arruntius, who was appointed supervisor of the games in 55 CE (Tacitus, *Ann.* 13.22). Wiseman (2013a: 69) gives some details about his prominent family and suggests that he was, at the time, one of the Praetorian Prefects, alongside Clemens (above, §37), which would explain how he could give the Germans orders, as reported here. True, Feldman observes that, having just mentioned and identified Euarestus Arruntius (§145), Josephus would not have mentioned another Arruntius without clearly distinguishing between the two; therefore he adopts L. A. Post's suggestion to emend καὶ Στήλας Ἀρούντιος into καταστείλας Ἀρούντιος, "By now Arruntius had got control" (Feldman 1965: 283). Feldman is followed by Kavanagh 2010: 1016. However, it appears both that the addition of "Stella" does distinguish between the two, and that if readers were meant to think only one Arruntius appears in the story, they would not understand why his arrival is reported twice (§§147–148)—a problem that, evidently, brought Dindorf (1865: 746, noted by Niese ad loc.) to follow the Latin "circumibat" and emend the verb at §148 from παρῆν into περιήει, the result being that Arruntius, instead of "arriving" twice, merely "wandered about." It seems simpler to assume two individuals are meant.

402 See the end of the preceding note.

403 Although διασαφέω frequently means merely "explain," "inform" (e.g. 18.71, 199), here it seems that, in light of all the rumors and lack of clarity, as well as the Germans' reputation for low intelligence (§120), the opening of διασαφοῦντες points to something more "thorough," in order to convince the Germans.

404 This seems to conflict with the statement, a few sections back (§§138–142), that the people in the theater were saved because the Germans were convinced by their pleading and therefore refrained from what they had intended to do, understanding that it was evil. Likewise, it seems to contradict the statement at §121 that they had already learned that Gaius had been killed, and that was the impetus for their rage. However, these generalizations need not point to the use of different sources; they may be no more than expressions of the author's desire to maintain tension, and in any case it is probable that the situation was ambiguous.

405 For this translation of εὔνοια (as opposed to the more literal "goodwill" at §§135–136), see the note on "loyalty to Gaius" at 18.124.

406 Ἀνεπιβούλευτος. See the note on "conspiracy" at §43.

407 Note that σαφοῦς ("clear") here confirms the success of διασαφοῦντες at §148.

408 For the gifts of money through which Gaius obtained their goodwill, see above, §121.

409 Wiseman (1992: 9) comments that the two possibilities mentioned were both well-founded: when the Princeps died with no heir, power was still expected to revert automatically to the Senate, but obviously it was possible that "some powerful individual might succeed in establishing himself, whether by bloodless coup or by civil war, in the autocratic position left vacant by the

Chaerea and   **(1.19) 153** Returning to Chaerea:[410] he was greatly afraid concerning Minucianus,[411] lest he
Minucianus   fall into the hands of the Germans and perish in their madness, and so he went to each
of the soldiers,[412] asking them to make an effort to see to his safety and making extensive
inquiries [to ascertain] that he had not perished. **154** Minucianus, indeed, had been brought
up[413] before Clemens,[414] who released him, testifying, together[415] with many other people
of senatorial rank,[416] both to the justice of the deed and to the valor of those who had
resolved upon it and who had not backed off in cowardice from carrying it out, as follows:

> **155** For tyranny arises out of the pleasure of hubris[417] but [lasts] only for a short time,
> and the tyrant's departure from life cannot be happy,[418] for [people of] virtue hate
> him.[419] **156** Rather, [a tyrant's end] comes with such misfortune as happened to Gaius,
> who, even before there was any initiative by the rebels and the plotters, had become a
> conspirator to attack himself. For he taught those who were his closest friends to make
> war upon him, by treating them outrageously and intolerably,[420] setting the protection
> of the law aside.[421] Now, accordingly, although nominally they are the ones who killed
> Gaius, in fact he lies there having destroyed himself utterly.

(1.20) 157 People were already getting up to leave the theater since the guards, who at first
had been very strict, had loosened up.[422] The one responsible for allowing the spectators so

---

defunct." Mentioning the two possibilities adumbrates the coming debate about restoring the Republic.

410 Chaerea has not been mentioned since the end of the long section on him at §§111–113, apart from the reference to his men at §115. It is unclear where he has been in the meantime. However, as Wiseman (2013a: 69) notes, it seems that unlike the preceding passages and those that follow (§§157ff.), the coming scene involving Chaerea, Vinicianus, and Clemens did not take place in the theater. Thus, this section cuts into the theater scene, and is one of the indications that suggest Josephus used more than one source; see the introduction to Book 19, at nn. 12–13.

411 I.e., Annius Vinicianus, one of the main conspirators; see above, §§18, 20, etc.

412 Not the Germans. As Wiseman notes (2013a: 69), the reference is probably to soldiers of Chaerea's own cohort.

413 I.e., for judgment. For such usage of ἀνάγω, see the note on "bring Aretas up" at 18.115.

414 Presumably, the commander of the Praetorian Guard, who was in on the conspiracy (see above, §§37–47).

415 This is the only occurrence of συμμαρτυρέω in Josephus.

416 Wiseman (2013a: 22) takes Josephus to mean that Clemens released the others just as Vinicianus, but that does not account for the prefix of συμμαρτυρῶν.

417 For Gaius's hubris, see the note on "hubris" at §1.

418 That is, a tyrant's death will never be a happy one, for virtue—and those who uphold it—will hate him. For the notion of a "happy" (εὐτυχής) death, which therefore

seems to refer to leaving a good reputation (see the note on "remembered" at 20.216), see also 20.18; contrast 19.270, where the reference to dying εὐδαιμόνως seems rather to apply to the victim's mood. The use of εὐτυχεῖς here sets up the contrast with μετὰ ... δυστυχίας in the next paragraph.

419 That is, they hate him in his lifetime and will revile his memory. For this formulation, μίσει χρωμένης, see also §146. Wiseman (2013a: 70) points to the similar opposition of tyranny and virtue in Tacitus, *Ann.* 16.21, where the tyrant Nero is said to have "conceived the ambition to extirpate virtue herself by killing Thrasea Paetus and Barea Soranus."

420 For his turning his friends into his enemies, see also below, §§203 and 211. Suetonius, *Cal.* 26.1 writes: "It would be trivial and pointless to add to this an account of his treatment of his relatives and friends ... [some examples] ... all these were rewarded for their kinship and their faithful services by a bloody death" (trans. Rolfe, LCL).

421 The rule of the tyrant is the opposite of rule based on the laws; see the note on "laws" at §15.

422 This verb, ὑπανίημι, appears elsewhere in Josephus only at 2.61, where the context is similar to here (prison guards relaxing their severity). As often, Niese retained the manuscripts' reading (ὑπανίσως) in his editio maior (1890a: 237) but since it is difficult to construe he offered a conjecture (ὑπανεισῶν) in its apparatus and adopted the latter in his editio minor (1890b: 203), followed by Feldman (1965: 286). For other suggestions, see *CCFJ* 4.236, s.v. ὑπανίημι.

energetically and completely to depart was Alcyon the physician,[423] who had been taken off to care for some wounded people.[424] He sent those with him off, ostensibly[425] to bring things that he needed to treat the wounded, but really to get them out of the danger that had come upon them.[426]

158 In the meantime[427] there was also a meeting of the Senate,[428] and the populace [too convened], where it was usual for them to assemble—in the Forum. They were [both] engaged in investigating the assassins of Gaius, but while the populace was really quite upset about it,[429] the Senate merely gave the [same] appearance.[430]

The People and the Senate Deliberate

159 Before the populace[431] there then appeared Valerius Asiaticus, who was of consular rank.[432] They were very tumultuous and behaving indignantly that those who had killed the emperor were still unknown, but when everyone was asking him insistently, who had done the act, he said: "Would that it had been I!" **160** And the consuls[433] proposed an edict[434]

---

423 He is probably to be identified with "Alcon the surgeon," mentioned by Pliny (*NH* 29.22) in the days of Claudius, and also mentioned by Martial (*Epigrams* 6.70; 11.84).

424 It is unclear who had taken Alc(y)on and whom he was expected to treat. Wiseman (2013a: 70) suggests he was taken by the Germans to treat some of their men, who may have been hurt in the struggle with Norbanus (see above, §§123–124).

425 Such contrasts between appearances and the truth are common in Josephus, and not least in this book; in the nature of things, tyranny requires both sides to dissimulate. See §§40–41, 97, 101, 130, 156–158, 166, 240, 246, 260, and the note on "private gain" at 18.7.

426 There is some lack of clarity here, for if the beginning of this paragraph reported that people were leaving because the Germans had loosened up, now we read of departure—of masses?—only via subterfuge. But situations like these need not be unambiguous.

427 Wiseman (2013a: 70–72) suggests that §§158–160, which interrupt the flow of the story, introduce Valerius Asiaticus as if he were a new character (see §102), include an inconsistency vis-à-vis §115 (see the note there on "beloved") and another vis-à-vis §161 (where the gathering of the consuls seems to contradict the consuls' edict reported at §160), and duplicate material at §189, are drawn from a separate source: "158–160 and 160 [i.e., 161, DRS]–89 probably represent two versions of the same debate ... the doublet suggests that Josephus has given a very compressed account of the Senate's debate from one source, followed by a longer one (though restricted almost entirely to Sentius' speech) from another."

428 Concerning this meeting of the Senate, Suetonius, *Cal.* 60, writes: "the Senate was so unanimously in favour of re-establishing the republic that the consuls called the

first meeting, not in the senate house, because it had the name Julia, but in the Capitol." Cassius Dio (60.1.1) too notes that, following the assassination, the Senate was convened in the Capitol, and so does Josephus himself in *War* 2.205. However, here in *Antiquities* Josephus does not state where the Senate convened. For the location of a later meeting of the Senate on the Capitoline Hill, see the note on "Jupiter Victor" at §248.

429 For the general populace's attitude, see the note on "beloved" at §115. Cassius Dio's account (59.30.1c), however, implies that the general public was quite happy about the assassination.

430 Here the point is to portray the Senate as hoping to make the most of the opportunity, but also to denigrate it as impractical: it does nothing to enforce its claim to rule, but arrogantly thinks it will fall into its hands of itself (§161). Cf. the introduction to Book 19.

431 In Dio's similar account (59.30.2), Asiaticus addresses the Praetorian Guard, not the general populace.

432 On Asiaticus, see the note at §102. As noted at the beginning of the preceding paragraph, this introduction as if he were new to readers is among the hints that the present brief account of what happened "in the meantime" may be based on a source different from whatever supplied the main narrative.

433 The consuls were Gnaeus Sentius Saturninus and Quintus Pomponius Secundus (see *War* 2.205 and Dio 59.30.3). They are mentioned below at §166 and §263, respectively.

434 Διάγραμμα; this term appears in Josephus only in *Ant.* 19, here and below, at §§274 and 279, and according to some mss. also in 285. For its use in the Roman period as one of the Greek terms for an *edictum*, see *GTRI* 127–128, who points also to Plutarch, *Marcellus* 24.7, *Pomp.* 48.4; and Appian, *B.C.* 2.126. For Hellenistic usage, cf. Welles 1934: 324.

in which they condemned Gaius, and ordered both the populace and the soldiers[435] to go home, promising the populace, on the one hand, the hope of much indulgence, and the soldiers, on the other hand, that they would receive honors if they remained orderly, as usual, and did not go out rampaging. For there was fear that if they went out wildly, the city too would bear its share of the evil, when they turned to robbing them[436] and despoiling[437] the temples.[438]

161 As for the senators, the whole multitude of them had already assembled earlier,[439] especially those who had joined together in the murder of Gaius; they were confident and very scornful [of the opponents and difficulties still standing in their way], as if [control of public] affairs[440] had [already] been transferred to them.[441]

The Army Chooses Claudius

(2.1) 162 While affairs were in that state, Claudius was suddenly snatched from the palace.[442] For the soldiers, after they held a meeting and discussed with one another what should be done,[443] saw that it was impossible for a democracy[444] to be in control of such a great

---

435 Wiseman (2013a: 72) identifies these soldiers as the urban cohorts. However, as mentioned in the note on "to the camp" at §226, other sources report that the urban cohorts were ordered to take control of the Forum and the Senate, and the city in general, which conflicts with the notion that they had been ordered to return to their quarters. It is possible, therefore, that these were the German bodyguards, whom Josephus had already described as governed by their tempers and killing indiscriminately (above, §§120–126, 149–152), and who, according to Cassius Dio (59.30.1b), had already fallen "to rioting and quarreling, with the result that there was much bloodshed"—which sounds like the fear expressed in the continuation of this paragraph.

436 The inhabitants of the city.

437 Apart from here, Josephus uses σύλησις only in *Ant.* 12.267, where it replaces βεβηλόω in 1 Macc 2:12. As there, where, concerning Jerusalem, Josephus (by moving from pollution to robbery) creates a parallelism between robbing the city and robbing the Temple, so too here he creates the same parallelism with regard to Rome. On ancient expectations concerning the horrors that follow the conquest of cities, cf. Paul 1982 and below, n. 805.

438 Josephus's narrative here omits much that is reported elsewhere: the consuls and Senate used the urban cohorts to take possession of the Forum and the Capitol (Suetonius, *Claud.* 10.3), entrusted to those cohorts the protection of the city (Josephus, *War* 2.205), and transferred the public treasury to the Capitol (Dio 59.30.3).

439 Contrast §249, where, the next day, only one hundred senators are said to have assembled. Correspondingly, the present emphasis on their confidence contrasts with the emphasis there (§248) on their fear and despair.

440 For use of πράγματα ("affairs") in the sense of "state," see Glass and Keddie 2020. In a Roman context, it often conforms to *res publica*. That meaning is certainly intended here, but I have adhered to the literal sense in order to reflect the word's repetition at the start of the next paragraph.

441 More scorn for the Senate; see the note on "appearance" at §158. At this point, readers expect to hear what was said at the Senate's meeting, but Josephus first brings us up to date about what happened in the real world, before he allows the senators even to begin their fine rhetoric at §166.

442 Lit. "from the house"; see the note on "the palace" at §8. Indeed, after his departure from the theater (§102), Claudius was last mentioned as having been in the palace (§103, βασίλειον), and later too we read that it was while searching the palace (§214, βασίλειον) that the Germans found Claudius (§217), just as Dio 60.1.2 says he hid within the palace (τὸ παλάτιον). Suetonius (*Claud,* 10.1) specifies that he hid in a specific room or apartment (*diaeta*) called the Hermaeum, which is also known from inscriptions; see Hurley 2001: 95–96 and Barrett 2019: 271.

443 Note the similar account of the soldiers' meeting below, at §214, where they are also identified as the those of the Praetorian Guard.

444 As at §§173 and 187, "democracy" is primarily a negative term, denoting rule without an emperor, as under the Republic; so too Cassius Dio 53.17.1–3; 66.12.2. Note also the adverb δημοκρατικῶς at 20.234, where too, as the noun here, it denotes rule without kings. Contrast *War* 2.205, where, in the present context, the Senate's goal is phrased positively, referring to what they do want, instead of an emperor: "aristocracy." This is in line with

state,[445] and that if a democracy ever did arrive it would not rule for their good. **163** But [they also realized that] if a single individual were to take hold of rule by himself, he would be very aggrieved with them for not having been collaborators in establishing his rule.[446] **164** Accordingly, [they thought] it was proper, so long as public affairs had not yet been decided, to choose Claudius as the ruler, for he was an uncle of the deceased,[447] and of those assembled in the Senate there was no one superior to him with regard to the dignity of his ancestors or the virtue and the education to which he had devoted himself[448]—**165** and after he was installed as emperor he would honor them as was customary and requite them[449] with gifts.[450] With those thoughts in mind, they did it immediately.[451] Thus Claudius, on the one hand, was snatched[452] by the soldiers.

166 But Gnaeus Sentius Saturninus,[453] on the other hand, although he had heard of the kidnapping of Claudius, and that he had laid claim[454] to rule (seemingly unwillingly, but in truth desiring it),[455] got up in the Senate and, not at all stricken by consternation, gave the following speech of exhortation,[456] as is appropriate to free and noble men:[457]

Sentius Saturninus's Speech in the Senate

Josephus's usual usage for rule by council (D. R. Schwartz 1983/84: 33–34)—in this case, the Senate.

445 For the same idea, see below, §225: "impossibility of the project" (ἀμήχανον τοῦ πράγματος) with regard to rule by the Senate. That statement accompanies another one (§224) that morally condemns the Senate; see the introduction to Book 19.

446 This fear is repeated at §225.

447 In Josephus's other account, the soldiers' reasoning emphasizes the popularity of Claudius's brother, Germanicus (§§217, 223). Cassius Dio (60.1.3), more generally, writes that they made him emperor because "he was of the imperial family and was regarded as suitable."

448 One may suspect that at least the last-named consideration was more important to Josephus, or to the literate author of his source, than to the soldiers themselves. For Claudius's devotion to learning, see the notes on "learning" and "Greek" at §213.

449 The expectation to be thus honored is also mentioned in the other version, below at §225. And, indeed, it is later reported that Claudius presented them with such rewards (§247). Suetonius (*Claud.* 10.4) reports Claudius's promises to give each soldier fifteen thousand sesterces if he were made emperor.

450 The quotation mark in Niese's edition here (1890a: 238) is apparently a printer's error.

451 As Wiseman (2013a: xiv–xv, 72–73, 84) notes, as part of his argument for Josephus's use of more than one source, in this account the soldiers had already decided to choose Claudius as emperor before they "snatched" him, whereas in the other account (§§212–225) the decision seems to have been reached only after he was "snatched."

452 By repeating the verb used at §162, ἁρπάζω, Josephus clarifies to readers that all that has been told since §162 is just the details of what was stated there.

453 Currently one of the consuls (41 CE), along with Q. Pomponius Secundus, who is mentioned below at §263. Sentius Saturninus is here introduced for the first time, and is not identified as a consul, but both consuls are mentioned as such and identified in this context in Josephus's narrative at *War* 2.205, as well as Dio 59.30.3. This Sentius Saturninus is probably to be identified with the Sentius who was, according to Tacitus (*Hist.* 4.7.2), a friend of Vespasian. He came from a very prominent family: his father, who bore the same name, was suffect consul in 4 CE and became governor of Syria in 17 CE (Tacitus, *Ann.* 2.74), and a generation earlier his grandfather, C. Sentius Saturninus, had been consul in 19 BCE and governor of Syria in 10–7 BCE (see *War* 1.554, 577; *Ant.* 16.280, 344, 368, 17.24, 89).

454 This is the only appearance of ἐπιδικάζω in Josephus.

455 For Claudius's reluctance to accept rule, see Dio 60.1.3a. Suetonius, in contrast, recounts how Claudius worked towards acquiring rule, in part by offering huge bribes to the soldiers (Suetonius, *Claud.* 10.4–11.1). Cf. the note on "ostensibly" at §157.

456 On παραίνεσις ("exhortation" to virtuous behavior) and speeches devoted to it, see Swancutt 2005 and Malherbe 1986: 68–79. On Sentius's speech, see esp. Timpe 1960: 482–486, Mason 2003c: 585–588, and Free 2017: 604–607.

457 There is some tension between this statement introducing Sentius's speech, with its emphasis that it was "appropriate to free and noble men," which echoes the major theme of the speech ("liberty"), as well as the large space Josephus devoted to quoting it (§§167–184), on the one hand, and the way Josephus's narrative undercuts the speech both by framing it between the army's creation of a fait accompli in §§162–165 (and see the

(2.2)167 Although it may be hard to believe, O Romans,[458] since it has come to us unhoped after so much time,[459] we have the dignity of free men. While it is unclear how long it will last, and that remains in the domain of the gods who bestowed it,[460] it suffices to cause celebration, for even if it will be taken away from us it brought us together in happiness. 168 Indeed, for those who know virtue it is sufficient to have lived, even if only for a single hour, a way of life with autonomous[461] thought under the independent jurisdiction[462] of the fatherland according to laws,[463] under which it once blossomed.[464] 169 I cannot remember the earlier liberty because I was born after it, but as I now fill myself up insatiably with the current liberty, I consider most blessed those who were born and grew up in it, and I consider no less worthy of honor than the gods these men who at least[465] now, if late and at such an age, have allowed us to taste of it. 170 Would that it remain unthreatened for all time to come! But if need be, even this one day suffices—both for our youths and for those of us who have grown old. For the old it shall be taken as if it were eternity, if only so they can die having had some familiarity with its boons, 171 while for the young it shall be a good lesson in the virtuous[466] way of life[467] of the men from whom we descend.[468] Now, therefore, for us too, given the present moment, nothing is more important for us than to live with virtue; for only it can devise,[469] for humanity,[470] the path to liberty. 172 For ancient things I know from hearsay, but these things I have come to know by direct contact, seeing them with my

---

note on "to them" at §161) and the little ring-scene (§185), right after Sentius concludes the speech, on the other. It appears that Josephus wants us both to recognize the values on behalf of which Sentius will speak and to realize that, in this world, they cannot be attained. That message corresponds to the heroic role attributed to Chaerea, who will be executed for his efforts.

458 Wiseman (2013a: 74) asserts the significance of this opening, in that Sentius, although speaking to the senators (so we would expect a Greek equivalent of "patres conscripti"), addresses, as it were, the entire Roman citizen body. Mason, somewhat similarly, suggests that he may be addressing the senators as "Romans" because the issue is the liberty and history of the Roman people (Mason 2016a: cxlii–cxliii). In any case, §185 shows that Sentius's audience was not limited to senators.

459 As we will soon see, for Sentius, liberty was lost with Julius Caesar (§173). Correspondingly, at §187 too, after the speech, the length of time that liberty was lost is given as one hundred years; that too seems to point back to Caesar's first consulship. See the note on "aside" at §187.

460 Cf. §219, where Gratus, the soldier who finds Claudius, tells him that the gods have taken rule from Gaius and granted it to him, also §§169, 175, 182, 233. As is noted in the introduction to Book 19, in the discussion of doubts concerning the Cluvius theory, Josephus does not hesitate to allow non-Jews to refer to gods.

461 In Josephus, αὐτοτελής appears only here and in quoting Strabo at *Ant.* 14.117. See the next note.

462 This is the only occurrence of αὐτόδικος in Josephus. As Mason notes, the only known occurrence of the word prior to Josephus comes, as here alongside αὐτοτελής, at Thucydides 5.18.2, in the context of the terms that ended the first phase of the Peloponnesian War. Although Thucydides is referring to a temple and Josephus, here, to a state, it is possible that he borrowed his phrasing from Thucydides, and that his readers would recognize it.

463 For tyranny being the opposite of rule based on the laws, see the note on "the laws" at §15.

464 For the same image, see *Ant.* 1.171 and below, §192.

465 On γοῦν, see the note on "at least" at 18.243.

466 ἀρετή, the Greek equivalent of the Latin *virtus*. For *virtus* as a most important Roman value, see Sallust, *Catiline* 6.5, 7.5. 53.4, and esp. Cicero, *Phil.* 4.13. For the Republican notion of *virtus*, its complexity, and its evolution, see McDonnell 2006. For the emperors' being in opposition to *virtus*, see below, §173; for Gaius's hostility to it, see §203.

467 For this translation of κατάστασις, see van Henten 2014: 188, n. 1752, on *Ant.* 15.267—a text which similarly contrasts a pristine ancient way of life (in that case: the Jews') to the corrupted form to which it had deteriorated.

468 This seems to refer to the forefathers of the Roman Republic.

469 Apart from 18.290, this is the only occurrence of ἐκφροντίζω in Josephus. Cf. the note on "agreement" at 18.203.

470 Cf. §41.

own eyes: with how many evils tyrannies fill states, blocking all virtue and depriving liberty of its high-mindedness,[471] appointing teachers of flattery and fear and leaving affairs not to the wisdom of the laws,[472] but to the wrath of those who are set above it.

173 For since the time when Julius Caesar resolved to destroy the democracy,[473] and—thoroughly doing violence to the good order of the laws[474]—upset the state entirely, being above justice but under the control of whatever brought pleasure[475] to him personally, there is not a single calamity that has not wearied[476] the city. **174** For all who succeeded him[477] as rulers have competed with one another in causing ancestral ways to disappear and as to who could leave the citizens more bereft of nobility. For they thought it was best for their own security to deal only with dishonest[478] men, while it was best not only to take down somewhat in their boasting,[479] but rather fully to decree the ruin, of all those who were believed to distinguish themselves in virtue.[480]

175 But although they were many in number, and each, as he ruled, showed himself to be intolerable[481] in his harshness,[482] one of them, Gaius, who today is dead, more than all [the others] displayed terrible behavior not only towards his fellow citizens;[483] he even let his unbridled rage loose against members of his family and his friends alike. Upon all, without distinction, he imposed even worse evils than those

---

471 That is, it forces free people to give up their high-mindedness. The same is said at §174, with regard to citizens bereft of nobility. Sentius is thus challenging the senators to live up to the demands of the liberty they claim.

472 On the laws' wisdom, see the note on "wisdom" at 18.16.

473 For "democracy" meaning rule without a king (and not necessarily some specific alternative), see the note on "democracy" at §162. For the view of Julius Caesar as a tyrant see e.g., Cicero, *De officiis* 2.23, 3.82–85; *Att.* 10.1.3, and for Caesar as the beginning of the end of the Republic see also Lucan, *Pharsalia* 7.691ff; Appian, *Preface* 6, and further the note on "set aside" at §187. As is pointed out by Wiseman (1992: 10), it was especially fitting to count from Caesar's first consulship, for the death of Gaius constituted the end of Caesar's dynasty. Tacitus (*Hist.* 1.1.1), in contrast, points to Augustus's victory at Actium, and so does Cassius Dio (53.17.1)—as already above at §75.

474 Cicero (*De Officiis* 3.83) describes Caesar's rule as "the destruction of law and liberty."

475 See the note on "pleasure" at §201. Below, at §201, Gaius is described as being "under the control of pleasure." Compare also 5.179: "once they [the Hebrews] deviated from the order of their constitution, they turned to living in accordance with pleasure and their own will"; see Mason 2016a: cxlix.

476 See the note on "harrying and plundering" at §2.

477 So too after Sentius's speech, at §187, and implicitly also at §230, all of Julius Caesar's successors are said

to have been tyrants. This harsh attack against Caesar and all the emperors who followed him, beginning with Augustus, may well have been meant to be taken by astute readers as veiled criticism of Domitian; see Mason 2003c: esp. 583–586 and idem 2005a: 271–274.

478 This adjective, κίβδηλος ("adulterated," used especially of counterfeit or debased coins), appears in Josephus only here.

479 Αὔχημα. In Josephus, only here and below at §250. Cf. the note on "greatness" at §81.

480 See the note on "virtuous" at §171. Something seems to be wrong with the text at the end of §174; Niese (1890a: 240) marks a lacuna.

481 This is the only occurrence of ἀνύποιστος in Josephus.

482 Βαρύτης is found in Josephus three times: here, below at §230, and at 18.371 concerning the harsh rule of Anileus in Babylonia.

483 For Gaius's treatment of citizens, see above, e.g., §§2–3, 12, 24–26. This is the only occurrence of συμπολίτης in Josephus, and the word may be a pointer toward the history of this narrative. Namely, simple πολίτης is the standard Greek way to refer not only to "citizen" but also to "fellow citizen" (see LSJ 1435a, top; Danker 2000: 846, s.v. [§2]), as also among Jews (e.g. 2 Macc 4:5, 50; *Letter of Aristeas* 3, 36; *Leg.* 211; see D. R. Schwartz 2008: 50–51), so συμπολίτης is hardly attested. LSJ 1685, s.v., cites only the present passage and a Roman inscription, along with the fact that the word was condemned by Phrynichus, for "to words like πολίτης, which imply fellowship, no Attic writer added σύν" (Rutherford 1881: 255–256). Similarly,

[imposed by] people who are unjustly enraged into exacting punishment, savagely treating men and the gods alike.[484] **176** Indeed, tyranny does not consider pleasure a [sufficient] profit even when it is misappropriated outrageously,[485] nor [is it satisfied by] the grief caused by [attacks on] property[486] and wives;[487] rather, [it insists on] the profit it derives from molesting[488] the entire households[489] of its enemies.

177 All liberty is the enemy of tyranny,[490] and even those who are willing to make light of whatever they have suffered cannot move [a tyrant] to goodwill. For [tyrants] know very well how they have fully afflicted them with evils, and even if they generously belittle their misfortune, the [tyrants] cannot ignore what they did to them, and so the only way they can believe they can attain immunity from those whom they suspect is by being able to eliminate them completely.[491]

178 Having gotten yourselves free[492] of such evils, and made yourselves beholden one to another—which is the most reliable of all constitutions, [promising] loyalty in

---

Pollux, *Onomasticon* 3.51 (ed. Bethe, 1.171), although noting that Euripides used the term, denounced it as οὐ δόκιμον ("not approved"). Originally, however, as Benveniste (1974) has shown, πολίτης, in contrast to the Latin *civis*, did not imply commonality; indeed, he observes (275, n. 2; 277, n. 2) that the meaning "fellow citizen" remained "peu frequent," "très rarement," in Greek. Thus, the use of συμπολίτης here might be a pedantic rendering of the Latin *civis* by a Roman translator who was aware of the nuance intended ("*fellow* citizen") but unaware, or not certain, that the same nuance was implied by the Greek πολίτης. Cf. the note on "civil life" at §306.

484 Compare Josephus's statement in his reflection—apropos of the reign of King Saul—on the corruption of the character of people who become kings or attain autocratic power: "they put on audacity, insanity, contempt of things human and divine" (*Ant.* 6.264). Cf. Plato, *Republic* 573c, concerning the tyrant: "And again the madman, the deranged man, attempts and expects to rule over not only men but gods."

485 With hubris; cf. §155 above: "tyranny arises out of the pleasure of hubris." For Gaius's *hubris*, see the note on it at §1.

486 On Gaius's attacks on property, see above, §§2–3, with the notes there, as well as Suetonius, *Cal.* 38–41 and Dio 59.10.7; 59.15; 59.21. On wives, see the next note. Cf. *Life* 80, where Josephus defends himself against the charge of having been a tyrant (see *Life* 260, 302) by insisting that he always abstained from molesting women and from accepting gifts.

487 As noted above on "Regulus" at §9, in 38 CE Gaius forced Publius Memmius Regulus to give him his wife, Lollia Paulina, in marriage, only to divorce her soon thereafter (Suetonius, *Cal.* 25.2; Dio 59.12.1). Other cases of such outrageous treatment of other men's wives are reported by Suetonius and Cassius Dio: he seduced Ennia Naevia, wife of Macro, the commander of the Praetorian

Guard (Suetonius, *Cal.* 12.2; but see Tacitus, *Ann.* 6.45; Dio 58.28.4; Philo, *Leg.* 39–40, 61, and Barrett 2019: 48–49); he took his sister, Drusilla—with whom, previously, he often had incestual relations—from her husband, the ex-consul L. Cassius Longinus, and treated her as his wife (Suetonius, *Cal.* 24.1–2); he took Livia Orestilla from her husband Gaius Piso, during their marriage ceremony, and divorced her within a few days (Suetonius, *Cal.* 25.1; Dio 59.8.7); see also Dio 59.3.3.

488 This verb, διοχλέω, is usually taken to mean "annoy exceedingly" (LSJ 435), which hardly fits here; that, together with the fact that it appears only twice in Josephus, here and 9.34, has attracted emendations, as Feldman (1965: 296, n. 3) notes. But the manuscripts are unanimous here (although they have the plural, διοχλουμένων; Niese [1890a: 241] follows Bekker in emending to the singular:—ου) and LSJ (ibid.) cites a first-century case of it referring to "pressing for payment" (P. Oxy. 286.13), which more or less fits here.

489 Πανοικεσίᾳ. Compare the harsh punishment executed by Herod against some conspirators and "their entire households (πανοικί)" (*Ant.* 15.290).

490 This contradiction between tyranny and liberty is the main point of this long speech. For this notion see also above, §§42, 79. As indicated in the note on "laws" at §15, according to the Roman view, "liberty is based on the laws" and the tyrant is the opposite of rule based on the laws; thus, the tyrant is the enemy of liberty. Tacitus, *Agricola* 3.1, plainly speaks of the incompatibility of the Principate with "liberty" (see also Lucan, *Pharsalia* 691–692). Cf. Wirszubski 1950: 124–171; Hammond 1963.

491 For such euphemistic use of αἴρω for killing, as also at §182, see *ThLJ* 13, where it is labeled as characteristic of *Ant.* 17–19. On such euphemistic usage in general, see the note on "to handle" at §14.

492 ἀπογίνομαι occurs in Josephus only here and at *Ant.* 5.1, where it means "to be dead."

the present and, for the future, lack of conspiracies[493] and the fame that is proper to the success of the city—it is right that you devote your attention to the benefit of all in common and declare a contrary opinion[494] if something already proposed[495] does not please you. 179 That does not at all entail any danger, for he who stands at the head[496] is not a despot[497] who need render no account[498] no matter how he damages the city and does away autocratically with those who have spoken.[499]

180 Indeed, what nurtured the tyranny was nothing new, only [our own] sloth and failure to speak out against anything that it wished.[500] 181 We have fallen under the pleasure[501] of peace[502] and have learned to live in the manner of prisoners,[503] and [all of us, namely], both those who have suffered irremediable evils and those who have [only] seen them [befall] those near[504] them[505]—[living] in fear of dying with virtue[506] we endure until we die with the most extreme shame.

182 But first we must confer the highest honors upon those who eliminated[507] the tyrant, especially Cassius Chaerea;[508] for this one man, together with the gods, has revealed himself as the provider, with his resolve and his hands,[509] of our liberty. 183 It is appropriate that we not forget him. Rather, since while we were still under tyranny he was the first[510] to devote his plans, and to endanger himself,[511] for our liberty,

---

493 Ἀνεπιβούλευτος; see the note on "conspiracy" at §43.

494 This is the only occurrence of ἀνταποφαίνω in Josephus. Wiseman (2013a: 76) points to the only earlier attestations, in Thucydides (3.38.2 and 3.67.3): "Josephus's word choice again points to his conscious borrowing from the master historian" (Steve Mason). Cf. the note on "jurisdiction" at §168.

495 Mason notes: "Josephus is the first known user of this double-compound verb, προεισηγέομαι, which does not appear again until late antiquity. The simpler εἰσηγέ-ομαι ('propose, introduce') is Thucydidean (3.20.1; 4.76.2; 6.99.2; 7.73.1), also common among Athenian philosophers and orators. It is easy to imagine Josephus applying a second prefix for this purpose."

496 This refers, in the present context, first of all to Sentius himself, but also more generally means that in the restored republic that will always be the case.

497 On "despot," see the note on "orders" at §68.

498 This is the only occurrence of ἀνεύθυνος in Josephus.

499 For this opposition of tyranny to free speech, compare Tacitus, *Agricola* 2.

500 An example of this senatorial silence is found in Cassius Dio 59.16.8–9. For this understanding, that tyrannical regimes are made possible by the silence and indolence of "good" people, see *War* 2.276, along with Mason's note ad loc. (2008: 225, n. 1762) on the virtue of honest and free speech as a civic duty, also Ananus's speech on the subject at *War* 4.163–192. Cf. the note on "with them" at 20.180.

501 Josephus employs τερπνός only here and at *War* 3.53. For the idea of "falling under pleasure," cf. the note on "passions for her" at §193.

502 Compare Tacitus, *Hist.* 1.88: "The leading men of the Senate were weak from old age and had grown inactive through a long peace."

503 For life under the emperors or tyrants as being the equivalent of slavery see also below, §227, where the senators are said to have "the ambition to get out from under the servitude that had been imposed upon them by the hubris of tyrants"; cf. Cassius Dio 46.32.1, 34.4. For the combination of the tranquility of peace and the willing acceptance of slavery, see also Sallust, *Hist.* 1 fr. 49.24–25; Tacitus, *Ann.* 1.2; Wirszubski 1950: 91–96.

504 This is the only occurrence of πέλας in Josephus.

505 For the same distinction, see §14.

506 That is, we live because we fear to die virtuously. On Roman *virtus*, see the note on "virtuous" at §171.

507 Cf. the note on "completely" at §177.

508 Throughout Josephus's narrative it is stressed that Chaerea was the hero of the assassination (§§23, 27, 37, 45, 70, 83–84, 105, and esp. §§111–113); cf. the note on "Chaerea" at §111.

509 Compare above, §113: the deed "should be accounted to the credit of Chaerea's will, his virtue, and the work of his hands."

510 I use this translation to reflect the emphatic prefixes of the two verbs here: προβεβουλευκότος ... προκεκιν-δυνευκότος. Again, compare above, §111–113: "he was the first to ponder how to do it ... and he was also the first to speak out boldly about it to others ... he was clearly the first who moved and took the assassination in hand courageously."

511 This is the only appearance of προκινδυνεύω in *Antiquities*, but it does appear several times in *War*.

now, when we are under liberty, declaring[512] him honors should be the first thing we decide as unsubjugated[513] men. **184** It is a most proper deed, appropriate to free men, to requite benefactors,[514] such as this man has been for all of us. He is not at all close, in comparison, to Cassius and Brutus who killed Gaius Julius,[515] for while they, after all, stirred up[516] civil strife[517] and wars in the city, he, along with the killing of the tyrant,[518] also freed the city from the terrors for which [the tyrant][519] had been responsible.

(2.3) **185** Those were Sentius's words, and they were well received by the senators and by all of the equites who were present. But then one Trebellius Maximus[520] jumped up and pulled off Sentius's ring, to which was attached a stone engraved with the image of Gaius,[521]

---

512 This use of ἀποφήνασθαι reminds readers of the admonition with ἀνταποφήνασθαι at §178.

513 This is the only occurrence of ἀνεπίτακτος in Josephus.

514 On benefactors, see the note on "benefit" at 18.95.

515 That is, the assassination of Julius Caesar on the Ides of March, 44 BCE. Josephus briefly mentioned Julius Caesar's assassination in *War* 1.218 and *Ant.* 14.270. Wiseman (2013a: 77) notes the rare form for Julius Caesar's name, Gaius Julius, here as well as in Tacitus, *Hist.* 1.50, instead of the more conventional Gaius Caesar, and suggests that it may have been used to avoid confusion with Gaius Caligula. But note "Julius Caesar" earlier in this same speech, above at §173. Such outright praise of the emperor/tyrant-killers and a positive comparison to the assassins of Julius Caesar was very problematic and dangerous during the Principate, and especially during the reigns of such emperors as Gaius, Nero, and Domitian. Authors were prosecuted for writing praise of Brutus and Cassius and their books were burned (Tacitus, *Ann.* 4.34–35), although those assassins were long dead, and the portraits of Brutus and Cassius could not even be shown in the funeral procession of Junia, Brutus's sister and Cassius's wife (Tacitus, *Ann.* 3.76); for similar reports, see *Ann.* 4.34 and 16.7. During Domitian's reign—at which time Josephus was writing this work—authors who wrote in praise of opponents of past emperors suffered a similar fate along with their works (Tacitus, *Agricola* 2; Suetonius, *Dom.* 10; Pliny, *Ep.* 7.19; Cassius Dio 67.13.2). Thus, this praise of the assassins of Caesar and even higher praise of those of Gaius, which Josephus puts at the very end of Sentius's speech, is significant and exceptional. Cf. Mason 2003c: esp. 559–560: idem 2005a: 252–254, 273–274.

516 This is the only occurrence of ἐπαναρριπίζω in extant ancient Greek literature. As often with the double prefix ἐπαν-, it may be that the nuance is "stirred up *again*," namely, the years of Julius Caesar's tyranny were peaceful but were preceded by civil strife and that

resumed after his death, while Gaius's reign was characterized by tyranny and Chaerea had now freed the city from that. Cf. Mason 2008, 215, n. 1673, on similar language in *War* 2.265.

517 Στάσις; see the note on "strife" at 18.8. Likewise, Suetonius reports that his father had told him "that Otho ... so loathed civil strife, that at the mere mention of the fate of Brutus and Cassius at a banquet he shuddered" (Suetonius, *Otho* 10.1, trans. Rolfe, LCL), and Cassius Dio (44.1) opens his narrative of the assassination of Julius Caesar by asserting that it "brought upon the Romans seditions and civil wars once more after a state of harmony. His slayers ... threw the city into disorder when at last it possessed a stable government" (trans. Cary, LCL). Indeed, the assassination of Julius Caesar led to renewed civil strife. However, the assassination of Gaius too brought Rome to the brink of civil war, as even the present scene shows (and see below, §§241–243 and *War* 2.205).

518 Τυραννοκτονία. See the note on "tyrannicide" at §63.

519 I renderedd ἐντεῦθεν according to its apparent sense here. A more natural reading would seem to imply that the assassination caused terrible things but Chaerea prevented them, but it does not seem that Josephus's narrative or interpretation supports such a claim.

520 Probably M. Trebellius Maximus, who was suffect consul in 55 or 56. He was sent with others to carry out an assessment of Gaul in 61 (Tacitus, *Ann.* 14.46), and was governor of Britain from 63 to 69 (Tacitus, *Hist.* 1.60; *Agricola* 16). Either this Trebellius or his father commanded Roman forces active in Cappadocia in 36 CE (Tacitus, *Ann.* 6.41).

521 A comprehensive description of the wearing of rings, as signets and as ornaments, is given by Pliny in *NH*, 33.8–13, 17–34, 41; 37.1–11. Pliny explains that golden rings were a mark distinguishing the equites from the plebs (33.29–34). Most important, for the present

which—so he assumed—[Sentius] had ignored,[522] being taken up with his zeal in speaking and planning what to do. The image was smashed into pieces. **186** It was now far into the night, and Chaerea asked the consuls for the password; they gave "liberty."[523] And they were amazed: what was happening[524] was nigh unbelievable! **187** For it was in [precisely[525]] the hundredth year, counting from when the democracy[526] had first been set aside,[527] that the giving of the password [had now reverted[528]] to the consuls. For before the city became subject to tyrants it was [the consuls] who had ruled the soldiers.[529]

188 Chaerea, having received the password, passed it on to the soldiers who had joined together with the Senate. They amounted to about four[530] cohorts,[531] for whom being

---

context, is Pliny's description of a first-century custom of wearing rings with effigies (33.41), including images of the emperor. On ancient and Roman rings see Marshall 1907: xv–xxi, and the descriptions of the rings engraved with figures on pp. 22–31, 39–49, 71–86. Especially with regard to Pliny's evidence, and the ring's function as suggesting status and power (but also hinting at effeminacy [cf. §30]), see Hawley 2007, also Spier 1992.

522 Barrett 2019: 272 points to this ring as evidence that Sentius could not have supported the republican ideals Josephus ascribed him. However, that seems to be only a remnant of the same passage in the first edition (1989: 174), in which Barrett also stated that Josephus reported that Sentius was himself a candidate to succeed Gaius. The latter, which is unfounded, was not repeated in the second edition, and probably some of the earlier skepticism should have gone with it. There is, however, some justification for Timpe's observation (1960: 476) that this scene subverts the speech's pathos ("eine hintergründige Entlarvung und Abwertung dieses Pathos"), as if to say that even senators who expressed the most high-sounding principles and opposition to imperial rule were not above kowtowing to it. See the introduction to Book 19. The effect is similar to that of the move from *Ant.* 15.423, where all are said to be so happy about Herod's completion of the reconstruction of the Sanctuary, to the very next lines, which report that Herod built a secret tunnel on the Temple Mount in order to provide himself with a means of escape in case a popular revolt broke out against him.

523 Above, at §54, Chaerea was said to have hopefully characterized Vinicianus, who was not a consul, as giving him this same password; now it really happens. See also Hammond 1963: 98.

524 For τὰ δρώμενα see also 20.191.

525 I have added this because the point seems to be that the number of years is striking particularly because it is so round. Cf. the note on "date" at §95.

526 I.e., the Republic; see the note on "democracy" at §162.

527 Above, at §173, the "democracy" was said to have been destroyed by Julius Caesar, but without specifying which point in his career, and a few points are possible. Thus, for example, Lucan points back to Caesar's defeat of Pompey in the battle of Pharsalus in 48 BCE (see Lucan, *Pharsalia* 7.691ff.), and apparently so does Appian (*Preface*, 6). However, as Wiseman asserts, the hundred years mentioned here point back to the establishment of the coalition between Julius Caesar, Pompey, and Crassus in 60 BCE (the first "triumvirate"), and/or to Julius Caesar's first consulate, in 59 BCE (cf. above, §173)—which is especially apposite insofar as Gaius was the last of his dynasty (Wiseman 1992: 10). Indeed, in 59 BCE Cicero wrote that the Republic is ruined and its "constitution is completely lost to us" (*rem publicum funditus amisimus*; Cicero, *Ep. Ad Quintum Fratrem* 1.2.15 and *Ep. Ad. Atticus* 2.21.1); see Wirszubski 1950: 74–76. See further the note on "democracy" at §173, where accounts that point instead to Augustus are also noted, and compare §228, where the days of Pompey are characterized as a period of civil strife.

528 It appears that a verb like this is missing from the Greek here; see Feldman 1965: 300, n. 5.

529 As is reported at Polybius 6.34.5–6.

530 Thackeray (*ThLJ* 221, s.v. εἰς) characterizes Josephus's use of εἰς with numbers as "occasional." Josephus seems to mean that the number of soldiers who came together as individuals, those who preferred the emperor-less situation, amounted to about the number of soldiers in four cohorts, that is, around 2000 men. However, the parallel at *War* 2.205 reports that *three* cohorts remained loyal to the Senate. That sounds like organized cohorts, not individuals. Indeed, Suetonius (*Claud.* 10.3), who speaks about this same event, explicitly reports that the urban cohorts were loyal to the Senate, and Tacitus reports (*Ann.* 4.5) that there were, at the time, three such cohorts. As for Josephus's datum here, referring to four: a fourth was added in Claudius's day, and it may be that Josephus, or his source, thought that was the case in Gaius's day as well. On the urban cohorts, see Southern 2007: 119.

531 For the use of σπεῖρα for a Roman *cohors*, a unit of around five hundred men (see Coello 1996: 1–11 and Webster 1998: 148–149), see GTRI 85, 163.

without a king[532] was viewed as more respectable than tyranny. **189** These then went off with the military tribunes, and the people too were already returning to their homes,[533] very joyous and in hope and good spirits about having regained rule of themselves, no more [being dependent] upon someone placed above them. And Chaerea was everything for them.[534]

Loose Ends: The Assassination of Gaius's Wife and Daughter

(2.4) 190 But Chaerea was very worried by the fact that Gaius's daughter[535] and wife[536] still survived, and that perdition had not befallen his whole family[537] along with him. For any one of them that survived would remain a threat of perdition to the city and the laws. Moreover, he was dead-set to complete his plan and fully to gratify his hatred for Gaius.[538] So he dispatched Julius Lupus, one of the tribunes,[539] to kill Gaius's wife and daughter. **191** They put Lupus in charge of this job because he was a relative of Clemens,[540] so that by taking part even to this [relatively minor] extent in the tyrannicide he might glory in virtue in the eyes of the public and be thought to have been a partner of those who from the outset began to conspire.[541] **192** True, a few of the conspirators thought it was even cruel for him to be bold against the woman, for Gaius had been following his own nature and not her advice in doing all the things he did—things that exhausted[542] the city[543] by the evils that took

---

532 Apart from here, ἀβασίλευτος appears in Josephus only at 18.44. On the negative phrasing of the issue, "being without a king," cf. the note on "democracy" at §162.

533 This partially parallels §160 above.

534 Earlier, in contrast, we read that the *hoi polloi* were in favor of the Principate in general and Gaius in particular (see above, §§115, 158–159, and below, §§227–228). But such generalizations are cheap, and anyway Josephus loves to complain about the fickleness of urban riffraff; cf. the note on "upon them" at §157.

535 Julia Drusilla; see the note on "daughter" at §11.

536 Gaius's wife was Milonia Caesonia (below, §195), towards whom Gaius appears to have had genuine affection. Suetonius (*Cal.* 25.3) describes her as "neither beautiful nor young," and says she was already the mother of three daughters by another man; Wardle (1998: 122–123), accordingly, suggests that Gaius married her because of her proven fertility, given his need for an heir. See further Barrett 2019: 132–135. On Gaius's previous wives, see Suetonius, *Cal.* 12, 25.1–2 and Wardle 1998.

537 Thus, below at §258, he also asks for the head of Claudius.

538 Barrett (2019: 260) argues that, in fact, their murder had been decided upon in advance, so that Caesonia would not "become a focus of resentment and resistance," and was carried out immediately after the assassination of Gaius. Therefore, he argues, Josephus's coming account of her lying alongside her husband's corpse is "a poetic elaboration." He argues that (a) Caesonia would certainly

have escaped and not remained near the corpse, (b) it is unlikely that the conspirators would have given her this window of time to escape, and (c) the palace appears to have been under the control of the Praetorian Guard very soon after the assassination.

539 This Julius Lupus is not otherwise known. Suetonius (*Cal.* 59) mentions a centurion, but does not name him. Perhaps he was the father of Tiberius Iulius Lupus, who was the Roman governor in Egypt in 72–73, known, *inter alia*, from *War* 7.420–434; see Bastianini 1975: 275 and Cotton and Geiger 1989: 62–67.

540 The commander of the Praetorian Guard.; see the note on "Clemens" at §37. Townend (1961: 57–58) suggested that Clemens may have been married to Lupus's sister.

541 Levick (1990: 37–38) takes Josephus here to mean that the purpose of using Lupus was to implicate Clemens in the conspiracy. Wiseman (2013a: 80) agrees that that was the actual historical motive, but emphasizes that Josephus himself is not clear about Clemens's involvement; see §§37–47. Be that as it may, it is clear that the present passage, by explaining Lupus's involvement as the result of some devious consideration, undercuts his role in comparison to that of Chaerea. For the same goal served in another way, see §§269–271.

542 ἀπαγορεύω, as at 18.366. For the same idea as here, see §§2, 246.

543 See the note on "harrying and plundering" at §2.

hold of it and destroyed any citizen who even only began to blossom.[544] **193** But others[545] charged that it was at her will that even such things [happened], laying upon her the guilt[546] for all those wicked things that had been done by Gaius, for [they said] she had given Gaius a drug that had been provided[547] [to her] in order to enslave his thoughts and secure[548] his passions for her,[549] and it drove him into insanity[550]—so she was the one who had fitted out the ship[551] against the fortunes of the Romans and of the world subject to them.[552]

194 In the end it was determined that she must die, for even the efforts of those who zealously opposed[553] it were without avail, and Lupus was sent. He did not at all delay in performing what he had to do, so as not to fulfill in proper time what he had been sent to take care of, for he desired in no way to be subject to censure[554] in performing what was of advantage to the populace. **195** Upon coming to the palace he encountered Caesonia, Gaius's wife, lying alongside the body of her husband, which was lying on the floor[555] without any of those things that the law graciously bestows upon the dead.[556] She was smeared[557] with blood from his wounds and suffering greatly; and her daughter had thrown herself down beside[558] her. In such a state nothing was heard apart from her blaming of Gaius, that he had not accepted as convincing what she had so often warned. **196** Even at the time that statement was taken both ways, and today as well those who hear of it may equally well give more weight to whichever interpretation they prefer. [Namely], some say the statement meant that she had advised him to give up his mad measures and cruelty to the citizens, instead ruling affairs moderately and virtuously, while he would destroy himself if he

---

544 That is, anyone who even only began to shine. Cf. the note on "blossomed" at §168.

545 Josephus's recourse to "others" here allows him to solve a problem. On the one hand, he loves to complain about wives who do not know their place and bring catastrophe upon their husbands, and in particular he (as others: see the note on "insanity" later in this paragraph) likes to report that they resort to drugs (15.222–229 [a double opportunity for Josephus, which allows him to condemn both Herod's conniving sister and his arrogant wife!], 18.352, 20.148); but on the other hand he does not want to portray Gaius as an innocent victim. By attributing the condemnation of Caesonia to others, Josephus has his cake and eats it too.

546 For the same collocation, see the note on "brought against" at §137.

547 For this sense of ψηφίζω, see also §43.

548 See the note on "secure" at §43.

549 Josephus likes to portray men who lose their heads over women and are thereby "enslaved" by them, such as David (7.130), Marcus Antonius (*War* 1.243) and Herod's brother Pheroras (*Ant.* 16.194–200). Note also the case of Mundus (18.68), along with the note on "more severe penalty" at 18.80.

550 That Caesonia gave Gaius an aphrodisiac drug that drove him to madness is reported by Suetonius, *Cal.* 50.2, and Juvenal (*Satires* 6.614–625) cites the case of Caesonia's poisoning of Gaius as an example of wives who use "Thessalian potions which enable a wife to confuse her husband's mind and beat him on the buttocks

with her sandal." Barrett (2019: 285) asserts that this claim should be discounted, suggesting that it "perhaps arose to explain Caesonia's strange hold over her husband," and H. Lindsay (1993: 156) suggests that it was propaganda by the conspirators intended to justify her murder.

551 Elsewhere, Josephus usually uses ναυπηγ- literally, of ship-building (*War* 1.280; *Ant.* 8.163 and 16.147). Here, however, it is used of the "ship of state"; for that image, see esp. Plato, *Republic* 6.488a–489d, along with Castillio 2010.

552 Cf. the note on "earth and sea" at §1.

553 This is the only occurrence of ἀποσπεύδω in Josephus.

554 This is the only occurrence of μεμπτός in Josephus.

555 This is the only occurrence of χαμαιπετής in Josephus.

556 The Roman custom was to wash, anoint, and dress the corpse according to the deceased person's status and place a coin in its mouth, then to lay it on a bed surrounded by torches, while family and servants sing the lamentation of the dead. This lying-in-state period would last a few days, followed by the funeral procession and the cremation (Toynbee 1971: 43–61, esp. 43–48). Some of these will later be done to Gaius's corpse by Agrippa (§237).

557 This is the only occurrence of ἀναφύρω in Josephus.

558 This is the only occurrence of παρρρίπτω in Josephus.

[continued to] behave according to his own nature. **197** Others, however, [think that] word of the conspirators had made its way around[559] and she had urged Gaius not at all to delay but, rather, immediately[560] to get rid of all of them, even if they had not done anything unjust, so as to leave himself free from dangers—and that that is what she now blamed him about, that he had been too soft to carry out what she had told him, in advance, that he should do. **198** That, then, is what Caesonia said and what people thought about it.

When she saw Lupus's approach she pointed to Gaius's corpse and called upon him, with wailing and tears, to come nearer.[561] **199** But when she saw that Lupus was firm in his attitude and was not at all approaching her as if it were for a task he found distasteful, she realized what he had come to do, bared her throat very willingly,[562] and, lamenting as is appropriate for those who have with full certainty given up on their lives, urged him not to put off the completion[563] of the drama they had composed for them.[564] **200** Thus she died there, bravely,[565] at the hand of Lupus; and along with her, her young daughter[566] too.[567] And Lupus hurried off to be the first to report it to Chaerea's men.

Gaius Caligula: Summng Up

(2.5) 201 This, then, was the way Gaius died, after ruling the Romans for four months short of four years.[568] He was a man who even prior to coming to power[569] had reached the peak of brutality[570] and malice, one who was under the control of pleasure[571] and a lover of

---

559 This is the same use of ἐπιφοιτάω as above at §134. For the possibility that word of the conspiracy had gotten around, see §§19, 46–47, 62, 91–92, 132–133.

560 On μηδὲν εἰς ἀναβολὰς ἀλλ᾽ ἐκ τοῦ ὀξέος, which combines (as at 17.187, 312; 18.107, 309) two of Josephus's favorite phrases, see the notes on "without delay" at 18.107 and on "immediately" at 18.58.

561 Josephus uses ἆσσον only here and at 1.328.

562 This is in stark contrast to Lupus's behavior at his own execution later—where it is contrasted explicitly with that of Chaerea: he "was cowardly about extending his neck" (below, §271). For the noble bravery evinced by baring one's own throat, cf. Josephus's accounts of Jews at 18.59, 271, also the note on "courage" at 18.333.

563 Τελειώσει. Compare Chaerea's determination to "complete (τελειώσασθαι) his plan," above at §190.

564 I.e., the "drama" that the conspirators had put together for her and her daughter. Josephus frequently uses συντίθημι of the conspirators' plotting; see §§45, 156, 191 (along with 20.54, 153, etc.). For its use for "composing" a literary work, see e.g., §208. In comparing the fate that the conspirators had assigned her to a "drama," Josephus's Caesonia plays with both senses.

565 For Josephus's admiration of those who know death is imminent and accept it with εὐψυχία, compare esp. 6.350 and 14.367. More generally, cf. the note on "courage" at 18.333.

566 Θυγάτριον. This is the only occurrence of this diminutive form in Josephus. Julia Drusilla was probably born in the summer of 39 (see the note on "daughter"

at §11), so she will have been about a year and a half old at this point.

567 According to Suetonius (*Cal.* 59), Caesonia was killed by being stabbed with a sword and Julia Drusilla's "brains were dashed out against the wall." Dio (59.29.7) simply mentions that they were murdered, without any details; so too Plutarch, *Antony* 87.4.

568 So too *War* 2.204. Counting from Tiberius's death (16 March 37) to Gaius's (24 Jan. 41), Suetonius's datum of three years, ten months and eight days (*Cal.* 59) is much more precise. Cassius Dio 59.30.1 gives three years, nine months, and twenty-eight days. For ambiguities concerning the date an emperor's rule began, see Mason 2008: 168, n. 1273. For the debate about the precise day of his death, see the note on "final day" at §77.

569 This is seemingly contradicted later in this same obituary, at §210, where Gaius is said to have been corrupted by his rise to power. Similarly, at 18.256, Josephus wrote that during the first two years of his reign Gaius ruled "very magnanimously," a view shared by others; see the note there on "respect for the divine."

570 Cf. the note on "brutal" at 18.44.

571 Compare above, Sentius's statement that Julius Caesar had been "under the control of whatever brought pleasure to him personally" (§173), also §§43, 176, 207, etc. On this common Josephan theme (see already 5.179: "once they [the Hebrews] deviated from the order of their constitution, they turned to living in accordance with pleasure and their own will"), see Mason 2016a: cxlviii–cxlix. The ninth book of Plato's *Republic* is the classic

slander,[572] terrorized by things that made him afraid[573] and therefore most murderous[574] against those he dared [to attack]. He endowed himself with full authority with only one single aim—to behave outrageously, treating with ridiculous generosity those who least deserved it[575] and supplying [it all] by murder and [other] illegal behavior. 202 He was anxious both to be and to seem greater than the deity[576] and the law,[577] although he was subservient to the multitude's[578] words of praise, and he considered virtuous[579] all acts for which the law, adjudging them shameful, imposes punishment.[580] 203 Nor would he recall friendship, no matter how great it had been[581] and for what great causes, and once he was angry at people he would strike out and punish them even for the most minor reason.[582] Anything that happened in consonance with virtue he considered hostile, and it was impossible to oppose him[583] about anything he felt an urge[584] to ordain.[585] 204 For that reason he even had sexual intercourse with his full sister[586]—on account of which the citizens' hatred for him began to grow even more vehement,[587] for the fact that for a great period of time nothing [of the kind] had ever been reported[588] invited [first] incredulity and [then] hostility toward the one who had done it. 205 No one could mention any great work or palace

---

ancient account of the tyrant as a pleasure-seeker; on it, see Nielsen 2019.

572 So too in Gaius's description by his contemporary Seneca (*Const.* 18.1).

573 For his extreme fearfulness, cf. Suetonius, *Cal.* 51.

574 Superlative of φονικός, which is used in *Antiquities* only here and at §34.

575 Gaius's favors to those he liked are the theme of Suetonius, *Cal.* 55; as the present passage, so too Suetonius focuses on those unworthy of such attention, such as an actor, some gladiators, and his horse (on whom see the note on "horses" at §257).

576 See §11 where, as at Suetonius, *Cal.* 33, he is said to have questioned which divinity was greater, Jupiter or himself. In general, on Gaius's divine pretensions, see the note on "mortal" at §4.

577 See the note on "laws" at §15; see also §§57, 156, 168, 173.

578 That is, he was enslaved by the need to be praised by the πλῆθος, which, our aristocratic author (Josephus or his source) believed, was in fact unworthy of anyone's respect; see the note on "multitude" at 18.26.

579 On the Roman notion of *virtus*, see the note on "virtuous" at §171.

580 For such a formulation of the radical contradiction between his behavior and the law, cf. Tacitus's condemnation of the Jews: "The Jews regard as profane all that we hold sacred; on the other hand, they permit all that we abhor" (*Hist.* 5.4.1, trans. Moore, LCL).

581 See above, §156: "he taught those who were his closest friends to make war upon him, by treating them outrageously and intolerably," and the note there, as well as below, §211.

582 For such brutality, see Suetonius, *Cal.* 26–33.

583 Josephus uses ἀναντίλεκτος elsewhere only at §24 and 3.5.

584 Josephus uses ἐπιθυμία with λαμβάνω for a passion for a woman at 7.134 and 20.142—which conforms to the use of ὅθεν at the outset of §204.

585 Compare his reply to his own grandmother, according to Suetonius (*Cal.* 29.1): "Remember that I have the right to do anything to anybody." See also ibid. 32.3 and 33.

586 For the use of γνήσιος to denote siblings who share both parents, see the note on "legitimate" at 18.40. Here the reference is to Julia Drusilla, Gaius's favorite sister. Both Cassius Dio (59.3.6, 26.5) and Suetonius (*Cal.* 24.1) report that Gaius had incestuous relations with all of his sisters, and Suetonius especially mentions his affection towards Drusilla, with whom he is said to have had relations already as a minor (cf. Dio 59.11.1). Barrett (2019: 117–121), although he accepts that Gaius was particularly attached to Drusilla. is skeptical about these reports of incest with his sisters, pointing to the fact that it is not mentioned by his contemporaries Philo and Seneca, nor by Tacitus—but even if it were, in the nature of things we would still wonder what those writers had for evidence, apart from their hostility. For this kind of vilification, cf. 20.145.

587 This again asserts popular antipathy toward Gaius in agreement with some other passages (§§189, 191, 272) and opposition to others (§§115, 158).

588 For such hyperbole, see the note on "recorded" at §1. For a previous instance, Wiseman (2013a: 205) points to reports that P. Clodius (first century BCE) had incestuous relations with his sisters (Plutarch, *Cicero* 29.4–5).

constructed by him for the benefit of his contemporaries,[589] nor for that of future generations, apart, of course, from [the harbor] around Rhegium and Sicily[590] that he planned
to build to receive the grain-bearing ships from Egypt. 206 That admittedly would have
been great and most useful for ship-goers. But it did not come to completion, but was left
half-done[591] because of the rather sluggish[592] way in which he pursued the project. 207
The reason was his zeal for useless things and for spending on pleasures that would benefit
him alone,[593] which undermined his ambition to do things that, as all agree,[594] would have
been greater.[595]

208 Nonetheless,[596] he was a topflight orator, quite practiced both in the Greek language
and in the ancestral language of the Romans, and he understood how to reply on the spot
to the [speeches] composed by others even if they had prepared them long in advance,
immediately showing himself more convincing than anyone else concerning a great
matter[597]—all that due to his natural ability[598] for this and to his bolstering its strength by
practicing[599] the effort. 209 For being the son of the son of the brother of Tiberius,[600] whose
successor he became, there was a great necessity of gaining education, for he himself[601] had
succeeded in it with first-class distinction,[602] and Gaius was just as enthusiastic [for educa-
tion], complying with the orders of the man who was both his relative and his ruler, and
[thus] he stood above and beyond the other citizens of his day.

---

589 Josephus exaggerates, for other sources do report quite a few building projects undertaken by Gaius. He is said to have attempted to build a canal across the Isthmus of Corinth (Pliny, *NH* 4.10; Suetonius, *Cal.* 21), and to have begun building necessary aqueducts in Rome that were ultimately finished by Claudius (Pliny, *NH* 36.122; Suetonius, *Cal.* 21; Frontinus, *Aq.* 13). Suetonius reports that "he built villas and country houses" and some other extravagant projects (*Cal.* 37.2–3), and also lists some projects he completed (the Temple of Augustus and the Theater of Pompey, of which construction began under Tiberius, and repairs of the city walls and temples at Syracuse) and others he planned: "to rebuild the palace of Polycrates at Samos, to finish the temple of Didymaean Apollo at Miletus, to found a city high up in the Alps" (*Cal.* 21). See further Barrett 2019: 223–246 ("Caligula the Builder").

590 Rhegium (modern Reggio Calabria) is located vis-à-vis Sicily at the western tip of the Italian "boot."

591 As I was kindly informed in July 2021 by the National Archaeological Museum of Reggio Calabria, there seem to be no known remains of the project.

592 See the note on "sluggish" at 18.173.

593 Dio (59.4.5) likewise describes him as spending money unsparingly, and Suetonius, *Cal.* 37, further details his costly extravagant lifestyle, such as drinking expensive pearls dissolved in vinegar and serving his guests food made of gold.

594 For Josephus's use of the post-classical ἀνομολο-γέομαι "agree" and the suggestion of "doubtless, undisputed" for the participial instance here, see *CCFJ* 1.137.

595 That is, all agree that Gaius had the potential for better—as §208 will now begin to demonstrate.

596 On Josephus's use of ἄλλως, see the note on "otherwise" at 18.19. Here it serves to open the "on the other hand" part of Josephus's summary. As Mason (2016a: cxliii) notes, Josephus frequently gives balanced "obituaries" when taking leave of major characters. Note, for example, his studied evenhandedness about Samson (*Ant.* 5.316–317), Salome (13.430–432), Mariamme (15.237–239), and Herod (17.191–192); for his extended discussion of how Herod could be both generous and cruel, see 16.150–159.

597 His oratorical skills are also noted by Suetonius (*Cal.* 53), who claimed that Gaius was very boastful of those skills, asserting that, in contrast to him, his contemporary Seneca "composed 'mere school exercises.'" Cassius Dio (59.19.3–8) also emphasizes this point and Gaius's claim "to surpass all the orators." See also Tacitus, *Ann.* 13.3. The *Suda* even attributes to Gaius a Latin book on oratory. See further Barrett 2019: 68–69 and Faur 1978.

598 This is the only occurrence of εὐκολία in Josephus.

599 For μελέτη in this sense, compare esp. §270.

600 Gaius's father, Germanicus, was the son of Tiberius's brother, Drusus the Elder.

601 Tiberius. Recall that Gaius spent years with Tiberius in Capri and elsewhere; Barrett 2019: 43–54.

602 For Tiberius's studies and education see Suetonius, *Tib.* 56, 57.1, 70; Philo, *Leg.* 142; Smallwood 1970: 227; Levick 1999: 15–18.

210 But all the boons that accrued to him via his education could not withstand the corruption that came upon him because of the authority [with which he was endowed upon becoming emperor];[603] indeed, for those for whom it is easy to act without being accountable,[604] the virtue of self-control[605] can be procured only with difficulty.[606] **211** In his beginnings he assiduously[607] cultivated friends and especially respectable ones, due to his education and his reputation for being zealous for greater things, until with the coming of hubris[608] he divested himself[609] of the goodwill that they had exhibited toward him[610]—and so when hatred grew up secretly in its stead,[611] he was killed as a result of their conspiracy.

(3.1) 212 As for Claudius,[612] already above[613] I have stated that there had been a parting[614] between his and Gaius's paths. When the palace was thrown into turmoil on account of the excitement attending upon Caesar's death, [Claudius], not knowing what to do [to ensure] his safety, and finding himself cut off[615] in a narrow passageway,[616] hid himself, although having no reason to suspect any danger, apart from his being a member of the

Soldiers Kidnap Claudius to the Imperial Throne

603 As noted, this is in tension with §201.

604 Elsewhere, Josephus uses ἀνυπεύθυνος only at 16.398 and *War* 1.469; ὑπεύθυνος appears at 2.146, 7.39 and 14.258.

605 On self-control, see the note at 18.66.

606 This is the only occurrence of δυσπόριστος in Josephus. For such general comments about human nature and life, cf. §§296, 319, also, for example, 6.341, *War* 1.208, and *Life* 80. For the theme that power corrupts good people, see Josephus's more elaborate statement at *Ant.* 6.262–267.

607 This is the only attested appearance of this compound verb, ὑποσπουδάζω. Feldman (1965: 312) suggests emending it into ὑπερσπουδάζω, for the prefix makes better sense, and the verb, although rare, does appear elsewhere in Josephus (15.69).

608 On such a turnabout in Gaius's character, see the note on "for the divine" at 18.256.

609 This is the only occurrence of ἀπαμφίασις in Josephus, and gave rise to variant readings and to the notation "dub[ious]" in LSJ 177, s.v., where it is rendered "putting off." The apparent meaning is that Gaius first enjoyed popular goodwill and it served to protect him, but eventually he behaved in a way that caused him to forfeit it.

610 Compare *Ant.* 6.267, in Josephus's statement mentioned in the note on "difficulty" at §210.

611 I.e., instead of the goodwill. Compare 15.44 (according to most witnesses), the only other occurrence of ὑποφύω in Josephus; there too the subject is μῖσος.

612 Josephus's readers, who of course know that Claudius succeeded Gaius on the imperial throne, will

recognize here not only a return to a thread of the narrative, but also the announcement of the next chapter of imperial history. At this point, the story changes from the struggle of liberty-seeking conspirators, supported by senators, against a tyrannical emperor, in which the Senate is on the right side, to the struggle between the army, which was powerful and desired an emperor, and the Senate, which unrealistically wanted to restore the Republic but did nothing but talk. On Claudius's rise to power, see Momigliano 1961: 20–22; Scramuzza 1940: 51–63; Levick 1990: 29–39. The first part of this narrative, concerning the discovery of Claudius, repeats some details already noted earlier in this book (§§162–165) and also presents some views—such as popular support for the Principate, and specifically for Claudius, along with scorn for the Senate—that contrast with the earlier narrative, as is noted by Wiseman 2013a: xiv–xv.

613 §103.

614 This is the only occurrence of ἀπόρρηξις in Josephus. The use of the noun allows Josephus to avoid saying who deviated from whom. According to §102–103, Claudius and his party took the usual route and Gaius departed from it.

615 "Cut off," suggested here by *CCFJ* 2.442, s.v. καταλαμβάνω, could refer to the assassins' intentional separation of the crowd from the emperor (see above §101 and Suetonius, *Cal.* 58.3). Suetonius, *Claud.* 10.3 reports explicitly that Claudius was shut out with the rest of the crowd.

616 Above, at §162, Claudius is only said to have been in the palace, just as Dio (60.1.2) simply writes that Claudius hid "in a dark corner somewhere." Suetonius (*Claud.* 10.1) specifies that Claudius withdrew to an

nobility.[617] **213** For he had conducted himself moderately as a private citizen, being content with what he had,[618] devoting himself to learning[619] and especially to Greek[620] and keeping himself far from anything that in any way tended to disorder. **214** But now panic took hold of the mob and the entire palace was filled with the soldiers' rage at the same time that the bodyguards[621] were taken over by a cowardice and disorderliness [appropriate to] private citizens.[622] They (those of them who were there), termed the "Praetorian Guard,"[623] who were the fittest[624] unit of the entire army, were in consultation as to what was to be done[625]—although they gave little consideration to avenging Gaius, for [they considered that] his fortune was just. **215** Rather, they were surveying their own[626] situation [in order to decide] what path would be proper,[627] just as the Germans[628] were busy punishing the assassins[629] more to satisfy their own cruelty than to serve the commonweal.[630]

---

apartment called the Hermaeum and "hid among the curtains which hung before the door" of a balcony there.

617 It is not clear whether this means that Claudius had no reason to fear danger, for he had given no offense, even apart from the fact that being a member of the nobility (and imperial family) meant no one would dare hurt him (cf. §102) or, rather, that although Claudius had no reason to fear danger on his own account, being a member of the nobility (and imperial family) could make him an object of indiscriminate violence in the wake of the assassination.

618 For Claudius's lack of political ambition, whether innate or after initial rebuffs, see also Suetonius, *Claud.* 5. Nevertheless, Claudius had held some offices of state, including the consulship for two months alongside Gaius (ibid. 6–7).

619 Claudius's devotion to learning is also mentioned above, at §164. Suetonius (*Claud.* 3.1) reports that from early on he devoted serious attention to liberal studies and published his work in various fields, also that he wrote a history, an autobiography, and a "Defense of Cicero," invented three new letters and published a book on their theory (ibid. 41) and another on the art of gaming (ibid. 33.2). Cassius Dio (60.2.1) also mentions his mental ability (cf. Tacitus, *Ann.* 6.46) and that he composed historical treatises. Pliny's references to Claudius as a source (e.g., *NH* 5.63; 6.27, 31) probably refer to his historical works; see the next note.

620 Suetonius reports that Claudius took "every occasion to declare his regard for that language and its superiority," replied to Greek envoys in Greek, quoted Homer from the tribune, and "even wrote historical works in Greek, twenty books of Etruscan history and eight of Carthaginian" (Suetonius, *Claud.* 42). His use of Greek, quoting of Homer, and writing of history are also attested in Seneca's satire, *Apocolocyntosis* (§5). See further Momigliano 1961: 1–19 and Levick 1990: 17–20, and recall that Claudius "grew up together" (18.165) with Agrippa I who, like his brother Herod, preferred Greek; see the note on "Romans" at §275.

621 As is explained immediately below, Josephus is referring here to the Praetorian Guards. See the note on "bodyguards" at §119.

622 As Thackeray notes (*ThLJ* 70, s.v. ἀπολαμβάνειν, fin), "text and meaning doubtful." Schalit (1963: 338) understands that the populace was afraid of the bodyguards, while Wiseman (2013a: 32) suggests that Josephus meant the populace was as cowardly as mercenaries. I have translated on the assumption that Josephus means that the Praetorians were at first at a loss as to what to do, although such indecision is what an aristocrat like Josephus would like to expect from lowly common citizens.

623 Here Josephus uses another term for the Praetorian Guard, στρατηγικός (see also *GTRI* 86), rather than σωματοφύλαξ, which he uses for the Guard at §§247 and 267, as is usual (*GTRI* 90, s.v.).

624 For such use of καθαρός (lit., "pure," here in the superlative) with regard to army units, see already Herodotus 1.211.2 and 4.135.2, cited in LSJ 850, s.v., §1,6.

625 This meeting of the Praetorian Guard was already mentioned above, at §§162–165.

626 Here the rough breathing (αὑτούς), as in Naber (1893: 242), seems preferable.

627 That is, what path would be to their best advantage, as at §§162–165 above.

628 The emperor's bodyguards (see above, §119).

629 See above, §§123–126.

630 Above, at §§121–122, vengeance appears to be their more prominent motive.

216 Claudius was upset by all of this, fearing for his safety,[631] especially after he saw the heads of Asprenas and his men[632] being carried by. So he stood in some little place accessible by a few stairs, drawing himself back into the darkness there.[633]

217 But Gratus,[634] one of the soldiers around the palace, saw him. Although he was not able to recognize his face exactly due to the darkness, he did not fail to adjudge properly that the being hiding[635] there was a person,[636] so he came closer, and, despite being asked [by Claudius] to go away, he lunged upon him and, grabbing hold of him, recognized him. "It is Germanicus,"[637] he said to those who came up after him; "let us carry him off and set him up as [Rome's] ruler!"[638] **218** Claudius, seeing that they were prepared to snatch him and afraid that he might die for the murder of Gaius,[639] asked that they spare him,[640] setting out before them the memory of his never having been overbearing[641] and that he had had no foreknowledge[642] of what had happened.[643] **219** But Gratus, smiling, took hold of his right hand and said: "Stop this small-minded talk[644] about your safety! You should be

---

631 Claudius's "terror" is also mentioned by Suetonius (*Claud.* 10.1).

632 See the note on "Asprenas and his men" at §142.

633 For his place of hiding, see the note on "passage-way" at §212.

634 Otherwise unknown. Suetonius, *Claud.* 10.2 speaks of "a common soldier," and Dio (60.1.2) speaks of "some soldiers who had entered the palace for the purpose of plundering."

635 Josephus uses ὑπολοχάω elsewhere only at *War* 6.366; Mason notes he is the only ancient writer known to have used this verb.

636 Suetonius, *Claud.* 10.2 writes that the soldier saw Claudius's feet.

637 Suetonius (*Claud.* 1.3; 2.1) reports that one of the honors that the Senate voted to convey to Drusus the Elder, Claudius's father, was the cognomen "Germanicus" for him and his descendants, and that Claudius too began using it when his elder brother, Germanicus (Gaius's father), was adopted into the Julian family.

638 This contrasts with §§164–165 above, where the soldiers are said to have planned in advance to enthrone Claudius, and then snatched him in order to realize their plan.

639 Niese reads καὶ δείσας, μὴ κατὰ φωνὴν ἀποθάνοι τὴν Γαΐου, but κατὰ φωνήν seems to be quite difficult to construe. Schreckenberg, who indeed brands that reading "unverständlich" (1977: 124, n. 5), suggested (1970: 73) that we emend κατὰ φωνήν into κατ᾽ ἐντολήν, as if Claudius were afraid that Gaius, prior to his death, had ordered the soldiers to kill Claudius. He supports his suggestion by reference to Josephus's use of ἐντολή for such deathbed orders (*War* 1.441–442, 579), also to the reasonable expectation that a dying Caligula would want to eliminate Claudius. Nevertheless, that is quite a radical emendation. Moreover, it does not explain the relevance

of Claudius's protest, in the continuation of this passage, that he had not been involved in the plot; if the dying Gaius ordered the death of Claudius, there is no reason to think that it was because of any suspicion that Claudius was involved in a plot to kill him. On both counts, it appears simpler to change only a single letter and read φονήν (as in Ambrosianus, followed by Feldman 1965: 60), or two letters, and read φόνον (so Naber 1893: 31), the former being a rare form of the latter, which is the usual term for shed blood or murder (according to a marginal note in A here, cited by Niese ad loc., φονή is a "poetic" form). Taking κατά with the accusative in its usual sense of "in accordance with," which turns into "for, because of" (LSJ 883, s.v., §IV), Josephus would mean that Claudius was afraid that the soldiers would kill him "for the blood of Gaius" or "for the murder of Gaius," as translated above. A discussion of this case as one in which the usual rules and preferences conflict appears just before the end of Part VI of the Introduction.

640 Suetonius (*Claud.* 10.2) writes that Claudius fell at the soldier's feet "in terror."

641 Interestingly, Josephus uses ἀνεπαχθής elsewhere only at *Ant.* 18.207 and 209, of Claudius's brother (and Gaius's father), Germanicus. Cf. the note on "imposed upon them" at §227.

642 Josephus uses ἀπρομηθής only here and at 18.175, in a passage concerning Tiberius; Mason notes that he is the earliest known user of the adjective.

643 See also above, §213: Claudius "had conducted himself moderately as a private citizen, being content with what he had ... and keeping himself far from anything that in any way tended to disorder."

644 Μικρολογέομαι. This is its only occurrence in Josephus; here it is obviously meant to contrast with the coming call upon him to think big (μεγαλοφρονεῖσθαι), which is much more appropriate for rulers; see, for

thinking great-mindedly about rule, which the gods who took it away from Gaius have, taking providential care of the universe,[645] agreed to grant to your virtue. So come and take over[646] the throne[647] of your ancestors!" 220 And he picked him up and carried him,[648] for he was not at all able to walk on his feet on account of his fear and his joy at what had been said.[649]

(3.2) 221 Many of the bodyguards[650] had in the meantime gathered around Gratus. Some, however, when they saw Claudius being led off as if he were being dragged away for punishment for what had occurred, although he had been an inactive man[651] throughout his entire life[652] and had met up with many dangers during Gaius's reign,[653] asked them to allow [him] a trial concerning his fate, before the consuls. 222 When the majority of the soldiers gathered,[654] however,[655] the mob[656] began to flee, but Claudius was unable to move forward because of his body's weakness[657] (and those who had been carrying his litter[658] had saved themselves by fleeing, when he was taken, considering the rescue of their master to be beyond hope).

example, *Ant.* 12.115, 122, 128 (Ptolemy II, Vespasian, and Titus) and 18.256 (Gaius). On the various senses of the verb, see the note on "high spirit" at 18.255.

645 Again, this seems to refer to the Roman perception of Rome's universal rule; see §14 and the note on "earth and sea" at §1.

646 Although ἀπολαμβάνω can have the sense of "regain, recover" (*ThLJ* 70), as at §313, Claudius had never been emperor. Perhaps for that reason, translators regularly offer "accept" (Schalit 1963: 338; Feldman 1965: 317). But that fails to reflect the opening ἀπό, and also portrays Claudius's role as very passive, whereas in fact Gratus is urging Claudius to become active. Possibly the verb is meant to refer to "taking back" rule for his dynasty, rather than letting it pass into the hands of the Senate—but the continuation seems to assume that, if not Claudius, someone else would sit on the imperial throne. It seems best, therefore, to render the verb in light of ἀντιλαμβάνεσθαι at §238.

647 Josephus usually uses θρόνος literally, of the royal seat itself (see, e.g., *Ant.* 11.235, 238, 17.201, 18.107). For such metonymous usage for ruling, cf. *Ant.* 7.356.

648 Josephus uses ἀναβαστάζω elsewhere only at §226.

649 Suetonius (*Claud.* 10.2) reports that the soldier who had found Claudius took him to his comrades, and they put him in a litter and carried it (cf. below, §222), while he was "in a state of despair and terror." Cf. §222. Josephus, however, as in his "obituaries" (see the note on "nonetheless" at §208), likes to present pictures that pull in both directions; cf. Mason 2003a (on "counterpoint") and Mason 2005a (on irony).

650 Determining who's who at §§221–222 is quite difficult, and the situation is exacerbated by an apparent lacuna—after ἀγόμενον (Feldman 1965: 316) or after ἕλκεσθαι (Niese 1890a: 249). I have translated on the

assumptions that the "bodyguards" are the Germans, who, outnumbering Gratus, would have dragged Claudius off to be punished for the assassination of Claudius; that the sight of that threat outraged "some" who are mentioned in this paragraph, who tried to get the Germans at least to agree to allow Claudius a trial before killing him; and that the next paragraph reports that so many more Praetorian Guards (Gratus's comrades) arrived that "the mob" of Germans dispersed.

651 I.e., in public affairs; on ἀπράγμων, cf. the note on "inactive life" at §32.

652 As is also stated at §§213, 231. Suetonius (*Claud.* 10.2) too reports that the people who saw Claudius being led off "pitied him, as an innocent man who was being hurried off to execution" (trans. Rolfe, LCL). However, Suetonius refers to onlookers in general, whereas Josephus is referring here to the "bodyguards"; see the note on "bodyguards" at §221.

653 This is the theme of Suetonius, *Claud.* 9. Cf. the note on "Claudius" at §13.

654 Note that συστρεφομένων here answers and trumps συνεστρέφοντο at §221: Germans gathered threateningly, Romans gathered protectively, and the Germans scattered. See the note on "mob," below, but also that on "bodyguards" at §221.

655 And so Gratus was no longer isolated.

656 That is, the Germans. This portrayal of the Praetorian Guards as respectable, while the German bodyguards are a barbaric mob (§§119–122, 138) who flee from real soldiers, was music to Roman ears. For the pejorative nuance of ὅμιλος, cf. 4.37 and 18.60.

657 Cf. just above, at §220, where he is said to have been unable "to walk on his feet on account of his fear and his joy at what had been said."

658 This seems to refer to his regular litter-bearers. Suetonius (*Claud.* 10.2) reports, similarly, that the soldiers

223 When they came to the open space of the Palatine—which the tradition about the city reports was the first part of the city of the Romans to be settled[659]—and were already coming up to the public space,[660] there was a yet larger gathering[661] of soldiers,[662] who reacted joyously to the sight of Claudius, and who were all for installing him as emperor on account of their goodwill toward Germanicus,[663] who had been his brother and had left behind a great reputation among all who had had dealings with him.[664] **224** They also took into account[665] the greed of those who held sway in the Senate[666] and how far it had gone astray for that reason during the previous regime.[667] **225** They also considered the impossibility of the project,[668] and that if everything passed back into the hands of one person it would be dangerous for them for [that] one person to have gained rule [without their support];[669] but it was possible that if Claudius received it by their assent[670] and goodwill he would remember them and requite them gratefully with honor, which would doubtless be commensurate with such things.[671]

(3.3) 226 These, then, were the things they went over in detail[672] with and among themselves and which they reported to those who were continually joining them. They, upon

---

placed Claudius in the litter and carried it themselves because Claudius's litter-bearers had absconded.

659 So too Dionysius of Halicarnassus, 1.87.3; Livy 1.7; Tacitus, *Ann.* 12.24. Cf. Richardson 1992: 280. For the Palatine in general and its development see ibid. 279–282. The fact that the Palatine is here introduced to readers as if it were not already familiar to them from §§75, 85–86, where it was not defined, is among the reasons to posit the use of more than one source.

660 True, τὸ δημόσιον (lit. "public [building]") can be used specifically of the Treasury, see 13.265–266 and 16.164, also *Life* 363, 370, along with *GTRI* 35. However, there seems to be no support for the notion that the treasury (*aerarium*) was located on the Palatine, and in fact what our story requires is a statement that those who had abducted Claudius in the inner passages of the imperial residence had now made their way out to where they might meet the general public.

661 Apart from 17.43, this is the only appearance of ἐπιφοίτησις in Josephus. But the verb, ἐπιφοιτάω, appears several times in these books (18.82, 241, 368; 19.134, 197).

662 Here the story continues the line begun with Gratus's grabbing of Claudius (§§217–220) and then the arrival of more soldiers at §222; they are the ones who make Claudius emperor.

663 Gaius's father and Claudius's older brother. For the surname "Germanicus" see above, §217.

664 For Germanicus's continued popularity, long after his death (19 CE; see above, 18.53–54) see 18.206; Cassius Dio 58.8.2, 59.3.8; Tacitus, *Ann.* 11.12, 12.2, 14.7; and the note on "elsewhere" at 18.54. For the people's goodwill

towards Claudius thanks to his older brother's reputation, see also Suetonius, *Claud.* 7.

665 Elsewhere Josephus uses ἀναλογισμός only at *War* 2.18, and there in a financial context.

666 The consideration cited at §225 is similar to that reported at §§162–165, but this one, the senators' greed, is new. It corresponds to the general tendency of this story, since the death of Gaius: to delegitimize the Senate and the possibility of its returning to rule as during the Republic.

667 I.e., whenever it ruled without an emperor, in the days of the Republic. This seems to be indicated by §228 as well, where the reference to greed is accompanied by an allusion to the days of Pompey; see Wiseman 2013a: 88–89. But the motif of greed leading rulers astray is universal. Cf. the observation Josephus attributes to Tiberius at 18.172, as well as his own frequent attribution of greed (πλεονεξία, as here) to wicked rulers; see the data assembled by Feldman 1998a: 203–204.

668 Of the state being ruled by the Senate, as opposed to a single individual—for which latter two options now follow.

669 Something is wrong with the text here; Niese (1890a: 251) marks a dittography.

670 Josephus uses ἐπιχώρησις only here and at §231. Similarly, the verb ἐπιχωρέω is frequent in this story (§§12, 107, 252), but appears elsewhere in Josephus's oeuvre only at 17.32, 300; 18.376. This is part of the distinctive lexicon of *Ant.* 17–19.

671 This consideration too was raised above, at §165.

672 See the note on "criss-crossed" at §122.

learning the news, enthusiastically received the marching orders;[673] closing ranks and wheeling about,[674] they took [Claudius] to the camp[675]—picking up the litter[676] and carrying it[677] so that it would not impede them in their haste.[678]

227 The opinions of the populace and of the senators diverged. The latter aspired to their former high status and, the moment[679] having supplied [the opportunity], had the ambition to get out from under the servitude[680] that had been imposed upon them[681] by the hubris of the tyrants.[682] 228 But the populace, being jealous of the Senate and knowing that the emperors had curbed[683] its greed[684] and were a refuge for itself, was happy at the seizure of Claudius, for they supposed that by installing him as emperor they would preserve themselves from civil strife, such as had transpired in the days of Pompey.[685]

Senators Talk, 1   229 The Senate, when it learned that Claudius had been brought to the camp by the soldiers, sent to him some of their members who were of preeminent virtue,[686] to instruct him

---

673 I have translated πρόκλησις here on the background of *War* 2.579, where Josephus uses it of a bugled order to soldiers to advance; see the next note.

674 *CCFJ* 3.394, s.v. περικλάω has only a question mark to offer for this verb here, and elsewhere in Josephus it appears only at 15.335, with regard to breaking waves. But Polybius (10.23.6; 11.12.4 and 23.2) uses it or the cognate noun of something like "wheeling about" or "breaking away" (from the former direction) by soldiers. For such maneuvers by Roman soldiers, see *War* 2.579 and 3.105, where Josephus uses περιαγωγή.

675 That is, to the Praetorian camp; so too Suetonius, *Claud.* 10.2. The Praetorian camp (*Castra Praetoria*) was built by Tiberius in 21–23 CE (Suetonius, *Tib.* 37.1; Tacitus, *Ann.* 4.2; Cassius Dio, 57.19.6) in the northeast corner of Rome, beyond its inhabited area, outside the Porta Viminalis, at one of the highest points in the city. See further Richardson 1992: 78–79. According to Suetonius (*Claud.* 10.3), "the consuls with the Senate and the city cohorts had taken possession of the Forum and the Capitol," and the urban cohorts' support for the Senate, at this time, also emerges from *War* 2.205, despite its vagueness; see Mason 2008: 170, n. 1281, and the note on "cohorts" at §188. Therefore, the Praetorians certainly could not remain within the city, and their camp was the safest place.

676 Φοράδην. Only occurrence in Josephus.

677 Ἀναβαστάζω, as at §220, above.

678 Since the usual litter-bearers had absconded when Claudius was taken (§222; Suetonius, *Claud.* 10.2).

679 For such a portrayal of time (χρόνος) as an actor, cf. §44.

680 See the note on "prisoners" at §181 above.

681 This use of ἔπακτον resonates well with the emphasis at §218 that Claudius, just as Germanicus (18.207, 209), had always been the opposite: ἀνεπαχθής.

682 For the hubris of tyrants see above §§155 and 176; for Gaius's, see §1. This succinctly summarizes some of the main points of Sentius's speech (§§167–184), including the view of all emperors as tyrants.

683 On ἐπιστόμισμα, see the note on "curbing" at 18.330.

684 As above, §224.

685 The reference to civil strife (στάσις) in the days of Pompey would seem to point to the civil war between him and Caesar in 49–48 BCE. It is interesting that the narrative here points to the days of Pompey, whereas above (§173, and by implication at §187) the "end of democracy" and the "upheaval of the state" are connected to Julius Caesar, just as the narrative above seems to count the end of the Republic from 60 or 59 BCE (§187). Are these divergent views as to when the Republic ended (cf. the notes on §§173 and 187)? Do these differences (Caesar or Pompey; 60/59 BCE or 49–48 BCE) attest to the use of different sources? Note too, that the view ascribed here to "the people" contradicts §189 above, where they are said to have been joyous to have regained "rule of themselves" (see also §191). Suetonius (*Claud.* 10.4) too writes that "the populace ... called for one ruler and expressly named Claudius." However, such general assessments need not point to the use of sources; they are putty in the eyes of the observer and conform to an author's needs at any particular juncture.

686 These delegates are identified below, at §234.

that he should not insist[687] on attaining power.[688] **230** Rather, [they were to argue that] he should defer to the Senate, as being an individual he should yield to the many, leaving it to the law to attend providentially to the good order of the commonwealth. [Moreover, they said,] remembering the terrible things the earlier tyrants had done to the city, and those done by Gaius that had endangered him too,[689] along with them, he should not—while hating the harshness[690] of the tyranny that had been practiced by others in their hubris[691]—of his own volition dare to act drunkenly[692] against the fatherland. **231** And if he agreed and indicated that his earlier virtue, of being uninvolved in public affairs,[693] would remain firm,[694] he would obtain honors, which would be voted him by free citizens, for with the permission of the law he would earn, both as ruler and as ruled, praise for his virtue.[695] **232** If, however, he were so out of his mind as not to be sobered[696] by Gaius's death, they, at least, would not concede to him; for they had a large army at their side, with a plenitude of arms and a multitude of slaves who would use them.[697] **233** And great is the contingent[698] constituted by hope and fortune,[699] for the gods ally themselves only with those who carry on the struggle for virtue and propriety, that is, those who fight for the liberty of the fatherland.

---

687 Feldman (1965:321) renders: "He must not take forcible action to put himself on the throne." That conforms to the etymology and usual sense of βιάζομαι; see Thackeray, *ThLJ* 104–105. However, if their appeal related specifically to the use of force, it would imply that the issue were only *how* Claudius should become emperor, the delegates' request being that he do so without violence, namely, by submitting to the Senate, which would then make him emperor, without violence. In fact, however, as §231 shows, they want him to return to uninvolvement in politics, that is, not to become emperor. Hence it seems preferable to assume that, in their opening statement, the delegates were diplomatic, and did not necessarily allude to the possibility of Claudius using force. Thackeray (ibid.) lists several passages, including this one, for βιάζομαι as plain "insist" (although some are less unambiguous than others); for this sense, see also 18.299 and Papone 1990.

688 Cassius Dio (60.1.4) reports that the *consuls* sent tribunes and others to instruct Claudius not to do anything in order to attain power, but rather to submit to the authority of the people, the Senate, and the laws. Here, however, the focus is on the Senate.

689 Same argument as above at §221.

690 Βαρύτης. See the note on "harshness" at §175.

691 This is reminiscent of the Senate's goals reported just above, at §227.

692 To this ἐπὶ παροινίᾳ θαρσεῖν compare §364: ὕβρεως καὶ παροινίας. Claudius was apparently a notoriously heavy drinker; see Suetonius, *Claud.* 5.1, 33.1, 40.1; and Dio

61.34.2. For Josephus's frequent use of drunkenness as a literal or metaphorical charge against those who relate recklessly to the body politic, see Mason 2008: 185–186, n. 1408.

693 See above, §§213 and 221.

694 On βέβαιος, see the note on "full-fledged" at 20.38.

695 On Roman *virtus,* see the note on "virtuous" at §171.

696 This translation of σωφρονίζω here is suggested by "drunkenly" at §230. Cf. 20.166.

697 The same argument is made again later by the Senate (§242). In *War* 2.205 Josephus wrote that the Senate "voted to make war against Claudius." The army mentioned here is certainly the three urban cohorts mentioned in *War* 2.205, which would amount to 1500 soldiers; cf. note on "four cohorts" at §188.

698 I.e., along with army and armed slaves, they can also count on the help of the gods. (For μέρος of a part of an army, see e.g., 12.295, 428; 13.95.) For a similar thought, see 18.363.

699 Wiseman (2013a: 90) sees this as "the most pointed of all his [i.e., Josephus'] Thucydidean reminiscences," for the arguments are the same as those used against Athenian power by the Melian commissioners in 415 BCE, according to Thucydides (5.102, 104). If so, the outcome of that debate, which was so catastrophic for the Melians, is, for readers familiar with that story, a powerful element in the portrayal of the Senate as pathetic. For Josephus's echoing of the Melian debate in *War* (2.355–357; 4.175–179; 5.364–367), see Mason 2008: 268.

(3.4) 234 The envoys, Veranius[700] and Brocchus,[701] both of them tribunes of the people,[702] used words like these and, falling before his knees as supplicants, implored him[703] not to throw the city into wars and evils—for they saw that Claudius was walled roundabout[704] by a large army, with which the consuls[705] could not be compared.[706] 235 If he aspired[707] to rule, it was [they said] to be received as a grant by the Senate, for he would rule more auspiciously[708] and more successfully if he obtained [authority] not via outrage but, rather, by the goodwill of those who bestowed it.[709]

Agrippa Intervenes, I

(4.1) 236 Claudius understood with what great stubborn arrogance they had been sent.[710] And although for the moment he was moved by their attitude to greater restraint,[711] he recuperated from his fear of them, thanks both to the boldness of the soldiers[712] and to urging

---

700 Quintus Veranius, later consul in 49 and governor of Britain in 57–58. See Tacitus, *Ann.* 14.29 and *Agricola* 14.

701 Brocchus's identity is unknown, and the manuscripts offer various spellings. For the suggestion to identify him as Sertorius Brocchus, who apart from being plebian tribune in 41 is also attested on a coin (*RPCSup* 1.103, no. 2101A) as governor of an eastern province, probably Bithynia, during the reign of Claudius, see Levick 1990: 31.

702 Mason notes that the Senate's mobilization of plebian tribunes, whose function had largely been eclipsed by the emperors' *tribunicia potestas*, itself pointed to the desire to restore the Republic.

703 For similar scenes and formulation, cf. 17.94 (προσπεσόντος … ἱκετεύοντος) and *War* 4.640 (προσπίπτοντες … καθικέτευσαν); cf. *Ant.* 14.481.

704 For such usage of φράσσω, comparing soldiers to walls, cf. §§74, 241.

705 That is, the forces supporting the consuls (and the Senate)—mostly: the urban cohorts (see the note on "to the camp" at §226).

706 That is, the tribunes themselves realized that the argument they had just presented, about the strength of the Senate's army (§232), was blatantly false. Indeed, the Praetorian Guard, which was now supporting Claudius (§§223–226), was made up of nine cohorts (Tacitus, *Ann.* 4.5.3)—three times the strength of the urban cohorts, who seem to have still remained loyal to the Senate (see the preceding note). In addition, the Praetorians were much better armed and trained.

707 Same verb as at §227.

708 Αἰσιώτερον, comparative of αἴσιος, which Josephus uses only here.

709 Note that Josephus reports no response to the Senate's delegates, nor that that they depart, while below, in the context of a story in which Agrippa I stars, we read

again that the Senate dispatched delegates to Claudius and they did receive a response and depart (§§244–247a), whereupon the story returns at §247b to Claudius (Κλαύδιος δέ). It is likely that Josephus's main source, which focused on Claudius, and his source which focused on Agrippa I, had different versions of the same delegation. See D. R. Schwartz 1990a: 28.

710 That is, the Senate's lack of strength made its stubbornness in voicing such demands arrogant, presumptuous. Here Josephus strikingly moves from the high-sounding speech to the facts of life, signing on, as author, to the realpolitical view that those who do not have power are arrogant if they persist in acting, or even in talking, as if they did; once again the Melian debate comes to mind (see the note on "fortune" at §233). For the same usage of αὐθάδεια (arrogance/stubbornness in the face of insuperable odds), see Titus's speech before Gischala at *War* 4.94, 96. On the word's range of senses and the difficulty of rendering it into English, see Spicq 1994: 1.229–230.

711 That is, at first, before "recuperating," he was somewhat intimidated by the Senate; perhaps this is the context of Suetonius's report (*Claud.* 10.3), that when Claudius was summoned to consult with the Senate, he replied, disingenuously, that he was being detained against his will. For Josephus's (and/or his source's) story it is important to portray Claudius as intimidated, for that enhances the importance of Agrippa's intervention, to which the story immediately turns. Cf. the notes on "empire" at §238 and on "Quintus" at §264.

712 Suetonius, *Claud.* 10.3–4, explains that the change in Claudius's attitude from fear to confidence resulted from the Senate's slowness in acting on its plans because of "the tiresome bickering of those who held divergent views," along with the support for his rule by the populace. This led him to allow "the armed assembly of the

by King Agrippa[713] that he not let slip through his hands[714] such a rule that had come to him of its own accord.[715] **237** Having first done for Gaius what was appropriate for a man whom [Gaius] had treated with honor[716] (for he had treated Gaius's corpse properly,[717] put it up on a bier, and covered it as best he could),[718] he went back to the bodyguards and reported to them that Gaius was alive, and saying that, since he was suffering seriously from wounds, physicians were on their way.[719] **238** On hearing of the abduction of Claudius by the soldiers, he pushed his way to him and, finding him troubled and about to defer to the Senate, he tried to rouse him, urging him to lay hold[720] of the empire.[721]

239 After saying that to Claudius he went home, and when the Senate sent for him[722] he anointed his head with fragrant oils as if he [were coming] from a banquet that had just dispersed,[723] came to it and asked the senators what Claudius had done. **240** When

---

soldiers to swear allegiance to him" (trans. Rolfe, LCL), and also to offer bribes to those soldiers: fifteen thousand sesterces each.

713 In *Antiquities* 19, this is the first mention of King Agrippa I, grandson of Herod the Great, who was one of the main characters in Book 18. Indeed, the last we heard of Agrippa he was in Rome, but that was so far back (18.289–300) that the fact that Josephus offers here no explanation as to why he was in Rome suggests a move to a source focused on Agrippa; see the introduction to Book 19, at n. 14. So do the very suddenness of the introduction of Agrippa here, the need for a flashback (down to §245a) to bring us up to date about his activities until now, and the fact that §236a now gives two explanations for Claudius's change of attitude; all this suggests that Josephus is here supplementing a source that focused on Claudius, the army, and the Senate, from one that focused on Agrippa. Agrippa's part in helping Claudius become emperor is reflected by a coin (see the note on "Romans" at §275) and mentioned briefly by Cassius Dio (60.8.2), but not by Suetonius. It is also claimed in *War* 2.206–217, although in writing that account Josephus seems not to have had access to the pro-Agrippan source he used to supplement his story here. See the next notes and D. R. Schwartz 1990a: 23–30.

714 Same expression as at §81.

715 I.e., rule that he had not sought out to obtain for himself. The notion seems to be that had it been his own initiative he could decide to give it up, but it would be disrespectful to the gods (or to "Time"; cf. §44) to spurn what they had sent his way.

716 Gaius had released Agrippa from prison and given him the first two-thirds of his kingdom; see *Ant.* 18.236–239, 252. For their friendship and the honor in which Gaius had held Agrippa, see *Ant.* 18. 289–301.

717 For περιέπω in this sense see *War* 3.408, 438; *Ant.* 10.53.

718 For Roman customs of dealing with the deceased, see the note on "the dead" at §195. Suetonius, *Cal.* 59,

reports that Gaius's corpse was taken in secret to the Lamian gardens, where it was only partly consumed on the pyre, "and buried beneath a light covering of turf," and that his sisters later dug it up and had it properly cremated and buried. The Lamian gardens, which are also mentioned in Philo, *Leg.* 351, have been identified south of the Piazza Vittorio Emanuele II and Piazza Dante (H. Lindsay 1993: 170; Richardson 1992: 199).

719 Compare above, §134. Here Josephus portrays Agrippa as cleverly hiding the fact of Gaius's death in order to allow his successor time to organize his takeover of power. For similar cases, cf. §353 (Agrippa I), also 13.400 (Alexander Janneus), *War* 1.666//*Ant.* 17.193 (Herod); and Cassius Dio 69.1.3–4 (Trajan).

720 See the notes on "take over" at §219 and on "lay claim" at 18.4.

721 The account here is significantly different from Josephus's report of these same events in *War* 2.205–210. There, after we hear nothing about an embassy from the Senate to Claudius and rather learn that the Senate "voted to make war against Claudius," Claudius appears to be more determined to rule and there is no hint that he considered deferring to the Senate. Correspondingly, Agrippa is a much more passive figure there: he does not initiate anything, is rather summoned for consultations by both Claudius and the Senate, and decides to go to Claudius first, "having fully understood that the Caesar was already in power." That is, Agrippa's enhanced role in our story entailed a weakening of Claudius. Cf. the note on "restraint" at §236.

722 As mentioned in the preceding note, *War* 2.206 reports that Agrippa had been summoned by the Senate already earlier, at the same time that he had been summoned—according to that account—by Claudius. According to §207, Agrippa went to the Senate immediately after his meeting with Claudius, the latter having sent him there "as an emissary."

723 On such practice, cf. Petronius, *Satyricon* 60.3 and 65.7, along with Schmeling 2011: 248, 270–271; he

they told him how things were and beyond that asked him[724] what his opinion was about the whole situation, he urged them—although he said he was[725] ready even to die for [the Senate's] good repute[726]—to set their eyes upon what was useful, disregarding all else even if it might lead to pleasure. 241 For [he said], those who strive for rule need to have both arms and soldiers, who can wall them roundabout,[727] lest they start out although unprepared and suffer failure for that reason.[728] 242 When the Senate replied that it had a great supply of weapons and would supply money, and something of an army that sided with it, and that it would be reinforced by the freeing of slaves,[729] Agrippa responded:

> May it be, O Senate, that you accomplish whatever you desire; but I must speak to you without hesitation because what I have to say pertains to survival [itself].[730] 243 Know that the army, which will fight on behalf of Claudius, has been prepared for bearing arms over a long time, while ours[731] will be a hodgepodge mob[732] who, having unexpectedly been freed from slavery, will also be hard to control.[733] We shall fight masters of the art, leading out [against them] men who do not even know how to draw their swords.[734] 244 Therefore, it seems to me [better] to send to Claudius to convince him to lay down the office—and I am willing to be sent on the mission.

(4.2) 245 That is what he said, and, when they agreed, he was sent with others—whereupon he privately told Claudius about the dismay in the Senate[735] and instructed him to answer in a fashion more appropriate to a ruler, employing the dignity of authority. 246 So Claudius, [responding to the delegates], said that he was not surprised that the Senate did not endure with pleasure the notion of being ruled, for it had been exhausted[736] by the cruelty of those who had previously wielded supreme power, but that they would taste fairness in his moderate days, for although nominally rule would be by one, in fact it would be held

---

cites Tibullus, *Elegies* 1.7.51, who "notes that scented oil in the hair is a mark of a party-person." Note also Martial, *Epigrams* 3.12 and Athenaeus 9.408e and 11.462d–the latter two cited by S. Lieberman (1955–1988: 1.95) in his commentary on *t. Berakhot* 5:29 ("it is not praiseworthy for a sage to depart with a fragrant head"), to which I was kindly referred by Yair Furstenberg. Cf. the note on "perfuming themselves" at §358.

724 This is the only occurrence of προσανέρομαι in Josephus.

725 Lit. "in his words (he replied)." Apparently Josephus is pointing out that, just as by spreading rumors (§237) and anointing his head (§239), so too in his response to the Senate, Agrippa was playing a double game. For more of the same, see the note on "ours" at §243. The opposition of "words" and "fact" is very common in this book; cf. the note on "ostensibly" at §157.

726 This is the only occurrence of εὐκλεής in *Antiquities*, but it appears a few times in *War*.

727 For this image, see above, §234.

728 Or perhaps: encounter such forces (serving the other side) and fail, as Schalit (1963: 340) translates.

729 The same list of assets appears in the Senate's appeal to Claudius at §232. For the freeing and arming of slaves in times of need, cf. Suetonius, *Aug.* 25.2.

730 The Greek employs no possessive adjective here. Various translations add "your," but perhaps "our" would fit Agrippa's pose better; see the next note.

731 Here, as at §§239–240, the author enjoys portraying Agrippa's duplicity: the senators are easy prey for his flattery and seductive words. As already at 18.146, 166–167, he is portrayed as something of a manipulator, who knows how to get along with the powerful to his own advantage. Note, in this context, that in arguing his case Agrippa totally ignores the urban cohorts, which are still on the Senate's side (see the note on "the camp" at §226).

732 For σύγκλυδες, cf. 18.37—the riffraff who settled in Tiberias.

733 This is the only appearance of δυσκράτητος in Josephus.

734 On Josephus's appreciation of the importance of military training, see the note on "training" at 18.367.

735 Cf. the note on "soldiers" at §236; the narrative now resumes from there, after the Agrippan interlude (see the note on "King Agrippa" at §236).

736 For such use of τρύω, cf. 18.175; for the same notion, see also 19.2, 192.

jointly,[737] equally available to all.[738] Since he had safely made his way through numerous vicissitudes,[739] before their eyes, they would do well not to disbelieve him.[740]

247 The ambassadors, having been conciliated by hearing these words, were sent on their way. Claudius, for his part, spoke to the assembled army and had it swear to remain loyal to him.[741] He gave each of the bodyguards[742] five thousand drachmas,[743] and proportionately higher sums to their officers,[744] and he promised similar gifts to all [soldiers], wherever they were encamped.[745]

(4.3) 248 The consuls convened the Senate in the Temple of Jupiter Victor;[746] it was still nighttime. Of the senators, those who were hiding in the city procrastinated when they heard it, while others had already gone off to their own country estates.[747] For seeing in advance how everything would turn out, and despairing of liberty, they thought it much better to live out their lives without the danger of slavery [and] in leisure rather than

Senators Talk, II

---

737 There might be some irony here on Josephus's part, reflecting common knowledge that actually the opposite was true: although nominally, during the Principate, it was still the Senate that ruled and the Princeps was only first among many, in fact the emperor ruled alone. Cf. Wallace-Hadrill 1982.

738 For εἰς μέσον in the sense of "accessible to all equally," see the note on "leave open" at §11. Claudius's argument here is, for the most part, paralleled in the account in *War*: he would rule moderately and not as a tyrant, he would be satisfied solely with the honor of his title, and he "would yield to all [of them] the deliberation over each [item] of public business" (*War* 2.208). Similar promises of moderation and intention to share power with the Senate were attributed to other emperors at the beginning of their rule; see Cassius Dio 59.6.1 (Gaius Caligula); Tacitus, *Ann.* 13.4 (Nero).

739 Cf. above, §§13, 67–68.

740 After Claudius's response, until this last sentence, has been conciliatory, promising the Senate its authority and his cooperation, here he ends up with something of a threat: since it seems clear that he enjoys good fortune, the senators should not imagine he might fail.

741 On such oaths, see the note on "loyalty to Gaius" at 18.124.

742 Here σωματοφύλαξ apparently refers to the Praetorian Guard. See the note on "Praetorian Guard" at §214. The Guard was also rewarded for its role in Claudius's accession by its depiction on two coin-types minted in his early years; see Levick 1990: 39.

743 Five thousand drachmas, i.e. 5/6 of a talent (see the note on "talents" at 18.160), were the equivalent of 20,000 sesterces, "an enormous sum" (Levick 1990: 32). Suetonius (*Claud.* 10.4), however, reports that Claudius promised each soldier 15,000 drachmas, commenting that by doing so Claudius was the first of the emperors

who resorted to bribery to assure himself of the soldiers' loyalty.

744 For officers receiving proportionately (ἀνάλογος) larger shares than soldiers, see also *War* 1.356.

745 As Levick (1990: 32–33) notes, this was probably intended to undermine the loyalty of the urban cohorts to the Senate. As we shall soon hear, that apparently worked.

746 Earlier it was assumed to have been on the Palatine, and that Josephus should have referred here to the Temple of Zeus on the Capitoline Hill (the "Capitolium"; see the notes on §4); see, for example, Mason 2008: 170–171, n. 1282. An epigraphical find changed that: "The temple of Jupiter Victor referred to by Josephus in his narrative of A.D. 41 is now firmly sited on the Capitol by a new fragment of calendar *fasti*" (Wiseman 2013b: 251). This location of the Senate's meeting tallies with other evidence for the Capitol being under the control of the consuls and the Senate at this point (Suetonius, *Claud.* 10.3), and that the consuls had already transferred the treasury there (Cassius Dio, 59.30.3). Indeed, the Capitoline Hill, and especially the Temple of Jupiter Capitolinus, was most defensible and, at times of particular importance, served as the meeting place of the Senate; cf. above, the note on "Senate" at §158. However, the question remains why the Senate would choose, for the meeting described here, this temple rather than the Capitolium. Be that as it may, note Suetonius's claim (*Cal.* 60) that the senators were so much in favor of reestablishing the Republic that the consuls deliberately convened the Senate not in its regular venue, the Curia Julia, in order to distance itself from that name's imperial association.

747 For this meaning of ἀγρός (lit. "field"), see also *Life* 422. For senators fleeing the city or hiding in the dangerous times following the killing of emperors, cf. Tacitus, *Hist.* 3.86 (following the death of Vitellius in 69) and Herodian 2.6.3 (after the murder of Pertinax in

struggling[748] or maintaining their fathers' dignity[749] while leaving themselves uncertain[750] with regard to their survival. **249** All the same, a hundred (no more) assembled;[751] but as they were exchanging views[752] about the matters at hand suddenly a shout went up from the army unit that was there with them,[753] demanding that the Senate choose a commander who would rule by himself[754] and not destroy the empire via polyarchy.[755] **250** And they[756] declared that their point was that rule should be granted[757] not to all, but rather to one; but they left it to them[758] to see who was worthy of such an authority.[759] So it happened that the Senate was even more in distress, because of both the failure of its boasting[760] about liberty and its fear of Claudius.

251 Nonetheless, there were some who contended [for power] on the basis of family dignity and marriage ties. Thus, for example, Marcus Minucianus[761]—who was highly respected (thanks to his own noble birth and to having married Julia, Gaius's sister[762]) and who was eager to compete for [control] of the state—was held back by the consuls, who

---

193), both cited along with our passage by Talbert 1984: 149. Contrast §161, which reports, concerning the Senate's deliberations on the day of the assassination, that "the whole multitude of them had already assembled earlier."

748 This is exactly the complacent behavior condemned by Sentius in his speech (above, §§180–181).

749 Compare above, §§2 and 164: "dignity of ancestors."

750 This is the only occurrence of ἀμφίβολος in *Antiquities*.

751 Out of a total of around 600 senators, probably no more than 400 might be expected to attend in the best of times; see Talbert 1984: 134–152. Having already mentioned the "confusion" in the Senate (§245), here Josephus appears to be rubbing in his accusation, in §248, that the majority of senators behaved like self-serving cowards.

752 Διαβουλεύω. Only here in Josephus.

753 I.e., the urban cohorts, which evidently were still loyal to the Senate. See Mason 2008: 170, n. 1281.

754 Here αὐτοκράτορα is an adjective, but, in context, it obviously refers to an emperor. Cf. the notes on "ancestors" at §123 and on "commander" at §256.

755 The only other occurrence of πολυαρχία in Josephus is at *Ant.* 4.297, where too the point is the impossibility of successful rule by many. Feldman ad loc. (2000: 462, n. 1018) aptly compares Thucydides's comments at 6.72.4 on the problem of too many generals issuing orders.

756 Although the coming words add nothing to the foregoing, they nevertheless seem to be the continuation of the soldiers' demand, not (as in Feldman 1965: 331) the Senate's response.

757 This is the only occurrence of ἐφέσιμος in Josephus.

758 The senators.

759 In the parallel account in *War*, the option of nominating an emperor was on the Senate's table from the outset, alongside the option of a return to the Republic

(*War* 2.205). Perhaps that is a consequence of Josephus's summarizing a longer narrative, as suggested there by Mason (2008: 171, n. 1287). Be that as it may, the present story makes the Senate look all the more pathetic insofar as it did not even consider, as a possibility, the option that, in short order, became the only one.

760 Αὔχημα. As above, §174, and cf. the note on "had been sent" at §236.

761 Niese (1890: 254) reads Μινουκιανὸς Μάρκον, but here I have followed Swan (1970: 153–154) in reading both names in the accusative (the object of "held back"), parallel to the opening accusative of §252. On Marcus Vinicianus, see the note on "Minucianus" at §102. Josephus introduces him fully here, carefully distinguishing him from Annius "Minucianus"—just as carefully as in the next paragraph, §252 where he identifies the latter "Minucianus" as "one of Gaius's assassins" although readers should already know that from §§18, 20, 49–50, 96, 153–154; that too clarifies that the reference in §252 is not to the person mentioned here, in §251. Niese followed the manuscripts and read the first name in the nominative, as if Josephus meant that "Minucianus [proposed?] Marcus," but several considerations argue against that: the absence of a verb (which led Niese [1890b: 217] to posit a lacuna here); readers' ignorance as to which "Marcus" would be meant; the failure to identify "Minucianus" here in contrast with the identification of Annius at §252 (we would have expected the opposite if both references were to the same person); and the fact that since Annius was among the conspirators (§§18, 20, 49–50, 96, 153–154), readers would be mystified by the notion that he now supported a candidate for emperor, rather than supporting the attempt to restore the Republic. Hence, from all points of view it appears wisest to follow Swan and conclude that the present passage refers to Marcus "Minucianus."

762 See the note on "sister's" at §102.

strung together[763] one pretext after another. **252** So too Valerius Asiaticus[764] was restrained from similar notions by Minucianus,[765] one of Gaius's assassins.[766] For there would have been a massacre no smaller than any [imaginable] if those who yearned for imperial rule had been allowed to array themselves [for combat] against Claudius. **253** Moreover, the gladiators too (of whom there was a considerable number),[767] as well as the soldiers of the night-watch[768] in the city[769] and many oarsmen[770] were streaming together to the camp,[771] so that those who were competing[772] for rule withdrew—some in order to spare the city, others out of fear for themselves.

(4.4) 254 At the first break of day both Chaerea and those with him arrived and attempted to speak with the soldiers. But when those in the crowd saw them hushing them with their hands and about to begin to speak, they tumultuously shouted out[773] so much that they did not allow them to speak, for they were all pushing to be ruled by a single ruler, and they demanded him who would rule them, as if they would not tolerate delays. **255** The Senate was now stymied,[774] both with regard to how it might rule and with regard to the form in which it could be ruled, for the soldiers did not accept them but the assassins of Gaius did not allow them to come to an agreement with the soldiers.

The Army Prevails

---

763 Cf. *ThLJ* 42, s.v. ἀναρτᾶν.

764 On Asiaticus, see the note on "Valerius Asiaticus" at §102.

765 I.e., Annius Vinicianus. See the note on "Minucianus" at §18. Here he is identified this way to distinguish him from Marcus Vinicianus, mentioned in the preceding paragraph.

766 According to Suetonius (*Galba* 7), the future emperor Galba was another such potential candidate now, but despite being urged by many to compete for the empire, he refused.

767 Although not as favored as the circus races, gladiators and gladiatorial shows were quite favored by Gaius. He gave several gladiatorial shows (see §130, also Suetonius, *Cal.* 18.1), he owned his own gladiatorial school (Pliny, *NH* 11.144, 245) and even took part in the contests (ibid. 32.2; 54.1), and he entrusted the command of his bodyguard to Thracian gladiators (ibid. 55.2). See further Barrett 2019: 65–66.

768 This is the only occurrence of νυκτοφυλακέω in Josephus, although νυκτοφύλαξ also appears once, in *War* 4.645. On watches, see the note on "watch" at 18.356.

769 The reference is, apparently, to the *cohortes vigilum*. Established by Augustus, these were seven cohorts, each responsible for two regions of the city. They were commanded by a prefect and originally consisted only of freedmen. Their duty was to prevent crime and especially fires in the city at night. Accordingly, they were armed only with staffs and whips, along with their fire-fighting equipment. See Suetonius, *Aug.* 30.1; Cassius Dio 55.26.4–5; Southern 2007: 119–20, and the more detailed discussions of Daugherty 1992 and Rainbird 1986. There is evidence that in the early third century each cohort numbered around a thousand men, but according to Rainbird (1986: 150) their numbers were doubled then, each cohort numbering originally 560 men. If so, at the time of Gaius and Claudius there would have been nearly 4,000 of them in Rome.

770 Ἐρέτης. In Josephus only here and in *War* 2.110. Some of the fleet was stationed in Ostia, and those oarsmen could have easily made their way to Rome (cf. Suetonius, *Vesp.* 8.3).

771 That is, the Praetorian camp, where Claudius was; see above, §226.

772 For this sense of μέτειμι, see also Plutarch, *Publ.* 11.1 and *Cicero* 1.3.

773 This is the only occurrence of ἀναθορυβέω in Josephus. It portrays the soldiers as a mob; cf. the note on "tumult" at 18.58.

774 Wiseman emphasizes the contrast with the Senate's determination the previous day, and notes that the consuls are not mentioned here; cf. §259, where they do not function. Thus, the Senate (i.e, the senators who dared remain) appears weak, lacks leadership, and wallows in dilemmas; cf. Suetonius's comment cited in the note on "soldiers" at §236.

256 When things were in this state, Chaerea, not restraining his rage at the soldiers' demand for an emperor, promised to give them a commander,[775] if someone would bring him a password from Eutychus.[776] 257 This Eutychus was a charioteer of the so-called Green [faction],[777] for which Gaius had been very enthusiastic,[778] and the soldiers had been vexed by the demeaning labors demanded of them in building the stables for his[779] horses.[780] 258 Chaerea upbraided them with that and many other similar (taunts), and [he also said] that [they] should bring the head of Claudius; for it would be terrible, [he said], if after insanity[781] they should now turn the supreme power over to derangement.[782]

259 But they were not turned aside[783] by those words. Rather, drawing their swords and raising the standards, they hurried off to Claudius to join those who had taken an oath to him.[784] That left the Senate desolate of defenders, the consuls differing in no way from private citizens.[785] 260 There was bewilderment and dejection, for the people[786] did not know how they might be treated, given the fact that Claudius was provoked against them, and they reviled one another and were affected by contrition.

261 But Sabinus, one of those who had killed Gaius,[787] stepped out before them all[788] and threatened to kill himself[789] first, rather than install Claudius as ruler and look on as slave-rule[790] took hold; and he rebuked Chaerea as suffering from [excessive] love of life, if after being the first to show scorn for Gaius he considered living to take precedence over

---

775 There seems to be something pointed in Chaerea's diction here: the soldiers wanted an αὐτοκράτωρ, by which they meant a commander, *imperator*, but he, knowing that in the meantime the word had come to refer to a tyrannical head of state (our "emperor"; see GTRI 119–120) and that was what he opposed, responded with the term, στρατηγός, that was appropriate for soldiers but not for states. On Josephus's usage of αὐτοκράτωρ, see the note on "ancestors" at §123.

776 This was an ironic taunt, as will immediately be explained. Josephus attributes to Chaerea simililar irony at §38.

777 There were four teams, or factions, in Roman chariot races, named by colors: green, white, red, and blue. On them, see Cameron 1976: 45–73.

778 Suetonius (*Cal.* 55.2–3) reports Gaius's enthusiastic devotion to the Green faction, saying that "he constantly dined and spent the night in their stable," and that he once gave Eutychus 2 million sesterces in gifts. Cf. Cassius Dio 59.14.5–6. For emperors with preferences for this or that faction, see Cameron 1976: 54.

779 Probably Gaius is meant, Josephus thinking of his most famous horse; see the next note.

780 On Gaius's pampering of his favorite horse, Incitatus, see Suetonius, *Cal.* 55.3, who lists ridiculous details under the heading of Gaius's "insania." Cf. Barrett 2019: 66–67. For the sources' tendency to generalize from single instances to the plural in order to condemn Gaius all the more, see Charlesworth 1933: 110–111.

781 For Gaius's "insanity" (μανία), see the notes on "insanity" at §1 and on "horses" at §257, also §284.

782 I have translated παραφροσύνη as at §§284 and 285, but there it applies to Gaius and is meant to

condemn him morally. Here, however, it seems that no more is needed than lack of good sense. Claudius was certainly not stupid, but rather very learned; see above, §213 and the note there. Nevertheless, Dio (60.2.4) writes that Claudius, because he was frequently ill and also out of fearfulness, "feigned a stupidity (εὐήθεια) greater than was really the case." Cf. Levick 1990: 13–15.

783 This is the only occurrence of διατρέπω in *Antiquities*.

784 That is, the Praetorian Guard, as at §247 above.

785 According to the parallel account (*War* 2.212), the one soldier who had started stirring those who were with the Senate (see the note, above at §249) led his fellow-soldiers to Claudius, and the senators, realizing their helpless situation, followed. In the short account in Dio 60.1.4, the soldiers' desertion of the Senate is likewise the turning point. According to the aristocratic view expressed here, "private citizens" (ἰδιῶται) are by definition pathetically ineffective, as they are described in the next sentence, cf. §214.

786 I.e., the senators.

787 See above, §§46 and 110.

788 For speakers stepping out εἰς μέσον in order to speak "in the eyes of all," see, for example, *Life* 37, 134, 251. Cf. the note on "to all" at §246.

789 As he will soon indeed do (below, §273).

790 In all of extant ancient Greek literature, δουλοκρατία appears only here and at §14. The latter uses it to refer to slaves ruling over their masters, and that seems to be the case here as well, given the characterization of Claudius as stupid—hence: easily misled—at §258. Cassius Dio (60.2.4–5) writes that the deterioration during Claudius's rule was mainly due to "the freedmen and

freedom, although liberty could not thus be restored to the fatherland.[791] **262** Chaerea said he had no thought at all of hesitating to die, but did want to sound out[792] Claudius's attitude.

(4.5) 263 That, then, is how things were for them.[793] At the camp,[794] however, people kept pushing forward to pay their respects.[795] And one of the consuls, Quintus Pomponius,[796] was especially guilty in the eyes of the soldiers, as one who had urged the Senate to [assert] liberty,[797] and they assailed him with drawn swords and would have done him in had Claudius not intervened and prevented it.[798] **264** After snatching the consul away from the danger, Claudius sat down next to him,[799] but he did not receive with similar honor those of the senators who were with Quintus.[800] Some of them even received blows from them[801] when pushing themselves forward to petition[802] him: Aponius[803] retreated, wounded, and it was dangerous for all of them.

265 King Agrippa, however, came forward to Claudius and asked him to take a kinder[804] stance toward the senators; for if any evil befell the Senate there would be no one else for him to rule.[805] **266** Claudius was convinced,[806] and he convened[807] the Senate upon the

Agrippa Intervenes, II

---

the women with whom he associated; for he … was ruled by slaves and by women," and commented that he himself "had become a slave." Similarly, Suetonius, *Claud.* 25.5, 28, 29.1. For this type of invective, see the note on "passion" at 18.350. On the influence of Claudius's freedmen, see the notes on "influence with him" at §362 and on "friends" at 20.135.

791 This is reminiscent of the implied charge against many of the senators above, at §248. But with regard to Chaerea it contradicts virtually all that we had been told about him, as the fearless leader and hero of the plot to assassinate Gaius and as a champion of "liberty"—including just above, at §258. Hence readers will expect Chaerea to deny the charge, as he immediately does.

792 So renders *ThLJ* 149; this is the only occurrence of διακωδωνίζω in Josephus.

793 I.e., for the senators. For transitional phrases such as this, which allow Josephus to toggle between one location and the other (and in the present case allows him to pick up the camp story from §247), cf. the note on "his many wounds" at §114.

794 That is, the Praetorian camp, where Claudius was; see above, §226.

795 To Claudius, as explicit in some manuscripts.

796 Q. Pomponius Secundus, suffect consul in 41, brother of P. Pomponius Secundus, and half-brother of Gaius's wife, Caesonia; see the note on "Pompedius" at §32. This Q. Pomponius eventually joined a rebellion against Claudius in 42 (Tacitus, *Ann.* 13.43).

797 For the consuls calling for liberty and/or assembling the Senate see above, §§160, 186–187, 248.

798 In the parallel narrative, in *War* 2.213, it is the leaders of the group in general who are in danger, and are saved by Claudius, after King Agrippa—who is not mentioned in the narrative here—made him aware of the situation and advised him to restrain the soldiers.

799 For this magnanimous gesture, cf. §333.

800 In *War* 2.214 Claudius is said to have "welcomed the Senate into the camp" and even "showed kindness towards them," whereas here he welcomes them only later, at the suggestion of Agrippa. For similar modifications of Claudius's attitude so as to enlarge Agrippa's role, see the note on "restraint" at §236. On Josephus's use of a pro-Agrippan source here but not in *War*, see the note on "Agrippa" at §236.

801 Evidently: from the soldiers.

802 On ἔντευξις see Guéraud 1931 and Spicq 1994: 2.6–10.

803 Aponius, who has not been mentioned above, is probably to be identified with Aponius Saturninus, who is said to have once unknowingly bought thirteen gladiators for a fortune of nine million sesterces at one of Gaius's auctions, after he fell asleep but kept nodding as the price went up (Suetonius, *Cal.* 38).

804 This is the only occurrence of ἤπιος in Josephus.

805 In *War* (2.213) this is phrased with a colorful image: Agrippa persuaded Claudius to intervene and restrain the soldiers' attack on the senators, lest, "after destroying those on whose account being supreme is impressive, he would be king of a desert." On that image, which also appears in Josephus's Herodian narrative at *War* 1.355//*Ant.* 14.484, see Mason 2008: 177, n. 1345.

806 According to *War* 2.214, Claudius welcomed the senators into the Praetorian camp, and then went out with them to offer sacrifices of thanksgiving for his accession. Here too, Mason (2008: 177, n. 1349) raises the possibility that *War* compresses the source of the present account. Cf. above, the note on "him" at §264.

807 Attentive readers will note that the repeated use of συγκαλέω, first for the consuls' "convening" of the Senate (§248) and now for Claudius's, underlines who won—the same point that he made by the very fact of

Chaerea's Fate

Palatine.[808] He was borne through the city accompanied by the soldiers, who were very nasty to the multitude [along the way]. **267** Of Gaius's assassins, Chaerea and Sabinus came forward quite openly, but on the orders of Pollio,[809] whom Claudius had shortly before selected to be praetorian prefect, they were prevented[810] from approaching [Claudius].

268 When Claudius arrived at the Palatine he called his companions[811] together and put the question of Chaerea['s fate] to a vote. They thought that his deed had been magnificent, but [nonetheless] accused the one who had done it of disloyalty[812] and thought it was proper to impose a punishment upon him as a deterrent for times to come. **269** He was therefore led off to be killed, and with him Lupus[813] and numerous [other] Romans.[814] It is said that Chaerea bore the suffering high-mindedly,[815] not only in his unfaltering[816] bearing but also in the way he rebuked Lupus, who had turned aside to weep. **270** Indeed, when Lupus, upon taking off his robe, complained about the cold,[817] [Chaerea] said that cold could never hurt a wolf.[818] With a multitude of people following to see the show,[819] when they arrived at the place [of execution][820] he asked the soldier whether he had experience with executions or this was the first time he bore the sword,[821] and he requested that he

convening the Senate himself, at a venue that *he* ordained, although it was already convened elsewhere.

808 Probably in the Temple of Apollo (so Talbert 1984: 117–118 and Wiseman 2013a: 97). That temple was completed and dedicated by Augustus in 28 BCE, in a part of his house on the Palatine that had been struck by lightning. The area was large enough to accommodate meetings of the Senate, and such meetings were indeed held there frequently (Suetonius, *Aug.* 29.1, 3; Cassius Dio 53.1.3; Tacitus, *Ann.* 2.37). See also Richardson 1992: 14.

809 Rufrius Pollio, who later accompanied Claudius on a campaign to Britain (43 CE), and was granted a seat in the Senate upon his return (Dio 60.23.2). As Wiseman points out (2013a: 97), after the assassination of Gaius, it was clear that the former commanders of the Guard could not retain their positions.

810 Here εἰργόμενοι is unambiguously passive. Cf. the note on "excluded" at 18.19.

811 For Claudius's ἑταῖροι ("companions," *amici principis*), also mentioned at §89 and referred to as his "freedmen and friends" at 20.135, who could function, as here, as an informal but nonetheless influential advisory council, see Musurillo 1954: 202–204 and Crook 1955: 40–45.

812 On Josephus's use of ἀπιστία for treachery, as also in *Ant.* 15.110, see D. R. Lindsay 1993: 108–110. According to Dio 60.3.4, Claudius executed Chaerea "as if he had caught Chaerea plotting against himself." For Claudius's need to preserve appearances by executing whoever assassinated Gaius, although he welcomed the act, cf. 15.61 (Herod's need to mourn, publicly and ostentatiously, the death of Aristobulus III, which he had arranged) and 18.236 (Gaius's need to avoid the impression that he was happy about Tiberius's death, although he was). On this topic see, in general, the note on "derangement" at §284.

813 On Lupus and his assassination of Gaius's wife and daughter see above, §§190–200. The fact that, in

contrast to Chaerea and Sabinus (§267), Lupus did not come forward bravely is part of the portrayal of him as a cowardly foil for Chaerea; see the note on "conspire" at §191 and on "willingly" at §199.

814 In contrast, Suetonius (*Claud.* 11.1) reports that, after establishing his power, Claudius pardoned all that had happened during the two days of the assassination and its aftermath, and executed only "a few of the tribunes and centurions who had conspired against Gaius ... both to make an example of them and because he knew that they had also demanded his own death." Similarly, Dio (60.3.4) speaks of the execution of Chaerea and "some others." Josephus's story has Agrippa's man, Claudius, behaving more humanely and also mentions that Claudius executed Chaerea "as if he had caught Chaerea plotting against himself." Cf. §§273–274.

815 For Josephus's emphasis that dying μεγαλόφρονως proves a man's heroic nature, note also the cases of Samson (5.317), Jonathan (6.127), and even Ahitophel (7.229). Cf. the note on "high spirit" at 18.255.

816 This is the only occurrence of ἀμετάπτωτος in Josephus.

817 Recall that this was taking place at the end of January, a few days after the execution of Gaius.

818 Playing with the Latin *lupus*, wolf. This is often taken to point to a Latin Vorlage, but see the introduction to Book 19.

819 For Roman executions as public spectacles, cf. the note on "the entire city" at 20.136.

820 Possibly the Campus Esquilinus, just outside the Esquiline Gate, which was a regular place of executions; see Tacitus, *Ann.* 2.32 and Suetonius, *Claud.* 25.3.

821 Niese (1890a: 257) and others note that there seems to be a lacuna here, for the soldier's reply is missing. But since Chaerea asks not only about the soldier's experience but also, specifically, about "the sword" (τὸ

bring [the sword]⁸²² with which he himself had done away with Gaius.⁸²³ He died in good spirits,⁸²⁴ by a single blow. **271** Lupus, in contrast,⁸²⁵ was despondent and did not make his departure very gracefully,⁸²⁶ [suffering] many blows because he was cowardly about extending his neck.⁸²⁷

(4.6) 272 When a few days later it was time to bring sacrifices,⁸²⁸ the multitude of Romans who brought sacrifices for their own [deceased relations] also honored Chaerea with portions they placed in the fire, calling upon him to be gracious and bear no grudge⁸²⁹ about their ingratitude toward him. Such, then, was the end of Chaerea's life.

The Aftermath

273 As for Sabinus,⁸³⁰ Claudius not only dropped the charge against him⁸³¹ but also allowed him to retain the position that he had.⁸³² However, thinking it unjust not to keep

---

ξίφος), which he obviously must have had, it may be that no answer was expected. Rather, in something of the same "highminded" joking spirit evinced by the reference to "wolf," Chaerea's question may have been meant only as a rhetorical opening for his coming request to bring his own sword, as if to say that "*my* sword has experience and so can be trusted to do the job."

822 On beheading by sword in the Principate (not an ax, as earlier, e.g., *War* 1.357—Antigonus), see Mommsen 1899: 917–918, 923–924. He also notes that, under the Principate, it was usually carried out by soldiers, as is reported here.

823 Readers are probably meant to take this as a matter of pride for Chaerea, and to remember that Chaerea's forerunner in tyrannicide, Cassius, to whom Chaerea was favorably compared at §184, was said to have taken his own life with the very dagger he had used in the assassination of Julius Caesar (Plutarch, *Caesar* 69.3). Readers seeking oracular ambiguity (such as that at *War* 6.312–314), may, however, recall that at §55 Chaerea said (prophesied?) that his sword would suffice for "both of us": in context, there, that means that one sword was enough for him and Vinicianus to kill Gaius, but here it turns out that it was sufficient to kill Gaius and him.

824 Although translators usually take εὐδαιμόνως here to mean that Chaerea "was fortunate" insofar as he was killed by a single blow (Feldman 1965: 339; Wiseman 2013a: 39), the contrast with Lupus, whose being despondent and cowardly multiplied his wounds, seems to indicate that in fact it is, first of all, the attitudes of the two that are being contrasted—as usual, to Chaerea's advantage; cf. the note on "his age" at §45, and on "conspire" at §191.

825 As mentioned above (in the note on "willingly" at §199), Lupus's uncourageous behavior here at his execution is in stark contrast, not only to the behavior of Chaerea, but also to that of Lupus's own victim, Caesonia, as well as to that of heroic Jews.

826 I have borrowed this translation of δεξιῶς (lit. "right-handedly," "dexterously") here from *ThLJ* 128; cf. the note on "invidious" at 20.266.

827 Cf. the end (§189) of Philo's *In Flaccum*, where the villain's desperate attempt to avoid the executioners' blows simply resulted in multiplying them. For a similar contrast between courageous and pathetic victims executed one after the other, in very similar circumstances, cf. Tacitus, *Ann*. 15.67–68.

828 I.e., the Feralia (or: Parentalia), the Roman festival of ancestors, on February 13–21 (see Ovid, *Fasti* 2.533–570).

829 This is the only occurrence of ἄμηνις in surviving ancient literature. But Josephus does use μῆνις several times—including 18.188, where it refers to a long-held "grudge"; so too elsewhere, including *Life* 392. Indeed, Ovid's text on the Feralia, mentioned in the preceding note, opens and closes with its definition as being an occasion to "appease" (*placare*) the souls of the dead. On "the powers of the dead" in ancient Rome, see King 2020: 89–127.

830 Sabinus had come forward and acknowledged his role in the assassination; see §§110, 267.

831 On Claudius's restraint in this regard, cf. the note on "derangement" at §284.

832 I.e., the office of military tribune (§46).

faith[833] with his fellow conspirators,[834] he killed himself,[835] falling forward upon his sword until the hilt[836] came up to the wound.[837]

Claudius's Arrangements upon Succession to the Throne

(5.1) 274 Claudius, having speedily removed from the military anyone who was suspect,[838] published an edict[839] confirming Agrippa's rule, which Gaius had given [him],[840] and relating to the king with praise. He also added to his realm all that had been ruled by King Herod,[841] who was his grandfather, namely Judea and Samaria. 275 These he restored to him as if he owed them to him because he belonged to the family [of Herod]. But he also gave him Lysanias's Abila[842] and, of his own property, all that he had in Mount Lebanon,[843]

---

833 This is the only occurrence of ἐκλειπία in surviving ancient literature.

834 Especially in light of his rhetoric at §261!

835 Dio too reports his suicide, writing that Sabinus did not desire "to live after his comrade had been executed" (60.3.5).

836 This is the only occurrence of κώπη in Josephus. Richards and Shutt 1939: 183 ironically comment on the use of μέχρι without τοῦ and suggest it has fallen out: "μέχρι … συνελθεῖν is, even for J., too strange: prob. μέχρι <τοῦ>." But given that, remarkably, no manuscript mentioned by Niese preserves that, although any scribe could have added it, perhaps we should suspect interference by a Latin phrase that comes, of course, without any article; see the next note.

837 Cf. Virgil, *Aeneid* 2.553 and 10.535–536: killing "capulo tenus" (by a sword-thrust "up to the hilt") testifies to power and decisiveness.

838 Feldman (1965: 341) translates "Claudius purged the army of all unreliable units," as if the reference is to something new, beyond what has been reported. But the text seems to refer to individuals, not to units, and it seems unlikely that Josephus would have his readers assume there were otherwise unmentioned units of the army that were suspected of being disloyal to the new emperor, and other sources fail to report anything of the kind. Rather, this line should be read as another summary that amounts to a transition from the preceding story (which reported the death of Charaea and Sabinus) to the next one; cf. the note on "his many wounds" at §114. While the next part of the sentence is paralleled at *War* 2.215–216, the removal of soldiers is not. Suetonius, *Claud.* 11.1 says that Claudius decreed that all should be forgiven and forgotten, apart from the execution of some tribunes and

centurions who were involved in the conspiracy against Gaius (see also Cassius Dio 60.3.4–5).

839 Διάγραμμα. See the note on "edict" at §160.

840 That is, Claudius confirmed Agrippa's rule of the territories Gaius gave Agrippa in 37 and 39, as reported at 18.237 and 252–255: the territories that previously formed Philip's tetrarchy (Batanea, Trachonitis, Auranitis, Gaulanitis, and the area around Panias), Lysanias's tetrarchy (Abila, some twenty km. northwest of Damascus, Souk Wadi Barada), and Herod Antipas's territories (in Galilee and Transjordan). However, in the next paragraph (§275) we read that Claudius *additionally* gave Agrippa Lysanias's Abila. That contradicts 18.237 but corresponds to *War,* where 2.181 does not mention Abila among Gaius's gifts to Agrippa in 37 and 2.215 mentions it among Claudius's. Barrett (1990: 284–285) suggests that following Gaius's death all of his *acta* were abolished and that would have included the client kings he appointed; therefore, client kings had to be reinstated by Claudius, and this may explain some of the confusion in Josephus. This suggestion is, however, rejected by D. Wardle 1992a; see the note on "Commagene" at §276. As noted on "Lysanias's tetrarchy" at 18.237, it seems simplest to suspect that 18.237 was wrong to include Abila. Cf. Kokkinos 1998: 280–281.

841 I.e., all that he did not yet rule. Herod's kingdom had been divided, for the most part, among three of his sons, and, in 37 and 39, Gaius had given Agrippa the lands of two of them, Philip (18.237) and Herod Antipas (18.252). Now Claudius gave him the rest, the real heartland of the kingdom.

842 See the note on "had given him" at §274.

843 On the emperor's property, and the problematic distinction between his *fiscus* and the imperial treasury (*aerarium*), see Millar 1977: 133–201; Osgood 2011: 312–313.

and he bound himself by oath[844] to Agrippa[845] in the middle of the forum of the city of the Romans.[846] **276** Taking away from Antiochus the kingdom which he had, he bestowed upon him [instead] a certain portion of Cilicia and also Commagene.[847] And he freed Alexander the Alabarch—an old friend of his who had been the administrator of [the property of] his mother, Antonia,[848] who had been imprisoned due to Gaius's anger, and whose son[849] married Agrippa's daughter, Berenice.[850] **277** But after Alexander's son, Marcus, died after he

---

844 For ὅρκια τέμνειν, see, for example, *Iliad* 2.124 and Polybius 21.24.3; "*Temnein horkia* means 'to make a treaty'; the primary meaning of this formula means cutting the pledges of the contract which has been sworn (*horkia*), viz., the sacramental victims, while the oath is being taken" (Bickerman 2007: 1.3). This ceremony is apparently commemorated by a coin, issued simultaneously by Agrippa and his brother, Herod of Chalicis, that shows them crowning Claudius; the inscription on the reverse mentions the "oath" (ὅρκια) that established Agrippa's alliance with the emperor, the Senate, and the people of Rome. See Meshorer 2001: 100–101 and Kropp 2013. Indeed, Cassius Dio (60.8.2–3; GLAJJ 2.367–368) writes that Claudius "enlarged the domain of Agrippa of Palestine, who, happening to be in Rome, had helped him to become emperor, and bestowed on him the rank of consul" (trans. Cary, LCL), and that he also gave Agrippa's brother, Herod, "the rank of praetor and a principality. And he permitted them to enter the Senate and to express their thanks to him in Greek." For a hint that Claudius's commitment to Agrippa I referred to his posterity as well, see the note on "oaths" at §362.

845 As stated in the preceding note, Cassius Dio mentions the two brothers together, and the coin at least shows them both (although only Agrippa is mentioned in the legend). Our passage, however, ignores Herod of Chalcis here, and at §277 will portray him as the beneficiary of Agrippa's intervention with the emperor, just as we will even see reluctance to call Herod "king" (see the note on "Chalcis" at §338). All of this points to use of a source that focused favorably upon Agrippa. Cf. the note on "Agrippa" at §236.

846 For this full formulation, instead of plain "Rome," which in this case might reflect *Forum Romanorum*, see the note on "Jerusalemites" at 20.11.

847 In 37 Gaius Caligula appointed Antiochus IV king over his father's former kingdom, Commagene, and also added the coast of Cilicia to his realm, after it had been annexed to Syria for close to two decades (Cassius Dio 59.8.2; cf. Bickerman 2007: 1.268–271). Therefore, Josephus's statement here means that Claudius deposed

Antiochus and then, seemingly immediately, reinstated him as king over the very same territories. That is quite odd. Dio, in contrast, writes that Antiochus was already deposed by Gaius, and was restored by Claudius in 41 (Dio 60.8.1). Feldman accepts Dio's report and assumes Josephus was confused. However, as Barrett notes, Dio reports this in his narrative about Claudius (Book 60), while in his chapters about Gaius (Book 59) there is no hint of any falling-out between Gaius and Antiochus. Consequently, Barrett upholds Josephus's report here, suggesting that Claudius's deposition of Antiochus had nothing to do with Antiochus himself, but was rather a part of a sweeping abolition of all of Gaius's *acta* (cf. Suetonius, *Claud.* 11.3; Dio 60.4.1), and that Dio did not understand the process and therefore assumed Gaius had deposed Antiochus (Barrett 1990: 285). D. Wardle (1992a) rejects Barrett's view, and asserts that in the early empire client kings were formally given their position by the Senate and therefore a general abolition of Gaius's *acta* would not have affected those kings' positions. Wardle further points out that the events of the year 40 in Dio's Book 59 survive only in the epitomes, and therefore their absence in that book does not mean much—so Gaius may have indeed deposed Antiochus in 40.

848 On Alexander, see the note on "Alabarch" at 18.159. For a particular implication of the present datum, that he was Antonia's guardian, see the note on "money" at 18.165. Probably what is meant here is that he managed her property in Egypt; so Evans 1995: 580. On that property, for which there is a good bit of papyrological evidence, see Rostovtzeff 1957: 1.292 and 2.670, n. 45, also Kokkinos 1992: 68–86. On the manuscript variant here that adds "Lysimachus" to Alexander's name, probably because of a misreading of Philo's *De Animalibus*, see Terian 1981: 25–28 and Evans 1995: 586–589.

849 The next line supplies the name of Alexander's son.

850 Julia Berenice, daughter of Agrippa and Cypros. Years later she would become Titus's lover. About her, see Krieger 1997; Mason 2008: 178, n. 1359; and Ilan 2022.

had taken her as a virgin,[851] Agrippa gave her to his brother Herod,[852] after asking Claudius that the kingdom of Chalcis be his.[853]

Claudius and the Jews of the Empire

(5.2) 278 At that time, Jews[854] were engaged in civil strife against[855] the Greeks in the city of the Alexandrians.[856] For when Gaius died, the Jewish nation, which during his rule had been humiliated and terribly outraged by the Alexandrians,[857] took heart and immediately

---

851 Although some have taken this passage to mean that she was a virgin when married by Herod (see *HJP* 1.572, n. 59), so had been only engaged to Marcus and their marriage was not consummated, that requires some clever punctuation of the text and also contradicts the plain meaning of the end of §276. Rather, it seems that all Josephus means is that she was first married, as a virgin, to Marcus, and then later, in a second marriage, to Herod; for similar use of παρθένον λαβών, as here, with regard to a first marriage as opposed to a second one, see 17.352. Josephus has, however, collapsed several events, for epigraphic evidence shows that Marcus was still alive in 43; see *CPJ* 2.197–200 and the note on "his reign" at §350. If Agrippa married her off to his brother Herod, that must have been between Marcus's death and Agrippa's, later in 43 or in 44—but that is well after the present context, 41 CE, when, according to both Josephus (here) and Cassius Dio (60.8.2–3), Claudius granted Herod the kingdom of Chalcis. We should conclude, accordingly, that Josephus's reference to Berenice's widowhood and second marriage appears here only to round out the presentation of Alexander the Alabarch, which does indeed belong to the present chronological context. The facts that §277 is out of chronological order, opens with a reference to "Alexander's son, Marcus" although the previous line referred to him with no name, and focuses on a marriage within the Herodian family, all suggest that this passage, like 20.104, is a snippet based on a Herodian family chronicle; see the note on "Herod" at 20.104.

852 Marriages with nieces seem to have been fairly widespread in Jewish antiquity—widespread enough to be taken for granted, even as a usual expectation, by tannaitic texts (*t. Qidd.* 1:4 [ed. Lieberman, 276]; *b. Yevamot* 62b–63a; *m. Nedarim* 8:7 and 9:10; the last two apparently assume the expectation was prevalent enough to require someone to bind himself by an oath if he wanted to evade it), and to be opposed by some Qumran texts; see esp. *Damascus Document* 5:8–11 and *Temple Scroll* 66:15–17. Josephus takes it for granted concerning Abraham and Sarah at *Ant.* 1.154, and mentions another case at 12.187–189. In general, see Mayer 1987: 55–56. In any case, royal

families often have their own needs and preferences when it comes to marriage, and the practice was fairly common in the Herodian family (see 20.103; *War* 1.563// *Ant.* 17.19; *Ant.* 16.194–196, 215, 18.110).

853 I.e., Herod's. Chalcis was in the Beqaa, the Lebanese (or "Massyas" [Strabo 16.2.10]) plain between the Lebanon and anti-Lebanon mountains; see *HJP* 1.571–573. That Claudius awarded this kingdom to Herod is also stated at *War* 2.217, but that does not say it was at Agrippa's behest; cf. the note on "Agrippa" at §275.

854 The lack of an article and the use of the genitive here ('Ιουδαίων) is perhaps meant to soften the report; not "the Jews," but only "[some] Jews," were engaged in the stasis. On Claudius's policies and dealings with the Jews, and their contradictory tendencies, see the note on "nation" at 20.12. On his involvement with the Jews of Alexandria, see Tcherikover in *CPJ* 1.69–74 and 2.36–55 (*CPJ* 153), Kasher 1985: 262–309, D. R. Schwartz 1990a: 74–77, Slingerland 1997: 143–150, and Ben Zeev 1998: 294–342.

855 It is possible that Josephus means only that there was a conflict "between Jews and Greeks" (Feldman 1965: 343; Schalit 1963: 343). However, given the explanation in the next sentence, that the Jews took up arms, this πρός + accusative should be given its full sense, which assigns the initiative to the Jews; see LSJ 1497, s.v. πρός, §III.C.4 and D. R. Schwartz 1990a: 102–103, n. 49. For a similar formulation, but with the shoe on the other foot in a later episode in Alexandria, see *War* 2.487: ἀεὶ μὲν ἦν στάσις πρὸς τὸ Ἰουδαϊκὸν τοῖς ἐπιχωρίοις. Thackeray (JLCL 2.543) renders merely "there had been incessant strife between the native inhabitants and the Jewish settlers," but Mason (2008: 350) renders more specifically, "there was ongoing civil strife among the natives *toward* the Judean [element]," and the continuation indeed goes on to portray the Jews as victims.

856 For this full formulation, rather than plain "Alexandria," see the note on "Jerusalemites" at 20.11.

857 For those terrible events of 38 CE, see 18.257–260, and especially Philo, *Flaccus* 26–107 and *Leg.* 120–137; Bergmann and Hoffmann 1987; Modrzejewski 1997: 165–173; Sanders 2016; Ritter 2015: 132–183; Alston 2020.

armed itself.[858] **279** So Claudius wrote the governor of Egypt[859] to put down the civil strife, and, upon the urging of Kings Agrippa and Herod, he also sent out an edict[860] written to Alexandria and Syria,[861] with the following text:[862]

---

858 It is perhaps surprising that Josephus here lays the initiative for the renewal of violence on the Jews, although he does emphasize how justified their grudge was. Moreover, this appears to contradict the quoted edict itself, which lays the blame on the Greeks (§284). This incongruity between the introduction to the edict and the edict itself is at the heart of discussions about the authenticity of the edict; see the note on "text" at §279. A solution proposed by a scholar who assumes the authenticity of the edict is that Josephus, in this introduction to the edict, was following "an independent Alexandrian Jewish source that did not survive," which dealt with the events that occurred later that same year and provoked Claudius's later letter, preserved on papyrus (*CPJ* 153), that was more negative towards the Jews; so Ben Zeev 1998: 313–315. As Ben-Zeev notes, that suggestion entails the conclusion that Josephus was either unaware of or did not care about the discrepancy in tone between the introduction and the edict. So does any other suggestion, unless one attempts to neutralize the opening of §278 by taking πρός as "with" (see the note there on "against"), by emphasizing its statement that the Jews had good reason to take up arms, and by arguing they did so only in self-defense, not in vengeance. Those are all possible.

859 The identity of this governor is not clear, for two reasons. First, there is a gap in the dated evidence for Roman governors of Egypt: for C. Vitrasius Pollio there are dated testimonies between October 38 and sometime in 40, while for his successor, L. Aemilius Rectus, the evidence begins with the opening of *CPJ* 153 in November 41 and goes down to April 42; see Bastianini 1975: 271–272. Thus, even if we were sure that the present text is authentic and was published shortly after Gaius's death in January 41 (as is suggested by §§278–279), we would not know who the governor was. Moreover, there is room to doubt that the document is authentic; it might be a Jewish version of *CPJ* 153; see the note on "text" at the end of the present paragraph.

860 Διάγραμμα. See the note on "edict" at §160.

861 Yet the following edict discusses the rights of Alexandrian Jews alone, and Josephus soon explicitly writes that it was addressed to Alexandria (§286). It is followed, beginning at §287, with one to the rest of the world. Probably Josephus refers to Syria here because that is the part of the rest of the world that will interest him in what follows; see esp. §§300–311.

862 The following two edicts, and especially the first one, which was addressed to Alexandria, have elicited extensive scholarly discussion. For references to some of the huge bibliography about this issue, see *CPJ* 2.36–37 and Ben Zeev 1998: 295–296; for reviews of scholarship, see Feldman 1965: 346–349 and Ritter 2015: 142–156. The debate was sparked especially by the discovery of a papyrus, first published in 1924 (Bell 1924 = *CPJ* 153 = Smallwood 1967, no. 370), that preserves a copy—a "very careless" private copy (Harker 2008: 26)—of a letter of Claudius addressed to the Alexandrians and dated to the same year; like the present edict, it deals with the clashes between Jews and their neighbors in Alexandria and with the rights of the Jews. That papyrus drew much scholarly attention for many reasons, but in the Jewish context was and is important especially because Claudius's attitude towards the Jews is distinctly more negative than in the edicts quoted here by Josephus. Thus, the present document opens by emphasizing that the Jews were longtime residents of Alexandria, were called "Alexandrians" and had "obtained equal civil status from the (Ptolemaic) kings" (§281) and that the Romans too had preserved their rights (§§282–283); it says nothing (apart from the hint that might be indicated by the closing call upon both sides to keep the peace [§285]) about Jewish violence; and it blames the Alexandrians for rising up against the Jews (§284), saying that that happened when Gaius, in his "great madness and derangement," persecuted the Jews (§284). All of that is music to Jewish ears. The papyrus letter, in contrast, is much more evenhanded, but expresses suspicion and hostility toward the Jews. "The tone of this version of the letter favours the Greeks. They are given a slap on the wrist for starting a 'war against the Jews,' while the Jews are castigated and given a series of prohibitions" (Harker 2008: 26): not to send two delegations (meaning unclear), not to infiltrate games in the city, not to bring in Jews from Syria or Egypt. Not only that, but Claudius also warns the Jews that if they do such things, which he characterizes as aiming for more than they have "in a foreign city" (l. 95), he will treat them "as fomenting a common plague for the whole world" (lines 98–100). Scholars have suggested, with various nuances, the two obvious solutions: either Claudius's attitude towards the Jews changed radically during his first year and both documents are authentic (e.g., Kasher 1985: 273–274, and—more cautiously—Ben Zeev 1998: 305–326; cf. Ritter 2015:

280 Tiberius Claudius Caesar Augustus Germanicus, of tribunician power,[863] says:
281 Whereas [a] I have known from the outset that the Jews in Alexandria, called
Alexandrians,[864] settled together[865] in the very earliest times[866] with the Alexandrians
and obtained equal civil status from the kings,[867] as has been made clear by the documents which they have and from the edicts,[868] and 282 [b] after Alexandria was subjected by Augustus to our own rule their rights were preserved by the prefects sent
there from time to time[869] and there was never any controversy regarding their rights,

---

153–156), or the edict quoted by Josephus is a Jewish forgery, or a Jewish "version" of Claudius's letter; so, for example, D. R. Schwartz 1990a: 99–106 and Harker 2008: 25–28.

863 *Tribunicia potestas.* Hudson (cited by Niese 1890a: 259 ad loc.) suggested correcting the text by adding to Claudius's titles here ἀρχιερεὺς μέγιστος, i.e., *pontifex maximus*, as appears in the following edict (§287) as well as in Claudius's letter to the Alexandrians (CPJ 153, lines 14–15). But perhaps we should not expect too much consistency. On the one hand, both of the latter documents include a consular title as well; and on the other hand, at 20.11 too there is no reference to Claudius's high-priestly office.

864 Writing that the Jews of Alexandria are "called 'Alexandrians'" implies that they enjoyed the same legal status as their Greek neighbors. This is one of the most significant contrasts with the aforementioned papyrus letter of Claudius (CPJ 153), which clearly distinguishes between the "Alexandrians" and "the Jews"—see lines 82–83, 88–89: "I conjure the Alexandrians (Ἀλεξανδρεῖς μέν) to behave gently and kindly towards the Jews ... The Jews, on the other hand (καὶ Ἰουδέοις δέ), I order ..." (see also Tcherikover's comments at CPJ 2.49). Ben Zeev (1998: 315–316), however, stresses that even Josephus's text of the edict here only says that the Jews were "*called* 'Alexandrians,'" suggesting that they were not so in the strict legal sense. Yet, the continuation of this sentence in the edict makes it explicit that the Jews enjoyed equal rights with the Alexandrians; whereas the papyrus letter mentions only the Jews' right to live according to their religious practices and customs (lines 85–87) but not any political rights, even admonishing them to be satisfied with that and not to seek more in a city that "is not their own" (lines 94–95). Twice more in Josephus's writings the Jews are referred to as "Alexandrians": (1) at *Ant.* 14.188 Julius Caesar is said to have made a bronze tablet declaring that the Jews of Alexandria were Alexandrian citizens (cf. *Apion* 2.35–37), and (2) at *Apion* 2.38 Josephus takes issue with Apion's amazement that the Jews "were called 'Alexandrians'"; see Barclay (2007: 188–189, n. 124, ad loc.). It seems that the Jews often claimed to be "Alexandrians," even if not all would agree they were entitled to that status and insisted, instead, that they were merely inhabitants of the city. This is implied by another papyrus, which

contains a petition of a Jewish man who called himself an "Alexandrian" but someone knocked that down to "a Jew from Alexandria" (CPJ 151, l. 2 [CPJ 2.30–32]). Cf. Feldman 1965: 344–346, n. d and Ritter 2015: 86–88. Kasher (1985: 274–278) suggests a rather complicated solution: that the term was used to stress that the Jews had a status equal to that of citizens of the *polis*; but they were not themselves citizens of the *polis*; rather, "they were *politai* of their own political organization, and because the existence of that organization in Alexandria was legally recognized, they could be called 'Alexandrians'" (p. 275). Presumably, not all would understand such usage and/or agree with it.

865 Συγκατοικίζω; LSJ: "colonize jointly, join in colonizing." In Josephus this term appears only here and in *Ant.* 17.352, and in the latter it is used metaphorically of marriage. *War* 2.487 asserts that Alexander the Great granted the Jews "the [privilege of] settling (μετοικέω) in the city."

866 As mentioned in the previous note, at *War* 2.487 Josephus asserts that the Jews settled in Alexandria already in Alexander's time, and he does so also in *Apion* 2.42. In contrast, in his papyrus letter to the Alexandrians, Claudius merely writes that the Jews "have inhabited the same city for many years" (lines 83–84).

867 I.e., the Ptolemaic kings. *War* 2.487–488 likewise mentions that Alexander's successors upheld his grant of equal rights to the Jews of Alexandria. See also *Apion* 1.189 (Pseudo-Hecataeus) on the Jews' rights in Alexandria upon settling in Egypt (τὴν κατοίκησιν αὐτῶν καὶ τὴν πολιτείαν) early in the Ptolemaic period.

868 These documents about the status of Jews in Alexandria, which presumably were collected by the Jews of Alexandria, have not survived and are not quoted by Josephus. See Motzo 1977: 751–753 and Ben Zeev 1998: 300–301. For the use of διάταγμα for "edict," as also below at §§285–286, 291–292, 304, 306–307, 310, see GTRI 36, s.v., also 127–128.

869 On the Roman governors of Egypt, see Bastianini 1975. But we have no evidence about their dealings with Jews prior to the fourth decade of the first century. On Roman rule in Egypt as it pertained to the Jews down to the days of Claudius, see Tcherikover in CPJ 1.55–69; Barclay 1996: 49–56; and Modrzejewski 1997: 161–173.

283 just as [c] when the Jews' ethnarch[870] died at the time when Aquila[871] was in Alexandria, Augustus did not prevent[872] (the appointment of additional) ethnarchs,[873] because of his desire that each [people] remain subject to its own customs and not be forced to violate its ancestral religion;[874] **284** and [d] the Alexandrians rose up[875] against the Jews among them[876] in the times of Gaius Caesar who, due to his great madness[877] and derangement[878] humiliated the Jewish nation because it did not want to violate its ancestral religion by addressing him as a god;[879] [therefore]

---

870 For the relatively rare title "ethnarch" see Sharon 2010. Among other known ethnarchs are the Hasmonean Hyrcanus II (e.g., *Ant.* 14.194, 196) and Herod's son Archelaus (*War* 2.93//*Ant.* 17.317; *War* 2.96; 111, 115, 167; *Ant.* 17.339; and a fragment of Nicolaus—*GLAJJ* 1.252, lines 73–74), as well as the "ethnarch of King Aretas" in or near Damascus mentioned in 2 Corinthians 11:32. On him, see Taylor 1992. An ethnarch of the Jews in Egypt is mentioned in a passage from Strabo cited by Josephus at *Ant.* 14.117 (and Philo, *Flacc.* 74, mentions a "genarch"); see Stern, *GLAJJ* 1.280–281.

871 Probably C. Iulius Aquila, who is known to have been the prefect of Egypt in 10/11 CE (Bastianini 1975: 269).

872 This implies, realistically enough, the assumption that even had Augustus wanted to put an end to the office he would not have put an end to an ethnarch's tenure but, rather, have waited until a more elegant opportunity presented itself. Cf. Tiberius's annexation of Philip's tetrarchy to the province of Syria upon the tetrarch's death (18.108) and Claudius's transformation of Judea into a province upon that of Agrippa I (19.360–363).

873 This seemingly contradicts Philo's statement in *Flacc.* 74 that, after the death of the *genarch* (a title which is apparently synonymous with ethnarch; see the hendiadys at Philo, *Who is the Heir* 279), Augustus appointed a *gerousia* to take charge of Jewish affairs. To resolve this apparent contradiction, Box (1939: 103) noted that Philo did not write that the office of ethnarch was abolished, and therefore suggests that all Philo meant is that Augustus now put the ethnarch at the head of the newly-formed *gerousia* (cf. Sharon 2010: 486). Another suggestion is that Claudius knew that there had been no ethnarchs since the day of Aquila but wanted to underline that that was not Augustus's fault; perhaps the deceased ethnarch was the last of a dynasty that died out. See van der Horst 2003a: 168–169; cf. D. R. Schwartz 1990a: 104 and Ben Zeev 1998: 302.

874 Ben Zeev (1998: 302–303) points to the existence of inscriptions and papyri that attest to Augustus's recognition of the rights of several subject peoples. On the translation of θρησκεία, see the note on "religion's"

at 18.287. For Josephus's claim that he himself followed the tolerant policy that he here ascribes to Augustus, see *Life* 113.

875 It seems that ἐπαρθῆναι implies both being moved to act and arrogance. Cf. 20.82 and *Life* 24.

876 This plain assignment of blame to the Alexandrians, not the Jews, goes well with the coming reference to Gaius in creating doubts about the authenticity of this document. Cf. the note on "text" at §279.

877 For ἀπόνοια, LSJ 211, s.v. offers "loss of all sense" and "madness." Cf. the note on "insanity" at §1.

878 Claudius refers to Gaius's παραφροσύνη in the next paragraph as well (§285). However, on the one hand Josephus himself uses it, as author, in §258 (as also at 12.112 and 14.101), and, on the other hand, its appearance in an official document, alongside "madness," in an emperor's characterization of his predecessor, appears suspicious, for Gaius was Claudius's nephew, and predecessor, and one might expect appearances to be maintained; cf. the note on "disloyalty" at §268. This is among the considerations that suggest the present document is a product of Jewish forgery or editing. Yakobson (1989: 50–65) portrays an ambiguous public attitude of Claudius vis-à-vis Gaius, underlining his punishment of Gaius's assassins (but not all of them; see §273), his refusal to impose damnatio memoriae (but surreptitious removal of Gaius's statues, at night [Cassius Dio 60.4.6]), and his failure to punish most of those who had collaborated with Gaius in his crimes. Similarly, in response to Ramage's (1983: 202–206) attempt to infer from numismatic evidence that Claudius used his coinage to attack Gaius, Levick (1990: 88–89) argued that that evidence has been wrongly interpreted, just as, more generally, she assembles other evidence for Claudius's usual abstention, early in his reign (to which the present document belongs), from attacks on his predecessor.

879 As S. R. F. Price (1984: 81) underlines, referring to *Leg.* 353, Gaius was the only significant exception to the rule that "the Roman emperors did not use *theos* of themselves when communicating in Greek with their subjects."

285 I desire that none of the rights of the Jewish nation shall be lost to them on account of Gaius's derangement; rather, their former privileges must be preserved for them although they maintain their own customs. And I demand[880] that both sides give the utmost forethought to [ensuring] that no disturbance occur after the publication of my edict.[881]

(5.3) 286 That, then, was the written text of the edict sent to Alexandria[882] on behalf of the Jews. The one to the rest of the inhabited world was as follows:[883]

287 Tiberius Claudius Caesar Augustus Germanicus, high priest, of tribunician power, elected consul for the second time,[884] says: **288** Since King[885] Agrippa and Herod, my closest friends,[886] have asked me to agree to preserve, also for the Jews living throughout the Romans' empire,[887] the same rights that [I guaranteed] the Jews in Alexandria, I am very happy to agree, not only [a] so as to be gracious to them who asked me [to do so], **289** but also [b] because I consider them too, on whose behalf the request was made,[888] to be worthy [of it] by virtue of their loyalty[889] and friendship to the Romans, and especially because [c] I consider it to be just that not even a Greek city[890] should forfeit these rights, after they were maintained for it during the days of the divine Augustus.[891]

---

880 Διακελεύομαι. This is its only occurrence in Josephus's writings. The papyrus letter uses plain κελεύω at the outset of its warning to the Jews (CPJ 153, line 89).

881 This last section is the operative section of the edict—Claudius's decision. Its call upon both sides to strive to avoid provocation contrasts somewhat with the rest of the document, which is wholly in favor of the Jews. But it is in line with Claudius's letter preserved on papyrus, CPJ 153: lines 86–88 demand that the Alexandrians allow the Jews "to keep their own ways"; lines 79–80 urge both sides to "stop this destructive and obstinate mutual enmity"; and in lines 100–102, near the end of the letter, Claudius writes: "If you both give up your present ways and are willing to live in gentleness and kindness with one another ...". So if Jewish forgers or editors were involved in formulating the present document, they were clever enough to allow the emperor an evenhanded conclusion.

882 Yet, in introducing the edict Josephus had said that it was addressed to both Alexandria and Syria (see above, §279).

883 On this edict, see the detailed dicussion in Ben Zeev 1998: 328–342.

884 Claudius's second consulate was in 42, so he was "cos. design. II" in 41—his first year as emperor. Ben Zeev 1998: 330 lists three letters of Claudius to various cities, all dated to 41, in which appear the same titles of Claudius as here.

885 Here in the singular, in contrast to the plural used at §279.

886 Τῶν φιλτάτων μοι. Ben Zeev (1998: 331) writes that this is a common expression in official Roman documents,

and mentions Millar's observation that Roman emperors used in their edicts "language which implies that these are essentially personal decisions and pronouncements," for which he cites this instance as an example (Millar 1977: 258–259). Yet, as Ben Zeev also notes, the friendship between Claudius and Agrippa was a real one; see the note on "along" at 18.143.

887 Intervention of leaders of Judea in favor of Jews of the Diaspora is recorded from the days of the ethnarch Hyrcanus II in the 40s BCE: for the Jews of Ephesus (Ant. 14.223–227) and of Laodicea (Ant. 14.241–243). Cf. Mendels 1997: 211–212; Sharon 2010: 481–482, 490. Personal friends often petitioned Roman leaders in order to secure rights and privileges, and, as at 20.12–13, Claudius often mentions personal friends in his speeches and edicts (Ben Zeev 1998: 335–336).

888 I.e., the Jews of the Roman Empire.

889 The loyalty (πίστις) of Hyrcanus II is mentioned as a reason for Julius Caesar's granting of rights to Hyrcanus and his children and the Jews in the first Roman document, among those cited by Josephus, that postdates the Roman takeover of Judea (Ant. 14.192). Loyalty and goodwill of peoples under Roman domination are often given as reasons for conferring rights upon them by Claudius; see Ben Zeev 1998: 331–332, 337–338.

890 This formulation, that assumes that the Jews have a stronger claim to their rights than Greek cities do to theirs, is another giveaway of the Jewish editing this document has undergone.

891 As Ben Zeev (1998: 338) observes and illustrates, "confirmation of the rights given by Augustus is a

290 And it is proper that the Jews in the entire world that we rule observe their ancestral customs[892] without any interference[893]—just as I myself call upon them now, in this benevolent edict[894] of mine, to behave more appropriately—observing their own laws and not expressing scorn[895] for the religions[896] of other nations. **291** And I desire that the rulers of the cities and colonies[897] and municipalities[898] in Italy and abroad, [as well as] kings and potentates, shall have this edict of mine inscribed by their own delegates and keep it posted[899] for at least thirty days in a place at which it can easily be read from the ground.[900]

---

common feature of the policy implemented by Claudius." So too in his letter to the Alexandrians, Claudius confirms the rights of the Alexandrians "in the same way that the god Augustus confirmed them" (*CPJ* 153, lines 57–59).

892 Τὰ πάτρια ἔθη. The same formulation as in Caesar's edicts in 14.194, 216 and the decree of Ephesus at 14.263. Below in this same section Claudius speaks, instead, of "their own laws" (νόμοι), just as such terms appear fairly indiscriminately in those earlier documents as well; see, for example, 14.195 (νόμοι), 216 (νόμιμα), 263 (νόμοι). While for Jews such distinctions could be very important (see, for example, 13.296–297 and Philo, *Hypothetica* 7.6, along with the note on "regulations" at 18.274), no one should expect a Roman emperor, or a formulator of Roman documents, to care much about them. In general, see Schröder 1996.

893 For similar use of ἀνεπικώλυτος in a Roman privilege for the Jews, see 16.169. Cf. the last verse of Acts: Paul is allowed to live and preach in Rome ἀκωλύτως. Of the present document, Ben-Zeev (1998: 332) writes that "this is the first unambiguous mention of rights applying to all the Jews living in the Roman world." But earlier texts do point in the same direction; see *Ant.* 16.162–165 (Augustus) and 14.194–195, 213–216 (Julius Caesar), as well as various letters by Roman magistrates to Greek cities (e.g., to Ephesus—*Ant.* 14.225–227; to Laodicea—14.241–243). See Sharon 2017: 125–135.

894 For this sense, referring to the document itself and not only to the value it expresses, see LSJ 1932, s.v. φιλανθρωπία §III. See also Ben Zeev (1998: 332), who quotes Benner's explanation that "a quality of the emperor is substituted for the actual manifestation of that quality, i.e., *beneficium* or *edictum*." For rulers' pride in this quality in Roman period, see esp. Bell 1949 and Spicq 1994: 3.160–171. Bell cites several cases of such use of φιλανθρωπία with a personal pronoun; see, for example, *SP* no. 217, in which the emperor Gallienus (267 CE) concludes a decision granting privileges to someone with the statement that the latter shall thereby enjoy τῆς ἐμῆς φιλανθρωπίας. Cf. the note on "benevolent" at §330.

895 This is the only occurrence of ἐξουθενίζω in Josephus.

896 Δεισιδαιμονίαι. Although the term can have a negative sense, "superstition" (see Mason 2008: 145, n. 1096, on *War* 2.174), in Josephus it is usually positive or neutral ("religion"); see Koets 1929: 21–24 and *ThLJ* 126, s.v. δεισιδαιμονία. Here too, as in other Roman documents with regard to the Jews (such as *Ant.* 14.228, 232, 234) and others, both with regard to those others and with regard to the Romans themselves, the term is not negative, and probably corresponds to *pietas* or *religio*; see Koets 1929: 23–24 and Ben Zeev 1998: 153, 332. True, translating ancient Latin "religio" into modern English "religion" is not without its pitfalls; but there does not seem to be a better alternative. Cf. Mason 2007: 482 and Barton and Boyarin 2016.

897 This is the only occurrence of κολωνία in Josephus. Usually he uses ἀποικία; the use of the transliterated Latin term (*colonia*), as the next noun too, gives the document some Latin flavor.

898 This is the only occurrence of μουνικίπιον in Josephus; cf. the preceding note.

899 This is the only occurrence of the otherwise common verb ἔκκειμαι in Josephus. As Katzoff (1982: 209–217) notes, although it was not usual to include instructions concerning publication in the body of an edict, reserving them instead for a cover letter to the relevant official, "Roman imperial practice was not consistent on this point" (216). The present document is one of two that he cites. For other such lack of consistency, see the note on "Dorites" at §303.

900 Feldman notes that the final requirement, that it should be published in a place where it may be read from the ground, is almost identical to a Latin formula—*ut de plano recte legi possi(n)t*; for texts with this and similar formulations about publication, see Ando 2000: 97–101. For Gaius's unfair practice in this regard, see the note on "upon them" at §25.

Agrippa I, King of Judea

Agrippa's Opening Gestures and Arrangements

(6.1) 292 With these edicts, then, sent to Alexandria and to the whole world, Claudius Caesar showed what his opinion was concerning the Jews.

And he immediately sent Agrippa[901] on his way, with magnificent honors, to take up his kingdom, ordering the provincial governors and procurators, in writing, to treat him cordially.[902]

293 He,[903] as appropriate for someone going back to better fortunes,[904] quickly returned.

Upon arriving in Jerusalem he completely carried out[905] thanksgiving sacrifices, omitting nothing that the law requires.[906] 294 For that reason he also arranged for[907] the "shaving"[908] of a very large number of Nazirites.[909] As for the golden chain, equal in weight to the iron chain with which his sovereign hands had been bound, that Gaius had given him as a

---

901 For the argument, that the section starting here and ending at §299 was mistakenly placed here by Josephus, and actually describes Agrippa's return to Judea following his first enthronement by Gaius in 37 (described in *Ant.* 18.237), see D. R. Schwartz 1990a: 11–14 and below, the note on "better" at §294. For criticism of that theory, see Kokkinos 1998: 282–284.

902 This is the only occurrence of ἐράσμιος in Josephus.

903 On Agrippa I, see Ciaceri 1917; Charlesworth 1936b: 3–30; *HJP* 1.442–453; Smallwood 1981: 187–200; D. R. Schwartz 1990a; Wilker 2007: 131–192.

904 In context, this refers to Claudius's enlargement of Agrippa's kingdom in 41 (above, §§274–275). Perhaps, however, it in fact alludes to Agrippa's release from prison and acquisition of Philip's realm in 37; see the note on "Agrippa" at §292.

905 This is the only occurrence of ἐκπληρόω ("fill up") in Josephus. It might refer to "fulfillment" of a vow (as at Acts 13:32–33), but no vow has been mentioned. Probably we need only assume an expectation that the safe conclusion of a voyage should entail some thanksgiving, and that can be expressed negligently or "fully." On this theme, see Kattan Gribetz 2017.

906 But Jewish law did not, apparently, require any thanksgiving sacrifices; they are voluntary. See Josephus, *Ant.* 3.228–229. Perhaps all that Josephus means is that when Agrippa offered such sacrifices he did so the way the law prescribes (as suggested by Feldman's expansive translation: "omitting none of the ritual enjoined by our law").

907 Paying for a Nazirite's sacrifices was a well-known type of charity. The Palestinian Talmud (*y. Ber.* 7:2, 11b//*y. Nazir* 5:5, 54b) narrates a story in which a Hasmonean king, Alexander Janneus, paid for 450 sacrificial animals for the sacrifices of 150 indigent Nazirites—three each,

as required by Numbers 6:14. Büchler (1897/98: 700–701) suggested that that story was in fact initially about Agrippa, as the present story—a suggestion rejected by Joshua Efron (1987: 147–50) but supported by Goodblatt 1987b: 16–23. Noam (2017) proposed a more nuanced view, according to which the talmudic story combined two traditions: an early story from Hasmonean times, not involving King Jannaeus, to which the story about Jannaeus was later added, perhaps on the basis of the story about Agrippa. That later Jewish tradition confused Jannaeus with Agrippa would not be surprising, especially since both were often mentioned in connection with a woman (Salome Alexandra/Berenice); cf. D. R. Schwartz 1981/82: 266–267.

908 Feldman (1965: 353) renders ξυρᾶσθαι here as "to be shorn" and Schalit too (1963; 344) refers to haircuts. But the biblical text that lies behind this, Num 6 (see the next note), refers literally to shaving (*glh*), as does Josephus's use of ξυρήσας at *Ant.* 7.129, where it is used of beards.

909 On this episode, see esp. Schumann 2021: 217–220. Since a main component of the Nazirite's vow was not to cut his hair (Numbers 6:5; Judges 16:17), the plain meaning of this section is that Agrippa ordered the violation of the vow of many Nazirites, which would not at all fit the context. Reference to Acts 21:23–24, where Paul is told to pay for four men who had taken vows, so they could "shave their heads," solves the problem: what is meant is that Agrippa and Paul covered the expenses of the offerings of some needy Nazirites—which would allow them to end the period of the vow and, therefore, to shave (Numbers 6:18–19). That the reference is to payment, which is clear in Acts but not in Josephus, accords with, and is explained by, the formlation preserved in the Mishnah, where the term *tiglaḥat* (lit. "shaving") is indeed used in the sense of "to bring the offerings of a Nazirite"; see *m. Nazir* 2:5, 6; Epstein 1938: 15–16; Feldman 1965: 352–353,

reminder of the bitter[910] misfortune [that had befallen him] and witness to its reversal for the better[911]—he hung it up within the courts of the Temple, over the treasury,[912] as an illustration of the truth that great power can at times collapse and that God can raise up the fallen.[913] **295** For the dedication of the chain demonstrated to all that King Agrippa had been stripped of his former dignity and jailed, but after only a short time, his fetters left behind, was elevated to a kingship even more magnificent than the previous one.[914] **296** May these things lead us to bear in mind, that it is part of the human condition that great things[915] slip away while declining powers can again achieve conspicuous heights.[916]

(6.2) 297 Having completely[917] worshipped God, Agrippa removed Theophilus, son of Ananus,[918] from the high priesthood, assigning his position to Simon[919] (whose surname was

---

n. c; D. R. Schwartz 1990a: 68 and n. 4. It is remarkable that Josephus, in the present short passage, both fails to recognize that his readers might not know what a "Nazirite" is (contrast 4.72, the only other occurrence of "Nazirites" in his writings, where he takes that into account and therefore adds "that is how they are called"; cf. the note on "named" at at 18.4) and also uses a verb that only Jews would understand properly in this context. (Note, in this context, the difficulties—Josephus's? copyists?—raised by the appearance of the same verb at *War* 2.313, set out by Mason 2008: 250, n. 2004). Whether these in-group formulations point to a Jerusalemite source or only to Josephus's own Jerusalemite vocabulary is unclear, but it certainly indicates a lack of attention on his part.

910 Στυγνός. Josephus uses this term only here and below at §318, in a similar phrase.

911 See 18.237 and the note on "better fortunes" at §293. This is the most convincing consideration in favor of the suggestion that this section describes Agrippa's first return to Judea following his enthronement by Gaius in 37 (see the note on "Agrippa" at §292). For why would Agrippa wait four years to commemorate his turn of fortune? And why, in 41 CE, would Agrippa think that anyone in Jerusalem would have been happy to see him dedicate, in the Temple, a gift emanating from an emperor who had, so recently, attempted to desecrate it?

912 On the temple treasury, cf. Hamilton 1964 and *HJP* 2.279–284.

913 For this common theme, of the great change of fortune, in Josephus's materials on Agrippa, see also 18.129, 197–202 and 239, below at §318 and just above at §292. The prominence and utility of this theme in Agrippa's story is reminiscent of two well-known biblical stories, that of Joseph in Egypt as related in Genesis and the story of the book of Esther (see further the note on "have in common" at 18.201 and D. R. Schwartz 1990a: 33–35). More

generally, on reversals of fortune in Josephus, see the note on "[to us all]" at 20.57.

914 Namely, after being king of Philip's territories since 37 (18.237) and Antipas's since 39 (18.252), he was now given Judea and Samaria as well, the heart of the country, along with additional territories (§§274–275). That is, this sentence reflects Josephus's opinion, reflected in this story's location here, that it refers to Agrippa's return to Judea after Claudius's ascent to the throne.

915 Niese (1890a: 261) reads καὶ πεσεῖν ὀλισθάνειν τὰ μεγέθη but brackets πεσεῖν and notes "mihi spurium aut corruptum uid[etur]." Feldman (1965: 354) would rescue the word by emending it, following two mansucripts, into πᾶσιν, rendering "for all grandeurs to glide away." But that dative is difficult to construe and anyway the point of the statement is that for some grandeur can be reachieved. Perhaps πεσεῖν was born as a gloss on the rare ὀλισθάνειν.

916 On this trope, see the note on "[to us all]" at 20.57.

917 This is the only occurrence of ἐντελῶς in Josephus. It corresponds to ἐξεπλήρωσε in §293.

918 For the beginning of his high priesthood, see 18.123.

919 Rabbinic tradition records the case of "Simon the Just," who heard a voice from the Holy of Holies announcing the death of Gaius and the cancellation of his decrees (*t. Sotah* 13:6; *y. Sotah* 9.24b; *Scholion to Megillat Ta'anit* for 22 Shebat [Noam 2003: 283]). If the name is not merely a stock name for a high priest of the mythic past (see A. Tropper 2013), then, as has been noted, the reference would be to this Simon Cantheras; see Winter 1954 and Noam 2003: 283–290. That would imply, however, that Simon was already high priest when Gaius died (cf. Winter loc cit., 73, n. 6), which is another reason for the suggestion that this entire section actually speaks of Agrippa's initial return to Judea after his enthronement by Gaius; see the note on "Agrippa" at §292.

Cantheras[920]), son of Boethus.[921] Simon had two brothers and his father Boethus—whose daughter, as I explained above,[922] had been married by King Herod. **298** Simon thus held the high priesthood, as did[923] his brothers and his father, just as earlier the three sons of Simon, son of Onias, held the position in the period of Macedonian rule,[924] as we related in earlier writings.[925]

(6.3) 299 Having thus taken care of the high priesthood, the king requited the Jerusalemites for their goodwill toward him. For he remitted to them that [tax] which they had to pay for each house,[926] considering it proper to repay the affection of those who loved him. As cavalry commander[927] of the entire army he appointed Silas, a man who had shared together[928] many tribulations with him.[929]

The Dora Affair and Petronius's Intervention

300 After a very short period of time went by, youths[930] of Dora,[931] who rated audacity higher than sanctity,[932] and who by nature had come to be extraordinarily bold,[933] brought a statue of Caesar and dedicated it[934] in the Jews' synagogue.[935] **301** This angered Agrippa

---

920 On this surname and its implications, see the note on "Cantheras" at 19.342.

921 I.e., of the Boethus clan; see the note on "Boethus" at 18.3. As for "Cantheras," see the note on "Cantheras" at §342 and Appendix 2.

922 See *Ant.* 15.320–322, recalled at 18.136.

923 I have rendered σύν here on the assumption that it does not imply any sharing of the office. Contrast *Ant.* 11.306, along with Spilsbury and Seeman 2017: 110, n. 1035.

924 "Macedonian" is Josephus's usual term for the Hellenistic period prior to the Hasmoneans; see the first and last paragraphs of *Ant.* 12.

925 This refers to *Ant.* 12.238, where Josephus gave the sons' names as Onias, Jesus/Jason, and Onias/Menelaus. That is apparently confused, both because it is unlikely that Simon had two sons named "Onias" and because of the much earlier evidence supplied by 2 Maccabees. Cf. the note on "Menelaus" at 20.235. This type of topic interested Josephus; cf. 20.197–198 on Ananus and his sons.

926 On this tax, perhaps reflected in *m. Bava Batra* 1:5 (which states that inhabitants of a town may be compelled to contribute to the building of the city walls and gates), see Udoh 2020: 177–180. For this type of gesture of goodwill, cf. the note on "remitted" at 18.90.

927 Most of the witnesses here read ἵππαρχον, lit. "commander of the cavalry." Since, however, Josephus says "of the entire army," Niese (1890a: 261; 1890b: 223) and Feldman (1965: 356) prefer the Ambrosianus's ἔπαρχον, "governor." But the manuscripts all read ἵππαρχος at §317 and ἱππαρχίας at §320. Rather than depending on a single manuscript here and correcting the text at §§317 and 320 (as is suggested by Dindorf [1865: 762] and followed by Niese [1890a: 261, 264–265] and Feldman [1965: 356, 362, 364]), it seems more prudent to read ἱππ- in all three

passages and conclude that the term could designate an officer with a broader command—as is already suggested by 18.237 (see the note there, on "cavalry commander"). Moreover, note that ἔπαρχος ("prefect"), when used without qualification, usually refers to provincial governors (as at 18.33; 19.363, 20. 193, 297), not to generals (for whom we would expect στρατηγός; cf. the note on "commander" at §256).

928 This is the only occurrence of συμμετέχω in *Antiquities*. Usually plain μετέχω is used (e.g. §§133, 191).

929 This apparently refers to the assistance Silas afforded Agrippa when he was imprisoned (18.204). This reward too thus points to a time close to Agrippa's release from prison and initial enthronement by Gaius, rather than after his second enthronement by Claudius; see the note on "Agrippa" at §292.

930 That the rowdies were youths is a standard topos; see the note on "our youths" at 18.10. On the present episode, see Kasher 1985: 264–267 and Krause 2017: 117–123.

931 The coastal city Dora, founded by Phoenicians, was located ca. 12 km. north of Caesarea. On it, see *HJP* 2.118–120 and Nitschke, Martin, and Shalev 2011.

932 This is the only occurrence of the form ὁσιότης in Josephus.

933 For such pejorative use of θρασύς, especially of youthful hotheads, see the note on "audacious" at 18.6.

934 Or: set it up; see the note on "installation of the statue" at 18.272. In Alexandria too, according to Philo (*Leg.* 134–135), the anti-Jewish violence in 38 CE included the introduction of portraits and statues of Gaius into the Jews' synagogues.

935 This is the earliest context in which Josephus mentions a synagogue in Palestine; others are mentioned in his narratives about the 60s CE (*War* 2.285–289; *Life*

greatly, for it amounted to[936] abrogation of his ancestral laws. Without delay[937] he went to Publius Petronius, who was the governor of Syria,[938] and denounced the Dorites. **302** And he, being upset no less [than Agrippa] about what had been done, for he too considered it to be impious to violate things ordained by law,[939] angrily[940] wrote the leaders[941] of the Dorites as follows:

> **303** Publius Petronius, legate[942] of Tiberius Claudius Caesar Augustus Germanicus, says [as follows] to the heads of the Dorites:[943] **304** Since [a] some of you have gone so far in their mindless audacity [i] not only not to obey the edict[944] published by Claudius Caesar Augustus Germanicus to the effect that the Jews are to be allowed to observe their ancestral practices, **305** but also [ii] to do that which is totally opposite, namely, prevent the Jews's synagogue from being one by transferring the[945] statue of Caesar into it, thus acting contrary to the law not only vis-à-vis the Jews, but also vis-à-vis the emperor, of whom the image would better be placed in his own temple than in a foreign one—certainly than in the place of the synagogue,[946] for according to nature it is just that each rule his own place,[947] in accordance with Caesar's

---

277–280). On synagogues in Josephus, see Krause 2017. More generally on synagogues in antiquity, see Levine 2005a; he discusses the present episode at pp. 66–67.

936 For this sense of δύνασθαι here, see *ThLJ* 194, s.v., §4.

937 This is the only occurrence of ἀμελλητί in Josephus. See the note on "without delay" at §341.

938 On Petronius, see 18.261ff. Josephus's introduction of him as a new character here, and his failure to relate in any way to the fact that this Petronius is the main actor in the long story related at 18.261–309, which in fact dealt with an issue very similar to the present one (the introduction of a statue of the emperor into a Jewish sacred site), is quite an egregious instance of the way stories have been thrown together in these books.

939 This is the only occurrence of ἔννομος in Josephus. The way it allows for vagueness as to whether the reference is to Jewish law or Roman law is very convenient for Josephus here. For a similar case, cf. Acts 18:12–16.

940 His anger would, historically, and perhaps for attentive readers, reflect his experience in the Temple-statue affair in Gaius's day and first-hand knowledge of the way it could threaten public order. As noted, however, it is quite remarkable that Josephus does not comment on that.

941 Although the manuscripts read τοῖς ἀποστάσι ("to the rebels"), this translation follows Niese's conjecture (1890a: 262): τοῖς προεστῶσι ("the leaders"). That fits the address at §303, also the assumption at §304 that not all of the addressees were guilty.

942 This (πρεσβευτής) is Petronius's title at 18.261 as well. It represents *legatus* but, as Eck (2008: 220) points out, when complemented only with the emperor's name, as here, it is not precise. Petronius, as governor of Syria,

was *legatus Augusti pro praetore*; for *pro praetore*, ἀντιστράτηγος would be expected (see *GTRI* 22, 106–107), as for example with regard to Vitellius at 15.407 (τῷ τῆς Συρίας ἀντιστρατήγῳ), according to Niese 1892: 405. As a glance at *CCFJ* 1.145 shows, witnesses and scholars differ frequently about Josephus's use of ἀντιστράτηγος.

943 Ben Zeev (1998: 351–352) notes the hybrid character of this document. It opens with the name of its writer, Petronius, his title, and the verb λέγει, all of which is, as at §§280, 287, characteristic of edicts; but then it names the addressees—which is, as at 20.11, a characteristic of letters. As she notes, however (following Katzoff 1980: 810, n. 7), this is not without parallel; see also the note on "posted" at §291. Moreover, even if it were unparalleled, it would be difficult, as is so often the case, to decide whether that more likely points to authenticity (and a careless chancellery) or, rather, to a negligent forgery.

944 The reference is, apparently, to Claudius's second, universal, edict cited above, §§286–291, for only it applied anywhere outside Alexandria. At §310, however, Petronius refers to both—perhaps to make his appeal all the weightier as it draws to a close.

945 The definite article here seems to mean no more than "the one that generated this dispute."

946 Tcherikover (1959: 306) stressed that this is the only document in which we find "a trace of the exemption of the Jews from the worship of the divine Caesar, but this emphasis had a special reason connected with contemporary events" (i.e., following Gaius's attempt to place his image in the Temple).

947 Cf. above, §283: "Augustus ... because of his desire that each [subject people] remain subject to its own customs and not be forced to violate its ancestral cult."

decree;[948] **306** and [since] [b] it would be silly for me to mention my own decree[949] after the emperor's edict that allows Jews to follow their own customs, although ordering them to share civil life[950] with the Greeks,[951] [therefore I proclaim]:

307 As for those who have dared to do such things against the august[952] [emperor's] edict, things concerning which even those who are thought to be prominent among them are upset and say they were not done at their own decision but, rather, by the impulse of the mob, I have ordered that they be brought up to me by the centurion, Proclus Vitellius,[953] to be held accountable for the things that were done.

308 And I advise[954] the chief leaders, that if they do not desire that it be thought that the injustice was done at their decision, let them point out the guilty parties to the centurion, without allowing there to be anything that might touch off civil strife or a battle—for that, I believe, is what [the criminals] are hunting for by such actions.

309 And as for me and my most honored friend, King Agrippa, we have nothing more in mind than to prevent that the Jewish nation, grasping some occasion, gather together on the pretext of self-defense and turn to desperation.[955]

310 And in order that it be all the better known, what the most august [emperor] too thinks of this whole business, I have attached his edicts that were published in Alexandria[956]—for although it seems that they are known to all, my most honored [friend] King Agrippa read them then out upon the podium when offering before me his legal argument that they[957] should not be deprived of the gifts[958] they had been given by the most august [emperor]. **311** As for the future, accordingly, I command that you seek no excuse for civil strife or rioting. Rather, each shall worship according to his own customs.

(6.4) 312 Thus did Petronius, for his part, direct his attention to making right the wrong that had already been done, and [to ensuring] that nothing similar would happen to them [again].[959]

---

948 Ἐπίκριμα here must reflect the Latin *decretum* (*GTRI* 46, 128–129). In Josephus's writings it appears only here and in the next line.

949 What decree is meant is unclear, for we do not know of another decree of Petronius. Ben Zeev (1998: 348–349) suggests that it refers to this message to Dora, but that does not see to be supported by the text here.

950 This is the only occurrence of συμπολιτεύω in Josephus; but συμπολίτης ("fellow citizens") also appears once, above at §175; see the note on it there. For the term see further Ben Zeev 1998: 354–355.

951 Here we have a statement of what we would term separation of religion and state: the Romans recognize that two sets of norms obligate the Jews, and expect them to go their own way (if they want) concerning their own but otherwise to follow those of the Greek cities in which they live. To the extent that the laws and customs of a Greek city included what we would term religious practices, this implies a recognition that Jews would be excluded from some of the city's norms due to their own religious norms—as is spelled out in some of the Roman documents assembled in *Ant.* 14 and 16. On those documents and rights, see Ben-Zeev 1998.

952 Here and in §310 I have translated σεβαστός rather than rendering it as "Augustus," as usual, because

it seems clear the reference is to Claudius's edict, cited at the outset (§304).

953 This Vitellius seems to be otherwise unknown.

954 On such polite usage of παραινέω, see the note on "urged" at 20.6.

955 ἀπόνοια. The sense here is as at 18.274, in a very similar context.

956 See the note on "edict" at §304.

957 The Jews of Dora.

958 Ben Zeev (1998: 350) remarks that "the choice of the term δωρεά to express Claudius' grants to the Jews is highly meaningful, since it shows that, in spite of the fact that the Jews had been accorded the right to follow their traditional customs already by Julius Caesar and then by Augustus, this right is still regarded by Petronius as 'a privilege,' which consequently can be revoked any time."

959 This parenthetical addition is required to avoid the implication that what had already happened had happened to others, not to Jews. Another way of dealing with that would be to accept the suggestion of Richards and Shutt (1939: 183) to emend εἰς αὐτούς into εἰσαῦθις ("again"), which occurs, for example, at 16.153 (two words), 17.115, and 18.200.

313 King Agrippa, for his part, took the high priesthood away from Simon Cantheras, reappointing to the position Jonathan,[960] the son of Ananus;[961] for he adhered to the view[962] that he was more worthy of the position.[963] But to the latter, taking back[964] such a great honor did not seem to be welcome,[965] and he begged off in the following words:

Agrippa and the High Priesthood

> **314** I am happy to have been honored by you, O king, cherishing in my soul this prize that your judgment has given me, although God in no way adjudged me worthy of the high priesthood. But I am content to have worn the holy vestment once;[966] for then I wore it more sacredly than if I were now to take it back.[967] **315** As for you, if you now wish to give the prize to someone more worthy than me, let [my] advice guide you: I have a brother who is pure of sin both toward God and toward you, O king. I recommend him as appropriate for this position.

316 The king, taking pleasure at these words, admired Jonathan's position on the matter, and gave the high priesthood to his brother, Matthias.[968] And not long thereafter Marsus[969] succeeded Petronius and [began to] rule[970] Syria.[971]

(7.1) 317 Silas, the king's commander,[972] who had always remained faithful to him through all turns of fortune,[973] never refusing[974] to share together[975] with him any danger, and often instead undertaking the most perilous burdens [on his behalf], was full of confidence, assuming that the stability of their friendship also entailed equal honor. **318** So he never took the back seat[976] to the king, and was unbridled in all his conversation with him, and

Agrippa and Silas

---

960 Jonathan, the brother of Theophilus whom Agrippa removed from that same post not much earlier, before appointing Simon Catheras (above, §297), had already been high priest prior to his brother's term (18.95) until he was deposed by Vitellius (18.123).

961 For Ananus see above, 18.26.

962 For the senses of ὁμολογέω (agreeing, confessing ...), see Tov 1999: 115–121.

963 The notion that a high priest should be "worthy" of the position is not to be taken for granted, for Bible and tradition make descent from Aaron, and from particular families among the Aaronites, the sole criterion. However, the notion is not an unnatural one (see already Malachi 2!), especially in a Hellenistic context in which the very word for priest (ἱερεύς) is derived from "holy," and such passages as Ben Sira's praise of Aaron (45:6), and 2 Maccabees' condemnation of Menelaus (4:25: "with nothing worthy of high priesthood"), show that it indeed was held here and there.

964 Although ἀπολαμβάνω need not imply recovery of something previously held (cf. the note on "take over" at §219), this translation, as for example at 15.180, seems to be indicated here by the repetition of the same verb at the end of §314; so *ThLJ* 70.

965 This is the only occurrence of ἀσμενιστός in Josephus.

966 If the reconstruction suggested in the note on "in Judea" at 18.90 is correct, the reference is probably to Passover of 37 CE. On the high-priestly vestments, see the note on "ornaments" at 18.90.

967 Jonathan's surprising response is among the reasons that led Smallwood (1981: 173) to suggest that when Vitellius deposed him (18.123), it was perhaps in accordance with Jonathan's own wishes.

968 On Matthias, cf. VanderKam 2004: 448.

969 C. Vibius Marsus was suffect consul in 17 CE. He had been considered for the governorship of Syria already in 19 CE, following Germanicus's death, but deferred to the seniority of his competitor, Cn. Sentius Saturninus (Tacitus, *Ann.* 2.74). Now, in 42 CE, Claudius gave him that office, from which he would later remove him, shortly after Agrippa I's death (see below, §20.1). During his tenure in Syria he was able to impede the aspirations of Vardanes, the Parthian king, to recover Armenia (Tacitus, *Ann.* 11.10.1; cf. below, §§20.69–73). See Dąbrowa 1998: 44–46 and *HJP* 1.263–264.

970 For διέπω of ruling a province, see the note on "administered" at 18.29.

971 For such bunching of changes in functionaries, see the note on "taking" at §342, the opening note at 20.103, and the note on "Phabes" at 20.179.

972 At §299 he was defined as "cavalry commander of the entire army."

973 See 18.204 and the note above, on §299.

974 Josephus uses ἀναίνομαι elsewhere only at 17.10.

975 As also at §299, although the Greek is different.

976 That is, he never accepted an inferior role. Josephus uses ὑποκατακλίνω only once more, at *Ant.* 12.210, where it refers to seating arrangements at a feast and the placement at the foot of the table implies inferior status.

in conversations he was burdensome insofar as he magnified himself⁹⁷⁷ immoderately and frequently reminded the king of the bitter⁹⁷⁸ moments of misfortune, so as then to point up his own devotion [to Agrippa]; without letup he would go on and on about how, going through so much [with Agrippa], he had exerted himself on his behalf.⁹⁷⁹ **319** Such expansion about these things seemed to be insulting, for which reason the king received the man's unrestrained⁹⁸⁰ frankness with hostility. For the memories of dishonorable times are not pleasant, and he who is continually pointing out how he had earlier been of service is a fool. **320** Indeed, in the end Silas so aroused the king's temper that, moved more by anger than by considered reasoning,⁹⁸¹ he not only removed Silas from his command⁹⁸² but also turned him over [to guards] and sent him, chained, to his own homeland.⁹⁸³

321 But in time his temper cooled and he submitted his judgment of the man to clearer⁹⁸⁴ thought, taking into consideration how much suffering Silas had endured⁹⁸⁵ on his behalf.⁹⁸⁶ Therefore, when celebrating his birthday,⁹⁸⁷ when there was joy for all whom he ruled and they were holding festivities,⁹⁸⁸ from one minute to the next he recalled Silas to sit⁹⁸⁹ and eat with him.⁹⁹⁰ **322** But [Silas], who was by nature independent, thought that he had appropriate cause for wrath, and he did not hide it from those who came for him, saying:

323 What honor is this for which the king recalls me, one that will shortly disappear? For he did not even preserve the rewards he earlier gave me for my loyalty toward him, but rather stripped them away⁹⁹¹ wantonly!⁹⁹² **324** Or did he think that I would desist from my frankness, which, after all I know, I will shout out even more?! How I saved him from such terrible situations, how much suffering I bore so as to provide him with security and honor—for which the reward I received is chains and a dark cell! **325** I am not [the kind of man who⁹⁹³] will ever forget these; perhaps my soul, even when

977 Σεμνύνω. As at §329.

978 Στυγνός. See the note on "bitter" at §294.

979 As reported at 18.204.

980 This adjective, ἀταμίευτος, appears in *Antiquities* only here and at §329. But Josephus frequently uses words of the same stem (ταμι-) in a similar sense. Readers might especially think of the frequent use of ταμίας for quaestor (*GTRI* 91), who was something like our "comptroller," whose job it was to keep things within their proper bounds.

981 For an otherwise thoughtful person's λογισμός being overcome by some baser emotion, cf. §107. However, §353 suggests that there was some larger background for Agrippa's removal of Silas.

982 Here all the manuscripts give ἱππαρχίας. Cf. the note on "cavalry commander" at §299,

983 Josephus does not identify Silas's homeland, but it seems likely that he hailed from the military colony of Babylonian Jews established by King Herod in Batanea (*Ant.* 17.23–31). Batanea was under Agrippa's rule and Josephus testifies that this colony continued to serve Agrippa, as well as his son, Agrippa II (ibid. §§28, 31). Moreover, Silas's name was shared by one "Silas the Babylonian" who, in the 60s, deserted the army of Agrippa II and joined the rebels (*War* 2.520; cf. 3.11, 19 and *Life* 54). See D. R. Schwartz 1990a: 70.

984 Lit. "purer." Josephus uses εἰλικρινής elsewhere only at *War* 2.345.

985 This is the only occurrence of ἀνατλῆναι in Josephus.

986 As above, §§299, 317.

987 Celebration of birthdays by Jews in antiquity is virtually unheard of; see Hoehner 1972: 160–161. But the coming scene is clearly reminiscent of Gen 40:20, where Pharaoh, celebrating his birthday, recalls a senior official whom he had imprisoned. This is, then, alongside 18.195–201 and 18.237, another case in which the story of Agrippa has been enriched by allusions to the biblical story of Joseph (cf. the note on "in common" at 18.201). That—perhaps reinforced by Agrippa's upbringing in Rome, where such celebrations were common (*HJP* 1. 346–348, n. 26)—can account for the current reference.

988 This is the only occurrence of θαλία in Josephus.

989 For the gesture, cf. §§264, 333.

990 This is the only occurrence of συνέστιος in Josephus; the verb συνεστιάω appears a few times.

991 Josephus uses ἀποσυλάω elsewhere only at 15.279—there in its literal sense, "to strip off."

992 For ὑβρίζω, to act with hubris, cf. the note on "hubris" at §1.

993 This seems to be implied by the heavy formulation opening this sentence: οὐκ ἐγώ.

it is separated from my flesh,[994] will take the memory of my excellence along with itself.[995]

These are the words that he screamed out and commanded [the king's agents] to tell the king. And he, seeing that [Silas] was incurable, again left him under guard.

(7.2) 326 He reinforced the walls of Jerusalem, facing the new city,[996] at public expense, both widening their breadth and raising their height.[997] Had he finished the work, he would have made them stronger than any human force;[998] [and that would have happened], had not Marsus,[999] the governor of Syria, reported to Claudius Caesar, in writing, about what was being done.[1000] 327 Suspecting some sort of a revolt,[1001] Claudius emphatically ordered Agrippa to stop the construction of the walls—and he did not think of disobeying.[1002]

Agrippa vs. Marsus, I

(7.3) 328 This king was by nature a benefactor[1003] in gifts and was proud to be generous to nations:[1004] in expending great masses of sums he made himself famous, enjoying being

Agrippa the Benefactor

---

994 Josephus frequently uses plain μεθίστημι of death (e.g. 18.31, 89; 19.66), but here the formulation (μεταστᾶσα τῆς σαρκὸς ἡ ψυχή) is fuller, given Silas's desire to speak of what would happen thereafter. The separation or liberation of the soul from the body is a phrase and notion found frequently in Josephus; see Sievers 1998: 27–31.

995 This is the only occurrence of συνεπιφέρω in Josephus. Josephus here allows Silas to speak as a Pharisee (18.14) or an Essene (*War* 2.154–155), not as a Sadducee who believes that the soul perishes along with the body (18.16). This is frequent for Josephus; see *War* 6.47 (a pre-battle speech by Titus), 7.344–348 (Eleazar b. Yair's second pre-suicide speech at Masada), *Apion* 2.203, 218, along with Sievers 1998 and Mason 2008: 124, n. 947 on the Platonic background.

996 At *War* 5.149–151, Josephus reports that the new area of the city was called Bezetha (Βεζεθά, best known from John 5:2) and was opposite the Antonia. He further writes there that the term Bezetha "might be translated into Greek as 'New Town,'" but that is wrong; for options as to forms of the name and what it means, see Mason 2008: 255, n. 2062. At *War* 2.530 Josephus formulated more accurately: "Bezetha, *also called* the 'New City.'"

997 The fortification of Jerusalem during Claudius's reign is also mentioned by Tacitus (*Hist.* 5.12.2). Josephus appears to discuss the building or reinforcement of this same wall in two other passages—*War* 2.218–219; 5.147–155—but there are significant divergences among the three. Here Josephus appears to speak of reinforcement of an already-existing wall that "faces" the "new city." In *War* 2.218–219 he says that Agrippa began to surround Jerusalem with a wall and does not mention the "new city," seemingly implying a new construction of a wall surrounding the entire city. Moreover, that passage says that construction came to a halt due to Agrippa's death, mentioning no Roman intervention. In *War* 5.147–155,

Josephus describes the "third wall" around Jerusalem, and says that it was "built" by Agrippa to encompass the new additions to the city, which had been outside of the previously existing walls and thus unprotected. In that description too, however, Josephus writes that the construction was not completed, and although he does not mention Marsus's involvement, he does report that Agrippa, wary lest Claudius view the construction of such an enormous wall as indicating that he had revolutionary intentions, suspended this wall's construction after merely laying its foundations. For these sources, remnants of the wall, and attempts to reconstruct its course, see D. R. Schwartz 1990a: 140–144; Mason 2008: 170–180, n. 1364; and Arbiv 2023.

998 This is a curious statement, insofar as it basically confirms that the Romans had some reason to worry about these walls. Cf. the note on "Romans' interests" at §341.

999 On Marsus, see the note at §316.

1000 For Jewish suspicion that a governor's reports about them to Rome might put them in a worse light than was justified, cf. Philo, *Leg.* 202.

1001 Compare §§338–342, where Marsus interferes with another project that, sincerely or maliciously, he took to betray more independence than a vassal should be allowed.

1002 For a similar formulation, see Philo, *Flacc.* 26.

1003 Josephus uses the adjective εὐεργετικός only three times. Here and at §330 it describes Agrippa, in contrast to Herod. But in *Ant.* 16.150 it is actually used to describe Herod, and is used in the superlative: "… he had a most beneficent (εὐεργετικοτάτη) nature," a passage which, however, as §329, contrasts Herod's beneficence towards most people with his ill-treatment of his subjects and relatives. On euergetism, and Josephus on euergetism, see the note on "benefit" at 18.95.

1004 While in Jewish Greek ἔθνη often means "*other* nations," corresponding to Hebrew *goyim*, and, as such,

gracious and rejoicing in living in good repute.[1005] His manner corresponded in no way to that of Herod, who was king before him, **329** for the latter had been evil in character, relentless in punishment and unrestrained[1006] against those toward whom he was hostile. [Herod] was, it was agreed, more at home among Greeks than Jews; indeed, he magnified gentiles' cities with gifts of moneys, building baths, theaters and other things: in some he erected temples and in others, porticos, but he did not think any Jewish city worthy even of a small bit of work or of any gift worthy of being recalled.[1007] **330** But Agrippa was gentle[1008] in nature and was similarly beneficent[1009] to all: to foreigners he was benevolent,[1010] but while he demonstrated to them his love of gift-giving, toward members of his own community[1011] he was, proportionately,[1012] all the more well-disposed and sympathetic. **331** Indeed, he took pleasure in [our[1013]] way of life and was continuously in Jerusalem,[1014] observing the ancestral practices in purity.[1015] Thus, he conducted himself in complete purity and no day passed him by deprived of the customary sacrifices.[1016]

Gentle Agrippa   **(7.4) 332** Thus, for example,[1017] there was among the Jerusalemites a native man named Simon who was thought to be very exacting about the [Judaic] regulations.[1018] He assembled[1019] a multitude at the time when the king was away on a trip to Caesarea, and

---

has something of a negative valence, that is too uncouth for Josephus, in general, and especially here, in light of the opening of §330. For a long catalogue of his uses of the word, see *ThLJ* 213–214.

1005 So already from the outset: 18.144–145.

1006 On ἀταμίευτος, see the note on "unrestrained" at §319.

1007 Given Herod's work in Jerusalem, this is a gross misstatement; contrast *War* 1.401–402; *Ant.* 15.380–425. Cf. Josephus's similarly hostile comment about Gaius Caligula at §§205–206.

1008 This occurrence of πραΰς is the opening bracket of the coming story; cf. πράως at §333 and πραότητα at §334. On the term, see Spicq 1994: 3.160–171.

1009 See the note on "benefactor" at §328.

1010 Just as Herod too was φιλάνθρωπος to foreign cities (15.327). On this quality, see the note on "edict" at §290.

1011 This use of τοῖς ὁμοφύλοις, borne out as it is by references to Agrippa's adherence to the appropriate rites of purity and offering of sacrifices, conforms to the impression gained elsewhere as well, that Josephus means something like "fellow religionists." See the note on "religion" at 18.64.

1012 For this sense of ἀναλόγως, compare the adjective at §247 and the adverb in *War* 1.356//14.486. Just as, in those two cases, each officer received more than each soldier, here Josephus apparently means that the amount of money Agrippa spent on his projects for Jews was, given their relatively small numbers, proportionately greater than what he spent for gentiles.

1013 This supplement seems to be indicated by the flow from the preceding paragraph.

1014 This is an obvious exaggeration, given all the time Agrippa spent in Rome, and the reports in the following sections about him being in Caesarea (the very next section), Beirut (§§335–337), and Tiberias (§§338–342), and then his death in Caesarea (§§343–350). In fact, Acts 12:19 reports that after Peter's escape from prison, Agrippa "went down from Judea to Caesarea, and remained there." For detailed skepticism about Josephus's claim here, see Lämmer 1981/82: 201–202.

1015 Cf. the note on "daughters" at §357.

1016 The formulation is reminiscent of §293. As there, probably the intention is not that he brought his own sacrifice(s) daily, which in fact the laws would not require, but, rather, that he undertook financial responsibility for some sacrifices (such as the Nazirites' sacrifices mentioned at §294)—as did various earlier benefactors, such as Seleucus IV (according to 2 Macc 3:3) and Augustus (according to Philo, *Leg.* 157).

1017 On καὶ δή as a way to introduce something that illustrates the preceding statement, see the note on "for example" at 18.257. In this case, the story is meant to illustrate Agrippa's "gentleness"; see §§330 and 334.

1018 This characterization of Simon has led some to assume he was a Pharisee. Indeed, Josephus often associates the Pharisees with "exact" interpretation of the laws (e.g., *War* 2.162; *Ant.* 17.41; *Life* 191); see A. I. Baumgarten 1982: 413–417. However, other religious virtuosi could well make the same claim, competing with the Pharisees; cf. *War* 2.145. For the suggestion that Simon's views here are "priestly" and that he was, therefore, closer to the Sadducees and/or Qumran than to the Pharisees, see the note on "by birth" at the end of this paragraph.

1019 This is the only occurrence of ἁλίζω in Josephus.

audaciously defamed him[1020] as not being holy: it was, [he said], proper to deny him entrance to the temple, which is the prerogative only of [Jews] by birth.[1021] **333** When the commander of the city[1022] wrote to the king and reported that Simon was inciting the people this way, the king sent for him and, since he was then sitting in the theater,[1023] asked him to sit down next to him. Calmly and gently, he said: "Tell me, what of the things happening here is against the law?" **334** He, having nothing to say, asked to be allowed forgiveness.[1024]

1020 The topos of critics of a king, clothed in the aura of religious authority, whose criticism is either malicious or turns out to be false (just as Simon's turns into naught at §§333–334), appears a few times in *Antiquities*: 13.288; 15.277–279; 17.41.

1021 Lit. "native-born." According to our notions, there is some tension between the claim that Agrippa was not "holy" (ὅσιος), which sounds like it applies to his behavior, and the complaint that his ancestry was improper. Earlier scholars thought, therefore, that the received text (τοῖς ἐγγενέσιν) should be emended, a notion that was reinforced by the assumption that Herod's (and therefore Agrippa's) Idumean ancestry could not have been an issue because, according to rabbinic Judaism, converts are considered full Jews. Accordingly, they thought Simon's complaint pertained to Agrippa's behavior (see below, the note on "theater" at §333), which was thought to make him impure, and they therefore preferred, beginning with Niese (1890a: 267), to emend the text and have it apply to those whose behavior is improper. However, on the one hand we now know that the word Niese suggested instead of ἐγγενέσιν here (and indeed adopted, as usual, in his editio minor [1890b: 227]), namely εὐαγέσιν (Feldman: "ritually clean"), and which was adopted by Alon (1977: 138–145) and Feldman (1965: 370–371, n. c), never appears elsewhere in Josephus (*CCFJ* 2.225). So although it is not impossible, it is not likely; while there are many words that appear only once each in Josephus, creation of another via emendation should be only a last resort. Moreover, the point of departure for the emendation was the rabbinic and traditional Jewish notion that converts are considered full Jews ("after he was baptized and emerged from the water he is an Israelite from all points of view" [*b. Yevamot* 47b]), something that Niese could have found in any handbook about Judaism in his day. Indeed, the Mishnah (*Soṭah* 7:6) explicitly indicates that although Agrippa was worried that his ancestry might be an issue, the rabbis reassured him that he was considered fully Jewish, just as *m. Bikkurim* 3:4 indicates the rabbis' assumption that Agrippa could enter the Temple (although it is not a report that that actually happened).

However, already during Niese's lifetime an inscription from the Temple Mount (*OGIS* 598 = *CII/P* 1, no. 2; Boffo 1994: 283–290 [no. 32]) was discovered that prohibited the entry of an ἀλλογενής (see the note on "secretly" at 18.30), and a few decades after his death the discovery of the Dead Sea Scrolls demonstrated more generally, but also in this particular connection, the existence of a type of Judaism in the late Second Temple period that put a heavy emphasis on pedigree. This was a priestly type of Judaism, for the basic distinction between priests and rabbis is that while rabbis choose to be rabbis, and are recognized as such by teachers, peers, and communities who choose to do so, Jewish priests (*kohanim*) are defined exclusively by their birth, as sons of male Aaronites; see the note on "priesthood" at 20.226. Accordingly, it made sense for priests, and members of priestly communities, to deny the possibility of conversion to Judaism, for that process is predicated on the assumption that it is people's decisions and commitments, not their descent, that define them. Indeed, evidence from the Dead Sea Scrolls shows that such natural priestly insistence on the importance of differential descent was alive and well late into the Second Temple period. See, for example, *Damascus Document* 14:3–6, which insists that priests, Levites, other Jews ("Israel"), and converts (*ha-gĕr*) sit in four separate sections in community meetings, which basically means that converts are not Jews. With regard to our particular issue in the present passage, note esp. two Qumran texts that restrict or condemn the entrance of converts into the Temple: *Temple Scroll* 39–40 and *4QFlorilegium* 1, 3–4. See D. R. Schwartz 1990a: 124–130 and 2013: 50–57, also, in general: Himmelfarb 2006 and Thiessen 2011. It appears, therefore, that we should retain the received text and infer that while Simon may well have had the reputation of being a strict observer of the law, his orientation was priestly, not Pharisaic/rabbinic.

1022 This seems to be the only reference to such a position in Jerusalem, perhaps comparable to the Roman *praefectus urbi* (see the note on "guardian of the city" at 18.169). Perhaps, however, the reference is to the "captain of the Temple" (*War* 2.409, 6.294; Acts 4:1, 5:24), who is probably the officer the rabbis termed "captain of the priests" (*m. Pesahim* 1:6; *m. Yoma* 7:1).

1023 On the theater in Caesarea, see *War* 1.415, *Ant.* 15.341, Segal 1995: 64–69; and Z. Weiss 2014: 16–17. Lämmer 1981/82: 206–209 assumes that Agrippa was attending games or a festival. For Jewish opposition to such games, and the attempt to interpret the present story in light of it, see Alon 1977: 138–145.

1024 For τυχεῖν... συγγνώμης see also 1.311 and *Life* 227.

And the king, faster than one would have expected,[1025] was reconciled with him—for in his judgment gentleness[1026] was more appropriate to kings than wrath,[1027] and he knew that kindness[1028] is more fitting than anger for the great. Indeed, he even awarded Simon some gift before sending him away.

Agrippa's Projects in Berytus

(7.5) 335 Although he instituted many things for many people,[1029] he especially honored the people of Berytus.[1030] For he built them a theater that outstripped many in expense and beauty, also an amphitheater[1031] at great expense, as well as baths and porticos; in none of these projects did he impair beauty or size by skimping on expenses. **336** He also generously lavished upon them dedication [festivities]: in the theater putting on spectacles including all sorts of musical works, which made for diversified delight, and in the amphitheater showing his magnanimity in the great number of gladiators [he presented].[1032] **337** There, desirous that the spectators might also delight in the confrontation of a large number of antagonists, he sent seven hundred men in to fight against another seven hundred, all of them being criminals that he had set aside for this event, so that while they would be punished, their acts of war might engender the pleasure of peace. Those, then, he utterly[1033] wiped out.

Agrippa vs. Marsus, II

(8.1) 338 After completing the abovementioned [projects] in Berytus, he moved on to Tiberias, a city of the Galilee.[1034] He was, it seems, admired by all of the other kings. At any rate, there came to him King Antiochus of Commagene;[1035] Sampsigeramus of Emesa;[1036] Cotys, who reigned in Armenia Minor;[1037] Polemo, who had obtained the rule

---

1025 Reading, with Hudson (Hudson and Havercamp 1726: 1.949, n. p) and Naber (1893: xxxiv), θᾶττον ἤ προσεδόκηησέν τις. Josephus likes comments like this, as may be seen in the way he adds them into accounts otherwise based on the Bible, such as 1.115 and 11.80. Cf. 18.309 and *Life* 394, where he uses similar phrases to finish up a story, also 20.86.

1026 That Agrippa was "gentle" is the point of the story; see the note on "gentle" at §330.

1027 This is part of a king's "high-mindedness"; see the note on "valor" at 18.326.

1028 On the senses of ἐπιείκεια, see Spicq 1994: 2.34–38 and Danker 1982: 351–352.

1029 Cf. the formulation above, §330.

1030 That Beirut was a Roman *colonia* since the days of Augustus ("a Latin island in a sea of Oriental Hellenism" [Mommsen 1885: 459; cf. Isaac 1998: 270–271]) made it an especially apt object of attention for Herodian euergetism; see Hall 2004: 62–64. The Herodian tradition of generosity towards the city began with Herod himself, who built a market (*War* 1.422); for Agrippa II's generosity towards this city, including the building of (another?) theater, see below, *Ant.* 20.211–212. On Beirut in this period, see Hall 2004: esp. 84–88.

1031 For Josephus's use of "amphitheater" for a hippodrome, see Weiss 2014: 24–28, hence Weiss's scare quotes (ibid. 68) with reference to the edifice mentioned here.

1032 On this episode, see Lämmer 1981/82: 209–214 and, for such spectacles in the Herodian period, Weiss 2014: 158–159.

1033 Elsewhere Josephus uses πασσυδί only at 5.161. Contrast the apparently positive description here to the condemnation of the same type of gladiatorial show by Herod in *Ant.* 15.274–275, as well as of Agrippa II's generosity towards Beirut in *Ant.* 20.211–212. Things like this are ad personam, rhetorical putty in Josephus's hands; cf. the note on "pregnant" at 20.18.

1034 For its foundation, see 18.36–38.

1035 King Antiochus IV of Commagene; see the note on "Commagene" at §276. Perhaps this visit was the occasion for the kings' agreement that Agrippa's daughter would marry Antiochus's son; see §355. The two kings probably knew each other already in Rome; see esp. Cassius Dio 59.24.1 (*GLAJJ*, no. 421).

1036 On Sampsigeramus II of Emesa, see Sullivan 1977b: 212–214. Agrippa's brother Aristobulus married Sampsigeramus's daughter Iotape (18.135).

1037 Armenia Minor (described by Strabo, *Geog.* 12.3.28), which was eventually ruled by a son of Herod of Chalcis (20.158) and then incorporated by Vespasian into Cappadocia, was near the Black Sea on the western side of the Euphrates, which divided it from the rest of Armenia. In general, see Mitford 1980. Here the reference is, apparently, to the son of Cotys, king of Thrace, who is mentioned by Tacitus in *Ann.* 2.67; the son was appointed

of Pontus;[1038] and also Herod, who was his own brother and ruled Chalcis.[1039] **339** He conversed with all of them when entertaining them and in friendly gatherings, especially demonstrating the height of his noble sentiment and, thereby, making it seem that it was indeed justified that he be honored by each king's[1040] arrival.

340 However, while they were still staying with him, Marsus, the governor of Syria, arrived. The king, taking care to show honor to the Romans, went out to meet him at a distance of seven furlongs from the city. **341** But this was, it seems, to become the beginning of his falling out with Marsus. For when he was sitting together in his carriage[1041] with the other kings, whom he also brought out with him, their harmony and such a degree of mutual friendship among them were suspect in Marsus's eyes, for he did not suppose that such concord among rulers could further the Romans' [interests].[1042] Therefore, he immediately sent to each of them some of his messengers and ordered them to return home without delay.[1043] **342** Agrippa took that with disgruntlement:[1044] toward Marsus, on the one hand, he was henceforth hostile,[1045] and, on the other hand, taking[1046] away the high priesthood from Matthias,[1047] he appointed Elioneus, the son of Cantheras,[1048] in his stead.

---

king of Armenia Minor by Gaius (Cassius Dio 59.12.2). Agrippa may well have known him from his days in Rome, where he too enjoyed the patronage of Antonia Minor; see the note on "along" at 18.143.

1038 On Polemo II of Pontus see Sullivan 1980: 925–30. At 20.145 Josephus refers to him as king of Cilicia. Indeed, according to Dio 60.8.2 Claudius granted him territory in Cilicia, around the same time he expanded Agrippa I's kingdom.

1039 For Herod's being made king of Chalcis by Claudius see above, §277 and *War* 2.217. It appears that Josephus, or his pro-Agrippan source, is somewhat begrudging about terming Herod a "king," a term he avoids here, at §353, and at 20.15. Cf. the note on "city of the Romans" at §275.

1040 Lit. "the king's," if the reading τοῦ βασιλέως is retained, with Niese (1890a: 268). My "each" is a way to avoid the other option, suggested by Hudson (as cited by Niese ad loc.): emending to τῶν βασιλέων. That is, if the opening of the paragraph refers to all the guests, the end of it praises Agrippa for making each one feel special.

1041 This is the only occurrence of the Homeric word ἀπήνη in Josephus.

1042 Josephus noted a similar suspicion on the part of Marsus in the story above about Agrippa's attempt to reinforce or build the "third wall" of Jerusalem (§§326–327). However, two factors suggest that, despite that basic similarity, Josephus probably derived them from different sources: (1) Josephus writes here that this episode was the origin of enmity between Marsus and Agrippa, a statement that seems not to be aware of the first episode; (2) the earlier story refers to Agrippa by name, confirms that the walls he was building would be impregnable, and reports that the emperor himself, to whom Marsus reported the conclave, viewed Agrippa's actions as suspicious and ordered him to desist, whereas here Agrippa is

referred to as "the king," Marsus's suspicions are said to be baseless, and the emperor is not mentioned. That is, the point of view from which the second episode is told is quite different from that of the first. See D. R. Schwartz 1990a: 15–16.

1043 This is the only time δίχα μελλήσεως appears anywhere in ancient literature. Usually, in *Antiquities*, Josephus prefers οὐδὲν εἰς ἀναβολάς; see the note on "without delay" at 18.107.

1044 This is the only appearance of ἀνιαρῶς in *Antiquities*, but cf. *Life* 377.

1045 As is illustrated by 20.1.

1046 Although this reads as if the change in the high priesthood expressed Agrippa's hostility toward Marsus, in fact it seems the two are unrelated. Rather, Josephus is simply taking the opportunity to bring us up to date about the high-priestly succession before turning to the last scene of Agrippa's life. On such bunching, see the note on "Syria" at §316. For a similar case, see 20.139.

1047 See §316.

1048 Niese (1890a: 269) retains Ambrosianus's τοῦ Κιθαίρου, but some witnesses read τοῦ Κανθερᾶ and it is usually assumed that the latter should be read here, as at 19.297 and 20.16. See, for example, Ilan 2002: 411 and VanderKam 2004: 449–451. Note also that, according to 20.16, "Cantheras" was his surname (like Simon's [§297]), i.e., not the name of his father. (For that usage, see the note on "Boethus" at 18.3.) That point goes together with the fact that the Mishnah refers to a high priest named Eliehoeinai b. HaQoph (*m. Parah* 3:5), where HaQoph probably corresponds to "Caiaphas"; Brody 1990 suggests that the Aramaic name Caiaphas and the Greco-Roman name Cantheras basically mean the same thing, namely, "porter, carrier of burdens." This implies that Eliehoeini and Simon were brothers of Joseph Caiaphas. For details, see Appendix 2.

Agrippa's Death   **(8.2) 343** When he had completed his third year as king of all of Judea,[1049] he came to the city of Caesarea, which was formerly called Strato's Tower.[1050] There he put on spectacles in honor of Caesar, knowing[1051] that it was a sort of festival in honor of his welfare.[1052] For this festival there gathered a multitude of people who held high positions in the province[1053] and had risen in dignity. **344** On the second day of the spectacles, wearing a garment made entirely out of silver, so that it was amazingly woven,[1054] he went to the theater as day was breaking. There the silver, when hit by the first rays of the sun,[1055] was caused to shine marvelously, and

---

1049 I.e., since Claudius's rise to the throne; see §274. Although readers, if they care about such details, might therefore infer that Agrippa died no earlier than late January 44, in fact we know from numismatic evidence that Agrippa counted his years from the autumn, so his first year ended in the autumn of 41 and the present datum, if it reflects Agrippa's practice, points to the autumn of 43. See esp. Stein 1981: 22–26; also D. R. Schwartz 1990a: 57–58; Kokkinos 1998: 285; Meshorer 2001: 91. Similarly, *War* 2.219 says that he died after reigning as king (of Judea) for three years, "having ruled the tetrarchies for three years before that," i.e., in Gaius's days. Cf. §351.

1050 Strato's Tower had been renamed Caesarea (Maritima) and built magnificently, with one of the largest harbors in the Mediterranean, by Herod the Great (see *War* 1.408–415; *Ant.* 15.331–341). On it, see the note on "Caesarea" at 18.55. When mentioning Caesarea, Josephus often adds its former name, as here; so at *Ant.* 13.313; 14.76; 15.293; 20.173. That might reflect the felt need to distinguish it from Caesarea Philippi, on which see 18.28 and 20.211.

1051 Reading ἐπιστάμενος with Niese's ed. maior (1890a: 269) and the manuscripts, followed by Feldman (1965: 376) and Kokkinos (1998: 378). But whereas Feldman renders simply as "knowing," Kokkinos renders "being informed" in order to serve his theory discussed in the next note. Others, including Niese in his ed. minor (1890b: 229) and Post as cited by Feldman, would emend to ἐνιστάμενος, making Agrippa the one who "instituted" the festival. This has everything to do with the question, who is "Caesar" in whose honor the festival was held; see the next note.

1052 Kokkinos (1998: 378) renders "There he then exhibited shows in honour of Caesar (i.e. Claudius), being informed that there would be a certain festival for his (i.e. the Emperor's) safety." He explains that the text means Agrippa learned of celebrations in honor of Claudius's safe return from Britain in the spring of 44 and, therefore, held a similar celebration in Caesarea in Claudius's honor—an interpretation that creates a late terminus post quem for Agrippa's death (see the note on "reign" at §350). However, ἐπίσταμαι means "to know," "to recognize" (cf. 18.201, 221; 19.236; 20.56, 70, 264), and if Agrippa is said to have known about the nature of the festival, the

implication is that the festival already existed. Rather than avoiding that conclusion by a forced translation or by emendation (see the preceding note), it seems preferable to follow it to evidence for a festival in Caesarea known as "Isactium"—games in honor of *Augustus*'s rise to power in the wake of his victory at Actium. For Josephus's use of plain "Caesar" for Augustus, see, for example, 18.32–32; for the evidence for such quadrennial games, established already by Herod (*War* 1.415; *Ant.* 16.136–141) upon the completion of Caesarea, see D. R. Schwartz 1992: 167–181, building on the reference to a Caesarean Ἰσάκτιον in *IGRR* 3.1012. If the festival was first celebrated in September (the month of Actium) of 10 BCE, upon the celebration of the construction of Caesarea (see *HJP* 1.293), the festival mentioned here will have been, in September 43, the fourteenth regular celebration. This also dovetails neatly with the conclusion, from numismatic evidence, that Agrippa counted his years from the autumn; see the note on "all of Judea" earlier in this paragraph. That means the end of his third year as king of all Judea will have been marked in the autumn of 43. Readers, who will certainly note that death came to Agrippa after he—as Gaius—was deified, might also note, already now or retrospectively, that death came to both in the context of spectacles in memory of Augustus (§75). On this episode, see also Lämmer 1981/82: 215–220.

1053 Here Josephus uses ἐπαρχία in a general way, reflecting Judea's usual status in the Roman period.

1054 In the parallel in Acts 12:21 it is said to have been a "royal garment." Cf. Dewar 2008: esp. 224–226, where Claudian's description of Honorius's glorious woven *toga picta* is cited and discussed, also Eusebius, *Life of Constantine* 3.10.3, on the emperor's grand entrance to the Council of Nicaea: "... and he finally walked along between them, like some heavenly angel of God, his bright mantle shedding lustre like beams of light, shining with the fiery radiance of a purple robe, and decorated with the dazzling brilliance of gold and precious stones" (trans. A. Cameron and S. G. Hall).

1055 On the association of Agrippa's appearance here with the usage of ἀνατολή (lit. "sunrise") for the appearance of rulers, see Siegert 2001: 279; he adduces *inter alia* Luke 1:78–79, which links messianic hopes to dawn and light. For similar solar imagery with regard to supernatural

it sparkled, glistening[1056] in a way that was somewhat fear- and awe-inspiring[1057] for those who fixed their eyes[1058] upon it. **345** Immediately the flatterers[1059] raised up their voices from every side,[1060] addressing him (not for his good!) as a god[1061] and going on to say: "May you be gracious[1062] to us, for if until now we have feared you as a man, from now on we admit that you are by nature above mortals."[1063] **346** The king neither reprimanded them nor rejected their impious flattery.[1064] But when looking up a little while later he saw the[1065] owl sitting on a rope over his own head.[1066] He immediately realized that it, although once a messenger[1067] of good tidings, was now one of bad ones;[1068] he felt distress across his heart, and an extreme pain, which began with vehemence and was severe already from its onset, started to grow in his abdomen.[1069] **347** Looking up toward his friends,[1070] he said: "I, who for you am a god, am already [now] ordered to lay down my life—so immediately

———

figures in a broader Jewish and Near Eastern context, see J. M. Baumgarten 2022: 152–174. For the motif of radiant garments indicating links to divinity, see esp. Warren 2016, a study that takes its point of departure from the description of Joseph's and Asenath's clothing in *Joseph and Asenath*, chs. 6 and 18. My thanks to Dr. Atar Livneh for her help with this note. As Mason notes, if we assume that the audience was sitting facing the Mediterranean to the west, and Agrippa was standing facing the audience, the rising sun would indeed have caused his silvery garment to shine remarkably. On the theater Herod built in Caesarea, and its orientation toward the sea, see Weiss 2014: 16–17.

1056 The last few words include three verbs that appear only here in Josephus: καταυγάζω, ἀποστίλβω, and μαρμαίρω.

1057 For the latter, φρικῶδες, cf. *War* 5.438, where the name of God is said to be φρικτός.

1058 This verb, ἀτενίζω, appears in Josephus only here and at *War* 5.517.

1059 This is the only occurrence of κόλαξ (flatterer) in Josephus, although he uses κολακεία and κολακεύω a dozen times each.

1060 For ἄλλος ἄλλοθεν see also *War* 3.384.

1061 For the common use of θεός of Hellenistic monarchs, see S. R. F. Price 1984: 81–82.

1062 For the expectation that God will be εὐμενής, cf. 2.161, 276; 3.72, 78, 80.

1063 A very similar story appears in Acts 12:21–23, where "King Herod" (= Agrippa) dies suddenly after a speech of his was received by the Caesarean crowd's shouts that his was "a voice of a god, not of a man." In Acts the story functions as his punishment for persecuting the apostles at the beginning of that same chapter. This episode figures prominently in the debate about Luke's use of Josephus; see the note on "Theudas" at 20.97.

1064 Feldman (1965: 378–379) thinks Josephus means that Agrippa did not reject the flattery "as impious," and therefore notes Richards's and Shutt's suggestion (1939:

183) to add ὡς (or emend Niese's ἀσεβοῦσαν into ἀσεβῆ οὖσαν). But Josephus could well be giving his own opinion, as author, that the flattery was impious.

1065 The definite article is to remind readers that Agrippa already saw the owl once, and its reappearance was promised long ago: 18.195.

1066 The rope over his head is part of the portent, an image presaging death.

1067 In a case like this, it is convenient that ἄγγελος can refer both to a mundane "messenger" (e.g. 20.87, 89) and to an "angel"; cf. *ThLJ* 3, s.v. Note that in Acts 12:23 no owl is mentioned, but it is said that "immediately an angel (ἄγγελος) of the Lord smote him."

1068 As was usual for Rome; see the note on "bubo" at 18.195.

1069 For stomach pains as the characteristic symptom of the death of wicked kings, often accompanied by worms (as Acts 12:23 specifically reports of Agrippa ["Herod"]), see Herodotus 4.205 (Pheretime), 2 Macc 9:9 (Antiochus Epiphanes), *War* 1.656//*Ant.* 17.169 (Herod), along with Nestle 1936; Africa 1982; and Spicq 1994: 3.266–267.

1070 Reading ἀναθεωρῶν with most of the witnesses (MWE and the Latin). That is, after §346, using a finite verb (εἶδεν), reported that Agrippa first saw the owl, here the participle indicates that Agrippa now looked, instead, at his friends. However, Niese (1890a: 269), Feldman (1965: 380), and Thackeray (*ThLJ* 35, svv. ἀναθεωρεῖν, ἀναθρῴσκειν) read ἀναθορών, "leaping up," following Ambrosianus. Neither verb appears elsewhere in Josephus, so the choice is difficult and perforce tentative. However, note that θεωρέω and related words are common, in Josephus as elsewhere, while θρῴσκω never appears in Josephus. Given Ambrosianus's frequent preference for colorful readings (see the note on "brought to him" at 20.5), it seems that the more pedestrian reading of the other manuscripts should be preferred, especially given the ease with which it can be coordinated with εἶδεν a few lines earlier.

does fate convict[1071] of untruth the voices that were just now raised about me, that he whom you called immortal is already being taken away to die. But what has been fixed by destiny[1072] is to be accepted,[1073] as God wills it—[especially by me] for, after all, I have lived not at all a base life,[1074] but, rather, one with the grandeur of being blessed."[1075] **348** As he was saying these words, he was suffering due to the intensification of the pain. With alacrity he was brought to the palace, and the word spread quickly to everyone, that, as things were,[1076] he would die in a very short time. **349** The multitude, together with wives and children, immediately sat in sackcloth, according to ancestral law,[1077] imploring God on behalf of the king; everything was filled with sobbing and lamentations. The king himself, lying high up in his bedroom and looking down on those fallen prostrate, did not remain tearless. **350** He passed away—done away[1078] by five days[1079] of continuous pain in his abdomen—in the fifty-fourth year of his life,[1080] the seventh of his reign.[1081] **351** For

---

1071 For the senses of ἐλέγχω (expose, reveal, convict, refute ...), see the note on "convict" at 20.266.

1072 For such use of πόρω, cf. 10.76 and *Apion* 1.247, 266 (where the story begins with a prophecy at 1.236).

1073 This is the only occurrence of δεκτέος in Josephus.

1074 For a φαῦλος life, cf. Josephus on Justus at *Life* 41, where Mason (2001: 46) renders "sordid."

1075 The point seems to be the standard religious sentiment that it is God's prerogative both to impose suffering and to bestow boons, and that especially one who has been the beneficiary of the latter should consider himself estopped from complaining about the former. Cf. Job 1:21 and *m. Berakhot* 9:5 ("one must bless God for the bad as for the good"). In referring to what destiny and God decreed, Agrippa naturally ignores the possibility that his death was a punishment for his hubris in accepting (perhaps even soliciting) deification.

1076 For ὡς ἔχοι, cf. 18.269 and 19.63.

1077 For the wearing of sackcloth as a traditional (πάτριος νόμος) accoutrement of Jewish petitioning of God in times of distress, see *Ant.* 12.300, where his source, at 1 Macc 3:47, written for Jews, needed to offer no such explanation. Indeed, it was common; cf. 20.123, Nehemiah 9:1, Esther 4:1–4, Jonah 3:5–8, Judith 4:10–14, 2 Macc 3:19 and 10:25, etc. Cf. the note on "ashes" at 20.123.

1078 Διεργάζομαι, See the note on "doing away" at §106.

1079 Precisely as was predicted at 18.200.

1080 For Latin influence on Josephus's formulation here, see Ward 2007: 636–637.

1081 Counting from his first installation as king, shortly after Tiberius died in March 37 (see 18.237), this places Agrippa's death "in" the year that began in the spring of 43 CE. This allows for our conclusion from the more specific statement at §343, that Agrippa's death came "when he completed" his third year as king of all of Judea, that it came in the autumn of 43; for the assumption that he counted his years according to an autumnal era, see the note on "Judea" at §343. See further, D. R. Schwartz

1990a: 107–111, 203–207. True, Kokkinos (1998: 378–380) rejected that early dating for Agrippa' death, offering four arguments in favor of the more usual 44. His main argument (1998: 302, n. 134) is based on an ostracon (*CPJ* 419d) that mentions Marcus (son of Alexander the Alabarch) in Claudius's fourth year: given that Claudius acceded to the imperial throne in January 41, that means Marcus was alive at least until late in January 44, and since §277 states that Agrippa I married Berenice off to his brother Herod after Marcus died, it follows that Agrippa too was still alive then. However, it appears that it was common, in Egypt, to count the years of Roman emperors according to the Egyptian civil year, which began on August 29 or 30, counting the time between the emperor's accession and the end of the following August, however long that time was, as his first year; see Bagnall and Worp 2004: 43. That moves the terminus post quem for Agrippa's death, supplied by this ostracon, back up to the end of August 43, which is prior (although not by much) to the September/October 43 date of death posited above. Moreover, note (with Fuchs 1947/49: 16–17) that the ostracon is a receipt issued in Marcus's name by his agents in a port distant from Alexandria, and may well have been issued some time after Marcus's death. Kokkinos's second argument is from the apparent nexus between Passover and Agrippa's death in Acts 12. However, on the one hand there really is not a chronological nexus between the two (see esp. Acts 12:19!), so even if Peter was arrested on Passover it could have been Passover of 43 (with Agrippa dying a half a year later), and, on the other hand, the Passover/liberation motif is so strong in the story in Acts (see D. R. Schwartz 1990: 120), while there is no reference at all to Passover in Josephus's story of Agrippa's death, despite the other similarities between the two accounts, that it is difficult to assign much historical weight to the dating in Acts. Concerning the third and fourth arguments offered by Kokkinos, see the notes on "welfare" at §343 and on "successor" at 20.1.

he had reigned for four years under Gaius Caesar,[1082] about three of them over Philip's tetrarchy[1083] and in the fourth additionally acquiring that of Herod [Antipas],[1084] and three more since Claudius Caesar had taken over the empire,[1085] during which he ruled as king over the aforementioned [regions] and also added Judea, Samaria and Caesarea.[1086] **352** He had great income from them, 1200 myriads [of drachmas],[1087] but he borrowed much additional money,[1088] for since he loved making gifts[1089] his expenses consumed his income; it was impossible to assuage his ambition.

(8.3) 353 While the multitude was still unaware[1090] that he had expired,[1091] Herod, who ruled[1092] Chalcis, and Helcias, the prefect and friend of the king,[1093] consulted together and sent Ariston, who was one of the most useful of the servants, and, as if the king had ordered it, killed Silas,[1094] for he was their enemy.[1095]

(9.1) 354 So King Agrippa left life that way, leaving behind him, as his family, his son Agrippa,[1096] who was in his seventeenth year, and three daughters, of whom Berenice—who was married to her father's brother Herod—was in her sixteenth year,[1097] while the other

---

1082 Josephus is writing in a general way, rounding up, for Gaius himself reigned somewhat less than four years; see above, §201. In *War* 2.219, Josephus instead rounded down, speaking just as generally of Agrippa's three years of rule prior to the additional kingship he received from Claudius.

1083 See *War* 2.181 and *Ant.* 18.237.

1084 See *War* 2.183 and *Ant.* 18.252.

1085 Counting from Claudius's ascent to the throne in January 41, this round figure is either somewhat high (if Agrippa died in the autumn of 43, as suggested in the note on "Judea" at §343) or somewhat low (if he died around Passover of 44, as suggested by Kokkinos; see the note on "reign" at §350). Neither would be unacceptable; the question as to when, precisely, he died must be decided on the basis of other considerations. In any case, readers who do not get into the details can content themselves here by noting that this datum, at the end of Josephus's account of Agrippa's death, corresponds precisely to the statement, at its opening at §343, that he died after completing three years as king of all of Judea.

1086 The separate reference to Caesarea, which is not mentioned at §§274–275, simply reflects the city's importance and the fact that Agrippa died there.

1087 As Feldman noted ad loc. (1965: 382, n. c.), the text here does not name the coinage, but "drachmas" should be understood. Momigliano (1934: 387–388) suggests that the very existence of the present figure reflects a Roman investigation into Agrippa's finances, and that the finding that his kingdom had a large deficit played a significant role in Claudius's decision to appoint a Roman governor,

rather than Agrippa's son, to succeed him. Cf. the note on "reasonable" at §362.

1088 There is some paronomasia here: he had income (προσωδεύσατο) but borrowed much more (προσεδανείσατο—this word's only occurrence in Josephus).

1089 Φιλόδωρος, as at §330; the same theme appeared already at 18.144–145.

1090 Josephus likes to discuss what those in the know do in the interval between a ruler's death and its becoming known; cf. the note on "way" at §237.

1091 Josephus uses ἐκπνοή only here and at §358; the verb ἐκπνέω appears six times, including twice in *Antiquities* (8.273 and 12.357).

1092 As at §338 above and 20.15 below, it seems like Josephus, or his source, is somewhat begrudging about terming Herod a "king."

1093 This is, probably, Helcias "the elder," who is mentioned above at 18.137 and 273; see the note on "Helcias the Elder" at 18.273. At 20.94 we read of Helcias the treasurer (of the Temple) in the next generation—probably this Helcias's son and the reason for specifying "the elder" here.

1094 For Silas's appointment by Agrippa as commander of his army, see §299; for his imprisonment, see §§317–325.

1095 It seems, accordingly, that there were other issues pertaining to Silas, and not merely his intemperate reminding of Agrippa of his past difficulties as claimed by the novelistic report at §§317–318.

1096 Agrippa I and Cypros had another son, Drusus, who died before growing up (see 18.132).

1097 See above, §277.

two, Mariamme and Drusilla, were virgins; the former was in her tenth year, while Drusilla was six.[1098] **355** They had been promised by their father in marriage: Mariamme to Julius Archelaus the son of Helcias;[1099] Drusilla to Epiphanes, who was the son of King Antiochus of Commagene.[1100]

356 But when it became known that Agrippa had passed away, the Caesareans and the Sebastenians,[1101] forgetting all the good things he had done,[1102] did the most hostile things. **357** They cast insults at the deceased,[1103] things that are not appropriate to say, and those who happened then to be in the army, who were numerous, went off to their quarters and, snatching[1104] the statues of the king's daughters,[1105] brought them with one accord[1106] to brothels and, setting them up on the roofs, outraged[1107] them as best they could, doing things too shameful to be reported. **358** Again, reclining in the public places they conducted public feasts while wearing crowns and perfuming themselves;[1108] and, pouring out offerings to Charon[1109] they drank with each other to the king's death. **359** They failed to remember not only Agrippa, who had bestowed upon them many acts of generosity, but also his

---

1098 A similar summary of his offspring is found in *War* 2.220.

1099 The same Helcias mentioned above at §353. His son, Julius Archelaus, remained prominent for decades; Josephus even names him, alongside Agrippa II and some "Herod," as one of the Jews who were well-versed in Greek wisdom, to whom he sold copies of his *War* (see *Apion* 1.51 and Stern 1976: 613). For this Archelaus see also Kokkinos 1998: 197. On the fruit of their marriage, and its dissolution, see 20.140, 147.

1100 For Antiochus IV of Commagene see above, at §276. Epiphanes was injured during the Roman civil war following the death of Nero, as he was cheering on the soldiers fighting for Otho (Tacitus, *Hist.* 2.25). For Epiphanes's significant role alongside the Romans, and against the Jews, in the Great Revolt, see *War* 5.460–465. Drusilla's engagement may have been contracted when Antiochus IV visited Agrippa in Tiberias, as reported above at §338. At 20.139, Josephus reports that Epiphanes eventually rejected the marriage because, despite his promise to convert to Judaism, he was unwilling to do so, whereupon Drusilla was given by her brother, Agrippa II, to Azizus, King of Emesa. Cf. 20.141–144.

1101 As §365 makes clear, the reference is to units of auxiliary troops recruited from these two major gentile cities in Judea. For some detail about their numbers, perhaps totaling around three thousand, see §365. On these units, of which the latter is known already from the days of Herod and Archelaus (*War* 2.52; *Ant.* 17.266), see Yankelevitch 1979/80; Shatzman 1991: 193; Lémonon 2007: 88–91; Eck 2007: 107; Mason 2008: 36, n. 318, and idem 2016c: 258–260. More generally, on Roman military in Judea between Herod's death and the rebellion of 66, see Dąbrowa 2015. For the background of hostility between Jews and Greeks in Caesarea, see also 20.173–178, 182–184, and Levine 1974.

1102 Agrippa's generosity towards these cities is mentioned again immediately below, at §359. However, apart from the spectacles which he put on in Caesarea in honor of the emperor (§343, above), Josephus does not mention any specific projects that Agrippa undertook for these two cities, and we have no other evidence for them.

1103 Of the six times Josephus uses κατοίχομαι, three are in this story (here and §§363–364).

1104 This verb, ἁρπάζω, implies the use of force; usually (e.g. 15.289; 20.214) it refers to the unauthorized seizing of someone or something. Here it underlines the heinous nature of the deed.

1105 In order to maintain Agrippa's image as a pious Jew (as at §331), Graetz (1905: 351) posits (arguing against Schürer and others) that the statues were set up not by Agrippa but, rather, by the gentile population of Caesarea; perhaps the flow of the present sentence indicates that they were located in the soldiers' baracks. However, the very existence of these statues, whether Agrippa himself set them up or only allowed others (the soldiers?) to do so, raises some doubts concerning the king's reputation for Jewish piety. More generally on such doubts, which are not allayed by Agrippa's image in rabbinic literature, see D. R. Schwartz 1990a: 132–134, 157–171.

1106 Josephus emphasizes that they were all despicable. On the high degree of unanimity implied by ὁμοθυμαδόν, see Spicq 1994: 2.580–582.

1107 This is the only occurrence of ἀφυβρίζω in Josephus. For the notion that bringing an image of someone into a brothel was a way of denigrating the person, see McGinn 2004: 86, who cites evidence, such as Suetonius, *Tiberius* 58, for Roman prosecution of those who brought images of emperors into latrines or brothels.

1108 Given the reference to "crowns," perhaps this too refers to their heads; cf. the note on "dispersed" at §239.

1109 The mythological ferryman of the underworld. See, for example, *Aenid* 6.295–336.

grandfather, Herod. For it was he who had founded their cities, fitting them out with ports and temples at magnificent expense.[1110]

(9.2) 360 The son of the deceased, Agrippa, was in Rome at the time, being raised by Claudius Caesar.[1111] 361 When Caesar learned that Agrippa had died, and that the Sebastenians and Caesareans had behaved outrageously toward him, he was aggrieved for him and wrathful toward those who had been ungrateful. 362 He was, accordingly, about to send the younger Agrippa immediately to take over the kingdom, wishing at the same time to fulfill[1112] the oaths[1113] that had been sworn between them. But the freedmen and friends, who had great influence with him,[1114] dissuaded him, saying it was risky to entrust to one who was wholly[1115] a youth, who had not even passed out of his childhood, a kingdom of such size. He would not, [they said], be able to bear all the cares of administration, for even for a fully-grown person a kingdom was a heavy burden.

Caesar thought that what they said was reasonable.[1116] 363 He therefore sent out Cuspius Fadus[1117] as prefect of Judea[1118] and the entire kingdom,[1119] giving the deceased respect insofar as he did not introduce Marsus, who had been hostile to him,[1120] into the kingdom.[1121]

Claudius's Arrangements after Agrippa's Death

1110 For Herod's lavish projects at Caesarea and Sebaste, see *War* 1.408–415; *Ant.* 15.331–341; *War* 1.403; *Ant.* 15.292–298.

1111 As Claudius himself mentions at 20.12; note also 20.135. For the Herodian practice of sending princes to be educated in Rome, see *Ant.* 15.342–343; 16.6; 18.143. For the same practice by other client kings, see 18.52 and the note on "hostages" at 18.42. According to §354, Agrippa II was sixteen when his father died.

1112 This is the only occurrence of ἐμπεδόω in Josephus.

1113 We know of only one oath between them: at the occasion of the confirmation of Agrippa I's kingship. See the note on "oath" at §275. But the use of ὅρκος in the plural is usual, even when only a single occasion is meant; compare, for example, 18.334 and 20.62. Perhaps the plural reflects the fact that the oath included more than one promise—including, apparently, some promise, however explicit or vague, that Agrippa I would be succeeded by his son.

1114 Claudius's dependence upon his freedmen is a common theme in Josephus and elsewhere (e.g., Suetonius, *Claud.* 25; Cassius Dio 60.2.4–5)—one that is apparently overstated; see Carney 1960 and Osgood 2011: 190–205. *War* 2.220 simply says that Claudius did not appoint Agrippa II "since he was altogether immature," and does not mention this influence. See also the note on "friends" at 20.135.

1115 There are only three appearances of κομιδῇ in Josephus, two in *Ant.* 19 (here and above at §136), and the third at *War* 1.203, where it pertains to Herod's being quite young (κομιδῇ νέον). Indeed, Josephus is quite consistent: the reference here is to Agrippa II at the age of sixteen

(§354), and the passage in *War* 1.203 is paralleled by *Ant.* 14.158, where Josephus reports that, at the time, Herod was fifteen. (Whether the latter datum is true is another issue; see Sharon 2014b.)

1116 The question, why Claudius decided to put an end to the kingdom and restored direct Roman rule, would seem not to be a difficult one. It is natural for empires to annex territories they have conquered, even if there need be no rush about it, and sometimes, as in the case of Judea, the process is held up for a while thanks to personal ties (such as those of Octavian and Marcus Antonius with Herod or of Gaius and Claudius with Agrippa I) or simply by the fact of continuing stable and submissive rule by the local vassal dynasty. Now, in the absence of such, history could take its natural course. Cf. the note on "of drachmas" at §352 and D. R. Schwartz 1990a: 149–151.

1117 Apart from the passing reference at *War* 2.220, he is known only from *Antiquities*.

1118 Thus, Judea was officially returned to provincial status. For the question whether it was a full-fledged "independent" province from 6, from now (44), or only from 66/67, see the note on "appendix to Syria" at 18.2.

1119 The formulation continues to distinguish between Judea and other parts of Herod's kingdom, despite their reunification under Agrippa I; cf. §351. This reflects the ambiguity of "Judea," which properly refers only to the region around Jerusalem but also designated the entire kingdom.

1120 I.e., Agrippa's enemy; see §§326–327, 341–342, and 20.1.

1121 Reading βασιλείαν with Niese (1890a: 272), who adopts Hudson's emendation of the manuscripts' βασίλειον ("palace"). This implies that, were it not for

364 And he decided to order Fadus, before doing anything else, to castigate the Caesareans and Sebastenians for their outrageous behavior toward the deceased and their drunken behavior[1122] toward [Agrippa's] female survivors; **365** to transfer to Pontus the cavalry wing[1123] of Caesareans and Sebastenians[1124] and the five cohorts,[1125] to do their military service there; and to choose the same number of soldiers from among the legions in Syria to fill their place.[1126] **366** But the troops that had been ordered to be transferred were not [transferred], for by sending emissaries to Claudius they appeased[1127] him and obtained [permission] to remain in Judea. And in times to come they were the source of the greatest troubles for the Judeans,[1128] sowing the seeds of the war under Florus.[1129] For this reason Vespasian, when he came to power, as we shall recount shortly,[1130] removed them from the province.

---

the enmity between Agrippa and Marsus, the latter would have been entrusted with the administration of Agrippa's kingdom. This corresponds to the assumption that between the suspension of Pilate in 37 and the installation of Agrippa as king of Judea in 41, Judea had had no governor of its own and had been ruled directly by the governor of Syria; Claudius would have returned Judea to that status quo ante were it not for the special consideration concerning Agrippa and Marsus. See also below, 20.1, on Agrippa's efforts to keep Marsus out. On Ed. Schwartz's theory about a later attempt of Claudius to attach Judea to Syria, see the note on "Jews" at 20.118. For the discussion of Judea's official status vis-à-vis Syria until the revolt of 66, see the note on "to Syria" at 18.2.

1122 For παροινία, cf. §230; for its combination specifically with ὕβρις, as here, see 17.254.

1123 In this period, Greek ἴλη usually represents the Roman *ala* ("wing"), but "in the literary writers tends to mean little more than 'a unit of horse' and it is up to the readers to deduce the Roman unit involved" (GTRI 56, 155). Probably here an auxiliary unit of five hundred is meant; see Webster 1998: 145–148. On the Roman garrison of Judea, see the note on "Sebastenians" at §356.

1124 At 20.122 and at *War* 2.236 Josephus refers to the "Sebastenian" wing, but here he refers to one composed of both Sebastenians and Caesareans. Probably it was indeed mixed (so, for example, HJP 1.364, n. 52), and perhaps that is reflected by the formulation at *War* 2.236, that it was (merely?) "called" (καλουμένην) Sebastenian. But it is not impossible that Josephus meant to refer, here, to one wing each.

1125 On "cohorts," see the note at §188.

1126 For such use of ἀναπληρόω for reassignment of troops after the movement of units, cf. *War* 5.43. For doubt that Claudius really intended to do what is described here, and the comment that Vespasian later did do it, thereby neutralizing to some extent the ethnic hostilities between the Judean population and the Roman military, see Mason 2016c: 270, 280.

1127 ἀπομειλίσσομαι appears in Josephus only here and at *War* 1.221.

1128 On the Judeans' future troubles with them, see *War* 2.236 and *Ant.* 20.122, where the procurator Cumanus, who preceded Florus by several years (48–52), is said to have used them against the Judeans, and at the time of Felix (52–60), during the Caesarean dispute the Caesarean and Sebastenian soldiers again stood against the Judeans (*Ant.* 20.176). The fact that Roman rule in Judea was enforced by units drawn from the non-Jewish population, which had its own interests and reasons for hostility toward the Jews, played a significant role in the rebellion; see Rappaport 1981 and Mason 2016c: 258–260.

1129 Here, prominently at the end of the book, by referring to Florus just as at the beginning of Book 18 (§25) and the end of Book 20 (§§252–258), Josephus reminds readers where this is all going.

1130 There is no such report in *Antiquities*, and it would in fact be surprising if Josephus, so far along in his work, of which the story ends in 66, really thought he might take it as far as Vespasian's accession to the imperial throne in 69. He did not do so, and the current promise, as several in Book 20 (§§48, 53, 96, 144, 147), is not fulfilled in Josephus's extant writings. Concerning them all, we can only wonder which to prefer: that, even this late in the work, he did not know where it would end; that he meant to refer to another projected work (such as the update of *War* mentioned at 20.267) but failed to make that clear; or that the reference came along as part of a passage he based on some other source, in which the topic was indeed discussed later on. In the present case, the reference here to "shortly" apparently excludes the second option; when Josephus wants to refer to another, projected, composition, he typically uses ἐν ἄλλοις or ἐν ἑτέροις ("elsewhere"; see, for example, 1.192 and 3.143). See the lists of such references in Drüner 1896: 82–94.

BOOK 20

(1.1) 1 After King Agrippa died, as we reported in the preceding book,[1] Claudius Caesar sent Cassius Longinus[2] as Marsus's successor[3]—thus showing respect to the memory of the king who, while alive, had written him several times asking him no longer to allow Marsus to continue to preside over affairs in Syria.[4] **2** Fadus,[5] when he arrived in Judea as procurator,[6] learned that the Judeans residing in Perea[7] were engaged in civil strife with the Philadelphians[8] over the boundaries of a village by the name of Zia,[9] which was filled with warlike men; indeed the Pereans,[10] without the approval of their leaders, had taken up arms and killed many of the Philadelphians. **3** What angered Fadus greatly, when he learned of this, was that they had not left it to him to adjudicate, [as they should have done] even though they considered themselves unjustly treated by the Philadelphians[11]—but had, rather, turned to weapons.[12] **4** Accordingly, after arresting three of their leaders, who were also responsible for the civil strife, he ordered they be kept in fetters; then he killed one of them, named Annibas,[13] and imposed exile upon the other two, Amaramus and Eleazar. **5** And not long thereafter the arch-brigand Tholomeus too was killed, after he was brought to him;[14] he had inflicted much trouble upon Idumea and the Arabs.[15] Thus was Judea purified of bands of brigands from then on, by virtue of Fadus's providential care and attention.

Fadus's Governorship

---

1 For such explicit reference to the division of *Antiquities* into different books, see also the openings of Books 8, 13–15, the statement at 20.267 that it includes twenty books, and the end of *Apion* 1. Along with the references at *Ant.* 13.173, 298 and 18.11 to "the second book" of *War*, they indicate that, in contrast to the works of some other authors, Josephus himself divided *Antiquities* into books, and so the book-divisions may be included among other considerations concerning the interpretation of his work.

2 On Cassius Longinus, governor of Syria ca. 44–50 but best known as a legal scholar, see *HJP* 1.264 and Dąbrowa 1998: 46–49. On the end of his term, cf. the note on "Quadratus" at §125.

3 According to Kokkinos (1998: 380), in his case for dating Agrippa's death to the spring of 44 (see the note on "reign" at 19.350), this passage means that Marsus was replaced "almost immediately" after Agrippa's death; since "Marsus threatened an attack on Vardanes shortly before the death of the Parthian king (Tacitus, *Ann.* 11.10)," and coins show Vardanes was alive as late as the autumn of 44, it follows that it is unlikely that Agrippa died a year earlier than that. However, Josephus does not say that Claudius removed Marsus from office immediately after Agrippa's death, and Tacitus's summary of Marsus's blocking of Vardanes and the latter's subsequent doings until his death does not require the inference that the former took place "shortly" before the latter. For the death of Vardanes in 45, or perhaps even 47/48, see Schippmann 2016.

4 For the hostility between Agrippa and Marsus, see 19.326, 340–341, 363.

5 On Fadus's term of office, see *HJP* 1.455–456; Smallwood 1981: 257–262.

6 On this title, see the note on "prefect" at 18.33.

7 The region of Jewish settlement in Transjordan, from the Dead Sea northward and bounded by the hinterlands of Decapolis cities to the east and north; see the note on "Perea" at 18.240.

8 Philadelphia is modern Amman; it was named after Ptolemy II Philadelphus, who refounded it. According to *War* 3.47, Philadelphia (or its surrounding villages, as here) marked the eastern frontier of Perea.

9 The manuscripts read ΜΙΑΣ, i.e., "one" village of which the name has been lost. The translation follows H. Relandus's (1714: 897) emendation to ΖΙΑΣ on the basis of Eusebius's reference (Klostermann 1904: 94, l. 3) to a village named Zia not far west of Philadelphia.

10 That is, "the Jews residing in Perea" mentioned a few lines earlier.

11 Josephus, of course, wants his readers to view this as a cynical and insincere declaration, similar to that at §126.

12 For this stock phrase, see also §120 and, for example, 5.150; 17.242; and *Life* 31, 391.

13 Ἀννίβας is the Greek form of "Hanibal"—hardly an expected name for a Jewish rebel; see the note on "Arabs" at §5. For Schlatter's suggestion on the basis of the Latin reading here, "Antibam," that "Antipas"—a name that makes some sense in this region—should be read, see Schalit 1968: 13, s.v. Ἀντίπας 3; Hengel 1989: 343, n. 163.

14 Ambrosianus and the Epitome (Niese 1887–1896: 349) add "in fetters," but fetters may be taken for granted (cf. §§102, 168). For other examples of such "useless" (Niese 1892: xxxiii) additions in Ambrosianus, see the notes on "leaped down" at §58, "killed himself" at §80, "very long" at §94, "inhabitants" at §114, "formed" at §180, "literature" at §263, "nations" at §264, and "odious" at §266, as also on "lie" at 18.194. In all of these cases, Niese rejected A's additions, but Feldman accepted them.

15 It seems that, with Hengel 1989: 343–344, we should understand that Tholomeus, Annibas, Amaramus,

6 Also at that time, having sent for the high priests and the leaders of the Jerusalemites, he urged[16] them to deposit the full-length tunic and the holy vestment, which according to custom only the high priest could wear, in the Antonia (which is a fortress[17]), so that it[18] would henceforth be deposited under Roman authority, as had been the case in the past.[19] **7** They did not dare to oppose him, but nevertheless they called upon Fadus, and also upon Longinus—for he too had come to Jerusalem, taking along with him a large force out of fear that Fadus's orders would force the Jewish population into rebellion[20]—to allow them, first of all, to send ambassadors to Caesar to ask him [to allow] them to have the holy vestment [remain] under their own authority, and then also to wait until it became known, what Claudius's response to that would be.[21] **8** They said they would allow the Jews to send out the ambassadors if they could take their children as hostages. When they readily agreed and turned them over, the ambassadors were sent out.

Claudius, Aggrippa II, and Herod of Chalcis

9 When they arrived in Rome, the younger Agrippa, son of the deceased [Agrippa], who (as I already said[22]) happened to be with Claudius Caesar, upon knowing the reason for their arrival, called upon Caesar to agree to what the Jews were asking concerning the sacred vestment, and to write to Fadus about the matter.

(1.2) 10 After summoning the ambassadors Claudius said that he agreed, and he instructed them to be grateful[23] to Agrippa, for it was he who had asked him to do these things. In addition[24] to his [oral] responses he also gave them the following letter:[25]

11 Claudius Caesar Germanicus—of tribunician power for the fifth time, consul designate[26] for the fourth time, and imperator for the tenth time,[27] father of his country[28]—to the rulers, council, and populace of the [city of] the Jerusalemites[29] and the

---

and Eleazar were all Jewish. Eleazar's name shows he was Jewish, and probably Ἀμάραμος (cf. Moses' father, Ἀμαράμης [2.210, 217, etc.]) does the same for him. Similarly, the fact that they are said to have been in conflict with Philadelphians, Idumeans, and Arabs associates them with the other antagonists—the Jews. Finally, the very fact that the next sentence says that *Judea* was thereby purged of brigands points toward the same conclusion.

16 Although παραινέω usually refers to urging (as, for example, at §32), when a ruler urges it can amount to an order (as at §§32, 109 and 19.308)—as is said more explicitly at §7.

17 Josephus also adds this gloss at §110, 18.91, and *Life* 20. The fortress is not mentioned frequently in *Antiquities* (and only that once in *Life*), and apparently Josephus thought the Roman-sounding name might mystify readers.

18 Here Josephus apparently thinks of the tunic and the sacred robe all as one item, called "the vestment" at §§7–9 (as also at 15.405–408 and 18.90–95).

19 See the survey of this topic in 18.91–95.

20 For intervention by the Roman governor of Syria in order to keep the peace in Judea, as for example at 18.88–89 and 20.125–133, see also Stern 1974a: 311–314; Eck 2007; 35–37, 45–48. The question whether (as Stern thought) such intervention was within a neighboring province (Judea) simply because Syria had legions, or rather (as

Eck argues) Judea was in fact still part of the province of Syria, is largely academic; see the note on "appendix to Syria" at 18.2.

21 For a similar issue and similar procedure, see §193.

22 At 19.360.

23 For χάριν εἰδέναι in this sense see also, for example, 4.261 and 14.182.

24 For this nuance of ἐπί with the dative, as also at §120, see Haenchen 1971: 62–63, n. 6.

25 On the procedure here, with the emperor's oral decision in Rome being transmitted via letter to the province, as is explicit at *War* 2.284, see Millar 1977: 218–219.

26 For much evidence of such use of ἀποδείκνυμι, see *GTRI* 24.

27 On the date, see the note on "July" at §14.

28 Claudius originally refused the honorific title "pater patriae," "the one honour that acknowledged the monarchic character of his rule" (Stevenson 2007: 119), but took it in 42; see Levick 1990: 41 and 204, n. 2 and Stevenson 2007: 123–124. For more Greek evidence for this title, see *GTRI* 74.

29 Such a full formulation of a city's name (rather than plain "Jerusalem"), as often in *Ant.* 20 (§§49–50, 95, 105, 133, 204, 244) and *Life* (§§130, 202, 237), is widespread in antiquity, and recurs elsewhere in Josephus as well, including of such cities as Rome (19.7, 275; 20.148), Alexandria (19.278),

entire nation of the Jews: greetings.[30] **12** My [dear] Agrippa, whom I have raised[31] and have here with me, has—since he is most pious—brought your ambassadors before me. After they thanked me for the solicitous care I have taken for your nation,[32] and asked, earnestly and emphatically, that the sacred vestment and the crown be under your authority, I have agreed, just as was once done by Vitellius,[33] who is an excellent person for whom I have the highest respect.[34] **13** I have concurred with that opinion first of all because of my own piety and my desire that each person practice religion[35] according to his own ancestral practice,[36] and furthermore because I know that in doing this I shall greatly please[37] King Herod himself and Aristobulus the Younger[38]—people with whom I have many authentic claims to friendship,[39] being excellent people whom I honor, and men whose loyalty to me I know [to be no less than][40] their enthusiasm on your behalf. **14** I have written about these matters to Cuspius Fadus, my procurator. Those who convey this letter [are]: Cornelius son of Ceron, Tryphon son of Theudion, Dorotheos son of Nathanael, and John the son of John.[41] Written on the fourth day prior to the calends of July[42] during[43] the consulship of Rufus and Pompeius Silvanus.

---

and Ptolemais/Akko (*Life* 214). Although sometimes it is taken to be more "grandiose" (Bagnall 1993: 333, n. 2), often, as here, that does not seem to be the case.

30 Although this formulation, with references to archons, *boulē* and *dēmos*, sounds as if Jerusalem were a *polis*, there is virtually no evidence for archons or a *boulē* in Jerusalem. It is, therefore, likelier to assume that this is just some official's, or some copyist's, notion of what is standard in such letters. See Tcherikover 1964. Cf. the note on "citizens" at 18.15.

31 See the note on "Claudius Caesar" at 19.360.

32 In the present context, this alludes to the documents preserved in 19.280–291. On Claudius and the Jews in general, see Momigliano 1961: 29–38, Tcherikover in *CPJ* 1.69–74, Stern, *GLAJJ* 2.113–117, D. R. Schwartz 1990a: 90–106, Botermann 1996, and Slingerland 1997 (with Linder 2000/2001). Note that Josephus nowhere mentions a most central item in that dossier (on which Botermann and Slingerland focus): Claudius's expulsion of the Jews of Rome (Cassius Dio 60.6.6; Suetonius, *Claud.* 25; Acts 18:2). Nor does Josephus give us any inkling of the fact that Claudius was perfectly capable of threatening to deal with the Jews "as fomenting a common plague for the whole world"; see the note on "following text" at 19.279. Rather, beginning with Claudius's benevolent treatment of the Jews of Alexandria (19.278–291) and Agrippa (§292) and the present incident, and then his disposition of the Jewish-Samaritan dispute reported later in this book (§§134–136), Claudius is portrayed as consistently friendly to the Jews, without exception. One may wonder whether this owes more to Josephus's desire to portray him schematically as the opposite of Gaius or, rather, to Josephus's dependence on Agrippan materials that had every reason to portray Agrippa's patron, whom Agrippa had helped to the throne, as good for the Jews. For the conflicting tendencies that affected Claudius's

attitude toward the Jews, of which Josephus shows us only one side, see esp. Momigliano 1961: 29–38.

33 See 15.405 and 18.91–95.

34 For the close relationship between Claudius and Lucius Vitellius, see esp. Suetonius, *Vitellius* 2, also *PIR¹*V500.

35 For the translation of θρησκεία (and so θρησκεύω) in this general sense, cf. the note on "their religion" at 18.287.

36 As in the documents cited at 19.283–285, 290.

37 The words "shall greatly please" (πάνυ χαριοῦμαι) are in the first edition, but not in the manuscripts, which (as noted by Niese 1890a: 278) apparently have a lacuna here; something like them is necessary.

38 "King Herod" is Herod of Chalcis (brother of Agrippa I). As for "Aristobulus the Younger": as Kokkinos (1998: 309) explains, he is probably that Herod's son, mentioned at 18.134. Cf. the last note on §104.

39 See the note on "friends" at 19.288.

40 The rhetoric seems to require this sense.

41 For a son to bear his father's name was not common, but not at all without parallel; cf. §197; *War* 5.534; *Life* 8, 33; Luke 1:59; Hachlili 1983/84: 192–194.

42 The name of the month did not survive in the Greek witnesses nor in what Niese considers the better Latin witnesses; "kal. Iulii" is found in some of the other Latin witnesses, and that translates into 28 June 45 CE. It seems, however, that in fact 29 July 45 is the correct date. Already Eck (1972: 264, n. 15) contemplated making the correction, and it was confirmed by Gallivan (1978: 408) on the basis of a text published just around when Eck wrote, which indicates that these consuls' predecessors were still in office in late June 45. The year, in any case, corresponds to the titles enumerated at §11.

43 For such use of ἐπί to denote "during the time of," see esp. Haenchen 1971: 62–63, n. 6; he also cites §§144,

(1.3) 15 Herod, the brother of the deceased Agrippa, who was at that time entrusted with the rule of Chalcis, also asked Claudius Caesar for authority over the Temple, and the sacred moneys, and the appointment of high priests—and received them all.[44] **16** Beginning with him, that authority remained with his descendants until the end of the[45] war.[46] Indeed, [utilizing this authority[47]], Herod transferred the man surnamed Cantheras out of the high priesthood,[48] bestowing in his stead the succession to the position upon Joseph the son of Camei.[49]

The Conversion of the Royal House of Adiabene

(2.1) 17 At that time[50] Queen Helena of the Adiabenians[51] and her son Izates came over to the Jewish way of life[52] under the following circumstances.[53] **18** Monobazus, king of the

---

228 and *Life* 37. See also see LSJ 621b, §11, and the note on "his" at §101.

44 This imperial mandate apparently explains not only appointments and removals of high priests but also such measures as those described at §§216–218, 222–223. For a detailed discussion of this authority, which is again mentioned at §222, see Wilker 2007: 205–252.

45 Use of the definite article here, at the opening of the final book of *Antiquities*, amounts to a reminder (like the one just above, at the very end of Book 19) as to where this story is going; cf. below, the note on "the" at §184.

46 The only descendant who actually inherited it from Herod of Chalcis was his nephew, Agrippa II. This is not mentioned specifically in the account of his inheritance of his uncle's kingdom (§104), but is clearly shown by his repeated appointment and removals of high priests (§§179, 196, 197, 203, 213, 223) and the stories at §§216–218, 222–223.

47 On καὶ δή, see the note on "for example" at 18.257.

48 On Elioneus b. Cantheras, see the note on "Cantheras" at 19.342.

49 Like so many high priests, whose names were no more than items on a list (see the Introduction, at n. 9), Josephus has no more to say about him, apart from his replacement at §103. But it might be that his name is among the names of high-priestly families that appear in a fragmentary Qumran text; see Eshel 2001: 133 and VanderKam 2004: 454–455.

50 That is, during the Judean governorship of Fadus, in the mid-40s. Presumably Josephus placed the story here because it resulted in Helena's pilgrimage to Jerusalem (§§49–53), which he dates at §101, perhaps on the basis of his own first-hand knowledge (for he was a youth in Jerusalem at the time), to the days of Fadus's immediate successor.

51 Adiabene was a small kingdom in northern Mesopotamia. For its historical geography, see esp. Marciak 2017: 257–271.

52 On this episode, see Täubler 1904: 62–65; Neusner 1984: 61–63; Schiffman 1987; Cohen 1987: 424–425; Gilbert 1990/91; Broer 1994; Mason 1998b: 90–95; Rajak 2001:

286–293; Livesey 2010: 35–40; Marciak 2014. On Helena in particular, see also Liebowitz 2018, also Kattan-Gribetz 2024. On the rabbinic version of the story, in *Gen. Rabbah* 46:10 (ed. Theodor-Albeck, 467–468), which shares some motifs with Josephus's story, see Ilan in Ilan and Noam 2017: 1.508–520; as Noam notes, ibid. 1.31, the fact that the midrash does not give Helena's name in this story, although she is well-known in rabbinic literature (including *m. Nazir* 3:6 and *m. Yoma* 3:10), suggests that it is not dependent on Josephus's account. Although Josephus, as usual, refers to adoption of Jewish practices rather than using a more abstract term (see the note on "practices" at 18.141), it is obvious that his story is very positive about what we term conversion to Judaism. It has been argued, however, especially by Cohen (loc. cit.), that usually Josephus is more embarrassed by this topic and circumspect about it, since it aroused antagonism and resentment in Rome; among Josephus's contemporaries, see for example, Seneca, *De superstitione*, as cited by Augustine, *City of God* 6.11; Tacitus, *Hist.* 5.5.1–2; Juvenal, *Satires* 14.96–106 (*GLAJJ*, nos. 186, 281, 301). If so, the presence of this story is to be understood as exceptional because it is based on a source that Josephus took over wholesale and/or because it relates to a region outside of the Roman Empire, concerning which he perhaps thought that he need not be worried about Roman antagonism and resentment. Mason, for his part, takes the story, Josephus's most sustained discussion of conversion, to be a major support for his impression that *Antiquities* was meant to encourage gentiles interested in Judaism. On the thin line between recognizing that Josephus, in *Antiquities*, is attempting to win respectability for Judaism, and the conclusion that he is actually missionizing for Judaism, see Sterling 1992: 306–308. On the story's function in Book 20, see the note on "providence" at §49.

53 For this formulation as a means of introducing material from a separate source into a narrative, especially when it comes together with "at this time" or the like, see the note on "circumstances" at 18.39. The use of a source for the story is also suggested by the unfulfilled

Adiabenians, surnamed Bazeus,[54] who was captivated by passion[55] for his sister Helena,
took her in marriage and made her pregnant.[56] And once it happened that, when sleeping
together with her, he rested his hand upon his wife's belly when she was asleep, whereupon
he thought he heard a voice[57] commanding him to remove his hand from her abdomen
and not exert any pressure upon the baby within it, who with God's providence had already
found a fortunate beginning and would find a fortunate end.[58] **19** Unsettled by the voice, he
woke up immediately and told his wife these things; and, indeed, he called the son Izates.[59]

20 Monobazus had an older son from Helena and other children from other wives, but it
was obvious that all of his goodwill was focused upon Izates, as if he were his only child.[60]
21 For this reason, jealousy toward the child grew among his brothers, who shared the same
father, and out of that there grew hatred, for all were grieved by the fact that their father
preferred Izates to them.[61] **22** Although the[ir] father clearly realized this, he forgave them,
on the one hand, as being afflicted by it[62] not out of wickedness, but rather out of their

cross-references at §§53, 96. Given the focus of the story
it is natural to think of a Mesopotamian or specifically
Adiabenian Jewish source, but there is little to go on; see
the notes on "pregnant" at §18, on "power" at §90, and on
"daughters" at §92.

54 Apparently a nickname ("hypocoristicon") based
on the latter part of his full name, similar to "Honyo"
for Yohanan.

55 Josephus likes expressions like this. Cf. the note on
"passion" at 18.350.

56 This is an egregious case of Josephan favoritism;
contrast §145, where merely the suspicion of such an
incestuous relationship is part of Josephus's case against
Agrippa I's daughters, and 19.204, where it functions as
part of the condemnation of Gaius Caligula. (For similar
double standards, cf. the notes on "wiped out" at 19.337
and on "squandering" at 20.211.) However, note that,
apart from the fact that Helena and Izates are heroes for
Josephus, while Agrippa's daughters and Caligula are at
the other pole, the relationship that is reported, and the
narrative's evident acceptance and approval of it, may
reflect Mesopotamian practice and a Mesopotamian
Jewish source that took such relationships for granted.
See Skjærvo 2013: "In Zoroastrian Middle Persian (Pahlavi)
texts, the term xwēdōodah (Av. xᮿaētuuadaϑa) is said to
refer to marital unions of father and daughter, mother
and son, or brother and sister (next-of-kin or close-kin
marriage, nuclear family incest), and to be one of the
most pious actions possible."

57 This formulation allows Josephus both to report
a heavenly voice and to avoid taking responsibility for
its reality. For another way of achieving the same end,
cf. 13.282: if here Josephus reports the voice himself but
says only that the king *thought* he heard it, there Josephus
reports that "they say" that Hyrcanus heard a heavenly

voice. These are both variations on his usual procedure
concerning miracles, namely, to tell the story but inform
readers they are free not to believe; see the note on "like"
at 19.108.

58 For such pre-birth annunciations concerning
infants who will enjoy divine favor, cf. Judges 13:3–5//
Ant. 5.277–278 and Luke 1:30–33. On this kind of story,
cf. Finlay 2005. On dying with a good reputation, see the
note on "remembered" at §216.

59 The emphatic καί γε ("indeed") implies that the
meaning of this name is somehow appropriate to what
was just said; indeed, "Izates" is (as was explained to me
by Michael Shenkar) a grecized form of the Parthian
yazad, "god." Various more or less similar names ("Zoitos,"
"Yazutos"...) appear in witnesses to the rabbinic version of
the story in *Gen. Rabbah* 46:10 (ed. Theodor-Albeck, 467).

60 On μονογενής as expressing especial endearment
(even if there are other children), see Winter 1953; at
p. 342, on Josephus's usage, Winter comments that the
present passage is exceptional, for usually he uses it
literally of someone without siblings (*Ant.* 1.222; 2.181;
5.264), while here it means "favorite," "best beloved."
However, on the one hand even the literal meaning
implies special affection (as in the first and third passages quoted), and, on the other hand, here too it is used
literally; the fact that Izates was not in fact the only son
is indicated by ὡς, "as if."

61 Josephus tells the story in a way reminiscent of
the biblical story of Joseph and his brothers (Gen 37//
Ant. 2.10–38), a story of which Josephus was fond; see the
notes on "before he died" at §24 and on "have in common" at 18.201. Cf. the similar motif in the Tobiad story,
at 12.202, 218.

62 That is, being afflicted by hatred.

desire to attain the affection of their father;[63] but as for the youth, on the other hand, he was very much in fear concerning him, lest he suffer something as a result of his brothers' hatred. Therefore, giving him many gifts, he sent him to Abennerigus,[64] the king of Charax Spasinou,[65] entrusting to him the boy's security. **23** Abennerigus was happy to receive the youth, and out of his great affection for him gave him his daughter, named Samacho, as a wife. He also gave him a gift of land, from which he would be able to derive great profits.

(2.2) 24 Monobazus, already being old and realizing that he had only a short time left to live, wanted his son to come before his eyes before he died.[66] Therefore he sent for him, welcomed him most enthusiastically, and gave him the land called Cardon.[67] **25** That land grows the greatest [amount] of good amomum;[68] and in it are also found the remnants of the ark in which, it is said, Noah survived the flood, which until today are pointed out to those who want to see them.[69] **26** So Izates remained in that land until the death of his father. But on the day that Monobazus died, Queen Helena sent for all of the great men and the satraps of the kingdom and those entrusted with the military forces. **27** To those who arrived, she said: "I think it is not unknown to you that my husband prayed[70] that his successor as king should be Izates, and that he considered him worthy [of that]; but all the same I await your decision. For happy is he who receives his rule not from one, but from many who so desire."

28 She said that in order to test what those who had been assembled were thinking. After hearing what she said, they first prostrated themselves before the queen, as is their custom,[71]

---

63 For love (usually of a woman, here of a father) as excusing misdeeds, cf. the note on "severe penalty" at 18.80.

64 The coins of Abinergaos I of Characene show he reigned 10/11–13/14 CE or later, and then, after an interruption, from 22/23; see Schuol 2000: 320–326.

65 "Spasines's Fort," named after its founder, Hyspaosines, a satrap of Antiochus IV. This city at the northwestern end of the Persian Gulf was capital of the kingdom that therefore became known as Characene. See esp. Pliny, *NH* 6.138–141, with Schuol 2000: 106–109, 278–279. On the political history of the kingdom, see ibid. 453–461. In Hebrew and Aramaic sources, the region is termed Meishan (Mesene) (Schuol 2000: 276–278); at *Ant.* 1.145, Josephus notes the equation.

66 This sounds like an allusion to Gen 45:28, in the biblical Joseph story, as does also *Life* 204; see the note on "to them" at §21.

67 The manuscripts and Niese (1890a: 280) read Καρρῶν, but that is otherwise unknown, hence the general acceptance of the seventeenth-century emendation to Καρδῶν, Gordyene, which, as the notes to §25 show, fits the coming references to amomum and to Noah's ark. See Marciak 2014: 197–198.

68 On this aromatic plant, which is difficult to identify today but was often mentioned in ancient literature and "in bestem Ansehen stand" (see, for example, Strabo, *Geog.* 16.1.24, in the context of his description of Gordyene), see P. Wagler, "Amomon," *PWRE* 1.1873–1874.

69 That Noah's ark, which according to Genesis 8:4 came to rest on "the mountains of Ararat," is still visible "in Armenia on the mountain of the Cordyaeans" (Gordyene) in Armenia, was stated by the Babylonian author Berossus (third-century BCE), as quoted by Josephus at *Ant.* 1.93 (where the next paragraph records references to the ark by other Hellenistic writers). Others held, however, that its remains were found near Apamea, in Phrygia; see Meshorer 1981.

70 Josephus, as others, uses εὔχομαι sometimes for swearing (as at *War* 2.313), sometimes for praying (e.g., 13.304; 14.22; 17.13; 18.211); see Spicq 1994: 2.147–154. Here, it seems the latter is to be preferred, for Helena would not want to put the nobles into the position of contemplating whether or not to do something contrary to Monobazus's oath. Moreover, Josephus typically uses ὅρκος with an auxiliary verb for the taking of oaths, as at §62 and 19.247, 362. True, sometimes (as Spicq notes, ibid. 150) εὔχομαι amounts to no more than "wish," and translators typically prefer the latter here (Feldman 1965: 405, "had set his heart"; Mathieu and Herrmann 1929: 257, "souhaitait"). It may well be, however, that Josephus, or his source, is deliberately portraying Helena as using religious language.

71 For this eastern alterity of *proskynesis*, cf. Feldman 1998a: 353–354: he shows how Josephus, in his version of the biblical story of Joseph, which includes several references to his brothers' bowing down to him (which

then they said they would ratify the king's decision and happily obey Izates, whom his father had rightly adjudged before the brothers in accordance with the prayers of all. **29** They also said they wanted preemptively to kill[72] Izates's brothers and relatives, so as to establish his rule securely.[73] For [they said], if they were destroyed it would eliminate all fear that might otherwise arise on account of their hatred and jealousy. **30** In response, Helena declared[74] that she thanked them for their goodwill toward her and Izates, but called upon them nevertheless to put off deciding about killing the brothers until Izates himself arrived and concurred. **31** Since despite their counsel they failed to convince her to put [the brothers and relations] to death, they urged her, for their own safety, to keep them fettered until Izates's arrival. And they also advised her to put at the head of the government, in the meantime, some guardian whom she especially trusted. **32** Helena was convinced of these things, and installed as king her eldest son, Monobazus. Crowning him with the diadem and giving him his father's signet ring and that [sword] which was called among them *sampsera*,[75] she bade him to administer the kingdom until his brother's arrival. **33** And [Izates], immediately upon hearing of his father's death, came and replaced his brother Monobazus, who withdrew from rule in his favor.

(2.3) 34 Now at the time when Izates was staying in Charax Spasinou, a certain Jewish merchant[76] named Ananias who had visited with the king's wives taught them to revere[77] God according to the ancestral custom of the Jews. **35** So it happened that, through them, he came to the notice of Izates and he too was similarly won over.[78] When Izates was recalled by his father to Adiabene,[79] Ananias went there with him, obeying his repeated request. And it had also happened that Helena too, after receiving similar instruction from some other Jew, had been brought over to their laws. **36** When Izates, upon taking over the kingdom and coming to Adiabene, saw his brothers and the other relatives in chains he was vexed about what had happened. **37** Thinking it impious to kill them or to keep them in fetters, but also considering it risky to keep them with him—resentful as they were—unfettered, he sent some of them with their children to Rome as hostages to Claudius Caesar, and others to Artabanus the Parthian, on the same pretext.[80]

---

the Septuagint renders with προσκυνέω at Genesis 42:6; 43:26, 28; 47:31) "carefully avoids all indication that anyone bows down to Joseph." For discussion of the meaning of the term and of the critical view of prostration as an abominable oriental practice in literature more or less contemporary with Josephus (Q. Curtius, Plutarch, and Arrian), see Balsdon 1950: 371–382. Correspondingly, Josephus usually uses προσκυνέω more generally, of showing respect, or worship; see, for example, §§49, 56, 65, 71; 20.164.

72 This is the only occurrence of προαποκτείνω in Josephus (just as many of the προ- words listed in *CCFJ* 3.516–517 appear only once each), and the earliest of those cited by LSJ 1469.

73 For such practice as standard operating procedure in royal courts, see the note on "to his death" at 18.187.

74 On the senses of ὁμολογέω see Tov 1999: 115–121.

75 For the tracing of this Greek version of the word (known also from Arrian and a papyrus) back to the Middle Persian *šamšēr*, see Brust 2005: 571–576.

76 For the evidence on Jewish inhabitants in the region, see Schuol 2000: 276–278, 326 and Oppenheimer 2005: 409–416.

77 This use of σέβειν is calculated, for it is the beginning of a discussion that will come to focus, at §§38–42, on the question whether it is enough to revere ("fear") God or whether one who does so should also convert to Judaism and thus become a Jew. Josephus, as others (such as Juvenal, *Satires* 14.96–106 = *GLAJJ*, no. 301) is very well aware of the distinction between sympathizers, who "fear God," and those who go all the way and convert to Judaism. See the note on "Jewish practices" at 18.82.

78 συναναπείθω appears in Josephus only here and in *Life* 424.

79 That is, by his father's testament; see §27.

80 That is, he claimed to use them to guarantee Adiabene's peaceable intentions vis-à-vis the two great powers, but his main motivation was to keep them far away from him. On diplomatic hostages, see the note on "hostages" at 18.42.

(2.4) **38** When he learned that his own mother was very pleased with the Jews' practices, he became enthusiastic about going over to them himself.[81] But considering that he could not be a full-fledged[82] Jew if he were not circumcised,[83] he was ready to do [that]. **39** When his mother learned this, however, she tried to prevent him, saying that it would bring danger upon him. For [she said], he was a king, and he would engender great discontent among his subjects if they were to learn that he was enthusiastic for customs that were foreign and strange for them, and they would not tolerate having a Jew as their king.

40 That is what she said, attempting in every way to dissuade him. He reported her words to Ananias, and he agreed with [Izates's] mother and at the same time threatened him, that if he did not agree [to abstain from circumcision] he would abandon [him] and depart—**41** for [he said], he was afraid that when the fact became known to all, he would be in danger of being punished as if he were responsible for these things and the king's teacher for such improper acts. Moreover, he said that [Izates] could revere the deity[84] even without circumcision, if indeed he had decided to be devoted to the Jews' ancestral practices—and that was more important[85] than being circumcised. **42** When he also said that God too would grant him forgiveness for not performing the act out of necessity and the fear of his subjects,[86] the king was convinced by [his] words, for a time. **43** However, he did not give up his enthusiasm[87] entirely, and when later on another Jew—from the Galilee, named Eleazar—arrived, one who was thought to be very exacting about the ancestral practices,[88] he encouraged [the king] to perform the act. **44** For when he entered to greet him and encountered him reading the law of Moses,[89] he said:

---

81 This passage apparently assumes the distinction between "revering God" (§34) and living according to Jewish laws (§35). Izates had already been won over to the former while in Charax Spasinou, while his mother, in Adiabene, had been won over to the latter (§35); now Izates too, having come to Adiabene, wants to accept the latter. See the note on "revere" at §34.

82 I take this sense of εἶναι βεβαίως Ἰουδαῖος from the comparison with *War* 2.263, where a sympathizer with Judaism is termed "mixed" (μεμιγμένον), from the Syrians' point of view, as opposed to a Jew who is βεβαίως ἀλλόφυλον ("an actual foreigner" [Mason 2008: 342]). Another sense, "stably" (as at 19.231), might also be indicated here, inasmuch as circumcision was, basically, thought to be irrevocable, although the operation known as "epispasm," that undoes circumcision, does begin to appear in the first century. See Hall 1988: 82 and D. R. Schwartz 2022: 157–158.

83 For circumcision as the sine qua non of a Jewish male, see esp. Thiessen 2011 and Livesey 2010. For the suggestion that there was significant contemplation in first-century Judaism of the possibility that a male gentile might convert to Judaism without circumcision, see the arguments offered by McEleney 1974 and the rebuttal by Nolland 1981. On rabbinic literature, which is later, and a survey of scholarly views, cf. esp. Porton 1994: 94–95.

84 This use of τὸ θεῖον, as opposed to τὸν θεόν at §§42, 44, 48, might be calculated: Ananias is urging Izates to

remain a non-Jew, and therefore uses a more general and universal term. See the note on "the deity" at 18.5.

85 For this meaning of κυριώτερον see, for example, 4.309 and *Apion* 1.19.

86 The use of a preposition here (ἐκ τῶν ὑπηκόων) is somewhat heavy, for only a plain genitive is needed; see, for example, 18.215; 19.51, 250. But this pleonasm is not infrequent in Josephus (e.g., 11.287; 13.356; 14.113; 20.220), as elsewhere (LSJ 1947, s.v. φόβος, §IIa).

87 To become a "full-fledged" Jew, as at §38.

88 On this phrase, see the note on "exacting about the regulations" at 19.332, where it is emphasized that this need not denote Pharisees. However, if there Simon apparently denied the efficacy of conversion, here Eleazar is positing it, and if Simon's position is priestly (see the note on "by birth" at 19.332), Eleazar's is not; his view corresponds with that followed by the Pharisees and the rabbis. On the latter, see Lavee 2018. In the present context, however, Josephus does not raise the questions, whether conversion is an effective process or whether circumcision is a sine qua non for it for males. All agree about both points. Rather, by contrasting Ananias (and Helena) to Eleazar he raises only the question whether conversion, which of course entails circumcision, is wise or safe for a king.

89 It is interesting to wonder what readers are supposed to think about where Izates found the book and in what language it was, but these are not questions that need concern edifying storytellers.

You are not aware, O king, that you are committing the gravest injustice against the laws and, through them, against God. For you should not only read the laws; rather, you should do, first of all, what is ordained by them. **45** How long will you remain uncircumcised?! But if you have not yet read the law about that,[90] read it now, so you will know what impiety it is [to which I refer].

46 Upon hearing these words, the king did not put off the act. Rather, moving into another room and summoning his physician, he executed that which was commanded. Then, calling for his mother and for his teacher, Ananias, he indicated[91] [to them] that the act had been done. **47** They were immediately affected by no little shock and fear, lest—if it were to become known[92] that the king had done the act—the king, on the on hand, would be in danger of losing rule [of the kingdom], for his subjects would not tolerate being ruled by a man who was a devotee of the customs of others, and they too, on the other hand, would be in danger, for they would be made to bear the guilt [for what Izates had done]. **48** But it was God[93] who prevented their fears from being realized. For he preserved Izates and his children when they fell into many dangers,[94] providing [them] with way[s] to be saved from impossible situations, demonstrating that for those who look away [from other considerations] to him, and put their faith[95] in him, the fruit of piety[96] is not denied. But these things I shall report later.[97]

(2.5) 49 When Helena, the king's mother, saw that the affairs of the kingdom were proceeding peacefully, her son being prosperous and envied among all,[98] including gentiles, due to God's providence,[99] she had a yearning to visit the city of the Jerusalemites so as to worship

Helena's Pilgrimage to Jerusalem

---

90 Genesis 17:9–14. There, however, as also at Leviticus 12:3, it is only the circumcision of male infants that is contemplated. Similarly, although Exodus 12:48 states that the circumcision of a gentile allows him to partake of the paschal sacrifice, it says nothing more general about becoming a Jew. For the argument that, accordingly, there were ancient Jews who denied the possibility of conversion to Judaism, by males, for circumcision later than the eighth day was ineffective, see esp. Thiessen 2011. For Josephus, however, it was clear that conversion was feasible and circumcision was, for males, a necessary condition; see *War* 2.454; *Ant.* 11.285; *Life* 113; also Cohen 1987: 421 and D. R. Schwartz 2007c: 94–96.

91 This use of ἐσήμαινεν, rather than plain "told," sounds mysterious, perhaps hinting either that he was so weakened by the operation that he could not talk but only gesture, or, perhaps, that he showed them what had been done.

92 For this sense of εἰς ἔλεγχον ἐλθούσης, cf. *Life* 91: εἰς ἔλεγχον ... ἀφικομένης.

93 This formulation indicates that Izates's advisers failed to dissuade him, which Josephus takes for granted.

94 For such usage, which juxtaposes the admission that sometimes things just happen with the belief that God's providence can protect against them, see Spicq 1994: 3.97–98.

95 On Josephus's usage here, see D. R. Lindsay 1993: 125: "the idea of believing or trusting in God results in a passive benefit for the believer."

96 For this metaphor, as already at Hosea 10:12, *Letter of Aristeas* 232, and Philippians 1:11, see esp. Satlow 2010.

97 Concerning Izates, see §§75–91. Concerning his children, see *War* 6.356–357—a story that Josephus perhaps hoped to retell (see below, §267).

98 This motivation for Helena's conversion is just the same as that given for Izates's brother and kinsmen (§75). Apparently it was important for Josephus to argue that conversion to Judaism need not arouse contempt. There was, indeed, plenty of contempt for Jewish proselytes in Rome in Josephus's day; see the note on "way of life" at §17.

99 This story's emphasis on divine providence (§§18, 48, 49, 72, 75, 81, 85, 91) is underlined by Gilbert 1990/91: 300. As he notes, it conforms to a basic theme of *Antiquities* (see the note on "of man" at 19.61) and, thereby, amounts to promising righteous converts that which Judaism promises righteous Jews. For readers who go on to read down to the end of Book 20, the point will be all the more reinforced (as Sarit Kattan Gribetz pointed out) when they realize the other half of the same notion: that while God providentially protects righteous converts even in Mesopotamia, he will "hide his face"

in the Temple of God that was spoken of [so highly] by all of humanity[100] and bring there sacrifices of thanksgiving.[101] So she asked her son for permission [to make the trip]. 50 After he approved most enthusiastically of what his mother had requested, preparing the great amount of supplies needed for the trip and giving [her] much money [for it], she went down[102] to the city of the Jerusalemites, her son accompanying her for a great distance.

51 Her arrival was very beneficial for the Jerusalemites, since a famine[103] was then pressing hard upon their city and many were being ruined by the[ir] lack of means; Queen Helena,[104] accordingly, sent some of her people to Alexandria to buy wheat[105] for large sums of money, and others to Cyprus to bring a shipload of dried figs.[106] 52 When they returned quickly, bringing [these], she distributed food to the destitute, thus leaving behind for herself the greatest name,[107] thanks to this benefaction[108] for our entire nation. 53 And when also her son, Izates, learned of the famine, he sent great sums of money to the leaders of the Jerusalemites, the distribution of which allowed many to recover from the severe duress of the famine. But we shall narrate after these [events] the good works done to our city by these kings.[109]

---

even from thoroughbred Jerusalemites if they stray from his ways; see esp. §166. Given the fairly obvious way in which the end of Book 19, where Agrippa is treated as a god, matches the opening of the book, where Gaius is, it is not difficult to imagine that Josephus, or his readers, would notice this point in the present book.

100 For similar phrases that proudly underline the worldwide fame of the Temple of Jerusalem, see 13.77, also 2 Macc 2:22 and 3:12; Philo, *Leg.* 191, 198. That fame cannot be distinguished from that of Jerusalem, the "longe clarissima urbium Orientis non Iudaeae modo" (Pliny, *NH* 5.70), "famosa urbs" (Tacitus, *Hist.* 5.2.1). On Jerusalem's fame in antiquity, see also Stern, *GLAJJ* 1.477–478 and idem 1991: 518–530.

101 This story is vaguely reminiscent of the Mishnah's report (*Nazir* 3:6) that she vowed to become a Nazir if her son returned safely from war. On Nazirites, see the note on "Nazirites" at 19.294.

102 H. van Herwerden was so bothered by this departure from usual Jewish—and Josephan—parlance about "going up" to Jerusalem (see the note on "went up" at 18.90) that he proposed (as is reported at *CCFJ* 1.83, following Naber 1893: xxxv) emending καταβαίνει into ἀναβαίνει. But the manuscripts are unanimous, and we can infer that Josephus simply referred to her westward voyage, in the direction of the Mediterranean, with the usual Greek phrase for "go down from the inland parts to the sea, esp. from central Asia" (LSJ 884, s.v. καταβαίνω, §I.2); cf. §116 and the note on "satrapies" at 18.100.

103 This famine is probably to be identified with the one in the late 40s mentioned at Acts 11:27–30 and at *Ant.* 3.320–321 as having been in the days of Claudius. (On the chronological problem raised by the latter passage, see D. R. Schwartz 2024a. On this famine, see Gapp 1935 and

Dupont 1955: 52–55. On the question, whether it really affected "the whole world" [Acts 11:28], see esp. Aus 2015: 167–199.) At §101 Josephus clarifies that it occurred in the days of Fadus's successor, Tiberius Julius Alexander; that is, Josephus has located the entire Adiabene story under Fadus (§§2, 97) but in including this episode it has moved beyond that timeframe.

104 The use of her title, as also the identification of Izates as her son at §53 (which is superfluous in general, and certainly after §§49–50), are remarkable. Perhaps it reflects Josephus's sense that their first appearance in the new geographical context requires something of a new introduction.

105 As did Herod in 25 BCE, in similar circumstances; see *Ant.* 15.306–308. Egypt was famous for its wheat in the Roman period; see, for example, Seneca, *Epistle* 77.1; Josephus, *War* 2.386; Rickman 1980; and Erdkamp 2005: 225–237. Ibid. 226–230 Erdkamp discusses Josephus's testimony at *War* 2.386: if Josephus claims that Egypt supplied Rome with a full third of its grain, Erdkamp argues that, in fact, it supplied most of it.

106 At §101, as also 3.321, Josephus mentions only the wheat from Egypt. On figs, which could easily be dried, stored, and shipped, and were therefore a standard item in famine relief, see Garnsey 1988: 53–55.

107 For "leaving behind (καταλείπω)" a reputation, cf. the note on "remembered" at §216.

108 For εὐποία, cf. 2.261–262; 15.405; and 19.356. For the concept, which is more usually expressed by εὐεργεσία and related words, see the note on "benefit" at 18.95.

109 Apart from a passing cross-reference back to here at §101, Josephus does not fulfill this promise, nor the one at §96, and we do not know what good works Josephus meant. Although it is possible that Josephus planned to

(3.1) 54 Artabanus, the king of the Parthians, upon discovering that his satraps had put together a conspiracy against him, and [therefore] not viewing it as safe to remain among them, decided to up and go to Izates, in the desire of finding there some means to survive and to return to rule, if he could.[110] **55** Indeed, he arrived [in Adiabene], taking along with him about a thousand relatives and servants, and as it happened, he encountered Izates while still on the way. **56** [Artabanus] knew quite well who he was, but he was not recognized by Izates. Standing near him, he first prostrated himself before him, according to the ancestral custom, and then said:

Izates Saves Artabanus

> O king, do not ignore me, your supplicant, nor be contemptuous of my request. For I have become humble due to a turn of fortune; from being a king I have become a private person, and need your succor. **57** Look, then, at the instability of fortune and that it is common [to us all],[111] and so consider what is providential for you too. For if my case is ignored and left unpunished, there will be many more audacious people [who will threaten] other kings as well.

58 He said that in tears and with his head bowed. As for Izates: when he heard the name and saw Artabanus standing as a supplicant to him, he leaped down[112] from his horse and **59** said:

> Be brave, O king, and do not let the present upset you as if it were incurable; for the reversal of your sad state will be swift.[113] You will find me to be a friend and ally even better than you hoped, for I will either restore you to the kingdom of the Parthians or abdicate my own.

(3.2) 60 Having said that, he put Artabanus back on his horse and himself accompanied him on foot, giving him this honor as the greater king. When Artabanus saw that, however,

---

write about this, whether in *Antiquities* or in a later work (see §267), the general assumption that this detailed narrative is based on a Mesopotamian Jewish source that focused panegyrically on the Adiabenian dynasty suggests that uncorroborated cross-references within the narrative derive from that source. Cf. the note on "shortly" at 19.366.

110 This episode, which for Josephus is important only insofar as it brought the Parthian king to seek Izates's help and occasioned a demonstration of the latter's gracious behavior towards his fallen overlord, is not simple to date. Usually it is placed between Artabanus II's agreement with Vitellius mentioned at 18.96–100 (late in Tiberius's reign or early in Gaius's; see the opening note on 18.4.4 [§96]) and Artabanus's death in 38 (see the note on "died" at §69); so Debevoise 1938: 165–166 and Schippmann 2011. However, that seems to derive only from the order of events in Josephus: from the fact that he records the meeting with Vitellius in Book 18. It seems likelier that the present reference is to the same flight of Artabanus II mentioned by Josephus at 18.99–100 among the events that *preceded* Artabanus's meeting with Vitellius. Note that in both cases Artabanus is said to have fled (i) from high-ranking internal opponents (there "men of the

first rank," here "satraps"), (ii) inland (there "to one of the upper satrapies," here to Adiabene), (iii) only temporarily, for he was soon able to return (although the explanations of how that happened are different). In any case, it is remarkable that Josephus makes no cross-reference here to the episode in Book 18, and if the two episodes are identical it is just as remarkable that he makes no reference there to the present story. See the Introduction, at n. 11.

111 For rhetorical usage of this motif, compare, for example, §61; 14.381; 19.296; and—with regard to Titus's ruminations when he saw Josephus fall from command to captivity—*War* 3.394–396. It is also a central element of Josephus's story of Agrippa I; see the note on "fallen" at 18.294. For its most famous occurrences, see Herodotus 1.86 (Cyrus regrets his decision to burn Croesus alive) and Polybius 38.21.1–3 (Scipio's tears at the destruction of Carthage); Polybius highlights this theme already at the opening of his work (1.1.2). Parallels and other cases are assembled by Grethlein 2013: 261–262.

112 Here Ambrosianus adds ὀξέως ("quickly"); see the note on "brought to him" at §5.

113 This recalls the German prisoner's speech to Agrippa at 18.197–200.

he took it badly, and he swore, by the fortune and the honor which had come upon him, that he would dismount unless [Izates] remounted and went before him. **61** Being persuaded, he leaped upon the horse and led him to the kingdom, allotting him every honor in its councils and the most prominent couches at banquets[114]—giving regard not to his current fortune but to his original dignity, and somehow also keeping in mind that reversals of fortune are common to [all] men. **62** He also wrote to the Parthians, urging them to re-accept Artabanus, offering his right hand[115] as security for an amnesty for the things that had been done, along with oaths and his [willingness to] mediate. **63** Since the Parthians did not wish to refuse to accept him, but said they could not because they had entrusted rule to another (Cinnamus was the name of the one who had succeeded) and that they were afraid, lest the move [to restore Artabanus] cause them to fall into the clutches of civil strife, **64** Cinnamus, learning of their preference [for Artabanus], wrote to Artabanus, for he had been brought up by him and was a gentleman by nature, and called upon him to trust him and come take over his rule. **65** And Artabanus, trusting [in Cinnamus], indeed came. Cinnamus met him and, after prostrating himself and calling him king, put the diadem on his head after taking it off his own.[116]

(3.3) 66 Thus was Artabanus restored to his reign by Izates, after having previously fallen from power on account of the [machinations] of the grandees. And he was not forgetful of the benefactions that he had received; rather, he repaid Izates with the greatest honors among them: **67** he allowed him to wear his tiara upright and to recline on a golden couch, which are dignities and symbols of the Parthian kings alone.[117] **68** He also gave him much good land, which he took away from the king of Armenia; the land was called Nisibis, within which the Macedonians had earlier founded the city of Antioch, to which they gave the surname Epimygdonia.[118] With such honors, then, did the Parthian king honor Izates.[119]

Izates vs. Vardanes

(3.4) 69 Not long thereafter, however, Artabanus died,[120] leaving the kingdom to his son Vardanes.[121] He came to Izates and—since he was planning to make war against the Romans—tried to convince him to fight together with him and to prepare an allied force.

---

114 See the note on "alone" at §67.

115 On the giving of the right hand, see the note on "for visitors" at 18.328.

116 For serious doubts about this whole story, beginning with Josephus being the only literary account of the Cinnamus story, Cinnamus not being a Parthian name, and there being no numismatic evidence for his existence, and also raising questions about the logic of the story, see Chaumont 2011.

117 As at §61. On the Parthian king's tiara, which is prominent in royal iconography, see Olbrycht 1997. As for καθεύδειν on a golden κλίνη: the verb appears (although with no explicit subject), in a similar context of rewarding at an eastern court, at 11.35, and there Spilsbury and Seeman (2017: 20) render "sleep upon a golden (bed)." However, although that is the usual meaning of the verb, it seems likelier that the reference here is to reclining on a couch, including at meals, as at §61; cf. Esther 1:6. On depictions of golden couches at Sasanian royal banquets,

see Minov 2021: 238–239 (to which I was kindly referred by Michael Shenkar).

118 As Mason notes, this is the only known reference to Epimygdonia in surviving ancient Greek. For the region's fertility, see Cameron 2019: 12–13; he cites, *inter alia*, Strabo, *Geog.* 16.1.23 and Pliny 6.117. Cameron notes (12, n. 50) concerning the present passage, "Josephus is confused," for, in fact, Nisibis was not a land (or "district"); it was a city, the same city also known as Epimygdonian Antioch. This Nisibis is to be distinguished from the more obscure one mentioned in the story of Asineus and Anileus; see the note on "Nisibis" at 18.312.

119 On such statements, which wrap up the preceding narrative before moving on to the next, see the note on "Petronius" at 18.288.

120 This is usually dated ca. 38 CE; so Debevoise 1938: 166 and Schippmann 2011.

121 Josephus here skips Artabanus's first successor, Gotarzes II, who reigned briefly (Tacitus, *Ann.* 11.8; see

70 But Izates was not at all convinced. For Izates, who knew the power and good fortune of the Romans,[122] thought that Vardanes was undertaking something impossible. 71 Furthermore, Izates had sent [to Judea[123]] both his sons (five in number), who were young in age, to learn our ancestral language and culture accurately, and his mother, to worship in the Temple, as I already said.[124] He was therefore all the more hesitant, and without letup attempted to dissuade Vardanes by telling him of the power and the deeds of the Romans,[125] thinking thereby to cause him to take fright and give up his enthusiasm to campaign against them. 72 The Parthian, angered at this, immediately declared war upon Izates. However, he did not reap any benefit from this campaign, God sundering all his hopes. 73 For when the Parthians learned what Vardanes had in mind and that he had decided to campaign against the Romans, they killed him and transferred rule to his brother, Cortades.[126] 74 When he too was killed not long thereafter, as the result of a plot against him, he was succeeded by his brother Vologeses,[127] who then assigned dominions to two brothers of his by the same father: Media to the older of the two, Pacorus, and Armenia to the younger, Tiridates.[128]

(4.1) 75 When the king's brother Monobazus and other kinsmen saw that Izates, thanks to his piety toward God, had become an object of universal envy,[129] they too became enthusiastic to abandon their ancestral practices and practice the Jews' customs. 76 But their doings were discovered by the [kingdom's] subjects. The grandees, although they took it very hard, did not display their anger; rather, they kept it to themselves while eagerly

Izates vs. Adiabenian Grandees, Arabs, and Parthians

Debevoise 1938: 166–167) before unhappy subjects called in Vardanes I, who successfully took over and reigned until ca. 45 or later (Schippmann 2016). For Gotarzes's return, see below, §73.

122 Rome's δύναμις and τύχη, as reasons not to oppose it, are (as opposed to the benefits of Roman rule) recurrent themes in *War*; note especially their collocation at 2.373 as explaining the Gauls' submissiveness, just as, at *Life* 17, Josephus claims that he himself pointed to Rome's τύχη along with its (successful) experience at war as reasons Judeans should abstain from rebellion. On Josephus's use of τύχη, see Lindner 1972: 89–94; on the way mobilization of it subtly undercuts Rome's merit, see Mason 2008: 289–290, n. 2354 (and the note on "Petronius" at 18.305). On Plutarch's resort to τύχη in explaining the success of Rome, see Swain 1989.

123 This is implied both by the nature of their studies and by the parallelism of the coming reference to Helena.

124 Above, §§49–53. That is, Izates claimed that if he were to join in war against the Romans it could endanger his mother and sons, who were in Roman territory.

125 Perhaps Josephus was thinking here of his own attempts to use similar arguments (*Life* 17–19) to avert war with Rome, or those of Agrippa II (*War* 2.345–401) and others, which all failed, just as did Izates's. In any case,

Josephus is evidently happy to show his Roman readers that pious Jews respect their empire.

126 I.e., Gotarzes II; see the note on "Vardanes" at §69. The reason Josephus gives for the Parthians' opposition to Vardanes is not found in Tacitus's account (*Ann.* 11.10), but Roman readers might be happy to read it.

127 According to Tacitus (*Ann.*12.14), (a) Gotarzes was first succeeded by a Vonones, who reigned only briefly before being replaced by Vologases, who (b) was in fact Gotarzes's son, not his brother (hence Artabanus's grandson, not his son). But Josephus is consistent; see below, §82. Debevoise (1938: 174) sides with Tacitus on the first issue (suggesting Josephus simply skipped Vonones because his reign was so short) and leaves the second one open; Schippmann (2016) takes the opposite options.

128 On these events, see Debevoise 1938: 170–174.

129 As above, §49. Interestingly, Josephus usually assumes that a ruler's success attracts envy that is hostile; so, for example, *Ant.* 6.193; 13.288//*War* 1.67; 14.163; 18.240; *War* 1.208; and *Life* 122. On that motif, see the note on "jealous" at 18.240. Here, however, Josephus, in consonance with the general message of this story, namely, that conversion to Judaism can enlist divine providence and thus promise well-being, asserts that those who observed Izates's success realized it was because of his piety, and so their envy brought them to desire to emulate him.

seeking an appropriate opportunity to punish them.[130] **77** Accordingly,[131] they wrote Abias, king of the Arabs,[132] promising to give him large sums of money if he would be willing to campaign against their king, and also stating that they would leave the king in the lurch in the first engagement. For, [they said], they wanted to punish him for having despised their own practices. Having bound themselves in their agreement with one another by oaths, they called upon [Abias] to act quickly. **78** The Arab agreed and, leading a large force, he came against Izates. On the verge of the first engagement, but before they came to blows,[133] all of the [grandees], upon a [prearranged] signal, abandoned Izates, as if they had been seized by panicky fear; turning their backs[134] to the enemy's soldiers, they fled. **79** Izates was not cowed, but when he realized that his grandees had betrayed him, he too turned back to the camp. When, upon investigation, he learned that the reason [for their flight] was that they had aligned themselves with the Arab, he executed those of them who were guilty; then, the next day, he attacked [the Arabs], killing many of them and forcing all [the others] to flee.[135] **80** As for the king himself, Izates pursued him and boxed him into a fortress named Arsamus;[136] in an intense attack upon the fortress he captured it, taking all the booty that was there, which was quite a lot. Then he turned back to Adiabene. He did not capture Abias alive, for after he was surrounded on all sides he killed himself.[137]

(4.2) 81 The Adiabenian grandees, who had had no luck in their first attempt, for God had given them up into the hands of the king, did not at all keep quiet.[138] Rather, they wrote again, this time to Vologeses, who was king of the Parthians, calling upon him to kill Izates, on the one hand, and to appoint for them, on the other hand, another ruler, even one of Parthian descent; for they said they hated their own king because he had abolished their ancestral practices, having become a devotee of foreign customs.

82 Hearing this, the Parthian was aroused[139] to war. But since he had no just pretext, he sent [a message] demanding [the return of] the honors that his father[140] had presented Izates,[141] and declaring[142] war if Izates refused. **83** Izates was not a little upset in his mind when he heard these things, because he thought that returning the gifts would make him look contemptible, for it would appear that he had done it out of fear. **84** Moreover, he

---

130 In the following two stories, Josephus fleshes out the fear mentioned at §§41, 47 and the divine protection promised at §48; see Marciak 2014: 111–112. As at 18.44, 99–100 and above, §54, the eastern grandees are portrayed as conspiratorial and conniving—a portrayal Romans would probably be happy to read.

131 As at the opening of §55, so too here καὶ δή moves from the statement of intention to report of consequent action. On such full translations of καὶ δή, see the note on "for example" at 18.257.

132 Retsö (2003: 414) argues that these Arabs lived west of the Tigris in northern Mesopotamia, and are probably the ones to whom Josephus refers in *War* 1.3 as well, alongside the people of Adiabene. See also Marciak 2014: 239, n. 47.

133 For εἰς χεῖρας ἐλθεῖν, cf. 5.73, 356; 15.149.

134 For τὰ νῶτα ἐντρέψαι see already Herodotus 7.211. Cf. *Ant.* 12.424 where Josephus, paraphrasing 1 Macc 9:10,

has Judas Maccabeus proudly refuse to show his back to his enemies.

135 A standard outcome; see the note on "to flee" at 18.87.

136 According to Retsö (2003: 414), Arsamus is probably the same as Arsham, known to have been between Mosul and Zakho.

137 Here, as elsewhere (see the note on "brought to him" at §5), Ambrosianus offers a superfluous expansion: "before he could be closed in upon by Izates."

138 On the coming episode, known only from Josephus, see Debevoise 1938: 177–178.

139 Cf. the note on "rose up" at 19.284.

140 Artabanus II; see the note on "Vologeses" at §74.

141 As reported at §§66–68.

142 I have translated according to the obvious meaning of καταγγέλλω above at §72, as also elsewhere. At times, however, the sense is rather "threatening," as, for

knew that even if the Parthian received the honors back he would not keep quiet. Therefore, he decided to turn over to the caring God [the handling of] the mortal danger to himself. **85** Considering him the best ally[143] he had, he deposited his children and his wives in his safest fortress, moved all the grain into fortresses,[144] and set fire to the grass and the pastures.[145] After making these preparations, he awaited the enemy's soldiers. **86** When the Parthian arrived with a large force of infantry and cavalry—sooner than expected,[146] for he had marched without pause—he set up a fortified camp on the river that borders on Adiabene and Media.[147] Izates too located his camp not far from there, having with him cavalry—six thousand in number. **87** A messenger sent by the Parthian came to Izates, informing him of the great power of the Parthian empire, of which the borders went from the Euphrates River until Bactria, and listing the kings subject to it, **88** and he threatened to punish Izates if he were to be ungrateful to his rulers, [stating that] even the God whom he revered would not be able to save him from the king's hands. **89** After the messenger had declared those things, Izates said he knew that the power of the Parthians greatly differed from his own, but he also knew, he said, that God is greater than all of humanity. Then, having given this response, he turned to supplication of God: throwing himself upon the ground and disheveling his hair with ashes,[148] together with his wife and children he fasted[149] and called upon God, saying:[150] **90** "If it is not in vain, O sovereign Lord, that I have experienced[151] your kindness,[152] and that I consider you rightly to be the only and first lord of all, come as an ally not only to defend me from my enemies, but also because they have contemptuously attacked your power."[153] **91** These words he cried out as a lament,

---

example, in 11.222, 229. In the present context, there is not much difference between an ultimatum and a threat of war.

143 For Josephus on God as an ally (βοηθός), see esp. Gafni 1989: 126–127 (where "allegiance" on p. 127 should be "alliance").

144 On the meaning of βᾶρις, see the note on "large building" at 18.91.

145 Such scorched-earth tactics by those retreating in the face of invasion were well-known in antiquity. See, for some examples, Herodotus 4.120; Xenophon, *Anabasis* 1.6; Caesar, *Gallic War* 7.14.

146 On θᾶττον ἐλπίδος, see the note on "expected" at 19.335.

147 The border between Adiabene and Media Atropatene (to its east) was marked by the Zagros Mountains (Marciak 2017: 270); the river is probably the Great Zab.

148 For such use of ashes cf. §123 and 7.171, 204. As here, it comes together with fasting at 1 Macc 3:47.

149 For fasting as reinforcing prayer, cf. 2 Samuel 12:16–23; Jonah 3:5; Esther 4:16; 1 Macc 3:47; 2 Macc 13:12; etc. Note esp. 1 Macc 3:17, which (echoing 1 Samuel 14) refers to soldiers who had not eaten. No explanation is given, but Josephus (*Ant.* 12.290) naturally explains this was pre-battle fasting. Cf. Hacham 1996.

150 On this prayer, see especially Jonquière 2007: 202–207. Prayers that attempt to motivate God to intervene on

behalf of the faithful by arguing that the attack on them is really on him are quite standard; see, for example, Exodus 32:12; Deut 32:27; Psalms 79:9–10; 115:1; Isaiah 37:15–20; Jeremiah 14:21; LXX Daniel 3:34, 43 (Prayer of Azariah); 2 Macc 8:15; 3 Macc 2:9, 14, 17–18; 2 Baruch 5:1; Johnson 1948: 38–41 ("An Appeal to God's Dignity or Pride"); Miller 1994: 120–126 (on "intimating that God's reputation is at stake"). See the next note.

151 The manuscripts' ἐγενόμην, maintained by Niese (1890a: 291), is somewhat difficult to render here, and has engendered emendations; see Feldman 1965: 434, n. 3. But in any case the logic of the appeal is clear: suffering a disaster is all the worse if it comes shortly after being the beneficiary of God's grace. For the same consideration, cf. 8.128, also Judith 4:3 and 2 Macc 13:11 and 14:36. In the present passage, the reference to the enemies as those who showed contempt for God (just as 2 Macc 13:11 refers to the blasphemous enemies), argues that such a quick reversal of fortunes, if God were to allow it, would also sully his own name. Cf. the preceding note.

152 On χρηστότης as characteristic of God, as of princes and rulers, see Spicq 1994: 3.512–513.

153 For a discussion of variant readings of this conclusion of the prayer, and the suggestion that in its original Aramaic it denounced Vologeses as one whose mouth arrogantly "speaks great things," echoing Daniel 7:8, 20, see Schalit 1965: 174–176.

with tears and wailing, and God indeed heeded: immediately, that same night, Vologeses received letters in which it was written that a great force[154] of Dahae and Sacae, holding him in contempt due to his absence, had invaded Parthia and were ravaging it. [Upon reading this], Vologeses immediately turned back, having accomplished nothing. Thus did Izates, by God's providence, escape the Parthian's threats.[155]

Deaths of Izates and Helena

(4.3) 92 Not long after, having completed fifty-five years since his birth and twenty-four years of reign, he passed away, leaving after him twenty-four male children[156] and twenty-four daughters,[157] 93 and having ordained that his brother Monobazus should succeed him as ruler. In this way he requited him for having faithfully preserved dominion for him when he was away from home after [their] father's death.[158] 94 When his mother, Helena, heard of the death of her child she took it very badly, as is proper when a mother loses a most pious[159] son; but she nevertheless had some consolation when she heard that the succession to the throne had passed to her elder son, and she hurried to go to him. But after she arrived in Adiabene she did not outlive her son Izates for very long.[160] 95 Monobazus sent her bones, and those of his brother, to Jerusalem, ordering that they be buried in the pyramids (three in number) that his mother had constructed at a distance of three furlongs from the city of the Jerusalemites.[161] 96 As for what King Monobazus did during his lifetime—that we shall recount later.[162]

---

154 On such use of χείρ, see the note on "force" at 18.261.

155 For this type of salvation, cf. 2 Kings 19:7//Isaiah 37:7. In his version of that story, at *Ant.* 9.14–18, Josephus too, as his biblical sources, underlines God's providential involvement. Contrast the very similar case at 1 Macc 6:55–57: while a religious author, like Josephus here (and Tilly 2015: 169) finds it important to assert divine string-pulling, the author of 1 Maccabees did not (nor did Josephus, who closely follows 1 Maccabees in his version of that story at *Ant.* 12.379–381). Cf. D. R. Schwartz 2022: 22–36.

156 See the note on "male [children]" at 18.132.

157 This repeated use of twenty-four, which is a very standard round hyperbolic number in aggadic literature (see Bergmann 1938: 367–368), clearly shows the folkloristic nature of Josephus's source for this report. Compare, for example, *b. Berakhot* 55b ("twenty-four dream interpreters in Jerusalem" all gave different interpretations) and *y. Sanhedrin* 10.29c (Israel was exiled after it split into twenty-four different sects).

158 See above, §32.

159 Josephus's statement, in this context, that Izates had been εὐσεβέστατος, is somewhat ambiguous: does it refer to his piety toward God or, rather, to his mother (on filial "piety" see esp. Feldman 1998a: 128–129)? But there is no need to choose between those two options. Contrast, for example, Absalom, who, in a situation similar to that of Izates, rebelled and sinned against both God and his father (7.198), whereupon David, quite appropriately, characterizes Absalom as ἀσεβής, aligning himself with God against him (7.209).

160 Here Ambrosianus has a long dramatic addition: "rather, crushed by old age and the pain of grief, she soon breathed her last." On such additions, see the note on "brought to him" at §5.

161 These monuments, which are mentioned (as "Helena's grave") as a landmark at *War* 5.55, 119, 147 (as also by later visitors to the Jerusalem; see *inter alia* Eusebius, *Church History* 2.12 and Jerome, *Letter* 108.9), must have been very impressive; Pausanias (*Description of Greece* 8.16.5 [GLAJJ 2.196–197]) expands on Helena's grave alongside his account of the Mausoleum at Halicarnassus that was considered one of the seven wonders of the world. Today the remains of these monuments are known as the "Tombs of the Kings," north of the wall of the Old City. Among the finds there were sarcophagi of which one, now in the Louvre, has inscriptions that apparently label the deceased as "queen," so it is thought to be that of Helena, or perhaps one of her relations. See HJP 3.164, n. 66, and esp. Marciak 2014: 139–162. On the question, whether other Jews from the region of Adiabene and Parthia customarily sought to be buried in Jerusalem (as burial in Palestine was common in later periods [Gafni 1997: 79–95]), see Shenkar 2014.

162 This promise remains unfulfilled; see the note on "these kings" at §53.

(5.1) 97 While Fadus was adminstering Judea, a charlatan[163] named Theudas[164] persuaded a great mob of people to take their possessions and follow him to the Jordan River.[165] For he said that he was a prophet, and said that with a command he would split the river, thus provding them easy passage across it.[166] 98 Saying such things, he deceived many people. But Fadus did not allow them to derive any benefit from their senselessness. Rather, he dispatched against them a wing[167] of cavalry; falling upon them unexpectedly, it killed many and took many others alive.[168] Also capturing Theudas himself, they cut off his head and brought it to Jerusalem.[169] 99 These, then, were the events that happened to the Judeans while Cuspius Fadus was procurator.

Theudas

(5.2) 100 As Fadus's successor there came Tiberius Alexander,[170] the son of Alexander who had both been alabarch in Alexandria[171] and had, in pedigree and wealth, exceeded all his

The Governorship of Tiberius Julius Alexander

---

163 On γόης as impostor/charlatan/deceiver, rather than "magician," see esp. Bloch 1999, followed by Barclay 2007: 248, n. 530. The former nuance emerges from Josephus's pairing of the term with ἀπατέων; see the note on "deceptive men" at §167.

164 Theudas is also mentioned at Acts 5:36–37, where he is apparently said to have preceded Judas the Galilean, although in fact Judas preceded Theudas by some four decades (18.4). That egregious error has been explained as the result of Luke's careless reading of the present passage, which mentions Judas at §102, a few lines after this report about Theudas. Given the fact, however, that this would be the most cogent item in the dossier showing that Luke read Josephus, and that other explanations of the error are possible (and that, indeed, the use of μετὰ τοῦτον in Acts 5:37, in introducing Judas after Theudas might mean only "furthermore," not "after him"), the case remains inconclusive. Not much has changed since, a century and a half ago, Schürer (1876: 582) concluded his study of "Lucas und Josephus" with the oft-quoted verdict that Luke either ignored Josephus or, having read Josephus, forgot what he read—although it is possible that he read Josephus, recalled the name "Theudas," and was not concerned about chronological details. See the detailed discussions in Schreckenberg 1980: 195–198 and Mason 2023: 465–469.

165 On this episode, see Hengel 1989: 229–230; Horsley and Hanson 1999: 164–167, and the commentaries to Acts 5:36. As Horsley and Hanson emphasize, it is not surprising that there was anti-Roman agitation in the years immediately following the Roman re-annexation of Judea. Nor is it surprising that Josephus is not explicit about that; see below, the note on "Jerusalem" at §98.

166 This promised miracle must have been understood in light of the fact that its biblical precedent (Josh 3:14–17//*Ant.* 5.16–19) constituted the closing bracket of a divinely-orchestrated story of redemption from foreign rule, and conquest of Palestine, that began with the splitting of the Red Sea (Exodus 14//*Ant.* 3.338–339). See the

note on "Jerusalem" at §98. To get to the Jordan River, Theudas and his followers had to enter the Judean desert; see the note on "providence of God" at §168.

167 See the note on "wing" at 19.365.

168 This collocation, with λαμβάνω, is a favorite in *Ant.* 20; see also §§122, 171, 177, 208 and *Life* 412, also καταλαβὼν ζῶντα at §80. It does not appear in Books 18–19. Indeed, elsewhere, Josephus prefers to let those not killed escape; see the note on "flee" at 18.87.

169 Josephus does not explain why a Roman governor would take an interest in such a self-proclaimed prophet and his followers, much less—why he punished them. Why should Fadus care about Theudas and some dupes who thought he could split the waters of the Jordan? It seems likely that Fadus, whether or not he knew that, according to Joshua 3, Joshua's splitting of the Jordan was a preliminary to the conquest of Canaan, would worry that any mass movement might turn into an anti-Roman rebellion. But Josephus says nary a word about that. For Josephus's attempt to hide, in *Antiquities*, the potentially dangerous links between religion and state, see also the note on "punished" at §168.

170 On Tiberius Julius Alexander and his highly successful career in Roman service in Judea and Egypt, eventually rising to the governorship of Egypt and then serving as Titus's commander-in-chief at the siege of Jerusalem (where he presided over the destruction of the Temple to which his father had so generously and piously donated [*War* 5.205] and to which his uncle Philo had made a pilgrimage [*On Providence* 2.64]), see A. Fuks in *CPJ* 2.188–197; Modrzejewski 1997: 185–190; Schimanowski 2007; Mason 2008: 181–182, n. 1378; Sterling 2020; and the new epigraphic material presented in *CPJ* 5, 185–188. See also the note on "alabarch there" at §147. As for the dating of Alexander's Judean governorship, see the note on "Alexander" at §103.

171 On this well-known figure, Philo's brother, see the note on "Alabarch" at 18.159.

contemporaries there. But Alexander differed from his father with regard to piety,[172] for he did not continue to adhere to the ancestral customs.[173] 101 In his[174] days [as governor of Judea] there occurred the great famine in Judea, at which time Queen Helena bought wheat at great expense from Egypt and distributed it to the destitute, as I have already reported.[175] 102 Additionally, Jacob and Simon, the sons of Judas the Galilean—who had brought the people to rebel against Rome at the time Quirinius assessed Judea, as I reported above[176]—were arrested,[177] and Alexander ordered that they be crucified.[178]

A Potpourri of Updates

103[179] King Herod of Chalcis, having removed Joseph the son of Camei from the high priesthood,[180] gave the succession to the office to Ananias the son of Nedebeus[181] in his

---

172 For Alexander's costly contribution to the Temple of Jerusalem, see *War* 5.205. For some Josephan elaboration on the point that the piety of sons can fall far from that of their fathers, see 6.33–34.

173 On the question of Tiberius's "apostasy," see Schimanowski 2007. Romans seem hardly to have been aware of his Jewish origin: Juvenal (*Satires* 1.127–131) alludes to him, apparently, as an Egyptian "arabarch" and Tacitus, who names him, identifies him once as an Egyptian (*Hist.* 1.11) and once as an "inlustris eques Romanus" (*Ann.* 15.28.1).

174 Reading ἐπὶ τούτου with Niese (1890a: 293; 1890b: 247), who followed the Epitome (Niese 1887–1896: 355). The manuscripts read a dative plural, ἐπὶ τούτοις, which has been taken to refer to the days of Fadus and Tiberius Julius Alexander; so esp. Schürer, *HJP* 1.457, n. 8. That could be preferable insofar as Josephus places the whole Adiabene story, including famine relief in Judea (§§51–53), within his "chapter" on Fadus, just as Acts (11:28) has the famine occur near Agrippa's death (ch. 12). However, either or both of the latter considerations could just as well be a reason for scribes to change the singular, here, into a plural. In fact, Josephus, in telling the whole Adiabene story as one long unit, may have departed some from the chronological context of Fadus's term of office (see the note on "famine" at §51), and the reference to the famine at Acts 11:28 is to a *prophecy* of the famine, which is said to have occurred sometime "in the days of Claudius." Moreover, if we read ἐπὶ τούτοις it could well be that it does not mean "in their days"; it could be not much more than "next." Cf. the note on "thereupon" at 18.104. Two considerations against taking ἐπὶ τούτοις to mean "in their days" are: (1) the use of ἐπί +dative of time is rare (LSJ 622, s.v. §B.II); (2) the only way readers could understand "their" here as referring back to Fadus is if they realize that all the text about Alexander, since his name appeared near the beginning of §100, was parenthetical. But ancient texts did not have parentheses and there seems to be nothing else in the text that could indicate to readers that "their" refers not to Alexander and his father

but, rather, to Alexander and his predecessor. In contrast, the reading ἐπὶ τούτου is unproblematic, for (1) ἐπί +genitive is usual with regard to time (see the note on "during" at §14) and (2) we expect to read, after the introduction of a new ruler, about what happened in his days. Cf. esp. 15.405, where, in a historical survey, the mention of Tiberius is followed by a report of what happened "in his days" (ἐπὶ τούτου), also, for example, although with other formulations, 18.29 and 20.105.

175 See §51, where, quite appropriately, more details are given.

176 At 18.4–9, 23–25.

177 Lit. "brought up," i.e., to the governor, for judgment; cf. the fuller formulations at §§5, 168. Josephus does not say why they were arrested. We must assume, from the governor's response, that they were involved in anti-Roman agitation or rebellion—just as in the next generation as well, a grandson (?) of Judas was a leader of the Sicarii and, eventually, the last commander of Masada (*War* 7.253). For the Sicarii as anti-Roman rebels, see the note on "Sicarii" at §186. On this family, see Stern 1973: 135–140, also the note on "Golanite" at 18.4.

178 On ἀνασταυρόω, see the note on "crucifixion" at 18.64.

179 In the next three sentences (§§1103–104) Josephus reports changes of personnel in the high priesthood, the Roman governorship of Judea, and the kingdom of Chalcis. As at 19.342, for example, these should not be understood as if they all happened at the same time, or as if there were some essential or literary relationship among them. Rather, Josephus is simply taking advantage of the transition between narratives to bring us up to date. For similar updating of various fronts between chapters of Judean history, compare 18.36–54, below §§137–159, and *Ant.* 11.346–347.

180 In accordance with the authority granted him by Claudius (above, §§15–16).

181 This Ananias is also known from the Talmud (*b. Pesaḥ.* 57a//*b. Keritot* 28a–b). On him, see VanderKam 2004: 454–463. VanderKam (as others, including *HJP*

stead. Cumanus came as the successor of Tiberius Alexander.[182] 104 Herod,[183] the brother of the elder king Agrippa,[184] died in the eighth year of the reign of Claudius Caesar,[185] leaving three sons: Aristobulus (who had been born to him by his first wife[186]) and—of Berenice, his brother's daughter[187]—Berenicianus and Hyrcanus. Claudius Caesar gave his reign to the younger Agrippa.[188]

(5.3) 105 While Cumanus[189] was administering the affairs of Judea, civil strife befell the city of the Jerusalemites, causing numerous Jews to perish. First I will recount the reason on account of which this happened. 106 When the holiday called *Pascha* (during which it is our custom that unleavened [breads] are served) was being observed,[190] such a large multitude

Cumanus's Stormy Governorship

2.231) assumes that Ananias remained high priest for around a decade, 48–59 CE. It might be, however, that although he remained influential after his tenure as high priest (§§205, 213; *War* 2.243; and note that two of his sons were captains of the Temple; see the note on "Ananus" at §131), that tenure itself lasted not much more than a year, ending with the end of Cumanus's governorship; see below, Appendix 1. True, a problem is raised by his designation as "high priest" at Acts 23:2 and 24:1, where he apparently chairs the trial of Paul sometime in the 50s. But it is perhaps no more difficult than his designation as "high priest" at *Ant.* 20.205, 208 and *War* 2.243, where it is clear that he was not the serving high priest. On such usage, see the note on "Joazar" at 18.3. For a former high priest identified as "the high priest" and presiding over a judicial process, cf. John 18:13–24.

182 Josephus does not specify the length of Tiberius Julius Alexander's tenure as Roman governor of Judea. Usually it is assumed that he lasted two years, on the one hand because the next sentence refers to Claudius's eighth year (48), on the other hand simply because it is attractively neat to assign Fadus 44–46 and then Tiberius Alexander 46–48. The notion that two years was a standard term of office reappears in standard reconstructions of the sixties, which assign Festus 60–62 and Albinus 62–64; some would also take Acts 24:27 as if it dated something "when Felix's two years" as governor were completed, as if that were the rule. But such a short tenure for Felix entails problems of its own (see Appendix 1, §§9–10) and, in any case would undermine the presumption concerning Festus; see, for example, Lambertz 1953: 224–225. Accordingly, for dating governorships in the second half of the forties and the first half of the sixties we basically have to do the same type of guesswork as for 6–15; see the note on "thereafter" at 18.31.

183 Although readers might infer from the next few words that Josephus is carefully distinguishing this Herod from "King Herod of Chalcis" who was mentioned at §102, in fact they were the same person. It seems that Josephus, in bringing us up to date on various fronts, is using diverse

materials and has not put much effort into editing them. In this case, the first snippet seems to have been drawn from a chronicle of the high priesthood (see the note on "Theophilus" at 18.123), while the second may derive from a family chronicle that focused on Agrippa I (see the note on "Herod the Elder" at 18.130).

184 This, rather than Agrippa "the Great," seems to be the best translation of τοῦ μεγάλου here, esp. given the reference to his son later in this paragraph. Cf. the note on "Agrippa the Elder" at 18.142.

185 I.e., the year that began in January 48. Agrippa II, who was appointed to replace his uncle, apparently began counting his regnal years a year later; see the note on "reign" at §257.

186 Mariamme (18.134).

187 Namely, the daughter of Agrippa I (*Ant.* 19.277, 354); on her, see Ilan 2022. On uncle-niece marriage, see the note on "Herod" at 19.277.

188 According to *Ant.* 19.362, when Agrippa I died, Claudius wanted to give his kingdom to Agrippa II but was dissuaded by his friends, who argued that Agrippa II, who was then around sixteen, was too young for the responsibility. Now, four or five years later, Claudius gave him another kingdom; for a further change a few years later, see §138. In general, on Agrippa II and his territories, see also *War* 2.223, 247 along with *HJP* 1.471–483 and Wilker 2007: 31–32. Kokkinos (1998: 309–310) points out that Herod of Chalcis's own son, Aristobulus (named "the Younger" at §13), was probably too young to succeed his father, which is why his kingdom was given to Agrippa II.

189 Apart from a reference in Tacitus, who fills his name out into Ventidius Cumanus and gives a different version of one of the coming stories (see the note on "Jews" at §118), Cumanus is known only from Josephus. Usually it is thought that he was governor between 48 and 52, but in §8 of Appendix 1 (and in more detail in D. R. Schwartz 1992: 218–242 and 2024a) it is argued that in fact 48–49 is more likely.

190 See the note on "*Pascha*" at 18.29.

[of Jews] had gathered for the holiday from all around[191] that Cumanus, who was afraid that some sort of uprising might develop among them,[192] ordered one unit of soldiers to take up its arms and position itself about the roofed colonnades of the Temple so as to put down the uprising, if such should indeed occur. **107** This had also been done, on the festivals, by those who administered Judea before him.[193]

108 On the fourth day of the festival a certain soldier exposed himself and displayed his private parts to the multitude. When they saw that, there ensued rage and wrath [among the Jews], who said that the act was not an offense against them but, rather, a display of impiety toward God.[194] Moreover, some of the more insolent [among them] defamed Cumanus, saying that the soldier had been put up to it by him. **109** But although Cumanus too was quite upset when he heard the defamations, he nevertheless urged those who were keen on [fomenting] rebellion to desist and not to inflame the state with civil strife during the festival.[195] **110** When, however, he did not succeed in convincing them, and instead they intensified their abuse of him,[196] he ordered the army to equip itself with full battle-dress and come to the Antonia, which (as I have earlier said[197]) is a fortress situated above the Temple. **111** When the multitude saw the soldiers upon their arrival they began to flee out of fear, but since all the exits were narrow and they thought they were being pursued by the soldiers, they were squashed together in their flight; many perished, crushed together[198] by one another.[199] **112** The number of those who perished in that episode of civil strife

---

191 See the note on "twenty thousand" at §112.

192 The intensity of nationalist feeling during pilgrimages, when large masses of Jews came together in what was once the capital of a sovereign Judean kingdom, and hence the likelihood of disorder on such occasions, is frequently mentioned by Josephus; see, for example, *Ant.* 13.372; 15.50–52; 17.213–218, 254; *War* 2.517.

193 This standard procedure is also mentioned at §192. Note, however, that in the parallel to the present passage at *War* 2.224 we read only the general statement that soldiers are usually posted around the colonnades on holidays. The reference here, to Cumanus's forerunners, is the type of detail we would expect to find in a brief defending Cumanus, insofar as it emphasizes that he did not do anything unusually provocative. See the note on "festival" at §109.

194 For a similar formulation, see 18.260.

195 This statement, which has no parallel at all in the version in *War* (2.224–227), underlines that Cumanus was not to be blamed for the subsequent violence. For the suggestion that the present version somehow reflects Cumanus's defense brief, at the hearing described below (§§134–136), see D. R. Schwartz 2012b; for a similar case concerning the other Judean governor of whose accusation we know, see the opening note at 18.55 (on 18.3.1). The notion that Josephus was following such an earlier document here conforms to Mason's observation (2008: 188, n. 1431) that *War* 2.229's version of the present story is awkwardly out of order, which suggests that Josephus, in

War, "is quickly condensing the longer account that will be given more space in *Ant.* 20."

196 The description here, reminiscent of that at 18.60–61 in Pilate's day, reinforces Cumanus's defense discussed in the preceding note by emphasizing the misbehavior of the Jewish mob.

197 Including at 15.292, 409, and 18.91. For the formulation here (ἐπικείμενον τῷ ἱερῷ), cf. esp. *War* 5.245 (φρούριον γὰρ ἐπέκειτο τῇ πόλει μὲν τὸ ἱερόν, τῷ ἱερῷ δ᾽ ἡ Ἀντωνία ["the Temple dominated the city, but Antonia dominated the Temple"]). For Josephus's appetite for such formulations, cf. *War* 1.112 (Salome "ruled the others, but the Pharisees ruled her"); *Ant.* 15.361 ("with regard to their goodwill toward him [Herod]: after [Marcus Vipsanius] Agrippa, Augustus honored no one more than Herod, just as after Augustus, Agrippa assigned Herod first place in his friendship"//*War* 1.400); and *War* 5.257 ("But I say, that although the stasis subdued the city, the Romans subdued the stasis.") As with the comparison at §§253–254, it could well be that Josephus, when composing *Antiquities*, remembered his catchier formulations in his earlier composition.

198 For a rabbinic expression of surprise that it happened only once that someone was crushed in the Temple on Passover, despite the crowds of pilgrims, see *b. Pesaḥim* 64b.

199 Note well: the Jews were not killed by the Romans, nor did the Romans even enter the Temple Mount. The Romans, according to the present story, kept their

was counted—twenty thousand.[200] And so there was henceforth mourning instead of festivity,[201] everyone abandoning the prayers and sacrifices and turning instead to lamentations and wailing[202]—so great were the sufferings engendered by the wanton behavior of a single soldier.[203]

(5.4) 113 Their first mourning had not even ended when another befell them.[204] For some of those who had gone over to fomenting rebellion held up[205] one Stephanus, an imperial slave,[206] as he was making his way on the public road about a hundred furlongs from the city, robbing him of all his property. **114** When Cumanus heard what had been done, he immediately sent soldiers, ordering them to pillage the nearby villages and to shackle and bring to him their most prominent inhabitants.[207] **115** After the pillage, one of the soldiers took [a scroll of] the laws of Moses that had been kept in one of the villages and, displaying it before all, he ripped it up[208] while uttering blasphemies[209] and expressing a plethora of ridicule.[210]

---

distance: they only showed themselves in battle gear in Antonia, the Roman bastion north of the Temple Mount, in order to intimidate the Jews. Compare *War* 2.226, which, at this point of the story, has Cumanus's soldiers pouring into the colonnades.

200 Thirty thousand according to the parallel at *War* 2.227. Such numbers are not to be pressed; what's a myriad here or there? Nevertheless, numerous sources put myriads of Jews in Jerusalem on the pilgrimage festivals (even if we discount the millions mentioned by Josephus [*War* 6.420–427] and the rabbinic parallel [*t. Pesaḥim* 4:15, ed. Lieberman, 166 = 4:3, ed. Zuckermandel, 163], on which see Y. Fisch in Ilan and Noam 2017: 2.812–821); see, for example, *Ant.* 14.337 and 17.214, 18.313, 20.187, *War* 2.515, Philo, *Special Laws* 1.69, Acts 2:1–11, and *m. Pesaḥim* 5:5, 7, also Jeremias 1969: 77–84 and Safrai 1976: 901–902.

201 This phrase, πένθος δ᾽ ἦν τὸ λοιπὸν ἀντὶ τῆς ἑορτῆς, sounds formulaic, perhaps inspired by Amos 8:10, which is echoed at 1 Macc 1:39 (and 9:41) and, very similarly, in the parallel to the present passage at *War* 2.227: γενέσθαι δὲ τὴν ἑορτὴν πένθος.

202 This is the only occurrence of κλαυθμός in Josephus.

203 Cf. the similar comment at *Ant.* 18.84. That comment excuses the Jews at large, the present one tends to clear Cumanus; see the note on "during the festival" at §109. For a more famous case of this tactic, cf. *War* 6.252 (the Temple was destroyed because a single soldier, ignoring his orders, vitiated Titus's decision, together with his most senior officers, to preserve it.)

204 As Norden (1913a: 642, n. 1) observed, Josephus's account of Cumanus, as that of Pilate, is presented as an unrelenting series of calamities. Introductions such as the present passage, just as 18.65 and 18.85, carry much of the burden. For another case, see the note on "unholiness" at §167.

205 The verb λῃστεύω, which also appears at §186, identifies the perpetrators as "brigands"—on whom see the note on "brigands" at 18.7.

206 On imperial slaves and freedmen in this period, see the collection of sources in Smallwood 1967: 56–59.

207 Here there is another "useless" but dramatic addition in Ambrosianus, telling us what we anyway can infer from the fact they were arrested: "so they could account for the things that had been done so insolently." Cf. the note on "brought to him" at §5.

208 Compare evidence for Roman soldiers tearing up Jewish scrolls at Masada: Cotton (1989): 160–161, with n. 23. On the severity of the offense in Jewish eyes, and the significance of the Torah scroll as a symbol of the Jews' identity, see S. Schwartz 2014: 1–3.

209 Although βλασφημία usually means "insult" or "slander" (e.g. at §109), here, where no human object is mentioned, it seems that whatever the soldier said in the context of destroying a scroll of the Torah would be construed as what we term "blasphemy." See the discussion of Greek and English usage in Danker 2000: 178, s.v. βλασφημία, §bγ.

210 The verb κατακερτομέω appears only twice elsewhere in Josephus, both of them, as here, together with πολλά (*Life* 323; *War* 6.172).

116 Jews having heard of this, many of them hastened together and went down[211] to Caesarea, where Cumanus happened to be, beseeching him to exact justice[212] not for them but, rather, for God, whose laws had been outraged.[213] [They said] they would be unable to go on living if their ancestral laws were so completely outraged.[214] 117 Cumanus, afraid that the masses might again foment rebellion,[215] and having consulted with his friends,[216] beheaded the soldier[217] who had outraged the laws, thus forestalling the civil strife that had been on the verge of breaking out a second time.

(6.1) 118 There was also [an outbreak of] hostility between the Samaritans and the Jews,[218] for the following reason. It was customary for the Galileans going to the holy

211 For "going down" to the coast see also, for example, *Ant.* 17.219//*War* 2.14 and Acts 12:19. Cf. §50.

212 This literal translation of ἐκδικέω (just as for the noun at §119, according to Ambosianus), seems to fit the context better than the usual "avenge," for the appropriate stance of provincials is to ask the governor to do what justice demands, not to dictate what that is. Cf. §§3, 126 and, for example, *Flacc.* 105–106 and Acts 25:16 along with Dupont 1961.

213 The same distinction as above, §108.

214 The Jews' devotion to their laws, even unto death, is a favorite Josephan theme; see the note on "accept death" at 18.59.

215 Same phrase as at §133. What "again" here, and "second time" at the end of this paragraph, refer to is not clear. Since the end of the paragraph refers to the fear that στάσις ("civil strife") would break out a second time, apparently we should infer that the first στάσις was the preceding episode, which is indeed termed στάσις at §112. But if so, usage of πάλιν νεωτερίσειεν here is hardly justified, for all we have there is a protest that ends with Jews in panic and flight; that is not something Josephus should refer to as "fomenting rebellion" or "rebelling," and only with difficulty can we call it "civil strife"; note that Feldman (1965: 449–451) renders στάσις by "revolution" and "uprising" at §117, but only by "disturbance" at §112. Probably we should infer that the allusion here is, nonetheless, to the angry Jewish complaints mentioned in §§108–109. Cumanus had every reason to make them seem as threatening, perhaps even violent, as possible, so as to counter any Jewish complaints that he used excessive force against the Jews. This suggests, in turn, that Josephus's formulation here reflects his use of a document written in Cumanus's defense. For Josephus's use of such materials regarding Pilate and Cumanus, see the next note.

216 For a Roman governor's *amici*, see the note on "friends" at 18.89. By noting their agreement here, Josephus's account defends Cumanus against potential complaints that he gave in to his subjects' demands after

they had been rebellious. For the *Sitz im Leben* of such a defense, cf. above, the note on "festival" at §109.

217 *War* 2.231 adds that this was done after he was led off "in the midst of his accusers"; on such demonstrative punishments, cf. the note on "dragged around" at §136.

218 On hostility between Samaritans and Jews, see the note on "Samaritan men" at 18.30. The present episode has been the object of intense study; see, among others, Momigliano 1934: 388–391; Aberbach 1949/50; Stern, *GLAJJ* 2.76–82 and 1974a: 374–376. This interest has been sparked especially by differences between it and Tacitus's report in *Ann.* 12.54 (*GLAJJ*, no. 288), in the context of 52 CE: although evidently referring to the same episode, it refers to Ventidius Cumanus as governor of the Galilee and to Felix (whom Josephus does not mention as being in Palestine until after Cumanus's term of office) as governor of Samaria, but mentions no governor of Judea. This, together with Tacitus's statement there, that Felix had already ruled Judea ("iam pridem Iudaeae impositus"), and his statement at *Ann.* 12.23.1 (*GLAJJ*, no. 287), in the context of 49 CE that, upon the death of Agrippa, Judea was annexed to the province of Syria, led E. Schwartz (1907: 286–287) to suggest that, although Josephus did not know it, Claudius embarked on an administrative experiment (*Verwaltungsexperiment*) upon the death of Agrippa I, subsuming the Judean heartland under the authority of the governor of Syria (hence no governor of Judea is mentioned in 12.54) and leaving other regions of Palestine under various officials (much as the situation we posited from 37–41; see the note on "commander" at 18.237). However, accepting Tacitus's testimony wholesale entails setting aside all of Josephus's detailed data about the governorships of Fadus, Tiberius Julius Alexander, and Cumanus, and Tacitus's blooper at 12.23.1, that Agrippa I died in 49 CE, inspires no confidence. With regard to Judea, at best we might conclude, with Stern (*GLAJJ* 2.75), that Tacitus is consistent in his error. However, it may well be that Felix was in Palestine in some secondary role already in the days of Cumanus; that could explain, for example, the fact that a prominent Judean high

city[219] on the festivals to make their way via the region of the Samaritans.[220] But once, while making their way, they were attacked by some people of a village called Ginae, which lies on the border between Samaria and the Great Plain,[221] who killed many of them.[222] **119** When they learned what had been done, the Galileans' leaders went to Cumanus and called upon him to investigate the murder of those who had been killed. But Cumanus, whom the Samaritans had convinced with money,[223] pooh-poohed[224] [the complaint].[225] **120** Upset by that, Galileans urged the multitude of Jews to turn to arms and stand their ground for liberty. For, they said, slavery is hard in and of itself, but is totally intolerable when it is compounded[226] by outrage.[227] **121** Although the leaders tried to calm them down and promised that they would convince Cumanus to punish the murderers,[228] the others did not pay them any attention.[229] [Rather], taking up arms and calling upon Eleazar the son of Deinaios,[230]

---

priest supported Felix's candidacy for the governorship (see §162). If, then, Felix had been in Palestine in some secondary position under Cumanus, then, since we know that the violence that ensued was between Galileans and Samaritans and we can see from §§134–137 that, when the dispute came to be adjudicated in Rome, Felix was the winner and Cumanus the loser, it is not too difficult to understand how Roman observers might gain the impression that each of the two had been charged with ruling one of those two regions. Apart from that, note Eck's position, cited in the note on "Syria" at 18.2, that Judea was always part of Provincia Syria until the rebellion of 66.

219 For this appellation (here: τὴν ἱερὰν πόλιν) for Jerusalem, elsewhere in Josephus, see *War* 2.397; *Ant.* 4.227; and *Apion* 1.282. It is found already in the Hebrew Bible (Isaiah 48:2 and 52:1; Nehemiah 11:1; Daniel 9:24); in literature of the Second Temple period it is found in such texts as Sirach 36:12, Tobit 13:9, 1 Macc 2:7, 2 Maccabees 1:2; 3:1; 9:14; 15:14, and Philo's *Flacc* 46 and *Leg* 281. The city's holiness derived from the Temple, a point reflected in the Qumran preference for *'ir hamiqdaš* ("city of the Temple"); so *Damascus Document* 12:1; *11QTemple* 45:11–12, 16–17; and 4Q248 (Broshi and Eshel 1997: 121). Cf. the note on "of Jerusalem" at 18.271.

220 As Mason (2008: 189–190, n. 1449), Josephus reports at *Life* 269 that, using this route, one could come from the Galilee to Jerusalem in three days; the same is indicated by *m. Bava Metzia* 2:6. But he also indicates, there, that it could be risky—as is suggested by Luke 9:52–53. As a result, or for other reasons, some pilgrims to Jerusalem from the north instead took the longer but safer Jordan Valley route, as Jesus is said to have done (Mark 10:46; 11:1). But the route via Samaria seems to have been the main one; see Safrai 1965: 116–117 (= Safrai 1981: 136–138).

221 Although Josephus's nomenclature concerning "the plain" and "the great plain" is not always unambiguous (see the note on "Great Plain" at 18.122), in this case the reference is clearly to the Esdraelon, which is between Samaria and Galilee, for *War* 3.48 specifically says that this village is on the northern border of Samaria; cf. *War* 2.232 (the village is "in the great plain of Samaria"). It is assumed to be at the site of modern Jenin, some 35 km. due east of Caesarea.

222 As the next paragraph makes clear, Josephus means that the Samaritans of Ginae killed many Galileans. At *War* 2.232, while some witnesses have only one Galilean being killed, three manuscripts say "many" were; Niese and Destinon (1894: 199), Thackeray (1926: 414, n. 1), and Mason (2008: 190, n. 1451, with detailed discussion) follow the former, assuming the latter are accommodating that text to ours.

223 A frequent complaint, as at §183 and 18.97.

224 Cf. 5.144 and 12.395, where, similarly, ὀλιγωρέω is used for belittling/ignoring—respectively, justice and oaths.

225 Niese (1890a: 296; 1890b: 249) leaves the verb ὀλιγωρέω with no explicit object, which is quite possible, as at 10.85. I have completed the thought *ad sensum*; other supplements are offered by Ambrosianus and the Epitome (Niese 1887–1896: 357).

226 See the note on "addition" at §10.

227 For the contrast between "liberty" and "slavery" and the rebels' use of it, see the notes on "enslavement" and "liberty" at 18.4.

228 For Josephus's frequent use of δίκας εἰσπράσσω παρά for "punishing someone," see §76 and *ThLJ* 224.

229 This is a frequent motif in Josephus, with an apologetic point: the elders, who represent legitimate and intelligent Jewish leadership, oppose rebellion and express faith in Roman justice, but hotheaded youths fail to listen to them. See the note on "youths" at 18.10.

230 On his end, see below, §161. He seems to be mentioned as a murderer in *m. Sotah* 9.9, also, in *Midrash Song of Song Rabba* 2.7, alongside Bar Kochva and others, as one who "pushed the End" (attempted to force a messianic redemption) and failed; see Ilan in Ilan and Noam 2017: 1.521–526.

a brigand who had spent many years in the mountains,[231] to aid them, they pillaged some of the Samaritans' villages after torching them.[232]

122 When word of what had happened came to Cumanus, he took the cavalry wing of Sebastenians[233] and four units[234] of infantry and, arming the Samaritans as well,[235] set out against the Jews; engaging them [in battle], he killed many of them and took many more alive.[236] **123** When the most prominent Jerusalemites, by position and birth, saw to what great calamities things had come, they bound themselves around with sackcloth, having covered their heads with ashes,[237] and, in every possible way, called upon the rebels and entreated them—portraying before their eyes how the fatherland would be destroyed, the Temple destroyed by fire, and they themselves, their wives, and their children would be sold into slavery—to change their disposition, throw down their arms, and henceforth return to their homes and keep the peace.[238] **124** Having said these things they were indeed persuasive: some dispersed, and[239] the brigands went off again to their strongholds—and from that point on, all of Judea was filled with bands of brigands.[240]

Ummidius Quadratus Intervenes

(6.2) 125 But the heads of the Samaritans went to Ummidius Quadratus,[241] who was then governing Syria and happened to be in Tyre, and they accused the Jews of torching their

---

231 For ἐν ὄρει in this general sense, see also 13.19, 159. Although those cases include a definite article (τῷ), it does not refer to any antecedent. Without the article, as here: Marcus Aurelius, *Meditations* 10.15.1.

232 Burning and looting villages is standard in this book; see also §§121, 125, 172, 185, and 187.

233 See the note on "Sebastenians" at 19.356.

234 Τάγμα usually means "legion" (*GTRI* 90, 163), but that is out of the question here. Probably "cohort" is meant, as at 19.119 (see the note there on "cohort") and *War* 4.645, where Josephus's τάγματα, referring to troops in Rome, corresponds to what Tacitus, in the same context, terms "cohortes" (*Hist.* 3.64). Since 19.366 indicates that all the Caesarean and Sebastenians auxiliaries totaled one or two (see the note on "Sebastenians" at §365) cavalry "wings" and five cohorts, the force described here constituted most of the troops at Cumanus's disposal; perhaps most of the others were still in Jerusalem (§106). Note, however, that the parallel at *War* 2.236 mentions no infantry at all, only the cavalry wing.

235 For another case of a Roman governor fielding a local militia under Claudius, see Tacitus, *Ann.* 12.49, cited (along with Tacitus, *Hist.* 2.12 and other passages), by Marquardt 1876: 520–521.

236 For this standard outcome of such clashes, see the note on "alive" at §98. According to *War* 2.236, however, the opposite was true. Here too, the present version shows Cumanus's restraint; see the note on "festival" at §109.

237 For the combination of sackcloth and ashes, cf. Isaiah 58:5; Esther 4:1, 3; Judith 4:10–15; 1 Macc 3:47;

2 Macc 10:25, Matthew 11:21//Luke 10:13, etc. Sometimes it is not clear whether σποδός refers to ashes (Heb. *'efer*) or dust (Heb. *'afar*); see Muraoka 2009: 631, s.v. Cf. the note on "law" at 19.349.

238 For similar appeals, meant to show readers that the Jewish leadership is responsible and recognizes Roman power, see the end of Agrippa II's long speech (*War* 2.400), the appeal by other dignitaries at *War* 2.416, and those by Josephus himself at *War* 5.361–419, 6.96–112, and *Life* 18.

239 In light of the problem addressed in the next note, it is tempting to translate "but." But the parallelism of the two clauses (coordinated with μέν ... δέ), both elaborating on the general statement that the peace-seeking speakers were persuasive, seems to exclude that.

240 How could the land become full of brigands if, after the prominent Jerusalemites had spoken so persuasively, they had all returned to their strongholds? It seems that Josephus is torn between two tendencies: the need, in the present story, to emphasize that the Jews, as represented by their legitimate leaders, were not responsible for further violence, and the more general need, in this book, to show a deterioration of the situation until it finally exploded into a rebellion; see the note on "downhill" at §160. Here, therefore, although admitting that the brigands returned to where they previously were, he portrays that restoration of the status quo ante as if it were a new filling of the country with brigands. For a similar case, cf. §215.

241 On Quadratus, governor of Syria from sometime in the middle of the first century until 60, see *HJP* 1.264.

villages and pillaging them.²⁴² **126** They said that they were upset not so much about what they had suffered, as about the way [the Jews] had shown contempt for the Romans—for [they said], even if [the Jews] had suffered injustice they should have taken the case to Roman justice, rather than running around roughshod as if they did not have Roman rulers. They said, accordingly, that they had come to him seeking justice.²⁴³ **127** Such, then, was the Samaritans' complaint. But the Jews said the Samaritans had been responsible for the civil strife and the battle, but above all that Cumanus [was to blame], for he had been corrupted by them with gifts and had, therefore, ignored the murder of those who had been killed.²⁴⁴ **128** Quadratus, after listening to them, postponed judgment, saying that he would declare [his verdict] after learning the truth more closely²⁴⁵ upon coming to Judea. **129** So they²⁴⁶ departed without accomplishing anything, but not long thereafter Quadratus came to Samaria; there, after holding a hearing,²⁴⁷ he came to believe that the Samaritans had been responsible for the outbreak. He also crucified those Samaritans and Jews who, he learned, had been involved in rebellion and had been taken prisoner by Cumanus.

130 Proceeding from there to a certain village, Lydda, which was not much smaller than a city,²⁴⁸ he sat upon a tribunal platform and, hearing the Samaritans through for a second time, learned from one of the Samaritans that one of the Jews' leaders, named Doetos,²⁴⁹

---

and Dąbrowa 1998: 49–53. It is often assumed that he began his term of service only in 50 or even 51. Schürer lists Quadratus's predecessor, Longinus, as having been in office until "c. 50" and infers from Tacitus's reference (*Ann.* 12.45) to Quadratus's functioning as governor of Syria in 51, only that "he may well have gone there in 50," and Dąbrowa (1998: 47) goes even further and suggests Longinus remained in office until 51. However, since the sparse numismatic evidence includes Longinus's latest coin as governor of Syria from 47/48 (Dąbrowa 1998: 46), the basis for a later terminus post quem is only the fact that Tacitus, in the course of a story he offers at *Ann.* 12.11–12 in his account of 49 (ibid. 12.5–24), refers to Longinus as the governor of Syria and his involvement in Parthian affairs; Schürer leaves that as is, while Dąbrowa suggests that Claudius probably asked Longinus to remain involved even after 49. However, Tacitus's account of this episode, in the course of his account of 49, opens at 12.10 with the appeal of a Parthian delegation that actually arrived already in 47 (*Ann.* 11.10), and it goes on until the report at 12.14 of the death of Gotarzes, which came in 51 or 52. That is, Tacitus has located, in his account of 49, a long story about Parthian affairs, and Longinus's role in it comes early on in the story, before the details and campaigns reported in 12.10–14; for details, see Schwartz 1992: 239–240. Accordingly, if Josephus's account, here and at *War* 2.223–244, indicates that Cumanus's term of office lasted no more than a year, 48/49 (see Appendix 1, §8), Quadratus's involvement would not contradict that.

242 Here Josephus repeats the formulation at §121, but astute readers will realize that that is only the end of the account that in fact began earlier, at §118, with Samaritan criminality: the wicked Samaritans fail to report both that they had begun the violence and that they had bribed Cumanus to punish the Jews. As at §3, readers are supposed to realize just how villainous the Samaritans are: after doing all those terrible things they dare to present themselves to the Romans, via a very selective and skewed version of the story, as the injured party—and also present themselves cynically, in the next few lines, as those who nonetheless are not so much upset about their own suffering as about the violation of Roman law and order; for a similar move by an earlier villain, cf. 2 Macc 14:8. For Josephus's portrayal of another manipulative Samaritan statement to the Romans, see the note on "Tirathana" at 18.88. For Josephus's fundamental antipathy toward Samaritans, see the note on "Samaritan men" at 18.30.

243 See the note on "exact justice" at §116.

244 This refers to the appeal reported at §119.

245 On the sense of ἀκριβέστερον, see the note on "detail" at 18.129.

246 The Samaritans and the Jews.

247 This verb, διακούω, appears four times in this story (§§129, 130, 135, 136), also at §195 and at *Life* 229, but only twice elsewhere in *Antiquities*, both in Book 14. It may be added to Thackeray's list of words common to *Ant.* 20 and *Life* (*ThLJ* ix).

248 On ancient Lydda (modern Lod, northwest of Jerusalem on the way to Tel-Aviv), see J. J. Schwartz 1991 and Oppenheimer 2005: 47–65.

249 This name occasioned an intricate chain of conjectures in Schalit 1968: 39–40, 129. Cf. Ilan 2002: 272, s.v. Διόδοτος.

along with some fellow rebels (four in number), had incited the populace to rebel against the Romans.[250]

131 Quadratus ordered that they be executed, and that the retinue of[251] Ananias the high priest, and the captain[252] Ananus,[253] should be sent up[254] in fetters to render account[255] to Claudius Caesar concerning what had occurred. **132** He also ordered the leaders of the Samaritans and Jews, as well as Cumanus (the procurator) and Celer, who was a military tribune,[256] to go off to Italy, to the emperor, to be judged by him[257] concerning their claims against one another.[258] **133** He himself, afraid lest the Jewish masses might again foment rebellion,[259] came to the city of the Jerusalemites—but found it peaceful and observing an ancestral festival of God.[260] Convinced that no rebelliousness might develop among them, he left them in their festivities and turned back toward Antioch.

Claudius Adjudicates

(6.3) 134 Cumanus's men and the Samaritans' leaders, who had been sent up to Rome, were assigned a day[261] by the emperor, at which time they were to speak about their disputes

---

250 Since the foregoing account of the strife between Judeans and Samaritans does not include this detail, perhaps readers are supposed to think it is a Samaritan calumny meant to enlist Roman support. That would be a welcome result for Josephus, similar to the one he seeks at §126; see the note on "pillaging them" at §125. But Josephus says simply, earlier in this sentence, not merely that a Samaritan said or accused or alleged that Doetos had incited rebellion, but that Quadratus, in a thorough hearing, *learned* that from the Samaritan, which sounds like Josephus confirms it was true and means that Quadratus was convinced by it. Correspondingly, §131 reports that Quadratus acted decisively on the basis of the information—but nothing here indicates that Josephus condemns Quadratus. Moreover, as the prominent Jerusalemites realized (§130), it was not possible, in Roman Judea, to fight with the Samaritans without fighting the Romans.

251 Literally, τοὺς περὶ Ἀνανίαν refers to those around Ananias, so might exclude the high priest himself. However, that is a very pedantic reading, and often it may be shown that the whole group is meant; see the notes on "Anileus's men" at 18.354 and on "around Chaerea" at 19.70. Moreover, in this case the parallel at *War* 2.243 explicitly includes Ananias among those sent to Rome. Those who insist, here, on leaving him in Judea do so in order to allow Ananias to continue serving as high priest until the appointment of Ishmael b. Phiabi which, they think, occurred much later, at the end of Felix's term of office (where notice of it is given: §§179–181). That, however, seems to reflect a misunderstanding of the way Josephus organizes his material; see the Introduction, at n. 16.

252 This temple official, mentioned also in *War* 2.409 and 6.294, Acts 4:1; 5:24, 26, is probably the same as the

s^egan hakohanim mentioned in rabbinic literature, e.g., *m. Sotah* 7:7 and *m. Yoma* 3:9. See *HJP* 2.277–279; Safrai 1976: 875–876.

253 The parallel at *War* 2.243 says Ananus was the son of Ananias the high priest. Such nepotism was common; note especially *War* 2.409, which reports that Ananus's brother was in the same position in 66 CE, and the bitter ditty preserved in *b. Pesahim* 57a//*t. Menahot* 13:21 (ed. Zuckermandel, 533).

254 On the use of "sending up," (ἀναπέμπω, as also at §§134, 161), namely to Rome (where else is there to be sent?!), as expressing a Roman point of view, see the note on "sent up" at 18.51.

255 For this phrasing (λόγον ὑφέξοντας) see also 14.180; 17.144; *Life* 13, 408.

256 On this use of χιλίαρχος, see *GTRI* 163. We are not told of what he was accused, which, judging from his fate (§136), must have been serious.

257 For the use of ἐπί with reference to a person in the genitive as referring to the one who shall judge (as also, for example, at *Life* 258, and Acts 25:9), see Schalit 1967/68.

258 According to Mommsen (1899: 241), referring to this passage and also to *Life* 3, it was relatively rare for local governors to send such cases to the emperor, if they did not involve Roman citizens (such as Paul: Acts 22:27–28; 25:11–12). In general, on Rome's handling of complaints against provincial governors, see Brunt 1961; on appeals to Caesar, see Jones 1968: 51–65.

259 The same phrase as §117.

260 Same type of idyllic scene: 18.90, 122.

261 Lit., "they received a day from the emperor" (λαμβάνουσι παρὰ τοῦ αὐτοκράτορος ἡμέραν). Cf. Claudius's statement to Alexandrian delegates: μερίσω σοι ταύτην τὴν ἡμέραν (*CPJ* 156a, col. 2, lines 12–13).

against one another.[262] **135** The greatest support was given to Cumanus and the Samaritans by Caesar's freedmen and friends,[263] and it would have been all over for the Jews had not, indeed, the younger Agrippa, who happened to have been in Rome,[264] and who saw how the Jewish leaders were being outrun, intensely implored Agrippina, the emperor's wife,[265] to convince her husband to hear out [the case] in a way appropriate to his own justice and punish those responsible for the rebellion.[266] **136** When Claudius, who had been made well-disposed by this appeal and heard the case through, found that the Samaritans had been the authors of the troubles, he ordered the execution of those of them who had come to him; he also imposed exile upon Cumanus, and ordered that Celer (the military tribune) be taken to Jerusalem and then executed, before the eyes of all, by being dragged around[267] the entire city.[268] **(7.1)**[269] **137** And he sent Claudius[270] Felix, Pallas's brother,[271] to be in charge of the affairs of Judea.[272]

---

262 This phrasing seems to preserve the memory of a dispute between Cumanus and the Samaritans, as at §125.

263 On the real or perceived influence of freedmen on Roman emperors, which peaked in the days of Claudius and Nero, and accordingly "the reactions to their wealth and power were virulent, and the historical tradition surrounding these individuals is exceptionally hostile," see Mouritsen 2011: 95–96. For such hostility, see also below, §183. On the freedmen's wealth, which often fanned jealous hostility, see also ibid. 109–118. On the traditional claim that Claudius was enslaved by his freedmen (and his wives), see the note on "great influence with him" at 19.362. On the way this functions well for a diasporic historian, here as at §182, see the note on "monarchy" at 18.377.

264 Agrippa II, born ca. 27 (19.354). He was raised in Rome (19.360; 20.12), as was common for princes of vassal kingdoms; see the note on "Claudius Caesar" at 19.360.

265 On Agrippina, who was Gaius Caligula's sister and Nero's mother, see Barrett 1996.

266 Josephus likes to report intervention by emperor's wives on the Jews' behalf; so too §195 and *Life* 16. Agrippina the Younger was the granddaughter of Antonia Minor, who had been a patron of Agrippa I (see above, 18.143, 164, 202–203); for the assumption that Agrippina supported Agrippa II's case in this instance because of her family's long association with his, see Barrett 1996: 126.

267 Lit. "before" (ἐπί); apparently what is meant is "before [the walls that encircle the] entire city."

268 For parallels for such public and demonstrative punishment, cf. *War* 2.231 and 6.359; Curtius Rufus 4.6 29; 2 Macc 4:38; Suetonius, *Cal.* 35.2. More generally, on "punishment parades" and punishment as a spectacle in late antiquity, see Lavan 2020: 1.184–191 and Carucci 2019. Mason (2008: 199, n. 1545) notes that such a terrible punishment for Celer may have been a move on Claudius's

part to assuage the Jews's anger, similar to what was done to the soldier who had ripped up the Torah scroll; see above, §117.

269 I have attached this paragraph to the preceding (as already Buchon 1836: 532), despite the traditional paragraphing, because the appointment of a new governor finishes up the disposition of Judea that Claudius began by exiling the incumbent governor; for a very similar passage, see 18.237. Moreover, it seems (as explained in the note on "Judea" at the end of the present sentence) that several years went by between the appointment of Felix and Claudius's twelfth year, which is mentioned in the next paragraph (§138). On the way indenting and translation here have been affected by that chronological issue, see the Introduction, beginning at n. 91. For another deviation from the traditional paragraphing, see below at §151.

270 Following the reading of the manuscripts here; see the Introduction, at n. 92.

271 On Pallas, a famous influential freedman, see the note on "slaves" at 18.182.

272 Josephus does not say how long Cumanus remained in office. Usually his tenure is thought to have extended from 48 CE (Claudius's eighth year, mentioned alongside the appointment of Cumanus at §§103–104) to 52 CE (Claudius's twelfth year, mentioned in the next paragraph [§138]); so, for example, *HJP* 1.458–459 and Smallwood 1981: 263–268; Mason 2008: 184, n. 1396. However, there is reason to think Cumanus was replaced after only a year, already in 48/49. This is suggested both by the very stormy account of his tenure in *War* 2.223–246, of which the natural reading is that it lasted only a year, and by other considerations, including the need to have a high priest named Ishmael (b. Phiabi), who was appointed in the days of Felix (20.179), serving, as is reported at *Ant.* 3.320, during the famine of the late forties (see the note on "famine" at §51). See Appendix 1, §8.

*Updates and
Gossip about
Herodians*

138 Upon the completion of the twelfth year of his reign,[273] he bestowed upon Agrippa Philip's tetrarchy[274] and also Batanea, adding to it Trachonitis together with Abila (which had been Lysanias's tetrarchy[275]). But he took Chalcis away from him, after he had ruled it for four years. **139** Upon receiving this gift from Caesar,[276] Agrippa married off his sister[277] Drusilla to Azizus, King of Emesa,[278] who was willing to be circumcised; for Epiphanes, the son of King Antiochus [of Commagene] had declined the marriage because he did not want to undertake Jewish practices, although earlier he had promised her father that he would do so.[279] **140** And he gave Mariamme to Archelaus, the son of Helcias,[280] to whom Agrippa the[ir] father had previously betrothed her; they had a daughter named Berenice.[281]

(7.2) 141 It befell Drusilla's marriage to Azizus to be dissolved not long thereafter[282] under the following circumstances.[283] **142** When Felix was administering Judea, he saw her and, since she was more beautiful than all others, he was taken by a desire for the woman. He sent to her one of his Jewish friends, named Atomus, who was a Cypriot by birth,[284] who pretended to be a magician,[285] and who attempted to persuade her to leave her husband and marry him, promising to make her happy[286] if she did not spurn him. **143** Since she was suffering and desirous of fleeing her sister Berenice's jealousy of her on account of her

---

273 I.e., late in 52 or early in 53. On Agrippa II's territories, see the note on "younger Agrippa" at §104.

274 According to 17.319 and 18.106, Philip's domain had indeed included Trachonitis, Gaulanitis, and Batanea. The fact that Trachonitis and Batanea are nevertheless listed separately here might suggest that some changes had been made over the years.

275 On which see 18.237 and 19.275, also *HJP* 1.567–569.

276 Although this sounds as if there is some causal relationship between the gift and the matchmaking, none is evident, and it seems, rather, that Josephus is just trying, artificially, to create some flow between disparate data that he has assembled here. For a similar case, see 19.342.

277 Josephus takes it for granted that after the death of the father his son inherits the responsibility for marrying off remaining daughters. So too Philo, *Spec. leg.* 3.67; cf. *Ant.* 4.246 and Schremer 2003: 127, n. 4.

278 Homs in northern Syria. Azizus, whose death is recorded at §158, was the son and successor of Sampsigeramus II, king of Emesa, who was Agrippa I's colleague (19.338) and his brother's father-in-law (18.135); see Sullivan 1977b: 215–216.

279 As is reported in 19.355. For the Herodians' insistence that men who marry their daughters be circumcised (as opposed to the Herodians' willingness to marry gentile women without any conversion process), see also, on the one hand, §145 and 16.225, and, on the other, 16.11; 18.109, 135, 139 along with Cohen 1999: 272 ("The biblical principle still applies: a gentile woman 'converts' by being

married to a Jewish husband"); Hadas-Lebel 1993; and Wilker 2007: 49–53.

280 On Helcias, see the note on "Helcias" at 19.355, where this engagement is reported.

281 On Mariamme's marriages and children, see also §147 and Kokkinos 1998: 198–199.

282 Indeed: the marriage was not contracted earlier than late 52 (above §§138–139), and Azizus managed not only to lose Drusilla but also to die by sometime in Nero's first year (§158), i.e., 54/55.

283 On this introductory phrase as indicating the introduction of material from a new source—in this case, one hostile to Agrippa II, as the following two stories show—see the note on "circumstances" at 18.39, also D. R. Schwartz 1981/82 and the note on "between the two" at §213.

284 On the Jews of ancient Cyprus, see van der Horst 2003b.

285 For silly women who fall for the promises of wily dissimulators, see also *Ant.* 17.41 and 18.65–84. Jewish magicians from Cyprus are also mentioned at Acts 13:6 and, apparently, by Pliny, *NH* 30.11; see van der Horst 2003b: 118–119. As Bloch notes (1998: 151), in the present passage Josephus shows no embarrassment concerning the notion that a Jew might be a magician or pretend to be one, just as in general he does not seem to have been worried by accusations concerning Jewish magic. Cf. the note on "charlatans" at §160 and, in general, Bohak 2008.

286 As Feldman notes (1965: 465, n. g), Thackeray suspected a pun here (*felix* = happy).

beauty[287] (for she abused her quite seriously on account of his proposal),[288] she was convinced to violate the ancestral regulations[289] and marry Felix. By him she gave birth to a son named Agrippa. **144** But as for how that youth and his wife disappeared at the time of the eruption of Mt. Vesuvius in the days of Titus Caesar—that I shall recount later.[290]

(7.3) 145 After the death of Herod,[291] who had been her husband and uncle, Berenice remained a widow[292] for a long time. But when a rumor circulated that she was living with[293] her brother,[294] she persuaded Polemo, who was king of Cilicia,[295] to be circumcised and marry her; in this way, she thought to convict the slanders of falsehood.[296] **146** Polemo agreed, especially on account of her wealth. But the marriage did not last long, for Berenice abandoned Polemo—out of licentiousness, it was said. And so he was

---

287 Josephus thus manages to begin his sniping at Berenice even before he turns his attention directly to her; see the note on "falsehood" at §145.

288 The construction of the first part of this sentence, with its several clauses, is difficult, and has attracted emendations and divergent translations. Niese (1890b: 253 marks a lacuna); for some suggestions, see Feldman (1965: 466a).

289 Josephus condemns Drusilla, first of all, for leaving one husband for another without divorce—as other Herodian women, Salome and Herodias, condemned earlier by Josephus (15.259 and 18.136), and as Drusilla's two sisters, mentioned in the next lines (§§146–147). (On this phenomenon, which might have been more acceptable in Roman eyes than in Josephus's, see Jackson 2005.) But the fact that nothing is said of Felix having been circumcised, in contrast to §§139, 145, makes it all the worse.

290 There is no such later report, and it is also difficult to imagine that Josephus thought he would continue his history as far as 79 CE, when Mt. Vesuvius erupted, destroying Pompei, for the logic of *Antiquities* has it stopping where it does, upon the outbreak of the war to which Josephus devoted another work. For the options, see the note on "shortly" at 19.366.

291 The death of Herod of Chalcis, in 48 CE, was reported at §104.

292 This is the only instance of ἐπιχηρεύω in Josephus. For the expectation that widows remain chaste and virtuous, cf. the note on "chastity" at 18.180. Here, Josephus will hasten to tell us that Berenice was no Antonia Minor.

293 The verb here, συνείη, appears in similarly incestuous contexts at 18.42 and 19.204.

294 Berenice often appeared together with Agrippa II as his "queen"; see Acts 25:13, 23; *War* 2.344, 402; and a Beirut inscription (Boffo 1994, no. 41 = *AE* 1928: no. 82). Note also 18.194 (and, for the suggestion that the "king and queen" mentioned at *b. Pesaḥim* 57a were Agrippa

II and Berenice: D. R. Schwartz 1981/82: 263–268 and Ilan 2022: 16–17). For the malicious rumor this could engender, especially after Berenice later achieved notoriety by her affair with Titus (on which see *GLAJJ* 2.9), see also Juvenal 6.153–160 (*GLAJJ*, no. 298), which refers to a gift that Agrippa once gave his "incestuous" sister (*incestae ... sorori*). For this kind of defamation, see also 19.204. Curiosity and the human tendency to conjectures about such relationships are not limited to antiquity; cf. Ilan (2022): 72–75.

295 See the note on "Pontus" at 19.338.

296 On the senses of ἐλέγχω, see the note on "convict" at §266. This whole report about Berenice is a masterpiece of innuendo: a rumor of incest, a pushy move to convince someone to marry her for her own purposes, and the ridiculous notion that entering into marriage could prove she had not been incestuous (not to mention the notion that her fellow Jews would hardly have been happy with her marriage to a gentile). And all that just warms readers up for the next lines, where Josephus, having stuck in the knife (as already at §143), begins to twist it, with a snide reference to Berenice's wealth and outright condemnation for licentiousness, which made divorce from her into liberation. What underlies Josephus's hostility to Berenice here, as opposed to the positive picture in *War* (esp. 2.309–314, also 2.333, 344, 402), is unknown. As Krieger (1997: 9) notes, the fact that between the compositon of *War* and that of *Antiquities* her relationship with Titus ended (and Titus died) might help explain why Josephus felt free to express his hostility. But that does does not explain what generated it. Krieger (ibid.) suspects that her image depends on that of Agrippa II, whom Josephus attacks (at §§189–190, 216–218) as part of his general claim, late in *Antiquities*, that it was criminal behavior by the Jewish aristocracy that led to the catastrophe. For the suggestion that this hostility draws on a source used by Josephus, whether primarily

concomitantly released[297] from marriage and from [the obligation to] persevere in the customs of the Jews. **147** At the same time Mariamme too,[298] who had divorced Archelaus,[299] married Demetrius, one of the most prominent Alexandrians in terms of family and wealth; at that time he also held the post of alabarch there.[300] She had a child by him, named Agrippinus. But I shall report in detail about each of these people later on.[301]

Nero's Succession to the Empire

(8.1) 148 Claudius Caesar died, having reigned for thirteen years, eight months, and twenty days.[302] There were some who said that his wife, Agrippina, killed him with a drug.[303] Her father had been Germanicus (Caesar's brother), and her previous husband had been Domitius Ahenobarbus, one of the prominent men of the city of Rome.[304] **149** After he died and she had remained a widow for a long time, Claudius took her as his wife along with her son,[305] named Domitius after his father. ([Claudius] had previously killed his wife Messalina out of jealousy.[306] From her he had children: Britannicus and Octavia. **150** Antonia was the

---

anti-Agrippan or primarily anti-Berenician, see, respectively, D. R. Schwartz 1981/82 and Ilan 2022: 76–85. Use of such a source could also explain the references in §§144, 147 to events beyond the scope of *Antiquities*. Be that as it may, it may be enough to point, here, to Josephus's usual hostility to pushy women (see the note on "demands" at 18.42) and to Berenice's bad reputation in Rome (see above, the note on "brother"), as another eastern princess who, as in the case of Cleopatra and Marcus Antonius, seduced and subjugated a Roman ruler.

297 Given that Josephus's usage here obviously relates to life according to Jewish customs as having been a burden suffered by Polemo, the use of the same verb for his "release" from Berenice is biting. For its use with regard to deliverance from shame or oppression (as at 18.371; 19.184, 243), see *ThLJ* 59, s.v. ἀπαλλάσσειν.

298 This use of καὶ Μαριάμμη, after a sentence about Polemo, is somewhat puzzling. Apparently it means that, for Josephus, this entire section, beginning with §139, is about Agrippa II's sisters, and now he has something to report about Mariamme too. Moreover, by using καὶ to remind readers of the other two sisters, Josephus primes them to expect a nasty story about her, and thus encourages them to read the coming story as a condemnation, although it is not as clearly heinous as those about Drusilla and Berenice. See the next note.

299 On this Archelaus, see above, §140. Here Josephus turns to similar condemnation of yet another sister of Agrippa II: pushy and a gold-digger, she took the initiative to get rid of her first husband in order to marry a richer one. For Josephus's explicit condemnation of such behavior, which (he claims) characterized all three daughters of Agrippa II, see the note on "ancestral rules" at §143.

300 See the note on "Alabarch" at 18.159. Given Josephus's description of the family, Demetrius may have been a brother of Tiberius Julius Alexander (20.103).

301 None of them reappears in the narrative; cf. the note on "recount later" at §144.

302 He died on 13 Oct. 54. Counting from the assassination of Gaius on 24 January 41, Josephus's statement is extremely precise: ten days short of thirteen years and nine months. For the same figure, which is "exactly correct" (Mason 2008: 202, n. 1558), see *War* 2.248 and Cassius Dio 60.34.2. For similar data about other emperors, see the note on "days of rule" at 18.32. Note that the last we heard of Claudius concerned his penultimate, twelfth, year (§138), which is where Josephus opened his excursus on the Herodians. Now, having completed that, Josephus finishes up his account of Claudius. This is a fairly usual procedure; see the Introduction, at n. 15.

303 See Tacitus, *Ann.* 12.66–67 and Suetonius, *Claud.* 44.2. Nasty rumors like this one are natural and can be neither proven nor disproven. For a review of the evidence, see Barrett 1996: 138–142. Josephus, in any case, was not about to pass up the opportunity to record such an accusation of a woman, even if, instead of reporting that Agrippina killed Claudius or stating (as at 19.110, 207) that "all agree" that she did, he hides behind "some" and "so it is said" (§151) and thereby avoids taking responsibility for it. Cf. the note on "others" at 19.193.

304 Consul in 32 CE, Domitius had married Agrippina in 28 CE. He was banished by Tiberius in the last year of the latter's reign, returned to Rome after Tiberius's death, but died late in 40; he "occupies a special place in history as the only one of Agrippina's husbands she was not accused of murdering" (Barrett 1996: 70).

305 That is, Claudius adopted her son, as is stated more clearly at §150 and by Tacitus at *Ann.* 12.26.

306 In 48 CE; see Barrett 1990: 64–67. The main source is Tacitus, *Ann.* 11.26–38.

eldest of the siblings,[307] having been born to him by Paetina, his first wife.[308]) Indeed,[309] he betrothed Octavia to Nero—which is how Caesar later called him,[310] after adopting him as a son.[311] (8.2) **151** Agrippina, however,[312] fearful that Britannicus, upon becoming a man,[313] might take over his father's rule,[314] and wanting to seize power preemptively for her own son,[315] arranged (so it is said)[316] the details of Claudius's death. **152** Immediately [thereafter], she sent Burrus, the prefect of the troops,[317] and along with him the military tribunes and the most powerful freedmen, to escort Nero to the camp and proclaim him emperor.

153 Having thus taken over rule, Nero killed Britannicus by drugs,[318] keeping this far from the public eye; but not much later he killed his own mother openly.[319] That was the way he repaid her not only for giving birth to him but also for the fact that it was through her machinations[320] that he came to succeed to the dominion of Rome. He also killed Octavia,[321] whom he had married, as well as many [other] dignified people, charging that they had instigated conspiracies against him.[322]

(8.3)[323] **154** But I can allow myself not to write much about those things, for many have composed the history of Nero.[324] Of these, some have been careless about the truth out of goodwill, having been well-treated by him, while others have so shamelessly caroused in

Josephus's Reflections on His Own Mandate

---

307 Claudius's children.

308 Actually, Aelia Paetina was Claudius's second wife; see Suetonius, *Claud.* 26.

309 On καὶ δή, see the note on "for example" at 18.257. Its use here means that Claudius not only took this son in, along with Agrippina (§149), but "indeed" also fully assimilated him into his family by betrothing him to his daughter.

310 Instead of "Domitius."

311 On the adoption (in 50) and the betrothal (in 53?), see Barrett 1996: 111, 135. For the evidence concerning Nero's old and new names, see ibid. 280, n. 61.

312 I have given this heavy translation of δέ here, and also abstained from indenting for the new paragraph, in order to reflect Josephus's logic here: having opened 8.1 with the suggestion that Agrippina murdered Claudius, he went on to report that although Claudius fully adopted Agrippina's son (see the note on "indeed" at §150), nevertheless she was worried that Nero might be passed over.

313 Britannicus was born early in 41. "Becoming a man" (ἀνδρωθείς) probably refers to the donning of the *toga virilis*, around the age of fifteen. Cf. Harrill 2002: 255–266.

314 Probably this refers not to a putsch, but to being designated heir.

315 The same stock motivation of pushy and wicked mothers was attributed at 18.41–42 to the wicked Thesmousa; contrast the virtuous Helena at 20.29–30.

316 As reported at §148.

317 I.e., prefect of the Praetorian Guard. For such usage of ἔπαρχος, see *GTRI* 138–140. Burrus's presence

alongside Nero, upon his accession, is reported by Tacitus too (*Ann.* 12.69). Burrus would later be counted, at least by rumor, among those murdered by Nero (Tacitus, *Ann.* 24.51; Suetonius, *Nero* 35.5). Cf. the note on "Beryllus" at §183.

318 Britannicus seems to have died in February or the early spring of 55. On the claim that Nero poisoned him, see Tacitus, *Ann.* 13.15–17 and esp. Cizek 1999.

319 Agrippina. For her death, in 59, see Tacitus, *Ann.* 14.1–13 and Barrett 1996: 181–195.

320 Josephus now gives up the pretense of merely relating a rumor (cf. §§148, 151). For such use of μηχανή, which characterizes what Agrippina did in a way that is apparently more devious or sinister than the plain δια-πράσσω ("brought about") did at §152, see the note on "engineered" at 18.41.

321 For the death of Octavia (Claudius's daughter and Nero's wife [§150]) in 62, see Tacitus, *Ann.* 14.63–64, Griffin 2000: 98–99, and Murgatroyd 2008.

322 Especially the Pisonian (Tacitus, *Ann.* 48–71) and Vinician (Suetonius, *Nero* 36–37) conspiracies. On these, and others, along with Nero's persecution of the Stoics, see Griffin 2000: 164–179 and Rutledge 2001: 166–173.

323 For similar passages, see the parallel at *War* 2.250–251, also 4.491–496; *Ant.* 14.1–3; 16.186–187.

324 For a survey of the earlier but lost sources that served such later authors as Tacitus, Suetonius, and Cassius Dio, see Griffin 2000: 235–237 and Hurley 2013: 29–31.

lies, out of hatred and hostility toward him, that it is appropriate to condemn them.[325] **155** It does not occur to me to wonder at those who lie about Nero,[326] for even when writing about his predecessors they did not take care to write the historical truth, although they had no hatred for them since so much time had gone by since them. **156** But let those who do not intend to write the truth be allowed to write as they desire, for that seems to be what makes them happy. **157** We, however, although we have set truth as our goal,[327] think it appropriate to recall only briefly matters that do not pertain to our present topic.[328] Things that befell us Jews, in contrast, we recount not at all marginally, abstaining from reporting neither suffering nor sins. Indeed, I shall now return the narrative to the story of our own events.[329]

More Updates about Herodians

(8.4) 158 When Azizus, ruler of Emesa,[330] died in the first year of Nero's reign, his brother, Sohaemus, succeeded him as ruler.[331] Aristobulus, the son of Herod King of Chalcis, was granted, by Nero, the rule of Armenia Minor.[332] **159** And Caesar gave Agrippa part of the Galilee as a gift, ordering Tiberias and Taricheae[333] to be subject to him, also giving him Julias (a city of the Perea) and fourteen villages around it.[334]

Felix's Governorship

(8.5)[335] 160 Affairs in Judea were continually and progressively going downhill.[336] The country was again filled with bands of brigands and charlatans who led the masses astray. **161** But Felix captured and killed many of them daily, along with the brigands. He also took alive Eleazar the son of Deinaios,[337] who had formed a band of brigands, by entrapping him.

---

325 For a very similar passage, see *Apion* 1.46. For the argument that here Josephus was thinking specifically of Cluvius Rufus as having flattered Nero, and Pliny as having been hostile toward him, see Gercke 1895: 254–261. According to Hurley (2013: 30), however, it is likely that already Cluvius joined in the chorus supporting "the new Flavian dynasty whose legitimacy was being defined by the illegitimacy of the deposed Nero and whose sobriety could be contrasted with the flamboyance of the reign just past." On Nero's image in antiquity, see Krüger 2012: 559–578 and Heerink and Meijer 2022, including Schulz 2022: 326: "The Flavian response [to Nero], the distance to Nero, as expressed in several media, is a conscious and well-calculated construction of Flavian identity. It is highly probable that Flavian historiography, which has not come down to us, portrayed Nero in a critical and negative way, too."

326 For ironic concessions like this to untruthful historians, which amount to condemnations, compare 16.186–187 and *Apion* 1.218.

327 As Josephus frequently emphasizes, e.g., 8.56; 14.1–3; 16.187; *War* 1.16; *Life* 40, 364; *Apion* 1.6, 23–27, 47–52, etc. See also below, §260. For the understanding of truthfulness as balance and impartiality, cf. Marincola 1997: 158–174 (168–169 on Josephus, although only in *War*). On *sine ira et studio* ("without anger or favor," Tacitus, *Ann.*1.1) as a professed ideal of ancient historians, along with a discussion of how it was often honored in the breach, see Heldmann 2011.

328 Here Josephus excuses himself for failing to offer any proof for the mud he just slung. By the time he was

writing, Nero's reputation seems to have been so bad that he could probably assume readers would readily accept his attitude. Cf. the note on "condemn them" at §154.

329 Actually, however, as at §§103–104, he first devotes two paragraphs that bring us up to date concerning ancillary matters.

330 Cf. above, note on "Emesa" at §139.

331 On Sohaemus, see Sullivan 1977b: 215–218. During the Judean war he sent troops to support the Romans (*War* 2.500–501 and 3.68; Tacitus, *Histories* 5.1.2).

332 See the note on "Armenia Minor" at 19.338.

333 Usually identified as Magdala, somewhat more than "thirty furlongs" (*Life* 157) north of Tiberias on the western coast of the Sea of Galilee, despite the fact that Pliny (*NH* 5.71) places it at the southern end of the Sea; see *HJP* 1.494–495, n. 44; Stern, *GLAJJ* 1.309 and 478; Kokkinos 2010; and Mason 2016c: 395–401.

334 The reference is apparently to the city founded by Herod Antipas; see the note on "wife" at 18.27. On "Perea," Transjordan north of the Dead Sea, see the note at 18.240.

335 On Felix's term of office in Judea, see *HJP* 1.459–466; Smallwood 1981: 269–270; Mason 2008: 206–221; D. R. Schwartz 2017: 377–387.

336 As already at §124, which the present passage virtually repeats, Josephus punctuates Book 20 with such reminders that the final explosion is in sight; see also §§172, 210 and 214. The result is a sense of inevitability, a remorseless deterioration toward catastrophe. For the thesis that Josephus, with his hindsight, has misled modern scholarship into accepting that assessment, see McLaren 1998.

337 See the note on "son of Deinaios" at §121.

Namely, after extending to him a guarantee that he would not suffer any harm, he convinced him to come to him, [whereupon] he sent him up to Rome[338] in fetters.[339]

162 Felix was also hostile toward Jonathan the high priest,[340] for he frequently admonished him to administer the affairs of Judea better, lest he himself incur popular censure; for he had asked Caesar that [Felix] be sent as the procurator of Judea.[341] [Therefore], he figured out an excuse for getting rid of [Jonathan], who had become a constant annoyance for him; for those who wish to do wrong find it difficult always to be admonished.[342] **163** Accordingly, for this reason Felix promised to give a large sum of money to Jonathan's most trusted friend, a Jerusalemite by birth named Doras, and thus convinced him[343] to bring in brigands[344] to kill Jonathan. Hearkening to their appeal, he organized the murder to be executed by the brigands in the following manner: **164** some of them came up[345] to the city as if to worship God, but mingled in around Jonathan,[346] with daggers under their clothes, and killed him.

165 Since the murder remained unavenged, henceforth the brigands continued to come up on festivals with complete impunity and, similarly hiding their weapons,[347] they mixed in among the crowds and killed people—some were their own enemies, others as a service for others, in return for payment—not only in the rest of the city but even a few within the Temple itself; even there did they dare to slaughter, not even there considering it an act of impiety![348] **166** It is for this reason, I believe,[349] that even God, hating their impiety, turned

---

338 See the note on "sent up" at §131.

339 In this passage Josephus has his cake and eats it too. On the one hand, it is good that a Jewish terrorist was apprehended, because that was at least a move in the right direction—the attempt to restore order. On the other hand, however, Josephus reports that the Jewish rebel was so successful that it was only via perfidy that the Romans could apprehend him. (For similar ambivalence in Josephus's depiction of rebels, see the note on "bizarre manners" at 18.23.) Although some readers might think that Eleazar was naïve to believe Felix's guarantee, Josephus's portrayal of the terrorist as a victim of perfidy nonetheless enlists readers' sympathy for him, for, as the Roman stereotypes of *graeca fides* and *punica fides* show (see Gruen 2011: 115–140) and whatever the true facts were, the Romans prided themselves on keeping their promises. Compare, for example, *War* 3.532–542, where Vespasian has to be convinced, against his moral qualms, to violate a promise of free passage, and even then is said to have framed his promise ambivalently (ἀμφίβο-λον); similarly, at *War* 2.450–456, where Jews violate their oath promising free passage to Roman soldiers, it is clear that Josephus condemns the Jews for that and views the Romans as innocent victims of a terrible crime. For a list of villains portrayed by Josephus as oath-breakers, see Mason 2008: 109–110, n. 842.

340 I.e., the former high priest (see 18.95, 123 and 19.314). For continued use of the title by and of former high priests, see the note on "Joazar" at 18.3.

341 Presumably Jonathan had the opportunity for such involvement during the hearings that led to the deposition of Cumanus, perhaps in the wake of prior

dealings with Felix, who (according to Tacitus, *Ann.* 12.54) had served in Palestine already during Cumanus's governorship; see the note on "the Jews" at §118.

342 For a similar comment, see 19.319.

343 For "convincing" by bribery, cf. the note on "money" at 18.97.

344 The parallel at *War* 2.254–256 calls them Sicarii, a term that Josephus first introduces, in this book, at §186. But neither passage asserts that the Sicarii first appeared at that time, and their roots seem to go back earlier. See the note at §186 on "Sicarii."

345 On "coming up" to Jerusalem, see the note on "went up" at 18.90.

346 For the assumption that a popular high priest might be surrounded by a large crowd of admirers, see also Ben Sira 50:5, *Ant.* 15.50–52, and *m. Yoma* 7:4 with *b. Yoma* 71b.

347 Lit. "their iron(s)." See the note on "weapons" at 19.56.

348 "[T]he defilement of the temple by bloodshed committed in or near it is an important leitmotif of *Jewish War* (4.150–51, 201, 215; 5.15–18, 100–105; 6.95–110). For Josephus, this bloodshed plays a particular role in bringing about the divine punishment that concludes the rebellion (cf. *Ant.* 20.165–166)" (Klawans 2010b: 291). Note also *Ant.* 9.168; 11.300–301; Matthew 23:35; and Klawans 2012: 126–129. More generally, on the importance, for Josephus, of the Temple's ritual purity (which also comes up in these books at 18.19, 29–30 and 19.332–334), see Mason 2013 and Hasselmann 2022: 144–147.

349 On Josephus's use of "I believe," cf. Daube 1976 (on *Ant.* 11.237). It appears to be a way of hedging, of

away from our city,[350] decided that the Temple was no more a pure residence for him[351] and to bring the Romans down upon us and purifying fire[352] down upon the city, and to impose slavery upon us along with our wives and children with the intention of bringing us to our senses via suffering.[353]

(8.6) 167 While the doings of the brigands filled up the city with such unholiness,[354] the impostors and the deceptive men[355] wheedled the multitude to follow them out into the desert. 168 For, they said, they would show them clear signs and wonders that would occur through the providence of God.[356] Many were persuaded and paid the penalty for their lack of sense, for Felix had them arrested and punished.[357]

---

telling readers that it is not required that they accept this datum, similar to his statements concerning miracles; cf. the note on "however they like" at 19.108.

350 Here, as at *War* 2.539, Josephus argues that God punished the Jews not directly but, rather, by "turning away" from them (suspending his providential supervision, thus allowing calamities to occur) on account of their sins, what the Bible calls "hiding his face" (Deut 31:17–18; 32:20; Isaiah 54:8; 2 Macc 5:17). On this theme, see Friedman 1977; Balentine 1983; and D. R. Schwartz 2008: 262 (on 2 Macc 5:17).

351 Here Josephus assumes the plain meaning of the Temple: as the Bible put it so frequently, it was God's house. For a most explicit version of this, see *War* 6.300// Tacitus, *Hist.* 5.13.1 (*GLAJJ*, no. 281). Elsewhere, of course, Josephus can evince more delicate formulations that give their due both to God's transcendence, on the one hand, and to the human perception that he is present or even resident in the Temple, on the other. See esp. *Ant.* 8.102, 106–108, 114, 119, also the note on "him" at 18.306.

352 For this notion, see esp. Krieger 1998.

353 For such use of σωφρονίζω in a similar context, interpreting suffering as meant to edify and reform (as in Deut 32 and 2 Macc 6:12–17), cf. 2.305 and 5.256; 18.128; D. R. Schwartz 2003; Werse 2018. Cf. "sobered" at 19.232.

354 For this kind of linkage of troubles, continued at §169 and then again at §172b, cf. the note on "befell them" at §113.

355 Josephus likes this collocation (γόητες καὶ ἀπατεῶ-νες); cf. *Apion* 2.145, 161, where he rebuffs the charge that Moses was one. Similar formulations are found at §188 (τοὺς ἀπατηθέντας ... ὑπὸ ... γόητος) and *Life* 40 (where he claims Justus of Tiberias successfully overcame his opponents γοητείᾳ καὶ ἀπάτῃ). Cf. the note on "charlatan" at §97.

356 These desert prophets are reminiscent of Theudas (above, §§97–99) and those mentioned at §188.

On such figures, and why the wilderness attracted them (no tax-collectors? inspiring quiet and purity?), see Longenecker 1998 and D. R. Schwartz 2000. For Josephus on providence, see the note on "of man" at 19.61. Readers will note, however, that, unlike the author, whose identification of the workings of divine providence are of course supposed to be accepted as true (such as recently at §§18, 49, 91; cf. the note on "of man" at 19.61), villains who make claims about divine providence can turn out to be wrong, with fateful consequences for those dupes who believe them.

357 As with Theudas (§§97–98), Josephus prefers not to say why the governor, who certainly did not believe the promised miracles would occur, bothered to intervene; see the note on "to Jerusalem" at §98. In the present case, we may point to Josephus's fuller account in *War* (2.259–260), where he explicitly says that the prophets fostered "revolutionary" changes by promising signs of "liberty," and Felix quite properly saw in such agitation an impetus to "rebellion" (νεωτερισμοὺς ... ἐλευθερίας ... ἀποστάσεως). That is, the promised miracles were meant to demonstrate divine support for a movement that aimed to put an end to Roman rule in Judea, and it was quite reasonable for a Roman governor to fear that the aroused multitude might pursue rebellion even if the miracles did not happen. It seems that in *War* Josephus told things the way they were, but in *Antiquities*, written more than a decade later, he tried to tell stories, even about pre-70 Judea, according to the separation of religion and state that Jewish life in the Diaspora required—so religious figures, such as prophets, should not be involved in anti-Roman agitation. If that leaves some of Josephus's stories somewhat opaque and incoherent, he must have thought it was worth it. See the notes on "images" at 18.55 and on "to us" at 18.264, also D. R. Schwartz 2013: 156–160.

169 At that time there came to Jerusalem, from Egypt, someone who said he was a prophet. He urged the urban multitude[358] of Jerusalem [to go with him] to the mountain that was called "[Mount] of Olives," which is located across from the city at a distance of five furlongs.[359] **170** For, he said, he wanted to show them from there how at his command the Jerusalemites'[360] walls would fall, through which he promised to allow them entry [into the city]. **171** But Felix, when he learned of these things, ordered his soldiers to take up their arms,[361] and with many cavalrymen and infantry he stormed out of Jerusalem and attacked the Egyptian's men; he killed four hundred of them and took two hundred alive. **172** The Egyptian himself escaped from the battle and disappeared.

But again the brigands incited the populace to war against Rome,[362] calling upon them not to be subject to them. Setting afire the villages of those who did not obey them, they also pillaged them.[363]

(8.7) 173 There was also civil strife of the Jews who lived in Caesarea, against the Syrians[364] there, concerning equality of civil status.[365] For the Jews demanded to rule[366] by virtue of the fact that the founder of Caesarea, their King Herod, was of Jewish descent.[367] The

The Caesarean Dispute, 1

---

358 On Josephus's aristocratic use of πλῆθος for this pathetically gullible multitude, cf. the note on "multitude" at 18.26.

359 That is, about a kilometer away from Jerusalem. This mountain is actually a long ridge, so the fact that elsewhere (*War* 5.70) Josephus estimates the distance at six furlongs is not surprising. See Mason 2008: 213, n. 1648.

360 On such usage, cf. the note on "Jerusalemites" at §11.

361 Here too, only the parallel in *War* explains why the Roman governor got involved: the prophet did not merely intend to order the walls of Jerusalem to fall. Rather, he intended to attack the city with his men, overcome the Roman garrison, and set himself up as ruler instead of the Romans. And that corresponds to the report in Acts 21:38, apparently in reference to this same Egyptian prophet, that his followers were Sicarii. None of that appears here. Rather, as with the preceding story, Josephus has leaned over backwards, even at the price of maiming a coherent story, in order to avoid revealing such pragmatic political involvement by Jewish religious figures.

362 Note well, here Josephus ascribes this program to "the brigands," last mentioned in §167, not to the prophets mentioned in the preceding two stories. As explained above, here Josephus keeps the latter at a distance from affairs of state; see the notes on "punished" at §168 and "arms" at §171. In the parallel at *War* 2.264, in contrast, Josephus, less concerned to separate religion from state, says the charlatans and the brigands joined forces.

363 Note that Josephus says the rebels wanted Jews not just to disobey Rome, but, rather, to obey *them*. This contributes to vilifying them.

364 As Mason (2008: 217, n. 1681) notes, in the parallel account in *War* 2 Josephus introduces the Judeans'

adversaries in Caesarea as "Syrians" (§266) but usually calls them "Greeks" (§§265, 267–268, 284–285), while the account in *Antiquities* uses only "Syrians" (§§173–175, 183–184). This, Mason suggests, should be correlated with the fact that in *War* the Syrians' argument focuses on the (Hellenistic) statues and shrines that Herod established in the city, in contrast to *Antiquities*, where that argument is absent and the debate pertains only to the question of who first resided in the city. On "Greeks and Syrians in Josephus" see also Rajak 2001: 140–141; she suggests that, in general (but without referring to the present passage), Josephus views the former as urban and the latter as rural. Andrade (2010: 343), similarly, argues that ethnic Syrians could refer to themselves (as Josephus here) as "Syrians" but preferred "Greeks" in discussions of the identity of the *polis*. Taking Rajak and Andrade together, one may wonder if Josephus, here, does not deliberately stick to "Syrians" (rather than "Greeks") in order to engender doubt about their claim on the *polis*.

365 On this episode, which is continued at §§182–184, see esp. Levine 1974, Kasher 1977/78, D. R. Schwartz 1992/93, and Andrade 2010. On the parallel but somewhat divergent account in *War* 2.266–270, see Mason 2008: 215–221.

366 This passage, which clarifies that the issue was who was to rule in Caesarea, undercuts Josephus's attempt, in the preceding sentence, to upgrade the issue as if it were about equality of civil rights (*isopoliteia*). Perhaps the choice to formulate the issue as one about equal rights reflects the needs of the Judean delegates when the matter came to be adjudicated in Rome.

367 The same argument is ascribed the Jews at *War* 2.266. For Herod's foundation of Caesarea, see 15.331–341. However, it is difficult to imagine that the type of Jews

Syrians, in response, while admitting that about Herod, said that Caesarea had earlier been called "Strato's Tower" and at that time the city had not had even a single Jewish resident. **174** When the country's[368] prefects[369] heard that, they arrested those from both sides who were responsible for the civil strife, and, by lashing them roughly, put an end to the tumult—but only for a little while, **175** for again the Jews of the city, confident on the basis of their wealth and for that reason scorning the Syrians, began to badmouth them in the expectation of provoking them.[370] **176** The latter, however, although they were not as rich [as the Jews], were emboldened[371] by the fact that most of those [recruited] by the Romans to serve in the army there were Caesareans and Sebastenians.[372] For a time they too insulted the Jews only with words, but later [those on both sides] began to throw rocks at each other, until, as it happened, many on both sides were wounded or even fell [dead]; but the Jews were victorious. **177** When Felix saw that the rivalry had taken warlike form, rushing forward, he called upon the Jews to desist, and when they did not heed him, he armed his soldiers and unleashed them—killing many of them and taking more alive. He also allowed them to loot some of the houses in the city, which were replete with large sums of money. **178** Those of the Jews who were more moderate,[373] and of higher rank, afraid for themselves, called upon Felix to call off the troops by bugle-call and mercifully allow them henceforth to express contrition about what had been done. Felix was [indeed] convinced to do so.[374]

---

who were willing to slug it out with gentiles in the streets of Caesarea looked back with any enthusiasm or sincerity at Herod as having been a Jew. More likely they viewed him as "a half-Jew" (*Ant.* 14.403; cf. *m. Sotah* 7:8; cf. the note on "by birth" at 19.332) and, in any case, condemned him for having kowtowed to Rome. But when disputes came before Roman officials the Jews (as the Samaritans of §126) had to find arguments that might work in such contexts. Josephus and his readers must have realized this, and so there is something ironically amusing about the present passage.

368 This reference is χώρα is somewhat mystifying (and is absent in the parallel at *War* 2.269, which refers to ἔπαρχοι with no further identification). Although at times Josephus uses χώρα in its Hellenistic sense as the "territory" belonging to a certain city (as at 18.311), usually he uses it with regard to an entire "country"; see, for example, 18.50, 121; 20.23–24, 118. 160, 204. That fits, to some extent, the use of ἔπαρχος; see the next note.

369 Josephus usually uses ἔπαρχος in the singular, of a province's *praefectus* (see the note on "prefect" at 18.33), so the use of the plural here is surprising. Given the fact that §177 takes Felix's presence for granted, perhaps Josephus means "the authorities" in general (so *CCFJ* 2.138) or "the prefect and those of his officers who were responsible for this region," the latter being the Roman officers who commanded auxiliary troops, whose duties included

maintaining law and order in the region. Correspondingly, Mason (2008: 220–221, n. 1705, on the parallel at *War* 2.269, also Mason 2016c: 274) suggests that Josephus is using the term of prefects of (auxiliary) cohorts; for such usage see, exceptionally, *War* 3.122 and 5.48.

370 Here Josephus condemns these Jews who, depending on their wealth, evinced scorn for their neighbors; he implies they got what they deserved. See the note on "the laws" at 18.59.

371 Such negative usage of μέγα φρονέω ("thinking *too* big" and therefore tending to misbehave) is especially characteristic of *Life* (17, 43, 52). For its positive sense, see the note on "high spirit" at 18.255.

372 On them, see the note on "Sebastenians" at 19.356. Given the fact that Josephus views the Caesarean dispute as generating the war (§184), it is apparently these troops' involvement here that Josephus was thinking of in the very last lines of *Ant.* 19, where he says they were "the source of the greatest troubles for the Judeans, sowing the seeds of the war under Florus."

373 This, or perhaps "generous," "kind," is the usual translation of ἐπιεικής, and I have adopted it here as also in the similar passage at §201. *CCFJ* 2.157, s.v. assigns it the meaning "eminent, distinguished" here, but that seems to be covered by the next words, προύχοντες κατὰ τὴν ἀξίωσιν.

374 For the continuation of this story, see below, §182.

(8.8) 179 At that time, King Agrippa gave the high priesthood to Ishmael, who was the son of Phabes.[375] **180** And there then broke out civil strife among the high priests,[376] both against the priests and against the heads of the Jerusalemite populace: each of them[377] had formed[378] a gang[379] of the most audacious and revolutionary people and made himself its leader, and when they clashed they badmouthed each other and threw stones.[380] But not a single person remonstrated with them.[381] Rather, as if they were in an ungoverned city, they did what they did with [total] license. **181** Such a degree of shamelessness and insolence

Stasis in Jerusalem

---

375 On this Ishmael b. Phiabi (as the name is vocalized in rabbinic literature, such as *m. Sotah* 9:15 and b. *Pes.* 57a; see Schalit 1968: 121 and Ilan 2002: 403), see VanderKam 2004: 463–475. He is not to be confused with his father or grandfather (see Appendix 2, n. 13), mentioned at 18.34. The present one might be identical with the Ishmael whose sons are referred to at *War* 6.114 as sons of a high priest; there we read that he was beheaded in Cyrene, perhaps in the context of post-rebellion disorder there (*War* 7.437–450; *Life* 424–425). Be that as it may, the dating of the present Ishmael's tenure as high priest is unclear. Josephus reports it here just before the end of Felix's governorship, but (1) it is not clear when that was (see the note on "successor" at §182) and (2) anyway it seems that Josephus bunches notices of this type between tenures of procurators (see the opening note at §103), so even if it occurred in the middle or beginning of Felix's tenure it would still be listed here. If indeed Cumanus lasted only one year in office (see Appendix 1, §8), and was replaced in 49/50 CE, this Ishmael could be identical with "Ishmael the high priest" in the days of Claudius mentioned in *Ant.* 3.320. Otherwise it is quite impossible to identify the latter. Moreover, as a secondary advantage, if we conclude that Ishmael was appointed around 49/50 and lasted in office until ca. 60 (see the note on "as hostages" at §195), our conclusion would tally with the talmudic report that he served as high priest for ten years (*b. Yoma* 9a). That report is wrong if, as the consensus has it, he was appointed only ca. 59; moreover, that consensus has Ishmael's predecessor, Ananias b. Nedebeus, serving more than a decade, but he is not mentioned in that talmudic list of long-serving high priests. It is not clear that much weight should be assigned to the talmudic list, but all things being equal, a reconstruction based on Josephus that conforms to the list's report is to be preferred to one that contradicts it regarding both Ishmael and Ananias. For a detailed discussion of the issues (including the interpretation of Acts 23:2–5, where Ananias is called "high priest" but Paul is said not to have realized that he is the high priest), see D. R. Schwartz 1992: 218–242 (and

Goodman 1987: 142, n. 5). For a detailed response that defends the conventional chronology, see VanderKam 2004: 455–475; for a rejoinder, see D. R. Schwartz 2024a.

376 There is some uncertainty about the text here, but the basic meaning, which pits the high priests, as villains, against the others, appears to be clear.

377 Namely, of the high priests, as is clarified by the opening of §180 and exemplified at §213.

378 Ambrosianus adds "and collected unto himself," which adds nothing to the statement that each man formed a group and was its leader; see the note on "brought to him" at §5.

379 For this pejorative translation of στῖφος in connection with brigands, cf. 8.204, *War* 3.450, *Life* 21 and Mason 2001: 32, n. 144 ("swarm").

380 For the same pair, see §213.

381 For this theme, that the good citizens of Jerusalem were cowed into silence by the troublemakers, see also *War* 2.276 and esp. Ananus b. Ananus's speech at *War* 4.163–192 and *Life* 20–23, also the note on "it wished" at 19.180. The same theme, basically, is also at the bottom of the string of three rabbinic stories about the destruction of Jerusalem in *b. Gittin* 55b–56a, where the first denounces rabbis who were afraid to open their mouths to protest improper behavior, the second denounces one who was afraid to make an extraordinary decision when the alternative would be to do nothing and let a calamity occur, and the third shows that even the rebels' commander was afraid to tell his men that the time had come to surrender and that his guards at the gates of Jerusalem failed to do their duty because of their fears of what people might say about them. See D. R. Schwartz 1997/98. This theme is an elegant solution to a dilemma: how to maintain the notion that the catastrophe came about on account of the Jews' sins but avoid claiming that all or even most Jews were wicked? Answer: by portraying them as basically good people whose sin was of omission, and that was due to fear: they erred insofar as they did not have the courage to speak out against the lawless and rebellious minority.

took over the high priests, that they even dared to send their slaves[382] to the threshing-floors to take the tithes[383] that were [in fact] due to the [common] priests,[384] and so it happened that the needy among the priests starved to death.[385] Thus did the violence of those engaged in civil strife overpower all that is just.[386]

The Caesarean Dispute, II

(8.9) 182 When Porcius Festus was sent by Nero as Felix's successor,[387] the leaders of the Jews residing in Caesarea went up to Rome[388] to accuse Felix.[389] He certainly would have had to pay the price for his unjust acts against the Judeans,[390] had Nero not acceded to the intense pleading on Felix's behalf by his brother, Pallas, who at that time was highly

---

382 For high priests' slaves who, in a similar context, are said to beat people up with their staves, see the angry ditty in *b. Pesaḥim* 57a.

383 On the loose use of δεκάτη (here and at §§206–207) to include not only tithes but also other offerings, including "heave-offerings" (*terumot*), in the context of the broader debate as to whether tithes were meant for Levites or (as here) for priests, see J. M. Baumgarten 2022: 205–212 (pp. 209–210 on Josephus's usage here).

384 On tithes in this period, see Oppenheimer 1977: 23–51. For reports of similar violence by high priests, see the stories in *b. Pesaḥim* 57a and *y. Sotah* 9.24a//*Maaser Sheni* 5.56d. For the topos of poor priests going to threshing-floors in order to collect their tithes, cf. *Midrash Proverbs* (ed. Buber) 59, where Prov 29:4 is taken to mean that one should prefer a judge who, like a king, is rich and therefore independent, and not one who is poor, like a priest who, for his livelihood, makes the rounds from one threshing-floor to another.

385 People apparently liked to tell stories like this, especially in reflection about the causes of the Destruction. A very similar story appears at §206, and a comparable tannaitic story appears in *b. Pesaḥim* 57a; on it, see Y. Fisch in Ilan and Noam 2017: 1.526–543. That tannaitic story does not mention Ishmael b. Phiabi, but it is followed (ibid.) by two other tannaitic traditions that do, and both—the first explicitly and the second ironically (see D. R. Schwartz 1981/82: 262–268)—condemn him, alongside other high priests of the first century, reflecting rabbinic thoughts about who was to blame for the Destruction. As the solution discussed in n. 381, so too this one: by focusing blame on a type of Jew who no longer exists (high priests), Josephus and the rabbis could maintain the notion that sin brings on suffering without blaming themselves and their own predecessors.

386 For similar comments about how a small number of villains can bring disaster on all, cf. §112 and 18.84.

387 There is, especially because of the reference in Acts 24:27 to Festus's arrival in Judea in the context of the trials of Paul, considerable controversy as to the date of Festus's appointment; see Saumagne 1966, Stern 1974b: 74–76, and Appendix 1, §9–10.

388 On "going up" to Rome, see the note on "sent up" at §131. This account is quite different from that provided by *War* 2.270, 284, for in that case delegates from both sides were sent by Felix and the decision came only after several years, while here we read of a delegation that went to Rome after the end of his term and received a swift response. As is argued by Schürer (*HJP* 1.467, n. 45) and Mason (2008: 221–222, n. 1721), probably the account in *War* is to be set aside (or read very loosely, with 2.284 opening with a flashback), both because, in general, such a delay is unlikely and because, specifically, of the consideration cited immediately below, in the note on "by Nero."

389 For complaints about governors after the conclusion of their terms of office, taken for granted at *Flacc.* 105 and *Leg.* 199, see Brunt 1961.

390 Josephus tells us, in *War* and *Antiquities*, next to nothing about unjust acts by Felix. While we can well imagine Jews who had their complaints about him, for example Jews in Caesarea who thought his repression of violence there (§177) was too heavy-handed, Josephus does not present it that way, but here he nevertheless signs on, as an author, to the condemnation. It seems, that is, that Josephus is torn between a narrative that portrayed Felix simply as wicked, as was to be expected from the brother of the wicked Pallas (such as that in Tacitus, *Ann.* 12.53–54 ["he thought he could do any evil acts with impunity"] and *Hist.* 5.9 ["every kind of barbarity and lust"]; cf. the next note), on the one hand, and his own growing desire, in *Antiquities*, to point to the Jews' sinfulness as explaining their suffering, on the other. Similar tension may be observed in Josephus's account of Albinus as well; see the note on "brigands" at §215.

honored by Nero.[391] **183** And the leaders of the Syrians of Caesarea convinced Beryllus[392] (who was Nero's tutor[393] and entrusted with his correspondence in Greek),[394] with a large sum of money,[395] to ask Nero [to give] them a letter abrogating the Jews' equality of civic rights[396] with them. **184** Beryllus, upon urging the emperor [as they desired], indeed succeeded in bringing about the composition of the letter[397]—which brought on the causes of the calamities that thereafter befell our nation. For when the Jews of Caesarea learned what had been written, they pursued their civl strife against the Syrians all the more, until it broke out into the[398] war.[399]

(8.10) 185 When Festus[400] arrived in Judea it was being ravaged by the brigands— all of its villages being set afire and pillaged.[401] **186** And the Sicarii[402] (as they were

Festus's Governorship

---

391 On Pallas and his influence, see the note on "slaves" at 18.182. Josephus likes to complain about the great influence of Greek freedmen; see the note on "friends" at §135. Pallas died in 62 CE (Tacitus, *Ann.* 14.65), and his death is said to have come at Nero's hands—all the more reason to reject the plain meaning of *War* 2.284, namely, that Nero's decision about Jewish rights in Caesarea, which here we read was urged by Pallas, came only in 66. E. Schwartz (1907: 285) doubts the truth of Josephus's statement here, because Pallas fell from grace shortly after Nero's rise to power (Tacitus, *Ann.* 13.14). However, Tacitus reports only that Pallas was removed from office, but emphasizes that he was not treated as a criminal, and he also retained great wealth, so whether or not he was still "highly honored" by Nero, it could well be that his influence helped save his brother. Cf. Oost 1958: 133–138.

392 Hudson (cited by Niese ad loc. [1890a: 307]) emended this to Burrus, thus equating him with the praetorian "prefect" mentioned at §152. But although Mommsen (1885: 529, n. 1) considers the identity of the two certain (*sicher*), and others too subscribe to it, there seems to be little to recommend it: there seems to be no manuscript evidence for the emendation and Josephus identifies the two in very different ways.

393 For Nero's having a *paedagogus*, see also Suetonius, *Nero* 22.1. On the position, see Bradley 1985.

394 On Beryllus's position as *ab epistulis graecis*, and his role in the present story, see Millar 1967: 15–16.

395 For "convincing with money" of bribery, see the note on "money" at 18.97.

396 See the note on "rule" at §173.

397 Griffin (2000: 55) states that Beryllus was here looking after "his Syrian compatriots," but offers no evidence regarding his roots. For the possibility that a Jewish critique of him has survived as a grafitto in Poppaea's villa in Torre Annunziata (near Pompei), see Ciardiello 2012.

398 On the definite article here (contrast the expected anarthrous appearance of στάσις with the same verb, ἐξάπτω, at §§109, 180), as again at § 224, cf. the notes on "downhill" at §160, on "brigands" at 18.7, and on "the" at §16.

399 For Josephus's thoughts on the catalysts of the war, see the survey in Bilde 1979. The contribution of the Caesarean conflict is similarly emphasized in *War* 2.284. That passage, however, raises a chronological difficulty; see the note on "to Rome" at §182. For more general thoughts about who was responsible for the catastrophe, see the notes on "with them" at §180 and on "starved to death" at §181, also Klawans 2010b and Price 2007.

400 On Festus's term of office in Judea, see *HJP* 1.459–466 and Smallwood 1981: 269–270. On its termini, apparently 60–62, see Appendix 1. Festus played a role in Paul's trial, according to Acts 25–26, but is otherwise unknown, apart from the brief parallel in *War* 2.271.

401 As is usual in this book (§§121, 125, 172, 187).

402 On the Sicarii, see esp. Stern 1973: 135–140; Hengel 1989: 76–145 and—on their commonalities with the Zealots—380–404; Mason 2008: 207–208, n. 1604; Brighton 2009; Rappaport 2011; and (on the way Josephus "vituperatively" used the term to arouse condemnation among Roman readers) Vandenberghe 2016. Cf. the note on "brigands" at §163. Given the fact that Eleazar b. Yair, the commander of the rebels at Masada in the early 70s, is specifically said, at *War* 7.253, to have been both a Sicarius and a "descendant" (grandson?) of Judas the Galilean (who led the rebellion against Rome at the time of the census of 6 CE [18.4–9, 23; *War* 2.118; Acts 5:37], and whose sons were executed as rebels in the forties [§102]), it is usually assumed that the movement goes back at least to the early first century, and is to be identified with what Josephus terms a "fourth philosophy" with regard to Judas (18.23; *War* 2.118). For that identification, see also the note

called[403]), who were brigands, were then especially numerous: using daggers that were very similar in size to the Persians' short swords,[404] but curved[405] like what the Romans' call *sicae*,[406] from which the[se] brigands got their name, they killed numerous people. 187 For on the festivals, when the multitude pours together into the city to [express] its piety,[407] they would mix themselves in (as we have already said[408]) and slaughter with ease whoever they wanted. Moreover, frequently they would descend, armed, upon the villages of their enemies, loot them and set them on fire. 188 Festus also sent a force of cavalry and infantry against those who had been led astray by some charlatan who had promised them salvation[409] and an end of [their] troubles if they were willing to follow him into the wilderness.[410] Those sent out after them wiped out both the charlatan himself and those who had followed him.

---

on "manners" at 18.23. Some scholars tend to play down the characterization of the Sicarii as anti-Roman rebels, emphasizing that they largely sat out the war at Masada and are known mostly for their attacks on other Jews and participation in what may be viewed as regional conflicts with the non-Jewish population of Palestine; see esp. Mason 2016: 255, who roundly states that, as opposed to other groups of rebels, "Josephus gives the *sicarii* no role in the war against Rome." However, such distinctions are difficult to make and, whatever explains the Sicarii's preference for Masada over Jerusalem during most of the war (for some speculation, see Rappaport 2011: 336), it is difficult to argue that Josephus or the Romans made such distinctions. Josephus lists the Sicarii alongside the other groups in his catalogue at *War* 7.262–274; the Sicarii's platform rested on a rejection of Roman authority (18.4//*War* 2.118, also 7.323, 410, 418–419), their attacks on other Jews are explained as punishment of them for submitting to Rome (§172//*War* 2.264–265; 7.254–255), many other Jews did join the Sicarii "in the war against the Romans" (*War* 7.257), at §102 Josephus takes it for granted that Judas of Galilee called for rebellion against Rome and that a Roman governor had good reason to kill Judas's sons, and regional conflict between Jews and non-Jews necessarily entailed rejection of Roman law and order in Judea; see §§2–5 and the note on "Romans" at §130. As for other sources, note a Roman officer's assumption, according to Acts 21:38, that Sicarii, even those who "go out into the desert," are involved in *stasis*, and the end of the next note; the fact that the rabbis' memories of the war against Rome included Sicarii in Jerusalem does not disprove Josephus's account, but it too indicates that the Sicarii were seen to be a group of rebels against Rome.

403 The term is probably of Roman origin, one that denounces them and categorizes them as the type of criminals addressed by the *Lex Cornelia de sicariis et veneficis* of 81 BCE; see Vandenberghe 2016 and Mason 2016c: 256–257. But Josephus treats them as a well-defined group; see esp. the catalogue at *War* 7.262–274. For references to them in rabbinic literature, of rebels in Jerusalem, see Hengel 1989: 50–53. Cf. the preceding note.

404 Feldman (1965: 489, n. d), who renders ἀκινάκης "scimitar," refers to Herodotus (3.118), Xenophon (*Anabasis* 1.2.27), and Horace (*Odes* 1.27.5–6: Medus acinaces). For Josephus's interest in such weapons, cf. 18.45.

405 This is the only occurrence of ἐπικαμπής in Josephus.

406 On *sicae*, which were often used by criminals and also by gladiators, see Hug 1923 and Rustoiu 2007 (with numerous illustrations). Two or three have been found in Judea; see Streckert and Seevers 2023: 306–307.

407 See the note on "twenty thousand" at §112. Here Josephus emphasizes the religious purpose of the pilgrimage, which makes the murders all the more heinous.

408 At §165.

409 On σωτηρία, which elsewhere often means "security" or "safety" (e.g. §§22, 48) but when prophesied refers to "salvation" by God, see Spicq 1994: 3.344–357. But that had political meaning in first-century Judea; note especially the rebels' coins from the rebellion of 66 that proclaim *ge'ullat Zion* ("the redemption of Zion"). As Hengel (1989: 117–118) points out, the same term (with "Israel") also appeared alongside of the unambiguously political "for the freedom (*ḥerut*) of Israel" (or: "of Jerusalem") on coins of the Bar-Kokhba rebellion.

410 That is, yet another of the type mentioned at §§97, 167.

(8.11) 189 At that time, King Agrippa built a room of unusual size[411] in the royal palace in Jerusalem,[412] near the Xystus.[413] **190** In earlier times the palace had [been built by] the sons of Asamonaios.[414] Since it was located upon a high site, it allowed those who wished to look down from it the most wonderful view of the city—which the king loved to do: while reclining,[415] he used to watch, from there, what was being done in the Temple. **191** When the foremost Jerusalemites saw this they were very upset, for it was not in accordance with ancestral practice that doings in the Temple—and especially the sacrificial worship—should be looked down upon.[416] So they erected a high wall upon the fore-hall[417] in the inner temple facing west. **192** When this was built, however, it cut off the view not only from the royal triclinium, but also from the western portico, which is in the outer part of the temple, where, on holidays, the Romans customarily kept watch throughout the temple.[418]

193 King Agrippa was upset about that, and especially Festus (the prefect) as well, and he ordered them to destroy [the wall]. But they asked him to give them permission to send an embassy concerning this to Nero,[419] for, they said, they could not go on living[420] if any part of the Temple were to be torn down.[421] **194** When Festus agreed, they sent from

Agrippa II vs. the Priests

---

411 Mason (2008: 264, n. 2162) suggests that an additional story is meant, which offered the enhanced view assumed by the following account.

412 On the Hasmoneans' palace, mentioned here as already at 14.7, which (according to §191) must have been on the eastern edge of the Upper City, opposite the Temple Mount, see Netzer 2018: 123, 126–127.

413 On what is meant by this—a "polished" terrace on the slope leading up to the Upper City?—see Mason's detailed discussion at *War* 2.344 (2008: 263–264, n. 2159).

414 That is, the members of the Hasmonean dynasty, which ruled Judea, first independently and later under Roman tutelage, from the mid-second century until the days of Herod; its story fills much of *Ant.* 12–14. The name does not appear in the Books of Maccabees or elsewhere in sources of the Second Temple period, but is not uncommon in rabbinic literature; see Noam 2018. For suggestions concerning its origin, see First 2015: 76–93. The phrasing here ("sons of") is a literal rendition of the Hebrew *b^enei Ḥashmonai,* as, for example, at *m. Middot* 1:6. Elsewhere too (11.111; 12.265; 14.490–491; 15.403; 16.187 and the high-priestly chronicle: 20.238, 247, 249, also *Life* 2, 4), *Antiquities* consistently identifies the dynasty as that of Asamonaios, including by the otiose "descendants of the sons of Asamonaios" at §238. In the more polished *War*, in contrast, the graecized substantive οἱ Ἀσαμωναῖοι is used (2.344 and 5.139).

415 Even just reclining, as if watching a show meant to entertain him, was disrespectful enough; in the Temple court itself, according to *y. Yoma* 3.40b//*b. Yoma* 25a, no one, with the possible exception of Davidic kings, was even allowed to sit. If Agrippa was not only reclining, but also eating (as κατάκειμαι often implies, as at 10.232 and 13.291), the outrage of those who protested would be all

the more understandable. However, the verb need not entail eating; see for example 6.363 and 19.349.

416 It seems that, as already suggested by such biblical texts as Numbers 4:20, the viewing of the sacred rituals or vessels, by gentiles or others who were unauthorized, was considered to be forbidden, perhaps because it somehow demeaned them; see 14.71–72, 482–483 and D. R. Schwartz 1986; Anderson 2009: 168–183; and Fraade 2009. Viewing the Temple service from above, literally "looking down" (κατοπτεύω) upon it, would be all the worse. If Agrippa was not aware of such sensitivities, or was but chose to ignore them, it is difficult to agree with Curran (2011: 73) that this episode shows that "Agrippa's intentions were further illustration of a committed interest in Judaism and its institutions," to which he compares Acts 25:22ff.

417 Apparently the present reference is to the hall mentioned at *War* 6.150, 220. Since it faced west, a wall on top of it could indeed block the view from the Hasmonean palace further to the west.

418 See above, §§106–107.

419 For a similar issue and procedure, see §7.

420 As at §116. So too Herodias at 18.242, but she is only a manipulative and self-centered woman. In contrast, Josephus loves to impute to the Jews and their spokesmen such seriousness about the law; see the note on "accept death" at 18.59.

421 Given the fact that they had themselves built the wall, what was really at stake here was the question, who was in control of the Temple—the prefect? the Temple's Herodian supervisor (§§15–16, 222)? Or the Jews (or priests) themselves? That also seems to be reflected by Nero's two-fold response, that he both approved of what they had done and allowed the wall to remain (§195); since all they had done, according to Josephus, was build

among themselves the first ten men,[422] and also Ishmael the high priest and Helcias the treasurer.[423] **195** Nero, after hearing them out, not only approved of what they had done but also agreed to allow the construction [to remain] as it was—thus responding graciously to his wife, Poppaea, for she was god-fearing[424] and had besought him concerning the Jews. She ordered the ten to depart, but kept Helcias and Ishmael with her as hostages.[425] **196** When the king learned this, he gave the high priesthood to Joseph, surnamed Cabi, who was the son of the high priest Simon.[426]

The Death of Jacob ("James"), Jesus's Brother

(9.1)[427] **197** When Caesar learned of Festus's death[428] he sent Albinus to Judea, as prefect. The king, for his part, took the high priesthood away from Joseph and, as successor to the office, gave it to the son of Ananus, who too was called Ananus.[429] **198** It is said that the elder Ananus was the most fortunate person, for he had five sons and it happened that all five of them served as high priests of God.[430] [Moreover,] that was after he himself had

---

the wall, the first clause suggests that there was also an argument about whether they needed anyone's permission to do that. Cf. esp. *War* 6.124–128, where Josephus has Titus emphasize the Romans' willingness to grant the Temple something like exterritorial status.

422 On the institution of municipal *deka protoi*, which appears in the first century, see Dmitriev 2005: 197–200. For Palestine, see esp. *War* 2.639 and *Life* 69168, along with Tcherikover 1964: 68–69, n. 13 and Mason 2001: 61, n. 376.

423 On Helcias, who belonged to a family that was close to the Herodians for generations, see the note on "Helcias the Elder" at 18.273. As for the treasurers of the Temple, see *HJP* 2.279–284 and, for rabbinic sources, Safrai 1976: 879–880.

424 There has been quite a bit of scholarly interest in Poppaea's involvement on the Jews' behalf and Josephus's characterization of her as god-fearing (θεοσε-βής), but apart from §252 and (in contrast) *Life* 16 there is very little to go on. It is not clear whether the adjective refers to her generally as pious or, rather, as sympathizing with Judaism (see the note at 18.82 on "Jewish practices"). Moreover, given her generally unsavory reputation in Roman sources, beginning in extant texts with Tacitus, *Ann.* 13.45–46 ("She was a woman possessed of all advantages but a character [*praeter honestum animum*] ... she paraded modesty, and practiced wantonness [*lascivia*]" [trans. Jackson, LCL]), it is not clear whether the adjective reflects anything more than Josephan flattery or ad hoc characterization in this case. Moreover, whatever Josephus thought, it is possible that the claim that Poppaea tended to Judaism originally functioned as yet another slur. See Williams 1988; Grüll and Benke 2011; Ciardiello 2012; Edelmann-Singer 2013; Hollander 2014: 59–63; and Baughman 2014.

425 Josephus does not date the delegates' departure for Rome. For the argument that it was ca. 60 CE, and that Ishmael was high priest until then, see Appendix 1, §9–10.

426 On this Joseph b. Simon, whose surname is given in different forms by different witnesses, see Schalit 1968: 70, s.v. Καμεί and VanderKam 2004: 475–476. He was, perhaps, a member of the same family as Joseph b. Camith (18.34) and Joseph b. Camei (20.16), assuming that "Cami" (or the like) was the name of their clan, not specifically of their father; see the note on "son of Boethus" at 18.3. Nothing is known about him. True, a "Joseph b. Simon" was among the aristocratic high priests who, like Josephus, were at first entrusted with the rule of a district at the beginning of the Jewish revolt against Rome (*War* 2.567), and a "Joseph" was among the "high priests" who eventually surrendered to the Romans (*War* 6.114). But the name is common; in the Babylonian Talmud (*Gittin* 24b), "Joseph b. Simon" is the equivalent of our "John Smith," a standard example of a name borne by more than one person.

427 On this episode, see Brandon 1967b; F. S. Jones 1990; McLaren 1991: 148–155; Bauckham 1999; McLaren 2001; Lambers-Petry 2002; Mason 2003b: 236–248; Painter 2004: 130–141; Eliav 2004; Martin 2006: 29–82 (a detailed commentary on §§197–203); Frey 2024. As opposed to the *Testimonium Flavianum* about Jesus (18.63–64), there is relatively little debate about the authenticity of the present passage, if only because of the reserved way in which it refers to Jesus, merely as "called Christ," at §200; see the note there on "Christ."

428 Of which Josephus has not informed us.

429 For sons who bear their father's name, see the note on "John" at §14.

430 For the first four, see above: 18.34, 95, 123; 19.316. For Josephus's natural interest in such recurrence of the

earlier enjoyed the position for a long time.[431] That did not happen to any of our other high priests.

199 The younger Ananus, who (as we said) took over the high priesthood, was daring in his nature and extraordinarily bold,[432] and belonged to[433] the school of the Sadducees, which is, with regard to judicial issues, more brutal than all the other Jews, as we have already reported.[434] **200** That being the way he was, Ananus thought he had an appropriate opportunity, given the death of Festus and Albinus still being en route [to Judea], to convene a council[435] of judges and bring before it the brother of the Jesus called

---

office in a given family, compare 19.297, which refers, in turn, to 12.238. In recognizing this family's important role in the high priesthood, we should also recall that Joseph Caiaphas, who served for quite a long time (see 18.35, 95), was (according to John 18:13) Ananus's son-in-law, just as Luke 3:1–2 and Acts 4:6 put them both in "the high-priestly family." Given the fact that Ananus ("Annas" in biblical translations) the father was significantly involved in the trial of Jesus (John 18:13, 19–24) and the apostles (Acts 4:5–6), while Ananus the son was responsible for the death of James, this family seems to exemplify the hostility of the Sadducean high priesthood toward the nascent church; on "the hatred of the house of Annas," see Gaechter 1947. Such hostility is taken for granted at Acts 4:1–3 and esp. 5:17, also Luke 20:27–40 and Acts 23:1–3. It is not difficult to think of reasons for it, be they the Christian focus on resurrection as opposed to the Sadducean denial of it (*Ant.* 18.16; Luke 20:27; Acts 4:2 and 23:8) or the Christian tendency to locate sanctity outside of the Temple (and/or to use the term "temple" as a metaphor), such as at John 2:21, 1 Corinthians 6:19, 2 Corinthians 6:16, Ephesians 2:19–22. The memory, in this connection, of Jesus's disruption of order in the Temple (Matthew 21:12–13// Mark 11:15–18) and prophecy of its destruction (Matthew 24:1–2//Mark 13:1–2) may well have contributed to Sadducean antipathy toward his followers; cf. Acts 6:13–14. See, in general, Le Moyne 1972: 401–406; B. Chilton in *ABD* 1.257–258; and Regev 2019: 42, 192.

431 Namely, ca. 6–15; see *Ant.* 18.26, 34, also VanderKam 2004: 420–424.

432 This is pejorative, as is shown by the reaction of the fairest and most law-observant residents of the city (§201); cf. θρασυτάτ- at §206, 213 and ἀναθαρρήσαντες at §210, also the note on "audacious" at 18.6. Josephus's negative picture of the younger Ananus, in the present episode, sharply contradicts his narrative in *War* 4.318–325, where this Ananus is the paragon and mainstay of respectability and law and order, and his murder, by villainous rebels, is taken to have been the point of no return on the road to catastrophe; Mason (2016b: 22–23) takes it, indeed, to be the very turning-point of the entire

work. While Rajak (2002: 131, n. 73) has taken this contradiction to show that the present passage is not authentic, it seems preferable to accept the passage as authentic and view the contradiction as indicating that, in *Antiquities'* retrospective view of the events of the revolt, Josephus was adopting a narrative that tended—esp. in the cases of Felix and Albinus—to blame the high priesthood in general and, accordingly, found it more difficult, or less functional, to distinguish between good guys and villains in their ranks. Cf. the notes on "with them" at §180 and on "starved to death" at §181. For such a narrative in rabbinic literature, see *b. Pesaḥim* 57a.

433 On μέτειμι, see the note on "belong" at 18.16.

434 Actually, Josephus never says this. But at *Ant.* 13.294 he reported that the Pharisees tend toward lenient punishments. The present passage thus indicates that Josephus thought of the Pharisees and Sadducees as a matched pair of binary opposites: what he posited for the one he denied for the other. Cf. the note on "in contrast" at 18.16.

435 "Council" renders the Greek "sanhedrin" (συνέδριον); so too at §202, also §216. That has led various scholars to see take the present passage as referring to the convening of "the Sanhedrin" (as Feldman 1965 translates in all three passages), a body mentioned in the New Testament and rabbinic literature but difficult to pin down historically. However, §§200, 202, 216 do not attach a definite article to συνέδριον, and the impression (as is noted by Grabbe 2008: 12 concerning §216) is one of an ad hoc assembly, not a regular institution; indeed, the present story suggests that one could not be convened without special authorization. In the numerous references in the Gospels and Acts, in contrast, a direct article is the rule and the impression is one of an institution that convenes regularly (and when John 11:47 refers, exceptionally, to the convening of a συνέδριον without a definite article, the impression is that it is an informal consulation.) That is part of the growth of a Christian narrative that presents the Jews as collectively and institutionally, not merely occasionally, hostile to Christianity. Similarly, the later rabbis would, for their own reasons, of course

"Christ,"[436] whose name was Jacob,[437] along with some others;[438] after accusing them of having violated the law,[439] he turned them over to be stoned.[440] 201 Those who were thought to be the most moderate[441] people in the city, and most exacting in the observance of the laws,[442] were very upset about this, and so they secretly sent to the king and called upon him to write to[443] Ananus, not to do anything like that again—for, [they said], he had not done his first act properly. 202 Some of them also went out to meet Albinus on his way

---

take it for granted that the Sanhedrin ("from which the Torah goes forth to all of Israel") was a regular institution (*m. Sanhedrin* 11:2; this Mishnah refers to "the Great Court that [sat in]the Chamber of Hewn Stone"; *m. Middot* 5:4, in turn, defines that court as "the Great Sanhedrin of Israel"). For surveys of the evidence and attempts to reconstruct the situation in the first century, see Safrai and Stern 1974: 379–400; McLaren 1991: 213–217; Sanders 1992: 472–490; and Grabbe 2008. Concerning ancient Jewish usage of συνέδριον (deliberative body? advisory body? court?), note also the debate among Wolfson 1945/46, Zeitlin 1945/46, and Hoenig 1946/47.

436 The contrast between the non-committal way in which Josephus here says only that Jesus was "called 'Christ,'" on the one hand, and "he was the Christ" and other declarations of Christian belief about Jesus in the *Testimonium Flavianum* (*Ant.* 18.63–64), on the other, is one of the reasons for the consensus that the present passage is authentic. See, for example, Winter 1973: 430–432; Whealey 2016: 353. Doubts have been expressed, nevertheless, by scholars who suspect the present text is a Christian interpolation; so Rajak (see the note on "bold" at §199) and Carrier 2012. Carrier suggests that originally the Jesus mentioned here was not identified more precisely and the person Josephus meant was not Jesus of Nazareth; rather, he suggests, Josephus referred to Jesus b. Damnaios, who is mentioned a few lines later (§203), and whose appointment as high priest, replacing Ananus, could be understood as Agrippa's taking sides in a feud between the two families. He argues that the current text, which identifies "Jesus" precisely the way he is identified at Matthew 1:16, a text quite familiar to Christian copyists, resulted (a) from misunderstanding by such copyists, who probably did not realize how common a name "Jesus" was, and (b) from Eusebius's quoting of Origen's citation of Josephus in a way that does not properly distinguish between Josephus's text and Origen's interpretation. Whatever one thinks of the latter arguments, it must be noted that the case would be more persuasive had Jesus b. Damnaios been mentioned before this passage, so readers could think of him when reading "Jesus" *simpliciter*.

437 As in the New Testament (Galatians 1:19; Acts 15:13; 21:18), so too here, Jesus's brother is named Jacob, which is usually rendered "James" in English (via the popular Latin "Jacomus"). On him, see Painter 2004. The

present passage is the only direct non-Christian evidence for him. Today it is usually assumed that a Jerusalem ossuary bearing the inscription "Jacob the son of Joseph the brother of Jesus," is a modern forgery, but even if not: (a) the names are common and need not refer to James the Just, and (b) it might be Joseph, rather than Jacob, who is referred to as Jesus's brother. See Goodblatt 2013.

438 Nothing is known about the identity of these others, not even whether they were associated with James or, rather, other non-conformists or dissidents that Ananus found threatening and took the opportunity to purge. Nor can we exclude the possibility that even if there was only one victim, James, Josephus might throw in some others gratis to make Ananus look worse.

439 This contrasts with the New Testament portrayal of James as adhering to Jewish law, a point that elicited some criticism from Paul; see Acts 21:18–24; Gal 2:12, and the apparent response to Paul (esp. Gal 3:1–14?) in James 2:8–26. It is not surprising, however, that someone to Paul's right, in this respect, might still be well to the left of Sadducees.

440 On stoning as a Jewish mode of execution see, *inter alia*, *Ant.* 4.264//16.365; 14.24; 17.216; *Life* 76; *Apion* 2.206; John 8:7, Acts 5:26; 14:19; 7:58–59, *m. Sanhedrin* 6:1; 7:1, 7, 9. For the argument, on the basis of biblical and rabbinic texts, that the choice of stoning indicates the charge was "blasphemy," see Lambers-Petry 2002: 102–104. Bauckham 1999 argues, instead, that the charge was based on the law of Deuteronomy 13 concerning a man who leads others into idolatry, which too was punishable by stoning, according to *m. Sanhedrin* 7:4, 10. For other traditions about the mode of James' death and his place of burial, see Eliav 2004.

441 See the note on "moderate" at §178.

442 This is often predicated of the Pharisees, as for example at *War* 2.162; *Life* 191; Acts 26:5 (and 22:3); see A. I. Baumgarten 1982 (he derives the name "Pharisee" from a Hebrew equivalent). Indeed, if the protesters were Pharisees it would fit their specific antagonism to the Sadducees here. But Josephus has no reason to suggest that among the Jews only some sectarians were outraged by this travesty of justice. See esp. McLaren 1991: 151–152, n. 3 and idem 2001: 6–12.

443 For such use of ἐπιστέλλω as straddling the field between writing and—given the status of the

from Alexandria,[444] and informed him that Ananus had no authority to convene a council without his approval.[445] 203 Albinus, convinced by what he had been told, wrote angrily to Ananus, threatening to punish him. And King Agrippa[446] therefore took the high priesthood away from him, after he had held it for three months, and installed Jesus the son of Damnaios [in his stead].

(9.2) 204 When Albinus[447] arrived in the city of the Jerusalemites, he applied all his energy and forethought to bringing peace to the land by stamping out many of the Sicarii.[448]

205 But the high priest Ananias was gaining in prestige day by day, and the people rewarded him magnificently with good-will and respect. For he was well-supplied with money,[449] and daily he cultivated Albinus and the high priest with gifts.[450] 206 And[451] he had servants who were very wicked, who—going about with the most insolent men—would go to the granaries and forcefully take the tithes that belonged to the priests; they did not draw back from beating those who refused.[452] 207 Moreover, the high priests did just like his slaves did,

Albinus's Governorship

High Priests and Sicarii

---

writer—ordering, compare, for example, 19.327, 341. Cf. the note on "orders" at 19.262.

444 For Alexandria as a usual port on the way between Rome and Judea, see also 14.376; 18.169; *Flacc.* 26, 28; Charlesworth 1936a: 42–43.

445 Here the reference is specifically to a council that exerts judicial authority, especially one that undertakes to impose a death penalty; for the Roman monopoly on capital jurisdiction, see John 18:31, *War* 2.117, and *y. Sanhedrin* 1.18a ("forty years before the destruction of the Temple capital jurisdiction was denied [to the Jews]"), also the note on "full authority" at 18.2. For doubts about that monopoly, see esp. Martin 2006. In any case, presumably Agrippa had no need to convene a council for purposes that were within his authority, such as the one described at §§216–218.

446 This full reference to Agrippa II, with his title, seems to have been typical of Josephus's source for the high-priestly succession; cf. the note on "Theophilus" at 18.123.

447 On Albinus's term of office in Judea, see *HJP* 1.468–470; Smallwood 1981: 280–282. On Josephus's account: D. R. Schwartz 2011. It appears that Albinus served from 62 or 63 (four years before the war and seven and a half years before the destruction—*War* 6.300, 308), until 64 or 65, for, according to §257, the outbreak of the war, in 66, came in Albinus's successor's second year. Albinus's name is often identified as the Lucceius Albinus whose later governorships, and death under Vitellius, are reported by Tacitus at *Hist.* 2.58–59; so, for example, *PIR* 2.400 (L264).

448 This is one of the more egregious differences between the accounts of the pre-war years in *War* and *Antiquities*. Whereas according to *War* 2.271–277, Festus was fine and tried to maintain law and order, Albinus was terrible but at least tried to hide his crimes, and Florus

was even worse and flaunted them, here—since Josephus wants to blame Jews—Albinus is rehabilitated and comes off wonderfully, thus serving as a foil for the Jews. Josephus will reproduce *War*'s account at §§252–254, and already §215 will show him struggling to coordinate his present narrative with it; see the note on "brigands" at §215. Here, however, in *Antiquities*' main narrative about Albinus, Josephus wants to condemn sinful Jews, esp. villainous high-priests, and Albinus is the beneficiary. See D. R. Schwartz 2011.

449 This is the only occurrence of πορστικός in Josephus; *CCFJ* 3.495 s.v. renders "clever at producing something for oneself," which sounds quite pejorative. Cf. the next note.

450 This characterization of Ananias is somewhat ambiguous, given the reference to the goodwill Ananias enjoyed, which sounds nice. Nevertheless, the emphasis upon his wealth, along with the report that he plied it daily upon the high priest and the governor, imply condemnation, and so it seems that the reference to the goodwill he garnered is ironic. Condemnation is implied by the immediate continuation as well.

451 Feldman (1965: 499) and Schalit (1963: 369) open this sentence with "but," as if Josephus meant Ananias was fine but his servants were wicked. That, however, seems to be the kind of harmonization that only the naïve might accept, so it is difficult to think that Josephus meant that. For similar harmonization, note Rashi's commentary on *b. Pesaḥim* 57a, s.v. Ishmael b. Phiabi: he thinks the text first condemns Ishmael's household (in a story similar to Josephus's) but then praises him. There too, it is easier to assume the latter is bitterly ironic; see D. R. Schwartz 1981/82: 263–266.

452 See the note on "starved to death" at §181; we have here a stock story about high-priestly magnates who preyed upon the poor. Readers may wonder whether

no one being able to prevent them. So it happened that some of the priests who used to live from the tithes died for lack of food.[453]

(9.3) 208 Again it happened, at the time of the festival,[454] which was then being celebrated, that the Sicarii entered the city by night[455] and, taking alive the scribe[456] of Eleazar (the captain of the Temple, who was a son of Ananias the high priest[457]), bound him and took him off with them. 209 Then they sent to Ananias and said they would release the scribe to him, if he would convince Albinus to release ten of their men who had been arrested. Ananias, under this duress, persuaded Albinus and obtained the request.[458] 210 This was the beginning of greater troubles, for the brigands managed one way or another to kidnap members of Ananias's household and, holding them in uninterrupted captivity, did not release them unless they received some Sicarii in return. Again growing to a not inconsiderable number, they took courage and ravaged the entire land.[459]

Agrippa II's Foreign Projects

(9.4) 211 At that time, King Agrippa, having built up greatly the Caesarea known as "Philipp's," named it Neronias in honor of Nero.[460] And in Berytus,[461] having constructed a theater for a large sum of money, he donated large sums for the annual festivities [there], squandering[462] on this many myriads of drachmas. 212 For he also gave out wheat to the populace and

Josephus remembered, when writing the present passage, that he had already used this story in the earlier context.

453 This too is at §181.

454 The use of the definite article here, without any specification as to which holiday is meant, is perplexing. Perhaps it reflects Hebrew usage, according to which *he-ḥag* ("the festival") was Tabernacles (so, for example, *m. Rosh Hashana* 1:2, *m. Bikkurim* 1:6). Contrast 18.122 and 20.133, where, when Josephus wants to be vague, he refers to "a festival" with neither a name nor a definite article, and cf. D. R. Schwartz 1997: 105–109, in connection with *War* 1.229//*Ant.* 14.285.

455 Cf. the note on "at night" at 18.56.

456 This Greek term, γραμματεύς, often refers generally to administrative officials, including as the Septuagint's translation not only of *sophēr* ("scribe") but also of *šoṭēr* ("officer"). Cf. D. R. Schwartz 1992: 89–101; Mandel 2017: 73–75. Indeed, lists of officials associated with the Temple in the first century do not include "scribes." See the detailed lists offered in *m. Sheqalim* 5:1–2//*t. Sheqalim* 2:14 (ed. Lieberman, 210–211), along with *b. Pesaḥim* 57a (a bitter ditty complaining about such officials); see Jeremias 1969: 165–166, 195–196. But the latter text does mention officials with "quills."

457 For such use of "high priest" of a member of the high-priestly aristocracy even if not currently the high priest, see the note on "Joazar" at 18.3.

458 Given the fact that this Eleazar was soon to be revealed as one of the major leaders of the anti-Roman rebels (*War* 2.409), it is not wild to speculate, with Smallwood (1981: 282), that he was colluding with the Sicarii in organizing such moves to coerce Albinus into releasing prisoners.

459 Another ominous generalization, alongside §§124, 160, and 214, marking the road to the final catastrophe.

460 On Caesarea Philippi, of which the founding was reported at 18.28, see *HJP* 2.169–171, Z. U. Maʻoz in *NEAEHL* 1.136–143, and M. Hartal, ibid. 5.1587–1594. "Caesarea Neronias" appears on coins of Agrippa II minted in 65/66 (*RPC* 1.4991), but was abandoned after Nero's death; see Meshorer 1985: 68–69 and Bernett 2007a: 353.

461 Agrippa II's contributions to Beirut continued a family tradition; see the note on "Berytus" at 19.335. Note especially Boffo 1994: 338–342 and Ilan 2022: 67–69 on a Beirut inscription (*AE* 1928: no. 82) honoring him and his sister, Berenice, for their restoration of a building originally donated by Herod.

462 For such a pejorative sense of ἀναλίσκω (rather than merely "spending"), cf. 2.88 and 18.145, also *War* 1.91. It is only natural that those who liked Herod and Agrippa would take pride in their generous support of important centers around the Mediterranean, while those who did not might view it as wasting the Judeans' wealth. Note especially the complaints at 16.158 and 19.329–330, in contrast to the praise at *War* 1.422–428. Presumably the latter should be traced to Nicolaus of Damascus (cf. Stern, *GLAJJ* 1.229–230). Cf. the note on "pregnant" at §18.

distributed oil, and he beautified the whole city by erecting statues and replicas of ancient models; he transferred to it almost all of the ornaments of his kingdom! For this reason, hatred of him grew among his subjects, because he was taking away that which was theirs in order to adorn a foreign city.[463]

213 Jesus the son of Gamaliel received the high-priestly succession from the king after he removed Jesus the son of Damnaios [from the office]. There ensued civil strife between the two:[464] making gangs of the most insolent men, they frequently slipped from badmouthing into stone-throwing.[465] But Ananias maintained his predominance, using his wealth to keep ahead of those willing to receive it. **214** Costobar and Saul themselves[466] assembled masses of scoundrels; and although they were of the royal family, and thanks to their closeness to Agrippa enjoyed [his] good will, they were violent men and ready to plunder those weaker than them.[467] Especially from that point in time it happened that our city was affected by sickness,[468] everything going downhill.[469]

More High-Priestly and Herodian Violence

(9.5) 215 When Albinus heard that Gessius Florus was arriving as his successor, he—desiring to be thought someone who had provided something [beneficial] for the Jerusalemites[470]—brought out all the prisoners and ordered the execution of all of those who were clearly worthy of death, but freed, in return for money, those who had been imprisoned only on some minor and incidental charge.[471] The result was that the prison was purged of prisoners, but the land was filled with brigands.[472]

Conclusion of Albinus's Governorship

---

463 And, of course, the financing of statues in particular will have aroused the Jews' ire. On the hostility to Agrippa II evinced here, see the next note.

464 As Hölscher notes (1916: 1990–1991), at *Life* 204 Josephus claims that Jesus b. Gamaliel was his good friend. Hölscher takes this as evidence that the present passage is based on a written source (whose nuance Josephus did not notice). See also the notes on "themselves" and on "than them" at §214. For the suggestion that such material hostile to the high priesthood and to Agrippa II derived from a source that focused on such themes, as also above at §§141–147, 179–181, see D. R. Schwartz 1981/82. But it is also congenial to Josephus's major theme in the present book, that things were going downhill on account of the Jews' own sins; see D. R. Schwartz 2011.

465 As at §180, and similar to §207.

466 Even without the emphatic addition of αὐτοί ("themselves"), and certainly with it, this passage seems to assume that readers already know who they are. But they do not, and even the explanation of their boldness, namely, that they were of the royal family and close to Agrippa, does not identify them. Contrast *War* 2.418, where they are properly introduced—as brothers who were relations of Agrippa II. It is difficult to avoid the conclusion that Josephus was either following a source that had previously introduced them, or else writing up his own notes with little thought for his readers. See also the next note.

467 Although *War* 2.418, 556 portrays these relatives of Agrippa as respectable citizens who fled Jerusalem

when the rebellion began, here they are portrayed as gangsters, which amounts to a swipe at Agrippa too, similar to those at his sisters (§§141–146), at the high priests he appointed, and personally at him as well (§§189–195, 216–218). Whether or not Agrippa II was already dead by the time *Ant.* 20 became available (see *HJP* 1.481–483, n. 45 and D. R. Schwartz 1992: 243–282), Josephus apparently wanted to include him more generally, and not only specifically at §216–218, among those responsible for the final deterioration and catastrophe.

468 For the Thucydidean metaphor of "sickness" with regard to stasis, see already Josephus's opening of *War*, with Price 2005b: 139*. Note also Mason 2008: 214, n. 1660 on *War* 2.264.

469 On this refrain, see the note on "downhill" at §160.

470 On such gestures, which can amount to bribes in order to suppress complaints about a governor's behavior, cf. Acts 24:27 and Tacitus, *Ann.* 13.31, along with Brunt 1961: 214–215. Compare Josephus's analysis of Herod's remission of taxes after a famine at *Ant.* 15.365: although the pretext was relief of his subjects' suffering, the real goal was conciliation of his opponents.

471 For διὰ μίκραν καὶ τὴν τυχοῦσαν αἰτίαν see also *Life* 13, where Josephus's point, as their advocate, is that those so charged should not have been imprisoned.

472 "The land was filled with brigands" continues a—or the—major theme of *Ant.* 20; see the note on "downhill" at §160. As Cohen (1979: 62) noted, however, "the tone of AJ 20.215 is particularly ambiguous and/or self-contradictory." How could the release of petty criminals

Agrippa II's Projects in the Temple and Jerusalem

(9.6) 216 Those of the Levites (a tribe) who were singers[473] convinced the king to convene a council[474] and allow them to wear linen vestments, just as the priests.[475] For, they said, it was appropriate that he make some innovation during the period of his reign, by which it would be remembered.[476] 217 And they did not fail to obtain their request, for the king, with the agreement of the members[477] of the council, agreed that the psalm-singers put aside the garments they had hitherto worn and, instead, wear linen as they desired. 218 And since a part of the tribe engaged in the cultic service in the Temple, he allowed them to learn the hymns[478] by heart, as they requested.[479] All of this contravened the ancestral laws, and once they had been violated it was impossible that judgment not be imposed.[480]

(9.7) 219 At that time the Temple too was completed.[481] The populace, seeing that the workers—numbering more than 18,000—were unemployed and would be without wages, for they had earned their upkeep by working on the Temple, 220 and also not wanting

---

fill the land with brigands, who are heinous criminals? And if the point is to show Albinus as doing something beneficial, why report that, when releasing these criminals, he took money, which sounds like bribery? It seems that Josephus, caught between his narrative in *War* 2.272–276, in which Albinus was terrible (and he will revert to that line shortly, at §252, after the excursus on the high-priestly succession), and his present narrative, which is devoted to showing that it was wicked Jews whose sins brought about the catastrophe, gives some of this and some of that. See D. R. Schwartz 2011. For such playing of both sides, cf. the notes on "brigands" at §124 and "others" at 19.193.

473 On the Levitical singers, see Safrai 1976: 872. Josephus's need to explain to his readers that "Levites" denotes a "tribe" reflects the general paucity of references to them in his works; while priests are mentioned very often, the last time "Levites" were mentioned was at 13.63, 73. Nor is the situation much different elsewhere: "On the whole the evidence about Levites is extraordinarily meagre" (Jeremias 1969: 213).

474 Although the term used is συνέδριον, as at §200 there is no definite article; see the note on "a council of judges" at §200. In a case like this, one would expect the priests to be involved; see the note on "office" at 18.17.

475 For the priests' linen vestments, see Exod 28:42 and 39:28, also *Ant.* 3.152–153; 8.93; and *War* 5.229. See also the note on "the Fast" at 18.94. As a rule, the sources record no special vestments for Levites, but note the strange exception at *Ant.* 8.94, where Josephus refers to linen garments for the Levite singers. For contextualization of the present episode on the background of other evidence for debates about the functions and relative status of the Levites as compared to priests, see Fraade 1999: 116–117, nn. 23–24. For Josephus's concern that priests

be allowed special clothing forbidden to others, see also *Ant.* 4.208.

476 That a king should want to be remembered is natural; see, for example, §§18, 52, also 6.343, 11.183, 15.380, and 19.223. But the present passage is terribly ironic for, as Josephus will emphasize at §218 (as already at 18.9), innovation in cultic ritual is the last thing a pious king should want to be associated with his name. See the note on "innovation" at 18.9.

477 This is the only occurrence of ἐποίχομαι in Josephus.

478 Probably referring to psalms; for the juxtaposition of David's "songs and hymns" and the Levites' songs and musical instruments, see also *Ant.* 7.305–306. For a survey of the sources on the recitation of psalms in the Second Temple, such as *m. Sukkot* 5:4 and *m. Tamid* 7:4, see Rendsburg 2014: 106–117.

479 This apparently means that he allowed Levites, whose clans were traditionally assigned particular roles in the Temple (see 1 Chr 9:17–18, 33; Ezra 2:41–42), to move into other positions. For such competition between Levites, see also the story in *Sifre Numbers* §116 (ed. Horovitz, 132)//*b. Arakhin* 11b): a Levite doorkeeper tells a Levite singer who wanted to help him to desist, "for you are among the singers, not the doorkeepers."

480 Cf. the note on "innovation" at *Ant.* 18.9.

481 Although Herod completed the renovation of the Temple already in the penultimate decade of the first century BCE (*Ant.* 15.380, 420–421), it seems clear that work continued, or was required by new circumstances, such as the damage inflicted in the "War of Varus" (*Ant.* 17.261–262; *Assumption of Moses* 6:9); note John 2:20–21, where, in the days of Jesus, reference is made to forty-six years of work having gone into the Temple. For post-Herodian work in Jerusalem, see Szanton et al. 2019 (on Pilate).

(due to fear of the Romans) to keep money on deposit,[482] urged the king to raise up the eastern portico, which would allow him both to be considerate of the workers and also to expend the treasury upon them, for if anyone worked even only a short time during the day he immediately received his pay for it.[483] **221** That portico was part of the outer Temple, located in a deep ravine; it had walls four hundred cubits [long] made of square stones that were exceedingly white,[484] each one twenty cubits long and six cubits high[485]—the work of King Solomon who was the first to build the entire Temple.[486] **222** The king, who had been entrusted by Claudius Caesar with the supervision of the Temple,[487] realizing that it is always easy to demolish something but difficult to [re]build it,[488] and especially in the case of this portico, for which much time and money would be needed for the work, rejected the request about that, but did not hinder the paving of the city with white stone.[489] **223** And taking the high priesthood away from Jesus son of Gamaliel he gave it to Matthias the son of Theophilus,[490] in whose time there also[491] began the Judeans' war against the Romans.

(10.1) 224 I consider it necessary, and appropriate to this history, to go into some detail[492] about the high priests[493]—how they began, who is allowed to be among those who hold

Summary of the High Priesthood

---

482 That the reference is to the Temple's treasury is evident both from the fact that hitherto the money had supported work on the Temple and from the explanation in §222 that Agrippa was the Temple's supervisor. On the money in the Temple treasury, see the note on "sacred moneys" at 18.60. For instances in which the Romans robbed it, see *Ant.* 14.105–109 (Crassus) and 17.264 (Sabinus), also *War* 2.293 (Florus); cf. 18.60–62, on Pilate's use of the Temple's money for public works, and already Cicero, *Pro Flacco* 28.66–69 (*GLAJJ* no. 68).

483 Here Josephus is evidently alluding to the law of Deuteronomy 24:15//Leviticus 19:13//*m. Bava Metzia* 9:11–12, which he states at *Ant.* 4.288; see Feldman 2000: 456–458.

484 Cf. the note on "white stone" at §222.

485 Although Josephus's "twenty cubits" (around ten meters) is an exaggeration, some of the stones in this wall were nonetheless huge, the largest being more than seven meters long (Mazar 2011: 145).

486 So too *War* 5.185. This portico is, correspondingly, known as "Solomon's Portico" in Acts 3:11 and 5:12. That Solomon built the eastern wall seems to be stated at 15.398 (on the text, see van Henten 2014: 302, n. 2829) and is clearly stated at *War* 5.185–187, where Josephus adds that the wall-building in Herod's days was on (the other) three sides. As Orit Peleg-Barkat kindly explained to me, since Herod did not expand the Temple Mount on its eastern side, its relative antiquity could give rise to the belief that its wall remained from the First Temple, Solomon's. Indeed, it seems that parts of the eastern wall originated in the First Temple period, but Herod's work on the wall, both on its northern and southern ends, was massive; see Mazar 2011: 275–276.

487 See §§15–16.

488 For the same notion, see also *Ant.* 15.380–390, as well as the talmudic story of Herod's reconstruction of the Temple (*b. Bava Batra* 3b–4a). The latter comes in the context of the law that one may not destroy a synagogue until a new one has been built, lest, for whatever reason, it prove impossible to build the new one.

489 On the use of Temple funds for public works in Jerusalem, see the note on "water" at 18.60. For Josephus's references to "white stone" in *Antiquities*, which is more accurate than "marble," which is mentioned in parallels in *War* (where this particular passage has, however, no parallel), see Fischer and Stein 1994. For the suggestion that it was the Roman notions (e.g. Suetonius, *Aug.* 28.3) of Josephus's assistants for *War* (*Apion* 1.50) that created that book's references to "marble," see D. R. Schwartz 2015a.

490 Perhaps the son of Theophilus b. Ananus (18.123; 19.297); see VanderKam 2004: 487.

491 That is, in addition to his serving as high priest; cf. 18.31.

492 For this sense of διηγέομαι, in other passages in which Josephus introduces lengthy excurses, see, for example, 18.129, 310.

493 That lists of high priests, and of other priests as well, were preserved over long periods of time is mentioned by Josephus, with some pride, at *Ant.* 13.78 and *Apion* 1.36, and reflected by his account of his own genealogy, as he found it "in the public documents" (*Life* 6). It is also reflected by such passages as Ezra 7:1–5. Note especially the opening of *Ant.* 11.297, where the reference to Jehoiarib b. Eliashib, concerning whose tenure Josephus has nothing to report and so his name functions

this office, and how many there were until the end of the war.[494] **225** To begin: it is said that Moses's brother Aaron was the first of all who served as high priests to God, and that when he died his sons immediately inherited the position, and that after them the office remained [the prerogative] of all of their descendants. **226** For that reason, it is also [our] ancestral tradition that no one may be high priest who is not of the blood of Aaron; a person of other descent, even if he should happen to be king, may not attain to the high priesthood.[495] **227** Now the number of all of the high priests, beginning with Aaron, who was (as we said) the first, down to Phanasus, the high priest appointed by those engaged in civil strife during the war,[496] is eighty-three. **228** Of these, [only[497]] thirteen served as high priests during the period from Moses's times in the desert, when the tabernacle Moses built for God stood, until the entry into Judea, where King Solomon erected the sanctuary to God.[498] **229** For at first they held the high priesthood until the end of their lives,[499] but later on they succeeded to it even from living [incumbents]. Those thirteen, being descendants of the two sons of Aaron,[500] received the position in succession.[501] And their constitution[502] was at first an aristocracy, thereafter a monarchy, and the third one was rule by kings.[503] **230** The number of years during which the thirteen ruled,[504] from the day our fathers left Egypt under the leadership of Moses until the construction of the sanctuary that King Solomon erected in Jerusalem, was six hundred and twelve years.[505]

only as a place-holder representing a generation, reflects Josephus's use of such a list; so too 18.34. On the present list, see esp. Hölscher 1940 and Gußmann 2008: 273–286. For a list of discrepancies between data in the pre-Herodian part of the present list and those found elsewhere in *Antiquities*, which shows that Josephus, at least for the early period, did not create the list by assembling his own data, and suggests he depended on another extant source, see Hölscher 1916: 1989–1990.

494 On the use of the definite article here with no further identification, cf. the note on "the" at §184. Actually, the present list goes until the destruction of the Temple (§250). Whatever was left of the war after that (as recounted in *War* 7, including the long Masada story), it left no place for high priests.

495 Here Josephus has simplified matters: since he is discussing only the high priesthood, he formulates the limitation to sons of Aaron as if it regarded the high priesthood alone. In fact, tradition allowed only sons of Aaron to be priests, not just high priests—as Josephus himself emphasizes, especially in his history of the divided kingdom; note his additions to the biblical text at *Ant.* 8.228//1 Kings 12:31 and *Ant.* 9.224//2 Chronicles 26:19.

496 For the story of this alleged country bumpkin, who was made high priest by sacrilegious rebels, see *War* 4.152–157, which has a rabbinic parallel at *t. Kippurim* 1:6 (ed. Lieberman, 222); see VanderKam 2004: 487–489, also D. Baratz in Ilan and Noam 2017: 2.665–672. Rajak (2002: 132–333) sees in the rabbinic accounts, which tend to negate Josephus's portrayal of him as a low-class boor, "a clear demonstration of the historian's prejudice."

497 This addition is entailed by §229, which explains why they were so few. For a similar case, see §§242–243.

498 The formulation is somewhat sloppy, as if Solomon built the Temple immediately after the entry into Judea. Josephus will clarify this at §230.

499 The early practice of holding the office for life explains how so few could fill such a long period.

500 I.e., the two surviving sons; see Lev 10:1–2//*Ant.* 3.209.

501 Given the opening of §228, Josephus seems to mean that each of these thirteen inherited the position only upon the death of his predecessor.

502 In line with a Greek tradition especially developed by Aristotle and Polybius, Josephus keeps track of the type of constitutions that characterized the Jewish polity; note especially *Ant.* 6.83–85, 11.111–113, and 14.41, 91; *Apion* 2.164; D. R. Schwartz 1983/84; Mason 2012: 136–147.

503 Josephus distinguishes here between the "aristocratic" constitution in the days of Moses and Joshua (as in *Ant.* 6.83); the rule of the Judges, who ruled "alone" (hence were "monarchs," as is explicit at §261 and 11.112) but not as kings; and the rule by kings, which began with Saul (*Ant.* 6.83, 11.112).

504 On such use of ἄρχω, which is common in this summary (§§238, 245, 246; note also the use of ἀρχή of the high priesthood at §249), as elsewhere in Josephus, see the note on "ruled" at §238.

505 But 1 Kings 6:1 states that 480 years went by between the Exodus from Egypt and Solmon's construction of the Temple. While the present figure, 612, reappears at *Apion* 2.19, at *Ant.* 8.61 the figure is 592, and the

(10.2) 231 After those thirteen high priests, the[506] eighteen[507] held the high priesthood in Jerusalem[508] from the days of King Solomon, passing it down one to the next[509] until Nebuchadnezzar, king of the Babylonians, campaigned against the city, burned the Temple, exiled our nation to Babylonia,[510] and took the high priest Josadakes[511] captive.[512] 232 The period of time during which they were high priests was four hundred and sixty-six years, six months and ten days[513]—during which period the Jews were ruled by kings.[514]

---

latter is also assumed by *Ant.* 10.147, which has the period from the Exodus to the destruction of the First Temple being 1062 years; since that same text says the Temple existed for 470 years, that leaves, as does 8.61, 592 years for the period from the Exodus until its construction. As for the discrepancy between 612 and 592, both of which are thus attested twice: if we do not simply assume that Josephus had two different traditions, which is unlikely, we might suspect that the data reflect some doubt concerning the length of the reign of Saul (concerning which the text of 1 Samuel 13:1 is notoriously problematic). Namely, at *Ant.* 10.143 Josephus assigned Saul only twenty years, but at 6.378 he assigned him 22 + 18 years, i.e., forty. At 6.378, however, the Latin version assigns him 2 + 18 years, i.e., twenty, as at 10.143. Perhaps, then, we should assume that (a) Josephus originally assigned Saul twenty years, and held the total period from the Exodus to the construction of the Temple was 592 years, but (b) Christian copyists, who preferred to assign Saul forty *as is stated at Acts 13:21*, corrected Josephus's text at *Ant.* 6.378 and correspondingly added twenty years to the total stated here and at *Apion* 2.19, but failed to correct the data at 8.61 and 10.147. For that suggestion, see Rappaport 1930: 51. For more discussion, see Milikowsky 2002: 191–197.

506 This definite article (οἱ) is puzzling, and several witnesses indeed omit it.

507 So too *Sifre Numbers* §131 (ed. Horovitz, 173); *y. Yoma* 1.38c; and *b. Yoma* 9a. At *Ant.* 10.151–153 Josephus gives their names—but only of seventeen, down to Josedek. Here he counts eighteen, because he includes Josedek's son Jesus among this first group, just as he excludes him from the "fifteen" mentioned at §234. How Josephus related, if he did, to 1 Chronicles 6:10–15, which lists only nine, is unknown.

508 Josephus's text here, Μετὰ δὲ τοὺς δεκατρεῖς ἀρχιερέας ἐκείνους οἱ δέκα καὶ ὀκτὼ τὴν ἀρχιερωσύνην ἔσχον ἀπὸ Σολόμωνος βασιλέως ἐν Ἱεροσολύμοις αὐτὴν διαδεξάμενοι, is somewhat ambiguous. Feldman (1965: 511) and Schalit (1963: 371) link "in Jerusalem" to Solomon, in accordance with the order of Josephus's words, but on the one hand, there is no apparent reason to specify that Solomon was king in Jerusalem and, on the other hand, we see at §237,

as elsewhere (e.g., 2 Macc 3:9; see D. R. Schwartz 2008: 193), the notion that the high priest was "of the city."

509 At *Ant.* 10.153, after listing all the high priests from Solomon until the destruction of the First Temple, Josephus emphasizes that "in all of these cases, sons succeeded their fathers to the high priesthood." For his pride about that, see also 13.78, as well as the formulaic repetitions in the list at 10.152–153. Cf. the note on "ancestral" at 18.172.

510 It is remarkable that here and at §233, Babylonia is rendered as Βαβυλών, rather than Βαβυλωνία, although the latter was usual in *Ant.* 18 (§§104, 310, 311, 313, 318, 331, 337, 379), apart from the two passages in which Josephus seems to be referring to the city of Babylon (18.359, 373; see the note on "Babylon" at 18.359). Apart from pointing to differential editing, it might be, given the nature of the present list, that ultimately it is the fact that Hebrew has only one topnym, *babel*, for both the country and the city, that lies behind the usage here.

511 A few witnesses give the name the same Hebrew way it is given in §234.

512 1 Chronicles 6:15//*Ant.* 10.150. Actually, as VanderKam (2004: 18–19) notes, Jehozadak's father was serving as high priest when the Temple was destroyed, so Jehozadak did not serve as high priest. But Josephus calls him high priest at 10.150, 154, as also here. On such general usage, see the note on "Joazar" at 18.3. In this case, moreover, the title imparts some desirable continuity; see the note on "Josedek" at §234.

513 Compare *Ant.* 10.143, where Josephus states that the Davidic dynasty reigned for six months more than 514 years, and that includes, as it states, twenty of Saul and, presumably, forty of David (*Ant.* 7.389). That leaves only 454 years for the period beginning with Solomon, less than the 466 mentioned here. Moreover, given that the construction of the temple took seven years and Solomon began the project only a few years into his reign (1 Kings 7:38; *Ant.* 10.99), the present figure should be even lower—bringing it close to the 410 years posited by the Talmud (*b. Yoma* 9a). Modern estimates are somewhat shorter.

514 As is said at §229. Here one sees clearly the distinction between the high-priestly leadership, on the one hand, and rule, on the other. Cf. the note on "high priests" at §251.

233 After a period of seventy years of captivity[515] under the Babylonians, Cyrus, king of the Persians, again released the Jews from Babylonia to their native land and allowed them to re-erect the sanctuary.[516] **234** Jesus the son of Josedek,[517] who was one of the captives who returned, then took over the high priesthood. He and his descendants—fifteen in all[518]—held [the position] until [the days of] King Antiochus Eupator—during which period, of four hundred and fourteen years,[519] they were governed democratically.[520]

(10.3) 235 It was first[521] the abovementioned Antiochus and his general Lysias who put an end to a high priesthood of Onias, who was also named Menelaus,[522] killing him in Beroea[523] and appointing Jacimus high priest: he was an Aaronite, but not of the [high-priestly]

---

515 The same number of years is stated quite prominently in the first line of *Ant.* 11. Actually, however, fewer than fifty years went by between the destruction of the First Temple (586 BCE) and Cyrus's proclamation (ca. 538 BCE). Josephus's figure is based, apparently, on the assumption that Jeremiah's prophecy of seventy years of exile (Jer 25:11–12; 29:10; *Ant.* 10.112) was fulfilled precisely, as he indeed emphasizes at the opening of *Ant.* 11.

516 As in his version of Cyrus's edict at 11.4, here too Josephus has Cyrus refer to the construction of the ναός. Usually, however, Josephus uses τὸ ἱερόν of the Temple in general, reserving ναός specifically for the Sanctuary (*hekhal*), its central building. See Joüon 1935 and the notes on "Temple" at 18.29 and on "God" at 18.261.

517 Evidently Josephus expects readers to realize that Jesus was the son of the last pre-exilic high priest (§231), thus indicating basic continuity. On this Jesus, see VanderKam 2004: 18–42.

518 For a reconstruction of the list, from Joiakim (who succeeded Jesus; see the note on "eighteen" at §231) to Alcimus, see VanderKam 2004: 491.

519 This figure, which in our terms takes us back from Antiochus Eupator's accession to the throne late in 164 BCE to 578 BCE, seems to be calculated, not from the return from Babylonian exile after Cyrus's edict but, rather, from the destruction of the First Temple a few decades earlier, which we date to 586 BCE. Similarly, at *Ant.* 13.301 Josephus states that 481 years (the parallel at *War* 1.70 reads 471) and three months went by between the return from Babylonia and Aristobulus I's accession to the throne in 104 BCE. If we assume that there too Josephus confused the return from Babylonia with the destruction of the First Temple, we arrive in the same vicinity. Elsewhere, however, it seems that Josephus—as other Jews (cf. Daniel 10:1 + 11:2–3; *b. Abodah Zarah* 9a)—thought the Persian period (the Second Temple period prior to the days of Alexander) was much shorter than it really was; see D. R. Schwartz 1990b: 184–185.

520 Contrast *Ant.* 11.111, which characterizes the constitution during this period as "aristocratic and oligarchic," a statement that Josephus explains as pointing to rule by high priests. It appears that δημοκρατία here has the negative meaning of "without kings" (contrast the end of §232), which is the way the term functions the other times it is used in *Antiquities* (19.162, 173, 187); see the note on "democracy" at 19.162.

521 The formulation seems to be clumsy, for what Josephus really means, and what he emphasizes by opening the sentence with πρῶτος, is that this was the first time anyone removed a serving high priest from office. Antiochus Eupator's priority in this is also emphasized, similarly, at 15.40–41, which also lists two later cases.

522 For this equation see also *Ant.* 12.239, 383; cf. the note on "as his father" at §236. But the identification of Menelaus as Onias has no basis in 2 Maccabees, which is our only other source about Menelaus, and the fact that Josephus himself claims at *Ant.* 12.237–239 that Menelaus had a brother named Onias (namely, Onias III) makes it highly unlikely that Menelaus too was named Onias. Rather, 2 Maccabees identifies Menelaus as the brother of Onias's rival, Simon, who in turn was identified as a Benjaminite (or, according to the Latin text, a member of the priestly clan of Bilgah; see 2 Macc 4:23 and 3:4, also D. R. Schwartz 2008: 95–96). As for the origin of Josephus's confusion, Stern (1991: 45–46) suggested that Josephus's source identified Menelaus as Onias IV's "uncle" (θεῖος) and Josephus assumed that meant "his father's brother" whereas in fact it meant "his mother's brother."

523 For the execution of Menelaus in Beroea (Aleppo), by Lysias (Antiochus V's vizier), see also *Ant.* 12.384–385 and 2 Macc 13:3–8. This is one of the few data in 2 Maccabees shared by Josephus although without parallel in 1 Maccabees; see D. R. Schwartz 2008: 86–87.

house.⁵²⁴ **236** For that reason Onias, who was the nephew of the deceased Onias and had the same name as his father,⁵²⁵ having gone to Egypt and been received in friendship by Ptolemy Philometor and his wife Cleopatra, convinced them to build in the Heliopolitan district⁵²⁶ a sanctuary to God, very similar to the one in Jerusalem, and to install him as [its] high priest.⁵²⁷ **237** But I have frequently reported about the temple constructed in Egypt.⁵²⁸ As for Jacimus, after three years⁵²⁹ in the high priesthood he died. He was not succeeded by anyone; rather, for seven years the city⁵³⁰ remained without a high priest.⁵³¹ **238** However, after the sons of Asamonaios had been entrusted with leadership of the nation and made war against the Macedonians, they appointed Jonathan as high priest,⁵³² and he

524 That Alcimus (as he is named in 1 Macc 7 and 2 Macc 14) was an Aaronite is explicit in 1 Macc 7:14; that he was not of the high-priestly family is explicit in *Ant.* 12.387.

525 That is, this Onias was, respectively, the son and nephew of two brothers named Onias. This corresponds to Josephus's statement at *Ant.* 12.237–238 that Onias III, the son of Simon, had two brothers, Jesus and Onias, of whom the former changed his name to Jason and the latter—to Menelaus. See the note on "Menelaus" at §235. At *War* 7.423, however, Josephus states that it was Onias son of Simon, that is, Onias III, who founded the Temple of Onias in Egypt. For detailed discussion of this issue, culminating in the suggestion that *War* is correct and Onias IV is only a figment of Josephan confusion, see Piotrkowski 2019: esp. 79–102.

526 Heliopolis, in the eastern Nile delta, north of Cairo. Concerning the location of the temple, of which no remains have yet been found, see Piotrkowski 2019: 346–350.

527 For Josephus's "overtly miso-Oniad" (Piotrkowski 2019: 54) version of Onias IV's appeal to the Egyptian monarchs (arguing that a multiplicity of temples engenders mutual hostility among their devotees and therefore asking for permission to build yet another one!) and their approval, see *Ant.* 13.65–71. It pertains only to permission to build the temple, not to the appointment of Onias as a high priest, but perhaps that should be taken for granted, given both his pedigree and his role as founder of the new temple.

528 See *War* 1.33; 7.421–436; *Ant.* 12.387–388; 13.62–73. On Onias's Temple in general, see Capponi 2007 and Piotrkowski 2019.

529 This probably means "in the third year." According to 1 Maccabees (7:1 and 9:54), Alcimus became high priest in 151 of the Seleucid Era (henceforth SE), i.e., 162/161 BCE, and died in 153 SE (160/159 BCE).

530 See the note on "in Jerusalem" at §231.

531 At *Ant.* 12.414 Josephus reports that Judas Maccabeus became high priest after Alcimus died, at 12.434 he says Judas served as high priest for three years until his death, and at 13.46 he notes that when Jonathan became high priest, it was after the position had been vacant for four years. That notion, which means seven years passed between the death of Alcimus and Jonathan's rise to the high priesthood, derives simply from the combination of 1 Macc 9:54 (Alcimus died in 153 SE [153/152 BCE]) and 1 Macc 10:1, 21 (Jonathan's appointment to the high priesthood in 160 SE). Here, however, we see that Josephus has given up his earlier claim (which has no basis in 1 or 2 Maccabees) that Judas was ever high priest, so the "intersacerdotium" has grown to seven years. For speculation about who (if anyone) was really high priest in Jerusalem during the seven-year "intersacerdotium," which of course comes along with speculation about why someone preferred to ignore him, and what that might have to do with the origin of the Qumran sect, see VanderKam 2004: 244–250 and D. R. Schwartz 2022: 313.

532 This does not suggest that the Hasmoneans had previously appointed a high priest and now did so again; in the Greek, "again" (πάλιν) opens the sentence, right after the statement that the city went for seven years without a high priest, and all it means it that again a high priest was appointed—namely, as the continuation reports, by the Hasmoneans. Note, however, that Jonathan, although indeed a Hasmonean, was not appointed by the Hasmoneans; he was appointed by Alexander Balas (1 Macc 10:20–21//*Ant.* 13.45–46). Hasmonean independence began only under his successor, Simon (1 Macc 13:41–42). For a similar inaccuracy, note 17.162, where Josephus states (in a speech ascribed to Herod) that the Hasmoneans ruled as kings (ἐβασίλευον) for 125 years prior to Herod. These might be innocent generalizations reflecting the knowledge that most Hasmonean rulers were sovereign. Perhaps, however, a role was played by the fact that Josephus's claim to be

ruled[533] for seven years.[534] **239** When he died as the result of a plot and an ambush engineered by Tryphon, as I explained somewhere above,[535] Simon his brother took over the high priesthood. **240** When he too was done away with by craft, by his son-in-law at a symposium,[536] a son, named Hyrcanus,[537] succeeded him after he had held the high priesthood for one year more than his brother.[538] Hyrcanus enjoyed the position[539] for thirty-one years;[540] when he died as an old man[541] he left the succession to Judas, who was also called Aristobulus.[542] **241** The latter was succeeded by his brother Alexander, after he died of a

---

linked to the Hasmoneans (*Ant.* 16.187) was via Jonathan's daughter (*Life* 2–4), a datum that will have made him especially unwilling to sully his credentials. (While in *Life* 4 it might well be that Josephus is confused and should have referred to Alexander Janneus, whose Hebrew name was Jonathan, he identifies her as the daughter of the Jonathan who was first Hasmonean high priest and was Simon's brother.)

533 This plain use of ἄρχω for serving as high priest, as elsewhere (see the note on "ruled" at §230), corresponds to the nature of things in the Hasmonean period, even before the Hasmoneans undertook such a quasi-title as ἡγούμενος (1 Macc 13:8; 14:41) or moved all the way to "king" (*Ant.* 13.301). For the real meaning of high priesthood for Jonathan, see esp. 1 Macc 10:21; for Simon, see 1 Macc 16:11–12. As Arenhoevel (1967: 45–46) observed, "the priestly office did not correspond well to what the family really did; that was probably recognized by the author of 1 Maccabees himself ... of high priesthood one notices [in 1 Maccabees] nothing but the title."

534 This statement contradicts the evidence of 1 Maccabees, which states at 10:21 that Jonathan began to serve as high priest in the autumn of 160 SE and, after reporting Jonathan's death at 13:23, goes on at 13:42 to define Simon's first year as 170 SE (as does Josephus, at *Ant.* 13.213), thus giving Jonathan a full decade of rule, ca. 152–142 BCE. Most take "seven" here to be an error; for a speculative suggestion as to how it could have been born from a scribal error, see Marcus in JLCL 7.332–333, n. b. But, although *we* can depend on 1 Maccabees, §240a shows that Josephus indeed meant seven; see the note on "brother" at §240. For the rejection of a suggestion that, despite 1 Macc 10:21, Jonathan in fact began to serve only in 150 BCE, see VanderKam 2004: 256–259.

535 *Ant.* 13.191–192, on the basis of 1 Maccabees 13.

536 In general, all that is meant is a dinner, but Josephus probably uses "symposium" (lit. "drinking together"), here as in 13.228, in recognition of the fact that, according to 1 Macc 16:16, Simon and his sons were drunk when Ptolemy killed them.

537 According to *War* 1.54 and *Ant.* 13.288, where he is first introduced into Josephus's narratives, his name was

John (Johanan), although he was also called Hyrcanus. Indeed, at *War* 1.67–58 he is just "John." In *Antiquities*, however, apart from that introduction, he is always (at 7.393 and some forty times in *Ant.* 13) just "Hyrcanus," as here. But Hyrcanus II (John's grandson) is also just "Hyrcanus" (as below at §§242–245), a fact that explains why 18.91 notes, although with some exaggeration, that there were "many" high priests named Hyrcanus. In rabbinic literature, in contrast, we consistently read of "John the high priest," not of Hyrcanus; see, for example, in the Mishnah: *Ma'aser Sheni* 5:15, *Sotah* 9:10, *Parah* 3:4, *Yadayim* 4:6.

538 That is, Simon served as high priest for eight years, as is said explicitly at *Ant.* 13.228—from 170 SE (1 Macc 13:42) until 177 SE (1 Macc 16:14), i.e., 143/2–136/5 BCE. See the note on "seven years" at §239.

539 Same phrase, τῆς τιμῆς ἀπολαύσας, above §198; for the high-priestly office as a τιμή, see the note on "office" at 18.17.

540 As is also said explicitly at *Ant.* 13.299–from 135/4 BCE (1 Macc 16:14) until 105/4; for details, see D. R. Schwartz 2022: 405, n. 5.

541 If indeed it was claimed, albeit maliciously, that John Hyrcanus was born to a mother who had been a captive in the days of Antiochus Epiphanes (*Ant.* 13.292), i.e., in the days of the Hasmonean revolt in the 160s, he will not have been much older than sixty at his death. It might be that Josephus's somewhat exaggerated phrasing means simply to reflect the fact that, as opposed to Jonathan, Simon, and Aristobulus, John died an untroubled death. Such a point would correspond well with John's general function, for Josephus, as the idyllic apogee of the Hasmonean dynasty; he achieved what no one else ever did (*Ant.* 13.299–300; //*War* 1.68–69), but after his death things quickly went downhill.

542 That Aristobulus was also called Judas is not stated elsewhere by Josephus, but has recently been confirmed by numismatic evidence; see Shaham 2020. It is interesting to wonder what led Josephus to introduce, here and in the next paragraph, a Hebrew name he ignores elsewhere, in the same context in which he refers both to Hyrcanus and Alexander without repeating

disease[543] after holding both the high priesthood and kingship—for Judas was the first to crown himself with a diadem[544]—for a single year.[545]

(10.4) 242 After Alexander ruled as king and served as high priest for twenty-seven years[546] he departed this life, allowing his wife to determine who would serve as high priest.[547] She gave the high priesthood to Hyrcanus,[548] while she herself ruled the kingdom for nine years, until she died.[549] Hyrcanus her son held the high priesthood for [only[550]] the same number of years. 243 For after her death, his brother Aristobulus fought him and, after defeating him, took that office away from him,[551] he himself ruling as king and as high priest of the nation. 244 When Pompey came and took the city of the Jerusalemites by force in the third year, and in the same number of months, of Aristobulus's reign,[552] he sent him with his children, in fetters, to Rome; restoring the high priesthood to Hyrcanus, he allowed him the leadership of the nation[553] but prevented him from wearing a crown. 245 Hyrcanus, in addition

their Hebrew names (John and Jonathan/Jannai, respectively), which are indeed stated elsewhere in *Antiquities* (13.228, 320).

543 For a dramatic ("pathetic") account of Aristobulus's disease and death, see *Ant.* 13.314–317.

544 Josephus underlines Aristobulus's taking of the royal crown very emphatically at *Ant.* 13.301//*War* 1.70.

545 104/103 BCE; for the termini, see D. R. Schwartz 2022: 405, n. 5. That Aristobulus ruled only one year is also stated by Josephus at *Ant.* 13.318//*War* 1.84. On the mistaken chronology at *War* 1.70//*Ant.* 13.301, see the note on "four hundred and fourteen years" at §234.

546 That Alexander reigned for 27 years (103–76 BCE) is also stated at *Ant.* 13.404//*War* 1.106.

547 That it was Alexander's widow, Salome Alexandra, who appointed Hyrcanus II to the high priesthood, is stated at *Ant.* 13.408//*War* 1.109. But Josephus's account of Alexander's deathbed instructions to his wife (13.400–404) focuses on relations with the Pharisees and does not address this point. The same is true of the talmudic parallel to the latter story; see *b. Sotah* 22b, along with T. Ilan in Ilan and Noam 2017: 1.308–317.

548 On his name, see above, the note on "Hyrcanus" at §240. Note, with Ilan 1987/88: 10–11, that we do not know that his Hebrew name was (as his grandfather) John (Johanan), nor, indeed, whether he in fact had a Hebrew name.

549 That Salome ruled for nine years (76–67 BCE) is also stated at *Ant.* 13.430//*War* 1.119.

550 As at §228, this assessment seems to be required by the explanatory γάρ ("for") that opens the next clause.

551 See *Ant.* 14.4–7, 97. Here, in this survey of the high-priestly succession, as also in that detailed discussion in

Ant. 14, Josephus fails to repeat the statement at *War* 1.121 that Hyrcanus was at least allowed to retain his honors as the "king's brother"; on that designation, and esp. for the argument that it did not denote any official status (and certainly not the high priesthood), see Schalit 1939.

552 In 63 BCE; for the date of Pompey's conquest of Jerusalem, see *Ant.* 14.66. At 14.97, however, Josephus states that Aristobulus was king and high priest for three years and *six* months—and that, together with the three months of rule Josephus assigns to Hyrcanus II after their mother's death (15.180), indeed fills up (as is noted by Marcus 1943: 450–451, n. c) the time between her death and Pompey's conquest of Jerusalem. Thus, the datum given here seems to be too short (as is emphasized by Sharon 2017: 395), and the fact that it is phrased, in the Greek, not as "after two years and three months" but, rather, as "in his third year and the same number of months," suggests there might be some confusion with Antigonus, who is assigned three years and three months (§246). It might also be, as Claude Eilers pointed out to me, that Josephus (or his sources) was inconsistent as to where to place the end of Aristobulus's term, perhaps once dating it according to his arrest (14.55–57) and once according to the end of the subsequent siege of the Temple, which came, according to *War* 1.149, in the third month of the siege.

553 In his "constitutional" discussions Josephus frequently refers to the *prostasia* of the people and locates it with the high priests; see esp. §251. Usually, this seems to be only a general manner of speaking, one that compares the Jews to a collegium, without any formal content; see D. R. Schwartz 1983/84. In the present case, however, there might be some formal content as well, since according

to his first nine years,[554] ruled another twenty-four.[555] Then, after the Parthian grandees Barzabanes and Pacorus crossed the Euphrates and made war upon Hyrcanus,[556] they took him captive[557] and installed Aristobulus's son, Antigonus, as king. **246** After he ruled three years and three months[558] he was besieged and overcome by Sosius[559] and Herod; Antonius killed him after he had been taken off to Antioch.[560]

(10.5) 247 When the Romans put the kingdom into Herod's hands, he no longer appointed high priests of the Hasmonean line.[561] Rather, he gave away the position to insignificant people[562] who were of merely priestly descent[563]—apart from one exception, Aristobulus. **248** [Namely], he gave the high priesthood to Aristobulus (grandson of Hyrcanus who had been taken off by the Parthians) after he married his sister, Mariamme, seeking to capture the goodwill of the masses toward him thanks to the memory of Hyrcanus. But when he later became afraid that all would tend away from him and toward Aristobulus,[564] he killed him

---

to documents preserved in *Ant.* 14 (including §§191, 194 [quite demonstratively], 196, 200, 209), Julius Caesar referred to Hyrcanus II as the Jews' "ethnarch" (as did also Marcus Antonius—14.306, 314, 317), and such a vague authority might well be associated with such a vague (not royal) title. True, it is not clear that already Pompey endowed Hyrcanus II with that title (as is proposed by several scholars; see Sharon 2017: 127, n. 27). But however that may be, Josephus might be thinking of it. On the title, see Sharon 2010.

554 While his mother ruled (§242).

555 At 15.180, Josephus states that after Pompey restored him to the high priesthood, Hyrcanus served in that position for another forty years. That is plainly wrong, for Hyrcanus was taken captive, and mutilated so as to disqualify him from the high priesthood (14.366), in 40 BCE, which is close to twenty-four years after Pompey's activity in Judea. For suggestions concerning the datum at 15.180 (typology? polemics?), see van Henten 2014: 120, n. 1067.

556 This clearly shows the provincial and high-priestly orientation of the present text (cf. the note on "high priesthood" at §226); the Parthians had other things on their mind. On the Parthian invasion of the Roman East, which began in winter/spring 41/40 BCE, see Debevoise 1938: 108–119; Reynolds 1982; Stern 1995: 249–255; and Lanser 2021.

557 Here Josephus omits the detail given in both of his works, that Antigonus himself mutilated Hyrcanus in order to ensure that, according to the terms of Leviticus 21:17–24, he would not be able to return to the high priesthood; see *War* 1.270 and *Ant.* 14.366.

558 For relevant calculations, see Sharon 2017: 427–428 (but cf. the note on "reign" at §244). On Antigonus's rule as king and high priest, 40–37 BCE, see VanderKam 2004: 385–393. For his coins, which are the most impressive of all the Hasmonean coins, see Meshorer 2001: 50–57.

559 Gaius Sosius, who is well known from a variety of evidence; see Stern, *GLAJJ* 1.367. It is not surprising that while Josephus refers here to Sosius and Herod, Roman observers tended, naturally, to credit the former alone; see Seneca, *Suasoriae* 2.21, Tacitus, *Hist.* 5.9.1, and Cassius Dio 49.22.3 (*GLAJJ*, nos. 149, 281, 414).

560 On the execution of Antigonus, which attracted attention and fostered rumors about Herod's personal involvement, see *War* 1.357; *Ant.* 14.489–490 and 15.8–10 (quoting Strabo); Cassius Dio 49.2.6; Stern, *GLAJJ* 1.284–285 and 2.359–362; and Schalit 2001: 691–692. On the possibility that Antigonus's bones were buried in Jerusalem, see Sharon 2017: 453–459.

561 On Herod's policy, which preferred high priests from new families, even from Jewish families from abroad, who would not compete with him, see Stern in Safrai and Stern 1974–76: 1.250; 604–608 and Stern 1982: 49–55. For details on the individual high priests under Herod, see VanderKam 2004: 394–416.

562 Cf. Josephus's assertion at the opening of his autobiography that he is not of a family that is ἄσημος but, rather, of one related to the Hasmonean high priests, and note esp. *Ant.* 15.22, where Josephus explains that since Herod did not want to appoint anyone τῶν ἐπισή-μων to the high priesthood, he imported from Babylonia a priest who was τῶν ἀσημοτέρων. Note that Josephus did not identify himself as a descendant of the Hasmoneans in *War*; the closest he comes is at *War* 5.419, where he says that he was of a distinguished family. Only in *Antiquities* (16.187) and its appendix (*Life* 2–4) does he claim the Hasmonean connection. Whatever brought him to do that, it functions, *inter alia*, as part of his critique of the high priests of his day; see the notes on "death" at §181 and on "bold" at §199.

563 See the note on "by descent" at 18.103.

564 See the scene depicted at *Ant.* 15.51–52//*War* 1.437.

by engineering his drowning while swimming in Jericho, as we have already reported.[565] **249** After that he no longer[566] entrusted the high priesthood to descendants of the sons of Asamonaios.

Archelaus, Herod's son, did the same concerning the appointment of priests, and [so did] the Romans after they took over the rule of the Judeans after him.[567] **250** And so there were a total of twenty-eight [men] who served as high priests from the times of Herod until the day when Titus took[568] the sanctuary and the city and put them to the torch—a period of one hundred and seven years.[569] **251** Some of them served in their office[570] while Herod was king or in the days of his son, Archelaus.[571] After their deaths,[572] however, the constitution became an aristocracy, with the leadership of the nation being entrusted to the high priests.[573]

Let that, then, be enough about the high priests.

(11.1) 252 Gessius Florus,[574] sent by Nero as Albinus's successor, deluged the Jews with numerous calamities. He was born in Clazomenae,[575] but was accompanied by his woman, Cleopatra, who did not at all lag behind him in wickedness; through her friendship with

*Florus's
Governorship:
The Conclusion
of the Narrative*

---

565 At *Ant.* 15.50–56. A shorter account appears at *War* 1.437.

566 The use of οὐκέτι here concerning the appointment of Hasmoneans, as at §247, signals, as a *Wiederaufnahme*, that the main narrative is resuming.

567 This statement concerning the continuity from Herod to Archelaus to the Romans, concerning the high priesthood, echoes a similar one at *Ant.* 18.93.

568 Josephus's use of ἑλών corresponds to that in *War*, where it is a leitmotif denoting the final conquest of each of the three theaters of the war (north, Perea, Jerusalem: *War* 4.120, 339; 6.435). See D. R. Schwartz 2015b.

569 Both the span of years and the number of high priests are accurate. Josephus counts from Herod's conquest of Jerusalem in 37 BCE to its destruction in 70 CE, and his narratives do indeed list twenty-eight high priests; see *HJP* 2.228–232, along with VanderKam 2004: 411, n. 42 and 488.

570 The use of πολιτεύομαι here is striking; while Josephus can no longer speak of high priests "ruling," as in the Hasmonean period (see the note on "ruled" at §238), he chose a word that suggests something of the political nature of the position. This conforms to the end of the present sentence, which states that after Herod and Archelaus, it was the high priests to whom "leadership" of the people reverted. So here the verb tends more to "serve in office" than merely its usual sense (2 Macc 6:1;

Acts 23:1; see Spicq 1994: 3.131–133) of "live according to the civic laws."

571 As at §244, Josephus carefully distinguishes here between Herod, who reigned as a king (βασιλεύοντος, singular), and Archelaus, who did not. Cf. the note on "as king" at 18.93.

572 Josephus is speaking loosely here, for concerning Archelaus what mattered was not his death but, rather, his exile (*Ant.* 17.342–344).

573 As *Ant.* 11.111, this sounds as if "aristocracy" were equated with rule by high priests; note *Apion* 1.30, where the priests are termed τοὺς ἀρίστους. However, both passages actually refer to the high priests holding *prostasia*, alongside of an aristocratic government. On *prostasia*, see the note on "leadership of the nation" at §244. On Josephus's use of "aristocracy" of government by council (as is clearest at 4.223; 5.135; and 14.91), see D. R. Schwartz 1983/84: 32–34. However, Josephus apparently refers not to any regular council, for the existence of which he gives no evidence. Rather, he seems to mean that, in the absence of a king, the priests and high priests were the highest authorities among the Jews. For Josephus's general preference for priestly rule, see *Ant.* 4.224 and *Apion* 2.185–187.

574 On Florus's governorship, see Smallwood 1981: 282–292.

575 A city in Ionia, not far from the Gulf of Izmir on the western coast of Turkey.

Poppaea, Nero's woman,[576] he had obtained the position.[577] **253** He was so evil and violent in the exercise of his authority that the Jews, in the depths of their sufferings, praised Albinus as if he had been a benefactor.[578] **254** For he had [at least] tried to hide his wickedness and taken care that it not be discovered by all, but Gessius Florus paraded his wickedness toward our nation as if he had been sent so as to demonstrate his wickedness, leaving aside no type of rapine nor of any unjust punishment.[579] **255** For he was merciless[580] in the face of [circumstances that should arouse] pity,[581] nor could any amount of gain satisfy him—for to him there was no difference between a lot and a little,[582] and he even made common cause with brigands. In fact, many did the same[583] fearlessly, secure in their knowledge that he would leave them safe in return for receiving his portion [of their takings]—and it was not at all middling.[584] **256** As for the unfortunate Jews—unable to endure the devastations

---

576 Given Josephus's frequent concern to distinguish between marriage and less formal liaisons (see the note on "wife" at 18.344), and given his characterization of this Cleopatra and Poppaea's reputation (see the note on "god-fearing" at §195), his use of γυνή rather than γαμετή for these women may be disparaging. Poppaea became Nero's wife in 62, after he divorced and killed his first wife, Claudius's daughter Octavia (above, §153). See Griffin 2000: 98–100.

577 That is, although Florus began far from Rome, his marriage opened up opportunities for him. For Florus's marriage as an example of the way eastern or Greek parvenus could advance themselves by marriage with spouses with the right connections in Rome, see Levick 1967: 105–106. On the phenomenon that although until the days of Claudius most Roman governors of Judea were of Italian origin, from then on Greeks become prominent among them, and on its implications (a natural sympathy for, and tendency to take the part of, the Syro-Greek population of Judea?), see Stern 1974a: 318–319. Such a tendency, to the extent it existed (Stern points to only three of the last seven prefects, Tiberius Julius Alexander, Felix, and Florus, and of them the first was of Jewish descent, even if he "became in all respects a Hellenized oriental"), would dovetail neatly with the natural tendency of auxiliary troops at the governor's disposal; see the note on "Judeans" at 19.366.

578 For this same type of comparison ("A was terrible, but B made even A look good"), cf. *War* 7.262–263. This same comparison of Albinus to Florus, including the following statement about Albinus hiding his crimes while Florus flaunted them, is found in *War* 2.277: Josephus reports that although Albinus had been terrible, in comparison to Florus he was wonderful. As we have seen, however, in *Antiquities* Josephus's main account of Albinus focuses on Jewish sinfulness and that improved Albinus's image; see the note on "Sicarii" at §204. Now, moving toward the end of his story, and after the long excursus on the high priesthood, Josephus reverts to his narrative line in *War*: Albinus and Florus goaded the Jews into rebellion. Compare Philo's assertion (*Leg.* 199) that a wicked governor might seek to provoke his subjects into

misbehaving so as to deny them the imperial goodwill necessary to allow them to accuse him of his misdeeds.

579 Note, with Smallwood (1981: 283–284) and McLaren (1998: 110–111), that Josephus gives, in *Antiquities*, no details to flesh out his broad condemnation of Florus here. Its purpose is to contribute to Josephus's effort to impart a sense of increasing unrest, and deterioration toward explosion, and to place the blame on Roman misgovernment; see esp. §257. (This assignment of blame, which is already found in *War*, competes with another, most prominent in *Antiquities*, that blames the Jews themselves; see the note on "Sicarii" at §204.) Note, moreover, that already at the outset of Roman rule, at 18.25, Josephus had informed his readers that things would explode under Florus, and he reminded them of that in a very prominent place, namely, the very end of Book 19 (§366); now, after punctuating Book 20 with numerous pointers to the deterioration toward explosion (§§124, 160, 172, 210, and 214), that circle is completed. For an egregious case of the tendency of modern scholarship, problematized by McLaren, to follow Josephus closely, not only in his reports of events, but also in his interpretation of them and evaluation of individuals, see *HJP* 1.470: this conclusion of Schürer's survey of the Roman governors of Judea is hardly more than a paraphrase of Josephus's account here and its brief parallel at *War* 2.277–279.

580 This adjective, ἀτεγκτος, appears elsewhere in Josephus only in *War* 5.417.

581 Florus thus appears to be even worse than Caligula (19.36, 38) and barbarian Germans (19.141–142).

582 I.e., nothing was too small for him to take lawlessly.

583 Apparently: engaged in brigandage.

584 The meaning of the last clause is not clear. Feldman (1965: 523) treats it as an independent sentence commenting on the whole situation: "There was no limit in sight" (or: "And this was intolerable"). It seems likelier, however, despite the move from plural to singular (μέρεσιν τοῦτο), that it characterizes the size of Florus's shares of the brigands' takings.

wrought by the brigands, they were all driven out of their homes[585] and forced to flee, considering it better to live among gentiles, no matter where. 257 What more need be said? For Florus forced us to start the war against the Romans,[586] since we considered it better to perish all at once rather than bit by bit. And so it happened[587] that the war began, in the second year of Florus's governorship, the twelfth of Nero's reign.[588] 258 But concerning those things we were forced to do or endured[589] as suffering[590]—those who want to know about such things in detail may read in the books I wrote about the Judean war.

(12.1) 259 Here, then, shall end my *Antiquities*,[591] after which I began to write the *War*.[592] It comprises that which has been passed down,[593] concerning the period from the first genesis of humanity until the twelfth year of Nero's rule, with regard to the things that happened to us Jews[594]—in Egypt, Syria and Palestine:[595] 260 what we suffered[596] at the

Conclusion of Antiquities

---

585 On this passage and its parallel in *War* 2.279, see D. R. Schwartz 2013: 39–43.

586 For this important apologetical theme, that the rebellion was forced upon the Jews by Florus, see already 1.6, also 20.258 and *Life* 27. Even Tacitus echoes this theme, noting at *Hist.* 5.9.3–10.1 that, despite all the terrors of Felix's days (see the note on "against the Judeans" at §182), the Judeans' patience lasted until Florus's governorship and only then did war break out. See Bilde 1979.

587 On καὶ δή as illustrating the preceding statement or what it implies, see the note on "for example" at 18.257.

588 For such dating in more than one way as a marker of an important historical moment, cf. 8.61–62, *War* 2.284, Luke 3:1–2, and Thucydides 2.2. That the war broke out in the twelfth year of Nero's reign is also stated at *War* 2.284, although there it is equated not to a year of Florus's tenure but, rather, to the seventeenth year of Agrippa II's reign. Nero's twelfth year began in October 65; counting back seventeen years places the beginning of Agrippa II's reign in 49/50 CE, which is about what we would expect on the basis of 20.104. See D. R. Schwartz 1992: 225 and Mason 2008: 183–184, n. 1394, and 231, nn. 1824–1825.

589 For such use of ὑπομένω, which combines both the passage of time (since the beginning of the war at the time mentioned in the preceding line) and suffering, cf. §§116, 193.

590 See the note on "what we suffered" at §260.

591 On this conclusion, see Laqueur 1920: 3–6 and Barish 1978. Laqueur thought that §§259–266 are the conclusion of a second edition of *Antiquities*, which appeared along with the *Life* (as is promised at §266) after the death of Agrippa II in 100 (since Agrippa's death is mentioned at *Life* 359–360), while §§267–268 are the conclusion of the first edition of 93/94. Barish, however, saw §§267–268 as merely concluding the present conclusion and doubted, as many others, that late date for Agrippa II's death, which basically derives only from the late testimony of Photius. For a review of the evidence and arguments, one that leans toward the later date for Agrippa II's death, see

D. R. Schwartz 1992: 243–282. But accepting the later date for Agrippa's death need not entail Laqueur's conclusion about two endings and two editions.

592 As is obvious from the end of the preceding sentence, as well as from other considerations (including the fact that according to *Life* 359–361 and *Apion* 1.50–51 he presented *War* to Vespasian, who died in 79), Josephus in fact wrote *War* well before *Antiquities*. What he means here must be only that *War* narrates events that occurred after those dealt with in *Antiquities*.

593 For dependence upon *paradosis* as legitimating, see A. I. Baumgarten 1987.

594 On Josephus's use of first-person plural of the Jews, as also below at §264, see the note on "among us" at 18.64.

595 For Josephus it is quite exceptional to refer to Judea as "Palestine." Feldman (1990: 11–12) states that Josephus almost always uses the term for Philistia, the only exception being the present passage. An obvious explanation for the exception is that his reference to *Ioudaioi* all over would have been perplexing had he gone on to refer to "Judea." That is, Josephus realized that his readers would tend to take *Ioudaioi* as if it referred to people resident in or from Judea, what we would call "Judeans," but wanted to avoid that, in recognition of their ubiquity. Therefore, when referring to those *Ioudaioi* who came from what he normally called "Judea," he chose a toponym that did not point out any special relationship between *Ioudaioi* and that place. A similar phenomenon may be seen among other writers of the first century, who seem to have had problems with "Judea" because of their awareness of *Ioudaioi* who were not there; they too prefer to use "Palaestina" or "Idumea" (facilitated by Herod's Idumean roots); see D. R. Schwartz 2005: 69. Indeed, within two generations Rome, following the Bar-Kokhba Revolt, would change the name of the province from Judea to Syria Palaestina. See Smallwood 1981: 463–464, and, on Hadrian's motives, Mason 2016c: 245.

596 While "happened to" at §259 need not imply passivity, the present summary of Jewish history, as if (as

hands of the Assyrians and the Babylonians, and how we were treated by[597] Persians and Macedonians—and after them, Romans. And I believe I have composed the whole work with complete accuracy[598] in every regard. **261** I have also striven to preserve the written list[599] of the high priests who served over two thousand years.[600] I have also done the same, without error, concerning the succession of kings and their acts, reporting[601] also the constitutions and rules of monarchs,[602] things concerning all of which the holy books contain the record—for that is what I promised to do at the outset of this history.[603]

262 And I might say, encouraged as I am by the completion of my undertaking, that no one else, neither Jew nor gentile, would have been able, even if he so desired, to present to the Greeks[604] a work[605] as accurate and detailed[606] as this one. **263** For I am—so agree the members of my people—far beyond them with regard to the native[607] learning,[608] and

---

already at §258) it is all a matter of suffering at the hands of others, unambiguously does. Cf. E. S. Gruen 2011.

597 Two manuscripts (AE) add δεινά, thus characterizing what the last three empires did to the Jews, or at least what the Persians and the Macedonians did to them, as "terrible"; Feldman (1965: 524–525) adopts the word and renders "the harsh treatment." That would allow all of the empires to come under the general statement about "what we suffered," but if that were the intention, why break up the list? Hence, it seems wiser to exclude the word, with Niese, and to conclude that Josephus summarizes Judean history of the First Temple period (when they had a state of their own) as one in which foreign empires were by definition oppressive, while the relations of the Judeans with the empires of the Second Temple period, when Judeans generally had no state of their own, were more nuanced.

598 Cf. the note on "truth as our goal" at §157.

599 For such written records, see the note on "high priesthood" at §224.

600 Not surprisingly, this is somewhat exaggerated, even according to Josephus's own data in the high-priestly summary (§§224–251), which total less than 1700.

601 Feldman (1965: 526) adopts here Ambrosianus's additional reference to the kings' ἀγωγή ("conduct"), but it is not clear to what that might refer in addition to their "acts," and at 18.169, the last time Josephus used the word, it had the concrete sense of being brought before an official. Niese (1890a: 319), following the other witnesses, and the *lectio brevior potior* principle, omits it here.

602 Given the juxtaposition to "kings" (βασιλεῖς), by "monarchs" (μονάρχες) Josephus probably means the biblical Judges; see esp. §229 and 11.112.

603 Given the reference to the holy books, Josephus is presumably referring here to his promise, at the beginning of his work (*Ant.* 1.5, 17) as elsewhere (4.196; 8.56; 10.218), not to add or detract from what is stated in the Bible, in fulfillment of the biblical admonition (Deut 4:2; 12:32). On this promise, which must be taken with a grain of salt (and anyway the biblical admonition applied to

laws, not to narrative), although conforming in general to a claim to be thorough and truthful, see Feldman 1998a: 37–46 and Cohen 1979: 27–28. For a similar claim concerning the post-biblical period, see the opening of *Ant.* 14. After documenting widespread use of the formula by others (citing esp. van Unnik 1949 and Schäublin 1974), Cohen remarks that since *Ant.* 1.17 "consists of historiographical commonplaces ... we may suppose these pronouncements are not to be taken very seriously. Probably none of the writers quoted above fulfilled his promise to present a translation only and not to add or omit anything." For the argument that Josephus, as others in his age, thought that repetition of a text required faithfulness to its content (as understood by the new writer) rather than its wording, see Inowlocki 2005.

604 Here is a clear statement about his intended audience, as already at 1.5, 9, and 10–17 (where he compares his project to that of the Jews who translated the Torah for Ptolemy Philadelphus), also, very explicitly, at 16.174. See the Introduction at nn. 34–35.

605 Here too Josephus is probably thinking of his introduction, which repeatedly terms the work a πραγματεία (1.5, 17, 25). But he uses the term the same way frequently, whether of his own works (4.198; 12.245; 13.173; *Apion* 1.50, 54) or of those of others (*Life* 336–337). For the history of this sense of the term, see Krebs 2015: 514.

606 For this full sense of ἀκριβῶς, see the note on "detail" at 18.129.

607 After τὴν ἐπιχώριον, Ambrosianus (again followed by Feldman [1965: 526] but not by Niese [1890a: 320]) adds καὶ παρ' ἡμῖν ("and among us"), but since only the next part of this paragraph refers to non-Jewish Greek learning, the result is that both of the first formulations refer only to Jewish learning, so nothing much is gained by adopting Ambrosianus's reading. Perhaps it reflects a misunderstanding inspired by παρ' ἡμῖν γάρ at the opening of the next paragraph, §264. Cf. the note on "brought to him" at §5.

608 Josephus makes similar assertions at *Life* 9 (precocious child), *War* 3.352 (priestly education as a biblical

I have also applied myself earnestly to studies of Greek literature,[609] after taking up the study of grammar—although with regard to accurate [oral] presentation,[610] ancestral habit was [admittedly] a hindrance.[611] **264** For among us, those who are commended[612] are not those who learn the language[s] of many nations,[613] for such practice is considered to be characteristic not only of the average free man[614] but also of those slaves who desire it.[615] Rather, [we][616] testify to the wisdom of such people who know our regulations accurately and can interpret the sense[617] of the sacred writings.[618] **265** For this reason, although many have struggled in the training for this, hardly two or three have achieved the goal—and immediately they received the fruits of their labors.

---

scholar), and *Apion* 1.218. On the latter, as Josephus's assertion of his superiority in comparison to other Jewish Hellenistic writers, see D. R. Schwartz 2007a. For studies of Josephus's education, which use fewer superlatives than he did, see S. Schwartz 1990: 23–57 and Tuval 2013: 115–128.

609　Here, since it is listed as a stage after "grammar" (τὴν γραμματικὴν ἐμπειρίαν), *grammata* refers to literature and not merely the letters of the alphabet. But *grammata* in that broader sense includes poetry, so (even if Josephus did want to claim knowledge of that), Ambrosianus's "and poetry" is superfluous. As in Ambrosianus's "plus" at §264 (see the note there on "nations"), it looks like some devotee of literature added details that interested him. Cf. the note on "brought to him" at §5. See also Destinon 1904: 25, n. 1 and 26; he underlines Josephus's striking failure to claim that he learned to *write* Greek, adducing it in support of his argument for Josephus's dependence upon assistants for much of his work. On such theories, see the Introduction, at nn. 48–54.

610　It is usual to translate προφορά here as "pronunciation," and it certainly includes that. But literally it is broader, and Dionysius of Halicarnassus uses it, at *Demosthenes* 22, of the delivery of a speech, including reference to tone and the moods the orator conveys. As Price (2005a: 105) observes, it might be that Josephus is apologizing, here, for some unwillingness to read from his work in public; on such recitations, by authors, see Ogilvie 1980: 12–13; Huitink and van Henten 2009; and Mason 2011. Cf. Pliny the Younger, *Ep.* 9.34, where the author, pointing to his own lack of proficiency in reading poetry, considers asking a freedman to do so in his stead. Similarly, Swain (1996: 43–51) shows that some first- and second-century intellectuals expressed anxiety even about their written Greek.

611　For a comparable case that sounds familiar to the present writer, see *Scriptores Historiae Augustae, Septimius Severus*, chs. 1 and 19: the African-born emperor, who began studying Greek and Latin as a youth and moved to Rome already around the age of eighteen, retained an African accent in Latin even in old age. So too Quintilian (*Inst.* 1.1.13) complains about the Latin pronunciation of those who first learned Greek when they were young and became too used to Greek formulations and intonation.

612　For this sense of ἀποδέχομαι (lit. "admit," "receive"), which, Thackeray noted, is characteristic of *Antiquities* (e.g. 8.206 and 12.108, where it is parallel, respectively, to reward and to praise), see *ThLJ* 67.

613　Here too Ambrosianus has a substantial but "useless" expansion ("or who adorn their style with smoothness of diction" [trans. Feldman 1965: 529]); cf. the note on "literature" at §263.

614　That is, even one who is not an aristocrat.

615　Cf. §§183–184 on a Greek expert in writing who was a terrible villain, also Josephus's attack on Justus in *Life* 40, where he admits Justus's dexterity in language and nevertheless condemns him; note also Josephus's general complaint in the first paragraph of *War*. For similar comments on Greeks, see the note on "philosophy" at 18.9. On learned slaves, see Forbes 1955 and Harris 1989: 247–248. In the present passage, Josephus basically aligns good pronunciation alongside linguistic skill as frills that, as opposed to knowledge and truthfulness, need not guarantee quality.

616　Lit. "they." On the translation of this paragraph, see n. 89 to the Introduction.

617　For this sense of δύναμις, see 3.90, where too it is the meaning of a text that is meant, as distinguished from its wording.

618　Josephus boasts about his own skill at interpreting the Bible at *War* 3.352 and *Apion* 1.54, in both cases linking his capability to his priestly descent. For the assumption that priests would best understand and teach the Torah, see, for example, Malachi 2:6–7; Ben Sira 45:17; *Testament of Levi* 13:2; *War* 2.417; *Ant.* 3.321, 4.304, etc.

266 Perhaps it will not be invidious[619] for me briefly to go through [some details] concerning my family and the events of my life,[620] so long as there are still alive people [who may want] to convict[621] [me][622] or, [alternatively], to testify [on my behalf].[623]

267 Having [said] that,[624] I shall conclude my *Antiquities*,[625] which is contained in twenty books—sixty thousand lines.[626] And if the deity allows it I will again write up, cursorily,[627]

---

619   Compare esp. *Apion* 2.147, 286–287; "Josephus is acutely conscious of the problem of self-praise," which can arouse envy (Barclay 2007: 330, n. 1152). This is part of a yet larger theme in Josephus, that success tends to arouse jealousy; see the note on "jealous" at 18.240. Here Ambrosianus again expands: "nor seem to many to be σκαιός." However, on the one hand this does not add much, and on the other it appears that, although elsewhere the adjective (lit. "left-handed") often means "gauche" or "awkward" (as Feldman [1965: 529], who adopts Ambrosianus's text, translates here), Josephus tends to use it more harshly. True, *CCFJ* (4.20) suggests "awkward" (as Feldman) or "unpleasant" for this passage, but this is the only such passage; five of the other six occurrences of the word, all in *Antiquities* (6.80; 9.232; 11.216; 18.44; and 19.201), are covered by its other suggestions, which are harsher: "bad, evil, wicked, brutal, harsh," and even for the sixth, at 14.267, it suggests nothing milder than "malicious, injudicious"; in the present volume, I rendered "brutal/ity" at 18.44 and 19.201, where it is used to describe the worst of villains. That is, it may be that Ambrosianus preserves here the contribution of an expansive copyist who used the adjective here in a sense that is usual elsewhere but not for Josephus. Cf. the note on "brought to him" at §5.

620   This amounts to an announcement of his *Life*. Indeed, formally that book is an appendix to the *Antiquities*; note not only the enclitic beginning ("As for me ... ") but also, and especially, the fact that *Life* ends at §430, with Josephus's statement that he hereby concludes *Antiquities*.

621   On the senses of ἐλέγχω (expose, reveal, convict, prove, refute, confute), see *ThLJ* 245. Here, as at §145 and 19.347, I have preferred "convict" in accordance with Josephus's other alternative here, "testify on behalf"; for Josephus's tendency to phrase attacks and defense in such juridical terms, cf. esp. *Against Apion*, along with Kasher 1996: 170–171.

622   As van der Horst 1979 notes, Josephus's δέ at the opening of the *Life* could be emphatic, signaling "a self-assertive counter-attack" on anyone who cast doubts on his priestly descent. Given the fact that Josephus's

Life polemicizes against Justus of Tiberius (§§336–367), Laqueur (1920: 270–271, followed by van der Horst) assumes that such doubts had been among the aspersions he cast on Josephus.

623   For Josephus's insistence on his own honesty, as shown by his willingness to publish his *War* while those who might contradict him were still alive, see his argument with Justus in *Life* 361–362 and his proud declaration at *Apion* 1.50. For *Life* as a work that presents (and defends) Josephus's character, see esp. Mason 2001: xlvii–l.

624   Cf. the note on "Thereupon" at 18.104.

625   On the question whether this is a new conclusion or just a peroration of the one that began at §259, see the note on "end my *Antiqities*" at §259.

626   Josephus thus estimates 3000 lines per book. For the usual length of lines in ancient manuscripts, around 34–38 letters per line, see Birt 1882: 194–204; Harris 1893: 15–16; and Finegan 1974: 39. The product of those two data, over all twenty books of the *Antiquities*, would yield a total of somewhat more than two million letters for the whole of the *Antiquities*. That is fairly accurate, not far from the 1.71 million letters estimated by Graux 1878 (non vidi; cited, although apparently with an extra zero, by Birt 1882: 204, n. 1); Graux's figure, in turn, is very close to the 1.68 million I arrived at by counting the letters in a random sample of six paragraphs (237 words) from *Antiquities* 18 and extrapolating on the basis of the total of 305,870 words in all of *Antiquities*, according to the online Perseus word study tool. As for words: dividing the latter total among twenty books yields an average of somewhat more than fifteen thousand words per book, which places the books of *Antiquities* squarely in the medium-length range of the chart for ancient Greek compositions. For comparative figures, see Burridge 1992: 118.

627   The present passage is the only citation in LSJ (1371, s.v. περιδρομή II) for κατὰ περιδρομήν in the sense of "cursorily"; Gutschmid (1893: 374) renders "breviter omnia percurrendo" ("briefly running through everything"). Laqueur (1920: 32–33, 1), however, who agrees that that is the expected sense but notes the difficulty of supporting it according to the received reading, suggests reading κατὰ παραδρομήν, for which he compares

a memoir concerning the war and what has happened to us until the present day,[628] which is in the thirteenth year of the rule of Domitian Caesar and the fifty-sixth since my own birth.[629] **268** I have also decided to compose, in four books, an account of the beliefs we Jews hold about God and his nature, and about the laws[630]—why, according to them, some things we are allowed to do, while others are forbidden.[631]

ἐκ παραδρομῆς in Polybius 21.34.2 and Plutarch, *On the Education of Children* 10 7c. Note also Aristotle, *Politics* 1336^{b}24, ἐν παραδρομῇ τοῦτον πεποιήμεθα τὸν λόγον.

628 Josephus expresses such a hope elsewhere as well (§§53, 96, 144, 147), but no such work, nor any hint of it, has been found. The closest he gets to an update of his history to cover the post-70 period is in the concluding section of his *Life*, which deals cursorily with his own personal affairs until the days of Domitian. By 93/94, when he finished the *Antiquities*, Josephus was pushing sixty, and as Thackeray noted (1929: 106–107), was likely getting tired of the project (and perhaps indicates as much in his prologue—1.7). Given the pressing need to defend himself against Justus (which engendered the *Life*) and to defend the *Antiquities* (which engendered *Against Apion*; see its opening lines), it would not be surprising if he never seriously began another work. See Petersen 1958.

629 Josephus was born in the first year of Gaius's reign (*Life* 5), i.e., 37 CE (and so was about thirty in 67—*Life*

80), and Domitian began to rule in 81; together, these data bring us to 93/94. For details, see Vincent 1911 and Jones 2002.

630 As with the hope to write another history (§267), in this case too there is no evidence that Josephus fulfilled or attempted to fulfill this hope, although it is expressed elsewhere as well (perhaps as early as *War* 5.237 and certainly at *Ant.* 1.25, 29; 3.94; 4.198, etc.). In general, on the topic of such unfulfilled plans, see Petersen 1958. For the suggestion that *Against Apion* (esp. 2.145ff.) is what resulted when Josephus sat down to write this projected work, see Altshuler 1978/79 and Gerber 1997: 64–65.

631 For this formulation summarizing the laws as they might be explained to gentiles, cf. *Letter of Aristeas* 143 (in the story to which Josephus points, at the opening of *Antiquities* [1.10–12], as justifying his own project): "there is a deep reason in each individual case why we abstain from the use of certain things and enjoy the common use of others" (trans. R. H. Charles).

APPENDICES

APPENDIX 1
CHRONOLOGICAL SURVEY OF THE ROMAN GOVERNORS OF JUDEA, 6–66 CE

The chronological scaffolding of the sixty years of Judean history covered in *Antiquities* 18–20, from the establishment of direct Roman rule in 6 CE to the outbreak of the rebellion in 66, is supplied by the frequent references to individuals who succeeded one another as Rome's governors of Judea.[1] In all, twelve are mentioned.[2] We know the names of the governors, their order, and the name of the emperor who appointed each of them. Since, however, Josephus never (with the two doubtful exceptions discussed below in paragraphs 4–5) tells us how many years a governor was in office, pinning down their tenures, sometimes even approximately, is a challenge. It has been addressed by numerous scholars over the generations, but for a long time it has been usual to follow Schürer's reconstruction;[3] see *HJP* 1.382–383, 455–470.

Apart from a very small amount of other evidence, most of the data can be derived, whether directly or by inference, only from Josephus. Consequently, reconstruction of this chronological backbone of the period, as of so much else reported by Josephus, depends on our notions of what he knew, what he inferred, and how he built his narrative. My conclusions differ at some points, in a few cases significantly, from Schürer's. In the following discussion, I will note Schürer's dates for the governors and my own, along with a summary of the main considerations and a reference to the relevant annotations to the translation. Since many of the data apply to transitions from one governor to the next, the end of one's tenure being the terminus post quem for that of his successor,[4] in several cases more than one governor will be discussed at a time.

1–3: *Coponius, Marcus Ambivulus. Annius Rufus.* According to 18.2, Coponius was sent to govern Judea upon the deposition and expulsion of Archelaus. Assuming that Herod died in 4 BCE (see *HJP* 1.326–328, n. 165 and the opening note on 18.1.1 at 18.1), *Ant.* 17.342, which reports that Archelaus ruled only ten years before being deposed, dates the end of that decade to 6 CE. That corresponds to 18.26, which reports that Quirinius—along with whom Coponius came to Judea (*Ant.* 17.355 and 18.1–2)—finished his census in Judea "in the thirty-seventh year after Antonius was defeated by Caesar at Actium," i.e., in 6 CE, within a year of his arrival.

According to 18.31–32, Coponius was succeeded first by Ambivulus and then by Rufus, with Augustus's death, in mid-August 14, coming in the course of the latter's governorship. Moreover, it seems, as we shall see in the next paragraph, that Rufus's successor was appointed not more than a year after Augustus's death. But we do not know how to divide the years between 6 and 15 among these three governors. Schürer's split of those nine years

---

1 On the conventional use of "governor," see the opening note at 18.31.

2 On Marcellus and Marullus, who are sometimes counted as governors, see below, after paras. 4–5. For a graphic presentation of how the governors' terms serve as the basic division of the narrative, see the table that precedes the Introduction.

3 See *HJP* 1.382–383, 455–470. Compare, for example, the detailed tables in Rhoads 1976: 184–185 and Horsley and Hanson 1999: 260–261, where the dates of the governors are all identical with Schürer's.

4 The terminus post quem but not necessarily the starting point, for while usually a governor remained in office until his successor arrived (see, for example, 20.103,

into three equal tenures of three years each (6–9; 9–12; 12–15; *HJP* 1.383) is only a conventional guess.

4–5: *Valerius Gratus and Pontius Pilate.* According to *Ant.* 18.177, Tiberius appointed these two Roman governors of Judea during his twenty-two years as emperor (Aug. 14–March 37), and at 18.89 we read that Pilate's term of office ended around the time of Tiberius's death. Since the text of Josephus as we have it states, at 18.35, 89, that Gratus was in office for eleven years and Pilate for ten, it follows that Gratus was appointed early in Tiberius's reign, and that we should assign Gratus 15–26 and Pilate—26–36/37; so *HJP* 1.382, n. 130. However, the numbers given at 18.35, 89, which state the length of their respective terms of office, are the only such data supplied for governors in *Antiquities*, and that creates some doubt about them; given Christian copyists' natural interest in dating Pilate,[5] one should hesitate to build much upon them. Rather, if we set those two data aside, we should find it striking that all that Josephus reports concerning Gratus in 18.34–35 sounds like it took no more than four or five years: upon arrival in Judea he removed the incumbent high priest and appointed one whom he fired "not long thereafter," whereupon he appointed two more for no more than a year each and, after appointing a fourth, returned to Rome. Anyone who reads thereafter, as we do at 18.35, that that all took eleven years should be very surprised. Moreover, Josephus locates within his "chapter" on Pilate accounts of the foundation of Tiberias (18.36–38), of the death of Germanicus (18.53–54), and of the expulsions from Rome of Jews and of the devotees of Isis (18.65–84), all four of which occurred in or about 19 CE (as we know from numismatics in the first case [see the note on "Gennesaritis" at 18.36] and from Tacitus in the other three). That all suggests that, in fact, Gratus was governor 15–18/19 and Pilate—beginning in 19. See the opening note on 18.3.1 at 18.55. Pilate is, therefore, as Josephus notes at 18.177, quite a good example for Tiberius's tendency to leave governors at their positions for a long time.

As for the end of Pilate's governorship: that it was around the time of Tiberius's death (March 37) emerges from 18.89, where we read that although Pilate hurried to Rome after Vitellius deposed him from office, he did not arrive there prior to Tiberius's death. A more precise dating depends on the identification of the Passover mentioned at 18.90, during which Vitellius visited Jerusalem just after removing Pilate from office (assuming the order of Josephus's narrative is reliable here). Although all agree that the festival of Vitellius's visit mentioned a few pages later, at *Ant.* 18.122–124, was in the spring of 37 (since news of Tiberius's death in mid-March 37 reached Vitellius during this visit), Schürer (*HJP* 1.387, n. 145) identifies it specifically as Passover 37 (for Shavuot [Pentecost] would be too late for such momentous news to reach the Roman governor of Syria). That forced Schürer to conclude that Vitellius's visit on the preceding Passover, mentioned explicitly at 18.90, was that of 36, so Pilate was removed from office in the spring of 36. That, however, leaves us wondering how Pilate could "hurry" to Rome (18.89), as was expected under the circumstances, and nonetheless not reach it by March 37. Rather, it seems likelier to assume that Josephus has preserved two separate accounts of the same visit on a festival from two different points of view (one that focused on matters of priestly interest, one that focused on Herod Antipas);

182, 215), in some cases circumstances could create a delay; for the clearest example, in which a governor died in office and so could be replaced only after the emperor learned of that and could send a successor, see 20.197–204.

5 Apart from the possibility that such copyists were simply mistaken, Eisler (1929/30: 1.128–130) noted that the circulation of anti-Christian "Acts of Pilate" that dated the Crucifixion to 21 CE may have encouraged Christians deliberately to postdate Pilate's arrival in Judea so as to pull out the carpet from under that text, as Eusebius does at *Church History* 1.9.

to identify the festival as Passover 37; and to conclude that Pilate was removed from office shortly before that festival. See the note on "Judea" at 18.90.

> [*Marcellus and Marullus,* mentioned in 18.89, 237. Schürer (*HJP* 1.383) assumes both were Roman governors of Judea, and leaves open the possibility that they were, in fact, despite the statement that Gaius "sent out" Marullus (which Schürer takes to be a general formulation), the same person. Whatever we think of the latter question, here it is important to note that neither is termed governor and that neither is said to have played any role (as a governor of Judea presumably would) in the Temple-statue affair of 39–41, although both Josephus and Philo give detailed accounts of it. Accordingly, it seems likely, instead, that they—just as Capito (Philo, *Leg.* 199)—were secondary officials in Judea who reported directly to the Roman governor of Syria when there was no Roman governor of Judea in the days of Gaius Caligula. See the note on "force" at 18.261.]

> [*Agrippa I* ruled Judea from his enthronement shortly after Gaius Caligula's death in January 41 (19.274) until his own death in 43 or 44. On the date of his death, see the note on "reign" at 19.350. Thereafter Claudius restored provincial rule.]

6–7: Cuspius Fadus and Tiberius Julius Alexander. We know that Claudius appointed Fadus as governor after the death of Agrippa I (*Ant.* 19.363), that he was in office in mid-45 (20.14), and that his successor was in office when King Herod of Chalcis died in Claudius's eighth year, i.e., 48 (20.103–104). But here too, as in the case of the first three governors, we have no guide to dividing the period among the two; Schürer's neat assignment of 44–46 to Fadus and 46–48 to Tiberius Julius Alexander (*HJP* 1.455–456) is, again, merely a conventional guess.

8: Ventidius Cumanus. Since Cumanus's appointment is mentioned alongside Herod of Chalcis's death in Claudius's eighth year (20.103–104), which was 48 CE, and his exile is reported just before a reference to Claudius's twelfth year (20.136–138), it is usual to date his tenure between those termini, i.e., 48–52 CE. So *HJP* 1.460, n. 17, which bolsters the date of the end of his term, and the appointment of his successor, Felix, by pointing to Tacitus's reference to Felix's governorship at *Ann.* 12.54, in the context of Tacitus's narrative for 52 CE. So too Feldman 1965: 461, n. e: "He was named procurator in c. A.D. 52." That conventional dating is possible. However, what Tacitus says is that Felix was already governor of Judea by then ("iam pridem Iudaeae impositus"), and, as with Josephus on Gratus (above), the contents of Josephus's report of Cumanus's days in Judea seem to fill a much shorter period. As Thackeray noted, "According to B[ellum], the disturbances described in this chapter must have extended over a whole year from one Passover (§224) to the next [§244, already after Cumanus was sent off to Rome]" (JLCL 2.419, n. c; so too Shatzman in Ullmann 2009: 248, n. 244 ["doubtless"]), and nothing indicates that his service began earlier than that year. That is, it seems preferable to date Cumanus's tenure to 48–49 CE. Moreover, Josephus locates his report of Agrippa II's appointment of Ishmael b. Phiabi to the high priesthood at 20.179, in the days of Cumanus's successor, Felix, and that should mean that it was during Felix's governorship that Agrippa appointed Ishmael; see the note on "Phabes" at 20.179 and, on such bunching of secondary material toward the end of a chapter on a governor, the Introduction, at nn. 14–16. But *Ant.* 3.320 reports that Ishmael was high priest during the famine in the days of Claudius, and other evidence locates that famine to ca. 48/49 (see the note on "famine" at 20.51). That too indicates that Felix was governor by then. The juxtaposition of the end of Cumanus's story, at 20.137, to a story about other people in Claudius's twelfth year, at 20.138, which goes along with the conventional start of a new chapter at §20.137, need not oblige us to assume chronological adjacency; see the introductory note on 20.7.1. at 20.137. Similarly, the fact that Tacitus (*Ann.* 12.11–12) refers to Longinus as governor of Syria in the context of his account of 49 CE need not imply that Quadratus, Longinus's successor, came only later than that, for Tacitus's story is a long one that was spread over several years; see the note on "Quadratus" at 20.125. For more detail, see the note on "Judea" at 20.137, also D. R. Schwartz 1992: 218–242 and 2024a.

9–10: *Antonius*[6] *Felix and Porcius Festus*. Assuming, as explained above, that Felix replaced Cumanus in 49 CE, and that Festus's successor, Albinus, was in office by 62 (see below), it remains to determine, first of all, when Festus replaced Felix. Some scholars place that as early as 55 or 56; so Lambertz 1953 and Saumagne 1966. Others, however, including HJP 1.465–466, n. 42 and Stern 1974b: 74–76, place it in 59 or 60. Josephus gives us next to nothing to go on, but Acts 24:27 reports that Festus arrived to replace Felix two years after the latter had imprisoned Paul; the issue is, therefore, discussed frequently in attempts to reconstruct Pauline chronology. There too, however, there is little to go on, whether in Acts or in Paul's epistles. The only explicit statements in the sources come in Armenian and Latin versions of Eusebius's *Chronicle*, which place Felix's recall in 54–56. Schürer, however, tends to reject the Eusebian evidence as conjectural, and Stern adds that Eusebius's chronological data for first-century Judea are often wrong. Rather, Schürer and Stern tend to date Festus's entrance into office ca. 60. True, Schürer's two main arguments are based, for the most part, on the assumption—which we have rejected—that Felix's tenure began only in 52: (a) Josephus's account of Felix's regime (20.160–181) gives the impression that it took several years, and (b) Acts 21:38 relates to an affair in Felix's regime (the Egyptian prophet: 20.169–172), which Schürer assumes occurred in the days of Nero, as being in the past even before the two years between Paul's imprisonment and Festus's arrival. But there is no particular reason to date the Egyptian prophet to Nero's reign, for Felix was appointed by Claudius; the fact that Josephus chose to follow Claudius to his death and then relate cursorily to his successor, Nero (20.148–159), before recounting the events of Felix's term of office, including that of the Egyptian prophet, does not at all imply that all of those events happened only after Nero's succession to the throne. In any case, if, as argued above, Felix was appointed in 49, Schürer's arguments lose their force. Stern, however, offers another argument in support of the late date: Josephus's statement (*Life* 13) that he went to Rome ca. 63/64 in order to lobby for the release of priests who had been imprisoned by Felix comports better with the assumption that Felix served until 60, rather than with a date half a decade earlier.

11–12: *Lucceius Albinus and Gessius Florus*. That Albinus was governor "four years before the war" is stated at *War* 6.300–305. Since Josephus dates the outbreak of the war to the spring/summer of Nero's twelfth year (*War* 2.284, 555; *Ant.* 20.257, 259), which began in October 65, it follows that Albinus was in office at least as early as 62. We do not know how long before that he was appointed; Schürer's decision to prefer 62 results only from his decision to date the start of Festus's tenure in 60 together with his impression that the events of Festus's regime (20.182–196) must have filled more than a year. But the decision is far from certain (see above) and the impression is no more than that. As for the transition from Albinus to Florus: since, as noted, Josephus repeatedly dates the outbreak of the rebellion to the spring/summer of Nero's twelfth year, which began in October 65, and according to *Ant.* 20.257 the rebellion broke out in the second year of Florus's governorship, we should date the outset of his term to sometime in 64 or 65.

---

6 On the question of Felix's gentilicium, see the Introduction, n. 92.

APPENDIX 2
ON POSSIBILITIES, PROBABILITIES, AND SIMON CANTHERAS'S PEDIGREE
(*ANT.* 19.297)

At *Ant.* 19.297–298, Josephus gives some details about Agrippa I's first appointee to the high priesthood, around 40 CE:[1]

> **297** Having completely worshipped God, Agrippa removed Theophilus, son of Ananus, from the high priesthood, assigning his position to Simon (whose surname was Cantheras), son of Boethus. Simon had two brothers and his father Boethus—whose daughter, as I explained above, had been married by King Herod. **298** Simon thus held the high priesthood, as did his brothers and his father, just as earlier the three sons of Simon, son of Onias, held the position in the period of Macedonian rule, as we related in earlier writings.

This brief report, which focuses on the remarkable recurrence of the high-priestly office within certain families (an interest that Josephus and others evince elsewhere as well[2]), raises several difficulties. They illustrate some of the choices historians must make when attempting to reconstruct "what really happened" on the basis of the relevant sources (which often are neither complete nor free of ambiguity) but without losing sight of what nature and experience indicate is likely. They will also illustrate, it seems, with regard to the use of "son of," the importance of familiarity with Hebrew idioms relevant to the Jerusalem priesthood within which Josephus was raised and spent his first three decades.[3]

According to the usual interpretation of this text,

a. It contains one plain but understandable error, namely, the statement that Herod's father-in-law was a high priest named "Boethus." On the one hand, since Josephus's supplies very full and consistent data about the succession of high priests in the Herodian-Roman period[4] but no high priest of that name is known, it is difficult to accept his statement about Boethus. On the other hand, Josephus does refer several times to "Simon b. Boethus" as longtime high priest in Herod's days, who was appointed when Herod married his daughter, Mariamme II (see *Ant.* 15.320; 17.78; also 18.109, 136, which mention Simon but not Boethus), and Josephus's remark, "as I explained above," gives us all the more confidence in assuming he is referring to that marriage. It is, therefore, widely agreed that Josephus's reference to "Boethus" is simply a slip for "Simon b. Boethus."

b. Simon Cantheras's two brothers who were also high priests, as was their father, were Joazar and Eleazar, who were appointed to the high priesthood one after the other just before Herod's death and just after it (*Ant.* 17.164, 339, 341). That conclusion is thought to be well-founded, for:

---

1 Josephus places it in 41 CE but it may be that it in fact came in 38; see the note on "Agrippa" at 19.292. This doubt is of no importance for the issue discussed in this appendix.

2 *Ant.* 12.238 (alluded to here) and 20.198. Cf. *b. Yoma* 47a//*Leviticus Rabbah* 20.11 (ed. Margaliot, 2: 470): "It is said that Qimḥit had seven sons and all served in the high priesthood."

3 For other examples of this, see the notes on "built of stones" at 18.93 and on "Nazirites" at 19.294.

4 At 20.250 he states that there were twenty-eight high priests from Herod until the destruction of the

(i)   that Joazar was of the Boethus family is stated explicitly at 17.339 and 18.3, where he is termed "son of Boethus," which need mean no more than "of the Boethus family;"[5]

(ii) that Eleazar was Joazar's brother is stated explicitly at 17.339; and

(iii) that Joazar (and hence Eleazar) was the brother of Mariamme II (and hence the son of Simon b. Boethus) is derived from 17.164, according to an interpretation to which we shall return below.

•••

This widespread reconstruction is offered in all the right places: in Feldman's note on *Ant.* 19.297 and in detailed discussions of the issue by Stern, Kokkinos, VanderKam, and Gußmann.[6] Note, however, that Gußmann, after first presenting the consensus without any hesitation, goes on, in a remarkable bit of understatement, to conclude his discussion with the following remark: "Ein chronologisches Problem bereiten die Angaben des Josephus, wonach Kantheras' Brüder bereits fünfzig Jahre früher regiert hätten und sein Sohn (Elionaius, Hp. 19) bereits drei Jahre nach ihm."[7] For a topic like this, the fact that there are remaining chronological problems created by Josephus's data—the only data that exist—means that the issue cannot be considered resolved.

Whatever we think of the second chronological problem raised by Gußmann, about Simon's son (to which we shall return), the first is difficult enough: it is not easy to believe that someone was appointed to the high priesthood some fifty years after his brothers (and although the number of years was probably closer to forty-five, that hardly changes anything). Moreover, the problem is severely exacerbated by Josephus's datum, followed by the consensus that those brothers had a sister, Mariamme II, who married Herod the Great already some twenty years before they were appointed to the high priesthood. True, we do not know precisely when the marriage took place; most scholars point to ca. 23 BCE, but Kokkinos argues for 29/28 BCE.[8] Nor do we know how old Mariamme II was at the time; at *Ant.* 15.321 Josephus terms her a "child" (παῖς) at the time of the engagement, but also reports that she was beautiful enough to be the talk of the town and for Herod to be "smitten" by her. No matter how late we place the marriage in the 20s BCE, and no matter how young we imagine the bride was, it is highly unlikely that she would have a brother young enough to be appointed high priest sixty-plus years later. It is much easier to suppose that Agrippa's appointee belonged to the next generation.

This problem is, of course, recognized by scholars who adhere to the consensus set out above. Their response is to insist that what I just characterized as "highly unlikely" is nevertheless possible. Thus Kokkinos, after following the above data to the conclusion that Simon b. Boethus could have been born as late as 61/60 BCE (if Mariamme II was born ca. 41, when he was twenty, and married at thirteen), puts the issue as follows:

Temple, and, indeed, historians have little difficulty in piecing together the list, especially in light of the fact that Josephus frequently gives their names not only when they are appointed but also when they are removed from office. See the note on "one hundred and seven years" at 20.250.

5 See below, n. 16.

6 Feldman 1965: 355–357, n. d; Stern 1976: 604–605; Kokkinos 1998: 217–223; VanderKam 2004: 443–447; Gußmann 2008: 422.

7 "A chronological problem is created by Josephus's data, according to which Cantheras's brothers served already fifty years before him and his son (Elioneus, high priest no. 19 [in Gußmann's list]) already three years after him."

8 Kokkinos 1998: 221–222.

> The question then is whether it is possible for him to have a son, Simon II Cantheras, who became high priest 100 years later ... The answer to that is that it is not impossible: If Cantheras was 50 on his appointment, his father would have had him when he was 50.[9]

Here I would respond, as a matter of historical method, that the question whether something is merely "possible" should not govern our reconstructions of history, and so the finding that something "is not impossible" is not enough to establish it as the preferred reconstruction. Outside of courts of law that insist on proof beyond all reasonable doubt, normally we do not do our business that way—neither when reconstructing history nor when doing most other things. Rather, we prefer that our reconstructions be probable, not only not excluded as impossible. In the present case, therefore, we should admit that although it is not impossible, a reconstruction that presumes that Simon b. Boethus fathered a son when he was fifty and that his son was appointed to the high priesthood when he was fifty is not at all probable. It would not be very probable today, when very few men have children at the age of fifty, and it would have been all the more unlikely in the Roman empire, in which, although there were exceptional cases of longevity,[10] average life expectancy was less than thirty,[11] less of a fifth of the people lived to fifty, and even among those who lived until twenty (and so might be appointed to the high priesthood) average life expectancy did not reach fifty.[12] And it becomes, of course, less and less probable the more we budge from the optimal hypotheses that Simon b. Boethus was only twenty when Mariamme II was born and that she married at thirteen.

The chronological difficulty does not totally exclude that reconstruction. But it does mean that its improbability should be weighed against that entailed by an alternate reconstruction that does not entail such a chronological improbability.

Before turning to that alternative, two other problems should be noted with regard to the consensus. The first concerns the assumption of patronymy, namely, that Simon b. Boethus was the father of Simon Cantheras. For although we can point to cases in Judea of the Second Temple period in which father and son had the same name—such as Josephus's brother Mattathias (*Life* 8), John b. John (20.14), Ananus b. Ananus (20.197), and the presumption of Luke 1:59—it seems nevertheless to have been relatively rare.[13] As Ilan put it (not in the present context, but on the basis of her familiarity with the full corpus), "a son bearing the same name as the father is not unheard of among Jews in Greco-Roman Palestine."[14] I would emphasize that "not unheard of," just as "not impossible," is not the kind of probability we would prefer to build on, if there is a likelier alternative.

---

9 Kokkinos 1998: 222. Similarly, VanderKam (2004: 445) notes my admission (1990a: 187) that "this would be possible, since Josephus does not tell us when Simon [Cantheras] was born." The continuation of my admission there is pessimistic, as below.

10 See Parkin 2003: 44–46.

11 See, for example, the chapter on "Age at Death" in van der Horst 1991: 73–84.

12 For the last two data, see the entries for 50 in the second column, and for 20 in the third column, in the table supplied by Frier 1983: 329.

13 Apart from royal dynasties, in which it was common, such as Herod and Herod Antipas, Agrippa I and Agrippa II, Joseph, Aristobulus (18.137), and Alexander (*Ant.* 18.134, 137, 139). For some additional cases (*War* 5.534; *Life* 33), see Stern 1991: 42, n. 45. Hachlili (1983/84: 192) posits an additional case: that Ishmael b. Phiabi I (high priest ca. 15 CE; *Ant.* 18.34) was the father of Ishmael b. Phiabi II (*Ant.* 20.179). It could well be, however, that the latter was the former's grandson. So Stern (1976: 608, "very likely"), on the basis of the usual assumption that the latter was appointed ca. 59 CE. Even if he is moved up a decade, as suggested in D. R. Schwartz 2024a, he might still be a grandson, not a son. Papponymy is much more prevalent than patronymy.

14 Ilan (2002): 33.

The second problem relates to the assumption that "Boethus" at *Ant.* 19.297 is merely a mistake for "Simon b. Boethus." Here I would underline that Josephus, in that paragraph, relates to Simon twice with regard to Boethus: τῷ δὲ Βοηθοῦ Σίμωνι ... τῷ Σίμωνι καὶ πατὴρ Βοηθός. Although the second time he is quite explicit, and wrong, the first formulation, which uses only the genitive but not "father," is precisely what Josephus uses for Joazar at 17.339, just as he uses "son of Boethus" (Βοηθοῦ παῖς) for some otherwise unknown Matthias, said to be of high-priestly descent, mentioned in a later context (*War* 5.527).[15] If we are not to conclude that Josephus is habitually in error about Boethus, which would undercut our entire endeavor, we should conclude, instead, that calling a priest Βοηθοῦ was a way of referring to him as a member of the Boethus clan, not specifically as a "son of [an individual named] Boethus." Indeed, that would correspond to regular Hebrew style, in which *ben* can indicate many relationships of belonging, apart from biological sonship.[16] That is, while we should agree that the statement in 19.297 that Simon Cantheras's father was named Boethus is wrong, we may retain the assumption that Simon belonged to the Boethus clan. For the Boethusides being considered a clan, we need go no further than a well-known ditty denouncing the high-priestly "houses": it denounces "the House of Boethus" alongside other "houses" of high priests.[17]

Turning now to the alternate reconstruction, let us ask whether it is difficult or easy to find Simon Cantheras a father and two brothers who were high priests closer to his own appointment to the office ca. 41 CE. The easier it is to do so, the more convincing that alternate reconstruction will be.[18]

Concerning the brothers, first of all, it turns out to be fairly easy, with the help of a focus on Simon's byname, "Cantheras." That is a rare and mystifying name, but it reappears in a context that is only slightly later: at 19.342 Josephus reports that Agrippa I's final appointment of a high priest, a few years after that of Simon Cantheras, was of "Elioneus b. Cantheras" (Ἐλιωναῖον τὸν τοῦ Κανθηρᾶ[19] παῖδα). Although that sounds as if Cantheras were Elioneus's father, at 20.16, where his removal from office is mentioned (so we can be sure the same individual is meant), Josephus terms him simply "the man surnamed Cantheras" (τὸν ἐπικαλούμενον Κανθήραν), basically the same formulation as that used of Simon at 19.297 (τούτῳ Κανθηρᾶς ἐπίκλησις ἦν). This indicates clearly that Cantheras is a byname, not specifically the name of Simon's or Elioneus's father. Both the use of surnames, and their representation as "son of," corresponding to common Hebrew usage of *ben*, are well-attested for the Second Temple period.[20]

---

15 On Matthias (actually: on whom he was not), see Stern 1976: 605–606 and VanderKam 2004: 448–449, n. 140.

16 With regard to priestly families, for which clans were very important, note, for example, "sons of Jehoiarib" (1 Macc 2:1; 14:29; cf. 1 Chron 24:7), "son of Haqqoz" (1 Macc 8:17; cf. 1 Chron 24:10), "sons of Zadok" (Ezek 44:15; Ben Sira 51 [Hebrew text]; *1QS* 5:2), and "priests of the sons of Hezir" (inscription on their tomb; Stern 1976: 594–595). For such usage in Jewish Greek, see also Danker 2000: 1024, s.v. υἱός, §2β ("of the individual members of a large and coherent group"). As for the use of *ben* to refer to a surname, which might relate to a quality or a characterization, not to the father's name, see, for example, ben Kalba Savua and ben Ṣiṣit HaKeset in the story at *b. Giṭṭin* 56a, along with the list of officials in *m. Sheqalim* 5:1, which juxtaposes "*ben*" names with "house" names.

On the broad usage of *ben* in biblical Hebrew, see Berlin 2009.

17 For references, see below, n. 27.

18 And this is a reason to reject Smallwood's suggestion (1962: 33–34) that Simon Cantheras was the son of Joazar or Eleazar, although not the brother of two high priests. That would resolve the chronological problem only by excluding one of the main elements of the puzzle.

19 Although Ambrosianus, followed by Niese (1890a: 269), reads τοῦ Κιθαίρου, most scholars agree that "Cantheras" (as in the Latin and in a marginal reading in Ambrosianus) is to be preferred, if only because that is the reading at 20.16, which is the next reference to the same person. See, for example, Feldman (1965: 376, n. a) and VanderKam 2004: 449, n. 141.

20 On the use of ἐπικαλέομαι for bynames that are not names of fathers, see, for example, *Ant.* 12.43 ("Simon,

If so, then our search for Simon Cantheras's brothers who too were high priests has easily brought us to one, Elioneus. And he, in turn, can easily bring us to the third brother—for the Mishnah (*Parah* 3:5) calls Elioneus, presumably the same person (given the rareness of the name), *ben haqqayyāf*, which shows that he was known by that Aramaic surname too.[21] But that Aramaic surname is shared, of course, by Joseph Caiaphas—and both Josephus (at 18.95: τὸν Καϊάφαν ἐπικαλούμενον) and the Gospels (Matt 26:3: τοῦ λεγομένου Καϊάφα) clearly refer to "Caiaphas" as a surname, not as the name of the high priest's father.[22]

That is, we can easily point to three men who served as high priests not a half century apart from each other but, rather, within a decade of each other (Joseph until 36/37 [*Ant.* 18.95], Simon ca. 41, and Elioneus ca. 43/44) and seem to have been brothers. True, we have no direct evidence about their father, but they are linked by their surname: Simon and Elioneus share the same Greek surname, Elioneus is known by that Greek surname and also by its Aramaic equivalent, and Joseph is known by the latter. It is, therefore, quite reasonable to conjecture that they were brothers. If, then, Josephus tells us at 19.297 that one of them, Simon, had two brothers who were high priests, and Joseph and Elioneeus are eligible candidates and we know they were high priests, it becomes very attractive, especially given the fact that the names of all first-century high priests are known,[23] to assume that these are the three brothers to whom Josephus is referring.

But what about their father, who too was a high priest, according to 19.297? Is it difficult or easy to find one for them, among the high priests of the preceding generation? This brings us to *Ant.* 17.164, where Josephus reports that Herod, in the final year of his life, removed Matthias b. Theophilus from the high priesthood and appointed Joazar—who is identified at 17.339 and 18.3 as "son of Boethus"—in his stead:

> He treated the others more mildly, but put an end to the priestly service of Matthias the high priest on the notion that he had been part of the cause of those events, and appointed (in his stead) as high priest Joazar, his wife's brother (ἀδελφὸν γυναικὸς τῆς αὐτοῦ).

As noted earlier in this appendix, scholars usually take "his" (τῆς αὐτοῦ) to mean that Joazar was the brother of Herod's wife, whom they take to be Mariamme II; the relationship between the two is thought to be demonstrated by the fact that she is identified as a daughter of Simon b. Boethus (*Ant.* 15.320; 17.78) and he as "son of Boethus" (17.339 and 18.3).

However, although, strangely, some scholars think it is simply obvious that 17.164 refers to Joazar as the brother of Herod's wife,[24] the fact is that not a few scholars have taken ἀδελφὸν γυναικὸς τῆς αὐτοῦ to mean that Joazar was the brother of *Matthias*'s wife. So, for example, Smallwood (1962: 33), Jeremias (1969: 154–155), and Horsley (1986: 32); so too Whiston.[25]

---

also called 'the Righteous'"), 13.62 ("Ptolemy, surnamed Philometor"), 222 ("Antiochus, surnamed Soter"), Acts 4:36 ("Joseph, surnamed Barnabas"),10:5, 32 ("Simon who was surnamed Peter"), 12:25 ("John, surnamed Mark"). In general, on surnames and this usage, see Spicq 1994: 2.41–43. As for the use of *ben* to refer to a surname, not the father's name, see above, n. 16.

21 Indeed, R. Brody (1990) has given a good philological explanation why the Greek *cantheras* might be rendered by that Aramaic designation. But even if that explanation is doubted (so, for example, Horbury 1994: 40), the fact remains that Elioneus bore both names.

22 For "Caiaphas" as a surname, not a patryonmic, see Metzner 2010: 36–37.

23 See above, n. 4.

24 Kokkinos 1998: 219: "The plain meaning of *Ant.* 17.164 is that Joazar was the brother of the wife of Herod (Mariamme II)..."

25 "... and made Joazar, who was Matthias's wife's brother, high priest in his stead" (Whiston 1878: 456).

Indeed, several arguments can be brought in favor of that reading. First, note that readers of *Antiquities* 17 had recently learned, at *Ant.* 17.19–22, that Herod then had nine wives, so if "his" means Herod's, a reference to "his wife" would not have been very helpful to readers. Second, such readers had also read, even more recently (17.78), that Mariamme II was no longer Herod's wife, the king having divorced her at the same time he installed Matthias as high priest (17.78), and that should have made it even harder to think of her when reading 17.164. Third, at *War* 1.599 we read that Herod had tortured Mariamme II's brothers, whereupon they denounced her, and it was that which brought Herod to divorce her and remove her son from his will. How likely is it that Herod, after torturing those brothers and humiliating their sister, would then appoint one of those brothers, and then another, to the high priesthood?[26]

If, however, 17.164 means instead that it was Matthias b. Theophilus whose wife's brothers (Joazar and Eleazar) were high priests of the House of Boethus—that is, that he was married to a woman who was of the Boethus clan—then, in the absence of any knowledge about Matthias's own family, it is reasonable to infer that his family was considered part of the House of Boethus. That is the way aristocracies work. Indeed, the famous talmudic text alluded to above complains that not only the sons, but also the sons-in-law, of the high-priestly houses received privileged treatment as members of them.[27] So all we need to do, in order to accommodate Josephus's data, is posit that Matthias b. Theophilus was married to a woman who belonged to the Boethus clan and that the three brothers we have located (Simon Cantheras, Elioneus Cantheras, and Josephus Caiaphas) were their sons.

•••

In the end, we must choose between two reconstructions. Both agree that Josephus erred at 19.297 when he states that Simon Cantheras's father was Boethus, father of Mariamme II; he should have written "Simon b. Boethus." Beyond that, we have to weigh the pros and cons of the two suggestions.

One, which is widespread, identifies Simon Cantheras as the brother of Herod's wife, Mariamme II; his father was Simon b. Boethus and his two brothers, according to this reconstruction, are two high priests late in Herod's day, Joazar and Eleazar, who are explicitly identified as Boethusides. That is all fine, as far as it goes, but making Simon their brother requires us to imagine that Simon was appointed to the high priesthood more than sixty

---

Whiston's case is different from the others, insofar as while the others, who were historians writing on the topic, may have been influenced by their attention to the passages that describe both Joazar and Mariamme as Boethusides (*Ant.* 15.320; 17.78, 339; 18.3), Whiston was probably simply translating the text one line after another in accordance with what he took to be its natural meaning.

26 Of those three arguments, VanderKam, in rejecting the reconstruction proposed here, fails to relate to the first two; he recognizes the third problem, but notes that "we do not know whether any future high priest was among the brothers so abused" (2004: 413, n. 47). He also

claims that the fact that Herod had divorced Mariamme II need not have prevented him from appointing her brother to the high priesthood. That is true, but beside the point; the question is how Josephus's readers would understand his text, or how he should have formulated it.

27 "For they are high priests and their sons are treasurers and their sons-in-law are officials and their servants beat the people with staves" (*b. Pes.* 57a//*t. Menaḥot* 13:21 [ed. Zuckermandel, 533]). Note, furthermore, the way John 18:13 identifies Caiaphas as son-in-law of the high priest, Annas. A high-priestly pedigree can explain Annas's willingness to let Caiaphas marry his daughter.

years after his sister married and more than forty years after two of his brothers were high priests; both, while "not impossible," are far beyond what anyone would normally suppose, even today, much less in antiquity. Moreover, that reconstruction requires us both to assume that Simon had the same first name as his father, which is only "not unheard of,"[28] and to read *Ant.* 17.164 in a way that should be difficult for readers of *Antiquities* 17, whether because they know that Herod had many wives or because they know Mariamme II was not among them at the time in question.

The other reconstruction avoids all three of those difficulties, but requires us first to find three brothers by inferences from their surnames: Simon Cantheras—Elioneus Canthera/Kayyafa—Joseph Caiaphas and then to link them all to the Boethus family (to which Josephus clearly links Simon Cantheras at 19.297) by assuming something otherwise unknown: that Matthias b. Theophilus had married a daughter of Simon b. Boethus, and they were the parents of Simon, Elioneus, and Joseph. That assumption, which allows us to read 17.164 in what seems to be a more natural way and also supplies us with three brothers and a father who were high priests, is only an assumption; that weakness of this second reconstruction must be weighed against the advantage it has insofar as it allows three brothers to be more or less contemporaries rather than leaving a gap of half a century between the high priesthoods of two and that of the third.

Making inferences from sources, on the basis of all the relevant considerations, is what historians do. As Momigliano (1980: 20) once put it:

> All of the historian's work is based on sources ... But nevertheless, the historian is not an interpreter of sources, although interpret he does. Rather, he is an interpreter of the reality of which the sources are indicative signs, or fragments.

That is, the proper understanding of texts is an historian's starting point, but the goal is to reconstruct what happened in the real world—and the limits concerning what can or cannot happen in that world are just as binding as the rules of grammar. True, even in a case in which what a text states contradicts the rules of nature, we should not interpret it (or emend it) to conform to our notions; ancient texts can be wrong, or have some ironic or other intention. But if the relevant texts (such as Βοηθοῦ at *Ant.* 19.297, τὸν τοῦ Κανθηρᾶ παῖδα at 19.342, and ἀδελφὸν γυναικὸς τῆς αὐτοῦ at 17.164) can reasonably be interpreted, on the basis of comparable evidence, in ways that do not entail a contradiction of nature, or do not even come so close to doing so that the best we can say about them is that what they posit is "not impossible," it appears to be preferable to take that route, unless and until further evidence becomes available.

---

28 See above, at n. 14.

APPENDIX 3
AN ANCIENT TABLE OF CONTENTS

Greek and Latin manuscripts of Josephus include, at the opening of each book of *Antiquities*, lists of its topics, sometimes termed *argumenta*; some Latin manuscripts include the respective entries at the beginning of each chapter. Sometimes they correspond fairly closely to Josephus's text and language, sometimes they depart from them, whether with regard to contents (e.g. 18.IX; 19.VIII) or order (see nn. 4, 7, 8). Nor is it easy to understand what is summarized, what ignored, and they often seem somewhat haphazard; at times the summaries give details of the same story (e.g., 18.I–III, XVII–XIX; 20.I–VII), whereas in other cases they are more like titles of chapters. Altogether not much is known about these lists or their provenance, not even whether they were authored by Josephus himself (whether prospectively, as an outline for his work, or retrospectively), as has been suggested especially on the basis of the lack of apparent Christian input,[1] or are rather of later origin, as has been suggested on the basis of differential vocabulary[2] and other considerations; see esp. Sievers 2007 and Nodet 2017. This appendix offers a translation of the lists for Books 18–20 as they appear in Niese 1890a. I added some notes to the translation, the italicized references at the end of each entry, and the italicized years at the end of the list for each book.

•••

These are the contents of the eighteenth book of Josephus's histories of Jewish antiquity:

I.   How Quirinius was sent by Augustus as the evaluator of Syria and Judea and to sell off Archelaus's property. *18.1*

II.   How Coponius, of the equestrian order, was sent as the prefect of Judea. *18.2*

III.   How Judas the Galilean persuaded the multitude not to register properties, until the high priest Joazar persuaded them instead to obey the Romans. *18.3*

IV.   What and how many sects of philosophers there are among the Jews and what [their] laws are. *18.11*

V.   How the tetrarchs Herod and Philip founded cities in honor of Caesar. *18.26*

VI.   How Samaritans scattered bones of the dead in the Temple, defiling the people[3] for seven days. *18.29*

VII.   How Herod's sister Salome died, leaving her (property) to Julia, Caesar's wife. *18.31*

VIII. How Pontius Pilate wished to bring busts of Caesar secretly into Jerusalem, but the population refused to accept them and was disorderly. *18.55*

IX.   What was done by the Samaritans [sic!] to the Jews in Rome at that time. *18.81*

X.   Pontius Pilate is accused before Vitellius by the Samaritans, and Vitellius requires him to go up to Rome to render account for what he had done. *18.88*

---

1 Note, for example, that the lists for Books 18–20 ignore Josephus's passages about Jesus (18.63–64), John the Baptist (18.116–119), and James the Just (20.197–203).

2 Note, for example, that although in his entire corpus Josephus uses ἐξορίζω only twice, both in *Apion* (1.257;2.191), it appears here at 18.XVI and 20.XVI.

3 Perhaps the reading found in two manuscripts, ναὸν ("sanctuary"), should be preferred instead of λαὸν. Note that there is a lacuna at 18.30 (see the note there on "throughout the Temple"); perhaps the reference here to "seven days" (cf. Numbers 19:16) points to the lost text.

XI. Herod the tetrarch [made] war against King Aretas of the Arabs and was defeated. *18.109–115*

XII. How Tiberius Caesar wrote Vitellius [and ordered him] both to persuade Artabanus the Parthian to send him hostages and to make war against Aretas..[4]*18.96, 115.*

XIII. Philip's death and how his tetrarchy became a province. *18.106–108.*

XIV. Agrippa sailed to Rome, and how he was put into chains upon the accusation of his own freedman. *18.126*

XV. In what manner he was freed by Gaius after Tiberius's death and became king of Philip's tetrarchy. *18.224*

XVI. How Herod, having gone up to Rome, was exiled and his tetrarchy bestowed upon Agrippa. *18.240*

XVII. Civil strife in Alexandria between Jews and Greeks and each side's delegation to Gaius. *18.257a*

XVIII. Accusation of the Jews by Apion, and other members of his delegation, that they do not have statues of Caesar. *18.257b*

XIX. How Gaius, becoming indignant, sent Petronius to Syria to make war upon the Jews if they do not agree to introduce his statue. *18.261*

XX. The ruin that was brought upon the Jews in Babylonia by the brothers Asineus and Anileus. *18.310*

The book encompasses a period of 32 years. *6–38 CE* (*?*)

•••

These are the contents of the nineteenth book of Josephus's histories of Jewish antiquity:

I. How Gaius Caesar, being the victim of a conspiracy, was killed by Chaerea, and how his uncle Claudius was forced by the army to take over rule [of the empire]. *19.1*

II. The struggle of the Senate and the people against him and the military forces that supported him. *19.227*

III. A delegation of King Agrippa to the Senate, and how the soldiers who were with the Senate made common cause to desert it for Claudius and make him the ruler of the state, so the Senate, left all alone, called upon Claudius to be reconciliated. *19.236*

IV. How Claudius Caesar restored to Agrippa his entire ancestral kingdom and also gave him Lysanias's tetrarchy. *19.274*

V. Claudius Caesar's proclamations in Alexandria about the Jews there and throughout his entire realm. *19.278*

VI. King Agrippa sets sail for Judea. *19.292*

VII. The letter of Publius Petronius, the governor of Syria, to the Dorites about the Jews. *19.300*

VIII. How King Agrippa built up the walls of Jerusalem at great expense but the project remained uncompleted because he died in its midst.[5] *19.326*

IX. What he did in three years, until his death, and in what matter he passed away. *19.328*

This book encompasses a period of three years and six months. *40/41–43/44 CE*

•••

---

4 This summary (XII) combines material reported by Josephus at 18.96 and 18.115; the stories summarized in XI and XIII come between those two passages.

5 According to *Ant.* 19.326–327, Agrippa desisted from the project at Claudius's behest.

These are the contents of the twentieth book of Josephus's histories of Jewish antiquity:

I.   How Claudius Caesar sent Fadus as procurator of Judea after the death of Agrippa. *20.1*

II.   Civil strife of the Philadelphians against the Jews who live in the Perea about the borders of a single village.[6] And how after many Philadelphians were killed by them Fadus, indignant against the Jews of Perea, captured and executed the three main men [of their numbers]. *20.2*

III.   How Tholomeus, the arch-brigand, who had been robbing the Arabs, was captured and, after being brought to Fadus, executed. *20.5*

IV.   How Fadus and Cassius Longinus (the governor of Syria), having come up to Jerusalem, ordered the most prominent among the Jews to deposit the full-length and holy vestment in the Antonia, under Roman authority, as was previously the case. *20.6*

V.   The Jew's petition to Fadus and Longinus, asking them to allow them to send a legation to Claudius Caesar about this matter. *20.7*

VI.   How Fadus, after taking hostages, gave them permission. *20.8*

VII.   How Claudius Caesar, having been called upon by the younger Agrippa, granted the Jews the things that they requested and wrote Fadus about them. *20.9*

VIII. In what manner Queen Helena of the Adiabenians and her sons, Monobazus and Izates, and their whole family became zealous for Jewish practices. *20.17*

IX.   How, upon the death of Herod, King of Chalcis, the younger Agrippa took over his realm, having been given it by Claudius Caesar.[7] *20.104*

X.   How Tiberius Alexander, having come to Judea as its procurator, punished the sons of Judas the Galilean who had led the multitude astray. *20.102*

XI.   About the famine that occurred in the country. *20.101*

XII.   The arrival of Cumanus in Judea, after he had been sent by Caesar as procurator. *20.104*

XIII. How a great number of Jews perished in the Temple in his day. *20.105*

XIV. Civil strife by Jews against Samaritans and how many of the Samaritans were killed. *20.118*

XV.   How [Ummidius] Quadratus, the governor of Syria, having heard that and having come up to Judea, ordered the most prominent among the Jews and the Samaritans to go up to Rome, along with Cumanus the procurator and Celer the military tribune, so as to render account to Claudius Caesar concerning what they had done, while he himself punished some of the Jews. *20.125*

XVI. How Claudius, having heard them, acquitted the Jews of the charge (having been called upon [to do so] by King Agrippa), but exiled Cumanus and punished Celer (the military tribune) and the most prominent of the Samaritans. *20.134*

XVII. How Felix, having been sent as procurator and finding the country being ravaged by the brigands, took care to wipe them out and establish peace in the country; he put the most prominent of the brigands, named Eleazar, into chains and sent him up to Rome. *20.160*

---

6 Reading μιᾶς. Cf. the note on "Zia" at 20.2.

7 The order of IX–XII deviates from that of the account at *Ant.* 20.101–104.

XVIII. How when a certain Egyptian charlatan came to visit [Judea] and many Jews were led astray by him, Felix sortied out against them and killed many of them. *20.169*

XIX.   How Felix the procurator put an end to the civil strife of the most prominent Jews in Caesarea against the Syrians. *20.173*

XX.   In what manner Nero succeeded to rule after Claudius died.[8] *20.148*

XXI.   How it happened that when Porcius Festus was sent to Judea to be procurator the land was being ravaged by the Sicarii. *20.185*

XXII. On the portico of the outer temple and the way the Jews raised it higher. *20.189*

XXIII. How Festus, indignant about that, sent the most prominent Jews to Rome, to Nero, to convince him about what they had done. *20.193*

XXIV. How, when Festus died in Judea, Albinus came as his successor. *20.197*

XXV.   How in his day the Sicarii stopped ravaging the country. *20.204*

XXVI. How Florus, having come as Albinus's successor, brought such great troubles upon the Jews that he forced them to turn to arms. *20.252*

XXVII. On Josephus, his family and his life as a citizen.[9] *Life*
This book encompasses a period of twenty-six years.[10] *44–70 CE*

---

8 Josephus's discussion of this, at *Ant.* 20.148–157, precedes the material summarized in XVII–XIX.

9 This somewhat strange use of πολιτεία is paralleled at *Life* 344 and perhaps is suggested by πολιτεύεσθαι at *Life* 12, just as this whole entry appears to be referring to the *Life*, treating it, in consonance with other evidence, as an appendix to *Antiquities*. Cf. the note on "my life" at 20.266.

10 So Niese, following most manuscripts. One reads "22," apparently calculating from Agrippa's death to the outbreak of the rebellion.

BIBLIOGRAPHY

Aberbach, M. (1949/50). "The Conflicting Accounts of Josephus and Tacitus Concerning Cumanus' and Felix' Terms of Office." *JQR* 40: 1–14.

Africa, T. (1982). "Worms and the Death of Kings: A Cautionary Note on Disease and History." *Classical Antiquity* 1: 1–17.

Albert, K. (1902). *Strabo als Quelle des Flavius Josephus*. Diss. Würzburg. Aschaffenburg: Schippnersehen Druckerei.

Alkier, S. and J. Zangenberg, ed. (2003). *Zeichen aus Text und Stein: Studien auf dem Weg zu einer Archäologie des Neuen Testaments*. Texte und Arbeiten zum neutestamentlichen Zeitalter 42. Tübingen: Francke.

Allen, J. (2006). *Hostages and Hostage-Taking in the Roman Empire*. Cambridge: Cambridge University Press.

Alon, G. (1977). *Jews, Judaism and the Classical World: Studies in Jewish History in the Times of the Second Temple and Talmud*. Jerusalem: Magnes.

Alston, R. (2020). "Ethnic Violence in Roman Alexandria: A Comparative Approach." *Acta Classica* 63: 1–29.

Altshuler, D. (1978/79). "The Treatise ΠΕΡΙ ΕΘΩΝ ΚΑΙ ΑΙΤΙΩΝ 'On Customs and Causes' by Flavius Josephus." *JQR* 69: 226–232.

Amorai-Stark, S. et al. (2018). "An Inscribed Copper-Alloy Finger Ring from Herodium Depicting a Krater." *IEJ* 68: 208–220.

Anderson, G. (2009). "Towards a Theology of the Tabernacle and Its Furniture." Pp. 159–194 in *Text, Thought, and Practice in Qumran and Early Christianity*, ed. R. Clements and D. R. Schwartz. STDJ 84. Leiden: Brill.

Ando, C. (2000). *Imperial Ideology and Provincial Loyalty in the Roman Empire*. Classics and Contemporary Thought 6. Berkeley: University of California Press.

Andrade, N. (2010). "Ambiguity, Violence, and Community in the Cities of Judaea and Syria." *Historia* 59: 342–370.

Annas, J. (2017). "Philo on Virtue and the Laws of Moses." Pp. 188–213 in eadem, *Virtue and Laws in Plato and Beyond*. Oxford: Oxford University Press.

Appelbaum, A. (2018). "A Fresh Look at Philo's Family." *SPA* 30: 93–113.

Arav, R. and R. A. Freund, ed. (1995–2009). *Bethsaida: A City by the Northern Shore of the Sea of* Galilee. 4 vols. Kirksville, Missouri: Thomas Jefferson University Press.

Arbiv, K. (2023). "Evidence of the Roman Attack on the Third Wall of Jerusalem at the End of the Second Temple Period." *Atiqot* 111: 103–118.

Arenhoevel, D. (1967). *Die Theokratie nach dem 1. und 2. Makkabäerbuch*. Walberberger Studien der Albertus-Magnus-Akademie: Theologische Reihe, 3. Mainz: Matthias-Grünewald.

Arnhart, L. (1983). "Statesmanship as Magnanimity: Classical, Christian and Modern." *Polity* 16: 263–283.

Atkinson, K. M. T. (1958). "The Governors of the Province Asia in the Reign of Augustus." *Historia* 7: 300–330.

Attridge, H. A. (1976). *The Interpretation of Biblical History in the Antiquitates Judaicae of Flavius Josephus*. HDR 7. Missoula: Scholars.

Aus, R. D. (2015). *Essays in the Judaic Background of Mark 11:12–14, 20–21; 15:23; Luke 1:37; John 19:28–30; and Acts 11:28*. Studies in Judaism. Lanham, Maryland: University Press of America.

Aviam, M. (2007). "The Archaeological Illumination of Josephus' Narrative of the Battles at Yodefat and Gamla." Pp. 372–384 in Rodgers 2007.

Avi-Yonah, M. (1950/51). "The Foundation of Tiberias." *IEJ* 1: 160–169.

Bagnall, R. S. (1993). *Egypt in Late Antiquity*. Princeton: Princeton University Press.

Bagnall, R. S. and K. A. Worp. (2004). *Chronological Systems of Byzantine Egypt*. Second edition. Leiden: Brill.

Balentine, S. E. (1983). *The Hidden God: The Hiding of the Face of God in the Old Testament*. Oxford Theological Monographs. Oxford: Oxford University Press.

Balsdon, J. P. V. D. (1950). "The 'Divinity' of Alexander." *Historia* 1: 363–388.

Bammel, E. (1974a). "Joasar." *ZDPV* 90: 61–68.

Bammel, E. (1974b). "Die Blutgerichtsbarkeit in der römischen Provinz Judäa vor dem ersten jüdischen Aufstand." *JJS* 25: 35–49.

Barag, D. (1992/93). "New Evidence on the Foreign Policy of John Hyrcanus I." *INJ* 12: 1–12.

Barclay, J. M. G. (1996). *Jews in the Mediterranean Diaspora from Alexander to Trajan (323 BCE–117 CE)*. Edinburgh: T. & T. Clark.

Barclay, J. M. G. (2007). *Against Apion*. FJTC 10. Leiden: Brill.

Bardet, S. (2002). *Le Testimonium Flavianum: Examen historique, considérations historiographiques*. Josèphe et son temps 5. Paris: du Cerf.

Barish, D. A. (1978). "The *Autobiography* of Josephus and the Hypothesis of a Second Edition of His *Antiquities*." HTR 71: 61–75.

Barkay, R. (2018). "The Origin of Aretas IV King of the Nabataeans." *ARAM* 30: 369–373.

Bar-Kochva, B. (1996). *Pseudo-Hecataeus* On the Jews: *Legitimizing the Jewish Diaspora*. HCS 21. Berkeley: University of California.

Barrett, A. A. (1989). *Caligula: The Corruption of Power*. London: Batsford.

Barrett, A. A. (1990). "Claudius, Gaius and the Client Kings." *CQ* 40: 284–286.

Barrett, A. A. (1996). *Agrippina: Sex, Power, and Politics in the Early Empire*. New Haven: Yale University Press.

Barrett, A. A. (2019). *Caligula: The Abuse of Power*. Second edition. Abingdon: Routledge.

Bartlett, J. R., ed. (2002). *Jews in the Hellenistic and Roman Cities*. London: Routledge.

Barton, C. A. and D. Boyarin (2016). *Imagine no Religion: How Modern Abstractions Hide Ancient Realities*. New York: Fordham University Press.

Bastianini, G. (1975). "Lista dei prefetti d'Egitto dal 30a al 299p." *ZPE* 17: 263–321.

Bauckham, R. (1999). "For What Offence Was James Put to Death?" Pp. 199–232 in *James the Just and Christian Origins*, ed. B. D. Chilton and C. A. Evans. Supplements to NovT 98. Leiden: Brill.

Baughman, K. E. (2014). "Poppaea Sabina, Jewish Sympathies, and the Fire of Rome." *Women in Judaism* 11: 1–18.

Baumbach, G. (1989). "The Sadducees in Josephus." Pp. 173–195 in Feldman and Hata 1989.

Baumbach, G. (1997). "Die Pharisäersdarstellung des Josephus: propharisäisch oder antipharisäisch?" *Franz-Delitzsch-Vorlesungen der Westfälischen Wilhelms-Universität Münster* 6: 3–42.

Baumgarten, A. I. (1982). "The Name of the Pharisees." *JBL* 102: 411–428.

Baumgarten, A. I. (1987). "The Pharisaic Paradosis." *HTR* 80: 63–78.

Baumgarten, A. I. (1994). "Josephus on Essene Sacrifice." *JJS* 45: 169–183.

Baumgarten, A. [I.]. (1998). "Graeco-Roman Voluntary Associations and Ancient Jewish Sects." Pp. 93–111 in *Jews in a Graeco-Roman World*, ed. M. Goodman. Oxford: Oxford University Press.

Baumgarten, A. I. (2016). "Josephus and the Jewish Sects." Pp. 261–272 in Chapman and Rodgers 2016.

Baumgarten, J. M. (1977). *Studies in Qumran Law*. SJLA 24. Leiden: Brill.

Baumgarten, J. M. (1982). "Hanging and Treason in Qumran and Roman Law." *EI* 16: 7*–16* (in English).

Baumgarten, J. M. (2022). *Studies in Qumran Law and Thought*, ed R. A. Clements and D. R. Schwartz. STDJ 138. Leiden: Brill.

Beall, T. S. (1988). *Josephus' Description of the Essenes Illustrated by the Dead Sea Scrolls*. SNTSMS 58. Cambridge: Cambridge University Press.

Beebe, H. K. (1983). "Caesarea Maritima: Its Strategic and Political Significance to Rome." *Journal of Near Eastern Studies* 42: 195–207.

Begg, C. T. and P. Spilsbury (2005). *Judean Antiquities Books 8–10*. FJTC 5. Leiden: Brill.

Beit-Arieh, I. (2008). "Malḥata, Tel." Pp. 1917–1918 in *NEAEHL* 5.

Beit-Arieh, I and L. Freud (2015). *Tel Malḥata: A Central City in the Biblical Negev*, I. Monograph Series of the Sonia and Marco Nadler Institute of Archaeology 32. Winona Lake, Indiana: Eisenbrauns.

Bekker, I. (1856). *Flavii Iosephi Opera Omnia*, IV. Lipsiae: Teubneri.

Bell, A. A., Jr. (1976/77). "Josephus the Satirist? A Clue to the Original Form of the 'Testimonium Flavianum.'" *JQR* 67: 16–22.

Bell, H. I. (1924). *Jews and Christians in Egypt*. London: British Museum.

Bell, H. I. (1949). "Philanthropia in the Papyri of the Roman Period." Pp. 31–37 in *Hommages à Joseph Bidez et à Franz Cumont*. Collection Latomus 2. Bruxelles: Latomus.

Bell, S. (2014). "Roman Chariot Racing: Charioteers, Factions, Spectators." Pp. 492–504 in *A Companion to Sport and Spectacle in Greek and Roman Antiquity*, ed. P. Christesen and D. G. Kyle. Chichester, West Sussex, UK: Wiley-Blackwell.

Bellen, H. (1981). *Die germanische Leibwache der römischen Kaiser des julisch-claudischen Hauses*. Abhandlungen der geistes- und sozialwissenschaftlichen Klasse Jg. 1981 Nr. 1. Mainz: Akademie der Wissenschaften und Literatur, and Wiesbaden: Steiner.

Benveniste, E. (1974). "Deux modèles linguistiques de la cité." Pages 272–280 in idem, *Problèmes de linguistique générale*, vol. 2. Bibliothèque des sciences humaines. Paris: Gallimard.

Ben-Yishai, S. (2006). "Book XIX of Josephus' *Jewish Antiquities* in Context." MA Thesis, The Hebrew University of Jerusalem.

Ben-Yishai, S. (2021). "'Brigands' and 'Tyrants' in Josephus' *Bellvm Jvdaicvm*." *CQ* 71: 902–907.

Ben Zeev, M. P. (1998). *Jewish Rights in the Roman World: The Greek and Roman Documents Quoted by Josephus Flavius.* Tübingen: Mohr Siebeck.

Berger, A. (1953). "Encyclopedic Dictionary of Roman Law." *Transactions of the American Philosophical Society* n.s. 43/2: 333–809.

Berger, S. (1992). *Revolution and Society in Greek Sicily and Southern Italy.* Historia Einzelschriften 71. Stuttgart: Steiner.

Bergmann, J. (1938). "Die runden und hyperbolischen Zahlen in der Agada." *MGWJ* 82: 361–376.

Bergmann, W. and C. Hoffmann (1987). "Kalkül oder 'Massenwahn'? Eine soziologische Interpretation der antijüdischen Unruhen in Alexandria 38 n. Chr." Pp. 15–46 in *Antisemitismus und jüdische Geschichte: Studien zu Ehren von Herbert A. Strauss*, ed. R. Erb and M. Schmidt. Berlin: Wissenschaftlicher Autorenverlag.

Bergmeier, R. (1993). *Die Essener-Berichte des Flavius Josephus: Quellenstudien zu den Essenertexten im Werk des judischen Historiographen.* Kampen: Kok Pharos.

Bergmeier, R. (2013). *Die Qumran-Essener-Hypothese: Die Handschriftenfunde bei Khirbet Qumran, ihr spezifischer Trägerkreis und die essenische Gemeinschaftsbewegung.* Biblisch-theologische Studien 133. Neukirchener Verlag.

Berkowitz, B. A. (2006). *Execution and Invention: Death Penalty Discourse in Early Rabbinic and Christian Cultures.* New York: Oxford University Press.

Berlin, A. (2009). "Rams and Lambs in Psalm 114:4 and 6: The Septuagint's Translation of X//בן Y Parallelisms." *Textus* 24: 107–117.

Bernett, M. (2007). *Der Kaiserkult in Judäa unter den Herodiern und Römern: Untersuchungen zur politischen und religiösen Geschichte Judäas von 30 v. bis 66 n. Chr.* WUNT 203. Tübingen: Mohr Siebeck.

Bernett, M. (2007a). "Roman Imperial Cult in the Galilee: Structures, Functions, and Dynamics." Pp. 337–356 in *Religion, Ethnicity and Identity in Ancient Galilee: A Region in Transition*, ed. J. Zangenberg, H. W. Attridge, and D. B. Martin. WUNT 210. Tübingen: Mohr Siebeck.

Berthelot, K. (2000). "The Use of Greek and Roman Stereotypes of the Egyptians by Hellenistic Jewish Apologists, with Special Reference to Josephus' *Against Apion*." Pp. 185–221 in *Internationales Josephus-Kolloquium Aarhus 1999*, ed. J. U. Kalms. MJS 6. Münster: LIT

Berthelot, K. (2021). *Jews and Their Roman Rivals: Pagan Rome's Challenge to Israel.* Princeton: Princeton University Press.

Bichler, R. (2018). "Benedikt Niese: Ein verkannter Handbuchautor?" Pp. 49–90 in *In solo barbarico ...: Das Seminar für alte Geschichte der Philipps-Universität Marburg von seinen Anfängen bis in die 1960er Jahre*, ed. V. Losemann and K. Ruffing. Münster: Waxmann.

Bickerman, E. J. (2007). *Studies in Jewish and Christian History: A New Edition in English including The God of the Maccabees*, ed. A. Tropper. 2 vols. AJEC 68. Leiden: Brill.

Bietenhard, H. (1977). "Die syrische Dekapolis von Pompeius bis Trajan." *ANRW* II/8: 220–261.

Bietenholz, P. G. (1994). *Historia and Fabula: Myths and Legends in Historical Thought from Antiquity to the Modern Age.* Brill's Studies in Intellectual History 59. Leiden: Brill.

Bigwood, J. M. (2004). "Queen Mousa, Mother and Wife (?) of King Phraatakes of Parthia: A Re-Evaluation of the Evidence." *Mouseion* III/4: 35–70.

Bikerman, E. (1938). *Institutions des Séleucides.* Service des Antiquités: Bibliothèque archéologique et historique 26. Paris: Geuthner.

Bilde, P. (1978). "The Roman Emperor Gaius (Caligula)'s Attempt to Erect his Statue in the Temple of Jerusalem." *Studia Theologica* 32: 67–93.

Bilde, P. (1979). "The Causes of the Jewish War according to Josephus." *JSJ* 10: 179–202.

Bilde, P. (1988). *Flavius Josephus between Jerusalem and Rome: His Life, His Works, and Their Importance.* Journal for the Study of the Pseudepigrapha Supplement Series 2. Sheffield: Sheffield Academic Press.

Bingham, S. (2013). *The Praetorian Guard: A History of Rome's Elite Special Forces.* London: Tauris.

Bird, H. W. (1994). *Liber de Caesaribus of Sextus Aurelius Victor.* Translated Texts for Historians 17. Liverpool: Liverpool University Press.

Bird, M. F. (2006). *Jesus and the Origins of the Gentile Mission.* Library of New Testament Studies 331. London: T. & T. Clark.

Birley, A. R. (2000). "Two Unidentified Senators in Josephus, *A.J.* 19." *CQ* 50: 620–623.

Birnbaum, E. (2004). "A Leader with Vision in the Ancient Jewish Diaspora: Philo of Alexandria." Pp. 1.57–90 in *Jewish Religious Leadership: Image and Reality*, ed. J. Wertheimer. 2 vols. New York: Jewish Theological Seminary.

Birt, T. (1882). *Das antike Buchwesen in seinem Verhältniss zur Litteratur.* Berlin: Hertz.

Bloch, R. (1999). "Mose und die Scharlatane: Zum Vorwurf γόης καὶ ἀπατεών in Contra Apionem 2.145–161." Pp. 142–157 in *Internationales Josephus-Kolloquium Brüssel 1998*, ed. J. U. Kalms and F. Siegert. MJS 4. Münster: LIT.

Bloch, R. (2006). "Josephus, Ant. Iud. 1,15: ἀσχήμων μυθολογία." *ZNW* 97: 131–133.

Boatwright, M. T. (2012). *Peoples of the Roman World*. Cambridge: Cambridge University Press.

Boffo, L. (1994). *Iscrizioni greche e latine per lo studio della Bibbia*. Brescia: Paideia.

Bohak, G. (2008). *Ancient Jewish Magic: A History*. Cambridge: Cambridge University Press.

Bohrmann, M. (1999). "Le voyage à Rome de Flavius Josèphe (*Vita* 13–16)." Pp. 222–229 in *Internationales Josephus-Kolloquium Brüssel 1998*, ed. J. U. Kalms and F. Siegert. MJS 4. Münster: LIT.

Bond, H. (1998). *Pontius Pilate in History and Interpretation*. SNTSMS 100. Cambridge: Cambridge University Press.

Bond, H. (2004). *Caiaphas: Friend of Rome and Judge of Jesus?* Louisville: Westminster John Knox.

Botermann, H. (1996). *Das Judenedikt des Kaisers Claudius: Römischer Staat und* Christiani *im 1. Jahrhundert*. Hermes Einzelschriften 71. Stuttgart: Steiner.

Bovon, F. (2000). "*Fragment Oxyrhynchus 840*, Fragment of a Lost Gospel, Witness of an Early Christian Controversy over Purity." *JBL* 119: 705–728.

Box, H. (1939). *Philonis Alexandrini: In Flaccum*. London: Oxford University Press.

Bradley, K. R. (1985). "Child Care at Rome: The Role of Men." *Historical Reflections/Réflections historiques* 12: 485–523.

Brandon, S. G. F. (1967a). *Jesus and the Zealots: A Study of the Political Factor in Primitive Christianity*. New York: Scribner's Sons.

Brandon, S. G. F. (1967b). "The Death of James the Just: A New Interpretation." Pp. 57–69 in *Studies in Mysticism and Religon Presented to Gershom G. Scholem on His Seventieth Birthday by Pupils, Colleagues, and Friends*, ed. E. E. Urbach, R. J. Z. Werblowsky, and C. Wirszubski. Jerusalem: Magnes Press.

Brann, M. (1873). *Die Söhne des Herodes: Eine biographische Skizze, zugleich ein Beitrag zur neutestamentliche Zeitgeschichte*. Breslau: Skutsch (reprint of six installments in *MGWJ* 22 [1873]).

Braund, D. (1983). "Four Notes on the Herods." *CQ* 33: 239–242.

Braund, D. (1984). *Rome and the Friendly King: The Character of the Client Kingship*. London: Croom Helm, and New York: St. Martin's Press.

Brenk, F. E. and F. C. de Rossi (2001). "The 'Notorious' Felix, Procurator of Judaea, and His Many Wives." *Biblica* 62: 410–417.

Brighton, M. A. (2009). *The Sicarii in Josephus's Judean War: Rhetorical Analysis and Historical Observations*. Early Judaism and Its Literature 27. Atlanta: Society of Biblical Literature.

Briscoe, J. (1971). "The Imperial Oath of Allegiance." *CR* 21 (1971): 260–263.

Brody, R. (1990). "Appendix IV: Caiaphas and Cantheras." Pp. 190–195 in D. R. Schwartz 1990a.

Broer, I. (1994). "Die Konversion des Königshauses von Adiabene nach Josephus (Ant XX)." Pp. 133–162 in *Nach den Anfängen Fragen: Herrn Prof. Dr. theol. Gerhard Dautzenberg zum 60. Geburtstag am 30. Januar 1994*, ed. C. Mayer, K. Müller, and G. Schmalenberg. Giessen: Fachbereich Evangelische Theologie und Katholische Theologie und deren Didaktik.

Broshi, M. and E. Eshel (1997). "The Greek King is Antiochus IV (4QHistorical Text = 4Q248)." *JJS* 48: 120–129.

Brown, A. Philip, II. (2013). "Chrysostom and Epiphanius: Long Hair Prohibited as Covering in 1 Corinthians 11:4, 7." *Bulletin for Biblical Research* 23: 365–376.

Brown, R. E. (1993). *The Birth of the Messiah: A Commentary on the Infancy Narratives in the Gospels of Matthew and Luke*. New updated edition. New York: Doubleday.

Brown, R. E. (1994). *The Death of the Messiah: From Gethsamene to the Grave*. 2 vols. Anchor Bible Reference Library. New York: Doubleday.

Bruce, F. F. (1963/65). "Herod Antipas, Tetrarch of Galilee and Peraea." *The Annual of Leeds University Oriental Society* 5: 6–23.

Brunt, P. A. (1961). "Charges of Provincial Maladministration under the Early Principate." *Historia* 10: 189–227.

Brunt, P. A. (1975). "The Administrators of Roman Egypt." *JRS* 65: 124–47.

Brunt, P. A. (1983). "Princeps and Equites." *JRS* 73: 42–75.

Brust, M. (2005). *Die indischen und iranischen Lehnwörter im Griechischen*. Innsbrucker Beiträge zur Sprachwissenschaft. Innsbruck: Institut für Sprachen und Literaturen der Universität Innsbruck.

Bruun, C. (1999). "Methodisches zu den pejorative Spitznamen in der Antike und im Mittelalter (am Beispiel Notkers des Stammlers)." *Archiv für Kulturgeschichte* 81: 259–282.

Buchon, J.-A.-C. (1836). *Œuvres complètes de Flavius Joseph*. Paris: Desrez.

Büchler, A. (1896/97). "The Sources of Josephus for the History of Syria." *JQR* o.s. 9: 311–349.

Büchler, A. (1897/98). "The Fore-Court of Women and the Brass Gate in the Temple of Jerusalem." *JQR* 10: 678–718.

Burkitt, F. C. (1931). "H. St. J. Thackeray and His Work." *JTS* 32: 225–227.

Burridge, R. A. (1992). *What are the Gospels? A Comparison with Graeco-Roman Biography*. Cambridge: Cambridge University Press.

Busink, T. A. (1970–1980). *Der Tempel von Jerusalem von Salomo bis Herodes: Eine archäologisch-historische Studie unter Berücksichtigung des westsemitischen Tempelbaus.* 2 vols. Leiden: Brill.

Byron, J. (2003). *Slavery Metaphors in Early Judaism and Pauline Christianity: A Traditio-Historical and Exegetical Examination.* WUNT II/162. Tübingen: Mohr Siebeck.

Cairns, F. (2012). *Roman Lyric: Collected Papers on Catullus and Horace.* Beiträge zur Altertumskunde 301. Berlin: De Gruyter.

Cameron, A. (1976). *Circus Factions: Blues and Greens at Rome and Byzantium.* Oxford: Clarendon Press.

Cameron, H. (2019). *Making Mesopotamia: Geography and Empire in a Romano-Iranian Borderland.* Impact of Empire 32. Leiden: Brill.

Capponi, L. (2005). *Augustan Egypt: The Creation of a Roman Province.* New York: Routledge.

Capponi, L. (2007). *Il tempio di Leontopli in Egitto: Identità politica e religiosa dei Giudei di Onia (c. 150 a.C.–73 d.C.).* Pubblicazioni della Facoltà di Lettere e Filosofia dell'Università di Pavia. Pisa: ETS.

Carlier, C. (2008). *La cite de Moïse: Le people juif chez Philon d'Alexandrie.* Monothéismes et philosophie. Turnhout: Brepols.

Carney, T. F. (1960). "The Changing Picture of Claudius." *Acta Classica* 3: 99–104.

Carrier, R. (2012). "Origen, Eusebius, and the Accidental Interpolation in Josephus, *Jewish Antiquities* 20.200." *Journal of Early Christian Studies* 20: 489–514.

Carucci, M. (2019). "The Spectacle of Justice in the Roman Empire." Pp. 212–233 in *The Impact of Justice on the Roman Empire: Proceedings of the Thirteenth Workshop of the International Network Impact of Empire (Gent, June 21–24, 2017),* ed. O. Hekster and K. Verboven. Leiden: Brill.

Castelli, S. (2002). *Il terzo libro delle* Antichità Giudaiche *di Flavio Giuseppe e la Bibbia: Problemi storici et letterari, Traduzione e commento.* Biblioteca di Athenaeum 48. Como: New Press.

Castillio, P. G. (2010). "Plato: The Ship of State." *Philosophical Inquiry* 32: 1–22.

Chancey, M. (2001). "The Cultural Milieu of Ancient Sepphoris." *NTS* 47: 127–145.

Chancey, M. A. (2005). *Greco-Roman Culture and the Galilee of Jesus.* Cambridge: Cambridge University Press.

Chapman, H. H. (2019). "Josephus's Jewish War and Late Republican Civil War." Pp. 292–219 in *The Historiography of Late Republican Civil War,* ed. C. H. Lange and F. J. Vervaet. Historiography of Rome and Its Empire 5. Leiden: Brill.

Chapman, H. H. and Z. Rodgers, ed. (2016). *A Companion to Josephus.* Blackwell Companions to the Ancient World. Chichester: Wiley-Blackwell.

Charlesworth, J. and W. Weaver, ed. (1992). *What Has Archaeology to do with Faith?* Valley Forge: Trinity Press International.

Charlesworth, M. P. (1933). "The Tradition about Caligula." *Cambridge Historical Journal* 4: 105–119.

Charlesworth, M. P. (1936a). *Trade-Routes and Commerce of the Roman Empire.* 2nd edition. Cambridge: Cambridge University Press.

Charlesworth, M. P. (1936b). *Five Men: Character Studies from the Roman Empire.* Martin Classical Lectures 6. Cambridge, Mass.: Harvard University Press.

Chaumont, M. L. (2011). "Cinnamus." *Encyclopædia Iranica* V/6: 593–594 (updated online version, accessed in January 2024).

Chrysostomus (1839). *The Homilies of S. John Chrysostom, Archbishop of Constantinople, on the First Epistle of St. Paul the Apostle to the Corinthians, Part II.* Oxford: Parker.

Ciaceri, E. (1916/17). "Agrippa I° e la politica di Roma verso la Giudea." *Atti del Reale Istituto Veneto di Scienze, Lettere ed Arti* 76/2: 687–724.

Ciardiello, R. (2012). "Beryllos, the Jews and the Villa of Poppaea in Oplontis (Torre Annunziata)." Pp. 265–281 in *Contested Spaces: Houses and Temples in Roman Antiquity and the New Testament,* ed. D. L. Balch and A. Weissenrieder. WUNT 285. Tübingen: Mohr Siebeck.

Cizek, E. (1999). "Britannicus a-t-il été empoisonné?" *Helmantica* 50: 173–183.

Clements, R. A. (2012). "Epilogue: 70 CE after 135 CE—The Making of a Watershed." Pp. 517–536 in *Was 70 a Watershed in Jewish History? On Jews and Judaism before and after the Destruction of the Second Temple,* ed. D. R. Schwartz, Z. Weiss, and R. A. Clements. AJEC 78. Leiden: Brill.

Coello, T. (1996). *Unit Sizes in the Late Roman Army.* BAR International Series 645. Oxford: Tempus Reparatum.

Cohen, N. G. (1975/76). "Asinaeus and Anilaeus: Additional Comments to Josephus' Antiquities of the Jews." *ASTI* 10: 30–37.

Cohen, S. J. D. (1979). *Josephus in Galilee and Rome: His Vita and Development as a Historian.* Columbia Studies in the Classical Tradition 8. Leiden: Brill.

Cohen, S. J. D. (1982/83). "Alexander the Great and Jaddus the High Priest according to Josephus." *AJS Review* 7–8: 41–68.

Cohen, S. J. D. (1987). "Respect for Judaism by Gentiles according to Josephus." *HTR* 80: 409–430.

Cohen, S. J. D. (1990). "The Modern Study of Ancient Judaism." Pp. 55–73 in *The State of Jewish Studies*, ed. S. J. D. Cohen and E. L. Greenstein. Detroit: Wayne State University Press.

Cohen, S. J. D. (1994). "ΙΟΥΔΑΙΟΣ ΤΟ ΓΕΝΟΣ and Related Expressions in Josephus." Pp. 23–38 in *Josephus and the History of the Greco-Roman Period: Essays in Memory of Morton Smith*, ed. F. Parente and J. Sievers; SPB 41; Leiden: Brill.

Cohen, S. J. D. (1999). *The Beginnings of Jewishness: Boundaries, Varieties, Uncertainties*. HCS 31. Berkeley: Univ. of California.

Cohen-Matlofsky, C. (2020). "Women at Qumran? Reconsidering the Textual and Archaeological Data." Pp. 143–165 in *Sacred Texts and Disparate Interpetations: Qumran Manuscripts Seventy Years Later*, ed. H. Drawnel. STDJ 133. Leiden: Brill.

Colautti, F. M. (2002). *Passover in the Work of Josephus*. JSJSup 75. Leiden: Brill.

Coleman, K. M. (1990). "Fatal Charades: Roman Executions Staged as Mythological Enactments." *JRS* 80: 44–73.

Collins, J. J. (2009). "Josephus on the Essenes: The Sources of His Information." Pp. 51–72 in *A Wandering Galilean: Essays in Honour of Seán Freyne,* ed. Z. Rodgers et al. JSJSup 132. Leiden: Brill.

Collins, M. F. (1972). "The Hidden Vessels in Samaritan Traditions." *JSJ* 3: 97–116.

Cook, J. G. (2019). "Raised on the Third Day According to the Scriptures: Hosea 6:2 in Jewish Tradition." Pp. 188–211 in *Paul and Scripture*, ed. S. E. Porter and C. D. Land. Pauline Studies 10. Leiden: Brill.

Cooley, A. E. (2009). *Res Gestae Divi Augusti: Text, Translation, and Commentary*. Cambridge: Cambridge University Press.

Cooper, G. C. (1998). *Attic Greek Prose Syntax*, I. Ann Arbor: University of Michigan Press.

Corbett, P. E. (1930). *The Roman Law of Marriage*. Oxford: The Clarendon Press.

Cotton, H. M. (1989). "The Date of the Fall of Masada: The Evidence of the Masada Papyri." *ZPE* 78: 157–162.

Cotton, H. M. (1999). "Some Aspects of the Roman Administration of Judaea/Syria-Palaestina." Pp. 75–91 in *Lokale Autonomie und römische Ordnungsmacht in den kaiserzeitlichen Provinzen vom 1.–3. Jahrhundert*, ed. Werner Eck. München: Oldenbourg.

Cotton, H. M. and J. Geiger (1989). *Masada, II: The Yigael Yadin Excavations 1963–1965, Final Reports: The Latin and Greek Documents*. Jerusalem: Israel Exploration Society and The Hebrew University of Jerusalem.

Cowan, J. A. (2018). "A Tale of Two *Antiquities*: A Fresh Evaluation of the Relationship between the Ancient Histories of T. Flavius Josephus and Dionysius of Halicarnassus." *JSJ* 49: 1–23.

Crook, J. (1955). *Consilium Principis: Imperial Councils and Counsellors from Augustus to Diocletian*. Cambridge: Cambridge University Press.

Cunliffe, B. (2011). "In the Fabulous Celtic Twilight." Pp. 190–210 in *The Barbarians of Ancient Europe: Realities and Interactions*, ed. L. Bonfante. Cambridge: Cambridge University Press.

Curran, J. (2011). "Flavius Josephus in Rome." Pp. 65–86 in *Flavius Josephus: Interpretation and History*, ed. J. Pastor, P. Stern, and M. Mor. JSJSup 146. Leiden: Brill.

Currie, H. MacL. (1989). "An Obituary Formula in the Historians." *Latomus* 48: 346–353.

Czajkowski, K. and B. Eckhardt (2021). *Herod in History: Nicolaus of Damascus and the Augustan Context*. Oxford: Oxford University Press.

Dąbrowa, E. (1998). *The Governors of Roman Syria from Augustus to Septimius Severus*. Antiquitas I/45. Bonn: Habelt.

Dąbrowa, E. (2011). "The Date of the Census of Quirinius and the Chronology of the Governors of the Province of Syria." *ZPE* 178: 137–142.

Dąbrowa, E. (2012). "The Arsacid Empire." Pp. 164–186 in *The Oxford Handbook of Iranian History*, ed. T. Daryaee. Oxford: Oxford University Press.

Dąbrowa, E. (2015). "The Roman Army in Action in Judea (4 BCE–66 CE)." Pp. 59–68 in *Ad fines imperii romani: Studia Thaddaeo Sarnowski septuagenario ab amicis, collegis discipulisque dedicata*, ed. A. Tomas. Varsoviae: Institute of Archaeology, University of Warsaw.

Danby, H. (1933). *The Mishnah*. Oxford: Oxford University Press.

Danker, F. W. (1982). *Benefactor: Epigraphic Study of a Graeco-Roman and New Testament Semantic Field*. St. Louis: Clayton Publishing House.

Danker, F. W., ed. (2000). *A Greek-English Lexicon of the New Testament and Other Early Christian Literature*. Third edition. Chicago: University of Chicago Press.

Daube, D. (1976). "'I Believe' in *Jewish Antiquities* xi.237." *JJS* 27 (1976): 142–146.

Daube, D. (1980). "Typology in Josephus." *JJS* 31: 18–36.

Daugherty, G. N. (1992). "The *Cohortes Vigilum* and the Great Fire of 64 AD." *CJ* 87: 229–240.

Debevoise N. C. (1938). *A Political History of Parthia*. Chicago: The University of Chicago Press.

Degrassi, A., ed. (1963). *Inscriptiones Italiae XIII/2: Fasti Anni Numami et Iuliani*. Roma: Istituto poligrafico dello stato.

Deines, R. (1993). *Jüdische Steingefässe und pharisäische Frömmigkeit: Ein archäologisch-historischer Beitrag zum Verständnis von Joh 2,6 und der jüdischen Reinheitshalacha zur Zeit Jesu*. WUNT II/52. Tübingen: Mohr Siebeck.

Denniston, J. D. (1954). *The Greek Particles*. 2nd edition. Oxford: Clarendon Press.

Dessau, H., ed. (1892). *Inscriptiones Latinae Selectae*, vol. I. Berlin: Weidmann.

Destinon, J. von (1904). *Untersuchungen zu Flavius Josephus*. Wissenschaftliche Beilage zur Jahresbericht des kgl. Gymnasiums zu Kiel. Kiel: Fienke.

Dewar, M. (2008). "Spinning the *Trabea*: Consular Robes and Propaganda in the Panegyrics of Claudian." Pp. 217–237 in *Roman Dress and the Fabrics of Roman Culture*, ed. J. Edmondson and A. Keith. Toronto: University of Toronto Press.

Dickey, E. (1996). *Greek Forms of Address: From Herodotus to Lucian*. Oxford: Clarendon Press.

Dindorf, G. (1865). *Flavii Iosephi Opera, græce et latine*. I. Parisiis: Didot.

Dittenberger, W., ed. (1903–1905). *Orientis graeci inscriptiones selectae*. 2 vols. Lipsiae: Hirzel.

Dittenberger, W., ed. (1960). *Sylloge Inscriptionum Graecarum*. 4th edition. 4 vols. Hildesheim: Olms.

Dmitriev, S. (2005). *City Government in Hellenistic and Roman Asia Minor*. Oxford: Oxford University Press.

Dodge, H. (2014). "Venues for Spectacle and Sport (other than Amphitheatres) in the Roman World." Pp. 561–577 in *A Companion to Sport and Spectacle in Greek and Roman Antiquity*, ed. P. Christesen and D. G. Kyle. Blackwell Companions to the Ancient World. Chichester: Wiley-Blackwell.

Domaszewski, A. von (1885). *Die Fahnen im römischen Heere*. Abhandlungen des archäologisch-epigraphischen Seminars der Universität Wien 5. Wien: Gerold.

Don-Yehiya, E. (1992). "Hanukkah and the Myth of the Maccabees in Zionist Ideology and Israeli Society." *Jewish Journal of Sociology* 34: 5–23.

Drüner, H. (1896). *Untersuchungen über Josephus*. Ph.D. Marburg. Marburg: Hamel.

Dueck, D. and J. Geiger (2013). "The Land of Israel through Greek Eyes: The Case of Dor." *Cathedra* 149: 7–24 (in Hebrew).

Dunkle, J. R. (1971). "The Rhetorical Tyrant in Roman Historiography: Sallust, Livy and Tacitus." *The Classical World* 65: 12–20.

Dupont, J. (1955). "Notes sur les Actes des Apôtres." *RB* 62: 45–59.

Dupont, J. (1961). "*Aequitas Romana:* Notes sur Actes 25, 16." *RSR* 49: 354–385.

Dyson, S. L. (2010). *Rome: A Living Portrait of an Ancient City*. Baltimore: Johns Hopkins University Press.

Eaton, J. (2011). "The Political Significance of the Imperial Watchword in the Early Empire." *Greece and Rome* 58: 48–63.

Eck, W. (1972). "M. Pompeius Silvanus, consul designatus tertium: Ein Vertrauter Vespasians und Domitians." *ZPE* 9: 259–276.

Eck, W. (2007). *Rom und Judaea: Fünf Vorträge zur römischen Herrschaft in Palaestina*. Jenaer Vorlesungen zu Judentum, Antike und Christentum 2. Tübingen: Mohr Siebeck.

Eck, W. and A. Ecker (2023). "Not a 'Signet Ring' of Pontius. Pilatus." *'Atiqot* 110: 89–96.

Eck, W. (2008). "Benennung von römischen Amtsträgern und politisch-militärisch-administrativen Funktionen bei Flavius Iosephus: Probleme der korrekten Identifizierung." *ZPE* 166: 218–226.

Eckstein, A. M. (1990). "Josephus and Polybius: A Reconsideration." *Classical Antiquity* 9: 175–208.

Edelmann-Singer, B. (2013). "Herrscherfrauen als Leitfiguren: Iulia Severa, Poppaea und die 'Matronage' der jüdischen Religion." Pp. 89–99 in *Matronage: Handlungsstrategien und soziale Netzwerke von Herrscherfrauen im Altertum in diachroner Perspektive*, ed. Ch. Kunst. Osnabrücker Forschungen zu Altertum und Antike-Rezeption 20. Rahden/Westfalen: Leidorf.

Eder, S. (2022). *Frauen, die sich einmischen: biblisch-politische Lektüren : Festgabe für Irmtraud Fischer aus Anlass ihres 65. Geburtstages*, ed. S. Eder et al. Stuttgart: Kohlhammer.

Efron, J. (1987). *Studies on the Hasmonean Period*. SJLA 39. Leiden: Brill.

Ehrenkrook, J. von (2011). "Effeminacy in the Shadow of Empire: The Politics of Transgressive Gender in Josephus's *Bellum Judaicum*." *JQR* 101: 145–163.

Eisler, R. (1929/30). *ΙΗΣΟΥΣ ΒΑΣΙΛΕΥΣ ΟΥ ΒΑΣΙΛΕΥΣΑΣ: Die messianische Unabhängigkeitsbewegung vom Auftreten Johannes des Täufers bis zum Untergang Jakobs des Gerechten nach der neuerschlossenen Eroberung von Jerusalem des Flavius Josephus und den christlichen Quellen*. 2 vols. Heidelberg: Winters.

Ekinci, E. B. (2018). "Fratricide in Ottoman Law." *Belleten* [of the Turkish Historical Society] 82: 1013–1046.

Eliav, Y. Z. (2004). "The Tomb of James, Brother of Jesus, as Locus Memoriae." *HTR* 97: 33–59.

Ellens, J. H. ed. (2014). *Bethsaida in Archaeology, History and Ancient Culture: A Festschrift in Honor of John T. Greene*. Newcastle upon Tyne: Cambridge Scholars Publishing.

Emonds, H. (1941). *Zweite Auflage im Altertum: Kulturgeschichtliche Studien zur Überlieferung der antiken Literatur*. Leipzig: Harrassowitz.

Epstein, J. N. (1938). "On the Terms of 'Naziriteship.'" Pp. 10–16 in *Magnes Anniversary Book*, ed. F. I. Baer et al. Jerusalem: Hebrew University Press (in Hebrew).

Erdkamp, P. (2005). *The Grain Market in the Roman Empire: A Social, Political and Economic Study*. Cambridge: Cambridge University Press.

Ernesti, J. A. (1795). *Observationes philologico-criticae in Aristophanis Nubes et Flav. Iosephi Antiq. Iud.* Lipsiae: Fritsch.

Eshel, H. (2001). "4Q348, 4Q343 and 4Q345: Three Economic Documents from Qumran Cave 4?" *JJS* 52: 132–135.

Evans, K. G. (1995). "Alexander the Alabarch: Roman and Jew." Pp. 576–594 in *Society of Biblical Literature 1995 Seminar Papers*, ed. E. H. Lovering, Jr. SBLSPS 34. Atlanta: Scholars Press.

Faur, J.-C. (1978). "Un discours de l'empereur Caligula au Sénat (Dion, Hist. rom. LIX, 16)." *Klio* 60: 439–447.

Fantasia, U. (2004). "ἀκριβής." Pp. 1.36–66 in *Lexicon Historiographicum Graecum et Latinum*, ed. C. Ampolo and U. Fantasia. 3 vols. Pisa: Edizioni della Normale, 2004–.

Feingold, M. (2015). "A Rake's Progress: William Whiston Reads Josephus." *Eighteenth-Century Studies* 49: 17–30.

Feldman, L. H. (1962). "The Sources of Josephus' 'Antiquities,' Book 19." *Latomus* 21: 320–333.

Feldman, L. H., ed. and trans. (1965). *Josephus IX: Jewish Antiquities, Books XVIII–XX*. LCL. London: Heinemann, and Cambridge, Mass.: Harvard University Press.[1]

Feldman, L. H. (1984a). *Josephus and Modern Scholarship (1937–1980)*. Berlin: De Gruyter.

Feldman, L. H. (1984b). "Flavius Josephus Revisited: The Man, His Writings, and His Significance." *ANRW* II/21.2: 763–862.

Feldman, L. H. (1990). "Some Observations on the Name of Palestine." *HUCA* 61: 1–23.

Feldman, L. H. (1998a). *Josephus's Interpretation of the Bible*. HCS 27. Los Angeles: University of California Press.

Feldman, L. H. (1998b). *Studies in Josephus' Rewritten Bible*. Leiden: Brill.

Feldman, L. H. (2000). *Judean Antiquities 1–4*. FJTC 3. Leiden: Brill.

Feldman, L. H. and G. Hata, ed. (1989). *Josephus, the Bible, and History*. Leiden: Brill.

Finckh, H. E. (1962). *Zinsrecht der gräko-ägyptischen Papyri*. Nürnberg: Staudacher.

Finegan, J. (1974). *Encountering New Testament Manuscripts: A Working Introduction to Textual Criticism*. Grand Rapids, Michigan: Eerdmans.

Finkelstein, L. (1962). *The Pharisees: The Sociological Background of Their Faith*. 3rd edition. 2 vols. Philadelphia: Jewish Publication Society of America.

Finlay, T. D. (2005). *The Birth Report Genre in the Hebrew Bible*. FAT II/12. Tübingen: Mohr Siebeck.

First, M. 2015. *Esther Unmasked: Solving Eleven Mysteries of the Jewish Holidays and Liturgy*. New York: Kodesh Press.

Fischer, J. B. (1958/59). "The Term ΔΕΣΠΟΤΗΣ in Josephus." *JQR* 49: 132–138.

Fischer, M. L. and A. Stein (1994). "Josephus on the Use of Marble in Building Projects of Herod the Great." *JJS* 45: 79–85.

Fishwick, D. (1978). "The Development of Provincial Ruler Worship in the Western Roman Empire." Pp. 1201–1253 in *ANRW* II/16.2.

Fitzmyer, J. A. (1981). *The Gospel According to Luke (I–IX)*. Anchor Bible 28. Garden City, NY: Doubleday.

Flatto, D. C. (2020). *The Crown and the Courts: Separation of Powers in the Early Jewish Imagination*. Cambridge, Mass.: Harvard University Press.

Flusser, D. (2009). "Did the Jewish People Obscure the Memory of the Maccabees in the Middle Ages?" Pp. 137–155 in idem, *Judaism of the Second Temple Period, vol. 2: The Jewish Sages and Their Literature*. Grand Rapids: Eerdmans; Jerusalem: Magnes; and Jerusalem: Jerusalem Pespectives.

Forbes, C. A. (1955). "The Education and Training of Slaves in Antiquity." *TAPA* 86: 321–360.

Forster, E. S. (1950). "Columella and His Latin Treatise on Agriculture." *Greece and Rome* 19: 123–128.

Fraade, S. D. (1999). "Shifting from Priestly to Non-Priestly Legal Authority: A Comparison of the Damascus Document and the Midrash Sifra." *Dead Sea Discoveries* 6: 109–125.

Fraade, S. D. (2009). "The Temple as a Marker of Jewish Identity before and after 70 CE: The Role of the Holy Vessels in Rabbinic Memory and Imagination." Pp. 237–265 in *Jewish Identities in Antiquity: Studies in Memory of Menahem Stern*, ed. L. I. Levine and D. R. Schwartz. Tübingen: Mohr Siebeck.

Fraschetti, A., ed. (1991). *La commemorazione di Germanico nella documentazione epigrafica*. Saggi di storia antica 14. Roma: "L'Erma" di Bretschneider.

Free, A. (2017). "Beobachtungen zu den Büchern 18–20 der *Antiquitates Iudaicae* des Flavius Josephus." *Klio* 99: 586–628.

Friedman, R. E. (1977). "The Biblical Expression *mastîr pānîm*." *Hebrew Annual Review* 1: 139–147.

---

1 I used and cite the 1969 reprint. Later printings divide Books 18–19 and 20 into two separate volumes: the pagination in the first is as in the one-volume edition; in the second, the pagination is as in the original but the page numbers are lower by 388. Moreover, at least once (at 20.140) the text of the "reprint" has been silently corrected.

Frier, B. (1983). "Roman Life Expectancy: The Pannonian Evidence." *Phoenix* 37: 328–344.

Frey, J., S. Gripentrog and D. R. Schwartz, ed. (2007). *Jewish Identity in the Greco-Roman World*. AJEC 71. Leiden: Brill.

Frey, J. (2022). *Qumran and Christian Origins*. Waco, Texas: Baylor University Press.

Frey, J. (2024). "Josephus's Account of the Martyrdom of James: A Source for the Position of the Jerusalem Community of Jesus Followers within Their Environment?" Pp. 262–278 in *A Vision of the Days (Dan 10:14): Studies in Early Jewish History and Historiography in Honor of Daniel R. Schwartz*, ed. R. Brody et al. Leiden: Brill.

Freyne, S. (1980). *Galilee from Alexander the Great to Hadrian 323 B.C.E.–135 C.E.: A Study of Second Temple Judaism*. Wilmington: Continuum International Publishing Group.

Freyne, S. (1998). *Galilee, Jesus and the Gospels, Literary Approaches and Historical Investigations*. Philadelphia: Fortress Press.

Frick, C. (1893a). Review of Niese 1890a, Niese 1892, etc. *Berliner philologische Wochenschrift* 13: 296–299.

Frick, C. (1893b). Review of Naber 1893. *Berliner philologische Wochenschrift* 13: 299–300.

Fuchs [i.e. Fuks], A. (1947/49). "Marcus Julius Alexander." *Zion* 13/14: 10–17 (in Hebrew).

Gaechter, P. (1947). "The Hatred of the House of Annas." *Theological Studies* 8: 3–34.

Gafni, I. M. (1989). "Josephus and 1 Maccabees." Pp. 116–131 in Feldman and Hata 1989.

Gafni, I. M. (1997). *Land, Center and Diaspora: Jewish Constructs in Late Antiquity*. JSPSup 21. Sheffield: Sheffield Academic Press.

Gafni, I. M. (2019). *Jews and Judaism in the Rabbinic Era: Image and Reality—History and Historiography*. TSAJ 173. Tübingen: Mohr Siebeck.

Gallivan, P. (1978). "The Fasti for the Reign of Claudius." *CQ* 28: 407–426.

Gapp, K. S. (1935). "The Universal Famine under Claudius." *HTR* 28: 258–265.

Gardner, G. (2007). "Jewish Leadership and Hellenistic Civic Benefaction in the Second Century B.C.E." *JBL* 126: 327–343.

Garnsey, P. (1988). *Famine and Food Supply in the Graeco-Roman World: Responses to Risk and Crisis*. Cambridge: Cambridge University Press.

Garzetti, A. (1956). "La data dell'incontro all'Eufrate di Artabano III con L. Vitellio legato di Siria." Pp. 1.211–229 in *Studi in onore di Aristide Calderini e Roberto Paribeni*. 3 vols. Milano: Ceschina.

Gasparini, V. (2017). "Negotiating the Body: Between Religious Investment and Narratological Strategies: Paulina, Decia Mundus and the Priests of Anubis." Pp. 385–405 in *Beyond Priesthood: Religious Entrepreneurs and Innovators in the Roman Empire*, ed. R. L. Gordon, G. Petridou, and J. Rüpke. Religionsgeschichtliche Versuche und Vorarbeiten 66. Berlin: De Gruyter.

Gasparro, G. S. (2018). "Anubis in the 'Isiac' Family in the Hellenistic and Roman World." *Acta Antiqua Academiae Scientiarum Hungaricae* 58: 529–548.

Gerber, C. (1997). *Ein Bild des Judentums für Nichtjuden von Flavius Josephus: Untersuchungen zu seiner Schrift, Contra Apionem*. AGAJU 40. Leiden: Brill.

Gercke, A. (1895). *Seneca-Studien*. Leipzig: Teubner.

Gertoux, G. (2015). "Herod the Great and Jesus: Chronological, Historical and Archaeological Evidence." (online; accessed in May 2020).

Ghiretti, M. (1985). "Lo 'status' della Giudea dall'età Augustea all'età Claudia." *Latomus* 44: 751–766.

Gibbs, J. G. and L. H. Feldman (1985/86). "Josephus' Vocabulary for Slavery." *JQR* 76: 281–310.

Giet, S. (1956). "Un procédé littéraire d'exposition: l'anticipation chronologique." *Revue des études Augustiniennes et patristiques* 2: 243–249.

Gilbert, G. (1990/91). "The Making of a Jew: 'God-fearer' or Convert in the Story of Izates." *USQR* 44: 299–313.

Gillman, F. M. (2003). *Herodias: At Home in That Fox's Den*. Interfaces. Collegeville, Minnesota: Liturgical Press.

Glare, P. G. W., ed. (2000). *Oxford Latin Dictionary*. Corrected ed. Oxford: Clarendon Press.

Glass, R. G. and G. A. Keddie (2020). "From the Ptolemies to the Romans: Empire in Jewish Literature from Egypt." *JSJ* 51: 179–207.

Goetz, G., ed. (1888). *Corpus glossariorum latinorum*, II. Lipsiae: Teubner.

Goldenberg, R. (1979). "The Jewish Sabbath in the Roman World up to the Time of Constantine the Great." *ANRW* II/19.1: 414–447.

González-Salinero, R. (2022). *Military Service and the Integration of Jews into the Roman Empire*. Brill Reference Library of Judaism 72. Leiden: Brill.

Goodblatt, D. (1987a). "Josephus on Parthian Babylonia (Antiquities XVIII, 310–379)." *JAOS* 107: 605–622.

Goodblatt, D. (1987b). "Agrippa I and Palestinian Judaism in the First Century." *Jewish History* 2/1 (Spring 1987): 7–32.

Goodblatt, D. (1989). "The Place of the Pharisees in First Century Judaism: The State of the Debate." *JSJ* 20: 12–30.

Goodblatt, D. (1996). "Priestly Ideologies of the Judean Resistance." *JSQ* 3: 115–249.

Goodblatt, D. (2013). "Who is the Brother of Jesus? On Tripartite Naming Formulas in Ancient Jewish and Middle Aramaic Inscriptions." Pp. 1.147–165 in *Envisioning Judaism: Studies in Honor of Peter Schäfer on the Occasion of His Seventieth Birthday*, ed. R. S. Boustan et al. 2 vols. Tübingen: Mohr Siebeck.

Goodenough, E. R. (1926). "Philo and Public Life." *Journal of Egyptian Archaeology* 12: 77–79.

Goodman, M. (1983). *State and Society in Roman Galilee, A.D. 132–212*. Totowa: Rowman and Allanheld.

Goodman, M. (1987). *The Ruling Class of Judaea: The Origins of the Jewish Revolt against Rome, A.D. 66–70*. Cambridge: Cambridge University Press.

Goodman, M. (1994). "Josephus as Roman Citizen." Pp. 329–338 in Parente and Sievers 1994.

Goodman, M. (2007a). *Rome and Jerusalem: The Clash of Ancient Civilizations*. London: Allen Lane.

Goodman, M. (2007b). *Judaism in the Roman World: Collected Essays*. AJEC 67. Leiden: Brill.

Goodman, M. D. and A. J. Holladay. (1986). "Religious Scruples in Ancient Warfare." *CQ* 36: 151–171.

Goranson, S. (1984). "'Essenes': Etymology from עשה." *RQ* 11: 483–498.

Goud, T. E. (1996). "The Sources of Josephus *Antiquities* 19." *Historia* 45: 472–482.

Grabbe, L. L. (2008). "Sanhedrin, Sanhedriyyot, or Mere Invention?" *JSJ* 39: 1–19.

Grabbe, L. L. (2021). *A History of the Jews and Judaism in the Second Temple Period, 4: The Jews under the Roman Shadow (4 BCE–150 CE)*. LSTS 99. London: T. & T. Clark.

Graetz, H. (1905). *Geschichte der Juden von den ältesten Zeiten bis auf die Gegenwart*, III/1. 5th edition. Leipzig: Leiner.

Gramaglia, P. A. (1998). "Il *Testimonium Flavianum*: Analisi linguistica." *Henoch* 20: 153–177.

Graux, C. (1878). "Nouvelles recherches sur la stichométrie." *Revue de Philologie, de littérature, et d'histoire anciennes*. 2: 97–143.

Gray, E. W. (1972). "Tiberius and the Provinces." *CR* 22: 383–385 (review of Orth 1970).

Greenhut, Z. (1992). "The 'Caiaphas' Tomb in North Talipiyot, Jerusalem." *'Atiqot* 21: 63–71.

Gregoratti, L. (2012). "Parthian Women in Flavius Josephus." Pp. 183–192 in *Jüdisch-hellenistische Literatur in ihrem interkulturellen Kontext*, ed. M. Hirschberger. Frankfurt am Main: Peter Lang Verlag.

Grethlein, J. (2013). *Experience and Teleology in Ancient Historiography: 'Futures Past' from Herodotus to Augustine*. Cambridge: Cambridge University Press.

Griffin, M. T. (2000). *Nero: The End of a Dynasty*. 2nd edition. New York: Routledge.

Grüll, T. and L. Benke (2011). "A Hebrew/Aramaic Graffito and Poppaea's Alleged Jewish Sympathy." *JJS* 62: 37–55.

Gruen, E. S. (2002). *Diaspora: Jews amidst Greeks and Romans*. Cambridge, Mass.: Harvard University Press.

Gruen, E. S. (2011). *Rethinking the Other in Antiquity*. Princeton: Princeton University Press.

Gruen, E. S. (2011). "Louis Feldman and the 'Lachrymose' Version of Jewish History." Pp. 227–231 in *Sacrifice, Scripture, and Substitution: Readings in Ancient Judaism and Christianity*, ed. A. W. Astell and S. Goodhart. Notre Dame, Ind.: University of Notre Dame.

Gruen, E. S. (2016). "Caligula, the Imperial Cult, and Philo's *Legatio*." Pp. 397–409 in idem, *Constructs of Identity in Hellenistic Judaism: Essays on Early Jewish Literature and History*. Deuterocanonical and Cognate Literature Studies 29. Berlin: De Gruyter.

Gruen, E. S. (2020). *Ethnicity in the Ancient World: Did It Matter?* Berlin: De Gruyter.

Grünbaum, P. (1887). *Die Priestergesetze bei Flavius Josephus: Eine Parallele zu Bibel und Tradition*. Diss. Halle.

Grünewald, T. (2004). *Bandits in the Roman Empire: Myth and Reality*. London: Routledge.

Guéraud, O. (1931). ΕΝΤΕΥΞΕΙΣ: *Requêtes et plaintes adressées au roi d'Égypte au IIIᵉ siècle avant J.-C.* Publications de la Société royale égyptienne de papyrologie: Textes et documents 1. Le Caire: Impr. de l'Inst. Français d'Archéologie Orientale.

Guillaumont, A. (1971). "A propos du célibat des Esséniens." Pp. 395–404 in *Hommages à André Dupont-Sommer*. Paris: Adrien-Maisonneuve.

Gußmann, O. (2008), *Das Priesterverständnis des Flavius Josephus*. TSAJ 124. Tübingen: Mohr Siebeck.

Gutschmid, A. von (1885). "Verzeichniss der Nabatäischen Könige." Pp. 81–89 in J. Euting, *Nabatäische Inschriften aus Arabien*. Berlin: Reimer.

Gutschmid, A. von (1888). *Geschichte Irans und seiner Nachbarländer von Alexander dem Grossen bis zum Untergang der Arsaciden*. Tübingen: Laupp.

Gutschmid, A. von (1893). "Vorlesungen über Josephos' Bücher gegen Apion." Pp. 336–589 in idem, *Kleine Schriften*, IV: *Schriften zur griechischen Geschichte und Literatur*, ed. F. Rühl. Leipzig: Teubner.

Haaland, G. (1999). "Jewish Laws for a Roman Audience: Toward an Understanding of Contra Apionem." Pp. 282–304 in *Internationales Josephus-Kolloquium Brüssel 1998*, ed. J. U. Kalms and F. Siegert. MJS 4. Münster: LIT. (I cite from the reprint in Haaland 2006, which shows the original page numbers).

Haaland, G. (2005). "Josephus and the Philosophers of Rome: Does *Contra Apionem* Mirror Domitian's Crushing of the Stoic Opposition?" Pp. 297–316 in *Josephus and Jewish History in Flavian Rome and Beyond*, ed. J. Sievers and G. Lembi. JSJSup 104. Leiden: Brill.

Haaland, G. (2006). *Beyond Philosophy: Studies in Josephus and His* Contra Apionem. Diss. Norwegian School of Theology.

Haaland, G. (2007). "What Difference Does Philosophy Make? The Three Schools as a Rhetorical Device in Josephus." Pp. 262–288 in Rodgers 2007.

Habicht, C. (1969). *Die Inschriften des Asklepieions*. Altertümer von Pergamon 8/3. Berlin: De Gruyter.

Hacham, N. (1996). "Communal Fasts in the Second Temple Period." M.A. thesis. The Hebrew University of Jerusalem (in Hebrew).

Hacham, N. (2007). "3 Maccabees and Esther: Parallels, Intertextuality, and Diaspora Identity." *JBL* 126: 765–785.

Hacham, N. and T. Ilan (2020–). *Corpus Papyrorum Judaicarum*. 3 vols. (vols. 4–6). Berlin: De Gruyter and Jerusalem: Magnes.

Hachlili, R. (1983/84): "Names and Nicknames of Jews in Second Temple Times." *Eretz-Israel* 17: 188–211 (in Hebrew).

Hadas-Lebel, M. (1993). "Les mariages mixtes dans la famille d'Hérode et la *halakha* prétalmudique sur la patrilinéarité." *REJ* 152: 397–404.

Hadas-Lebel, M. (2002). "Alexandre Jannée a-t-il crucifié ses opposants pharisiens? Etude de σταυρός, ἀνασταυρόω chez Flavius Josèphe." Pp. 59–71 in *Internationales Josephus-Kolloquium Paris 2001*, ed. F. Siegert and J. U. Kalms. MJS 12. Münster: LIT.

Hall, L. J. (2004). *Roman Berytus: Beirut in Late Antiquity*. London: Routledge.

Hall, R. G. (1988). "Epispasm and the Dating of Ancient Jewish Writings." *JSP* 2: 71–86.

Hamilton, N. Q. (1964) "Temple Cleansing and Temple Bank." *JBL* 83: 365–372.

Hammond, M. (1963). "Res olim dissociabiles: Principatus ac Libertas: Liberty under the Early Roman Empire." *Harvard Studies in Classical Philology* 67: 93–113.

Hammond, N. G. L. and G. T. Griffith (1979). *A History of Macedonia, II: 550–336 B.C.* Oxford: Clarendon Press.

Hansen, G. C. (1998). "Textkritisches zu Josephus." Pp. 144–158 in *Internationales Josephus-Kolloquium Münster 1997*, ed. F. Siegert and J. U. Kalms. MJS 2. Münster: LIT.

Harker, A. (2008). *Loyalty and Dissidence in Roman Egypt: The Case of the* Acta Alexandrinorum. Cambridge: Cambridge University Press.

Harnack, A. (1913). "Der jüdische Geschichtsschreiber Josephus und Jesus Christus." *Internationale Monatsschrift für Wissenschaft, Kunst und Technik* 7: 1037–1067.

Harris, J. R. (1893). *Stichometry*. London: Clay.

Harris, W. V. (1989). *Ancient Literacy*. Cambridge, Mass.: Harvard.

Harrison, R. (2013). *Heritage: Critical Approaches*. New York: Routledge.

Hartmann, M. (2001). *Der Tod Johannes' des Täufers: Eine exegetische und rezeptionsgeschichtliche Studie auf dem Hintergrund narrativer, intertextueller und kulturanthropologischer Zugänge*. SBB 45. Stuttgart: Katholisches Bibelwerk.

Hasselmann, M. (2022). *Konstruktion sozialer Identität: Studien zum Reinheitsvorschriften im antiken Judentum und im Neuen Testament*. AJEC 115. Leiden: Brill. I

Hata, G. (1994). "Imagining Some Dark Periods in Josephus' Life." Pp. 309–328 in Parente and Sievers 1994.

Hawley, R. 2007. "Lords of the Rings: Ring-Wearing, Status, and Identity in the Age of Pliny the Elder." Pages 103–111 in *Vita Vigilia Est: Essays in Honour of Barbara Levick*, ed. E. Bispham and G. Rowe. Bulletin of the Institute of Classical Studies Supplement 100. London: Institute of Classical Studies, School of Advanced Study, University of London.

Head, B. V. (1911). *Historia Numorum: A Manual of Greek Numismatics*. Oxford: Clarendon Press.

Heerink, M. and E. Meijer, ed. (2022). *Flavian Responses to Nero's Rome*. Amsterdam: Amsterdam University Press.

Held, W. (2002). "Die Residenzstädte der Seleukiden: Babylon, Seleukia am Tigris, Ai Khanum, Seleukia in Pieria, Antiocheia am Orontes." *Journal des deuschen archäologischen Instituts* 117: 217–249.

Heldmann, K. (2011). *sine ira et studio: Das Subjectivitätsprinzip der römischen Geschichtsschreibung und das Selbstverständnis antiker Historiker*. Zetemata 139. München: Beck.

Hengel, M. (1977). *Crucifixion in the Ancient World and the Folly of the Message of the Cross*. Philadelphia: Fortress Press.

Hengel, M. (1989). *The Zealots: Investigations into the Jewish Freedom Movement in the Period from Herod I until 70 A.D.* Edinburgh: T. & T. Clark.

Hennig, D. (1975). *L. Aelius Seianus: Untersuchungen zur Regierung des Tiberius*. Vestigia 21. München: Beck.

Henning, O. (1922). "Römische Stücke aus Josephus." Diss. Tübingen.

Henten, J. W. van (2011). "Constructing Herod as a Tyrant: Assessing Josephus' Parallel Passages." Pp. 193–216 in *Flavius Josephus: Interpretation and History,* ed. J. Pastor, P. Stern, and M. Mor. JSJSup 146. Leiden: Brill.

Henten, J. W. van (2014). *Judean Antiquities 15.* FJTC 7b. Leiden: Brill.

Henten, J. W. van (2018). "Josephus as Narrator." Pp. 121–150 in *Autoren in religiösen literarischen Texten der späthellenistischen und der frühkaiserzeitlichen Welt: Zwölf Fallstudien,* ed. E.-M. Becker and J. Rüpke. Culture, Religion, and Politics in the Greco-Roman World 3. Tübingen: Mohr Siebeck.

Henten, J. W. van (2020). "Testimonium Flavianum." Pp. 365–370 in *From Paul to Josephus: Literary Receptions of Jesus in the First Century* CE, ed. H. K. Bond (= *The Reception of Jesus in the First Three Centuries* 1). London: T. & T. Clark.

Herman, G. (2006). "Iranian Epic Motifs in Josephus' Antiquities (XVIII, 314–370)." *JJS* 57: 245–268.

Herman, G. (2012). "The Jews of Parthian Babylonia." Pp. 141–150 in *The Parthian Empire and Its Religions: Studies in the Dynamics of Religious Diversity,* ed. P. Wick and M. Zehnder. Pietas 5. Gutenberg: Computus.

Herrmann, P. (1968). *Der römische Kaisereid: Untersuchungen zu seiner Herkunft und Entwicklung.* Hypomnemata 20. Göttingen: Vandenhoeck und Ruprecht.

Herwerden, H. van (1893). "Commentationes Flavianae duae." *Mnemosyne* 21 (1893): 225–263.

Heyn, M. K. (2008). "Sacerdotal Activities and Parthian Dress in Roman Palmyra." Pp. 170–193 in *Reading a Dynamic Canvas: Adornment in the Ancient Mediterranean World,* ed. C. S. Colburn and M. K. Heyn. Newcastle: Cambridge Scholars.

Hicks, E. L. (1889). "Inscriptions from Casarea, Lydae, Patara, Myra." *JHS* 10: 46–85.

Himmelfarb, M. (2006). *A Kingdom of Priests: Ancestry and Merit in Ancient Judaism.* Jewish Culture and Contacts. Philadelphia: University of Pennsylvania.

Höffken, P. (2007). "Überlegungen zum Leserkreis der 'Antiquitates' des Josephus." *JSJ* 38: 328–341.

Hoehner, H. W. (1972). *Herod Antipas.* SNTSMS 17. Cambridge: Cambridge University Press.

Hölscher, G. (1904). *Die Quellen des Josephus für die Zeit vom Exil bis zum jüdischen Kriege.* Leipzig: Teubner.

Hölscher, G. (1916). "Josephus." *PWRE* XI/2: 1934–2000.

Hölscher, G. (1940). *Die Hohenpriesterliste bei Josephus und die evangelische Chronologie.* Sitzungsberichte der Heidelberger Akademie der Wissenschaften, philos.-hist. Klasse 30/3, 1939. Heidelberg: Winter.

Hoenig, S. B. (1946/47). "Synedrion in the Attic Orators, the Ptolemaic Papyri and Its Adoption by Josephus, the Gospels and the Tannaim." *JQR* 37: 179–187.

Holladay, C. R. (1983). *Fragments from Hellenistic Jewish Authors, I: Historians.* Chico: Scholars Press.

Hollander, W. den (2014). *Josephus, the Emperors, and the City of Rome.* AJEC 86. Leiden: Brill.

Holwerda, [J. H.]. (1853). "Observationes criticae in Flavii Iosephi Antiquitatum Iudaicarum librum XVIII." *Mnemosyne* 2: 111–141.

Holzmeister, U. (1920). "Der Hohepriester jenes Jahres." *Zeitschrift für katholische Theologie* 44: 306–312.

Holzmeister, U. (1932). "Wann war Pilatus Prokurator von Judaea?" *Biblica* 13: 228–232.

Hooff, A. J. L. van (1990). *From Autothanasia to Suicide: Self-Killing in Classical Antiquity.* London: Routledge.

Horbury, W. (1994). "The 'Caiaphas' Ossuaries and Joseph Caiaphas." *PEQ* 126: 32–48.

Horsley, R. A. (1986). "High Priests and the Politics of Roman Palestine: A Contextual Analysis of the Evidence of Josephus." *JSJ* 17: 23–55.

Horsley, R. A. (1995). *Galilee: History, Politics, People.* Valley Forge: Trinity Press International.

Horsley, R. A. and J. S. Hanson (1999). *Bandits, Prophets and Messiahs: Popular Movements in the Time of Jesus.* Harrisburg, Pennsylvania: Trinity Press International.

Horsley, R. A. (2022). *The Pharisees and the Temple-State of Judea.* Eugene, Oregon: Cascade Books.

Horst, P. W. van der (1979). "Some Late Instances of Inceptive ΔE." *Mnemosyne* 32: 377–378.

Horst, P. W. van der (1991). *Ancient Jewish Epitaphs: An Introductory Survey of a Millennium of Jewish Funerary Epigraphy (300 BCE–700 CE).* Contributions to Biblical Exegesis and Theology 2. Kampen: Kok Pharos.

Horst, P. W. van der (2003a). *Philo of Alexandria: Philo's* Flaccus*: The First Pogrom.* Philo of Alexandria Commentary Series 2. Leiden: Brill.

Horst, P. W. van der (2003b). "The Jews of Ancient Cyprus." *Zutot* 3: 110–120.

Horst, P. W. van der (2012). "*Philosophia Epeisaktos*: Some Notes on Josephus, *A.J.* 18.9." Pp. 311–322 in *The Jewish Revolt against Rome: Interdisciplinary Perspectives,* ed. M. Popović. JSJSup 154. Leiden: Brill.

Houston, G. W. (1985). "Tiberius on Capri." *GR* 27: 179–196.

Hug, A. (1923). "Sica." *PWRE* IIA/2: 2184–2185.

Hudson, J. and S. Havercamp (1726). *Flavii Josephi quae reperiri potuerunt Opera Omnia, græce e latine.* 2 vols. Amstelaedami: Wetstenios; Lugd. Bat.: Luchtmans; and Ultrajecti: Broedelet.

Huitink, L. and J. W. van Henten (2009). "The Publication of Josephus' Works and Their Audiences." *Zutot* 6 (2009): 49–60.

Humphrey, J. H. (1986). *Roman Circuses: Arenas for Chariot Racing.* Revised edition, Berkeley: University of California Press.

Hunt, A. S. and C. C. Edgar (1934). *Select Papyri,* 2. LCL. Cambridge: Harvard University Press and London: Heinemann.

Hurley, D. W. ed. (2001). *Suetonius: Divus Claudius.* Cambridge: Cambridge University Press.

Hurley, D. W. (2013). "Biographies of Nero." Pp. 29–44 in *A Companion to the Neronian Age,* ed. E. Buckley and M. T. Dinter. Blackwell Companions to the Ancient World. Chichester: Wiley-Blackwell.

Ilan, T. (1987/88). "The Greek Names of the Hasmoneans." *JQR* 78: 1–20.

Ilan, T. (1992). "'Man Born of Woman …' (Job 14:1): The Phenomenon of Men Bearing Metronymes at the Time of Jesus." *NovT* 34: 23–45.

Ilan, T. (1995). *Jewish Women in Greco-Roman Palestine: An Inquiry into Image and Status.* Tübingen: J.C.B. Mohr.

Ilan, T. (1999). *Integrating Women into Second Temple History.* Tübingen: J.C.B. Mohr.

Ilan, T. (2002). *Lexicon of Jewish Names in Late Antiquity, Part I: Palestine 330 BCE–200 CE.* TSAJ 91. Tübingen: Mohr Siebeck.

Ilan, T. (2016). "Josephus on Women." Pp. 210–221 in Chapman and Rodgers 2016.

Ilan, T. (2022). *Queen Berenice: A Jewish Female Icon of the First Century CE.* Studies in Theology and Religion 29. Leiden: Brill.

Ilan, T. and V. Noam, et al., ed. (2017). *Josephus and the Rabbis,* ed. T. Ilan, V. Noam et al. 2 vols. Between Bible and Mishnah: The David and Jemima Jeselsohn Library. Jerusalem: Yad Ben-Zvi (in Hebrew).

Inowlocki, S. (2005). "'Neither Adding nor Omitting Anything': Josephus' Promise Not to Modify the Scriptures in Greek and Latin Context." *JJS* 56: 48–65.

Isaac, B. (1998). *The Near East under Roman Rule: Selected Papers.* MnemSup 177. Leiden: Brill.

Jachowski, R. J. (2015). "The Death of Herod the Great and the Latin Josephus: Re-examining the Twenty-Second Year of Tiberius." *JGRChJ* 11: 9–18.

Jackson, B. S. (2005). "The Divorces of the Herodian Princesses: Jewish Law, Roman Law or Palace Law?" Pp. 343–368 in *Josephus and Jewish History in Flavian Rome and Beyond,* ed. J. Sievers and G. Lembi. JSJSup 104. Leiden: Brill.

Jacoby, K. (1893) Review of Naber's 1892–1893 editions of *Ant.* 11–20. *Wochenschrift für klassische Philologie.* 10:1003–1007.

Jastrow, M. (1950). *A Dictionary of the Targumim, the Talmud Babli and Yerushalmi, and the Midrashic Literature.* New York: Pardes Publishing House.

Jensen, M. H. (2007). "Josephus and Antipas: A Case Study of Josephus' Narratives on Herod Antipas." Pp. 289–312 in Rodgers 2007.

Jensen, M. H. (2010). *Herod Antipas in Galilee: The Literary and Archaeological Sources on the Reign of Herod Antipas and Its Socio-Economic Impact on Galilee.* 2nd edition. WUNT II/215. Tübingen: Mohr Siebeck.

Jeremias, J. (1969). *Jerusalem in the Time of Jesus: An Investigation into Economic and Social Conditions during the New Testament Period.* Philadelphia: Fortress.

Jeremias, J. (1982). *Jesus' Promise to the Nations.* Philadelphia: Fortress Press.

Johnson, A. C., P. R. Coleman-Norton, and F. C. Bourne. (1961). *Ancient Roman Statutes: A Translation with Introduction, Commentary, Glossary and Index.* Austin: University of Texas Press.

Johnson, N. B. (1948). *Prayer in the Apocrypha and Pseudepigrapha: A Study of the Jewish Concept of God.* JBL Monograph Series 2. Philadelphia: Society of Biblical Literature and Exegesis.

Jones, A. H. M. (1931). "The Urbanization of Palestine." *Journal of Roman Studies* 21: 78–85.

Jones, A. H. M. (1968). *Studies in Roman Government and Law.* New York: Barnes and Noble.

Jones, B. W. (1984). *The Emperor Titus.* New York: Palgrave Macmillan.

Jones, B. W. (1992). *The Emperor Domitian.* New York: Routledge.

Jones, C. P. (2002). "Towards a Chronology of Josephus." SCI 21: 113–22.

Jones, F. S. (1990). "The Martyrdom of James in Hegesippus, Clement of Alexandria, and Christian Apocrypha, Including Nag Hammadi: A Study of the Textual Relations." *Society of Biblical Literature Seminar Paper Series* 29: 322–335.

Jones, K. R. (2011). *Jewish Reactions to the Destruction of Jerusalem in A.D. 70.: Apocalypses and Related Pseudepigrapa.* JSJSup 151. Leiden: Brill.

Jonquière, T. M. (2007). *Prayer in Josephus.* AJEC 70. Leiden: Brill.

Joüon, P. (1935). "Les mots employés pour designer 'le Temple' dans l'Ancien Testament, le Nouveau Testament et Josèphe." *RSR* 25: 329–343.

Kadman, L. (1960). *The Coins of the Jewish War of 66–73 C.E.* Jerusalem: Schocken Publishing House.

Kahrstedt, U. (1950). *Artabanos III. und seine Erben*. Dissertationes Bernenses I/2. Bernae: A. Francke.

Kajava, M. (1998). "Visceratio." *Arctos* 32: 109–131.

Kampen, J. (1986). "A Reconsideration of the Name 'Essene' in Greco-Jewish Literature in Light of Recent Perceptions of the Dead Sea Sect." *HUCA* 57: 61–81.

Kasher, A. (1977/78). "The *Isopoliteia* Question in Caesarea Maritima." *JQR* 68: 16–27.

Kasher, A. (1985). *The Jews in Hellenistic and Roman Egypt: The Struggle for Equal Rights.* TSAJ 7. Tübingen: Mohr.

Kasher, A. (1996). "Polemic and Apologetic Methods of Writing in *Contra Apionem*." Pp. 143–186 in *Josephus' Contra Apionem: Studies in Its Character and Content with a Latin Concordance to the Portions Missing in Greek.* AGAJU 34. Leiden: Brill.

Kattan Gribetz, S. (2017). "'Lead Me Forth in Peace': The Origins of the Wayfarer's Prayer and Rabbinic Rituals of Travel in the Roman World." Pp. 297–327 in *Journeys in the Roman East: Imagined and Real*, ed. M. R. Niehoff. Culture, Religion and Politics in the Greco-Roman World 1. Tübingen: Mohr Siebeck.

Kattan Gribetz, Sarit. (2024). "Queen Helena of Adiabene through the Centuries." Pp. 195–236 in *Constructions of Gender in Religious Traditions of Late Antiquity*, ed. S. Sheinfeld, J. Hoppe, and K. Ehrensperger. Lanham: Rowman & Littlefield.

Katzoff, R. (1980). "Sources of Law in Roman Egypt: The Role of the Prefect." *ANRW* II/13: 807–844.

Katzoff, R. (1982). "Prefectural Edicts and Letters." *ZPE* 48: 209–217.

Kavanagh, B. J. (2001a). "Asiaticus, Seneca, and Caligula's Assassination." Pp. 105–117 in *In Altum: Seventy-Five Years of Classical Studies in Newfoundland*, ed. M. Joyal. St. Johns: Memorial University.

Kavanagh, B. J. (2001b). "The Conspirator Aemilius Regulus and Seneca's Aunt's Family." *Historia* 50: 379–384.

Kavanagh, B. J. (2010). "The Identity and Fate of Caligula's Assassin, Aquila." *Latomus* 69: 1007–1017.

Keddie, A. (2019). *Class and Power in Roman Palestine: The Socioeconomic Setting of Judaism and Christian Origins.* Cambridge: Cambridge University Press.

Kellner, H. (1888). "Die römischen Statthalter von Syrien und Judäa zur Zeit Christi und der Apostel." *Zeitschrift für katholische Theologie* 12: 460–486, 630–655.

Kidd, I. G. (1988). *Posidonius: II. The Commentary: (i) Testimonia and Fragments 1–149.* Cambridge: Cambridge University Press.

Kienast, D. (1996). *Römische Kaisertabelle: Grundzüge einer römischen Kaiserchronologie.* 2nd revised edition. Darmstadt: Wissenschaftliche Buchgesellschaft.

Kiernan, V. G. (1957). "Foreign Mercenaries and Absolute Monarchy." *Past and Present* 11: 66–86.

King, C. W. (2020). *The Ancient Roman Afterlife: Di Manes, Belief, and the Cult of the Dead.* Ashley and Peter Larkin Series in Greek and Roman Culture. Austin: University of Texas Press.

Klawans, J. (2009). "Josephus on Fate, Free Will, and Ancient Jewish Types of Compatibilism." *Numen* 56: 44–90.

Klawans, J. (2010a). "The Dead Sea Scrolls, the Essenes, and the Study of Religious Belief: Determinism and Freedom of Choice." Pp. 264–283 in *Rediscovering the Dead Sea Scrolls: An Assessment of Old and New Approaches and Methods*, ed. M. L. Grossman. Grand Rapids: Eerdmans.

Klawans, J. (2010b). "Josephus, the Rabbis, and Responses to Catastrophes Ancient and Modern." *JQR* 100: 278–309.

Klawans, J. (2012). *Josephus and the Theologies of Ancient Judaism.* New York: Oxford University Press.

Kletter, K. M. (2016). "The Christian Reception of Josephus in Late Antiquity and the Middle Ages." Pp. 368–381 in Chapman and Rodgers 2016.

Kletter, R., I. Ziffer, and W. Zwickel (2011). "The History and Archaeology of Yavneh." Pp. 1–13 in *Yavneh I: The Excavation of the 'Temple Hill' Repository Pit and the Cult Stands*, ed. R. Kletter, I. Ziffer, and W. Zwickel. OBOSA 30. Fribourg: Academic Press.

Kloppenborg, J. S. (2009). "Unsocial Bandits." Pp. 451–484 in *A Wandering Galilean: Essays in Honour of Seán Freyne*, ed. Z. Rodgers et al. JSJSup 132. Leiden: Brill.

Klostermann, E., ed. (1904). *Eusebius: Das Onomastikon der biblischen Ortnamen.* Leipzig: Hinrichs.

Koestermann, E. (1958). "Die Mission des Germanicus im Orient." *Historia* 7: 331–375.

Koets, P. J. (1929). *Δεισιδαιμονία: A Contribution to the Knowledge of the Religious Terminology in Greek.* Purmerend: Muusses.

Kogon, A. J. and J.-P. Fontanille (2018). *The Coinage of Herod Antipas: A Study and Die Classification of the Earliest Coins of Galilee.* AJEC 102. Leiden: Brill.

Kokkinos, N. (1990). "A Fresh Look at the *gentilicium* of Felix Procurator of Judaea." *Latomus* 49: 126–141.

Kokkinos, N. (1992). *Antonia Augusta: Portrait of a Great Roman Lady.* London: Routledge.

Kokkinos, N. (1998). *The Herodian Dynasty: Origins, Role in Society and Eclipse.* Sheffield: Sheffield Academic.

Kokkinos, N. (2008). "The Foundation of Bethsaida-Julias by Philip the Tetrarch." *JJS* 59: 236–251.

Kokkinos, N. (2010). "The Location of Tarichaea: North or South of Tiberias?" *PEQ* 142: 7–23.

Korzeniewski, D. (1974). "Trinkspruch auf eine großzügige Gastgeberin." *Gymnasium* 81: 513–519.

Kovács, P. (2009). *Marcus Aurelius' Rain Miracle and the Marcomannic Wars.* MnemSup 308. Leiden: Brill.

Krause, A. R. (2017). *Synagogues in the Works of Flavius Josephus: Rhetoric, Spatiality, and First-Century Jewish Institutions.* AJEC 97. Leiden: Brill.

Krauter, S. (2007). "Die Beteiligung von Nichtjuden am Jerusalemer Tempelkult." Pp. 55–74 in *Jewish Identity in the Greco-Roman World*, ed. J. Frey et al. AJEC 71. Leiden: Brill.

Krebs, C. B. (2015). "The Buried Tradition of Programmatic Titulature among Republican Historians: Polybius' ΠΡΑΓΜΑΤΕΙΑ, Asellio's Res Gestae, and Sisenna's Redefinition of Historiae." *AJP* 106: 503–524.

Krieger, K.-S. (1992). "Die Problematik chronologischer Rekonstruktion zur Amtszeit des Pilatus." *BN* 61: 27–32.

Krieger, K.-S. (1993a). "Chronologische Problem in der Geschichte der ersten fünf Statthalter der Provinz Judä." *BN* 68: 18–23.

Krieger, K.-S. (1993b). "Zur Frage nach der Hauptquelle über die Geschichte der Provinz Judä in den Antiquitates des Flavius Josephus." *BN* 63: 37–41.

Krieger, K.-S. (1997). "Berenike, die Schwester König Agrippas II., bei Flavius Josephus." *JSJ* 28: 1–11.

Krieger, K.-S. (1998). "Das reinigende Feuer: Die Zerstörung des Zweiten Tempels in der Darstellung des Josephus." *Bibel und Kirche* 1998: 73–78.

Krieger, K.-S. (2002). "A Synoptic Approach to B 2:117–283 and A 18–20." Pp. 90–100 in *Internationales Josephus-Kolloquium Paris 2001: Studies on the Antiquities of Josephus*, ed. F. Siegert and J. U. Kalms. MJS 12. Münster: LIT.

Kropp, A. J. T. M. (2013). "Crowning the Emperor: An Unorthodox Image of Claudius, Agrippa and Herod of Chalkis." *Syria* 90: 377–389.

Krüger, J. (2012). *Nero: Der römische Kaiser und seine Zeit.* Köln: Böhlau.

Kruse, H. (1959). "Noch einmal zur Josephus-Stelle Antiqu. 18,1,5." *VT* 9: 31–39.

Kuhn, H.-W. (2015). *Betsaida/Bethsaida—Julias (et-Tell): Die ersten 25 Jahre der Ausgrabung (1987–2011) mit Nachträgen bis 2013/The First Twenty-Five Years of Excavations (1987–2011) with Postscripts until 2013.* NTOA Series Archaologica 4. Göttingen: Vandenhoeck und Ruprecht.

Lämmer, M. (1981/82). "Griechische Agone und römische Spiele unter der Regierung des jüdischen Königs Agrippa I." *Kölner Beiträge zur Sportwissenschaft* 10/11: 199–237.

Lambers-Petry, D. (2002). "How to Become a Christian Martyr: Reflections on the Death of James as Described by Josephus and in Early Christian Literature." Pp. 101–124 in *Internationales Josephus-Kolloquium Paris 2001: Studies on the Antiquities of Josephus*, ed. F. Siegert and J. U. Kalms. MJS 12. Münster: LIT.

Lambertz, M. (1953). "Porcius Festus." *PWRE* Halbband 43: 220–227.

Lans, Birgit van der. (2015). "The Politics of Exclusion: Expulsion of Jews and Others from Rome." Pp. 33–77 in *People under Power: Early Jewish and Christian Responses to the Roman Empire*. Amsterdam: Amsterdam University Press.

Lanser, R. D. (2021). "The Parthian War Paradigm and the Reign of Herod the Great." *Near Eastern Archaeological Society Bulletin* 66: 21–36.

Lapin, H., ed. (1998). *Religious and Ethnic Communities in Later Roman Palestine.* Bethesda, Maryland: University Press.

Laqueur, R. (1913). *Polybius.* Leipzig: Teubner.

Laqueur, R. (1920). *Der jüdische Historiker Flavius Josephus: Ein biographischer Versuch auf neuer quellenkritischer Grundlage.* Giessen: Münchow.

Lavan, L. (2020). *Public Space in the Late Antique City.* 2 vols. Late Antique Archaeology Supplementary Series 5. Leiden: Brill.

Lavee, M. (2018). *The Rabbinic Conversion of Judaism: The Unique Perspective of the Bavli on Conversion and the Construction of Jewish Identity.* AJEC 99. Leiden: Brill.

Lee, J. A. L. (1972). "ἈΠΟΣΚΕΥΗ in the Septuagint." *JTS* n.s. 23: 430–437.

Lemaire, A. (2002). "L'expérience essénienne de Flavius Josèphe." Pp. 138–151 in *Internationales Josephus-Kolloquium Paris 2001: Studies on the Antiquities of Josephus*, ed. F. Siegert and J. U. Kalms. MJS 12. Münster: LIT.

Lembi, G. (2001). "Il *Testimonium Flavianum*, Agrippa I e i fratelli Asineo e Anileo: Osservazioni sul libro XVIII delle *Antichità* di Giuseppe." *Materia Giudaica* 6: 53–68.

Lémonon, J.-P. (1992). "Ponce Pilate: Documents profanes, Nouveau Testament et traditions ecclésiales." *ANRW* II/26.1: 741–778.

Lémonon, J.-P. (2007). *Ponce Pilate.* Paris: Éditions de l'Atelier/Éditions Ouvrières. (second ed. of idem, *Pilate et le gouvernement de la Judée: Textes et monuments.* Paris: Gabalda, 1981.)

Le Moyne, J. (1972). *Les Sadducéens.* ÉtB. Paris: Lecoffre/Gabalda.

Lenschau, T. (1939). "Orodes 3." *PWRE* Halbband 35: 1142–1143,

Leon, H. J. (1995). *The Jews of Ancient Rome*. Updated ed. Peabody, Mass.: Hendrickson.

Leoni, T. (2009). "The Text of Josephus's Works: An Overview." *JSJ* 40: 149–184.

Leoni, T. (2016). "The Text of the Josephan Corpus: Principal Greek Manuscripts, Ancient Latin Translations, and the Indirect Tradition." Pp. 307–321 in Chapman and Rodgers 2016.

Levick, B. (1967). *Roman Colonies in Southern Asia Minor*. Oxford: Clarendon Press.

Levick, B. (1990). *Claudius*. London: B. T. Batsford Ltd.

Levick, B. (1999). *Tiberius the Politician*. 2nd edition. London: Routledge.

Levick, B. (2013). "Cluvius Rufus." Pp. 1.549–560 and 2.1036–1041 in *The Fragments of the Roman Historians*, ed. T. J. Cornell. 3 vols. Oxford: Oxford University Press.

Levine, L. I. (1974). "The Jewish-Greek Conflict in First-Century Caesarea." *JJS* 25: 381–397.

Levine, L. I. (1975). *Caesarea under Roman Rule*. SJLA 7. Leiden: Brill.

Levine, L. I. (1978). "R. Simeon b. Yohai and the Purification of Tiberias: History and Tradition." *HUCA* 49: 143–185.

Levine, L. I., ed. (1981). *Ancient Synagogues Revealed*. Jerusalem: Israel Exploration Society.

Levine, L. I., ed. (1992). *The Galilee in Late Antiquity*. New York: The Jewish Theological Seminary of America.

Levine, L. I. (2005a). *The Ancient Synagogue: The First Thousand Years*. 2nd edition. New Haven: Yale University Press.

Levine, L. I. (2005b). "Figural Art in Ancient Judaism." *Ars Judaica* 1: 9–26

Levine, L. I. (2012). *Visual Judaism in Late Antiquity: Historical Contexts of Jewish Art*. New Haven: Yale University Press.

Lévystone, D. (2014). "Plato, Socratics and the Tyrannical Personality." *Journal of Greco-Roman Studies* 53(3): 33–52.

Lewy, H. (1920–1945).[2] Hans (Johanan) Lewy's hand-annotated copy of Niese 1890b, in Bloomfield Library of the Hebrew University of Jerusalem, Mt. Scopus; JMS. Barcode: 0168693-004-001.

Lichtenberger, A. (2003). *Kulte und Kultur der Dekapolis: Untersuchungen zu numismatischen, archäologischen und epigraphischen Zeugnissen*. Wiesbaden: Harrassowitz.

Liddell, H. G., R. Scott, and H. S. Jones. (1992). *A Greek-English Lexicon*. Oxford: Clarendon Press (reprint of revised 9th edition of 1940, includes 1968 *Supplement*).

Lieberman, S. (1955–1988). *Tosefta Ki-fshuṭah: A Comprehensive Commentary on the Tosefta*. 10 vols. New York: Jewish Theological Seminary of America (in Hebrew).

Liebowitz, E. (2018). "A New Perspective on Two Jewish Queens in the Second Temple Period: Alexandra of Judaea and Helene of Adiabene." Pp. 41–65 in *Sources and Interpretation in Ancient Judaism: Studies for Tal Ilan at Sixty*, ed. M. M. Piotrkowski, G. Herman, and S. Dönitz. AJEC 104. Leiden: Brill.

Liempt, L. van (1927). "De testimonio Flaviano." *Mnemosyne* n.s. 55: 109–116.

Lifshitz, B. (1977). "Césarée de Palestine: Son histoire et ses institutions." *ANRW* II/.8: 490–518.

Linder, A. (2000/2001). Review of Slingerland 1997. *JQR* 91: 232–236.

Lindner, H. (1972). *Die Geschichtsauffassung des Flavius Josephus im Bellum Judaicum*. AGAJU 12. Leiden: Brill.

Lindsay, D. R. (1993). *Πίστις and Πιστεύειν as Faith Terminology in the Writings of Flavius Josephus and the New Testament*. AGAJU 19; Leiden: Brill.

Lindsay, H., ed. (1993). *Suetonius: Caligula, Edited with Introduction and Commentary*. London: Bristol Classical Press.

Livesey, N. E. (2010). *Circumcision as a Malleable Symbol*. WUNT II/295. Tübingen: Mohr Siebeck.

Lloyd, A. B. (1976). *Herodotus, Book II: Commentary 1–98*. Études préliminaires aux religions orientales dans l'empire romain 43. Leiden: Brill.

Lo Cascio, Elio. (1999). "Census provinciale, imposizione fiscale e amministrazioni cittadine nel Principato." Pp. 197–211 in *Lokale Autonomie und römische Ordnungsmacht in den kaiserzeitlichen Provinzen vom 1.–3. Jahrhundert*, ed. Werner Eck. München: Oldenbourg.

Lofberg, J. O. L. (1917?). *Sycophancy in Athens*. n.p.: Collegiate Press.

Loftus, F. (1977/78). "The Anti-Roman Revolts of the Jews and the Galileans." *JQR* 68: 78–98.

Longenecker, B. W. (1998). "The Wilderness and Revolutionary Ferment in First-Century Palestine: A Response to D. R. Schwartz and J. Marcus." *JSJ* 29: 322–336.

Lott, J. B. (2012). *Death and Dynasty in Early Rome: Key Sources, with Text, Translation, and Commentary*. Cambridge: Cambridge University Press.

---

2 Lewy was born in 1904 and died in 1945. I do not know when he wrote his marginalia in this volume, but it was no earlier than 1920, as is shown by his reference, at p. 269, to Laqueur 1920.

Luraghi, N. (2018). "The Discourse of Tyranny and the Greek Roots of the Bad King." Pp. 11–26 in *Evil Lords: Theories and Representations of Tyranny from Antiquity to the Renaissance*, ed. Nikos Panou and Hester Schadee. New York: Oxford University Press.

Magness, J. (2002). *The Archaeology of Qumran and the Dead Sea Scrolls*. Grand Rapids, Michigan: Eerdmans.

Magness, J. (2011). *Stone and Dung, Oil and Spit: Jewish Daily Life in the Time of Jesus*. Grand Rapids, Michigan: Eerdmans.

Mahieu, B. (2012). *Between Rome and Jerusalem: Herod the Great and His Sons in Their Struggle for Recognition. A Chronological Investigation of the Period 40 BC–39 AD with a Time Setting of New Testament Events*. Orientalia Lovaniensia Analecta 208. Leuven: Peeters.

Maier, G. (1971). *Mensch und freier Wille nach den jüdischen Religionsparteien zwischen Ben Sira und Paulus*. WUNT 12. Tübingen: Mohr (Siebeck).

Maier, P. L. (1971). "The Fate of Pontius Pilate." *Hermes* 99: 362–371.

Main, E. (1990). "Sadducéens vus par Flavius Josèphe." *RB* 97 (1990): 161–206.

Maione, V. (2016). *Parco archeologico sommerso di Baia: The Underwater Archeology Park of Baia*. Napoli: Valtrend.

Malherbe, A. J. (1986). *Moral Exhortation: A Greco-Roman Sourcebook*. Library of Early Christianity 4. Philadelphia: Westminster Press.

Malloch, S. J. V. (2001). "Gaius' Bridge at Baiae and Alexander-*Imitatio*." *CQ* 51: 206–217.

Mandel, P. (1992). "Birah as an Architectural Term in Rabbinic Literature." *Tarbiz* 61: 195–217 (in Hebrew).

Mandel, P. (2006). "The Loss of Center: Changing Attitudes towards the Temple in Aggadic Literature." *HTR* 99: 17–35.

Mandel, P. (2007). "Scriptural Exegesis and the Pharisees in Josephus." *JJS* 58: 19–32.

Mandel, P. D. (2017). *The Origins of Midrash: From Teaching to Text*. JSJSup 180. Leiden: Brill.

Mandell, S. (1984). "Who Paid the Temple Tax When the Jews Were under Roman Rule?" *HTR* 77: 223–232.

Manns, F. and E. Alliata, ed. (1993). *Early Christianity in Context: Monuments and Documents*. Jerusalem: Franciscan Printing Press.

Marciak, M. (2014). *Izates, Helena, and Monobazos of Adiabene: A Study on Literary Traditions and History*. Philippika 66. Wiesbaden: Harrassowitz.

Marciak, M. (2017). *Sophene, Gordyene, and Adiabene: Three Regna Minora of Northern Mesopotamia between East and West*. Impact of Empire 26. Leiden: Brill.

Marcus, R. (1943). *Josephus VII: Jewish Antiquities, Books XII–XIV*. LCL. London: Heinemann, and Cambridge, Mass.: Harvard.

Marcus, R. (1954). "Pharisees, Essenes, and Gnostics." *JBL* 73: 157–161.

Marcus, R. and A. Wikgren, ed. and trans. (1963). *Josephus VIII: Jewish Antiquities, Books XV–XVII*. LCL. London: Heinemann.

Marincola, J. (1997). *Authority and Tradition in Ancient Historiography*. Cambridge: Cambridge University Press.

Marquardt, J. (1876). *Römische Staatsverwaltung*, II. Handbuch der römischen Alterthümer 5. Leipzig: Hirzel.

Marshall, F. H. (1907). *Catalogue of the Finger Rings, Greek, Etruscan, and Roman, in the Departments of Antiquities, British Museum*. London: British Museum.

Martin, R. (2006). *Understanding Local Autonomy in Judaea between 6 and 66 CE*. Lewiston: Mellon.

Mason, H. J. (1974). *Greek Terms for Roman Institutions: A Lexicon and Analysis*. American Studies in Papyrology 13. Toronto: Hakkert.

Mason, S. (1988). "Priesthood in Josephus and the 'Pharisaic Revolution.'" *JBL* 107: 657–661.

Mason, S. (1991). *Flavius Josephus on the Pharisees: A Composition-Critical Study*. SPB 39. Leiden: Brill.

Mason, S. (1992). *Josephus and the New Testament*. Peabody, Mass.: Hendrickson Publishers.

Mason, S. (1998a). "An Essay in Character: The Aim and Audience of Josephus's *Vita*." Pp. 31–77 in *Internationales Josephus-Kolloquium Münster 1997*, ed. F. Siegert and J. U. Kalms. MJS 2. Münster: LIT.

Mason, S. (1998b). "'Should Any Wish to Enquire Further' (*Ant.* 1.25): The Aim and Audience of Josephus's *Judean Antiquities/Life*." Pp. 64–103 in *Understanding Josephus: Seven Perspectives*, ed. S. Mason. JSPSup 32: Sheffield: Sheffield Academic Press.

Mason, S. (2001). *Life of Josephus: Translation and Commentary*. FJTC 9. Leiden: Brill.

Mason, S. (2003a). "Contradiction or Counterpoint? Josephus and Historical Method." *Review of Rabbinic Judaism* 6: 145–188.

Mason, S. (2003b). *Josephus and the New Testament*. Second edition. Peabody, Mass.: Hendrickson.

Mason, S. (2003c). "Flavius Josephus in Flavian Rome: Reading on and between the Lines." Pp. 559–589 in *Flavian Rome: Culture, Image, Text*, ed. A. J. Boyle and W. J. Dominik. Leiden: Brill.

Mason, S. (2005a). "Figured Speech and Irony in T. Flavius Josephus." Pp. 243–288 in *Flavius Josephus and Flavian Rome*, ed. J. Edmondson, S. Mason, and J. Rives. Oxford: Oxford University Press.

Mason, S. (2005b). "Of Audience and Meaning: Reading Josephus's *Bellum Judaicum* in the Context of a Flavian Audience." Pp. 71–100 in *Josephus and Jewish History in Flavian Rome and Beyond*, ed. J. Sievers and G. Lembi. JSJSup 104. Leiden: Brill.

Mason, S. (2007a). "Essenes and Lurking Spartans in Josephus' *Judean War*: From Story to History." Pp. 219–261 in Rodgers 2007.

Mason, S. (2007b). "Jews, Judaeans, Judaizing, Judaism: Problems of Categorization in Ancient History." *JSJ* 38: 487–512.

Mason, S. (2008). *Judean War 2*. FJTC 1b. Leiden: Brill.

Mason, S. (2011a). "Josephus, Publication, and Audiences: A Response." *Zutot* 8: 81–94.

Mason, S. (2011b). "The Historical Problem of the Essenes." Pp. 201–252 in *Celebrating the Dead Sea Scrolls: A Canadian Collection*, ed. P. W. Flint, J. Duhaime, and K. S. Baek. Atlanta: Society of Biblical Literature.

Mason, S. (2012). "The Importance of the Latter Half of Josephus's *Judaean Antiquities* for his Roman Audience." Pp. 129–55 in *Pentateuchal Traditions in the Late Second Temple Period*, ed. A. Moriya and G. Hata. JSJSup 158. Leiden: Brill.

Mason, S. (2013). "Pollution and Purification in Josephus's *Judean War*." Pp. 181–207 in *Purity, Holiness, and Identity in Judaism and Christianity: Essays in Memory of Susan Haber*, ed. C. Ehrlich, A. Runesson, and E. Schuller. WUNT 305. Tübingen: Mohr Siebeck.

Mason, S. (2016a). Review of Wiseman 2013a. *Histos* 10: cxxxix–cliv.

Mason, S. (2016b). "Josephus's *Judean War*." Pp. 13–35 in Chapman and Rodgers 2016.

Mason, S. (2016c). *A History of the Jewish War, A. D. 66–74*. Cambridge: Cambridge University Press.

Mason, S. (2021). "Josephus's Pharisees." Pp. 80–111 in *The Pharisees*, ed. J. Sievers and A.-J. Levine. Grand Rapids: Eerdmans.

Mason, S. (2022a). "Jewish Sources: Flavius Josephus." Pp. 160–166 in *The Jesus Handbook*. Edited by J. Schröter and C. Jacobi. Grand Rapids, MI: Eerdmans.

Mason, S. (2022b). *Judean War 4*. FJTC 2a. Leiden: Brill.

Mason, S. (2023). *Jews and Christians in the Roman World: From Historical Method to Cases*. AJEC 116. Leiden: Brill.

Massey, P. T. (2007). "The Meaning of κατακαλύπτω and κατὰ κεφαλῆς ἔχων in 1 Corinthians 11.2–16." *NTS* 53: 502–523.

Mathieu, G. and L. Herrmann, (1929). *Antiquités judaïques, Livres XVI–XX*. Œuvres complètes de Flavius Josèphe 4. Paris: Leroux.

Mayer, G. (1987). *Die jüdische Frau in der hellenistisch-römischen Antike*. Stuttgart: Kohlhammer.

Mazar, E. (2011). *The Walls of the Temple Mount*. 2 vols. Shoham Academic Research and Publication.

McCracken, G. (1940). "Tiberius and the Cult of the Dioscuri at Tusculum." *CJ* 35: 486–488.

McDonnell, M. (2006). *Roman Manliness: "Virtus" and the Roman Republic*. Cambridge: Cambridge University Press.

McEleney, N. (1974). "Conversion, Circumcision, and the Law." *NTS* 20: 319–341.

McGing, B. C. (1998). "Bandits, Real and Imagined." *Bulletin of the American Society of Papyrologists* 35: 159–183.

McGinn, T. A. J. (2004). *The Economy of Prostitution in the Roman World: A Study of Social History and the Brothel*. Ann Arbor: University of Michigan Press.

McLaren, J. S. (1991). *Power and Politics in Palestine: The Jews and the Governing of Their Land 100 BC–AD 70*. JSNTSup 63. Sheffield: Sheffield Academic Press.

McLaren, J. S. (1998). *Turbulent Times? Josephus and Scholarship on Judaea in the First Century CE*. JSPSup 29. Sheffield: Sheffield Academic Press.

McLaren, J. S. (2000). "Josephus' Summary Statements Regarding the Essenes, Pharisees and Sadducees." *Australian Biblical Review* 40 (2000): 31–46.

McLaren, J. S. (2001). "Ananus, James, and the Earliest Christianity: Josephus' Account of the Death of James." *JTS* 52: 1–25.

McLaren, J. S. (2004). "Constructing Judaean History in the Diaspora: Josephus's Accounts of Judas." Pp. 90–108 in *Negotiating Diaspora: Jewish Strategies in the Roman World*, ed. J. M. G. Barclay. LSTS 45. London: T. & T. Clark International.

Mealand, D. I. (1975). "Community of Goods at Qumran." *Theologische Zeitschrift* 31: 129–139.

Meinhold, A. (1976). "Die Gattung der Josephsgeschichte und des Estherbuches: Diasporanovelle II." *Zeitschrift für die alttestamentliche Wissenschaft* 88: 72–93.

Mendels, D. (1997). *The Rise and Fall of Jewish Nationalism*. 2nd edition. Grand Rapids: Eerdmans.

Meshorer, Y. (1981). "An Ancient Coin Depicts Noah's Ark." *Biblical Archaeology Review* 7:5: 38–39.

Meshorer, Y. (1984/85). "The Coins of Caesarea Paneas." *INJ* 8: 37–58.

Meshorer, Y. (1985). *City-Coins of Eretz-Israel and the Decapolis in the Roman Period*. Jerusalem: Israel Museum.

Meshorer, Y. (1996). "Coins of Sepphoris." Pp. 195–198 in *Sepphoris in Galilee: Crosscurrents of Culture*, ed. R. M. Nagy et al. Raleigh: North Carolina Museum of Art.

Meshorer, Y. (2001). *A Treasury of Jewish Coins from the Persian Period to Bar Kokhba*. Jerusalem: Yad Ben-Zvi; Nyack, NY: Amphora.

Metzner, R. (2010). *Kaiphas: Der Hohepriester jenes Jahres*. AJEC 75. Leiden: Brill.

Meyers, E. M. (1998). "The Early Roman Period at Sepphoris: Chronological, Archaeological, Literary and Social Considerations." Pp. 343–355 in *Hesed Ve-Emet: Studies in Honor of Ernest S. Frerichs*, ed. J. Magness and S. Gitin. Brown Judaic Studies 320. Atlanta: Scholars Press.

Meyers, E. M., ed. (1999). *Galilee through the Centuries: Confluence of Cultures*. Winona Lake: Eisenbrauns.

Meyers, E. M. (2002). "Sepphoris: City of Peace." Pp. 110–120 in *The First Jewish Revolt: Archaeology, History, and Ideology*, ed. A. M. Berlin and J. A. Overman. New York: Routledge.

Meyers, E. M. (2010). "Khirbet Qumran and Its Environs." Pp. 21–45 in *The Oxford Handbook of the Dead Sea Scrolls*, ed. T. H. Lim and J. J. Collins. Oxford: Oxford University Press.

Michael, J. H. (1924). "The Jewish Sabbath in the Latin Classical Writers." *American Journal of Semitic Languages and Literatures* 40: 117–124.

Milikowsky, C. (2002). "Josephus between Rabbinic Culture and Hellenistic Historiography." Pp. 159–200 in *Shem in the Tents of Japhet: Essays on the Encounter of Judaism and Hellenism*, ed. J. L. Kugel. JSJSup 74. Leiden: Brill.

Millar, F. (1967). "Emperors at Work." *JRS* 57: 9–19.

Millar, F. (1977). *The Emperor in the Roman World (31 BC–AD 337)*. London: Duckworth.

Miller, P. D. (1994). *They Cried to the Lord: The Form and Theology of Biblical Prayer*. Minneapolis: Fortress.

Miller, S. S. (1984). *Studies in the History and Traditions of Sepphoris*. Leiden: Brill.

Miller, S. S. (1987). "Intercity Relations in Roman Palestine: The Case of Sepphoris and Tiberias." *AJS Review* 12: 1–24.

Miller, S. S. (1999). "Those Cantankerous Sepphoreans Revisited." Pp. 543–573 in *Ki Baruch Hu: Ancient Near East, Biblical and Judaic Studies in Honor of Baruch A. Levine*, ed. R. Chazan et al. Winona Lake, Indiana: Eisenbrauns.

Miller, S. S. (2001). "Josephus on the Cities of Galilee: Factions, Rivalries and Alliances in the First Jewish Revolt." *Historia* 50: 453–467.

Miller, S. S. (2015). *At the Intersection of Texts and Material Finds: Stepped Pools, Stone Vessels, and Ritual Purity among the Jews of Roman Galilee*. Journal of Ancient Judaism Supplements 16. Göttingen: Vandenhoeck und Ruprecht.

Minov, S. (2021). *Memory and Identity in the Syriac Cave of Treasures: Rewriting the Bible in Sasanian Iran*. Jerusalem Studies in Religion and Culture 26. Leiden: Brill.

Miraldi, L. (1998). *Antichità giudaiche di Giuseppe Flavio*. 2 vols. Torino: Unione Tipografico-Editrice Torinese.

Mitford, T. B. (1980). "Cappadocia and Armenia Minor: Historical Setting of the *Limes*." *ANRW* II/7.2: 1169–1228.

Modrzejewski, J. M. (1997). *The Jews of Egypt: From Rameses II to Emperor Hadrian*. Corrected edition. Princeton: Princeton University Press.

Moehring, H. R. (1961). "Josephus on the Marriage Customs of the Essenes." Pp. 120–127 in *Early Christian Origins: Studies in Honor of Harold R. Willoughby*, ed. A. Wikgren. Chicago: Quadrangle Books.

Möller, C. and G. Schmitt. (1976). *Siedlungen Palästinas nach Flavius Josephus*. Wiesbaden: Reichert.

Momigliano, A. (1932). "Osservazioni sulle fonti per la storia di Caligola, Claudio, Nerone." *Rendiconti della R. Accademia Nazionale dei Lincei: Classe di Scienze morali, storiche e filologiche* VI/8.5–6. I use the reprint as pp. 2.799–836 in idem, *Quinto contributo alla storia degli studi classici e del mondo antico*. 2 vols. Storia e letteratura 135–136. Roma: Storia e letteratura, 1975, which shows the original pagination.

Momigliano, A. (1934). "Ricerche sull'organizzazione della Giudea sotto il dominio romano (63 a.C.–70 d. C.)." *Annali della R. Scuola Normale Superiore di Pisa: Lettere, Storia e Filosofia* II/3: 183–221, 347–396. I use the reprint as a single volume (Amsterdam: Hakkert, 1967), but cite according to the original pagination, which is shown in the reprint.

Momigliano, A. (1961). *Claudius: The Emperor and His Achievement*. Oxford: Clarendon Press.

Momigliano, A. (1980). "Le regole del giuoco nello studio della storia antica." In idem, *Sesto contributo alla storia degli studi classici e del mondo antico* (2 vols. Storia e letteratura 149. Roma: Storia e letteratura, 1980), 1: 13–22.

Mommsen, T. (1870). "Cornelius Tacitus und Cluvius Rufus." *Hermes* 4: 295–325.

Mommsen, T. (1885). *Römische Geschichte, V: Die Provinzen von Caesar bis Diocletian*. Berlin: Weidmann.

Mommsen, T. (1899). *Römisches Strafrecht*. Systematisches Handbuch der deutschen Rechtswissenschaft I/4. Leipzig: Duncker und Humblot.

Mommsen, T. (1910). *Historische Schriften*, III (= *Gesammelte Schriften*, VI). Berlin: Weidmann.

Moore, G. F. (1929). "Fate and Free Will in the Jewish Philosophies according to Josephus." *HTR* 22: 371–289.

Morrison, C. E. (2021). "Interpreting the Name 'Pharisee.'" Pages 3–19 in *The Pharisees*, ed. J. Sievers and A.-J. Levine. Grand Rapids: Eerdmans.

Motzo, R. B. (1977). *Richerche sulla letteratura e la storia giudaico-ellenistica*, ed. F. Parente. Roma: Centro editoriale internazionale.

Mouritsen, H. (2011). *The Freedman in the Roman World*. Cambridge: Cambridge University Press.

Muraoka, T. (2009). *A Greek-English Lexicon of the Septuagint*. Louvain: Peeters.

Murgatroyd, P. (2008). "Tacitus on the Death of Octavia." *Greece and Rome* 55: 263–273.

Musurillo, H. (1954). *The Acts of the Pagan Martyrs:* Acta Alexandrinorum. Oxford: Clarendon.

Nabel, J. (2017). "The Seleucids Imprisoned: Arsacid-Roman Hostage Submission and Its Hellenistic Precedents." Pp. 25–50 in *Arsacids, Romans, and Local Elites: Cross-Cultural Interactions of the Parthian Empire*, ed. J. M. Schlude and B. B. Rubin. Oxford: Oxbow Books.

Naber, S. A. (1892). *Flavii Josephi opera omnia post Immanuelem Bekkerum*, III. Lipsiae: Teubneri.

Naber, S. A. (1893). *Flavii Josephi opera omnia post Immanuelem Bekkerum*, IV. Lipsiae: Teubneri.

Nagy, R. M. et al., ed. (1996). *Sepphoris in Galilee: Crosscurrents of Culture*. Raleigh: North Carolina Museum of Art.

Nestle, E. (1936). "Legenden vom Tod der Gottesverächter." *Archiv für Religionswissenschaft* 33: 246–269.

Netzer, E. (2018). *The Palaces of the Hasmoneans and Herod the Great*. Reprinted and expanded edition. Jerusalem: Yad Ben-Zvi and Israel Exploration Society.

Netzer, E. (2001). *Hasmonean and Herodian Palaces at Jericho: Final Reports of the 1973–1987 Excavations, Volume 1: Stratigraphy and Architecture*. Jerusalem: Israel Exploration Society and the Institute of Archaeology of the Hebrew University of Jerusalem.

Neusner, J. (1984). *A History of the Jews in Babylonia, 1: The Parthian Period*. BJS 62. Chico, Calif.: Scholars Press. (Third printing of volume published originally in 1969).

Nicolet, C. (1991). *Space, Geography, and Politics in the Early Roman Empire*. Ann Arbor: University of Michigan Press.

Nicols, J. (1975). "Antonia and Sejanus." *Historia* 24: 48–58.

Nielsen, K. M. (2019). "The Tyrant's Vice: *Pleonexia* and Lawlessness in Plato's Republic." *Philosophical Perspectives* 33: 146–169.

Niese, B. (1887–1896). *Flavii Iosephii Antiquitatum Iudaicarum Epitoma*. Marburgi Chattorum: Robert Friedrich.

Niese, B. (1888). *Flavii Iosephi Opera*, I (editio minor). Berolini: apud Weidmannos.

Niese, B. and J. von Destinon (1894). *Flavii Iosephi Opera*, VI. Berlin: apud Weidmannos.

Niese, B. (1890a). *Flavii Iosephi Opera*, IV (editio maior). Berolini: apud Weidmannos.

Niese, B. (1890b). *Flavii Iosephi Opera*, IV (editio minor). Berolini: apud Weidmannos.

Niese, B. (1892). *Flavii Iosephi Opera*, III (editio maior). Berolini: apud Weidmannos.

Niese, B. (1894). "De testimonio Christiano quod est apud Josephum antiq. Iud. XVIII 63 sq. disputatio." Pp. iii–x in *Indices lectionum et publicarum et privatarum quae in Academia Marpurgensi per semestre hibernum...habendae proponuntur*. Marpurgi: R. Friedrich.

Niese, B. (1895). *Flavii Iosephi Opera*, VI (editio minor). Berolini: apud Weidmannos.

Nilsson, M. P. (1958). Review of G. François, *Le polythéisme et l'emploi au singulier des mots ϑεός, δαίμων dans la littérature grecque d'Homère à Platon* (1957). *L'Antiquité Classique* 27: 528–530.

Nir, R. (2009). "Josephus's Account of John the Baptist: A Re–Examination." Pp. 157–186 in *Israel's Land: Papers Presented to Israel Shatzman on His Jubilee*, ed. J. Geiger, H. M. Cotton, and G. D. Stiebel. Raanana: Open University of Israel (in Hebrew).

Nitschke, J. (2006). *Dignitas und auctoritas— Der römische Senat und Augustus: Prosopographische Überlegungen zur Karriere der Konsuln und Statthalter 30 v. Chr. bis 14 n. Chr.* 2nd edition. Quellen und Forschungen zur antiken Welt 39; München: Utz.

Nitschke, J. L., S. R. Martin, and Y. Shalev (2011). "Between Carmel and the Sea—Tel Dor: The Late Periods." *Near Eastern Archaeology* 74: 132–153.

Noam, V. (2003). *Megillat Ta'anit: Versions, Interpretation, History, with a critical edition*. Jerusalem: Yad Ben-Zvi (in Hebrew).

Noam, V. (2017). "Agrippa/Jannaeus and the Nazirites' Offerings." Pp. 1.493–507 in Ilan and Noam 2017.

Noam, V. (2018). *Shifting Images of the Hasmoneans: Second Temple Legends and Their Reception in Josephus and Rabbinic Literature*. Oxford: Oxford University Press.

Nodet, E. (1985). "Jésus et Jean-Baptiste selon Josèphe." *RB* 92: 321–348.

Nodet, E. (2018). *The Hebrew Bible of Josephus: Main Features*. CRB 92. Leuven: Peeters.

Nolland, J. (1981). "Uncircumcised Proselytes?" *JSJ* 12: 173–194.

Norden, E. (1913a). "Josephus und Tacitus über Jesus und eine messianische Prophetie." *Neue Jahrbücher für das klassische Altertum* 31: 637–666.

Norden, E. (1913b). *Agnostos Theos: Untersuchungen zur Formengeschichte religiöser Rede.* Leipzig: Teubner.

North, H. F. (1966). *Sophrosyne: Self-Knowledge and Self-Restraint in Greek Literature.* Ithaca, NY: Cornell University Press.

Noy, D. (1995). *Jewish Inscriptions of Western Europe, vol. 2: The City of Rome.* Cambridge: Cambridge University Press.

Oakley, S. P. (2019). "The Expansive Scale of the *Roman Antiquities.*" Pp. 127–160 in *Dionysius of Halicarnassus and Augustan Rome,* ed. R. Hunter and C. C. de Jonge. Greek Culture in the Roman World. Cambridge: Cambridge University Press.

Ogg, G. (1967/68). "The Quirinius Question To-day." *Expository Times* 79: 231–236.

Ogilvie, R. M. (1980). *Roman Literature and Society.* Brighton, Sussex: Harvester Press, and Totowa, New Jersey: Barnes and Noble Books.

Olbrycht, M. J. (1997). "Parthian King's Tiara: Numismatic Evidence and Some Aspects of Arsacid Political Ideology." *Notae numismaticae* 2: 27–57.

Olbrycht, M. J. (2012). "The Political-Military Strategy of Artabanos/Ardawān II in AD 34–37." *Anabasis* 3: 216–237.

Olbrycht, M. J. (2014). "The Genealogy of Artabanus II (AD 8/9–39/40), King of Parthia." *Miscellanea Anthropologica et Sociologica* 15: 92–97.

Oldfather, C. H., trans. (1939). *Diodorus of Sicily,* III. LCL. London: Heinemann and Cambridge, Mass.: Harvard.

Oliver, J. H. (1989). *Greek Constitutions of Early Roman Emperors from Inscriptions and Papyri.* Memoirs of the American Philosophical Society 178. Philadelphia: American Philosophical Society.

Olson, K. A. (1999). "Eusebius and the 'Testimonium Flavianum.'" *CBQ* 61: 305–322.

Olson, K. A. (2013). "A Eusebian Reading of the *Testimonium Flavianum.*" Pp. 97–114 in *Eusebius of Caesarea: Tradition and Innovations.* Edited by A. Johnson and J. Schott. Cambridge, Mass.: Harvard University Press for the Center for Hellenic Studies.

Olsson, B. and M. Zetterholm, ed. (2003). *The Ancient Synagogue: From Its Origins until 200 C.E.* Stockholm: Almqvist & Wiksell.

Oost, S. I. (1958). "The Career of M. Antonius Pallas." *AJP* 79: 113–139.

Opelt, I. (1966). "Eule (Uhu, Käuzchen)." *RAC* 6.890–900.

Oppenheimer, A. (1977). *The 'Am Ha-Aretz: A Study in the Social History of the Jewish People in the Hellenistic-Roman Period.* ALGHJ 8. Leiden: Brill.

Oppenheimer, A. (1983). *Babylonia Judaica in the Talmudic Period.* Beihefte zum Tübinger Atlas des vorderen Orients B47. Wiesbaden: Reichert.

Oppenheimer, A. (2005). *Between Rome and Babylon: Studies in Jewish Leadership and Society,* ed. N. Oppenheimer. TSAJ 108. Tübingen: Mohr Siebeck.

Orth, W. (1970). *Die Provinzialpolitik des Tiberius.* Diss. München.

Osgood, J. (2011). *Claudius Caesar: Image and Power in the Early Roman Empire.* Cambridge: Cambridge University Press.

Otto, W. F. (1913). *Herodes: Beiträge zur Geschichte des letzten jüdischen Königshauses.* Stuttgart: Metzler.

Overduin, F. (2015). *Nicander of Colophon's* Theriaca: *A Literary Commentary.* MnemSup 374. Leiden: Brill.

Painter, J. (2004). *Just James: The Brother of Jesus in History and Tradition.* 2nd edition. Studies on Personalities of the New Testament. Columbia: University of South Carolina Press.

Papone, P. (1990). "Il regno dei cieli soffre violenza? (Mt 11, 12)." *Rivista biblica* 38: 375–376.

Parente, F. and J. Sievers, ed. (1994). *Josephus and the History of the Greco-Roman Period: Essays in Memory of Morton Smith.* SPB 41. Leiden: Brill.

Parker, R. (2002). "A New Euphemism for Death in a Manumission Inscription from Chaironeia." *ZPE* 139: 66–68.

Parkin, T. G. (2003). *Old Age in the Roman World: A Cultural and Social History.* Baltimore: Johns Hopkins University Press.

Patrich, J. (1982). "A Sadducean Halakha and the Jerusalem Aqueduct." *Jerusalem Cathedra* 2: 25–39.

Patrich, J. (2001). "The *Carceres* of the Herodian Hippodrome/Stadium at Caesarea Maritima and Connections with the Circus Maximus." *JRA* 14: 269–283.

Patrich, J. (2011). *Studies in the Archaeology and History of Caesarea Maritima: Caput Judaeae, Metropolis Palaestinae.* AJEC 77. Leiden: Brill.

Paul, G. M. (1982). "'*Urbs capta*': Sketch of an Ancient Literary Motif." *Phoenix* 36: 144–155.

Pease, A. S. (1935). *Publi Vergili Maronis Aeneidos Liber Quartus.* Cambridge, Mass.: Harvard University Press.

Peleg-Barkat, O. (2017). *Herodian Architectural Decoration and King Herod's Royal Stoa.* The Temple Mount Excavations in Jerusalem, 1968–1978, Directed by Benjamin Mazar, Final Reports 5. Jerusalem: Hebrew University of Jerusalem, Institute of Archaeology.

Pelletier, A. (1962). *Flavius Josèphe, adaptateur de la lettre d'Aristée: Une réaction atticisante contre la Koinè*. Études et commentaires 45. Paris: Klincksieck.

Petersen, H. (1958). "Real and Alleged Literary Projects of Josephus." *AJP* 79: 259–274.

Petrochilos, N. K. (1974). *Roman Attitudes to the Greeks*. S. Saripolos's Library 25. Athens: National and Capodistrian University of Athens, Faculty of Arts.

Phang, S. E. (2008). *Roman Military Service: Ideologies of Discipline in the Late Republic and Early Principate*. Cambridge: Cambridge University Press.

Pilhofer, P. (1990). *Presbyteron Kreitton: Der Altersbeweis der judischen und christlichen Apologeten und seine Vorgeschichte*. WUNT II/39; Tübingen: Mohr (Siebeck).

Piotrkowski, M. (2019). *Priests in Exile: The History of the Temple of Onias and Its Community in the Hellenistic Period*. Berlin: De Gruyter.

Poehlmann, W. (1992). "The Sadducees as Josephus Presents Them, or The Curious Case of Ananus." Pp. 87–100 in *All Things New: Essays in Honor of Roy A. Harrisville,* ed. A. J. Hultgren, D. H. Juel, and J. D. Kingsbury. St. Paul, MN: Luther Northwestern Theological Seminary.

Pomeroy, S. B. (1994). *Xenophon, Oeconomicus: A Social and Historical Commentary*. Oxford: Clarendon Press.

Porton, G. G. (1994). *The Stranger within Your Gates: Converts and Conversion in Rabbinic Literature*. Chicago Studies in the History of Judaism. Chicago: University of Chicago Press.

Potter, D. (1994). *Prophets and Emperors: Human and Divine Authority from Augsutus to Theodosius*. Revealing Antiquity 7. Cambridge, Mass.: Harvard University Press.

Potter, D. S. (1999). *Literary Texts and the Roman Historian*. Approaching the Ancient World. London: Routledge.

Powell, J. E. (1936). "Josephus, *Ant. Jud.* XVIII 6, 5 § 172." *Classical Review* 50: 11.

Powell, L. (2013). *Germanicus: The Magnificent Life and Mysterious Death of Rome's Most Popular General*. Barnsely: Pen and Sword.

Price, J. J. (1992). *Jerusalem under Siege: The Collapse of the Jewish State, 66–70 C.E.* Brill's Series in Jewish Studies 3. Leiden: Brill.

Price, J. J. (2005a). "The Provincial Historian in Rome." Pp. 101–118 in *Josephus and Jewish History in Flavian Rome and Beyond*, ed. J. Sievers and G. Lembi. JSJSup 104. Leiden: Brill.

Price, J. J. (2005b). "Josephus' First Sentence and the Preface to *Bellum Judaicum*." Pp. 131*–144* in *For Uriel: Studies in the History of Israel in Antiquity Presented to Professor Uriel Rappaport*, ed. M. Mor et al. Jerusalem: Zalman Shazar Center.

Price, J. J. (2007). "Josephus and the Dialogue on the Destruction of the Temple." Pp. 181–194 in *Josephus und das Neue Testament: Wechselseitige Wahrnehmungen*, ed. C. Böttrich and J. Herzer. Tübingen: Mohr Siebeck.

Price, J. J. (2011). "Josephus' Reading of Thucydides: A Test Case in the Bellum Iudaicum." Pages 79–98 in *Thucydides—A Violent Teacher? History and Its Representations*, ed. G. Rechenauer and V. Pothou. Göttingen: V&R Unipress.

Price, S. R. F. (1984). "Gods and Emperors: The Greek Language of the Roman Imperial Cult." *JHS* 104: 79–95.

Puech, É. (1993). *La croyance des Esséniens en la vie future: Immortalité, résurrection, vie éternelle? Histoire d'une croyance dans le judaïsme ancien*. 2 vols. ÉtB n.s. 21–22. Paris: Lecoffre.

Pummer, R. (2009). *The Samaritans in Flavius Josephus*. TSAJ 129. Tübingen: Mohr Siebeck.

Purcell, N. (1995). "Literate Games: Roman Urban Society and the Game of *Alea*." *Past and Present* 147: 3–37.

Qedar, S. (1986/87). "Two Lead Weights of Herod Antipas and Agrippa II and the Early History of Tiberias." *INJ* 9: 29–35.

Raban, A. and K. G. Holum, ed. (1996). *Caesarea Maritima: A Retrospective after Two Millennia*. Leiden: Brill.

Radin, M. (1917/18). "Roman Knowledge of Jewish Literature." *CJ* 13: 149–176.

Radin, M. (1927/28). Review of JLCL 1. *CJ* 23: 230–235.

Radin, M. (1929). "The Pedigree of Josephus." *CP* 24: 193–196.

Rainbird, J. S. (1986). "The Fire Stations of Imperial Rome." *Papers of the British School at Rome* 54: 147–169.

Rajak, T. (1998). "The *Against Apion* and the Continuities in Josephus's Political Thought." Pp. 222–246 in *Understanding Josephus: Seven Perspectives*, ed. S. Mason. JSPSup32. Sheffield: Sheffield Academic Press.

Rajak, T. (2001). *The Jewish Dialogue with Greece and Rome: Studies in Cultural and Social Interaction*. AGAJU 48. Leiden: Brill.

Rajak, T. (2002). *Josephus: The Historian and His Society*. 2nd edition. London: Duckworth.

Ramage, E. S. (1983). "Denigration of Predecessor under Claudius, Galba, and Vespasian." *Historia* 32: 201–214.

Rappaport, S. (1930). *Agada und Exegese bei Flavius Josephus*. Veröffentlichungen der Oberrabiner Dr. H. P. Chajes-Preisstiftung und der Israelitisch-theologischen Lehranstalt in Wien 3. Wien: Alexander Kohut Memorial Foundation.

Rappaport, U. (1981). "Jewish-Pagan Relations and the Revolt against Rome in 66–70 C.E." *Jerusalem Cathedra* 1: 81–95.

Rappaport, U. (2011). "Who Were the Sicarii?" Pp. 323–342 in *The Jewish Revolt against Rome: Interdisciplinary Perspectives*, ed. M. Popović. JSJSup 154. Leiden: Brill.

Rappaport, U. (2013). *The House of the Hasmoneans: The People of Israel in the Land of Israel in the Hasmonean Period*. Jerusalem: Yad Izhak Ben-Zvi (in Hebrew).

Rawson, E. (1987). "*Discrimina Ordinum*: The *Lex Julia Theatralis*." *Papers of the British School at Rome* 55: 83–114.

Reed, J. L. (2000). *Archaeology and the Galilean Jesus*. Harrisburg, Pennsylvania: Trinity Press International.

Regev, E. (2008). "Cherchez les femmes: Were the *yaḥad* Celibates?" *Dead Sea Discoveries* 15: 253–284.

Regev, E. (2019). *The Temple in Early Christianity: Experiencing the Sacred*. New Haven: Yale University Press.

Reinach, T. (1893). *Revue critique d'histoire et de littérature* n.s. 35: 123–124 (review of Niese's and Naber's editions of Josephus).

Reinach, T. (1897). "Josèphe sur Jésus." *Revue des études juives* 35: 1–18.

Reinhold, M. (1970). *History of Purple as a Status Symbol in Antiquity*. Collection Latomus 116. Bruxelles: Latomus.

Reinhold, M. (1980). "Roman Attitudes toward Egyptians." *The Ancient World* 3: 97–103.

Reiter, S. (1927). "ΑΡΕΤΗ und der Titel von Philo's 'Legatio'." Pp. 228–237 in ΕΠΙΤΥΜΒΙΟΝ *Heinrich Swoboda dargebracht*. Reichenberg: Stiepel.

Relandus, H. (1714). *Palaestina ex monumentis veteribus illustrata*, II. Trajecti Batavorum: Broedelet.

Rendsburg, G. A. (2014). "The Psalms as Hymns in the Temple of Jerusalem." Pp. 95–122 in: *Jesus and the Temple: Textual and Archaeological Explorations*, ed. J. H. Charlesworth. Minneapolis: Fortress Press.

Rengstorf, K. H. (1973–1983). *The Complete Concordance to Flavius Josephus*. 4 vols. Leiden: Brill.[3]

Retsö, J. 2003. *The Arabs in Antiquity: Their History from the Assyrians to the Umayyads*. London and New York: RoutledgeCurzon.

Rey-Coquais, J.-P. (1978). "Syrie romaine, de Pompée à Dioclétien." *JRS* 68: 44–73.

Reynolds, J. M. (1982). *Aphrodisias and Rome: Documents from the Excavation of the Theatre at Aphrodisias Conducted by Professor Kenan T. Erim, together with some related texts*. JRS Monograph 1. London: Society for the Promotion of Roman Studies.

Reynolds, J. M. and R. Tannenbaum. (1987). *Jews and God-Fearers at Aphrodisias: Greek Inscriptions with Commentary: Texts from the Excavations at Aphrodisias Conducted by Kenan T. Erim*. Cambridge Philological Society Supplementary Volume 12. Cambridge: Cambridge Philological Society.

Rhoads, D. M. (1976). *Israel in Revolution, 6–74 C.E.: A Political History Based on the Writings of Josephus*. Philadelphia: Fortress Press.

Rhoads, J. H. (2011). "Josephus Misdated the Census of Quirinius." *Journal of the Evangelical Theological Society* 54: 65–87.

Richards, G. C. (1939). "The Composition of Josephus' Antiquities." *CQ* 33: 36–40.

Richards, G. C. and R. J. H. Shutt. (1937). "Critical Notes on Josephus' Antiquities." *CQ* 31: 170–177.

Richards, G. C. and R. J. H. Shutt. (1939). "Critical Notes on Josephus' Antiquities, II." *CQ* 33: 180–183.

Richardson, L. (1992). *A New Topographical Dictionary of Ancient Rome*. Baltimore: Johns Hopkins University Press.

Richardson, P. (2004). *Building Jewish in the Roman East*. Waco, Texas: Baylor University Press.

Rickman, G. E. (1980). "The Grain Trade under the Roman Empire." *Memoirs of the American Academy in Rome* 36: 261–275.

Ringel, J. (1975). *Césarée de Palestine: Étude historique et archéologique*. Paris: Ophrys.

Ritschl, F. (1873). "Eine Berichtigung der republicanischen Consularfasten: Zugleich als Beitrag zur Geschichte der römisch-jüdischen internationalen Beziehungen." *RhM* n. F. 28: 586–614.

Ritter, B. (2015). *Judeans in the Greek Cities of the Roman Empire: Rights, Citizenship and Civil Discord*. JSJSup 170. Leiden: Brill.

Ritter, H. W. (1972). "Cluvius Rufus bei Josephus? Bemerkungen zu Ios. *Ant.* 19, 91f." *RhM* 115: 85–91.

Rocca, S. (2022). *In the Shadow of the Caesars: Jewish Life in Roman Italy*. Brill Reference Library of Judaism 74. Leiden: Brill.

Rodgers, Z., ed. (2007). *Making History: Josephus and Historical Method*. JSJSup 110. Leiden: Brill.

Rogers, R. S. (1932). "Fulvia Paulina C. Sentii Saturnini." *AJP* 53: 252–256.

Rolfe, J. C. (1933). "On *hoc age*, Plautus Capt. 144." *CP* 28: 47–50.

---

3 I used the two-volume corrected reprint published by Brill in 2002, but cite according to the original volume- and page-numbers, which are reproduced in the reprint.

Roller, D. W. (2018). *Cleopatra's Daughter and Other Royal Women of the Augustan Era.* Oxford: Oxford University Press.

Roller, M. B. (2017). *Dining Posture in Ancient Rome: Bodies, Values, and Status.* Princeton: Princeton University Press.

Roman Provincial Coinage. http://rpc.ashmus.ox.ac.uk/.

Rostovtzeff, M. (1957). *The Social and Economic History of the Roman Empire.* 2nd edition, revised by P. M. Fraser. 2 vols. Oxford: Clarendon Press.

Rühl, F.[4] (1893). Reviews of Naber's 1892–1893 editions of *Ant.* 11–20. *Literarisches Centralblatt für Deutschland* 1893: 182–183, 1191–1192.

Rustoiu, A. (2007). "Thracian *Sica* and Dacian *Falx*: The History of a 'National' Weapon." Pp. 67–82 in *Dacia Felix: Studia Michaeli Bărbulescu Oblata*, ed. S. Nemeti et al. Cluj-Napoca: Universitatea Babeş-Bolyai.

Rutgers, L. V. (1994). "Roman Policy towards the Jews: Expulsions from the City of Rome in the First Century C.E." *CA* 13: 56–74.

Rutgers, L. V. (1998). *The Hidden Heritage of Diaspora Judaism.* Biblical Exegesis and Theology 20. Leuven: Peeters.

Rutherford, W. G. (1881). *The New Phrynichus, being a revised text of the Ecloga of the grammarian Phrynichus.* London: Macmillan.

Rutledge, S. H. (2001). *Imperial Inquisitions: Prosecutors and Informants from Tiberius to Domitian.* London: Routledge.

Rzepka, J. (2012). "How Many Companions Did Philip II Have?" *Electra* 19: 131–135.

Safrai, S. (1963). "The Avoidance of Public Office in Papyrus Oxy. 1477 and in Talmudic Sources." *JJS* 14: 67–70.

Safrai, S. (1965). *Pilgrimage at the Time of the Second Temple.* Tel Aviv: Am Hassefer (in Hebrew).

Safrai, S. (1981). *Die Wallfahrt im Zeitalter des Zweiten Tempels.* Forschungen zum jüdisch-christlichen Dialog 2. Neukirchen-Vluyn: Neukirchener Verlag.

Safrai, S. (1976). "The Temple." Pp. 2.865–907 in Safrai and Stern 1974–1976.

Safrai, S. and M. Stern (1974). "Jewish Self-Government." Pp. 1.377–419 in Safrai and Stern 1974–1976.

Safrai, S. and M. Stern (1974–1976). *The Jewish People in the First Century.* 2 vols. Compendia Rerum Iudaicarum ad Novum Testamentum 1. Assen: Van Gorcum.

Sanders, E. P. (1992). *Judaism: Practice and Belief.* London: SCM Press.

Sanders, E. P. (2009). "Covenantal Nomism Revisited." *JSQ* 16: 23–55.

Sanders, L. J. (2016). "The Causes of the Alexandrian Pogrom and the Visit of Agrippa I to Alexandria in 38 CE." Pp. 2–30 in *History, Memory, and Jewish Identity*, ed. I. Robinson, N. S. Cohn, and L. DiTommaso. North American Jewish Studies. Boston: Academic Studies Press.

Sandmel, S. (1962). "Parallelomania." *JBL* 81: 1–13.

Sartre, M. (2005). *The Middle East under Rome.* Cambridge, Mass.: Belknap Press of Harvard University Press.

Satlow, M. L. (2010). "'Fruit and the Fruit of Fruit': Charity and Piety among Jews in Late Antique Palestine." *JQR* 100: 244–277.

Saulnier, C. (1984). "Hérode Antipas et Jean le Baptiste: Quelques remarques sur les confusions chronologique de Flavius Josèphe." *RB* 91: 362–376.

Saumagne, C. (1966). "Saint Paul et Félix, procurateur de Judée." Pp. 3.1373–1386 in *Mélanges d'archéologie et d'histoire offerts à André Piganiol*, ed. R. Chevallier. 3 vols. Paris: S.E.V.P.E.N.

Schäublin, C. (1974). "Μήτε προσθεῖναι μήτ' ἀφελεῖν." *Museum Helveticum* 31: 144–149.

Schalit, A. (1939). "Has Hyrcanus Been Appointed 'Brother of the King'?" *Bulletin of the Jewish Palestine Exploration Society* 6: 145–148 (in Hebrew).

Schalit, A. (1944). *Josephus: Antiquities, Books 1–10.* 2 vols. Jerusalem: Bialik Institute (in Hebrew).

Schalit, A. (1963). *Flavii Josephi Antiquitates Judaicae, Libri XI–XX, in linguam hebraicam vertit annotationibus amplissimis illustravit et proeoemio instruxit.* Jerusalem: Bialik Institute (in Hebrew).

Schalit, A. (1965). "Evidence of an Aramaic Source in Josephus' 'Antiquities of the Jews.'" *ASTI* 4: 163–188.

Schalit, A. (1967/68). "Zu Apg 25,9." *ASTI* 6: 106–113.

Schalit, A. (1968). *Namenwörterbuch zu Flavius Josephus.* CCFJ Supplement 1. Leiden: Brill.

Schalit, A. (1973). *Zur Josephus-Forschung.* Wege der Forschung 84. Darmstadt: Wissenschaftliche Buchgesellschaft.

Schalit, A. (1979). Unpublished typescript of German annotations to *Ant.* 11.1–208. Ms. V3640 in Manuscript Division of the National Library of Israel, Jerusalem. See D. R. Schwartz 2020c.

Schalit, A. (2001). *König Herodes: Der Mann und sein Werk.* 2nd edition. Berlin: De Gruyter.

---

4 For the identification of this reviewer, I rely on Schreckenberg 1972: 39.

Schemann, F. (1887). *Die Quellen des Flavius Josephus in der jüdischen Archaeologie Buch XVIII–XX = Polemos II, Cap. VII–XIV, 3*. Diss. Marburg. Hagen: Butz.

Scherberich, K. (2001). "Josephus und seine Quellen im 19. Buch der *Antiquitates Iudaicae* (ant. Iud. 19,1–273)." *Klio* 83: 134–151.

Schiffman, L. H. (1984/85). "The Samaritans in Tannaitic Halakhah." *JQR* 75: 323–350.

Schiffman, L. H. (1987). "The Conversion of the Royal House of Adiabene in Josephus and Rabbinic Sources." Pp. 293–312 in *Josephus, Judaism, and Christianity*, ed. L. H. Feldman and G. Hata. Detroit: Wayne State University Press.

Schimanowski, G. (2007). "Die jüdische Integration in der Oberschicht Alexandriens und die angebliche Apostasie des Tiberius Julius Alexanders." Pp. 111–135 in *Jewish Identity in the Greco-Roman World*, ed. J. Frey et al. AJEC 71. Leiden: Brill.

Schippmann, K. (2011). "Artabanus (Arsacid Kings)." *Encyclopædia Iranica* II/6: 647–650 (updated online version, accessed in April 2020).

Schippmann, K. (2016). "Arsacids ii: The Arsacid Dynasty." *Encyclopaedia Iranica* II/5: 525–536 (1987; updated online version, accessed in May 2020).

Schlatter, A. (1913). *Die hebräischen Namen bei Josephus*. Gütersloh: Bertelsmann.

Schlude, J. M. (2020). *Rome, Parthia, and the Politics of Peace: The Origins of War in the Ancient Middle East*. Abingdon, Oxon: Routledge.

Schmeling, G. with A. Setaioli. (2011). *A Commentary on the* Satyrica *of Petronius*. Oxford: Oxford University Press.

Schoenfeld, A. J. (2006). "Sons of Israel in Caesar's Service: Jewish Soldiers in the Roman Military." *Shofar* 24/3 (Spring 2006): 115–126.

Schofield, M. (2000). "Epicurean and Stoic Political Thought." Pp. 435–456 in *The Cambridge History of Greek and Roman Political Thought*, ed. C. Rowe and M. Schofield. Cambridge: Cambridge University Press.

Schorch, S. (2010). "Jacob's Ladder and Aaron's Vestments: Traces of Mystical and Magical Traditions in the Book of Wisdom." Pp. 183–195 in *Studies in the Book of Wisdom*, ed. G. G. Xeravits and J. Zsengellér. JSJSup 142. Leiden: Brill.

Schreckenberg, H. (1970). "Einige Vermutungen zum Josephustext." *Theokratia* 1: 64–75.

Schreckenberg, H. (1972). *Die Flavius-Josephus-Tradition in Antike und Mittelalter*. ALGHJ 5. Leiden: Brill.

Schreckenberg, H. (1977). *Rezeptionsgeschichtliche und textkritische Untersuchungen zu Flavius Josephus*. ALGHJ 10. Leiden: Brill.

Schreckenberg, H. (1980). "Flavius Josephus und die lukanischen Schriften." Pp. 179–209 in *Wort in der Zeit: Neutestamentliche Studien: Festgabe für Karl Heinrich Rengstorf zum 75. Geburtstag*, ed. W. Laubeck and M. Baumann. Leiden: Brill.

Schreckenberg, H. (2012). "Textkritisches zu den *Antiquitates Judaicae* des Flavius Josephus." *JSJ* 43: 42–57.

Schremer, A. 2003. *Male and Female He Created Them: Jewish Marriage in the Late Second Temple, Mishnah and Talmud Periods*. Jerusalem: Zalman Shazar Center (in Hebrew).

Schröder, B. (1996). *Die 'väterlichen Gesetze': Flavius Josephus als Vermittler von Halachah an Griechen und Römer*. TSAJ 53. Tübingen: Mohr (Siebeck).

Schrömbges, P. (1988). "Caligulas Wahn: Zur Historizität eines Topos." *Tyche* 3: 171–190.

Schürer, E. (1876). "Lucas und Josephus." *ZWT* 19: 574–582.

Schürer, E. (1890). Review of Niese 1890a. *TLZ* 15: 644–645.

Schürer, E. (1892). Review of Niese 1892. *TLZ* 17: 514–516.

Schürer, E. (1973–1987). *The History of the Jewish People in the Age of Jesus Christ (175 B.C.–A.D. 135)*, I–III. New English ed. by G. Vermes et al. Edinburgh: T. & T. Clark.

Schulz, V. (2022). "Historiographical Responses to Flavian Responses to Nero." Pp. 325–349 in Heerink and Meijer 2022.

Schumann, D. (2021). *Gelübde im antiken Judentum und frühesten Christentum*. AJEC 111. Leiden: Brill.

Schuol, M. (2000). *Die Charakene: Ein mesopotamisches Königsreich in hellenistisch-parthischer Zeit*. Oriens et Occidens 1. Stuttgart: Steiner.

Schwartz, D. G. (2006). *Roll the Bones: The History of Gambling*. New York: Gotham Books.

Schwartz, D. R. (1981). "Priesthood and Priestly Descent: Josephus, *Antiquities* 10. 80." *JTS* 32: 129–135.

Schwartz D. R. (1981/82). "ΚΑΤΑ ΤΟΥΤΟΝ ΤΟΝ ΚΑΙΠΟΝ: Josephus' Source on Agrippa II." *JQR* 72: 241–268.

Schwartz, D. R. (1983a). "Josephus and Philo on Pontius Pilate." *Jerusalem Cathedra* 3: 26–45.

Schwartz, D. R. (1983b). "Josephus and Nicolaus on the Pharisees." *JSJ* 14: 157–171.

Schwartz, D. R. (1983/84). "Josephus on the Jewish Constitutions and Community." *SCI* 7: 30–52.

Schwartz, D. R. (1986). "Viewing the Holy Utensils (P. Oxy. V, 840)." *NTS* 32: 153–159.

Schwartz, D. R. (1989/90). "On Drama and Authenticity in Philo and Josephus." *SCI* 10: 113–129.

Schwartz, D. R. (1990a). *Agrippa I: The Last King of Judaea*. TSAJ 23. Tübingen: Mohr.

Schwartz, D. R. (1990b). "On Some Papyri and Josephus' Sources and Chronology for the Persian Period." *JSJ* 21: 175–199.

Schwartz, D. R. (1992). *Studies in the Jewish Background of Christianity*. WUNT 60. Tübingen: J. C. B. Mohr.

Schwartz, D. R. (1992/93). "Felix and Isopoliteia, Josephus and Tacitus." *Zion* 58: 265–286 (in Hebrew).

Schwartz, D. R. (1994). "Josephus on Hyrcanus II." Pp. 210–232 in *Josephus and the History of the Greco-Roman Period: Essays in Memory of Morton Smith*, ed. F. Parente and J. Sievers. SPB 41. Leiden: Brill.

Schwartz, D. R. (1996). "God, Gentiles, and Jewish Law: On Acts 15 and Josephus' Adiabene Narrative." Pp. 263–282 in *Geschichte—Tradition—Reflexion: Festschrift für Martin Hengel zum 70. Geburtstag, Band I: Judentum*, ed. P. Schäfer. Tübingen: Mohr (Siebeck).

Schwartz, D. R. (1997). "Cassius' Chronology and Josephus' Vagueness." *SCI* 16: 102–112.

Schwartz, D. R. (1997/98). "More on 'Zechariah ben Avkules: Humility or Zealotry?.'" *Zion* 53: 313–316 (in Hebrew).

Schwartz, D. R. (1999). "From the Maccabees to Masada: On Diasporan Historiography of the Second Temple Period." Pp. 29–40 in *Jüdische Geschichte in hellenistisch-römischer Zeit: Wege der Forschung–Vom alten zum neuen Schürer*, ed. A. Oppenheimer. München: Oldenbourg.

Schwartz, D. R. (2000). "Whence the Voice? A Response to Bruce W. Longenecker." *JSJ* 31: 42–46.

Schwartz, D. R. (2002). "Rome and the Jews: Josephus on 'Freedom' and 'Autonomy.'" Pp. 65–81 in *Representations of Empire: Rome and the Mediterranean World*, ed. A. K. Bowman et al. Proceedings of the British Academy 114. Oxford: Oxford University Press.

Schwartz, D. R. (2003). "Divine Punishment in Second Maccabees: Vengeance, Abandonment or Loving Discipline?" Pp. 109–116 in *Der Mensch vor Gott: Forschungen zum Menschenbild in Bibel, antikem Judentum und Koran: Festschrift für Hermann Lichtenberger zum 60. Geburtstag,* ed. U. Mittmann-Richert, F. Avemarie, and G. S. Oegema. Neukirchen-Vluyn: Neukirchener Verlag.

Schwartz, D. R. (2005). "Herodians and *Ioudaioi* in Flavian Rome." Pp. 63–78 in *Flavius Josephus and Flavian Rome*, ed. J. Edmondson, S. Mason, and J. Rives. Oxford: Oxford University Press.

Schwartz, D. R. (2006). "'Stone House', *Birah*, and Antonia during the Time of Jesus." Pp. 341–348 in *Jesus and Archaeology*, ed. J. H. Charlesworth. Grand Rapids, Michigan: Eerdmans.

Schwartz, D. R. (2007a). "Josephus on His Jewish Forerunners (*Contra Apionem* 1.218)." Pp. 195–206 in *Studies in Josephus and the Varieties of Ancient Judaism: Louis H. Feldman Jubilee Volume*. ed. S. J. D. Cohen and J. J. Schwartz. AJEC 67. Leiden: Brill.

Schwartz, D. R. (2007b). "Composition and Sources in *Antiquities* 18: The Case of Pontius Pilate." Pp. 125–146 in Rodgers 2007.

Schwartz, D. R. (2007c). "Doing Like Jews or Becoming a Jew? Josephus on Women Converts to Judaism." Pp. 93–109 in Frey 2007.

Schwartz, D. R. (2008). *2 Maccabees*. Commentaries on Early Jewish Literature. Berlin: De Gruyter.

Schwartz, D. R. (2009). "One Temple and Many Synagogues: On Religion and State in Herodian Judaea and Augustan Rome." Pp. 385–398 in: *Herod and Augustus*, ed. D. M. Jacobson and N. Kokkinos. IJS Studies in Judaica 6. Leiden: Brill.

Schwartz, D. R. (2010). "Emending Josephus to Conform to the Mishnah—A Century Later." *JQR* 100: 529–543.

Schwartz, D. R. (2011). "Josephus on Albinus: The Eve of Catastrophe in Changing Retrospect." Pp. 291–309 in *The Jewish Revolt against Rome: Interdisciplinary Perspectives*, ed. M. Popović. JSJSup 154. Leiden: Brill.

Schwartz, D. R. (2012a). "Philo and Josephus on the Violence in Alexandria in 38 C.E." *SPA* 24: 149–66.

Schwartz, D. R. (2012b). "Sources and Composition in Josephus: The Episode of the Galileans and the Samaritans in Cumanus' Days." Pp. 125–146 in *Israel and the Diaspora in the Time of the Second Temple and the Mishnah: Aryeh Kasher Memorial Volume*, ed. Y. Shahar. Te'uda 25. Ramat Aviv: Tel-Aviv University (in Hebrew).

Schwartz, D. R. (2013). *Reading the First Century: On Reading Josephus and Studying Jewish History of the First Century*. WUNT 300. Tübingen: Mohr Siebeck.

Schwartz, D. R. (2014). *Judeans and Jews: Four Faces of Dichotomy in Ancient Jewish History*. Kenneth Michael Tanenbaum Series in Jewish Studies. Toronto: University of Toronto Press.

Schwartz, D. R. (2015a). "On Herod's and Josephus' Building Materials." *Eretz-Israel* 31: 421–425 (Ehud Netzer Volume, ed. Z. Weiss et al.): 421–425 (in Hebrew).

Schwartz, D. R. (2015b). "Josephus between the Flavians and God: On the Duality of *The Judean War*." Pp. 33–41 in *Milestones: Essays in Jewish History Dedicated to Zvi (Kuti) Yekutiel*, ed. I. Etkes, D. Assaf, and Y. Kaplan. Jerusalem: Zalman Shazar Center (in Hebrew).

Schwartz, D. R. (2016). "Many Sources but a Single Author: Josephus's *Jewish Antiquities*." Pp. 36–58 in Chapman and Rodgers 2016.

Schwartz, D. R. (2017). "'Going up to Rome' in Josephus's *Antiquities*." Pp. 373–388 in *Journeys in the Roman East: Imagined and Real*, ed. M. R. Niehoff. Culture, Religion and Politics in the Greco-Roman World 1. Tübingen: Mohr Siebeck.

Schwartz, D. R. (2018). "Malthace, Archelaus, and Herod Antipas: Between Genealogy and Typology." Pp. 32–40 in *Sources and Interpretation in Ancient Judaism: Studies for Tal Ilan at Sixty*, ed. M. M. Piotrkowski, G. Herman, and S. Dönitz. AJEC 104. Leiden: Brill.

Schwartz, D. R. (2020a). "On Triads, Teleology, and Tensions in *Antiquities* 18–20." *Religions* 11 (online).

Schwartz, D. R. (2020b). "Josephus on Paneion." *Jerusalem and Eretz Israel* 20 (= *The Joshua Schwartz Volume*): 55*–68.*

Schwartz, D, R. (2020c). "Hellenism, Judaism, and Apologetics; Josephus's *Antiquities* according to an Unpublished Commentary by Abraham Schalit." *Jewish Studies Internet Journal* 19: 1–20.

Schwartz, D. R. (2022). *1 Maccabees*. Anchor Yale Bible 41C. New Haven: Yale University Press.

Schwartz, D. R. (2023). "Reinach and Stephanus, Philo and Josephus: A Note on the Testimonium Flavianum." Pp. 205–218 in *Essays on Jews and Christians in Late Antiquity in Honour of Oded Irshai*, ed. B. Bitton-Ashkelony and M. Goodman. Cultural Encouners in Late Antiquity and the Middle Ages 40. Turnhout: Brepols.

Schwartz, D. R. (2024a, forthcoming). "Once Again on Josephus, Tacitus, and the Chronology of Judea in the Mid-First Century." Pp. 130–146 in *L'univers de Flavius Josèphe: Judaïsmes et christianismes au début de l'Empire romain: Mélanges offerts à Étienne Nodet, o.p.*, ed. M. Leroy. Cahiers de la Revue Biblique 96. Leuven: Peeters.

Schwartz, D. R. (2024b). "Josephus and Nicolaus on Arabs and Arabia." Pp. 140–156 in *Looking in, Looking out: Jews and Non-Jews in Mutual Contemplation: Essays for Martin Goodman on His 70th Birthday*, ed. K. Czajkowski and D. A. Friedman. Leiden: Brill.

Schwartz, D. R. (2024c, forthcoming). "God's Power and Man's Efforts: Josephus, *Antiquities* 18.18." *Meghillot: Studies in the Dead Sea Scrolls* 17 (in Hebrew).

Schwartz, D. R. (2025, forthcoming). "Thinking Big in Josephus." In *Bridging Educational Virtues and Values: Greco-Roman, Jewish, and Early Christian Paideia and Its Relevance in Past and Present*, ed. G. Gelardini, K. S. Fuglseth, and P. J. Bekken. Religious Diversity and Education in Europe. Münster: Waxmann.

Schwartz, E. (1907). "Zur Chronologie des Paulus." *Nachrichten von der königlichen Gesellschaft der Wissenschaften zu Göttingen: philologisch-historische Klasse aus dem Jahre 1907*: 263–299.

Schwartz, J. J. (1991). *Lod (Lydda), Israel: From Its Origins through the Byzantine Period, 5600 B.C.E.–640 C.E.* British Archaeological Reports, International Series 571. Oxford: Tempus Reparatum.

Schwartz, S. (1984). "T. Mucius Clemens, Commander of the Army of Agrippa II: An Epigraphical Note." *ZPE* 56: 240–242.

Schwartz, S. (1990). *Josephus and Judaean Politics*. Columbia Studies in the Classical Tradition 18. Leiden: Brill.

Schwartz, S. (2009). "Euergetism in Josephus and the Epigraphic Culture of First-Century Jerusalem." Pp. 75–92 in *From Hellenism to Islam: Cultural and Linguistic Change in the Roman Near East*, ed. H. Cotton et al. Cambridge: Cambridge University Press.

Schwartz, S. (2009/10). "Sunt Lachrymae Rerum" (review of Goodman 2007a). *JQR* 99: 55–64.

Schwartz, S. (2014). *The Ancient Jews from Alexander to Muhammed*. Key Themes in Ancient History. Cambridge: Cambridge University Press.

Scott, H. M. (1897). Review of Büchler 1896/97. *American Journal of Theology* 1: 848–850.

Scramuzza, V. M. (1940). *The Emperor Claudius*. Cambridge: Harvard University Press.

Segal, A. (1995). *Theatres in Roman Palestine and Provincia Arabia*. MnemSup 140. Leiden: Brill.

Shaham, H. (2020). "Yehudah Aristobulus Die Study Reveals Hasmonean Mint Chronology and Supports Josephus' Narrative." *Israel Numismatic Research* 15: 61–88.

Sharon, N. (2010). "The Title *Ethnarch* in Second Temple Period Judea." *JSJ* 41: 472–493.

Sharon, N. (2013/14). "Three Notes on the Life and Death of Mattathias Antigonus and the Names of the Last Hasmoneans." *Zion* 79: 93–97 (in Hebrew).

Sharon, N. (2014a). "The Conquests of Jerusalem by Pompey and Herod: On Sabbath or 'Sabbath of Sabbaths?'" *JSQ* 21: 193–220.

Sharon, N. (2014b). "Herod's Age When Appointed *Strategos* of Galilee: Scribal Error or Literary Motif?" *Biblica* 95: 49–63.

Sharon, N. (2017). *Judea under Roman Domination: The First Generation of Statelessness and Its Legacy*. Early Judaism and Its Literature 46. Atlanta: Society of Biblical Literature.

Shatzman, I. (1991). *The Armies of the Hasmonaeans and Herod: From Hellenistic to Roman Frameworks*. TSAJ 25. Tübingen: Mohr (Siebeck).

Shatzman, I. (1999). "The Integration of Judaea into the Roman Empire." *SCI* 18: 49–84.

Shatzman, I. (2002). "Success Followed by Envy: The Greek Tradition and Josephus." Pp. 36–54 in *Words in Memory of Menahem Stern Ten Years after His Death, and Studies in the Wake of His Research*. Jerusalem: Israel Academy of Sciences and Humanities (in Hebrew).

Shaw, B. D. (1993). "Tyrants, Bandits and Kings: Personal Power in Josephus." *JJS* 44: 176–204.

Shenkar, M. (2014). "*Yosef bar El'asa Artaka* and the Elusive Jewish Diaspora of Pre-Islamic Iran and Central Asia." *JJS* 65: 58–76.

Sherwin-White, A. N. (1963). *Roman Society and Roman Law in the New Testament*. Oxford: Oxford University Press.

Shutt, R. J. H. (1961). *Studies in Josephus*. London: S.P.C.K.

Shutt, R. J. H. (1980). "The Concept of God in the Works of Flavius Josephus." *JJS* 31: 171–189.

Sidwell, B. (2010). "Gaius Caligula's Mental Illness." *Classical World* 103: 183–206.

Siegert, F. (2001). *Zwischen Hebräischer Bibel und Altem Testament: Eine Einführung in die Septuaginta*. MJS 9. Münster: LIT.

Siegert, F., H. Schreckenberg, and M. Vogel et al., ed. (2001). *Flavius Josephus: Aus meinem Leben (Vita)—Kritische Ausgabe, Übersetzung und Kommentar*. Tübingen: Mohr Siebeck.

Sievers, J. (1998). "Josephus and the Afterlife." Pp. 20–31 in *Understanding Josephus: Seven Perspectives*, ed. S. Mason. JSPSup 32: Sheffield: Sheffield Academic Press.

Sievers, J. (2001). *Synopsis of the Greek Sources for the Hasmonean Period: 1–2 Maccabees and Josephus, War 1 and Antiquities 12–14*. Subsidia Biblica 20. Roma: Pontificio Istituto Biblico.

Sievers, J. (2014). Review of Mahieu 2012. *Biblica* 95: 470–472.

Sigismund, M. (2007). "Small Change? Coins and Weights as a Mirror of Ethnic, Religious and Political Identity in First and Second Century C.E. Tiberias." Pp. 315–336 in *Religion, Ethnicity and Identity in Ancient Galilee: A Region in Transition*, ed. J. Zangenberg, H. W. Attridge, and D. B. Martin. WUNT 210. Tübingen: Mohr Siebeck.

Sittl, C. (1890). *Die Gebärden der Griechen und Römer*. Leipzig: Teubner.

Skjærvo, P. O. (2013). "Marriage II: Next of Kin Marriage in Zoroastrianism." *Encylopædia Iranica* (online, accessed in August 2022).

Slingerland, H. D. (1997). *Claudian Policymaking and the Early Imperial Repression of Judaism in Rome*. SFSHJ 160. Atlanta: Scholars.

Smallwood, E. M. (1954). "The Date of the Dismissal of Pontius Pilate from Judaea." *JJS* 5: 12–21.

Smallwood, E. M. (1962). "High Priests and Politics in Roman Palestine." *JTS*. 13: 14–34.

Smallwood, E. M. (1963). Review of Shutt 1961. *CR* 13: 290–291.

Smallwood, E. M. (1967). *Documents Illustrating the Principates of Gaius, Claudius, and Nero*. Cambridge: Cambridge University Press.

Smallwood, E. M. (1970). *Philonis Alexandrini Legatio ad Gaium*. 2nd edition. Leiden: Brill.

Smallwood, E. M. (1981). *The Jews under Roman Rule, From Pompey to Diocletian: A Study in Political Relations*. Corrected reprint of 1976 original. Leiden: Brill.

Smallwood, E. M. (1987). "Philo and Josephus as Historians of the Same Events." Pp. 114–129 in *Josephus, Judaism, and Christianity*, ed. L. H. Feldman and G. Hata. Detroit: Wayne State University Press.

Smith, M. (1958). "The Description of the Essenes in Josephus and the Philosophumena." *HUCA* 29: 273–313.

Smith, M. D. (1999). "A Tale of Two Julias: Julia, Julias, and Josephus." Pp. 2.333–345 in Arav and Freund 1995–2009.

Sokoloff, M. (1992). *A Dictionary of Jewish Palestinian Aramaic of the Byzantine Period*. 2nd printing. Ramat Gan, Israel: Bar-Ilan University Press.

Sokoloff, M. (2002). *A Dictionary of Jewish Babylonian Aramaic of the Talmudic and Geonic Periods*. Ramat Gan, Israel: Bar-Ilan University Press.

Southern, P. (2007). *The Roman Army: A Social and Institutional History*. Oxford: Oxford University Press.

Speidel, M. P. (1994). *Riding for Caesar: The Roman Emperors' Horse Guards*. Cambridge, Mass.: Harvard University Press.

Sperber, D. (1977). "On the Office of the *agoranomus* in Roman Palestine." *ZDMG* 127: 227–243.

Spicq, C. (1994). *Theological Lexicon of the New Testament*. 3 vols. Peabody, Mass.: Hendrickson.

Spier, J. (1992). *Ancient Gems and Finger Rings: Catalogue of the Collections*. Malibu CA: J. Paul Getty Museum Publications.

Spilsbury, P. and C. Seeman (2017). *Judean Antiquities 11*. FJTC 6a. Leiden: Brill.

Spivey, N. (2013). *Greek Sculpture*. New York: Cambridge University Press.

Stacey, D. (2004). *Excavations at Tiberias, 1973–1974: The Early Islamic Period*. IAA Reports 21. Jerusalem: Israel Antiquities Authority.

Stegemann, H. (1998). *The Library of Qumran: On the Essenes, Qumran, John the Baptist and Jesus*. Leiden: Brill.

Stein, A. (1981). "Some Notes on the Chronology of the Coins of Agrippa I." *INJ* 5: 22–26.

Stein, A. (1992). "Gaius Iulius, an Agoranomos from Tiberias." *ZPE* 93: 144–148.

Stein, E. (1937). *De Woordenkeuze in het Bellum Judaïcum van Flavius Josephus*. Diss. Leiden. Amsterdam: Paris.

Steinmann, A. E. (2009). "When Did Herod the Great Reign?" *NovT* 51: 1–29.

Stelten, L. F., ed. (1990). *Flavius Vegetius Renatus: Epitoma Rei Militaris*. American University Studies 17/2. New York: Lang.

Sterling, G. E. (1992). *Historiography and Self-Definition: Josephos, Luke-Acts and Apologetic Historiography*. Supplements to NovT 64. Leiden: Brill.

Sterling, G. E. (2020). "'Pre-eminent in Family and Wealth:' Gaius Julius Alexander and the Alexandrian Jewish Community." Pp. 259–279 in *Israel in Egypt: The Land of Egypt as Concept and Reality for Jews in Antiquity and the Early Medieval Period*, ed. A. Salvesen, S. Pearce, and M. Frenkel. AJEC 110. Leiden: Brill.

Stern, E., et al. (1993–2008). *The New Encyclopedia of Archaeological Excavations in the Holy Land*, ed. E. Stern et al. 5 vols. Jerusalem: Israel Exploration Society, and Washington, D.C.: Biblical Archaeology Society.

Stern, M. (1973). "Zealots." Pp. 135–152 in *Encyclopedia Judaica Year Book 1973: Events of 1972*. Jerusalem: Keter.

Stern, M. (1974a). "The Province of Judaea." Pp. 1.308–376 in Safrai and Stern 1974–1976.

Stern, M. (1974b). "The Sources." Pp. 1.1–77 in Safrai and Stern 1974–1976.

Stern, M. (1974c). "The Reign of Herod and the Herodian Dynasty." Pp. 1.216–307 in Safrai and Stern 1974–1976.

Stern, M. (1974–1984). *Greek and Latin Authors on Jews and Judaism*. 3 vols. Jerusalem: The Israel Academy of Sciences and Humanities.

Stern, M. (1976). "Aspects of Jewish Society: The Priesthood and Other Classes." Pp. 2.561–630 in Safrai and Stern 1974–1976.

Stern, M. (1982). "Social and Political Realignments in Herodian Judaea." *Jerusalem Cathedra* 2: 40–62.

Stern, M. (1987). "Josephus and the Roman Empire as Reflected in *The Jewish War*." Pp. 71–80 in *Josephus, Judaism, and Christianity*, ed. L. H. Feldman and G. Hata. Detroit: Wayne State University Press.

Stern, M. (1988). "Antisemitism in Rome." Pp. 13–25 in *Antisemitism through the Ages*, ed. S. Almog. Studies in Antisemitism. Oxford: Pergamon Press.

Stern, M. (1991). *Studies in Jewish History: The Second Temple Period*. Ed. M. Amit, I. Gafni, and M. D. Herr. Jerusalem: Yad Izhak Ben-Zvi (in Hebrew).

Stern, M. (1995). *Hasmonaean Judaea in the Hellenistic World: Chapters in Political History*, ed. D. R. Schwartz. Jerusalem: Zalman Shazar Center (in Hebrew).

Stevenson, T. (2007). "Roman Coins and Refusals of the Title *'Pater Patriae'*." *Numismatic Chronicle* 167: 119–141.

Stewart, A. (1990). *Greek Sculpture: An Exploration*. 2 vols.; New Haven: Yale University Press.

Stowasser, M. (2008). "Pontius Pilatus in der Darstellung des Bellum Iudaicum." *Protokolle zur Bibel* 17: 91–103.

Strange, J. F. et al. (1994–1995). "Excavations at Sepphoris: The Location and Identification of Shikhin." *IEJ* 44: 216–227; 45: 171–187.

Streckert, K. H. and B. V. Seevers (2023). "Militaria." Pp. 300–312 in *The Excavations at Khirbet el-Maqatir: 1995–2001 and 2009–2016: Volume 2: The Late Hellenistic, Early Roman, and Byzantine Periods*, edited by Scott Stripling and M. A. Hassler. Summertown, Oxford: Archaeopress.

Strickert, F. M. (1995). "The Coins of Philip." Pp. 1.165–189 in Arav and Freund 1995–2009.

Strickert, F. (2002). "Josephus' Reference to Julia, Caesar's Daughter: Jewish Antiquities 18.27–28." *JJS* 53: 27–34.

Strickert, F. (2010). "The Founding of the City of Julias by the Tetrarch Philip in 30 CE." *JJS* 61: 220–233.

Strickert, F. M. (2011). *Philip's City: From Bethsaida to Julias*. Collegeville, Minn.: Liturgical Press.

Strickert, F. (2014). "A Fresh Analysis of Josephus' Portrayal of Herodias, Wife of Herod's Sons." In Ellens 2014: 360–393.

Strugnell, E. (2008). "Thea Musa, Roman Queen of Parthia." *Iranica Antiqua* 43: 275–298.

Strugnell, J. (1958). "Flavius Josephus and the Essenes: *Antiquities* XVIII.18–22." *JBL* 77: 106–115.

Sullivan, R. D. (1977a). "The Dynasty of Commagene." *ANRW* II/8: 732–798.

Sullivan, R. D. (1977b). "The Dynasty of Emesa." *ANRW* II/8: 198–219.

Sullivan, R. D. (1980). "Dynasts in Pontus." *ANRW* II/7.2: 913–930.

Swain, S. (1989). "Plutarch: Chance, Providence, and History." *AJP* 110: 272–302.

Swain, S. (1996). *Hellenism and Empire: Language, Classicism, and Power in the Greek World*, AD 50–250. Oxford: Clarendon.

Swan, M. (1970). "Josephus, *A. J.*, XIX, 251–252: Opposition to Gaius and Claudius." *AJP* 91: 149–164.

Swan, P. M. (1976). "A Consular Epicurean under the Early Principate." *Phoenix* 30: 54–60.

Swan, P. M. (2004). *The Augustan Succession: An Historical Commentary on Cassius Dio's* Roman History, *Books 55–56 (9 B.C.–A.D. 14)*. American Classical Studies 47. Oxford: Oxford University Press.

Swancutt, D. M. (2005). "Paraenesis in Light of Protrepsis: Troubling the Typical Dichotomy." Pp. 113–153 in *Early Christian Paraenesis in Context*, ed. J. Starr and T. Engberg-Perdersen. Berlin: De Gruyter.

Syme, R. (1956). "Some Pisones in Tacitus." *JRS* 46: 17–21.

Syme, R. (1958). *Tacitus*. 2 vols. Oxford: Clarendon.

Syme, R. (1964). "The Stemma of the Sentii Saturnini." *Historia* 13: 156–166.

Syme, R. (1979). "Domitius Corbulo." Pp. 805–824 in idem, *Roman Papers*, II, ed. E. Badian. Oxford: Clarendon Press.

Syme, R. (1984). *Roman Papers*, III, ed. A. R. Birley. Oxford: Clarendon Press.

Syme, R. (1986). *The Augustan Aristocracy*. Oxford: Clarendon.

Szanton, N. et al. (2019). "Pontius Pilate in Jerusalem: The Monumental Street from the Siloam Pool to the Temple Mount." *Tel Aviv* 46: 147–166.

Täubler, E. (1904). *Die Parthernachrichten bei Josephus*. Diss. Berlin. Berlin: Ebering.

Täubler, E. (1916). "Die nicht bestimmbaren Hinweise bei Josephus und die Anonymushypothese." *Hermes* 51: 211–232.

Takács, S. A. (1995). *Isis and Serapis in the Roman World*. RGRW 124. Leiden: Brill.

Talbert, R. J. A. (1984). *The Senate of Imperial Rome*. Princeton: Princeton University Press.

Taylor, J. (1992). "The Ethnarch of King Aretas at Damascus: A Note on 2 Cor 11,32–33." *RB* 99: 719–728.

Taylor, J. (2001). "The Community of Goods among the First Christians and among the Essenes." Pp. 147–164 in *Historical Perspectives: From the Hasmoneans to Bar Kokhba in Light of the Dead Sea Scrolls: Proceedings of the Fourth International Symposium of the Orion Center for the Study of the Dead Sea Scrolls and Associated Literature, 27–31 January, 1999*, ed. D. Goodblatt, A. Pinnick, and D. R. Schwartz. STDJ 37. Leiden: Brill.

Taylor, J. E. (2012). *The Essenes, the Scrolls, and the Dead Sea*. Oxford: Oxford University Press.

Taylor, J. E. (2016). "Imagining Judean Priestly Dress: The Berne Josephus and Judaea Capta Coinage." Pp. 195–212 in *Dressing Judeans and Christians in Antiquity*, ed. K. Upson-Saia, C. Daniel-Hughes, and A. J. Batten. London: Routledge.

Tcherikover, V. (1957). "Jewish Apologetic Literature Reconsidered." *Eos* 48/3 (= *Symbolae Raphaeli Taubenschlag Dedicatae*, III): 169–193.

Tcherikover, V. (1959). *Hellenistic Civilization and the Jews*. Philadelphia: The Jewish Publication Society of America; Jerusalem: Magnes Press.

Tcherikover, V. A., A. Fuks and M. Stern, ed. (1957–1964). *Corpus Papyrorum Judaicarum*. 3 vols. Cambridge, Mass.: Harvard.

Tcherikover, V. A. (1964). "Was Jerusalem a 'Polis'?" *IEJ* 14: 61–78.

Terian, A. (1981). *Philonis Alexandrini De Animalibus: The Armenian Text with an Introduction, Translation, and Commentary*. Studies in Hellenistic Judaism: Supplements to *Studia Philonica* 1. Chico, California: Scholars Press.

Thackeray, H. St. J. (1919). *Selections from Josephus*. Translations of Early Documents, Series 2. London: Society for Promoting Christian Knowledge.

Thackeray, H. St. J., ed. and trans. (1926). *Josephus*, I (LCL), Cambridge, Mass.: Harvard University Press and London: Heinemann.

Thackeray, H. St. J. (1929). *Josephus: The Man and the Historian*. New York: Jewish Institute of Religion Press.

Thackeray, H. St. J. and R. Marcus (1930–1955). *A Lexicon to Josephus*. 4 parts. Paris: Librairie Orientaliste Paul Geuthner.

Thackeray, H. St. J. (1932). "On Josephus' Statement of the Pharisees' Doctrine of Fate (ANTIQ. xviii. 1,3)." *HTR* 25: 93.

Thiel, N. (2020). "The Use of the Term "Galileans" in the Writings of Flavius Josephus Revisited." *JQR* 110: 221–244.

Thiessen, M. (2011). *Contesting Conversion: Genealogy, Circumcision, and Identity in Ancient Judaism and Christianity*. New York: Oxford University Press.

Tilly, M. (2015). *1 Makkabäer*. Herders Theologischer Kommentar zum Alten Testament. Freiburg: Herder.

Timpe, D. (1960). "Römische Geschichte bei Flavius Josephus." *Historia* 9: 474–502.

Tov, E. (1999). *The Greek and Hebrew Bible: Collected Essays on the Septuagint*. VTSup 72. Leiden: Brill.

Townend, G. B. (1960). "The Sources of the Greek in Suetonius." *Hermes* 88: 98–120.

Townend, G. [B.]. (1961). "Some Flavian Connections." *JRS* 51: 54–62.

Townend, G. B. (1964). "Cluvius Rufus in the *Histories* of Tacitus." *AJP* 85: 337–377.

Toynbee, J. M. C. (1971). *Death and Burial in the Roman World*. Ithaca: Cornell University Press.

Troiani, L. (1986). "I lettori della *Antichità Giudaiche* di Giuseppe: Prospettive e problemi." *Athenaeum* 64: 343–353.

Troiani, L. (2005). "Il Gesù de Flavio Giuseppe." *Ricerche storico bibliche* 17/2 (2005): 137–147.

Tromp, J. (2008). "John the Baptist according to Flavius Josephus, and His Incorporation in the Christian Tradition." Pp. 135–149 in Empsychoi Logoi—*Religious Innovations in Antiquity: Studies in Honour of Pieter Willem van der Horst*, ed. A. Houtman, A. de Jong, and M. Misset-van de Weg. AJEC 73. Leiden: Brill.

Tropper, A. (2013). *Simeon the Righteous in Rabbinic Literature: A Legend Reinvented*. AJEC 84. Leiden: Brill.

Tropper, D. (1972/73). "Bet Din shel Kohanim." *JQR* 63: 204–221.

Tsur, Y. (2021). "Political Tenure, Term Limits, and Corruption." *Social Science Research Network*, June 2021 (online, accessed 9 March 2023).

Tuval, M. (2013). *From Jerusalem Priest to Roman Jew: On Josephus and the Paradigms of Ancient Judaism.* WUNT II/357. Tübingen: Mohr Siebeck.

Udoh, F. E. (2002). "Jewish Antiquities XIV, 205, 207–208 and 'The Great Plain'." *PEQ* 134: 130–143.

Udoh, F. E. (2020). *To Caesar What is Caesar's: Tribute, Taxes, and Imperial Administration in Early Roman Palestine.* 2nd edition. BJS 343. Providence, Rhode Island: Brown Judaic Studies.

Ullmann, L. (trans.) (2009). *Yosef ben Matityahu/[Titus] Flavius Josephus: History of the Jewish War against the Romans.* Jerusalem: Carmel (in Hebrew).

Unnik, W. C. van (1949). "De la règle Μήτε προσθεῖναι μήτε ἀφελεῖν dans l'histoire du canon." *Vigiliae Christianae* 3: 1–36.

Unnik, W. C. van (1974). "Josephus' Account of the Story of Israel's Sin with Alien Women in the Country of Midian (Num. 25:11ff.)." Pp. 241–261 in *Travels in the World of the Old Testament: Studies Presented to Professor M. A. Beek on the Occasion of his 65th Birthday*, ed. M. S. H. G. Heerma van Voss, P. H. J. Houwink ten Cate, and N. A. van Uchelen. Studia Semitica Neerlandica 16. Assen: Van Gorcum.

VanderKam, J. C. (2004). *From Joshua to Caiaphas: High Priests after the Exile.* Minneapolis: Fortress, and Assen: Van Gorcum.

Verdenius, W. J. (1974). "Inceptive ΔE again." *Mnemosyne* (ser. 4) 27: 173–174.

Vermes, G. (1960). "The Etymology of 'Essenes.'" *RQ* 2: 427–443.

Victor, U. (2010). "Das *Testimonium Flavianum*: Ein authentischer Text des Josephus." *NovT* 52: 72–82.

Villalba i Varneda, P. (1986). *The Historical Method of Flavius Josephus.* ALGHJ 19. Leiden: Brill.

Vincent, H. (1911). "Chronologie des oeuvres de Josèphe." *RB* 8: 366–383.

Visi, T. (2020). "The Chronology of John the Baptist and the Crucifixion of Jesus of Nazareth: A New Approach." *Journal for the Study of the Historical Jesus* 18: 1–34.

Vitelli, M. (2018). "La più antica testimonianza letteraria non-cristiana su Gesù: Considerazioni sul *Testimonium Flavianum* (Ant. XVIII 63–64)." *Mosaico* 5: 1–35.

Voorst, R. van (2000). *Jesus outside the New Testament.* Grand Rapids, Mich.: Eerdmans.

Wächter, L. (1969). "Die unterschiedliche Haltung der Pharisäer, Sadduzäer und Essener zur Heimarmene nach dem Bericht des Josephus." *ZRGG* 21: 97–114.

Walbank, F. W. (1957–1979). *A Historical Commentary on Polybius.* 3 vols. Oxford: Clarendon Press.

Walcot, P. (1991). "On Widows and Their Reputation in Antiquity." *Symbolae Osloenses* 66: 5–26.

Walker, J. (2000). *Rhetoric and Poetics in Antiquity.* New York: Oxford University Press.

Wallace-Hadrill, A. (1982). "Civilis Princeps: Between Citizen and King." *JRS* 72: 32–48.

Ward, J. S. (2007). "Roman Greek: Latinisms in the Greek of Flavius Josephus." *CQ* 57: 632–649.

Wardle, D. (1991). "When Did Gaius Caligula Die?" *Acta Classica* 34: 158–165.

Wardle, D. (1992a). "Caligula and the Client Kings." *CQ* 42: 437–443.

Wardle, D. (1992b). "Cluvius Rufus and Suetonius." *Hermes* 120: 466–482.

Wardle, D. (1997). "An Allusion to the Kaisereid in Tacitus *Annals* 1. 42?" *CQ* 47: 609–613.

Wardle, D. (1998). "Caligula and His Wives." *Latomus* 57: 109–126.

Wardle, D. (2007). "Caligula's Bridge of Boats—AD 39 or 40?" *Historia* 56: 118–20.

Warren, M. (2016). "A Robe Like Lightning: Clothing Changes and Identification in *Joseph and Asenath*." Pp. 137–153 in *Dressing Judeans and Christians in Antiquity*, ed. K. Upson-Saia, C. Daniel-Hughes, and A. J. Batten. London: Routledge.

Weaver, P. R. C. (1983). Review of Bellen 1981. *Gnomon* 55: 436–441.

Weaver, P. R. C. (1994). "Epaphroditus, Josephus, and Epictetus." *CQ* 44: 468–479.

Webster, G. (1998). *The Roman Imperial Army of the First and Second Centuries A.D.* 3rd edition. Norman: University of Oklahoma Press.

Weingärtner, D. G. (1969). *Die Ägyptenreise des Germanicus.* Papyrologische Texte und Abhandlungen 11. Bonn: Habelt.

Weinreich, O. (1911). *Der Trug des Nektanebos: Wandlungen eines Novellenstoffs.* Leipzig: Teubner.

Weiss, H. (1998). "The Sabbath in the Writings of Josephus." *JSJ* 29: 363–390.

Weiss, Z. (1999). "Adopting a Novelty: The Jews and the Roman Games in Palestine." Pp. 23–49 in *The Roman and Byzantine Near East, II: Some Recent Archaeological Research*, ed. J. H. Humphrey. Portsmouth: JRA.

Weiss, Z. (2007). "Josephus and Archaeology on the Cities of the Galilee." Pp. 385–414 in Rodgers 2007.

Weiss, Z. (2014) *Public Spectacles in Roman and Late Antique Palestine.* Revealing Antiquity 21. Cambridge, Mass.: Harvard University Press.

Welles, C. B. (1934). *Royal Correspondence in the Hellenistic Period: A Study in Greek Epigraphy*. New Haven: Yale University Press.

Wells, P. S. (2011). "The Ancient Germans." Pp. 211–232 in *The Barbarians of Ancient Europe: Realities and Interactions*, ed. L. Bonfante. Cambridge: Cambridge University Press.

Wendland P. (1892). *Deutsche Literaturzeitung* 13: 1265–1268 (review of vols. 3–4 of Niese's editio maior and vol. 3 of his editio minor).

Werse, N. R. (2018). "Exile, Restoration, and the Question of Postexilic Suffering in Josephus." *JSJ* 49: 390–403.

Whealey, A. (2003). *Josephus on Jesus: The Testimonium Flavianum Controversy from Late Antiquity to Modern Times*. Studies in Biblical Literature 36. New York: Lang.

Whealey, A. (2016). "The *Testimonium Flavianum*." Pp. 345–355 in Chapman and Rodgers 2016.

Whiston, W., trans. (1878).[5] *The Works of Flavius Josephus*. London: Ward, Lock and Co.

Whiston, W., trans. (1889). *The Works of Flavius Josephus: Whiston's Translation Revised by the Rev. A. R. Shilleto, M. A.*, III. London: Bell.

Wilcken, U. (1912). *Grundzüge und Chrestomathie der Papyruskunde*, I/2. Leipzig: Teubner.

Wilhelm, A. (1894). "Kietis: Zu Tacitus und Josephus." *Archäologisch-epigraphische Mittheilungen aus Österreich-Ungarn* 17: 1–6.

Wilhelm, A. (1943). "Beschluß zu Ehren des Demetrios ὁ μέγας." *Jahreshefte des Österreichischen Archäologischen Institutes in Wien* 35: 157–163.

Wilker, J. (2007). *Für Rom und Jerusalem: Die herodianische Dynastie im 1. Jahrhundert n. Chr*. Studien zur Alten Geschichte 5. Frankfurt am Main: Antike.

Wilkinson, S. (2005). *Caligula*. London: Routledge.

Wilkinson, S. (2012). *Republicanism during the Early Roman Empire*. London: Continuum.

Williams, M. H. (1988). "θεοσεβὴς γὰρ ἦν: The Jewish Tendencies of Poppaea Sabina." *JTS* n.s. 39: 97–111.

Williamson, H. G. M. (1977). "The Historical Value of Josephus' *Jewish Antiquities* xi. 297–301." *JTS* n.s. 28: 49–66.

Willrich, H. (1903). "Caligula." *Klio* 3: 397–470.

Wills, L. M. (1990). *The Jew in the Court of the Foreign King: Ancient Jewish Court Legends*. HDR 26. Minneapolis: Fortress.

Wink, W. (1968). *John the Baptist in the Gospel Tradition*. SNTSMS 7. London: Cambridge University Press.

Winter, P. (1953). "ΜΟΝΟΓΕΝΗΣ ΠΑΡΑ ΠΑΤΡΟΣ." *ZRGG* 5: 335–365.

Winter, P. (1954). "Simeon der Gerechte und Caius Caligula." *ZRGG* 6: 72–74.

Winter, P. (1973). "Excursus II: Josephus on Jesus and James." In *HJP* 1.428–441.

Winterling, A. (2011). *Caligula: A Biography*. Berkeley: University of California Press.

Winterling, A. (2018). "Imperial Madness in Ancient Rome." Pp. 61–80 in *Evil Lords: Theories and Representations of Tyranny from Antiquity to the Renaissance*, ed. by N. Panou and H. Schadee. New York: Oxford University Press.

Wirszubski, C. (1950). *Libertas as a Political Idea at Rome during the Late Republic and Early Principate*. Cambridge: Cambridge University Press.

Wiseman, T. P. (1985). *Catullus and His World: A Reappraisal*. Cambridge: Cambridge University Press.

Wiseman, T. P. (1987). "Josephus on the Palatine." Pp. 167–175 in idem, *Roman Studies: Literary and Historical*. Liverpool: Francis Cairns Ltd.

Wiseman, T. P. (1992). "Killing Caligula." Pp. 1–13 in idem, *Talking to Virgil: A Miscellany*. Exeter: Univ. of Exeter.

Wiseman, T. P. (2013a). *The Death of Caligula: Josephus Ant. Iud. XIX 1–273, Translation and Commentary*. Liverpool: Liverpool University Press.

Wiseman, T. P. (2013b). "The Palatine, from Evander to Elgabalus." *JRS* 103: 234–268.

Wolfson, H. A. (1945/46). "Synedrion in Greek Jewish Literature and Philo." *JQR* 36: 303–306.

Woodman, A. J. (1998). *Tacitus Reviewed*. Oxford: Clarendon Press.

Woods, D. (2008). "Tiberius, Tacfarinas, and the Jews." *Arctos* 42: 267–284.

Woods, D. (2018). "Caligula, Asprenas, and the Bloodied Robe." *Mnemosyne* 71: 873–880.

Yakobson, A. (1989). "The Attitude of Roman Emperors to Their Predecessors, from Tiberius to the 'Englightened Emperors.'" Unpublished M.A. Thesis, The Hebrew University of Jerusalem (in Hebrew).

Yakobson, A. (1998). "The Princess of Inscriptions: Senatus Consultum de Cn. Pisone Patre and the Early Years of Tiberius' Reign." *SCI* 17: 206–224 (review article).

---

5 The date of publication is not stated in the volume; various libraries list it as 1878 or 1879.

Yakobson, A. (2003). "*Maiestas*, the Imperial Ideology and the Imperial Family: The Evidence of the Senatus Consultum de Cn. Pisone Patre." *Eutopia* 3: 75–107.

Yankelevitch, R. (1979/80). "The Auxiliary Troops from Caesarea and Sebaste: A Decisive Factor in the Rebellion against Rome." *Tarbiz* 49: 33–42 (in Hebrew).

Yavetz, Z. (1969). *Plebs and Princeps*. London: Oxford University Press.

Yavetz, Z. (1996). "Caligula, Imperial Madness and Modern Historiography." *Klio* 78: 105–129.

Yechezkel, A., Y. Negev, A. Frumkin, and U. Leibner (2021). "The Shaft Tunnel of the Biar Aqueduct of Jerusalem: Architecture, Hydrology, and Dating." *Geoarchaeology* 2021 (online).

Yerushalmi, Y. H. (1976). *The Lisbon Massacre of 1506 and the Royal Image in the* Shebet Yehudah. HUCA Supplements 1. Cincinnati: Hebrew Union College—Jewish Institute of Religion.

Zeitlin, S. (1945/46). "Synedrion in the Judeo-Hellenistic Literature and Sanhedrin in the Tannaitic Literature." *JQR* 36: 307–315.

OPENING NOTE ABOUT THE INDEXES

The increasing accessibility of electronic resources that allow ancient sources, and also books such as this one, to be read and searched online, allows readers to do, by themselves, what indexes used to do for them. Any reader with access to an electronic file who wants to know if some ancient or modern person or place is mentioned in this book can find such passages faster by searching the volume than by consulting an index in the back of it and then flipping back to the appropriate page. I have, nevertheless, included an *index of subjects*, since many of the entries in it could not be created simply by searching for this or that term, and, as is traditional, I have separated out from it, in a separate index, the *ancient names and places*. Together, those indexes can allow readers a good idea of what is discussed in the book, beyond the analytic table of the Josephan text at pp. xxi–xxiii. Those who want more detail can use Schalit 1968 or the copious index in Feldman 1965. An *index of modern scholars* is also included, for it complements the bibliography and invites readers to follow scholarly debates relevant to this volume. In contrast, but following the lead of other volumes in this series, I have depended on readers' access to *CCFJ* and to electronic resources as reason to abstain from including indexes of ancient Greek and other words and of ancient texts cited in this volume. Its annotations include more than two hundred references each to Suetonius and to Josephus's *War* 2, hundreds more to other passages in Josephus's oeuvre, more than a hundred each to Cassius Dio and Luke-Acts, and scores each to 1–2 Maccabees, Strabo, Philo, Seneca, Pliny, Plutarch, the Hebrew Bible, the Gospels, and the Mishnah, along with a host of other ancient authors and texts that are cited less often. Experience shows that, already today, readers who are interested in comparing the ancient sources prefer to find them electronically.

INDEX OF SUBJECTS

afterlife 53–56, 130, 132
alabarch 106, 125, 235, 236, 279, 292
Ambrosianus 23, 53, 79, 112, 126, 143, 194, 219, 244, 256, 263, 323, 324
apostasy 100, 101, 280
aqueduct 74, 216
Aramaic 66, 139, 140, 143, 144, 253, 268, 277, 337
aristocracy 55, 116, 161, 162, 204, 291, 308, 312, 319
aristocrat, Josephus as 53, 67, 118, 122, 162, 166, 169, 181, 186, 196, 198, 215, 230, 297, 323
assistants (Josephus's) 21–23, 311, 323
"at that time" xvii, 8
auxiliary troops 11, 126, 258, 260, 286, 298, 320

birthdays 64, 117, 182, 248
bloodshed 295
bones 62, 63, 67, 278, 318
bribery 10, 102, 205, 225, 227, 287, 295, 301, 309, 310
brigands 10, 29, 138, 149, 263, 264, 283, 286, 294–302, 307–310, 320–321
busts 72, 74, 105

cannibalism 193
capital jurisdiction 46, 307
celibacy 58–59
constitutions 102, 207, 208, 211, 214, 312, 314, 317, 319, 322
converts and conversion 8, 29, 32, 33, 76, 101, 251, 266, 270, 271, 275, 290
crucifixion 76, 77, 80, 93, 188, 189, 280, 287, 330

democracy 178, 204, 205, 207, 211, 212, 222, 314
desert 231, 279, 296, 312
destruction of Temple 2, 15, 49, 80, 82, 93, 129, 180, 277, 299, 300, 305, 307, 312, 314, 333
diptych 74–75
divorce 62, 92, 99, 100, 107, 208, 291, 292, 320, 338

edition, second 22, 325
equites 46, 78, 166, 180, 186, 189, 196, 210, 280
Essenes 14, 28, 51–59
euergetism 86, 250, 252

famine 49, 167, 272–280, 289, 309, 331
fatigue 11, 325
Forth Philosophy 13, 26, 47, 50–52, 59, 60, 178, 301

freedmen 102, 110, 114, 181, 229–232, 259, 289, 293, 301
freedom, liberty 47, 58, 50, 111, 69, 96, 131, 161, 170, 171, 177–179, 185, 189, 205–211, 223, 227, 228, 231, 285, 296, 302

Galileans 59, 61, 66, 284, 285
gladiators 159, 173, 195–198, 215, 229, 231, 252, 302
"go up" 16, 93, 272, 284, 288, 295, 300

Hebrew 17, 89, 99, 119, 140, 250, 303, 306, 308, 313, 316–317, 336
"high priest" 46, 281, 299, 308
holy city 36, 128, 284–285
horoscopes 117
hostages 68, 70, 85, 89, 259, 264, 269, 304
hyperbole 75, 137, 165, 215

inscriptions 45, 46, 63, 72, 82, 96, 102, 106, 138, 251, 291, 308
irony 11, 26, 48, 60, 108, 122, 150, 163, 169, 192, 220, 227, 230, 294, 307, 310, 339
Isactium 254
Isis 78–81

"Jew" xiv, 33
Judea—provincial status 46, 62, 64, 264, 284
"Judean" xiv, 46, 112
juridical language 324

lectio brevior potior 24, 27, 322
lectio difficilior 24, 25, 53, 60
litotes 77, 172
Luke—used Josephus? 255, 279

marble 311
messiah, messianism 76, 188, 255, 285
mob, masses, *hoi polloi* 55, 61, 70, 75, 212, 297

Nazirites 17, 242, 243, 272, 333

oaths 96, 142, 180, 230, 235, 236, 259, 268, 29
ornithoscopy 126

Passover, *Pascha* 62, 84, 95, 96, 247, 256, 257, 271, 281, 282, 330
patronymy 335
Pharisees 14, 47, 50–56, 59, 129, 249, 251, 252, 270, 282, 305, 306, 317
philosophy 48–54, 57–60, 125, 130, 323

pilgrims, pilgrimage 49, 62, 63, 114, 138, 282, 285
poisoning 71, 145, 147, 181, 213, 292, 293
priestly Judaism 55, 86, 101, 251–252, 316
prophets, prophecy 58, 77, 78, 97, 279, 296, 297, 332
prostasia 317, 319
providence, divine 113, 122, 135, 136, 143, 180, 188, 266, 267, 271, 273, 275, 278, 279, 296

Quellenforschung, Quellenkritik 21

"religion" 32, 33, 101, 132, 241 250
resurrection 54, 76–78, 305

Sabbath 86, 139, 140
sackcloth 256, 286
sacrifices 17, 56, 57, 119, 144, 182, 231, 233, 242, 250, 272
Sadducees 14, 51–56, 129, 251, 305, 306
Samaritans 14, 63, 82–84, 101, 284–289, 298
schematic numbers 278
Second Commandment 73
Senate, senators 6, 13, 45, 52, 71, 110, 115, 119, 136, 159–162, 165, 166, 180, 186, 196, 201–205, 209, 211, 217–232, 235
Sicarii 10, 49, 59, 60, 280, 295, 297, 301–302, 307–308, 320, 5
slaves, slavery 58, 110, 112, 145, 169, 170, 230, 231, 283
"sloppiness" 3, 312
stichometry 324
suicide 47, 64, 103, 135, 171, 188, 234, 249

Testimonium Flavianum 9, 14, 75–77, 304, 306
toggling 112, 193, 231
triads 51, 102, 120, 165, 171, 172
tyrants, tyranny 49, 107, 110, 118, 132, 161, 162, 165–171, 174–177, 180, 181, 185, 187, 191, 195, 197–199, 202, 203, 207–212, 217, 222, 223, 227, 230, 233

"under the following circumstances" 67–68, 85, 137, 266, 283, 290

vagueness 95, 139, 222, 245
vestments, high-priestly 17, 55, 84–86, 247, 264, 269, 310

Wiederaufnahme 13, 60, 319
women 32, 55, 58, 68, 69, 78–81, 99, 101, 106, 124, 138, 143, 144, 147, 159, 170, 174–176, 186, 197–198, 208, 213, 231, 290–292, 320

INDEX OF ANCIENT PERSONS AND PLACES

Aaron   59, 247, 312
Abdagases   142
Abennerigus   268
Abias (king of Arabs)   276
Abila, Abilene   30, 120, 234, 290
Actium   61, 85, 145, 207, 254, 329
Adiabene   5, 12, 18, 101, 266–278, 280
Agrippa I   97–123, 132–135, 224–263
     passim
Agrippa II   97, 98, 257, 259, 264–266,
     275, 281, 286, 289–290, 294, 299,
     303, 306–311, 321, 331
Agrippina   68, 69, 102, 172, 190, 289,
     292, 293
Albinus, Lucceius   7, 9–10, 17, 20, 35, 81,
     281, 300, 304–310, 320
Alcyon/Alcon   203
Alexander Janneus   116, 225, 242, 316
Alexander the Alabarch   106, 125, 235,
     236, 256, 351
Alexander the Great   95, 231, 168, 184,
     188, 238, 248, 352
Alexandria   49, 81, 106, 121, 124, 149, 185,
     236–240, 244, 245, 256, 264, 265,
     307, 341
Alexas   100
Amaramus (brigand)   263
Ambivulus, Marcus   64, 329
Ananias (merchant)   269–271
Ananias b. Nedebeus   3, 7, 269–271,
     280, 281, 288, 299, 307–309
Ananus (captain of Temple)   288
Ananus (high priest)   61, 65, 66, 244,
     304, 305
Ananus b. Ananus   304–307
Ananus b. Seth   61, 65
Anileus   26, 69, 80, 137–149, 207, 274,
     288
Annas see Ananus
Annibas (brigand)   263
Anthedon   105
Antigonus   174, 233, 317, 318
Antioch   86, 126, 149
Antiochus III of Commagene   14, 71, 72
Antiochus III   95
Antiochus IV Epiphanes   95, 150, 176,
     316
Antiochus IV of Comagene   100, 132,
     235
Antiochus V Eupator   314
Antiochus VII Sidetes   6
Antium   185
Antonia (fortress)   85–86, 249, 264,
     282, 283
Antonia Minor   6, 102 105–111, 114, 120,
     190, 235, 289, 291
Antonius, Marcus   60, 64, 70, 85, 102,
     145, 213, 259, 292, 318, 329
Anubis   79

Apion   96, 124
Aponius   231
Archelaus   45, 85, 258, 319, 329
Aretas IV   91–97, 103, 202, 239, 341
Aristobulus (brother of Agrippa I)   99,
     104, 105, 128
Aristobulus (father of
     Agrippa I)   97–99, 102, 121
Aristobulus (son of Herod of
     Chalcis)   3, 99, 100, 265, 281, 294
Aristobulus I   314–317
Aristobulus II   172, 317, 318
Aristobulus III   232, 318
Ariston   257
Armenia   71, 87, 88, 100, 247, 268, 275,
     294, 362
Arruntius, Euarestus   200
Arruntius, Stella   201
Artabanus II   5, 70, 71, 87–89, 112, 123,
     141–143, 146, 149, 269, 273, 274
Aruntius, Paullus   190
Asamonaios   303, 315, 319
Asineus   80, 137, 138, 140–145, 274, 341
Asprenas   186, 189
Atomus (a Cypriot)   290
Augustus (emp.)   14, 16, 61, 67–71, 86,
     96, 110, 112, 162, 183, 186, 194, 195,
     211, 229, 238–241, 246, 350, 252,
     254, 282
Azizus   3, 115, 258, 290, 294

Babylon, Babylonia(n)   89, 137–151, 165,
     207, 248, 268, 313, 314, 318, 322
Baiae   122, 123, 167
Batanea   30, 90, 234, 248, 290
Bathybius   157, 187
Berenice (daughter of Agrippa I   69,
     98, 112, 235, 242, 256, 257, 281, 291,
     292
Berenice (mother of Agrippa I)   99,
     102, 105–107
Beryllus   181, 293, 301
Berytus (Beirut)   46, 250, 252, 291, 308,
     354
Betharamaphta   61
Bethlehem   45, 74
Bethsaida   62, 344, 350, 357, 352, 372
Bezetha   249
Boethus   65, 66, 244, 333–339
Britannicus   292, 293
Brocchus   224
Brutus   210

Caesarea Maritima   49, 72–74, 188,
     250–259, 284–285, 297–301
Caesarea Philippi ("Neronias")   62, 308
Caesonia   165, 169, 212, 213, 214, 213, 233
Caiaphas   65, 66, 71, 86, 253, 305,
     337–339

Callistus   181
Camith   65, 304
Cantheras   3, 66, 243, 247, 253, 266,
     333–339
Capito, Herennius   331
Capitolium   167, 169, 182, 227
Cappadocia   100, 210
Capri   106–110, 114, 216
Caspian Gates   88
Cassius   210
Celer   288, 289, 342
Chaerea, Cassius   13, 48, 160, 161,
     171–193, 202, 206, 209–214,
     229–233, 288
Chalcis   3, 4, 7, 30, 98, 99, 235, 236, 257,
     266, 280, 281, 290
Charax Spasinou   268, 269
Cietis   100
Cilicia   71, 101, 235, 291
Cinyras   188
Claudius (emp.)   passim, esp. 204–266,
     288–292
Clazomenae   319
Clemens, M. Arrecinus   176–178
Cleopatra (Florus's wife)   319
Cleopatra (Herod's wife)   61
Cleopatra VII   145, 292
Cluvius Rufus   18, 156–162, 187, 206, 294
Commagene   14, 71, 72, 100, 132, 234,
     235, 258, 290, 372
Coponius   45, 46, 62, 64, 329, 340
Corinth   216
Cornelius Sabinus   178, 191, 192, 195,
     230, 232–234
Cortades   275
Costobar (gangster)   309
Cotys   252
Crassus   16, 70, 125, 188, 211
crucifixion   76, 77, 23, 280, 354, 374
Ctesiphon   70, 150
Cumanus, Ventidius   3, 4, 14, 19, 30, 31,
     75, 260, 281–289, 299, 331, 332, 342
Cypros (wife of Agrippa I)   32, 97–100,
     103, 106, 235, 257
Cyprus   98, 188, 290

David   54, 217, 278, 313
Demetrius (alabarch)   292
Dicearcheia   4, 6, 106, 122, 167
Dionysius of Halicarnassus   155
Doetos   287
Domitian (emp.)   176, 207, 210, 325
Dora   244–246
Drusilla (Caligula's daughter)   169, 212,
     214
Drusilla (Caligula's sister)   169, 172,
     208, 215
Drusilla (daughter of Agrippa I)   3, 98,
     115, 258, 290–292

Drusus (son of Agrippa I)   98, 257
Drusus the Elder   71, 102, 109, 110, 115–117, 190, 216, 219
Drusus the Younger   94, 102, 107, 110, 112, 114, 117

Eleazar (Galilean)   270
Eleazar (giant)   89
Eleazar b. Ananus   65
Eleazar b. Deinaios   285, 294, 295
Elioneus b. Cantheras   3, 253, 266, 334–339
Epimygdonia   274
Epiphanes (of Commagene)   290
Esdraelon   95, 285
Esther   16, 133, 134, 150, 243
Euodos   116
Euphrates River   12, 18, 87, 89, 126, 137, 277, 318

Fadus, Cuspius   8, 259, 260, 263–266, 272, 279, 280, 281, 284, 331, 342
Felix   7, 8, 17, 20, 30, 31, 36, 115, 281, 284, 285, 289–291, 294–300, 305, 320, 331, 332
Festus, Porcius   7, 10, 81, 281, 300–307, 332, 343
Flaccus (gov. of Egypt)   197
Flaccus (gov. of Syria)   104–105
Florus, Gessius   10, 15, 60, 260, 298, 307, 309, 311, 319–321, 332
Fortunatus   122
Fulvia   80–81

Gabalis   92
Gaius Caligula   passim, esp. 107, 119–136, 155–217
Galilee   5, 47, 59, 61, 66, 121, 234, 253, 270, 284, 285, 294, 302
Gamala   17, 47, 136
Gaulanitis (Golan)   47, 47, 59, 90, 234, 280, 290
Gerizim, Mt.   82
Germanicus   16, 65, 71, 72, 102, 106, 114–116, 190, 194, 197, 205, 216, 219, 221, 222, 292, 330
Ginae   285
Golan   47, 59, 280
Gordyene   268
Gratus (soldier)   206, 219, 220
Gratus, Valerius   64–67, 72, 109, 330
Great Plain   95, 285

Hasmoneans ("sons of Asamonaios")   303
Helcias   100, 128, 257, 258, 290, 304
Helena   68, 266–272, 275, 278, 280, 293
Herod (the Great)   2, 45, 46, 55, 62, 65, 67, 85 91, 96–103, 105, 117, 138, 145, 166, 188, 195, 208, 211, 216, 225, 234, 244, 248–255, 258, 259, 272, 280–282, 297, 298, 303, 308, 311, 315, 318, 319, 329, 333, 334, 338, 339
Herod Antipas   4, 6, 12, 18, 32, 61, 62, 66, 71, 84, 85, 87–95, 103, 121–124, 263, 294, 331, 335

Herod of Chalcis   3, 4, 6–8, 98, 218, 235–237, 240, 256, 257, 258, 265, 266, 291, 331
Herodias   17, 32, 48, 69, 91–94, 99–100, 103,121–124, 147, 291, 303
Hyrcanus II   171, 172, 239, 240, 316, 317, 318

Iotape   99, 100
Ishmael b. Phabes (Phiabi) I   65, 335
Ishmael b. Phiabi II   7, 8, 288, 289, 299, 300, 304, 307, 331, 335
Ishmael b. Phiabi   335
Isis   78–80
Izates   5, 33, 80, 101, 112, 266–278

Jacob (rebel)   280
James (Jacob, brother of Jesus)   305, 306
Jamneia (Jabneh)   64, 105, 124
Jesus b. Damnaios   307
Jesus b. Gamaliel   309, 311
Jesus of Nazareth   2, 3, 23, 45, 54, 75–78, 93, 285, 304–306, 310, 340
Joazar b. Boethus   46, 61, 333–338
John b. John   265, 335
John Hyrcanus I   85, 116, 267, 316, 317
John of Gischala   175
John the Baptist   6, 45, 91–94, 340
Jonathan (Hasmonean)   315, 316
Jonathan b. Ananus   86, 95, 247, 295
Jordan River, Jordan Valley   62, 64, 95, 279, 285
Joseph (biblical figure)   113, 120, 248
Joseph b. Camith/Camei   3, 66, 266, 280, 304
Joshua   61, 242, 279, 312, 370, 374
Judas Maccabeus   194, 276, 315
Judas the Galilean   5, 6, 47, 48, 50, 59–61, 279, 280, 301, 302
Julias   61, 61, 91, 294
Julius Caesar   16, 64, 112, 160, 183, 195, 196, 206–207, 210, 211, 214, 222, 233, 238, 240, 241, 246, 318??
Jupiter see Zeus

Lepidus, Marcus Aemilius   172, 179, 190
Livia (Julia, Augustus's wife)   61, 62, 64, 105, 183, 208
Longinus, Cassius   85, 208, 263, 264, 287, 331
Lugdunum   123
Lupus, Julius   158, 159, 212, 213, 214, 232, 233
Lydda   287
Lysanias   120, 234, 290
Lysias   314

Machaerus   92–94, 121
Macro   111, 114, 208
Malatha   103
Malthace   61, 91
Marcellus   83, 125, 203, 329, 331
Marcus (son of Alexander the Alabarch)   235, 256

Mariamme (Agrippa I's daughter)   98, 258, 290, 292, 333–339
Mariamme I (Herod's wife)   69, 97, 98, 145, 163, 216, 318
Mariamme II (Herod's wife)   91, 99, 333–339
Marsus, Vibius   3, 247, 249, 253, 259, 260, 263
Marsyas   105, 114, 119
Marullus   83, 120, 125, 329, 331
Masada   17, 47, 136, 161, 249, 280, 283, 301, 302, 312
Matthias b. Ananus   247
Matthias b. Theophilus   311, 337–339
Media   70
Menelaus (high priest)   304
Minucianus, Annius   171–172, 178–180, 189, 202, 229
Minucianus, Marcus   190, 228
Misenum   167
Mithridates   146–148
Monobazus   266–269, 275, 278, 342
Moses   54, 55, 58, 80, 82, 83, 85, 101, 265, 270, 283, 296, 310, 312, 344
Mundus, Decius   78, 79, 80, 213
Myrrha   78, 188

Nabatea   91, 92
Nebuchadnezzar   313
Nehardea   15, 137, 138, 148, 151
Nero (emp.)   7, 8, 64, 69, 100, 155–158, 171, 182, 187, 195, 202, 210, 227, 289, 293–294, 300–304, 308, 319, 332
Nicolaus of Damascus   1, 5, 46, 55, 64, 71, 90, 91, 181, 239, 308
Nisibis   15, 137, 151, 274
Norbanus   34, 196, 203

Octavia (daughter of Claudius)   292, 293, 320
Olives, Mt. of   297
Orodes   69–72, 87

Pacorus   275, 318
Palatine Hill   160, 173, 182–187, 194, 221, 227, 232
Palestine   321
Pallas   30, 110, 181, 289, 300, 301
Paneas see Caesarea Philippi   62
Papinus   176
Parthia   12, 18, 67, 87, 88, 89, 138, 278
Paulina   78, 79, 81, 168, 208
Pella   95
Perea   62, 93, 121, 263, 294, 319, 342
Petra   92–97
Petronius, Publius   5, 13, 26, 95, 125–136, 165, 245–246
Philadelphia   121, 263, 264, 342
Philip (son of Herod)   61, 100
Philip II of Macedon   188
Philo   124–125
Phraataces   67–69, 89
Phraates IV   67–70
Pilate, Pontius   1, 7, 13, 14, 19, 36, 64–66, 72–77, 82–86, 128, 137, 162, 260, 283, 284, 310, 330–331

Piso, Gn. Calpurnius 16, 71, 104, 107, 119, 208, 293
Pliny 294
Polemo, king of Cilicia 291
Polybius 312
Polydeuces 169
Pompedius 175
Pompey 89, 160, 165, 188, 211, 221, 222, 317, 318
Pomponius 175, 205, 231
Pontus 253, 260, 291
Pontus 260
Poppaea 301, 304, 320
Protos 105, 107
Ptolemais 95, 105, 126, 265
Puteoli, Pozzuoli 4, 6, 106, 167

Quadratus, Ummidius 73, 175, 263, 286, 287, 288, 331, 342
Quirinius 6, 45, 46, 47, 60, 61, 62, 175, 280, 329, 340
Qumran 56, 58, 59, 236, 251, 266, 285, 315

Regulus, Aemilius 34, 168, 171, 208
Regulus, Memmius 168
Rhegium 216
Rufus, Annius 64, 65, 329–330

Sadok the Pharisee 47–50
Salome (Herod's sister) 64, 67, 98, 99, 291
Salome Alexandra 151, 216, 242, 282, 317
Samaria 63, 234, 243, 257, 284, 285, 287
Sampsigeramus 99, 252, 290

Sardinia 81
Saturninus (Roman husband[s?]) 78, 81
Saul (gangster) 309
Sea of Galilee, Gennesaritis 62
Sejanus 102, 110, 111, 123
Seleucia 49, 70, 89, 137, 149, 150, 151
Seneca 171
Sentius Saturninus 159–162, 173, 203, 205–211
Sepphoris 61
Septimius Severus (emp.) 323
Sharon (plain) 95
Silanus 71
Silas 114, 120, 244, 247, 248, 249, 257
Simon (Hasmonean) 316
Simon (pious Jerusalemite) 251–252
Simon (rebel) 280
Simon b. Boethus 91, 333
Simon b. Camith 65
Simon b. Onias 244
Simon Cantheras 243, 333–349
Solomon 54–55, 311–313
Sosius, Gaius 318
Stephanus 283
Stoecheus 114
Strabo 59, 117
Syracuse 216

Taricheae 294
Thallos 107
Theophilus b. Ananus 95, 243
Thesmousa/Theamousa 68, 293
Theudas 255, 279, 296
Tholomeus (brigand) 263

Tiberias 7, 14, 61, 66–67, 71–72, 103, 128, 130, 226, 250, 253, 258, 294, 296, 330
Tiberius (emp.) passim, esp. until p. 120
Tiberius Alexander 3
Tiberius Gemellus 107, 111–118
Timidius 175
Tirathana 82, 82, 287
Tiridates 149, 275
Titus (emp.) 182, 220, 249, 291, 304, 319
"Tombs of the Kings" 278
Trachonitis 30, 90, 100, 138, 234, 290
Trebellius 33, 210
Tusculum 109
Tyre 103, 137, 286

Valerius, Asiaticus 190, 203, 229
Vardanes 247, 263, 274, 275
Veranius 224
Vespasian (emp.) 7, 11, 46, 47, 100, 113, 156, 165, 205, 220, 260, 295, 321
Vesuvius, Mt. 291
Vinicianus see Minucianus
Vitellius, L. 6, 82–90, 93–97, 125, 245, 247, 265, 273, 330
Vologeses 275–278
Vonones 69–71, 275

Xystus 303

Zeus (Jupiter) 126, 166–169, 191, 203, 215, 227
Zia 263, 285, 301, 311, 342

INDEX OF MODERN AUTHORS

This index was prepared by Ayala Schwartz.

Aberbach, M.   284
Africa, T.   255
Albert, K.   59
Allen, J.   68
Alon, G.   2, 65, 251, 252
Alston, R.   236
Altshuler, D.   325
Anderson, G.   303
Ando, C.   241
Andrade, N.   297
Annas, J.   127
Appelbaum, A.   106
Arav, R.   62
Arbiv, K.   249
Arenhoevel, D.   316
Arnhart, L.   123
Atkinson, K. M. T.   196
Attridge, H. A.   22, 180
Aus, R. D.   272
Aviam, M.   47
Avi-Yonah, M.   66

Bagnall, R. S.   256, 265
Balentine, S. E.   296
Balsdon, J. P. V. D.   269
Bammel, E.   1, 46, 61, 64
Barag, D.   6
Baratz, D.   312
Barclay, J. M. G.   28, 57, 58, 60, 80, 124, 125, 238, 279, 324
Bardet, S.   75
Barish, D. A.   321
Barkay, R.   91
Bar-Kochva, B.   96
Barrett, A. A.   passim, esp. in Book 19
Barton, C. A.   241
Bastianini, G.   111, 212, 237, 238, 239
Bauckham, R.   304, 306
Baughman, K. E.   304
Baumbach, G.   51
Baumgarten, A. I.   51, 52, 54, 56, 57, 97, 251, 306, 321
Baumgarten, J. M.   56, 57, 58, 59, 76, 255, 300
Beall, T. S.   51, 59
Beebe, H. K.   72
Begg, C. T.   178, 192
Beit-Arieh, I.   103
Bekker, I.   60, 116, 157, 208
Bell, A. A.   78
Bell, H. I.   241
Bell, S.   173
Bellen, H.   195
Ben Zeev, M. P.   236, 237, 238, 239, 240, 241, 245, 246
Benke, L.   304
Benveniste, E.   208

Ben-Yishai, S.   162, 166, 171
Berger, S.   49
Bergmann, J.   278
Bergmann, W.   236
Bergmeier, R.   51
Berlin, A.   336
Bernett, M.   124, 308
Berthelot, K.   165, 186
Bichler, R.   23
Bickerman(n), E. J.   63, 77, 181, 235
Bietenholz, P. G.   88
Bigwood, J. M.   67
Bikerman, E.   69, 149
Bilde, P.   15, 21, 124, 135, 136, 301, 321
Bingham, S.   174
Bird, H. W.   166, 167
Bird, M. F.   76
Birley, A. R.   175, 187
Birnbaum, E.   125
Birt, T.   324
Bloch, R.   279, 290
Boffo, L.   45, 46, 63, 72, 82, 120, 251, 291, 308
Bohak, G.   290
Bond, H.   66, 72
Botermann, H.   265
Bourne, F. C.   66, 72, 96, 131
Bovon, F.   64
Box, H.   239
Boyarin, D.   241
Bradley, K. R.   301
Brandon, S. G. F.   304
Braund, D.   68, 123
Brenk, F. E.   30
Brighton, M. A.   48, 301
Briscoe, J.   96
Brody, R.   140, 253, 337
Broer, I.   266
Broshi, M.   285
Brown, A. Philip, II.   182
Brown, R. E.   45, 76
Brunt, P. A.   20, 108, 166, 196, 288, 300, 309
Brust, M.   269
Bruun, C.   176
Buchon, J.-A.-C.   31, 289
Büchler, A.   11, 242
Burkitt, F. C.   28
Burridge, R. A.   324
Busink, T. A.   85
Byron, J.   48

Cairns, F.   133
Cameron, A.   76, 173, 230, 254
Cameron, H.   274
Capponi, L.   133
Carlier, C.   128

Carney, T. F.   259
Carrier, R.   306
Carucci, M.   289
Castelli, S.   85
Castillio, P. G.   213
Chancey, M.   61
Chapman, H. H.   49
Charlesworth, M. P.   102, 119, 155, 191, 230, 242, 307
Chaumont, M. L.   247
Ciaceri, E.   91, 242
Ciardiello, R.   301, 304
Cizek, E.   293
Clements, R. A.   93
Coello, T.   211
Cohen, N. G.   137, 144
Cohen, S. J. D.   3, 10, 33, 66, 80, 89, 95, 101, 128, 144, 266, 271, 290, 322
Cohen-Matlofsky, C.   58
Colautti, F. M.   62
Coleman, K. M.   88
Collins, J. J.   51
Collins, M. F.   82
Cook, J. G.   77
Cooper, G. C.   141
Corbett, P. E.   80
Cotton, H. M.   46, 212, 283
Cowan, J. A.   155
Crook, J.   232
Cunliffe, B.   195
Curran, J.   303
Currie, H. MacL.   194
Czajkowski, K.   5

Dąbrowa, E.   45, 71, 82, 87, 88, 104, 125, 247, 258, 263, 287
Danker, F. W.   26, 49, 63, 76, 86, 87, 89, 96, 105, 115, 127, 140, 146, 173, 174, 207, 252, 283, 336
Daube, D.   83, 113, 295
Daugherty, G. N.   229
Debevoise N. C.   67, 68, 69, 70, 87, 89, 273, 274, 275, 276, 318
Degrassi, A.   183, 185
Deines, R.   86
Denniston, J. D.   111, 124
Destinon, J. von.   22, 70, 114, 155, 172, 193, 285, 323
Dewar, M.   254
Dickey, E.   189
Dindorf, G.   92, 157, 201, 244
Dmitriev, S.   304
Dodge, H.   173
Domaszewski, A. von   72
Don-Yehiya, E.   2
Drüner, H.   11, 73, 260
Dunkle, J. R.   168, 198

Dupont, J.   272, 284
Dyson, S. L.   185

Eaton, J.   186
Eck, W.   46, 62, 64, 65, 72, 73, 245, 258, 264, 265
Ecker, A.   72
Eckhardt, B.   5
Eckstein, A. M.   50, 148
Edelmann-Singer, B.   304
Eder, S.   69
Efron, J.   242
Ehrenkrook, J. von.   175
Eisler, R.   76, 330
Ekinci, E. B.   111
Eliav, Y. Z.   304, 306
Ellens, J. H.   62
Emonds, H.   22
Epstein, J. N.   242
Erdkamp, P.   103, 272
Ernesti, J. A.   25, 108
Eshel, E.   285
Eshel, H.   266
Evans, K. G.   106, 235

Fantasia, U.   97
Faur, J.-C.   216
Feingold, M.   76
Feldman, L. H.   passim
Finegan, J.   324
Finkelstein, L.   55
Finlay, T. D.   267
First, M.   303
Fisch, Y.   62, 283, 300
Fischer, J. B.   60, 182
Fischer, M. L.   311
Fishwick, D.   124
Fitzmyer, J. A.   45
Flatto, D. C.   155, 162
Flusser, D.   2
Fontanille, J.-P.   61, 66
Forbes, C. A.   323
Forster, E. S.   89
Fraade, S. D.   303, 310
Fraschetti, A.   72
Free, A.   118, 155, 157, 187, 205
Freud, I.   103
Freund, R. A.   62
Frey, J.   51, 304
Frick, C.   23, 24
Friedman, R. E.   296
Frier, B.   335
Frumkin, A.   74
Fuchs [i.e. Fuks], A.   256

Gaechter, P.   305
Gafni, I. M.   47, 130, 277, 278
Gallivan, P.   158, 187, 265
Gapp, K. S.   272
Gardner, G.   86, 173
Garnsey, P.   272
Garzetti, A.   87
Gasparini, V.   78
Gasparro, G. S.   79
Geiger, J.   212
Gerber, C.   325

Gercke, A.   294
Gertoux, G.   45
Ghiretti, M.   46
Gibbs, J. G.   58, 146
Giet, S.   9
Gilbert, G.   266, 271
Gillman, F. M.   91
Glass, R. G.   204
Goetz, G.   185
Goldenberg, R.   139
González-Salinero, R.   81
Goodblatt, D.   55, 60, 137, 143, 144, 149, 242, 306
Goodenough, E. R.   125, 175
Goodman, M.   15, 49, 51, 57, 140, 299
Goud, T. E.   155, 157, 158, 160
Grabbe, L. L.   15, 48, 305, 306
Graetz, H.   258
Gramaglia, P. A.   75
Graux, C.   324
Gray, E. W.   108
Greenhut, Z.   66
Gregoratti, L.   67
Grethlein, J.   273
Griffin, M. T.   243, 301, 320
Griffith, G. T.   189
Gruen, E. S.   81, 124, 138, 295, 322
Grüll, T.   304
Grünbaum, P.   85
Grünewald, T.   48
Guéraud, O.   231
Guillaumont, A.   58
Gußmann, O.   85, 312, 334
Gutschmid, A. von   9, 25, 67, 76, 91, 134, 139, 146, 324

Haaland, G.   48, 50, 51
Hacham, N.   133, 277
Hachlili, R.   47, 265, 335
Hadas-Lebel, M.   76, 290
Hall, L. J.   252
Hall, R. G.   270
Hamilton, N. Q.   243
Hammond, M.   208, 211
Hammond, N. G. L.   189
Hanson, J. S.   279, 329
Harker, A.   237, 238
Harnack, A.   9, 75, 77
Harris, J. R.   324
Harris, W. V.   323
Hartmann, M.   93
Hasselmann, M.   295
Hata, G.   51, 148
Havercamp, S.   25, 26, 78, 107, 157, 176, 187, 252
Hawley, R.   211
Heerink, M.   294
Held, W.   149
Heldmann, K.   294
Hengel, M.   47, 59, 81, 263, 279, 301, 302
Hennig, D.   110
Henning, O.   155
Henten, J. W. van.   16, 63, 75, 76, 85, 90, 131, 145, 170, 171, 206, 311, 318, 323

Herman, G.   137, 138, 141, 143, 146
Herrmann, L.   27, 28, 30, 31, 63, 69, 86, 92, 97, 103, 111, 125, 174, 183, 192, 199, 268
Herrmann, P.   96
Herwerden, H. van.   272
Heyn, M. K.   70
Hicks, E. L.   136
Himmelfarb, M.   252
Hoehner, H. W.   61, 66, 92, 93, 99, 121, 123, 248
Hoenig, S. B.   306
Höffken, P.   16
Hoffmann, C.   236
Holladay, A. J.   140
Holladay, C. R.   107
Hollander, W. den.   304
Hölscher, G.   8, 56, 57, 155, 158, 159, 309, 312
Holwerda, [J. H.].   50, 174, 183
Holzmeister, U.   65, 84
Hooff, A. J. L. Van   135
Horbury, W.   337
Horsley, R. A.   53, 279, 329, 337
Horst, P. W. van der   45, 50, 111, 169, 239, 290, 324, 335
Houston, G. W.   106
Hudson, J.   25, 26, 48, 78, 107, 131, 133, 148, 150, 157, 172, 176, 183, 187, 238, 252, 253, 259, 301
Hug, A.   302
Huitink, L.   16, 323
Humphrey, J. H.   173
Hurley, D. W.   204, 293, 294

Ilan, T.   66, 132, 138, 197, 235, 253, 266, 281, 285, 287, 291, 292, 299, 308, 317, 285
Inowlocki, S.   322
Isaac, B.   252

Jachowski, R. J.   90
Jackson, B. S.   100, 195, 291, 304
Jacoby, K.   23
Jensen, M. H.   66
Jeremias, J.   76, 283, 308, 310, 337
Johnson, N. B.   277
Jones, A. H. M.   61, 65, 105, 288
Jones, C. P.   325
Jones, F. S.   304
Jones, K. R.   17
Jonquière, T. M.   277
Joüon, P.   62, 214

Kahrstedt, U.   70
Kajava, M.   198
Kampen, J.   51
Kasher, A.   38, 47, 236, 237, 238, 244, 247, 324
Kattan Gribetz, S.   242, 266, 271
Katzoff, R.   100, 241, 245
Kavanagh, B. J.   171, 187, 190, 201
Keddie, A.   84
Keddie, G. A.   204
Kiernan, V. G.   197
King, C. W.   233

Klawans, J.   17, 52, 53, 54, 56, 71, 180,
      295, 301
Kletter, K. M.   2
Kletter, R.   105
Kloppenborg, J. S.   129
Klostermann, E.   263
Koestermann, E.   71
Koets, P. J.   241
Kogon, A. J.   61, 66
Kokkinos, N.   passim
Korzeniewski, D.   133
Kovács, P.   132
Krause, A. R.   51, 244, 245
Krauter, S.   95
Krebs, C. B.   322
Krieger, K.-S.   10, 20, 64, 84, 95, 235,
      291, 296
Kropp, A. J. T. M.   235
Krüger, J.   294
Kruse, H.   59
Kuhn, H.-W.   62

Lambers-Petry, D.   304, 306
Lambertz, M.   281, 332
Lämmer, M.   250, 252, 254
Lans, Birgit van der   81
Lanser, R. D.   318
Laqueur, R.   22, 67, 321, 324
Lavan, L.   289
Lavee, M.   33, 101
Le Moyne, J.   54, 305
Lee, J. A. L.   150
Lembi, G.   80, 119, 123, 137, 144, 145
Lémonon, J.-P.   46, 72, 73, 74, 83, 129,
      258
Lenschau, T.   70
Leon, H. J.   80
Leoni, T.   24
Levick, B.   passim
Levine, L. I.   50, 67, 72, 73, 245, 258, 297
Lewy, H.   56, 88, 119, 120
Lieberman, S.   29, 66, 146, 220, 236, 283,
      308, 312
Liebowitz, E.   266
Liempt, L. van   75, 76, 77
Lifshitz, B.   72
Linder, A.   265
Lindner, H.   71, 275
Lindsay, D. R.   232, 271
Lindsay, H.   167, 172, 185, 213, 225
Livesey, N. E.   266, 270
Lloyd, A. B.   138
Lofberg, J. O. L.   169
Loftus, F.   59
Longenecker, B. W.   296
Lott, J. B.   71, 102, 110
Luraghi, N.   171

Magness, J.   55, 86
Mahieu, B.   45, 66
Maier, G.   83
Maier, P. L.   52
Main, E.   51
Maione, V.   122

Malherbe, A. J.   205
Malloch, S. J. V.   168
Mandel, P.   53, 85, 308
Mandell, S.   137
Marciak, M.   266, 268, 276, 277, 278
Marcus, R.   57, 90, 126, 131, 316, 312
Marincola, J.   294
Marquardt, J.   286
Marshall, F. H.   211
Martin, R.   46, 304, 307
Martin, S. R.   244
Mason, H. J. (*GTRI*)   passim
Mason, S.   passim
Massey, P. T.   182
Mathieu, G.   25, 27, 28, 30, 31, 63, 69,
      86, 92, 97, 103, 111, 125, 174, 183, 192,
      199, 268
Mayer, G.   236
Mazar, E.   311
McCracken, G.   109
McDonnell, M.   206
McEleney, N.   270
McGing, B. C.   129
McGinn, T. A. J.   258
McLaren, J. S.   15, 51, 60, 74, 294, 304,
      306, 320
Mealand, D. I.   58
Meijer, E.   294
Meinhold, A.   120, 133
Mendels, D.   240
Meshorer, Y.   61, 62, 72, 90, 235, 254,
      268, 308
Metzner, R.   66, 86, 337
Michael, J. H.   139, 267, 274
Milikowsky, C.   313
Millar, F.   166, 168, 173, 181, 182, 194, 195,
      234, 240, 264, 301
Miller, P. D.   277
Miller, S. S.   61, 66, 86
Minov, S.   274
Miraldi, L.   31
Modrzejewski, J. M.   236, 238, 279
Moehring, H. R.   58
Momigliano, A.   155, 217, 218, 257, 265,
      284, 339
Mommsen, T.   18, 23, 113–114, 156–157,
      187, 195, 233, 252, 288, 301
Moore, G. F.   52, 198, 215
Morrison, C. E.   52
Motzo, R. B.   238
Mouritsen, H.   289
Muraoka, T.   286
Murgatroyd, P.   293
Musurillo, H.   232

Nabel, J.   68
Naber, S. A.   23, 24, 27, 84, 116, 117, 126,
      138, 157, 174, 183, 192, 218, 219, 252,
      272
Nagy, R. M.   61
Negev, Y.   74
Nestle, E.   255
Netzer, E.   85, 92, 303
Neusner, J.   137, 266

Nicolet, C.   165
Nicols, J.   110
Nielsen, K. M.   215
Niese, B.   passim
Nilsson, M. P.   115
Nir, R.   93
Nitschke, J.   45
Nitschke, J. L.   244
Noam, V.   2, 54, 62, 124, 132, 180, 242,
      243, 266, 283, 285, 300, 303, 312, 317
Nodet, E.   35, 93, 94, 340
Nolland, J.   270
Norden, E.   9, 14, 18, 49, 74, 76, 157, 283
North, H. F.   78
Noy, D.   80, 208

Oakley, S. P   97
Ogg, G.   45
Ogilvie, R. M.   323
Olbrycht, M. J.   69, 87, 88, 274
Oldfather, C. H   195
Oliver, J. H.   178
Olson, K. A.   75, 76
Oost, S. I.   110, 301
Opelt, I.   112
Oppenheimer, A.   137, 147, 151, 269, 287,
      300
Orth, W.   108, 174
Osgood, J.   234, 259
Otto, W. F.   8, 84
Overduin, F.   200

Painter, J.   304, 306
Papone, P.   223
Parker, R.   170
Parkin, T. G.   52, 335
Patrich, J.   72, 73, 74
Paul, G. M.   204, 242, 242, 281, 299, 306
Pease, A. S.   112
Peleg-Barkat, O.   63, 311
Pelletier, A.   35
Petersen, H.   11, 21, 68, 97, 183, 325
Phang, S. E.   148
Pilhofer, P.   49
Piotrkowski, M.   315
Poehlmann, W.   51
Porton, G. G.   270
Potter, D.   117
Potter, D. S.   21
Powell, J. E.   108
Powell, L.   71
Price, J. J.   21, 49, 301, 309, 323
Price, S. R. F.   239, 255
Puech, É.   56
Pummer, R.   16, 62, 63, 82
Purcell, N.   134

Qedar, S.   103

Radin, M.   17, 22, 27, 28, 29, 121, 185
Rainbird, J. S.   229
Rajak, T.   9, 21, 86, 132, 198, 266, 297,
      305, 306, 312
Ramage, E. S.   239

Rappaport, S.   313
Rappaport, U.   60, 103, 260, 301, 302
Rawson, E.   186
Regev, E.   58, 305
Reinach, T.   23, 27, 76
Reinhold, M.   23, 80, 186
Reiter, S.   127
Relandus, H.   263
Rendsburg, G. A.   310
Rengstorf, K. H.   34
Retsö, J.   276
Rey-Coquais, J.-P.   45, 126
Reynolds, J. M.   80, 318
Rhoads, D. M.   329
Rhoads, J. H.   45
Richards, G. C.   22, 24, 26, 89, 94, 102, 129, 132, 234, 246
Richardson, L.   167, 182, 194, 221, 222, 225, 232
Rickman, G. E.   272
Ringel, J.   72
Ritschl, F.   22
Ritter, B.   236, 237, 238
Ritter, H. W.   155, 158
Rogers, R. S.   80, 81
Rolfe, J. C.   169, 191, 202, 210, 220, 225
Roller, D. W.   64, 67
Roller, M. B.   133
Rostovtzeff, M.   235
Rühl, F.   23
Rustoiu, A.   302
Rutgers, L. V.   80, 81
Rutherford, W. G.   207
Rutledge, S. H.   119, 198, 293
Rzepka, J.   188

Safrai, S.   64, 129, 283, 285, 288, 304, 306, 310, 318
Sanders, E. P.   56, 85, 306
Sanders, L. J.   121, 124, 236
Sandmel, S.   156
Sartre, M.   71
Satlow, M. L.   271
Saulnier, C.   91
Saumagne, C.   300, 332
Schalit, A.   passim
Schäublin, C.   322
Schemann, F.   18, 112, 128, 155
Scherberich, K.   5, 155
Schiffman, L. H.   63, 266
Schimanowski, G.   63, 266
Schippmann, K.   67, 70, 263, 273, 274, 275
Schlatter, A.   263
Schlude, J. M.   87
Schmeling, G.   225
Schoenfeld, A. J.   81
Schofield, M.   175
Schorch, S.   85
Schreckenberg, H.   23, 24, 27, 45, 126, 219, 179, 367
Schremer, A.   290
Schröder, B.   49, 241
Schrömbges, P.   165

Schürer, E. (HJP)   passim
Schulz, V.   294
Schumann, D.   242
Schuol, M.   268, 269
Schwartz, D. G.   134
Schwartz, D. R.   passim
Schwartz, E.   284, 301
Schwartz, J. J.   287
Schwartz, S.   15, 16, 30, 86, 283, 323
Scott, H. M.   11
Scramuzza, V. M.   217
Seeman, C.   113, 244, 274
Seevers, B. V.   302
Segal, A.   252
Setaioli, A.   225
Shaham, H.   316
Shalev, Y.   244
Sharon, N.   48, 86, 95, 239, 240, 241, 259, 317, 318
Shatzman, I.   121, 165, 258, 331
Shaw, B. D.   137, 141
Shenkar, M.   267, 274, 278
Sherwin-White, A. N.   45
Shutt, R. J. H.   21, 24, 26, 48, 52, 71, 89, 94, 102, 129, 132, 234, 247, 255
Sidwell, B.   124, 165
Siegert, F.   60, 254
Sievers, J.   35, 45, 249, 340
Sigismund, M.   103
Sittl, C.   200
Skjærvo, P. O.   267
Slingerland, H. D.   236, 265
Smallwood, E. M.   passim
Smith, M.   58
Smith, M. D.   62
Sokoloff, M.   139, 140
Southern, P.   211, 229
Speidel, M. P.   195
Sperber, D.   103
Spicq, C.   passim
Spier, J.   211
Spilsbury, P.   113, 192, 244, 274
Spivey, N.   168
Stein, A.   21
Stein, E.   103, 104, 254, 311
Steinmann, A. E.   90
Stelten, L. F.   138, 146, 148
Sterling, G. E.   16, 106, 266, 279
Stern, M.   passim
Stevenson, T.   264
Stewart, A.   168
Stowasser, M.   72
Streckert, K. H.   302
Strickert, F. M.   61, 62, 90, 91
Strugnell, E.   68, 89
Strugnell, J.   56
Sullivan, R. D.   71, 99, 290, 294
Swain, S.   275, 323
Swan, M.   171, 190, 228
Swan, P. M.   112, 175
Swancutt, D. M.   205
Syme, R.   21, 45, 81, 104, 155, 157, 158, 159, 161, 190
Szanton, N.   72, 310

Takács, S. A.   78
Talbert, R. J. A.   228, 232
Tannenbaum, R.   80
Täubler, E.   11, 64, 71, 87, 88, 266
Taylor, J.   58, 62, 239
Taylor, J. E.   57, 58, 85
Tcherikover, V.   17, 53, 106, 236, 238, 245, 265, 304
Terian, A.   235
Thackeray, H. St. J.   passim
Thiel, N.   59
Thiessen, M.   252, 270, 271
Tilly, M.   278
Timpe, D.   18, 155, 157, 158, 160, 205, 211
Tov, E.   247, 269
Townend, G. B.   18, 212
Toynbee, J. M. C.   213
Troiani, L.   16
Tromp, J.   93
Tropper, A.   243
Tropper, D.   55
Tsur, Y.   108
Tuval, M.   20, 73, 101, 130, 323

Udoh, F. E.   84, 95, 129, 244
Ullmann, L.   331
Unnik, W. C. van.   144, 322

VanderKam, J. C.   passim
Verdenius, W. J.   45
Victor, U.   75, 227
Villalba i Varneda, P.   7, 71
Vincent, H.   325
Visi, T.   76, 92, 93
Vitelli, M.   76
Voorst, R. van.   75, 107

Wächter, L.   56
Walbank, F. W.   187
Walcot, P.   110
Walker, J.   83
Wallace-Hadrill, A.   227
Ward, J. S.   159, 256
Wardle, D.   96, 158, 168, 184, 185, 187, 212, 234, 235
Warren, M.   255
Weaver, P. R. C.   195
Webster, G.   211, 260
Weingärtner, D. G.   71
Weiss, H.   139
Weiss, Z.   61, 66, 73, 252, 255
Welles, C. B.   85, 203
Wendland P.   23, 24
Werse, N. R.   296
Whealey, A.   75, 306
Whiston, W.   27, 28, 29, 32, 45, 76, 135, 337, 338
Wikgren, A.   131
Wilcken, U.   131
Wilhelm, A.   100, 101, 102
Wilker, J.   46, 61, 66, 90, 242, 266, 281, 290
Wilkinson, S.   123
Williams, M. H.   304

Williamson, H. G. M.   11, 68
Willrich, H.   171
Wills, L. M.   120, 133
Winter, P.   75, 76, 77, 243, 267, 306
Winterling, A.   165
Wirszubski, C.   170, 177, 208, 209, 211
Wiseman, T. P.   25, passim in Bk. 19

Wolfson, H. A.   306
Woodman, A. J.   108
Woods, D.   81, 186, 191
Worp, K. A.   256

Yakobson, A.   71, 119, 239
Yankelevitch, R.   258

Yavetz, Z.   165, 166, 181, 198
Yechezkel, A. Y.   74
Yerushalmi, Y. H.   150

Zeitlin, S.   306
Ziffer, I.   105
Zwickel, W.   105